TREASURY
EDITION

The
McGraw-Hill
Literature Series

Focus
Perception
Insights
Encounters

American Literature:
A Chronological Approach

American Literature:
A Thematic Approach

English Literature:
A Chronological Approach

British and Western Literature:
A Thematic Approach

G. Robert Carlsen
General Editor

Editors

G. Robert Carlsen
Iowa City, Iowa

Miriam Gilbert
Iowa City, Iowa

Contributors

Lee Davis, Westhampton, New York
Lorraine Labate, Stamford, Connecticut
Bea Rockstroh, Clayton, Missouri

ADVISORS

Michael Hannigan, Waterbury, Connecticut
Ann T. Cook, Tampa, Florida
Paula N. Nikla, Tampa, Florida
Ellen Oberfelder, Baltimore, Maryland
Robert Sarli, Bethpage, New York
Evelyn Stanton, Charlotte, North Carolina
Joy Averett, Oxford, North Carolina
Marietta Hickman, Wake Forest,
North Carolina
Mary Stamler, Youngstown, Ohio
Sherry Morgan, Sand Springs, Oklahoma
Sr. Therese Dougherty, Carbondale,
Pennsylvania

Judith Frederick, Ulysses, Pennsylvania
Joy Johnson, Webster, South Dakota
Glen Smith, San Antonio, Texas
Anita Arnold, San Antonio, Texas
Gale Calelly, Houston, Texas
Gayle Lemmond, Hampton, Virginia
Beth Rich, Salt Lake City, Utah
Cynthia Masincup, Woodstock, Virginia
B. J. Davis, Culpeper, Virginia
Robert Lambriola, Virginia Beach, Virginia
Anna Cooke, Staunton, Virginia
Sharon Clemont, Kennewick, Washington

BRITISH AND WESTERN LITERATURE

A Thematic Approach

G. Robert Carlsen • Miriam Gilbert

TREASURY EDITION

WEBSTER DIVISION, McGRAW-HILL BOOK COMPANY
New York, St. Louis, San Francisco, Dallas, Atlanta

Cover Art:
The Houses of Parliament
Claude Monet
Musèe du Jeu de Paume, Paris
RMN and SPADEM

Editorial Direction: John A. Rothermich
Editors: Martha Alderson and Steven Griffel
Editing and Styling: Robert Towns
Design Supervision: Virginia Copeland and Valerie Greco
Production: Tom Goodwin

Photo Editor: Alan Forman
Photo Research: C. Buff Rosenthal and Alan Forman
Text and Cover Design: Blaise Zito Associates, Inc.
Cover Concept: Alan Forman

This book was set in Caledonia by Typographic Sales, Inc. The color
separation was done by Typographic Sales, Inc.

Library of Congress Cataloging in Publication Data
Main entry under title:

British and Western literature.

(The McGraw-Hill literature series)
"Treasury edition."
Bibliography: p.
Includes index.
    Summary: A thematically arranged anthology of poems,
short stories, plays, and novellas from western literature
for the twelfth-grade reader.
    1. Literature—Collections. [1. Literature—
Collections] I. Carlsen, G. Robert, date
II. Gilbert, Miriam. III. Series.
PN6014.B732   1985   808.8   84-755
ISBN 0-07-009821-2

ISBN 0-07-009821-2

Contents

Conflict of Wills

Medieval British Poetry: Understanding Poetry

Renaissance British Poetry: The Elizabethan Age

Choice and Consequence

Seventeenth- and Eighteenth-Century British Poetry: An Age of Contradictions

Foibles

Nineteenth-Century British Poetry: Revolution and Imagination

Critics of Society

Twentieth-Century British Poetry:
The Present and the Past

Know Thyself

CONFLICT OF WILLS

COMBAT BETWEEN THE GIAOUR AND THE PASHA *Eugène Delacroix* *Courtesy of the Art Institute of Chicago*

Any story is based on conflict, whether it is a brief tale, such as de Maupassant's "The Necklace," or a novel that runs to a thousand pages, such as Tolstoy's *War and Peace.* The struggle

1

between two forces forms the pattern of the story, giving it a beginning, a development, and a conclusion.

There are four main kinds of conflict. First, we have struggles between people and the forces of nature: floods, fires, drought, cold, and heat. Second, there are conflicts between a person and such elements of the social order as prejudice, customs, or tyranny. Third, there is the conflict that lies within an individual's mind, when conscience is at war with desire. Last, conflict arises between two individuals when each attempts to force his or her will on the other. Such conflict of wills between two persons is the central issue in this opening theme.

Conflict in real life may be unpleasant, but in literature readers find it exciting. People in conflict stand out clearly and sharply for what they are. In a crisis, we sharpen our thinking and our actions. Tales of conflict bring to the surface problems concerning the meaning and values of life, and the reader is forced to evaluate the situation:

Why, at times, is it impossible for two individuals to agree?

Where does the right lie?

As the conflict is resolved, the writer may show us a tragic view of life or may end on a comic or optimistic note. In any case, readers see a reflection of their own problems and gain insight into themselves.

The writers of this theme, CONFLICT OF WILLS, range in time from the fifth century B.C. to our own day. Some force us to ponder the tragic in life; others focus our attention on the humorous and the ridiculous. The theme of conflict between individuals serves not only to unify each piece of literature, but also to explore an aspect of human experience.

SOPHOCLES

496-406 B.C.

Sophocles[1] is one of three Greek tragic dramatists whose plays have been preserved for modern times. (Of the more than one hundred plays he wrote, complete copies of only seven remain.) He was born at Colonus,[2] near Athens. At the age of sixteen he was chosen to lead a chorus of boys in the celebration of Athens' great naval victory over the Persians at Salamis.[3] During his career he served his city in many posts at home and abroad and at the age of fifty-five became a general during the Samian War.[4]

We do not know exactly when Sophocles first entered plays in the annual dramatic competition at Athens. We do know, however, that he took the top prize for the first time when he was only twenty-eight. In that competition he defeated the great writer Aeschylus.[5] During his

Sophocles, playwright of the Golden Age of Greece, performed many public duties in addition to his creative life as an artist. Born in 496 B.C., Sophocles lived for ninety years. At his birth, Athens was a young democracy experimenting with the new machinery of popular government. By the time of his death, Athens had been drained by the conflicts resulting from the Peloponnesian War.

---

1. **Sophocles** (sof′ə klēz′).
2. **Colonus** (kə lō′nəs).
3. **Salamis** (sal′ə məs), ancient capital of the island of Cyprus.
4. **Samian** (sā′mē ən), from the Aegean island of Samos.
5. **Aeschylus** (es′kə ləs), 525–456 B.C.

life he was awarded the first prize about twenty times, and he never placed lower than second in the contest.

Sophocles, like many great playwrights, was an innovator. For one thing, he introduced more elaborate scene-painting to the Greek theater. A more important contribution, however, was the addition of a third actor to the cast of his plays. Before Sophocles' time all the parts in the Greek plays (except the chorus) were taken by only two actors—a severe limitation. In adding the third actor, Sophocles opened new possibilities for a more complicated and flexible arrangement of the stage action.

Antigone

Antigone[1] is a drama in which a strong-willed woman and her powerful uncle, both fiercely believing themselves to be right, clash on a matter of principle. It is also one of the great and enduring works of our cultural heritage. The play belongs to that class of literature known as *tragedy*, which the ancient Greek dramatists developed to great heights.

Tragedy

There is a legend in Greek mythology of a magnificent bird which is born from fire and ashes. Ancient Greeks named the bird the phoenix.[2] It is a strange conception: strength and life rising out of destruction. This conception was carried by the Greeks into an art form—the tragic drama—recognized as one of the most difficult yet enriching experiences of Western culture.

The subject of a tragedy is the downfall of a hero, usually ending with her or his destruction or death. Readers or playgoers who submit themselves to tragedy share the emotions of the tragic characters. This emotional tension increases almost to the breaking point. Then, as the hero faces the final, horrible truth, the audience experiences a release, a release not granted to the hero of the play. This release is reminiscent of the phoenix, since from the ashes of devastating emotion there rises a feeling of calm, a sense of harmony in the universe. The Greeks called this emotional effect *catharsis*.[3]

There are many theories about tragedy. Most of them stem from the work of the great Greek critic and philosopher Aristotle.[4] He examined the Greek tragedies and described them in his *Poetics*, a book still widely read today. The following are a few of the statements that have been made about tragedy, and for which there is general agreement among critics.

1. *Tragedy arouses the emotions of pity and fear, wonder and awe.* Readers watch the hero move toward destruction; they have pity for the hero; they share the hero's fear and suffering; they experience wonder and awe before the forces of Fate. The emotional impact of

A *member of the National Theater of Greece, Aphrodite Gregoriadou, appears in a production of the classic theater filmed in Delphi.*

---

1. **Antigone** (an tig′ə nē).
2. **phoenix** (fē′niks), this legend is thought to relate to the sun as it dies in flames at sunset and rises in the fiery dawn.
3. **catharsis** (kə thär′sis).
4. **Aristotle** (ar′ə stot′l), 384–322 B.C.

Portrait sculpture of the Greek philosopher Aristotle, pupil of Plato, and through him of Socrates.
The ruins of the ancient theater at Hipeiros, sharing its valley with the cultivated fields of modern Greece.

tragedy is two-pronged: (a) readers turn their thoughts inward to ponder their own fate; (b) readers are moved to consider momentarily the fate of all human beings.

2. *A tragic hero must be a man or woman capable of great suffering.* Tragic heroes are often kings, queens, warriors, or persons of noble spirit and high position. They are not merely "upset" by the small annoyances and misfortunes of life. They are larger than life. Thus in the great suffering of unusually sensitive and noble persons, the reader can see more clearly the vast reaches of the human spirit.

3. *Tragedy explores the question of the ways of God to Mortals.* We have always been disturbed about why God permits us to suffer, often (from a human point of view) so needlessly. Tragedy does not propose a solution to this problem. It presents the question in dramatic form for us to contemplate.

4. *Tragedy purifies the emotions.* It purges the baser emotions so that the better ones shine forth. This is the doctrine of catharsis as formulated by Aristotle. Readers experience mounting anguish which builds to a peak like gathering flood waters. Suddenly they feel as if a flood gate has been opened releasing the pent-up emotions, and in the place of the raging flood, flows a quiet, gentle stream. The point at which this happens in tragedy is called the climax.

5. *Tragedy shows how the hero is brought to disaster by a single flaw in character.* Each person's nature is composed not only of the noble, the dignified, and the godlike but also of the base, the ignoble, the bestial. Tragedy shows us a person who has noble attributes, but whose character is marred by a flaw which ultimately leads to a downfall.

There have been very few masters of tragic drama. Three of them—Aeschylus, Sophocles, and Euripides[5]—wrote within a period of a few years during the "Golden Age" in ancient Greece. A fourth, William Shakespeare, wrote in our own language. In this book you will have an opportunity to read and compare two great tragedies; Shakespeare's *Macbeth* and Sophocles' *Antigone* are different in their styles and

---

5. **Euripides** (yu̇ rip′ə dēz′), approximately 480–406 B.C.

techniques, but alike in producing the impact of tragedy.

The Greek Theater

Today, we think of the theater as a place of amusement. The Greek tragedies, however, were produced as part of an annual religious festival in Athens. Each year new plays were presented before the entire populace of the city, and an award was given to the playwright who presented the best series of three dramas. Sophocles received the prize often during his long, productive life.

The plays were put on beneath the bright skies of Greece, in huge outdoor amphitheaters, somewhat like modern football stadiums cut in half. Built upon hillsides, they seated as many as 40,000 people at a time. The stage was a slightly raised platform in the open area upon the ground. We do not know for certain all the details of the Greek theater. Scholars believe that the stage was backed by a structure with pillars and columns which could represent a palace or the walls of a city. All of the actors were men. They wore masks which may have

Two scenes from the revival of the classic drama Electra *performed at Epidavros by the National Theater of Greece during the Epidavros Festival, 1961.*

contained built-in megaphones to send their voices through the vast theater. Platform shoes gave them added height.

Thus the play depended more on the *words* the actors spoke than on subtle effects of facial expression or gesture. The actors' movements had to be broad and bold. This kind of theater has little relation to the *realistic* style of drama we expect today.

One aspect of the Greek theater which often confuses modern readers is the chorus. We still find the chorus in our musical comedies, but it is rare in "serious" plays and films. The Greek chorus was a group of actors who moved and sang together. Actually the plays themselves developed from a kind of community sing when bit by bit a chorus grew up that told stories in song and verse. To this an actor was added who carried on a dialogue with the chorus. Then a second actor was added, and a third. With each additional actor, the chorus shrank in size and importance.

In Sophocles' time the chorus did many things. It could set the mood of the story with its poetic songs. It could represent the common people, the townspeople, the citizen in the street. Sometimes the chorus sided with one or another character in the play. Sometimes it warned a character of impending disaster.

Often the chorus, with its folk truths and its common sense, created a contrast with the loftier passions and thoughts of the hero. The one thing the chorus did *not* do was mouth directly the ideas of the author. The modern reader of Greek drama must remember that the chorus functions as a character in the play.

The Greek theater developed certain *conventions* or standard ways of presenting action. All theaters have their conventions. For example, in a modern movie we accept a convention that shows an actor in London, New York, and Hong Kong all within the space of a minute or two. This movement of a person through time and space would have bewildered the ancient Greeks.

The Greek tragedy usually followed conventions requiring *unity* of time, place, and action. A play took place within a single day's time. The scene did not change; it usually remained in the courtyard of the palace or in the main square of the city. Unity of action meant that the writer concentrated on *one* story line at a time. There were no subplots or diversions.

The Greeks felt that physical horror was so repulsive to see that it ruined the artistic effect of the drama. Therefore, all violent actions took place offstage. They were reported to the audience by messengers.

The Greek tragic dramatists seldom invented original stories or characters. Over and over again, they went back to the old legends and epics of their people. Sophocles' audience knew the outcome of the story before arriving at the theater. Thus Greek writers had little need to create suspense. Instead, they concentrated on character portrayal, on ideas, and on poetry. The center of the story was the emotions of the characters.

The Background of *Antigone*

Antigone is a play complete in itself, but it is part of a series of three plays Sophocles wrote about the city of Thebes[1] and the family of Oedipus.[2] The other two are *Oedipus Rex* (*Oedipus the King*) and *Oedipus at Colonus.*

From the tragic conclusion to Oedipus Rex *comes this scene of Alexis Minotis as Oedipus. The Greek National Theater production at Delphi.*

The series follows the destiny of a family haunted by a curse that follows them from generation to generation.

The curse began with a prophecy by the oracle at Delphi[3] to the King and Queen of Thebes that their son (Oedipus) would kill his father and marry his own mother. To escape this fate, the parents left their baby alone in the mountains to die. But the child was found by a shepherd and eventually was adopted by the King and Queen of Corinth[4] and brought up as

---

1. **Thebes** (thēbz).
2. **Oedipus** (ed′ə pəs) *or* (ē′də pəs).
3. **Delphi** (del′fī).
4. **Corinth** (kôr′inth) *or* (kor′inth).

In dramatic mask and costume, Douglas Campbell played Oedipus to an American audience at the Stratford Shakespearean Festival, Ontario, Canada.

their son—unaware of his real birth. Years later, grown to adulthood, Oedipus unknowingly fulfilled the prophecy by killing his real father in an accidental meeting. Then he went on to Thebes, where he won the hand of the Queen, Jocasta,[5] and became King of the city. The play *Oedipus Rex* tells how, years later, he discovered the horrible truth about himself, put out his own eyes, and cast himself into exile. He left his brother-in-law, Creon,[6] as regent of Thebes, to look after his two sons, Polyneices and Eteocles,[7] and his daughters, Antigone and Ismene.[8] The death of Oedipus is the subject of *Oedipus at Colonus*.

Before he died, Oedipus had directed his sons to share the kingship of Thebes by occupying the throne in alternate years. However, after his initial reign, Eteocles refused to step down and banished his brother. Polyneices fled to Argos[9] where he married the daughter of King Adrastus and enlisted seven Argive chieftains to join him in an attack on Thebes. During the battle, the two brothers killed each other in a hand-to-hand fight. Their uncle,

Creon, was now King of Thebes. Maintaining that Eteocles had defended Thebes, Creon ordered him buried with all religious rites and honors. But Polyneices had brought an enemy force against the gates of Thebes, and so he must be regarded as a rebel and as such denied a religious burial. His body was to be left lying uncovered in the fields for beasts and birds to feed upon.

Antigone, the sister of both warriors, was appalled by Creon's order, since the ancient Greeks believed that the soul could not rest until the body had been properly buried. As Antigone saw it, her obligations to her dead brother and to the sacred laws of Heaven demanded that she see his body buried, regardless of the laws of the state.

So the curse on the royal house of Thebes moves forward. Conflict is set in motion between two sincere and strong-willed people, Antigone and her uncle Creon, now the King.

---

5. **Jocasta** (jō kas′tə).
6. **Creon** (krē′on).
7. **Polyneices** (pol′ə nī′sēz). **Eteocles** (e tē′ə klēz′).
8. **Ismene** (is mē′nə).
9. **Argos** (är′gŏs), a city state in south central Greece (adj. **Argive**).

Antigone

a tragedy,
first produced in Athens,
about 441 B.C.
Translated into English verse
by H. D. F. Kitto

Characters

ANTIGONE,
*daughter of the former King, Oedipus,
and niece of the present ruler, Creon*
ISMENE, *her sister*
CREON, *now King of Thebes*
HAEMON, *his son*
A GUARD
TEIRESIAS, *a blind seer*
EURYDICE, *Creon's wife*
MESSENGERS
CHORUS OF THEBAN NOBLES

The Scene
Thebes, before the royal palace.

Enter, from the palace, ANTIGONE *and* ISMENE.

ANTIGONE. Ismene, my own sister, dear
　　Ismene,
　How many miseries our father caused!
　And is there one of them that does not
　　fall
　On us while yet we live? Unhappiness,
　Calamity, disgrace, dishonour—which　　5
　Of these have you and I not known? And
　　now
　Again: there is the order which they say
　Brave Creon has proclaimed to all the
　　city.
　You understand? or do you not yet know
　What outrage threatens one of those we
　　love?　　10

ISMENE. Of them, Antigone, I have not
　　heard
　Good news or bad—nothing, since we
　　two sisters
　Were robbed of our two brothers on one
　　day
　When each destroyed the other. During
　　the night
　The enemy has fled: so much I know,　　15
　But nothing more, either for grief or
　　joy.
ANTIGONE. I knew it; therefore I have
　　brought you here,
　Outside the doors, to tell you secretly.
ISMENE. What is it? Some dark shadow is
　　upon you.
ANTIGONE. Our brothers' burial.—Creon
　　has ordained　　20
　Honour for one, dishonour for the other.
　Eteocles, they say, has been entombed
　With every solemn rite and ceremony
　To do him honour in the world below;
　But as for Polyneices, Creon has ordered　　25
　That none shall bury him or mourn for
　　him;
　He must be left to lie unwept, unburied,
　For hungry birds of prey to swoop and
　　feast
　On his poor body. So he has decreed,
　Our noble Creon, to all the citizens:　　30
　To you, to me. To me! And he is coming
　To make it public here, that no one may
　Be left in ignorance; nor does he hold it
　Of little moment: he who disobeys
　In any detail shall be put to death　　35
　By public stoning in the streets of
　　Thebes.
　So it is now for you to show if you
　Are worthy, or unworthy, of your birth.
ISMENE. O my poor sister! If it has come
　　to this
　What can I do, either to help or hinder?　　40

From *Sophocles: Three Tragedies,* translated by H. D. F. Kitto. Copyright © 1962 by Oxford University Press. Reprinted by permission.

Haemon (hē′mon).
Teiresias (tī rē′si əs).
Eurydice (yù rid′ə sē).

ANTIGONE. Will you join hands with me and share my task?

ISMENE. What dangerous enterprise have you in mind?

ANTIGONE. Will you join me in taking up the body?

ISMENE. What? Would you bury him, against the law?

ANTIGONE. No one shall say *I* failed him! I will bury 45
My brother—and yours too, if you will not.

ISMENE. You reckless girl! When Creon has forbidden?

ANTIGONE. He has no right to keep me from my own!

ISMENE. Think of our father, dear Antigone,
And how we saw him die, hated and scorned, 50
When his own hands had blinded his own eyes
Because of sins which he himself disclosed;
And how his mother-wife, two names in one,
Knotted a rope, and so destroyed herself.
And, last of all, upon a single day 55
Our brothers fought each other to the death
And shed upon the ground the blood that joined them.
Now you and I are left, alone; and think:
If we defy the King's prerogative
And break the law, our death will be more shameful 60
Even than theirs. Remember too that we
Are women, not made to fight with men. Since they
Who rule us now are stronger far than we,
In this and worse than this we must obey them.
Therefore, beseeching pardon from the dead, 65
Since what I do is done on hard compulsion,
I yield to those who have authority;

For useless meddling has no sense at all.

ANTIGONE. I will not urge you. Even if you should wish
To give your help I would not take it now. 70
Your choice is made. But I shall bury him.
And if I have to die for this pure crime,
I am content, for I shall rest beside him;
His love will answer mine. I have to please
The dead far longer than I need to please 75
The living; with them, I have to dwell for ever.
But you, if so you choose, you may dishonour
The sacred laws that Heaven holds in honour.

ISMENE. I do them no dishonour, but to act
Against the city's will I am too weak. 80

ANTIGONE. Make that your pretext! I will go and heap
The earth upon the brother whom I love.

ISMENE. You reckless girl! I tremble for your life.

ANTIGONE. Look to yourself and do not fear for me.

ISMENE. At least let no one hear of it, but keep 85
Your purpose secret, and so too will I.

ANTIGONE. Go and denounce me! I shall hate you more
If you keep silent and do not proclaim it.

ISMENE. Your heart is hot upon a wintry work!

ANTIGONE. I know I please whom most I ought to please. 90

ISMENE. But can you do it? It is impossible!

ANTIGONE. When I can do no more, then I will stop.

ISMENE. But why attempt a hopeless task at all?

ANTIGONE. O stop, or I shall hate you! He will hate
You too, for ever, justly. Let me be, 95
Me and my folly! I will face the danger
That so dismays you, for it cannot be

So dreadful as to die a coward's death.
ISMENE. Then go and do it, if you must. It is
Blind folly—but those who love you love
    you dearly.   100

Exeunt severally.

FIRST ODE

Strophe 1

CHORUS. Welcome, light of the Sun, the
    fairest
Sun that ever has dawned upon
Thebes, the city of seven gates!
At last thou art arisen, great
Orb of shining day, pouring   105
Light across the gleaming water of
    Dirkê.[1]
Thou hast turned into headlong flight,
Galloping faster and faster, the foe who
Bearing a snow-white shield in full
Panoply came from Argos.   110

He had come to destroy us, in Polyneices'
Fierce quarrel. *He* brought them against
    our land;
And like some eagle screaming his rage
From the sky he descended upon us,
With his armour about him, shining like
    snow,   115
    With spear upon spear,
And with plumes that swayed on their
    helmets.

Antistrophe 1

Close he hovered above our houses,
Circling around our seven gates, with
Spears that thirsted to drink our blood.   120
He's gone! gone before ever his jaws
Snapped on our flesh, before he sated
Himself with our blood, before his blaz-
    ing fire-brand
Seized with its fire our city's towers.
Terrible clangour of arms repelled him,   125

*This bronze statue of a "Draped Warrior" is a
beautiful example of classic Greek restraint.*
Courtesy of Wadsworth Antheneum, Hartford, Conn.

Driving him back, for hard it is to
Strive with the sons of a Dragon.[2]

For the arrogant boast of an impious
    man
Zeus[3] hateth exceedingly. So, when he
    saw
This army advancing in swollen flood   130
In the pride of its gilded equipment,

---

1. **Dirkê** (dėr′kĕ), a spring named after Dirce, daughter
of the sun-god. She was a mythical queen of Thebes, of
tragic significance.
2. **Dragon**, the emblem of Thebes.
3. **Zeus** (züs), the most important and powerful god of
the Greeks.

He struck them down from the rampart's
    edge
    With a fiery bolt
In the midst of their shout of "Triumph!"

Strophe 2

Heavily down to the earth did he fall,
    and lie there,   135
He who with torch in his hand and pos-
    sessed with frenzy
    Breathed forth bitterest hate
    Like some fierce tempestuous wind.
      So it fared then with him;
And of the rest, each met his own ter-
    rible doom,   140
Given by the great War-god, our de-
    liverer.

Seven foemen appointed to our seven
    gates[4]
Each fell to a Theban, and Argive arms
Shall grace our Theban temple of Zeus:
Save two, those two of unnatural hate, 145
Two sons of one mother, two sons of one
    King;
They strove for the crown, and shared
    with the sword
Their estate, each slain by his brother.

Antistrophe 2

Yet do we see in our midst, and acclaim
    with gladness,
Victory, glorious Victory, smiling, wel-
    come.   150
    Now, since danger is past,
    Thoughts of war shall pass from our
      minds.
    Come! let all thank the gods,
Dancing before temple and shrine all
    through the night,
Following Thee, Theban Dionysus.[5]   155

CHORUS-LEADER. But here comes Creon, the
    new king of Thebes,

In these new fortunes that the gods have
    given us.
What purpose is he furthering, that he
Has called this gathering of his Coun-
    sellors?

Enter CREON, *attended.*

CREON. My lords: for what concerns the
    state, the gods   160
Who tossed it on the angry surge of strife
Have righted it again; and therefore you
By royal edict I have summoned here,
Chosen from all our number. I know well
How you revered the throne of Laïus;[6] 165
And then, when Oedipus maintained our
    state,
And when he perished, round his sons
    you rallied,
Still firm and steadfast in your loyalty.
Since they have fallen by a double doom
Upon a single day, two brothers each   170
Killing the other with polluted sword,[7]
I now possess the throne and royal
    power
By right of nearest kinship with the
    dead.
    There is no art that teaches us to know
The temper, mind or spirit of any man 175
Until he has been proved by government
And lawgiving. A man who rules a state
And will not ever steer the wisest course,
But is afraid, and says not what he
    thinks,
That man is worthless; and if any holds 180
A friend of more account than his own
    city,
I scorn him; for if I should see destruc-
    tion

---

4. Polyneices led seven chieftains from Argos against the seven gates of Thebes.
5. **Dionysus** (dī'ə nī'səs), the Greek god said to be the son of Zeus and Semele of Thebes. The drama is supposed to have been developed to honor his fall festivals.
6. **Laïus** (lā'əs), the father of Oedipus.
7. Each sword was polluted by the blood of fratricide (brother murder).

Threatening the safety of my citizens,
I would not hold my peace, nor would I count
That man my friend who was my country's foe,   185
Zeus be my witness. For be sure of this:
It is the city that protects us all;
She bears us through the storm; only when she
Rides safe and sound can we make loyal friends.

   This I believe, and thus will I maintain   190
Our city's greatness.—Now, conformably,
Of Oedipus' two sons I have proclaimed
This edict: he who in his country's cause
Fought gloriously and so laid down his life,
Shall be entombed and graced with every rite   195
That men can pay to those who die with honour;
But for his brother, him called Polyneices,
Who came from exile to lay waste his land,
To burn the temples of his native gods,
To drink his kindred blood, and to enslave   200
The rest, I have proclaimed to Thebes that none
Shall give him funeral honours or lament him,
But leave him there unburied, to be devoured
By dogs and birds, mangled most hideously.
Such is my will; never shall I allow   205
The villain to win more honour than the upright;
But any who show love to this our city
In life and death alike shall win my praise.
CHORUS-LEADER. Such is your will, my lord; so you requite
Our city's champion and our city's foe.   210

You, being sovereign, make what laws you will
Both for the dead and those of us who live.
CREON. See then that you defend the law now made.
CHORUS-LEADER. No, lay that burden on some younger men.[8]
CREON. I have appointed guards to watch the body.   215
CHORUS-LEADER. What further charge, then, do you lay on us?
CREON. Not to connive at those that disobey me.
CHORUS-LEADER. None are so foolish as to long for death.
CREON. Death is indeed the price, but love of gain
Has often lured a man to his destruction.   220

Enter a GUARD.

GUARD. My lord: I cannot say that I am come
All out of breath with running. More than once
I stopped and thought and turned round in my path
And started to go back. My mind had much
To say to me. One time it said "You fool!   225
Why do you go to certain punishment?"
Another time "What? Standing still, you wretch?
You'll smart for it, if Creon comes to hear
From someone else." And so I went along
Debating with myself, not swift nor sure.   230
This way, a short road soon becomes a long one.
At last this was the verdict: I must come
And tell you. It may be worse than nothing; still,
I'll tell you. I can suffer nothing more

---

8. The chorus was composed of elderly men. Like Antigone, they are shocked at the outrage to the body; but they are not prepared to oppose Creon's authority.

Large masks such as this helped actors project their tragic or comic characters throughout huge amphitheaters. Fifth century B.C.

No sign of digging; the earth was hard
    and dry
And undisturbed; no wagon had been
    there;   250
He who had done it left no trace at all.
So, when the first day-watchman showed
    it to us,
We were appalled. We could not see the
    body;
It was not buried but was thinly covered
With dust, as if by someone who had
    sought   255
To avoid a curse. Although we looked,
    we saw
No sign that any dog or bird had come
And torn the body. Angry accusations
Flew up between us; each man blamed
    another,
And in the end it would have come to
    blows,   260
For there was none to stop it. Each
    single man
Seemed guilty, yet proclaimed his igno-
    rance
And could not be convicted. We were
    all
Ready to take hot iron in our hands,
To walk through fire,[9] to swear by all the
    gods   265
We had not done it, nor had secret
    knowledge
Of any man who did it or contrived it.
We could not find a clue. Then one man
    spoke:
It made us hang our heads in terror, yet
No one could answer him, nor could we
    see   270
Much profit for ourselves if we should
    do it.
He said "We must report this thing to
    Creon;
We dare not hide it"; and his word pre-
    vailed.

Than what is in my fate. There is my
    comfort!   235
CREON. And what is this that makes you so
    despondent?
GUARD. First for myself: I did not see it
    done,
    I do not know who did it. Plainly then,
    I cannot rightly come to any harm.
CREON. You are a cautious fellow, building
    up   240
    This barricade. You bring unpleasant
    news?
GUARD. I do, and peril makes a man pause
    long.
CREON. O, won't you tell your story and be
    gone?
GUARD. Then, here it is. The body: someone
    has
    Just buried it, and gone away. He
    sprinkled   245
    Dry dust on it, with all the sacred rites.
CREON. What? Buried it? What man has so
    defied me?
GUARD. How can I tell? There was no mark
    of pickaxe,

---

9. According to certain primitive justice an innocent person was supposed to be uninjured after a trial by fire.

I am the unlucky man who drew the prize
When we cast lots, and therefore I am come   275
Unwilling and, for certain, most unwelcome:
Nobody loves the bringer of bad news.
CHORUS-LEADER. My lord, the thought has risen in my mind:
Do we not see in this the hand of God?
CREON. Silence! or you will anger me. You are   280
An old man: must you be a fool as well?
Intolerable, that you suppose the gods
Should have a single thought for this dead body.
What? should they honour him with burial
As one who served them well, when he had come   285
To burn their pillared temples, to destroy
Their treasuries, to devastate their land
And overturn its laws? Or have you noticed
The gods prefer the vile? No, from the first
There was a muttering against my edict,   290
Wagging of heads in secret, restiveness
And discontent with my authority.
I know that some of these perverted others
And bribed them to this act.[10] Of all vile things
Current on earth, none is so vile as money.   295
For money opens wide the city-gates
To ravishers, it drives the citizens
To exile, it perverts the honest mind
To shamefulness, it teaches men to practise
All forms of wickedness and impiety.   300
These criminals who sold themselves for money
Have bought with it their certain punishment;
For, as I reverence the throne of Zeus,

I tell you plainly, and confirm it with
My oath: unless you find, and bring before me,   305
The very author of this burial-rite
Mere death shall not suffice; you shall be hanged
Alive, until you have disclosed the crime,
That for the future you may ply your trade
More cleverly, and learn not every pocket   310
Is safely to be picked. Ill-gotten gains
More often lead to ruin than to safety.
GUARD. May I reply? Or must I turn and go?
CREON. Now, as before, your very voice offends me.
GUARD. Is it your ears that feel it, or your mind?   315
CREON. Why must you probe the seat of our displeasure?[11]
GUARD. The rebel hurts your mind; I but your ears.
CREON. No more of this! You are a babbling fool!
GUARD. If so, I cannot be the one who did it.
CREON. Yes, but you did—selling your life for money!   320
GUARD. It's bad, to judge at random, and judge wrong!
CREON. You judge my judgement as you will—but bring
The man who did it, or you shall proclaim
What punishment is earned by crooked dealings.
GUARD. God grant he may be found! But whether he   325
Be found or not—for this must lie with chance—
You will not see me coming *here* again.

---

10. Creon is obsessed with suspicions about rebellious responses to his edict. He imagines that everyone has been corrupted by bribery.
11. **our** in reference to Creon is the "royal" plural form, affected by kings.

Alive beyond my hope and expectation,
I thank the gods who have delivered me.

Exeunt severally CREON *and* GUARD.

SECOND ODE

Strophe 1

CHORUS. Wonders are many, yet of all   330
  Things is Man the most wonderful.
    He can sail on the stormy sea
      Though the tempest rage, and the
        loud
    Waves roar around, as he makes his
    Path amid the towering surge.   335

  Earth inexhaustible, ageless, he wearies,
      as
  Backwards and forwards, from season
      to season, his
    Ox-team drives along the plough-
      share.

Antistrophe 1

  He can entrap the cheerful birds,
  Setting a snare, and all the wild   340
  Beasts of the earth he has learned to
      catch, and
  Fish that teem in the deep sea, with
  Nets knotted of stout cords; of
  Such inventiveness is man.
  Through his inventions he becomes
      lord   345
  Even of the beasts of the mountain: the
      long-haired
  Horse he subdues to the yoke on his
      neck, and the
  Hill-bred bull, of strength untiring.

Strophe 2

  And speech he has learned, and
      thought
  So swift, and the temper of mind   350
  To dwell within cities, and not to lie
      bare

Amid the keen, biting frosts
Or cower beneath pelting rain;
Full of resource against all that comes
    to him
Is Man. Against Death alone   355
He is left with no defence.
But painful sickness he can cure
    By his own skill.

Antistrophe 2

Surpassing belief, the device and
Cunning that Man has attained,   360
And it bringeth him now to evil, now
    to good.
If he observe Law, and tread
The righteous path God ordained,
Honoured is he; dishonoured, the man
    whose reckless heart
Shall make him join hands with sin: 365
May I not think like him,
Nor may such an impious man
    Dwell in my house.

Enter GUARD, *with* ANTIGONE.

CHORUS-LEADER. What evil spirit is abroad?
    I know
  Her well: Antigone. But how can I   370
  Believe it? Why, O you unlucky
    daughter
  Of an unlucky father, what is this?
  Can it be you, so mad and so defiant,
  So disobedient to a King's decree?
GUARD. Here is the one who did the deed,
    this girl;   375
  We caught her burying him.—But where
    is Creon?
CHORUS-LEADER. He comes, just as you need
    him, from the palace.

Enter CREON, *attended.*

CREON. How? What occasion makes my
    coming timely?
GUARD. Sir, against nothing should a man
    take oath,
  For second thoughts belie him. Under
    your threats   380

That lashed me like a hailstorm, I'd
  have said
I would not quickly have come here
  again;
But joy that comes beyond our dearest
  hope
Surpasses all in magnitude. So I
Return, though I had sworn I never
  would,   385
Bringing this girl detected in the act
Of honouring the body. This time no lot
Was cast; the windfall is my very own.
And so, my lord, do as you please: take
  her
Yourself, examine her, cross-question
  her.   390
I claim the right of free and final quit-
  tance.
CREON. Why do you bring this girl? Where
  was she taken?
GUARD. In burying the body. That is all.
CREON. You know what you are saying? Do
  you mean it?
GUARD. I saw her giving burial to the corpse   395
  You had forbidden. Is that plain and
  clear?
CREON. How did you see and take her so
  red-handed?
GUARD. It was like this. When we had
  reached the place,
  Those dreadful threats of yours upon
  our heads,
  We swept aside each grain of dust that
  hid   400
  The clammy body, leaving it quite bare,
  And sat down on a hill, to the windward
  side
  That so we might avoid the smell of it.
  We kept sharp look-out; each man
  roundly cursed
  His neighbour, if he should neglect his
  duty.   405
So the time passed, until the blazing sun
Reached his mid-course and burned us
  with his heat.
Then, suddenly, a whirlwind came from
  heaven

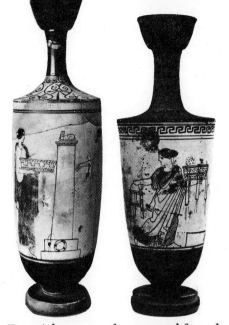

*From Athens come these two red-figured vases.
Left, a woman brings offerings to a tomb;
right, mourners come.*

And raised a storm of dust, which
  blotted out
The earth and sky; the air was filled with
  sand   410
And leaves ripped from the trees. We
  closed our eyes
And bore this visitation as we could.
At last it ended; then we saw the girl.
She raised a bitter cry, as will a bird
Returning to its nest and finding it   415
Despoiled, a cradle empty of its young.
So, when she saw the body bare, she
  raised
A cry of anguish mixed with impreca-
  tions
Laid upon those who did it; then at once
Brought handfuls of dry dust, and raised
  aloft   420
A shapely vase of bronze, and three
  times poured
The funeral libation for the dead.[12]

___

12. This is part of the prescribed burial rituals.

We rushed upon her swiftly, seized our
    prey,
And charged her both with this offence
    and that.
She faced us calmly; she did not disown   425
The double crime. How glad I was!—
    and yet
How sorry too; it is a painful thing
To bring a friend to ruin. Still, for me,
My own escape comes before every-
    thing.
CREON. You there, who keep your eyes
    fixed on the ground,   430
Do you admit this, or do you deny it?
ANTIGONE. No, I do not deny it. I admit it.
CREON [to GUARD]. Then you may go; go
    where you like. You have
Been fully cleared of that grave accusa-
    tion.

Exit GUARD.

You: tell me briefly—I want no long
    speech: 435
Did you not know that this had been
    forbidden?
ANTIGONE. Of course I knew. There was a
    proclamation.
CREON. And so you dared to disobey the
    law?
ANTIGONE. It was not Zeus who published
    this decree,
Nor have the Powers who rule among
    the dead   440
Imposed such laws as this upon man-
    kind;
Nor could I think that a decree of
    yours—
A man—could override the laws of
    Heaven
Unwritten and unchanging. Not of today
Or yesterday is their authority;   445
They are eternal; no man saw their birth.
Was I to stand before the gods' tribunal
For disobeying *them*, because I feared
A man? I knew that I should have to die,
Even without your edict; if I die   450

Before my time, why then, I count it
    gain;
To one who lives as I do, ringed about
With countless miseries, why, death is
    welcome.
For me to meet this doom is little grief;
But when my mother's son lay dead, had
    I   455
Neglected him and left him there un-
    buried,
That would have caused me grief; this
    causes none.
And if you think it folly, then perhaps
I am accused of folly by the fool.
CHORUS-LEADER. The daughter shows her
    father's temper—fierce,   460
Defiant; she will not yield to any storm.
CREON. But it is those that are most ob-
    stinate
Suffer the greatest fall; the hardest iron,
Most fiercely tempered in the fire, that is
Most often snapped and splintered. I
    have seen   465
The wildest horses tamed, and only by
The tiny bit. There is no room for pride
In one who is a slave! This girl already
Had fully learned the art of insolence
When she transgressed the laws that I
    established;   470
And now to that she adds a second out-
    rage—
To boast of what she did, and laugh at
    us.
Now she would be the man, not I, if she
Defeated me and did not pay for it.
But though she be my niece, or closer
    still   475
Than all our family, she shall not escape
The direst penalty; no, nor shall her
    sister:
I judge her guilty too; she played her
    part
In burying the body. Summon her.
Just now I saw her raving and distracted   480
Within the palace. So it often is:
Those who plan crime in secret are be-
    trayed

Despite themselves; they show it in their
  faces.
But this is worst of all: to be convicted
And then to glorify the crime as virtue.   485

Exeunt some GUARDS.

ANTIGONE. Would you do more than simply
  take and kill me?
CREON. I will have nothing more, and noth-
  ing less.
ANTIGONE. Then why delay? To me no
  word of yours
Is pleasing—Heaven forbid it should be
  so!—
And everything in me displeases you.   490
Yet what could I have done to win re-
  nown
More glorious than giving burial
To my own brother? These men too
  would say it,
Except that terror cows them into
  silence.
A king has many a privilege: the
  greatest,   495
That he can say and do all that he will.
CREON. You are the only one in Thebes to
  think it!
ANTIGONE. These think as I do—but they
  dare not speak.
CREON. Have you no shame, not to conform
  with others?
ANTIGONE. To reverence a brother is no
  shame.   500
CREON. Was he no brother, he[13] who died
  for Thebes?
ANTIGONE. One mother and one father gave
  them birth.
CREON. Honouring the traitor, you dishonour *him.*
ANTIGONE. He will not bear this testimony,
  in death.
CREON. Yes! if the traitor fare the same as
  he.   505
ANTIGONE. It was a brother, not a slave who
  died!
CREON. He died attacking Thebes; the
  other saved us.

ANTIGONE. Even so, the god of Death demands these rites.
CREON. The good demand more honour
  than the wicked.
ANTIGONE. Who knows? In death they may
  be reconciled.   510
CREON. Death does not make an enemy a
  friend!
ANTIGONE. Even so, I give both love, not
  share their hatred.
CREON. Down then to Hell! Love there, if
  love you must.
While I am living, no woman shall have
  rule.

Enter GUARDS, *with* ISMENE.

CHORUS-LEADER. See where Ismene leaves
  the palace-gate,   515
In tears shed for her sister. On her brow
A cloud of grief has blotted out her sun,
And breaks in rain upon her comeliness.
CREON. You, lurking like a serpent in my
  house,
Drinking my life-blood unawares; nor
  did   520
I know that I was cherishing two fiends,
Subverters of my throne: come, tell me
  this:
Do you confess you shared this burial,
Or will you swear you had no knowledge
  of it?
ISMENE. I did it too, if she allows my claim;   525
I share the burden of this heavy charge.
ANTIGONE. No! Justice will not suffer that;
  for you
Refused, and I gave you no part in it.
ISMENE. But in your stormy voyage I am
  glad
To share the danger, travelling at your
  side.   530
ANTIGONE. Whose was the deed the god of
  Death knows well;
I love not those who love in words alone.
ISMENE. My sister, do not scorn me, nor
  refuse

---

13. Creon now refers to Eteocles.

That I may die with you, honouring the dead.

ANTIGONE. You shall not die with me, nor claim as yours 535
What you rejected. My death will be enough.

ISMENE. What life is left to me if I lose you?

ANTIGONE. Ask Creon! It was Creon that you cared for.

ISMENE. O why taunt me, when it does not help you?

ANTIGONE. If I do taunt you, it is to my pain. 540

ISMENE. Can I not help you, even at this late hour?

ANTIGONE. Save your own life. I grudge not your escape.

ISMENE. Alas! Can I not join you in your fate?

ANTIGONE. You cannot: you chose life, and I chose death.

ISMENE. But not without the warning that I gave you! 545

ANTIGONE. Some thought *you* wise; the dead commended me.

ISMENE. But my offence has been as great as yours.

ANTIGONE. Be comforted; you live, but I have given
My life already, in service of the dead.

CREON. Of these two girls, one has been driven frantic, 550
The other has been frantic since her birth.

ISMENE. Not so, my lord; but when disaster comes
The reason that one has cannot stand firm.

CREON. Yours did not, when you chose to partner crime![14]

ISMENE. But what is life to me, without my sister? 555

CREON. Say not "my sister": sister you have none.

ISMENE. But she is Haemon's bride—and can you kill her?

CREON. Is she the only woman he can bed with?

ISMENE. The only one so joined in love with him.

CREON. I hate a son to have an evil wife. 560

ANTIGONE. O my dear Haemon! How your father wrongs you!

CREON. I hear too much of you and of your marriage.

ISMENE. He is your son; how can you take her from him?

CREON. It is not I, but Death, that stops this wedding.

CHORUS-LEADER. It is determined, then, that she must die? 565

CREON. For you, and me, determined. [*To the* GUARDS.] Take them in
At once; no more delay. Henceforward let
Them stay at home, like women, not roam abroad.
Even the bold, you know, will seek escape
When they see death at last standing beside them. 570

Exeunt ANTIGONE *and* ISMENE *into the palace, guarded.* CREON *remains.*

THIRD ODE

Strophe 1

CHORUS. Thrice happy are they who have never known disaster!
Once a house is shaken of Heaven, disaster
Never leaves it, from generation to generation.
'Tis even as the swelling sea,
When the roaring wind from Thrace[15] 575
Drives blustering over the water and makes it black:

---

14. To become a partner in Antigone's crime.

15. **Thrace** (thrās), the ancient region bordering the Black Sea roughly from the mouth of the Danube south to northeastern Greece.

It bears up from below
A thick, dark cloud of mud,
And groaning cliffs repel the smack of
    wind and angry breakers.

Antistrophe 1

I see, in the house of our kings, how
    ancient sorrows   580
Rise again; disaster is linked with di-
    saster.
Woe again must each generation inherit.
    Some god
Besets them, nor will give release.
On the last of royal blood
There gleamed a shimmering light in the
    house of Oedipus.   585
    But Death comes once again
With blood-stained axe, and hews
The sapling down; and Frenzy lends her
    aid, and vengeful Madness.

Strophe 2

Thy power, Zeus, is almighty! No
Mortal insolence can oppose Thee!   590
Sleep, which conquers all else, cannot
    overcome Thee,
    Nor can the never-wearied
Years, but throughout
Time thou art strong and ageless,
    In thy own Olympus[16]   595
Ruling in radiant splendour.
For today, and in all past time,
And through all time to come,
This is the law: that in Man's
Life every success brings with it some
    disaster.   600

Antistrophe 2

Hope springs high, and to many a man
Hope brings comfort and consolation;
Yet she is to some nothing but fond
    illusion:
Swiftly they come to ruin,
As when a man   605

Treads unawares on hot fire.
    For it was a wise man
First made that ancient saying:
To the man whom God will ruin
One day shall evil seem   610
Good, in his twisted judgement
He comes in a short time to fell di-
    saster.

CHORUS-LEADER. See, here comes Haemon,
    last-born of your children,
    Grieving, it may be, for Antigone.
CREON. Soon we shall know, better than
    seers can tell us.   615

Enter HAEMON.

My son:
You have not come in rage against your
    father
Because your bride must die? Or are you
    still
My loyal son, whatever I may do?
HAEMON. Father, I am your son; may your
    wise judgement   620
Rule me, and may I always follow it.
No marriage shall be thought a greater
    prize
For me to win than your good govern-
    ment.
CREON. So may you ever be resolved, my
    son,
In all things to be guided by your
    father.   625
It is for this men pray that they may
    have
Obedient children, that they may re-
    quite
Their father's enemy with enmity
And honour whom their father loves to
    honour.
One who begets unprofitable children   630
Makes trouble for himself, and gives his
    foes
Nothing but laughter. Therefore do not
    let

---

16. **Olympus** (ō lim′pəs), a lofty mountain in northeast
Greece, the legendary home of Zeus and the gods.

Your pleasure in a woman overcome
Your judgement, knowing this, that if
    you have
An evil wife to share your house, you'll
    find   635
Cold comfort in your bed. What other
    wound
Can cut so deep as treachery at home?
So, think this girl your enemy; spit on
    her,
And let her find her husband down in
    Hell!
She is the only one that I have found   640
In all the city disobedient.
I will not make myself a liar. I
Have caught her; I will kill her. Let her
    sing
Her hymns to Sacred Kinship! If I breed
Rebellion in the house, then it is certain   645
There'll be no lack of rebels out of doors.
No man can rule a city uprightly
Who is not just in ruling his own house-
    hold.
Never will I approve of one who breaks
And violates the law, or would dictate   650
To those who rule. Lawful authority
Must be obeyed in all things, great or
    small,
Just and unjust alike; and such a man
Would win my confidence both in
    command
And as a subject; standing at my side   655
In the storm of battle he would hold his
    ground,
Not leave me unprotected. But there is
No greater curse than disobedience.
This brings destruction on a city, this
Drives men from hearth and home, this
    brings about   660
A sudden panic in the battle-front.
Where all goes well, obedience is the
    cause.
So we must vindicate the law; we must
    not be
Defeated by a woman. Better far
Be overthrown, if need be, by a man   665
Than to be called the victim of a woman.

CHORUS-LEADER. Unless the years have
    stolen away our wits,
All you say is said most prudently.
HAEMON. Father, it is the gods who give
    us wisdom;
No gift of theirs more precious. I can-
    not say   670
That you are wrong, nor would I ever
    learn
That impudence, although perhaps
    another
Might fairly say it. But it falls to me,
Being your son, to note what others say,
Or do, or censure in you, for your glance   675
Intimidates the common citizen;
He will not say, before your face, what
    might
Displease you; I can listen freely, how
The city mourns this girl. "No other
    woman,"
So they are saying, "so undeservedly   680
Has been condemned for such a glori-
    ous deed.
When her own brother had been slain
    in battle
She would not let his body lie unburied
To be devoured by dogs or birds of
    prey.
Is not this worthy of a crown of gold?"—   685
Such is the muttering that spreads
    everywhere.
    Father, no greater treasure can I have
Than your prosperity; no son can find
A greater prize than his own father's
    fame,
No father than his son's. Therefore let
    not   690
This single thought possess you: only
    what
You say is right, and nothing else. The
    man
Who thinks that he alone is wise, that
    he
Is best in speech or counsel, such a man
Brought to the proof is found but empti-
    ness.   695
There's no disgrace, even if one is wise,

In learning more, and knowing when to
    yield.
See how the trees that grow beside a
    torrent
Preserve their branches, if they bend;
    the others,
Those that resist, are torn out, root and
    branch.   700
So too the captain of a ship; let him
Refuse to shorten sail, despite the
    storm—
He'll end his voyage bottom uppermost.
No, let your anger cool, and be per-
    suaded.
If one who is still young can speak with
    sense,   705
Then I would say that he does best who
    has
Most understanding; second best, the
    man
Who profits from the wisdom of another.
CHORUS-LEADER. My lord, he has not spoken
    foolishly;
You each can learn some wisdom from
    the other.   710
CREON. What? men of our age go to school
    again
And take a lesson from a very boy?
HAEMON. If it is worth the taking. I am
    young,
But think what should be done, not of
    my age.
CREON. What should be done! To honour
    disobedience!   715
HAEMON. I would not have you honour
    criminals.
CREON. And is this girl then not a criminal?
HAEMON. The city with a single voice
    denies it.
CREON. Must I give orders then by their
    permission?
HAEMON. If youth is folly, this is child-
    ishness.   720
CREON. Am I to rule for them, not for my-
    self?
HAEMON. That is not government, but
    tyranny.

CREON. The king is lord and master of his
    city.
HAEMON. Then you had better rule a desert
    island!
CREON. This man, it seems, is the ally of the
    woman.   725
HAEMON. If you're the woman, yes! I fight
    for you.
CREON. Villain! Do you oppose your
    father's will?
HAEMON. Only because you are opposing
    Justice.
CREON. When I regard my own preroga-
    tive?
HAEMON. Opposing God's, you disregard
    your own.   730
CREON. Scoundrel, so to surrender to a
    woman!
HAEMON. But not to anything that brings
    me shame.
CREON. Your every word is in defence of
    her.
HAEMON. And me, and you—and of the
    gods below.
CREON. You shall not marry her this side
    the grave!   735
HAEMON. So, she must die—and will not
    die alone.
CREON. What? Threaten me? Are you so
    insolent?
HAEMON. It is no threat, if I reply to folly.
CREON. The fool would teach me sense!
    You'll pay for it.
HAEMON. I'd call you mad, if you were not
    my father.   740
CREON. I'll hear no chatter from a woman's
    plaything.
HAEMON. Would you have all the talk, and
    hear no answer?
CREON. So?
    I swear that you shall not bandy
    words
With me and not repent it! Bring her
    out,   745
That loathsome creature! I will have her
    killed

At once, before her bridegroom's very
    eyes.
HAEMON. How can you think it? I will not
    see that,
Nor shall you ever see my face again.
Those friends of yours who can must
    tolerate   750
Your raging madness; I will not endure
    it.

Exit HAEMON.

CHORUS-LEADER. How angrily he went, my
    lord! The young,
When they are greatly hurt, grow des-
    perate.
CREON. Then let his pride and folly do their
    worst!
He shall not save these women from
    their doom.   755
CHORUS-LEADER. Is it your purpose then to
    kill them both?
CREON. Not her who had no part in it.—I
    thank you.
CHORUS-LEADER. And for the other: how is
    she to die?
CREON. I'll find a cave in some deserted
    spot,
And there I will imprison her alive   760
With so much food—no more—as will
    avert
Pollution and a curse upon the city.[17]
There let her pray to Death, the only
    god
Whom she reveres, to rescue her from
    death,
Or learn at last, though it be late, that it   765
Is wanton folly to respect the dead.

CREON *remains on the stage.*

FOURTH ODE

Strophe

CHORUS. Invincible, implacable Love, O
    Love, that makes havoc of all wealth;
    That peacefully keeps his night-watch

On tender cheek of a maiden: 770
The Sea is no barrier, nor
Mountainous waste to Love's flight; for
No one can escape Love's domination,
Man, no, nor immortal god. Love's
Prey is possessed by madness.   775

Antistrophe

By Love, the mind even of the just
Is bent awry; he becomes unjust.
So here: it is Love that stirred up
This quarrel of son with father.
The kindling light of Love in the soft   780
Eye of a bride conquers, for
Love sits on his throne, one of the great
    Powers;
Nought else can prevail against
Invincible Aphrodite.[18]

Enter ANTIGONE, *under guard. (From
this point up to the end of the fifth ode
everything is sung, except the two
speeches in blank verse.)*

CHORUS. I too, when I see this sight, cannot
    stay   785
Within bounds; I cannot keep back my
    tears
Which rise like a flood. For behold, they
    bring
Antigone here, on the journey that all
Must make, to the silence of Hades.

COMMOS

Strophe 1

ANTIGONE. Behold me, O lords of my native
    city!   790
Now do I make my last journey;

---

17. Creon has announced that anyone burying Polyneices would be put to death by public stoning (line 36),
but now he feels that the direct execution of Antigone
might bring a curse on the city.
18. **Aphrodite** (af′rə dī′tē), (in Latin, **Venus**) the Greek
goddess of beauty and love.

Now do I see the last
Sun that ever I shall behold.
Never another! Death, that lulls
All to sleep, takes me while I live   795
Down to the grim shore of Acheron.[19]
    No wedding day can be
    Mine, no hymn will be raised to
      honour
    Marriage of mine; for I
Go to espouse the bridegroom, Death.   800
CHORUS. Yet a glorious death, and rich in
    fame
Is yours; you go to the silent tomb
Not smitten with wasting sickness, nor
Repaying a debt to the sharp-edged
    sword;
But alone among mortals you go to the
    home   805
Of the dead while yet you are living.

Antistrophe 1

ANTIGONE. They tell of how cruelly she did
    perish,
Niobe, Queen in Thebes;[20]
For, as ivy grows on a tree,
Strangling it, so she slowly turned to   810
Stone on a Phrygian mountain-top.[21]
Now the rain-storms wear her away—
    So does the story run—and
Snow clings to her always:
Tears fall from her weeping eyes for   815
Ever and ever. Like to hers, the
Cruel death that now awaits me.
CHORUS. But she was a goddess, and born
    of the gods;
We are but mortals, of mortals born.
For a mortal to share in the doom of a
    god,   820
That brings her renown while yet she
    lives,
And a glory that long will outlive her.

Strophe 2

ANTIGONE. Alas, they laugh! O by the gods
    of Thebes, my native city,

Mock me, if you must, when I am gone,
    not to my face!
O Thebes my city, O you lordly men of
    Thebes!   825
O water of Dirkê's stream! Holy soil
    where our chariots run!
You, you do I call upon; you, you shall
    testify
How all unwept of friends, by what
    harsh decree,
They send me to the cavern that shall be
    my everlasting grave.
Ah, cruel doom! to be banished from
    earth, nor welcomed   830
Among the dead, set apart, for ever!
CHORUS. Too bold, too reckless, you af-
    fronted
Justice. Now that awful power
Takes terrible vengeance, O my child.
For some old sin you make atonement.   835

Antistrophe 2

ANTIGONE. My father's sin! There is the
    source of all my anguish.
Harsh fate that befell my father! Harsh
    fate that has held
Fast in its grip the whole renowned race
    of Labdacus![22]
O the blind madness of my father's and
    my mother's marriage!
O cursed union of a son with his own
    mother!   840
From such as those I draw my own un-
    happy life;

---

19. **Acheron** (ak′ə ron′), a river in Hades, the land of the dead.
20. **Niobe** (nī′ō bē′), a legendary queen of Thebes who angered the gods Apollo and Artemis by pointing out that their mother, Leto, had only two children while she, Niobe, had twelve. The offended gods brought about the early death of all of her children and prevented their burial. Niobe lamented their fate, fasting and weeping, until Zeus turned her to stone.
21. **Phrygian** (frij′ē ən), of Phrygia, Niobe's native country in western Asia Minor.
22. **Labdacus** (lab′də kəs), a king of Thebes, father of Laïus, and ancestor of Oedipus.

This third century B.C. relief, "Menander Contemplating Comic Masks," helps us imagine the actor's role by taking us behind the scenes of classic drama.

And now I go to dwell with them, un-
    wedded and accursed.
O brother, through an evil marriage[23]
    you were slain; and I
Live—but your dead hand destroys me.
CHORUS. Such loyalty is a holy thing.   845
    Yet none that holds authority
    Can brook disobedience, O my child.
    Your self-willed pride has been your
    ruin.

Epode

ANTIGONE. Unwept, unwedded and unbe-
    friended,
    Alone, pitilessly used,   850
    Now they drag me to death.
    Never again, O thou Sun in the heavens,
    May I look on thy holy radiance!
    Such is my fate, and no one laments it;
    No friend is here to mourn me.   855

CREON. Enough of this! If tears and lamen-
    tations
Could stave off death they would go on
    for ever.
Take her away at once, and wall her up
Inside a cavern, as I have commanded,
And leave her there, alone, in solitude.   860

Her home shall be her tomb; there she
    may live
Or die, as she may choose: my hands are
    clean;[24]
But she shall live no more among the
    living.
ANTIGONE. O grave, my bridal-chamber,
    everlasting
Prison within a rock: now I must go   865
To join my own, those many who have
    died
And whom Persephone[25] has welcomed
    home;
And now to me, the last of all, so young,
Death comes, so cruelly. And yet I go
In the sure hope that you will welcome
    me,   870
Father, and you, my mother; you, my
    brother.
For when you died it was my hands that
    washed
And dressed you, laid you in your
    graves, and poured
The last libations. Now, because to you,
Polyneices, I have given burial,   875
To me they give a recompense like this!
Yet what I did, the wise will all approve.
For had I lost a son, or lost a husband,
Never would I have ventured such an
    act
Against the city's will. And wherefore
    so?   880
My husband dead, I might have found
    another;
Another son from him, if I had lost
A son. But since my mother and my
    father
Have both gone to the grave, there can
    be none
Henceforth that I can ever call my
    brother.   885

23. **evil marriage**, a reference to Polyneices' marriage to a princess of Argo, which led to his alliance with the Argive chieftains whom he led against Thebes.
24. See note 17.
25. **Persephone** (pər sef′ə nē), queen of the underworld.

It was for this I paid you such an honour,
Dear Polyneices, and in Creon's eyes
Thus wantonly and gravely have of-
    fended.
So with rude hands he drags me to my
    death.
No chanted wedding-hymn, no bridal-
    joy,   890
But like an outcast, and without a friend,
No tender care of children can be mine;
They take me to the cavernous home of
    death.
What ordinance of the gods have I trans-
    gressed?
Why should I look to Heaven any more 895
For help, or seek an ally among men?
If this is what the gods approve, why
    then,
When I am dead I shall discern my
    fault;
If theirs the sin, may they endure a
    doom
No worse than mine, so wantonly in-
    flicted!   900
CHORUS. Still from the same quarter the
    same wild winds
  Blow fiercely, and shake her stubborn
    soul.
CREON. And therefore, for this, these men
    shall have cause,
  Bitter cause, to lament their tardiness.
CHORUS. I fear these words bring us closer
    yet   905
    To the verge of death.
CREON. I have nothing to say, no comfort
    to give:
  The sentence is passed, and the end is
    here.
ANTIGONE. O city of Thebes where my
    fathers dwelt,
  O gods of our race,   910
Now at last their hands are upon me!
You princes of Thebes, O look upon me,
The last that remain of a line of kings!
How savagely impious men use me,
For keeping a law that is holy.   915

Exit ANTIGONE, *under guard.* CREON *remains.*

FIFTH ODE

Strophe 1

CHORUS. There was one in days of old who
    was imprisoned
  In a chamber like a grave, within a
    tower:
  Fair Danaë, who in darkness was held,
    and never saw the pure day-
    light.[26]
  Yet she too, O my child, was of an an-
    cient line,
  Entrusted with divine seed that had
    come in shower of gold.   920
  Mysterious, overmastering, is the power
    of Fate.
  From this, nor wealth nor force of arms
    Nor strong encircling city-walls
    Nor storm-tossed ship can give de-
    liverance.

Antistrophe 1

Close bondage was ordained by Dio-
    nysus   925
For one who in a frenzy had denied
His godhead: in a cavern Lycurgus,[27]
    for his sin, was imprisoned.
In such wise did his madness bear a bit-
    ter fruit,
Which withered in a dungeon. So he
    learned it was a god
He had ventured in his blindness to re-
    vile and taunt.   930
    The sacred dances he had tried

---

26. **Danaë** (da′na ē), was imprisoned by her father, king
of Argos, to keep her from suitors, since an oracle had
proclaimed he would be killed by his grandson. But Zeus
visited her in the form of a golden rain, and she gave
birth to the hero Perseus who did kill the king.
27. **Lycurgus** (lī kėr′gəs), a king of Thrace had doubted
Dionysus' divinity when his rites were newly introduced
from the East. He was driven mad and imprisoned by
Zeus.

To quell, and end the Bacchic rite,[28]
Offending all the tuneful Muses.

Strophe 2

There is a town by the rocks where a
    sea meets another sea,
Two black rocks by the Bosphorus,[29]   935
    near the Thracian coast,
Salmŷdessus;[30] and there a wife had
    been spurned,
    Held close in bitter constraint.
    Then upon both her children
A blinding wound fell from her cruel
    rival:
With shuttle in hand she smote the open
    eyes with sharp   940
And blood-stained point, and brought
    to Phineus'
Two sons a darkness that cried for ven-
    geance.

Antistrophe 2

In bitter grief and despair they be-
    wailed their unhappy lot,
Children born to a mother whose mar-
    riage proved accursed.
Yet she came of a race of ancient kings,   945
    Her sire the offspring of gods.
    Reared in a distant country,
    Among her fierce, northern father's
    tempests,
She went, a Boread,[31] swift as horses,
    over the lofty
Mountains. Yet not even she was   950
Safe against the long-lived Fates, my
    daughter.

Enter TEIRESIAS, *led by a boy.*

TEIRESIAS. My lords, I share my journey
    with this boy
Whose eyes must see for both; for so
    the blind
Must move abroad, with one to guide
    their steps.
CREON. Why, what is this? Why are *you*
    here, Teiresias?   955

TEIRESIAS. I will explain; you will do well
    to listen.
CREON. Have I not always followed your
    good counsel?
TEIRESIAS. You have; therefore we have
    been guided well.
CREON. I have had much experience of
    your wisdom.
TEIRESIAS. Then think: once more you
    tread the razor's edge.   960
CREON. You make me tremble! What is it
    you mean?
TEIRESIAS. What divination has revealed to
    me,
    That I will tell you. To my ancient seat
Of augury I went, where all the birds
Foregather. There I sat, and heard a
    clamour   965
Strange and unnatural—birds scream-
    ing in rage.
I knew that they were tearing at each
    other
With murderous claws: the beating of
    their wings
Meant nothing less than that; and I was
    frightened.
I made a blazing fire upon the altar   970
And offered sacrifice: it would not burn;
The melting fat oozed out upon the
    embers
And smoked and bubbled; high into the
    air
The bladder spirted gall, and from the
    bones
The fatty meat slid off and left them
    bare.   975

---

28. **Bacchic** (bak′ik), rites honoring Dionysus (Bacchus).
29. **Bosphorus** (bos′fər əs), eighteen-mile strait between
Turkey in Asia and Turkey in Europe connecting the Sea
of Marmara with the Black Sea.
30. **Salmŷdessus** (sal′mi des′əs), country in Thrace ruled
by **Phineus** (fin′ē əs), who abandoned his first wife to
marry a savage and vindictive second who blinded her
stepsons and imprisoned their mother.
31. **Boread** (bôr′ē əd), a spirit of the north wind, Boreas,
father of the rejected queen.

Such omens, baffling, indistinct, I learned
From him who guides me, as I am guide to others.
Sickness has come upon us, and the cause
Is you: our altars and our sacred hearths
Are all polluted by the dogs and birds   980
That have been gorging on the fallen body
Of Polyneices. Therefore heaven will not
Accept from us our prayers, no fire will burn
Our offerings, nor · will birds give out clear sounds,
For they are glutted with the blood of men.   985
Be warned, my son. No man alive is free
From error, but the wise and prudent man
When he has fallen into evil courses
Does not persist, but tries to find amendment.
It is the stubborn man who is the fool.   990
Yield to the dead, forbear to strike the fallen;
To slay the slain, is that a deed of valour?
Your good is what I seek; and that instruction
Is best that comes from wisdom, and brings profit.
CREON. Sir, all of you, like bowmen at a target,   995
Let fly your shafts at me. Now they have turned
Even diviners on me! By that tribe
I am bought and sold and stowed away on board.
Go, make your profits, drive your trade
In Lydian silver or in Indian gold,[32]   1000
But him you shall not bury in a tomb,
No, not though Zeus' own eagles eat the corpse
And bear the carrion to their master's throne:
Not even so, for fear of that defilement,

Will I permit his burial—for well I know   1005
That mortal man cannot defile the gods.
But, old Teiresias, even the cleverest men
Fall shamefully when for a little money
They use fair words to mask their villainy.
TEIRESIAS. Does any man reflect, does any know . . .   1010
CREON. Know *what?* Why do you preach at me like this?
TEIRESIAS. How much the greatest blessing is good counsel?
CREON. As much, I think, as folly is his plague.
TEIRESIAS. Yet with this plague you are yourself infected.
CREON. I will not bandy words with any prophet.   1015
TEIRESIAS. And yet you say my prophecies are dishonest!
CREON. Prophets have always been too fond of gold.
TEIRESIAS. And tyrants, of the shameful use of power.
CREON. You know it is your King of whom you speak?
TEIRESIAS. King of the land I saved from mortal danger.   1020
CREON. A clever prophet—but an evil one.
TEIRESIAS. You'll rouse me to awaken my dark secret.
CREON. Awaken it, but do not speak for money.
TEIRESIAS. And do you think that I am come to *that?*
CREON. You shall not buy and sell *my* policy.   1025
TEIRESIAS. Then I will tell you this: you will not live
Through many circuits of the racing sun
Before you give a child of your own body

---

32. Silver and gold from the foreign countries of **Lydia** (lid′ē ə), in southwest Asia Minor and India. Creon suggests that Teiresias may have been paid to be disloyal.

29

To make amends for murder, death for
    death;
Because you have thrust down within
    the earth   1030
One who should walk upon it, and have
    lodged
A living soul dishonourably in a tomb;
And impiously have kept upon the earth
Unburied and unblest one who belongs
Neither to you nor to the upper gods   1035
But to the gods below, who are de-
    spoiled
By you. Therefore the gods arouse
    against you
Their sure avengers; they lie in your path
Even now to trap you and to make you
    pay
Their price.—Now think: do I say *this*
    for money?   1040
Not many hours will pass before your
    house
Rings loud with lamentation, men and
    women.
Hatred for you is moving in those cities
Whose mangled sons had funeral-rites
    from dogs[33]
Or from some bird of prey, whose wings
    have carried   1045
The taint of dead men's flesh to their
    own homes,
Polluting hearth and altar.
These are the arrows that I launch at
    you,
Because you anger me. I shall not miss
My aim, and you shall not escape their
    smart.   1050
Boy, lead me home again, that he may
    vent
His rage upon some younger man, and
    learn
To moderate his violent tongue, and
    find
More understanding than he has today.

Exit TEIRESIAS.

CHORUS-LEADER. And so, my lord, he leaves
    us, with a threat   1055

Of doom. I have lived long, but I am
    sure
Of this: no single prophecy that he
Has made to Thebes has gone without
    fulfilment.
CREON. I know it too, and I am terrified.
    To yield is very hard, but to resist   1060
And meet disaster, that is harder still.
CHORUS-LEADER. Creon, this is no time for
    wrong decision.
CREON. What shall I do? Advise me; I will
    listen.
CHORUS-LEADER. Release Antigone from
    her rock-hewn dungeon,
And lay the unburied body in a tomb.   1065
CREON. Is this your counsel? You would
    have me yield?
CHORUS-LEADER. I would, and quickly. The
    destroying hand
Of Heaven is quick to punish human
    error.
CREON. How hard it is! And yet one can-
    not fight
Against Necessity.—I will give way.   1070
CHORUS-LEADER. Go then and do it; leave it
    not to others.
CREON. Just as I am I go. — You men-at-
    arms,
You here, and those within: away at once
Up to the hill, and take your implements.
Now that my resolution is reversed   1075
I who imprisoned her will set her free.—
    I fear it may be wisest to observe
Throughout one's life the laws that are
    established.
Exit CREON.

SIXTH ODE

Strophe 1

CHORUS. Thou Spirit whose names are
    many, Dionysus,

---

33. The warriors who fell with Polyneices were also
left unburied.

Born to Zeus the loud-thunderer,   1080
Joy of thy Theban mother-nymph,
Lover of famous Italy:
King art thou in the crowded shrine
Where Demeter has her abode, O
Bacchus! Here is thy mother's home, 1085
Here is thine, by the smooth Is-
    mênus' flood, here where the
    savage
Dragon's teeth had offspring.[34]

Antistrophe 1

Thou art seen by the nymphs amid the
    smoky torchlight,
   Where, upon Parnassus' height,[35]   1090
   They hold revels to honour Thee
   Close to the spring of Castaly.[36]
   Thou art come from the ivy-clad
   Slopes of Asian hills, and vineyards
   Hanging thick with clustering grapes. 1095
   Mystic voices chant: "O
   Bacchus! O Bacchus!" in
   The roads and ways of Thebê.

Strophe 2

Here is thy chosen home,
   In Thebes above all lands,   1100
   With thy mother, bride of Zeus.
   Wherefore, since a pollution holds
   All our people fast in its grip,
O come with swift healing across the
    wall of high Parnassus,
   Or over the rough Eurîpus.[37]   1105

Antistrophe 2

Stars that move, breathing flame,
   Honour Thee as they dance;
   Voices cry to Thee in the night.
   Son begotten of Zeus, appear!
   Come, Lord, with thy company,   1110
Thy own nymphs, who with wild, night-
    long dances praise Thee,
   Bountiful Dionysus!

Enter a MESSENGER.

MESSENGER. You noblemen of Thebes, how
    insecure
   Is human fortune! Chance will over-
    throw
   The great, and raise the lowly; nothing's
    firm,   1115
   Either for confidence or for despair;
   No one can prophesy what lies in store.
   An hour ago, how much I envied Creon!
   He had saved Thebes, we had accorded
    him
   The sovereign power; he ruled our land 1120
   Supported by a noble prince, his son.
   Now all is lost, and he who forfeits joy
   Forfeits his life; he is a breathing corpse.
   Heap treasures in your palace, if you
    will,
   And wear the pomp of royalty; but if 1125
   You have no happiness, I would not give
   A straw for all of it, compared with joy.
CHORUS-LEADER. What is this weight of
    heavy news you bring?
MESSENGER. Death! — and the blood-guilt
    rests upon the living.
CHORUS-LEADER. Death? Who is dead? And
    who has killed him? Tell me.   1130
MESSENGER. Haemon is dead, and by no
    stranger's hand.
CHORUS-LEADER. But by his father's? Or was
    it his own?
MESSENGER. His own—inflamed with anger
    at his father.
CHORUS-LEADER. Yours was no idle proph-
    ecy, Teiresias!

---

34. **Dionysus** (Bacchus, Iacchus, etc.) See footnote 5. It is hoped that Bacchus can deliver Thebes from its tragedy. **Italy** may refer to Icaria in Attica where early festivals for Bacchus were held. **Demeter** (di mē′tər), (in Latin, **Ceres**) was the goddess of agriculture. Dionysus' worship was connected with that of Demeter at Eleusis. **Ismênus** (is mē′nəs), a river near Thebes. **Dragon's teeth**, according to ancient myth, were sowed to produce the first men of Thebes.
35. **Parnassus** (pär nas′əs), a mountain in central Greece on which is Delphi, the shrine Dionysus shared with Apollo.
36. **Castaly** (kas′tə lē), a spring on Mt. Parnassus.
37. **Eurîpus** (yủ rī′pəs), a strait between Boeotia, the region in northeast Greece in which Thebes was the chief city, and the island Euboea.

Reminiscent of the great battle at the gates of Thebes is this ancient relief sculpture of horsemen.

MESSENGER. That is my news. What next, remains with you.   1135

CHORUS-LEADER. But look! There is his wife, Eurydice;

She is coming from the palace. Has she heard

About her son, or is she here by chance?

Enter EURYDICE.

EURYDICE. You citizens of Thebes, I overheard

When I was standing at the gates, for I   1140

Had come to make an offering at the shrine

Of Pallas,[38] and my hand was on the bar

That holds the gate, to draw it; then there fell

Upon my ears a voice that spoke of death.

My terror took away my strength; I fell   1145

Into my servants' arms and swooned away.

But tell it me once more; I can endure

To listen; I am no stranger to bad news.

MESSENGER. Dear lady, I was there, and I will tell

The truth; I will not keep it back from you.   1150

Why should I gloss it over? You would hear

From someone else, and I should seem a liar.

The truth is always best.

        I went with Creon

Up to the hill where Polyneices' body

Still lay, unpitied, torn by animals.   1155

We gave it holy washing, and we prayed

To Hecate and Pluto[39] that they would

Restrain their anger and be merciful.

And then we cut some branches, and we burned

What little had been left, and built a mound   1160

Over his ashes of his native soil.

Then, to the cavern, to the home of death,

The bridal-chamber with its bed of stone.

One of us heard a cry of lamentation

From that unhallowed place; he went to Creon   1165

And told him. On the wind, as he came near,

Cries of despair were borne. He groaned aloud

In anguish: "O, and are my fears come true?

Of all the journeys I have made, am I

To find this one the most calamitous?   1170

It is my son's voice greets me. Hurry, men;

Run to the place, and when you reach the tomb

Creep in between the gaping stones and see

If it be Haemon there, or if the gods

Are cheating me." Upon this desperate order   1175

We ran and looked. Within the furthest chamber

We saw her hanging, dead; strips from her dress

Had served her for a rope. Haemon we saw

---

38. **Pallas**, or Pallas Athene (pal′əs ə thē′nə), a Greek goddess, guardian of cities.
39. **Hecate** (hek′ə tē), a goddess of the underworld, and **Pluto** (plü′tō), chief god of the dead.

Embracing her dead body and lamenting

His loss, his father's deed, and her destruction.   1180

When Creon saw him he cried out in anguish,

Went in, and called to him: "My son! my son!

O why? What have you done? What brought you here?

What is this madness? O come out, my son,

Come, I implore you!" Haemon glared at him   1185

With anger in his eyes, spat in his face,

Said nothing, drew his double-hilted sword,

But missed his aim as Creon leapt aside.

Then in remorse he leaned upon the blade

And drove it half its length into his body.   1190

While yet the life was in him he embraced

The girl with failing arms, and breathing hard

Poured out his life-blood on to her white face.

So side by side they lie, and both are dead.

Not in this world but in the world below 1195

He wins his bride, and shows to all mankind

That folly is the worst of human evils.

Exit EURYDICE.

CHORUS-LEADER. What can we think of this? The Queen is gone

Without one word of good or evil omen.

MESSENGER. What can it mean? But yet we may sustain   1200

The hope that she would not display her grief

In public, but will rouse the sad lament

For Haemon's death among her serving-women

Inside the palace. She has true discretion,

And she would never do what is unseemly.   1205

CHORUS-LEADER. I cannot say, but wild lament would be

Less ominous than this unnatural silence.

MESSENGER. It *is* unnatural; there may be danger.

I'll follow her; it may be she is hiding

Some secret purpose in her passionate heart.   1210

Exit MESSENGER, *into the palace.*

CHORUS. Look, Creon draws near, and the burden he bears

Gives witness to his misdeeds; the cause Lies only in his blind error.

Enter CREON *and the* GUARDS, *with the body of* HAEMON.

Strophe 1

CREON. Alas!

The wrongs I have done by ill-counselling!   1215

Cruel and fraught with death.

You behold, men of Thebes,

The slayer, the slain; a father, a son.

My own stubborn ways have borne bitter fruit.

My son! Dead, my son! So soon torn from me,   1220

So young, so young!

The fault only mine, not yours, O my son.

CHORUS-LEADER. Too late, too late you see the path of wisdom.

CREON. Alas!

A bitter lesson I have learned! The god   1225

Coming with all his weight has borne down on me.

And smitten me with all his cruelty;

My joy overturned, trampled beneath his feet.

What suffering besets the whole race of men!

Enter MESSENGER, *from the palace.*

MESSENGER. My master, when you came you brought a burden 1230
Of sorrow with you; now, within your house,
A second store of misery confronts you.
CREON. Another sorrow come to crown my sorrow?
MESSENGER. The Queen, true mother of her son, is dead;
In grief she drove a blade into her heart. 1235

Antistrophe 1

CREON. Alas!
Thou grim hand of death, greedy and unappeased,
Why so implacable?
Voice of doom, you who bring
Such dire news of grief, O, can it be true? 1240
What have you said, my son? O, you have slain the slain!
Tell me, can it be true? Is death crowning death?
My wife! my wife!
My son dead, and now my wife taken too!

EURYDICE's *body is discovered.*

CHORUS-LEADER. But raise your eyes: there is her lifeless body. 1245
CREON. Alas!
Here is a sorrow that redoubles sorrow.
Where will it end? What else can Fate hold in store?
While yet I clasp my dead son in my arms
Before me there lies another struck by death. 1250
Alas cruel doom! the mother's and the son's.
MESSENGER. She took a sharp-edged knife, stood by the altar,

And made lament for Megareus[40] who was killed
Of old, and next for Haemon. Then at last,
Invoking evil upon you, the slayer 1255
Of both her sons, she closed her eyes in death.

Strophe 2

CREON. A curse, a thing of terror! O, is there none
Will unsheathe a sword to end all my woes
With one deadly thrust? My grief crushes me.
MESSENGER. She cursed you for the guilt of Haemon's death 1260
And of the other son who died before.
CREON. What did she do? How did she end her life?
MESSENGER. She heard my bitter story; then she put
A dagger to her heart and drove it home.
CREON. The guilt falls on me alone; none but I 1265
Have slain her; no other shares in the sin.
'Twas I dealt the blow. This is the truth, my friends.
Away, take me away, far from the sight of men!
My life now is death. Lead me away from here.
CHORUS-LEADER. That would be well, if anything is well. 1270
Briefest is best when such disaster comes.

Antistrophe 2

CREON. O come, best of all the days I can see,

---

40. **Megareus** (mə gar'ē əs), elder brother of Haemon, who sacrificed himself to save Thebes during the Argive siege to fulfill a prophecy that a man of pure Theban stock—descended from the warriors who sprang from the dragon's teeth—must die.

Warriors in combat, black-figured amphora.

The last day of all, the day that brings
    death.
O come quickly! Come, thou night with
    no dawn!
CHORUS-LEADER. That's for the future; here
    and now are duties   1275
That fall on those to whom they are al-
    lotted.
CREON. I prayed for death; I wish for noth-
    ing else.
CHORUS-LEADER. Then pray no more; from
    suffering that has been
Decreed no man will ever find escape.
CREON. Lead me away, a rash, a misguided
    man,   1280
Whose blindness has killed a wife and a
    son.
O where can I look? What strength can I
    find?
On me has fallen a doom greater than I
    can bear.

Exeunt CREON *and* GUARDS *into the pal-
    ace.*

CHORUS. Of happiness, far the greatest part
Is wisdom, and reverence towards the
    gods.   1285
Proud words of the arrogant man, in the
    end,
Meet punishment, great as his pride was
    great,
Till at last he is schooled in wisdom.

I

HOW INSECURE IS HUMAN FORTUNE

Antigone vividly presents the conflict of two
strong-willed people, each acting according to a
personal sense of duty and conscience, each seeing
the situation from a different point of view. There
is no escape from the dilemma because both
staunchly maintain their positions—until it is too
late. The result of the conflict is the destruction of
both of the antagonists: Antigone through death,
Creon through the loss of his son and wife and
the crushing of his stubborn pride. The only note
of hope is the humility and self-knowledge Creon
gains at the end of the play.

II
IMPLICATIONS

1. In a great piece of literature the thoughts and
questions of the author and the problems of the
characters continue to have deep meaning through
the ages. Consider the following statements from
the play. Has time made them "antiquated" or do
they still have meaning for us today? (The character who speaks is named in parentheses.)

    a. But why attempt a hopeless task at all?
        (Ismene)

    b. . . . love of gain
        Has often lured a man to his destruction.
        (Creon)

    c. Nor could I think that a decree of yours—
        A man—could override the laws of Heaven
        Unwritten and unchanging. (Antigone)

    d. No man can rule a city uprightly
        Who is not just in ruling his own household.
        (Creon)

    e. There's no disgrace, even if one is wise,
        In learning more, and knowing when to yield.
        (Haemon)

    f. . . . how insecure
        Is human fortune! Chance will overthrow
        The great, and raise the lowly. . . .
        (Messenger)

2. In real life it is often hard to know people's
true motives for their actions. But in a work of
literature the author can show us the minds and
hearts of the characters. Which of the following
motives or qualities could belong to Antigone and
which to Creon?

courage	loyalty to family	selfishness
duty	religious belief	stubborness
pride	patriotism	revenge
logic	power	anger

After you have made lists of motives and qualities
for the two characters, answer these questions.

    a. Does your examination of Creon's and Anti-
gone's motives indicate that either one is all right
or all wrong? Is there some right on each side?

b. Which motives do you consider the better ones?

3. The statements that follow should be considered thoughtfully. On the basis of the drama you have just read, would you agree or disagree?

a. The playwright shows Creon as a typical villain and gives him no "saving virtues."

b. Sophocles presents Antigone as both unfeeling and aggressive. Support your opinion with lines from the play.

c. The Chorus, representing the opinion of the townspeople, sides sometimes with Creon and sometimes with Antigone.

d. The conflict of wills in this play results from the conflicting motives of the characters. Use one of these pairs to demonstrate your opinion.

Antigone and Ismene
Creon and Haemon
Creon and Teiresias

III
TECHNIQUES

Any piece of writing contains two elements: "content"—that is, what the writing is *about*—and "form"—the *way* in which the author has shaped the content and set it down in words. Throughout this book, in sections labeled "Techniques," you will be asked to formulate ideas about content and form. Two aspects of technique will be emphasized for each theme. In this opening section, CONFLICT OF WILLS, special attention is given to *Identification* and *Diction*.

Identification

Reading has been called a form of daydreaming. Of course, it is more than that; but it is an escape from our dull, average routine into a more exciting, heightened life. Reading offers conflict, adventure, romance, and an examination of problems and values. The escape we find in literature comes about through a process of *identification*. One part of us knows that the characters in a book are fictitious, not "real"; but another part of us assumes the role of the hero. We identify with the characters, and suffer or rejoice as they do. By thus actually *experiencing* the lives of the characters we can plumb new depths of awareness of others. We also arrive at new understandings about ourselves.

Authors plan their stories around this literary identification. They carefully choose which characters in the story will be the major ones. They set up a very personal relationship between reader and character. Sometimes authors allow the audience to identify with more than a single person in the story. They may also shift the reader's sympathy from one figure to another; and with the shift of sympathy may come a shift in reader identification.

1. As you read the play did you identify with Antigone? With Creon? With both?

2. Is there any shift in your sympathy as the play progresses?

3. Try to imagine what the play would have been like if Sophocles had chosen either Haemon or Ismene as his major character.

Diction

Words are the essential material with which writers work. The words which they choose can be precise or blurred, sharp or dull. In great literature the words must be exactly right for the particular emotion, story, tone, and idea of the work. It is obvious, for example, that in the translation of *Antigone*, American slang would have been jarring. Literary critics use the term *diction* to refer to an author's choice of language.

What choices are open? The author must ask: Shall my vocabulary here be abstract or concrete? Should the language of this poem (or play or novel) be formal or colloquial? How colloquial? Can I include slang? Should the speech be plain, literal, direct? Or should it be rich, and filled with figures of speech? Should it be modern or archaic?

In looking at *Antigone*, of course, we must remember that we are dealing with a translation, not with the original Greek. The translator, Professor Kitto, is one of England's leading classical scholars. We may assume that the English he chooses gives us a good indication of the original Greek.

Below are five quotations from the play. From each pair of adjectives that follow, choose the word that best describes each quotation.

plain — flowery
conversational — oratorical
abstract — concrete

a. Know *what?* Why do you preach at me like this?

b. For, as ivy grows on a tree,
Strangling it, so she slowly turned to
Stone on a Phrygian mountain-top.

c. . . . Lawful authority
Must be obeyed in all things, great or small,
Just and unjust alike.

d. Thou spirit whose names are many, Dionysus,
Born to Zeus the loud-thunderer,
Joy of thy Theban mother-nymph,
Lover of famous Italy:
King art thou in the crowded shrine
Where Demeter has her abode . . .

e. Then think: once more you tread the razor's
edge.

IV

WORDS

A. Frequently, the apparent meaning of a word group can lead us to a reasonable guess about the meanings of individual unfamiliar words. Thus, if we meet with a sentence about "tornadoes, hurricanes, and monsoons," we may safely conclude that a *monsoon* is a violent storm, without knowing the exact details.

Examine the first speech of Antigone (lines 1–10), and notice that the context—surrounding words—would lead us to good guesses about the meanings of *calamity* and *proclaim* if they were unfamiliar. By using context clues followed by a dictionary check, determine the meaning of the following words in *Antigone*.

prerogative (line 59)	*requite* (line 209)
pretext (line 81)	*connive* (line 217)
sated (line 122)	*belie* (line 380)
edict (line 163)	*imprecations* (line 418)

B. Words can have many meanings and carry a wide range of suggestions which change from use to use. Consider the way Antigone uses the word *ordained* in connection with Creon's order in line 20. Compare the usage of this word in line 363 where it relates to God's guidance of mortals. What does the word now imply about Creon's decisions?

1. What does Antigone mean by calling Creon "brave"? (line 8)

2. What is the special meaning of *pure* in "this *pure* crime"? (line 72)

3. What does a "double doom" mean? (line 169)

4. Explain "graced with every rite." (line 195)

C. It is the function of the poet, dramatist, or other writer to illumine thoughts, to make them vivid and striking, through the use of comparisons. To be effective, these comparisons must point out likenesses in things which are in essence unlike. Comparisons made for literary effect are of two kinds: *simile* and *metaphor*. (See also p. 105.)

A *simile* is a figure of speech which, using the words *like* or *as*, states a resemblance between things essentially unlike: To illustrate, in line 115, the chorus sings of Polyneices' men in armor "shining like snow." Note that this line fulfills the two requirements of simile: it uses *like* in stating the comparison; and it compares unlike things—armor and snow—which are alike in that both shine in the sunlight.

A *metaphor* is a figure of speech which, omitting *like* or *as*, implies a likeness between things essentially unlike.

Find some of the similes and metaphors in *Antigone*.

D. Good writing is likely to involve an alteration—a playing back and forth—between general or abstract wording on one hand, and specific or concrete wording on the other.

It often happens that specific, concrete wording creates a vivid image. Note the effect in line 54 of "knotted a rope." Notice your own reaction in lines 121–122 to the words, "before ever his jaws snapped on our flesh."

Where else in *Antigone* do you find similarly striking effects produced by specific detail expressed in concrete wording?

E. Notice in line 105 that the sun is referred to as a "great orb of shining day." The word *orb* rarely occurs, except in the poetry of an earlier period. The dictionary gives it the following usage label: *archaic*. It is bookish, learned, and unusual in ordinary English.

Perhaps you may feel that some of the following are like *orb* in being bookish:

entombed (line 22)	*beseeching* (line 65)
unwept (line 27)	*panoply* (line 110)

Make your own list of bookish words. Look up these words in the dictionary to see whether the dictionary assigns a special usage status to each word that you have felt to be bookish.

No one is suggesting that you use bookish words in your speech; rather, it is hoped that you will become better aware of such words in your reading.

COLUMNS OF THE PARTHENON

THE GOLDEN AGE OF GREECE

For a brief period of about a hundred years, the mountainous peninsula of Greece was the scene of the first great period of Western civilization. This was a Golden Age which had roots extending far back in time. The small city-state of Athens was the center of Greek achievement in philosophy, science, government, and the arts. In the span of a few generations, Athens was the home of the philosophers Socrates, Plato, and Aristotle; the government leaders Themistocles, Pericles, and Solon; the sculptors Phydias and Praxiteles; the historians Herodotus and Xenophon; and the architects who built the Parthenon.

Legends of the gods and goddesses, and of their half-human descendants, the demigods, play a prominent part in Greek art. Hermes, lower right, known in Roman mythology as Mercury, was the herald of the gods. He holds the infant Dionysus, son of Zeus.

Zeus and Poseidon (scholars are not certain which one the bronze at left represents) were, respectively, the ruler of the gods and the god of the sea.

HERMES
(*marble*)
Praxiteles

BRONZE HEAD OF ZEUS *or* POSEIDON

39

BRONZE YOUTH FROM ANTICYTHERA

One of the Greek goals was a sane mind in a sound body. The athlete was honored as an ideal of bodily grace and beauty, and was a favorite subject for sculptors. Great athletic contests held at Olympia and Delphi had a semireligious function. So important were these contests that even in time of war a month's truce was called to let Greeks from all parts of the peninsula participate. The prizes were decorated pottery vases or ornamental bronze jars such as the water jar pictured here.

Delphi, on the slopes of Mount Parnassus, was the site of the oldest and most sacred shrine of Greek religion. Here the world-famous oracle of Apollo made prophetic pronouncements. Questions that deeply disturbed the Greeks were referred to the sacred oracle of Apollo. The mysterious prophecies of the oracle were interpreted by the priests of the shrine so loosely and poetically that whatever occurred could be said to have been part of the prophecy.

The hero Hercules, at right, was deified as a son of Zeus, indicating the honor awarded strength.

RUINS OF A SMALL TEMPLE
AT DELPHI

BRONZE WATER JAR
*Prize from the games in honor
of the goddess Hera*

HERCULES
AS AN ARCHER

Athena Nike, the victorious Athena, is represented in this figure found on the island of Samothrace. Swirling, gallant, elaborately detailed, the statue is usually attributed to a period later than the more restrained Golden Age. Nevertheless, it reflects the dignity and power of that great age.

THE WINGED VICTORY
OF SAMOTHRACE

GIRL WITH PIGEONS
*Grave relief
from the Island of Paros*

From the Island of Paros comes the earlier, quieter marble of a young girl with pigeons. This memorial relief has rare sweetness and sadness. In these contrasting works, we see something of the range of the creative Greek spirit.

VIEW OF THE ACROPOLIS

THE RUINS OF THE ACROPOLIS
The Porch of the Maidens at center

During the height of the Athenian civilization, the top of the hill above the city was splendid with noble civic buildings and crowned with the most famous building of all times, the Parthenon, temple of Athena, patron goddess of the city. Even in ruins the majesty of the Acropolis is inspiring and continues to influence Western art and thought.

During foreign occupations, the Parthenon had been converted first to a Christian church and then to a Turkish mosque, but until 1687 it remained largely intact. In the fall of 1687, while being used as a powder storehouse, it was blown up by the Venetians who overthrew the Turks.

43

THE ERECHTEUM
Porch of the Maidens

Part of the Acropolis is the temple
to Erechtheus, ancestral god
of Attica. The renowned porch above
is supported by pillars in the form
of female figures called caryatids,
after the priestesses of the temple
of Diana at Caryae in Laconia.

MARBLE HORSES
Frieze from a sarcophagus in Lycia

From ancient Greece to the museums
of the world have gone innumerable
pieces of sculpture such as
this handsome relief of prancing
horses, which was once part
of a splendid tomb in Lycia.

SOCRATES

Self-taught and eccentric, stonecutter and soldier, Socrates goaded his contemporaries to examine their actions and their values. He left us an enduring image of the rational mind.

General and scholar, Pericles was the leader of Athens at the pinnacle of its power. During his forty years as head of the government, this great leader established an ideal city-state in which artists and philosophers flourished.

The vase is a fine example of the artistry of the period.

WARRIORS
Black figured vase

PERICLES

45

GIOVANNI GUARESCHI

Giovanni Guareschi[1] (1908–1968) was one of Italy's leading cartoonists and humorists, who found his inspiration in the village life of his country. His best-known stories are about a continuing battle between the village priest, Don Camillo, and the Communist mayor, Peppone. During World War II, Guareschi spent three years in a concentration camp as a prisoner of war. He wrote, "When I returned to Italy I found that many things were changed, especially the Italians, and I spent a good deal of time trying to figure out whether they had changed for the better or for the worse. In the end I discovered that they had not changed at all and then I became so depressed that I shut myself in my house. Shortly thereafter a new magazine called *Candido* was established in Milan[2] and, in working for it, I found myself up to my eyes in politics although I was then, and still am, an independent. Nevertheless the magazine values my contributions very highly— perhaps because I am editor in chief. The people in these stories are true to life and the stories are so true that more than once, after I had written a story, the thing actually happened and one read it in the news. In fact the truth surpasses the imagination. I once wrote a story about the Communist Peppone who was annoyed during a political meeting by an airplane which threw down pamphlets of the opposition. Peppone took up a machine gun but he could not bring himself to fire on the plane. When I wrote this I said to myself, 'This is too fantastic.' Some months later at Spilimberg not only did the Communists fire on an airplane that distributed anti-Communist pamphlets but they shot it down. I have nothing more to say about *The Little World of Don Camillo*. You can't expect that after a poor fellow has written a book he should also understand it?"

The Little World of Don Camillo

The little world of Don Camillo is to be found somewhere in the valley of the Po River. It is almost any village on that stretch of plain in Northern Italy. There, between the Po and the Apennines,[1] the climate is always the same. The landscape never changes and, in country like this, you can stop along any road for a moment and look at a farmhouse sitting in the midst of maize and hemp—and immediately a story is born.

Why do I tell you this instead of getting on with my story. Because I want you to understand that, in the Little World between the river and the mountains, many things can happen that cannot happen anywhere else. Here, the deep, eternal breathing of the river freshens the air, for both the living and the dead, and even the dogs, have souls. If you keep this in mind, you will easily come to know the village priest, Don Camillo, and his adversary Peppone, the Communist Mayor. You will not be surprised that Christ watches the goings-on from a big cross in the village church and not

1. **Giovanni Guareschi** (jō vä′nē gwə res′kē).
2. **Milan** (mi lan′), a large city in northeastern Italy.

1. **Apennines** (ap′ə nīnz), a mountain range in central Italy.

infrequently talks, and that one man beats the other over the head, but fairly—that is, without hatred—and that in the end the two enemies find they agree about essentials.

And one final word of explanation before I begin my story. If there is a priest anywhere who feels offended by my treatment of Don Camillo, he is welcome to break the biggest candle available over my head. And if there is a Communist who feels offended by Peppone, he is welcome to break a hammer and sickle[2] on my back. But if there is anyone who is offended by the conversations of Christ, I can't help it; for the one who speaks in this story is not Christ but my Christ—that is, the voice of my conscience.

Rivalry

A big shot from the city was going to visit the village, and people were coming from all the surrounding cells. Therefore, Peppone decreed that the ceremony was to be held in the big square. He had a large platform decorated with red erected and got one of those trucks with four great loudspeakers and all the electric mechanism inside it for amplifying the voice.

And so, on the afternoon of that Sunday, the public square was crammed with people and so also was the church square, which happened to be next to it. Don Camillo shut all the doors and withdrew into the sacristy, so as to avoid seeing or hearing anything which would put him in a temper. He was actually dozing when

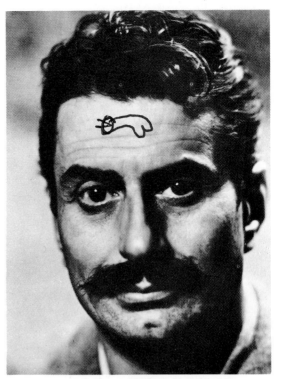

Giovanni Guareschi, Italian humorist, author of The Little World of Don Camillo, *and creator of the accompanying drawings.*

a voice like the wrath of God roused him with a jerk as it bellowed: "COMRADES! ..."

It was as though the walls had melted away.

Don Camillo went to work off his indignation at the high altar. "They must have aimed one of their accursed loudspeakers directly at the church," he exclaimed. "It is nothing short of violation of domicile."

"What can you do about it, Don Camillo? It is progress," replied Christ.

After a few generalizations, the voice got down to business and, since the speaker was an extremist, he made no bones about it. "*We must remain within the law and we shall do so! Even at the cost of taking up our weapons and using the firing squad on all the enemies of the people. ...*"

---

2. **hammer and sickle,** the Communist emblem.

47

Don Camillo was pawing the ground like a restive horse. "Lord, only listen to him!"

"I hear him, Don Camillo. I hear him only too well."

"Lord, why don't You drop a thunderbolt on all that rabble?"

"Don Camillo, let us remain within the law. If your method of driving the truth into the head of one who is in error is to shoot him down, what was the use of My crucifixion?"

Don Camillo shrugged. "You are right, of course. We can do nothing but wait for them to crucify us too."

Christ smiled. "If instead of speaking first and then thinking over what you have said, you thought first and did the speaking afterwards, you might not have to regret the foolish things you say."

Don Camillo bowed his head.

"... *as for those who, hiding in the shadow of the Crucifix, attempt with the poison of their ambiguous words to spread dissension among the masses of the workers....*" The voice of the loudspeaker, borne on the wind, filled the church and shook the bright-colored glass in the Gothic windows. Don Camillo grabbed a heavy bronze candlestick and brandishing it like a club, made for the church door.

"Don Camillo, stop! You will not leave the church until everyone has gone away."

"Oh, very well," replied Don Camillo, putting the candlestick back on the altar. "I obey." He marched up and down the church and finally stopped in front of Christ. "But in here I can do as I please?"

"Naturally, Don Camillo. Here you are in your own house and free to do exactly as you wish. Short of climbing up to a window and firing at the people below."

Three minutes later, Don Camillo, leaping and bounding cheerfully in the bell chamber of the church tower, was performing the most infernal carillon that had ever been heard in the village.

The orator was forced to interrupt his speech and turned to the local authorities who were standing with him on the platform. "He must be stopped!" the big shot cried indignantly.

Peppone agreed gravely, nodding his head. "He must indeed," he replied, "and there are just two ways of stopping him. One is to explode a mine under the church tower and the other is to bombard it with heavy artillery."

The orator told him to stop talking nonsense. Surely it was easy enough to break in the door of the tower and climb the stairs.

"Well," said Peppone calmly, "you go up by ladders from landing to landing. Look, comrade, do you see those projections just by the big window of the belfry? They are the steps that the bellringer has removed as he went up. By closing the trap door of the top landing, he is cut off from the world."

"We might try firing at the windows of the tower!" suggested Smilzo.

"Certainly," agreed Peppone, "but we would have to knock him out with the first shot, otherwise he'd begin firing and then there might be trouble."

The bells stopped ringing for a moment, and the orator resumed his speech; all went well so long as he was careful to say nothing of which Don Camillo disapproved. Otherwise, Don Camillo immediately began a counterargument with his bells. In the end, the speech was merely pathetic and patriotic and was therefore respected by the threatening bells.

That evening, Peppone met Don Camillo. 'Watch out, Don Camillo. This baiting could bring you to a bad end."

"There is no baiting involved," replied Don Camillo calmly. "You blow your trumpets and we ring our bells. That, comrade, is democracy. If on the other hand, only one person is allowed to perform, that is a dictatorship."

Peppone held his peace, but one morning Don Camillo got up to find a merry-go-round, a swing, three shooting galleries, a ferris wheel, and an indefinite number of other booths set up, within exactly one foot of the line that divided the public square from the church square.

The owners of the "amusement park" showed him their permits, duly signed by the Mayor, and Don Camillo retired without comment to the rectory. That evening all hell broke loose in the form of barrel organs, loudspeakers, gunfire, shouting and singing, bells, whistling, screaming and bellowing.

Don Camillo went to protest to Christ. "This shows a lack of respect for the house of God."

"Is there anything that is immoral or scandalous?" asked Christ.

"No—merry-go-rounds, swings, little motor cars—chiefly children's amusements."

"Well then, it is simply democracy."

"But this infernal din?" protested Don Camillo.

"The din is democracy too, provided it remains within the law. Outside Church territory, the Mayor is in command, my son."

One side of the rectory adjoined the square, and exactly underneath one of its windows a strange apparatus had been erected. This immediately aroused Don Camillo's curiosity. It was a small column about three feet high, topped by a kind of stuffed mushroom covered with leather. Behind it was another column, taller and more slender, which had a large dial with numbers from 1 to 1000. A blow was struck at the mushroom, and the dial recorded its force. Don Camillo, squinting through the cracks of the shutters, began to enjoy himself.

By eleven o'clock in the evening, the highest number recorded was 750 and that stood to the credit of Badile, the Gretti's cowman, who had fists like sacks of potatoes. Then suddenly Comrade Peppone made his appearance, surrounded by his satellites. All the people came running to watch, crying, "Go on, Peppone, whack it!" Peppone removed his jacket, rolled up his sleeves and took his stand opposite the machine, measuring the distance with his clenched fist. There was total silence, and even Don Camillo felt his heart hammering.

Peppone's fist sailed through the air and struck the mushroom.

"Nine hundred and fifty," yelled the owner of the machine. "I've seen only one other man get that score and he was a longshoreman in

Genoa."[3] The crowd howled enthusiastically.

Peppone put on his coat again, raised his head and looked up at the shuttered window where Don Camillo was hiding. "To whom it may concern," he remarked loudly, "I might say that a blow that registers nine hundred and fifty is no joke."

Everyone looked up at the rectory window and laughed. Don Camillo went to bed with his legs shaking under him. The next evening he was there again, peeking from behind his window and waiting feverishly for the clock to strike eleven. Once again, Peppone arrived with his staff, took off his coat, rolled up his sleeves and aimed a mighty blow at the mushroom.

"Nine hundred and fifty-one!" howled the crowd. And once again they looked up at Don Camillo's window and snickered. Peppone also looked up.

"To whom it may concern," he remarked loudly, "I might say that a blow that registers nine hundred and fifty-one is no joke!"

Don Camillo went to bed that night with a temperature.

Next day, he went and knelt before Christ. "Lord," he sighed, "I am being dragged over the precipice!"

"Be strong and resist, Don Camillo!"

That evening, Don Camillo went to his peep-hole in the window as though he were on his way to the scaffold. The story of Peppone's feat had spread like wildfire, and the whole countryside had come to see the performance. When Peppone appeared there was an audible whisper of "Here he is!" Peppone looked up, jeering, took off his coat, raised his fist and there was silence.

"Nine hundred and fifty-two!"

Don Camillo, when he saw a million eyes fixed on his window, lost the light of reason and hurled himself out of the room.

"To whom . . ." Peppone did not have time to finish; Don Camillo already stood before him. The crowd bellowed and then was suddenly silent.

Don Camillo threw out his chest, took a firm stance, threw away his hat and crossed him-

self. Then he raised his formidable fist and struck hard.

"One thousand!" yelled the crowd.

"To whom it may concern, I might say that a blow that registers one thousand is no joke," remarked Don Camillo.

Peppone had grown rather pale, and his satellites were glancing at him doubtfully, hesitating between resentment and disappointment. Other bystanders were chuckling delightedly. Peppone looked Don Camillo straight in the eye and took off his coat again. He stepped in front of the machine and raised his fist.

"Lord!" whispered Don Camillo hastily.

Peppone's fist sailed through the air.

"One thousand," bawled the crowd and Peppone's bodyguard rejoiced.

"At one thousand all blows are formidable," observed Smilzo. "I think we'll leave it at that."

Peppone went triumphantly in one direction while Don Camillo walked off triumphantly in the other.

"Lord," said Don Camillo when he knelt before the crucifix. "I thank you. I was scared to death."

"That you wouldn't make a thousand?"

"No, that that pig-headed fool wouldn't make it too. I would have had it on my conscience."

"I knew it, and it was lucky that I came to your help," replied Christ, smiling. "Moreover, Peppone, as soon as he saw you, nearly died for

_____

3. **Genoa** (jen'ō ə), a seaport southwest of Milan.

fear you wouldn't reach nine hundred and fifty-two."

"Possibly!" muttered Don Camillo, who now and then liked to appear skeptical.

I
CONFLICT AND COMEDY

Though one is comedy and one is tragedy, the conflicts in *Antigone* and *Don Camillo* are similar. Like Creon, Peppone gives his highest allegiance to the State; like Antigone, Don Camillo gives his allegiance to an older tradition. Sophocles' drama ends in catastrophe and death; Guareschi, with his background as a cartoonist, distorts and exaggerates until his story bubbles over with laughter.

II
IMPLICATIONS

Explain why you agree or disagree with the following statements.

1. Peppone and Don Camillo are basically alike in temperament and character.

2. The story shows that it is possible to fight in public an individual that you respect in private.

3. Conflict is intensified when people try to prove themselves right.

4. It is not easy to see that an opponent's point of view has any validity.

III
TECHNIQUES

Identification

1. What characteristics of Don Camillo tend to make the reader identify with him?

2. Are there points in the story in which you identify with Peppone?

3. How do the dialogues with Christ make you *more* or *less* sympathetic with Don Camillo?

Diction

The previous selections in this book have been serious in tone. But the reader of "Rivalry" knows from the opening words: "A big shot from the city . . ." that this is to be a comic or light-hearted story. From the list that follows, select the adjectives that best describe the kind of language Guareschi uses. (Assume that the translation is a fair reflection of the original Italian.) Then find examples in the story to support your choices.

1. Slangy
2. Visually precise
3. Exaggerated
4. Colloquial
5. Archaic
6. Delicate
7. Simple, straightforward

LUIGI PIRANDELLO

Luigi Pirandello[1] (1867–1936), who won the Nobel Prize in 1934,
distinguished himself in three areas of literature: the short story,
the novel, and the drama. At nineteen he left his country home in Sicily for Rome
and stayed there five years. But in 1891 he moved to Bonn, Germany,[2] where he took
a degree in philosophy. Until 1923 he taught in a girls' high school in Rome,
writing part time. Starting with verse in 1894, he was persuaded to try his hand
at fiction. His first novel was published in 1901; this was followed by a series
of short stories. Most of his characters come from the Italian lower-middle class.
In 1912 a dramatist urged him to try his hand at converting one of his short stories
into a one-act play. This attempt was so successful that he proceeded to write
a large number of plays with tremendous enthusiasm. At first his dramas were criticized
for being too "cerebral" and not showing life as it really is. But gradually the impact
of Pirandello's philosophy trickled through. He said of his writing in 1920,
"I think that life is a very sad piece of buffoonery; because we have in ourselves,
without being able to know why, wherefore and whence, the need to deceive ourselves
constantly by creating a reality (one for each and never the same for all),
which from time to time is discovered to be vain and illusory."

The Jar

translated by Arthur and Henrie Mayne

The olive crop was a bumper one that year: the trees had flowered luxuriantly the year before, and, though there had been a long spell of misty weather at the time, the fruit had set well. Lollo Zirafa had a fine plantation on his farm at Primosole.[1] Reckoning that the five old jars of glazed earthenware which he had in his wine cellar would not suffice to hold all the oil of that harvest, he had placed an order well beforehand at Santo Stefano di Camastra, where they are made. His new jar was to be of greater capacity—breast-high and pot-bellied; it would be the mother superior to the little community of five other jars.

I need scarcely say that Don Lollo Zirafa had had a dispute with the potter concerning this jar. It would indeed be hard to name anyone with whom he had not picked a quarrel; for every trifle—be it merely a stone that had fallen from his boundary wall, or a handful of straw—he would shout out to the servants to saddle his mule, so that he could hurry to the town and file a suit. He had half ruined himself, because of the large sums he had had to spend on court fees and lawyers' bills, bringing actions against one person after another, which always ended in his having to pay the costs of both sides. People said that his legal adviser grew so tired of seeing him appear two or three times a week that he tried to reduce the frequency of his visits by making him a present of a volume

---

---

1. **Luigi Pirandello** (lwē′jē′ pir′ən del′ō).
2. **Bonn** (bon), in West Germany, is the site of a well-known university.

---

1. **Lollo Zirafa** (lō′lō zer′ä fä). **Primosole** (prim′ō sō′ lä).

which looked like a prayer book; it contained the judicial code—the idea being that he should take the trouble to see for himself what the rights and wrongs of the case were before hurrying to bring a suit.

Previously, when anyone had a difference with him, they would try to make him lose his temper by shouting out: "Saddle the mule!" but now they changed it to: "Go and look up your pocket code!" Don Lollo would reply: "That I will and I'll break the lot of you, you swine!"

In course of time, the new jar, for which he had paid the goodly sum of four florins,[2] duly arrived; until room could be found for it in the wine cellar, it was lodged in the crushing-shed[3] for a few days. Never had there been a finer jar. It was quite distressing to see it lodged in that foul den, which reeked of stale grape juice and had that musty smell of places deprived of light and air.

It was now two days since the harvesting of the olives had begun, and Don Lollo was almost beside himself, having to supervise not only the men who were beating down the fruit from the trees, but also a number of others who had come with mule loads of manure to be deposited in heaps on the hillside, where he had a field in which he was going to sow beans for the next crop. He felt that it was really more than one man could manage. He was at his wits' ends whom to attend to. Cursing like a trooper, he vowed he would exterminate, first this man and then that, if an olive—one single olive—was missing. He almost talked as if he had counted them one by one, on his trees. Then he would turn to the muleteers and utter the direst threats as to what would happen, if any one heap of manure were not exactly the same size as the others. A little white cap on his head, his sleeves rolled up and his shirt open at the front, he rushed here, there, and everywhere; his face was a bright red and poured with sweat, his eyes glared about him wolfishly, while his hands rubbed angrily at his shaven chin, where a fresh growth of beard always sprouted the moment the razor had left it.

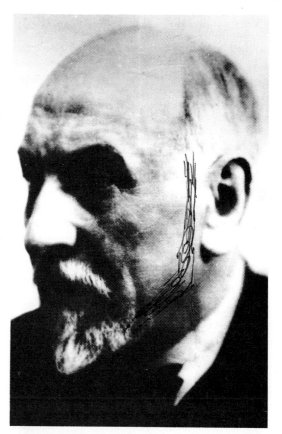

Luigi Pirandello,
Sicilian author and 1934 winner
of the Nobel Prize for Literature.

At the close of the third day's work, three of the farm hands—rough fellows with dirty, brutish faces—went to the crushing-shed; they had been beating the olive trees and went to replace their ladders and poles in the shed. They stood aghast at the sight of the fine new jar in two pieces, looking for all the world as if some one had caught hold of the bulging front and cut it off with a sharp sweep of the knife.

"Oh, my Heaven! look! look!"

"How on earth has that happened?"

"My holy aunt! When Don Lollo hears of it! The new jar! What a pity, though!"

---

2. **florins** (flôr′ənz), old gold coins first struck in Florence, Italy, but no longer minted.
3. **the crushing-shed**, where grapes were crushed into juice to begin the making of wine.

The first of the three, more frightened than his companions, proposed to shut the door again at once and to sneak away very quietly, leaving their ladders and poles outside leaning up against the wall; but the second took him up sharply.

"That's a stupid idea! You can't try that on Don Lollo. As like as not he'd believe we broke it ourselves. No, we will stay here!"

He went out of the shed and, using his hands as a trumpet, called out:

"Don Lollo! Oh! Don LOLLOOOOO!"

When the farmer came up and saw the damage, he fell into a towering passion. First he vented his fury on the three men. He seized one of them by the throat, pinned him against the wall, and shouted:

"By Jove, you'll pay for that!"

The other two sprang forward in wild excitement, fell upon Don Lollo and pulled him away. Then his mad rage turned against himself; he stamped his feet, flung his cap on the ground, and slapped his cheeks, bewailing his loss with screams suited only for the death of a relation.

"The new jar! A four-florin jar! Brand new!"

Who could have broken it? Could it possibly have broken of itself? Certainly some one must have broken it, out of malice or from envy at his possession of such a beauty. But when? How? There was no sign of violence. Could it conceivably have come in a broken condition from the pottery? No, it rang like a bell on its arrival.

As soon as the farm hands saw that their master's first outburst of rage was spent, they began to console him, saying that he should not take it so to heart, as the jar could be mended. After all, the break was not a bad one, for the front had come away all in one piece; a clever riveter could repair it and make it as good as new. Zi'[4] Dima Licasi was just the man for the job: he had invented a marvelous cement made of some composition which he kept a strict secret —miraculous stuff! Once it had set, you couldn't loosen it, even with a hammer. So they suggested that, if Don Lollo agreed, Zi' Dima Licasi should turn up at daybreak and—as sure

as eggs were eggs—the jar would be repaired and be even better than a new one.

For a long time Don Lollo turned a deaf ear to their advice—it was quite useless, there was no making good the damage—but in the end he allowed himself to be persuaded, and punctually at daybreak Zi' Dima Licasi arrived at Primosole with his outfit in a basket slung on his back. He turned out to be a misshapen old man with swollen crooked joints, like the stem of an ancient Saracen olive tree. To extract a word from him, it looked as if you would have to use a pair of forceps on his mouth. His ungraceful figure seemed to radiate discontent or gloom, due perhaps to his disappointment that no one had so far been found willing to do justice to his merits as an inventor. For Zi' Dima Licasi had not yet patented his discovery; he wanted to make a name for it first by its successful application. Meanwhile he felt it necessary to keep a sharp lookout, lest some one steal the secret of his process.

"Let me see that cement of yours," began Don Lollo in a distrustful tone, after examining him from head to foot for several minutes.

Zi' Dima declined, with a dignified shake of the head.

"You'll see its results."

"But, will it hold?"

Zi' Dima put his basket on the ground and took out from it a red bundle composed of a large cotton handkerchief, much the worse for wear, wrapped round and round something. He began to unroll it very carefully, while they all stood round watching him with close attention. When at last, however, nothing came to light save a pair of spectacles with bridge and sides broken and tied up with string, there was a general laugh. Zi' Dima took no notice, but wiped his fingers before handling the spectacles, then put them on and, with much solemnity, began his examination of the jar, which had been brought outside onto the threshing floor. Finally he said:

"It'll hold."

_____
4. **Zi'** (zē), from *zio* meaning "uncle."

"But I can't trust cement alone," Don Lollo stipulated. "I must have rivets as well."

"I'm off," Zi' Dima promptly replied, standing up and replacing his basket on his back.

Don Lollo caught hold of his arm:

"Off? Where to? You've got no more manners than a pig! . . . Just look at this pauper putting on an air of royalty! . . . Why! you wretched fool, I've got to put oil in that jar, and don't you know that oil oozes? Yards and yards to join together, and you talk of using cement alone! I want rivets—cement and rivets. It's for me to decide."

Zi' Dima shut his eyes, closed his lips tightly and shook his head. People were all like that— they refused to give him the satisfaction of turning out a neat bit of work, performed with artistic thoroughness and proving the wonderful virtues of his cement.

"If," he said, "the jar doesn't ring as true as a bell once more. . . ."

"I won't listen to a word," Don Lollo broke in. "I want rivets! I'll pay you for cement and rivets. How much will it come to?"

"If I use cement only . . ."

"My God! what an obstinate fellow! What did I say? I told you I wanted rivets. We'll settle the terms after the work is done. I've no more time to waste on you."

And he went off to look after his men.

In a state of great indignation Zi' Dima started on the job and his temper continued to rise as he bored hole after hole in the jar and in its broken section—holes for his iron rivets. Along with the squeaking of his tool went a running accompaniment of grunts which grew steadily louder and more frequent; his fury made his eyes more piercing and bloodshot and his face became green with bile. When he had finished that first operation, he flung his borer angrily into the basket and held the detached portion up against the jar to satisfy himself that the holes were at equal distances and fitted one another; next he took his pliers and cut a length of iron wire into as many pieces as he needed rivets, and then called to one of the men who were beating the olive trees to come and help him.

"Cheer up, Zi' Dima!" said the laborer, seeing how upset the old man looked.

Zi' Dima raised his hand with a savage gesture. He opened the tin which contained the cement and held it up towards heaven, as if offering it to God, seeing that men refused to recognize its value. Then he began to spread it with his finger all round the detached portion and along the broken edge of the jar. Taking his pliers and the iron rivets he had prepared, he crept inside the open belly of the jar and instructed the farm hand to hold the piece up, fitting it closely to the jar as he had himself done a short time previously. Before starting to put in the rivets, he spoke from inside the jar:

"Pull! Pull! Tug at it with all your might! . . . You see it doesn't come loose. Curses on people who won't believe me! Knock it! Yes, knock it! . . . Doesn't it ring like a bell, even with me inside it? Go and tell your master that!"

"It's for the top-dog to give orders, Zi' Dima," said the man with a sigh, "and it's for the underdog to carry them out. Put the rivets in. Put 'em in."

Zi' Dima began to pass the bits of iron through adjacent holes, one on each side of the crack, twisting up the ends with his pliers. It took him an hour to put them all in, and he poured with sweat inside the jar. As he worked he complained of his misfortune, and the farm hand stayed near, trying to console him.

"Now help me to get out," said Zi' Dima, when all was finished.

But large though its belly was, the jar had a distinctly narrow neck—a fact which Zi' Dima had overlooked, being so absorbed in his grievance. Now, try as he would, he could not manage to squeeze his way out. Instead of helping him, the farm hand stood idly by, convulsed with laughter. So there was poor Zi' Dima, imprisoned in the jar which he had mended and— there was no use in blinking at the fact—in a jar which would have to be broken to let him out, and this time broken for good.

Hearing the laughter and shouts, Don Lollo came rushing up. Inside the jar Zi' Dima was spitting like an angry cat.

"Let me out," he screamed, "I want to get out! Be quick! Help!"

Don Lollo was quite taken aback and unable to believe his own ears.

"What? Inside there? He's riveted himself up inside?"

Then he went up to the jar and shouted out to Zi' Dima:

"Help you? What help do you think I can give you? You stupid old dodderer, what d'you mean by it? Why couldn't you measure it first? Come, have a try! Put an arm out . . . that's it! Now the head! Up you come! . . . No, no, gently! . . . Down again . . . Wait a bit! . . . Not that way . . . Down, get down . . . How on earth could you do such a thing? . . . What about my jar now? . . .

"Keep calm! Keep calm!" he recommended to all the onlookers, as if it was they who were becoming excited and not himself. . . . "My head's going round! Keep calm! This is quite a new point! Get me my mule!"

He rapped the jar with his knuckles. Yes, it really rang like a bell once again.

"Fine! Repaired as good as new. . . . You wait a bit!" he said to the prisoner; then instructed his man to be off and saddle the mule. He rubbed his forehead vigorously with his fingers, and continued:

"I wonder what's the best course. That's not a jar, it's a contrivance of the devil himself. . . . Keep still! Keep still!" he exclaimed, rushing up to steady the jar, in which Zi' Dima, now in a towering passion, was struggling like a wild animal in a trap.

"It's a new point, my good man, which the lawyer must settle. I can't rely on my own judgment. . . . Where's that mule? Hurry up with the mule! . . . I'll go straight there and back. You must wait patiently; it's in your own interest. . . . Meanwhile, keep quiet, be calm! I must look after my own rights. And, first of all, to put myself in the right, I fulfill my obligation. Here you are! I am paying you for your work, for a whole day's work. Here are your five lire.[5] Is that enough?"

"I don't want anything," shouted Zi' Dima. "I want to get out!"

"You shall get out, but meanwhile I, for my part, am paying you. There they are—five lire."

He took the money out of his waistcoat pocket and tossed it into the jar, then enquired in a tone of great concern:

"Have you had any lunch? . . . Bread and something to eat with it, at once! . . . What! You don't want it? Well, then, throw it to the dogs! I shall have done my duty when I've given it to you."

Having ordered the food, he mounted and set out for the town. His wild gesticulations made those who saw him galloping past think that he might well be hastening to shut himself up in a lunatic asylum.

As luck would have it, he did not have to spend much time in the anteroom before being admitted to the lawyer's study; he had, however, to wait a long while before the lawyer could finish laughing after the matter had been related to him. Annoyed at the amusement he caused, Don Lollo said irritably:

"Excuse me, but I don't see anything to laugh at. It's all very well for your Honor, who is not the sufferer, but the jar is my property."

The lawyer, however, continued to laugh and then made him tell the story all over again. just as it had happened, so that he could raise another laugh out of it.

"Inside, eh? So he's riveted himself inside?" And what did Don Lollo want to do? . . . "To ke . . . to ke . . . keep him there inside—ha! ha! ha! . . . keep him there inside, so as not to lose the jar?"

"Why should I lose it?" cried Don Lollo, clenching his fists. "Why should I put up with the loss of my money, and have people laughing at me?"

"But don't you know what that's called?" said the lawyer at last. "It's called 'wrongful confinement.'"

5. **lire** (lir'ā), Italian coins, the five were worth about one dollar.

"Confinement? Well, who's confined him? He's confined himself! What fault is that of mine?"

The lawyer then explained to him that the matter gave rise to two cases: on the one hand he, Don Lollo, must straightway liberate the prisoner, if he wished to escape from being prosecuted for wrongful confinement; while, on the other hand, the riveter would be responsible for making good the loss resulting from his lack of skill or his stupidity.

"Ah!" said Don Lollo, with a sigh of relief. "So he'll have to pay me for my jar?"

"Wait a bit," remarked the lawyer. "Not as if it were a new jar, remember!"

"Why not?"

"Because it was a broken one, badly broken, too."

"Broken! No, Sir. Not broken. It's perfectly sound now and better than ever it was—he says so himself. And if I have to break it again, I shall not be able to have it mended. The jar will be ruined, Sir!"

The lawyer assured him that that point would be taken into account and that the riveter would have to pay the value which the jar had in its present condition.

"Therefore," he counselled, "get the man himself to give you an estimate of its value first."

"I kiss your hands," Don Lollo murmured, and hurried away.

On his return home towards evening, he found all his laborers engaged in a celebration around the inhabited jar. The watch dogs joined in the festivities with joyous barks and capers. Zi' Dima had not only calmed down, but had even come to enjoy his curious adventure and was able to laugh at it, with the melancholy humor of the unfortunate.

Don Lollo drove them all aside and bent down to look into the jar.

"Hallo! Getting along well?"

"Splendid! An open-air life for me!" replied the man. "It's better than in my own house."

"I'm glad to hear it. Meanwhile I'd just like you to know that that jar cost me four florins when it was new. How much do you think it is worth now?"

"With me inside it?" asked Zi' Dima.

The rustics laughed.

"Silence!" shouted Don Lollo. "Either your cement is of some use or it is of no use. There is no third possibility. If it is of no use you are a fraud. If it is of some use, the jar, in its present condition, must have a value. What is that value? I ask for your estimate."

After a space for reflection, Zi' Dima said:

"Here is my answer: if you had let me mend it with cement only—as I wanted to do—first of all I should not have been shut up inside it and the jar would have had its original value, without any doubt. But spoilt by these rivets, which had to be done from inside, it has lost most of its value. It's worth a third of its former price, more or less."

"One-third? That's one florin, thirty-three cents."

"Maybe less, but not more than that."

"Well," said Don Lollo. "Promise me that you'll pay me one florin—thirty-three cents."

"What?" asked Zi' Dima, as if he did not grasp the point.

"I will break the jar to let you out," replied Don Lollo. "And—the lawyer tells me—you are to pay me its value according to your own estimate—one florin thirty-three."

"I? Pay?" laughed Zi' Dima, "I'd sooner stay here till I rot!"

With some difficulty he managed to extract from his pocket a short and peculiarly foul pipe and lighted it, puffing out the smoke through the neck of the jar.

Don Lollo stood there scowling. The possibility that Zi' Dima would no longer be willing to leave the jar had not been foreseen either by himself or by the lawyer. What step should he take now? He was on the point of ordering them to saddle the mule, but reflected that it was already evening.

"Oh ho!" he said. "So you want to take up your abode in my jar! I call upon all you men as witnesses to his statement. He refuses to come out, in order to escape from paying. I am quite prepared to break it. Well, as you insist on staying there, I shall take proceedings against you tomorrow for unlawful occupancy of the jar and for preventing me from my rightful use of it."

Zi' Dima blew out another puff of smoke and answered calmly:

"No, your Honor. I don't want to prevent you at all. Do you think I am here because I like it? Let me out and I'll go away gladly enough. But as for paying, I wouldn't dream of it, your Honor."

In a sudden access of fury Don Lollo made to give a kick at the jar but stopped in time. Instead he seized it with both hands and shook it violently, uttering a hoarse growl.

"You see what fine cement it is," Zi' Dima remarked from inside.

"You rascal!" roared Don Lollo. "Whose fault is it, yours or mine? You expect me to pay for it, do you? You can starve to death inside first. We'll see who'll win."

He went away, forgetting all about the five lire which he had tossed into the jar that morning. But the first thing Zi' Dima thought of doing was to spend that money in having a festive evening, in company with the farm hands, who had been delayed in their work by that strange accident, and had decided to spend the night at the farm, in the open air, sleeping on the threshing floor. One of them went to a neighboring tavern to make the necessary purchases. The moon was so bright that it seemed almost day—a splendid night for their carousal.

Many hours later Don Lollo was awakened by an infernal din. Looking out from the farmhouse balcony, he could see in the moonlight what looked like a gang of devils on his threshing floor; his men, all roaring drunk, were holding hands and performing a dance round the jar, while Zi' Dima, inside it, was singing at the top of his voice.

This time Don Lollo could not restrain himself, but rushed down like a mad bull and, before they could stop him, gave the jar a push which started it rolling down the slope. It continued on its course, to the delight of the intoxicated company, until it hit an olive tree and cracked in pieces, leaving Zi' Dima the winner in the dispute.

I
GRAND EMOTIONS FROM TINY CAUSES

Some conflicts are of towering importance. They sweep through nations and cities with violence and bitterness. The same dark motives that cause these conflicts operate on a simple level, where a group of people gather for a cookout or the village gossips stand on a corner of Main Street. Conflict among simple villagers is the subject of "The Jar." Pirandello lends a touch of absurdity to the dark motives of his people. He turns it into a ludicrous tale that tweaks our conscience as it reminds us that we all share in the same defects.

II
IMPLICATIONS

Would you agree or disagree with the following statements?

1. Pirandello illustrates this point: sometimes the "letter of the law" applied rigidly becomes ridiculous.

2. "Life is a very sad piece of buffoonery."

3. The conflict in "The Jar" is triggered because Don Lollo and Zi' Dima have similar personalities.

4. While this story is amusing, it contains no "truth" of general human significance.

III
TECHNIQUES

Identification

In "The Jar" do you feel a sense of identification with any of the characters? With none of them? How do the appearances and personalities of the two main characters affect your sense of identification with them?

Diction

1. Compare the kind of language used by the author himself with that used by his characters. What distinctions do you find?

2. Find examples of the way in which Pirandello chooses words to bring action and vivid pictures into his prose. For example: "His eyes glared about him wolfishly. . . ."

3. What is the earliest point in the story at which the choice of language suggests that "The Jar" will probably be a comic tale?

IV
WORDS

A. Examine the following clauses and phrases from the preceding two stories for context clues to the italicized words.

1. ". . . to spread *dissension* among the masses of the workers . . ."

2. "Possibly!" muttered Don Camillo, who now and then liked to appear *skeptical*.

3. Don Lollo *stipulated*. "I must have rivets. . . ."

4. In a state of great *indignation* Zi' Dima started on the job and his temper continued to rise. . . .

5. The moon was so bright that it seemed almost day—a splendid night for their *carousal*.

6. It continued on its course, to the delight of the *intoxicated* company, until it hit an olive tree. . . .

B. Try several synonyms for the italicized words following. What effect would your choices have had in each phrase?

1. . . . the most *infernal* carillon . . .

2. . . . Peppone . . . surrounded by his *satellites*.

3. The crowd *bellowed*. . . .

4. . . . a *dispute* with the potter concerning this jar.

5. Along with the *squeaking* of his tool went a running accompaniment of grunts which grew louder. . . .

6. . . . he complained of his misfortune, and the farm hand stayed near, trying to *console* him.

C. Guareschi says that "Don Camillo was pawing the ground like a restive horse." Pirandello says that "Zi' Dima was spitting like an angry cat." What other similes do Guareschi and Pirandello use?

SAKI (H. H. Munro)

Hector Hugo Munro (1870–1916), better known to readers as Saki, "spoofed" the British society of Victoria's time, but in such a delicate and disarmingly simple way that the sting was removed, though the truth stands out clear and bright. Born in Burma of British parents, Munro was brought to England when he was two, to be raised by his grandmother and two stern, autocratic aunts. It was a devastatingly strict regime, and it is small wonder that one of Munro's favorite subjects for satire was aunts. In 1893 he obtained a post in Burma with the Military Police, and there his fondness for animals, both wild and domestic, could be indulged to the fullest. But after seven fevers in thirteen months, Munro's poor health forced him to return to England. After a period spent recuperating in the Devonshire countryside, he moved to London where he found to his delight that he could earn a living by writing. He began by writing political satires for the *Westminster Gazette* and moved on to satirizing British society. When war was declared in 1914, Munro immediately enlisted; he was killed in 1916 by a sniper's bullet. To try and pin down the elusive charm of Saki's tales is like trying to explain your fondness for a particular food. It is a matter of taste. Christopher Morley comments: "There is no greater compliment to be paid the right kind of friend than to hand him Saki, without a comment. Particularly to those less familiar with the mysterious jungles of English humour, a savage country with birds of unexpected plumage . . . There are certain social types whom Saki cooks and serves for us as absolutely perfect as asparagus and hollandaise." His pen name Munro was borrowed from the *Rubaiyat of Omar Khayyàm*, in which the cupbearer was named Saki. This English Saki brings pure delight to his followers as he shines his light upon the conflict between a "pseudo" aunt and her imaginative nephew.

The Lumber Room

The children were to be driven, as a special treat, to the sands at Jagborough. Nicholas was not to be of the party; he was in disgrace. Only that morning he had refused to eat his wholesome bread-and-milk on the seemingly frivolous ground that there was a frog in it. Older and wiser and better people had told him that there could not possibly be a frog in his bread-and-milk and that he was not to talk nonsense; he continued, nevertheless, to talk what seemed the veriest nonsense, and described with much detail the coloration and markings of the alleged frog. The dramatic part of the incident was that there really was a frog in Nicholas' basin of bread-and-milk; he had put it there himself, so he felt entitled to know something about it. The sin of taking a frog from the garden and putting it into a bowl of wholesome bread-and-milk was enlarged on at great length, but the fact that stood out clearest in the whole affair, as it presented itself to the mind of Nicholas, was that the older, wiser, and better people had been proved to be profoundly in error in matters about which they had expressed the utmost assurance.

"You said there couldn't possibly be a frog in my bread-and-milk; there *was* a frog in my bread-and-milk," he repeated, with the insistence of a skilled tactician who does not intend to shift from favorable ground.

So his boy-cousin and girl-cousin and his quite uninteresting younger brother were to be taken to Jagborough sands that afternoon and he was to stay at home. His cousins' aunt, who insisted, by an unwarranted stretch of imagination, in styling herself his aunt also, had hastily invented the Jagborough expedition in order to impress on Nicholas the delights that he had justly forfeited by his disgraceful conduct at the breakfast table. It was her habit, whenever one of the children fell from grace, to improvise something of a festival nature from which the offender would be rigorously debarred; if all the children sinned collectively they were suddenly informed of a circus in a neighboring town, a circus of unrivalled merit and uncounted elephants, to which, but for their depravity, they would have been taken that very day.

A few decent tears were looked for on the part of Nicholas when the moment for the departure of the expedition arrived. As a matter-of-fact, however, all the crying was done by his girl-cousin, who scraped her knee rather painfully against the step of the carriage as she was scrambling in.

"How she did howl," said Nicholas cheerfully, as the party drove off without any of the elation of high spirits that should have characterized it.

"She'll soon get over that," said the *soi-disant*[1] aunt; "it will be a glorious afternoon for racing about over those beautiful sands. How they will enjoy themselves!"

"Bobby won't enjoy himself much, and he won't race much either," said Nicholas with a grim chuckle; "his boots are hurting him. They're too tight."

"Why didn't he tell me they were hurting?" asked the aunt with some asperity.

"He told you twice, but you weren't listening. You often don't listen when we tell you important things."

"You are not to go into the gooseberry garden," said the aunt, changing the subject.

"Why not?" demanded Nicholas.

"Because you are in disgrace," said the aunt loftily.

Nicholas did not admit the flawlessness of the reasoning; he felt perfectly capable of being in disgrace and in a gooseberry garden at the same moment. His face took on an expression of considerable obstinacy. It was clear to his aunt that he was determined to get into the gooseberry garden, "only," as she remarked to herself, "because I have told him he is not to."

Now the gooseberry garden had two doors by which it might be entered, and once a small person like Nicholas could slip in there he could effectually disappear from view amid the masking growth of artichokes, raspberry canes, and fruit bushes. The aunt had many other things to do that afternoon, but she spent an hour or two in trivial gardening operations among flower beds and shrubberies, whence she could keep a watchful eye on the two doors that led to the forbidden paradise. She was a woman of few ideas, with immense powers of concentration.

Nicholas made one or two sorties[2] into the front garden, wriggling his way with obvious stealth of purpose towards one or other of the doors, but never able for a moment to evade the aunt's watchful eye. As a matter-of-fact, he had no intention of trying to get into the gooseberry garden, but it was extremely convenient for him that his aunt should believe that he had; it was a belief that would keep her on self-imposed sentry duty for the greater part of the afternoon. Having thoroughly confirmed and fortified her suspicions, Nicholas slipped back into the house and rapidly put into execution a plan of action that had long germinated in his brain. By standing on a chair in the library one could reach a shelf on which reposed a fat, important-looking key. The key was as important as it looked; it was the instrument which kept the mysteries of the lumber room[3] secure from unauthorized intru-

1. **soi-disant,** French for so-called, self-styled.
2. **sorties** (sôr′tēz), military missions.
3. **lumber room,** a storeroom.

sion, which opened a way only for aunts and suchlike privileged persons. Nicholas had not had much experience of the art of fitting keys into keyholes and turning locks, but for some days past he had practised with the key of the schoolroom door; he did not believe in trusting too much to luck and accident. The key turned stiffly in the lock, but it turned. The door opened, and Nicholas was in an unknown land, compared with which the gooseberry garden was a stale delight, a mere material pleasure.

Often and often Nicholas had pictured to himself what the lumber room might be like, that region that was so carefully sealed from youthful eyes and concerning which no questions were ever answered. It came up to his expectations. In the first place it was large and dimly lit, one high window opening on to the forbidden garden being its only source of illumination. In the second place it was a storehouse of unimagined treasures. The aunt-by-assertion was one of those people who think that things spoil by use and consign them to dust and damp by way of preserving them. Such parts of the house as Nicholas knew best were rather bare and cheerless, but here there were wonderful things for the eye to feast on. First and foremost there was a piece of framed tapestry that was evidently meant to be a fire screen. To Nicholas it was a living, breathing story; he sat down on a roll of Indian hangings, glowing in wonderful colors beneath a layer of dust, and took in all the details of the tapestry picture. A man, dressed in the hunting costume of some remote period, had just transfixed a stag with an arrow; it could not have been a difficult shot because the stag was only one or two paces away from him; in the thickly growing vegetation that the picture suggested it would not have been difficult to creep up to a feeding stag, and the two spotted dogs that were springing forward to join in the chase had evidently been trained to keep to heel till the arrow was discharged. That part of the picture was simple, if interesting, but did the huntsman see, what Nicholas saw, that four galloping wolves were coming in his direction through the wood? There might be more than

four of them hidden behind the trees, and in any case would the man and his dogs be able to cope with the four wolves if they made an attack? The man had only two arrows left in his quiver, and he might miss with one or both of them; all one knew about his skill in shooting was that he could hit a large stag at a ridiculously short range. Nicholas sat for many golden minutes revolving the possibilities of the scene; he was inclined to think that there were more than four wolves and that the man and his dogs were in a tight corner.

But there were other objects of delight and interest claiming his instant attention: there were quaint twisted candlesticks in the shape of snakes, and a teapot fashioned like a china duck, out of whose open beak the tea was supposed to come. How dull and shapeless the nursery teapot seemed in comparison! And there was a carved sandalwood box packed tight with aromatic cotton wool, and between the layers of cotton wool were little brass figures, humpnecked bulls, and peacocks and goblins, delightful to see and to handle. Less promising in appearance was a large square book with plain black covers; Nicholas peeped into it, and, behold, it was full of colored pictures of birds. And such birds! In the garden, and in the lanes when he went for a walk, Nicholas came across a few birds, of which the largest were an occasional magpie or wood pigeon; here were herons and bustards, kites, toucans, tiger bitterns, brush turkeys, ibises, golden pheasants, a whole portrait gallery of undreamed-of creatures. And as he was admiring the coloring of the mandarin duck and assigning a life history to it, the voice of his aunt in shrill vociferation of his name came from the gooseberry garden without. She had grown suspicious at his long disappearance, and had leapt to the conclusion that he had climbed over the wall behind the sheltering screen of the lilac bushes; she was now engaged in energetic and rather hopeless search for him among the artichokes and raspberry canes.

"Nicholas, Nicholas!" she screamed, "you are to come out of this at once. It's no use trying to hide there; I can see you all the time."

It was probably the first time for twenty years that any one had smiled in that lumber room.

Presently the angry repetitions of Nicholas' name gave way to a shriek, and a cry for somebody to come quickly. Nicholas shut the book, restored it carefully to its place in a corner, and shook some dust from a neighboring pile of newspapers over it. Then he crept from the room, locked the door, and replaced the key exactly where he had found it. His aunt was still calling his name when he sauntered into the front garden.

"Who's calling?" he asked.

"Me," came the answer from the other side of the wall; "didn't you hear me? I've been looking for you in the gooseberry garden, and I've slipped into the rain-water tank. Luckily there's no water in it, but the sides are slippery and I can't get out. Fetch the little ladder from under the cherry tree—"

"I was told I wasn't to go into the gooseberry garden," said Nicholas promptly.

"I told you not to, and now I tell you that you may," came the voice from the rain-water tank, rather impatiently.

"Your voice doesn't sound like aunt's," objected Nicholas; "you may be the Evil One tempting me to be disobedient. Aunt often tells me that the Evil One tempts me and that I always yield. This time I'm not going to yield."

"Don't talk nonsense," said the prisoner in the tank; "go and fetch the ladder."

"Will there be strawberry jam for tea?" asked Nicholas innocently.

"Certainly there will be," said the aunt, privately resolving that Nicholas should have none of it.

"Now I know that you are the Evil One and not aunt," shouted Nicholas gleefully; "when we asked for strawberry jam yesterday she said there wasn't any. I know there are four jars of it in the store cupboard, because I looked, and of course you know it's there, but *she* doesn't, because she said there wasn't any. Oh, Devil, you *have* sold yourself!"

There was an unusual sense of luxury in being able to talk to an aunt as though one was talking to the Evil One, but Nicholas knew, with childish discernment, that such luxuries were not to be overindulged in. He walked noisily away, and it was a kitchenmaid, in search of parsley, who eventually rescued the aunt from the rain-water tank.

Tea that evening was partaken of in a fearsome silence. The tide had been at its highest when the children had arrived at Jagborough Cove, so there had been no sands to play on—a circumstance that the aunt had overlooked in the haste of organizing her punitive expedition. The tightness of Bobby's boots had had disastrous effect on his temper the whole of the afternoon, and altogether the children could not have been said to have enjoyed themselves. The aunt maintained the frozen muteness of one who has suffered undignified and unmerited detention in a rain-water tank for thirty-five minutes. As for Nicholas, he, too, was silent, in the absorption of one who has much to think about; it was just possible, he considered, that the huntsman would escape with his hounds while the wolves feasted on the stricken stag.

I
LOGICAL ILLOGICALNESS

In his own way, Nicholas is perfectly logical when he says there is a frog in his cereal, when he refuses to cry at being left at home, when he will not take a ladder into the gooseberry garden, and when he claims the voices from the garden must be the devil. The aunt is logical in her own way. She believes firmly in discipline and that the best form of punishment is to take something pleasurable away from the culprit. The conflict of wills continues because each of the arguments has traces of illogicalness built into it. What are they?

II
IMPLICATIONS

Use the details in the story or your own experiences in discussing these statements:

1. The story could have been called "The Gooseberry Garden" instead of "The Lumber Room."

2. The fact that things work out in unexpected ways for the aunt is her own fault.

3. Nicholas is the kind of child whom it is fun to read about, but who would be difficult to handle in real life.

Identification

If you think of the story as a play, who is on stage the most? How do the descriptions of Nicholas and the aunt make the one more appealing than the other?

Diction

Examine the opening paragraph. Look at the following phrases in their context and then try to express what the choice of words does to the style.

> wholesome bread-and-milk
> seemingly frivolous ground
> older and wiser and better people
> veriest nonsense
> the alleged frog
> profoundly in error
> utmost assurance

IV

WORDS

A. Reread these phrases from the story. Use context clues here and in the story to determine the meaning of each italicized word.

1. ". . . he . . . described with much detail the coloration and markings of the *alleged* frog."

2. ". . . with the insistence of a skilled *tactician* who does not intend to shift from favorable ground."

3. ". . . from which the offender would be rigorously *debarred*."

4. " 'Why didn't he tell me they were hurting?' asked the aunt with some *asperity*."

5. "His face took on an expression of considerable *obstinacy*."

6. "Nicholas . . . put into execution a plan of action that had long *germinated* in his brain."

7. ". . . one of those people who think that things spoil by use and *consign* them to dust and damp by way of preserving them."

8. ". . . the voice of his aunt in shrill *vociferation* of his name. . . ."

9. ". . . a circumstance that the aunt had overlooked in the haste of organizing her *punitive* expedition."

B. The author uses the italicized words in these phrases to convey certain images. Substitute other words with similar meanings and then decide why the author chose the words he did.

1. "scraped her knee . . . as she was *scrambling* in."

2. ". . . a shelf on which *reposed* a fat, important-looking key."

3. ". . . one high window being its only source of *illumination*."

4. "A man . . . had just *transfixed* a stag with an arrow. . . ."

5. ". . . two spotted dogs that were *springing* forward to join in the chase. . . ."

6. "She . . . had *leapt* to the conclusion that he had climbed over the wall. . . ."

7. "His aunt was still calling his name when he *sauntered* into the front garden."

8. "Tea that evening was *partaken* in a fearsome silence."

V

COMPOSITION

The author causes the reader to have certain feelings about the main characters through the descriptions of them. Here are some descriptions that give the reader an idea of Nicholas' aunt's personality.

> "She was a woman of few ideas, with immense powers of concentration."

> "The aunt-by-assertion was one of those people who think that things spoil by use and consign them to dust and damp by way of preserving them."

The author does not describe Nicholas in so many words, but the reader has a good picture of him through the descriptions of his actions. Write a paragraph describing Nicholas' personality.

ROALD DAHL

Roald Dahl[1] (1916–   ) is a free-lance writer said by some to have added a new dimension to the Gothic tale. He was born in Llandaff, South Wales, and was educated in England. He went to work for Shell Oil Company in Tanganyika in 1932. When World War II began, he joined the Royal Air Force and became a wing commander. After the war's end, he discovered that he could publish the stories he had been telling. His short stories have been most successful and have been compared to Thurber's stories, to Charles Addams' cartoons, and to nightmares. A critic says, "One comes away from a Dahl story uncertain of the implied profundity. . . . Dahl maintains anonymity with respect to his stories, but the immediate presence of a narrator is replaced by the 'grinning skull' quality of the narration. One never consciously sees—or even wishes to see—the motivation behind that grin, but the reader is constantly aware of an extremely skillful literary architecture."

After 25 years of writing adult stories, Dahl has now turned to writing screen plays and children's stories. He says, "I write children's books primarily for my own children. Had I not had any children I would never have written these books, nor would I have been capable of so doing. . . . I now infinitely prefer writing long stories for children. It is no easier, certainly, but it is more fun and it evokes a far greater response." He wrote the screen play for *Charlie and the Chocolate Factory*, one of his books for children.

In 1953, Dahl married English actress Patricia Neal who has won an Academy Award. In 1965 she suffered a stroke that left her paralyzed and speechless. Dahl's dramatization for television of her triumphant recovery from this illness won critical acclaim.

The Way Up to Heaven

All of her life, Mrs. Foster had had an almost pathological fear of missing a train, a plane, a boat, or even a theater curtain. In other respects, she was not a particularly nervous woman, but the mere thought of being late on occasions like these would throw her into such a state of nerves that she would begin to twitch. It was nothing much—just a tiny vellicating[1] muscle in the corner of the left eye, like a secret wink—but the annoying thing was that it refused to disappear until an hour or so after the train or plane or whatever it was had been safely caught.

It is really extraordinary how in certain people a simple apprehension about a thing like catching a train can grow into a serious obsession. At least half an hour before it was time to leave the house for the station, Mrs. Foster would step out of the elevator all ready to go, with hat and coat and gloves, and then, being quite unable to

---

1. **Roald Dahl** (rü′ôl dôl′).

1. **vellicating** (vel′ə kāt′ing), twitching.

sit down, she would flutter and fidget around from room to room until her husband, who must have been well aware of her state, finally emerged from his privacy and suggested in a cool dry voice that perhaps they had better get going now, had they not?

Mr. Foster may possibly have had a right to be irritated by this foolishness of his wife's, but he could have had no excuse for increasing her misery by keeping her waiting unnecessarily. Mind you, it is by no means certain that this is what he did, yet whenever they were to go somewhere, his timing was so accurate—just a minute or two late, you understand—and his manner so bland that it was hard to believe he wasn't purposely inflicting a nasty private little torture of his own on the unhappy lady. And one thing he must have known—that she would never dare to call out and tell him to hurry. He had disciplined her too well for that. He must also have known that if he was prepared to wait even beyond the last moment of safety, he could drive her nearly into hysterics. On one or two special occasions in the later years of their married life, it seemed almost as though he had *wanted* to miss the train simply in order to intensify the poor woman's suffering.

Assuming (though one cannot be sure) that the husband was guilty, what made his attitude doubly unreasonable was the fact that, with the exception of this one small irrepressible foible, Mrs. Foster was and always had been a good and loving wife. For over thirty years, she had served him loyally and well. There was no doubt about this. Even she, a very modest woman, was aware of it, and although she had for years refused to let herself believe that Mr. Foster would ever consciously torment her, there had been times recently when she had caught herself beginning to wonder.

Mr. Eugene Foster, who was nearly seventy years old, lived with his wife in a large six-story house on East Sixty-second Street, and they had four servants. It was a gloomy place, and few people came to visit them. But on this particular morning in January, the house had come alive and there was a great deal of bustling about. One maid was distributing bundles of dust sheets to every room, while another was draping them over the furniture. The butler was bringing down suitcases and putting them in the hall. The cook kept popping up from the kitchen to have a word with the butler, and Mrs. Foster herself, in an old-fashioned fur coat and with a black hat on the top of her head, was flying from room to room and pretending to supervise these operations. Actually, she was thinking of nothing at all except that she was going to miss her plane if her husband didn't come out of his study room and get ready.

"What time is it, Walker?" she said to the butler as she passed him.

"It's ten minutes past nine, madam."

"And has the car come?"

"Yes, madam, it's waiting. I'm just going to put the luggage in now."

"It takes an hour to get to Idlewild,"[2] she said. "My plane leaves at eleven. I have to be there half an hour beforehand for the formalities. I shall be late. I just *know* I'm going to be late."

"I think you have plenty of time, madam," the butler said kindly. "I warned Mr. Foster that you must leave at nine-fifteen. There's still another five minutes."

"Yes, Walker, I know, I know. But get the luggage in quickly, will you please?"

She began walking up and down the hall, and whenever the butler came by, she asked him the time. This, she kept telling herself, was the *one* plane she must not miss. It had taken months to persuade her husband to allow her to go. If she missed it, he might easily decide that she should cancel the whole thing. And the trouble was that he insisted on coming to the airport to see her off.

"Dear God," she said aloud, "I'm going to miss it. I know, I *know* I'm going to miss it." The little muscle beside the left eye was twitching madly now. The eyes themselves were very close to tears.

---

2. **Idlewild,** New York City's major airport, now called John F. Kennedy International Airport.

"What time is it, Walker?"

"It's eighteen minutes, past, madam."

"Now I really *will* miss it!" she cried. "Oh, I wish he would come!"

This was an important journey for Mrs. Foster. She was going all alone to Paris to visit her daughter, her only child, who was married to a Frenchman. Mrs. Foster didn't care much for the Frenchman, but she was fond of her daughter, and more than that, she had developed a great yearning to set eyes on her three grandchildren. She knew them only from the many photographs that she had received and that she kept putting up all over the house. They were beautiful, these children. She doted on them, and each time a new picture arrived, she would carry it away and sit with it for a long time, staring at it lovingly and searching the small faces for signs of that old satisfying blood likeness that meant so much. And now, lately, she had come more and more to feel that she did not really wish to live out her days in a place where she could not be near these children, and have them visit her, and take them for walks, and buy them presents, and watch them grow. She knew, of course, that it was wrong and in a way disloyal to have thoughts like these while her husband was still alive. She knew also that although he was no longer active in his many enterprises, he would never consent to leave New York and live in Paris. It was a miracle that he had ever agreed to let her fly over there alone for six weeks to visit them. But, oh, how she wished she could live there always, and be close to them!

"Walker, what time is it?"

"Twenty-two minutes past, madam."

As he spoke, a door opened and Mr. Foster came into the hall. He stood for a moment, looking intently at his wife, and she looked back at him—at this diminutive but still quite dapper old man with the huge bearded face that bore such an astonishing resemblance to those old photographs of Andrew Carnegie.[3]

---

3. **Andrew Carnegie** (1835–1919), an American steel manufacturer.

"Well," he said, "I suppose perhaps we'd better get going fairly soon if you want to catch that plane."

"Yes, dear—*yes!* Everything's ready. The car's waiting."

"That's good," he said. With his head over to one side, he was watching her closely. He had a peculiar way of cocking the head and then moving it in a series of small, rapid jerks. Because of this and because he was clasping his hands up high in front of him, near the chest, he was somehow like a squirrel standing there—a quick clever old squirrel from the Park.

"Here's Walker with your coat, dear. Put it on."

"I'll be with you in a moment," he said. "I'm just going to wash my hands."

She waited for him, and the tall butler stood beside her, holding the coat and the hat.

"Walker, will I miss it?"

"No, madam," the butler said. "I think you'll make it all right."

Then Mr. Foster appeared again, and the butler helped him on with his coat. Mrs. Foster hurried outside and got into the hired Cadillac. Her husband came after her, but he walked down the steps of the house slowly, pausing halfway to observe the sky and to sniff the cold morning air.

"It looks a bit foggy," he said as he sat down beside her in the car. "And it's always worse out there at the airport. I shouldn't be surprised if the flight's cancelled already."

"Don't say that, dear—*please.*"

They didn't speak again until the car had crossed over the river to Long Island.

"I arranged everything with the servants," Mr. Foster said. "They're all going off today. I gave them half pay for six weeks and told Walker I'd send him a telegram when we wanted them back."

"Yes," she said. "He told me."

"I'll move into the club tonight. It'll be a nice change staying at the club."

"Yes dear. I'll write to you."

"I'll call in at the house occasionally to see that everything's all right and to pick up the mail."

"But don't you really think Walker should stay there all the time to look after things?" she asked meekly.

"Nonsense. It's quite unnecessary. And anyway, I'd have to pay him full wages."

"Oh yes," she said. "Of course."

"What's more, you never know what people get up to when they're left alone in a house," Mr. Foster announced, and with that he took out a cigar and, after snipping off the end with a silver cutter, lit it with a gold lighter.

She sat still in the car with her hands clasped together tight under the rug.

"Will you write to me?" she asked.

"I'll see," he said. "But I doubt it. You know I don't hold with letter writing unless there's something specific to say."

"Yes, dear, I know. So don't you bother."

They drove on, along Queens Boulevard, and as they approached the flat marshland on which Idlewild is built, the fog began to thicken and the car had to slow down.

"Oh, dear!" cried Mrs. Foster. "I'm *sure* I'm going to miss it now! What time is it?"

"Stop fussing," the old man said. "It doesn't matter anyway. It's bound to be cancelled now. They never fly in this sort of weather. I don't know why you bothered to come out."

She couldn't be sure, but it seemed to her that there was suddenly a new note in his voice, and she turned to look at him. It was difficult to observe any change in his expression under all that hair. The mouth was what counted. She wished, as she had so often before, that she could see the mouth clearly. The eyes never showed anything except when he was in a rage.

"Of course," he went on, "if by chance it *does* go, then I agree with you—you'll be certain to miss it now. Why don't you resign yourself to that?"

She turned away and peered through the window at the fog. It seemed to be getting thicker as they went along, and now she could only just make out the edge of the road and the margin of grassland beyond it. She knew that her husband was still looking at her. She glanced back at him

again, and this time she noticed with a kind of horror that he was staring intently at the little place in the corner of her left eye where she could feel the muscle twitching.

"Won't you?" he said.

"Won't I what?"

"Be sure to miss it now if it goes. We can't drive fast in this muck."

He didn't speak to her any more after that. The car crawled on and on. The driver had a yellow lamp directed onto the edge of the road, and this helped him to keep going. Other lights, some white and some yellow, kept coming out of the fog toward them, and there was an especially bright one that followed close behind them all the time.

Suddenly, the driver stopped the car.

"There!" Mr. Foster cried. "We're stuck. I knew it."

"No, sir," the driver said, turning around. "We made it. This is the airport."

Without a word, Mrs. Foster jumped out and hurried through the main entrance into the building. There was a mass of people inside, mostly disconsolate passengers standing around the ticket counters. She pushed her way through and spoke to the clerk.

"Yes," he said. "Your flight is temporarily postponed. But please don't go away. We're expecting this weather to clear any moment."

She went back to her husband who was still sitting in the car and told him the news. "But don't you wait, dear," she said. "There's no sense in that."

"I won't," he answered. "So long as the driver can get me back. Can you get me back, driver?"

"I think so," the man said.

"Is the luggage out?"

"Yes, sir."

"Good-bye, dear," Mrs. Foster said, leaning into the car and giving her husband a small kiss on the coarse grey fur of his cheek.

"Good-bye," he answered. "Have a good trip."

The car drove off, and Mrs. Foster was left alone.

The rest of the day was a sort of nightmare for her. She sat for hour after hour on a bench, as close to the airline counter as possible, and every thirty minutes or so she would get up and ask the clerk if the situation had changed. She always received the same reply—that she must continue to wait, because the fog might blow away at any moment. It wasn't until after six in the evening that the loudspeakers finally announced that the flight had been postponed until eleven o'clock the next morning.

Mrs. Foster didn't quite know what to do when she heard this news. She stayed sitting on her bench for at least another half hour, wondering, in a tired, hazy sort of way, where she might go to spend the night. She hated to leave the airport. She didn't wish to see her husband. She was terrified that in one way or another he would eventually manage to prevent her from getting to France. She would have liked to remain just where she was, sitting on the bench the whole night through. That would be the safest. But she was already exhausted, and it didn't take long to realize that this was a ridiculous thing for an elderly lady to do. So in the end she went to a phone and called the house.

Her husband, who was on the point of leaving for the club, answered it himself. She told him the news, and asked whether the servants were still there.

"They've all gone," he said.

"In that case, dear, I'll just get myself a room somewhere for the night. And don't you bother yourself about it at all."

"That would be foolish," he said. "You've got a large house here at your disposal. Use it."

"But, dear, it's *empty*."

"Then I'll stay with you myself."

"There's no food in the house. There's nothing."

"Then eat before you come in. Don't be so stupid, woman. Everything you do, you seem to want to make a fuss about it."

"Yes," she said. "I'm sorry. I'll get myself a sandwich here, and then I'll come on in."

Outside the fog had cleared a little, but it was still a long, slow drive in the taxi, and she didn't arrive back at the house on Sixty-second Street until fairly late.

Her husband emerged from his study when he heard her coming in. "Well," he said, standing by the study door, "how was Paris?"

"We leave at eleven in the morning," she answered. "It's definite."

"You mean if the fog clears."

"It's clearing now. There's a wind coming up."

"You look tired," he said. "You must have had an anxious day."

"It wasn't very comfortable. I think I'll go straight to bed."

"I've ordered a car for the morning," he said. "Nine o'clock."

"Oh, thank you, dear. And I certainly hope you're not going to bother to come all the way out again to see me off."

"No," he said slowly. "I don't think I will. But there's no reason why you shouldn't drop me at the club on your way."

She looked at him, and at that moment he seemed to be standing a long way off from her, beyond some borderline. He was suddenly so small and far away that she couldn't be sure what he was doing, or what he was thinking, or even what he was.

"The club is downtown," she said. "It isn't on the way to the airport."

"But you'll have plenty of time, my dear. Don't you want to drop me at the club?"

"Oh, yes—of course."

"That's good. Then I'll see you in the morning at nine."

She went up to her bedroom on the third floor, and she was so exhausted from her day that she fell asleep soon after she lay down.

Next morning, Mrs. Foster was up early, and by eight-thirty she was downstairs and ready to leave.

Shortly after nine, her husband appeared. "Did you make any coffee?" he asked.

"No, dear. I thought you'd get a nice breakfast at the club. The car is here. It's been waiting. I'm all ready to go."

They were standing in the hall—they always

seemed to be meeting in the hall nowadays—she with her hat and coat and purse, he in a curiously cut Edwardian jacket with high lapels.

"Your luggage?"

"It's at the airport."

"Ah, yes," he said. "Of course. And if you're going to take me to the club first, I suppose we'd better get going fairly soon, hadn't we?"

"Yes!" she cried. "Oh, yes—*please!*"

"I'm just going to get a few cigars. I'll be right with you. You get in the car."

She turned and went out to where the chauffeur was standing, and he opened the car door for her as she approached.

"What time is it?" she asked him.

"About nine-fifteen."

Mr. Foster came out five minutes later, and watching him as he walked slowly down the steps, she noticed that his legs were like goat's legs in those narrow stovepipe trousers that he wore. As on the day before, he paused halfway down to sniff the air and to examine the sky. The weather was still not quite clear, but there was a wisp of sun coming through the mist.

"Perhaps you'll be lucky this time," he said as he settled himself beside her in the car.

"Hurry, please," she said to the chauffeur. "Don't bother about the rug. I'll arrange the rug. Please get going. I'm late."

The man went back to his seat behind the wheel and started the engine.

"*Just* a moment!" Mr. Foster said suddenly. "Hold it a moment, chauffeur, will you?"

"What is it, dear?" She saw him searching the pockets of his overcoat.

"I had a little present I wanted you to take to Ellen," he said. "Now, where on earth is it? I'm sure I had it in my hand as I came down."

"I never saw you carrying anything. What sort of present?"

"A little box wrapped up in white paper. I forgot to give it to you yesterday. I don't want to forget it today."

"A little box!" Mrs. Foster cried. "I never saw any little box!" She began hunting frantically in the back of the car.

Her husband continued searching through the pockets of his coat. Then he unbuttoned the coat and felt around in his jacket. "Confound it," he said. "I must've left it in my bedroom. I won't be a moment."

"Oh, *please!*" she cried. "We haven't got time! *Please* leave it! You can mail it. It's only one of those silly combs anyway. You're always giving her combs."

"And what's wrong with combs, may I ask?" he said, furious that she should have forgotten herself for once.

"Nothing, dear, I'm sure. But . . ."

"Stay here!" he commanded. "I'm going to get it."

"Be quick, dear! Oh, *please* be quick!"

She sat still, waiting and waiting.

"Chauffeur, what time is it?"

The man had a wristwatch, which he consulted. "I make it nearly nine-thirty."

"Can we get to the airport in an hour?"

"Just about."

At this point, Mrs. Foster suddenly spotted a corner of something white, wedged down in the crack of the seat on the side where her husband had been sitting. She reached over and pulled out a small paper-wrapped box, and at the same time she couldn't help noticing that it was wedged down firm and deep, as though with the help of a pushing hand.

"Here it is!" she cried. "I've found it! Oh, dear, and now he'll be up there forever searching for it! Chauffeur, quickly—run in and call him down, will you please?"

The chauffeur, a man with a small rebellious Irish mouth, didn't care very much for any of this, but he climbed out of the car and went up the steps to the front door of the house. Then he turned and came back. "Door's locked," he announced. "You got a key?"

"Yes—wait a minute." She began hunting madly in her purse. The little face was screwed up tight with anxiety, the lips pushed outward like a spout.

"Here it is! No—I'll go myself. It'll be quicker. I know where he'll be."

She hurried out of the car and up the steps to

the front door, holding the key in one hand. She slid the key into the keyhole and was about to turn it—and then she stopped. Her head came up, and she stood there absolutely motionless, her whole body arrested right in the middle of all this hurry to turn the key and get into the house, and she waited—five, six, seven, eight, nine, ten seconds, she waited. The way she was standing there, with her head in the air and the body so tense, it seemed as though she were listening for the repetition of some sound that she had heard a moment before from a place far away inside the house.

Yes—quite obviously she was listening. Her whole attitude was a *listening* one. She appeared actually to be moving one of her ears closer and closer to the door. Now it was right up against the door, and for still another few seconds she remained in that position, head up, ear to door, hand on key, about to enter but not entering, trying instead, or so it seemed, to hear and to analyze these sounds that were coming faintly from this place deep within the house.

Then, all at once, she sprang to life again. She withdrew the key from the door and came running back down the steps.

"It's too late!" she cried to the chauffeur. "I can't wait for him, I simply can't. I'll miss the plane. Hurry now, driver, hurry! To the airport!"

The chauffeur, had he been watching her closely, might have noticed that her face had turned absolutely white and that the whole expression had suddenly altered. There was no longer that rather soft and silly look. A peculiar hardness had settled itself upon the features. The little mouth, usually so flabby, was now tight and thin, the eyes were bright, and the voice, when she spoke, carried a new note of authority.

"Hurry, driver, hurry!"

"Isn't your husband travelling with you?" the man asked, astonished.

"Certainly not! I was only going to drop him at the club. It won't matter. He'll understand. He'll get a cab. Don't sit there talking, man. *Get going!* I've got a plane to catch for Paris!"

With Mrs. Foster urging him from the back seat, the man drove fast all the way, and she caught her plane with a few minutes to spare. Soon she was high up over the Atlantic, reclining comfortably in her airplane chair, listening to the hum of the motors, heading for Paris at last. The new mood was still with her. She felt remarkably strong and, in a queer sort of way, wonderful. She was a trifle breathless with it all, but this was more from pure astonishment at what she had done than anything else, and as the plane flew farther and farther away from New York and East Sixty-second Street, a great sense of calmness began to settle upon her. By the time she reached Paris, she was just as strong and cool and calm as she could wish.

She met her grandchildren, and they were even more beautiful in the flesh than in their photographs. They were like angels, she told herself, so beautiful they were. And every day she took them for walks, and fed them cakes, and bought them presents, and told them charming stories.

Once a week, on Tuesdays, she wrote a letter to her husband—a nice, chatty letter—full of news and gossip, which always ended with the words "Now be sure to take your meals regularly, dear, although this is something I'm afraid you may not be doing when I'm not with you."

When the six weeks were up, everybody was sad that she had to return to America, to her husband. Everybody, that is, except her. Surprisingly, she didn't seem to mind as much as one might have expected, and when she kissed them all good-bye, there was something in her manner and in the things she said that appeared to hint at the possibility of a return in the not too distant future.

However, like the faithful wife she was, she did not overstay her time. Exactly six weeks after she had arrived, she sent a cable to her husband and caught the plane back to New York.

Arriving at Idlewild, Mrs. Foster was interested to observe that there was no car to meet her. It is possible that she might even have been a little amused. But she was extremely calm and did not overtip the porter who helped her into a taxi with her baggage.

New York was colder than Paris, and there were lumps of dirty snow lying in the gutters of the streets. The taxi drew up before the house on Sixty-second Street, and Mrs. Foster persuaded the driver to carry her two large cases to the top of the steps. Then she paid him off and rang the bell. She waited, and there was no answer. Just to make sure, she rang again, and she could hear it tinkling shrilly far away in the pantry, at the back of the house. But still no one came.

So she took out her own key and opened the door herself.

The first thing she saw as she entered was a great pile of mail lying on the floor where it had fallen after being slipped through the letter hole. The place was dark and cold. A dust sheet was still draped over the grandfather clock. In spite of the cold, the atmosphere was peculiarly oppressive, and there was a faint but curious odor in the air that she had never smelled before.

She walked quickly across the hall and disappeared for a moment around the corner to the left, at the back. There was something deliberate and purposeful about this action; she had the air of a woman who is off to investigate a rumor or to confirm a suspicion. And when she returned a few seconds later, there was a little glimmer of satisfaction on her face.

She paused in the center of the hall, as though wondering what to do next. Then, suddenly, she turned and went across into her husband's study. On the desk she found his address book, and after hunting through it for a while she picked up the phone and dialled a number.

"Hello," she said. "Listen—this is Nine East Sixty-second Street . . . Yes, that's right. Could you send someone round as soon as possible, do you think? Yes, it seems to be stuck between the second and third floors. At least, that's where the indicator's pointing . . . Right away? Oh, that's very kind of you. You see, my legs aren't

any too good for walking up a lot of stairs. Thank you so much. Good-bye."

She replaced the receiver and sat there at her husband's desk, patiently waiting for the man who would be coming soon to repair the elevator.

I
THE BREAKING POINT
An elderly, wealthy couple seemingly live a life of amiability and sophistication. But there is a conflict of wills operating here. Mrs. Foster has a deep fear of missing trains, planes, and even theater curtains. Her husband, on the other hand, dawdles and procrastinates when there is a time deadline to make. Does he do this deliberately to torment his wife? After years of marriage, she becomes suspicious as she notices little things: his seeming delight in the fog; his peering intently at her twitching eye; and finally, her discovery of the missing box shoved down behind the seat. Then the story moves to its surprising end. When did you first guess what is ultimately revealed at the end?

II
IMPLICATIONS
Discuss the following statements:

1. The conflict that is operating between husband and wife is shown only by the muscle twitching in Mrs. Foster's eye.

2. A repeated annoyance usually brings one to a point of eruption either with words or actions.

3. The title is ironic.

III
TECHNIQUES
Identification

Another writer might have made Mrs. Foster's anxiety about being on time ridiculous and her husband's antics in frustrating her, amusing. The story would then have been a comedy instead of a grim tale. With such a change, the reader's sympathies could have been with the husband. How does the author in this story make you side with the wife?

Diction

Read the phrases that follow and then reread the first four paragraphs to see the phrases in context.

Discuss the effect that Dahl's choice of words has on you as a reader. What quality does it give to the telling?

It was nothing much—. . . .

It is really extraordinary. . . .

Mr. Foster may possibly have had a right. . . .

Mind you, it is by no means certain. . . .

He had disciplined her. . . .

Assuming (though one cannot be sure). . . .

. . . there had been times recently. . . .

IV
WORDS

A. Use context clues here and in the story to define each italicized word.

1. "All her life, Mrs. Foster had had an almost *pathological* fear of missing a train, a plane, a boat, or even a theater curtain."

2. "It is really extraordinary how in certain people a simple *apprehension* . . . can grow into a serious obsession."

3. ". . . with the exception of this one small irrepressible *foible*, Mrs. Foster was . . . a good and loving wife."

4. "There was a mass of people inside, mostly *disconsolate* passengers standing around the ticket counters."

5. "In spite of the cold, the atmosphere was peculiarly *oppressive*. . . ."

B. The chart that follows lists words under Noun or Verb indicating how they were used in the story. Complete the chart by writing either the noun or verb form of each word.

Noun	Verb
obsession	_____
_____	discipline
_____	distribute
_____	supervise
operation	_____
resemblance	_____
suspicion	_____

V
COMPOSITION

The conflict between Mr. Foster and Mrs. Foster has grown over the years of their married life. Each has some reason to be annoyed with the other.

1. Write a paragraph explaining why Mr. Foster is justified in his actions.

2. Write a second paragraph explaining why Mrs. Foster is justified in her actions.

3. Write a final paragraph explaining why you think either Mr. Foster or Mrs. Foster is more at fault.

GEORGE ORWELL

George Orwell (1903–1950) was the pen name of Eric Blair, a tall, gentle Englishman who wrote in bitter, satiric fashion of the things he hated: Communists, leftists, intellectuals, cruelty in life. Born in Burma, he was educated at Eton and later served in the Indian Imperial Police in Burma. He fought in the Spanish Civil War and acquired an undying hatred of Communism which inspired his novels *Animal Farm* and *Nineteen Eighty-Four*. Orwell felt that people must act decently toward themselves and toward their fellow human beings if liberty and justice are to be achieved. This intense feeling is one cause of the conflict of wills in the following essay about a true experience.

Shooting an Elephant

In Moulmein,[1] in lower Burma, I was hated by large numbers of people—the only time in my life that I have been important enough for this to happen to me. I was subdivisional police officer of the town, and in an aimless, petty kind of way an anti-European feeling was very bitter. No one had the guts to raise a riot, but if a European woman went through the bazaars[2] alone somebody would probably spit betel juice over her dress. As a police officer I was an obvious target and was baited whenever it seemed safe to do so. When a nimble Burman tripped me up on the football[3] field and the referee (another Burman) looked the other way, the crowd yelled with hideous laughter. This happened more than once. In the end the sneering yellow faces of young men that met me everywhere, the insults hooted after me when I was at a safe distance, got badly on my nerves. The young Buddhist priests were the worst of all. There were several thousands of them in the town and none of them seemed to have anything to do except stand on street corners and jeer at Europeans.

All this was perplexing and upsetting. For at that time I had already made up my mind that imperialism was an evil thing and the sooner I chucked up my job and got out of it the better. Theoretically—and secretly, of course—I was

all for the Burmese and all against their oppressors, the British. As for the job I was doing, I hated it more bitterly than I can perhaps make clear. In a job like that you see the dirty work of Empire at close quarters. The wretched prisoners huddling in the stinking cages of the lockups, the gray, cowed faces of the long-term convicts, the scarred buttocks of men who had been flogged with bamboos—all these oppressed me with an intolerable sense of guilt. But I could get nothing into perspective. I was young and ill-educated and I had to think out my problems in the utter silence that is imposed on every Englishman in the East. I did not know that the British Empire is dying, still less did I know that it is a great deal better than the younger empires that are going to supplant it. All I knew was that I was stuck between my hatred of the empire I served and my rage against the evil-spirited little beasts who tried to make my job impossible. With one part of my mind I thought of the British Raj as an unbreakable tyranny, as something clamped down, in *saecula saeculorum*,[4] upon the will of prostrate peoples, with another

---

1. **Moulmein** (mūl′mān′), a coastal city.
2. **bazaar** (bə zär′), an oriental market, consisting of many shops and stalls. The **betel** (bē′təl) **palm**, an Asiatic palm whose leaves and nuts are chewed much as Americans chew gum.
3. **football**, the game we usually call "soccer."
4. **Raj** (räj), rule, domination. **In saecula saeculorum,** "forever and forever."

From *Shooting an Elephant and Other Essays* by George Orwell, copyright 1950 by Sonia Brownell Orwell; renewed 1978 by Sonia Pitt-Rivers. Reprinted by permission of Harcourt Brace Jovanovich, Inc.

part I thought that the greatest joy in the world would be to drive a bayonet into a Buddhist priest's guts. Feelings like these are the normal by-product of imperialism; ask any Anglo-Indian[5] official, if you can catch him off duty.

One day something happened which in a roundabout way was enlightening. It was a tiny incident in itself, but it gave me a better glimpse than I had had before of the real nature of imperialism—the real motives for which despotic governments act. Early one morning the sub-inspector at a police station the other end of the town rang me up on the phone and said that an elephant was ravaging the bazaar. Would I please come and do something about it? I did not know what I could do, but I wanted to see what was happening and I got onto a pony and started out. I took my rifle, an old .44 Winchester and much too small to kill an elephant, but I thought the noise might be useful *in terrorem*.[6] Various Burmans stopped me on the way and told me about the elephant's doings. It was not, of course, a wild elephant, but a tame one which had gone "must."[7] It had been chained up, as tame elephants always are when their attack of "must" is due, but on the previous night it had broken its chain and escaped. Its mahout,[8] the only person who could manage it when it was in that state, had set out in pursuit, but had taken the wrong direction and was now twelve hours' journey away, and in the morning the elephant had suddenly reappeared in the town. The Burmese population had no weapons and were quite helpless against it. It had already destroyed somebody's bamboo hut, killed a cow, and raided some fruit stalls and devoured the stock; also it had met the municipal rubbish van and, when the driver jumped out and took to his heels, had turned the van over and inflicted violences upon it.

The Burmese sub-inspector and some Indian constables were waiting for me in the quarter where the elephant had been seen. It was a very poor quarter, a labyrinth of squalid huts, thatched with palm leaf, winding all over a steep hillside. I remember it was a cloudy, stuffy morning at the beginning of the rains. We began questioning the people where the elephant had gone and, as usual, failed to get any definite information. That is invariably the case in the East; a story always sounds clear enough at a distance, but the nearer you get to the scene of events the vaguer it becomes. Some of the people said that the elephant had gone in one direction, some said that it had gone in another, some professed not even to have heard of any elephant. I had made up my mind that the whole story was a pack of lies, when I heard yells a little distance away. There was a loud, scandalized cry of "Go away, child! Go away this instant!" and an old woman with a switch in her hand came round the corner of a hut, violently shooing away a crowd of naked children. Some more women followed, clicking their tongues and exclaiming; evidently there was something the children ought not to have seen. I rounded the hut and saw a man's dead body sprawling in the mud. He was an Indian, a black Dravidian coolie,[9] almost naked, and he could not have been dead many minutes. The people said that the elephant had come suddenly upon him round the corner of the hut, caught him with its trunk, put its foot on his back, and ground him into the earth. This was the rainy season and the ground was soft, and his face had scored a trench a foot deep and a couple of yards long. He was lying on his belly with his arms crucified and head sharply twisted to one side. His face was coated with mud, the eyes wide open, the teeth bared and grinning with an unendurable agony. (Never tell me, by the way, that the dead look peaceful. Most of the corpses I have seen looked devilish.) The friction of the great beast's foot had stripped the skin from his back as neatly as one skins a rabbit. As soon as I saw the dead man I sent an orderly to a friend's house nearby to borrow an elephant rifle. I had already sent back

5. **Anglo-Indian,** designating or pertaining to an Englishman serving in Indian or adjacent areas.
6. **.44,** a rifle of moderate caliber. **In terrorem,** "in case of fright."
7. **must,** frenzied and out of control.
8. **mahout** (mə hout'), an elephant driver and tender.
9. **Dravidian** (drə vid'ē ən), the ancient inhabitants of southern India. **coolie,** a Far Eastern laborer.

the pony, not wanting it to go mad with fright and throw me if it smelt the elephant.

The orderly came back in a few minutes with a rifle and five cartridges, and meanwhile some Burmans had arrived and told us that the elephant was in the paddy[10] fields below, only a few hundred yards away. As I started forward practically the whole yellow population of the quarter flocked out of the houses and followed me. They had seen the rifle and were all shouting excitedly that I was going to shoot the elephant. They had not shown much interest in the elephant when he was merely ravaging their homes, but it was different now that he was going to be shot. It was a bit of fun to them, as it would be to an English crowd; besides they wanted the meat. It made me vaguely uneasy. I had no intention of shooting the elephant—I had merely sent for the rifle to defend myself if necessary—and it is always unnerving to have a crowd following you. I marched down the hill, looking and feeling a fool, with the rifle over my shoulder and an ever growing army of people jostling at my heels. At the bottom, when you got away from the huts, there was a metaled road[11] and beyond that a miry waste of paddy fields a thousand yards across, not yet plowed but soggy from the first rains and dotted with coarse grass. The elephant was standing eight yards from the road, his left side toward us. He took not the slightest notice of the crowd's approach. He was tearing up bunches of grass, beating them against his knees to clean them, and stuffing them into his mouth.

I had halted on the road. As soon as I saw the elephant I knew with perfect certainty that I ought not to shoot him. It is a serious matter to shoot a working elephant—it is comparable to destroying a huge and costly piece of machinery—and obviously one ought not to do it if it can possibly be avoided. And at that distance, peacefully eating, the elephant looked no more dangerous than a cow. I thought then and I think now that his attack of "must" was already passing

10. **paddy** (pad′ē), rice fields.
11. **metaled road,** one with surfaces reinforced with metal strips or slabs.

off; in which case he would merely wander harmlessly about until the mahout came back and caught him. Moreover, I did not want in the least to shoot him. I decided that I would watch him a little while to make sure that he did not turn savage again, and then go home.

But at that moment I glanced round at the crowd that had followed me. It was an immense crowd, two thousand at the least and growing every minute. It blocked the road for a long distance on either side. I looked at the sea of yellow faces above the garish clothes—faces all happy and excited over this bit of fun, all certain that the elephant was going to be shot. They were watching me as they would watch a conjurer about to perform a trick. They did not like me, but with the magical rifle in my hand I was momentarily worth watching. And suddenly I realized that I would have to shoot the elephant after all. The people expected it of me and I had got to do it; I could feel their two thousand wills pressing me forward irresistibly. And it was at this moment, as I stood there with the rifle in my hands, that I first grasped the hollowness, the futility of the white man's dominion in the East. Here was I, the white man with his gun, standing in front of the unarmed crowd—seemingly the leading actor of the piece; but in reality I was only an absurd puppet pushed to and fro by the will of those yellow faces behind. I perceived in this moment that when the white man turns tyrant it is his own freedom that he destroys. He becomes a sort of hollow, posing dummy, the conventionalized figure of a sahib.[12] For it is the condition of his rule that he shall spend his life in trying to "impress the natives," and so in every crisis he has got to do what the "natives" expect of him. He wears a mask, and his face grows to fit it. I had got to shoot the elephant. I had committed myself to doing it when I sent for the rifle. A sahib has got to act like a sahib; he has got to appear resolute, to know his own mind and do definite things. To come all that way, rifle in hand, with two thousand people marching at my heels, and then to

12. **sahib** (sä′ ib), a European master or gentleman.

trail feebly away, having done nothing—no, that was impossible. The crowd would laugh at me. And my whole life, every white man's in the East, was one long struggle not to be laughed at.

But I did not want to shoot the elephant. I watched him beating his bunch of grass against his knees, with that preoccupied grandmotherly air that elephants have. It seemed to me that it would be murder to shoot him. At that age I was not squeamish about killing animals, but I had never shot an elephant and never wanted to. (Somehow it always seems worse to kill a large animal.) Besides, there was the beast's owner to be considered. Alive, the elephant was worth at least a hundred pounds; dead, he would only be worth the value of his tusks, five pounds, possibly. But I had got to act quickly. I turned to the experienced-looking Burmans who had been there when we arrived, and asked them how the elephant had been behaving. They all said the same thing; he took no notice of you if you left him alone, but he might charge if you went too close to him.

It was perfectly clear to me what I ought to do. I ought to walk up to within, say, twenty-five yards of the elephant and test his behavior. If he charged, I could shoot; if he took no notice of me, it would be safe to leave him until the mahout came back. But I also knew that I was going to do no such thing. I was a poor shot with a rifle and the ground was soft mud into which one would sink at every step. If the elephant charged and I missed him, I should have about as much chance as a toad under a steam roller. But even then I was not thinking particularly of my own skin, only of the watchful yellow faces behind. For at that moment, with the crowd watching me, I was not afraid in the ordinary sense, as I would have been if I had been alone. A white man mustn't be frightened in front of "natives"; and so, in general, he isn't frightened. The thought in my mind was that if anything went wrong those two thousand Burmans would see me pursued, caught, trampled on, and reduced to a grinning corpse like that Indian up the hill. And if that happened it was quite prob-

able that some of them would laugh. That would never do. There was only one alternative. I shoved the cartridges into the magazine and lay down on the road to get a better aim.

The crowd grew very still, and a deep, low, happy sigh, as of people who see the theater curtain go up at last, breathed from innumerable throats. They were going to have their bit of fun after all. The rifle was a beautiful German thing with cross-hair sights. I did not know then that in shooting an elephant one would shoot to cut an imaginary bar running from earhole to earhole. I ought, therefore, as the elephant was sideways on, to have aimed straight at his earhole; actually I aimed several inches in front of this, thinking the brain would be further forward.

When I pulled the trigger I did not hear the bang or feel the kick—one never does when a shot goes home—but I heard the devilish roar of glee that went up from the crowd. In that instant, in too short a time, one would have thought, even for the bullet to get there, a mysterious, terrible change had come over the elephant. He neither stirred nor fell, but every line of his body had altered. He looked suddenly stricken, shrunken, immensely old, as though the frightful impact of the bullet had paralyzed him without knocking him down. At last, after what seemed a long time—it might have been five seconds, I dare say—he sagged flabbily to his knees. His mouth slobbered. An enormous senility seemed to have settled upon him. One could have imagined him thousands of years old. I fired again into the same spot. At the second shot he did not collapse but climbed with desperate slowness to his feet and stood weakly erect, with legs sagging and head drooping. I fired a third time. That was the shot that did for him. You could see the agony of it jolt his whole body and knock the last remnant of strength from his legs. But in falling he seemed for a moment to rise, for as his hind legs collapsed beneath him he seemed to tower upward like a huge rock toppling, his trunk reaching skywards like a tree. He trumpeted for the first and only time. And then down he came, his belly toward me, with a crash that seemed to shake the ground even where I lay.

I got up. The Burmans were already racing past me across the mud. It was obvious that the elephant would never rise again, but he was not dead. He was breathing very rhythmically with long rattling gasps, his great mound of a side painfully rising and falling. His mouth was wide open—I could see far down into caverns of pink throat. I waited a long time for him to die, but his breathing did not weaken. Finally I fired my two remaining shots into the spot where I thought his heart must be. The thick blood welled out of him like red velvet, but still he did not die. His body did not even jerk when the shots hit him, the tortured breathing continued without a pause. He was dying, very slowly and in great agony, but in some world remote from me where not even a bullet could damage him further. I felt that I had got to put an end to that dreadful noise. It seemed dreadful to see the great beast lying there, powerless to move and yet powerless to die, and not even to be able to finish him. I sent back for my small rifle and poured shot after shot into his heart and down his throat. They seemed to make no impression. The tortured gasps continued as steadily as the ticking of a clock.

In the end I could not stand it any longer and went away. I heard later that it took him half an hour to die. Burmans were bringing dahs[13] and baskets even before I left, and I was told they had stripped his body almost to the bones by afternoon.

Afterwards, of course, there were endless discussions about the shooting of the elephant. The owner was furious, but he was only an Indian and could do nothing. Besides, legally I had done the right thing, for a mad elephant has to be killed, like a mad dog, if its owner fails to control it. Among the Europeans, opinion was divided. The older men said I was right, the younger men said it was a shame to shoot an elephant for killing a coolie, because an elephant

---

13. **dahs** (däz), bowls.
14. **Coringhee** (kō ring′gē), Southern Indian.

was worth more than any Coringhee[14] coolie. And afterwards I was very glad that the coolie had been killed; it put me legally in the right and gave me a sufficient pretext for shooting the elephant. I often wondered whether any of the others grasped that I had done it solely to avoid looking a fool.

I
THE PUBLIC AND THE PRIVATE LIFE

In this essay, George Orwell makes clear the conflicts that may confront one who lives in a world of political and cultural tensions. Orwell is a person of strong private principles, but he is also a police official whose role is a public one. What are the conflicts Orwell faces in this essay?

II
IMPLICATIONS

How do the following quotations show the conflict of wills in the situation?

1. ". . . I was stuck between my hatred of the empire I served and my rage against the evil-spirited little beasts who tried to make my job impossible."

2. ". . . I could feel their two thousand wills pressing me forward irresistibly."

3. "And my whole life, every white man's in the East, was one long struggle not to be laughed at."

4. "But I did not want to shoot the elephant."

III
TECHNIQUES

Identification

The reader's feelings about the situation and about the author are not likely to be simple. What qualities of Orwell's personality did you find admirable? What ones did you find offensive or unsympathetic? How would you sum up your opinion of him?

Diction

In the first two paragraphs, Orwell uses several almost slang expressions, such as "No one had the guts to. . . ." What qualities does the inclusion of such phrases give to the writing? Does it make it more or less formal?

GUY DE MAUPASSANT

A great French writer known for his short stories, Guy de Maupassant[1] (1850–1893) spent his childhood at his grandfather's estate in Normandy. Many of his stories realistically present the landscape and the people of that area. At thirteen, he attended a Catholic school but felt no regret at being expelled less than two years later. Sent then to Rouen's *lycée*, he spent Sundays at the house of his father's friend, Gustave Flaubert, listening to him discuss writing with the poet Louis Bouilhet. These sessions may have fostered de Maupassant's interest in writing. After the outbreak of the Franco-Prussian War, he interrupted his law studies to enlist. When he returned, he took a post as a clerk in the Ministry of Marine; this gave him first-hand insights into the life of office workers. Both experiences provided materials for his later short stories. While working as a clerk, de Maupassant divided his spare time between rowing on the Seine and writing. He showed everything he wrote to Flaubert, a tough taskmaster who emphasized the need for acute observation and realistic portrayals. When de Maupassant's story, "Boule de suif," was published in a collection of stories by French writers, critics declared it a masterpiece. In the next ten years, de Maupassant published some three hundred short stories and six novels—enough fiction to fill thirty books. Beset by agonizing headaches, eye trouble, and a growing fear of madness, he worked at a frantic pace, exercised too violently, and used drugs to escape. Finally, early in 1892, the pain became so unbearable that de Maupassant attempted suicide. He was then confined to a mental hospital, where he died. De Maupassant is noted for his skill in presenting men and women just as he saw them, using great objectivity and never expressing his own judgment of them. Conciseness, strength, and realism are the hallmarks of his works.

The Prisoners

translated by Artine Artinian

No noise in the forest, save for the light tremor of snow falling upon the trees. It had been coming down since noon, a fine snow which powdered the branches with a frozen froth, which threw over the dead leaves of the thickets a silvery roof, spread out on the roads an immense soft white rug, and increased the boundless silence of that ocean of trees.

In front of the ranger's house a barearmed young woman was chopping wood on a rock. She was tall, slender, and strong, a daughter of the woods, daughter and wife of rangers.

A voice called from within the house. "We are alone tonight, Berthine. You've got to come in. It's almost dark—Prussians and wolves may be about."

The woodchopper answered as she split a stump with vigorous blows, each of which lifted her chest with the upward thrust of her arms.

"I've finished, Mamma. I'm coming, I'm coming. Don't worry, it's still light."

---

1. **Guy de Maupassant** (gē′də mō′pə sänt).

Guy de Maupassant

She brought in kindling and logs, stacked them by the fireplace, went out again to close the enormous oak shutters, and, inside at last, closed the heavy bolts on the door.

Her mother, a wrinkled old woman whom age had made timorous, was spinning near the fire. "I don't like it when Papa is out. Two women aren't strong."

The young woman answered, "Oh! I guess I could kill a wolf or a Prussian." And she glanced at a large revolver hanging over the hearth.

Her husband had been taken into the army at the beginning of the Prussian invasion,[2] and the two women had remained alone with the father, the old ranger Nicolas Pichon,[3] called "High Horse," because he had obstinately refused to leave his home to go to the greater security of the city.

The nearest city was Rethel,[4] ancient fortress perched on a rock. The Rethelois were patriots.

They had decided to resist the invaders, to shut themselves in and withstand a siege according to the tradition of their city. Twice already, under Henry IV[5] and under Louis XIV,[6] the people of Rethel had distinguished themselves by their heroic stands. They would do it again this time, by God, or else they would burn within their walls!

So they had bought cannon and guns, equipped a militia, formed battalions and companies, and practiced every day on the central square. Everyone—bakers, grocers, butchers, notaries, lawyers, carpenters, bookdealers, even druggists—drilled in turn, at regular times, under the command of M. Lavigne, former noncommissioned officer of dragoons, now a dry-goods merchant, having married the daughter and inherited the shop of M. Revaudon, Sr.

He had taken the rank of major, commanding officer of the square, and, with all the young men away in the regular army, he had enlisted all the others and was training them for the resistance. Fat men no longer idled in the streets but walked briskly to reduce their fat and to improve their wind. Weak men carried loads to strengthen their muscles.

The Prussians were expected but did not arrive. And yet they were not far away; for twice already their scouts had come through the woods as far as the house of the ranger Nicolas Pichon, known as High Horse.

The old ranger, who could still run like a fox, had come to warn the city. They had set the cannon, but the enemy had not appeared.

The home of High Horse served as advance post in the forest of Aveline. Twice a week he would go to the city for provisions and would bring news of the country to the city dwellers.

He had left that very day to report that a small detachment of German infantry had stopped at his house the day before about two o'clock in the afternoon, and had left almost immediately. The noncommissioned officer in charge spoke French.

---

2. **Prussian invasion,** the setting is that of the Franco-Prussian War (1870–1871).
3. **Pichon** (pē shôn′).
4. **Rethel** (rə tel′), town in southern France.

5. **Henry IV,** king of France from 1589 to 1610.
6. **Louis XIV,** king of France from 1643 to 1715.

When the old man left home, he took along his two dogs, two lion-jawed watchdogs, for fear of the wolves, which were becoming savage, and he left his two women with the admonition to barricade themselves in the house as soon as it became dark.

His daughter feared nothing, but the old woman always shuddered and kept saying over and over, "All this will turn out bad. You'll see it will turn out bad."

That evening she was even more anxious than usual. "Do you know what time Papa'll get home?" she asked.

"Oh! Not before eleven o'clock, for sure. When he has dinner with the major, he always gets back late." And she hooked the kettle over the fire to make soup. A moment later she stopped stirring to listen to a vague noise which came to her through the chimney. She murmured, "I hear footsteps in the woods—seven or eight men, at least."

The terrified mother stopped her spinning wheel, stammering, "Oh! My goodness! And Papa not here."

She had not finished speaking when violent blows shook the door. As the women did not reply, a strong guttural voice shouted, "Open!"

Then, after a silence, the same voice continued, "Open! Or I break the door!"

Berthine slipped the big revolver into the pocket of her skirt, then pressing her ear to the door, she asked, "Who's there?"

The voice answered, "The detachment that came by the other day."

"What do you want?"

"I have been lost in the woods since this morning with my detachment. Open or I break the door."

She had no choice. Quickly she slipped the large bolt, then pulling the heavy door, she saw six men in the pale darkness of the snow, six Prussian soldiers, the same who had gone by the day before. She said firmly, "What have you come for at this hour?"

The noncommissioned officer repeated, "I am lost, completely lost. I recognized the house. Not eaten since this morning; my men either."

Berthine declared, "But Mamma and me are all alone tonight."

The soldier, who seemed like a good sort, replied, "It doesn't matter. I will not harm you, but you will give us something to eat. We are dead tired and starved."

The young woman stepped back. "Come in," she said.

They came in, covered with snow, their helmets topped by a kind of frothy cream which made them look like meringues, and they appeared worn out, exhausted.

She showed them the wooden benches along the two sides of the large table. "Sit down," she said. "I'll make you some soup. It's true you look all in." Then she closed the bolts of the door.

She added water to her kettle, put in more butter and potatoes, then unhooking a piece of bacon hanging in the fireplace, she cut half of it and dropped it in the soup.

The six men's eyes followed her every movement with aroused hunger. They had stacked their guns and helmets in a corner, and they were waiting, well-behaved like children on school benches.

The mother had begun to spin again, casting frequent apprehensive glances at the invaders. Nothing more was heard but the light whir of the spinning wheel and the crackling of the fire and the murmur of the simmering water.

But all of a sudden a strange noise made them all start, something like labored breathing at the door, an animal's breathing, strong and loud.

The German officer had darted toward the guns. The ranger's daughter stopped him with a gesture, and said smiling, "It's the wolves. They are like you, they prowl and are hungry."

The man, incredulous, wished to have a look, and as soon as he opened the upper panel of the door, he saw two big gray beasts streaking away. He muttered as he resumed his place, "I wouldn't have believed it." And he waited for his stew to be ready.

They ate it voraciously, with mouths stretched back to the ears to swallow the more, eyes opening wide at the same time as jaws, and throat noises like the gurgling in a drainpipe.

The two women silently watched the rapid movements of the big red beards; and the potatoes disappeared into the moving fleeces.

As they were thirsty, Berthine went to the cellar to draw cider. She was gone for some time; it was a small vaulted wine cellar which, it was said, had served as prison and hiding place during the Revolution. One had access to it by means of a narrow spiral stairway closed by a trap door in the rear of the kitchen.

When Berthine reappeared, she was laughing, she was laughing to herself in a sly way. And she gave the Germans her full pitcher.

Then she ate too, with her mother, at the other end of the kitchen.

The soldiers had finished eating, and all six of them fell asleep around the table. From time to time a forehead would fall onto the table with a thud, whereupon the man, rudely awakened, would straighten.

Berthine said to the officer, "Lie down before the fire, why don't you? There's room enough for six. I'm going up to my room with Mamma."

The two women went up to the second floor. The men heard them lock their door, walk about a bit; then they made no more noise.

The Prussians stretched out on the tile floor, their feet toward the fire, their heads on their rolled up coats, and all six were soon snoring, on six different keys, sharp or sonorous, but steady and powerful.

They had been sleeping for some time when a shot rang out, so loud that one would have thought it directed against the walls of the house. The soldiers were on their feet at once. But two more detonations burst out, followed by three others.

The upstairs door opened suddenly, and Berthine appeared, barefoot, in her nightgown, a candle in her hand, looking scared to death. She stammered, "That's the French, there are at least two hundred of them. If they find you here, they'll burn the house down. Go down to the cellar, quick, and don't make any noise. If you make any noise, we're lost."

"All right, we will. How do we go down?"

The young woman hurriedly lifted the narrow square trap door, and the six men disappeared by the little spiral staircase, disappearing into the ground one after another, descending backwards for surer footing.

But when the point of the last helmet had gone out of sight, Berthine slammed the heavy oak board, thick as a wall, hard as steel, held by hinges and a lock worthy of a prison cell, and turned the key twice in the lock. Then she began to laugh silently and ecstatically, with a mad desire to dance over the heads of her prisoners.

They made no noise whatever, enclosed as if in a box, a box of stone, with air entering only through a barred vent.

Berthine immediately relit her fire, put her kettle on again, and made more soup, saying to herself, "Papa will be tired tonight."

Then she sat down and waited. The only sound to break the silence was the regular tick-tock of the grandfather clock. From time to time she glanced impatiently at the clock, as if to say, "It sure is slow tonight."

But soon she thought she could hear murmuring below. Indistinct voices reached her through the stone vault of the cellar. The Prussians were beginning to suspect her ruse, and soon the officer climbed the little staircase and struck the trap door with his fists. Again he shouted, "Open!"

She rose, came close and, imitating his accent, said, "What do you want?"

"Open!"

"I won't."

The man was getting angry. "Open, or else I break the door!"

She began to laugh. "Break away, my good man, break away!"

So he began to strike the butt of his gun against the oaken trap door closed over his head. But it would have resisted blows from a catapult.

The ranger's daughter heard him go down again. Then, one after another, the soldiers came to try their strength and to inspect the trap door. But, doubtless judging their attempts futile, they all descended once more into the cellar and began to talk among themselves as before.

Berthine listened to them, then went to open the outside door and listened to the night.

A distant bark reached her. She began to whistle like a hunter, and almost instantly, two enormous dogs rose up in the dark and jumped playfully upon her. She grasped them by the neck and held them to keep them from running. Then she shouted with all her strength, "Hi, Papa!"

A voice replied, still far off, "Hi, Berthine."

She waited for a few seconds, then called again, "Hi, Papa!"

The voice, nearer now, answered, "Hi, Berthine!"

"Don't go past the vent," she said. "There are some Prussians in the cellar."

And suddenly the man's tall silhouette was outlined to the left, standing between two tree trunks. "Prussians in the cellar? What are they up to?"

His daughter began to laugh. "It's them that were here yesterday. Lost in the forest. I put them in the cellar to cool their heels." And she related the adventure, how she had scared them with revolver shots and locked them up in the cellar.

The old man, still serious, asked, "What do you expect me to do with them at this hour?"

She answered, "Go and get M. Lavigne and his men. He'll make them prisoners. Will he be glad!"

Old man Pichon smiled. "That's so. He will be glad!"

His daughter continued, "There's some soup for you. Eat it quick, then go."

The old ranger sat down and began to eat the soup after placing two full dishes on the floor for his dogs.

The Prussians, hearing the voices above, were now silent.

High Horse left a quarter of an hour later. And Berthine, head in hands, waited.

The prisoners began to move about again. They shouted now and beat incessantly with furious blows of their gun butts the solid trap door of the cellar. Then they began to shoot through the vent, doubtless hoping to be heard should some German detachment be passing in the neighborhood.

The ranger's daughter did not stir; but all this noise annoyed her, made her nervous. A devilish anger was beginning to get hold of her. She had a mind to murder them, the scoundrels, just to make them quiet.

Then, her impatience increasing, she started to look at the clock, counting the minutes.

The father had left an hour and a half ago. He had reached the city by now. She could picture him telling M. Lavigne about it, and the major was turning pale with emotion, and ringing for his maid to bring his uniform and his arms. She could hear the drummer running through the streets. Frightened heads appeared at the windows. The citizen-soldiers left their houses, half-dressed, out of breath, buckling their belts, and rushing towards their commander's house.

Then the troops, with High Horse leading, began to march in the night, in the snow, towards the forest.

She looked at the clock. "They can get here in an hour."

A nervous impatience consumed her. The minutes seemed interminable. How long it was!

At last the time she had set for their arrival was indicated on the dial.

And she opened the door again to listen to their coming. She saw a shadow walking warily. She was frightened and cried out. It was her father. He said. "They sent me to see if there was anything new."

"No, nothing."

Whereupon he gave a prolonged, strident blast on his whistle into the night. And soon they saw something brown coming slowly under the trees: the vanguard of ten men.

High Horse repeated over and over, "Don't go in front of the cellar vent." And the first-comers showed the others the dreaded vent.

The main body of the troop finally appeared, two hundred men in all, each one with two hundred rounds of ammunition.

M. Lavigne, on edge, excited, placed them in

such a way as to completely surround the house, while leaving a large open space in front of the little black hole level with the ground, through which the cellar received air.

Then he entered the house and inquired about the strength and disposition of the enemy, now so quiet that one would have thought them vanished, passed out or escaped through the vent.

M. Lavigne kicked the trap door with his foot and called out, "Mr. Prussian officer?"

The German did not reply.

The major continued, "Mr. Prussian officer?" But his efforts were vain. For twenty minutes he summoned the silent officer to surrender with arms and effects, promising him and his soldiers safety and military honors. But he obtained no sign either of consent or hostility. The situation was becoming difficult.

The militiamen stamped their feet in the snow, clapped their shoulders vigorously, the way coachmen do to keep warm, and they watched the vent with an increasing and childish urge to go near it.

Finally one of them, named Potdevin, who was very agile, decided to risk it. He leaped forward like a deer. His attempt succeeded. The prisoners seemed to be dead.

A voice shouted, "Nobody's there!"

And another soldier crossed the open space before the dangerous hole. Now it became a game. Every second a man would dash from one group to the other, as children do at prisoner's base, and he would churn the snow in his wild sprint. They had made several fires to warm themselves, and this running profile of the national guard appeared illuminated in its swift trip from the right camp to the left.

Someone shouted, "Your turn, Maloison!"

Maloison was a fat baker whose girth caused merriment among his pals.

He hesitated. They made fun of him. When he finally made up his mind, he set out on the double, in a regular rhythm which nevertheless made him pant and which shook his heavy paunch.

The entire detachment laughed till the tears came. They cried out in encouragement, "Bravo, bravo, Maloison!"

He had covered about two thirds of his distance when a sudden long red flame burst from the vent. A detonation thundered, and the corpulent baker fell on his face with a dreadful cry.

No one rushed up to help him. And they watched him drag himself painfully on all fours in the snow, groaning the while, until, the fateful passage behind him, he fainted.

He had a bullet in the fat of his thigh, high up.

After the first surprise and the first terror, laughter broke out again.

But Major Lavigne appeared on the threshold of the ranger's house. He had just drawn up his plan of attack. He commanded in a vibrant voice, "Tinsmith Planchut and his men!"

Three men stepped forward. "Take down the gutters of the house."

And in a quarter of an hour they had brought the major twenty meters of gutter. Whereupon, with a thousand measures of precaution, he had them bore a small round hole in the edge of the trap door, and starting a flow of water from the pump to this opening, he declared in high glee, "We shall treat the Germans to a drink."

A frenzied hurrah of admiration burst forth, followed by joyous shouts and laughs. And the major organized work platoons which would relieve each other every five minutes. Then he commanded, "Pump!"

And the iron handle having been put into motion, a slight noise glided along the length of the gutters and soon fell into the cellar, from step to step, with the cadence of a waterfall.

They waited.

An hour went by, then two, then three.

The French officer walked back and forth feverishly in the kitchen, putting his ear to the floor from time to time, trying to guess what the enemy was doing, wondering if he would soon capitulate.

He was stirring now, the enemy. They could hear him moving barrels, speaking, splashing.

Toward eight o'clock in the morning a voice came from the vent. "I wish to speak to the French officer."

Lavigne replied from the window, without thrusting his head out too far, "Do you surrender?"

"I surrender."

"In that case, hand over the guns."

They saw a gun fall from the hole into the snow, then two, then three, all of them. And the same voice declared, "I haven't any more. Hurry. I'm drowning."

The major commanded, "Cease pumping." The pump handle fell motionless. And having filled the kitchen with soldiers fully armed, he slowly lifted the oaken trap door.

Four soaked heads appeared, four blond heads with long light hair, and soon the other two—six shaking, dripping, frightened Germans came out of the trap door.

They were seized and tied. Then, as the French feared a surprise, they left at once, in two companies, one carrying Maloison on a mattress with poles.

They marched triumphantly into Rethel.

M. Lavigne was decorated for having captured a Prussian vanguard, and the fat baker was awarded the military medal for wounds received at the hands of the enemy.

I
CONFLICT OF WILLS IN WAR

Unlike the bitter personal conflicts between individuals that erupt in such selections as *Antigone* and "The Jar," war breeds a generalized animosity between the people of one nation and the people of another. Berthine has no personal dislike of the six soldiers. They behave themselves in a well-mannered fashion even though they are desperately tired. Yet because of their nationality, they are her enemies, and she sets out to capture them. As a reader, you are probably on her side and want her to succeed. Why?

II
IMPLICATIONS

Discuss the following propositions, using the selection to support your opinions whenever possible.

1. It is hard to conceive of Berthine and her mother being so very different.

2. The Prussians do not realize the kind of person that Berthine is.

3. The story is a good illustration of Hemingway's definition of courage: "grace under pressure."

4. It is surprising that Berthine is not decorated for her part in the capture of the Prussians.

5. The last paragraph of the story is intentionally ironic.

III
TECHNIQUES

Identification

The reader's center of interest in the story is Berthine. Do you identify with her, or do you find her to be an interesting stranger?

Diction

Just as individual writers have characteristic ways of writing, so certain word choices or expressions seem characteristic of the period in which they were written. Since this is a nineteenth-century story, it contains phrases, such as those following, that would be expressed differently by a modern author. Try to rephrase them in modern diction.

1. A daughter of the woods.

2. A wrinkled old woman whom age had made timorous.

3. An admonition to barricade themselves in the house.

4. . . . . they were waiting, well-behaved like children on school benches.

5. It would have resisted blows from a catapult.

6. The way coachmen do to keep warm.

EVELYN WAUGH

Evelyn Waugh (1903–1966) was born into a family of writers. His father was a
scholar and a writer. His older brother, Alec, was a novelist. So Evelyn came early to a
deep and intense interest in art and prose. Waugh had experienced Oxford
in the twenties, schoolmastering, country life in England and Ireland,
and mad parties with bright young women. Satirizing the life of the English
upper classes, his stories seem to be about a universe that is completely
without reason. People behave in an outrageous fashion without regard
for the consequences. He used macabre and atrocious situations, such as the operation
of an animal funeral parlor in Southern California and a cocktail party given
by a dying woman in her hospital room. A telling piece of Waugh philosophy
is summed up in a speech by one of the characters in a story, who says, "It would be
very wicked to do anything to fit a boy for the modern world." A friend
described him in his college days as "so demure and yet so wild." This is also
the quality of his writing: so demure and yet so wild. He seemed to see life
as a gigantic circus taking place inside a tent set up in the midst
of the modern wasteland. Every now and then a wind blows back a flap of the tent
so that the wasteland is glimpsed through the clowns' act.

On Guard

EVELYN WAUGH

I

Millicent Blade had a notable head of
naturally fair hair; she had a docile and affectionate disposition, and an expression of face
which changed with lightning rapidity from
amiability to laughter and from laughter to respectful interest. But the feature which, more
than any other, endeared her to sentimental
Anglo-Saxon manhood was her nose.

It was not everybody's nose; many prefer one
with greater body; it was not a nose to appeal
to painters, for it was far too small and quite
without shape, a mere dab of putty without
apparent bone structure; a nose which made it
impossible for its wearer to be haughty or imposing or astute. It would not have done for
a governess or a 'cellist or even a post-office
clerk, but it suited Miss Blade's book perfectly,
for it was a nose that pierced the thin surface

crust of the English heart to its warm and pulpy
core; a nose to take the thoughts of English
manhood back to its schooldays, to the doughy-
faced urchins on whom it had squandered its
first affection, to memories of changing room
and chapel and battered straw boaters.[1] Three
Englishmen in five, it is true, grow snobbish
about these things in later life and prefer a nose
that makes more show in public—but two in
five is an average with which any girl of modest
fortune may be reasonably content.

Hector kissed her reverently on the tip of
this nose. As he did so, his senses reeled and in
momentary delirium he saw the fading light
of the November afternoon, the raw mist
spreading over the playing fields; overheated
youth in the scrum; frigid youth at the touch-

From *Charles Ryder's Schooldays and Other Stories* by Evelyn Waugh. Copyright 1936, 1964 by Evelyn Waugh. First appeared in *Mr. Loveday's Little Outing*. By permission of Little, Brown and Company.

1. **boater**, stiff straw hat.

Evelyn Waugh

line, shuffling on the duckboards,[2] chafing their fingers and, when their mouths were emptied of biscuit crumbs, cheering their house team to further exertion.

"You will wait for me, won't you?" he said.

"Yes, darling."

"And you will write?"

"Yes, darling," she replied more doubtfully, "sometimes . . . at least I'll try. Writing is not my best thing, you know."

"I shall think of you all the time Out There,"[3] said Hector. "It's going to be terrible—miles of impassable wagon track between me and the nearest white man, blinding sun, lions, mosquitoes, hostile natives, work from dawn until sunset single-handed against the forces of nature, fever, cholera . . . But soon I shall be able to send for you to join me."

"Yes, darling."

"It's bound to be a success. I've discussed it all with Beckthorpe—that's the chap who's selling me the farm. You see, the crop has failed every year so far—first coffee, then sisal, then tobacco, that's all you can grow there, and the year Beckthorpe grew sisal, everyone else was making a packet[4] in tobacco, but sisal was no good; then he grew tobacco, but by then it was coffee he ought to have grown, and so on. He stuck it nine years. Well if you work it out mathematically, Beckthorpe says, in three years one's bound to strike the right crop. I can't quite explain why, but it is like roulette and all that sort of thing, you see."

"Yes, darling."

Hector gazed at her little, shapeless, mobile button of a nose and was lost again . . . "Play up, play up," and after the match the smell of crumpets being toasted over a gas-ring[5] in his study . . .

---

2. **scrum . . . touchline . . . duckboards,** refer to Rugby, English football.

3. **Out There,** Hector is going to a British territory in Africa.

4 **packet,** much money.

5. **gas-ring,** a small gas stove with a single burner.

Later that evening he dined with Beckthorpe, and, as he dined, he grew more despondent.

"Tomorrow this time I shall be at sea," he said, twiddling his empty port glass.

"Cheer up, old boy," said Beckthorpe.

Hector filled his glass and gazed with growing distaste round the reeking dining room of Beckthorpe's club. The last awful member had left the room and they were alone with the cold buffet.

"I say, you know, I've been trying to work it out. It *was* in three years you said the crop was bound to be right, wasn't it?"

"That's right, old boy."

"Well, I've been through the sum and it seems to me that it may be eighty-one years before it comes right."

"No, no, old boy, three or nine, or at the most twenty-seven."

"Are you sure?"

"Quite."

"Good . . . you know it's awful leaving Milly behind. Suppose it *is* eighty-one years before the crop succeeds. It's the devil of a time to expect a girl to wait. Some other blighter[6] might turn up, if you see what I mean."

❋   ❋   ❋

"Tell you what, old boy. You ought to give her something."

"I'm always giving her things. She either breaks them or loses them or forgets where she got them."

"You must give her something she will always have by her, something that will last."

"Eighty-one years?"

"Well, say twenty-seven. Something to remind her of you."

"I could give her a photograph—but I might change a bit in twenty-seven years."

"No, no, that would be most unsuitable. A photograph wouldn't do at all. I know what I'd give her. I'd give her a dog."

"Dog?"

"A healthy puppy that was over distemper and looked like living a long time. She might even call it Hector."

"Would that be a good thing, Beckthorpe?"

"Best possible, old boy."

So next morning, before catching the boat train,[7] Hector hurried to one of the mammoth stores of London and was shown the livestock department. "I want a puppy."

"Yes, sir. "Any particular sort?"

"One that will live a long time. Eighty-one years, or twenty-seven at the least."

The man looked doubtful. "We have some fine healthy puppies of course," he admitted, "but none of them carry a guarantee. Now if it was longevity you wanted, might I recommend a tortoise? They live to an extraordinary age and are very safe in traffic."

"No, it must be a pup."

"Or a parrot?"

"No, no, a pup. I would prefer one named Hector."

They walked together past monkeys and kittens and cockatoos to the dog department which, even at this early hour, had attracted a small congregation of rapt worshippers. There were puppies of all varieties in wire-fronted kennels, ears cocked, tails wagging, noisily soliciting attention. Rather wildly, Hector selected a poodle and, as the salesman disappeared to fetch him his change, he leant down for a moment's intense communion with the beast of his choice. He gazed deep into the sharp little face, avoided a sudden snap and said with profound solemnity, "You are to look after Milly, Hector. See that she doesn't marry anyone until I get back."

And the pup Hector waved his plume of tail.

III

Millicent came to see him off, but, negligently, went to the wrong station; it could not have mattered, however, for she was twenty

---

6. **blighter** (blī′tər), fellow.
7. **boat train,** train making connections with a boat.

minutes late. Hector and the poodle hung about the barrier[8] looking for her, and not until the train was already moving did he bundle the animal into Beckthorpe's arms with instructions to deliver him at Millicent's address. Luggage labelled for Mombasa,[9] *Wanted on the voyage,* lay in the rack above him. He felt very much neglected.

That evening as the ship pitched and rolled past the Channel lighthouses, he recieved a radiogram: MISERABLE TO MISS YOU WENT PADDINGTON LIKE IDIOT THANK YOU THANK YOU FOR SWEET DOG I LOVE HIM FATHER MINDS DREADFULLY LONGING TO HEAR ABOUT FARM DONT FALL FOR SHIP SIREN ALL LOVE MILLY.

In the Red Sea he received another. BEWARE SIRENS PUPPY BIT MAN CALLED MIKE.

After that Hector heard nothing of Millicent except for a Christmas card which arrived in the last days of February.

IV

Generally speaking, Millicent's fancy for any particular young man was likely to last four months. It depended on how far he had got in that time whether the process of extinction was sudden or protracted. In the case of Hector, her affection had been due to diminish at about the time that she became engaged to him; it had been artificially prolonged during the succeeding three weeks, during which he made strenuous, infectiously earnest efforts to find employment in England; it came to an abrupt end with his departure for Kenya. Accordingly the duties of the puppy Hector began with his first days at home. He was young for the job and wholly inexperienced; it is impossible to blame him for his mistake in the matter of Mike Boswell.

This was a young man who had enjoyed a wholly unromantic friendship with Millicent since she first came out. He had seen her fair hair in all kinds of light, in and out of doors, crowned in hats in succeeding fashions, bound with ribbon, decorated with combs, jauntily stuck with flowers; he had seen her nose up-

lifted in all kinds of weather, had even, on occasions, playfully tweaked it with his finger and thumb, and had never for one moment felt remotely attracted by her.

But the puppy Hector could hardly be expected to know this. All he knew was that two days after receiving his commission, he observed a tall and personable man of marriageable age who treated his hostess with the sort of familiarity which, among the kennel maids with whom he had been brought up, meant only one thing.

The two young people were having tea together. Hector watched for some time from his place on the sofa, barely stifling his growls. A climax was reached when, in the course of some barely intelligible backchat, Mike leant forward and patted Millicent on the knee.

It was not a serious bite, a mere snap, in fact; but Hector had small teeth as sharp as pins. It was the sudden, nervous speed with which Mike withdrew his hand which caused the damage; he swore, wrapped his hand in a handkerchief, and at Millicent's entreaty revealed three or four minute wounds. Millicent spoke harshly to Hector and tenderly to Mike, and hurried to her mother's medicine cupboard for a bottle of iodine.

Now no Englishman, however phlegmatic, can have his hand dabbed with iodine without, momentarily at any rate, falling in love.

Mike had seen the nose countless times before, but that afternoon, as it was bowed over his scratched thumb, and as Millicent said, "Am I hurting terribly?", as it was raised towards him, and as Millicent said, "There. Now it will be all right," Mike suddenly saw it transfigured as its devotees saw it and from that moment, until long after the three months of attention which she accorded him, he was Millicent's besotted suitor.

The pup Hector saw all this and realized his

8. **barrier,** the gate separating passengers from bystanders.
9. **Mombasa** (mom bä′sə), an island off the coast of Kenya in East Africa.

89

mistake. Never again, he decided, would he give Millicent the excuse to run for the iodine bottle.

V

He had on the whole an easy task, for Millicent's naturally capricious nature could, as a rule, be relied upon, unaided, to drive her lovers into extremes of irritation. Moreover, she had come to love the dog. She received very regular letters from Hector, written weekly and arriving in batches of three or four according to the mails. She always opened them; often she read them to the end, but their contents made little impression upon her mind and gradually their writer drifted into oblivion so that when people said to her, "How is darling Hector?" it came naturally to her to reply, "He doesn't like the hot weather much I'm afraid, and his coat is in a very poor state. I'm thinking of having him plucked," instead of, "He had a go[10] of malaria and there is black worm in his tobacco crop."

Playing upon this affection which had grown up for him, Hector achieved a technique for dealing with Millicent's young men. He no longer growled at them or soiled their trousers; that merely resulted in his being turned from the room; instead, he found it increasingly easy to usurp the conversation.

Tea was the most dangerous time of day, for then Millicent was permitted to entertain her friends in her sitting room; accordingly, though he had a constitutional preference for pungent, meaty dishes, Hector heroically simulated a love of lump sugar. Having made this apparent, at whatever cost to his digestion, it was easy to lead Millicent on to an interest in tricks; he would beg and "trust," lie down as though dead, stand in the corner and raise a forepaw to his ear.

"What does s-u-g-a-r spell?" Millicent would ask, and Hector would walk round the tea table to the sugar-bowl and lay his nose against it, gazing earnestly and clouding the silver with his moist breath.

"He understands everything," Millicent would say in triumph.

When tricks failed Hector would demand to be let out of the door. The young man would be obliged to interrupt himself to open it. Once on the other side Hector would scratch and whine for readmission.

In moments of extreme anxiety Hector would affect to be sick—no difficult feat after the unwelcome diet of lump sugar; he would stretch out his neck, retching noisily, till Millicent snatched him up and carried him to the hall, where the floor, paved in marble, was less vulnerable—but by that time a tender atmosphere had been shattered and one wholly prejudicial to romance created to take its place.

This series of devices spaced out through the afternoon and tactfully obtruded whenever the guest showed signs of leading the conversation to a more intimate phase, distracted young man after young man and sent them finally away, baffled and despairing.

Every morning Hector lay on Millicent's bed while she took her breakfast and read the daily paper. This hour from ten to eleven was sacred to the telephone and it was then that the young men with whom she had danced overnight attempted to renew their friendship and make plans for the day. At first Hector sought, not unsuccessfully, to prevent these assignations by entangling himself in the wire, but soon a subtler and more insulting technique suggested itself. He pretended to telephone too. Thus, as soon as the bell rang, he would wag his tail and cock his head on one side in a way that he had learned was engaging. Millicent would begin her conversation and Hector would wriggle up under her arm and nuzzle against the receiver.

"Listen," she would say, "*someone* wants to talk to you. Isn't he an angel?" Then she would hold the receiver down to him and the young man at the other end would be dazed by a shattering series of yelps. This accomplishment appealed so much to Millicent that often she would not even bother to find out the name of

---

10. **go,** an attack.

the caller but, instead, would take off the receiver and hold it directly to the black snout, so that some wretched young man half a mile away, feeling, perhaps, none too well in the early morning, found himself barked to silence before he had spoken a word.

At other times, young men badly taken with the nose would attempt to waylay Millicent in Hyde Park when she was taking Hector for exercise. Here at first, Hector would get lost, fight other dogs and bite small children to keep himself constantly in her attention, but soon he adopted a gentler course. He insisted upon carrying Millicent's bag for her. He would trot in front of the couple and whenever he thought an interruption desirable he would drop the bag; the young man was obliged to pick it up and restore it first to Millicent and then, at her request, to the dog. Few young men were sufficiently servile to submit to more than one walk in these degrading conditions.

In this way two years passed. Letters arrived constantly from Kenya, full of devotion, full of minor disasters—blight in the sisal, locusts in the coffee, labour troubles, drought, flood, the local government, the world market. Occasionally Millicent read the letters aloud to the dog, usually she left them unread on her breakfast tray. She and Hector moved together through the leisurely routine of English social life. Wherever she carried her nose, two in five marriageable men fell temporarily in love; wherever Hector followed their ardour changed to irritation, shame and disgust. Mothers began to remark complacently that it was curious how that fascinating Blade girl never got married.

VI

At last in the third year of this régime a new problem presented itself in the person of Major Sir Alexander Dreadnought, Bart., M.P.,[11] and Hector immediately realized that he was up against something altogether more formidable than he had hitherto tackled.

Sir Alexander was not a young man; he was forty-five and a widower. He was wealthy, popular and preternaturally patient; he was also mildly distinguished, being joint-master of a Midland pack of hounds and a junior minister;[12] he bore a war record of conspicuous gallantry. Millie's father and mother were delighted when they saw that her nose was having its effect on him. Hector took against him from the first, exerted every art which his two-and-a-half years' practice had perfected, and achieved nothing. Devices that had driven a dozen young men to frenzies of chagrin seemed only to accentuate Sir Alexander's tender solicitude. When he came to the house to fetch Millicent for the evening he was found to have filled the pockets of his evening clothes with lump sugar for Hector; when Hector was sick Sir Alexander was there first, on his knees with a page of *The Times;* Hector resorted to his early, violent manner and bit him frequently and hard, but Sir Alexander merely remarked, "I believe I am making the little fellow jealous. A delightful trait."

For the truth was that Sir Alexander had been persecuted long and bitterly from his earliest days—his parents, his sisters, his schoolfellows, his company-sergeant and his colonel, his colleagues in politics, his wife, his joint-master, huntsman and hunt secretary, his election agent, his constituents, and even his parliamentary private secretary had one and all pitched into Sir Alexander, and he accepted this treatment as a matter of course. For him it was the most natural thing in the world to have his eardrums outraged by barks when he rang up the young woman of his affections; it was a high privilege to retrieve her handbag when Hector dropped it in the Park; the small wounds that Hector was able to inflict on his ankles and wrists were to him knightly scars. In his more ambitious moments he referred to Hector in Millicent's hearing as "my little rival." There could be no doubt whatever of his intentions and when he asked Millicent and her mama to

---

11. **Bart.,** baronet, a minor noble. **M.P.,** member of Parliament.
12. . . . **junior minister.** He was distinguished as both a hunter and minor government official.

visit him in the country, he added at the foot of the letter, *"Of course the invitation includes little Hector."*

The Saturday to Monday visit to Sir Alexander's was a nightmare to the poodle. He worked as he had never worked before; every artifice by which he could render his presence odious was attempted and attempted in vain. As far as his host was concerned, that is to say. The rest of the household responded well enough, and he received a vicious kick when, through his own bad management, he found himself alone with the second footman, whom he had succeeded in upsetting with a tray of cups at tea time.

Conduct that had driven Millicent in shame from half the stately homes of England was meekly accepted here. There were other dogs in the house—elderly, sober, well-behaved animals at whom Hector flew; they turned their heads sadly away from his yaps of defiance, he snapped at their ears. They lolloped sombrely out of reach and Sir Alexander had them shut away for the rest of the visit.

There was an exciting Aubusson carpet[13] in the dining room to which Hector was able to do irreparable damage; Sir Alexander seemed not to notice.

Hector found a carrion in the park and conscientiously rolled in it—although such a thing was obnoxious to his nature—and, returning, fouled every chair in the drawing room; Sir Alexander himself helped Millicent wash him and brought some bath salts from his own bathroom for the operation.

Hector howled all night; he hid and had half the household searching for him with lanterns; he killed some young pheasants and made a sporting attempt on a peacock. All to no purpose. He staved off an actual proposal, it is true—once in the Dutch garden, once on the way to the stables and once while he was being bathed—but when Monday morning arrived and he heard Sir Alexander say, "I hope Hector enjoyed his visit a little. I hope I shall see him here *very, very* often," he knew that he was defeated.

It was now only a matter of waiting. The evenings in London were a time when it was impossible for him to keep Millicent under observation. One of these days he would wake up to hear Millicent telephoning to her girl friends, breaking the good news of her engagement.

Thus it was that after a long conflict of loyalties he came to a desperate resolve. He had grown fond of his young mistress; often and often when her face had been pressed down to his he had felt sympathy with that long line of young men whom it was his duty to persecute. But Hector was no kitchen-haunting mongrel. By the code of all well-born dogs it is money that counts. It is the purchaser, not the mere feeder and fondler, to whom ultimately loyalty is due. The hand which had once fumbled with the fivers in the live-stock department of the mammoth store now tilled the unfertile soil of equatorial Africa, but the sacred words of commission still rang in Hector's memory. All through the Sunday night and the journey of Monday morning, Hector wrestled with his problem; then he came to the decision. *The nose must go.*

VII

It was an easy business; one firm snap as she bent over his basket and the work was accomplished. She went to a plastic surgeon and emerged some weeks later without scar or stitch. But it was a different nose; the surgeon in his way was an artist and, as I have said above, Millicent's nose had no sculptural qualities. Now she has a fine aristocratic beak, worthy of the spinster she is about to become. Like all spinsters she watches eagerly for the foreign mails and keeps carefully under lock and key a casket full of depressing agricultural intelligence; like all spinsters she is accompanied everywhere by an ageing lapdog.

---

13. **Aubusson carpet** (ō′bə sōn′), a rug woven to show figures and scenery as in a tapestry.

I
WOMAN'S BEST FRIEND?

Antigone was commanded by her conscience to set herself against the edicts of the state. Don Camillo felt keenly a responsibility to a particular set of ideals. Hector, the pup, is equally faithful to his conscience and his responsibilities, but the fact that Hector is a dog makes his extreme dedication laughable. Waugh's fascination with the bizarre is strongly evident in this tale full of his special brand of lunatic logic.

II
IMPLICATIONS

State your reaction to the following statements.

1. The conflict of wills reaches the heights of ridiculousness in this story because one of the antagonists is a dog.

2. A conflict of wills must result in violence.

3. Waugh is a critic of British society. In this story he is attacking one, two, all, or none of the following:

a. British womanhood

b. The courting habits of the British

c. The position of a dog in a society household

d. The ineffectiveness of the British male

III
TECHNIQUES

Identification

1. By making the reader identify with a dog, how does Waugh bring out the absurdity of the situation?

2. Where does your sympathy shift from Hector to Millicent?

Diction

Read the names of the characters out loud. How well do the names fit the characters?

IV
WORDS

In this story by Waugh, how would you describe the language of the characters depicted? How does the device of suiting language to character add to the effectiveness of the story?

MARTIN ANDERSEN NEXØ

Martin Andersen Nexø[1] (1869–1954), who was named Martin Andersen at birth, was born in the slums of Copenhagen. The Andersens were a large family, and Martin was the fourth of eleven children. He was always nervous and delicate. The children were terrorized by their drunkard father, who, fortunately, was often away looking for work. Their mother scrubbed stairways to earn money, and Martin's older sister cared for him until he was old enough to help sell fritters and cherries by pushcart. After the Franco-Prussian War the Andersens moved to squalid quarters in the father's original hometown, Nexø, on the Baltic island of Bornholm. There life was even harder, but the children loved the sea. For the first time, Nexø felt happy, working as a herd tender and going to school. Later in life, he annexed the name of this town to his own name, becoming Martin Andersen Nexø. From the age of twelve, he dabbled in various types of work—from farmhand to shoemaker to church builder. In the process, his proletarian class consciousness was awakened. Then, the widow of a poet helped him go to school and become a teacher. He started writing poetry and sketches telling of workers' hardships. While convalescing from an illness, he did a great deal of traveling on foot, living among peasants and slum dwellers. This experience prompted his decision to devote his life to the defense of the poor. Nexø's first novel, *Pelle the Conqueror* (1901), depicts his own life and tells of the struggles of the Danish working class. *Ditte*, a sequel, is about a proletarian worker of even humbler origin. After the publication of *Ditte*, he wrote a book almost every year. Nexø's eightieth birthday was declared a national festival in Copenhagen. Two years later he moved to East Germany, and in 1954 he died in Dresden.

Life Sentence

translated from the Danish

Mattis Lau was the sole child of early-spent parents. His mother was in her forties when he was born, his father ten years older; he did not come as God's gift to a young, hot-blooded couple, but as a somewhat tardy hand-out to two people already in fear of age. Every child more or less carries the weight of the grown-ups' years; it is not exactly lessened if the child is born as late as in this case. When Mattis came, his parents had used up the rest of their surplus vitality. He had enough for all three of them, but it was hard to keep a fire blazing under the wails of his mother and his father's bleary eyes.

They never understood the urge in his play, but let it wither. He was allowed to do neither this nor that—neither to write with charcoal

1. **Andersen Nexø** (än'dər sən nek'sē).

on the loam walls of the tumble-down fisherman's hut, nor under any circumstances to pound the rough spruce-wood table with one of the things that only had to fall into his busy little hands to turn into tools. Like most parents, they rated dead things above the living child; and little Mattis soon saw clearly that he was the most worthless thing on earth. It certainly was owing only to the parents' infinite goodness that a small boy got permission to stay alive after breaking a tooth off the rake, or tearing a few knots in the old fishing net. By rights he should have been beaten to pulp long ago.

Actually Mattis' parents weren't such bad child-beaters. They just let him know on sufficient occasions that justice was again being tempered with mercy. The stick hung over his childhood like a constant threat.

At an early age he had to do his share of work —which did not bother him at all. He merely wished to be alone with it; then, as it went on, his work turned quite of its own accord into the most fascinating play. But if his father and mother were present it soon became galling toil, as it long was for the parents.

Despite all, he grew up to be a real boy, who preferred the harbor and the beach to the schoolhouse and learned much that might come in handy once he got out into the world. And he would get out into the world! He was afraid of no boy in the fishing village, and the parents whimpered when they heard of his recklessness and his foolhardy pranks. They liked best to see him sit by the window in his free time, with a copybook in his hand; then they knew where he was, and he neither ruined nor ate so much. When somebody called, he had to show how good he was at reading and writing. Perhaps they were trying to make up somehow, through him, for their own failure to obtain an education; at any rate, he never made them so happy as on the day when he came home and reported that he was to stand first on the church platform.

After confirmation, most of the boys in his class were scattered to the four winds. Poor people's children take to the air early; down there

Martin Andersen Nexø

by the beach, it was customary for the young to leave the nest as soon as they had the pastor's blessing to cease being children. The ones who had something in them went to sea; the others took jobs in the capital or on the far side of the island—but fly they must! Only stick-in-the-muds remained at home to care for the soil. From long ago there were two kinds of men on the beach: those who had been to sea in their young days and now were plying the fisherman's trade, and then the stove-warmers who were working the land.

Throughout his childhood, Mattis had known that he wanted to go to sea when the time came —far out, where none knew its depth and where Father and Mother could not watch him from shore, clucking like troubled hens. And yet he resigned himself to staying at home and doing more and more of the two oldsters' work.

Between times, if he ever harbored plans to break out, they clung to him with trembling hands. His father led him round about the tiny patch of land, talked of it as though it were a patrimony[2] and begged him not to desert all this. And his mother would confide with a chuckle that someone or other wasn't sleeping nights, on his account. One could always find him a nice girl with money way back in the closet, if only he continued to stay at home.

Mattis couldn't care less about the promises and fine words. The shack wasn't a mite too good to put a match to it, and the girls he'd never seen were more alluring than the ones he knew. He was longing to get out—out where the rolling waves tossed the great tarred, oaken cradles from port to port.

And getting out was not even so very difficult. Often enough, when he came in with a catch of sea bass and lay alongside the windjammers to sell a fish, the captains offered him hire—all he had to do was climb aboard and let the dory drift ashore with the tide. But when the crucial moment came he stayed. Duty, toward the two old grumblers in the shack, held him fast—he could not escape.

"I have to wait till they're dead," he thought, pulling the heavy oars.

It always was easier for Mattis to row out to sea than back home; and he knew the reason quite well. The way home was the sour way of duty; that made it so arduous. He didn't feel a trace of filial love; it did not warm his heart to care for the two old people, who under cover of the parental name had always cramped his life. He would not mind if death were to deliver them. But it could never occur to him to desert them.

So he stayed at home and took the load off his gouty old father's back, looked after the nets and tilled the bit of soil—joylessly, yet so that there was enough to eat. He milked the two shaggy cows for his mother, cut nettles for the pigs and twice annually made a pilgrimage to town to pay the taxes. Inwardly he did not get richer, fooling around like this. He became close-mouthed and sluggish.

On one thing his mind was firmly made up:

not to be caught by some wench. Once his parents died, he wanted to be his own master and free to go wherever in the world it drew him.

The Laus hailed from the interior of the island—from the Lauenhof, a farm situated a mile inland. It belonged to Hans Lau, an uncle of Mattis. Since he was the only one with a farm, he was regarded as the head of the family.

He was arrogant and ruthless by nature and took various liberties, while the Laus otherwise strictly observed the proprieties, as befits little people. He was reputed to be reckless at cards and a rake; the poor relations could not help admiring this, as big-farmer manners.

The farm was neither big nor good, by the way; most of its soil was rock. But it was still a farm, and all the Laus took pride in being farm-owner's children. It even flickered in the corners of the eyes of Mattis' used-up, shriveled father.

Hans Lau was well advanced in years, and as he had no children—at least in a manner of speaking—the question was to which of his nephews and nieces he would choose to leave his farm. Each family entertained a well-founded belief that it was the preferred one, and secretly acted on it. Thus the Laus came to draw apart from the rest of the poor in the district; there was something in their bearing as though they were merely disguised, and might take it into their heads one fine day to doff the poor man's garb. It was said of them that they were riding the high horse.

One day the Lauenhof owner turned up quite unexpectedly under his brother's low roof. Mattis was out behind the woodshed, tarring an old boat. He saw Hans Lau coming but he went on with his work; it angered him to see everything stood on its head if the uncle so much as showed himself.

Shortly after, his mother came round the corner of the house, on the run; he had not seen her so quick on her feet in a long time. "It's you he's come to see," she panted and pulled his sleeve; "now you'll probably be picked to own the farm. Be a little nice now!"

2. **patrimony** (pat′rə mō′nē), an estate inherited from one's father or ancestor.

Mattis looked after his work and let his mother prattle; he did not seem to know that she was there. She had to watch out for his motions with the tar-brush. But she kept nagging and pestering, and followed him round about the boat, undaunted: "You should put your time to use and drop your grouchiness just this once," she persisted. "Uncle Hans wants to talk it over with you personally. Can't you show a little manners for once!" When he still didn't answer, she ran inside again, to catch as much of what went on there as possible; her skirts flopped about her heels. It was the greatest day in her life.

Mattis did not look up, but he heard his mother bustling and he got mad. What did he care for Uncle Hans and his farm and the whole business? He only saw his relatives when he needed them, Uncle Hans did. When his mother promptly came back, Mattis threw some tools on his shoulder and withdrew toward the beach.

However, she had stated the case quite correctly. Hans Lau wanted to make the farm over to Mattis. It was to be transferred after his death, and until then he would pay Mattis and his parents one hundred thalers[3] a year—on the one condition that Mattis marry at once. For his wife, Uncle Hans had chosen Bodil, the Lauenhof housekeeper, a good, faithful girl who had sacrificed the best part of her youth to him and the farm. To reward her loyalty, Hans Lau wished to see her well married and to know that she'd be on the farm, as its mistress, when he was called away—in a little while.

Mattis had set his heart on being his own master, once he were rid of his duty to support the parents. It was hard to budge him. But the old people did not let him rest. They nagged him from dawn to dusk, tempted him with the prospect of one day being a big farmer and the head of the family. When this did not help, they whined that he would not lift a finger to lighten his old, toil-worn parents' old age. They sighed

whenever he approached, and at meal-times their talk inevitably turned to parents who had worn themselves out for their children and reaped the blackest ingratitude in return.

Soon all this became too much for Mattis; it was something he couldn't get around. Duty had left deep tracks in him, in which it was always easy to tread again. He was used to having to make sacrifices, and one day he yielded. It was merely as if the one porthole into the light and the world were being slammed shut.

His uncle strangely revived after the wedding, to the great indignation of the two oldsters. They had a long way to go yet, before being farm-owners! As for Mattis, he didn't care. He kept to himself, and it did not make him more sociable that Bodil hastened to present him with a little boy. It just meant somebody else to stay clear of.

Mattis was not kind to the boy, nor did anyone expect him to be. To see him was to get a splinter into his eye. It angered him to witness the child's careless joy and it angered him when, cautioned by experience, it shunned him—it only had to come before his eyes for wrath to flare up in him. He did not exactly account to himself for the causes of his feeling toward the child. There had to be an explanation for everything—to oneself, too; and he explained his conduct to himself as being about that of a strict but just pedagogue. If the others winked at the youngster's first boyish pranks, he took firm, heavy-handed action. His youth had been hard; he was passing the legacy on now.

Bodil dared not oppose him; she had no very clear idea anyway of whether and how he might be handled. He never reproached her, but she was nonetheless afraid of him; there was something in his eyes that told her to watch her step.

It would have served no purpose either, to dispute with Mattis about his treatment of the child—he suffered enough under it. His inability to find a way out turned the very pangs of his conscience against little Hans. One day Mattis caught him. The boy was standing out in the shed, letting the grindstone whir, so that a bright waterspout stood between the stone and

---

3. **thalers** (tä′lərz), a thaler was a German silver coin used from the fifteenth to the nineteenth centuries; it served as the German dollar.

the floor; he was so absorbed in the game that he sensed nothing until his father had him by the neck. He cried out insanely with fear when he saw the father above him, and this cry paralyzed something in Mattis and stayed his heavy hand. Bewildered, he flung the boy into a pile of hay and staggered to work, dazed by the youngster's horrible dread of him.

The boy's desperate, plaintive wails rang over to him as he worked, drowned out the blows of his axe and incessantly trickled at him, like an indictment. He struck more forcefully, to deaden the sound, but he could not get rid of it. Finally he could not stand it any longer; he threw the axe away and rose, irately—wasn't there a stick around so the brat could be shut up once and for all! He was blind with rage.

And suddenly it was as if the whole had burst —his rage and everything else—and collapsed within him. He led his hand over his eyes and fearfully stared over at the wall of the shed. The tortured small boy lying there, huddled and trembling and trying to swallow his tears so he wouldn't get a worse licking—that was he, Mattis! And the grindstone—why, he had just sneaked in and let it whir, because the spurting water was such fun when the stone really moved. Speed, speed! Nothing delighted his childish heart more, at the time, than to set something in rapid motion, that the sparks flew roundabout. But you weren't allowed to do that and so you did it in secret, as everything else that was worth while. It wetted the floor, and some day retribution fearfully caught up with you—as it now did with him. The floor was loam and couldn't be damaged; young as he was then, he had realized and understood that there was something called a curdled disposition. And now? His whole life had consisted of surrenders, piece by piece, until he too had become an embittered, shriveled sourpuss like his own father. Now he himself stalked the innocent joys of the child, catchpoll[4] that he was.

---

4. **catchpoll** (kach′pōl), sheriff's deputy; one who makes arrests for debts. Mattis likens himself to a cruel jailer.

The choked, broken sobs hurled accusation after accusation at him; they shattered him, until his heart ached and he could not breathe any more—he *had* to silence that sound! He looked round, helpless, bewildered, as if searching for the stick again, and then he suddenly rushed over to the boy and lifted him up. Mattis wasn't accustomed to embracing anyone; the little body surprised his palms and filled them with a tender warmth. How strangely dear it was to embrace someone! He took the boy on his knees and tried to get the small, dirty hands out of his face; he had never noticed them before; they were like a pair of little shovels, bearing every trace of their surroundings and hard inside, exactly like his own. He was a real boy who didn't spare his fists.

Silently the youngster let his hands be removed from his face—in fear, perhaps. But he would not look at Mattis' eyes; he turned his face away and kicked, to get down.

Mattis did not know what to do; it occurred to him to take the boy inside the shed, to the grindstone, and whirl it round till the water splashed over the floor. The boy was suspicious and kept close to the door, but his eyes could not resist; they stole out secretly, eager to catch something. And when a spray flew all the way across to his feet, it made him laugh.

"Well, how about splashing Father?" Mattis said and stood by the door—it was the first time that he gave this name to himself. The boy, still somewhat diffident, thrust himself over to the grindstone; soon the game was in full swing. It amused even Mattis, this play with the opaline water that stood in the air like a cock's tail and then suddenly burst into sprays. Here by the grindstone—a little late—he recaptured a piece of his childhood and vied with the boy in laughter.

At first Hans was still timid, and it was up to Mattis to come to him. The boy's distrust hurt and, at times, even angered him, but he had no choice. He humbled himself and went to look for the little chap and inveigle him. When nothing else worked, he could always win him over by tempting him with the grindstone.

Soon, however, the tot came quite by himself and put his little hand into the big one, and Mattis marveled how quickly a child's soul can forgive and forget—and was ashamed of himself. There was not much to be done about it now; his own soul had long congealed and no longer could be transformed. But it seemed to him as though in being with the boy he lived the other side of his childhood, as it were—the one that might have been. And this was why he could not be without him.

Everything, both play and earnest, started with the grindstone. When Hans got bigger, the stone was overshadowed by other and more fascinating things. Hans learned to fish and run a sailboat, and he helped his father till the soil. The boy was right behind Mattis all the time; they could not stand being apart, and in time grew strangly close to each other. Toward everyone else Mattis was and remained the surly grouch, and added to it was the fact now that he had the boy to defend.

"He's not going to live my life," Mattis told himself and saw to it that the boy was restrained as little as possible. When the others laid plans as to what he should become, Mattis cut off the debate with the curt statement that he was to have the right to make his own choice when the time came.

Mattis knew what the boy would choose— long before Hans knew it himself—and the knowledge made him anything but glad. But he sealed his feelings within himself, and after Hans' confirmation he himself took him to town and saw to it that he hired on with the right crew. When he got home he went out into the shed; there he sat almost the whole day, sunk in rumination, while his hard thumbnail chiseled and chiseled at the soft grindstone. He did not see the sense of everything.

It was not until the boy, too, came home after some weeks, explaining that he had been laid off because the sloop had sprung a leak and was to be laid up, that his existence began to have a meaning again. Mattis knew well that an explanation also was required for the fact that the boy came home instead of looking for another seagoing job—but he did not love him any less for it.

Working together, they frequently talked about having to listen round for a new hire for Hans, and on Mattis' part the talk was meant sincerely. He would have been the last to stand in the way of the boy's future.

However, the winter passed without anything turning up, and in the spring Hans declared that he would learn carpentry and then sail as a carpenter; this promised higher wages. Mattis had some objections but there was no real weight in them, and the boy's wish prevailed.

In the following summer the Lauenhof owner died at last. Mattis' parents were still living but they were very old and decrepit; the prospect of a Lauenhof residence had kept life in them far beyond a reasonable time. Mattis himself would have liked to sell the farm, but the old couple and Bodil objected. So he let them move up; he himself remained in the shack. He had nothing to do with the farm, and very little with the three of them, aside from their having imprisoned him. Now—at last—he was rid of all pressing bonds. He was not free and never became free; he felt that he had been imprisoned for too long a time to be able to become free again. But the bonds that held him now did not cut into his flesh. Here in the shack he had all that tied him to life: the sea which had sung its song in him since he was born, and the boy.

The boy remained living with him during his apprenticeship, and Mattis sunned himself in his young mind. He could not bear to think of it that he and Hans would have to part sooner or later; the boy was his link to the world, through which he lived and breathed. He no longer had any wish for his own future; quite imperceptibly, everything had turned into blind devotion and admiration for the lad. He no longer yearned for distant spaces, either. What he could still expect of life now had to be fulfilled through the boy.

Hans was to experience life for him. All that he himself had missed in his youth should be bestowed on the lad—gladly. But then, he could not even let him go.

Gradually this feeling grew into a gnawing hidden pain, into self-reproach for accepting the sacrifice of the boy and holding him back at home. One day the full, hard thought dawned on Mattis: he stood in Hans' way precisely as others had once stood in his. It cut him to the quick, but it terrified him to think of the only way out—for that led back into loneliness. He himself was to turn away the one being that had warmed his heart and gladdened him. Mattis, long accustomed to renunciation, fought a hard fight this time before he won.

One Sunday morning he took Hans out to sea. For several hours they dragged for bass, over the "grounds," where the "grass bass" keep themselves; then they rowed about and offered them for sale on various ships that lay at anchor, brought here by the land breeze. Mattis went aboard and bargained with the skippers while Hans remained in the boat to weigh the fish.

From one of the vessels, a large bark, Mattis climbed back into the boat with such strange movements that for a moment Hans thought, "They surely poured him some, there on board." But he suppressed the idea at once; his father never drank liquor. Mattis seated himself on the bench and stared in front of him; his expression was terribly serious, almost petrified.

"You'd better go aboard right away," he said in a hoarse voice. "They need a carpenter, and they offer good wages."

A sudden joy lit up the face of the son—until he caught the old man's lightless glance.

"But you—Father?" he asked slowly.

"I?—I'll row back and pack your stuff. I'll be back before nightfall—and the wind won't turn till then." Mattis stared up at the clouds.

"Yes, but I mean you, yourself. What'll you do then?"

"What I'll do? Well—I—" Mattis spoke tonelessly and fell abruptly silent.

"Come along, Father! You've got nothing to keep you here. We'll hire on together, here or on another ship. Let's go to sea together, you!"

Mattis sat there, withdrawn as if hearing nothing or listening to far-off music. Suddenly he straightened up. "Yes, we'll hire on together, you and I," he said and gripped Hans' hand. "Now go aboard."

"And you come with two bedrolls," Hans called down from the rail. Mattis nodded. Two bedrolls! Did the boy really mean it?

Could his youth not demand an end to having to drag a weight on his leg? He had been a good and loving son, he who had turned up in the nest as unexpectedly as a young cuckoo. Mattis had received his due from him and more; and now it had to be done with. There wasn't room for him on board.

He packed his son's sea chest and bedding, and let someone else row it out; he himself couldn't. He followed the boat with his eyes till it was alongside the ship; then he went into the tool-shed and set out to mend a net. He felt the wind beginning to turn, knew that the bark and the other sailboats out there were now weighing anchor. But he did not look up.

He had returned to his prison—what was the use of looking back!

I
THE POINT OF NO RETURN

At the end of the story, Mattis is described as going back into his prison. It might be interesting to speculate about the following question: At what point did Mattis receive his life sentence? At birth? At the

moment he accepted his uncle's offer? Or at some point in between? Did he actually assist in his own imprisonment by his lack of will?

II
IMPLICATIONS

What is your reaction to the following statements?

1. This story is a classic picture of the conflict between parents and child.

2. People tend to do to others exactly what they hated having done to them at an earlier time.

3. Hans is really not as eager to go to sea as his father seems to believe.

4. There is a profound difference between the quality of Mattis's sacrifice in letting Hans go and his sacrifices for his parents and wife.

III
TECHNIQUES

Identification

The reader's sympathies are definitely with Mattis and against his parents. What has Andersen Nexø done to make the reader feel this way? What might he have done if he had wanted readers to identify with the parents?

Diction

This selection frequently uses the *balanced sentence*, a sentence in which the first part presents an idea that the second part offsets. Point out the balanced elements in the sentences that follow.

1. . . . he did not come as God's gift to a young, hot-blooded couple, but as a somewhat tardy hand-out to two people already in fear of age.

2. At an early age he had to do his share of work—which did not bother him at all.

3. He was afraid of no boy in the fishing village, and the parents whimpered when they heard of his recklessness and his foolhardy pranks.

4. The ones who had something in them went to sea; the others took jobs in the capital or on the far side of the island. . . .

This kind of sentence gives a certain quality to the writing. What is that quality?

Conflict of Wills

CONFLICT AND THE STORY

Here are pairs of people who were pitched in opposition to each other in CONFLICT OF WILLS.

Creon and Antigone
Don Camillo and Peppone
Don Lollo and Zi' Dima
Nicholas and the aunt
Mr. Foster and Mrs. Foster
Berthine and her prisoners
Mattis and his parents

Take any one of the pairs and answer the following questions in relation to that pair.

1. What were the issues that set these antagonists against one another?

2. What were the motives of each opponent?

3. Was the apparent issue complicated by personality traits or submerged desires of the opponents?

4. Were these antagonists destroyed by their conflict? If not, why not?

5. Did the opponents try to understand each other's point of view?

6. Did you feel a sense of rightness about the resolution of the conflict?

IMPLICATIONS

Discuss the following statements by citing examples from the selections you have just read. This will require you to exercise your own observation and logic.

1. While a conflict of wills may be settled, the individuals involved never really change their opinions about what they believe.

2. The most devastating kinds of conflict spring from emotions rather than from reason.

3. Conflict is the means by which we test our own values.

4. A conflict of wills may be humorous to the observer, but it is never so to the people involved.

TECHNIQUES

Identification

1. For each selection, describe the person or persons with whom you most closely identified.

2. Take *one* of the selections. Discuss the approach or approaches by which the writer involves your sympathies with the leading character. Is it by:

a. selection of incident?

b. reactions of others toward him or her?

c. description?

d. direct comments about him or her?

Diction

Answer the following questions for one of the previous selections.

1. Is the dialogue realistic? stilted? fantastic? or . . . ?

2. How vivid are the descriptive passages?

3. In a few words, describe the total effect of this piece of writing.

WRITING FROM READING

1. In this unit you have been considering how writers make you identify with a central character in a story. Think back to the conflict between Creon and Antigone. With this conflict in mind, think of another that might occur today between two people of different ages. Write a page or two of dialogue (conversation) between the two in which they take opposite sides on an argument. Be sure the characters can discuss it from different points of view. By the choice of words, make your audience identify with one of the characters.

2. Write two paragraphs about getting up this morning. In the first, be matter of fact, objective, and factual. In the second, using the same material, choose your language to express your mood. Try to convey your feelings by words and sentence structure.

3. Write a paragraph using specific sensory words (color, smell, temperature, etc.,) to catch a momentary picture of a landscape, building, school room, or whatever. Before you start writing, decide the mood you wish to create with this picture. Into the scene you have created, introduce two people performing one swift action: a slap, a kiss, a comment, whatever comes to your mind. Use only a sentence or two for this description. What happened to the mood you tried to create?

MEDIEVAL BRITISH POETRY: Understanding Poetry

Approaching a Poem

The speaker of Shakespeare's "Sonnet 18" asks, "Shall I compare thee to a summer's day?" He thus prepares us for a series of comparisons between his beloved and the beauty of summer. But the poet is doing something beyond this, too. He is really asking the question all poets ask: "What is the most expressive way of conveying my feelings?" In this particular poem, before talking about his feelings, the poet alerts us to the problem of finding the right expression. He is looking for words, sounds, images, ideas, that will be both adequate and appropriate.

Poetry begins, then, with the combination of a feeling and an intense desire to creatively express that feeling. Indeed, it sometimes seems that the interest in form precedes the feeling or the idea. Poets are fascinated by the colors and textures of language, whether simple or ornate; by the varieties of meter, rhymes, rhyme schemes, stanza forms; by the infinite possibilities of imagery. We sometimes call such subjects "formal" or "technical," implying that such considerations are separate from the poet's main interest. But they are not. Rather, these considerations *are* the poem, for poetry distinguishes itself from prose by its emphasis on these matters. The reader's reactions to poetry are frequently similar to those evoked by other genres, but the ways in which the reader is asked to respond are both similar and different.

Therefore, as we look at poems from medieval times to the present, we need to become aware not just of *what* is said, but of *how* it is said. We need to learn how to respond to the many different techniques a poet can use.

The first step in approaching a poem is to read it aloud, because poetry is meant to be heard as well as understood. The next step is to ask the following questions:

1. *Who* is the speaker in the poem? What are we told about the speaker?

2. *Whom* is the speaker addressing? The reader? Another person in the poem? God? A specific group? An unsuspected audience?

3. *Where* does the poem take place? During a certain period in history? In a certain place? At a certain time of year?

4. *What* is the subject of the poem? A beloved? A place? An ambition? An emotion?

These questions deal with what might be called the facts of the poem. They can usually be answered quite definitely and specifically, although we need to read carefully since some of the answers are clear only by implication. Just as we must determine the basic facts of characterization, setting, and plot when reading a play or a short story, so we need to make sure that we have a clear idea of these elements in a poem.

After we have figured out "the plain sense of a poem," we can start to explore the poet's experience as well as our reaction to the poem. To do so, we need to ask two more questions:

How does the poem get its idea across?

Why does the poem exist?

The first question focuses on form; the second, on meaning; but they are really inseparable and should be thought of together. The more fully we understand, for example, the metaphors chosen by the poet, the more we will know why they affect us as they do. The better able we are to sense the changes in rhythm created by the varying lengths of lines or by a particular stanza form, the better we can follow the experience of the poem. *What* the poet is trying to convey to us—be it intellectual concept, sarcastic observation, lyrical outpouring, frightening narrative, or beautiful picture—is known fully only when we see *how* that experience is created, detail by detail.

Let's begin with a short lyric poem from the fifteenth century. This is an anonymous poem, so we know nothing about its author other than the feelings so vividly evoked.

Western Wind

Western wind, when will thou blow,
The small rain down can rain?
Christ, if my love were in my arms
And I in my bed again!

We know that the poet is a lover, separated from a beloved, and we recognize immediately the feelings of loneliness, of longing, even of desperation. But *how* do we know? *How* does the poet convey these feelings so movingly that this little four-line poem is still remembered, quoted, and anthologized? In formal terms, the poem's effect comes from striking use of language, personification, understatement, and subtle metrical variations. Let us look at these formal elements in more detail and then come back to the poem.

The Language
of Poetry

Poets have no special group of words reserved for them. Rather it is their *use* of language that transforms even the simplest words into something special, something remembered. Of course, poets have, at times, chosen particular words for their exotic flavor. In Milton's description of Satan being thrown out of heaven, "to dwell / In adamantine chains and penal fire," the word *adamantine* attracts our attention. It stretches itself out; it impresses us with the sense of something extremely strong.

Shakespeare, too, often employs exotic words. One such example is the following passage, in which Macbeth describes the effect his bloody hand will have on the ocean if he tries to wash away his guilt. Note the combination of two long Latinate words in one line:

. . . Thus my hand will rather
The multitudinous seas incarnadine,
Making the green one red.

The enormity of Macbeth's crime is felt through the lengthy words that seem crowded together owing to multiple syllables and internal rhymes.

The last line of Macbeth's speech illustrates the opposite way in which poetic language may work. In that line there are one-syllable words, familiar and common, rather than strange and exotic. Their very ordinariness contrasts with the extraordinary spectacle they describe: a bloody hand turning the green ocean red. Here poetic language works through simplicity, or more accurately, through the contrast between complex words in the second line and simple words in the third line.

In dealing with the words of any poem, we need to remember that their meanings exist simultaneously on at least two levels. The first level, *denotation*, is the literal meaning, the definition of the word. Because a word may have several meanings, readers should always consult a dictionary to resolve any questions about a word's meaning. Furthermore, when reading poems written before modern times, we need to check for word meanings that may now be obsolete. In "Western Wind," for example, "small" rain means "gentle" rain, a meaning of *small* that has disappeared from current use. A good place to find out what a word used to mean is an unabridged dictionary or the *Oxford English Dictionary*, which traces the historical development of each word.

Beyond the denotative level is the *connotative* level, the associations we bring to a word or that a word carries along with it. To understand *connotation*, let us look again at Shakespeare's "Shall I compare thee to a summer's day?" If the connotations of summer were hot, humid, scorching, and blazing, it is clear that the line would suddenly become satiric or, possibly, bitter. But the poet assumes that we will bring the connotations of warm, gentle, soft, and beautiful to the idea of summer. Perhaps, because he is English rather than South American, Shakespeare knows only a summer that is warm, not hot. However, he is depending not on the *actual* meaning of summer or even on the real feeling of a summer's day as we might know it, but on the familiar, accepted, *conventional* connotation of summer as a time of loveliness and beauty.

Thus, in reading a poem, we need to be aware of both the literal and the connotative meanings for a word. Knowing which of these meanings should be screened out, or in, is a matter of practice and of careful reading. We cannot be too quick to leave out associations which may be there for surprise effects. Nor can we be too eager to bring in all associations, no matter how distant. Usually the poem itself sets the limits, by creating a world with internal connections and consistency.

Imagery in Poetry

Much of what we know we learn from sense data—from seeing, hearing, smelling, tasting, and touching. The information we gather from our senses is so direct and immediate that often we *know* something without having to think about it. Poets use **images**—words that evoke or recall sensory experience—because they want us to have this intense, concrete, yet suggestive understanding. Since there are so many ways of sensing and so many ideas which can be expressed, a number of different relationships between the image and the thing it suggests have been defined. Here are some of the most important ones. You may recall meeting the terms *simile* and *metaphor* earlier in the text (p. 38), where they were defined as literary comparisons between things that are in essence unlike.

Simile comes from the Latin word for *like*. A simile is an image in which the poet says, "My love is like a red, red rose," with the word *like* making the comparison clear to us. Sometimes the comparison may be of two things which seem much less closely related: "When the evening is spread out against the sky / Like a patient etherized upon a table." The point of the simile is to get us to see the connection between the first part of the line, which is less well known (or sometimes more abstract), and the second part, which is the concrete sensory detail.

In a *metaphor*, which derives from the Greek word for *transfer*, we again compare two things, but without the connecting word *like* or *as*. Instead, we transfer the qualities of one thing to something else. The anonymous author of "Sir Patrick Spens" manages to transform the drinking of a cup of wine into a sinister, foreshadowing moment through the use of an adjective as a metaphor: "The king sits in Dumferline town, / Drinking the blude-reid [bloodred] wine." Wine and blood are both red liquids, but using the word *blood* to modify *red* transfers other connotations from blood to wine, specifically the idea of blood spilling out in death. Another example of the use of metaphor is Shakespeare's definition of love in "Sonnet 116":

> . . . it is an ever-fixéd mark,
> That looks on tempests and is never shaken;
> It is the star to every wandering bark,
> Whose worth's unknown, although his height
>   be taken.

Here the metaphors *ever-fixéd mark* and *star* serve to define the constancy and guidance of true love. Those qualities are made strong by the mention of *tempests*, *shaken*, and *wandering bark*, words which give us, through contrast, feelings of change and instability.

A particular kind of metaphor is *personification*, a literary technique in which a nonliving object is addressed or described as if it were alive. The connection may be made simply with an adjective, "And trouble deaf heaven with my bootless cries," or with direct address, "Western wind, when will thou blow." It can also be made with a combination of human actions, features, and feelings: "With how sad steps, O Moon, thou climb'st the skies, / How silently, and with how wan a face." Personification creates a direct, often intimate relationship between the speaker and the object or idea described.

Allusion, another form of metaphor, is the mentioning of something well known, frequently from past literature, as a way of describing something else. When Macbeth is described as "Bellona's bridegroom," we need to know that Bellona was the Roman goddess of war. The allusion thus reminds us not of Macbeth's marital status, but of his ability as a warrior.

Imagery is constantly at work in poetry, sometimes through single words, sometimes through extended descriptions, but always by appealing to our knowledge of one thing in an effort to lead us to knowledge of something else.

Meter in Poetry

In English, we pronounce some words and syllables more loudly than others. In the word *about*, for example, we say *a* softly and *bout* more loudly. The words or syllables that are pronounced more loudly than those on either side of them are called *accented* syllables. The soft sounds are *unaccented* syllables. Because of this quality of language, we can set up a rhythmic beat to language just as we have a beat in music. In poetry we call the beat the *meter*. The meter is organized by the number and arrangement of the unaccented, or soft, syllables in relationship to the accented, or loud, syllables. The five types of meter include soft-loud, loud-soft, soft-soft-loud, loud-soft-soft, and loud-loud. In rare cases other beats are made up of two softs, two louds, or sometimes of a soft-loud-soft.

In the ancient Greek theater, dance steps were composed of similar patterns from the steps taken on tip-toe and steps taken on the bottom of the foot. From this ancient description, the basic unit of a rhythmic pattern is called a *foot*, and the technical names used to describe them are the old Greek dance terms. The five most common are as follows:

the *iamb* (iambic): one light and one heavy stress (tŏ / níght)
the *trochee* (trochaic): the reverse of iambic. One heavy and one light stress (snéak / ĕr)
the *anapest* (anapestic): two light stresses followed by a heavy stress (ĭn / tĕr / fére)
the *dactyl* (dactylic): the reverse of anapestic. A heavy stress followed by two light ones (Flór / ĭ / dă)
the *spondee* (spondaic): two heavy stresses (arm / cháir)

Patterns in poetry are built not only by the kind of foot that the poem uses, but also by the number of feet (the number of units) to a line. For example, the ballad stanza is often composed of a four-foot, a three-foot, a four-foot, and a three-foot line. Lines of a given number of feet are called by the following terms:

monometer: one foot (very rare)
dimeter: two feet (rare)
trimeter: three feet
tetrameter: four feet
pentameter: five feet
hexameter: six feet

Because normal English conversation most often follows a pattern of soft and loud syllables, the most natural meter of English poetry is the iamb. And pentameter lines seem to be the length line used in an unusual amount of great English poetry. Such is the line:

Onĕ dáy / Ĭ wróte / hĕr náme / ŭpón / thĕ sánd

When compared with other languages, English has a relatively small number of rhyming words. Therefore, it is very difficult to sustain a long English poem with rhyming patterns. It seems monotonous and often forced. As a consequence, one of the great verse forms in English is *blank verse*, which consists of unrhymed iambic pentameter lines. It is not surprising that some of the greatest English poetry, that of Shakespeare and Milton, shows extensive use of blank verse.

Clearly, there can be no rhythm without a regular beat. But if the meter of a poem is too regular, it will produce a monotonous "rocking horse" effect. Therefore, a good poet knows how to bring variety into metrics. The simplest way of achieving variety is to substitute one kind of foot for another. In the following line Wordsworth has put a trochee in place of an iamb in the first foot:

Earth hăth / nŏt án / ўthĭng / tŏ shów / more fáir

A poem which stops short at the end of each line can also become monotonous. Skillful poets introduce an occasional run-on line for variety, as did Shakespeare at the beginning of his "Sonnet 116." The first line runs over into the second, and the second into the third; but the third and fourth lines are end-stopped:

Let me not to the marriage of true minds
Admit impediments. Love is not love
Which alters when it alteration finds,
Or bends with the remover to remove.

Still another device for achieving variety of rhythm is a *caesura*, or pause in the middle of a line. In this line from Wordsworth a caesura comes in the middle of the fourth foot:

Thĕ wórld / ĭs tóo / mŭch wíth / ŭs; ‖ láte / and sóon

In this tetrameter line from Blake a caesura follows the second foot:

Whát thĕ / hámmĕr? ‖ Whát thĕ / cháin?

Many poets, mostly in the twentieth century, have abandoned regular schemes of meter for *free verse*. But even when free, good verse has a rhythm or beat.

Understanding "Western Wind"

When we come back to "Western Wind" and consider it in relation to the ideas just discussed, we find ways of understanding the impact of this short poem. Let us look again at the poem.

Western wind, when will thou blow,
The small rain down can rain?
Christ, if my love were in my arms
And I in my bed again!

The emotional center of the poem comes in a single word, *Christ*, and that word has force because it is so unexpected. The poet has been using simple familiar words that relate to weather. Suddenly we find a word from another kind of vocabulary, and we are made aware that the speaker's feelings cannot be expressed merely through small talk about wind and rain. That word, *Christ*, with all its associations, seems at first out of place and then amazingly right. We may hear the word spoken angrily, longingly, impatiently—whatever the tone, we know that the speaker calls to Christ for comfort because there is no human being who can help.

Meter works here to give added emphasis to this central word. The poem's meter is not perfectly regular; yet we hear an iambic pattern in the first two lines:

Wĕstérn / wínd, / whĕn wíll / thŏu blów,

Thĕ smáll / ráin dŏwn / căn ráin?

Then, in the third line, the first word forms a foot by itself, forcing a shift in the pattern:

Chríst, / ĭf mў lóve / wĕre ín / mў árms /

The fourth line returns to a more familiar pattern, emphasizing by contrast the heavy beat on *Christ:*

Ănd Í / ĭn mў béd / ăgáin!

Note how the poet has combined varying metrical rhythms to suggest emotional restlessness. The anapestic syllables ("if my love," "in my bed") break up the iambic pattern and create a less secure, less ordered beat to the lines.

Note also how the combination of personification and understatement works to create the sense of loneliness. We hear the speaker addressing the wind in the first line and personifying the rain as "small" in the second. By the third line, we realize that this is a desperate attempt to create human contact even if from natural forces. The lost love seems even more desirable when we come to the last line. The speaker wishes to be in bed—with the lover, we may assume —but also because being in bed represents a warmth and comfort not found in wind and rain. The speaker, of course, does not spell out this contrast, and therein lies the force of the poem. The poem has—through language, through meter, through imagery, and through understatement—made us move with the speaker's feelings.

Medieval Lyrics

"Western Wind" is one of the most personal and moving
of medieval lyrics. The following lyrics
deal with emotions that are more generalized but nonetheless real.
"Now Go'th Sun Under Wood" is from
the early thirteenth century, "I Sing of a Maiden" is from
the early fifteenth century, and "The Corpus Christi Carol" is
from the early sixteenth century.

Now Go'th Sun Under Wood

Now goth[1] sonne under wode[2]—
Me reweth,[3] Marie, thy faire rode.[4]
Now goth sonne under tree—
Me reweth, Marie, thy sone and thee.

---

1. **goth,** goeth.
2. **wode,** wood.
3. **me reweth,** literally, it is rueful to me; therefore, I pity.
4. **rode,** face.

I Sing of a Maiden

I sing of a maiden
    That is makeless:[1]
King of alle kinges
    To[2] her son she ches.[3]

He came also[4] stille   5
    Where his mother was
As dew in Aprille
    That falleth on the grass.

He came also stille
    To his mother's bower[5]   10
As dew in Aprille
    That falleth on the flower.

He came also stille
    Where his mother lay
As dew in Aprille   15
    That falleth on the spray.

Mother and maiden
    Was never none but she—
Well may such a lady
    Godes mother be.   20

---

1. **makeless**, there are two meanings here: mateless
and matchless.
2. **to**, for.
3. **ches**, chose.
4. **also**, as.
5. **bower**, room, and, figuratively, womb.

Now Go'th Sun Under Wood

1. Some editions give this poem the title "Sunset on Calvary." Why doesn't the speaker just refer to that moment? What details create that reference?

2. This poem is made up of two couplets that are similar, but not exactly the same. What is the emotional force of the repeated words? What is the emotional force of the different words?

I Sing of a Maiden

1. What are the details in the poem which imply that the maiden is really the Virgin Mary? Why is that revelation kept for the last line?

2. The second, third, and fourth stanza are very much alike, with only a slight variation in the metaphor. What is the emotional effect of those three stanzas?

The Corpus Christi [1] Carol

Lully lullay, lully, lullay
The falcon hath born my make[2] away.

He bore him up, he bore him down,
He bore him into an orchard brown.

In that orchard there was a hall   5
That was hanged with purple and pall.[3]

And in that hall there was a bed,
It was hanged with gold so red.

And in that bed there lieth a knight,
His woundes bleeding day and night.   10

By that bed's side there kneeleth a may[4]
And she weepeth both night and day.

And by that bed's side there standeth a stone,
Corpus Christi written thereon.

---

1. **Corpus Christi,** the body of Christ.
2. **make,** mate.
3. **purple and pall,** rich purple cloth.
4. **may,** maiden.

The Corpus Christi Carol

1. The poem begins with a refrain that we are intended to hear after each of the stanzas. What effect does the refrain create?

2. What is the actual situation implied in the poem? What details might suggest a religious significance in that situation?

3. What is the emotional force of: "an orchard brown," "purple and pall," "gold so red"?

4. One might describe this poem in cinematic terms: The camera (speaker's voice) moves closer and closer to the scene, focusing first on the setting, then on the characters, and finally on the stone and its inscription. What is the effect of this progression?

Narrative and Drama in Poetry

So far we have considered poetry primarily as the expression of emotion through language, rhythm, metaphor, and understatement. Yet poetry is also related to other forms of expression, especially narrative and drama. When we speak of the implied situation in "Western Wind," we are constructing a small plot with a setting and two characters. When we talk of the speaker's feelings, we move toward the idea of a character revealing himself or herself to us. Poetry shares many elements with fiction, drama, and essays. We should look, then, at the interplay of forms and at how their qualities complement each other.

The characteristic compression of poetry is an enormous help to a storyteller. Suspense can be built, as we will see in "Edward," by *not* giving an explanation for the young man's strange actions. Or the storyteller can focus on particular scenes and leave out others, as in "Sir Patrick Spens," where the central action occurs outside the words of the poem—with chilling effect. Narrative tends to expand, to explain, to amplify, while poetry tends to compress. Thus a story told in poetry feels especially sharp and controlled. We have to fill in the explanations ourselves or, more simply, to concentrate on the actions that are presented.

Rhyme and meter create particular tension in narrative poetry. A poem's pattern is created by stanza divisions, the lengths of lines, the rhyme scheme, and the repetition of a refrain. Once a pattern has been established within a poem, it does not usually change.

The poem's form controls its pace, which proceeds in a predictable manner, even though individual lines may change rhythm. This predictability of poetry contrasts with the variety of paces that a story may have—a variety so great that we cannot guess whether the opening will be leisurely or fast, whether the events will be described with a great deal of detail or just a little, or whether the ending will come as a complete surprise in the last line or be gradually prepared for. When a story is told through poetry, two different paces are established—that of the poem and that of the story—and the poet may choose to exploit the difference between them. The writers of ballads frequently relate sensational stories of love and murder; yet they repeat phrases, insert refrains, and delay the climax so that the story fights to get told. The ballad pulls us simultaneously forward and backward, and the result is a pleasurable tension.

Drama, with dialogue as its characteristic form, also contributes to the variety of poetry. Dialogue implies that we are hearing true characterization. We feel as though we are eavesdropping on a conversation and so are privy to the real motives and thoughts of the people involved and not just to the masks they choose to present. Even a monologue is, in a sense, overheard (as is "Western Wind"). One might then argue that every poem is spoken and every poem becomes a small play. Sometimes most of the action is offstage, as in "The Corpus Christi Carol," where only the scene is presented and the characters are in fixed poses. Sometimes dialogue ultimately reveals the characters, as in "Edward." Sometimes, too, in a deliberately constructed monologue, the speaker talks to an unseen, silent character, as in many love poems. In some dramatic monologues, the speaker unwittingly reveals his or her true character. Browning's "My Last Duchess," which you will read in a later unit, is a well-known example of this type of dramatic monologue.

It is often helpful to view a poem as a short story, a condensed play, or a dramatic monologue. At the same time, we need to remember that a writer who chooses to make a *poem* is using a variety of literary strategies to influence our response.

The following poems include a long monologue ("The Wanderer"), a short narrative ("Sir Patrick Spens"), and a cryptic dialogue ("Edward")—all by anonymous authors and all carefully structured. As you read these poems, look not only at the story or the characterization but also at the interplay of language and sounds, of rhythm and refrain, and, most importantly, of forward narrative movement and repeated poetic structure.

This Old English poem, from a collection called *The Exeter Book*,
was probably written in the early tenth century. It was originally written in a
proselike form, probably to save costly parchment pages.
But it is planned in two half-line units that are frequently joined
by alliteration (see page 117). The speech of the Wanderer
is framed by a short introduction and conclusion. The major portion of the poem
is the sad meditation of this lonely man,
isolated from all his friends and seeing the destruction
of the culture he once loved.

The Wanderer [1]

Oft to the Wanderer,   weary of exile,
Cometh God's pity,   compassionate love,
Though woefully toiling   on wintry seas
With churning oar   in the icy wave,
Homeless and helpless   he fled from Fate.[2]   5
Thus saith the Wanderer   mindful of misery,
Grievous disasters,   and death of kin:
   "Oft when the day broke,   oft at the dawning,
Lonely and wretched   I wailed my woe.
No man is living,   no comrade left,   10
To whom I dare fully   unlock my heart.
I have learned truly   the mark of a man
Is keeping his counsel   and locking his lips,
Let him think what he will!   For, woe of heart
Withstandeth not Fate;   a failing spirit   15
Earneth no help.   Men eager for honor
Bury their sorrow   deep in the breast.
   So have I also,   often in wretchedness
Fettered my feelings,   far from my kin,
Homeless and hapless,   since days of old,   20
When the dark earth   covered my dear lord's face
And I sailed away   with sorrowful heart,
Over wintry seas,   seeking a gold-lord,[3]
If far or near   lived one to befriend me
With gift in the mead-hall   and comfort for grief.   25

---

1. **The Wanderer,** *Anhaga,* the Old English word originally used in line 1, really means "solitary one." And in line 6, the translator uses the title form instead of the literal translation of the Old English *eardstapa,* "earth walker."

2. **Fate,** the Old English word is *wyrd,* which actually means "what comes to pass." It is not as deterministic a word as our usual meaning of fate.
3. **gold-lord,** the head of the household frequently gave gifts of gold and other treasure to his followers.

Who bears it, knows   what a bitter companion,
Shoulder to shoulder,   sorrow can be,
When friends are no more.   His fortune is exile,
Not gifts of fine gold;   a heart that is frozen,
Earth's winsomeness dead.   And he dreams of the hall-men,   30
The dealing of treasure,   the days of his youth,
When his lord bade welcome   to wassail[4] and feast.
But gone is that gladness,   and never again
Shall come the loved counsel   of comrade and king.
    Even in slumber   his sorrow assaileth,   35
And, dreaming he claspeth   his dear lord again,
Head on knee, hand on knee,   loyally laying,
Pledging his liege[5]   as in days long past.
Then from his slumber   he starts lonely-hearted,
Beholding gray stretches   of tossing sea,   40
Sea-birds bathing,   with wings outspread,
While hailstorms darken,   and driving snow.
Bitterer then   is the bane[6] of his wretchedness,
The longing for loved ones: his grief is renewed.
The forms of his kinsmen   take shape in the silence;   45
In rapture he greets them;   in gladness he scans
Old comrades remembered.   But they melt into air
With no word of greeting   to gladden his heart.
Then again surges   his sorrow upon him;
And grimly he spurs   his weary soul   50
Once more to the toil   of the tossing sea.
   No wonder therefore,   in all the world,
If a shadow darkens   upon my spirit
When I reflect   on the fates of men—
How one by one   proud warriors vanish   55
From the halls that knew them,   and day by day
All this earth ages   and droops unto death.
No man may know wisdom   till many a winter
Has been his portion.   A wise man is patient,
Not swift to anger,   nor hasty of speech,   60
Neither too weak,   nor too reckless, in war,
Neither fearful nor fain,[7]   nor too wishful of wealth,
Nor too eager in vow[8]—   ere he know the event.
   A wise man will ponder   how dread is that doom
When all the world's wealth   shall be scattered and waste   65
As now, over all,   through the regions of earth,
Walls stand rime-covered[9]   and swept by the winds.

---

4. **wassail** (wŏs′əl), festive drink (ale, mead) associated
with good-luck toasts.
5. **liege** (lēj), sovereign lord.
6. **bane** (bān), poison (literally, death or harm).

7. **fain** (fān), desirous. The implication is that one should
not be cowardly or foolishly eager in battle.
8. **vow**, here, probably a boastful promise.
9. **rime-covered**, frost-covered.

The battlements crumble,   the wine-halls decay;
Joyless and silent   the heroes are sleeping
Where the proud host fell   by the wall they defended.   70
Some battle launched   on their long, last journey;
One a bird[10] bore   o'er the billowing sea
One the gray wolf[11] slew;   one a grieving eorl[12]
Sadly gave   to the grave's embrace.
The Warden of men   hath wasted this world   75
Till the sound of music   and revel is stilled,
And these giant-built structures[13]   stand empty of life.
    He who shall muse   on these mouldering ruins,
And deeply ponder   this darkling life,
Must brood on old legends   of battle and bloodshed,   80
And heavy the mood   that troubles his heart:
Where now is the warrior?   Where is the war horse?
Bestowal of treasure,   and sharing of feast?
Alas! the bright ale-cup,   the byrny-clad[14] warrior,
The prince in his splendor   those days are long sped   85
In the night of the past,   as if they never had been!
And now remains only,   for warriors' memorial,
A wall wondrous high   with serpent shapes carved.
Storms of ash-spears   have smitten the eorls,
Carnage of weapon,   and conquering Fate.   90
    Storms now batter   these ramparts of stone;
Blowing snow   and the blast of winter
Enfold the earth;   night-shadows fall
Darkly lowering,   from the north driving
Raging hail   in wrath upon men.   95
Wretchedness fills   the realm of earth,
And Fate's decrees   transform the world.
Here wealth is fleeting,   friends are fleeting,
Man is fleeting,   maid is fleeting;
All the foundation of earth   shall fail!"   100
    Thus spake the sage   in solitude pondering.
Good man is he   who guardeth his faith.
He must never too quickly   unburden his breast
Of its sorrow, but eagerly   strive for redress;
And happy the man   who seeketh for mercy   105
From his heavenly Father,   our Fortress and Strength.

ANONYMOUS
translated by C. W. Kennedy

---

10. **bird,** Old English literature frequently talks of the eagle or the raven as a battlefield scavenger.
11. **gray wolf,** another battlefield scavenger.
12. **eorl,** man, warrior.

13. **giant-built structures,** possibly Roman ruins, but the allusion is to buildings of former times, when heroic figures lived.
14. **bryny-clad,** dressed in coat of mail.

The incident recounted in this poem
is grounded in history. In 1281, the King of Scotland
forced Sir Patrick Spens to sail a ship bearing
the King's daughter, Princess Margaret, to her husband, the King of Norway.
On the return voyage, Sir Patrick and the Scots lords
who accompanied the Princess were drowned.

Sir Patrick Spens

The king sits in Dumferline town,
  Drinking the blude-reid[1] wine:
"O whar will I get a guid sailor
  To sail this ship of mine?"

Up and spak an eldern knicht,[2]   5
  Sat at the king's richt knee:
"Sir Patrick Spens is the best sailor
  That sails upon the sea."

The king has written a braid[3] letter
  And signed it wi' his hand,   10
And sent it to Sir Patrick Spens,
  Was walking on the sand.

The first line that Sir Patrick read,
  A loud lauch[4] lauched he;
The next line that Sir Patrick read,   15
  The tear blinded his ee.

"O wha is this has done this deed,
  This ill deed done to me,
To send me out this time o' the year,
  To sail upon the sea?   20

"Make haste, make haste, my mirry men all,
  Our guid ship sails the morn."
"O say na sae,[5] my master dear,
  For I fear a deadly storm.

"Late late yestre'en I saw the new moon   25
  Wi' the auld moon in her arm,[6]
And I fear, I fear, my dear master,
  That we will come to harm."

O our Scots nobles were richt laith[7]
  To weet[8] their cork-heeled shoon,[9]   30
But lang owre a' the play were played
  Their hats they swam aboon.[10]

O lang, lang may their ladies sit,
  Wi' their fans into their hand,
Or e'er they see Sir Patrick Spens   35
  Come sailing to the land.

O lang, lang may the ladies stand,
  Wi' their gold kembs[11] in their hair,
Waiting for their ain[12] dear lords,
  For they'll see thame na mair.[13]   40

Half o'er,[14] half o'er to Aberdour
  It's fifty fadom[15] deep,
And there lies guid Sir Patrick Spens,
  Wi' the Scots lords at his feet.

ANONYMOUS

---

6. yestre'en . . . auld moon in her arm, yesterday evening. The illusion of an old moon within the new one
was thought to be an omen of a great storm.
7. richt laith, right (very) loath.
8. weet, wet.
9. shoon, shoes.
10. owre, before; a' the play, all the play before the
business ended; aboon, above.
11. kembs, combs.
12. ain, own.
13. thame na mair, them no more.
14. half o'er, over (half way).
15. fadom, fathom.

---

1. blude-reid, blood-red.
2. eldern knicht, old knight.
3. braid, broad, plainspoken.
4. lauch, laugh.
5. na sae, not so.

Edward

"Why does your brand sae drap wi' bluid,[1]
    Edward, Edward?
Why does your brand sae drap wi' bluid,
  And why sae sad gang ye, O?"
"O I ha'e killed my hawk sae guid,   5
    Mither, mither,[2]
O I ha'e killed my hawk sae guid,
  And I had nae mair but he, O."

"Your hawkes bluid was never sae reid,[3]
    Edward, Edward.   10
Your hawkes bluid was never sae reid,
  My dear son I tell thee, O."
"O I ha'e killed my reid-roan steed,
    Mither, mither,
O I ha'e killed my reid-roan steed,   15
  That erst[4] was sae fair and free, O."

"Your steed was auld and ye ha'e gat mair,[5]
    Edward, Edward.
Your steed was auld and ye ha'e gat mair:
  Some other dule ye dree,[6] O."   20
"O I ha'e killed my fader[7] dear,
    Mither, mither,
"O I ha'e killed my fader dear,
  Alas and wae[8] is me, O!"

"And whatten penance wul ye dree[9] for that, 25
    Edward, Edward?
And whatten penance wul ye dree for that,
  My dear son, now tell me, O?"
"I'll set my feet in yonder boat,
    Mither, mither,   30
I'll set my feet in yonder boat,
  And I'll fare over the sea, O."

---

1. **brand sae drap wi' bluid**, sword so drip with blood.
2. **mither**, mother.
3. **reid**, red.
4. **erst**, used to be.
5. **ye ha'e gat mair**, you have more horses.
6. **dule ye dree**, some other sorrow you suffer.
7. **fader**, father.
8. **wae**, woe.
9. **whatten . . . wul ye dree**, what penance will you suffer?

"And what wul ye do wi' your towers and
        your ha',[10]
        Edward, Edward?
And what wul ye do wi' your towers and
        your ha',   35
    That were sae fair to see, O?"
"I'll let thame stand til they down fa',
        Mither, mither,
I'll let thame stand till they down fa',
    For here never mair maun I be, O."   40

"And what wul ye leave to your bairns[11] and
        your wife,
        Edward, Edward?
And what wul ye leave to your bairns and
        your wife,
    Whan ye gang over the sea, O?"
"The warldes room late them beg thrae
        life,[12]   45
        Mither, mither,
The warldes room late them beg thrae life,
    For thame never mair wul I see, O."

"And what wul ye leave to your ain mither
        dear,
        Edward, Edward?   50
And what wul ye leave to your ain mither
        dear,
    My dear son, now tell me, O?"
"The curse of hell frae me sal[13] ye bear,
        Mither, mither,
The curse of hell frae me sal ye bear,   55
    Sic counseils[14] ye gave to me, O."

ANONYMOUS

---

10. ha', hall, castle.
11. bairns, children.
12. warldes . . . thrae life, let them beg throughout the
whole world for life.
13. frae me sal, from me shall.
14. sic counseils, such advice.

The Wanderer

1. What are the positive images that the Wanderer remembers? What kind of life does he value?

2. What are the natural images in lines 1–51 that suggest the Wanderer's state of mind?

3. What advice does the Wanderer offer for coping with life's sorrows?

4. Lines 78–100 are built on a familiar medieval motif referred to as *ubi sunt?* ("where are they now?"). Why do you think this melancholy listing comes near the end of the poem?

5. Consider the following statements from the poem. Do you agree or disagree with them? Why?
   a. I have learned truly   the mark of a man
      Is keeping his counsel   and locking his lips,
      Let him think what he will!
   b. No man may know wisdom   till many a winter
      Has been his portion.
   c. Wretchedness fills   the realm of earth,
      And Fate's decrees   transform the world.

Sir Patrick Spens

1. How does the picture of the king, told in the first two lines, show his attitude toward the job he is assigning? What is the significance of the fact that the king does not seem to know the best sailor in his kingdom? Who suggests the name of Sir Patrick to the king? Why is it significant that he "sat at the king's right knee"?

2. The fourth stanza has a vivid contrast between the first two lines and the last two. How has Sir Patrick's attitude changed in the last two lines?

3. Is Sir Patrick really asking a question in the fifth stanza or is he simply raging against an unjust fate?

4. Why doesn't the narrator describe the storm? How do the images in the eighth stanza convey the scene and the emotional effect of the drowning?

5. Where do the narrator's sympathies lie?

6. Is the basic conflict between the king and Sir Patrick or between Sir Patrick and the elder knight? Is it between a simple man of action and a group of politicians or between duty and common sense? Or is it between each of these pairs?

7. Ballads often represent the voice of the common people protesting against the social order in which they live. If you look at this ballad from this point of view, what is it saying?

Edward

1. Dialogue makes up the whole poem. Who are the two speakers?

2. What is Edward's rank in society? What lines in the song supply this information?

3. Is the mother really seeking information? Or does she know the answer all along?

4. Why does Edward try to avoid telling the truth to his mother?

5. The poem represents an intense moment of conflict between mother and son, but not the whole story that led to this moment. Can you reconstruct the essential story from hints given in the poem? What kind of woman is the mother? What do you suppose were her motives?

Sound Effects

Sound effects is the last matter to be considered in our discussion of the formal aspects of poetry. The words of a poem are bound together not merely in stanza patterns visible to the eye, but in sound patterns as well. Poets use several types of sound effects to enhance the form and meaning of their poems.

Alliteration is the repetition of initial sounds, usually consonants. It can be seen joining the half-line units of "The Wanderer":

"Oft to the Wanderer,   weary of exile."

Assonance is the repetition of vowel sounds. It gives an internal music to lines such as:

Sadly gave   to the grave's embrace.
The Warden of men   hath wasted this
   world

Onomatopoeia is a device in which the sound of a word imitates or suggests the meaning. Consider these examples from "The Wanderer": churning, wailed, surges, batter, blast, blowing, raging. In a memorable line, "the sound must seem an echo to the sense," Alexander Pope summed up the idea. He then wrote a series of couplets brilliantly demonstrating his point:

> Soft is the strain when Zephyr gently blows,
> And the smooth stream in smoother numbers
>   flows:
> But when loud surges lash the sounding
>   shore,
> The hoarse, rough verse should like the
>   torrent roar:

> When Ajax strives some rock's vast weight to
>   throw,
> The line too labors, and the words move
>   slow;
> Not so, when swift Camilla scours the plain,
> Flies o'er th' unbending corn, and skims
>   along the main.

The sounds a poem makes, like its shape, work on us both consciously and unconsciously. When we make ourselves pay conscious attention to sound, we do so in order to hear more, to see more, to feel more.

GEOFFREY CHAUCER

1340?-1400

Geoffrey Chaucer, after a painting
by T. Occleve in the National Portrait
Gallery of London, England. This
fourteenth-century poet was widely
traveled, a diplomat, and servant of two
kings. From the experiences of his own
long life, he created the frame for his
sequence of Canterbury Tales. Most of the
portraits of the famous pilgrims are thought to
have been drawn from personages recognizable
to his contemporaries.

In the fourteenth century, Geoffrey Chaucer, the dominant literary figure in England, almost single-handedly brought to England the high literary culture of the early European renaissance. This man, said John Dryden, another famous English poet, was a "perpetual fountain of good sense . . . He must have been a man of a most wonderful comprehensive nature, because, as it has been truly observed of him, he has taken into the compass of his *Canterbury Tales* the various manners and humours (as we now call them) of the whole English nation, in his age. Not a single character escaped him. All his pilgrims are severally distinguished from each other. The matter and manner of their tales and of their telling are so suited to their different educations, humours and callings, that each of them would be improper in any other mouth. Even the grave and serious characters are distinguished by their several sorts of gravity . . . Some of his persons are vicious, and some virtuous, some are unlearned, or (as Chaucer calls them) lewd, and some are learned . . . 'Tis sufficient to say, according to the proverb, that here is God's plenty. We have our forefathers and great-granddames all before us, as they were in Chaucer's days: their general characters are still remaining in mankind, for mankind is ever the same, and nothing lost out of Nature, though everything is altered."

Geoffrey Chaucer was the son of a prominent bourgeois wine merchant, whose apparent success at his trade gave him contacts with the royal court. As was common in the Middle Ages, Chaucer's father placed the boy at about thirteen as a page in a great household, that of the Countess of Ulster. Here his tasks and training gave him an education in manners and provided him an opportunity to observe court life and society at first hand.

In 1360, Chaucer was captured in France during one of those endless campaigns that the English kings were then conducting. He was ransomed by King Edward III for about $1,200. Sometime during the period from 1360 to 1367, Chaucer joined the household of the king, and during those years he seems to have served the king as a trusted messenger and a minor diplomat.

From 1367 to 1386, the poet apparently prospered greatly. He was frequently sent to the continent "on the King's secret affairs." In 1372, he was sent to Genoa, Italy, to negotiate trade agreements, the first of several trips to Italy. On these, he undoubtedly became acquainted with the works of Boccaccio, Petrarch, and Dante, the three greatest Italian writers of the early Renaissance period.

In 1374, Chaucer was made Controller of Customs and Subsidy on Wools, Skins and Hides for the Port of London. In this job, he had an opportunity to meet many different kinds of people: ship captains, business leaders, dockhands, sailors. In 1382, he also became Controller of Customs of Wines, a trade about which he must have learned a good deal from his father.

In 1386, Chaucer moved from his residence in Aldgate, London, to a new home in the County of Kent. He represented Kent in the Parliament of 1386. Early in the reign of young King Richard II, he was appointed clerk of the King's Works, where he was responsible for construction and repairs affecting royal residences, parks, walls, and bridges. Since he had to pay laborers before the Treasury paid him, he had to keep dunning the Treasury for funds already paid out of his own pocket. In 1390, he was twice robbed and once beaten up, because he was known to carry large sums. Nearly two years of this, and Chaucer must have requested and received a new job as deputy forester of one of the King's forests. During these years and probably till his death, Chaucer was continually in financial difficulties, but it is a tribute to his diplomacy that he kept in the good graces of three succeeding monarchs in a troublesome time. He died on October 25, 1400.

Of Chaucer's personal life we know little, except what he reveals in his poems. Presumably, he led the life of a family man. His wife, Phillipa, appears in one of his poems, *The House of Fame,* as a woman whose tone of voice and manner in walking the poet compares unfavorably with that of an eagle. Chaucer also pictures himself in his poems as a round, jolly man, innocent but eager to learn. He once described what must have been his routine after balancing his customs accounts:

> For when your labor all is done
> And your accounts are all set true
> In place of rest or something new
> Home to your house you go alone
> And just as dumb as any stone
> You sit to read another book
> Until you wear that glassy look,
> And thus live a hermit's life
> Although your abstinence is slight.

Chaucer wrote many poems, but the two works for which he holds his place as one of the wisest and most broadly talented of English poets are *The Canterbury Tales* (of which two parts are reprinted here: The *Prologue,* and part of the *Pardoner's Tale*) and *Troilus and Criseyde,* one of the finest long narrative love poems in the English language.

Chaucer's life helps us to explain some of the qualities of his work. His strong, practical bent of mind is not surprising in a man whose business experience required him to be talented at detecting smugglers. His naïve innocence, which is the character he gives himself in his poems, is obviously a literary pose, a mask he uses to allow his readers to make their own evaluations of the people and situations he presents. This mask may also have been the protective disguise of the diplomat and the poet who had to live and deal with arrogant kings, shrewd merchants, and sophisticated diplomats. His knowledge and insight into the characters of many different kinds of people is a knowledge essential for those who would succeed in the world of business, diplomacy, and, for that matter, any world.

The values of studying Chaucer's poetry are the values of studying humankind. The English poet Blake summed up his favorite poet: "Chaucer's characters live age after age. Every age is a Canterbury Pilgrimage; we all pass on, each sustaining one of these characters, nor can a child be born, who is not one of these characters of Chaucer."

Chaucer's Language

Nations and languages, like people, have moments of creative power, when they declare their genius. Geoffrey Chaucer was lucky enough to have lived at such a moment in the history of England. The Norman Conquest of 1066 was long past, and the English people had developed a language and a culture that combined much of what was best in their Anglo-Saxon ancestors and their French conquerors. By 1340, which is approximately the year of Chaucer's birth, the English language had become a tongue which derived its strength from a Germanic grammar and its grace from the sweet-sounding and wide ranging words it borrowed from French. The English language had become a rich and musical tongue for a poet who had to read poetry aloud.

Chaucer's poetry was fresh and lively and close to the spoken language of his time. Chau-

cer wrote in the dialect of the city of London and his popularity was, in fact, one of the reasons that this dialect became the ancestor of modern standard British English (and thus of modern standard American English). Dryden, who had lost the secret of reading Chaucer's English, once said he had the "rude sweetness of a Scotch tune." Actually his language and his rhythm are quite smooth, once one knows the secret of reading Middle English (English of the period 1066–1500).

In the poetry below, you can examine the opening lines of the Prologue in the original Middle English. Though it looks like a foreign language, its proper pronunciation sounds like a more familiar, but quaint and primitive, version of English, which it is. The best way to learn to speak Chaucer's English with accuracy is to hear and imitate an experienced reader of Middle English. For this your class may wish to listen to the passages from *The Canterbury Tales* read in Middle English recorded on "The Changing English Language."*

Here are the first eighteen lines of the "Prologue" to *The Canterbury Tales* in Chaucer's English. Compare them with the translation on page 123.

Whan that Aprille with his shoures soote
The droghte of Marche hath percéd to the roote,
And bathed every veyne in swich licour,
Of which vertu engendred is the flour;
Whan Zephirus eek with his swete breeth
Inspiréd hath in every holt and heeth
The tendre croppes, and the yonge sonne
Hath in the Ram his halfe cours y-ronne,
And smale fowles maken melodye,
That slepen al the night with open yë,
(So priketh hem nature in hir corages),
Than longen folk to goon on pilgrimages
(And palmers for to seken straunge strondes)
To ferne halwes, couthe in sondry londes;
And specially, from every shires ende
Of Engelond, to Caunterbury they wende,
The holy blisful martir for to seke,
That hem hath holpen, whan that they were seke.

---

* "The Changing English Language," Gott and McDavid, Copyright, 1965, by McGraw-Hill, Inc.

THE PROLOGUE

When Chaucer set out to write what is now his most famous work, *The Canterbury Tales*, he wished to present a dramatic sequence of stories in prose and verse. He conceived of a group of travelers on a pilgrimage. To pass the time, each of his pilgrims was to tell two tales going to and two tales coming back from the shrine of Thomas à Becket at Canterbury. While he never even completed this framework with more than one tale for each of his pilgrims, he left a sufficient fragment to give us a good idea of his talents and to assure himself of a permanent place in English literature.

Chaucer's device of framing his tales within a pilgrimage gives him opportunity for dramatic action and for the development of character through the portraits of the pilgrims in the "Prologue" as well as through the story which each pilgrim chooses to tell.

The "General Prologue" which introduces *The Canterbury Tales* is a portrait gallery of English society from the lowest class up to the Knight. Only royalty—the top of the social ladder—is omitted. Unlike a modern playwright, who merely lists a cast of characters, Chaucer introduces them to us in detail. As you read the prologue, note the ways Chaucer has varied his portraits, arranging them in ways that suggest contrasts. Some move from top to toe, some highlight the character's past experience, some point out their most characteristic habits and actions. He enlivens and

complicates our reaction to each character by including his own apparently simple-minded evaluations of each one.

While most of the characters are types, Chaucer gives them an appearance of hard reality by recording them in detail: their clothing, their features, their scruples, their opinions, their characters. This seemingly infinite series of details is actually a tight-knit pattern that sums up a human personality. In order to read the prologue well, you must weigh the meaning of every detail and assess the combined effect of all details.

Perhaps the most important character in the prologue is the poet himself, who in the court of medieval England used to read his poems aloud. In the prologue, Chaucer gives a parody of himself. The character, Chaucer, is a plump, bumbling man, eager to please, and generally uncritical. This fictional substitute has a fatal overconfidence in his own ability to see things as they are. Thus, Chaucer the poet often uses Chaucer the guide to put over a joke on the reader. It is his way of asking the reader to look behind appearances. He tells us: Don't accept the world at face value, and don't accept the judgment of others; *evaluate everything for yourself.*

No wonder Chaucer was such a successful diplomat: He has given us his vision of reality, of the world around us, and he has made us think it is our own.

In the Middle Ages, pilgrimages were a popular form of entertainment and devotion—a combined religious and social outing. Every spring, as the roads of England became passable once more, pilgrims descended in throngs upon the shrine of England's famous Archbishop and martyr, Thomas à Becket. As we meet the Canterbury pilgrims, there are some thirty or so gathered one evening in the Tabard Inn, run by a genial host, Harry Bailly, in Southwark (ˈsəˈthark) in the suburbs of London. They are preparing for their journey on horseback next morning to the shrine of St. Thomas, some 55 miles to the southwest. After Thomas à Becket was brutally murdered by the followers of King Henry II in 1170, his blood, preserved in vials, was thought to work miracles in healing the sick, thus making his shrine a popular one from the fourteenth century to our own day. T. S. Eliot wrote his famous verse play *Murder in the Cathedral* to commemorate the Archbishop's martyrdom.

THE CANTERBURY TALES

TRANSLATED BY NEVILLE COGHILL

Prologue

When in April the sweet showers fall
And pierce the drought of March to the
    root, and all
The veins are bathed in liquor of such
    power
As brings about the engendering of the
    flower,
When also Zephyrus[1] with his sweet
    breath   5
Exhales an air in every grove and heath
Upon the tender shoots, and the young
    sun
His half-course in the sign of the *Ram*[2]
    has run,
And the small fowl are making melody
That sleep away the night with open eye   10
(So nature pricks them and their heart
    engages)
Then people long to go on pilgrimages
And palmers[3] long to seek the stranger
    strands
Of far-off saints, hallowed in sundry lands,
And specially, from every shire's end   15
In England, down to Canterbury they
    wend
To seek the holy blissful martyr, quick
To give his help to them when they were
    sick.
    It happened in that season that one day
In Southwark, at *The Tabard,* as I lay   20
Ready to go on pilgrimage and start

For Canterbury, most devout at heart,
At night there came into that hostelry[4]
Some nine and twenty in a company
Of sundry folk happening then to fall   25
In fellowship, and they were pilgrims all
That towards Canterbury meant to ride.
The rooms and stables of the inn were
    wide;
They made us easy, all was of the best.
And shortly, when the sun had gone to
    rest,   30
By speaking to them all upon the trip
I soon was one of them in fellowship
And promised to rise early and take the
    way
To Canterbury, as you heard me say.
    But none the less, while I have time and
        space,   35
Before my story takes a further pace,
It seems a reasonable thing to say
What their condition was, the full array
Of each of them, as it appeared to me
According to profession and degree,   40
And what apparel they were riding in;
And at a Knight I therefore will begin.

---

1. **Zephyrus** (zef'ər əs), the west wind.
2. **the Ram,** a zodiac sign often called Aries. During April the sun passes through the first part of this constellation.
3. **palmers,** travelers bearing crossed palm leaves to proclaim their religious pilgrimages.
4. **hostelry** (hos'tl rē), inn. The Tabard Inn existed in Chaucer's time. The inn sign was a tabard, or knight's tunic, with emblazoned arms.

Prologue to *The Canterbury Tales,* tr. Neville Coghill. Reprinted by permission of Penguin Books, Ltd.

The Knight

There was a *Knight,* a most distinguished
    man,
Who from the day on which he first began
To ride abroad had followed chivalry,   45
Truth, honour, generousness and courtesy.
He had done nobly in his sovereign's war
And ridden into battle, no man more,
As well in christian as in heathen places,
And ever honoured for his noble graces.   50

    When we took Alexandria,[5] he was
      there.
He often sat at table in the chair
Of honour, above all nations, when in
    Prussia.
In Lithuania he had ridden, and Russia,
No christian man so often, of his rank.[6]   55
When, in Granada, Algeciras sank
Under assault, he had been there, and in
North Africa, raiding Benamarin;
In Anatolia he had been as well
And fought when Ayas and Attalia fell,[7]   60
For all along the Mediterranean coast
He had embarked with many a noble host.
In fifteen mortal battles he had been
And jousted for our faith at Tramissene[8]
Thrice in the lists, and always killed his
    man.   65
This same distinguished knight had led
    the van
Once with the Bey of Balat,[9] doing work
For him against another heathen Turk;
He was of sovereign value in all eyes.
And though so much distinguished, he
    was wise   70
And in his bearing modest as a maid.
He never yet a boorish thing had said
In all his life to any, come what might;
He was a true, a perfect gentle-knight.[10]

    Speaking of his equipment, he possessed   75
Fine horses, but he was not gaily dressed.
He wore a fustian tunic[11] stained and dark
With smudges where his armour had left
    mark;

Just home from service, he had joined our
    ranks
To do his pilgrimage and render thanks.   80

The Squire

    He had his son with him, a fine young
    Squire,
A lover and cadet, a lad of fire
With locks as curly as if they had been
    pressed.
He was some twenty years of age, I
    guessed.
In stature he was of a moderate length,   85
With wonderful agility and strength.
He'd seen some service with the cavalry
In Flanders and Artois and Picardy[12]
And had done valiantly in little space
Of time, in hope to win his lady's grace.   90
He was embroidered like a meadow bright
And full of freshest flowers, red and white.
Singing he was, or fluting all the day;
He was as fresh as is the month of May.
Short was his gown, the sleeves were long
    and wide;   95
He knew the way to sit a horse and ride.
He could make songs and poems and recite,

---

5. Alexandria in Egypt was captured by Christian forces in 1365.
6. Chaucer's knight had taken part in many "religious" wars—perhaps too many to be actual fact. Teutonic knights fought Slavic forces in the Baltic areas, Prussia and Lithuania, and in Russia.
7. **Algeciras** (al′jə sir′əs), was captured from the Moors in **Granada** (grə nä′də), in southern Spain in 1344. **Benamarin** was a Moorish kingdom in northwest Africa. **Anatolia** (an′ə tō′lē ə), a part of Turkey in Asia Minor. **Ayas** (ä′yäs), near Antioch, a port in southwest Turkey, won from the Turks in 1367. **Attalia** (ä täl′ē ə), scene of a Turkish defeat in 1361.
8. **jousted** (just′əd) *or* (joust′əd) **at Tramissene,** single combats between picked champions are common in medieval literature.
9. **Bey of Balat** (bal′ät), a Turkish chieftain.
10. **gentle-knight,** proper knight, a member of the gentry.
11. **fustian** (fus′chən) **tunic,** a cotton and linen overblouse, usually belted.
12. **Flanders, Artois, Picardy,** sections of France.

Knew how to joust and dance, to draw and
    write.
He loved so hotly that till dawn grew pale
He slept as little as a nightingale.   100
Courteous he was, lowly and serviceable,
And carved to serve his father at the table.

The Yeoman

There was a *Yeoman*[13] with him at his
    side,
No other servant; so he chose to ride.
This Yeoman wore a coat and hood of
    green,   105
And peacock-feathered arrows, bright and
    keen
And neatly sheathed, hung at his belt the
    while
—For he could dress his gear in yeoman
    style,
His arrows never drooped their feathers
    low—
And in his hand he bore a mighty bow.   110
His head was like a nut, his face was brown.
He knew the whole of woodcraft up and
    down.
A saucy brace[14] was on his arm to ward
It from the bow-string, and a shield and
    sword
Hung at one side, and at the other slipped   115
A jaunty dirk, spear-sharp and well-
    equipped.
A medal of St Christopher[15] he wore
Of shining silver on his breast, and bore
A hunting-horn, well slung and burnished
    clean,
That dangled from a baldrick[16] of bright
    green.   120
He was a proper forester I guess.

The Prioress

There also was a *Nun,* a Prioress.
Her way of smiling very simple and coy.
Her greatest oath was only "By St Loy!"
And she was known as Madam Eglan-
    tyne.[17]   125
And well she sang a service, with a fine

Intoning through her nose, as was most
    seemly,
And she spoke daintily in French, ex-
    tremely,
After the school of Stratford-atte-Bowe;[18]
French in the Paris style she did not know. 130
At meat her manners were well taught
    withal;
No morsel from her lips did she let fall,
Nor dipped her fingers in the sauce too
    deep;
But she could carry a morsel up and keep
The smallest drop from falling on her
    breast.   135
For courtliness she had a special zest,
And she would wipe her upper lip so clean
That not a trace of grease was to be seen
Upon the cup when she had drunk; to eat,
She reached a hand sedately for the meat.   140
She certainly was very entertaining,
Pleasant and friendly in her ways, and
    straining
To counterfeit a courtly kind of grace,
A stately bearing fitting to her place,
And to seem dignified in all her dealings.   145

---

13. **yeoman** (yō′mən), from the class below the gentry household.
14. **a saucy brace,** a fancy leather wristguard for archers.
15. **St. Christopher,** possession of this medal was believed to protect travelers. The legend tells of Christopher who ferried people across a river on his shoulders. One day he carried a strangely heavy child. The child was Jesus and the saint was blessed by the contact.
    Note translator's English punctuation: no period following St.
16. **baldrick** (bôl′drik), a shoulder cord or band.
17. **St. Loy** (loy) or **Eligius** (ə lij′ē əs), a seventh-century French goldsmith who became a renowned church figure. Both the man and his name were suitably elegant for the lady Prioress. Coming from a prosperous family, the Prioress was the director—Mother Superior—of her Priory or convent. As such she was under oath not to leave the convent. **Eglantyne** (eg′lən tīn), the name means "sweetbriar"; it is a name often given to ladies in medieval romances.
18. **Stratford-atte-Bowe,** refers to Bow, an area in East London but at that time about two miles outside London. The Prioress speaks French with the accent of an English finishing school rather than in the Parisian French manner.

As for her sympathies and tender feelings,
She was so charitably solicitous
She used to weep if she but saw a mouse
Caught in a trap, if it were dead or bleed-
    ing
And she had little dogs she would be feed-
    ing   150
With roasted flesh, or milk, or fine white
    bread.
And bitterly she wept if one were dead
Or someone took a stick and made it smart;
She was all sentiment and tender heart.
Her veil was gathered in a seemly way,   155
Her nose was elegant, her eyes glass-grey;
Her mouth was very small, but soft and red,
Her forehead, certainly, was fair of spread,
Almost a span across the brows, I own;
She was indeed by no means undergrown.   160
Her cloak, I noticed, had a graceful charm.
She wore a coral trinket on her arm,
A set of beads, the gaudies[19] tricked in
    green,
Whence hung a golden brooch of brightest
    sheen
On which there first was graven a crowned
    A,   165
And lower, *Amor vincit omnia*.[20]
    Another *Nun*, the chaplain at her cell,
Was riding with her, and *three Priests* as
    well.

The Monk

    A *Monk* there was, one of the finest sort
Who rode the country;[21] hunting was his
    sport.   170
A manly man, to be an Abbot able;
Many a dainty horse he had in stable.
His bridle, when he rode, a man might
    hear
Jingling in a whistling wind as clear,
Aye, and as loud as does the chapel bell   175
Where my lord Monk was Prior of the cell.
The Rule of good St Benet or St Maur[22]
As old and strict he tended to ignore;
He let go by the things of yesterday

And took the modern world's more spacious
    way.   180
He did not rate that text at a plucked hen
Which says that hunters are not holy men
And that a monk uncloistered is a mere
Fish out of water, flapping on the pier,
That is to say a monk out of his cloister.   185
That was a text he held not worth an oyster;
And I agreed and said his views were
    sound;
Was he to study till his head went round
Poring over books in cloisters? Must he toil
As Austin[23] bade and till the very soil?   190
Was he to leave the world upon the shelf?
Let Austin have his labour to himself.
    This Monk was therefore a good man to
    horse;
Greyhounds he had, as swift as birds, to
    course.
Hunting a hare or riding at a fence   195
Was all his fun, he spared for no expense.
I saw his sleeves were garnished at the
    hand
With fine grey fur, the finest in the land,
And on his hood, to fasten it at his chin
He had a wrought-gold cunningly fash-
    ioned pin;   200
Into a lover's knot it seemed to pass.
His head was bald and shone like looking-
    glass;

---

19. **gaudies**, the prayer-counting beads of a rosary.
20. **Amor vincit omnia**, love conquers all.
21. **rode the country**, the monk was an "out-rider," in charge of the estates of the monastery and, as such, less confined than other monks.
22. **Rule of good St Benet . . .** St. Benedict originated the Benedictine order in Italy in the sixth century. His disciple, St. Maurus, brought the order to France. Members of this order take vows of poverty and obedience. They are to remain cloistered, apart from the world, and devoted to scholarship and prayer. This reference identifies the monk's own order as well as its ancient rules and duties—among them edicts against hunting—which he took so lightly.
23. **Austin**, St. Augustine of the fifth century was credited with the rule that all members of religious orders who are able should do manual work. The monk's argument that follows is: how will the world be served (the clergy had many official posts) if all the capable religious isolate themselves from it?

So did his face, as if it had been greased.
He was a fat and personable priest;
His prominent eyeballs never seemed to
   settle.   205
They glittered like the flames beneath a
   kettle;
Supple his boots, his horse in fine condition.
He was a prelate fit for exhibition,
He was not pale like a tormented soul.
He liked a fat swan best, and roasted
   whole.   210
His palfrey was as brown as is a berry.

The Friar

There was a *Friar,* a wanton one and
   merry,
A Limiter,[24] a very festive fellow.
In all Four Orders[25] there was none so
   mellow
So glib with gallant phrase and well-turned
   speech.   215
He'd fixed up many a marriage, giving each
Of his young women what he could afford
   her.
He was a noble pillar to his Order.
Highly beloved and intimate was he
With County folk within his boundary, 220
And city dames of honour and possessions;
For he was qualified to hear confessions,
Or so he said, with more than priestly
   scope;
He had a special license from the Pope.
Sweetly he heard his penitents at shrift 225
With pleasant absolution, for a gift.
He was an easy man in penance-giving
Where he could hope to make a decent liv-
   ing;
It's a sure sign whenever gifts are given
To a poor Order that a man's well shriven, 230
And should he give enough he knew in
   verity
The penitent repented in sincerity.
For many a fellow is so hard of heart
He cannot weep, for all his inward smart.
Therefore instead of weeping and of prayer 235

One should give silver for a poor Friar's
   care.
He kept his tippet[26] stuffed with pins for
   curls,
And pocket-knives, to give to pretty girls.
And certainly his voice was gay and sturdy,
For he sang well and played the hurdy-
   gurdy.   240
At sing-songs he was champion of the
   hour.[27]
His neck was whiter than a lily-flower
But strong enough to butt a bruiser down.
He knew the taverns well in every town
And every innkeeper and barmaid too 245
Better than lepers, beggars and that crew,
For in so eminent a man as he
It was not fitting with the dignity
Of his position, dealing with a scum
Of wretched lepers; nothing good can come 250
Of dealings with the slum-and-gutter
   dwellers,
But only with the rich and victual-sellers.
But anywhere a profit might accrue
Courteous he was and lowly of service too.
Natural gifts like his were hard to match. 255
He was the finest beggar of his batch,
And, for his begging-district, payed a rent;
His brethren did no poaching where he
   went.
For though a widow mightn't have a shoe,
So pleasant was his holy how-d'ye-do 260
He got his farthing from her just the same
Before he left, and so his income came
To more than he laid out. And how he
   romped,
Just like a puppy! He was ever prompt
To arbitrate disputes on settling days[28] 265

---

24. **Limiter,** a friar given the right to beg for alms within a limited district.
25. **all Four Orders,** the four main religious orders of mendicant friars, under vows of poverty, chastity, and obedience are: Franciscan, Dominican, Carmelite, and Augustinian. These orders lived in the secular field (not in monastic solitude) by begging alms, preaching, and hearing confessions.
26. **tippet** (tip′it), a hanging end of a sleeve or hood.
27. He was best among the group for ballad singing.
28. **settling days,** days set aside to settle disputes out of court.

(For a small fee) in many helpful ways,
Not then appearing as your cloistered
    scholar
With threadbare habit hardly worth a dol-
    lar,
But much more like a Doctor or a Pope.
Of double-worsted was the semi-cope   270
Upon his shoulders, and the swelling fold
About him, like a bell about its mould
When it is casting, rounded out his dress.
He lisped a little out of wantonness[29]
To make his English sweet upon his
    tongue.   275
When he had played his harp, or having
    sung,
His eyes would twinkle in his head as
    bright
As any star upon a frosty night.
This worthy's name was Hubert, it ap-
    peared.

The Merchant

There was a *Merchant* with a forking
    beard   28
And motley[30] dress; high on his horse he
    sat,
Upon his head a Flemish beaver hat
And on his feet daintily buckled boots.
He told of his opinions and pursuits
In solemn tones, and how he never lost.   285
The sea should be kept free at any cost[31]
(He thought) upon the Harwich-Holland
    range,[32]
He was expert at currency exchange.[33]
This estimable Merchant so had set
His wits to work, none knew he was in
    debt,   290
He was so stately in negotiation,
Loan, bargain and commercial obligation.
He was an excellent fellow all the same;
To tell the truth I do not know his name.[34]

The Oxford Student

An *Oxford Cleric,* still a student though,   295
One who had taken logic long ago,[35]

Was there; his horse was thinner than a
    rake,
And he was not too fat, I undertake,
But had a hollow look, a sober stare;
The thread upon his overcoat was bare.   300
He had found no preferment in the church
And he was too unworldly to make search
For secular employment. By his bed
He preferred having twenty books in red
And black, of Aristotle's philosophy,   305
To having fine clothes, fiddle or psaltery.[36]
Though a philosopher, as I have told,
He had not found the stone for making
    gold.[37]
Whatever money from his friends he took[38]
He spent on learning or another book   310
And prayed for them most earnestly, re-
    turning

---

29. **wantonness** meant gaity but it also carried the modern sense of decadence. Both the affected lisp and the white neck were commonly used symbols of depravity.
30. **motley** was multicolored or figured cloth. The various guilds had distinctive fabrics for their clothing, and this reference may suggest the membership of the merchant in a guild of those who exported wools and skins.
31. **at any cost,** piracy was a constant threat to sea trade. To guard the seas, the king hired private ships paid for by taxes on merchandise.
32. **Harwich-Holland** (har′ij) **range,** this originally referred to the old English port of Orwell, and the range is the sea between it and the Dutch coast.
33. The suggestion is that the merchant carried on speculative money exchange.
34. This may indicate contempt for the merchant class or, since many figures were drawn from life, it may be a barrier to possible identification.
35. **taken logic long ago,** according to the medieval university course of study, this would indicate that the cleric (used here to apply to a student preparing for the Church) had completed a bachelor's degree and was engaged in advanced study.
36. **twenty books . . . to . . . psaltery,** the number of books is merely suggestive of a library unusually large and expensive in those times. Such a collection might have cost more than three fine houses, obviously leaving the student unable to afford such luxuries as a psaltery (sôl′tər ē), a zitherlike instrument.
37. **making gold,** a play on "philosopher," which also meant "alchemist"—the medieval chemist who attempted to turn base metal into gold.
38. Giving alms to a student was considered a reverent act. Students were often supported by such patronage.

Thanks to them thus for paying for his
    learning.
His only care was study, and indeed
He never spoke a word more than was
    need,
Formal at that, respectful in the extreme, 315
Short, to the point, and lofty in his theme.
The thought of moral virtue filled his
    speech
And he would gladly learn, and gladly
    teach.

The Lawyer

A *Serjeant at the Law* who paid his calls,
Wary and wise, for clients at St Paul's[39] 320
There also was, of noted excellence.
Discreet he was, a man to reverence,
Or so he seemed, his sayings were so wise.
He often had been Justice of Assize[40]
By letters patent, and in full commission.[41] 325
His fame and learning and his high position
Had won him many a robe and many a fee.
There was no such conveyancer as he;
All was fee-simple to his strong digestion,[42]
Not one conveyance could be called in
    question; 330
Nowhere there was so busy a man as he;
But was less busy than he seemed to be.
He knew of every judgment, case and crime
Recorded, ever since King William's time.[43]
He could dictate defences or draft deeds; 335
No one could pinch a comma from his
    screeds,[44]
And he knew every statute off by rote.
He wore a homely parti-coloured coat[45]
Girt with a silken belt of pin-stripe stuff;
Of his appearance I have said enough. 340

The Franklin

There was a *Franklin*[46] with him, it ap-
    peared;
White as a daisy-petal was his beard.
A sanguine man, high-coloured and be-
    nign,[47]
He loved a morning sop of cake in wine.

He lived for pleasure and had always done, 345
For he was Epicurus' very son,[48]
In whose opinion sensual delight
Was the one true felicity in sight.
As noted as St Julian was for bounty[49]
He made his household free to all the
    County. 350
His bread, his ale were finest of the fine
And no one had a better stock of wine.
His house was never short of bake-meat
    pies
Of fish and flesh, and these in such supplies
It positively snowed with meat and drink 355
And all the dainties that a man could think.
According to the seasons of the year
Changes of dish were ordered to appear.
He kept fat partridges in coops, beyond
Many a bream[50] and pike were in his pond. 360

39. **Serjeant at the Law** is a lawyer of long experience and high estate appointed to serve the king. . . . **at St. Paul's.** The reference is disputed, but the porch of St. Paul's Cathedral in London seems to have been a meeting place for lawyers and their clients.
40. **Assize** (ə sīz´), justices for the periodic circuit courts were assigned by the king from among the elite group of sergeants at law.
41. **letters patent** (pat´nt) **and . . . commissions,** a public appointment as judge in an open letter from the king. The latter is a direct letter giving the judge wide power to hear all sorts of cases.
42. **conveyancer** (kən vā´ən sər), one who prepares deeds for transfer of property. The reference also suggests that the lawyer was a buyer of land in his own name rather than merely an agent. At this time many in the legal profession were becoming members of the landed class through new wealth and their ability to break old inherited land titles. **Fee simple** means *with clear title* and refers to the ability to arrange for the removal of inherited land claims, thus causing wide resentment of lawyers by the old gentry.
43. Some scholars suggest this is an exaggeration, since available records did not go back to the time of William the Conqueror (1066–87).
44. **screeds,** his writing was above reproach.
45. **homely parti-colored coat,** a plain striped coat.
46. **Franklin,** traveling companion to the lawyer; he was a wealthy landowner, a country gentleman of rank but not of noble birth.
47. **sanguine . . . benign,** he has a cheerful disposition and is ruddy in appearance.
48. **Epicurus** (ep´ə kyūr´əs), Greek philosopher, 342?–270 B.C., associated with luxurious living.
49. **St. Julian,** the legendary patron of hospitality.
50. **bream,** carp.

Woe to the cook whose sauces had no sting
Or who was unprepared in anything!
And in his hall a table stood arrayed
And ready all day long, with places laid.
As Justice at the Sessions[51] none stood higher;   365
He often had been Member for the Shire.[52]
A dagger and a little purse of silk
Hung at his girdle, white as morning milk.
As Sheriff he checked audit, every entry.[53]
He was a model among landed gentry.   370

The Five Tradesmen

A *Haberdasher*, a *Dyer*, a *Carpenter*,
A *Weaver* and a *Carpet-maker* were
Among our ranks, all in the livery
Of one impressive guild-fraternity.[54]
They were so trim and fresh their gear would pass   375
For new. Their knives were not tricked out with brass
But wrought with purest silver, which avouches
A like display on girdles and on pouches.
Each seemed a worthy burgess, fit to grace
A guild-hall with a seat upon the dais.[55]   380
Their wisdom would have justified a plan
To make each one of them an alderman;[56]
They had the capital and revenue,
Besides their wives declared it was their due.
And if they did not think so, then they ought;   385
To be called "*Madam*" is a glorious thought,
And so is going to church and being seen
Having your mantle carried like a queen.

The Cook

They had a *Cook* with them who stood alone
For boiling chicken with a marrow-bone,   390
Sharp flavouring-powder and a spice for savour.
He could distinguish London ale by flavour,
And he could roast and seethe and broil and fry,
Make good thick soup and bake a tasty pie.
But what a pity—so it seemed to me,   395
That he should have an ulcer on his knee.
As for blancmange, he made it with the best.

The Ship's Captain

There was a *Skipper* hailing from far west;
He came from Dartmouth, so I understood.
He rode a farmer's horse as best he could,   400
In a woollen gown that reached his knee.
A dagger on a lanyard[57] falling free
Hung from his neck under his arm and down.
The summer heat had tanned his colour brown,
And certainly he was an excellent fellow.   405
Many a draught of vintage, red and yellow,
He'd drawn at Bordeaux, while the trader snored.[58]
The nicer rules of conscience he ignored.
If, when he fought, the enemy vessel sank,
He sent his prisoners home; they walked the plank.   410
As for his skill in reckoning his tides,
Currents and many another risk besides,
Moons, harbours, pilots, he had such dispatch
That none from Hull to Carthage[59] was his match.

---

51. **Sessions,** sittings of the Justice of the Peace, a lower court than the assize of the knight's authority.
52. **Member . . .,** Member of Parliament for his county.
53. The Franklin was also a county auditor.
54. Their common costume suggests a unifying social or religious organization.
55. **up on the dais,** these were citizens prominent enough for the raised seats of honor in the guild hall.
56. **an alderman** had to have a certain amount of property. These men were sufficiently wealthy.
57. **lanyard** (lan′yərd), a cord around the neck.
58. **Bordeaux** (bôr dō′), a seaport in southern France. The suggestion is that he'd stolen the wine.
59. **Hull to Carthage,** seaports from England to Spain (Carthagena).

Hardy he was, prudent in undertaking; 415
His beard in many a tempest had its shak-
    ing,
And he knew all the havens as they were
From Gottland to the Cape of Finisterre,[60]
And every creek in Brittany and Spain;
The barge he owned was called *The*
    Maudelayne. 420

The Doctor

A *Doctor* too emerged as we proceeded;
No one alive could talk as well as he did
On points of medicine and of surgery,
For, being grounded in astronomy,
He watched his patient's favourable star 425
And, by his Natural Magic,[61] knew what
    are
The lucky hours and planetary degrees
For making charms and magic effigies.
The cause of every malady you'd got
He knew, and whether dry, cold, moist or
    hot;[62] 430
He knew their seat, their humour and con-
    dition.
He was a perfect practising physician.
These causes being known for what they
    were,
He gave the man his medicine then and
    there.
All his apothecaries in a tribe[63] 435
Were ready with the drugs he would pre-
    scribe,
And each made money from the other's
    guile;
They had been friendly for a goodish while.
He was well-versed in Esculapius[64] too
And what Hippocrates and Rufus knew 440
And Dioscorides, now dead and gone,
Galen and Rhazes, Hali, Serapion,
Averroes, Avicenna, Constantine,
Scotch Bernard, John of Gaddesden, Gil-
    bertine.
In his own diet he observed some measure; 445
There were no superfluities for pleasure,
Only digestives, nutritives and such.
He did not read the Bible very much.

In blood-red garments, slashed with blu-
    ish-grey
And lined with taffeta, he rode his way; 450
Yet he was rather close as to expenses
And kept the gold he won in pestilences.
Gold stimulates the heart, or so we're told.
He therefore had a special love of gold.

The Wife of Bath

A worthy *woman* from beside *Bath* city 455
Was with us, somewhat deaf, which was a
    pity.
In making cloth she showed so great a bent
She bettered those of Ypres and of Ghent.[65]
In all the parish not a dame dared stir
Towards the altar steps in front of her, 460
And if indeed they did, so wrath was she
As to be quite put out of charity.[66]
Her kerchiefs were of finely woven ground;
I dared have sworn they weighed a good
    ten pound,
The ones she wore on Sunday, on her head. 465
Her hose were of the finest scarlet red
And gartered tight; her shoes were soft and
    new.
Bold was her face, handsome, and red in
    hue.
A worthy woman all her life, what's more
She'd have five husbands, all at the church
    door,[67] 470

---

60. **Gottland, Finisterre** (fin′i ster′), from Sweden to Brittany.
61. **Natural Magic,** a legitimate study as opposed to black magic. The medical ideas are from astrology rather than astronomy.
62. **. . . hot,** the balance of the "humours" in the body was thought to be the key to health and disease.
63. This is an old jibe implying a moneymaking alliance between doctors and druggists.
64. The doctor was familiar with all the current medical authorities from the Greeks, real and legendary, through the Arabs to contemporary Europeans and the English.
65. **Ypres** (ē′prə), **Ghent** (gent), Flemish cities renowned for weaving.
66. The good wife was angry if any offerings were made in church before she brought up her gifts of lacework.
67. **church door,** where many medieval weddings were performed.

Apart from other company in youth;
No need just now to speak of that, forsooth.
And she had thrice been to Jerusalem,
Seen many strange rivers and passed over
    them;
She'd been to Rome and also to Boulogne, 475
St James of Compostella and Cologne,[68]
And she was skilled in wandering by the
    way.
She had gap-teeth, set widely, truth to say.
Easily on an ambling horse she sat
Well wimpled up,[69] and on her head a hat 480
As broad as is a buckler or a shield;
She had a flowing mantle that concealed
Large hips, her heels spurred sharply under
    that.
In company she liked to laugh and chat
And knew the remedies for love's mis-
    chances, 485
An art in which she knew the oldest dances.

The Parson

A holy-minded man of good renown
There was, and poor, the *Parson* to a town,
Yet he was rich in holy thought and work.
He also was a learned man, a clerk,[70] 490
Who truly knew Christ's gospel and would
    preach it
Devoutly to parishioners, and teach it.
Benign and wonderfully diligent,
And patient when adversity was sent
(For so he proved in great adversity) 495
He much disliked extorting tithe or fee,[71]
Nay rather he preferred beyond a doubt
Giving to poor parishioners round about
From his own goods and Easter offerings.
He found sufficiency in little things. 500
Wide was his parish, with houses far
    asunder,
Yet he neglected not in rain or thunder,
In sickness or in grief, to pay a call
On the remotest, whether great or small,
Upon his feet, and in his hand a stave.[72] 505
This noble example to his sheep he gave,
First following the word before he taught
    it,

And it was from the gospel he had caught
    it.
This little proverb he would add thereto
That if gold rust, what then will iron do? 510
For if a priest be foul in whom we trust
No wonder that a common man should
    rust;
And shame it is to see—let priests take
    stock—
A filthy shepherd and a snowy flock.
The true example that a priest should give 515
Is one of cleanness, how the sheep should
    live.
He did not set his benefice to hire[73]
And leave his sheep encumbered in the
    mire
Or run to London to earn easy bread
By singing masses for the wealthy dead, 520
Or find some Brotherhood and get enrolled.
He stayed at home and watched over his
    fold
So that no wolf should make the sheep mis-
    carry.
He was a shepherd and no mercenary.
Holy and virtuous he was, but then 525
Never contemptuous of sinful men,
Never disdainful, never too proud or fine,
But was discreet in teaching and benign.
His business was to show a fair behaviour
And draw men thus to Heaven and their
    Saviour, 530
Unless indeed a man were obstinate;
And such, whether of high or low estate,
He put to sharp rebuke to say the least.

---

68. . . . **Cologne**, she had been on pilgrimages to many shrines.
69. **wimpled**, veiled with a loose covering similar to a hood around the head and under the chin.
70. **clerk**, scholar.
71. It was an accepted custom to excommunicate or to refuse church comforts to parishioners who did not pay their church dues. Instead, the parson offered charity to his poor followers from his own funds.
72. **stave**, a walking stick.
73. It was a common abuse that clergy of the parson's rank would leave their rural posts for more comfortable city dwellings and hire substitutes.

The Wife of Bath

The Parson

The Miller

I think there never was a better priest.
He sought no pomp or glory in his dealings,   535
No scrupulosity had spiced his feelings.
Christ and His Twelve Apostles and their
     lore
He taught, but followed it himself before.

The Plowman

There was a *Plowman* with him there, his
     brother.
Many a load of dung one time or other   540
He must have carted through the morning
     dew.
He was an honest worker, good and true,
Living in peace and perfect charity,
And, as the gospel bade him, so did he,
Loving God best with all his heart and
     mind   545
And then his neighbour as himself, repined
At no misfortune, slacked for no content,
For steadily about his work he went
To thrash his corn, to dig or to manure
Or make a ditch; and he would help the
     poor   550
For love of Christ and never take a penny
If he could help it, and, as prompt as any,
He paid his tithes[74] in full when they were
     due

On what he owned, and on his earnings too.
He wore a tabard smock and rode a mare.[75]   555
     There was a *Reeve*, also a *Miller*, there,
A College *Manciple* from the Inns of Court,
A papal *Pardoner* and, in close consort,
A Church-Court *Summoner*, riding at a
     trot,[76]
And finally myself—that was the lot.   560

The Miller

The *Miller* was a chap of sixteen stone,[77]
A great stout fellow big in brawn and bone.
He did well out of them, for he could go
And win the ram at any wrestling show.
Broad, knotty and short-shouldered, he
     would boast   565

---

74. **This plowman is exceptional,** an idealized and rather
well-to-do worker. Having "tithes" to pay indicates some
property.
75. **tabard smock,** a loose belted smock. A **mare** was an
unfashionable mount.
76. **Reeve,** the supervisor of an English manor house.
Manciple (man′sə pəl), a steward and food buyer. **Pardoner,** a seller of clerical pardons for sins. **Summoner,** a
minor officer of the clerical courts who summoned people to answer to charges.
77. **sixteen stone,** 224 pounds. The stone is a British unit
equal to 14 pounds.

The Manciple   *The Knight*   *The Prioress*

He could heave any door off hinge and post,
Or take a run and break it with his head.
His beard, like any sow or fox, was red
And broad as well, as though it were a
 spade;
And, at its very tip, his nose displayed   570
A wart on which there stood a tuft of hair
Red as the bristles in an old sow's ear.
His nostrils were as black as they were
 wide.
He had a sword and buckler at his side,
His mighty mouth was like a furnace door.   575
A wrangler and buffoon, he had a store
Of tavern stories, filthy in the main.
His was a master-hand at stealing grain.
He felt it with his thumb and thus he knew
Its quality and took three times his due—   580
A thumb of gold, by God, to gauge an oat![78]
He wore a hood of blue and a white coat.
He liked to play his bagpipes up and down
And that was how he brought us out of
 town.

The Manciple

The *Manciple* came from the Inner
 Temple,[79]   585
All caterers might follow his example
In buying victuals; he was never rash

Whether he bought on credit or paid cash.
He used to watch the market most pre-
 cisely
And got in first, and so he did quite nicely. 590
Now isn't it a marvel of God's grace
That an illiterate fellow can outpace
The wisdom of a heap of learned men?
His masters—he had more than thirty
 then—
All versed in the abstrusest legal knowl-
 edge,   595
Could have produced a dozen from their
 College
Fit to be stewards in land and rents and
 game
To any Peer in England you could name,
And show him how to live on what he had
Debt-free (unless of course the Peer were
 mad)[80]   600
Or be as frugal as he might desire,
And they were fit to help about the Shire

---

78. Millers were proverbially dishonest and here
Chaucer plays on an old saying "An honest miller has
a golden thumb." The Miller's thumb is gold from his
profits.
79. **the Inner Temple,** the Manciple worked for one of
the London Inns of Court, or legal colleges.
80. Some members of the lawyer's society managed
large estates.

The Reeve

The Merchant

The Clerk

In any legal case there was to try;
And yet this Manciple could wipe their
    eye.[81]

The Reeve

The *Reeve* was old and choleric[82] and
    thin;   605
His beard was shaven closely to the skin,
His shorn hair came abruptly to a stop[83]
Above his ears, and he was docked on top
Just like a priest in front; his legs were lean,
Like sticks they were, no calf was to be
    seen.   610
He kept his bins and garners[84] very trim;
No auditor could gain a point on him.
And he could judge by watching drought
    and rain
The yield he might expect from seed and
    grain.
His master's sheep, his animals and hens,   615
Pigs, horses, dairies, stores and cattle-pens
Were wholly trusted to his government.
And he was under contract to present
The accounts, right from his master's earli-
    est years.
No one had ever caught him in arrears.   620
No bailiff, serf or herdsman dared to kick,

He knew their dodges, knew their every
    trick;
Feared like the plague he was, by those
    beneath.
He had a lovely dwelling on a heath,
Shadowed in green by trees above the
    sward.   625
A better hand at bargains than his lord,
He had grown rich and had a store of
    treasure
Well tucked away, yet out it came to
    pleasure
His lord with subtle loans or gifts of
    goods,[85]
To earn his thanks and even coats and
    hoods.   630
When young he'd learnt a useful trade and
    still
He was a carpenter of first-rate skill.
The stallion-cob he rode at a slow trot

---

81. **wipe their eye,** defraud them.
82. **choleric,** a complexion indicating a sharp and irritable disposition.
83. The shorn hair was a sign that the Reeve was a serf, here, undoubtedly chief of the manor's peasants.
84. **garner,** granary.
85. The treasures that he loaned for thanks had been taken from the lord in the first place.

The Summoner

The Monk

The Franklin

Was dapple-grey and bore the name of
    Scot.
He wore an overcoat of bluish shade   635
And rather long; he had a rusty blade
Slung at his side. He came, as I heard tell,
From Norfolk, near a place called Baldes-
    well.
His coat was tucked under his belt and
    splayed.
He rode the hindmost of our cavalcade.[86]   640

The Summoner

There was a *Summoner* with us in the
    place
Who had a fire-red cherubinnish face,[87]
For he had carbuncles. His eyes were nar-
    row,
He was as hot and lecherous as a sparrow.
Black, scabby brows he had, and a thin
    beard.   645
Children were afraid when he appeared.
No quicksilver, lead ointments, tartar
    creams,
Boracic, no, nor brimstone, so it seems,
Could make a salve that had the power to
    bite,

Clean up or cure his whelks of knobby
    white   650
Or purge the pimples sitting on his cheeks.
Garlic he loved, and onions too, and leeks,
And drinking strong wine till all was hazy.
Then he would shout and jabber as if crazy,
And wouldn't speak a word except in Latin 655
When he was drunk, such tags as he was
    pat in;[88]
He only had a few, say two or three,
That he had mugged up out of some decree;
No wonder, for he heard them every day.
And, as you know, a man can teach a jay   660
To call out "Walter" better than the Pope.[89]
But had you tried to test his wits and grope
For more, you'd have found nothing in the
    bag.
Then *"Questio quid juris"* was his tag.[90]
He was a gentle varlet and a kind one,   665
No better fellow if you went to find one . . .

---

86. In his place at the rear of the procession the Reeve
was farthest from his traditional enemy, the Miller.
87. Red as the face of a cherub in medieval painting.
88. He knew a few terms from familiar decrees.
89. The jay was trained to say "Walter," much as a
parrot is taught "Polly."
90. This Latin phrase means "The question is what
legal point is involved."

The Shipman

The Serjeant at the Law

The Friar

The Pardoner

He and a gentle *Pardoner* rode together,
A bird from Charing Cross[91] of the same
  feather,
Just back from visiting the Court of Rome.
He loudly sang *"Come hither, love, come
  home!"*   670
The Summoner sang deep seconds to this
  song,
No trumpet ever sounded half so strong.
This Pardoner had hair as yellow as wax,
Hanging down smoothly like a hank of flax.
In driblets fell his locks behind his head   675
Down to his shoulders which they over-
  spread;
Thinly they fell, like rat-tails, one by one.
He wore no hood upon his head, for fun;
The hood inside his wallet had been
  stowed,
He aimed at riding in the latest mode;   680
But for a little cap his head was bare
And he had bulging eye-balls, like a hare.
He'd sewed a holy relic on his cap;
His wallet lay before him on his lap,
Brimful of pardons come from Rome all
  hot.   685
He had the same small voice a goat has got.

His chin no beard had harboured, nor
  would harbour,
Smoother than ever chin was left by bar-
  ber. . . .
There was no pardoner of equal grace,
For in his trunk he had a pillow-case   690
Which he asserted was Our Lady's veil.
He said he had a gobbet[92] of the sail
Saint Peter had the time when he made
  bold
To walk the waves, till Jesu Christ took
  hold.
He had a cross of metal set with stones   695
And, in a glass, a rubble of pigs' bones.
And with these relics, any time he found
Some poor up-country parson to astound,
On one short day, in money down, he drew
More than the parson in a month or two,   700
And by his flatteries and prevarication
Made monkeys of the priest and congrega-
  tion.
But still to do him justice first and last
In church he was a noble ecclesiast.

---

91. **Charing Cross,** a place outside London near a
familiar religious organization. More pardoners claimed
to belong to it than was actually the case.
92. **gobbet,** piece.

How well he read a lesson or told a story!   705
But best of all he sang an Offertory,[93]
For well he knew that when that song was
    sung
He'd have to preach and tune his honey-
    tongue
And (well he could) win silver from the
    crowd.
That's why he sang so merrily and loud.   710

   Now I have told you shortly, in a clause,
The rank, the array, the number and the
    cause
Of our assembly in this company
In Southwark, at that high-class hostelry
Known as *The Tabard*, close beside *The
    Bell*.[94]   715
And now the time has come for me to tell
How we behaved that evening; I'll begin
After we had alighted at the Inn,
Then I'll report our journey, stage by stage,
All the remainder of our pilgrimage.   720
But first I beg of you, in courtesy,
Not to condemn me as unmannerly
If I speak plainly and with no concealings
And give account of all their words and
    dealings,
Using their very phrases as they fell.   725
For certainly, as you all know so well,
He who repeats a tale after a man
Is bound to say, as nearly as he can,
Each single word, if he remembers it,
However rudely spoken or unfit,   730
Or else the tale he tells will be untrue,
The things invented and the phrases new.
He may not flinch although it were his
    brother,
If he says one word he must say the other.
And Christ Himself spoke broad in Holy
    Writ,   735
And as you know there's nothing there un-
    fit,
And Plato says, for those with power to
    read,
"The word should be as cousin to the
    deed."
Further I beg you to forgive it me

If I neglect the order and degree   740
And what is due to rank in what I've
    planned.
I'm short of wit as you will understand.

Harry Bailly, the Host

   Our *Host* gave us great welcome; every-
    one
Was given a place and supper was begun.
He served the finest victuals you could
    think,   745
The wine was strong and we were glad to
    drink.
A very striking man our Host withal,
And fit to be a marshal in a hall.
His eyes were bright, his girth a little wide;
There is no finer burgess in Cheapside.[95]   750
Bold in his speech, yet wise and full of tact,
There was no manly attribute he lacked,
What's more he was a merry-hearted man.
After our meal he jokingly began
To talk of sport, and, among other things   755
After we'd settled up our reckonings,
He said as follows: "Truly, gentlemen,
You're very welcome and I can't think when
—Upon my word I'm telling you no lie—
I've seen a gathering here that looked so
    spry,   760
No, not this year, as in this tavern now.
I'd think you up some fun if I knew how.
And, as it happens, a thought has just oc-
    curred
And it will cost you nothing, on my word.
You're off to Canterbury—well, God speed!   765
Blessed St Thomas answer to your need!
And I don't doubt, before the journey's
    done
You mean to while the time in tales and fun.

---

93. **offertory,** psalms sung or chanted during the ritual
presentation of the bread and wine for communion or
during the collection after the sermon. Here the sermon
came between offertory and offering.
94. **The Bell,** another inn; unlike The Tabard, it cannot
be historically identified.
95. **Cheapside,** a major street in London.

Indeed, there's little pleasure for your
    bones
Riding along and all as dumb as stones.   770
So let me then propose for your enjoyment,
Just as I said, a suitable employment.
And if my notion suits and you agree
And promise to submit yourselves to me
Playing your parts exactly as I say   775
Tomorrow as you ride along the way,
Then by my father's soul (and he is dead)
If you don't like it you can have my head!
Hold up your hands, and not another
    word."
    Well, our consent of course was not de-
    ferred,   780
It seemed not worth a serious debate;
We all agreed to it at any rate
And bade him issue what commands he
    would.
"My lords," he said, "now listen for your
    good,
And please don't treat my notion with dis-
    dain.   785
This is the point. I'll make it short and
    plain.
Each one of you shall help to make things
    slip
By telling two stories on the outward trip
To Canterbury, that's what I intend,
And, on the homeward way to journey's
    end   790
Another two, tales from the days of old;
And then the man whose story is best told,
That is to say who gives the fullest measure
Of good morality and general pleasure,
He shall be given a supper, paid by all,   795
Here in this tavern, in this very hall,
When we come back again from Canter-
    bury.
And in the hope to keep you bright and
    merry
I'll go along with you myself and ride
All at my own expense and serve as guide.   800
I'll be the judge, and those who won't obey
Shall pay for what we spend upon the way.
Now if you all agree to what you've heard
Tell me at once without another word,

And I will make arrangements early for it."   805
    Of course we all agreed, in fact we swore
    it
Delightedly, and made entreaty too
That he should act as he proposed to do,
Become our Governor in short, and be
Judge of our tales and general referee,   810
And set the supper at a certain price.
We promised to be ruled by his advice
Come high, come low; unanimously thus
We set him up in judgement over us.
More wine was fetched, the business being
    done;   815
We drank it off and up went everyone
To bed without a moment of delay.

I
PORTRAITS IN A FRAME

Generally, Chaucer portrays characters from the top of the social and moral scale to the bottom. If you were assembling a group of people from modern life, what people would you choose as modern equivalents for each of the pilgrims?

II
IMPLICATIONS

The following questions and propositions require you to shape opinions, to assess arguments, and to draw valid conclusions. Be sure you can cite evidence to support your conclusions from your reading of the "Prologue."

1. Chaucer the poet does not admire the monk as completely as does Chaucer the pilgrim.

2. From his portraits of the religious figures on the pilgrimage, we can be sure that Chaucer admired the Church of his time wholeheartedly.

3. One of the most famous poems of the twentieth century, T. S. Eliot's *The Waste Land*, opens also with a passage about April and spring:

April is the cruellest month, breeding
Lilacs out of the dead land, mixing
Memory and desire, stirring
Dull roots with spring rain

Contrast this with the opening of the "Prologue." What are the implications of each as to the attitudes of the twentieth century and the attitudes of the fourteenth toward nature, spring, and love?

III
TECHNIQUES

Characterization and Contrast

The trained eye not only observes details with accuracy but also sees the inner meaning that details suggest. Chaucer's genius rested very largely on his ability to discover and record our complex human nature with precision and humor. Though one would never guess it on first reading, Chaucer's descriptions of people rely heavily on his knowledge of human character as described in medieval books on rhetoric, medicine, and astrology. In order to fully appreciate Chaucer's portrait sketches, it is helpful to see what attributes these medieval psychologists emphasized in their catalog of human characteristics:

Name.

Nature—place of origin, family, age, sex, bodily appearance: a special medieval study relating complexion to disposition indicating whether bright or dull, affable or rude, and all the qualities of mind and body bestowed by nature.

Manner of Life—occupation or trade, and the character of a person's home life.

Fortune—rich or poor, success or failure, and social rank.

Habit—characteristic habit or action, and some special knowledge or bodily skill achieved through training or practice.

Feeling—any fleeting passion: joy, fear, etc.

Interests—subjects of special importance to a person, hobbies and enthusiasms.

Purposes—plans or ambitions.

Achievements—deeds accomplished in which the person takes pride.

Accidents—current and past happenings.

Conversation.

Moral Nature—individual moral sensibilities or chief moral weaknesses.

These attributes, combined with a knowledge of medieval medicine and astrology, provided the basis of Chaucer's analysis of human character. It is astounding that he can record so much about a person so casually and yet so completely.

1. Chaucer varies the attributes he selects for his characters making one typical and general and another individual and specific, as he chooses. To fully appreciate his portrayal of human character, write an analysis of at least one of the pairs of characters listed below. Use the list of attributes to guide you. Decide what is the total impression of a character Chaucer wishes to give. Notice how he uses different combinations of these attributes to achieve the desired impression. On this basis, compare or contrast his rich thumbnail portraits of the following pilgrims:

a. The Knight and the Squire (accomplishments, rank, ages, clothing, feeling, habit)

b. The Nun and the Monk (conversation, feeling, manner of life, interests, moral nature vs. interests, achievements)

c. The Oxford Cleric and the Franklin (purposes and manner of life)

d. The Haberdasher, Dyer, Carpenter, Weaver, and Carpet-maker and the Wife of Bath (This will compare Chaucer's only group portrait with his most individual one.)

e. The Friar and the Parson (These are both religious portraits but opposite in nature.)

f. The Reeve and the Pardoner (These two lower-class portraits are much alike.)

2. Which pilgrims are presented without satire or irony in their portraits?

This portion of "The Pardoner's Tale" is the exemplum—an anecdote from the Pardoner's long sermon. The story is to bring home forcefully his favorite text: Avarice is the root of evil. Actually, the origins of this story are lost in antiquity; a haunting venture into the supernatural, the plot is one whose universal appeal has made it popular in different versions from China to modern Germany. Dealing with the ultimate mysteries of life, its power comes from its simplicity. In Chaucer's time, it would have been reminiscent of the Black Death which had made merry England a somber, eerie country earlier in the fourteenth century. Consider the Pardoner as he is described in the "Prologue." How is this story an expression of the character Chaucer intended for the Pardoner himself?

The
Pardoner's
Tale

But, sirs, I have a story to relate.
  It's of three rioters I have to tell
Who long before the morning service bell
Were sitting in a tavern for a drink.
And as they sat, they heard the hand-bell
  clink   5
Before a coffin going to the grave;
One of them called the little tavern-knave
And said "Go and find out at once—look
  spry!
Whose corpse is in that coffin passing by;
And see you get the name correctly too."   10
"Sir," said the boy, "no need, I promise you;
Two hours before you came here I was told.
He was a friend of yours in days of old,
And suddenly, last night, the man was slain,
Upon his bench, face up, dead drunk again. 15
There came a privy[1] thief, they call him
  Death,

Who kills us all round here, and in a breath
He speared him through the heart, he never
  stirred.
And then Death went his way without a
  word.
He's killed a thousand in the present
  plague,   20
And, sir, it doesn't do to be too vague
If you should meet him; you had best be
  wary.
Be on your guard with such an adversary,
Be primed to meet him everywhere you go,
That's what my mother said. It's all I
  know."   25
  The publican[2] joined in with, "By St
  Mary.
What the child says is right; you'd best be
  wary,
This very year he killed, in a large village
A mile away, man, woman, serf at tillage,
Page in the household, children—all there
  were.   30
Yes, I imagine that he lives round there.
It's well to be prepared in these alarms,
He might do you dishonour." "Huh, God's
  arms!"

"The Pardoner's Tale," tr. Neville Coghill. Reprinted by permission of Penguin Books, Ltd.

1. **privy** (priv′ē), secretive, stealthy.
2. **publican** (pub′lə kən), innkeeper.

The rioter said, "Is he so fierce to meet?
I'll search for him, by Jesus, street by street. 35
God's blessed bones! I'll register a vow!
Here, chaps! The three of us together now,
Hold up your hands, like me, and we'll be
    brothers
In this affair, and each defend the others,
And we will kill this traitor Death, I say! 40
Away with him as he has made away
With all our friends. God's dignity! To-
    night!"
    They made their bargain, swore with
        appetite,
These three, to live and die for one another
As brother-born might swear to his born
    brother. 45
And up they started in their drunken rage
And made towards this village which the
    page
And publican had spoken of before.
Many and grisly were the oaths they swore,
Tearing Christ's blessed body to a shred;[3] 50
"If we can only catch him, Death is dead!"
    When they had gone not fully half a mile,
Just as they were about to cross a stile,
They came upon a very poor old man
Who humbly greeted them and thus began, 55
"God look to you, my lords, and give you
    quiet!"
To which the proudest of these men of riot
Gave back the answer, "What, old fool?
    Give place!
Why are you all wrapped up except your
    face?
Why live so long? Isn't it time to die?" 60
    The old, old fellow looked him in the
        eye[4]
And said, "Because I never yet have found,
Though I have walked to India, searching
    round
Village and city on my pilgrimage,
One who would change his youth to have
    my age. 65
And so my age is mine and must be still
Upon me, for such time as God may will.
    "Not even Death, alas, will take my life;
So, like a wretched prisoner at strife

Within himself, I walk alone and wait 70
About the earth, which is my mother's gate,
Knock-knocking with my staff from night
    to noon
And crying, 'Mother, open to me soon!
Look at me, Mother, won't you let me in?
See how I wither, flesh and blood and skin! 75
Alas! When will these bones be laid to rest?
Mother, I would exchange—for that were
    best—
The wardrobe in my chamber, standing
    there
So long, for yours! Aye, for a shirt of hair
To wrap me in!' She has refused her grace, 80
Whence comes the pallor of my withered
    face.
    "But it dishonoured you when you began
To speak so roughly, sir, to an old man,
Unless he had injured you in word or deed.
It says in holy writ, as you may read, 85
'Thou shalt rise up before the hoary head
And honour it.' And therefore be it said
'Do no more harm to an old man than you,
Being now young, would have another do
When you are old'—if you should live till
    then. 90
And so may God be with you, gentlemen,
For I must go whither I have to go."
    "By God," the gambler said, "you shan't
        do so,
You don't get off so easy, by St John!
I heard you mention, just a moment gone, 95
A certain traitor Death who singles out
And kills the fine young fellows hereabout.
And you're his spy, by God! You wait a bit.
Say where he is or you shall pay for it,
By God and by the Holy Sacrament! 100
I say you've joined together by consent
To kill us younger folk, you thieving
    swine!"
    "Well, sirs," he said, "if it be your design
To find out Death, turn up this crooked way
Towards that grove. I left him there to-day 105

---

3. **to a shred**, they swore by various parts of Christ's
body.
4. Note that this figure has symbolic meaning.

Under a tree, and there you'll find him wait-
　　ing.
He isn't one to hide for all your prating.
You see that oak? He won't be far to find.
And God protect you that redeemed man-
　　kind,
Aye, and amend you!" Thus that ancient
　　man.　　　　　　　　　　　　　　110
　　At once the three young rioters began
To run, and reached the tree, and there
　　they found
A pile of golden florins on the ground,
New-coined, eight bushels of them as they
　　thought.
No longer was it Death those fellows
　　sought.　　　　　　　　　　　　115
For they were all so thrilled to see the sight,
The florins were so beautiful and bright,
That down they sat beside the precious
　　pile.
The wickedest spoke first after a while.
"Brothers," he said, "you listen to what I
　　say.　　　　　　　　　　　　　120
I'm pretty sharp although I joke away.
It's clear that Fortune has bestowed this
　　treasure
To let us live in jollity and pleasure.
Light come, light go! We'll spend it as we
　　ought.
God's precious dignity! Who would have
　　thought　　　　　　　　　　　125
This morning was to be our lucky day?
　　"If one could only get the gold away,
Back to my house, or else to yours, per-
　　haps—
For as you know, the gold is ours, chaps—
We'd all be at the top of fortune, hey?　　130
But certainly it can't be done by day.
People would call us robbers—a strong
　　gang,
So our own property would make us hang.
No, we must bring this treasure back by
　　night
Some prudent way, and keep it out of sight.　135
And so as a solution I propose
We draw for lots and see the way it goes.
The one who draws the longest, lucky man,

Shall run to town as quickly as he can
To fetch us bread and wine—but keep
　　things dark—　　　　　　　　　140
While two remain in hiding here to mark
Our heap of treasure. If there's no delay,
When night comes down we'll carry it
　　away,
All three of us, wherever we have planned."
　　He gathered lots and hid them in his
　　hand　　　　　　　　　　　　145
Bidding them draw for where the luck
　　should fall.
It fell upon the youngest of them all,
And off he ran at once towards the town.

　　As soon as he had gone the first sat down
And thus began a parley with the other:　　150
"You know that you can trust me as a
　　brother;
Now let me tell you where your profit lies;
You know our friend has gone to get sup-
　　plies
And here's a lot of gold that is to be
Divided equally amongst us three.　　　155
Nevertheless, if I could shape things thus
So that we shared it out—the two of us—
Wouldn't you take it as a friendly turn?"
　　"But how?" the other said with some con-
　　cern,
"Because he knows the gold's with me and
　　you;　　　　　　　　　　　　160
What can we tell him? What are we to
　　do?"
　　"Is it a bargain," said the first, "or no?
For I can tell you in a word or so
What's to be done to bring the thing
　　about."
"Trust me," the other said, "you needn't
　　doubt　　　　　　　　　　　165
My word. I won't betray you, I'll be true."
　　"Well," said his friend, "you see that we
　　are two,
And two are twice as powerful as one.
Now look; when he comes back, get up in
　　fun
To have a wrestle; then, as you attack,　　170
I'll up and put my dagger through his back

While you and he are struggling, as in
    game;
Then draw your dagger too and do the
    same.
Then all this money will be ours to spend,
Divided equally of course, dear friend.   175
Then we can gratify our lusts and fill
The day with dicing at our own sweet will."
Thus these two miscreants agreed to slay
The third and youngest, as you heard me
    say.
    The youngest, as he ran towards the
    town,   180
Kept turning over, rolling up and down
Within his heart the beauty of those bright
New florins, saying, "Lord, to think I might
Have all that treasure to myself alone!
Could there be anyone beneath the throne 185
Of God so happy as I then should be?"
    And so the Fiend, our common enemy,
Was given power to put it in his thought
That there was always poison to be bought,
And that with poison he could kill his
    friends.   190
To men in such a state the Devil sends
Thoughts of this kind, and has a full per-
    mission
To lure them on to sorrow and perdition;
For this young man was utterly content
To kill them both and never to repent.   195
    And on he ran, he had no thought to
    tarry,
Came to the town, found an apothecary
And said, "Sell me some poison if you will,
I have a lot of rats I want to kill
And there's a polecat[5] too about my yard 200
That takes my chickens and it hits me hard;
But I'll get even, as is only right,
With vermin that destroy a man by night."
    The chemist answered, "I've a prepara-
    tion
Which you shall have, and by my soul's sal-
    vation   205
If any living creature eat or drink
A mouthful, ere he has the time to think,
Though he took less than makes a grain of
    wheat,

You'll see him fall down dying at your feet;
Yes, die he must, and in so short a while   210
You'd hardly have the time to walk a mile,
The poison is so strong, you understand."
    This cursed fellow grabbed into his hand
The box of poison and away he ran
Into a neighbouring street, and found a
    man   215
Who lent him three large bottles. He with-
    drew
And deftly poured the poison into two.
He kept the third one clean, as well he
    might,
For his own drink, meaning to work all
    night
Stacking the gold and carrying it away.   220
And when this rioter, this devil's clay,
Had filled his bottles up with wine, all
    three,
Back to rejoin his comrades sauntered he.
    Why make a sermon of it? Why waste
    breath?
Exactly in the way they'd planned his death 225
They fell on him and slew him, two to one.
Then said the first of them when this was
    done,
"Now for a drink. Sit down and let's be
    merry.
For later on there'll be the corpse to bury."
And, as it happened, reaching for a sup,   230
He took a bottle full of poison up
And drank; and his companion, nothing
    loth,
Drank from it also, and they perished both.

I
A SHORT STORY IN VERSE
    Chaucer's remarkable gifts as a storyteller are
particularly visible in his control of a story's pace,
in his mastery of dialogue, in his patterning of the
right details to create a mood. Chaucer quickly
and picturesquely established the chilly setting of
his tale in the predawn tavern scene with the three

5. **polecat,** a European carnivorous animal like a ferret,
not the American skunk.

rioters. He is acutely sensitive, as one forced to read his poems to a live audience must be, to the necessity for a fast-moving tale. As John Dryden remarked of Chaucer's narrative skill: "As he knew what to say, so he knows also when to leave off—a continence which is practiced by few writers." Find examples of this restraint in the story.

II
IMPLICATIONS

Be prepared to defend or to refute any of the propositions below. Check the story, if you are not sure of your grounds.

1. The portrait of the Pardoner in the "Prologue" doesn't suit a person who could tell such a sensitive tale as this.

2. The details given about the old man in the story clearly indicate that he is Death.

III
TECHNIQUES
The Short Story, Dialogue, Details

Note that the whole story takes only 233 lines. Two-thirds of these are dialogue. The third which is not dialogue generally introduces some conversation. Thus, Chaucer sets his mood, develops his characters, and advances his plot almost totally by dialogue. Yet he is able to give distinctive characters to the tavern-knave, the old man, the publican, and each of the three rioters.

By his patterning of details, Chaucer manages to keep a sense of doom hanging heavy over his tale. Reread the story to see how the following factors contribute to this: the plague; the predawn setting; the clinking bell; the simple and restrained utterances of the boy and the old man; the bravado and the dramatic ironies of the rioter's speech that suggest so forcefully that from within the rioters shall come the flame which will devour them. If you remember Poe's criteria for the short story—singleness of effect, inevitability of action, singleness of theme—then Chaucer's tale seems a perfect example, written some 400 years before Poe's time.

1. The characters in this story have ironic speeches. Cite several instances where they are saying far more than they think they are.

2. Explain how the simple, natural dialogue increases the terror of the supernatural forces that are effortlessly achieving their end.

3. How can Chaucer's power to give meaning to details be seen in the first rioter's excuse to the apothecary when asking for poison?

rats

IV
WORDS

A. Determine the meaning of these italicized words from the context of Chaucer's "Prologue."

1. the *engendering* of the flower;

2. their heart *engages;*

3. into that *hostelry;*

4. that dangled from a *baldric* of bright green;

5. so charitably *solicitous* she used to weep;

6. he knew in *verity;*

7. a profit might *accrue;*

8. too unworldly to make search for *secular* employment.

After examining the expressions look up the italicized words to verify your guesses.

B. From period to period, words shift in their meanings; that is, they undergo *semantic* change. The original work of Chaucer would demonstrate this fact very clearly, but even the translation you have uses words with meanings no longer common, such as these from the "Prologue":

bathed in *liquor* of such power;
to seek the stranger *strands;*
had followed *chivalry;*
a perfect *gentle-knight;* a lover and *cadet;*
embroidered like a meadow bright;
a *saucy* brace;
a *proper* forester I guess;
to *counterfeit* a courtly kind of grace.

Use your dictionary to be sure that you know what meanings are intended in this selection. (Some dictionaries give older meanings first, but many put them after the current meanings.) Especially in reading older literature, make it a habit to notice when words have changed their meanings.

On the other hand, the translator has tried to use words that suggest in modern English what was originally intended in Chaucer's language.

C. The Knight is said to be "modest as a maid." The Squire is "embroidered like a meadow bright" and "fresh as is the month of May." What other similes do you find in the "Prologue"?

RENAISSANCE BRITISH POETRY:
The Elizabethan Age

From the time of the Norman (French) Conquest of England in 1066, the English culture and language underwent many changes. The Germanic tribal-based society (small groups separated from each other) became a European culture with a large city as the capital (London) and a royal court setting the fashion in dress, food, and the arts. The Germanic base of the English language was enriched and transformed by words from Latin, French, and Italian. At this time, also, English poets began to experiment with a variety of stanzaic and metrical forms borrowed from their readings in the classical poets (Greek and Latin) and from their French and Italian contemporaries.

During the Middle Ages, cities arose in England, trade was begun with other countries, and, in 1454, the printing press was invented. The influence of Gutenberg's invention is probably incalculable. No longer did books have to be slowly copied by hand; now a number of copies of the same text could be quickly produced. A reading public was created, now that access to both classical and contemporary texts was possible. A collection and retelling of many of the great stories surrounding King Arthur was printed by William Caxton in 1485. Thus, the myths of the past became the property of the present. Caxton also printed Chaucer's *The Canterbury Tales* and *Troilus and Criseyde* as well as works by Gower and Lydgate and a number of translations.

In addition to the changes in society, in language, and in availability of books, we must consider the influence of individual figures in the shaping of English poetry. It is noticeable that all the poems from before the Norman Conquest are by anonymous writers; we value the poems, but we know nothing about the writers. In fact, it might be said that the idea of a writer, as such, did not exist in England before the Norman Conquest. But as society changed, particularly in the fourteenth century, individual writers of genius arose. One such author was the *Pearl*-poet, whose name we do not know but who was identifiable as a writer in northern England who composed *Pearl* and *Sir Gawain and the Green Knight*. Another was William Langland, who wrote the long moral poem *Vision of William concerning Piers the Plowman*. And most important was Geoffrey Chaucer.

From the end of the fourteenth century the list grew, until at the end of the sixteenth century a major group of writers emerged: Wyatt, Surrey, Sidney, Spenser, Marlowe, Raleigh, Drayton, and, of course, William Shakespeare. A poetic tradition began to establish itself, and poets started to borrow not only from continental models but from each other. A context existed in which poetry was appreciated, considered fashionable, talked about. Such a context occurred during Chaucer's lifetime, during the reign of Edward III; another occurred, more splendidly, during the second half of the sixteenth century at the courts ruled over by Henry VIII (himself a poet and composer of songs), Mary I, and Elizabeth I. Because of Elizabeth's encouragement of poets and playwrights, we call this exciting literary period the "Elizabethan Age." Also known as the English Renaissance—literally a rebirth of interest in learning, language, travel, and foreign literature—this period was the source of a seemingly never-ending flow of great poems and plays.

But before we turn to poems of the English Renaissance, we need to know something of the forms these poets used. The most complicated yet most frequently used form was the *sonnet.* This form, popularized by the Italian poet Petrarch, consists of a fourteen-line poem divided into an eight-line beginning, the *octave,* and a six-line closing, the *sestet.* The rhyme scheme (pattern of rhymed lines) is *a b b a a b b a* and *c d c d c d* or *c d e c d e.*

The Italian, or Petrarchan, sonnet is fairly easy to write in Italian or French because both languages have multiple rhymes. In English, however, there is an enormous strain in finding two rhymes which can sustain the eight lines of the octave. The English sonnet, frequently called the Shakespearean sonnet, solves the rhyme problem by introducing more rhymes into the prescribed fourteen lines. The typical pattern is *a b a b c d c d e f e f g g.*

The appeal of the sonnet form is not easy to explain. Perhaps it lies in the combination of brevity (fourteen lines) and complexity (a prescribed rhyme scheme). For the Renaissance poets this form was both severely limited and highly flexible; they never tired of writing sonnets. Indeed, the sonnet as a form challenges writers in every century.

SIR THOMAS WYATT

Sir Thomas Wyatt (1503–1542) followed what seems to be the normal career for an Elizabethan courtier: education (at Cambridge), travel to Italy and France, and then the diplomatic service. He was charged with treason and imprisoned but acquitted before his death. Rumor has it that he was in love with Anne Boleyn before her marriage to Henry VIII. Whatever the truth, he certainly presents himself as a rejected lover in "Blame Not My Lute." Richard Tottel, the Elizabethan editor of a poetic miscellany where some of Wyatt's poems first appeared, tried to smooth out the irregular metrical beat of his lines. Modern editors go back to manuscripts to find what Wyatt really wrote, preferring the less polished but more interesting (and in some ways more timely) versions.

Blame Not My Lute

Blame not my lute, for he must sound
Of this or that as liketh me,
For lack of wit the lute is bound
To give such tunes as pleaseth me.
Though my songs be somewhat strange 5
And speaks such words as touch thy change,
  Blame not my lute.

My lute, alas, doth not offend,
Though that perforce he must agree
To sound such tunes as I intend, 10
To sing to them that heareth me.
Then, though my songs be somewhat plain,
And toucheth some that use to feign[1]
  Blame not my lute.

My lute and strings may not deny 15
But as I strike they must obey:
Break not them then so wrongfully,
But wreak[2] thyself some wiser way.
And though the songs which I indite[3]
Do quit[4] thy change with rightful spite, 20
  Blame not my lute.

1. **use to feign** (yüz'tü fān'), customarily deceive.
2. **wreak** (rēk), avenge.
3. **indite** (in dīt'), compose; write.
4. **quit**, requite.

147

Spite asketh spite and changing change,
And falséd faith must needs be known.
The fault so great, the case so strange,
Of right it must abroad be blown.[5]   25
Then since that by thine own desért[6]
My songs do tell how true thou art,
  Blame not my lute.

Blame but thyself that has misdone
And well deserved to have blame,   30
Change thou thy way so evil begun
And then my lute shall sound that same.
But if till then my fingers play,
By thy desért, their wonted[7] way,
  Blame not my lute.   35

Farewell, unknown, for though thou brake
My strings in spite, with great disdain,
Yet have I found out for thy sake
Strings for to string my lute again.
And if perchance this foolish rhyme   40
Do make thee blush at any time,
  Blame not my lute.

---

5. **blown,** made known.
6. **desert** (di zèrt'), deserving.
7. **wonted** (wun'tid), accustomed.

HENRY HOWARD, EARL OF SURREY

Henry Howard, Earl of Surrey (1517–1547), a friend of Wyatt's, was also a
courtier during the reign of Henry VIII. Surrey's cousin Catherine became
Henry's fifth wife, and, like Catherine, Surrey was executed for treason. His
poetry is much smoother, both in rhythm and in emotional tone, than Wyatt's.
His writing, both in his translation of the *Aeneid* and in his own poems,
represents a step toward the controlled, sophisticated style of Sir Philip Sidney.

The Soote Season

The soote[1] season, that bud and bloom forth brings,
With green hath clad the hill and eke[2] the vale;
The nightingale with feathers new she sings;
The turtle[3] to her make[4] hath told her tale.
Summer is come, for every spray now springs;   5
The hart hath hung his old head on the pale:[5]
The buck in brake[6] his winter coat he flings,
The fishes float with new repaired scale;
The adder all her slough[7] away she slings,
The swift swallow pursueth the flies small;   10
The busy bee her honey now she mings.[8]
Winter is worn, that was the flowers' bale.[9]
And thus I see among these pleasant things,
Each care decays, and yet my sorrow springs.

---

1. **soote** (sùt'ə), sweet.
2. **eke** (ēk), also.
3. **turtle,** turtledove.
4. **make,** mate.
5. **pale** (pāl), fence of an
enclosure.
6. **brake** (brāk), thicket.
7. **slough** (sluf), snakeskin.
8. **mings** (mingz), remembers.
9. **bale** (bāl), harm.

CHRISTOPHER MARLOWE

Christopher Marlowe (1564–1593) was born in the same year as William
Shakespeare. His short career as a playwright was ended by a tavern brawl in
which he was stabbed. Some scholars think that the brawl was a
deliberately planned attempt to kill Marlowe, perhaps because of his secret
work in the political service, perhaps because of his reputation as an atheist.
His great plays, *Tamburlaine*, *Dr. Faustus*, *The Jew of Malta*, and
Edward II, are remarkable for establishing blank verse as the foremost medium
for Elizabethan drama. They also created the notion of the "overreacher"—
the figure who strives like Tamburlaine to conquer the entire world,
or like Faustus to control all knowledge. Marlowe's delightful poem "The
Passionate Shepherd to His Love" shows another side of Marlowe—the
Elizabethan poet, securely in control of the conventions of the pastoral world,
playing a lighthearted role as traditional wooer.

The Passionate Shepherd to His Love

Come live with me and be my love,
And we will all the pleasures prove[1]
That valleys, groves, hills, and fields,
Woods, or steepy mountain yields.

And we will sit upon the rocks,   5
Seeing the shepherds feed their flocks,
By shallow rivers to whose falls
Melodious birds sing madrigals.

And I will make thee beds of roses
And a thousand fragrant posies,   10
A cap of flowers, and a kirtle
Embroidered all with leaves of myrtle;

A gown made of the finest wool
Which from our pretty lambs we pull;
Fair lined slippers for the cold,   15
With buckles of the purest gold;

A belt of straw and ivy buds,
With coral clasps and amber studs:
And if these pleasures may thee move,
Come live with me, and be my love.   20

The shepherds' swains shall dance and sing
For thy delight each May morning:
If these delights thy mind may move,
Then live with me and be my love.

---

1. **prove,** experience.

149

SIR WALTER RALEIGH

Sir Walter Raleigh (1552–1618) was a courtier, an explorer, a soldier, and, like
so many court figures, also a poet. He wrote a long poem in praise of
Queen Elizabeth (of which we possess only a fragment), a long prose
History of the World, and a number of delightful lyrics. His answer to
Marlowe's poem is as clever and as controlled as the original.

The Nymph's Reply to the Shepherd

If all the world and love were young,
And truth in every shepherd's tongue,
These pretty pleasures might me move,
To live with thee and be thy love.

Time drives the flocks from field to fold,   5
When rivers rage, and rocks grow cold;
And Philomel[1] becometh dumb;
The rest complain of cares to come.

The flowers do fade, and wanton fields
To wayward winter reckoning yields;   10
A honey tongue, a heart of gall,
Is fancy's spring, but sorrow's fall.

Thy gowns, thy shoes, thy beds of roses,
Thy cap, thy kirtle, and thy posies,
Soon break, soon wither, soon forgotten;   15
In folly ripe, in reason rotten.

Thy belt of straw and ivy buds,
Thy coral clasps and amber studs,
All these in me no means can move,
To come to thee and be thy love.   20

But could youth last, and love still breed,
Had joys no date, nor age no need,
Then these delights my mind might move
To live with thee and be thy love.

---

1. **Philomel,** the nightingale.

Blame Not My Lute

1. What is the implied dramatic situation in this
poem? What is the speaker's relationship to the
listener? What actions are implied in the poem or
between the lines?

2. What changes of tone do you hear in the poem?
How are they signaled?

3. What is the effect of the repeated short line
"Blame not my lute" in terms of the poet's argument? In terms of his emotional state?

4. With whom in the poem do you sympathize?
Why?

The Soote Season

How would you demonstrate the inadequacy of
the following statements about "The Soote Season"?

1. The sonnet merely lists details about spring
in a random order.

2. The sonnet is limited because there are only
two rhyming sounds.

3. The sonnet is an impersonal description and
tells us nothing about the poet's feelings.

The Passionate Shepherd to His Love and
The Nymph's Reply to the Shepherd

Do the following statements seem true or false
or neither?

1. One of the poems expresses the point of
view of a dreamer; the other, that of a realist.

2. Most men in love are impractical like the
shepherd; most women remain practical like the
nymph.

3. True love fares better if both parties retain
a mixture of romance and realism.

4. Marlowe leaves himself open to Raleigh's
reply. He deserves the implied criticism.

SIR PHILIP SIDNEY

Sir Philip Sidney (1554–1586) became a legend. Born into a noble family, he studied at Oxford, traveled abroad, and, as was the custom, served as a diplomat and a soldier. It was as a soldier that he died, fighting the Spanish in defense of Holland. Not only did Sidney have a splendid public career, but he was also a gifted writer whose works include an impassioned and important defense of poetry, a poignant sonnet sequence, and a long philosophical romance. So successful was he in so many areas that friends and later generations saw him as the living embodiment of the Renaissance ideal. His courtesy, his learning, his loving, his charm all seemed part of that ideal of aristocratic, careless grace. In the following sonnet from *Astrophel and Stella* we see the combination of intense feeling and poetic skill that Sidney was known for.

Sonnet 31
from Astrophel and Stella

With how sad steps, Oh Moon, thou climb'st the skies, *A*
How silently, and with how wan a face! *B*
What, may it be that even in heav'nly place *B*
That busy archer[1] his sharp arrows tries? *A*
Sure, if that long-with-love-acquainted eyes *A*   5
Can judge of love, thou feel'st a lover's case; *B*
I read it in thy looks: thy languished grace, *B*
To me that feel the like, thy state descries.[2]
Then even of fellowship, Oh Moon, tell me,
Is constant love deemed there but want of wit?   10
Are beauties there as proud as here they be?
Do they above love to be loved, and yet
Those lovers scorn whom that love doth possess?
Do they call virtue there ungratefulness?

1. **busy archer,** Cupid.
2. **descries,** perceives.

Sonnet 31

1. The section on Imagery (page 105) mentions the first two lines of this sonnet as an example of personification. What other details in the poem help to personify the Moon?

2. "Sonnet 31" demonstrates Sidney's version of the sonnet form. What is the formal structure he chooses? How is this particular structure related to his argument?

3. How would you describe the tone of the last six lines? Is that tone different from the tone of the opening lines? In what ways?

From an illustrated edition of The Faerie Queene

EDMUND SPENSER

Edmund Spenser (1552–1599) did not have the advantage of wealth and a courtly background as did Surrey and Sidney. Instead, he was a civil servant and spent most of his life in Ireland. Spenser's major work, an epic poem called *The Faerie Queene*, is an extremely complex piece, showing the poet's skill with narrative, vivid description, and variation of emotional effect. It stands as one of the major allegorical poems in English. Although he completed only six books, Spenser originally planned to write twelve (the standard number for epics). In each book he planned to treat one of the twelve moral virtues specified by Aristotle. Each book centers around a knight who represents one of these virtues. Each book is simultaneously a story and an allegory—an adventure that represents a spiritual experience. The hero of the first book is the Red Cross Knight, who begins as a "tall clownish young man" but who will end as the Knight of Holiness. In fact, he will discover that his name is St. George; he thus is the patron saint of England. When we first meet Red Cross in Canto I, he is riding with Una (whose name means "one," and who represents Truth) and her servant-dwarf; their mission is to rescue Una's parents and her land from a horrible monster. But before he reaches that last symbolic fight, Red Cross must be tested in a number of ways. In the episode in the Wandering Wood and the fight with Error, we see how much Red Cross has to learn. The passage contains many characteristics of Spenser's poem: archaic language deliberately chosen to give the epic a fairy-tale quality, lurid description of Error and her brood, spiritual dimension of the fight—and even an unexpected humorous touch when the monster spits out books and papers as well as frogs and toads.

from *The Faerie Queene*

BOOK I, CANTO I

7

Enforced to seek some covert nigh at hand,
A shady grove not far away they spied
That promised aid the tempest to withstand.
Whose lofty trees y-clad[1] with summer's pride
Did spread so broad that heaven's light did hide,   5
Not pierceable with power of any star.
And all within were paths and alleys wide,
With footing worn and leading inward far.
Fair harbor that them seems,[2] so in they entered are.

1. **y-clad,** dressed. Spenser is deliberately using an archaic form here.

2. **that them seems,** seems to them.

8

And forth they pass, with pleasure forward led,   10
Joying to hear the birds' sweet harmony,
Which therein shrouded from the tempest dread
Seemed in their song to scorn the cruel sky.
Much can[3] they praise the trees so straight and high:
The sailing pine[4], the cedar proud and tall,   15
The vine-prop elm, the poplar never dry,
The builder oak, sole king of forests all,
The aspen good for staves, the cypress funeral.

3. **can,** did.
4. **The sailing pine,** etc., the catalogue of trees, each identified with a particular use (the pine for shipbuilding, the elm for staking up grapes in vineyards, and so on) is a familiar classical and medieval literary device.

9

The laurel, meed[5] of mighty conquerors
And poets sage, the fir that weepeth still,[6]   20
The willow worn of forlorn paramours,
The yew[7] obedient to the bender's will,
The birch for shafts, the sallow[8] for the mill,
The myrrh sweet bleeding in the bitter wound,
The warlike beech, the ash for nothing ill,   25
The fruitful olive, and the platan[9] round,
The carver holm,[10] the maple seldom inward sound.

5. **meed,** reward.
6. **still,** always.

7. **yew,** used for making bows.
8. **sallow,** willow.

9. **platan,** plane tree.
10. **holm,** oak, used for carving.

10

Led with delight, they thus beguile the way
Until the blustering storm is overblown;
When weening[11] to return whence they did stray,   30
They cannot find that path which first was shown,
But wander to and fro in ways unknown,
Furthest from end then when they nearest ween,
That makes them doubt[12] their wits be not their own.
So many paths, so many turnings seen,   35
That which of them to take in diverse[13] doubt they been.

11. **weening,** expecting.

12. **doubt,** believe.

13. **diverse,** differing, distracting.

11

At last resolving forward still to fare
Till that some end they find or[14] in or out,
That path they take that beaten seemed most bare
And like to lead the labyrinth about;[15]   40
Which when by tract[16] they hunted had throughout,
At length it brought them to a hollow cave
Amid the thickest woods. The champion stout
Eftsoons[17] dismounted from his courser brave,[18]
And to the dwarf awhile his needless spear he gave.   45

14. **or,** either.

15. **about,** out of.
16. **tract,** tracks.

17. **Eftsoons,** then.
18. **brave,** splendid.

12

"Be well aware," quoth then that lady mild,
"Lest sudden mischief ye too rash provoke.
The danger hid, the place unknown and wild,
Breeds dreadful doubts. Oft fire is without smoke,
And peril without show. Therefore your stroke,   50
Sir knight, withhold till further trial made."
"Ah lady," said he, "shame were to revoke
The forward footing for[19] an hidden shade.
Virtue gives herself light through darkness for to wade."

19. **for,** because of.

13

"Yea, but," quoth she, "the peril of this place   55
I better wot[20] than you, though now too late
To wish you back return with foul disgrace;
Yet wisdom warns, whilst foot is in the gate,
To stay the step ere forced to retreat.
This is the Wandering Wood,[21] this Error's den,   60
A monster vile whom God and man does hate.
Therefore I read[22] beware." "Fly, fly," quoth then
The fearful dwarf, "this is no place for living men."

20. **wot,** know.

21. **Wandering Wood,** wandering has here both a literal and a moral sense; they are lost and can't find the right way—nor can they find the right. The monster Error is named from the Latin verb, *errare,* which means to wander.
22. **read,** advise.

14

But full of fire and greedy hardiment,[23]
The youthful knight could not for aught be stayed,
But forth unto the darksome hole he went
And lookèd in. His glistering armor made
A little glooming light, much like a shade,
By which he saw the ugly monster plain,
Half like a serpent horribly displayed;
But th'other half did woman's shape retain,[24]
Most loathsome, filthy, foul, and full of vile disdain.

23. **greedy hardiment,** eager courage, although the implication of greedy for glory is also present.

24. **woman's shape retain,** like many classical monsters, Error combines both animal and human features. Error is the first of three monsters that Red Cross will fight; another will emerge from the Castle of Orgoglio (Excessive Pride) and the final monster, again a dragon, keeps Una's parents in captivity.

15

And as she lay upon the dirty ground,
Her huge long tail her den all overspread,
Yet was in knots and many boughts[25] upwound,
Pointed with mortal sting. Of her there bred
A thousand young ones, which she daily fed,
Sucking upon her poisonous dugs,[26] each one
Of sundry shapes, yet all ill-favorèd.
Soon as that uncouth[27] light upon them shone,
Into her mouth they crept, and sudden all were gone.

25. **boughts,** coils.

26. **dugs,** breasts.

27. **uncouth,** unaccustomed.

16

Their dam[28] upstart, out of her den affrayed,[29]
And rushed forth, hurling her hideous tail
About her cursed head, whose folds displayed
Were stretched now forth at length without entrail.[30]
She looked about, and seeing one in mail
Armèd to point,[31] sought back to turn again;
For light she hated as the deadly bale,[32]
Aye[33] wont in desert darkness to remain,
Where plain none might her see, nor she see any plain.

28. **dam,** mother.
29. **affrayed,** frightened.

30. **entrail,** coils.

31. **to point,** completely.
32. **bale,** evil.

33. **Aye,** always.

17

Which when the valiant elf[34] perceived, he leapt
As lion fierce upon the flying prey,
And with his trenchant blade her boldly kept
From turning back and forced her to stay.
Therewith enraged she loudly gan to bray,
And turning fierce, her speckled tail advanced,
Threatening her angry sting, him to dismay.
Who nought aghast, his mighty hand enhanced;[35]
The stroke down from her head unto her shoulder glanced.

34. **elf,** man.

35. **enhanced,** raised.

18

Much daunted with that dint,[36] her sense was dazed,   100
Yet, kindling rage, herself she gathered round,[37]
And all at once her beastly body raised
With doubled forces high above the ground.
Tho[38] wrapping up her wreathèd stern[39] around,
Leapt fierce upon his shield, and her huge train[40]   105
All suddenly about his body wound,
That hand or foot to stir he strove in vain.
God help the man so wrapped in Error's endless train.[41]

36. **dint,** stroke.
37. **gathered round,** coiled up.

38. **Tho,** then.
39. **stern,** coiled tail.
40. **train,** tail.

41. **train,** deceit.

19

His lady, sad to see his sore constraint,
Cried out, "Now, now, sir knight, show what ye be;   110
Add faith unto your force and be not faint!
Strangle her, else she sure will strangle thee."
That when he heard, in great perplexity,
His gall did grate[42] for grief and high disdain,
And knitting all his force got one hand free,   115
Wherewith he gripped her gorge[43] with so great pain
That soon to loose her wicked bands did her constrain.

42. **gall did grate,** he was enraged.

43. **gorge,** throat.

20

Therewith she spewed out of her filthy maw[44]
A flood of poison horrible and black,
Full of great lumps of flesh and gobbets raw.   120
Which stunk so vildly[45] that it forced him slack
His grasping hold and from her turn him back.
Her vomit full of books and papers was,
With loathly frogs and toads which eyes did lack,
And creeping sought way in the weedy grass.   125
Her filthy parbreak[46] all the place defilèd has.

44. **maw,** stomach.

45. **vildly,** vilely.

46. **parbreak,** vomit.

21

As when old Father Nilus gins[47] to swell
With timely[48] pride above th' Egyptian vale,
His fatty[49] waves do fertile slime outwell,
And overflow each plain and lowly dale.   130
But when his later spring[50] gins to avale,[51]
Huge heaps of mud he leaves, wherein there breed
Ten thousand kinds of creatures, partly male
And partly female, of his fruitful seed;
Such ugly monstrous shapes elsewhere may no man read.[52]   135

47. **gins,** begins.
48. **timely,** seasonal.
49. **fatty,** rich.

50. **later spring,** last flood.
51. **avale,** sink.

52. **read,** see.

22

The same so sore annoyèd has the knight,
That well-nigh chokèd with the deadly stink,
His forces fail, ne[53] can no lenger[54] fight.
Whose courage when the fiend perceived to shrink,
She poured forth out of her hellish sink   140
Her fruitful[55] cursed spawn of serpents small,
Deformèd monsters, foul and black as ink;
Which swarming all about his legs did crawl,
And him encumbered sore, but could not hurt at all.

23

As gentle shepherd in sweet eventide,   145
When ruddy Phoebus gins to welk[56] in west,
High on an hill his flock to viewen wide
Marks which do bite their hasty supper best,
A cloud of cumbrous[57] gnats do him molest,
All striving to infix their feeble stings,   150
That from their noyance he nowhere can rest,
But with his clownish[58] hands their tender wings
He brusheth oft, and oft doth mar their murmurings.

53. **ne,** no.
54. **lenger,** longer.

55. **fruitful,** numerous.

56. **welk,** fade.

57. **cumbrous,** harassing.

58. **clownish,** rustic. It is worth noting that Red Cross is also described as a "tall clownish young man."

From an illustrated edition of
The Faerie Queene

24

Thus ill bestead,[59] and fearful more of shame
Than of the certain peril he stood in,   155
Half furious[60] unto his foe he came,
Resolved in mind all suddenly to win
Or soon to lose before he once would lin;[61]
And struck at her with more than manly force,
That from her body full of filthy sin   160
He reft her hateful head without remorse.
A stream of coal-black blood forth gushed from her corse.[62]

59. **bestead**, situated.

60. **furious**, insane.

61. **lin**, leave off.

62. **corse**, body.

25

Her scattered brood, soon as their parent dear
They saw so rudely falling to the ground,
Groaning full deadly, all with troublous fear   165
Gathered themselves about her body round,
Weening their wonted[63] entrance to have found
At her wide mouth; but being there withstood,
They flocked all about her bleeding wound
And sucked up their dying mother's blood,   170
Making her death their life and eke her hurt their good.

63. **wonted**, accustomed.

26

That detestable sight him much amazed,
To see th'unkindly imps[64] of[65] heaven accursed
Devour their dam. On whom while so he gazed,
Having all satisfied their bloody thirst,   175
Their bellies swollen he saw with fulness burst,
And bowels gushing forth. Well worthy end
Of such as drunk her life the which them nursed.
How needeth him no lenger labor spend;
His foes have slain themselves with whom he should contend. 180

64. **imps**, children.
65. **of**, by.

The Faerie Queene

1. Spenser is famous for his descriptive passages, yet one might argue that the catalogue of trees (stanzas 8–9) is not really useful for the narrative. Can you justify the inclusion of these two stanzas?

2. Sometimes Spenser lets a character announce the allegorical level very plainly as when Una says, "This is the Wandering Wood." But by the time she says where they are, the reader has already been warned that the characters are lost. What words and phrases in stanzas 7–12 suggest this symbolic world?

3. What qualities of Red Cross make him vulnerable to Error? And what does he need to help him escape from her clutches?

4. The description of Error and her progeny is full of vivid details. Which of these imply a symbolic value as well?

WILLIAM SHAKESPEARE

William Shakespeare (1564–1616) needs no real introduction here, although he is simultaneously the best-known English writer and one of the most mysterious figures in English literature. Nowhere is that mystery more tantalizing than in his 154 sonnets. These sonnets first appeared in 1609, although most scholars believe that they were written earlier, possibly between 1593 and 1596. We do not know to whom the sonnets were written or whether they reflect real events in the poet-dramatist's life. Nor need we search for the identity of the dark lady so bluntly described in "Sonnet 130" or worry about the young man who seems to be addressed in the first twenty sonnets, usually being encouraged to father children. The real value of the sonnets, whether they are read individually or in sequence, lies in their timeless evocation of human feelings. We find a wide range of feeling here, from happiness to sorrow, from belief to cynicism, from bitterness to playfulness. Shakespeare takes the sonnet form—so prescribed, seemingly so limited—and rings endless changes on it. His depth of feeling and the virtuosity of his poetic craft have lured readers back again and again.

Sonnet 18

Shall I compare thee to a summer's day?
Thou art more lovely and more temperate:
Rough winds do shake the darling buds of May,
And summer's lease hath all too short a date:
Sometime too hot the eye of heaven shines,   5
And often is his gold complexion dimmed;
And every fair from fair sometimes declines,
By chance or nature's changing course untrimmed;[1]
But thy eternal summer shall not fade,
Nor lose possession of that fair thou ow'st;[2]   10
Nor shall death brag thou wander'st in his shade,
When in eternal lines to time thou grow'st:
So long as men can breathe, or eyes can see,
So long lives this, and this gives life to thee.

1. **untrimmed,** unchecked.
2. **ow'st,** you own.

Sonnet 18

What is your reaction to the following statements?

1. The poet knows that nature's beauty passes.

2. The poet's real need is to preserve his own feelings about the woman, not her beauty.

3. The fact that you are reading this poem more than 350 years after it was written indicates that Shakespeare succeeded in his purpose.

Sonnet 29

When in disgrace with Fortune and men's eyes,
I all alone beweep my outcast state,
And trouble deaf heaven with my bootless[1] cries,
And look upon myself and curse my fate,
Wishing me like to one more rich in hope,   5
Featured like him, like him with friends possessed,
Desiring this man's art, and that man's scope,
With what I most enjoy contented least;
Yet in these thoughts myself almost despising,
Haply[2] I think on thee, and then my state,   10
Like to the lark at break of day arising
From sullen earth, sings hymns at heaven's gate;
For thy sweet love rememb'red such wealth brings,
That then I scorn to change my state with kings.

1. **bootless**, useless.
2. **haply**, perchance.

Sonnet 65

Since brass, nor stone, nor earth, nor boundless sea,
But sad mortality o'er-sways their power,
How with this rage shall beauty hold a plea,
Whose action is no stronger than a flower?
O, how shall summer's honey breath hold out   5
Against the wreckful siege of battering days,
When rocks impregnable are not so stout,
Nor gates of steel so strong, but Time decays?
O fearful meditation! where, alack,
Shall Time's best jewel from Time's chest lie hid?   10
Or what strong hand can hold his swift foot back?
Or who his spoil of beauty can forbid?
    O, none, unless this miracle have might,
    That in black ink my love may still shine bright.

Sonnet 116

Let me not to the marriage of true minds
Admit impediments. Love is not love
Which alters when it alteration finds,
Or bends with the remover to remove:
Oh, no! it is an ever-fixed mark,   5
That looks on tempests and is never shaken;
It is the star to every wandering bark,
Whose worth's unknown, although his height be taken.
Love's not Time's fool, though rosy lips and cheeks
Within his bending sickle's compass come;   10
Love alters not with his brief hours and weeks,
But bears it out even to the edge of doom.
If this be error and upon me proved,
I never writ, nor no man ever loved.

Sonnet 130

My mistress' eyes are nothing like the sun;
Coral is far more red than her lips' red;
If snow be white, why then her breasts are dun;[1]
If hairs be wires, black wires grow on her head.
I have seen roses damask'd,[2] red and white,   5
But no such roses see I in her cheeks;
And in some perfumes is there more delight
Than in the breath that from my mistress reeks.
I love to hear her speak, yet well I know
That music hath a far more pleasing sound;   10
I grant I never saw a goddess go;
My mistress, when she walks, treads on the ground.
And yet, by heaven, I think my love as rare
As any she belied with false compare.

---

1. **dun,** dull grayish brown.
2. **damask'd** (dam'əskt), varied in color.

Sonnet 29

1. Do you think the details of unhappiness in the first eight lines are causes of the poet's sorrow or results of it?

2. The poet needs to convince us that his mood has changed in the last six lines. How does he do this through language, imagery, and sentence structure?

Sonnet 65

1. What things does Shakespeare mention in the poem which we ordinarily think of as being permanent?

2. What are the contrasting things he mentions which are usually thought of as fragile or fleeting?

3. Do you agree that both sets of objects—those that seem fragile and those that seem permanent—are ultimately destroyed?

4. Do you agree or disagree that the "miracle" the poet seeks has come to pass? That is, that his love ("Time's best jewel") still shines brightly more than 300 years later?

Sonnet 116

1. What metaphors does Shakespeare use to express love's permanence?

2. In lines 1–4, the poet says that love will not change if it is really true love. In lines 5–8, he indicates that love is a permanent guide. In lines 9–12, he says that time cannot shift love. What one element is common to all three groups? What value is the poet seeking from love?

3. Do you have any doubts about the poet's confidence in love's constancy? Does he?

Sonnet 130

1. This poem might be considered a parody of poems which praise (or overpraise) the loved one's beauty. What are the words and phrases that specifically suggest this humorous/satiric tone?

2. What feeling is built up by the poet's series of negatives?

3. How does this feeling help the effect of the final couplet?

162 CHOICE AND CONSEQUENCE

CHOICE AND CONSEQUENCE

Gaunt and forbidding, the Rocky Mountains loom high above the plains, forming the Great Divide of the continent. On one slope of this craggy prominence the waters fall away to the Pacific; and on the other, the rivers flow toward the Atlantic. Travelers struggling on foot through a rough mountain pass are hard pressed to pinpoint the exact moment when they move from one slope to the other. It comes as a slowly dawning awareness of a change of angle, of direction, or of movement.

Just so are the phases of a person's life separated from one another. Childhood merges with adolescence; young adult life moves toward middle age; a happy marriage deteriorates into a dull, nagging emptiness. The moment of the turning point between these phases may be as indistinct and vague as the traveler's awareness of the actual moment of crossing the Great Divide. Only when looking back in time does one suddenly realize that a change has occurred; somewhere a decision has been made which can never be revoked. A new slope, a new phase of life, has been reached.

In attempting to find patterns in the chaotic world around them, writers have always tried to isolate the turning points of people's lives. Literature abounds in tales of how an apparently insignificant moment of choice brings consequences which reverberate throughout a lifetime. Sometimes the results that follow upon a choice cannot be foreseen: The choice of action seems like a stroke of blind fate. At other times the moment of choice is determined by a person's character. Then, as in the case of Socrates, the consequences of an action may be clearly seen in advance.

CHOICE AND CONSEQUENCE examines the ways in which our actions in the present touch our lives in the future. It is an exciting and thought-provoking theme, reflected here in the writings of some of the greatest authors of all time.

WILLIAM SHAKESPEARE

1564–1616

WILLIAM SHAKESPEARE, HIS METHOD OF WORK
Max Beerbohm

*This cartoon refers to the ever-
recurring controversy about
Shakespeare's actual authorship of the
famous works that bear his name.
Here the suggestion credits Francis Bacon.
Vigorous cases have been built for many
other behind-the-scenes authors.
Despite equally vigorous defenses,
the game of discrediting the Stratford
poet goes on and on. Cartoon
courtesy of G. Kearns.*

One of the great mysteries of literary history has been created by the lack of information about the writer called William Shakespeare. We know less about Shakespeare's life than we know of any other major writer, except Homer. More important than the minor details of his life, however, is the fact that he left about thirty-seven magnificent plays (authorities can't quite agree on the number) and a large amount of poetry including a sequence of 154 sonnets. In Shakespeare's time, the Elizabethan Age, the authors of most "good" literature were either university graduates or nobility. Shakespeare was neither: he was an actor and business manager from a family of moderate means in the country town of Stratford-on-Avon. Genius, however, cannot be too neatly accounted for; and in spite of all the attempts to prove that someone else *must* have written these plays, most scholars agree that *Macbeth* and *Hamlet* were indeed written by the actor Shakespeare. His friend Ben Jonson said of him that he was "not of an age, but for all time."

Shakespeare was born in 1564. He probably attended the free grammar school at Stratford which offered him excellent training in writing and in the classics. More important than his schooling is the fact that Shakespeare—like any great writer—observed the world around him intensely. He came to know life in the country and life in the city; he knew the ways of beggars and thieves as well as the ways of royalty; most of all he knew the complex workings of the human mind and heart. To this store of observation he brought a great poet's gift of language, and an actor-producer's knowledge of the stage.

Little is known of Shakespeare's early life, except that at the age of eighteen he married Ann Hathaway, by whom he had three children. We next hear of him in London in the early 1590's, beginning to make a name for himself as an actor, poet, and playwright. During the next twenty years he was connected with the Lord Chamberlain's Men (later the King's Men), a company of actors who worked mostly at the Globe Theater. During these two decades (from about 1591 to 1611) he wrote all the works by which we know him. By 1610 Shakespeare had earned himself a comfortable fortune in the theater, and in that year he retired to Stratford where he died in 1616.

A few of Shakespeare's plays were published during his lifetime, probably without his permission. They are thought to be "pirated" editions and are not very reliable. It seems strange to us today to think that a great writer would not carefully preserve his manuscripts and publish accurate texts of his writings. Seven years after his death, however, some of his associates in the theater realized the importance of Shakespeare's work and brought out a carefully edited volume, *Mr. William Shakespeare's Comedies, Histories and Tragedies.* This important volume is known as the First Folio.

The great Shakespearean roles—such as Hamlet, Cleopatra, Lear, Falstaff, and Lady Macbeth—have for more than three centuries been the ultimate challenge to actors and actresses. His characters emerge on the stage or from the printed page as complicated individuals. Comedy and tragedy stand side by side, even as we find them in life. A grim, tense scene is followed by a lively, amusing one; a moment of quiet and poetry may be succeeded by the noise of a full-scale battle. All of this is set forth in magnificent, forceful poetry—a flow of language which fits the action of each moment as a good lyric fits the music of a song.

The Theater of Shakespeare's Day

It seems fortunate that Shakespeare was born into the height of the Elizabethan Age. England was in the midst of a period of color, curiosity, exploration, expansion, riches. Shakespeare's plays became a gaudy mirror of the time, silvered with his genius. During the twenty years before Shakespeare arrived on the scene, there had been a great blossoming of popular theater. The London stage seemed to have been preparing itself for a great poet and playwright. The drama in England had its beginnings in simple religious pageants and morality plays, such as *Everyman,* performed in the market squares of the towns. Later, strolling players began to give crude comedies and tragedies in the great halls of castles and on platforms set up in the courtyards of inns. The first public theater in England was built in 1576, only about fifteen years before Shakespeare's first play was performed. Soon good writers began to appear—writers like Thomas Kyd and Christopher Marlowe—who developed a style of rapid action combined with blank verse. A large popular audience developed, composed of both aristocracy and commoners.

When Shakespeare began to write he found ready and waiting for him an eager audience and a vital, new, experimental theater. It is particularly important to note that he did not write for the "few"—the learned only—but for a large audience made up of scholars and illiterates, of rich and poor. Much of the richness of his plays lies in the fact that they could—and still do—satisfy all portions of the audience at once.

The stage of the Globe Theater, 1599.

The Elizabethan Stage

Macbeth contains twenty-eight separate scenes. Most of these scenes take only ten minutes or so to perform; many take less. Action shuttles rapidly back and forth between indoors and out; from one castle to another; from battlefields to witches' caves. The fast pace of a Shakespearean play depended in part upon the kind of stage on which it was performed.

The theater building itself was a kind of enclosed courtyard open to the skies (Shakespeare in *Henry V* calls it "this wooden O"). The stage was a simple platform jutting out into the audience. At the rear were doors for exits and entrances, and there may also have been a small curtained alcove in which "interior" scenes could be played. There was probably a balcony above the stage, from which kings could address armies, and from which Juliet could look down upon Romeo. The basic materials of this theater were imagination and language: there was no elaborate scenery as we know it today—no trees, no houses or buildings, no rooms filled with furniture. Because there was no need to shift the sets, the scenes followed each other in a rapid continuous action like that of a movie. Often, at the start of a scene, Shakespeare has a character speak lines that tell the audience the time of day and year, the place of action, and who the speaker is. If lines such as these disturb the modern reader,

it must be remembered that these plays are first meant to be seen, not read. The reader's responsibility is to make the action come alive, as in a theater.

In writing *Macbeth*, Shakespeare made use of some common beliefs of his age. First, Shakespeare's audience accepted the concept of the Divine Right of Kings, namely that a ruler's power came directly from God. Therefore, anyone who killed a king (as Macbeth kills Duncan) was, in effect, at war with God. Second, ghosts and witches were accepted as real by Shakespeare's audience. Third, the play has a political purpose: King James of Scotland had come to the throne of England shortly before *Macbeth* was produced. Banquo was supposed to have been a remote ancestor of James Stuart. Therefore, the play was a tribute to the King by Shakespeare, who glorifies the Stuart family and its right to rule. Shakespeare found the germ of his story in Holinshed's *Chronicles,* but used his writer's privilege of changing events to serve his dramatic purpose.

Macbeth as Tragedy

Antigone and *Macbeth* are both tragedies. Both plays are profound examinations of human life, of suffering, and of evil. But in tone and atmosphere the two plays are not alike. *Antigone* is a drama in which the players seem larger and more noble than in life: they are heroic in stature and representatives of all humanity, rather than individual characters. In *Macbeth*, characters are more individualized. The action is more complicated, and the feelings of the characters are more familiar.

Here, then, is *Macbeth*, one of Shakespeare's greatest tragedies. It is the story of a man who, finding himself faced with a moment of choice, lets the dark forces of his nature predominate. From that moment on, the good within him no longer has the power to control events. He heads step by step into a total disintegration of mind and spirit. The play begins with Macbeth at the height of success and honor, and follows him down the long, dark path to despair.

Generations of playgoers have felt horror and fear
in watching the story of Macbeth; but they have also been moved to pity
because of the anguish in Macbeth's soul. Shakespeare makes us look at ourselves
and ponder the potential for good and evil that lies in each of us.
Where will that moment come in our own lives when a choice may push us
in a new direction? Will we be able to control our fate better than did Macbeth?
Will we recognize the turning point of our lives?

The Tragedy of
MACBETH

Cast of Characters

DUNCAN   MALCOLM, DONALBAIN   MACBETH, BANQUO
King of Scotland   *his sons*   *generals of the King's Army*

MACDUFF, LENNOX, ROSS, MENTEITH, ANGUS, CAITHNESS
noblemen of Scotland

FLEANCE   SIWARD   YOUNG SIWARD   SEYTON
son to Banquo   *Earl of   his son   an officer
Northumberland,   attending
general of the   Macbeth*
English forces*

Boy, *son to Macduff,* an English Doctor, a Scotch Doctor, a Sergeant
a Porter, an Old Man

LADY MACBETH   LADY MACDUFF

Gentlewoman *attending on Lady Macbeth*

HECATE *and* three Witches

Lords, Gentlemen, Officers, Soldiers, Murderers, Attendants, and Messengers
The Ghost of Banquo and other Apparitions

Scene:
Scotland; England; the eleventh century

✿ Act I

Scotland. A desert place.

Thunder and lightning. Enter THREE WITCHES.

FIRST WITCH. When shall we three meet again
    In thunder, lightning, or in rain?
SECOND WITCH. When the hurlyburly's[1] done,
    When the battle's lost and won.
THIRD WITCH. That will be ere the set of sun.   5
FIRST WITCH. Where the place?
SECOND WITCH.   Upon the heath.
THIRD WITCH. There to meet with Macbeth.
FIRST WITCH. I come, Graymalkin![2]
SECOND WITCH. Paddock[3] calls.
THIRD WITCH.   Anon!
ALL. Fair is foul, and foul is fair.   10
    Hover through the fog and filthy air.

    Exeunt.[4]

1. **hurlyburly,** uproar, as of battle.

2. **Graymalkin** (grā mäl′kin), usually an old cat, figuratively an untidy old woman. The demons of the witches were thought to take the forms of cats, toads, etc.
3. **Paddock** (pad′ək), a toad or frog, animals used in conjuring witchcraft.
4. **Exeunt,** the plural form of exit meaning "they leave."

A camp near Forres.

Alarum within. Enter King DUNCAN, MALCOLM,
    DONALBAIN, LENNOX, *with Attendants,*
    meeting a bleeding SERGEANT.

KING. What bloody man is that? He can report,
    As seemeth by his plight, of the revolt
    The newest state.
MALCOLM.   This is the sergeant
    Who like a good and hardy soldier fought
    Gainst my captivity. Hail, brave friend!
    Say to the King the knowledge of the broil[5]   5
    As thou didst leave it.
SERGEANT.   Doubtful it stood,
    As two spent swimmers that do cling together
    And choke their art.[6] The merciless Macdonwald—
    Worthy to be a rebel, for to that   10
    The multiplying villainies of nature
    Do swarm upon him—from the western isles
    Of kerns and gallowglasses[7] is supplied;
    And fortune, on his damnèd quarrel smiling,[8]
    Showed like a rebel's whore. But all's too weak;   15

5. **broil,** battle.

6. **choke their art,** prevent themselves from swimming.
7. **kerns** (kėrnz) **and gallowglasses** (gal′ō glas′əz), Both terms mean Irish or Scottish foot soldiers. The latter were more heavily armed.
8. **fortune . . . smiling,** success personified. The quarrel is Macdonwald's contention or cause.

For brave Macbeth,—well he deserves that name,—
Disdaining fortune, with his brandished steel,
Which smoked with bloody execution,
Like valor's minion, carved out his passage
Till he faced the slave;[9]   20
Which ne'er shook hands nor bade farewell to him
Till he unseamed him from the nave to the chaps[10]
And fixed his head upon our battlements.

KING. O valiant cousin! worthy gentleman!

SERGEANT. As whence the sun 'gins his reflection   25
Shipwracking storms and direful thunders break,
So from that spring whence comfort seemed to come
Discomfort swells. Mark, King of Scotland, mark:
No sooner justice had, with valor armed,
Compelled these skipping kerns to trust their heels   30
But the Norweyan lord, surveying vantage,[11]
With furbished arms and new supplies of men,
Began a fresh assault.

KING.   Dismayed not this
Our captains, Macbeth and Banquo?

SERGEANT.   Yes,
As sparrows eagles, or the hare the lion.   35
If I say sooth, I must report they were
As cannons overcharged with double cracks;[12] so they
Doubly redoubled strokes upon the foe.
Except they meant to bathe in reeking wounds,
Or memorize another Golgotha,[13]   40
I cannot tell—
But I am faint; my gashes cry for help.

KING. So well thy words become thee as thy wounds;
They smack of honor both. Go get him surgeons.

Exit SERGEANT, *attended.*

Enter ROSS.

Who comes here?

MALCOLM.   The worthy thane[14] of Ross.   45

LENNOX. What a haste looks through his eyes! So should
he look
That seems to speak things strange.

ROSS.   God save the King!

KING. Whence cam'st thou, worthy thane?

ROSS.   From Fife, great
King,
Where the Norweyan banners flout the sky
And fan our people cold.   50
Norway himself, with terrible numbers,
Assisted by that most disloyal traitor

9. **slave,** merely a term of abuse: low character, villain. The hand shaking refers to the formalities of dueling.
10. **unseamed . . . to the chaps,** cut apart from navel to jaws.

11. **Norweyan . . . surveying vantage,** Norwegian seeing his advantage.

12. **double cracks,** double charges.

13. **memorize another Golgotha** (gol′gə thə), kill so many as to make a place of killing as renowned as was Golgotha in Jerusalem when Jesus was crucified.

14. **thane,** a Scots nobleman, as a baron.

The thane of Cawdor, began a dismal conflict,
Till that Bellona's bridegroom, lapped in proof,[15]
Confronted him with self-comparisons,
Point against point, rebellious arm 'gainst arm,
Curbing his lavish[16] spirit; and to conclude,
The victory fell on us.

KING.   Great happiness!

ROSS.   That now
Sweno, the Norways' king, craves composition;[17]
Nor would we deign him burial of his men
Till he disbursèd, at Saint Colme's Inch,[18]
Ten thousand dollars to our general use.

KING. No more that thane of Cawdor shall deceive
Our bosom interest.[19] Go pronounce his present death
And with his former title greet Macbeth.

ROSS. I'll see it done.

KING. What he hath lost, noble Macbeth hath won.

Exeunt.

15. **Bellona's** (bə lō'nəz), **bridegroom . . .**, the reference is to Macbeth whose great skill in battle makes him seem like the bridegroom of the Roman war goddess. . . . **lapped in proof**, dressed for battle.
16. **lavish**, great, rebellious, defiant.

17. **craves composition**, seeks an armistice.

18. **Saint Colme's inch**, an island, now Inchcolm in the Firth of Forth off Edinburgh. Dollars, of course, were not the coinage of Macbeth's time. This is an anachronism.
19. **bosom interest**, Cawdor cannot interfere again in the king's vital concerns.

SCENE 3

A heath near Forres.

Thunder. Enter the THREE WITCHES.

FIRST WITCH. Where hast thou been, sister?

SECOND WITCH. Killing swine.

THIRD WITCH. Sister, where thou?

FIRST WITCH. A sailor's wife had chestnuts in her lap,
And munched and munched and munched. "Give me."
quoth I.
"Aroint thee, witch!" the rump-fed ronyon[20] cries.
Her husband's to Aleppo[21] gone, o' the *Tiger;*
But in a sieve I'll thither sail,
And, like a rat without a tail,
I'll do, I'll do, and I'll do.

SECOND WITCH. I'll give thee a wind.

FIRST WITCH. Thou'rt kind.

THIRD WITCH. And I another.

FIRST WITCH. I myself have all the other;
And the very ports they blow,[22]
All the quarters that they know
I' the shipman's card.[23]
I will drain him dry as hay.
Sleep shall neither night nor day
Hang upon his penthouse lid;[24]
He shall live a man forbid.
Weary se'nnights,[25] nine times nine,

20. **Aroint . . . ronyon**, Get away . . . fat and seedy creature.
21. **Aleppo** (ə lep'ō), a Syrian city.

22. **very ports**, this may be read **various points** or to blow out of all harbors. Witches traditionally could control the four winds and here she means to keep the *Tiger* tossing and out of port.
23. **card**, compass.

24. **penthouse lid**, upper lid. The roof of the eye.

25. **se'nnights**, seven-night periods, weeks.

Shall he dwindle, peak,[26] and pine;
Though his bark cannot be lost,
Yet it shall be tempest-tossed.   25
Look what I have.
SECOND WITCH. Show me, show me.
FIRST WITCH. Here I have a pilot's thumb,[27]
Wrecked as homeward he did come.

Drum within.

THIRD WITCH. A drum, a drum!   30
Macbeth doth come.
ALL. The weird sisters, hand in hand,
Posters[28] of the sea and land,
Thus do go about, about:
Thrice to thine, and thrice to mine,   35
And thrice again, to make up nine.
Peace! The charm's wound up.

Enter MACBETH *and* BANQUO.

MACBETH. So foul and fair a day I have not seen.
BANQUO. How far is't called to Forres? What are these,
So withered, and so wild in their attire,   40
That look not like the inhabitants o' the earth,
And yet are on't? Live you? or are you aught
That man may question? You seem to understand me,
By each at once her choppy finger laying
Upon her skinny lips. You should be women,   45
And yet your beards forbid me to interpret
That you are so.
MACBETH.   Speak, if you can. What are you?
FIRST WITCH. All hail, Macbeth! Hail to thee, thane of
 Glamis!
SECOND WITCH. All hail, Macbeth! Hail to thee, thane of
 Cawdor!
THIRD WITCH. All hail, Macbeth, that shalt be King here-
after!   50
BANQUO. Good sir, why do you start and seem to fear
Things that do sound so fair? I' the name of truth,
Are ye fantastical,[29] or that indeed
Which outwardly ye show? My noble partner
You greet with present grace and great prediction   55
Of noble having and of royal hope,
That he seems rapt withal: to me you speak not.
If you can look into the seeds of time,
And say which grain will grow and which will not,
Speak then to me, who neither beg nor fear   60
Your favors nor your hate.

26. **peak,** become peaked.

27. **pilot's thumb,** according to witchcraft parts of bodies used in black magic were especially powerful if they came from one who had suffered a violent death.

28. **posters,** those who post about, travelers.

29. **Are ye fantastical?** Banquo asks the witches if they are creatures of the imagination or as real as they seem.

FIRST WITCH. Hail!
SECOND WITCH. Hail!
THIRD WITCH. Hail!
FIRST WITCH. Lesser than Macbeth, and greater,   65
SECOND WITCH. Not so happy, yet much happier.
THIRD WITCH. Thou shalt get[30] kings, though thou be
    none.
    So all hail, Macbeth and Banquo!
FIRST WITCH. Banquo and Macbeth, all hail!
MACBETH. Stay, you imperfect speakers, tell me more!   70
    By Sinel's death[31] I know I am thane of Glamis,
    But how of Cawdor?[32] The thane of Cawdor lives,
    A prosperous gentleman; and to be King
    Stands not within the prospect of belief,
    No more than to be Cawdor. Say from whence   75
    You owe this strange intelligence, or why
    Upon this blasted heath you stop our way
    With such prophetic greeting? Speak, I charge you.

    WITCHES *vanish*.

BANQUO. The earth hath bubbles, as the water has,
    And these are of them. Whither are they vanished?   80
MACBETH. Into the air, and what seemed corporal melted
    As breath into the wind. Would they had stayed!
BANQUO. Were such things here as we do speak about?
    Or have we eaten on the insane root[33]
    That takes the reason prisoner?   85
MACBETH. Your children shall be kings.
BANQUO.   You shall be King.
MACBETH. And thane of Cawdor too. Went it not so?
BANQUO. To the selfsame tune and words. Who's here?

    Enter ROSS *and* ANGUS.

ROSS. The King hath happily received, Macbeth,
    The news of thy success; and when he reads   90
    Thy personal venture in the rebels' fight,
    His wonders and his praises do contend
    Which should be thine or his. Silenced with that,
    In viewing o'er the rest o' the selfsame day,
    He finds thee in the stout Norweyan ranks,   95
    Nothing afeard of what thyself didst make,
    Strange images of death. As thick as hail
    Came post with post,[34] and every one did bear
    Thy praises in his kingdom's great defense
    And poured them down before him.
ANGUS.   We are sent   100
    To give thee from our royal master thanks;

30. **get**, beget. Banquo was the legendary ancestor of the royal Stuarts.

31. **Sinel's death**, Sinel was Macbeth's father.

32. **Cawdor?**, Macbeth had not learned about Cawdor's treason. The history here is complicated, and the play seems to have condensed three different campaigns.

33. **insane root**, a legendary root which could cause insanity when eaten. Hemlock is one possibility.

34. **post with post**, report after report.

Only to herald thee into his sight,
Not pay thee.

ROSS. And for an earnest[35] of a greater honor,
He bade me, from him, call thee thane of Cawdor;
In which addition,[36] hail, most worthy thane!
For it is thine.

BANQUO.   What, can the devil speak true?

MACBETH. The thane of Cawdor lives. Why do you dress me
In borrowed robes?

ANGUS.   Who was the thane lives yet;
But under heavy judgment bears that life
Which he deserves to lose. Whether he was combined
With those of Norway, or did line the rebel
With hidden help and vantage, or that with both
He labored in his country's wreck, I know not;
But treasons capital, confessed and proved,
Have overthrown him.

MACBETH.   (*Aside*) Glamis, and thane of Cawdor!
The greatest is behind.[37] (*To* ROSS *and* ANGUS) Thanks
for your pains.

(*Aside to* BANQUO) Do you not hope your children
shall be kings,
When those that gave the thane of Cawdor to me
Promised no less to them?

BANQUO.   That, trusted home,[38]
Might yet enkindle you unto the crown,
Besides the thane of Cawdor. But 'tis strange;
And oftentimes, to win us to our harm,
The instruments of darkness tell us truths,
Win us with honest trifles, to betray's
In deepest consequence.

Cousins, a word, I pray you. (*To* ROSS *and* ANGUS, *who*
approach.)

MACBETH.   (*Aside*) Two truths are told,
As happy prologues to the swelling act
Of the imperial theme.[39]—I thank you, gentlemen.—
(*Aside*) This supernatural soliciting
Cannot be ill; cannot be good. If ill,
Why hath it given me earnest of success,
Commencing in a truth? I am thane of Cawdor.
If good, why do I yield to that suggestion
Whose horrid image doth unfix my hair,
And make my seated heart knock at my ribs,
Against the use of nature?[40] Present fears
Are less than horrible imaginings.
My thought, whose murder yet is but fantastical,

105

110

115

120

125

130

135

35. **earnest,** a token as a pledge.

36. **in which addition,** with which new rank.

37. **behind,** still to come.

38. **trusted home,** taken seriously; Banquo jests.

39. **imperial theme,** the prophecy that Macbeth will be king.

40. **against the use of nature,** unnaturally. Macbeth does not ordinarily feel fear, but imagining the murder of Duncan stands his hair on end.

Shakes so my single state of man that function   140
Is smothered in surmise, and nothing is
But what is not.[41]

BANQUO.   Look, how our partner's rapt.

MACBETH. (*Aside*) If chance will have me King, why,
     chance may crown me,
Without my stir.[42]

BANQUO.   New honors come upon him,
Like our strange garments, cleave not to their mold   145
But with the aid of use.[43]

MACBETH.   (*Aside*) Come what come may,
Time and the hour runs through the roughest day.

BANQUO. Worthy Macbeth, we stay upon your leisure.[44]

MACBETH. Give me your favor.[45] My dull brain was
     wrought
With things forgotten. Kind gentleman, your pains   150
Are registered where every day I turn
The leaf to read them. Let us toward the King.
     (*To* BANQUO) Think upon what hath chanced; and,
     at more time,
The interim having weighed it, let us speak
Our free hearts each to other.

BANQUO.   (*To* MACBETH) Very gladly.   155

MACBETH. Till then, enough. Come, friends.

Exeunt.

SCENE 4

Forres. A room in the Palace.

Flourish. Enter King DUNCAN, MALCOLM, DONALBAIN, LEN-
NOX, *and Attendants.*

KING. Is execution done on Cawdor? Are not
Those in commission yet returned?

MALCOLM.   My liege,
They are not yet come back. But I have spoke
With one that saw him die who did report
That very frankly he confessed his treasons,   5
Implored your Highness' pardon and set forth
A deep repentance. Nothing in his life
Became him like the leaving it. He died
As one that had been studied in his death,
To throw away the dearest thing he owed   10
As 'twere a careless trifle.

KING.   There's no art
To find the mind's construction in the face.[46]

41. **but what is not,** the ideas occurring to Macbeth are so wild that he feels paralyzed by them. His imaginings seem more real than the world about him.

42. **without my stir,** without my efforts.

43. **aid of use,** Macbeth's new honors like new clothes are still sitting stiffly on him rather than being comfortably adjusted.

44. **upon your leisure,** we are waiting for you.

45. **favor,** pardon me. Macbeth excuses himself for being preoccupied with forgotten business.

46. **face,** no one is able to read a person's purpose or character in his or her face.

174 CHOICE AND CONSEQUENCE

He was a gentleman on whom I built
An absolute trust.

Enter MACBETH, BANQUO, ROSS, *and* ANGUS.

                O worthiest cousin,
The sin of my ingratitude even now   15
Was heavy on me! Thou art so far before,[47]
That swiftest wing of recompense is slow
To overtake thee. Would thou hadst less deserved,
That the proportion both of thanks and payment
Might have been mine! Only I have left to say,   20
More is thy due than more than all can pay.
MACBETH. The service and the loyalty I owe,
In doing it, pays itself. Your Highness' part
Is to receive our duties; and our duties
Are to your throne and state, children and servants,   25
Which do but what they should, by doing everything
Safe toward your love and honor.
KING.   Welcome hither.
I have begun to plant thee and will labor
To make thee full of growing. Noble Banquo,
That hast no less deserved, nor must be known   30
No less to have done so, let me infold thee
And hold thee to my heart.
BANQUO.   There if I grow,
The harvest is your own.
KING.   My plenteous joys,
Wanton in fullness, seek to hide themselves
In drops of sorrow.[48] Sons, kinsmen, thanes,   35
And you whose places are the nearest, know
We[49] will establish our estate upon
Our eldest, Malcolm, whom we name hereafter
The Prince of Cumberland;[50] which honor must
Not unaccompanied invest him only,   40
But signs of nobleness, like stars, shall shine
On all deservers. From hence to Inverness,[51]
And bind us further to you.
MACBETH. The rest is labor, which is not used for you.
I'll be myself the harbinger, and make joyful   45
The hearing of my wife with your approach;
So, humbly take my leave.
KING.   My worthy Cawdor!
MACBETH. (*Aside*) The Prince of Cumberland! That is a
    step
On which I must fall down, or else o'erleap,
For in my way it lies. Stars, hide your fires;   50
Let not light see my black and deep desires.

47. **before,** Macbeth's services are so far ahead of Duncan's rewards that he cannot thank him adequately.

48. **drops of sorrow,** tears of joy. Here **wanton** means perverse.

49. **we,** Duncan uses the royal plural for himself.

50. Duncan thus establishes his son as his heir. At this period in Scottish history, the line of succession was rarely father to son. But the Scottish lords are pledged to support the royal claim of the Prince of Cumberland. According to some early accounts, Macbeth had a legitimate claim to the throne. By this announcement Duncan rules out the possibility that Macbeth could succeed "without stir." Duncan concludes that his followers shall also benefit from this move.

51. **to Inverness,** Macbeth's castle where Duncan will be further indebted as a guest.

The eye wink at the hand; yet let that be,
Which the eye fears, when it is done, to see.

Exit.

KING. True, worthy Banquo: he is full so valiant,
And in his commendations I am fed;   55
It is a banquet to me. Let's after him,
Whose care is gone before to bid us welcome.
It is a peerless kinsman.

Flourish. Exeunt.

SCENE 5

Inverness. MACBETH's *Castle.*

Enter MACBETH's *Wife, alone, reading a letter.*

LADY MACBETH. "They met me in the day of success; and I
have learned by the perfectest report they have more
in them than mortal knowledge. When I burned in
desire to question them further, they made themselves air, into which they vanished. Whiles I stood   5
rapt in the wonder of it, came missives from the
King, who all-hailed me 'thane of Cawdor,' by
which title, before, these weird sisters saluted me,
and referred me to the coming on of time with 'Hail,
King that shalt be!' This have I thought good to de-   10
liver thee, my dearest partner of greatness, that thou
mightst not lose the dues of rejoicing by being ignorant of what greatness is promised thee. Lay it to
thy heart, and farewell."

Glamis thou art, and Cawdor, and shalt be   15
What thou art promised. Yet do I fear thy nature;
It is too full o' the milk of human kindness
To catch the nearest way.[52] Thou wouldst be great;
Art not without ambition, but without
The illness should attend it. What thou wouldst highly, 20
That wouldst thou holily;[53] wouldst not play false,
And yet wouldst wrongly win. Thou'ldst have, great
   Glamis,
That which cries "Thus thou must do," if thou have it;
And that which rather thou dost fear to do
Than wishest should be undone. Hie thee hither,   25
That I may pour my spirits in thine ear
And chastise with the valor of my tongue
All that impedes thee from the golden round[54]

52. **the nearest way,** murder is the quickest way to the throne, but Lady Macbeth thinks her husband has too gentle a disposition for it.
53. **holily,** Lady Macbeth feels that Macbeth prefers to behave as a saint while she feels that ambition and saintliness are not compatible.

54. **golden round,** crown.

Which fate and metaphysical aid[55] doth seem
To have thee crowned withal.

Enter MESSENGER.

                              What is your tidings? 30
MESSENGER. The King comes here tonight.
LADY MACBETH.   Thou'rt mad to say it!
  Is not thy master with him? who, were't so,
  Would have informed for preparation.[56]
MESSENGER. So please you, it is true. Our thane is coming.
  One of my fellows had the speed of him,[57] 35
  Who, almost dead for breath, had scarcely more
  Than would make up his message.
LADY MACBETH.   Give him tending;
  He brings great news.

Exit MESSENGER.

                         The raven himself is hoarse[58]
  That croaks the fatal entrance of Duncan
  Under my battlements. Come, you spirits[59] 40
  That tend on mortal thoughts, unsex me here,
  And fill me, from the crown to the toe, top-full
  Of direst cruelty! Make thick my blood;[60]
  Stop up the access and passage to remorse,
  That no compunctious visitings of nature[61] 45
  Shake my fell purpose, nor keep peace between[62]
  The effect and it! Come to my woman's breasts
  And take my milk for gall, you murdering ministers,
  Wherever in your sightless substances
  You wait on nature's mischief! Come, thick night, 50
  And pall thee in the dunnest smoke of hell,[63]
  That my keen knife see not the wound it makes,
  Nor heaven peep through the blanket of the dark
  To cry "Hold, hold!"

Enter MACBETH

                    Great Glamis! worthy Cawdor!
  Greater than both, by the all-hail hereafter! 55
  Thy letters have transported me beyond
  This ignorant present, and I feel now
  The future in the instant.[64]
MACBETH.   My dearest love,
  Duncan comes here tonight.
LADY MACBETH.   And when goes hence?
MACBETH. Tomorrow, as he purposes.
LADY MACBETH.   O, never 60
  Shall sun that morrow see!
  Your face, my thane, is as a book where men

55. . . . **aid,** supernatural help—the witches' prophecy.

56. Duncan's visit at this time seems incredible, like fate playing into her hands. Lady Macbeth suggests that if the visit were to be as announced, she would have had notice from Macbeth.
57. **had the speed of him,** went faster than he did.

58. **raven . . . hoarse,** the wild birds seem unusually excited. Birds of ill-omen occur repeatedly in this play.
59. **spirits,** Lady Macbeth asks to join forces with evil spirits that seem to be propelling the action and understand murderous designs.
60. **thick my blood,** this would give her a melancholy fierceness.
61. That no natural compassion deflect her plan.
62. Peace would indicate an interference between her plan and the action.

63. **and pall thee,** make for yourself a thick cover.

64. **instant,** at present.

May read strange matters. To beguile the time,
Look like the time;[65] bear welcome in your eye,
Your hand, your tongue; look like the innocent flower,   65
But be the serpent under't. He that's coming
Must be provided for; and you shall put
This night's great business into my dispatch,[66]
Which shall to all our nights and days to come
Give solely sovereign sway and masterdom.   70
MACBETH. We will speak further.
LADY MACBETH.   Only look up clear.
  To alter favor ever is to fear.
  Leave all the rest to me.

Exeunt.

SCENE 6

Inverness. Before MACBETH'S *Castle.*

Hautboys[67] and torches. Enter King DUNCAN, MALCOLM,
  DONALBAIN, BANQUO, LENNOX, MACDUFF, ROSS, ANGUS,
  and Attendants.

KING. This castle hath a pleasant seat.[68] The air
  Nimbly and sweetly recommends itself
  Unto our gentle senses.
BANQUO.   This guest of summer,
  The temple-haunting martlet,[69] does approve
  By his loved mansionry that the heaven's breath   5
  Smells wooingly here. No jutty, frieze,
  Buttress, nor coign of vantage,[70] but this bird
  Hath made his pendent bed and procreant cradle.
  Where they most breed and haunt, I have observed
  The air is delicate.

Enter LADY MACBETH.

KING.   See, see, our honored hostess!   10
  The love that follows us sometime is our trouble,
  Which still we thank as love. Herein I teach you
  How you shall bid God 'ield[71] us for your pains
  And thank us for your trouble.
LADY MACBETH.   All our service
  In every point twice done, and then done double,   15
  Were poor and single business to contend
  Against those honors deep and broad wherewith
  Your Majesty loads our house. For those of old,
  And the late dignities heaped up to them,
  We rest your hermits.[72]

65. **look like the time,** act as you would normally at this time.

66. **into my dispatch,** into my hands; leave it to me.

67. **Hautboys** (hō′boiz) *or* (ō′boiz), instruments related to oboes, played in the King's honor.

68. **seat,** site.

69. The fact that the martlet, the European swallow, stays near this mansion shows that it is as pleasant as a temple.

70. On every projection of the building, overhang, or advantageous angle this bird has built its hanging nest.

71. **bid God 'ield,** yield, repay us.

72. **dignities . . . hermits,** for the recent titles; we will gratefully pray for you as do those humble servants, "hermits," poor people committed to a life of prayer.

KING.   Where's the thane of Cawdor?   20
We coursed[73] him at the heels and had a purpose
To be his purveyor;[74] but he rides well,
And his great love, sharp as his spur, hath holp[75] him
To his home before us. Fair and noble hostess,
We are your guest tonight.

LADY MACBETH.   Your servants ever   25
Have theirs, themselves, and what is theirs, in compt,
To make their audit at your Highness' pleasure,
Still to return your own.[76]

KING.   Give me your hand;
Conduct me to mine host. We love him highly
And shall continue our graces towards him   30
By your leave, hostess.

Exeunt.

73. **coursed,** chased.
74. **purveyor,** to precede him and announce him.
75. **holp,** helped.

76. **theirs . . . return your own,** this is a hostess's courtesy: "My house is yours." It reminds the king that all nobles hold their possessions and servants by his permission and that Macbeth and his lady stand ready to repay him at any time.

SCENE 7

Inverness. Inside MACBETH's *Castle.*

Hautboys. Torches. Enter a Sewer[77] and other Servants with dishes and table service. They cross over the stage. Then enter MACBETH.

77. **sewer,** a butler who serves meals.

MACBETH. If it were done when 'tis done, then 'twere well
It were done quickly. If the assassination
Could trammel up the consequence,[78] and catch,
With his surcease, success; that but this blow
Might be the be-all and the end-all here,   5
But here, upon this bank and shoal of time,
We'd jump the life to come.[79] But in these cases
We still have judgment here, that we but teach
Bloody instructions, which, being taught, return
To plague the inventor. This even-handed justice   10
Commends the ingredients of our poisoned chalice
To our own lips. He's here in double trust:[80]
First, as I am his kinsman and his subject,
Strong both against the deed; then, as his host,
Who should against his murderer shut the door,   15
Not bear the knife myself. Besides, this Duncan
Hath borne his faculties so meek,[81] hath been
So clear in his great office, that his virtues
Will plead like angels, trumpet-tongued, against
The deep damnation of his taking-off;   20
And pity, like a naked new-born babe,
Striding the blast, or heaven's cherubim, horsed
Upon the sightless couriers of the air,
Shall blow the horrid deed in every eye,

78. **trammel up the consequence,** hold or prevent the evil results—punishment, damnation, the likelihood of being murdered in his own turn. Macbeth rehearses the reasons against the murder.

79. **life to come,** Macbeth feels that for the gamble in this lifetime he'd be risking eternity, as well as teaching others how to murder him in his turn.

80. **double trust,** Macbeth weighs his responsibilities as a protector of the king.

81. **faculties so meek,** Duncan is gentle and Macbeth realizes that the king's virtues make his murder especially gross.

That tears shall drown the wind.[82] I have no spur   25
To prick the sides of my intent, but only
Vaulting ambition, which o'erleaps itself
And falls on the other.[83]

Enter LADY MACBETH.

                                        How now! What news?
LADY MACBETH. He has almost supped. Why have you left
    the chamber?
MACBETH Hath he asked for me?
LADY MACBETH.   Know you not he has?   30
MACBETH. We will proceed no further in this business.
    He hath honored me of late, and I have bought
    Golden opinions from all sorts of people,
    Which would be worn now in their newest gloss,[84]
    Not cast aside so soon.
LADY MACBETH.   Was the hope drunk   35
    Wherein you dressed yourself? Hath it slept since?
    And wakes it now, to look so green[85] and pale
    At what it did so freely? From this time
    Such I account thy love. Art thou afeard
    To be the same in thine own act and valor   40
    As thou art in desire? Wouldst thou have that
    Which thou esteem'st the ornament of life,
    And live a coward in thine own esteem,
    Letting "I dare not" wait upon "I would,"
    Like the poor cat i' the adage?[86]
MACBETH.   Prithee peace!   45
    I dare do all that may become a man.
    Who dares do more is none.
LADY MACBETH.   What beast was't then
    That made you break this enterprise to me?[87]
    When you durst do it, then you were a man;
    And to be more than what you were, you would   50
    Be so much more the man. Nor time nor place
    Did then adhere,[88] and yet you would make both.
    They have made themselves, and that their fitness
        now
    Does unmake you. I have given suck, and know
    How tender 'tis to love the babe that milks me.   55
    I would, while it was smiling in my face,
    Have plucked my nipple from his boneless gums,
    And dashed the brains out, had I so sworn as you
    Have done to this.
MACBETH.   If we should fail?
LADY MACBETH.   We fail!
    But screw your courage to the sticking-place,[89]   60

82. **drown the wind,** tears falling like heavy rain will halt the storm winds.

83. **other,** side. His ambition is like a too-eager rider who leaps over the horse rather than onto it. Macbeth feels without a spur such as hate for Duncan, his ambition to leap onto the throne will only cause others to seek to topple him.

84. **newest gloss,** Macbeth would not throw away his growing reputation.

85. . . . **green,** sallow, sickly. Lady Macbeth mocks Macbeth's clothing of "golden opinions" as being less than his "drunken" hope for royal robes. She continues to berate him as unreliable and cowardly.

86. **cat i' the adage,** the proverb is an old one that says in effect: If the cat would catch fish it must wet its feet.

87. **beast . . . to me,** Macbeth has stated that he is as brave as anyone and implied that only a wild beast could do more. Lady Macbeth picks up his expression to taunt him: it was a beast, then, who told me of the plan to kill Duncan.
88. **then adhere,** when Macbeth wrote his letter giving rise to her hope the circumstances were not at hand as they are now.

89. **sticking-place,** the metaphor is of a crossbow which was screwed tight to fit the bowstring before it could be shot.

*Maurice Evans as Macbeth
and Judith Anderson
as Lady Macbeth.*

And we'll not fail. When Duncan is asleep—
Whereto the rather[90] shall his day's hard journey
Soundly invite him—his two chamberlains
Will I with wine and wassail[91] so convince
That memory, the warder of the brain,   65
Shall be a fume, and the receipt of reason
A limbeck only.[92] When in swinish sleep
Their drenched natures lie as in a death,
What cannot you and I perform upon
The unguarded Duncan? what not put upon   70
His spongy officers, who shall bear the guilt
Of our great quell?[93]

MACBETH.   Bring forth men-children only;
For thy undaunted mettle should compose
Nothing but males. Will it not be received,[94]
When we have marked with blood those sleepy two   75
Of his own chamber and used their very daggers,
That they have done't?

LADY MACBETH.   Who dares receive it other,
As we shall make our griefs and clamor roar
Upon his death?

MACBETH.   I am settled and bend up
Each corporal agent[95] to this terrible feat.   80
Away, and mock the time with fairest show;
False face must hide what the false heart doth know.

Exeunt.

90. **whereto the rather**, to which very readily. (Duncan is tired from travel.)
91. **wassail** (wos′əl), technically, a spiced ale.

92. **limbeck** (lim′bek), the cap of a still into which fumes rise. The metaphor is that a drunken person is like a still full of alcoholic fumes instead of consciousness.

93. **quell**, killing, murder.

94. **received**, accepted, believed.

95. **each corporal agent**, each bodily part and faculty. That he "bend up" to the feat refers back to the metaphor of the crossbow.

ACT I

TEMPTATION IN A PROPHECY

1. What are we told about Macbeth's life and character up to the time the play begins? What opinion do others have of him?

2. Look carefully at the witches' original prophecy to Macbeth and Banquo. Do the witches indicate that they have any power to turn their predictions into reality?

a. If you were in Macbeth's and Banquo's positions, what meaning would you draw from the witches' prophecies?

b. What is the difference in Macbeth's and Banquo's reactions to the witches?

3. How does Shakespeare contrast Macbeth's character with that of Lady Macbeth in Scenes 5 and 7? What arguments does Lady Macbeth use to force Macbeth to a decision?

4. What choices does Macbeth make during this act?

5. How is the Macbeth we see at the end of this act different from the Macbeth we saw and heard about at the outset of the play?

WORDS

A. The "Prologue to the Canterbury Tales" and "The Pardoner's Tale" were translations of Chaucer's Middle English into Modern English—the version you read was not the original one; but *Macbeth* is given almost as Shakespeare wrote it over three hundred and fifty years ago. In the older selections from English literature there are special difficulties about using the method of context clues to find the meanings of words. But perhaps you can guess the meanings of the italicized words in the following context from Act I.

1. . . . With *furbished* arms and new supplies of men. . . .

2. . . . With hidden help and *vantage*. . . .

3. . . . the fatal entrance of Duncan/Under my *battlements*.

B. One great problem in reading older literature comes from the way words change their meanings—undergo semantic change. Thus, today the word *cousin* means a son or daughter of an aunt or uncle but in Shakespeare's day it was used for almost any relative. The following words, from Act I of *Macbeth,* show semantic change; find out what they meant in Shakespeare's usage:

Scene II: *broil, quarrel, slave, survey, memorize, dismal, lavish, composition, present;*
Scene III: *poster, fantastical, post, earnest, addition, line, soliciting.*

The footnotes and the glossary of this book will help, but you will also need a large (unabridged) dictionary that gives more complete information. In selecting the meanings to interpret Shakespeare, you may have to guess about the one that fits best.

C. Shakespeare uses many similes and metaphors. The valor of Macbeth and Banquo is described in a simile: the Norwegians dismayed them as (no more than) sparrows dismay eagles.

Many metaphors and similes are easy to interpret. Now and then, a line may contain not only a simile or metaphor but also an archaic or obsolete word. Then, even the learned may have to pause to weigh the meaning of the line.

When we are told that Macbeth "Like valor's minion, carved out his passage," we must understand that *valor* is a personification, that *minion* means favorite or darling, and that *carved out* involves a metaphor.

Be prepared to explain the following lines.

1. I must report they were/As cannons overcharged with double cracks. . . .

2. Where the Norweyan banners flout the sky/And fan our people cold.

3. Sleep shall neither night nor day/Hang upon his penthouse lid. . . .

D. Look up these words and notice what status or usage label (obs. or archaic) the dictionary uses to describe them: *kern, gallowglass, minion, withal, coign.*

E. Shakespeare's English was not pronounced exactly as modern English is pronounced. It takes years of intense study to understand the principles underlying Shakespearean pronunciation, and even then one finds puzzling situations. In a general way, however, many of the words were pronounced with greater mouth opening than we would use today. Thus most words spelled with *ea*—like *heat* and *mean*—were pronounced with what we call a long a (ā) sound. *Weak* sounded like modern English *wake*, not like modern English *week*. In the first lines of Act I, *heath, weak,* and *unseamed* would all have been pronounced with the ā sound. Try reading several lines of *Macbeth* aloud pronouncing *ea* words with the ā sound.

❧ Act II

Inverness. Court of MACBETH's *Castle.*

Enter BANQUO, *and* FLEANCE *bearing a torch before him.*

BANQUO. How goes the night, boy?

FLEANCE. The moon is down; I have not heard the clock.

BANQUO. And she goes down at twelve.

FLEANCE.   I take't, 'tis later, sir.

BANQUO. Hold, take my sword. There's husbandry[1] in
    heaven;

    Their candles are all out. Take thee that too.   5

    A heavy summons[2] lies like lead upon me,

    And yet I would not sleep. Merciful powers,

    Restrain in me the cursèd thoughts that nature

    Gives way to in repose!

Enter MACBETH, *and a Servant with a torch.*

               Give me my sword.

    Who's there?   10

MACBETH. A friend.

BANQUO. What, sir, not yet at rest? The King's abed.

    He hath been in unusual pleasure, and

    Sent forth great largess to your offices.[3]

    This diamond he greets your wife withal   15

    By the name of most kind hostess, and shut up[4]

    In measureless content.

MACBETH.   Being unprepared,

    Our will became the servant to defect,

    Which else should free have wrought.[5]

BANQUO.   All's well.

    I dreamt last night of the three weird sisters.

    To you they have showed some truth.   20

MACBETH.   I think not of them.

    Yet, when we can entreat an hour to serve,

    We would spend it in some words upon that business,

    If you would grant the time.

BANQUO.   At your kind'st leisure.

MACBETH. If you shall cleave to my consent, when 'tis,   25

    It shall make honor for you.

BANQUO.   So I lose none

    In seeking to augment it, but still keep

    My bosom franchised and allegiance clear,[6]

    I shall be counseled.

1. **husbandry,** thrift.

2. **summons**—to sleep, drowsiness.

3. **great largess to your offices,** gifts and rewards for the servants of Macbeth's household; **offices** were the areas of work —the kitchen, etc.

4. **shut up,** concluded with great contentment.

5. Macbeth says he would have lodged the king more suitably if he'd had notice to prepare.

6. **franchised . . . clear,** above reproach, stainless. Banquo would be glad for further honor if he can get it honorably.

MACBETH.   Good repose the while!

BANQUO. Thanks, sir. The like to you!   30

Exeunt BANQUO *and* FLEANCE.

MACBETH. Go bid thy mistress, when my drink is ready,
She strike upon the bell. Get thee to bed.

Exit Servant.

Is this a dagger which I see before me,
The handle toward my hand? Come, let me clutch
    thee.
I have thee not, and yet I see thee still.   35
Art thou not, fatal vision, sensible
To feeling as to sight?[7] or art thou but
A dagger of the mind, a false creation,
Proceeding from the heat-oppressèd brain?
I see thee yet, in form as palpable   40
As this which now I draw.
Thou marshal'st me the way that I was going,
And such an instrument I was to use.
Mine eyes are made the fools o' the other senses,
Or else worth all the rest. I see thee still;   45
And on thy blade and dudgeon gouts[8] of blood,
Which was not so before. There's no such thing.
It is the bloody business which informs
Thus to mine eyes. Now o'er the one half-world
Nature seems dead, and wicked dreams abuse   50
The curtained sleep. Witchcraft celebrates
Pale Hecate's offerings;[9] and withered murder,
Alarumed by his sentinel, the wolf,
Whose howl's his watch,[10] thus with his stealthy pace,
With Tarquin's ravishing strides,[11] towards his design 55
Moves like a ghost. Thou sure and firm-set earth,
Hear not my steps, which way they walk, for fear
Thy very stones prate of my whereabout
And take the present horror from the time,
Which now suits with it. Whiles I threat, he lives;   60
Words to the heat of deeds too cold breath gives.

A bell rings.

I go, and it is done. The bell invites me.
Hear it not, Duncan, for it is a knell
That summons thee to heaven, or to hell.
Exit.

SCENE 2

The same.

Enter LADY MACBETH.

7. **sensible to feeling as to sight,** tangible, can the dagger be felt?

8. **dudgeon** (duj′ən), handle; **gouts** (gauts), great drops.

9. **Hecate** (hek′ə tē), a classical goddess of witchcraft and magic. Witches were still thought to make sacrifices to the devil.
10. **his watch,** the howl of the wolf is the time signal for murder.
11. **strides,** murder moves on like an infamous Roman king.

LADY MACBETH. That which hath made them drunk hath
    made me bold;
What hath quenched them hath given me fire. Hark!
    Peace!
It was the owl that shrieked, the fatal bellman[12]
Which gives the stern'st good-night. He is about it.
The doors are open, and the surfeited grooms
Do mock their charge with snores. I have drugged
    their possets,[13]
That death and nature do contend about them
Whether they live or die.
MACBETH.   (*Within*) Who's there? What, ho?
LADY MACBETH. Alack, I am afraid they have awaked,
    And 'tis not done. The attempt, and not the deed,
Confounds us. Hark! I laid their daggers ready;
He could not miss 'em. Had he not resembled
My father as he slept, I had done't.

Enter MACBETH.

                  My husband!
MACBETH. I have done the deed. Didst thou not hear a
    noise?
LADY MACBETH. I heard the owl scream and the crickets
    cry.
    Did you not speak?
MACBETH.   When?
LADY MACBETH.   Now.
MACBETH.   As I descended?
LADY MACBETH. Ay.
MACBETH. Hark!
    Who lies i' the second chamber?
LADY MACBETH.   Donalbain.
MACBETH. (*Looking on his hands.*) This is a sorry sight.
LADY MACBETH. A foolish thought, to say a sorry sight.
MACBETH. There's one did laugh in's sleep, and one cried
    "Murder!"
That they did wake each other. I stood and heard
    them.
But they did say their prayers, and addressed them
Again to sleep.
LADY MACBETH.   There are two lodged together.[14]
MACBETH. One cried "God bless us!" and "Amen" the
    other,
As they had seen me with these hangman's hands.
List'ning their fears,[15] I could not say "Amen,"
When they did say "God bless us!"
LADY MACBETH. Consider it not so deeply.

12. **fatal bellman,** one who, according to ancient London custom, rang the bell for prisoners the night before their execution.

13. **possets** (pos′its), hot wine drinks customarily taken before going to bed.

14. **together,** Lady Macbeth confirms that Donalbain had had to share a room with another guest.

15. **As they had seen . . . list'ning their fear,** as if they had seen Macbeth listening to their fearful exclamations.

MACBETH. But wherefore could not I pronounce "Amen"?
I had most need of blessing, and "Amen"
Stuck in my throat.
LADY MACBETH.   These deeds must not be thought
After these ways; so, it will make us mad.
MACBETH. Methought I heard a voice cry "Sleep no more!   35
Macbeth does murder sleep"—the innocent sleep,
Sleep that knits up the raveled sleave[16] of care,
The death of each day's life, sore labor's bath,
Balm of hurt minds, great nature's second course,[17]
Chief nourisher in life's feast—
LADY MACBETH.   What do you mean?   40
MACBETH. Still it cried "Sleep no more!" to all the house;
"Glamis hath murdered sleep, and therefore Cawdor
Shall sleep no more; Macbeth shall sleep no more!"
LADY MACBETH. Who was it that thus cried? Why, worthy
    thane,
You do unbend your noble strength to think   45
So brainsickly of things. Go get some water
And wash this filthy witness from your hand.
Why did you bring these daggers from the place?
They must lie there. Go carry them and smear
The sleepy grooms with blood.
MACBETH.   I'll go no more.   50
I am afraid to think what I have done;
Look on't again I dare not.
LADY MACBETH.   Infirm of purpose!
Give me the daggers. The sleeping and the dead
Are but as pictures. 'Tis the eye of childhood
That fears a painted devil. If he do bleed,   55
I'll gild the faces of the grooms withal,
For it must seem their guilt.

Exit. Knocking within.

MACBETH.   Whence is that knocking?
How is't with me, when every noise appalls me?
What hands are here? Ha! they pluck out mine eyes!
Will all great Neptune's ocean wash this blood   60
Clean from my hand? No. This my hand will rather
The multitudinous seas incarnadine,[18]
Making the green one red.

Reenter LADY MACBETH.

LADY MACBETH. My hands are of your color, but I shame
To wear a heart so white. (*Knocking within.*) I hear a
    knocking   65
At the south entry. Retire we to our chamber;
A little water clears us of this deed.

16. **raveled sleave,** tangled floss.

17. **second course,** sleep is the second and heavier course in life's feast.

*Jean Vilar as Macbeth in a scene
from a French staging.*

18. **incarnadine** (in kär′nə dən), color red.

How easy is it then! Your constancy
Hath left you unattended. (*Knocking within.*) Hark!
  more knocking.
Get on your nightgown, lest occasion call us   70
And show us to be watchers. Be not lost
So poorly in your thoughts.
MACBETH. To know my deed, 'twere best not know
  myself.

                    (*Knocking within.*)
Wake Duncan with thy knocking! I would thou
  couldst!

Exeunt.

SCENE 3

The same.

Enter a PORTER. *Knocking within.*

PORTER. Here's a knocking indeed! If a man were porter
  of hell gate, he should have old[19] turning the key.
  (*Knocking within.*) Knock, knock, knock! Who's
  there, i' the name of Beelzebub? Here's a farmer that
  hanged himself on the expectation of plenty. Come   5
  in time! Have napkins enow about you; here you'll
  sweat for't.[20] (*Knocking within.*) Knock, knock!
  Who's there, in the other devil's name? Faith, here's
  an equivocator,[21] that could swear in both the scales
  against either scale; who committed treason enough   10
  for God's sake, yet could not equivocate to heaven.
  O, come in, equivocator! (*Knocking within.*) Knock,
  knock, knock! Who's there? Faith, here's an English
  tailor come hither for stealing out of a French hose.
  Come in, tailor. Here you may roast your goose.[22]   15
  (*Knocking within.*) Knock, knock! Never at quiet!
  What are you? But this place is too cold for hell. I'll
  devil-porter it no further. I had thought to have let in
  some of all professions that go the primrose way to
  the everlasting bonfire. (*Knocking within.*) Anon,   20
  anon! (*Opens the gate.*) I pray you remember the
  porter.[23]

Enter MACDUFF *and* LENNOX.

MACDUFF. Was it so late, friend, ere you went to bed,
  That you do lie so late?
PORTER. Faith, sir, we were carousing till the second
  cock;[24] and drink, sir, is a great provoker.   25
MACDUFF. I believe drink gave thee the lie last night.

*Macduff and the porter, played by
George Wilson and Daniel Sorano.*

19. **have old,** have a lot to do, **old** is a
term of emphasis.

20. **sweat for't,** ironically, the porter is
playing at being a porter at hell's gate
letting in familiar types of sinners. The
farmer committed suicide at the thought
of a break in wheat prices. Food speculation was a traditional subject for condemnation.
21. **The other devil's name . . . equivocator** (i kwiv′ə kā′tər), the porter can only
remember the name **Beelzebub**; Mephistopheles, etc., escape his muddled brain.
The **equivocator** was Shakespeare's gibe
at those who held that religious reserva-
tions justified disloyalty to the English
crown.
22. **roast your goose,** this is a pun on the
fact that a tailor's iron was called a tailor's
goose. The tailor is damned for imitating
tight French styles and stealing ends of
fabrics.
23. **remember the porter** —with a tip.

24. **second cock,** the first cock cried at
midnight, the second at three A.M.

PORTER. That it did, sir, i' the very throat on me; but I
    requited him for his lie; and, I think, being too strong
    for him, though he took up my legs sometime, yet I
    made a shift to cast him.   30
MACDUFF. Is thy master stirring?

   Enter MACBETH.

Our knocking has awaked him; here he comes.
LENNOX. Good morrow, noble sir.
MACBETH.   Good morrow, both.
MACDUFF. Is the King stirring, worthy thane?
MACBETH.   Not yet.
MACDUFF. He did command me to call timely on him;   35
    I have almost slipped the hour.
MACBETH.   I'll bring you to him.
MACDUFF. I know this is a joyful trouble to you;
    But yet 'tis one.
MACBETH. The labor we delight in physics pain.[25]   25. **physics pain,** cures.
    This is the door.
MACDUFF.   I'll make so bold to call,   40
    For 'tis my limited service.

   Exit.

LENNOX. Goes the King hence today?
MACBETH.   He does; he did appoint so.
LENNOX. The night has been unruly. Where we lay,
    Our chimneys were blown down; and, as they say,
    Lamentings heard i' the air, strange screams of death,   45
    And prophesying with accents terrible,
    Of dire combustion and confused events
    New hatched to the woeful time. The obscure bird[26]   26. **the obscure bird,** the bird of dark-
    Clamored the livelong night. Some say the earth   ness, the owl.
    Was feverous and did shake.
MACBETH.   'Twas a rough night.   50
LENNOX. My young remembrance cannot parallel
    A fellow to it.

   Reenter MACDUFF.

MACDUFF. O horror, horror, horror! Tongue nor heart
    Cannot conceive nor name thee!
MACBETH AND LENNOX.   What's the matter?
MACDUFF. Confusion now hath made his masterpiece!   55
    Most sacrilegious murder hath broke ope
    The Lord's anointed temple and stole thence
    The life o'the building![27]   27. **o' the building,** the body was the
MACBETH.   What is't you say? the life?   temple of the soul and the king was the
LENNOX. Mean you his Majesty?   Lord's anointed.

MACDUFF. Approach the chamber, and destroy your sight   60
  With a new Gorgon.[28] Do not bid me speak.
  See, and then speak yourselves.

  Exeunt MACBETH *and* LENNOX.

                      Awake, awake!
  Ring the alarum bell. Murder and treason!
  Banquo and Donalbain! Malcolm! awake!
  Shake off this downy sleep, death's counterfeit,[29]   65
  And look on death itself! Up, up, and see
  The great doom's image! Malcolm! Banquo!
  As from your graves rise up and walk like sprites,[30]
  To countenance this horror! Ring the bell!

  Bell rings.

  Enter LADY MACBETH.

LADY MACBETH. What's the business.   70
  That such a hideous trumpet calls to parley
  The sleepers of the house? Speak, speak!
MACDUFF.   O gentle lady,
  'Tis not for you to hear what I can speak.
  The repetition, in a woman's ear,
  Would murder as it fell.

  Enter BANQUO.

             O Banquo, Banquo,   75
  Our royal master's murdered!
LADY MACBETH.   Woe, alas!
  What, in our house?
BANQUO.   Too cruel anywhere.
  Dear Duff, I prithee contradict thyself
  And say it is not so.

  Reenter MACBETH, LENNOX, *and* ROSS.

MACBETH. Had I but died an hour before this chance,   80
  I had lived a blessed time; for from this instant
  There's nothing serious in mortality;[31]
  All is but toys; renown and grace is dead;
  The wine of life is drawn, and the mere lees[32]
  Is left this vault to brag of.   85

  Enter MALCOLM *and* DONALBAIN.

DONALBAIN. What is amiss?
MACBETH.   You are, and do not know't.
  The spring, the head, the fountain of your blood
  Is stopped; the very source of it is stopped.
MACDUFF. Your royal father's murdered.
MALCOLM.   O, by whom?

28. **Gorgon** (gôr′gən), one of the hideous sisters in Greek mythology whose looks turned one to stone.

29. **counterfeit,** sleep imitates death.

30. **sprites,** ghosts.

31. **in mortality,** there is nothing worthwhile in life.

32. **lees,** the metaphor is of a wine cellar (vault) from which Duncan, the good wine, has been removed leaving only sediment, dregs.

LENNOX. Those of his chamber, as it seemed, had done't. 90
   Their hands and faces were all badged[33] with blood;
   So were their daggers, which unwiped we found
   Upon their pillows.
   They stared, and were distracted; no man's life
   Was to be trusted with them. 95
MACBETH. O, yet I do repent me of my fury,
   That I did kill them.
MACDUFF.   Wherefore did you so?
MACBETH. Who can be wise, amazed, temp'rate, and
      furious,
   Loyal and neutral, in a moment? No man.
   The expedition of my violent love 100
   Outrun the pauser, reason. Here lay Duncan,
   His silver skin laced with his golden blood,
   And his gashed stabs looked like a breach in nature
   For ruin's wasteful entrance; there, the murderers,
   Steeped in the colors of their trade, their daggers 105
   Unmannerly breeched with gore. Who could refrain
   That had a heart to love, and in that heart
   Courage to make's love known?
LADY MACBETH.   Help me hence, ho!
   Faints.

MACDUFF. Look to the lady.
MALCOLM.   (*Aside to* DONALBAIN) Why
      do we hold our tongues,
   That most may claim this argument for ours? 110
DONALBAIN. (*Aside to Malcolm*) What should be spoken
      here, where our fate,
   Hid in an auger-hole,[34] may rush, and seize us?
   Let's away;
   Our tears are not yet brewed.
MALCOLM. (*Aside to* DONALBAIN)
                     Nor our strong sorrow
   Upon the foot of motion.[35]
BANQUO.   Look to the lady. 115

   LADY MACBETH *is carried out.*

   And when we have our naked frailties hid,[36]
   That suffer in exposure, let us meet,
   And question this most bloody piece of work,
   To know it further. Fears and scruples shake us.
   In the great hand of God I stand, and thence 120
   Against the undivulged pretense I fight
   Of treasonous malice.[37]
MACDUFF.   And so do I.
ALL.   So all.

33. **badged,** marked as if with a crest.

34. **auger-hole,** Donalbain, as a royal heir, is fearful for his own safety; he says that danger may lurk in any place. Witches were believed capable of hiding even in small drilled holes.

35. **foot of motion,** our grief has not yet begun to show or act.

36. **. . . hid,** Banquo reminds the others that they're still in night clothes.

37. **treasonous malice,** Banquo senses but can't define the motive for such treason.

MACBETH. Let's briefly put on manly readiness
　And meet i' the hall together.
ALL.　　　　　　　　　　Well contented.

　　Exeunt all but MALCOLM *and* DONALBAIN.

MALCOLM. What will you do? Let's not consort with them.　125
　To show an unfelt sorrow is an office
　Which the false man does easy. I'll to England.
DONALBAIN. To Ireland I. Our separated fortune
　Shall keep us both the safer. Where we are,
　There's daggers in men's smiles; the near in blood,[38]　130
　The nearer bloody.
MALCOLM.　　　　This murderous shaft that's shot
　Hath not yet lighted,[39] and our safest way
　Is to avoid the aim. Therefore to horse;
　And let us not be dainty of leave-taking,
　But shift away. There's warrant in that theft　135
　Which steals itself when there's no mercy left.

　　Exeunt.

38. **near in blood,** the royal heirs are most in danger.

39. **not yet lighted,** there's more murder to come.

SCENE 4

Outside MACBETH'S *Castle.*

Enter ROSS *with an* OLD MAN.

OLD MAN. Threescore and ten I can remember well;
　Within the volume of which time I have seen
　Hours dreadful and things strange; but this sore night
　Hath trifled former knowings.[40]
ROSS.　　　　　　　　Ah, good father,
　Thou seest the heavens, as troubled with man's act,　5
　Threaten his bloody stage. By the clock 'tis day,
　And yet dark night strangles the traveling lamp.[41]
　Is't night's predominance, or the day's shame,
　That darkness does the face of earth entomb,
　When living light should kiss it?
OLD MAN.　　　　　　　'Tis unnatural,　10
　Even like the deed that's done. On Tuesday last
　A falcon, tow'ring in her pride of place,
　Was by a mousing owl hawked at and killed.[42]
ROSS. And Duncan's horses—a thing most strange and
　　　certain—
　Beauteous and swift, the minions of their race,　15
　Turned wild in nature, broke their stalls, flung out,
　Contending 'gainst obedience, as they would make
　War with mankind.

40. **trifled former knowings,** has made unimportant everything I knew before.

41. **traveling lamp,** the sun.

42. **falcon . . . killed,** it is another indication of how "time is out of joint" that a mere owl should kill a hunting falcon instead of its usual prey of mice.

OLD MAN.   'Tis said they eat each other.

ROSS. They did so, to the amazement of mine eyes
  That looked upon't.

  Enter MACDUFF.

                  Here comes the good Macduff.   20
  How goes the world, sir, now?

MACDUFF.   Why, see you not?

ROSS. Is't known who did this more than bloody deed?

MACDUFF. Those that Macbeth hath slain.

ROSS.   Alas, the day!
  What good could they pretend?[43]

MACDUFF.   They were suborned.[44]   25
  Malcolm and Donalbain, the King's two sons,
  Are stol'n away and fled, which puts upon them
  Suspicion of the deed.

ROSS.   'Gainst nature still!
  Thriftless ambition, that will ravin up[45]
  Thine own life's means! Then 'tis most like
  The sovereignty will fall upon Macbeth.   30

MACDUFF. He is already named, and gone to Scone[46]
  To be invested.

ROSS.   Where is Duncan's body?

MACDUFF. Carried to Colmekill,[47]
  The sacred storehouse of his predecessors
  And guardian of their bones.

ROSS.   Will you to Scone?   35

MACDUFF. No, cousin, I'll to Fife.[48]

ROSS.   Well, I will thither.

MACDUFF. Well, may you see things well done there.
  Adieu!
  Lest our old robes sit easier than our new![49]

ROSS. Farewell, father.

OLD MAN. God's benison go with you, and with those   40
  That would make good of bad, and friends of foes!

  Exeunt.

43. **pretend,** how could they put forth a reasonable excuse?

44. **suborned,** bribed; Macduff suggests that they had been paid to do the murder.

45. **ravin** (rā′vin), eat up.

46. **Scone,** the legendary coronation place for Scottish kings.

47. **Colmekill,** the island where ancient Scottish kings were buried.

48. **Fife,** Macduff's home.

49. Macduff hopes Macbeth's coming rule will not be threatening to the other nobles.

ACT II
A KING IS KILLED

1. If you were staging a production of *Macbeth*, would you have the dagger that Macbeth sees in Scene 1 visible to the audience?

2. How does Macbeth's conscience react before and during the murder? And Lady Macbeth's conscience? After the murder how does each of them react?

3. Why does Lady Macbeth faint?

4. What evidence is there that Banquo, Macduff, and others do not trust Macbeth?

5. Why do Duncan's sons flee rather than remain to inherit the crown?

❦ Act III

SCENE 1

Forres. The Palace.[1]

Enter BANQUO.

BANQUO. Thou hast it now: King, Cawdor, Glamis, all,
  As the weird women promised; and I fear
  Thou play'dst most foully for't. Yet it was said
  It should not stand in thy posterity,
  But that myself should be the root and father   5
  Of many kings. If there come truth from them—
  As upon thee, Macbeth, their speeches shine[2]—
  Why, by the verities on thee made good,
  May they not be my oracles as well
  And set me up in hope? But, hush, no more!   10

Trumpets sound a fanfare. Enter MACBETH, *as King;*
LADY MACBETH, *as Queen;* LENNOX, ROSS, *Lords and*
Attendants.

MACBETH. Here's our chief guest.

LADY MACBETH.   If he had been
    forgotten,
  It had been as a gap in our great feast,
  And all-thing unbecoming.[3]

MACBETH. Tonight we hold a solemn supper, sir,
  And I'll request your presence.[4]

BANQUO.   Let your Highness   15
  Command upon me,[5] to the which my duties
  Are with a most indissoluble tie
  For ever knit.

MACBETH.   Ride you this afternoon?

BANQUO. Ay, my good lord.

MACBETH. We should have else desired your good advice,   20
  Which still hath been both grave and prosperous,
  In this day's council; but we'll take tomorrow.
  Is't far you ride?

BANQUO. As far, my lord, as will fill up the time
  'Twixt this and supper. Go not my horse the better,   25
  I must become a borrower of the night[6]
  For a dark hour or twain.

MACBETH.   Fail not our feast.

BANQUO. My lord, I will not.

MACBETH. We hear our bloody cousins are bestowed
  In England and in Ireland, not confessing   30
  Their cruel parricide,[7] filling their hearers

1. Some months later. Suspicions are mounting about Macbeth.

2. **speeches shine,** the witches' prophecies are glowingly fulfilled.

3. **all-thing,** altogether.

4. **solemn supper . . .,** formal banquet. **I'll,** Macbeth uses **I** rather than the royal we as a gesture of special friendship.
5. **Command upon me,** Banquo replies formally, "your request is my command."

6. **. . . borrower of the night,** unless my horse is faster than expected, I'll be riding in the dark for several hours.

7. **cousins . . . parricide,** Malcolm and Donalbain are in England, denying the murder of their father and with "strange invention" accusing Macbeth.

With strange invention. But of that tomorrow,
When therewithal we shall have cause of state
Craving us jointly.[8] Hie you to horse. Adieu,
Till you return at night. Goes Fleance with you?   35
BANQUO. Ay, my good lord. Our time does call upon's.
MACBETH. I wish your horses swift and sure of foot,
And so I do commend you to their backs.
Farewell.

Exit BANQUO.

Let every man be master of his time   40
Till seven at night. To make society
The sweeter welcome, we will keep ourself
Till supper time alone; while then, God be with you!

Exeunt all but MACBETH *and an* ATTENDANT.

Sirrah, a word with you. Attend those men
Our pleasure?   45
ATTENDANT. They are, my lord, without the palace gate.
MACBETH. Bring them before us.

Exit ATTENDANT.
                                        To be thus is nothing,
But to be safely thus.[9] Our fears in Banquo
Stick deep, and in his royalty of nature
Reigns that which would be feared. 'Tis much he dares,   50
And, to that dauntless temper of his mind
He hath a wisdom that doth guide his valor
To act in safety. There is none but he
Whose being I do fear; and under him
My genius is rebuked, as it is said   55
Mark Antony's was by Caesar.[10] He chid the sisters
When first they put the name of King upon me,
And bade them speak to him. Then, prophet-like,
They hailed him father to a line of kings.
Upon my head they placed a fruitless crown   60
And put a barren scepter in my gripe,[11]
Thence to be wrenched with an unlineal hand,[12]
No son of mine succeeding. If't be so,
For Banquo's issue have I filed[13] my mind;
For them the gracious Duncan have I murdered;   65
Put rancors in the vessel of my peace[14]
Only for them, and mine eternal jewel[15]
Given to the common enemy of man,
To make them kings, the seed of Banquo kings!
Rather than so, come, Fate, into the list[16]   70
And champion me to the utterance! Who's there?

Reenter ATTENDANT, *with two* MURDERERS.

194 CHOICE AND CONSEQUENCE

8. **cause of state craving us jointly,** serious matter requiring our mutual attention.

9. **safely thus,** it is pointless to be king unless the throne is safe.

10. **genius is rebuked . . . by Caesar,** Banquo's fortune puts to shame Macbeth's guardian spirits just as Anthony was forewarned by a fortune-teller (according to Plutarch) that he would be overwhelmed by Caesar.

11. **gripe** (grīp), grip.
12. **unlineal hand,** out of direct line of hereditary descent.

13. **filed,** defiled.

14. **rancors in . . . peace,** poisoned his easy conscience.
15. **mine eternal jewel,** my soul—Macbeth has sold out to the devil only to benefit Banquo's heirs.

16. **list,** tournament ground.

Now go to the door and stay there till we call.

Exit ATTENDANT.

Was it not yesterday we spoke together?
MURDERERS. It was, so please your Highness.
MACBETH.   Well then, now
Have you considered of my speeches? Know   75
That it was he, in the times past, which held you
So under fortune,[17] which you thought had been
Our innocent self. This I made good to you
In our last conference, passed in probation with you,
How you were borne in hand, how crossed, the instru-
    ments,   80
Who wrought with them, and all things else that might
To half a soul and to a notion crazed
Say "Thus did Banquo."
FIRST MURDERER.   You made it known to us.
MACBETH. I did so; and went further, which is now
Our point of second meeting. Do you find   85
Your patience so predominant in your nature
That you can let this go? Are you so gospeled[18]
To pray for this good man and for his issue,
Whose heavy hand hath bowed you to the grave
And beggared yours for ever?
FIRST MURDERER.   We are men, my liege.   90
MACBETH. Ay, in the catalogue ye go for men,
As hounds and greyhounds, mongrels, spaniels, curs,
Shoughs, water-rugs, and demi-wolves are clept[19]
All by the name of dogs. The valued file[20]
Distinguishes the swift, the slow, the subtle,   95
The housekeeper, the hunter, every one
According to the gift which bounteous nature
Hath in him closed, whereby he does receive
Particular addition, from the bill
That writes them all alike; and so of men.   100
Now, if you have a station in the file,
Not i' the worst rank of manhood, say't;
And I will put that business in your bosoms
Whose execution takes your enemy off,
Grapples you to the heart and love of us,   105
Who wear our health but sickly in his life,
Which in his death were perfect.
SECOND MURDERER.   I am one, my liege,
Whom the vile blows and buffets of the world
Have so incensed that I am reckless what
I do to spite the world.

17. Macbeth has recruited for murderers Scottish gentlemen in dire straits who before had held Macbeth responsible for their troubles. He has convinced them that Banquo was the source of their grievances and so set up the murder to look like a grudge killing.

18. **gospeled**, so taught.

19. **shoughs** (shufs), lapdogs; **water-rugs**, water spaniels; **clept** (klept), called.
20. **file**, top group, first class.

FIRST MURDERER.   And I another,   110
   So weary with disasters, tugged with fortune,
   That I would set my life on any chance,
   . To mend it or be rid on't.
MACBETH.   Both of you
   Know Banquo was your enemy.
MURDERERS.   True, my lord.
MACBETH. So is he mine; and in such bloody distance   115
   That every minute of his being thrusts
   Against my near'st of life; and though I could
   With barefaced power sweep him from my sight
   And bid my will avouch it,[21] yet I must not,
   For certain friends that are both his and mine,   120
   Whose loves I may not drop, but wail his fall
   Who I myself struck down. And thence it is
   That I to your assistance do make love,
   Masking the business from the common eye
   For sundry weighty reasons.
SECOND MURDERER.   We shall, my lord,   125
   Perform what you command us.
FIRST MURDERER.   Though our lives—
MACBETH. Your spirits shine through you. Within this
     hour at most
   I will advise you where to plant yourselves,
   Acquaint you with the perfect spy o' the time,[22]
   The moment on't; for't must be done tonight,   130
   And something from the palace; always thought
   That I require a clearness; and with him—
   To leave no rubs nor botches in the work—
   Fleance his son, that keeps him company,
   Whose absence is no less material to me   135
   Than is his father's, must embrace the fate
   Of that dark hour. Resolve yourselves apart;
   I'll come to you anon.
MURDERERS.   We are resolved, my lord.
MACBETH. I'll call upon you straight. Abide within.

   Exeunt MURDERERS.

It is concluded. Banquo, thy soul's flight,   140
If it find heaven, must find it out tonight.

   Exit.

21. . . . **avouch it,** Macbeth admits that he could authorize Banquo's death by his kingly rights.

22. **spy o' the time,** information about the perfect moment for the murder.

SCENE 2

The Palace.

Enter LADY MACBETH *and a* SERVANT.

LADY MACBETH. Is Banquo gone from court?

SERVANT. Ay, madam, but returns again tonight.

LADY MACBETH. Say to the King, I would attend his leisure
  For a few words.

SERVANT.   Madam, I will.

  Exit.

LADY MACBETH.   Naught's had, all's spent,   5
  Where our desire is got without content.
  'Tis safer to be that which we destroy
  Than by destruction dwell in doubtful joy.[23]

  Enter MACBETH.

  How now, my lord? Why do you keep alone,
  Of sorriest fancies your companions making,
  Using those thoughts which should indeed have died   10
  With them they think on? Things without all remedy
  Should be without regard; what's done is done.

MACBETH. We have scotched[24] the snake, not killed it.
  She'll close[25] and be herself, whilst our poor malice
  Remains in danger of her former tooth.   15
  But let the frame of things disjoint,[26] both the worlds
    suffer,
  Ere we will eat our meal in fear, and sleep
  In the affliction of these terrible dreams
  That shake us nightly. Better be with the dead,
  Whom we, to gain our peace, have sent to peace,   20
  Than on the torture of the mind to lie
  In restless ecstasy. Duncan is in his grave;
  After life's fitful fever he sleeps well.
  Treason has done his worst: nor steel nor poison,
  Malice domestic, foreign levy,[27] nothing,   25
  Can touch him further.

LADY MACBETH.   Come on;
  Gentle my lord, sleek o'er your rugged looks;
  Be bright and jovial among your guests tonight.

MACBETH. So shall I, love; and so, I pray, be you.
  Let your remembrance apply to Banquo;   30
  Present him eminence[28] both with eye and tongue:
  Unsafe the while, that we
  Must lave our honors in these flattering streams,
  And make our faces vizards[29] to our hearts,
  Disguising what they are.

LADY MACBETH.   You must leave this.   35

MACBETH. O, full of scorpions is my mind, dear wife!
  Thou know'st that Banquo, and his Fleance, lives.

LADY MACBETH. But in them Nature's copy's not eterne.[30]

MACBETH. There's comfort yet; they are assailable;
  Then be thou jocund. Ere the bat hath flown   40

23. **doubtful joy,** Lady Macbeth shares Macbeth's worry about Banquo.

24. **scotched,** injured.

25. **close,** the snake (the threat) may become whole again.

26. **frame of things disjoint,** heaven and hell may come apart and both perish before Macbeth will live with this fear.

27. **levy** (le′vē), an invading army.

28. **eminence,** praise Banquo.

29. **vizard** (viz′ərd), the shield of a medieval helmet, masking the face.

30. **eterne** (ē tẻrn′), eternal, immortal; a human being's lease from nature is not a permanent one.

197

His cloistered flight, ere to black Hecate's summons
The shard-borne beetle[31] with his drowsy hums
Hath rung night's yawning peal, there shall be done
A deed of dreadful note.
LADY MACBETH.   What's to be done?
MACBETH. Be innocent of the knowledge, dearest chuck,   45
Till thou applaud the deed. Come, seeling night,[32]
Scarf up the tender eye of pitiful day,
And with thy bloody and invisible hand
Cancel and tear to pieces that great bond
Which keeps me pale! Light thickens, and the crow   50
Makes wing to the rooky wood.[33]
Good things of day begin to droop and drowse,
Whiles night's black agents to their preys do rouse.
Thou marvell'st at my words; but hold thee still:
Things bad begun make strong themselves by ill.   55
So prithee go with me.

Exeunt.

SCENE 3

A park near the Palace.

Enter three MURDERERS.

FIRST MURDERER. But who did bid thee join with us?
THIRD MURDERER.   Macbeth.
SECOND MURDERER. He needs not our mistrust, since he
     delivers
Our offices,[34] and what we have to do,
To the direction just.
FIRST MURDERER.   Then stand with us.
The west yet glimmers with some streaks of day.   5
Now spurs the lated traveler apace
To gain the timely inn,[35] and near approaches
The subject of our watch.
THIRD MURDERER.   Hark! I hear horses.
BANQUO. (*Within*) Give us a light there, ho!
SECOND MURDERER.   Then 'tis he. The rest
That are within the note of expectation   10
Already are i' the court.

FIRST MURDERER.   His horses go about.
THIRD MURDERER. Almost a mile; but he does usually—
So all men do—from hence to the palace gate
Make it their walk.[36]
SECOND MURDERER.   A light, a light!

Enter BANQUO, *and* FLEANCE *with a torch.*

31. **shard-borne,** borne aloft on scaly wings.

32. **seel** (sēl), to close the eyes; to blind. This entire metaphor comes from the hooding of falcons to tame them before training.

33. **rooky wood,** the forest filled with rooks (crows).

34. **offices,** duties, instructions.

35. **lated traveler . . . timely inn,** the evening traveler hurries to reach the inn before it is too dark.

36. Banquo and Fleance, as is customary, dismount some distance from the palace and walk the last stretch alone. Their servants take the horses to stable them. This, of course, makes the attack easier.

THIRD MURDERER.   'Tis he.

FIRST MURDERER. Stand to't.   15

BANQUO. It will be rain tonight.

FIRST MURDERER.   Let it come down!

They set upon BANQUO.

BANQUO. O treachery! Fly, good Fleance, fly, fly, fly!
    Thou mayst revenge. O slave!

Dies. FLEANCE *escapes.*

THIRD MURDERER. Who did strike out the light?

FIRST MURDERER.   Was't not the way?

THIRD MURDERER. There's but one down; the son is fled.

SECOND MURDERER.   We have lost   20
    Best half of our affair.

FIRST MURDERER. Well, let's away, and say how much is
    done.

Exeunt.

SCENE 4

Hall in the Palace.

A *banquet prepared. Enter* MACBETH, LADY MACBETH,
ROSS, LENNOX, LORDS *and Attendants.*

MACBETH. You know your own degrees,[37] sit down. At
    first
    And last the hearty welcome.

LORDS.   Thanks to your Majesty.

MACBETH. Ourself will mingle with society
    And play the humble host.
    Our hostess keeps her state,[38] but in best time   5
    We will require her welcome.

LADY MACBETH. Pronounce it for me, sir, to all our friends,
    For my heart speaks they are welcome.

Enter FIRST MURDERER *to the door.*

MACBETH. See, they encounter thee with their hearts'
    thanks.
    Both sides are even: here I'll sit i' the midst.   10
    Be large in mirth; anon we'll drink a measure
    The table round. (*Approaching* MURDERER *at door*)
    There's blood upon thy face.

MURDERER. 'Tis Banquo's then.

MACBETH. 'Tis better thee without than he within.
    Is he dispatched?   15

MURDERER. My lord, his throat is cut. That I did for him.

MACBETH. Thou art the best o' the cutthroats! Yet he's
    good

Maria Casares and Jean Vilar as the crowned Macbeths.

37. **own degrees,** relative ranks that determine protocol in seating at the table.

38. **her state,** Macbeth chooses to leave his royal seat and sit with his guest; Lady Macbeth stays on the raised throne.

That did the like for Fleance. If thou didst it,
Thou art the nonpareil.

MURDERER.   Most royal sir,
Fleance is 'scaped.   20

MACBETH. (*Aside*) Then comes my fit again. I had else
    been perfect,
Whole as the marble, founded as the rock,
As broad and general as the casing air.[39]
But now I am cabined, cribbed, confined, bound in
To saucy doubts and fears.—But Banquo's safe?   25

MURDERER. Ay, my good lord. Safe in a ditch he bides,
With twenty trenched gashes on his head,
The least a death to nature.

MACBETH.   Thanks for that!
(*Aside*) There the grown serpent lies; the worm that's
    fled
Hath nature that in time will venom breed,[40]   30
No teeth for the present. Get thee gone. Tomorrow
We'll hear ourselves again.

    Exit MURDERER.

LADY MACBETH.   My royal lord,
You do not give the cheer. The feast is sold
That is not often vouched,[41] while 'tis a-making,
'Tis given with welcome. To feed were best at home. 35
From thence, the sauce to meat is ceremony;
Meeting were bare without it.

The GHOST OF BANQUO *enters, and sits in* MACBETH'S
place.

MACBETH.   Sweet remembrancer!
Now good digestion wait on appetite,
And health on both!

LENNOX.   May't please your Highness sit.

MACBETH. Here had we now our country's honor roofed, 40
Were the graced person of our Banquo present;
Who may I rather challenge for unkindness
Than pity for mischance!

ROSS.   His absence, sir,
Lays blame upon his promise. Please't your Highness
To grace us with your royal company?   45

MACBETH. The table's full.

LENNOX.   Here is a place reserved, sir.

MACBETH. Where?

LENNOX. Here, my good lord. What is't that moves your
    Highness?

MACBETH. Which of you have done this?

LORDS.   What, my good lord?

39. **rock . . . casing air,** as solid as a rock and as free as the surrounding air.

40. **venom breed,** Macbeth refers to Banquo's offspring escaping.

41. **vouched** (voucht), without the host's constant attention, welcome, and cheer, a dinner is as one bought in an inn.

MACBETH. Thou canst not say I did it. Never shake 50
   Thy gory locks at me.
ROSS. Gentlemen, rise. His Highness is not well.
LADY MACBETH. Sit, worthy friends. My lord is often
   thus,[42]
   And hath been from his youth. Pray you keep seat.
   The fit is momentary; upon a thought 55
   He will again be well. If much you note him,
   You shall offend him and extend his passion.
   Feed, and regard him not.—Are you a man?
MACBETH. Ay, and a bold one, that dare look on that
   Which might appall the devil.
LADY MACBETH.   O proper stuff! 60
   This is the very painting of your fear;
   This is the air-drawn dagger which, you said,
   Led you to Duncan. O, these flaws and starts,
   Imposters to true fear, would well become
   A woman's story at a winter's fire, 65
   Authorized by her grandam.[43] Shame itself!
   Why do you make such faces? When all's done,
   You look but on a stool.
MACBETH. Prithee, see there! behold! look! lo! how say
   you?
   Why, what care I? If thou canst nod, speak too. 70
   If charnel-houses and our graves must send
   Those that we bury back, our monuments
   Shall be the maws of kites.[44]

   Exit GHOST.

LADY MACBETH.   What, quite unmanned in folly?
MACBETH. If I stand here, I saw him.
LADY MACBETH.   Fie, for shame!
MACBETH. Blood hath been shed ere now, i' the olden
   time, 75
   Ere humane statute purged the gentle weal;[45]
   Ay, and since too, murders have been performed
   Too terrible for the ear. The time has been,
   That, when the brains were out, the man would die,
   And there an end! But now they rise again, 80
   With twenty mortal murders on their crowns,
   And push us from our stools. This is more strange
   Than such a murder is.
LADY MACBETH.   My worthy lord,
   Your noble friends do lack you.
MACBETH.   I do forget.[46]
   Do not muse at me, my most worthy friends. 85
   I have a strange infirmity, which is nothing

42. **often thus,** Macbeth was subject to fits of hallucinations.

43. . . . **grandam,** "old wives tales."

44. **charnel-houses** (chär'nl), burial places for ancient bones; **maws of kites,** stomachs of carrion birds—if the dead return we'd do better to leave their bodies to birds of prey than to put up monuments.

45. **the gentle weal,** before laws against murder made the savage state gentle, civilized.

46. Macbeth remembers his guests.

To those that know me. Come, love and health to all!
Then I'll sit down. Give me some wine, fill full.

GHOST *reenters*.

I drink to the general joy o' the whole table,
And to our dear friend Banquo, whom we miss;   90
Would he were here! To all, and him, we thirst,
And all to all.
LORDS.   Our duties, and the pledge.
MACBETH. Avaunt! and quit my sight! let the earth hide
    thee!
Thy bones are marrowless, thy blood is cold;
Thou hast no speculation[47] in those eyes   95   47. **speculation,** power of sight.
Which thou dost glare with.
LADY MACBETH.   Think of this, good peers,
But as a thing of custom. 'Tis no other;
Only it spoils the pleasure of the time.
MACBETH. What man dare, I dare.
Approach thou like the rugged Russian bear,   100
The armed rhinoceros, or the Hyrcan[48] tiger;   48. **Hyrcan** (hėr′kən), from an ancient
Take any shape but that, and my firm nerves   Asian country near the Caspian Sea.
Shall never tremble. Or be alive again
And dare me to the desert with thy sword.
If trembling I inhabit then,[49] protest me   105   49. **inhabit then,** prove (myself) a
The baby of a girl. Hence, horrible shadow!   weakling.
Unreal mock'ry, hence!

Exit GHOST.

                    Why, so; being gone,
I am a man again. Pray you, sit still.
LADY MACBETH. You have displaced the mirth, broke the
    good meeting
With most admired disorder.
MACBETH.   Can such things be,   110
And overcome us like a summer's cloud,
Without our special wonder? You make me strange
Even to the disposition that I owe,[50]   50. **disposition that I owe,** Macbeth is
When now I think you can behold such sights,   bewildered by this change in his brave
And keep the natural ruby of your cheeks,   115   nature.
When mine is blanched with fear.
ROSS.   What sights, my lord?
LADY MACBETH. I pray you speak not. He grows worse
    and worse;
Question enrages him. At once, good night.
Stand not upon the order of your going,[51]   51. **order of your going,** do not wait
But go at once.   upon the order of rank for leaving.
LENNOX.   Good night, and better health   120   Ordinarily the highest noble would leave
Attend his Majesty!   first.

LADY MACBETH.   A kind good night to all!

Exeunt all but MACBETH *and* LADY MACBETH.

MACBETH. It will have blood. They say blood will have
    blood.
    Stones have been known to move and trees to speak;
    Augures and understood relations have
    By maggot-pies and choughs and rooks brought forth[52]   125
    The secret'st man of blood. What is the night?
LADY MACBETH. Almost at odds with morning, which is
    which.
MACBETH. How say'st thou, that Macduff denies his
    person[53]
    At our great bidding?
LADY MACBETH.   Did you send to him, sir?
MACBETH. I hear it by the way, but I will send.   130
    There's not a one of them but in his house
    I keep a servant fee'd.[54] I will tomorrow,
    And betimes I will, to the weird sisters.
    More shall they speak; for now I am bent to know,
    By the worst means, the worst. For mine own good   135
    All causes shall give way. I am in blood
    Stepped in so far that, should I wade no more,
    Returning were as tedious as go o'er.
    Strange things I have in head, that will to hand,
    Which must be acted ere they may be scanned.[55]   140
LADY MACBETH. You lack the season of all natures, sleep.
MACBETH. Come, we'll to sleep. My strange and self-
    abuse
    Is the initiate fear that wants hard use.
    We are yet but young in deed.

    Exeunt.

52. **augures** (ô′gyûrz), auguries, predictions of soothsayers have revealed murders by means of birds—magpies and
crows.

53. Macduff refuses Macbeth's calls.

54. **fee'd**, paid by Macbeth as a spy.

55. **scanned,** Macbeth considers strange
things that must be acted on before they
are carefully thought out.

SCENE 5

A heath.

Thunder. The THREE WITCHES *enter, meeting* HECATE.

FIRST WITCH. Why, how now, Hecate? You look angerly.
HECATE. Have I not reason, beldams[56] as you are,
    Saucy and overbold? How did you dare
    To trade and traffic with Macbeth
    In riddles and affairs of death;   5
    And I, the mistress of your charms,
    The close contriver of all harms,
    Was never called to bear my part,
    Or show the glory of our art?

56. **beldams** (bel′dəmz), old hags.

And, which is worse, all you have done
Hath been but for a wayward son,
Spiteful and wrathful, who, as others do,
Loves for his own ends, not for you.
But make amends now. Get you gone,
And at the pit of Acheron[57]
Meet me i' the morning. Thither he
Will come to know his destiny.
Your vessels and your spells provide,
Your charms and everything beside.
I am for the air; this night I'll spend
Unto a dismal and a fatal end.
Great business must be wrought ere noon.
Upon the corner of the moon
There hangs a vaporous drop profound.[58]
I'll catch it ere it comes to ground;
And that distilled by magic sleights,
Shall raise such artificial sprites
As by the strength of their illusion
Shall draw him on to his confusion.
He shall spurn fate, scorn death, and bear
His hopes 'bove wisdom, grace, and fear;
And you all know security
Is mortals' chiefest enemy.

*Music and a song within: "Come away, come away,"
etc.*

Hark! I am called; my little spirit, see
Sits in a foggy cloud, and stays for me.

Exit.

FIRST WITCH. Come, let's make haste. She'll soon be back
  again.

Exeunt.

SCENE 6

Forres. The Palace.

Enter LENNOX *and another* LORD.

LENNOX. My former speeches have but hit your thoughts,
  Which can interpret farther. Only I say
  Things have been strangely borne. The gracious
    Duncan
  Was pitied of Macbeth; marry, he was dead.[59]
  And the right-valiant Banquo walked too late;
  Whom, you may say, if't please you, Fleance killed,
  For Fleance fled. Men must not walk too late.

57. **Acheron** (ak′ə ron′), river leading to the classical underworld of the dead, Hades; **the pit** probably refers to a Scottish cavern.

58. **drop profound,** according to an ancient magic the moon gave off drops of venom under certain enchantments.

59. . . . **was dead,** Macbeth pitied Duncan after he was dead.

Who cannot want the thought[60] how monstrous
It was for Malcolm and for Donalbain
To kill their gracious father? Damnèd fact! 10
How it did grieve Macbeth! Did he not straight,
In pious rage, the two delinquents tear,
That were the slaves of drink and thralls of sleep?
Was not that nobly done? Ay, and wisely too;
For 'twould have angered any heart alive 15
To hear the men deny't. So that, I say,
He has borne all things well; and I do think
That, had he Duncan's sons under his key—
As, an't please heaven, he shall not—they should find
What 'twere to kill a father; so should Fleance. 20
But, peace! for from broad words,[61] and 'cause he failed
His presence at the tyrant's feast, I hear
Macduff lives in disgrace. Sir, can you tell
Where he bestows himself?
LORD.   The son of Duncan,
From whom this tyrant holds[62] the due of birth, 25
Lives in the English court, and is received
Of the most pious Edward with such grace
That the malevolence of fortune nothing
Takes from his high respect. Thither Macduff
Is gone to pray the holy king, upon his aid 30
To wake Northumberland and warlike Siward;[63]
That by the help of these—with Him above
To ratify the work—we may again
Give to our tables meat, sleep to our nights,
Free from our feasts and banquets bloody knives, 35
Do faithful homage and receive free honors—
All which we pine for now. And this report
Hath so exasperate the King that he
Prepares for some attempt of war.
LENNOX.   Sent he to Macduff?
LORD. He did; and with an absolute "Sir, not I!" 40
The cloudy[64] messenger turns me his back,
And hums, as who should say, "You'll rue the time
That clogs me with this answer."[65]
LENNOX.   And that well might
Advise him to a caution to hold what distance
His wisdom can provide. Some holy angel 45
Fly to the court of England and unfold
His message ere he come, that a swift blessing

60. **Who cannot want the thought,** who could keep from thinking?

61. **broad words,** outspoken statements against Macbeth.

62. **holds,** withholds.

63. **Siward,** the earl of Northumberland.

64. **cloudy,** gloomy.

65. The messenger mutters as if protesting having to carry the unwelcome news.

May soon return to this our suffering country
Under a hand accursed!

LORD.   I'll send my prayers with him.

Exeunt.

ACT III
MOUNTING CONSEQUENCES

1. What is the difference between Macbeth's behavior in the murder of Duncan and his behavior in the murder of Banquo? What changes in the character of Macbeth does this show?

2. What signs are there that Macbeth's conscience is troubling him?

3. How has the relationship of Macbeth and Lady Macbeth changed?

4. What unforeseen consequences have followed the choices Macbeth has made?

5. What signs are there that Macbeth's character and personality are beginning to crumble?

WORDS

A. Find the following phrases and clauses in Acts II and III of *Macbeth* and unlock them by means of context clues.

1. . . . the *surfeited* grooms/Do mock their charge with snores.

2. This my hand will rather/The *multitudinous* seas incarnadine. . . .

3. Those that Macbeth hath slain. . . . They were *suborned.*

4. God's *benison* go with you. . . .

5. Upon my head they placed a fruitless crown/And put a barren *scepter* in my gripe. . . .

6. . . . Then be thou *jocund.*

7. If thou didst it,/Thou art the *nonpareil.*

B. What did the following italicized words mean in Shakespeare's day?

my bosom *franchised*
sensible to feeling as to sight
do mock their *charge*
the night has been *unruly*
of dire *combustion*

C. Some of the similes and metaphors in Acts II and III of *Macbeth* are much admired.

Explain the following:

1. Sleep that knits up the raveled sleave of care. . . .

2. The wine of life is drawn. . . .

3. There's daggers in men's smiles. . . .

4. We have scotched the snake, not killed it.

5. Scarf up the tender eye of pitiful day. . . .

6. . . . wicked dreams abuse/The curtained sleep.

7. . . . destroy your sight/With a new Gorgon.

D. In Act II, scene 2, note that Shakespeare uses an abundance contrasted by a lack of specific detail to emphasize the difference between the highly imaginative Macbeth and his matter-of-fact wife.

Beginning with Macbeth's line, "One cried, 'God bless us!'" count the specific statements that reveal Macbeth's horror at the sight of his bloodstained hands. Consider his four successive speeches.

In contrast, what one command does his wife give concerning those same hands?

E. In Macbeth's soliloquy, Act II, scene 1, beginning "Is this a dagger that I see before me?" the obsolete Middle English word, *dudgeon,* is of semantic interest.

Originally dudgeon was the name of the kind of wood which woodturners and cutlers used for the haft (handle) of a dagger. In time, the haft itself was called the dudgeon. It is thus that Shakespeare uses it: "on thy blade and dudgeon gouts (drops) of blood."

Is the above movement an example of the broadening or the narrowing of the meaning of a word?

F. In reconstructing the pronunciation of the English of Shakespeare's day, scholars have concluded that words like *bake* and *take,* now pronounced with ā, were then pronounced *back* and *tack,* with a sustained short a (ă) sound.

In keeping with the above semantic trend, how did Elizabethans pronounce the following: fade, made, hate, rate?

❦ Act IV

SCENE 1

A cavern. In the middle, a boiling cauldron.

Thunder. Enter the THREE WITCHES.

FIRST WITCH. Thrice the brinded cat[1] hath mewed.
SECOND WITCH. Thrice, and once the hedge-pig whined.
THIRD WITCH. Harpier[2] cries, " 'Tis time, 'tis time."
FIRST WITCH. Round about the cauldron go;
  In the poisoned entrails throw.   5
  Toad, that under cold stone
  Days and nights has thirty-one
  Swelter'd venom sleeping got,
  Boil thou first i' the charmèd pot.
ALL. Double, double, toil and trouble;   10
  Fire burn and cauldron bubble.
SECOND WITCH. Fillet of a fenny snake,
  In the cauldron boil and bake;
  Eye of newt and toe of frog,
  Wool of bat and tongue of dog,   15
  Adder's fork and blind-worm's sting,
  Lizard's leg and howlet's wing,
  For a charm of powerful trouble,
  Like a hell-broth boil and bubble.
ALL. Double, double, toil and trouble;   20
  Fire burn, and cauldron bubble.
THIRD WITCH. Scale of dragon, tooth of wolf,
  Witches' mummy, maw and gulf
  Of the ravined salt-sea shark,
  Root of hemlock digged i' the dark,   25
  Liver of blaspheming Jew,
  Gall of goat and slips of yew
  Slivered in the moon's eclipse,
  Nose of Turk and Tartar's lips,
  Finger of birth-strangled babe   30
  Ditch-delivered by a drab,
  Make the gruel thick and slab.
  Add thereto a tiger's chaudron,[3]
  For the ingredients of our cauldron.
ALL. Double, double, toil and trouble;   35
  Fire burn and cauldron bubble.
SECOND WITCH. Cool it with a baboon's blood,
  Then the charm is firm and good.

Enter HECATE.

1. **brinded cat** (brin′dəd), streaked, another of the animals like Graymalkin who are associates of the witches.
2. **Harpier** (här′pē ər), another of the witches' demons.

3. **chaudron** (chô′drən), entrails.

HECATE. O, well done! I commend your pains,
    And every one shall share i' the gains.   40
    And now about the cauldron sing,
    Like elves and fairies in a ring,
    Enchanting all that you put in.

Music and a song "Black spirit," etc. HECATE *retires.*

SECOND WITCH. By the pricking of my thumbs,
    Something wicked this way comes.   45
         Open locks,
         Whoever knocks!

Enter MACBETH.

MACBETH. How now, you secret, black, and midnight
    hags!
    What is't you do?
ALL.   A deed without a name.
MACBETH. I conjure you, by that which you profess,   50
    Howe'er you come to know it, answer me.
    Though you untie the winds and let them fight
    Against the churches; though the yesty waves
    Confound and swallow navigation up;
    Though bladed corn be lodged and trees blown down;   55
    Though castles topple on their warders' heads;
    Though palaces and pyramids do slope
    Their heads to their foundations; though the treasure
    Of nature's germens[4] tumble all together,
    Even till destruction sicken; answer me   60
    To what I ask you.
FIRST WITCH.   Speak.
SECOND WITCH.   Demand.
THIRD WITCH.   We'll answer.
FIRST WITCH. Say, if thou'dst rather hear it from our
    mouths,
    Or from our masters?
MACBETH.   Call 'em! Let me see 'em.
FIRST WITCH. Pour in sow's blood, that hath eaten
    Her nine farrow; grease that's sweaten   65
    From the murderer's gibbet throw
    Into the flame.
ALL.   Come, high or low;
    Thyself and office deftly show!

Thunder. First Apparition: an Armed Head.

MACBETH. Tell me, thou unknown power—
FIRST WITCH.   He knows thy thought.
    Hear his speech, but say thou naught.   70

4. **germens** (jėr′menz), all the seeds of the future.

FIRST APPARITION. Macbeth! Macbeth! Macbeth! Beware
    Macduff;
    Beware the thane of Fife. Dismiss me. Enough.

Descends.

MACBETH. Whate'er thou art, for thy good caution thanks;
    Thou hast harped[5] my fear aright. But one word
    more—

FIRST WITCH. He will not be commanded. Here's another,   75
    More potent than the first.

Thunder. Second Apparition: a Bloody Child.

SECOND APPARITION. Macbeth! Macbeth! Macbeth!
MACBETH. Had I three ears, I'ld hear thee.
SECOND APPARITION. Be bloody, bold and resolute; laugh
    to scorn
    The power of man, for none of woman born   80
    Shall harm Macbeth.

Descends.

MACBETH. Then live, Macduff; what need I fear of thee?
    But yet I'll make assurance double sure
    And take a bond of fate. Thou shalt not live;
    That I may tell pale-hearted fear it lies,   85
    And sleep it spite of thunder.

*Thunder. Third Apparition: a Child crowned, with a
tree in his hand.*

                  What is this,
    That rises like the issue of a king,
    And wears upon his baby-brow the round
    And top of sovereignty?
ALL.   Listen, but speak not to't.
THIRD APPARITION. Be lion-mettled, proud, and take no
    care   90
    Who chafes, who frets, or where conspirers are.
    Macbeth shall never vanquished be until
    Great Birnam wood to high Dunsinane hill
    Shall come against him.

Descends.

MACBETH.   That will never be.
    Who can impress[6] the forest, bid the tree   95
    Unfix his earth-bound root? Sweet bodements![7] good!
    Rebellion's head, rise never, till the wood
    Of Birnam rise, and our high-placed Macbeth
    Shall live the lease of nature,[8] pay his breath
    To time and mortal custom. Yet my heart   100
    Throbs to know one thing. Tell me, if your art

5. **harped,** sounded the very chord of my fears.

6. **impress,** forcibly enlist.

7. **bodements** (bōd'mənts), prophecies.

8. **lease of nature,** a full lifetime ending with a natural death.

Can tell so much—shall Banquo's issue ever
Reign in this kingdom?

ALL.   Seek to know no more.

MACBETH. I will be satisfied. Deny me this,
And an eternal curse fall on you! Let me know.   105
Why sinks that cauldron? and what noise is this?

Hautboys.

FIRST WITCH. Show!

SECOND WITCH. Show!

THIRD WITCH. Show!

ALL. Show his eyes, and grieve his heart;   110
Come like shadows, so depart!

A show of eight Kings, the last with a glass in his hand;
BANQUO'S GHOST *following.*

MACBETH. Thou art too like the spirit of Banquo. Down!
Thy crown does sear mine eyeballs. And thy hair,
Thou other gold-bound brow, is like the first.
A third is like the former. Filthy hags!   115
Why do you show me this? A fourth! Start, eyes!
What, will the line stretch out to the crack of doom?
Another yet! A seventh! I'll see no more.
And yet the eighth appears,[9] who bears a glass
Which shows me many more; and some I see   120
That twofold balls and treble[10] scepters carry.
Horrible sight! Now I see 'tis true;
For the blood-boltered Banquo smiles upon me
And points at them for his.[11] What? Is this so?

Apparitions vanish.

FIRST WITCH. Ay, sir, all this is so. But why   125
Stands Macbeth thus amazedly?
Come, sisters, cheer we up his sprites,
And show the best of our delights.
I'll charm the air to give a sound
While you perform your antic round,   130
That this great king may kindly say
Our duties did his welcome pay.

Music. The WITCHES *dance, and vanish.*

MACBETH. Where are they? Gone? Let this pernicious
    hour
Stand aye accursèd in the calendar!
Come in, without there!

Enter LENNOX.

LENNOX.   What's your grace's will?   135

MACBETH. Saw you the weird sisters?

9. **eighth appears,** the eight kings of the Stuart dynasty, Robert II, III, and six Jameses to James I (1604), the first Stuart king to rule England.

10. **twofold and treble,** symbols of rule over increasing kingdoms.

11. The murdered Banquo is the ancestor of the royal Stuart line.

LENNOX.   No, my lord.

MACBETH. Came they not by you?

LENNOX.   No, indeed, my lord.

MACBETH. Infected be the air whereon they ride,
And damned all those that trust them! I did hear
The galloping of horse. Who was't came by?   140

LENNOX. 'Tis two or three, my lord, that bring you word
Macduff is fled to England.

MACBETH.   Fled to England?

LENNOX. Ay, my good lord.

MACBETH. (*Aside*) Time, thou anticipatest my dread ex-
ploits.
The flighty purpose never is o'ertook   145
Unless the deed go with it. From this moment
The very firstlings of my heart shall be
The firstlings of my hand. And even now,
To crown my thoughts with acts, be it thought and
done.
The castle of Macduff I will surprise;   150
Seize upon Fife; give to the edge o' the sword
His wife, his babes, and all unfortunate souls
That trace him in his line. No boasting like a fool;
This deed I'll do before this purpose cool.
But no more sights!—Where are these gentlemen?[12]   155
Come, bring me where they are.

Exeunt.

12. **Where are these gentlemen?**, those who bring news of Macduff's escape.

SCENE 2

Fife. MACDUFF's *Castle.*

Enter LADY MACDUFF, *her* SON, *and* ROSS.

LADY MACDUFF. What had he done, to make him fly the
land?

ROSS. You must have patience, madam.

LADY MACDUFF.   He had none.
His flight was madness. When our actions do not,
Our fears do make us traitors.

ROSS.   You know not
Whether it was his wisdom or his fear.   5

LADY MACDUFF. Wisdom? To leave his wife, to leave his
babes,
His mansion and his titles, in a place
From whence himself does fly? He loves us not;
He wants the natural touch. For the poor wren,
The most diminutive of birds, will fight,   10
Her young ones in her nest, against the owl.

All is the fear and nothing is the love;
As little is the wisdom, where the flight
So runs against all reason.
ROSS.   My dearest coz,
I pray you school yourself. But, for your husband,   15
He is noble, wise, judicious, and best knows
The fits o' the season. I dare not speak much further;
But cruel are the times, when we are traitors
And do not know ourselves; when we hold rumor[13]
From what we fear, yet know not what we fear,   20
But float upon a wild and violent sea
Each way and move. I take my leave of you.
Shall not be long but I'll be here again.
Things at the worst will cease, or else climb upward
To what they were before. My pretty cousin,[14]   25
Blessing upon us!
LADY MACDUFF. Fathered he is, and yet he's fatherless.
ROSS. I am so much a fool, should I stay longer,
It would be my disgrace and your discomfort.
I take my leave at once.

Exit.

LADY MACDUFF.   Sirrah, your father's dead;   30
And what will you do now? How will you live?
SON. As birds do, mother.
LADY MACDUFF.   What, with worms and flies?
SON. With what I get, I mean; and so do they.
LADY MACDUFF. Poor bird! thou'ldst never fear the net nor
lime,
The pitfall nor the gin.[15]   35
SON. Why should I, mother? Poor birds they are not set
for.
My father is not dead, for all your saying.
LADY MACDUFF. Yes, he is dead. How wilt thou do for a
father?
SON. Nay, how will you do for a husband?
LADY MACDUFF. Why, I can buy me twenty at any market.   40
SON. Then you'll buy 'em to sell again.
LADY MACDUFF. Thou speak'st with all thy wit; and yet,
i' faith,
With wit enough for thee.
SON. Was my father a traitor, mother?
LADY MACDUFF. Ay, that he was!   45
SON. What is a traitor?
LADY MACDUFF. Why, one that swears, and lies.
SON. And be all traitors that do so?

13. **hold rumor,** believe in every fear.

14. **cousin,** Ross has turned from Lady Macduff to her son.

15. **net nor lime . . . gin** (jin), all traps: nets, sticky birdlime, and other snares.

LADY MACDUFF. Every one that does so is a traitor, and
  must be hanged. 50
SON. And must they all be hanged that swear and lie?
LADY MACDUFF. Every one.
SON. Who must hang them?
LADY MACDUFF. Why, the honest men.
SON. Then the liars and swearers are fools; for there are 55
  liars and swearers enow to beat the honest men and
  hang up them.
LADY MACDUFF. Now, God help thee, poor monkey! But
  how wilt thou do for a father?
SON. If he were dead, you'ld weep for him. If you would 60
  not, it were a good sign that I should quickly have a
  new father.
LADY MACDUFF. Poor prattler, how thou talk'st!

Enter a MESSENGER.

MESSENGER. Bless you, fair dame! I am not to you known,
  Though in your state of honor I am perfect.[16] 65
  I doubt[17] some danger does approach you nearly.
  If you will take a homely[18] man's advice,
  Be not found here. Hence, with your little ones.
  To fright you thus, methinks I am too savage;
  To do worse to you were fell cruelty, 70
  Which is too nigh your person. Heaven preserve you!
  I dare abide no longer.

Exit.

LADY MACDUFF.   Whither should I fly?
I have done no harm. But I remember now
I am in this earthly world, where to do harm
Is often laudable, to do good sometime 75
Accounted dangerous folly. Why then, alas,
Do I put up that womanly defense,
To say I have done no harm?—What are these faces?

Enter MURDERERS.

FIRST MURDERER. Where is your husband?
LADY MACDUFF. I hope, in no place so unsanctified 80
  Where such as thou mayst find him.
FIRST MURDERER.   He's a traitor.
SON. Thou liest, thou shag-eared villain!
FIRST MURDERER.   What, you egg!

Stabbing him.

Young fry of treachery!

16. **am perfect,** the messenger says, "Though you don't know me I know you well, honorable lady."
17. **doubt,** fear.
18. **homely,** simple, of no rank.

213

SON.   He has killed me, mother.
Run away, I pray you!

Dies.

Exit LADY MACDUFF, *crying "Murder!"* MURDERERS *follow her.*

                    SCENE 3

England. Before the King's Palace.

Enter MALCOLM *and* MACDUFF.

MALCOLM. Let us seek out some desolate shade, and there
    Weep our sad bosoms empty.
MACDUFF.   Let us rather
    Hold fast the mortal sword and, like good men,
    Bestride our downfall'n birthdom.¹⁹ Each new morn
    New widows howl, new orphans cry, new sorrows   5
    Strike heaven on the face, that it resounds
    As if it felt with Scotland and yelled out
    Like syllable of dolor.²⁰
MALCOLM.   What I believe, I'll wail;
    What know, believe; and what I can redress,
    As I shall find the time to friend, I will.   10
    What you have spoke, it may be so perchance.
    This tyrant, whose sole name blisters our tongues,
    Was once thought honest; you have loved him well;
    He hath not touched you yet. I am young; but something
    You may deserve of him through me, and wisdom   15
    To offer up a weak, poor, innocent lamb
    T'appease an angry god.
MACDUFF. I am not treacherous.
MALCOLM.   But Macbeth is.
    A good and virtuous nature may recoil
    In an imperial charge.²¹ But I shall crave your pardon;   20
    That which you are, my thoughts cannot transpose.
    Angels are bright still, though the brightest fell.²²
    Though all things foul would wear the brows of grace,
    Yet grace must still look so.
MACDUFF.   I have lost my hopes.
MALCOLM. Perchance even there where I did find my
        doubts.   25
    Why in that rawness left you wife and child,
    Those precious motives, those strong knots of love,
    Without leave-taking? I pray you,
    Let not my jealousies be your dishonors,

19. **birthdom,** native land.

20. **dolor** (dō′lər), sorrow; heaven itself cries out like suffering Scotland.

21. **imperial charge,** king's order; Malcolm cannot quite trust Macduff and feels he may be an agent for Macbeth.
22. **brightest fell,** the reference is to the fall of the angel Lucifer; Macduff may yet be honest and loyal though his brilliant chieftain Macbeth proved corrupt.

But mine own safeties.[23] You may be rightly just,
Whatever I shall think.   30

MACDUFF.   Bleed, bleed, poor country!
Great tyranny, lay thou thy basis sure,
For goodness dare not check thee. Wear thou thy
    wrongs;
The title is affeered.[24] Fare thee well, lord.
I would not be the villain that thou think'st   35
For the whole space that's in the tyrant's grasp
And the rich East to boot.

MALCOLM.   Be not offended.
I speak not as in absolute fear of you.
I think our country sinks beneath the yoke;
It weeps, it bleeds, and each new day a gash   40
Is added to her wounds. I think withal
There would be hands uplifted in my right;
And here from gracious England have I offer
Of goodly thousands. But, for all this,
When I shall tread upon the tyrant's head   45
Or wear it on my sword, yet my poor country
Shall have more vices than it had before,
More suffer and more sundry ways than ever,
By him that shall succeed.

MACDUFF.   What should he be?

MALCOLM. It is myself I mean; in whom I know   50
All the particulars of vice so grafted
That, when they shall be opened, black Macbeth
Will seem as pure as snow, and the poor state
Esteem him as a lamb, being compared
With my confineless harms.

MACDUFF.   Not in the legions   55
Of horrid hell can come a devil more damned
In evils to top Macbeth.

MALCOLM.   I grant him bloody,
Luxurious, avaricious, false, deceitful,
Sudden, malicious, smacking of every sin
That has a name. But there's no bottom, none,   60
In my voluptuousness. Your wives, your daughters,
Your matrons and your maids, could not fill up
The cistern of my lust, and my desire
All continent impediments would o'erbear,
That did oppose my will. Better Macbeth   65
Than such an one to reign.

MACDUFF.   Boundless intemperance
In nature is a tyranny; it hath been
The untimely emptying of the happy throne,
And fall of many kings. But fear not yet

23. **safeties,** Malcolm apologizes for his suspicions and reminds Macduff that it is his life that is at stake.

24. **is affeered,** even good people fear to challenge Macbeth's title; therefore it is confirmed.

215

To take upon you what is yours. You may   70
Convey your pleasures in a spacious plenty,
And yet seem cold, the time you may so hoodwink.
We have willing dames enough; there cannot be
That vulture in you, to devour so many
As will to greatness dedicate themselves,   75
Finding it so inclined.

MALCOLM.   With this there grows
In my most ill-composed affection such
A stanchless avarice that, were I king,
I should cut off the nobles for their lands,
Desire his jewels, and this other's house;   80
And my more-having would be as a sauce
To make me hunger more, that I should forge
Quarrels unjust against the good and loyal,
Destroying them for wealth.

MACDUFF.   This avarice
Sticks deeper, grows with more pernicious root   85
Than summer-seeming lust, and it hath been
The sword of our slain kings. Yet do not fear;
Scotland hath foisons[25] to fill up your will
Of your mere own. All these are portable,
With other graces weighed.[26]   90

MALCOLM. But I have none. The king-becoming graces,
As justice, verity, temperance, stableness,
Bounty, perseverance, mercy, lowliness,
Devotion, patience, courage, fortitude,
I have no relish of them, but abound   95
In the division of each several crime,
Acting it many ways. Nay, had I power, I should
Pour the sweet milk of concord into hell,
Uproar the universal peace, confound
All unity on earth.

MACDUFF.   O Scotland, Scotland!   100

MALCOLM. If such a one be fit to govern, speak.
I am as I have spoken.

MACDUFF.   Fit to govern?
No, not to live. O nation miserable!
With an untitled tyrant bloody-sceptered,
When shalt thou see thy wholesome days again,   105
Since that the truest issue of thy throne
By his own interdiction stands accursed,
And does blaspheme his breed? Thy royal father
Was a most sainted king; the queen that bore thee,
Oft'ner upon her knees than on her feet,   110
Died every day she lived.[27] Fare thee well!
These evils thou repeat'st upon thyself

25. **foisons** (foi′zənz), great abundance.

26. **graces weighed,** things are bearable considering your great virtues.

27. **died every day she lived,** lived with such religious devotions as to consider death daily.

Have banished me from Scotland. O my breast,
Thy hope ends here!

MALCOLM.   Macduff, this noble passion,
  Child of integrity, hath from my soul   115
  Wiped the black scruples, reconciled my thoughts
  To thy good truth and honor. Devilish Macbeth
  By many of these trains hath sought to win me
  Into his power; and modest wisdom plucks me
  From over-credulous haste; but God above   120
  Deal between thee and me! for even now
  I put myself to thy direction, and
  Unspeak mine own detraction, here abjure
  The taints and blames I laid upon myself,
  For strangers to my nature. I am yet   125
  Unknown to woman, never was forsworn,
  Scarcely have coveted what was mine own,
  At no time broke my faith, would not betray
  The devil to his fellow, and delight
  No less in truth than life. My first false speaking 130
  Was this upon myself. What I am truly,
  Is thine and my poor country's to command;
  Whither indeed, before thy here-approach,
  Old Siward, with ten thousand warlike men
  Already at a point, was setting forth.   135
  Now we'll together, and the chance of goodness
  Be like our warranted quarrel! Why are you silent?

MACDUFF. Such welcome and unwelcome things at once
  'Tis hard to reconcile.

Enter a DOCTOR.

MALCOLM. Well, more anon. Comes the King forth, I pray
  you?   140

DOCTOR. Ay, sir; there are a crew of wretched souls
  That stay his cure. Their malady convinces
  The great assay of art;[28] but at his touch,
  Such sanctity hath heaven given his hand,
  They presently amend.

MALCOLM.   I thank you, doctor.   145

Exit DOCTOR.

MACDUFF. What's the disease he means?

MALCOLM.   'Tis called the evil:
  A most miraculous work in this good King,
  Which often, since my here-remain in England,
  I have seen him do. How he solicits heaven,
  Himself best knows; but strangely-visited people, 150
  All swoln and ulcerous, pitiful to the eye,

28. The reference is to the legendary cures wrought by King Edward. By touching diseased persons he was claimed to have wrought cures that baffled medical science.

The mere despair of surgery, he cures,
Hanging a golden stamp about their necks,
Put on with holy prayers; and 'tis spoken,
To the succeeding royalty he leaves 155
The healing benediction. With this strange virtue
He hath a heavenly gift of prophecy,
And sundry blessings hang about his throne
That speak him full of grace.

Enter ROSS.

MACDUFF.   See, who comes here.
MALCOLM. My countryman; but yet I know him not. 160
MACDUFF. My ever gentle cousin, welcome hither.
MALCOLM. I know him now. Good God, betimes remove
   The means that makes us strangers![29]
ROSS.   Sir, amen.
MACDUFF. Stands Scotland where it did?
ROSS.   Alas, poor country!
   Almost afraid to know itself! It cannot 165
   Be called our mother, but our grave; where nothing,
   But who knows nothing, is once seen to smile;
   Where sighs and groans and shrieks that rend the air,
   Are made, not marked; where violent sorrow seems
   A modern ecstasy. The dead man's knell 170
   Is there scarce asked for who; and good men's lives
   Expire before the flowers in their caps,
   Dying or ere they sicken.
MACDUFF.   O, relation
   Too nice, and yet too true!
MALCOLM.   What's the newest grief?
ROSS. That of an hour's age doth hiss the speaker; 175
   Each minute teems a new one.
MACDUFF.   How does my wife?
ROSS. Why, well.
MACDUFF.   And all my children?
ROSS.   Well too.
MACDUFF. The tyrant has not battered at their peace?
ROSS. No, they were well at peace when I did leave 'em.
MACDUFF. Be not a niggard of your speech. How goes't? 180
ROSS. When I came hither to transport the tidings,
   Which I have heavily borne, there ran a rumor
   Of many worthy fellows that were out;
   Which was to my belief witnessed the rather,
   For that I saw the tyrant's power afoot. 185
   Now is the time of help. Your eye in Scotland
   Would create soldiers, make our women fight,
   To doff their dire distresses.

29. Malcolm prays for a change that will let him go home and be again familiar with his fellow Scots.

MALCOLM.   Be't their comfort
We are coming thither. Gracious England hath
Lent us good Siward and ten thousand men;   190
An older and a better soldier none
That Christendom gives out.
ROSS.   Would I could answer
This comfort with the like! But I have words
That would be howled out in the desert air,
Where hearing should not latch them.
MACDUFF.   What concern they? 195
The general cause? or is it a fee-grief[30]
Due to some single breast?
ROSS.   No mind that's honest
But in it shares some woe, though the main part
Pertains to you alone.
MACDUFF.   If it be mine,
Keep it not from me, quickly let me have it.   200
ROSS. Let not your ears despise my tongue for ever,
Which shall possess them with the heaviest sound
That ever yet they heard.
MACDUFF.   Hum! I guess at it.
ROSS. Your castle is surprised; your wife and babes
Savagely slaughtered. To relate the manner   205
Were, on the quarry of these murdered deer,
To add the death of you.
MALCOLM.   Merciful heaven!
What, man! ne'er pull your hat upon your brows.
Give sorrow words. The grief that does not speak
Whispers the o'erfraught heart and bids it break.   210
MACDUFF. My children too?
ROSS.   Wife, children, servants, all
That could be found.
MACDUFF.   And I must be from thence?
My wife killed too?
ROSS.   I have said.
MALCOLM.   Be comforted.
Let's make us medicines of our great revenge,
To cure this deadly grief.   215
MACDUFF. He has no children.[31] All my pretty ones?
Did you say all? O hell-kite! All?
What, all my pretty chickens and their dam
At one fell swoop?
MALCOLM. Dispute it like a man.
MACDUFF.   I shall do so;   220
But I must also feel it as a man.
I cannot but remember such things were
That were most precious to me. Did heaven look on

30. **fee-grief**, a personal sorrow.

31. **no children**, Macbeth has no children to let him feel the enormity of this crime.

219

And would not take their part? Sinful Macduff,
They were all struck for thee! Naught that I am,   225
Not for their own demerits, but for mine,
Fell slaughter on their souls. Heaven rest them now!

MALCOLM. Be this the whetstone[32] of your sword. Let grief
Convert to anger; blunt not the heart, enrage it.

MACDUFF. O, I could play the woman with mine eyes,   230
And braggart with my tongue! But, gentle heavens,
Cut short all intermission. Front to front
Bring thou this fiend of Scotland and myself.
Within my sword's length set him; if he 'scape,
Heaven forgive him too!

MALCOLM.   This tune goes manly.   235
Come, go we to the King. Our power is ready;
Our lack is nothing but our leave. Macbeth
Is ripe for shaking, and the powers above
Put on their instruments. Receive what cheer you may;
The night is long that never finds the day.   240

Exeunt.

32. **whetstone**, stone on which to sharpen your sword: your will to act.

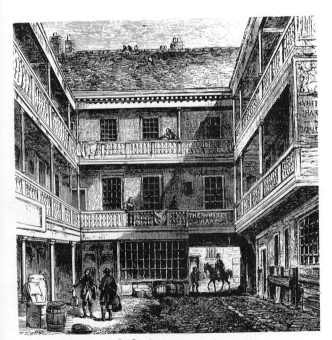

*An inn yard, the forerunner
of the early playhouse.*

ACT IV
MURDER COMPOUNDED

1. What are the three new prophecies the witches make to Macbeth? What questions do they refuse to answer? What is the meaning of the three apparitions Macbeth sees in the witches' cave?

2. Explain these lines:

"From this moment
The very firstlings of my heart shall be
The firstlings of my hand."

3. How does the murder of Macduff's family differ from the murder of Duncan? From the murder of Banquo?

4. What has happened to the Kingdom of Scotland since Macbeth took the crown?

5. In this act, is Macbeth acting with greater decision than in Act I? Is he more or less in control of himself and of events?

⟐Act V

SCENE 1

Dunsinane. Ante-room in the castle

Enter a DOCTOR OF PHYSIC *and a* WAITING-GENTLEWOMAN.

DOCTOR. I have two nights watched with you, but can perceive no truth in your report. When was it she last walked?

GENTLEWOMAN. Since his Majesty went into the field,[1] I have seen her rise from her bed, throw her nightgown upon her, unlock her closet, take forth paper, fold it, write upon't, read it, afterwards seal it, and again return to bed; yet all this while in a most fast sleep.

DOCTOR. A great perturbation in nature, to receive at once the benefit of sleep and do the effects of watching! In this slumbery agitation, besides her walking and other actual performances, what, at any time, have you heard her say?

GENTLEWOMAN. That, sir, which I will not report after her.

DOCTOR. You may to me, and 'tis most meet you should.

GENTLEWOMAN. Neither to you nor any one, having no witness to confirm my speech.

Enter LADY MACBETH, *with a lighted taper.*

Lo you, here she comes! This is her very guise,[2] and, upon my life, fast asleep! Observe her; stand close.

DOCTOR. How came she by that light?

GENTLEWOMAN. Why, it stood by her. She has light by her continually; 'tis her command.

DOCTOR. You see, her eyes are open.

GENTLEWOMAN. Ay, but their sense is shut.

DOCTOR. What is it she does now? Look, how she rubs her hands.

GENTLEWOMAN. It is an accustomed action with her, to seem thus washing her hands. I have known her continue in this a quarter of an hour.

LADY MACBETH. Yet here's a spot.

DOCTOR. Hark! she speaks. I will set down what comes from her, to satisfy my remembrance the more strongly.

LADY MACBETH. Out, damned spot! out, I say! One; two: why, then 'tis time to do't. Hell is murky. Fie, my lord, fie! a soldier, and afeard? What need we fear who knows it, when none can call our power to ac-

1. **into the field,** since Macbeth has been fighting his various enemies.

2. **her very guise,** her accustomed behavior.

Maria Casares as Lady Macbeth.

count? Yet who would have thought the old man to
have had so much blood in him?   40

DOCTOR. Do you mark that?

LADY MACBETH. The thane of Fife had a wife. Where is
she now? What, will these hands ne'er be clean? No
more o' that, my lord, no more o' that. You mar all
with this starting.   45

DOCTOR. Go to, go to! You have known what you should
not.

GENTLEWOMAN. She has spoke what she should not, I am
sure of that. Heaven knows what she has known.

LADY MACBETH. Here's the smell of the blood still. All the   50
perfumes of Arabia will not sweeten this little hand.
Oh, oh, oh!

DOCTOR. What a sigh is there! The heart is sorely charged.

GENTLEWOMAN. I would not have such a heart in my
bosom for the dignity of the whole body.   55

DOCTOR. Well, well, well,—

GENTLEWOMAN. Pray God it be, sir.

DOCTOR. This disease is beyond my practice. Yet I have
known those which have walked in their sleep who
have died holily in their beds.   60

LADY MACBETH. Wash your hands, put on your nightgown, look not so pale!—I tell you yet again, Banquo's buried. He cannot come out on 's grave.

DOCTOR. Even so?

LADY MACBETH. To bed, to bed! There's knocking at the   65
gate. Come, come, come, come, give me your hand.
What's done cannot be undone. To bed, to bed, to
bed!

Exit.

DOCTOR. Will she go now to bed?

GENTLEWOMAN. Directly.   70

DOCTOR. Foul whisperings are abroad. Unnatural deeds
Do breed unnatural troubles. Infected minds
To their deaf pillows will discharge their secrets.
More needs she the divine than the physician.
God, God forgive us all! Look after her;   75
Remove from her the means of all annoyance,[3]   3. **annoyance**, harm.
And still keep eyes upon her. So good night.
My mind she has mated, and amazed my sight.
I think, but dare not speak.

GENTLEWOMAN.   Goodnight, good doctor.   80

Exeunt.

222 CHOICE AND CONSEQUENCE

The country near Dunsinane.

Drum and colors. Enter MENTEITH, CAITHNESS, ANGUS, LENNOX *and Soldiers.*

MENTEITH. The English power is near, led on by Malcolm,
His uncle Siward, and the good Macduff.
Revenges burn in them; for their dear causes
Would to the bleeding and the grim alarm
Excite the mortified man.⁴

ANGUS.   Near Birnam wood   5
Shall we well meet them; that way are they coming.

CAITHNESS. Who knows if Donalbain be with his brother?

LENNOX. For certain, sir, he is not. I have a file
Of all the gentry. There is Siward's son,
And many unrough youths that even now   10
Protest their first of manhood.

MENTEITH.   What does the tyrant?

CAITHNESS. Great Dunsinane he strongly fortifies.
Some say he's mad; others, that lesser hate him,
Do call it valiant fury; but, for certain,
He cannot buckle his distempered cause   15
Within the belt of rule.⁵

ANGUS.   Now does he feel
His secret murders sticking on his hands;
Now minutely revolts upbraid his faith-breach;⁶
Those he commands move only in command,
Nothing in love. Now does he feel his title   20
Hang loose about him, like a giant's robe
Upon a dwarfish thief.

MENTEITH.   Who then shall blame
His pestered senses to recoil and start,
When all that is within him does condemn
Itself for being there?

CAITHNESS.   Well, march we on,   25
To give obedience where 'tis truly owed.
Meet we the medicine of the sickly weal;
And with him pour we, in our country's purge,
Each drop of us.⁷ Or so much as it needs
To dew the sovereign flower⁸ and drown the weeds.   30

LENNOX.   Make we our march towards Birnam.
Exeunt, marching.

4. **mortified man,** even a nearly dead or paralyzed person would be roused by the cause against Macbeth.

5. . . . **belt of rule,** Macbeth's cause is so diseased that he has no control over it.

6. **minutely . . . faith-breach,** every minute nobles revolt against Macbeth reminding him of his own disloyalty.

7. **each drop of us,** every drop of blood is pledged to Malcolm.
8. **sovereign flower,** Malcolm.

SCENE 3

Dunsinane. A room in the Castle.

Enter MACBETH, DOCTOR, *and Attendants.*

MACBETH. Bring me no more reports. Let them fly all!
  Till Birnam wood remove to Dunsinane,
  I cannot taint with fear. What's the boy Malcolm?
  Was he not born of woman? The spirits that know
  All mortal consequences have pronounced me thus: 5
  "Fear not, Macbeth. No man that's born of woman
  Shall e'er have power upon thee." Then fly, false
    thanes,
  And mingle with the English epicures.[9]
  The mind I sway by and the heart I bear
  Shall never sag with doubt nor shake with fear.   10

Enter SERVANT.

  The devil damn thee black, thou cream-faced loon!
  Where got'st thou that goose look?
SERVANT. There is ten thousand—
MACBETH.   Geese, villain?
SERVANT.   Soldiers, sir.
MACBETH. Go prick thy face and over-red thy fear,
  Thou lily-livered boy. What soldiers, patch?[10]   15
  Death of thy soul! Those linen cheeks of thine
  Are counselors to fear. What soldiers, whey-face?
SERVANT. The English force, so please you.
MACBETH. Take thy face hence.

  Exit SERVANT.

                    Seyton!—I am sick at heart,
  When I behold—Seyton, I say!—This push   20
  Will cheer me ever, or disseat me now.
  I have lived long enough. My way of life
  Is fallen into the sere, the yellow leaf;
  And that which should accompany old age,
  As honor, love, obedience, troops of friends,   25
  I must not look to have; but, in their stead,
  Curses, not loud but deep, mouth-honor,[11] breath,
  Which the poor heart would fain deny, and dare not.
  Seyton!

  Enter SEYTON.

SEYTON. What's your gracious pleasure?
MACBETH.   What news more?   30
SEYTON. All is confirmed, my lord, which was reported.
MACBETH. I'll fight, till from my bones my flesh be hacked.
  Give me my armor.
SEYTON.   'Tis not needed yet.
MACBETH. I'll put it on.
  Send out moe horses, skirr[12] the country round;   35

9. **epicures,** the Scots regarded the English as luxury lovers.

10. **patch,** fool.

11. **mouth-honor,** lip service, not allegiance of the heart.

12. **skirr,** fly, scurry, scour for enemies.

Hang those that talk of fear. Give me mine armor.
How does your patient, doctor?

DOCTOR.   Not so sick, my lord,
As she is troubled with thick-coming fancies
That keep her from her rest.

MACBETH.   Cure her of that.
Canst thou not minister to a mind diseased,   40
Pluck from the memory a rooted sorrow,
Raze out the written troubles of the brain,
And with some sweet oblivious antidote
Cleanse the stuffed bosom of that perilous stuff
Which weighs upon the heart?

DOCTOR.   Therein the patient   45
Must minister to himself.

MACBETH. Throw physic to the dogs, I'll none of it!
Come, put mine armor on. Give me my staff.
Seyton, send out. Doctor, the thanes fly from me.
Come, sir, dispatch. If thou couldst, doctor, cast   50
The water of my land,[13] find her disease
And purge it to a sound and pristine health,
I would applaud thee to the very echo,
That should applaud again.—Pull't off, I say.—
What rhubarb, senna, or what purgative drug,   55
Would scour these English hence? Hear'st thou of
    them?

DOCTOR. Ay, my good lord. Your royal preparation
Makes us hear something.

MACBETH.   Bring it after me.
I will not be afraid of death and bane
Till Birnam forest come to Dunsinane.   60

DOCTOR. (*Aside*) Were I from Dunsinane away and clear,
Profit again should hardly draw me here.

Exeunt.

13. **cast the water of my land,** diagnose
Scotland's disease.

SCENE 4

Country near Birnam Wood.

Drum and colors. Enter MALCOLM, SIWARD, *and his* SON,
    MACDUFF, MENTEITH, CAITHNESS, ANGUS, LENNOX, ROSS,
    and Soldiers, marching.

MALCOLM. Cousins, I hope the days are near at hand
That chambers will be safe.

MENTEITH.   We doubt it nothing.

SIWARD. What wood is this before us?

MENTEITH.   The wood of Birnam.

MALCOLM. Let every soldier hew him down a bough
  And bear't before him. Thereby shall we shadow   5
  The numbers of our host, and make discovery
  Err in report of us.
SOLDIERS.   It shall be done.
SIWARD. We learn no other but the confident tyrant
  Keeps still in Dunsinane, and will endure
  Our setting down before't.
MALCOLM.   'Tis his main hope;   10
  For where there is advantage to be given,
  Both more and less have given him the revolt;
  And none serve with him but constrainèd things,
  Whose hearts are absent too.
MACDUFF.   Let our just censures
  Attend the true event,[14] and put we on   15   14. **Attend the true event,** judgment can
  Industrious soldiership.   wait for the outcome, now we must be
SIWARD.   The time approaches   skillful soldiers.
  That will with due decision make us know
  What we shall say we have, and what we owe.
  Thoughts speculative their unsure hopes relate,[15]   15. Until we've won we're only guess-
  But certain issue strokes must arbitrate;   20   ing.
  Toward which advance the war.

  Exeunt, marching.

                    SCENE 5

Dunsinane. Within the Castle.

Enter MACBETH, SEYTON, *and Soldiers, with Drums and
  Colors.*

MACBETH. Hang out our banners on the outwards walls.
  The cry is still, "They come!" Our castle's strength
  Will laugh a siege to scorn. Here let them lie
  Till famine and the ague eat them up.
  Were they not forced[16] with those that should be ours,   5   16. **forced,** reinforced.
  We might have met them dareful, beard to beard,
  And beat them backward home.

  A cry of women, within.

                              What is that noise?
SEYTON. It is the cry of women, my good lord.

  Exit.

MACBETH. I have almost forgot the taste of fears.
  The time has been, my senses would have cooled   10
  To hear a night-shriek, and my fell of hair
  Would at a dismal treatise rouse and stir

As life were in't. I have supped full with horrors;
Direness, familiar to my slaughterous thoughts,
Cannot once start me.

Reenter SEYTON.

        Wherefore was that cry? 15
SEYTON. The Queen, my lord, is dead.
MACBETH. She should have died hereafter;
  There would have been a time for such a word.
  Tomorrow, and tomorrow, and tomorrow
  Creeps in this petty pace from day to day 20
  To the last syllable of recorded time;
  And all our yesterdays have lighted fools
  The way to dusty death. Out, out, brief candle!
  Life's but a walking shadow, a poor player,
  That struts and frets his hour upon the stage 25
  And then is heard no more. It is a tale
  Told by an idiot, full of sound and fury,
  Signifying nothing.

Enter a MESSENGER.

  Thou com'st to use thy tongue. Thy story quickly.
MESSENGER. Gracious my Lord, 30
  I should report that which I say I saw,
  But know not how to do it.
MACBETH.   Well, say, sir.
MESSENGER. As I did stand my watch upon the hill,
  I looked toward Birnam, and anon, methought
  The wood began to move.
MACBETH.   Liar and slave! 35
MESSENGER. Let me endure your wrath if't be not so.
  Within this three mile may you see it coming;
  I say, a moving grove.
MACBETH.   If thou speak'st false,
  Upon the next tree shalt thou hang alive,
  Till famine cling thee. If thy speech be sooth, 40
  I care not if thou dost for me as much.
  I pull in resolution, and begin
  To doubt the equivocation of the fiend,[17]
  That lies like truth: "Fear not, till Birnam wood
  Do come to Dunsinane." And now a wood 45
  Comes toward Dunsinane. Arm, arm, and out!
  If this which he avouches does appear,
  There is nor flying hence nor tarrying here.
  I 'gin to be aweary of the sun,
  And wish the estate o' the world were now undone. 50

17. **doubt the equivocation of the fiend,** begins to suspect that the devil has been misleading him by double meanings.

Ring the alarum bell! Blow, wind! come, wrack!
At least we'll die with harness on our back.

Exeunt.

SCENE 6

Dunsinane. Before MACBETH's *Castle.*

Drum and colors. Enter MALCOLM, SIWARD, MACDUFF, *and
    their army, with boughs.*

MALCOLM. Now near enough. Your leavy[18] screens throw
        down,
    And show like those you are. You, worthy uncle,
    Shall with my cousin, your right noble son,
    Lead our first battle. Worthy Macduff and we
    Shall take upon's what else remains to do,   5
    According to our order.
SIWARD.   Fare you well.
    Do we but find the tyrant's power tonight,
    Let us be beaten, if we cannot fight.
MACDUFF. Make all our trumpets speak; give them all
        breath,
    Those clamorous harbingers of blood and death.   10

    Exeunt. Alarums continued.

18. **leavy**, leafy.

SCENE 7

Another part of the field.

Enter MACBETH.

MACBETH. They have tied me to a stake; I cannot fly,
    But bearlike I must fight the course.[19] What's he
    That was not born of woman? Such a one
    Am I to fear, or none.

    Enter YOUNG SIWARD.

YOUNG SIWARD. What is thy name?
MACBETH.   Thou'lt be afraid to hear it.   5
YOUNG SIWARD. No; though thou call'st thyself a hotter
        name
    Than any is in hell.
MACBETH.   My name's Macbeth.
YOUNG SIWARD. The devil himself could not pronounce a
        title
    More hateful to mine ear.
MACBETH.   No, nor more fearful.

19. **fight the course,** Macbeth likens
himself to a chained bear being baited.
The course is a round or bout; here, the
battle.

YOUNG SIWARD. Thou liest, abhorrèd tyrant; with my
    sword   10
  I'll prove the lie thou speak'st.

They fight, and YOUNG SIWARD *is slain.*

MACBETH.   Thou wast born of woman.
  But swords I smile at, weapons laugh to scorn,
  Brandished by man that's of a woman born.

Exit.

Alarums. Enter MACDUFF.

MACDUFF. That way the noise is. Tyrant, show thy face!
  If thou be'st slain and with no stroke of mine,   15
  My wife and children's ghosts will haunt me still.
  I cannot strike at wretched kerns, whose arms
  Are hired to bear their staves. Either thou, Macbeth,
  Or else my sword with an unbattered edge
  I sheathe again undeeded. There thou shouldst be;   20
  By this great clatter, one of greatest note
  Seems bruited.[20] Let me find him, fortune!   20. **bruited,** reported, rumored.
  And more I beg not.

Exit. Alarums.

Enter MALCOLM *and* SIWARD.

SIWARD. This way, my lord; the castle's gently rendered:[21]   21. **rendered,** yielded, surrendered
  The tyrant's people on both sides do fight;   without great struggle.
  The noble thanes do bravely in the war;   25
  The day almost itself professes yours,[22]   22. **professed yours,** claims to be yours.
  And little is to do.
MALCOLM.   We have met with foes
  That strike beside us.[23]   23. **strike beside us,** Macbeth's followers
SIWARD.   Enter, sir, the castle.   seem deliberately to miss Malcolm's men.
                                                        They are halfhearted in their cause.

Exeunt. Alarum.

SCENE 8

Another part of the field.

Enter MACBETH.

MACBETH. Why should I play the Roman fool and die
  On mine own sword? Whiles I see lives, the gashes
  Do better upon them.

Enter MACDUFF.

MACDUFF.   Turn, hell-hound, turn!
MACBETH. Of all men else I have[24] avoided thee.   24. **have,** would have.
  But get thee back. My soul is too much charged   5
  With blood of thine already.

MACDUFF.   I have no words;
  My voice is in my sword, thou bloodier villain
  Than terms can give thee out!

  They fight.

MACBETH.   Thou losest labor.
  As easy mayst thou the intrenchant air
  With thy keen sword impress as make me bleed.   10
  Let fall thy blade on vulnerable crests;
  I bear a charmèd life, which must not yield
  To one of woman born.
MACDUFF.   Despair thy charm,
  And let the angel whom thou still hast served
  Tell thee, Macduff was from his mother's womb   15
  Untimely ripped.
MACBETH. Accursèd be that tongue that tells me so,
  For it hath cowed my better part of man!
  And be these juggling fiends no more believed,
  That palter[25] with us in a double sense,   20   25. **palter,** trick, deceive.
  That keep the word of promise to our ear,
  And break it to our hope. I'll not fight with thee.
MACDUFF. Then yield thee, coward,
  And live to be the show and gaze o' the time.[26]   26. **gaze o' the time,** the public spec-
  We'll have thee, as our rarer monsters are,   25   tacle of the age.
  Painted upon a pole, and underwrit,
  "Here may you see the tyrant."
MACBETH.   I will not yield,
  To kiss the ground before young Malcolm's feet
  And to be baited with the rabble's curse.
  Though Birnam wood be come to Dunsinane,   30
  And thou opposed, being of no woman born,
  Yet I will try the last. Before my body
  I throw my warlike shield. Lay on, Macduff,
  And damned be him that first cries "Hold, enough!"

  Exeunt, fighting. Alarums.

  Retreat. Flourish. Enter, with drum and colors, MAL-
  COLM, SIWARD, THANES, *and Soldiers.*

MALCOLM. I would the friends we miss were safe arrived.   35
SIWARD. Some must go off;[27] and yet, by these I see,   27. **go off,** be lost, killed.
  So great a day as this is cheaply bought.
MALCOLM. Macduff is missing, and your noble son.
ROSS. Your son, my lord, has paid a soldier's debt.
  He only lived but till he was a man;   40
  The which no sooner had his prowess confirmed
  In the unshrinking station where he fought
  But like a man he died.

SIWARD.   Then he is dead?

ROSS. Ay, and brought off the field. Your cause of sorrow
    Must not be measured by his worth, for then   45
    It hath no end.

SIWARD.   Had he his hurts before?

ROSS. Ay, on the front.

SIWARD.   Why then, God's soldier be he!
    Had I as many sons as I have hairs,
    I would not wish them to a fairer death.
    And so his knell is knolled.

MALCOLM.   He's worth more sorrow,   50
    And that I'll spend for him.

SIWARD.   He's worth no more.
    They say he parted well and paid his score;
    And so, God be with him! Here comes newer comfort.

Reenter MACDUFF, *with* MACBETH's *head.*

MACDUFF. Hail, King! for so thou art. Behold where
      stands
    The usurper's cursed head. The time is free.   55
    I see thee compassed with thy kingdom's pearl,[28]
    That speak my salutation in their minds;
    Whose voices I desire aloud with mine:
    Hail, King of Scotland!

ALL.   Hail, King of Scotland!

Flourish.

MALCOLM. We shall not spend a large expense of time   60
    Before we reckon with your several loves,
    And make us even with you.[29] My thanes and kinsmen,
    Henceforth be earls, the first that ever Scotland
    In such an honor named. What's more to do,
    Which would be planted newly with the time,   65
    As calling home our exiled friends abroad
    That fled the snares of watchful tyranny,
    Producing forth the cruel ministers
    Of this dead butcher and his fiendlike queen,
    Who, as 'tis thought, by self and violent hands   70
    Took off her life; this, and what needful else
    That calls upon us, by the grace of Grace
    We will perform in measure, time and place.
    So thanks to all at once and to each one,
    Whom we invite to see us crowned at Scone.   75

Flourish. Exeunt.

28. **kingdom's pearl,** the royal jewels of Scotland.

29. **even with you,** we (I) will reward you promptly.

THE PROPHECY FULFILLED

1. What are the memories that Lady Macbeth cannot rid herself of?

2. Trace Macbeth's changes of mood throughout this act. How does Macbeth react to his wife's death? What does this suggest about the changed relationship between them? What does it show about Macbeth's own character at this point?

3. How is each of the witches' prophecies fulfilled?

4. How do Macbeth's better qualities—such as courage and humaneness—show themselves during this act? Does this make *Macbeth* a greater and more interesting play than if Shakespeare had let Macbeth become nothing else but a villain who is out of control?

5. With what change of mood does the play end? What indications are there of the kind of king Malcolm will be?

WORDS

A. Use context clues to try to guess the meanings of the italicized words in the following phrases and clauses from Act IV:

1. Sweet *bodements!* good!

2. While you perform your *antic* round. . . .

3. Let this *pernicious* hour/Stand aye accursed. . . .

4. I . . . here *abjure*/The taints and blames I laid upon myself.

Look up each of these words in your dictionary and check your surmises against the definitions.

B. For reasonably full understanding of the play, to what extent do you need to know the exact meanings of the following words from Scene 1, Act IV: *entrails, fillet, fenny, newt, adder, maw, gall, yew, chaudron?* In general, when is it essential that you learn the meaning of a word new to you? When can you safely skip looking up a word? Find other words from Acts IV and V whose full meanings you do not need to know.

C. It will be obvious to you that in modern English many a common word has many different meanings. The *setting* of the sun is not like the *setting* of a trap. A musical *round* is not like a *round* of golf or a *round* of applause. A *break* in the weather is not like a *break* in a fabric or in a window pane. When a drama critic comments that

an actor "*played* the king as though somebody else was going to *play* the ace," the critic humorously changes the meanings of the words *play* and *king*. Before we can interpret a simile or a metaphor we must, of course, realize in what *sense* to interpret each of the words used. We cannot interpret common phrases of English correctly if we do not assign appropriate rather than inappropriate meanings to the words used. "To suffer a *check*" means little if we interpret *check* as a *bank account check* or as a *checked pattern* in a fabric. "Not worth a *hill* of beans" becomes a rather odd expression if one does not understand that *hill* means a little mound of earth around a growing plant. This problem besets us as we try to read Shakespeare. When the doctor says of Lady Macbeth, "My mind she has mated," he is not using *mate* in the sense of "join or couple" but *mate* as it is used in chess to mean *subdue* or *conquer*. What do the following expressions mean in Shakespeare? Pay particular attention to the italicized words in these quotations.

1. That I may tell pale-hearted fear it *lies*. . . .

2. Though all things foul would wear the brows of *grace*. . . .

3. All the particulars of vice so *grafted*. . . .

4. . . . that I should *forge*/Quarrels unjust. . . .

5. What, all my pretty chickens and their *dam*. . . .

6. But certain issue *strokes* must arbitrate. . . .

7. Direness . . . cannot once *start* me.

8. But bearlike I must fight the *course*.

9. They say he parted well and paid his *score*. . . .

10. . . . the cruel *ministers*/Of this dead butcher. . . .

I
TRAGEDY OF AMBITION

All people bear the seeds of both good and evil within them. *Macbeth* is the story of a brave and loyal soldier who allows his ambition to place him on the road to his own destruction. But Macbeth is not merely a "villain," that is, a character who is wholly evil. Throughout the play we see that Macbeth suffers from a deeply troubled conscience. Neither he nor his wife finds any pleasure or comfort in their "borrowed robes" as King and Queen. Macbeth, like most tyrants, becomes wilder and bloodier in his tyranny. The price he pays for power is a heavy one: the crumbling of his own personality. At the end of the play he rises again to majesty by returning to his noble self—a brave warrior. But by now his cause is lost.

Macbeth and Lady Macbeth demonstrate how our choices can bring about appalling consequences beyond our control.

1. Trace some of the choices made by characters in *Macbeth* and show the consequences that sprang from them.

2. Discuss *Macbeth* as a tragedy. Base your discussion on the description of tragedy on pages 4–5.

II
IMPLICATIONS

A. Words spoken by a character in a play must be considered within the context of the drama. For example, in Act II, Scene 3, Macbeth has slaughtered Duncan's servants to hide the fact that he himself has killed the King: He cries:

> Who can be wise, amazed, temp'rate, and
>   furious,
> Loyal and neutral, in a moment? No man.

There is wisdom in these words, but we must understand that Macbeth does not intend to utter a "truth" but is here speaking out of sheer hypocrisy. Apart from the dramatic context, however, there is a great deal of truth and universal meaning in many Shakespearean lines. Do you find any valid meaning today in these lines from *Macbeth*?

1.   But 'tis strange:
> And oftentimes, to win us to our harm,
> The instruments of darkness tell us truths,
> Win us with honest trifles, to betray's
> In deepest consequence.

2. False face must hide what the false heart doth know.

3. Words to the heat of deeds too cold breath gives.

4. To show an unfelt sorrow is an office
Which the false man does easy.

5.   Naught's had, all's spent,
Where our desire is got without content.

6. 'Tis safer to be that which we destroy
Than by destruction dwell in doubtful joy.

7.   Things without all remedy
Should be without regard: what's done is done.

8. They say, blood will have blood.

B. Are the following statements true or false? Find support for your opinion in the selection.

1. Macbeth was led into evil almost solely because of Lady Macbeth's determination.

2. Macbeth's indecision to commit the murder shows only that he is weak.

3. The murder actually drives Macbeth and Lady Macbeth apart.

4. Once the first murder is committed, the other murders are inevitable.

5. Macbeth could have been a force for great and positive good.

6. This play demonstrates that a move in the wrong direction must be followed by acts leading in the same direction.

7. Shakespeare wanted his audience to feel sympathy with Macbeth.

8. If tragedy shows characters experiencing great anguish of spirit which gives a feeling of release and purification to the beholder, then *Macbeth* is not tragedy.

9. Unlike the tragic Creon, Macbeth never really repents his actions.

III
TECHNIQUES
Character Development

In this section, attention is directed to the author's skill in handling two elements of his art: the way in which he creates and develops character and the way in which he uses imagery in his language.

Characters in a story may be said to be flat or round. Flat characters are those labeled by the writer as particular kinds of people; they never change: Nothing is added or subtracted from their original definition throughout the telling of the story. An example of a flat character is the porter in *Macbeth*. Short-story writers often depend on flat characters, especially for background characters whom they do not have time to develop. In novels or plays, many of the secondary characters fall within this category. Round characters are those who develop and grow; they are not all good or all bad. New facets of their personalities, their moral standards, their motivations are revealed as the story progresses. Usually the heroes of a novel or play—at least of a *good* novel or play—are fully rounded characters; even in a short story, the leading characters may have a three-dimensional quality.

The terms "flat" and "round" imply an evaluation by the reader and, obviously, characters may fall somewhere between the two stated divisions. It would be false to assume that all flat characterizations are poor and all round ones splendid. Mr. Micawber in Dickens' *David Copperfield* is a memorable example of a flat character.

How then do writers make characters seem to be alive, real people? They may reveal characters in several ways: first, by either directly describing characters or allowing people in the story to do so; second, by allowing the reader to judge characters through their interactions with others in the story; third, by letting characters reveal themselves through soliloquies or by letting the reader slip inside the characters' minds.

1. What in Macbeth's character makes him susceptible to the witches' prophecies?

2. Read the following lines. Write on a sheet of paper a word or two to tell what each succeeding quotation reveals or reinforces about Macbeth's character.

Sergeant, Act I, *scene* 2
For brave Macbeth—well he deserves that name,—

Duncan, Act I, *scene* 2
What he hath lost, noble Macbeth hath won.

Lady Macbeth, Act I, *scene* 5
                Yet do I fear thy nature;
It is too full o' the milk of human kindness
To catch the nearest way. Thou wouldst be great,
Art not without ambition, but without
The illness should attend it.

Macbeth, Act I, *scene* 7
                I have no spur
To prick the sides of my intent, but only
Vaulting ambition, . . .

Macbeth, Act I, *scene* 7
We will proceed no further in this business.

Macbeth, Act II, *scene* 1
Is this a dagger which I see before me,
The handle toward my hand?

Macbeth, Act II, *scene* 2
But wherefore could not I pronounce "Amen"?

Macbeth, Act III, *scene* 2
              Better be with the dead,
Whom we, to gain our peace, have sent to peace,

Than on the torture of the mind to lie
In restless ecstasy.

Macbeth, Act III, *scene* 2
Things bad begun make strong themselves by ill.

Macduff, Act IV, *scene* 3
                Not in the legions
Of horrid hell can come a devil more damned
In evils to top Macbeth.

Macbeth, Act V, *scene* 3
I will not be afraid of death and bane
Till Birnam forest come to Dunsinane.

Macbeth, Act V, *scene* 5
She should have died hereafter;
There would have been a time for such a word.

Macbeth, Act V, *scene* 8
                Lay on, Macduff,
And damned be him that first cries "Hold, enough!"

3. Do Macbeth's actions spring from his personality or are they seemingly unrelated? How many different methods has Shakespeare used to reveal Macbeth's character?

4. Reread Scenes 5 and 7 in Act I, and Scenes 1 and 2 in Act II. From these write a paragraph giving your impression of Lady Macbeth. Share these descriptions in class. Considering the general class picture of Lady Macbeth, do you think Shakespeare prepared you for Lady Macbeth's madness at the end of the play?

5. Do you think Shakespeare made the following characters round or flat?

  a. Banquo

  b. Malcolm

  c. Macduff

Imagery

Shakespeare is one of the greatest of English poets and his lines sparkle with fascinating images. In a few words he can call up a visual picture which communicates a complicated emotion. He might have had Macbeth say merely, "O, my mind is troubled, and full of ugly thoughts." Instead, he used a brilliant *image*: "O, full of scorpions is my mind, dear wife." Imagery is basic to poetry, and it is most commonly found in metaphors and similes. The only real difference between these is that a simile is usually introduced by the word *like* or *as*. An example of a simile is Lady Macbeth's

Your face, my thane, is as a book, where men
May read strange matters.

An example of metaphor is Macbeth's

I have supped full with horrors.

Note the simple yet vivid language. By using the word "supped," Shakespeare has compared Macbeth's evil deeds and thoughts to food at a banquet. But Shakespeare implies that the soul can become stuffed with evil as the body can with food. The idea has gained dimension, complication, color, by use of the comparison. And it has been expressed in only a few words. (For a further discussion of imagery in poetry see page 105.)

A series of quotations from *Macbeth* follows. Use the lines as a springboard. Discuss what picture, emotion, mood each image generates, and how effective you find it.

1. The earth hath bubbles, as the water has,
   And these are of them.

2. Sleep that knits up the raveled sleeve of care. . . .

3. There's daggers in men's smiles. . . .

4. We have scotched the snake, not killed it.

5.   look like the innocent flower,
   But be the serpent under't.

6. Macbeth is ripe for shaking. . . .

7.   My way of life
   Is fallen into the sere, the yellow leaf. . . .

8.   Out, out, brief candle!
   Life's but a walking shadow, a poor player,
   That struts and frets his hour upon the stage
   And then is heard no more. It is a tale
   Told by an idiot, full of sound and fury,
   Signifying nothing.

The London of Shakespeare's day. The Globe Theater, lower center, is on the Bankside in Southwark, south of the River Thames.

EDITH HAMILTON

While two of her books became classics during her lifetime, Edith Hamilton
(1867–1963) did not begin to write until she was nearly sixty. Educated as a
scholar, she was taught to read Latin at seven and soon was reading
both Latin and Greek for pleasure, as easily as English. Widely educated,
Hamilton was head of the Bryn Mawr School, a preparatory school
in Baltimore, from 1896 until 1922. It was after she retired from this position
that she began her second profession—that of a writer. A friend working on
Theatre Arts magazine suggested that she write an article on tragedy
for that periodical. The essay became the first chapter of her book,
The Greek Way, 1930. Critics have accused her of overlooking the unpleasant
details of ancient Greek life. To this charge she answered that she judged the Greeks
by their own standards, not by those of modern life, and she found the two standards
not interchangeable. Her life was crowned by a moment of exuberant pleasure
when at the age of eighty-nine the King of Greece decorated her and proclaimed her
an honorary citizen of Athens as she stood in the ancient theater of
Herodes Atticus[1] at the foot of the Acropolis. In loud, clear tones, for all to hear,
she shouted, "I am an Athenian! I am an Athenian! This is the proudest
day of my life!"

Witness to the Truth: Socrates

Socrates never tried to put the truth he had
found into words. He thought as Christ did that
it was impossible to tell men[2] what it was and
then expect them to know it. He too had no ordered philosophy or theology and he too never
wrote a word down. Like Christ he lived his
truth and died for it. A life can be more lasting
than systems of thought. Socrates has outlasted
two millenniums.

He was a witness to all that is contained in
the word goodness, to its reality and its power.
It was said of a great English scientist, "He
made it easy for people to believe in goodness."
This Socrates did as few since the beginning of
history. No one who knew him could doubt
that, as he said, "Goodness has a most real and
actual existence." He left the memory of a life
which conquered through it, which was never
defeated though he was imprisoned and put to
death, and which has been kept in men's memories among the things that are eternal. During
the four hundred years between his death and
Christ's the Greek and the Roman world turned
to him to learn how to live, and ever since men
have seen through him the changelessness of
the truth, the enduring verity of what he lived
by. "That which existing among men is the form
and likeness of God," Plato said.

Reprinted from *Witness to the Truth* by Edith Hamilton. By
permission of W. W. Norton & Company, Inc. Copyright
1948, © 1957 by W. W. Norton & Company, Inc. Copyright
renewed 1975 by Dorian F. Fielding.

1. **Herodes Atticus** (hə rō′dēz at′ə kəs), a Greek scholar
responsible for the building of the theater in Athens in
the second century A.D.
2. Throughout the selection, Hamilton uses *man* in its
original sense of *person* or *human being*.

He lived during the great age of Greece, in Athens of the fifth century B.C. No figure was more familiar there than his. He did not teach from some pulpit or teacher's desk, withdrawn from men in order to think great thoughts or to find God. The busy life of the city was his life. He knew everybody and everybody knew him. Wherever men met he was at home. In a sense he did not teach at all. He just talked spontaneously on anything that happened to come up as he walked the streets or went into a gymnasium or dined with a friend. He never thought, or at any rate he never spoke, about mankind or humanity or society or the public. What he was interested in was each individual he met. He felt an intense, overwhelming desire for the good of that particular person. Nothing could have been farther from him than the idea that for hundreds of years after his death people would turn to him for light. He never gave a thought to the future. He wanted good things for the Athenians whom he saw every day and whom he knew and loved and understood, and he wanted, so greatly, to open, at least a little bit, the eyes of that delightful young fellow who had just come up to him, or speak a word to that anxious father who was troubled about his son.

Athens was more and more hard pressed during his later life; she was at war and hardships were the order of the day but there was always time to stop and hear what Socrates was saying. He had a genius for conversation and the keen-witted Athenians were an eager audience. They were fighting, but they were thinking too, and ideas were very important. One of Plato's dialogues in which Socrates is the speaker begins: "Yesterday evening I got back from the army and I went straight to the gymnasium near the Archon's[1] porch and found a number of people I knew. I was quite unexpected and they all greeted me and asked, 'However did you escape?' 'Well,' I replied, 'you see I am here.' 'It's reported that the battle went badly and many people we knew fell.' 'Not far from the truth,' I said. 'You were there?' 'Yes.' 'Well then, do sit down and tell us all about it.' So I

Edith Hamilton, whose writing career began after she retired from twenty-six years as teacher and administrator of the Bryn Mawr School.

sat down and gave them the news from the army. But when there had been enough of this I began to ask them how things were going on at home, especially how the pursuit of philosophy was prospering."

That is what Athens was like during the greater part of Socrates' life. The importance of "philosophy," the search for wisdom, for the truth, never lapsed or receded into the background, and he was happy and at home there. But later a change came over the city. The war with Sparta lasted twenty-seven years and ended in total defeat for the Athenians. It shook the moral and spiritual foundations of Athens and brought a great part of them crashing down. The old ideas of right and wrong seemed shown up as false or at least futile. The Spartan idea of what was good and desirable was quite unlike the Athenian, and the Spartans won the war. By every realistic standard they proved that what they thought was right and what the Athenians thought was wrong. The great

---

1. **Archon** (är′kon), a chief magistrate or ruling officer.

historian of the war, Thucydides,[2] says the whole point of view in Athens changed, the very meaning of words was altered, vices were praised, virtues despised. The reckless disregard of life was held to be fine and courageous; kindness and generosity were scorned as proofs of softness and weakness.

The lowest depth was reached when the city put Socrates to death. That was in 399, five years after the war ended, when he was seventy years old. The charge was "Impiety," that he had induced the young men of the city to give up believing in the state religion which was still Homer's jovial, amoral Olympians,[3] impossible for any thinking person to take seriously. The indictment ran: "Socrates is an evil-doer and a corrupter of young men because he does not receive the gods the state receives, but introduces new divinities." In all the history of Athens we know of only four persons who were persecuted for their opinions and of the four, Socrates alone suffered the death penalty. But by that time Athens was ruined, overwhelmed by all that a crushing defeat brings to a proud people. The Athenians had lost their faith in everything they had stood for, their courage, too. They were a crushed, humiliated people, and they were afraid. They could not face the future; they could only look back, with an agony of regret for what they had lost. The passion for freedom, the instinct for reasonableness, which had marked them beyond all other qualities, were swept away in a wave of reaction. Socrates had new ideas; the gods he believed in had not the slightest resemblance to the old, and only the old was dear at that moment of Athens' misery. The city which had been given to hospitality to men of all sorts and conditions of opinions, and which hundreds of years later, St. Paul reported, was desirous of nothing so much as to hear something new, condemned to death her best and greatest citizen because he taught a new religion. And for a moment Athens was satisfied that she had taken a step back to the familiar and the safe and away from the dark menace of the future.

As a teacher of religion Socrates was a very odd figure, an evangelist such as there has never been before or since. He lived in an evil day, but he never denounced any of the evils. He never thundered anathemas as the men of righteousness have had the habit of doing against the wickedness of their times. Nothing could appear less like Isaiah and Jeremiah and all the other passionate reformers through the ages than he does as we see him in Plato's pages, so gentle, urbane, and companionable, thinking only of winning men over, persuading them, convincing them, never denouncing or threatening them.

His temper of mind was all the other way. He did not look at people with stern disapproval; he liked them. Their ways did not irritate or anger him; they did often amuse him. He had a gay spirit; he saw the world with a humorous eye. "Bless me," he said, looking around in the market where all an Athenian wanted lay piled in glowing profusion, "what a lot of things there are a man can do without." In the brilliant society of Periclean[4] Athens he was welcomed everywhere as the best of company. He had but to enter a gymnasium, that Athenian equivalent of a club, and eager young men gathered around him, greeting him as a boon companion, joking with him and making fun of him, with an undertone of loving delight in him. They really caught a glimpse of something lofty and beautiful in him never seen before.

He had a wonderful gift for making people feel at home with him. He did not seem to be trying to instruct them; he put forward no claim to know better than they did. He had a most disarming way of talking, a great taste for homely illustration and a great distaste for high-sounding talk, out of which, however, he got much amusement when anybody indulged in it. No one could be less pretentious. He seemed always to imply, "I know I may be

---

2. **Thucydides** (thü sid'ə dēz'), a Greek historian whose dates are approximately 470–400 B.C.
3. **Olympians,** gods and goddesses.
4. **Periclean** (per'ə klē'ən), relating to Pericles, the Athenian leader and general who died in 429 B.C.

quite wrong." And this was not merely his manner; he really had no fixed creed, no set of doctrines, which he felt he must make others believe. He had a profound conviction which ruled his life and which it was the effort of his life to communicate, but it did not present itself to him as a series of truths which it was imperative for all to accept. As a Greek his mind did not work that way. Greek religion was developed not by priests or prophets or saints, but by poets and artists and philosophers, all of them people who instinctively leave thought free. An Athenian's dearest right was to think for himself and he used it to the full.

So Socrates was only going along with his hearers when he declined to do their thinking for them. What he wanted was something much more difficult than that. Aristotle says happiness is activity of soul. It is a precise description of Socrates' way of making men happy. "God has sent me to attack this city," he told the Athenians, "as if it were a great horse sluggish from its size, which needs to be aroused by a gadfly. I think I am that gadfly. I will never cease from exhorting you: Are you not ashamed of caring so much for money and for reputation and for honour? Will you not think about wisdom and truth and what is good for your souls?" He would sting them into activity to see for themselves; he would not show them what they ought to see. His talks with them usually ended in some such fashion, as, "This may be true, but is also quite likely to be untrue, and therefore I would not have you too easily persuaded. Reflect well—and when you have found the truth, come and tell me."

No one less dogmatic ever lived. He spent his life in the search for the truth; it was all-important to him, but he did not leave behind him one hard and fast definition. He never stated, he only suggested—with a question mark. In his speech at his trial he spoke of "a divine agency which comes to me, a sign, a kind of a voice, which I was first conscious of as a child. It never commands me to do anything, but it does forbid me." That was all. He made no attempt to clarify or classify the ex-

perience; he knew he could not imprison within a formula the truth he saw. "To find the Maker and Father of all is hard," he said, "and having found him it is impossible to utter him."

But underneath this inconclusiveness was a clear purpose and a definite method. "The unexamined life is not worth living," he said. Each man must examine his own, look at himself, at what he is, in the light of the truth he could find if he sought for it. Socrates never offered to lead him to it. As he saw it, that would mean little. Only what each man discovered for himself could be actually true to him. The truth he accepted at secondhand on the word of another remained always unreal to him. The one way to help men was to make them want to find. "Although my mind is far from wise," he said, "some of those who come to me make astonishing progress. They discover for themselves, not from me—and yet I am an instrument in the hands of God."

He was always the seeker, inquiring, not instructing, but his questions upset men's confidence in themselves and the comfortable conventions they lived by. "Laches,[5] you are a soldier. Tell me, if you can, what is courage." "Indeed, Socrates, that is not difficult. He is courageous who does not run from the enemy, but stays at his post and fights." "Very good Laches, but I see I did not express myself clearly. May not another man who fights by running from the enemy also be courageous?" "Why, Socrates, I do not understand." "Well, Laches, the Scythians[6] fight by flying as well as by pursuing." "You are right, Socrates, but they are cavalry, not the heavy-armed Greek I was speaking of." "Yes, Laches, and I see I put my question badly. I meant to ask not only about the courage of heavy-armed soldiers, but of cavalry too, and not only those courageous in war, but in perils by sea and in disease and in poverty, and also those who have courage against their own desires as well as against

---

5. **Laches** (lā′chēz).
6. **Scythians** (sith′ē ənz), a people of what is now South Russia. They fired over their shoulders in a retreating strategem.

fear and pain. What is that quality common to all these cases which we call courage?"

The first effect he had upon his hearers was usually perplexity and bewilderment, sometimes it was extreme distress. Alcibiades,[7] most brilliant in that brilliant town, told the company at the dinner table in the *Symposium*, "I have heard Pericles and other great orators, but they never troubled me or made me angry at living a life no more worth living than a slave's life. But this man has often brought me to such a pass that I could hardly endure to go on as I was, neglecting what my soul needs. I have sometimes wished that he was dead."

That is how he could shake men's dispositions, although he himself would have said, It is not I. It is that they have found within themselves the light and in that clear shining they see the darkness they are living in and the meanness of their souls.

What he really was doing as he talked so easily and familiarly and humourously to the men of Athens, as he lived day by day so courteously and modestly and unobtrusively in his city that he loved, was establishing a new standard for the world. He believed with an unshakeable conviction that goodness and truth were the fundamental realities and that every human being had the capacity to attain to them. All men had within them a guide, a spark of the true light which could lead them to the full light of truth. This was Socrates' basic belief, in the words of the Gospel of John, "The true Light which lighteth every man that cometh into the world." His own mission he believed was to open blind eyes, to make men realize the darkness of their ignorance and evil and so to arouse in them a longing for the light; to induce them to seek until they caught a glimpse of the eternal truth and goodness "without variableness or shadow of turning" which underlay life's confusions and futilities. If once they could be shown them, could behold them in their beauty, they would inevitably, irresistibly, seek for a fuller and fuller sight. When men have attained to a perception of what Aristotle called "Excellence, much la-

boured for by the race of mortals," they do not let the vision go. Great thoughts endure. The false and the trivial pass away. And what is true of the race of men is true of the individual. Men are not able, it is not in them as human beings, if once they see the shining of the truth, to blot it out completely and forget it. We needs must love the highest when we see it. That is the great Socratic dogma.

Outside, in the wretched war-wracked city, all was in confusion, but everyone could create order in the one part of the world which was actually his own, his soul. The laws and the authority of the state might break down, but the laws of the life within, self-mastery, self-control, could not be touched by anything outside. And he who realized the divine order in himself made the great contribution toward bringing it into existence in the world. As St. Paul was to say four hundred years later, "The law of God after the inward man."

This was a new religion. Its centre was the soul. In that world of shaken moral values where people were saying, "Life is too short to find out if there are gods or not. Let us eat and drink, for tomorrow we die," Socrates came declaring that morality had an unshakeable foundation. The good, "that through whose presence the good are good," could be found by all. Morality was "of the nature of things"—human nature. "A good man in his dark strivings is somehow conscious of the right way." Goethe[8] was truly Socratic when he said that. Each soul, Socrates believed, had the seed of divinity, the potentiality of finding the underlying reality, which in another aspect is God, and of realizing the moral order. Therefore, each was of supreme importance. "The things of men," he said, were what a man should be concerned about. Cicero[9] understood him when he wrote, "He brought philosophy down from heaven

---

7. **Alcibiades** (al′sə bī′ə dēz′), a young relation of Pericles, a general and politician.
8. **Goethe** (gā′tə), 1749–1832, German poet and dramatist.
9. **Cicero** (sis′ə rō′), 106–43 B.C., Roman orator and author.

into the cities and homes of men." He himself would altogether have agreed. Yes, he would have said, because those are the places of importance, the places where men dwell. Philosophy, which is the love of the truth, must come down and live with mankind, the only seekers and discoverers of it. Men have the highest destiny. They can know the truth.

It was the one concern of his life that they should find it. They were so made that only then, only when they had beheld the truth and their souls were penetrated by its goodness and its beauty, could they really live, fulfilling at last their own nature, in harmony with reality, with God. Centuries later St. Augustine said: "Thou hast made us for thyself and restless are our hearts until they rest in thee."

But it is not only or even chiefly through his faith in man and in God that he has lived for nearly two thousand five hundred years. It is because of what he himself was. He proved the truth of what he said by his life and even more by his death. He showed men what they could become, their own spiritual possibilities, and he showed them how they could meet "the mighty stranger, death." This great lesson was not obscured by later legends of marvels and miracles. No magical doings were ever related of Socrates.

Strongest of all was the overpowering impression made by the last days of his life. Throughout them he had as throughout his life a heart at leisure from itself. When he was arrested and taken to court he met his accusers in a spirit of kindly good will. He refused to save his life by promising to give up teaching, but he did so with complete courtesy.

When the sentence of death had been pronounced he ended his reply to it by comforting his judges for condemning him.

In his prison cell he was serene, sometimes humourous, always perfectly natural, just himself, sweetly thoughtful of the men who loved him and of what they were suffering for him, but showing no suffering on his own behalf. He was ready to meet death peacefully, entirely fearless. One who was there with him said to

another who had been away from the city at the time: "I could not pity him. He seemed to me beyond that. I thought of him as blessed. I thought that he would be happy in the other world. What I felt was a strange mixture of pleasure and pain."

In prison a devoted friend, Crito, came to him, begging him, "O my beloved Socrates, let me entreat you to escape. Let us who can well afford it, bribe your way out of prison. Oh, be persuaded." Socrates answered serenely, "No. That cannot be. No one may do wrong intentionally. I will not break the law to save my life. I shall die, but I shall die innocent of wrong. This, dear Crito, is what a voice I seem to hear says to me and it prevents me from hearing any other. Yet speak, if you have something to say." "Socrates, I have nothing to say." "Then leave me, Crito, to fulfill the will of God and to follow whither he leads."

* * *

Some fifty years after his death Aristotle, who knew him well through Plato, surely had him in mind when he wrote: "There is a life which is higher than the measure of humanity. Men live it not by virtue of their humanity, but by virtue of something in them that is divine." Looking at Socrates, the Greek and Roman world knew that that had been done. A human life had been lived divinely and they took courage for their own lives.

* * *

I

IS AN IDEA WORTH DYING FOR?

Socrates, that strange, ugly man who buzzed about Athens asking thought-provoking questions of anyone who would listen, lived during the same Golden Age in Greece which produced Sophocles. Each in his way sought for the truth and attempted to transmit it to the Greek public. Sophocles used the drama to carry his ideas; Socrates, trained as a stonecutter, wrote nothing, but relied on his continual questioning. When Socrates at his trial refused to say that he would give up his teaching, he knew exactly what the consequences of such a choice would be. Yet, as often happens in human affairs, it may have been this final choice that has helped to make his ideas important to those who have followed. Because he was willing to die for what he believed in, his ideas and teachings stand forth clear-cut and noble through the passage of centuries. Things worth dying for must be worth living by. . . .

How do the following statements of philosophy from Socrates' biography apply to modern life?

1. Goodness has a most real and actual existence.

2. What a lot of things there are a man can do without.

3. Happiness is activity of soul.

4. The unexamined life is not worth living.

5. . . . goodness and truth are the fundamental realities and every human has the ability to attain to them.

6. The false and the trivial pass away.

7. Men have the highest destiny. They can know the truth.

8. No one may do wrong intentionally.

II
IMPLICATIONS

You may agree or disagree with the following statements, but whatever your opinion, be sure you can support your view by examples from the selection.

1. Socrates' choice (to die) was based solely on logic . . . conscience and emotion played no part in it.

2. Socrates' teachings are not for the ordinary person.

3. Socrates' death demonstrates his credo that it is better to undergo evil than to perform it.

4. It took tremendous courage to "choose" to die.

III
TECHNIQUES
Character Development

Write down everything you know about Socrates' personality and character. Now look back at Edith Hamilton's essay and see how many different devices she used to convey this picture.

Imagery

Socrates often explained abstract ideas by reference to specific things. How do the metaphors in these Socratic statements help make his ideas clear and vivid?

1. I think I am that gadfly.

2. The mighty stranger, death. . . .

3. And like the bee, leave my sting in you before I die. . . .

PLATO

One of the many young disciples who gathered around Socrates was Plato (427?–347 B.C.), son of an ancient and wealthy family. After Socrates' death, Plato carried on his teacher's search for truth and founded the academy at Athens. This gathering of teachers and students, devoted to a systematic search for philosophical and scientific truth, could be called the first European university. The great philosopher Aristotle was in turn Plato's student. Actually, Socrates never wrote about his philosophic ideas; what is known of his work has come to us through Plato's dialogues. Since Socrates taught by a question and answer method, Plato wrote the dialogues as a series of dramatic conversations; but, there is no way of knowing whether the words Plato attributes to Socrates were really spoken by him. Illness prevented Plato from being present at Socrates' death. Of course, he must have questioned those who were present about every detail and about every word that was spoken. When he came to reconstruct the scene in writing, years later, he cast his work in the form of a dialogue between a stranger, Echecrates, and Phaedo,[1] who had witnessed the scene. The method of execution in Athens was to give the prisoner a cup of hemlock—a poison—to drink.

The Death of Socrates

from the *Phaedo*

Benjamin Jowett, translator

I will begin [said Phaedo] at the beginning . . . On the previous days we had been in the habit of assembling early in the morning at the court in which the trial took place, and which is not far from the prison. There we used to wait talking with one another until the opening of the doors (for they were not opened very early); then we went in and generally passed the day with Socrates. On the last morning we assembled sooner than usual, having heard on the day before when we quitted the prison in the evening that the sacred ship had come from Delos;[2] and so we arranged to meet very early at the accustomed place. On our arrival the jailer who answered the door, instead of admitting us, came out and told us to stay until he called us. "For the Eleven," he said, "are now with Socrates; they are taking off his chains, and giving orders that he is to die today." He soon returned and said that we might come in.

On entering we found Socrates just released from chains, and Xanthippe,[3] whom you know, sitting by him and holding his child in her arms. When she saw us she uttered a cry and said, as women will, "O Socrates, this is the last time that either you will converse with your friends, or they with you."

Socrates turned to Crito and said: "Crito, let some one take her home." Some of Crito's people accordingly led her away, crying out and beating herself. And when she was gone . . . he arose and went into a chamber to bathe; Crito followed him, and told us to wait. So we

---

1. **Echecrates** (e chek′rə tēz′). **Phaedo** (fē′dō).
2. **Delos** (dē′los), an island in the Aegean Sea. No execution could take place until the ship returned from the ritual voyage to Apollo's island. This spring ceremony had begun the day before Socrates' trial and the winds had delayed it.
3. **Xanthippe** (zan tip′ē), wife of Socrates.

Plato, pupil of Socrates and founder of the Academy.

remained behind, talking and thinking . . . he was like a father of whom we were being bereaved, and we were about to pass the rest of our life as orphans. When he had taken his bath his children were brought to him—(he had two young sons and an elder one); and the women of the family also came, and he talked to them and gave them a few directions in the presence of Crito; then he dismissed them and returned to us.

Now the hour of sunset was near, for a good deal of time had passed while he was within. When he came out, he sat down with us again after his bath, but not much was said. Soon the jailer, who was the servant of the Eleven, entered and stood by him saying:—To you,

Socrates, whom I know to be the noblest and gentlest and best of all who ever came to this place, I will not impute the angry feelings of other men, who rage and swear at me, when, in obedience to the authorities, I bid them drink the poison—indeed, I am sure that you will not be angry with me for others, as you are aware, and not I, are to blame. And so fare you well, and try to bear lightly what must needs be— you know my errand. Then bursting into tears he turned away and went out.

Socrates looked at him, and said: I return your good wishes, and will do as you bid. Then turning to us, he said, How charming the man is: since I have been in prison he has always been coming to see me, and at times he would talk to me, and was as good to me as could be, and now see how generously he sorrows on my account. We must do as he says, Crito; and therefore let the cup be brought, if the poison is prepared; if not, let the attendant prepare some.

Yet, said Crito, the sun is still upon the hilltops, and I know that many a one has taken the draught late, and after the announcement had been made to him, he has eaten and drunk, and enjoyed the society of his beloved; do not hurry —there is time enough.

Socrates said: Yes, Crito, and they of whom you speak are right in so acting, for they think that they will be gainers by the delay; but I am right in not following their example, for I do not think that I should gain anything by drinking the poison a little later; I should only be ridiculous in my own eyes for sparing and saving a life which is already forfeit. Please then to do as I say, and not to refuse me.

Crito made a sign to the servant, who was standing by; and he went out, and having been absent for some time returned with the jailer carrying the cup of poison. Socrates said: You, my good friend, who are experienced in these matters, shall give me directions how I am to proceed. The man answered: You have only to walk about until your legs are heavy, and then to lie down, and the poison will act. At the same time he handed the cup to Socrates, who

*Socrates takes the cup of hemlock in this
painting of the "Death of Socrates"
by Jacques Louis David.*

in the easiest and gentlest manner, without the least fear or change of colour or feature, looking at the man with all his eyes . . . as his manner was, took the cup and said: What do you say about making a libation out of this cup to any god? May I, or not? The man answered: We only prepare, Socrates, just so much as we deem enough. I understand, he said: but I may and must ask the gods to prosper my journey from this to the other world—even so—and so be it according to my prayer. Then raising the cup to his lips, quite readily and cheerfully he drank off the poison. And hitherto most of us had been able to control our sorrow; but now when we saw him drinking, and saw too that he had finished the draught, we could no longer forbear, and in spite of myself my own tears were flowing fast; so that I covered my face and wept, not for him, but at the thought of my own calamity in having to part from such a friend. Nor was I the first; for Crito, when he found himself unable to restrain his tears, had got up, and I followed; and at that moment, Apollodorus,[4] who had been weeping all the

time, broke out in a loud and passionate cry which made cowards of us all.

Socrates alone retained his calmness: What is this strange outcry? he said. I sent away the women mainly in order that they might not misbehave in this way, for I have been told that a man should die in peace. Be quiet then, and have patience.

When we heard his words we were ashamed, and refrained our tears; and he walked about until, as he said, his legs began to fail, and then he lay on his back, according to the directions, and the man who gave him the poison now and then looked at his feet and legs; and after a while he pressed his foot hard, and asked him if he could feel; and he said, No; and then his leg, and so upwards and upwards, and showed us that he was cold and stiff. And he felt them himself, and said: When the poison reaches the heart, that will be the end.

---

4. **Apollodorus** (ə pol'ə dôr'əs).

245

He was beginning to grow cold about the groin, when he uncovered his face, for he had covered himself up, and said—they were his last words—he said: Crito, I owe a cock to Asclepius;[5] will you remember to pay the debt? The debt shall be paid, said Crito; is there anything else? There was no answer to this question; but in a minute or two a movement was heard, and the attendants uncovered him; his eyes were set, and Crito closed his eyes and mouth.

Such was the end . . . of our friend; concerning whom I may truly say, that of all the men of his time whom I have known, he was the wisest and justest and best.

I
"WE WERE LAUGHING AND WEEPING BY TURNS"

The *Phaedo* combines a sense of joy and sadness. Socrates' own calm spirit of justice and acceptance rises above the tears and moanings of his friends. Plato's account has a great impact on the reader because emotion and anguish lie just below the calm surface of the words.

What is revealed about the speakers of the following words:

1. . . . we were about to pass the rest of our lives as orphans. (Phaedo)

2. I do not think that I should gain anything by drinking the poison a little later. (Socrates)

3. Crito, I owe a cock to Asclepius; will you remember to pay the debt? (Socrates)

II
IMPLICATIONS

What is your reaction to the following statements? Do you agree or disagree?

1. Once a choice is made, it is best to accept the consequences immediately.

2. If Socrates had chosen to give up his teaching in order to save his life, he would have discredited his own ideas and probably would not be remembered today.

---

5. **Asclepius** (as klē′pē əs), the god of medicine and healing. Crito was to sacrifice the cock to his honor.

III
TECHNIQUES
Character Development

1. Are there any new aspects of Socrates' character that you find in this section from the *Phaedo* which you did not find in Edith Hamilton's biography?

2. How does Plato create a sense of Socrates' personality in the scene?

IV
WORDS

A. Following are several phrases and clauses taken from the Edith Hamilton selection:

1. Socrates has outlasted two *millenniums*.

2. . . . the enduring *verity* of what he lived by.

3. . . . the state religion which was still Homer's jovial, *amoral* Olympians. . . .

4. The *indictment* ran: "Socrates is an evildoer. . . ."

5. He never thundered *anathemas*. . . .

6. . . . so gentle, *urbane*, and companionable. . . .

7. . . . piled in glowing *profusion*. . . .

What does each of the italicized words mean? For which words are context clues a help and for which do you have to use your dictionary?

B. The preceding selections contain a number of famous names. Identify each of the following, explain what the use of each name suggests, and give adjectives, such as *platonic*, which have been derived from the proper nouns.

Plato   Homer   Jeremiah   Aristotle
Athens   St. Paul   Pericles   Goethe
Thucydides   Isaiah   Alcibiades St. Augustine

C. Edith Hamilton skillfully uses connotations (emotional associations) and suggestions of words. What are the connotations as well as the denotations (the precise meanings) of the italicized words in the following phrases?

no *ordered* philosophy;
false or at least *futile*;
the *instinct* for reasonableness;
all the other *passionate* reformers;
a *witness* to all that is contained in the word goodness;
a great taste for *homely* illustration;
he could not imprison within a *formula* the truth he saw.

GRAHAM GREENE

Graham Greene was born in 1904 in Hertfordshire, England, and began
his writing career as an editor for the London *Times*. Though perhaps better known
for his psychological thrillers such as *Orient Express*, *The Third Man*, and *Our Man
in Havana*, he has also written serious novels exploring the modern person's relation
to God. Greene probes the inner twistings and turnings of his characters' minds,
and reveals how these twistings affect their spirit and behavior. This makes
his characters grow and change as the story progresses. The reader's interest is held
by the revelation of personality. Greene once wrote, "We are saved or damned
by our thoughts not our actions." Hence the movements of his stories tend to be
subtle and intricate, presenting a kind of delicate dilemma that might face
each of us in our inner lives. The choice in "The Hint of an Explanation" hinges
on a delicate matter of conscience.

The Hint of an Explanation

A long train journey on a late December evening, in this new version of peace, is a dreary experience. I suppose that my fellow traveller and I could consider ourselves lucky to have a compartment to ourselves, even though the heating apparatus was not working, even though the lights went out entirely in the frequent Pennine tunnels[1] and were too dim anyway for us to read our books without straining our eyes, and though there was no restaurant car to give at least a change of scene. It was when we were trying simultaneously to chew the same kind of dry bun bought at the same station buffet that my companion and I came together. Before that we had sat at opposite ends of the carriage, both muffled to the chin in overcoats, both bent low over type we could barely make out, but as I threw the remains of my cake under the seat our eyes met, and he laid his book down.

By the time we were half-way to Bedwell Junction we had found an enormous range of subjects for discussion; starting with buns and

the weather, we had gone on to politics, the government, foreign affairs, the atom bomb, and, by an inevitable progression, God. We had not, however, become either shrill or acid. My companion, who now sat opposite me, leaning a little forward, so that our knees nearly touched, gave such an impression of serenity that it would have been impossible to quarrel with him, however much our views differed, and differ they did profoundly.

I had soon realized I was speaking to a Catholic, to someone who believed—how do they put it?—in an omnipotent and omniscient Deity, while I was what is loosely called an Agnostic. I have a certain intuition (which I do not trust, founded as it may well be on childish experiences and needs) that a God exists, and I am surprised occasionally into belief by the extraordinary coincidences that beset our path like the traps set for leopards in the jungle, but intellectually I am revolted at the whole notion of such a God who can so abandon his

From *21 Stories* by Graham Greene. Copyright 1947, renewed 1975 by Graham Greene. Reprinted by permission of Viking Penguin Inc.

1. **Pennine tunnels,** tunnels in the Pennines (pen′ĭnz), a range of low mountains in northwestern England.

Graham Greene

looked across the compartment at my fellow traveller, but his face was already again in shadow. I said weakly, "When you think what God—if there is a God—allows. It's not merely the physical agonies, but think of the corruption, even of children. . . ."

He said, "Our view is so limited," and I was disappointed at the conventionality of his reply. He must have been aware of my disappointment (it was as though our thoughts were huddled as closely as ourselves for warmth), for he went on, "Of course there is no answer here. We catch hints . . ." and then the train roared into another tunnel and the lights again went out. It was the longest tunnel yet; we went rocking down it, and the cold seemed to become more intense with the darkness like an icy fog (perhaps when one sense—of sight— is robbed of sensation, the others grow more sensitive). When we emerged into the mere grey of night and the globe lit up once more, I could see that my companion was leaning back on his seat.

I repeated his last words as a question, "Hints?"

"Oh, they mean very little in cold print—or cold speech," he said, shivering in his overcoat. "And they mean nothing at all to a human being other than the man who catches them. They are not scientific evidence—or evidence at all for that matter. Events that don't, somehow, turn out as they were intended—by the human actors I mean, or by the thing behind the human actors."

"The thing?"

"The word Satan is so anthropomorphic."

I had to lean forward now: I wanted to hear what he had to say. I am—I really am, you know—open to conviction.

He said, "One's words are so crude, but I sometimes feel pity for that thing. It is so continually finding the right weapon to use against its Enemy and the weapon breaks in its own breast. It sometimes seems to me so—power-

creatures to the enormities of Free Will. I found myself expressing this view to my companion, who listened quietly and with respect. He made no attempt to interrupt; he showed none of the impatience or the intellectual arrogance I have grown to expect from Catholics; when the lights of a wayside station flashed across his face that had escaped hitherto the rays of the one globe working in the compartment, I caught a glimpse suddenly of—what? I stopped speaking, so strong was the impression. I was carried back ten years, to the other side of the great useless conflict, to a small town, Gisors[2] in Normandy. I was again, for a moment, walking on the ancient battlements and looking down across the grey roofs, until my eyes for some reason lit on one grey stony "back" out of the many, where the face of a middle-aged man was pressed against a windowpane (I suppose that face has ceased to exist now, just as I believe the whole town with its medieval memories has been reduced to rubble). I remembered saying to myself with astonishment, "That man is happy—completely happy." I

2. **Gisors** (jē′zôr′), a French town in an area fought over in World War II.

less. You said something just now about the corruption of children. It reminded me of something in my own childhood. You are the first person—except for one—that I have thought of telling it to, perhaps because you are anonymous. It's not a very long story, and in a way it's relevant."

I said, "I'd like to hear it."

"You mustn't expect too much meaning. But to me there seems to be a hint. That's all. A hint."

He went slowly on, turning his face to the pane, though he could have seen nothing real in the whirling world outside except an occasional signal lamp, a light in a window, a small country station torn backwards by our rush, picking his words with precision. He said, "When I was a child they taught me to serve at Mass. The church was a small one, for there were very few Catholics where I lived. It was a market town in East Anglia,[3] surrounded by flat, chalky fields and ditches—so many ditches. I don't suppose there were fifty Catholics all told, and for some reason there was a tradition of hostility to us. Perhaps it went back to the burning of a Protestant martyr in the sixteenth century—there was a stone marking the place near where the meat stalls stood on Wednesdays. I was only half aware of the enmity, though I knew that my school nickname of Popey Martin had something to do with my religion, and I had heard that my father was nearly excluded from the Constitutional Club when he first came to the town.

"Every Sunday I had to dress up in my surplice and serve Mass. I hated it—I have always hated dressing up in any way (which is funny when you come to think of it), and I never ceased to be afraid of losing my place in the service and doing something which would put me to ridicule. Our services were at a different hour from the Anglican,[4] and as our small, far-from-select band trudged out of the hideous chapel the whole of the townsfolk seemed to be on the way past to the proper church—I always thought of it as the proper church. We had to pass the parade of their

eyes, indifferent, supercilious, mocking; you can't imagine how seriously religion can be taken in a small town, if only for social reasons.

"There was one man in particular; he was one of the two bakers in the town, the one my family did not patronize. I don't think any of the Catholics patronized him because he was called a free-thinker—an odd title, for, poor man, no one's thoughts were less free than his. He was hemmed in by his hatred—his hatred of us. He was very ugly to look at, with one wall-eye and a head the shape of a turnip, with the hair gone on the crown, and he was unmarried. He had no interests, apparently, but his baking and his hatred, though now that I am older I begin to see other sides to his nature —it did contain, perhaps, a certain furtive love. One would come across him suddenly sometimes on a country walk, especially if one were alone and it was Sunday. It was as if he rose from the ditches, and the smear of chalk on his clothes reminded one of the flour on his working overalls. He would have a stick in his hand and stab at the hedges, and if his mood were very black he would call out after one strange abrupt words like a foreign tongue—I know the meaning of those words, of course, now. Once the police went to his house because of what a boy said he'd seen, but nothing came of it except that the hate shackled him closer. His name was Blacker and he terrified me.

I think he had a particular hatred of my father—I don't know why. My father was manager of the Midland Bank, and it's possible that at some time Blacker may have had unsatisfactory dealings with the bank; my father was a very cautious man who suffered all his life from anxiety about money—his own and other people's. If I try and picture Blacker now I see him walking along a narrow path between high windowless walls, and at the end of the path stands a small boy of ten—me. I don't know whether it's a symbolic picture or the memory

---

3. **East Anglia,** the peninsula making up Norfolk and Suffolk northeast of London.
4. **the Anglican** (ang'glə kən), the Protestant Church of England.

of one of our encounters—our encounters somehow got more and more frequent. You talked just now about the corruption of children. That poor man was preparing to revenge himself on everything he hated—my father, the Catholics, the God whom people persisted in crediting—and that by corrupting me. He had evolved a horrible and ingenious plan.

"I remember the first time I had a friendly word from him. I was passing his shop as rapidly as I could when I heard his voice call out with a kind of sly subservience as though he were an under servant. 'Master David,' he called, 'Master David,' and I hurried on. But the next time I passed that way he was at his door (he must have seen me coming) with one of those curly cakes in his hand that we called Chelsea buns. I didn't want to take it, but he made me, and then I couldn't be other than polite when he asked me to come into his parlour behind the shop and see something very special.

"It was a small electric railway—a rare sight in those days, and he insisted on showing me how it worked. He made me turn the switches and stop and start it, and he told me that I could come in any morning and have a game with it. He used the word 'game' as though it were something secret, and it's true that I never told my family of this invitation and of how, perhaps twice a week those holidays, the desire to control that little railway became overpowering, and looking up and down the street to see if I were observed, I would dive into the shop."

Our larger, dirtier, adult train drove into a tunnel and the light went out. We sat in darkness and silence, with the noise of the train blocking our ears like wax. When we were through we didn't speak at once and I had to prick him into continuing. "An elaborate seduction," I said.

"Don't think his plans were as simple as that," my companion said, "or as crude. There was much more hate than love, poor man, in his make-up. Can you hate something you don't believe in? And yet he called himself a free-thinker. What an impossible paradox, to be free

and to be so obsessed. Day by day all through those holidays his obsession must have grown, but he kept a grip; he bided his time. Perhaps that thing I spoke of gave him the strength and the wisdom. It was only a week from the end of the holidays that he spoke to me on what concerned him so deeply.

"I heard him behind me as I knelt on the floor, coupling two coaches. He said, 'You won't be able to do this, Master David, when school starts.' It wasn't a sentence that needed any comment from me any more than the one that followed. 'You ought to have it for your own, you ought,' but how skilfully and unemphatically he had sowed the longing, the idea of a possibility. . . . I was coming to his parlour every day now; you see, I had to cram every opportunity in before the hated term started again, and I suppose I was becoming accustomed to Blacker, to that wall-eye, that turnip head, that nauseating subservience. The Pope, you know, describes himself as 'the servant of the servants of God,' and Blacker—I sometimes think that Blacker was 'the servant of the servants of . . .,' well, let it be.

"The very next day, standing in the doorway watching me play, he began to talk to me about religion. He said, with what untruth even I recognized, how much he admired the Catholics; he wished he could believe like that, but how could a baker believe? He accented 'a baker' as one might say a biologist, and the tiny train spun round the gauge 0 track. He said, 'I can bake the things you eat just as well as any Catholic can,' and disappeared into his shop. I hadn't the faintest idea what he meant. Presently he emerged again, holding in his hand a little wafer. 'Here,' he said, 'eat that and tell me. . . .' When I put it in my mouth I could tell that it was made in the same way as our wafers for communion—he had got the shape a little wrong, that was all—and I felt guilty and irrationally scared. 'Tell me,' he said, 'what's the difference?'

" 'Difference?' I asked.

" 'Isn't that just the same as you eat in church?'

"I said smugly, 'It hasn't been consecrated.'

"He said, 'Do you think, if I put the two of them under a microscope, you could tell the difference?'

"But even at ten I had the answer to that question. 'No,' I said, 'the—accidents don't change,' stumbling a little on the word 'accidents' which had suddenly conveyed to me the idea of death and wounds.

"Blacker said with sudden intensity, 'How I'd like to get one of your ones in my mouth—just to see. . . .'

"It may seem odd to you, but this was the first time that the idea of transubstantiation really lodged in my mind. I had learned it all by rote; I had grown up with the idea. The Mass was as lifeless to me as the sentences in *De Bello Gallico;*[5] communion a routine like drill in the school-yard, but here suddenly I was in the presence of a man who took it seriously, as seriously as the priest whom naturally one didn't count—it was his job. I felt more scared than ever.

"He said, 'It's all nonsense, but I'd just like to have it in my mouth.'

"'You could if you were a Catholic,' I said naïvely.

"He gazed at me with his one good eye, like a Cyclops. He said, 'You serve at Mass, don't you? It would be easy for you to get at one of those things. I tell you what I'd do—I'd swap this electric train for one of your wafers—consecrated, mind. It's got to be consecrated.'

"'I could get you one out of the box,' I said. I think I still imagined that his interest was a baker's interest—to see how they were made.

"'Oh, no,' he said, 'I want to see what your God tastes like.'

"'I couldn't do that.'

"'Not for a whole electric train, just for yourself? You wouldn't have any trouble at home. I'd pack it up and put a label inside that your dad could see: "For my bank manager's little boy from a grateful client." He'd be pleased as punch with that.'

"Now that we are grown men it seems a trivial temptation, doesn't it? But try to think back to your own childhood. There was a whole circuit of rails there on the floor at our feet, straight rails and curved, and a little station with porters and passengers, a tunnel, a footbridge, a level crossing, two signals, buffers, of course—and, above all, a turntable. The tears of longing came into my eyes when I looked at the turntable. It was my favorite piece—it looked so ugly and practical and true. I said weakly, 'I wouldn't know how.'

"How carefully he had been studying the ground! He must have slipped several times into Mass at the back of the church. It would have been no good, you understand, in a little town like that, presenting himself for communion. Everybody there knew him for what he was. He said to me, 'When you've been given communion you could just put it under your tongue a moment. He serves you and the other boy first, and I saw you once go out behind the curtain straight afterwards. You'd forgotten one of those little bottles.'

"'The cruet,' I said.

"'Pepper and salt.' He grinned at me jovially, and I—well, I looked at the little railway which I could no longer come and play with when term started. I said, 'You'd just swallow it, wouldn't you?'

"'Oh, yes,' he said. 'I'd just swallow it.'

"Somehow I didn't want to play with the train any more that day. I got up and made for the door, but he detained me, gripping my lapel. He said, 'This will be a secret between you and me. Tomorrow's Sunday. You come along here in the afternoon. Put it in an envelope and post it me. Monday morning the train will be delivered bright and early.'

"'Not tomorrow,' I implored him.

"'I'm not interested in any other Sunday,' he said. 'It's your only chance.' He shook me gently backwards and forwards. 'It will always have to be a secret between you and me,' he said. 'Why, if anyone knew they'd take away the train and

---

5. **De Bello Gallico,** *The Gallic War* (written by Julius Caesar), often used as a translation exercise in Latin classes.

there'd be me to reckon with. I'd bleed you something awful. You know how I'm always about on Sunday walks. You can't avoid a man like me. I crop up. You wouldn't ever be safe in your own house. I know ways to get into houses when people are asleep.' He pulled me into the shop after him and opened a drawer. In the drawer was an odd looking key and a cut-throat razor. He said, 'That's a master key that opens all locks and that—that's what I bleed people with.' Then he patted my cheek with his plump floury fingers and said, 'Forget it. You and me are friends.'

"That Sunday Mass stays in my head, every detail of it, as though it had happened only a week ago. From the moment of the Confession to the moment of Consecration it had a terrible importance; only one other Mass has ever been so important to me—perhaps not even one, for this was a solitary Mass which would never happen again. It seemed as final as the last Sacrament when the priest bent down and put the wafer in my mouth where I knelt before the altar with my fellow server.

"I suppose I had made up my mind to commit this awful act—for, you know, to us it must always seem an awful act—from the moment when I saw Blacker watching from the back of the church. He had put on his best black Sunday clothes and, as though he could never quite escape the smear of his profession, he had a dab of dried talcum on his cheek, which he had presumably applied after using that cut-throat of his. He was watching me closely all the time, and I think it was fear—fear of that terrible undefined thing called bleeding—as much as covetousness that drove me to carry out my instructions.

"My fellow server got briskly up and, taking the paten,[6] preceded Father Carey to the altar rail where the other communicants knelt. I had the Host[7] lodged under my tongue: it felt like a blister. I got up and made for the curtain to get the cruet that I had purposely left in the sacristy. When I was there I looked quickly round for a hiding place and saw an old copy of the *Universe* lying on a chair. I took the Host

from my mouth and inserted it between two sheets—a little damp mess of pulp. Then I thought: perhaps Father Carey has put out the paper for a particular purpose and he will find the Host before I have time to remove it, and the enormity of my act began to come home to me when I tried to imagine what punishment I should incur. Murder is sufficiently trivial to have its appropriate punishment, but for this act the mind boggled at the thought of any retribution at all. I tried to remove the Host, but it stuck clammily between the pages, and in desperation I tore out a piece of the news-paper and, screwing the whole thing up, stuck it in my trousers pocket. When I came back through the curtain carrying the cruet my eyes met Blacker's. He gave me a grin of encourage-ment and unhappiness—yes, I am sure, unhap-piness. Was it perhaps that the poor man was all the time seeking something incorruptible?

"I can remember little more of that day. I think my mind was shocked and stunned, and I was caught up too in the family bustle of Sunday. Sunday in a provincial town is the day for relations. All the family are at home, and unfamiliar cousins and uncles are apt to arrive, packed in the back seats of other people's cars. I remember that some crowd of the kind descended on us and pushed Blacker tempo-rarily out of the foreground of my mind. There was somebody called Aunt Lucy, with a loud hollow laugh that filled the house with me-chanical merriment like the sound of recorded laughter from inside a hall of mirrors, and I had no opportunity to go out alone even if I had wished to. When six o'clock came and Aunt Lucy and the cousins departed and peace re-turned, it was too late to go to Blacker's, and at eight it was my own bed-time.

"I think I had half forgotten what I had in my pocket. As I emptied my pocket the little screw of newspaper brought quickly back the Mass, the priest bending over me, Blacker's grin. I laid the packet on the chair by my bed

---

6. **paten,** plate.
7. **the Host,** the consecrated wafer used in the Mass.

and tried to go to sleep, but I was haunted by the shadows on the wall where the curtains blew, the squeak of furniture, the rustle in the chimney, haunted by the presence of God there on the chair. The Host had always been to me —well, the Host. I knew theoretically, as I have said, what I had to believe, but suddenly, as someone whistled in the road outside, whistled secretively, knowingly, to me, I knew that this which I had beside my bed was something of infinite value—something a man would pay for with his whole peace of mind, something that was so hated one could love it as one loves an outcast or a bullied child. These are adult words, and it was a child of ten who lay scared in bed, listening to the whistle from the road, Blacker's whistle, but I think he felt fairly clearly what I am describing now. That is what I meant when I said this Thing, whatever it is, that seizes every possible weapon against God, is always, everywhere, disappointed at the moment of success. It must have felt as certain of me as Blacker did. It must have felt certain too of Blacker. But I wonder, if one knew what happened later to that poor man, whether one would not find again that the weapon had been turned against its own breast.

"At last I couldn't bear that whistle any more and got out of bed. I opened the curtains a little way, and there right under my window,

the moonlight on his face, was Blacker. If I had stretched my hand down, his fingers reaching up could almost have touched mine. He looked up at me, flashing the one good eye, with hunger—I realize now that near-success must have developed his obsession almost to the point of madness. Desperation had driven him to the house. He whispered up at me. 'David, where is it?'

"I jerked my head back at the room. 'Give it me,' he said. 'Quick. You shall have the train in the morning.'

"I shook my head. He said, 'I've got the bleeder here, and the key. You'd better toss it down.'

" 'Go away,' I said, but I could hardly speak for fear.

" 'I'll bleed you first and then I'll have it just the same.'

" 'Oh, no, you won't,' I said. I went to the chair and picked it—Him—up. There was only one place where He was safe. I couldn't separate the Host from the paper, so I swallowed both. The newsprint stuck like a prune skin to the back of my throat, but I rinsed it down with water from the ewer. Then I went back to the window and looked down at Blacker. He began to wheedle me. 'What have you done with it, David? What's the fuss? It's only a bit of bread,' looking so longingly and pleadingly up

at me that even as a child I wondered whether he could really think that, and yet desire it so much.

"'I swallowed it,' I said.

"'Swallowed it?'

"'Yes,' I said. 'Go away.'

"Then something happened which seems to me now more terrible than his desire to corrupt or my thoughtless act: he began to weep—the tears ran lopsidedly out of the one good eye and his shoulders shook. I only saw his face for a moment before he bent his head and strode off, the bald turnip head shaking, into the dark. When I think of it now, it's almost as if I had seen that Thing weeping for its inevitable defeat. It had tried to use me as a weapon, and now I had broken in its hands and it wept its hopeless tears through one of Blacker's eyes."

The black furnaces of Bedwell Junction gathered around the line. The points switched and we were tossed from one set of rails to another. A spray of sparks, a signal light changing to red, tall chimneys jetting into the grey night sky, the fumes of steam from stationary engines —half the cold journey was over, and now remained the long wait for the slow cross-country train. I said, "It's an interesting story. I think I should have given Blacker what he wanted. I wonder what he would have done with it."

"I really believe," my companion said, "that he would first of all have put it under his microscope—before he did all the other things I expect he had planned."

"And the hints," I said. "I don't quite see what you mean by that."

"Oh, well," he said vaguely, "you know for me it was an odd beginning, that affair, when you come to think of it," but I never should have known what he meant had not his coat, when he rose to take the bag from the rack, come open and disclosed the collar of a priest.

I said, "I suppose you think you owe a lot to Blacker."

"Yes," he said, "you see, I am a very happy man."

THE POWER OF DARKNESS

The semidarkness of the train, the momentary flashes of light from outside, and the indistinctness of the listener make us feel personally involved, almost as if the priest's story is being told directly to us. The little boy's struggle is terrible in its inner intensity. The evil seems almost alive to the priest, grasping with terrifying strength at the boy's future. The consequences of the boy's choice are not immediately apparent. It is not until we weigh the last statement that we realize how far-reaching the choice was.

IMPLICATIONS

Discuss the implications of these quotations from the story:

1. "You can't imagine how seriously religion can be taken in a small town, if only for social reasons."

2. "Was it perhaps that the poor man was all the time seeking something incorruptible?"

3. "When I think of it now, it's almost as if I had seen that Thing weeping for its inevitable defeat."

(What does the priest mean by "that Thing"?)

TECHNIQUES

Character Development

1. What do you know about the narrator of the story—that is, the man to whom the priest is telling his tale?

2. Why does the narrator withhold the fact that the man in the railroad carriage is a priest until the end of the story? Would your impression of the story have been different if you had known he was a priest at the beginning?

Imagery

How effective are the following metaphors as used in the story? Could the ideas have been better expressed in "straight" prose?

1. . . . our thoughts were huddled as closely as ourselves for warmth.

2. "He was very ugly to look at, with one wall-eye and a head the shape of a turnip. . . ."

3. ". . . he had sowed the longing, the idea of a possibility. . . ."

KAREL ČAPEK

Karel Čapek[1] (1890–1938), the son of a country doctor, was born in Male
Svatonovice, Bohemia (which became a part of Czechoslovakia in 1949). He
studied in Prague, Berlin, and Paris, receiving a doctor of philosophy
degree from the University of Prague. After attaining his degree, Čapek
worked as a journalist and a stage manager. He wrote stories, plays,
and essays which were so well-received that he became the chief writer for the
Czech national theater. Čapek was a liberal and a humanist. His work
reflects a belief in the natural order of things as well as love and
concern for the common person. His essays were inspired by his travels in
a Europe of a now-bygone era. Most of Čapek's writing lightly protests
society's emphasis on material and technological matters rather than spiritual
values. In the United States, his best-known play is *R.U.R.* This play is set
in a future time when robots (a word created by Čapek) have been built to do
all of humankind's work. The robots rise in rebellion and conquer their human
masters, who have become soulless. But the robots soon realize that if
they are to survive, they must learn how to develop souls.

The Stamp Collection

translated from the Czech by Paul Selver

"There's no getting away from it," said old
Mr. Karas, "If a man were to rummage in his
past, he'd find material in it for a whole different
set of lives. One day, either by mistake, or because he felt inclined to, he chose just one of
them and went on with it to the end; but the
worst of it is, that those other lives, the ones
he might have lived, are not entirely dead.
And sometimes it happens that you feel a pain
in them, like a leg that has been cut off.

"When I was a boy of about ten, I began to
collect stamps; my father didn't altogether approve of it; he thought it'd make me neglect my
lessons, but I had a chum, Lojzik Cepelka, and
we used to share our passion for foreign stamps.
Lojzik's father used to play a barrel-organ, and
he was an untidy lad with freckles, a regular

ragamuffin, but I was fond of him, in the way
that schoolboys are fond of their chum. You
know, I'm an old man; I've had a wife and children, but I must say that none of our feelings
are finer than friendship. But you're only capable of it when you're young, later on, you get
sort of crusty and selfish. A friendship of that
sort I mean springs simply and solely from enthusiasm and admiration, from excess of vitality,
from abundance and overflow of emotion; you've
got so much of it, that you simply have to give
it away to somebody. My father was a lawyer,
the chief man among the local bigwigs, a most
dignified and severe person, and I had chummed
up with Lojzik, whose father was a drunken
organ-grinder and his mother a downtrodden
laundress, and yet I venerated and idolized
Lojzik, because he was smarter than myself,
because he could shift for himself and was as
plucky as they make them, because he had
freckles on his nose and could throw stones left-
handed—in fact, I can't remember all the things

1. **Karel Čapek** (kär′l chäp′ək).

Mr. and Mrs. Karel Čapek

that made me so attached to him; but it was certainly the closest attachment I have ever had.

"And so Lojzik was my trusty comrade when I began to collect stamps. I suppose that the craze for collecting things must be a survival of an instinct dating back to the times when every warrior collected the heads of enemies, the spoils of war, bearskins, stags' antlers, and, in fact, anything that could be captured as booty. But a stamp collection possesses one quality which makes it a perpetual adventure; it somehow excites you to touch a bit of some distant country, such as Bhutan,[2] Bolivia or the Cape of Good Hope; it brings you into a sort of personal and intimate touch with these foreign countries. So there is something about stamp-collecting which suggests travel by land and sea, and deeds of derring-do, in general. It's very much the same as the crusades.

"As I was saying, my father didn't exactly approve of it; as a rule, fathers don't approve of it, if their sons do something different from what they themselves have done; as a matter of fact, I'm just the same with my own sons. This business of being a father is a sort of mixed feeling, there's a great deal of affection in it, but there's also a certain prejudice, mistrust, hostility or whatever you may choose to call it; the more affection you have for your children, the more there is of this other feeling. Anyway, I had to hide my stamp collection in the attic, so that my father couldn't catch me with it; in the attic there was an old chest, a sort of flour-bin, and we used to crawl into it, like a couple of mice to have a look at each other's stamps. Look here, this is a Netherlands, this is an Egyptian, this is Sverige or Sweden. And because we had to hide our treasures like that, there was something deliciously sinful about it. The way I got hold of those stamps was also an adventurous business: I used to go round to families I knew and those I didn't, and beg and pray of them to let me soak the stamps off their old letters. Now and then I came across people who'd got drawers crammed full of old papers stored away, in an attic or a writing-table; those were my most delightful hours when, sitting on the floor, I sorted out those dusty piles of litter to try and find stamps I hadn't already got—you see, I was silly enough not to collect duplicates, and when I happened to come across an old Lombardy[3] or one of those tiny German states or free cities, why, the thrill I had was perfectly agonizing—every vast happiness has a sweet pang about it. And in the meantime Lojzik was waiting for me outside, and when at last I crept out, I whispered right in the doorway, 'Lojzik, Lojzik, I found a Hanover[4] there!'—'Have you got it?'—'Yes.' And away we ran with our booty, home to our treasure chest.

"In our town there were factories which turned out all sorts of trash, jute, calico, cotton,

---

2. **Bhutan** (bü tän′), an Asian country in the Himalayas on the northeast border of India.

3. **Lombardy** (lom′bər dē), a region of northern Italy.
4. **Hanover** (han′ō vər), a former state of northwestern Germany; a kingdom from 1814 to 1866; a Prussian province from 1866 to 1945.

and shoddy wool. . . . They used to let me ransack their waste-paper baskets, and that was my happiest hunting-ground; there I came across stamps from Siam and South Africa, China, Liberia, Afghanistan, Borneo, Brazil, New Zealand, India, the Congo—I wonder whether the mere sound of the names gives you the same sense of mystery and glamour as it does me. Good heavens, what joy, what frantic joy I felt when I found a stamp from, say, the Straits Settlements, or Korea or Nepal or New Guinea or Sierra Leone or Madagascar! I tell you, that particular rapture can be realized only by a hunter or a treasure-seeker or an archeologist who's doing excavations. To seek and to find—that's the greatest thrill and satisfaction which a man can get out of life. Everybody ought to seek something, if not stamps, then truth or golden ferns or at least stone arrowheads and ash-trays.

"Well, those were the happiest years of my life, my friendship with Lojzik and stamp-collecting. Then I had scarlet fever and they wouldn't let Lojzik come to see me, but he used to stand in the passage and whistle so that I could hear him. One day they must have taken their eyes off me or something; at all events, I got out of bed, and slipped upstairs to the attic to have a look at my stamps. I was so feeble that I could hardly lift the lid of the trunk. But the trunk was empty; the box containing the stamps was gone.

"I can't describe to you how distressed and horror-stricken I was. I think I must have stood there as if I'd been turned to stone, and I couldn't even cry, there was such a lump in my throat. First of all, it was appalling to me that my stamps, my greatest joy, were gone—but what was more appalling was that Lojzik, the only friend I had, must have stolen them while I was ill. I felt overwhelmed, dismayed, dumb-founded, woebegone—you know, it's amazing how much a child can suffer. How I got out of that attic, I don't know; but after that I had high fever again and during my clearer moments I pondered in despair. I never said a word about this to my father or my aunt—I had no mother.

I knew that they simply wouldn't understand me and through that I became rather estranged from them; from that time onwards my feelings for them ceased to be close and childlike. Lojzik's treachery affected me terribly, it was the first time anyone had played me false, 'A beggar,' I said to myself, 'Lojzik's a beggar and that's why he steals; it serves me right for chumming up with a beggar.' And this hardened my heart; it was then I began to draw a distinction between one person and another—I forfeited my state of social innocence; but at the time I didn't realize what a shock it had been to me and how much damage it had caused.

"When I had got over my fever, I also got over my distress at the loss of my stamp collection, though my heart still ached when I saw that Lojzik had now found new friends; but when he came running up to me, rather sheepishly because it was so long since we'd seen each other, I said to him in a curt, grown-up tone: 'You sling your hook, I've finished with you.' Lojzik turned red and presently replied: 'All right, then.' And from that time onward he hated me as thoroughly as the underdog can hate.

"Well, that was the incident which affected my whole life. The world I lived in was, so to speak, desecrated; I lost my faith in people; I learned how to hate and despise. After that I never had a friend; and when I grew up, I began to assume that because I was by myself, I needed nobody and would show favour to nobody. Then I discovered that nobody liked me; I used to put this down to the fact that I despised affection and was proof against all sentimentality. And so I became an aloof and purposeful man, very fussy about myself, very punctilious, and the kind of person who always wants to do the right thing. I was cantankerous and harsh towards my subordinates; I did not love the woman I married; I brought up my children to obey and fear me, and by my industry and sense of duty I gained quite a reputation. Such was my life, my whole life; I attended to nothing except my duty. When my time comes, the newspapers will say what valuable work I did and what an exemplary character I had. But if people only knew how much solitude, mistrust, and self-will there is about it all.

"Three years ago my wife died. I never admitted to myself or to anybody else, but I was terribly upset; and in my distress I rummaged about among all sorts of family keepsakes which had been left by my father and mother; photographs, letters, my old school exercise-books —I felt like choking when I saw how carefully my stern father had arranged and kept them; I think that, after all, he must have been fond of me. The cupboard in the attic was filled with these things, and at the bottom of a drawer was a box sealed with my father's seals; when I opened it, I discovered the stamp collection I had made fifty years earlier.

"I'm not going to keep anything back from you: I burst into tears and I took the box into my room like a man who has found a treasure. So *that's* what happened, suddenly flashed across my mind; while I was ill, somebody must have found my stamp collection and my father confiscated it, so that I should not neglect my lessons. He oughtn't to have done it, but it was all because of his concern and affection for me; I don't know how it was, but I began to feel sorry for him and for myself.

"And then I remembered: so Lojzik never stole my stamps. Good heavens, how I had wronged him! Again I saw the freckled and untidy urchin before me, and I wondered what had become of him and whether he was still alive. I tell you, I felt so wretched and ashamed when I looked back on it all. Because of a single false suspicion I had lost my only friend; because of that I had wasted my childhood. Because of that I had begun to despise the lower orders; because of that I had been so self-opinionated; because of that I never became attached to anyone. Because of that the very sight of a postage-stamp always made me feel annoyed and disgusted. Because of this I never wrote to my wife, either before or after our marriage, and I explained this away by pretending to be above what I chose to call gush; and my wife felt this keenly. Because of that I

was harsh and aloof. Because of that, only because of that, I had so fine a career and performed my duties in such an exemplary manner.

"I saw my whole life afresh; suddenly it seemed a different life, was the thought which struck me. If that hadn't happened, I should have been so full of enthusiasm and dash, affection, chivalry, wit and resourcefulness, strange and unruly things of that sort—why, good heavens, I might have been almost anything else, an explorer or an actor or a soldier! Why, I might have felt some affection for my peers, I might have drunk with them, understood them, oh, there's no knowing what I mightn't have done. I felt as if ice were thawing inside me. I went through the collection, stamp by stamp, they were all there, Lombardy, Cuba, Siam, Hanover, Nicaragua, the Philippines, all the places which I had wanted to go to and which I shall now never see. On each of these stamps there was a scrap of something, which might have been and never was. I sat brooding over them all night and took stock of my life. I realized that it had been an artificial and impersonal life, which did not belong to me, and that my proper life had never come into existence." Mr. Karas shook his head sadly. "When I consider all I might have been, and how I wronged Lojzik———"

Father Voves, on hearing these words, looked very downcast and forlorn; most likely he had remembered something in his own life. "Mr. Karas," he said pityingly, "don't think about it; it's no use, you can't put it right now, you can't make a fresh start———"

"No," sighed Mr. Karas with a slight flush. "But you know, anyhow—anyhow, I've started collecting stamps again."

I
CAN THE NARRATOR BE TRUSTED?

When reading a story told in the first person, you have to decide to what degree the speaker is telling the truth. Karas, an old man remembering his youth, is telling his story to a priest. Is Karas trying to find some justification for the kind of person he has become in the hope of shifting blame away from himself? If he had made a different choice—talked to Lojzik about his suspicions—would his life really have turned out differently?

II
IMPLICATIONS

From your own experience and from the story itself, do you think the following statements are right, wrong, or a bit of both?

1. The friendship between boys of such different backgrounds would have broken up sooner or later.

2. Modern communications methods have made the world so small that names of distant places no longer evoke the emotions that are recorded in this story.

3. A single traumatic experience can radically change one's personality.

4. Karas says that we all could lead many different lives. At some point, though—whether by chance or by inclination—we choose one way of life. Still, the others are never entirely dead.

5. Karas says that the shock of Lojzik's supposed betrayal caused him to lose his social innocence,

but this loss is something that everyone experiences in growing up.

III
TECHNIQUES

Characterization

1. List the things that Karas tells you about himself, past and present.

2. What do his voice and his manner of telling the story add to the picture?

Imagery

In the following excerpts, Čapek has created vivid images. What is unusual in the combination of words or items that he puts together?

1. ". . . why, the thrill I had was perfectly agonizing—every vast happiness has a sweet pang about it."

2. "Everybody ought to seek something; if not stamps, then truth or golden ferns or at least stone arrow-heads and ash-trays."

3. ". . . I rummaged about among all sorts of family keepsakes which had been left by my father and mother; photographs, letters, my old school exercise-books. . . ."

❦ COLETTE

Sidonie Gabrielle Claudine Colette[1] (1873–1954) was hailed during her life as
one of France's greatest writers, and when she died, she was given
a state funeral. As a young girl at school, Colette was always a top performer
and excelled in composition, which she said was as easy as "frying eggs."
At twenty, homesick and lonely in a new town, she married a thirty-four-
year-old friend of the family, Henri Gauthier-Villars, better known as
Willy. A music critic and author of breezy light novels, he found
sharp-tongued, rude, and mischievous Colette little help in his aspirations for
social advancement. But he quickly realized her marvelous ability for
observation and characterization and her insight into human behavior. So Willy
listened while Colette regaled him with delightful tales of her escapades
as a girl. He spiced these up a bit, and they published their first
co-authored novel, *Claudine at School*. The book was an instant success and
led to others in the series. But Colette and Willy's divorce ended their
authorial collaboration. Colette then continued to write on her own and for
some time published a book a year. Glenway Wescott said that her writing
was a wonderful combination of sensuousness, elegance, brevity,
clarity— "and those turns of phrase, speedy and forceful and neat, and with a
sense of fun, for which the French have the word *esprit*." Americans know
Colette best for *Gigi*, which was made into a musical comedy often replayed
on the television screen. Invalided with arthritis in later years, Colette
hobbled to the meeting of the Goncourt Academy when she was elected to
become one of the ten "living literary immortals" who annually award
the coveted Prix Goncourt for fiction. When reporters asked what her hopes
for the future were, she replied that they were simple: "to love . . . to live
a little . . . to have flowers . . . strawberries . . . to live in a more tranquil
universe." A plaque now hangs on the garden wall of her apartment house,
where she lived with her favorite books, her photographs, and her adored cats.
The plaque reads: "Here lived, here died Colette, whose work is a
window wide-open on life."

The Little Bouilloux Girl

translated from the French

The little Bouilloux[2] girl was so lovely that
even we children noticed it. It is unusual for
small girls to recognize beauty in one of themselves and pay homage to it. But there could be
no disputing such undeniable loveliness as hers.
Whenever my mother met the little Bouilloux
girl in the street, she would stop her and bend
over her as she was wont to bend over her yellow

1. **Colette** (kə let′).
2. **Bouilloux** (bwē yü′).

tea rose, her red flowering cactus or her Azure Blue butterfly trustfully asleep on the scaly bark of the pine tree. She would stroke her curly hair, golden as a half-ripe chestnut, and her delicately tinted cheeks, and watch the incredible lashes flutter over her great dark eyes. She would observe the glimmer of the perfect teeth in her peerless mouth, and when, at last, she let the child go on her way, she would look after her, murmuring, "It's prodigious!"

Several years passed, bringing yet further graces to the little Bouilloux girl. There were certain occasions recorded by our admiration: a prize giving at which, shyly murmuring an unintelligible recitation, she glowed through her tears like a peach under a summer shower. The little Bouilloux girl's first communion caused a scandal: the same evening, after vespers, she was seen drinking a half pint at the *Café du Commerce*, with her father, the sawyer,[3] and that night she danced, already feminine and flirtatious, a little unsteady in her white slippers, at the public ball.

With an arrogance to which she had accustomed us, she informed us later, at school, that she was to be apprenticed.

"Oh! Who to?"

"To Madame Adolphe."

"Oh! And are you to get wages at once?"

"No. I'm only thirteen, I shall start earning next year."

She left us without emotion, and coldly we let her go. Already her beauty isolated her and she had no friends at school, where she learned very little. Her Sundays and her Thursdays brought no intimacy with us; they were spent with a family that was considered "unsuitable," with girl cousins of eighteen well known for their brazen behavior, and with brothers, cartwright apprentices, who sported ties at fourteen and smoked when they escorted their sister to the Parisian shooting gallery at the fair or to the cheerful bar that the widow Pimolle had made so popular.

The very next morning on my way to school I met the little Bouilloux girl setting out for the dressmaker's workrooms, and I remained mo-

Colette

tionless, thunderstruck with jealous admiration, at the corner of the Rue des Soeurs, watching Nana Bouilloux's retreating form.

She had exchanged her black pinafore and short childish frock for a long skirt and a pleated blouse of pink sateen. She wore a black alpaca apron and her exuberant locks, disciplined and twisted into a "figure of eight," lay close as a helmet about the charming new shape of a round imperious head that retained nothing childish except its freshness and the not yet calculated impudence of a little village adventuress.

That morning the upper forms hummed like a hive.

"I've seen Nana Bouilloux! In a long dress, my dear, would you believe it? And her hair in a chignon! She had a pair of scissors hanging from her belt too!"

At noon I flew home to announce breathlessly:

"Mother! I met Nana Bouilloux in the street! She was passing our door. And she had on a long dress! Mother, just imagine, a long dress! And her hair in a chignon! And she had high heels and a pair of ———"

"Eat, Minet-Chéri,[4] eat, your cutlet will be cold."

---

3. **sawyer,** someone who saws wood in a sawmill.
4. **Minet-Chéri,** a term of endearment.

"And an apron, mother, such a lovely alpaca apron that looked like silk! Couldn't I possibly ———"

"No, Minet-Chéri, you certainly couldn't."

"But if Nana Bouilloux can ———"

"Yes, Nana Bouilloux, at thirteen, can, in fact she should, wear a chignon, a short apron and a long skirt—it's the uniform of all little Bouilloux girls throughout the world, at thirteen—more's the pity."

"But ———"

"Yes, I know you would like to wear the complete uniform of a little Bouilloux girl. It includes all that you've seen, and a bit more besides: a letter safely hidden in the apron pocket, an admirer who smells of wine and of cheap cigars; two admirers, three admirers and a little later on plenty of tears . . . and a sickly child hidden away, a child that has lain for months crushed by constricting stays. There it is, Minet-Chéri, the entire uniform of the little Bouilloux girls. Do you still want it?"

"Of course not, mother, I only wanted to see if a chignon ———"

But my mother shook her head, mocking but serious.

"No, no! You can't have the chignon without the apron, the apron without the letter, the letter without the high-heeled slippers, or the slippers without . . . all the rest of it! It's just a matter of choice!"

My envy was soon exhausted. The resplendent little Bouilloux girl became no more than a daily passer-by whom I scarcely noticed. Bareheaded in winter and summer, her gaily colored blouses varied from week to week, and in very cold weather she swathed her elegant shoulders in a useless little scarf. Erect, radiant as a thorny rose, her eyelashes sweeping her cheeks or half revealing her dark and dewy eyes, she grew daily more worthy of queening it over crowds, of being gazed at, adorned and bedecked with jewels. The severely smoothed crinkliness of her chestnut hair could still be discerned in little waves that caught the light in the golden mist at the nape of her neck and round her ears. She

always looked vaguely offended with her small, velvety nostrils reminding one of a doe.

She was fifteen or sixteen now—and so was I. Except that she laughed too freely on Sundays, in order to show her white teeth, as she hung on the arms of her brothers or her girl cousins, Nana Bouilloux was behaving fairly well.

"For a little Bouilloux girl, very well indeed!" was the public verdict.

She was seventeen, then eighteen; her complexion was like a peach on a south wall, no eyes could meet the challenge of hers and she had the bearing of a goddess. She began to take the floor at fetes and fairs, to dance with abandon, to stay out very late at night, wandering in the lanes with a man's arm round her waist. Always unkind, but full of laughter, provoking boldness in those who would have been content merely to love her.

Then came a St. John's Eve[5] when she appeared on the dance floor that was laid down on the *Place du Grand-Jeu* under the melancholy light of malodorous oil lamps. Hobnailed boots kicked up the dust between the planks of the "floor." All the young men, as was customary, kept their hats on while dancing. Blonde girls became claret-colored in their tight bodices, while the dark ones, sunburned from their work in the fields, looked black. But there, among a band of haughty workgirls, Nana Bouilloux, in a summer dress sprigged with little flowers, was drinking lemonade laced with red wine when the Parisians arrived on the scene.

They were two Parisians such as one sees in the country in summer, friends of a neighboring landowner, and supremely bored; Parisians in tussore[6] and white serge, come for a moment to mock at a village midsummer fete. They stopped laughing when they saw Nana Bouilloux and sat down near the bar in order to see her better. In low voices they exchanged comments which she pretended not to hear, since her pride as a beau-

---

5. **St. John's Eve,** the feast of St. John the Baptist is celebrated as a holiday in France on June 24.
6. **tussore** (tus'ôr), a tan silk.

tiful creature would not let her turn her eyes in their direction and giggle like her companions. She heard the words: "A swan among geese! A Greuze![7] A crime to let such a wonder bury herself here . . ." When the young man in the white suit asked the little Bouilloux girl for a waltz she got up without surprise and danced with him gravely, in silence. From time to time her eyelashes, more beautiful than a glance, brushed against her partner's fair mustache.

After the waltz the two Parisians went away, and Nana Bouilloux sat down by the bar, fanning herself. There she was soon approached by young Leriche, by Houette, even by Honce the chemist, and even by Possy the cabinetmaker, who was ageing, but none the less a good dancer. To all of them she replied, "Thank you, but I'm tired," and she left the ball at half-past ten o'clock.

And after that, nothing more ever happened to the little Bouilloux girl. The Parisians did not return, neither they, nor others like them. Houette, Honce, young Leriche, the commercial travelers with their gold watch chains, soldiers on leave and sheriff's clerks vainly climbed our steep street at the hours when the beautifully coiffed sempstress, on her way down it, passed

them by stiffly with a distant nod. They looked out for her at dances, where she sat drinking lemonade with an air of distinction and answered their importunities with "Thank you very much, but I'm not dancing, I'm tired." Taking offense, they soon began to snigger: "Tired! Her kind of tiredness lasts for thirty-six weeks!" and they kept a sharp watch on her figure. But nothing happened to the little Bouilloux girl, neither that nor anything else. She was simply waiting, possessed by an arrogant faith, conscious of the debt owed by the hazard that had armed her too well. She was awaiting . . . not the return of the Parisian in white serge, but a stranger, a ravisher. Her proud anticipation kept her silent and pure; with a little smile of surprise, she rejected Honce, who would have raised her to the rank of chemist's lawful wife, and she would have nothing to say to the sheriff's chief clerk. With never another lapse, taking back, once and for all, the smiles, the glances, the glowing bloom of her cheeks, the red young lips, she awaited her kingdom and the prince without a name.

Years later, when I passed through my native village, I could not find the shade of her who had so lovingly refused me what she called "The uniform of little Bouilloux girls." But as the car bore me slowly, though not slowly enough—never slowly enough—up a street where I have now no reason to stop, a woman drew back to avoid the wheel. A slender woman, her hair well dressed

---

7. **Greuze** (groiz). Nana Bouilloux is compared to a portrait by the French painter Jean Baptiste Greuze (1725–1805).

in a bygone fashion, dressmaker's scissors hanging from a steel "châtelaine"[8] on her black apron. Large, vindictive eyes, a tight mouth sealed by long silence, the sallow cheeks and temples of those who work by lamplight; a woman of forty-five or . . . Not at all; a woman of thirty-eight, a woman of my own age, of exactly my age, there was no room for doubt. As soon as the car allowed her room to pass, "the little Bouilloux girl" went on her way down the street, erect and indifferent, after one anxious, bitter glance had told her that the car did not contain the long-awaited ravisher.

I
CHOICES AND TURNING POINTS

There are times when we make a choice that we instantly realize has changed the direction of our lives. But usually it is only by looking backward that we can see that point in time when a particular choice gradually shifted the direction in which our lives were moving. The narrator suggests that Nana reached such a turning point at the midsummer fête when one dance with a Parisian changed her attitude toward the local young men. Did Nana make as deliberate a choice as the narrator thinks?

II
IMPLICATIONS
Give your reaction to the following statements.
1. Nana's beauty is really a curse.

---

8. **châtelaine** (shat′l ān), a hooklike clasp worn at a woman's waist.

2. People usually resent a person who is too physically attractive.

3. Nana chooses the impossible dream over humdrum reality.

4. We tend to think the worst of those we envy.

5. The mother says, "You can't have the hair-do without the rest of the costume. . . . It is just a matter of choice."

III
TECHNIQUES
Characterization

Nana changes in the course of the story. Are the changes convincing? Why or why not?

Imagery

Reread the first paragraph. What are the images used to communicate the unusual beauty of the little Bouilloux girl?

Throughout the story, only certain features of Nana are mentioned. Which ones can you recall without looking back at the selection?

IV
WORDS
Mama uses an unusual word to describe Nana's beauty: *prodigious*. We usually associate this word with greatness in size or extent. But as used here, it echoes the now obsolete meaning of its Latin forebear, *prōdigiōsus:* portentous, ominous.

Several times in describing the girl, the narrator uses the word *arrogant*, which means overly convinced of one's own importance. There is some irony here because it is obvious that the little Bouilloux girl is of a lower social class than is the narrator.

CHOICE AND CONSEQUENCE

The moments of crisis and decision captured in the gallery of paintings, drawings, and sculpture on the following pages reflect the concern that artists, as well as writers, have shown in this major theme of human life.

The French painter Delacroix portrays Christopher Columbus at one of the decisive moments of his life. Columbus stares at a fifteenth-century chart of the world that hangs above the head of his young son, Diego, whom he is entrusting to the care of the Dominicans of La Rabida on the eve of his great adventure. Here, Columbus is a symbol of the restless, questing spirit of Western civilization.

COLUMBUS AND HIS SON AT LA RABIDA *Eugène Delacroix*
Courtesy of The National Gallery of Art, Washington, D.C.,
Chester Dale Collection

265

THE BUILDING OF THE TROJAN HORSE
Giovanni Domenico Tiepolo
Courtesy of Wadsworth Antheneum,
Hartford, Conn.

The Greeks, who for nine
years had beseiged Troy, prepare
their master strategy, the wooden
horse, pretended gift to Athena.
Inside the horse, the Greeks
concealed their greatest heroes.
At night, after the Trojans
had dragged the horse
inside the city walls,
the Greek heroes issued forth,
opened the gates to the beseigers,
and Troy was destroyed.

The great German engraver
and painter Dürer movingly portrays
the prodigal son at his lowly task
of feeding swine. In anguish,
the prodigal said, "I will arise and go
to my father, and will say unto him,
'Father, I have sinned against heaven
and before thee, and am no more
worthy to be called thy son: make me
as one of Thy servants.' And he
arose and went to his father."

THE PRODIGAL SON
Albrecht Dürer
Courtesy of The National Gallery of Art,
Washington, D.C.,
Rosenwald Collection

Goethe, Marlowe, and Thomas Mann are among the many writers who have left versions of the legend of Faust, the scholar and sorcerer who sold his soul to the devil in return for knowledge, power, and youth.

Brutus, as Rome's first Consul, condemned his own sons to death for plotting to overthrow the state.
David portrays the drama of personal suffering in a parent who placed patriotism above family loyalties.

THE LICTORS BRING HOME TO BRUTUS
THE BODIES OF HIS SONS   *Jacques Louis David*
Courtesy of Wadsworth Atheneum, Hartford, Conn.

THE LAST OF ENGLAND
Ford Madox Brown
*Reproduced by courtesy
of the Trustees
of the Tate Gallery,
London*

The poverty caused by England's
Industrial Revolution forced thousands
of English citizens to emigrate to
Australia and America. The
Victorian painter Ford Madox Brown
depicts a moment of intense emotion
as an English couple leaves
the familiar shores of England
to begin life anew in a foreign land.

In the fourteenth century, Calais, France, under seige for more than a year,
was starving. Six citizens offered themselves to the enemy as hostages in return
for mercy for their city. Five hundred years later, the citizens of Calais commissioned
the French sculptor Rodin to create this monument to these brave burghers.

THE BURGHERS
OF CALAIS
Auguste Rodin

Bullfighting is a cruel sport in the eyes of many.
The Spanish, however, see it as a test of bravery
in the face of death. The French painter Manet shows
the fate of one man who chose to fight the brave bulls. The repose
of the figure and the calm of the painting itself emphasize,
by contrast, the moment of violence that has just passed.

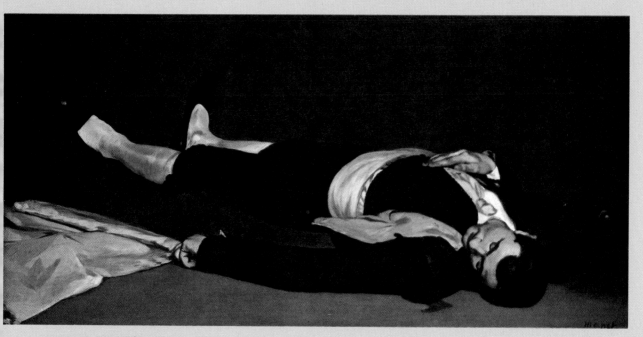

THE DEAD TOREADOR
Edouard Manet
Courtesy of The National Gallery of Art,
Washington, D.C., Widener Collection

THOMAS HARDY

Thomas Hardy (1840–1928) is one of the few great literary figures
who have achieved an important reputation as a writer of both prose and
poetry. To his own age he was a major novelist who dabbled in verse.
Modern critics, however, give increasingly greater emphasis to his poems. In both
prose and poetry his work is dark and pessimistic; he saw Nature as cruel
or indifferent to Humanity, and found life more often than not filled with bitter twists
of fate. Hardy was born near the wild heaths of the English county of Dorsetshire—
which he called Wessex in his novels. This landscape and its towns form the background
for his best work—such as *The Return of the Native; Jude, the Obscure;* and *The Mayor
of Casterbridge.* Hardy was popular in his own time, but his life was a series
of battles against forces that attacked him for the honesty and frankness
of his writing. His last novel, *Jude, the Obscure* (1896), raised such a storm
of protest that he resolved never again to write fiction, a resolution which he
faithfully kept. He returned to his first love, poetry, and produced hundreds
of lyric and narrative poems, as well as *The Dynasts,* a long epic drama in verse
of the Napoleonic Wars. Hardy has been called a fatalist because he so often shows
his characters helpless before the inflexible, crushing movement of life. In his own
defense Hardy replied that a novel is an impression of life, not an argument,
and that the artist must represent truly what he or she feels. The force and beauty
of his writing—especially his scenes of landscapes and country people—brought Hardy
great honor by the time of his death in 1928. He seemed to many the last
of the "Great Victorians," and he was buried among England's poets
in Westminster Abbey.

To Please His Wife

The interior of St. James's Church, in Havenpool Town, was slowly darkening under the
close clouds of a winter afternoon. It was Sunday: service had just ended, the face of the
parson in the pulpit was buried in his hands,
and the congregation, with a cheerful sigh of
release, were rising from their knees to depart.

For the moment the stillness was so complete
that the surging of the sea could be heard outside the harbour-bar. Then it was broken by
the footsteps of the clerk going towards the
west door to open it in the usual manner for the
exit of the assembly. Before, however, he had
reached the doorway, the latch was lifted from
without, and the dark figure of a man in a
sailor's garb appeared against the light.

The clerk stepped aside, the sailor closed the
door gently behind him, and advanced up the
nave till he stood at the chancel-step. The
parson looked up from the private little prayer
which, after so many for the parish, he quite
fairly took for himself, rose to his feet, and
stared at the intruder.

"I beg your pardon, sir," said the sailor, addressing the minister in a voice distinctly audible to all the congregation. "I have come here
to offer thanks for my narrow escape from shipwreck. I am given to understand that it is a
proper thing to do, if you have no objection?"

The parson, after a moment's pause, said
hesitatingly, "I have no objection; certainly. It
is usual to mention any such wish before ser-

vice, so that the proper words may be used in the General Thanksgiving. But, if you wish, we can read from the form for use after a storm at sea."

"Aye, sure; I ain't particular," said the sailor.

The clerk thereupon directed the sailor to the page in the prayer-book where the collect of thanksgiving would be found, and the rector began reading it, the sailor kneeling where he stood, and repeating it after him word by word in a distinct voice. The people, who had remained agape and motionless at the proceeding, mechanically knelt down likewise; but they continued to regard the isolated form of the sailor, who, in the precise middle of the chancel-step, remained fixed on his knees, facing the east, his hat beside him, his hands joined, and he quite unconscious of his appearance in their regard.

When his thanksgiving had come to an end he rose; the people rose also; and all went out of church together. As soon as the sailor emerged, so that the remaining daylight fell upon his face, old inhabitants began to recognize him as no other than Shadrach Jolliffe, a young man who had not been seen at Havenpool for several years. A son of the town, his parents had died when he was quite young, on which account he had early gone to sea, in the Newfoundland trade.

He talked with this and that townsman as he walked, informing them that, since leaving his native place years before, he had become captain and owner of a small coasting-ketch, which had providentially been saved from the gale as well as himself. Presently he drew near to two girls who were going out of the churchyard in front of him; they had been sitting in the nave at his entry, and had watched his doings with deep interest, afterwards discussing him as they moved out of church together. One was a slight and gentle creature, the other a tall, large-framed, deliberative girl. Captain Jolliffe regarded the loose curls of their hair, their backs and shoulders, down to their heels, for some time.

Thomas Hardy

"Who may them two maids be?" he whispered to his neighbour.

"The little one is Emily Hanning; the tall one, Joanna Phippard."

"Ah, I recollect 'em now, to be sure."

He advanced to their elbow, and genially stole a gaze at them.

"Emily, you don't know me?" said the sailor, turning his beaming brown eyes on her.

"I think I do, Mr. Jolliffe," said Emily shyly.

The other girl looked straight at him with her dark eyes.

"The face of Miss Joanna I don't call to mind so well," he continued. "But I know her beginnings and kindred."

They walked and talked together, Jolliffe narrating particulars of his late narrow escape, till they reached the corner of Sloop Lane, in which Emily Hanning dwelt, when, with a nod and smile, she left them. Soon the sailor parted also from Joanna, and, having no especial errand or appointment, turned back towards Emily's house. She lived with her father, who called himself an accountant, the daughter, however, keeping a little stationery-shop as a supplemental provision for the gaps of his somewhat

271

uncertain business. On entering, Jolliffe found father and daughter about to begin tea.

"Oh, I didn't know it was tea-time," he said. "Aye, I'll have a cup with much pleasure."

He remained to tea and long afterwards, telling more tales of his seafaring life. Several neighbours called to listen, and were asked to come in. Somehow Emily Hanning lost her heart to the sailor that Sunday night, and in the course of a week or two there was a tender understanding between them.

One moonlight evening in the next month Shadrach was ascending out of the town by the long straight road eastward, to an elevated suburb where the more fashionable houses stood—if anything near this ancient port could be called fashionable—when he saw a figure before him whom, from her manner of glancing back, he took to be Emily. But, on coming up, he found she was Joanna Phippard. He gave a gallant greeting, and walked beside her.

"Go along," she said, "or Emily will be jealous."

He seemed not to like the suggestion, and remained.

What was said and what was done on that walk never could be clearly recollected by Shadrach; but in some way or other Joanna contrived to wean him away from her gentler and younger rival. From that week onwards, Jolliffe was seen more and more in the wake of Joanna Phippard and less in the company of Emily; and it was soon rumoured about the quay that old Jolliffe's son, who had come home from sea, was going to be married to the former young woman, to the great disappointment of the latter.

Just after this report had gone about, Joanna dressed herself for a walk one morning, and started for Emily's house in the little cross-street. Intelligence of the deep sorrow of her friend on account of the loss of Shadrach had reached her ears also, and her conscience reproached her for winning him away.

Joanna was not altogether satisfied with the sailor. She liked his attentions, and she coveted the dignity of matrimony; but she had never been deeply in love with Jolliffe. For one thing, she was ambitious, and socially his position was hardly so good as her own, and there was always the chance of an attractive woman mating considerably above her. It had long been in her mind that she would not strongly object to give him back again to Emily if her friend felt so very badly about him. To this end she had written a letter of renunciation to Shadrach, which letter she carried in her hand, intending to send it if personal observation of Emily convinced her that her friend was suffering.

Joanna entered Sloop Lane and stepped down into the stationery shop, which was below the pavement level. Emily's father was never at home at this hour of the day, and it seemed as though Emily were not at home either, for the visitor could make nobody hear. Customers came so seldom hither that a five minutes' absence of the proprietor counted for little. Joanna waited in the little shop, where Emily had tastefully set out—as women can—articles in themselves of slight value, so as to obscure the meagreness of the stock-in-trade; till she saw a figure pausing without the window apparently absorbed in the contemplation of the sixpenny books, packets of paper, and prints hung on a string. It was Captain Shadrach Jolliffe, peering in to ascertain if Emily were there alone. Moved by an impulse of reluctance to meet him in a spot which breathed of Emily, Joanna slipped through the door that communicated with the parlour at the back. She had frequently done so before, for in her friendship with Emily she had the freedom of the house without ceremony.

Jolliffe entered the shop. Through the thin blind which screened the glass partition she could see that he was disappointed at not finding Emily there. He was about to go out again, when Emily's form darkened the doorway, hastening home from some errand. At sight of Jolliffe she started back as if she would have gone out again.

"Don't run away, Emily, don't!" said he. "What can make 'ye afraid?"

"I'm not afraid, Captain Jolliffe. Only—only I saw you all of a sudden, and—it made me jump!" Her voice showed that her heart had jumped even more than the rest of her.

"I just called as I was passing," he said.

"For some paper?" She hastened behind the counter.

"No, no, Emily; why do you get behind there? Why not stay by me? You seem to hate me."

"I don't hate you. How can I?"

"Then come out, so that we can talk like Christians."

Emily obeyed with a fitful laugh, till she stood again beside him in the open part of the shop.

"There's a dear," he said.

"You mustn't say that, Captain Jolliffe; because the words belong to somebody else."

"Ah! I know what you mean. But, Emily, upon my life I didn't know till this morning that you cared one bit about me, or I should not have done as I have done. I have the best of feelings for Joanna, but I know that from the beginning she hasn't cared for me more than in a friendly way; and I see now the one I ought to have asked to be my wife. You know, Emily, when a man comes home from sea after a long voyage he's as blind as a bat—he can't see who's who in women. They are all alike to him, beautiful creatures, and he takes the first that comes easy, without thinking if she loves him, or if he might not soon love another better than her. From the first I inclined to you most, but you were so backward and shy that I thought you didn't want me to bother 'ee, and so I went to Joanna."

"Don't say any more, Mr. Jolliffe, don't!" said she, choking. "You are going to marry Joanna next month, and it is wrong to—to——"

"O, Emily, my darling!" he cried, and clasped her little figure in his arms before she was aware.

Joanna, behind the curtain, turned pale, tried to withdraw her eyes, but could not.

"It is only you I love as a man ought to love the woman he is going to marry; and I know

this from what Joanna has said, that she will willingly let me off! She wants to marry higher I know, and only said 'Yes' to me out of kindness. A fine, tall girl like her isn't the sort for a plain sailor's wife; you be the best suited for that."

He kissed her and kissed her again, her flexible form quivering in the agitation of his embrace.

"I wonder—are you sure—Joanna is going to break off with you? Oh, are you sure? Because ——"

"I know she would not wish to make us miserable. She will release me."

"Oh, I hope—I hope she will! Don't stay any longer, Captain Jolliffe."

He lingered, however, till a customer came for a penny stick of sealing-wax, and then he withdrew.

Green envy had overspread Joanna at the scene. She looked about for a way of escape. To get out without Emily's knowledge of her visit was indispensable. She crept from the parlour into the passage, and thence to the front door of the house, where she let herself noiselessly into the street.

The sight of that caress had reversed all her resolutions. She could not let Shadrach go. Reaching home she burnt the letter, and told her mother that if Captain Jolliffe called she was too unwell to see him.

Shadrach, however, did not call. He sent her a note expressing in simple language the state of his feelings; and asked to be allowed to take advantage of the hints she had given him that her affection, too, was little more than friendly, by cancelling the engagement.

Looking out upon the harbour and the island beyond, he waited and waited in his lodgings for an answer that did not come. The suspense grew to be so intolerable that after dark he went up the High Street. He could not resist calling at Joanna's to learn his fate.

Her mother said her daughter was too unwell to see him, and to his questioning admitted that it was in consequence of a letter received from himself, which had distressed her deeply.

"You know what it was about, perhaps, Mrs. Phippard?" he said.

Mrs. Phippard owned that she did, adding that it put them in a very painful position. Thereupon Shadrach, fearing that he had been guilty of an enormity, explained that if his letter had pained Joanna it must be owing to a misunderstanding, since he had thought it would be a relief to her. If otherwise, he would hold himself bound by his word, and she was to think of the letter as never having been written.

Next morning he received an oral message from the young woman, asking him to fetch her home from a meeting that evening. This he did, and while walking from the Town Hall to her door, with her hand in his arm, she said:

"It is all the same as before between us, isn't it, Shadrach? Your letter was sent in mistake?"

"It is all the same as before," he answered, "if you say it must be."

"I wish it to be," she murmured, with hard lineaments, as she thought of Emily.

Shadrach was a religious and scrupulous man, who respected his word as his life. Shortly afterwards the wedding took place, Jolliffe having conveyed to Emily as gently as possible the error he had fallen into when estimating Joanna's mood as one of indifference.

II

A month after the marriage Joanna's mother died, and the couple were obliged to turn their attention to very practical matters. Now that she was left without a parent, Joanna could not bear the notion of her husband going to sea again, but the question was, what could he do at home? They finally decided to take on a small grocer's shop in the High Street, the good-will and stock of which were waiting to be disposed of at that time. Shadrach knew nothing of shopkeeping, and Joanna very little, but they hoped to learn.

To the management of this grocery business they now devoted all their energies, and continued to conduct it for many succeeding years,

without great success. Two sons were born to them, whom their mother loved to idolatry, although she had never passionately loved her husband; and she lavished upon them all her forethought and care. But the shop did not thrive, and the large dreams she had entertained of her sons' education and career became attenuated in the face of realities. Their schooling was of the plainest, but, being by the sea, they grew alert in all such nautical arts and enterprises as were attractive to their age.

The great interest of the Jolliffes' married life, outside their own immediate household, had lain in the marriage of Emily. By one of those odd chances which lead those that lurk in unexpected corners to be discovered, while the obvious are passed by, the gentle girl had been seen and loved by a thriving merchant of the town, a widower, some years older than herself, though still in the prime of life. At first Emily had declared that she never, never could marry any one; but Mr. Lester had quietly persevered, and had at last won her reluctant assent. Two children also were the fruit of this union, and, as they grew and prospered, Emily declared that she had never supposed that she could live to be so happy.

The worthy merchant's home, one of those large, substantial brick mansions frequently jammed up in old-fashioned towns, faced directly on the High Street, nearly opposite to the grocery shop of the Jolliffes, and it now became the pain of Joanna to behold the woman whose place she had usurped out of pure covetousness looking down from her position of comparative wealth upon the humble shop window with its dusty sugarloaves, heaps of raisins, and canisters of tea, over which it was her own lot to preside. The business having so dwindled, Joanna was obliged to serve in the shop herself, and it galled and mortified her that Emily Lester, sitting in her large drawing-room over the way, could witness her own dancings up and down behind the counter at the beck and call of wretched twopenny customers, whose patronage she was driven to welcome gladly; persons to whom she was compelled to be civil in the street, while Emily was bounding along with her children and her governess, and conversing with the genteelest people of the town and neighbourhood. This was what she had gained by not letting Shadrach Jolliffe, whom she had so faintly loved, carry his affection elsewhere.

Shadrach was a good and honest man, and he had been faithful to her in heart and in deed. Time had clipped the wings of his love for Emily in his devotion to the mother of his boys; he had quite lived down that impulsive earlier fancy, and Emily had become in his regard nothing more than a friend. It was the same with Emily's feelings for him. Possibly, had she found the least cause for jealousy, Joanna would almost have been better satisfied. It was in the absolute acquiescence of Emily and Shadrach in the results she herself had contrived that her discontent found nourishment.

Shadrach was not endowed with the narrow shrewdness necessary for developing a retail business in the face of many competitors. Did a customer inquire if the grocer could really recommend the wondrous substitute for eggs which a persevering bagman[1] had forced into his stock, he would answer that "when you did not put eggs into a pudding it was difficult to taste them there"; and when he was asked if his "real Mocha coffee" was real Mocha, he would say grimly, "as understood in small shops." The way to wealth was not by this route.

One summer day, when the big brick house opposite was reflecting the oppressive sun's heat into the shop, and nobody was present but husband and wife, Joanna looked across at Emily's door, where a wealthy visitor's carriage had drawn up. Traces of patronage had been visible in Emily's manner of late.

"Shadrach, the truth is, you are not a business man," his wife sadly murmured. "You were not brought up to shopkeeping, and it is impossible for a man to make a fortune at an occupation he has jumped into, as you did into this."

Jolliffe agreed with her, in this as in everything else. "Not that I care a rope's end about making a fortune," he said cheerfully. "I am happy enough, and we can rub on somehow."

She looked again at the great house through the screen of bottled pickles.

"Rub on—yes," she said bitterly. "But see how well off Emmy Lester is, who used to be so poor! Her boys will go to College, no doubt; and think of yours—obliged to go to the Parish School!"[2]

Shadrach's thoughts had flown to Emily.

"Nobody," he said good-humouredly, "ever did Emily a better turn than you did, Joanna, when you warned her off me and put an end to that little simpering nonsense between us, so as to leave it in her power to say 'Aye' to Lester when he came along."

This almost maddened her.

"Don't speak of bygones!" she implored, in stern sadness. "But think, for the boys' and my sake, not for your own, what are we to do to get richer?"

"Well," he said, becoming serious, "to tell the truth, I have always felt myself unfit for this business, though I've never liked to say so. I seem to want more room for sprawling; a more open space to strike out in than here among friends and neighbours. I could get rich as well as any man, if I tried my own way."

"I wish you would! What is your way?"

"To go to sea again."

She had been the very one to keep him at home, hating the semi-widowed existence of sailors' wives. But her ambition checked her instincts now, and she said:

"Do you think success really lies that way?"

"I am sure it lies in no other."

"Do you want to go, Shadrach?"

"Not for the pleasure of it, I can tell 'ee. There's no such pleasure at sea, Joanna, as I can find in my back parlour here. To speak honest, I have no love for the brine. I never had much. But if it comes to a question of a fortune for you and the lads, it is another thing.

---

1. **bagman,** a traveling peddler.
2. **Parish School,** a regional school maintained by the Church for poorer boys.

That's the only way to it for one born and bred a seafarer as I."

"Would it take long to earn?"

"Well, that depends; perhaps not."

The next morning Shadrach pulled from a chest of drawers the nautical jacket he had worn during the first months of his return, brushed out the moths, donned it, and walked down to the quay. The port still did a fair business in the Newfoundland trade, though not so much as formerly.

It was not long after this that he invested all he possessed in purchasing a part-ownership in a brig, of which he was appointed captain. A few months were passed in coast-trading, during which interval Shadrach wore off the land-rust that had accumulated upon him in his grocery phase; and in the spring the brig sailed for Newfoundland.

Joanna lived on at home with her sons, who were now growing up into strong lads, and occupying themselves in various ways about the harbour and quay.

"Never mind, let them work a little," their fond mother said to herself. "Our necessities compel it now, but when Shadrach comes home they will be only seventeen and eighteen, and they shall be removed from the port, and their education thoroughly taken in hand by a tutor; and with the money they'll have they will perhaps be as near to gentlemen as Emmy Lester's precious two, with their algebra and their Latin!"

The date for Shadrach's return drew near and arrived, and he did not appear. Joanna was assured that there was no cause for anxiety, sailing-ships being so uncertain in their coming; which assurance proved to be well grounded, for late one wet evening, about a month after the calculated time, the ship was announced as at hand, and presently the slip-slop step of Shadrach as the sailor sounded in the passage, and he entered. The boys had gone out and had missed him, and Joanna was sitting alone.

As soon as the first emotion of reunion between the couple had passed, Jolliffe explained the delay as owing to a small speculative contract, which had produced good results.

"I was determined not to disappoint 'ee," he said; "and I think you'll own that I haven't!"

With this he pulled out an enormous canvas bag, full and rotund as the money-bag of the giant whom Jack slew, untied it, and shook the contents out into her lap as she sat in her low chair by the fire. A mass of sovereigns and guineas[3] (there were guineas on the earth in those days) fell into her lap with a sudden thud, weighing down her gown to the floor.

"There!" said Shadrach complacently. "I told 'ee, dear, I'd do it; and have I done it or no?"

Somehow her face, after the first excitement of possession, did not retain its glory.

"It is a lot of gold, indeed," she said. "And—is this *all*?"

"All? Why, dear Joanna, do you know you can count to three hundred in that heap? It is a fortune!"

"Yes—yes. A fortune—judged by sea; but judged by land——"

However, she banished considerations of the money for the nonce. Soon the boys came in, and next Sunday Shadrach returned thanks to God—this time by the more ordinary channel of the italics in the General Thanksgiving. But a few days after, when the question of investing the money arose, he remarked that she did not seem so satisfied as he had hoped.

"Well you see, Shadrach," she answered, "*we* count by hundreds; *they* count by thousands" (nodding towards the other side of the street). "They have set up a carriage-and-pair since you left."

"Oh, have they?"

"My dear Shadrach, you don't know how the world moves. However, we'll do the best we can with it. But they are rich, and we are poor still!"

The greater part of a year was desultorily spent. She moved sadly about the house and

---

3. **the guinea** (gin′ē), was an English coin worth 21 shillings, minted from 1663 to 1813.

shop, and the boys were still occupying themselves in and around the harbour.

"Joanna," he said, one day, "I see by your movements that it is not enough."

"It is not enough," said she. "My boys will have to live by steering the ships that the Lesters own; and I was once above her."

Jolliffe was not an argumentative man, and he only murmured that he thought he would make another voyage. He meditated for several days, and coming home from the quay one afternoon said suddenly:

"I could do it for 'ee, dear, in one more trip for certain, if—if——"

"Do what, Shadrach?"

"Enable 'ee to count by thousands instead of hundreds."

"If what?"

"If I might take the boys."

She turned pale.

"Don't say that, Shadrach," she answered hastily.

"Why?"

"I don't like to hear it! There's danger at sea. I want them to be something genteel, and no danger to them. I couldn't let them risk their lives at sea. Oh, I couldn't ever, ever!"

"Very well, dear, it shan't be done."

Next day, after a silence, she asked a question:

"If they were to go with you it would make a great deal of difference, I suppose, to the profit?"

" 'Twould treble what I should get from the venture single-handed. Under my eye they would be as good as two more of myself."

Later on she said: "Tell me more about this."

"Well, the boys are almost as clever as master-mariners in handling a craft, upon my life! There isn't a more cranky place in the Northern Seas than about the sandbanks of this harbour, and they've practised here from their infancy. And they are so steady. I couldn't get their steadiness and their trustworthiness in half a dozen men twice their age."

"And is it *very* dangerous at sea; now, too, there are rumours of war?" she asked uneasily.

"Oh, well, there be risks. Still . . ."

The idea grew and magnified, and the mother's heart was crushed and stifled by it. Emmy was growing *too* patronizing; it could not be borne. Shadrach's wife could not help nagging him about their comparative poverty. The young men, amiable as their father, when spoken to on the subject of a voyage of enterprise, were quite willing to embark; and though they, like their father, had no great love for the sea, they became quite enthusiastic when the proposal was detailed.

Everything now hung upon their mother's assent. She withheld it long, but at last gave the word: the young men might accompany their father. Shadrach was unusually cheerful about it: Heaven had preserved him hitherto, and he had uttered his thanks. God would not forsake those who were faithful to him.

All that the Jolliffes possessed in the world was put into the enterprise. The grocery stock was pared down to the least that possibly could afford a bare sustenance to Joanna during the absence, which was to last through the usual "new-f'nland spell." How she would endure the weary time she hardly knew, for the boys had been with her formerly; but she nerved herself for the trial.

The ship was laden with boots and shoes, readymade clothing, fishing-tackle, butter, cheese, cordage, sailcloth, and many other commodities; and was to bring back oil, furs, skins, fish, cranberries, and what else came to hand. But much speculative trading to other ports was to be undertaken between the voyages out and homeward, and thereby much money made.

III

The brig sailed on a Monday morning in spring; but Joanna did not witness its departure. She could not bear the sight that she had been the means of bringing about. Knowing this, her husband told her overnight that they were to sail some time before noon next day;

hence when, awakening at five the next morning, she heard them bustling about downstairs, she did not hasten to descend, but lay trying to nerve herself for the parting, imagining they would leave about nine, as her husband had done on his previous voyage. When she did descend she beheld words chalked upon the sloping face of the bureau; but no husband or sons. In the hastily-scrawled lines Shadrach said they had gone off thus not to pain her by a leave-taking; and the sons had chalked under his words: "Good-bye, mother!"

She rushed to the quay and looked down the harbour towards the blue rim of the sea, but she could only see the masts and bulging sails of the *Joanna*; no human figures. " 'Tis I have sent them!" she said wildly, and burst into tears. In the house the chalked "Good-bye" nearly broke her heart. But when she had re-entered the front-room, and looked across at Emily's, a gleam of triumph lit her thin face at her anticipated release from the thraldom of subservience.

To do Emily Lester justice, her assumption of superiority was mainly a figment of Joanna's brain. That the circumstances of the merchant's wife were more luxurious than Joanna's, the former could not conceal; though whenever the two met, which was not very often now, Emily endeavoured to subdue the difference by every means in her power.

The first summer lapsed away; and Joanna meagrely maintained herself by the shop, which now consisted of little more than a window and a counter. Emily was, in truth, her only large customer; and Mrs. Lester's kindly readiness to buy anything and everything without questioning the quality had a sting of bitterness in it, for it was the uncritical attitude of a patron, and almost of a donor. The long dreary winter moved on; the face of the bureau had been turned to the wall to protect the chalked words of farewell, for Joanna could never bring herself to rub them out; and she often glanced at them with wet eyes. Emily's handsome boys came home for the Christmas holidays; the University was talked of for them;

and still Joanna subsisted, as it were, with held breath, like a person submerged. Only one summer more, and the "spell" would end. Towards the close of the time Emily called on her quondam friend. She had heard that Joanna began to feel anxious; she had received no letter from husband or sons for some months. Emily's silks rustled arrogantly when, in response to Joanna's almost dumb invitation, she squeezed through the opening of the counter and into the parlour behind the shop.

"*You* are all success, and *I* am all the other way!" said Joanna.

"But why do you think so?" said Emily. "They are to bring back a fortune, I hear."

"Ah! will they come? The doubt is more than a woman can bear. All three in one ship— think of that! And I have not heard of them for months!"

"But the time is not up. You should not meet misfortune half-way."

"Nothing will repay me for the grief of their absence!"

"Then why did you let them go? You were doing fairly well."

"I *made* them go!" she said, turning vehemently upon Emily. "And I'll tell you why! I could not bear that we should be only muddling on, and you so rich and patronizing! Now I have told you, and you may hate me if you will!"

"I shall never hate you, Joanna."

And she proved the truth of her words afterwards. The end of autumn came, and the brig should have been in port; but nothing like the *Joanna* appeared in the channel between the sands. It was now really time to be uneasy. Joanna Jolliffe sat by the fire, and every gust of wind caused her a cold thrill. She had always feared and detested the sea; to her it was a treacherous, restless, slimy creature, glorying in the griefs of women. "Still," she said, "they *must* come!"

She recalled to her mind that Shadrach had said before starting that if they returned safe and sound with success crowning their enterprise, he would go, as he had gone after his shipwreck, and kneel with his sons in the church and offer sincere thanks for their deliverance. She went to church regularly morning and afternoon, and sat in the most forward pew, nearest the chancel-step. Her eyes were mostly fixed on that step, where Shadrach had knelt in the bloom of his young manhood; she knew to an inch the spot which his knees had pressed twenty winters before; his outline as he had knelt, his hat on the step beside him. God was good. Surely her husband must kneel there again: a son on each side, as he had said; George just here, Jim just there. By long watching the spot as she worshipped, it became as if she saw the three returned ones there kneeling; the two slim outlines of her boys, the more bulky form between them; their hands clasped, their heads shaped against the eastern wall. The fancy grew almost to an hallucination: she could never turn her worn eyes to the step without seeing them there.

Nevertheless they did not come. Heaven was merciful, but it was not yet pleased to relieve her soul. This was her purgation for the sin of making them the slaves of her ambition. But it became more than purgation soon, and her mood approached despair. Months had passed since the brig had been due, but it had not returned.

Joanna was always hearing or seeing evidences of their arrival. When on the hill behind the port, whence a view of the open channel could be obtained, she felt sure that a little speck on the horizon, breaking the eternally level waste of waters southward, was the truck of the *Joanna's* mainmast. Or when indoors, a shout or excitement of any kind at the corner of the Town Cellar, where the High Street joined the quay, caused her to spring to her feet and cry: "'Tis they!"

But it was not. The visionary forms knelt every Sunday afternoon on the chancel-step, but not the real. Her shop had, as it were, eaten itself hollow. In the apathy which had resulted from her loneliness and grief she had ceased to take in the smallest supplies, and thus had sent away her last customer.

In this strait Emily Lester tried by every means in her power to aid the afflicted woman; but she met with constant repulses.

"I don't like you! I can't bear to see you!" Joanna would whisper hoarsely when Emily came to her and made advances.

"But I want to help and soothe you, Joanna," Emily would say.

"You are a lady, with a rich husband and fine sons! What can you want with a bereaved crone like me!"

"Joanna, I want this: I want you to come and live in my house, and not stay in this dismal place any longer."

"And suppose they come and don't find me at home? You wish to separate me and mine! No, I'll stay here. I don't like you, and I can't thank you, whatever kindness you do me!"

However, as time went on Joanna could not afford to pay the rent of the shop and house without an income. She was assured that all hope of the return of Shadrach and his sons was vain, and she reluctantly consented to accept the asylum of the Lesters' house. Here she was allotted a room of her own on the second floor, and went and came as she chose, without contact with the family. Her hair greyed and whitened, deep lines channelled her forehead, and her form grew gaunt and stooping. But she still expected the lost ones, and when she met Emily on the staircase she would say morosely: "I know why you've got me here! They'll come and be disappointed at not finding me at home and perhaps go away again; and then you'll be revenged for my taking Shadrach away from 'ee!"

Emily Lester bore these reproaches from the griefstricken soul. She was sure—all the people of Havenpool were sure—that Shadrach and his sons had gone to the bottom. For years the vessel had been given up as lost. Nevertheless, when awakened at night by any noise, Joanna would rise from bed and glance at the shop opposite by the light from the flickering lamp, to make sure it was not they.

It was a damp and dark December night, six years after the departure of the brig *Joanna*.

The wind was from the sea, and brought up a fishy mist which mopped the face like moist flannel. Joanna had prayed her usual prayer for the absent ones with more fervor and confidence than she had felt for months, and had fallen asleep about eleven. It must have been between one and two when she suddenly started up. She had certainly heard steps in the street, and the voices of Shadrach and her sons calling at the door of the grocery shop. She sprang out of bed, and, hardly knowing what clothing she dragged on herself, she hastened down Emily's large and carpeted staircase, put the candle on the hall table, unfastened the bolts and chain, and stepped into the street. The mist, blowing up the street from the quay, hindered her seeing the shop, although it was so near; but she had crossed to it in a moment. How was it? Nobody stood there. The wretched woman walked wildly up and down with her bare feet—there was not a soul. She returned and knocked with all her might at the door which had once been her own—they might have been admitted for the night, unwilling to disturb her till the morning. It was not till several minutes had elapsed that the young man who now kept the shop looked out of an upper window, and saw the skeleton of something human standing below half dressed.

"Has anybody come?" asked the form.

"Oh, Mrs. Jolliffe, I didn't know it was you," said the young man kindly, for he was aware how her baseless expectations moved her. "No: nobody has come."

I
A DOMESTIC TRAGEDY

This story is performed in an atmosphere like that of *Macbeth*—foreboding and dimly lighted. Hardy's Joanna does not have the same heroic passion of Lady Macbeth, but her motives spring from the same dark, ugly source. In both cases the devastation is total; yet there is a difference. In *Macbeth* the murder is premeditated; in "To Please His Wife" Joanna plays into the shadowy hands of Fate.

Are either of the following statements a fair summary of "To Please His Wife"?

1. People create their own "heaven" or "hell" in life.

2. We are powerless before the impassive, crushing movement of Fate.

II
IMPLICATIONS

How do you feel about the following statements? Do you think the selection proves or disproves them?

1. The fatal choice of Joanna's life came at the moment when she decided to marry Jolliffe out of jealousy.

2. The happiness or unhappiness resulting from any action is in direct proportion to the good and evil of the motive that sets the action in motion.

3. Joanna's madness is caused by the same pressures as was Lady Macbeth's.

4. This is a moral story intended to teach a lesson more than to amuse or give pleasure.

5. Hardy's pessimism shows through the story.

III
TECHNIQUES

Character Development

1. Give the incidents in which Hardy builds a picture of Joanna.

2. How does Hardy use Emily to accentuate Joanna's personality?

3. What is your impression of Jolliffe in the scene with Emily in the store? Does the rest of the story reinforce or change this impression?

Imagery

Hardy relies on vivid details and imagery to create atmosphere and mood. A reader often has almost a physical sensation from the scenes. Consider now the last scene beginning on page 279: "It was a damp and dark December night. . . ." Select the phrases that convey:

1. The quality of the night.

2. The street scene.

3. Joanna's appearance.

VIRGINIA WOOLF

The daughter of Leslie Stephen, a critic and scholar,
Virginia Woolf (1882–1941) educated herself by reading in her father's
vast library. She was born into an upper-class English society that was interested
in the arts and literature. Most of her life was lived in London, surrounded
by other writers, critics, and painters. In 1912, she married Leonard Woolf,
and with him founded the Hogarth Press, which published her own books
and the books of many younger writers, such as T. S. Eliot. Outwardly,
Virginia Woolf lived a comfortable life; she was known as a witty writer and talker
and as a warm friend. But her inner life was turbulent, and she had many periods
of depression, as can be seen from her journals published after her death
as *A Writer's Diary*. Virginia Woolf's greatest achievement was as a novelist,
two of her best books being *Mrs. Dalloway* and *To the Lighthouse*. She revolted
against the heavy English novel of her day in which thousands of physical details
were piled one upon another. She wanted to write about the interior worlds
of her characters, and found the "stream of consciousness" technique the right one
for her multilayered vision of human life.

The Duchess and the Jeweller

Oliver Bacon lived at the top of a house overlooking the Green Park. He had a flat; chairs jutted out at the right angles—chairs covered in hide. Sofas filled the bays of the windows—sofas covered in tapestry. The windows, the three long windows, had the proper allowance of discreet net and figured satin. The mahogany sideboard bulged discreetly with the right brandies, whiskeys, and liqueurs. And from the middle window he looked down upon the glossy roofs of fashionable cars packed in the narrow straits of Piccadilly.[1] A more central position could not be imagined. And at eight in the morning he would have his breakfast brought in on a tray by a man-servant: the man-servant would unfold his crimson dressing-gown; he would rip his letters open with his long pointed nails and would extract thick white cards of invitation upon which the engraving stood up roughly from duchesses, countesses, viscountesses, and Honourable Ladies. Then he would wash; then he would eat his toast; then he would read his paper by the bright burning fire of electric coals.

"Behold Oliver," he would say, addressing himself. "You who began life in a filthy little alley, you who . . ." and he would look down at his legs, so shapely in their perfect trousers; at his boots; at his spats. They were all shapely, shining; cut from the best cloth by the best scissors in Savile Row.[2] But he dismantled himself often and became again a little boy in a dark alley. He had once thought it the height of his ambition—selling stolen dogs to fashionable women in Whitechapel. And once he had been done.[3] "Oh, Oliver," his mother had wailed. "Oh, Oliver! When will you have sense, my son?" . . . Then he had gone behind a counter; had sold cheap watches; then he had taken

1. **Piccadilly,** a fashionable section of London.
2. **Savile Row,** a London street containing many expensive tailoring establishments.
3. **done,** cheated.

Virginia Woolf

a wallet to Amsterdam. . . . At that memory he would chuckle—the old Oliver remembering the young. Yes, he had done well with the three diamonds; also there was the commission on the emerald. After that he went into the private room behind the shop in Hatton Garden; the room with the scales, the safe, the thick magnifying glasses. And then . . . and then. . . . He chuckled. When he passed through the knots of jewellers in the hot evening who were discussing prices, gold mines, diamonds, reports from South Africa, one of them would lay a finger to the side of his nose and murmur, "Hum-m-m," as he passed. It was no more than a murmur; no more than a nudge on the shoulder, a finger on the nose, a buzz that ran through the cluster of jewellers in Hatton Garden on a hot afternoon—oh, many years ago now! But still Oliver felt it purring down his spine, the nudge, the murmur that meant, "Look at him—young Oliver, the young jeweller—there he goes." Young he was then. And he dressed better and better; and had, first a hansom cab; then a car; and first he went up to the dress circle, then down into the stalls.[4] And he had a villa at Richmond,[5] overlooking

the river, with trellises of red roses; and Mademoiselle used to pick one every morning and stick it in his buttonhole.

"So," said Oliver Bacon, rising and stretching his legs. "So . . ."

And he stood beneath the picture of an old lady on the mantelpiece and raised his hands. "I have kept my word," he said, laying his hands together, palm to palm, as if he were doing homage to her. "I have won my bet." That was so; he was the richest jeweller in England; but his nose, which was long and flexible, like an elephant's trunk, seemed to say by its curious quiver at the nostrils (but it seemed as if the whole nose quivered, not only the nostrils) that he was not satisfied yet; still smelt something under the ground a little further off. Imagine a giant hog in a pasture rich with truffles; after unearthing this truffle and that, still it smells a bigger, a blacker truffle under the ground further off. So Oliver snuffed always in the rich earth of Mayfair[6] another truffle, a blacker, a bigger further off.

Now then he straightened the pearl in his tie, cased himself in his smart blue overcoat; took his yellow gloves and his cane; and swayed as he descended the stairs and half snuffed, half sighed through his long sharp nose as he passed out into Piccadilly. For was he not still a sad man, a dissatisfied man, a man who seeks something that is hidden, though he had won his bet?

He swayed slightly as he walked, as the camel at the zoo sways from side to side when it walks along the asphalt paths laden with grocers and their wives eating from paper bags and throwing little bits of silver paper crumpled up on to the path. The camel despises the grocers; the camel is dissatisfied with its lot; the camel sees the blue lake and the fringe of palm trees in front of it. So the great jeweller, the greatest jeweller in the whole world, swung down Piccadilly, perfectly dressed, with his

4. **dress circle,** the better seats in the orchestra of a theater; **stalls,** private theater boxes.
5. **Richmond,** a suburb of London.
6. **Mayfair,** another fashionable section of London.

gloves, with his cane; but dissatisfied still, till he reached the dark little shop, that was famous in France, in Germany, in Austria, in Italy, and all over America—the dark little shop in the street off Bond Street.[7]

As usual, he strode through the shop without speaking, though the four men, the two old men, Marshall and Spencer, and the two young men, Hammond and Wicks, stood straight and looked at him, envying him. It was only with one finger of the amber-coloured glove, waggling, that he acknowledged their presence. And he went in and shut the door of his private room behind him.

Then he unlocked the grating that barred the window. The cries of Bond Street came in; the purr of the distant traffic. The light from reflectors at the back of the shop struck upwards. One tree waved six green leaves, for it was June. But Mademoiselle had married Mr. Pedder of the local brewery—no one stuck roses in his buttonhole now.

"So," he half sighed, half snorted, "so—"

Then he touched a spring in the wall and slowly the panelling slid open, and behind it were the steel safes, five, no, six of them, all of burnished steel. He twisted a key; unlocked one; then another. Each was lined with a pad of deep crimson velvet; in each lay jewels—bracelets, necklaces, rings, tiaras, ducal coronets; loose stones in glass shells; rubies, emeralds, pearls, diamonds. All safe, shining, cool, yet burning, eternally, with their own compressed light.

"Tears!" said Oliver, looking at the pearls.

"Heart's blood!" he said, looking at the rubies.

"Gunpowder!" he continued, rattling the diamonds so that they flashed and blazed.

"Gunpower enough to blow Mayfair—sky high, high, high!" He threw his head back and made a sound like a horse neighing as he said it.

The telephone buzzed obsequiously in a low muted voice on his table. He shut the safe.

"In ten minutes," he said. "Not before." And he sat down at his desk and looked at the heads of the Roman emperors that were graved on his sleeve links. And again he dismantled himself and became once more the little boy playing marbles in the alley where they sell stolen dogs on Sunday. He became that wily astute little boy, with lips like wet cherries. He dabbled his fingers in ropes of tripe; he dipped them in pans of frying fish; he dodged in and out among the crowds. He was slim, lissome, with eyes like licked stones. And now—now—the hands of the clock ticked on, one, two, three, four. . . . The Duchess of Lambourne waited his pleasure; the Duchess of Lambourne, daughter of a hundred Earls. She would wait for ten minutes on a chair at the counter. She would wait his pleasure. She would wait till he was ready to see her. He watched the clock in its shagreen case. The hand moved on. With each tick the clock handed him—so it seemed—pâté de foie gras, a glass of champagne, another of fine brandy, a cigar costing one guinea. The clock laid them on the table beside him as the ten minutes passed. Then he heard soft slow footsteps approaching; a rustle in the corridor. The door opened. Mr. Hammond flattened himself against the wall.

"Her Grace!" he announced.

And he waited there, flattened against the wall.

And Oliver, rising, could hear the rustle of the dress of the Duchess as she came down the passage. Then she loomed up, filling the door, filling the room with the aroma, the prestige, the arrogance, the pomp, the pride of all the Dukes and Duchesses swollen in one wave. And as a wave breaks, she broke, as she sat down, spreading and splashing and falling over Oliver Bacon, the great jeweller, covering him with sparkling bright colours, green, rose, violet; and odours; and iridescences; and rays shooting from fingers, nodding from plumes, flashing from silk; for she was very large, very fat, tightly girt in pink taffeta, and past her

---

7. **Bond Street,** a London street containing many fashionable stores.

prime. As a parasol with many flounces, as a peacock with many feathers, shuts its flounces, folds its feathers, so she subsided and shut herself as she sank down in the leather armchair.

"Good morning, Mr. Bacon," said the Duchess. And she held out her hand which came through the slit of her white glove. And Oliver bent low as he shook it. And as their hands touched the link was forged between them once more. They were friends, yet enemies; he was master, she was mistress; each cheated the other, each needed the other, each feared the other, each felt this and knew this every time they touched hands thus in the little back room with the white light outside, and the tree with its six leaves, and the sound of the street in the distance and behind them the safes.

"And today, Duchess—what can I do for you today?" said Oliver, very softly.

The Duchess opened her heart, her private heart, gaped wide. And with a sigh but no word she took from her bag a long wash-leather pouch—it looked like a lean yellow ferret. And from a slit in the ferret's belly she dropped pearls—ten pearls. They rolled from the slit in the ferret's belly—one, two, three, four—like the eggs of some heavenly bird.

"All that's left me, dear Mr. Bacon," she moaned. Five, six, seven—down they rolled, down the slopes of the vast mountain sides that fell between her knees into one narrow valley— the eighth, the ninth, and the tenth. There they lay in the glow of the peach-blossom taffeta. Ten pearls.

"From the Appleby cincture," she mourned. "The last . . . the last of them all."

Oliver stretched out and took one of the pearls between finger and thumb. It was round, it was lustrous. But real was it, or false? Was she lying again? Did she dare?

She laid her plump padded finger across her lips. "If the Duke knew . . ." she whispered. "Dear Mr. Bacon, a bit of bad luck. . ."

Been gambling again, had she?

"That villain! That sharper!" she hissed.

The man with the chipped cheek bone? A bad 'un. And the Duke was straight as a poker;

with side whiskers; would cut her off, shut her up down there if he knew—what I know, thought Oliver, and glanced at the safe.

"Araminta, Daphne, Diana," she moaned. "It's for *them*."

The ladies Araminta, Daphne, Diana—her daughters. He knew them; adored them. But it was Diana he loved.

"You have all my secrets," she leered. Tears slid; tears fell; tears, like diamonds, collecting powder in the ruts of her cherry blossom cheeks.

"Old friend," she murmured, "old friend."

"Old friend," he repeated, "old friend," as if he licked the words.

"How much?" he queried.

She covered the pearls with her hand.

"Twenty thousand," she whispered.

But was it real or false, the one he held in his hand? The Appleby cincture—hadn't she sold it already? He would ring for Spencer or Hammond. "Take it and test it," he would say. He stretched to the bell.

"You will come down tomorrow?" she urged, she interrupted. "The Prime Minister—His Royal Highness. . ." She stopped. "And Diana . . ." she added.

Oliver took his hand off the bell.

He looked past her, at the backs of the houses in Bond Street. But he saw, not the houses in Bond Street, but a dimpling river; and trout rising and salmon; and the Prime Minister; and himself too, in white waistcoat; and then, Diana. He looked down at the pearl in his hand. But how could he test it, in the light of the river, in the light of the eyes of Diana? But the eyes of the Duchess were on him.

"Twenty thousand," she moaned. "My honour!"

The honour of the mother of Diana! He drew his cheque book towards him; he took out his pen.

"Twenty—" he wrote. Then he stopped writing. The eyes of the old woman in the picture were on him—of the old woman his mother.

"Oliver!" she warned him. "Have sense! Don't be a fool!"

"Oliver!" the Duchess entreated—it was "Oliver" now, not "Mr. Bacon." "You'll come for a long week-end?"

Alone in the woods with Diana! Riding alone in the woods with Diana!

"Thousand," he wrote, and signed it.

"Here you are," he said.

And there opened all the flounces of the parasol, all the plumes of the peacock, the radiance of the wave, the swords and spears of Agincourt,[8] as she rose from her chair. And the two old men and the two young men, Spencer and Marshall, Wicks and Hammond, flattened themselves behind the counter envying him as he led her through the shop to the door. And he waggled his yellow glove in their faces, and she held her honour—a cheque for twenty thousand pounds with his signature—quite firmly in her hands.

"Are they false or are they real?" asked Oliver, shutting his private door. There they were, ten pearls on the blotting-paper on the table. He took them to the window. He held them under his lens to the light. . . . This, then, was the truffle he had routed out of the earth! Rotten at the centre—rotten at the core!

"Forgive me, oh, my mother!" he sighed, raising his hand as if he asked pardon of the old woman in the picture. And again he was a little boy in the alley where they sold dogs on Sunday.

"For," he murmured, laying the palms of his hands together, "it is to be a long week-end."

I
"FORGIVE ME, OH, MY MOTHER"

The jeweller's cry is known to most of us, for we are all guilty of doing things we know our parents may disapprove; yet the rewards seem so important that we forget the warnings. While the basic response is universal, the cynical warning in this story is hardly common. Virginia Woolf has

clearly delineated a rich, successful, envied business owner who is still dissatisfied. Here is the ever-present dilemma of life . . . though we may achieve one goal, the next is always out there in the distance beckoning us forward.

Discuss what the story implies about each of the following:

a. Human greed

b. The falseness of society

c. Status-seeking

d. Our inability to be satisfied

II
IMPLICATIONS

How do you feel about the following statements? Considering the story, are they true? False? Neither?

1. Bacon deceived himself about the pearls' being real because he was a status seeker.

2. Bacon knows that the pearls are false before he makes out the check.

3. Status is more important than money.

III
TECHNIQUES

Characterization

1. Consider Bacon's character:

a. What are the reactions of other people toward him?

b. What do Bacon's thoughts about his childhood reveal about his drives and interests?

c. Is he round or flat as a character?

2. Now try to describe the Duchess. How has the author conveyed her character?

Imagery

1. The author has used a great deal of imagery. Oliver's nose is compared to an elephant's; Oliver himself to a giant hog; his walk to a camel's; his sound as he views the jewels to a horse's neigh. What does this use of animals in describing Oliver Bacon seem to say about him?

2. Consider the images used to describe the jewels as Bacon views them. How does this imagery expand your awareness of the inner person?

3. The entrance and exit of the Duchess are rich with imagery. Reread these descriptions and list the metaphors used. What kind of feeling do you get from these images?

8. **Agincourt** (aj′in kôrt), a village in northwest France at which English forces under Henry V decisively defeated a much larger French army in 1415.

ALBERT CAMUS

Albert Camus (1913–1960), one of the youngest writers
ever to receive the Nobel prize for literature, was born in Algiers and grew up
in surroundings of the most intense poverty. He studied philosophy
at the University of Algiers, then worked as a journalist and in the theater
as an actor, director, and playwright. His first great work was the play *Caligula.*
During the Second World War, he worked with and wrote for the French underground
paper *Combat.* After the war, he entered into the midst of French intellectual
and literary activity, writing novels, plays, and essays until his sudden death
in an automobile accident. *The Stranger,* his first major work of fiction,
emphasizes the feeling (common to so much modern literature) that life is meaningless
and in isolation. *The Plague,* a masterpiece of fiction, probes the individual's
responsibility to the community. Camus struggles always to find answers
for the intellectual and spiritual problems that beset humankind, and in this struggle,
his tremendous compassion for human suffering, his condemnation of violence and
tyranny shine in his language. All of these concerns are found in "The Guest."
This story takes place during the years when Algeria was a colony of France
and the Arabs were engaged in a long, bitter, and bloody war for independence.

The Guest

translated by Justin O'Brien

The schoolmaster was watching the two men climb toward him. One was on horseback, the other on foot. They had not yet tackled the abrupt rise leading to the schoolhouse built on the hillside. They were toiling onward, making slow progress in the snow, among the stones, on the vast expanse of the high, deserted plateau. From time to time the horse stumbled. Without hearing anything yet, he could see the breath issuing from the horse's nostrils. One of the men, at least, knew the region. They were following the trail although it had disappeared days ago under a layer of dirty white snow. The schoolmaster calculated that it would take them half an hour to get onto the hill. It was cold; he went back into the school to get a sweater.

He crossed the empty, frigid classroom. On the blackboard the four rivers of France, drawn with four different colored chalks, had been flowing toward their estuaries for the past three days. Snow had suddenly fallen in mid-October after eight months of drought without the transition of rain, and the twenty pupils, more or less, who lived in the villages scattered over the plateau had stopped coming. With fair weather they would return. Daru now heated only the single room that was his lodging, adjoining the classroom and giving also onto the plateau to the east. Like the class windows, his window looked to the south too. On that side the school was a few kilometers from the point where the plateau began to slope toward the south. In clear weather could be seen the purple mass of the mountain range where the gap opened onto the desert.

Somewhat warmed, Daru returned to the window from which he had first seen the two men. They were no longer visible. Hence they must have tackled the rise. The sky was not so dark, for the snow had stopped falling during the night. The morning had opened with a dirty light which had scarcely become brighter as the ceiling of clouds lifted. At two in the afternoon it seemed as if the day were merely beginning. But still this was better than those three days when the thick snow was falling amidst unbroken darkness with little gusts of wind that rattled the double door of the classroom. Then Daru had spent long hours in his room, leaving it only to go to the shed and feed the chickens or get some coal. Fortunately the delivery truck from Tadjid, the nearest village to the north, had brought his supplies two days before the blizzard. It would return in forty-eight hours.

Besides, he had enough to resist a siege, for the little room was cluttered with bags of wheat that the administration left as a stock to distribute to those of his pupils whose families had suffered from the drought. Actually they had all been victims because they were all poor. Every day Daru would distribute a ration to the children. They had missed it, he knew, during these bad days. Possibly one of the fathers or big brothers would come this afternoon and he could supply them with grain. It was just a matter of carrying them over to the next harvest. Now shiploads of wheat were arriving from France and the worst was over. But it would be hard to forget that poverty, that army of ragged ghosts wandering in the sunlight, the plateaus burned to a cinder month after month, the earth shriveled up little by little, literally scorched, every stone bursting into dust under one's foot. The sheep had died then by thousands and even a few men, here and there, sometimes without anyone's knowing.

In contrast with such poverty, he who lived almost like a monk in his remote schoolhouse, nonetheless satisfied with the little he had and with the rough life, had felt like a lord with his white-washed walls, his narrow couch, his unpainted shelves, his well, and his weekly provision of water and food. And suddenly this snow, without warning, without the foretaste

Albert Camus

of rain. This is the way the region was, cruel to live in, even without men—who didn't help matters either. But Daru had been born here. Everywhere else, he felt exiled.

He stepped out onto the terrace in front of the schoolhouse. The two men were now halfway up the slope. He recognized the horseman as Balducci, the old gendarme he had known for a long time. Balducci was holding on the end of a rope an Arab who was walking behind him with hands bound and head lowered. The gendarme waved a greeting to which Daru did not reply, lost as he was in contemplation of the Arab dressed in a faded blue jellaba,[1] his feet in sandals but covered with socks of heavy raw wool, his head surmounted by a narrow, short *chèche*.[2] They were approaching. Balducci was holding back his horse in order

---

1. **jellaba** (jel ab′ə), a short-sleeved cloak with a hood.
2. **chèche** (shā shā′), a cylindrical skull cap.

not to hurt the Arab, and the group was advancing slowly.

Within earshot, Balducci shouted: "One hour to do the three kilometers from El Ameur!" Daru did not answer. Short and square in his thick sweater, he watched them climb. Not once had the Arab raised his head. "Hello," said Daru when they got up onto the terrace. "Come in and warm up." Balducci painfully got down from his horse without letting go the rope. From under his bristling mustache he smiled at the schoolmaster. His little dark eyes, deep-set under a tanned forehead, and his mouth surrounded with wrinkles made him look attentive and studious. Daru took the bridle, led the horse to the shed, and came back to the two men, who were now waiting for him in the school. He led them into his room. "I am going to heat up the classroom," he said. "We'll be more comfortable there." When he entered the room again, Balducci was on the couch. He had undone the rope tying him to the Arab, who had squatted near the stove. His hands still bound, the *chèche* pushed back on his head, he was looking toward the window. At first Daru noticed only his huge lips, fat, smooth, almost Negroid; yet his nose was straight, his eyes were dark and full of fever. The *chèche* revealed an obstinate forehead and, under the weathered skin now rather discolored by the cold, the whole face had a restless and rebellious look that struck Daru when the Arab, turning his face toward him, looked him straight in the eyes. "Go into the other room," said the schoolmaster, "and I'll make you some mint tea." "Thanks," Balducci said. "What a chore! How I long for retirement." And addressing his prisoner in Arabic: "Come on, you." The Arab got up and, slowly, holding his bound wrists in front of him, went into the classroom.

With the tea, Daru brought a chair. But Balducci was already enthroned on the nearest pupil's desk and the Arab had squatted against the teacher's platform facing the stove, which stood between the desk and the window. When he held out the glass of tea to the prisoner,

Daru hesitated at the sight of his bound hands. "He might perhaps be untied." "Sure," said Balducci. "That was for the trip." He started to get to his feet. But Daru, setting the glass on the floor, had knelt beside the Arab. Without saying anything, the Arab watched him with his feverish eyes. Once his hands were free, he rubbed his swollen wrists against each other, took the glass of tea, and sucked up the burning liquid in swift little sips.

"Good," said Daru. "And where are you headed?"

Balducci withdrew his mustache from the tea. "Here, son."

"Odd pupils! And you're spending the night?"

"No. I'm going back to El Ameur. And you will deliver this fellow to Tinguit. He is expected at police headquarters."

Balducci was looking at Daru with a friendly little smile.

"What's this story?" asked the schoolmaster. "Are you pulling my leg?"

"No, son. Those are the orders."

"The orders? I'm not . . ." Daru hesitated, not wanting to hurt the old Corsican. "I mean, that's not my job."

"What! What's the meaning of that? In wartime people do all kinds of jobs."

"Then I'll wait for the declaration of war!"

Balducci nodded.

"O.K. But the orders exist and they concern you too. Things are brewing, it appears. There is talk of a forthcoming revolt. We are mobilized, in a way."

Daru still had his obstinate look.

"Listen, son," Balducci said. "I like you and you must understand. There's only a dozen of us at El Ameur to patrol throughout the whole territory of a small department and I must get back in a hurry. I was told to hand this guy over to you and return without delay. He couldn't be kept there. His village was beginning to stir; they wanted to take him back. You must take him to Tinguit tomorrow before the day is over. Twenty kilometers shouldn't faze a husky fellow like you. After that, all will be over. You'll come back to your pupils and your comfortable life."

Behind the wall the horse could be heard snorting and pawing the earth. Daru was looking out the window. Decidedly, the weather was clearing and the light was increasing over the snowy plateau. When all the snow was melted, the sun would take over again and once more would burn the fields of stone. For days, still, the unchanging sky would shed its dry light on the solitary expanse where nothing had any connection with man.

"After all," he said, turning around toward Balducci, "what did he do?" And, before the gendarme had opened his mouth, he asked: "Does he speak French?"

"No, not a word. We had been looking for him for a month, but they were hiding him. He killed his cousin."

"Is he against us?"

"I don't think so. But you can never be sure."

"Why did he kill?"

"A family squabble, I think. One owed the other grain, it seems. It's not at all clear. In short, he killed his cousin with a billhook. You know, like a sheep, *kreezk!*"

Balducci made the gesture of drawing a blade across his throat and the Arab, his attention attracted, watched him with a sort of anxiety. Daru felt a sudden wrath against the man, against all men with their rotten spite, their tireless hates, their blood lust.

But the kettle was singing on the stove. He served Balducci more tea; hesitated, then served the Arab again, who, a second time, drank avidly. His raised arms made the jellaba fall open and the schoolmaster saw his thin, muscular chest.

"Thanks, kid," Balducci said. "And now, I'm off."

He got up and went toward the Arab, taking a small rope from his pocket.

"What are you doing?" Daru asked dryly.

Balducci, disconcerted, showed him the rope. "Don't bother."

The old gendarme hesitated. "It's up to you. Of course, you are armed?"

"I have my shotgun."

"Where?"

"In the trunk."

"You ought to have it near your bed."

"Why? I have nothing to fear."

"You're crazy, son. If there's an uprising, no one is safe, we're all in the same boat."

"I'll defend myself. I'll have time to see them coming."

Balducci began to laugh, then suddenly the mustache covered the white teeth.

"You'll have time? O.K. That's just what I was saying. You have always been a little cracked. That's why I like you, my son was like that."

At the same time he took out his revolver and put it on the desk.

"Keep it; I don't need two weapons from here to El Ameur."

The revolver shone against the black paint of the table. When the gendarme turned toward him, the schoolmaster caught the smell of leather and horseflesh.

"Listen, Balducci," Daru said suddenly, "every bit of this disgusts me, and first of all your fellow here. But I won't hand him over. Fight, yes, if I have to. But not that."

The old gendarme stood in front of him and looked at him severely.

"You're being a fool," he said slowly. "I don't like it either. You don't get used to putting a rope on a man even after years of it, and you're even ashamed—yes, ashamed. But you can't let them have their way."

"I won't hand him over," Daru said again.

"It's an order, son, and I repeat it."

"That's right. Repeat to them what I've said to you: I won't hand him over."

Balducci made a visible effort to reflect. He looked at the Arab and at Daru. At last he decided.

"No, I won't tell them anything. If you want to drop us, go ahead; I'll not denounce you. I have an order to deliver the prisoner and I'm doing so. And now you'll just sign this paper for me."

"There's no need. I'll not deny that you left him with me."

"Don't be mean with me. I know you'll tell the truth. You're from hereabouts and you are a man. But you must sign, that's the rule."

Daru opened his drawer, took out a little square bottle of purple ink, the red wooden penholder with the "sergeant-major" pen he used for making models of penmanship, and signed. The gendarme carefully folded the paper and put it into his wallet. Then he moved toward the door.

"I'll see you off," Daru said.

"No," said Balducci. "There's no use being polite. You insulted me."

He looked at the Arab, motionless in the same spot, sniffed peevishly, and turned away toward the door. "Good-by, son," he said. The door shut behind him. Balducci appeared suddenly outside the window and then disappeared. His footsteps were muffled by the snow. The horse stirred on the other side of the wall and several chickens fluttered in fright. A moment later Balducci reappeared outside the window leading the horse by the bridle. He walked toward the little rise without turning around and disappeared from sight with the horse following him. A big stone could be heard bouncing down. Daru walked back toward the prisoner, who, without stirring, never took his eyes off him. "Wait," the schoolmaster said in Arabic and went toward the bedroom. As he was going through the door, he had a second thought, went to the desk, took the revolver, and stuck it in his pocket. Then, without looking back, he went into his room.

For some time he lay on his couch watching the sky gradually close over, listening to the silence. It was this silence that had seemed painful to him during the first days here, after the war. He had requested a post in the little town at the base of the foothills separating the upper plateaus from the desert. There, rocky walls, green and black to the north, pink and lavender to the south, marked the frontier of eternal summer. He had been named to a post farther north, on the plateau itself. In the be-

ginning, the solitude and the silence had been hard for him on these wastelands peopled only by stones. Occasionally, furrows suggested cultivation, but they had been dug to uncover a certain kind of stone good for building. The only plowing here was to harvest rocks. Elsewhere a thin layer of soil accumulated in the hollows would be scraped out to enrich paltry village gardens. This is the way it was: bare rock covered three quarters of the region. Towns sprang up, flourished, then disappeared; men came by, loved one another or fought bitterly, then died. No one in this desert, neither he nor his guest, mattered. And yet, outside this desert neither of them, Daru knew, could have really lived.

When he got up, no noise came from the classroom. He was amazed at the unmixed joy he derived from the mere thought that the Arab might have fled and that he would be alone with no decision to make. But the prisoner was there. He had merely stretched out between the stove and the desk. With eyes open, he was staring at the ceiling. In that position, his thick lips were particularly noticeable, giving him a pouting look. "Come," said Daru. The Arab got up and followed him. In the bedroom, the schoolmaster pointed to a chair near the table under the window. The Arab sat down without taking his eyes off Daru.

"Are you hungry?"

"Yes," the prisoner said.

Daru set the table for two. He took flour and oil, shaped a cake in a frying-pan, and lighted the little stove that functioned on bottled gas. While the cake was cooking, he went out to the shed to get cheese, eggs, dates, and condensed milk. When the cake was done he set it on the window sill to cool, heated some condensed milk diluted with water, and beat up the eggs into an omelette. In one of his motions he knocked against the revolver stuck in his right pocket. He set the bowl down, went into the classroom, and put the revolver in his desk drawer. When he came back to the room, night was falling. He put on the light and served the Arab. "Eat," he said. The Arab took a piece of the cake, lifted it eagerly to his mouth, and stopped short.

"And you?" he asked.

"After you. I'll eat too."

The thick lips opened slightly. The Arab hesitated, then bit into the cake determinedly.

The meal over, the Arab looked at the schoolmaster. "Are you the judge?"

"No, I'm simply keeping you until tomorrow."

"Why do you eat with me?"

"I'm hungry."

The Arab fell silent. Daru got up and went out. He brought back a folding bed from the shed, set it up between the table and the stove, perpendicular to his own bed. From a large suitcase which, upright in a corner, served as a shelf for papers, he took two blankets and arranged them on the camp bed. Then he stopped, felt useless, and sat down on his bed. There was nothing more to do or to get ready. He had to look at this man. He looked at him, therefore, trying to imagine his face bursting with rage. He couldn't do so. He could see nothing but the dark yet shining eyes and the animal mouth.

"Why did you kill him?" he asked in a voice whose hostile tone surprised him.

The Arab looked away.

"He ran away. I ran after him."

He raised his eyes to Daru again and they were full of a sort of woeful interrogation. "Now what will they do to me?"

"Are you afraid?"

He stiffened, turning his eyes away.

"Are you sorry?"

The Arab stared at him openmouthed. Obviously he did not understand. Daru's annoyance was growing. At the same time he felt awkward and self-conscious with his big body wedged between the two beds.

"Lie down there," he said impatiently. "That's your bed."

The Arab didn't move. He called to Daru: "Tell me!"

The schoolmaster looked at him.

"Is the gendarme coming back tomorrow?"

"I don't know."

"Are you coming with us?"

"I don't know. Why?"

The prisoner got up and stretched out on top of the blankets, his feet toward the window. The light from the electric bulb shone straight into his eyes and he closed them at once.

"Why?" Daru repeated, standing beside the bed.

The Arab opened his eyes under the blinding light and looked at him, trying not to blink.

"Come with us," he said.

In the middle of the night, Daru was still not asleep. He had gone to bed after undressing completely; he generally slept naked. But when he suddenly realized that he had nothing on, he hesitated. He felt vulnerable and the temptation came to him to put his clothes back on. Then he shrugged his shoulders; after all, he wasn't a child and, if need be, he could break his adversary in two. From his bed he could observe him, lying on his back, still motionless with his eyes closed under the harsh light. When Daru turned out the light, the darkness seemed to coagulate all of a sudden. Little by little, the night came back to life in the window where the starless sky was stirring gently. The schoolmaster soon made out the body lying at his feet. The Arab still did not move, but his eyes seemed open. A faint wind was prowling around the schoolhouse. Perhaps it would drive away the clouds and the sun would reappear.

During the night the wind increased. The hens fluttered a little and then were silent. The Arab turned over on his side with his back to Daru, who thought he heard him moan. Then he listened for his guest's breathing, become heavier and more regular. He listened to that breath so close to him and mused without being able to go to sleep. In this room where he had been sleeping alone for a year, this presence bothered him. But it bothered him also by imposing on him a sort of brotherhood he knew well but refused to accept in the present circumstances. Men who share the same rooms, soldiers or prisoners, develop a strange alliance as if, having cast off their armor with their clothing, they fraternized every evening, over and above their differences, in the ancient community of dream and fatigue. But Daru shook himself; he didn't like such musings, and it was essential to sleep.

A little later, however, when the Arab stirred slightly, the schoolmaster was still not asleep. When the prisoner made a second move, he stiffened, on the alert. The Arab was lifting himself slowly on his arms with almost the motion of a sleepwalker. Seated upright in bed, he waited motionless without turning his head toward Daru, as if he were listening attentively. Daru did not stir; it had just occurred to him that the revolver was still in the drawer of his desk. It was better to act at once. Yet he continued to observe the prisoner, who, with the same slithery motion, put his feet on the ground, waited again, then began to stand up slowly. Daru was about to call out to him when the Arab began to walk, in a quite natural but extraordinarily silent way. He was heading toward the door at the end of the room that opened into the shed. He lifted the latch with precaution and went out, pushing the door behind him but without shutting it. Daru had not stirred. "He is running away," he merely thought. "Good riddance!" Yet he listened attentively. The hens were not fluttering; the guest must be on the plateau. A faint sound of water reached him, and he didn't know what it was until the Arab again stood framed in the doorway, closed the door carefully, and came back to bed without a sound. Then Daru turned his back on him and fell asleep. Still later he seemed, from the depths of his sleep, to hear furtive steps around the schoolhouse. "I'm dreaming! I'm dreaming!" he repeated to himself. And he went on sleeping.

When he awoke, the sky was clear; the loose window let in a cold, pure air. The Arab was asleep, hunched up under the blankets now, his mouth open, utterly relaxed. But when Daru shook him, he started dreadfully, staring at Daru with wild eyes as if he had never seen him and such a frightened expression that the schoolmaster stepped back. "Don't be afraid. It's me. You must eat." The Arab nodded his head and said yes. Calm had returned to his face, but his expression was vacant and listless.

The coffee was ready. They drank it seated together on the folding bed as they munched their pieces of the cake. Then Daru led the Arab under the shed and showed him the faucet where he washed. He went back into the room, folded the blankets and the bed, made his own bed and put the room in order. Then he went through the classroom and out onto the terrace. The sun was already rising in the blue sky, a soft, bright light was bathing the deserted plateau. On the ridge the snow was melting in spots. The stones were about to reappear. Crouched on the edge of the plateau, the schoolmaster looked at the deserted expanse. He thought of Balducci. He had hurt him, for he had sent him off in a way as if he didn't want to be associated with him. He could still hear the gendarme's farewell and, without knowing why, he felt strangely empty and vulnerable. At that moment, from the other side of the schoolhouse, the prisoner coughed. Daru listened to him almost despite himself and then, furious, threw a pebble that whistled through the air before sinking into the snow. That man's stupid crime revolted him, but to hand him over was contrary to honor. Merely thinking of it made him smart with humiliation. And he cursed at one and the same time his own people who had sent him this Arab and the Arab too who had dared to kill and not managed to get away. Daru got up, walked in a circle on the terrace, waited motionless, and then went back into the schoolhouse.

The Arab, leaning over the cement floor of the shed, was washing his teeth with two fingers. Daru looked at him and said: "Come." He went back into the room ahead of the prisoner. He slipped a hunting-jacket on over his sweater and put on walking-shoes. Standing, he waited until the Arab had put on his *chèche* and sandals. They went into the classroom and the schoolmaster pointed to the exit, saying: "Go ahead." The fellow didn't budge.

"I'm coming," said Daru. The Arab went out. Daru went back into the room and made a package of pieces of rusk, dates, and sugar. In the classroom, before going out, he hesitated a second in front of his desk, then crossed the threshold and locked the door. "That's the way," he said. He started toward the east, followed by the prisoner. But, a short distance from the schoolhouse, he thought he heard a slight sound behind them. He retraced his steps and examined the surroundings of the house; there was no one there. The Arab watched him without seeming to understand. "Come on," said Daru.

They walked for an hour and rested beside a sharp peak of limestone. The snow was melting faster and faster and the sun was drinking up the puddles at once, rapidly cleaning the plateau, which gradually dried and vibrated like the air itself. When they resumed walking, the ground rang under their feet. From time to time a bird rent the space in front of them with a joyful cry. Daru breathed in deeply the fresh morning light. He felt a sort of rapture before the vast familiar expanse, now almost entirely yellow under its dome of blue sky. They walked an hour more, descending toward the south. They reached a level height made up of crumbly rocks. From there on, the plateau sloped down, eastward, toward a low plain where there were a few spindly trees and, to the south, toward outcroppings of rock that gave the landscape a chaotic look.

Daru surveyed the two directions. There was nothing but the sky on the horizon. Not a man could be seen. He turned toward the Arab, who was looking at him blankly. Daru held out the package to him. "Take it," he said. "There are dates, bread, and sugar. You can hold out for two days. Here are a thousand francs too." The Arab took the package and the money but kept his full hands at chest level as if he didn't know what to do with what was being given him. "Now look," the schoolmaster said as he pointed in the direction of the east, "there's the way to Tinguit. You have a two-hour walk. At Tinguit you'll find the administration and the police. They are expecting you." The Arab looked toward the east, still holding the package and the money against his chest. Daru took his elbow and turned him rather roughly toward the south. At the foot of the height on which they stood could be seen a faint path. "That's the trail across the plateau. In a day's walk from here you'll find pasturelands and the first nomads. They'll take you in and shelter you according to their law." The Arab had now turned toward Daru and a sort of panic was visible in his expression. "Listen," he said. Daru shook his head: "No, be quiet. Now I'm leaving you." He turned his back on him, took two long steps in the direction of the school, looked hesitantly at the motionless Arab, and started off again. For a few minutes he heard nothing but his own step resounding on the cold ground and did not turn his head. A moment later, however, he turned around. The Arab was still there on the edge of the hill, his arms hanging now, and he was looking at the schoolmaster. Daru felt something rise in his throat. But he swore with impatience, waved vaguely, and started off again. He had already gone some distance when he again stopped and looked. There was no longer anyone on the hill.

Daru hesitated. The sun was now rather high in the sky and was beginning to beat down on his head. The schoolmaster retraced his steps, at first somewhat uncertainly, then with decision. When he reached the little hill, he was bathed in sweat. He climbed it as fast as he could and stopped, out of breath, at the top. The rock-fields to the south stood out sharply against the blue sky, but on the plain to the east a steamy heat was already rising. And in that slight haze, Daru, with heavy heart, made out the Arab walking slowly on the road to prison.

A little later, standing before the window of the classroom, the schoolmaster was watching the clear light bathing the whole surface of the plateau, but he hardly saw it. Behind him on the blackboard, among the winding French rivers, sprawled the clumsily chalked-up words he had just read: "You handed over our brother.

You will pay for this." Daru looked at the sky, the plateau, and, beyond, the invisible lands stretching all the way to the sea. In this vast landscape he had loved so much, he was alone.

I
FREEDOM IS RESPONSIBILITY

The title of the story is double-edged. The Arab prisoner becomes Daru's guest. But—even though Daru has been born in this country—as a member of the French Colonial minority he is also a "guest" in this harsh, stony landscape. In spite of the fact that he is just and compassionate, it is clear at the end of the story that he is no longer welcome. The entire story settles on the final word "alone."

II
IMPLICATIONS

Do you agree with these statements? Defend your answer by referring to the story.

1. A good citizen would have handed over the prisoner as requested.

2. An individual is always alone in the world.

3. Many people like to avoid responsibility. It requires courage to act freely and according to your beliefs.

4. The Arab's reasons for choosing the road to prison are clear.

5. Daru suffers the consequences of the Arab's choice.

III
TECHNIQUES

Characterization

Camus gives the reader little direct information about Daru. We come to know the teacher because we are allowed to see everything through his eyes, and to follow his thought process. What do the following details reveal about Daru?

1. His mode of life and the kind of clothes he wears.

2. His untying the Arab's hands and giving him tea.

3. His handling of the revolver.

4. His waiting when the Arab arises during the night.

5. The choice he gives to the prisoner.

6. His feeling for the landscape.

Imagery

The dividend that springs from the use of imagery is the multitude of ideas that can be generated with a few words. Take any one of the sentences given below and use it as a springboard to your own thoughts. What did you see, smell, feel, think when you read this line? Let your ideas flow freely. The thoughts produced need not have logical relationship to the story.

1. A faint wind was prowling around the schoolhouse.

2. The only plowing here was to harvest rocks.

3. The snow was melting faster and faster and the sun was drinking up the puddles at once.

LEO TOLSTOY

Born into a family of Russian nobility, Tolstoy (1828–1910) was orphaned at nine and sent to the home of elderly female relatives in Kazan. In 1844 he entered the University at Kazan, but he spent more time in a social whirl than in intellectual pursuits. After a few years he quit school and returned to his family's estate to farm and look after his serfs. His previous training had not prepared him for such tasks, and he failed miserably. After a stretch of the aimless life, typical of many wealthy young men, he joined the army as an officer. His first story, *Childhood,* was published in 1852. He retired from the army in 1857, and in 1861 he married Sophie Behrs, a woman sixteen years younger than himself. He had been trembling on the brink of an inner philosophical crisis, but his happy marriage postponed serious consideration of his attitudes toward life. During this period, he wrote two of his masterpieces, *War and Peace* and *Anna Karenina,* great realistic novels, whose countless characters are viewed from both the outside and the inside. In 1876 Count Tolstoy became troubled at his unreflecting and prosperous life. He thought of death and this, in turn, made him seek some religious justification for his life. He rejected established religions although he believed in a Supreme Being. He came to feel that we can only achieve happiness by loving all people and rejecting greed, lust, and anger. All violence he saw as criminal. The great gulf between the rich and the poor seemed to him in violation of all morality. He condemned the practice whereby landowners actually owned other people (their serfs) like property. When Tolstoy evolved his new concept of life, he also changed his attitude toward his writing. In his tract "What Is Art" (1896), he stated that "art is a means of emotional communion," a means by which the artist "infects other people with feelings he has himself experienced. If this infection does not take place, there is no art." The following story is from Tolstoy's later period, when he wrote only with the purpose of directly teaching a moral lesson. Although Tolstoy continued to live at his estate, he became estranged from his family because of his desire to give away his (and their) property, because of his vegetarian diet, and his sympathy for peasants and wandering pilgrims. In 1910 he secretly left home with his daughter Alexandra, intending never to return, but they got only as far as the railway station at Astapovo where he became ill and died in the stationmaster's room.

How Much Land Does a Man Need?

1

An older sister from town came to visit her younger sister in the country. The elder had married a merchant in town; the younger a peasant in the country. Drinking tea, the sisters chatted. The elder began to brag—to boast of her life in town; how spaciously and comfortably she lived, how well she dressed the children, how nicely she ate and drank, and how she went for drives, excursions, and to the theater.

The younger sister became offended and began disparaging the merchant's life and exalting her peasant life.

"I wouldn't trade my life for yours," she said. "Our life is rough, I grant you, but we haven't a worry. You may live more neatly, and, perhaps, earn a lot at your trade, but you may lose it all. Remember the proverb: loss is gain's big brother. It often goes like that: one day you're rich and the day after, you're begging in the streets. But our peasant life is more stable: a meager life, but a long one. We won't be rich, but we'll always eat."

The old sister began to speak:

"Eat—like the pigs and calves! No elegance, no manners! No matter how hard your man works, you'll live and die in manure and so will your children!"

Leo Tolstoy in the peasant garb he wore toward the end of his life.

"What of it," said the younger; "that's our way. Our life may be hard, but we bow to no one, are afraid of no one. While you in town are surrounded by temptations. It's all right now, but tomorrow it may turn ugly—suddenly you'll find your man tempted by cards, or wine, or some young charmer, and everything will turn to ashes. That's what often happens, doesn't it?"

Pakhom, lying on top the stove, listened to the women babbling.

"It's the absolute truth," he said. "We're so busy tilling mother earth from infancy, we don't get such nonsense in our heads. There's just one trouble—too little land! If I had all the land I wanted, I wouldn't fear the Devil himself!"

The women finished their tea, chatted some more about dresses, cleared the dishes, and went to bed. But the Devil sitting behind the stove had heard everything. He was delighted that the peasant wife had induced her husband to boast and, particularly, to boast that if he had enough land even the Devil could not get him.

"All right," he thought, "we'll have a tussle, you and I; I'll give you plenty of land. And then I'll get you through your land."

2

Next to the peasants there lived a small landowner. She had three hundred and twenty-five acres of land. And she had always lived in peace with the peasants—never abusing them. Then she hired as overseer a retired soldier who began to harass the peasants with fines. No matter how careful Pakhom was, either his horses wandered into her oats, or his cattle got into her garden, or his calves strayed onto her meadow—and there was a fine for everything.

Pakhom would pay up and then curse and beat his family. Many were the difficulties Pakhom suffered all summer because of that overseer. Come winter, he was glad to stable the cattle—he begrudged them the fodder, but at least he was free from worry.

It was rumored that winter that the lady was selling her land, and that the innkeeper on the main road was arranging to buy it. The peasants heard this and groaned. "Well," they thought, "if the innkeeper gets the land, he'll pester us with worse fines than the lady. We can't get along without this land; we live too close."

A delegation of peasants representing the commune came to ask the lady not to sell the land to the innkeeper, but to give it to them. They promised to pay more. The lady agreed. The peasants started making arrangements for the commune to buy the land; they held one meeting and another meeting—but the matter was still unsettled. The Evil One divided them, and they were completely unable to agree. Then the peasants decided that each would buy individually as much as he could. To this, also, the lady agreed. Pakhom heard that his neighbor had bought fifty-five acres from the lady, and that she had loaned him half the money for a year. Pakhom became envious. "They're buying up all the land," he thought, "and I'll be left with nothing." He consulted his wife.

"People are buying," he said, "so we must buy about twenty-five acres, too. Otherwise we can't exist—the overseer is crushing us with fines."

They figured out how they could buy. They had one hundred rubles put aside, and they sold the colt and half the bee swarm, hired out their son as a worker, borrowed from their brother-in-law, and raised half the money.

Pakhom gathered up the money, chose his land—forty acres including a little woods—and went to bargain with the lady. He drove a bargain for his forty acres, and sealed it with his hand and a deposit. They went to town and signed the deed with half the money paid down and the rest due in two years.

So Pakhom had his own land. He borrowed seed, sowed the land he had bought: it produced well. In a year, he had settled his debts with both the lady and his brother-in-law. And so Pakhom became a landowner: he plowed and sowed his own land, mowed hay on his own land, cut timber from his own land, and pastured his herd on his own land. When Pakhom went out to plow the land which he now owned forever, or when he happened to glance over the sprouting fields and meadows, he could not rejoice enough. It seemed to him that the grass grew and the flowers flowered in a new way. When he had walked across this land before, it had been land like any land; now it had become completely exceptional.

3

So Pakhom lived and was pleased. Everything would have been fine, had the peasants not begun trespassing on his fields and meadows. He begged them politely to stop, but the trespassing continued. Either the cowherds let the cattle into the meadows, or the horses got into the wheat while grazing at night. Time after time, Pakhom chased them out and forgave without pressing charges; then he became tired of it and started to complain to the district court. And he knew the peasants did not do these things deliberately, but only because they were crowded, yet he thought: "One still mustn't let them or they'll ravage everything. They must be taught."

To teach them, he sued once, and then again; one was fined, then another. Pakhom's neighbors began to hold a grudge against him; they started to trespass on purpose from time to time. One went to the grove at night and cut down a dozen linden trees for *bast*.[1] When Pakhom walked through the woods, he looked and saw a white glimmer. He approached—there lay the discarded peelings, and there stood the little stumps. If the villain had only cut the edges of the bush, or left one standing, but he had razed them all, one after the other. Pakhom was enraged. He thought and thought: "It must be Semon," he thought. He went to search Semon's farm, found nothing, and quarreled with him. And Pakhom was even more

---

1. **bast** (bast), wood fiber used to make ropes, etc.

certain Semon had done it. He filed a petition. Semon was called into court. The case dragged on and on; the peasant was acquitted for lack of evidence. Pakhom felt even more wronged and abused the elder and the judges.

"You're hand and hand with thieves," he said. "If you led honest lives, you wouldn't let thieves go free."

Pakhom quarreled with both the judges and his neighbors. The peasants started threatening to set fire to his place. Although Pakhom had more land than before, his neighbors were closing in on him.

Just then, there was a rumor that people were moving to new places. And Pakhom thought: "I have no reason to leave my land, but if some of us go, there'll be more space. I could take their land, add it to my place; life would be better. It's too crowded now."

Once when Pakhom was sitting at home, a peasant passing through dropped in. Pakhom put him up for the night, fed him, talked to him, and asked him where, pray, he came from. The peasant said he came from below, beyond the Volga, where he had been working. One thing led to another and the peasant gradually started telling how people were going there to settle. He told how his own people had gone there, joined the community, and divided off twenty-five acres a man.

"And the land is so good," he said, "that they sowed rye, and you couldn't see a horse in the stalks, it was so high; and so thick, that five handfuls make a sheaf. One peasant," he said, "who hadn't a thing but his bare hands, came there and now has six horses, two cows."

Pakhom's heart took fire. He was thinking: "Why be poor and crowded here if one can live well there? We'll sell the house and land here; with this money, I'll build myself a house there and set up a whole establishment. There's only trouble in this crowded place. But I had better make the trip and look into it myself."

That summer he got ready and went. He sailed down the Volga to Samara[2] in a steamer, then walked four hundred versts[3] on foot. When he arrived, everything was just as described. The peasants were living amply on twenty-five acres per head, and they participated willingly in the activities of the community. And whoever had money could buy, in addition to his share, as much of the very best land as he wanted at a ruble[4] an acre; you could buy as much as you wanted!

After finding out everything, Pakhom returned home and began selling all he owned. He sold the land at a profit, sold his own farm, sold his entire herd, resigned from the community, waited for spring, and set off with his family for the new place.

4

Pakhom arrived at the settlement with his family, and joined the community. He stood the elders drinks and put all the papers in order. They accepted Pakhom, divided off one hundred and twenty-five acres of land in various fields as his portion for his family of five—in addition to the use of the pasture. Pakhom built himself a farm and acquired a herd. His part of the common land alone was three times as large as before. And the land was fertile. He lived ten times better than in the past. You had arable land and fodder at will. And you could keep as many cattle as you wanted.

At first, while he was busy building and settling himself, he was content; but after he became used to it, he felt crowded on this land, too. The first year, Pakhom sowed wheat on his share of the common land—it grew well. He wanted to sow wheat again, but there was not enough common land. And what there was, was not suitable. In that region, wheat is sown only on grassland or wasteland. They sow the land for a year or two, then leave it fallow until the grass grows back again. And there are

2. **Samara** (sə mär′ə), city southeast of Moscow where the Volga and Samara rivers join; now called Kuibyshev.
3. **versts** (vèrstz), a Russian unit of distance about two-thirds of a mile.
4. **ruble**, a Russian monetary unit made up of 100 kopecks.

many wanting that kind of land, and not enough of it for all. There were disputes over it, too; the richer peasants wanted to sow it themselves, while the poor people wanted to rent it to dealers to raise tax money. Pakhom wanted to sow more. The following year, he went to a dealer and rented land from him for a year. He sowed more—it grew well; but it was far from the village—you had to cart it about fifteen versts. He saw the peasant-dealers living in farmhouses and growing rich. "That's the thing," thought Pakhom; "if only I could buy land permanently for myself and build a farmhouse on my land. Everything would be at hand." And Pakhom began pondering over how he could buy freehold land.

So Pakhom lived for three years. He rented land and sowed wheat on it. The years were good ones, and the wheat grew well, and the surplus money accumulated. But Pakhom found it annoying to rent land from people every year and to have to move from place to place. Whenever there was a good piece of land, the peasants immediately rushed to divide up everything; if Pakhom did not hurry to buy, he had no land to sow. The third year, he and a dealer rented part of the common pasture from some peasants; he had already plowed when the peasants sued and the work was wasted. "If it had been my own land," he thought, "I'd bow to no one and there'd be no trouble."

And Pakhom began to inquire where land could be bought permanently. And he came across a peasant. The peasant had bought one thousand three hundred and fifty acres, then gone bankrupt, and was selling cheaply. Pakhom began talking terms with him. They haggled and haggled and agreed on fifteen hundred rubles, half of it payable later. They had just reached an agreement when a traveling merchant stopped at the farm for something to eat. They drank and talked. The merchant said he was returning from the far-off Bashkir[5] country. There, he said, he bought thirteen thousand five hundred acres of land from the Bashkirs. And all for one thousand

rubles. Pakhom began asking questions. The merchant recounted.

"You just have to be nice to the old men," he said. "I distributed about a hundred rubles' worth of oriental robes and carpets and a case of tea, and gave wine to whoever wanted it. And I got the land for less than ten kopecks an acre." He showed Pakhom the deed. "The land," it read, "lies along a river, and the steppe is all grassland."

Pakhom began asking him how, where, and what.

"The land there—" said the merchant, "you couldn't walk around it in a year. The Bashkirs own it all. And the people are as silly as sheep. You can almost get it free."

"Well," Pakhom thought, "why should I buy thirteen hundred and fifty acres for my thousand rubles and saddle myself with a debt as well, when I can really get something for a thousand rubles."

5

Pakhom asked the way to the Bashkirs and as soon as he had escorted the merchant to the door, he began getting ready to go himself. He left the house in his wife's charge, made preparations, and set off with his hired hand. They went to town, bought a case of tea, gifts, wine—everything just as the merchant had said. They traveled and traveled, traversing five hundred versts. The seventh fortnight, they arrived at a Bashkir camp. Everything was just as the merchant had said. They all lived in felt tents on the steppe near a stream. They themselves neither plowed nor ate bread, but their cattle and horses wandered over the steppes in herds. Twice a day they drove the mares to the colts tethered behind the huts; they milked the mares and made *kumiss*[6] out of it. The women beat the *kumiss* and made cheese, while all the

---

5. **Bashkir** (bash kir′), of or relating to a Turkish people living between the Volga River and Ural Mountains.
6. **kumiss** (kü′mis), a drink made of fermented mare's milk.

men did was drink tea and *kumiss* and eat mutton and play reed pipes. They were all polite and jolly and they made merry all summer. A completely backward people, with no knowledge of Russian, but friendly.

As soon as the Bashkirs saw Pakhom, they came out of their tents and surrounded their guest. An interpreter was found; Pakhom told him he had come for land. The Bashkirs were delighted, seized Pakhom, conducted him to one of the best tents, placed him on a carpet, put feather pillows under him, sat down in a circle around him, and began serving him tea and *kumiss*. They slaughtered a sheep and fed him mutton. Pakhom fetched his gifts from the wagon and began distributing them among the Bashkirs. When Pakhom finished presenting his gifts to them, he divided up the tea. The Bashkirs were delighted. They jabbered and jabbered among themselves, then asked the interpreter to speak.

"They ask me to tell you that they like you," said the interpreter, "and that it is our custom to give a guest every satisfaction, and to render gifts in kind. You have presented us with gifts; now tell us what we have that you like, so we can give a gift to you."

"What I like most of all," said Pakhom, "is your land. Our land is crowded, and, furthermore, all of it has been tilled, while your land is plentiful and good. I've never seen the like."

The interpreter translated. The Bashkirs talked and talked among themselves. Pakhom did not understand what they were saying, but he saw that they were merry, were shouting something, and laughing. Then they became silent, turned to Pakhom, and the interpreter said, "They asked me to tell you that in return for your kindness they will be glad to give you as much land as you want. Just point it out and it will be yours."

They started to talk again and began to quarrel about something. Pakhom asked what the quarrel was about. And the interpreter said, "Some say the elder must be consulted about the land, that it can't be done without him. But others say it can be done."

6

The Bashkirs were still quarreling when, suddenly, out came a man in a fox fur cap. Everyone fell silent and stood up. And the interpreter said:

"That's the elder himself."

Pakhom immediately fetched the best robe and brought it to the elder along with five pounds of tea. The elder accepted and sat down in a seat of honor. And the Bashkirs immediately started telling him something. The elder listened and listened, requested silence with a nod, and said to Pakhom in Russian:

"Well," he said. "It can be done. Choose whatever you like. Land's plentiful."

"What does that mean: take what I want," thought Pakhom. "It has to be secured somehow. Or they'll say it's yours, then take it away."

"Thank you," he said, "for your kind words. You do have a lot of land, and I need only a little. But I'd like to know which is mine. It must be measured off somehow, and secured as mine. Our lives and deaths are in God's hands. What you, good people, are giving, your children may take back."

"You're right," said the elder; "it can be secured."

Pakhom said:

"I heard there was a merchant here. You gave him a little piece of land too, and made a deed. I should have the same thing."

The elder understood.

"It can all be done," he said. "We have a scribe, and we'll go to the town to affix the seals."

"And what is the price?" said Pakhom.

"We've only one price: a thousand rubles a day."

Pakhom did not understand.

"What kind of measure is that—a day? How many acres does it have?"

"That," he said, "we don't know. But we sell by the day; as much as you can walk around in a day is yours, and the price is a thousand rubles a day."

Pakhom was astonished.

"But look," he said, "a day's walking is a lot of land."

The elder laughed.

"It's all yours!" he said. "There's just one condition: if you're not back where you started in a day, your money is lost."

"And how," Pakhom said, "will you mark where I go?"

"Well, we'll stand on the spot you choose, and stay there while you walk off a circle; and you'll take a spade with you and, where convenient, dig holes to mark your path and pile the dirt up high; then we'll drive a plow from pit to pit. Make your circle wherever you want. What you walk around is all yours, as long as you're back where you started by sundown."

Pakhom was delighted. They decided to start off early. They chatted, drank more *kumiss*, ate mutton, drank tea again; night came on. They laid down a feather bed for Pakhom, and the Bashkirs dispersed, promising to assemble the next day at dawn to set out for the starting point before sunrise.

7

Pakhom lay on the feather bed, unable to sleep for thinking about the land. "I'll grab off a big piece of my own," he thought. "I can walk fifty versts in a day. The days are long now; there'll be quite a bit of land in fifty versts. What's poorest, I'll sell or let to the peasants, and I'll pick out the best to settle on myself. I'll get a plow and two oxen, and hire two laborers; I'll plow over a hundred acres and put cattle to graze on the rest."

All night Pakhom lay awake, drifting off to sleep only just before dawn. No sooner had he fallen asleep than he started to dream. He saw himself lying in that same hut and heard someone chuckling outside. And he wanted to see who was laughing, got up, went out of the hut, and there sat the Bashkir elder himself in front of the hut with both hands holding his sides, rocking back and forth, laughing at something.

Pakhom approached him and asked: "What are you laughing at?" Then he saw that it was not the Bashkir elder, but the merchant of the other day who had come to him and told him about the land. And he had barely asked the merchant, "Have you been here long?"—when it was no longer the merchant, but the peasant who had come on foot from the south long ago. Then Pakhom saw that it was not the peasant, but the Devil himself, laughing, horns, hoofs, and all; and in front of him lay a barefoot man in shirt and trousers. And Pakhom looked closer to see what sort of man he was. He saw it was a corpse and that it was—he himself. Horrified, Pakhom woke up. "The things one dreams," he thought. He looked around; through the open door he saw the dawn; it was already turning white. "Must rouse the people," he thought; "time to go." Pakhom got up, woke his hired hand who was asleep in the wagon, ordered the horses harnessed, and went to wake the Bashkirs.

"It's time," he said, "to go to the steppe to measure off the land."

The Bashkirs got up, assembled everything, and the elder arrived. The Bashkirs began drinking *kumiss* again, and offered Pakhom tea, but he did not want to linger.

"If we're going, let's go," he said. "It's time."

8

The Bashkirs assembled, climbed on horseback and in wagons and set off. Meanwhile, Pakhom took a spade and set off with his laborer in his own wagon. They arrived at the steppe just as day was breaking. They went up a hillock (known as a *shikhan* in Bashkir). The Bashkirs climbed out of their wagons, slid down from their horses, and gathered in a group. The elder went to Pakhom and pointed.

"There," he said; "everything the eye encompasses is ours. Take your pick."

Pakhom's eyes glowed. It was all grassland, level as the palm of the hand, black as a poppy seed, and wherever there was a hollow, there was grass growing chest-high.

The elder took off his fox cap and put it on the ground.

"That," he said, "will be the marker. Leave from here; return here. Whatever you walk around will be yours."

Pakhom drew out his money, placed it on the cap, unfastened his belt, took off his outer coat, girded his belt tightly over his stomach again, put a bag of bread inside his jacket, tied a flask of water to his belt, drew his bootlegs tight, took the spade from his laborer, and got set to go. He pondered and pondered over which direction to take—it was good everywhere. He was thinking: "It's all the same: I'll head toward the sunrise." He turned to face the sun and paced restlessly, waiting for it to appear over the horizon. He was thinking: "I must lose no time. And walking's easier while it's still cold." As soon as the sun's rays spurted over the horizon, Pakhom flung the spade over his shoulder and started off across the steppe.

He walked neither quickly nor slowly. He covered a verst; stopped, dug out a hole, and piled the turf up so it could be seen. He walked further. He loosened up and lengthened his stride. He covered still more ground; dug still another pit.

Pakhom glanced back. The *shikhan* was clearly visible in the sun, and the people stood there, and the hoops of the cart wheels glittered. Pakhom guessed that he had covered about five versts. It was getting warmer; he took off his jacket, flung it over his shoulder, and went on. He covered another five versts. It was warm. He glanced at the sun—already breakfast time.

"One lap finished," thought Pakhom. "But there are four in a day; it's too early to turn around yet. I'll just take my boots off." He sat down, took them off, stuck them in his belt, and went on. Walking became easier. He thought, "I'll just cover about five more versts, then start veering left. This is a very nice spot, too good to leave out. The farther away it is, the better it gets." He walked straight on. When he glanced around, the *shikhan* was barely visible, the people looked like black ants, and there was something faintly glistening on it.

"Well," thought Pakhom, "I've taken enough on this side; I must turn. Besides, I've been sweating—I'm thirsty." He stopped, dug a bigger hole, stacked the turf, untied his flask, and drank. Then he veered sharply to the left. On and on he went; the grass grew taller and it became hot.

Pakhom began to feel tired; he glanced at the sun—it was already lunch time. He stopped; sat on the ground; ate bread and drank water, but did not lie down. "Lie down and you'll fall asleep," he thought. After a while, he walked on. Walking was easy at first. Eating had increased his strength. But it had gotten very hot and he was becoming sleepy. Still he pressed on, thinking—an hour of suffering for a lifetime of living.

He walked a long way in this direction too, and when he was about to turn left, he came to a damp hollow, too nice to overlook. "Flax will grow well there," he thought. Again he went straight on. He took possession of the hollow, dug a hole beyond it, and turned the second corner. Pakhom glanced back at the *shikham*: it was hazy from the heat, something seemed to be wavering in the air, and through the haze the people were barely visible on top of the *shikham*—fifteen versts away. "Well," thought Pakhom, "I've taken long sides, I must take this one shorter." As he walked the third side, he increased his stride. He looked at the sun—it was already approaching tea-time, and he had only covered two versts on the third side. And it was still fifteen versts to the starting point. "No," he thought, "I'll have a lopsided place, but I must go straight back so I'll arrive in time. And not take any more. There's lots of land already." Pakhom shoveled out a hole as quickly as he could and turned straight toward the *shikhan.*

9

As Pakhom walked straight toward the *shikhan,* he began having difficulties. He was perspiring, and his bare legs were cut and bruised and were beginning to fail him. He wanted to rest but could not—otherwise he would not arrive before sunset. The sun would not wait; it continued sinking, sinking. "Ah," he thought, "if only I haven't made a mistake and taken too much! What if I don't make it?" He glanced ahead at the *shikhan*, looked at the sun: the starting point was far away, and the sun was nearing the horizon.

So Pakhom went on with difficulty; he kept increasing and increasing his stride. He walked, walked—and was still far away; he broke into a trot. He threw off his jacket, dropped his boots and flask; he threw off his cap, keeping only his spade to lean on. "Ah," he thought, "I've been too greedy, I've ruined the whole thing, I won't get there by sundown." And fear shortened his breath even more. Pakhom ran; his shirt and trousers clung to his body with sweat; his mouth was parched. His chest felt as though it had been inflated by the blacksmith's bellows; a hammer beat in his heart; and his legs no longer seemed to belong to his body— they were collapsing under him. Pakhom began to worry about dying of strain.

He was afraid of dying, but unable to stop. "I've run so far," he thought. "I'd be a fool to stop now." He ran and ran, and was very close when he heard a screeching—the Bashkirs shrieking at him—and his heart became even more inflamed by their cries. Pakhom pressed forward with his remaining strength, but the sun was already reaching the horizon; and, slipping behind a cloud, it became large, red, and bloody. Now it was beginning to go down. Although the sun was close to setting, Pakhom was no longer far from the starting point either. He could already see the people on the *shikhan* waving their arms at him, urging him on. He saw the fox cap on the ground and the money on it; and he saw the elder sitting on the ground, holding his sides with his hands. And Pakhom remembered his dream. "There is plenty of land," he thought, "if it please God to let me live on it. Oh, I've ruined myself," he thought. "I won't make it."

Pakhom glanced at the sun, but it had touched the earth and had already begun to slip behind the horizon which cut it into an arc. Pakhom overreached his remaining strength, driving his body forward so that his legs could barely move fast enough to keep him from falling. Just as Pakhom ran up to the base of the *shikhan*, it suddenly became dark. He glanced around—the sun had already set. Pakhom sighed. "My work has fallen through," he thought. He was about to stop when he heard the Bashkirs still shrieking. And he remembered that though it seemed below that the sun had set, it would still be shining on top of the *shikhan*. Pakhom took a deep breath and ran up the *shikhan*. It was still light there. As Pakhom reached the top, he saw the elder sitting in front of the cap, chuckling, holding his sides with his hands. Pakhom remembered his dream and groaned; his legs gave way, and he fell forward, his hands touching the cap.

"Aiee, good man!" cried the elder. "You have acquired plenty of land!"

Pakhom's laborer ran to lift him, but the blood was flowing from his mouth and he lay dead.

The Bashkirs clicked their tongues in commiseration.

The laborer took up the spade, dug Pakhom a grave just long enough to reach from his feet to his head—six feet in all—and buried him.

I
ARE WE OUR OWN EXECUTIONERS?

Pakhom was a hardworking man of the people until his greed for land corrupted his personality, his life, and his spirit and eventually caused his death. Tolstoy has used terse, staccato, almost abrupt language to tell this tale. Through "tracts" such as this story published for the Russian peasants, Tolstoy attempted to infect the Russian people with his vision of life.

From reading this story what do you know about:

1. The Russian land system of that day.
2. The spirit and mind of the Russian peasant.

II
IMPLICATIONS

Discuss the following statements which relate to the story. Do you agree or disagree with them?

1. It was Pakhom's motive, not the fact of his owning land, that was bad.

2. This story directly contradicts the premise that one should never be satisfied: that to be satisfied is to die.

III
TECHNIQUES

Character Development

Tolstoy gives a number of pictures of Pakhom through specific incidents. What do you know about Pakhom through:

1. His behavior toward his family when he had to pay fines?

2. His reactions toward his first piece of property bought from the woman?

3. His relations with the peasants whose animals trespassed on his land?

4. His change in attitude from the period when he buys into the new commune until he decides he must buy land permanently.

5. His decision to go to the Bashkirs and try to buy 13,000 acres instead of 1,350.

6. His attitudes as he is hiking to buy his "one" day of land?

Would you call this a flat or a rounded picture of Pakhom?

Imagery

1. Tolstoy creates vivid scenes. These, too, are a kind of image, leaving a picture in the reader's mind. Describe in a sentence what you remember of the following:

a. The scene between the two sisters as they discuss the virtues of their particular kinds of life.

b. The scene in the court when the verdict goes against Pakhom.

c. The scene in which Pakhom listens to the merchant describe the Bashkir's land.

d. Pakhom's arrival with gifts for the Bashkirs.

e. The last moments of the race.

2. One of the effects Tolstoy creates is the vision of the land. Discuss briefly:

a. The first piece of land Pakhom owns.

b. The peasant's description of the commune land.

c. Pakhom's view of the Bashkir's land just before he begins his walk.

d. The overall image of the Russian landscape.

IV
WORDS

A. Of the four preceding stories, the first has the most uncommon words and the third and fourth fewer than average. Which story is the easiest to read and which the most difficult? What factors other than uncommon words contribute to the level of difficulty?

B. Each of the preceding stories has some local color words. Hardy, for instance, uses architectural references. What is the *nave* of a church? What are *chancel-steps?*

Sailing ships are natural to this story. What is a *coasting-ketch?* A *brig?* What can you discover about the coins called *sovereigns* and *guineas?* When were they last minted?

What place names has Hardy chosen? How do they contribute to your picture of the setting?

"The Duchess and the Jeweler" naturally contains some words and phrases that suggest wealth and social position in London. Where, in London, is each of the following, and what does each place name suggest?

Piccadilly	*Richmond*
Savile Row	*Mayfair*
Whitechapel	*Bond Street*

Explain the meaning of the following:

dress circle	*obsequiously*
stalls	*graved*
the sword of Agincourt	*astute*
viscountess	*lissome*
tiara	*shagreen*
coronet	*cincture*

"The Guest" has as its setting that part of North Africa that was formerly a French colony. Consequently, the story contains a few French terms. Look up the meaning and pronunciation of the following:

gendarme   *kilometer*   *department*

"How Much Land Does a Man Need?" contains the following terms proper to a story of the Russia of the Czars. Find the meaning of each.

commune	*ruble*
steppe	*kumiss*
verst	

What conclusions can you draw concerning the effect of local color words and references upon the reader?

C. The authors studied have used metaphors as follows:

Hardy:

"the face of the parson . . . was buried in his hands"

"he dismantled himself"

Camus:

"the earth shriveled up little by little"

"Balducci was already enthroned on the nearest pupil's desk"

Tolstoy:

"Pakhom's heart took fire"

"the sun's rays spurted over the horizon"

Where else do these authors use verbs rather than nouns and adjectives in metaphoric language?

An author may delineate personality either by inserting figurative language into the characters' speeches or by omitting it. In "To Please His Wife," how does the presence or absence of figurative language in dialogue characterize each of the following: Shadrach, Joanna, Emily?

SUMMING UP

Choice and Consequence

THEME

Ideas about Fate, Destiny, Chance have been one of the major preoccupations of writers in all ages and in all nations. The questions that arise are too big to receive quick and simple answers. In the selections in CHOICE AND CONSEQUENCE you have had the chance to read what several great writers have written about this serious and haunting theme. Now consider and discuss these propositions in the light of what you have read:

1. For the sake of drama, writers often present life as something that comes in sections which are hinged together like a screen. Actually, life has no clear-cut divisions, but unrolls like a continuous bolt of fabric.

2. Which of the characters in these selections are completely aware of the fact that they are making important choices? Which characters make choices without being aware of the importance these decisions can have for their lives?

3. In which selections did the choices bring about *expected* consequences? In which were the characters surprised by the results of their choices?

4. Do any of the writers imply that Fate sends humans consequences which are unfair or unjust? Which consequences are portrayed as just rewards for strengths or for flaws of character?

5. Moments of choice bring out the strength or weakness in a person's character.

TECHNIQUES
Character Development

1. In which selections do the authors pass judgments on their characters directly? In which do they give their views indirectly by letting the reader build a picture of the characters?

2. Choose one or two characters in this unit who seemed real and convincing to you. In a short essay, try to explain the literary means by which the author was successful in presenting the characters. Or reverse the problem—tell why you think one of these authors has *failed* with the characters.

3. For each of these characters, select what you think to be his or her major moment of choice. What motives made them choose the way they did? Did the actions spring from their characters as portrayed by the author?

a. Macbeth	**d.** Karas
b. Socrates	**e.** Nana
c. The priest	**f.** Joanna
("The Hint of an	**g.** Daru
Explanation")	**h.** Pakhom

Imagery

Some of the greatest writers of all time have been collected in this unit. All of them are skilled in the ability to call up vivid pictures through the use of imagery. The total effect is to present writing which is rich and colorful, but also writing which is precise and packed with meaning. When readers have finished a story, poem, or play, it should leave them with a definite impression. Take each selection in this unit and find one or two adjectives that best describe its effect on you. Then share these answers in a class discussion.

SEVENTEENTH- AND EIGHTEENTH- CENTURY BRITISH POETRY:
An Age of Contradictions

The seventeenth and eighteenth centuries were characterized by contrasts, contradictions, and paradoxes. The dichotomy of this period can be seen in the two pictures of John Donne on the opposite page. They serve as useful emblems for the age's two opposing literary traditions: the worldly tradition and the religious tradition. The young John Donne, painted as a melancholy lover, suggests Donne's own love poems as well as a style of poetry that was elegant, witty, courtly, sometimes cynical, and always defiantly secular. In contrast, the old John Donne, a living effigy clothed in a shroud, reminds us of Donne's later poems, the "Holy Sonnets," of his religious meditations, and of the seventeenth century's attention to the next world.

The first half of the seventeenth century was a time of conflict between forms of government (the king versus Parliament) and forms of worship (Anglican versus Catholic, Anglican versus Puritan). Such conflicts are reflected in the two major traditions of seventeenth-century poetry and, as in the case of Donne, may appear within the writings of a single poet.

In the worldly tradition, we find Donne's *Songs and Sonnets* and the calm, controlled poems of Ben Jonson. Jonson, a superbly educated writer, turned to classical models and produced epigrams, satires, and odes—all marked by his style of grace and wit. The "tribe of Ben" poets who were influenced by his style include Richard Lovelace, Robert Herrick, and the other "cavalier" poets (so called because their poems reflect values associated with the Royalist Party in the Civil War, 1642–1660). The most accomplished of these poets was Andrew Marvell, who, like Donne, possessed intellect, passion, and wit.

The religious tradition, with its peculiar blend of love imagery and religious themes, found its most moving expression in the poetry of George Herbert. But the major religious poet of the century was John Milton, a Puritan writer. In later life he was blind and lived in isolation, having fallen out of public favor after the restoration of the monarchy (1660). In his seclusion, he composed the long religious poem *Paradise Lost*. Like Jonson, Milton turned to classical tradition, using as his models the great epics of Homer and Virgil.

John Dryden, the other major poet of the last half of the seventeenth century, was also a dramatist, a literary critic, and a translator. Unlike Milton, Dryden became a follower of Charles II and so enjoyed a respected position in society; he even attained the position of Poet Laureate. Dryden's major poems are satires that analyze the political, literary, and religious questions of the time. His controlled comic portraits are reminiscent of Chaucer's work.

Though England was not again troubled with revolution as bloody as the civil war of the seventeenth century, it was still a place of intense political, religious, and philosophic controversy during the eighteenth century. The rise of science, as exemplified in the Royal Society (founded about 1660), stressed empirical thought and plain language. The novel became an important form. Writers such as Daniel Defoe, Samuel Richardson, and Henry Fielding used the novel's wide scope to create pictures of society that ranged from realistic to sentimental to satiric. These perspectives also

John Donne as a young adventurer

the voice of the poet is usually witty, polished, urbane, without the rough desperation characteristic of Donne or the religious fervor found in Herbert.

Just as the portraits of Donne suggest the paradox of the seventeenth century, so the painting on page 414, by William Hogarth, reflects the eighteenth-century domination by public subject matter, seen not romantically or spiritually, but satirically. In the bustle of the election procession and the grim, satirical details, we find the energy of the eighteenth century and its own ironic self-awareness.

exist in the poetry of the period, with the satiric mode becoming dominant. Satire was polite but cutting. Its surface was polished and its edge sharpened by the crisp rhythm of the heroic couplet (two rhyming lines of iambic pentameter), which succinctly juxtaposed conflicting ideas.

Poets in the eighteenth century, of whom Alexander Pope was the most skillful, used the heroic couplet for satiric portraits, literary criticism, and social commentary. Their poems seem primarily public in nature, dealing with humans as social animals. Their forms (satire, ode, epigram, pastoral) are imitations of classical models and give this period the label "neoclassical." For most of the eighteenth century,

John Donne in his death shroud

307

JOHN DONNE

John Donne's life (1572–1631) followed the classic "sinner to saint" pattern described by St. Augustine. As a young man he studied law, traveled abroad, and took an office at court. He also married secretly, and when his new father-in-law discovered the marriage, Donne lost his position at court. He lived in retirement for some time, then became ordained as a priest, and finally became Dean to St. Paul's Cathedral in London. He was known to his contemporaries for his religious writings, especially his sermons. His earlier nonreligious poems (*Songs and Sonnets*) were not published until after his death. Many of his works mingle two vocabularies so that we find love spoken of in religious/spiritual terms and religion described through romantic/secular images.

The Bait

Come live with me and be my love,
And we will some new pleasures prove
Of golden sands, and crystal brooks,
With silken lines, and silver hooks.

There will the river whispering run   5
Warm'd by thy eyes, more than the Sun;
And there the enamour'd fish will stay,
Begging[1] themselves they may betray.

When thou wilt swim in that live bath,
Each fish, which every channel hath,   10
Will amorously to thee swim,
Gladder to catch thee, than thou him.

If thou, to be so seen, be'st loath,
By Sun, or Moon, thou dark'nest both,
And if myself have leave to see,   15
I need not their light, having thee.

---

1. **begging,** begging that.

Let others freeze with angling reeds,
And cut their legs, with shells and weeds,
Or treacherously poor fish beset,
With strangling snare, or windowy net: 20

Let coarse bold hands, from slimy nest
The bedded fish in banks out-wrest,
Or curious traitors, sleavesilk[2] flies,
Bewitch poor fishes' wand'ring eyes.

For thee, thou need'st no such deceit,   25
For thou thyself art thine own bait;
That fish, that is not catch'd thereby,
Alas, is wiser far than I.

---

2. **sleavesilk,** fine silk thread.

Death, Be Not Proud

Death, be not proud, though some have called thee
Mighty and dreadful, for thou art not so;
For those whom thou think'st thou dost overthrow
Die not, poor death, nor yet canst thou kill me.
From rest and sleep, which but thy pictures be,   5
Much pleasure, then from thee much more must flow,
And soonest our best men with thee do go,
Rest of their bones, and soul's delivery.
Thou art slave to Fate, chance, kings, and desperate men,
And does with poison, war, and sickness dwell,   10
And poppy, or charms can make us sleep as well,
And better than thy stroke; why swell'st thou then?
One short sleep past, we wake eternally,
And death shall be no more; death, thou shalt die.

A Hymn to God the Father[1]

Wilt Thou forgive that sin where I begun,
 Which is my sin, though it were done before?
Wilt Thou forgive that sin through which I run,
 And do run still, though still I do deplore?
  When Thou has done, Thou has not done,   5
  For I have more.

Wilt Thou forgive that sin by which I have won
 Others to sin? and made my sin their door?
Wilt Thou forgive that sin which I did shun
 A year or two, but wallowed in a score?[2]   10
  When Thou hast done, Thou hast not done,
  For I have more.

I have a sin of fear, that when I have spun
 My last thread, I shall perish on the shore;
Swear by Thy self, that at my death Thy Son   15
 Shall shine as he shines now and heretofore;
  And, having done that, Thou hast done,
  I fear no more.

---

1. This poem was written during a serious illness in 1623.
2. **score**, twenty.

The Bait

1. What is "the bait"?

2. What is the difference in fishing as an activity suggested by stanzas 1 and 2 and by stanzas 5 and 6? How does the language imply the difference?

3. What does the last stanza tell you about the poet's attitude?

4. What changes in attitude toward the woman can you find when you look at his poem in comparison to Marlowe's "The Passionate Shepherd"?

Death, Be Not Proud

1. What relationship is implied between the speaker and death?

2. What reasons does the speaker give for not being afraid of death?

3. How does the speaker persuade you (or himself) of the truth of the last four words?

A Hymn to God the Father

1. What are the major puns used in the poem?

2. The occasion on which the poem was written and the subject suggest a serious poem. Do the puns support or contradict that seriousness?

3. Both "Death, Be Not Proud" and "A Hymn to God the Father" concern themselves with death. What differences in attitude do you find in the poems?

BEN JONSON

Ben Jonson (1572–1637) was a contemporary of both John Donne and William Shakespeare. He was, unlike Shakespeare, extremely well-educated, and his poems are frequently based on Latin models which he knew in the original language. His great satiric comedies, *Volpone* (1606), *The Alchemist* (1610), and *Bartholomew Fair* (1614), treat with energy and amusement such subjects as greed, ambition, religious zeal, stupidity, and corruption. Though his poetry seems less personal than Donne's, we still hear a distinctive voice coping with matters as diverse as court life and the death of his first son.

On Court-Worm

All men are worms: but this no man. In silk
'Twas brought to court first wrapped, and white as milk;
Where, afterwards, it grew a butterfly:
Which was a caterpillar. So t'will die.

Still to Be Neat

Still to be neat, still to be dressed,
As you were going to a feast;
Still to be powdered, still perfumed;
Lady, it is to be presumed,
Though art's hid causes are not found,   5
All is not sweet, all is not sound.

Give me a look, give me a face
That makes simplicity a grace;
Robes loosely flowing, hair as free;
Such sweet neglect more taketh me   10
Then all th' adulteries of art.
They strike mine eyes, but not my heart.

On My First Son

Farewell, thou child of my right hand,[1] and joy;
My sin was too much hope of thee, loved boy.
Seven years thou wert lent to me, and I thee pay,
Exacted by thy fate, on the just day.[2]
O, could I lose all father now! For why   5
Will man lament the state he should envy?
To have so soon 'scaped world's and flesh's rage,
And, if no other misery, yet age?
Rest in soft peace, and asked, say here doth lie
BEN. JONSON, his best piece of poetry:[3]   10
For whose sake, henceforth, all his vows be such,
As what he loves may never like too much.

1. Jonson's son died of the plague in 1603; he, too, was named Benjamin, which in Hebrew means "son of the right hand."
2. **just day,** both "the Day of Judgment" and a reference to the fact that the boy died on his seventh birthday.
3. **poetry,** is used in the sense of its Greek root, "making," or "creation."

311

Hall of Mirrors, Palace of Versailles. Its splendor is representative of the seventeenth century's ornate architectural style.

Though I Am Young and Cannot Tell

Though I am young, and cannot tell
Either what Death or Love is well,
Yet I have heard they both bear darts,
And both do aim at human hearts.
And then again, I have been told   5
Love wounds with heat, as Death with cold;
So that I fear they do but bring
Extremes to touch, and mean one thing.

As in a ruin we it call
One thing to be blown up, or fall;   10
Or to our end like way may have
By a flash of lightning, or a wave;
So Love's inflamed shaft or brand
May kill as soon as Death's cold hand;
Except Love's fires the virtue have   15
To fright the frost out of the grave.

GEORGE HERBERT

George Herbert (1593–1633), like Donne, had both a political career (as Public Orator at Cambridge University and as a Member of Parliament) and a religious career (as pastor at Bemerton). His poems, collected and published after his death, reflect his constant attempts to find a comfortable and lasting relationship between himself and God. These attempts were frustrated by Herbert's sense of his own sinfulness and his belief that human beings were inherently unworthy of God's love. Herbert's poetry is notable for its craft. In the 164 poems that make up *The Temple*, no stanzaic form or rhyme scheme is repeated exactly from one poem to the next.

Easter Wings

Lord, who createdst man in wealth and store,[1]
Though foolishly he lost the same,
Decaying more and more
Till he became
Most poor:
With thee
O let me rise
As larks, harmoniously,
And sing this day thy victories:
Then shall the fall further the flight in me.

My tender age in sorrow did begin;
And still with sicknesses and shame
Thou didst so punish sin,
That I became
Most thin.
With thee
Let me combine,
And feel this day thy victory;
For, if I imp[2] my wing on thine,
Affliction shall advance the flight in me.

1. **store,** abundance.
2. **imp,** a term from falconry; to engraft feathers in the damaged wing of a bird so as to restore or improve its powers of flight.

The Collar

I struck the board[1] and cried, "No more;
    I will abroad!
What? Shall I ever sigh and pine?
My lines and life are free, free as the road,
    Loose as the wind, as large as store.[2]   5
        Shall I be still in suit?
   Have I no harvest but a thorn
   To let me blood, and not restore
What I have lost with cordial[3] fruit?
        Sure there was wine   10
  Before my sighs did dry it; there was corn
    Before my tears did drown it.
  Is the year only lost to me?
    Have I no bays[4] to crown it,
No flowers, no garlands gay? All blasted?   15
        All wasted?
  Not so, my heart; but there is fruit,
    And thou hast hands,
  Recover all thy sigh-blown age
On double pleasures: leave thy cold dispute   20
Of what is fit and not. Forsake thy cage,
    Thy rope of sands,
Which petty thoughts have made, and made to thee
  Good cable to enforce and draw,
    And be thy law,   25
  While thou didst wink and wouldst not see.
    Away! take heed;
    I will abroad.
Call in thy death's head there; tie up thy fears.
    He that forbears   30
   To suit and serve his need,
    Deserves his load."
But as I raved and grew more fierce and wild
    At every word,
Methought I heard one calling *Child!*   35
    And I replied, *My Lord.*

---

1. **board**, literally table, but also perhaps the Communion Table.
2. **store**, abundance.
3. **cordial**, life-giving, with a pun on its root meaning, "from the heart."
4. **bays**, a garland of laurels, signifying honor or renown.

The Pulley

When God at first made man,
Having a glass of blessings standing by,
   "Let us," said he, "pour on him all we can.
Let the world's riches, which dispersed lie,
   Contract into a span."   5

So strength first made a way;
Then beauty flowed, then wisdom, honor, pleasure.
   When almost all was out, God made a stay,
Perceiving that, alone of all his treasure,
   Rest in the bottom lay.   10

   "For if I should," said he,
"Bestow this jewel also on my creature,
   He would adore my gifts instead of me,
And rest in Nature, not the God of Nature;
   So both should losers be.   15

   "Yet let him keep the rest,
But keep them with repining restlessness.
   Let him be rich and weary, that at least,
If goodness lead him not, yet weariness
   May toss him to my breast."   20

Love (III)

Love bade me welcome: yet my soul drew back,
   Guilty of dust and sin.
But quick-eyed Love, observing me grow slack
   From my first entrance in,
Drew nearer to me, sweetly questioning   5
   If I lacked anything.

"A guest," I answered, "worthy to be here":
   Love said, "You shall be he."
"I, the unkind, ungrateful? Ah, my dear,
   I cannot look on thee."   10
Love took my hand, and smiling did reply,
   "Who made the eyes but I?"

"Truth, Lord, but I have marred them; let my shame
   Go where it doth deserve."
"And know you not," says Love, "who bore the blame?"   15
   "My dear, then I will serve."
"You must sit down," says Love, "and taste my meat."
   So I did sit and eat.

On Court-Worm

1. How does Jonson connect the metaphor to his real subject? What words are appropriate for both?

2. What change does Jonson make in the natural cycle? Why?

Still to Be Neat

1. What is the attitude toward beauty expressed here? What words best show the poet's real feelings?

2. Look at the balanced phrases in the poem. How is the last one different from the others? Why?

On My First Son

1. What reasons does Jonson use to comfort himself for the loss of his son? What development is there in these reasons?

2. The last two lines are difficult to understand, but somewhat easier if you add the suppressed "he" to the last line: "As what he loves (he) may never like too much." Can you see a connection between this line and line 2? What is the speaker's final attitude?

Though I Am Young and Cannot Tell

1. What are the similarities between Love and Death in this poem?

2. What are the differences between the two? What is the most important difference?

Easter Wings

1. What connections can you find between the shape of the poem and the subject?

2. Why are "wings" an appropriate image?

The Collar

1. What is the speaker rebelling against?

2. The speaker seems to be conducting an argument with himself. What are the major divisions—the problems and the potential solutions—of this argument?

3. How do the last four lines, through meaning and rhythm, work to resolve the poem?

The Pulley

1. What are the good things God gave to humankind?

2. What is the one thing God withheld? Why?

3. What is the significance of the title?

4. *Rest* is a word with two meanings: *"remainder"* and *"repose."* How does Herbert use both of these meanings?

Love (III)

1. What is the dramatic situation implied in the poem? How would you characterize the speaker?

2. What details in the poem lead you to identify "Love" and "the Lord"? What is gained by using "Love" throughout?

3. Why is the speaker so reluctant to accept Love's welcome? Why does he change his mind?

4. This poem is the last one in the collection of Herbert's poems called *The Temple*. What makes it seem a concluding poem?

Implications (George Herbert)
Consider the following statements. What does the poet think? What do you think?

1. The way to find salvation involves much painful struggle.

2. The way to find salvation involves simple acceptance of God's love.

3. Playing games with words is a form of praising God.

ROBERT HERRICK

Robert Herrick (1591–1674), although he was a priest, became widely known for his decidedly secular verse. An admirer of Ben Jonson, Herrick achieved the same elegant wit and used some of the same poetic forms as Jonson.

The Argument of His Book

I sing of brooks, of blossoms, birds, and bowers,
Of April, May, of June, and July flowers.
I sing of Maypoles, hock carts,[1] wassails, wakes,[2]
Of bridegrooms, brides, and of their bridal cakes.
I write of youth, of love, and have access   5
By these to sing of cleanly wantonness.
I sing of dews, of rains, and, piece by piece,
Of balm, of oil, of spice, and ambergris.[3]
I sing of times trans-shifting, and I write
How roses first came red and lilies white.   10
I write of groves, of twilights, and I sing
The court of Mab[4] and of the fairy king.
I write of hell; I sing (and ever shall)
Of heaven, and hope to have it after all.

---

1. **hock carts,** carts used to carry in the last load of the harvest.
2. **wakes,** parish festivals as well as watches over the dead.
3. **ambergris** (am'bər gris) substance from whales used in making perfume.
4. **Mab** (mab) the queen of the fairies (see *Romeo and Juliet*, I:4:39–79, Mercutio's famous speech describing her activities).

Delight in Disorder

A sweet disorder in the dress
Kindles in clothes a wantonness.
A lawn about the shoulders thrown
Into a fine distraction;
An erring lace, which here and there   5
Enthralls the crimson stomacher;
A cuff neglectful, and thereby
Ribbons to flow confusedly;
A winning wave, deserving note,
In the tempestuous petticoat;   10
A careless shoestring, in whose tie
I see a wild civility;
Do more bewitch me than when art
Is too precise in every part.

RICHARD LOVELACE

Richard Lovelace (1618–1658) lived a life of social, educational, and
personal success until the civil war in England. Then he was twice
imprisoned by the Puritan government, and he died in obscurity. His
famous lyric "To Lucasta, On Going to the Wars" expresses both personal
and political commitment in a combination that exalts them both.

*The sunken gardens at Kensington Palace, London, are representative of the
elaborate formal gardens and water displays typical of the eighteenth century.*

To Lucasta, On Going to the Wars

T ell me not, sweet, I am unkind
That from the nunnery
Of thy chaste breast and quiet mind,
To war and arms I fly.

True, a new mistress now I chase,   5
The first foe in the field;
And with a stronger faith embrace
A sword, a horse, a shield.

Yet this inconstancy is such
As you too shall adore;   10
I could not love thee, dear, so much,
Loved I not honor more.

The Argument of His Book

1. Herrick is making a list of various subjects he will write about. How random is his order? Can you detect any structure in his list? Any progression? Why does he begin where he does and end where he does?

2. The poem is noticeable for its great number of nouns and small number of adjectives. What effect is gained by using so many nouns?

Delight in Disorder

1. Again, the question of order becomes important. Why does the speaker list the details in the order he does?

2. What words suggest "delight" on the part of the speaker?

3. What sense do you get of the personality of the woman described?

4. Look back at Jonson's "Still To Be Neat" (page 311). How would you distinguish the two poets' views on the subject of careful art and neglected beauty?

To Lucasta, On Going to the Wars

1. What has Lucasta said to the poet to evoke the answer that forms this poem? Is the answer the complete answer, or is the speaker really motivated by other desires as well?

2. To some, this poem might imply that women think of the immediate, while men think of life on a larger scale. To others, it might imply that men tend to falsely equate war with honor, while women are concerned with more important human values. Do you agree with either of these views?

3. The pattern of the poem is logical argument. How is this pattern achieved?

ANDREW MARVELL

Andrew Marvell (1621–1678) managed to have a public career both under the
Puritan Interregnum and under the monarchy. In his poetry, he also
combined two traditions: the classical background and smooth texture of Ben
Jonson, and the witty intellectual passion of John Donne.

To His Coy Mistress

Had we but world enough, and time,
This coyness, lady, were no crime.
We would sit down, and think which way
To walk, and pass our long love's day.
Thou by the Indian Ganges' side   5
Shouldst rubies find; I by the tide
Of Humber[1] would complain. I would
Love you ten years before the flood,
And you should, if you please, refuse
Till the conversion of the Jews.[2]   10
My vegetable[3] love should grow
Vaster than empires and more slow;
An hundred years should go to praise
Thine eyes, and on thy forehead gaze;
Two hundred to adore each breast,   15
But thirty thousand to the rest;
An age at least to every part,
And the last age should show your heart.
For, lady, you deserve this state,[4]
Nor would I love at lesser rate.   20
    But at my back I always hear
Time's winged chariot hurrying near;
And yonder all before us lie
Deserts of vast eternity.
Thy beauty shall no more be found;   25
Nor, in thy marble vault, shall sound
My echoing song; then worms shall try
That long-preserved virginity,
And your quaint[5] honor turn to dust,
And into ashes all my lust: 30
The grave's a fine and private place,
But none, I think, do there embrace.
    Now therefore, while the youthful hue
Sits on thy skin like morning dew,
And while thy willing soul transpires[6]   35
At every pore with instant fires,
Now let us sport us while we may,
And now, like amorous birds of prey,
Rather at once our time devour
Than languish in his slow-chapped[7] power   40
Let us roll all our strength and all
Our sweetness up into one ball,
And tear our pleasures with rough strife
Thorough[8] the iron gates of life:
Thus, though we cannot make our sun   45
Stand still, yet we will make him run.[9]

---

1. **Humber,** the river that flows through Marvell's
hometown, Hull.
2. **conversion of the Jews,** supposed to occur, according to Christian tradition, at the end of history; therefore, a long time away.
3. **vegetable,** growing as slowly as vegetation.
4. **state,** dignity; ceremonial treatment.
5. **quaint,** fastidious.
6. **transpires,** breathes out.

7. **slow-chapped,** slow-jawed; personifying Time as
devouring love.
8. **thorough,** through.
9. Two biblical allusions are in the last two lines:
Joshua commanded the sun to stand still (Joshua 9),
while in Psalms 19:5, the sun is described "as a bridegroom coming out of his chamber, [who] rejoiceth as
a strong man to run a race."

Satan wounded, from an illustrated edition of Paradise Lost

JOHN MILTON

John Milton (1608–1674) was a writer of fierce conviction and passionate
intelligence who set out to accomplish, in his words, "things unattempted yet
in prose or rhyme." He succeeded, as *Paradise Lost* proves. Furthermore,
Milton's influence on later writers can hardly be measured. While he
was still a young man, he studied at Cambridge and traveled abroad, learning
Italian, Greek, Hebrew, Aramaic, French, and Spanish. During this
time, he wrote poems such as "L'Allegro" and "Il Penseroso." In his public
career as Latin Secretary for Cromwell's government (international
debate was still being conducted in Latin), he wrote many public statements,
including a justification for the beheading of Charles I. Milton also
wrote pamphlets on education, divorce, and freedom of the press, as well as
treatises on Christian doctrine. After the Restoration, Milton lived
a retired life. He had been blind since about 1652, and he had fallen out of
public favor with the monarchy. He devoted his enormous intellectual
and creative energies to his great work *Paradise Lost*, in which he undertook
to "justify the ways of God to men." For his form, he turned to the
epics of Homer, Virgil, and Dante. But while those epics were about mortals,
Milton's characters were Satan, God, Christ, Adam and Eve, and a
supporting cast of devils and angels. Milton's decision to start the story of the
Fall of Humanity with the Fall of Satan is not merely a following
of the epic convention that the story should start "in the middle." Rather,
Milton had to create Satan as *the* adversary, a great opponent to both God and
Adam, an antagonist of such stature that victory (by God) or defeat
(of Adam) would nonetheless be a heroic struggle. Milton's reliance on
Latin- and Greek-based words and his inversion of regular English sentence
structure can also be seen as his attempt to create a grand style
worthy of his theme. The following excerpts from Book I of *Paradise Lost*
describe the fall of Satan and Satan's reaction to his plight.

from *Paradise Lost*

... Him[1] the Almighty Power
Hurled headlong flaming from the ethereal sky
With hideous ruin[2] and combustion down
To bottomless perdition, there to dwell
In adamantine[3] chains and penal fire,   5
Who[4] durst defy the omnipotent to arms.
Nine times the space that measures day and night
To mortal men, he with his horrid crew[5]
Lay vanquished, rolling in the fiery gulf
Confounded[6] though immortal. But his doom   10
Reserved him to more wrath; for now the thought
Both of lost happiness and lasting pain
Torments him; round he throws his baleful eyes,
That witnessed[7] huge affliction and dismay
Mixed with obdurate pride and steadfast hate.   15
At once as far as angels' ken[8] he views
The dismal situation waste and wild:
A dungeon horrible, on all sides round
As one great furnace flamed, yet from those flames
No light, but rather darkness visible   20
Served only to discover sights of woe,
Regions of sorrow, doleful shades, where peace
And rest can never dwell, hope never comes[9]
That comes to all; but torture without end
Still urges,[10] and a fiery deluge, fed   25
With ever-burning sulphur, unconsumed:
Such place eternal justice had prepared
For those rebellious, here their prison ordained
In utter darkness, and their portion set
As far removed from God and light of heaven   30
As from the center thrice to the utmost pole.

. . . .

1. **Him,** Satan.
2. **ruin,** literally, falling.
3. **adamantine** (ad'ə man'tēn), adamant was an imaginary stone of impenetrable hardness.
4. **who,** he who.
5. **horrid crew,** all the other angels, now devils, who revolted with Satan against God and fell with him.

6. **confounded,** literally, poured together; hence, confused.
7. **witnessed,** expressed; revealed.
8. **ken,** range of vision.
9. **hope never comes,** an echo of Dante's Hell, which bore the legend "Abandon hope all ye who enter here."
10. **still urges,** continually provokes.

"Is this the region, this the soil, the clime,"
Said then the lost archangel, "this the seat[11]
That we must change for heaven, this mournful gloom
For that celestial light? Be it so, since he   35
Who now is sovereign can dispose and bid
What shall be right: farthest from him is best,
Whom reason hath equalled, force hath made supreme
Above his equals. Farewell, happy fields,
Where joy for ever dwells: hail, horrors! hail,   40
Infernal world! and thou, profoundest hell,
Receive thy new possessor: one who brings
A mind not to be changed by place or time.
The mind is its own place, and in itself
Can make a heaven of hell, a hell of heaven.   45
What matter where, if I be still the same,
And what I should be, all but less than he[12]
Whom thunder hath made greater? Here at least
We shall be free; the Almighty hath not built
Here for his envy, will not drive us hence;   50
Here we may reign secure, and in my choice
To reign is worth ambition, though in hell;
Better to reign in hell than serve in heaven.

———————

11. **seat,** established place; residence.
12. **all but less than he,** all but equal to.

On His Blindness

When I consider how my light is spent,
   Ere half my days, in this dark world and wide,
   And that one talent[1] which is death to hide,
   Lodged with me useless, though my soul more bent
To serve therewith my Maker, and present   5
   My true account, lest he returning chide;
   "Doth God exact day-labor, light denied?"
   I fondly[2] ask; but Patience to prevent
That murmur, soon replies, "God doth not need
   Either man's work or his own gifts; who best   10
   Bear his mild yoke, they serve him best. His state
Is kingly. Thousands at his bidding speed
   And post[3] o'er land and ocean without rest:
   They also serve who only stand and wait."

———————

1. **talent,** in part, an allusion to the parable of the
talents, Matthew 25:14–30.
2. **fondly,** foolishly.
3. **post,** travel.

To His Coy Mistress

1. The poem is written in three verse paragraphs. What is the central point of each one?

2. List the hyperboles in the first twenty lines. What do they tell us about the speaker and his attitude toward the lady?

3. What does the word *coy* mean? What sense do you get of the lady's interest (or lack of interest) in the speaker?

4. How seriously do you think we should take this poem? Why?

5. Consider the following statements. Which do you find strongest evidence for?

a. The poet is an old man who is afraid of death and who is deeply in love with a young woman.

b. The poet is a young man who uses the inevitability of death to scare the woman into responding to him.

Paradise Lost

1. What are the major oppositions Milton sets up in these passages?

2. In lines 1–31, what words are particularly important for creating Hell in a physical sense? In a moral sense?

3. In lines 32–53, we hear Satan talking to Beelzebub, another fallen angel. What arguments does Satan use to convince Beelzebub (and himself) that the demons are not really defeated?

4. What do you think of Satan's arguments? Are they convincing? Can you find any evidence that he is just rationalizing and trying to make the best of a bad situation?

On His Blindness

1. This sonnet takes the form of an internal conversation. The speaker asks himself a question and then answers it. In what mood does he ask the question? In what mood does he answer it?

2. *Talent* is a word with two meanings: the modern meaning of "ability" and the Biblical meaning of "a coin." The Biblical story tells of a servant who was given money (a talent) to keep for his master and who buried the money for safekeeping. His master scolded him for not investing it so that its value would increase. In this sonnet, is *talent* used in both the Biblical and the modern sense? What was Milton's "one talent"? Why would it be "death" to hide it?

3. How does Patience describe those who best serve God?

4. Does the last line imply that the best way to live would be to cease all activity?

JOHN DRYDEN

John Dryden (1631–1700) was successful at every literary form he tried, and he tried all except the novel. At first Dryden wrote "occasional poetry"— poems to mark a particular occasion. Then he turned to playwriting and wrote highly successful heroic tragedies and social comedies. He also wrote a famous and enduring commentary on dramatic theory and did translations (with his own critical introductions) of Homer, Virgil, Juvenal, and others. Dryden is best known for his satiric poems, written in polished, balanced couplets. The excerpts that follow are from two of his longer poems. The first, *MacFlecknoe*, attacks a literary and political rival; the second, *Absalom and Achitophel*, exposes the corruption of powerful government figures.

from *Macflecknoe* [1]

All human things are subject to decay,
And when fate summons, monarchs must obey.
This Flecknoe found, who, like Augustus,[2] young
Was called to empire, and had governed long;
In prose and verse, was owned, without dispute,   5
Through all the realms of Nonsense, absolute.
This aged prince, now flourishing in peace,
And blest with issue of a large increase,
Worn out with business, did at length debate
To settle the succession of the state;   10
And, pondering which of all his sons was fit
To reign, and wage immortal war with wit,[3]
Cried: "'Tis resolved; for nature pleads that he
Should only rule, who most resembles me.
Sh——[4] alone my perfect image bears,   15
Mature in dullness from his tender years:
Sh—— alone, of all my sons, is he
Who stands confirmed in full stupidity.
The rest to some faint meaning make pretense,
But Sh—— never deviates into sense.   20
Some beams of wit on other souls may fall,
Strike through, and make a lucid interval;
But Sh——'s genuine night admits no ray,
His rising fogs prevail upon the day.
Besides, his goodly fabric fills the eye,   25
And seems designed for thoughtless majesty:
Thoughtless as monarch oaks that shade the plain,
And, spread in solemn state, supinely reign.

---

1. **MacFlecknoe,** means "son of Flecknoe." Richard Flecknoe was an Irish poet, known for being tedious and prolific. By grafting the object of his attack, the comic playwright Thomas Shadwell, to the family line of Flecknoe, Dryden transfers Flecknoe's bad qualities to Shadwell. Dryden's attack on Shadwell had political origins: Dryden had written several political satires against the Earl of Shaftesbury (see the following poem) and Shadwell had replied with a satire against Dryden.

2. **Augustus,** (ô gus'təs), Augustus Caesar, who became emperor of Rome when he was thirty-two and ruled for forty years.
3. **wit,** an important and multifaceted word for the seventeenth and eighteenth centuries. It means "intellect, poetic imagination, general liveliness of mind, and articulateness."
4. **Sh––,** A half-hearted attempt to ensure anonymity, which fooled no one.

from *Absalom and Achitophel*[1]

Of these the false Achitophel was first;
A name to all succeeding ages cursed:
For close designs, and crooked counsels fit;
Sagacious, bold, and turbulent of wit;
Restless, unfixed in principles and place;   5
A fiery soul, which, working out its way,
Fretted the pygmy body to decay,
And o'er-informed the tenement of clay.[2]
A daring pilot in extremity;
Pleased with the danger, when the waves went high,   10
He sought the storms; but, for a calm unfit,
Would steer too nigh the sands, to boast his wit.
Great wits[3] are sure to madness near allied,
And thin partitions do their bounds divide;
Else why should he, with wealth and honor blest,   15
Refuse his age the needful hours of rest?
Punish a body which he could not please,
Bankrupt of life, yet prodigal of ease?
And all to leave what with his toil he won,
To that unfeathered two-legged thing,[4] a son;   20
Got,[5] while his soul did huddled[6] notions try;
And born a shapeless lump, like anarchy.
In friendship false, implacable in hate,
Resolved to ruin or to rule the state.
To compass this the triple bond[7] he broke,   25
The pillars of the public safety shook,
And fitted Israel[8] for a foreign yoke;
Then seized with fear, yet still affecting[9] fame,
Usurped a patriot's all-atoning name.
So easy still it proves in factious[10] times,   30
With public zeal to cancel private crimes.

---

1. *Absalom and Achitophel* takes its title, plot structure, and character names from II Samuel 13–18, the story of Absalom's revolt against his father, King David. Dryden is writing about the political situation in which the Earl of Shaftesbury (Achitophel) had urged King Charles's illegitimate son to seek the succession to the throne. This excerpt is the first description of Shaftesbury/Achitophel.
2. **o'er-informed the tenement of clay,** overanimated his body.
3. **wits,** geniuses.
4. **unfeathered and two-legged thing,** an allusion to Plato's definition of humans.
5. **got,** begotten, sired.
6. **huddled,** confused.
7. **triple bond,** alliance of England, Sweden, and the Dutch Republic against France.
8. **Israel,** England.
9. **affecting,** here, both "desiring" and "pretending to."
10. **factious** (fak′shəs), split by factions.

William Hogarth's "Beer Street" conveys the satiric
spirit of the eighteenth century, a spirit found in
the poets of the age, particularly Alexander Pope.

ALEXANDER POPE

Alexander Pope (1688–1744), though small (4 ft 6 in) and sickly, was the eighteenth century's most brilliant poet. In a poetic style composed of witty, graceful couplets, Pope treated many and disparate topics. He dealt with literary theory and practice in the *Essay on Criticism* and with philosophical problems in the *Essay on Man*. He wrote English verse translations of the *Iliad* and the *Odyssey* and attacked current writers in *The Dunciad*. The inspiration for his most famous poem was a society joke in which a curl was cut off from a lady's head. In an effort to placate the wounded feelings of the lady, Pope wrote *The Rape of the Lock*, first as a poem in two cantos, then in an extended five-canto version. The extended version contains elements of mock heroics, an epic battle (in the form of a card game), and a final appeal to the Muse: "This lock the Muse shall consecrate to fame, / And 'midst the stars inscribe Belinda's name."
In the two excerpts that follow, we meet Belinda getting up in the morning, and then follow her to Hampton Court, the scene of the fatal "assault."

from *The Rape of the Lock*

"BELINDA GETS DRESSED" (CANTO I)

And now, unveiled, the toilet[1] stands displayed,
Each silver vase in mystic order laid.
First, robed in white, the nymph[2] intent adores,
With head uncovered, the cosmetic powers.
A heavenly image in the glass[3] appears;   5
To that she bends, to that her eyes she rears.
The inferior priestess,[4] at her altar's side,
Trembling begins the sacred rites of pride.
Unnumbered treasures ope at once, and here
The various offerings of the world appear.   10
From each she nicely culls with curious toil,
And decks the goddess[5] with the glittering spoil.
This casket India's glowing gems unlocks,
And all Arabia[6] breathes from yonder box.

---

1. **toilet,** the dressing table and the equipment for make-up, etc.
2. **nymph** (nimf), Belinda.
3. **glass,** mirror.
4. **inferior priestess,** Belinda's maid.
5. **goddess,** Belinda.
6. **Arabia,** source of perfume (see *Macbeth* V:1:51).

The tortoise here and elephant unite,   15
Transformed to combs, the speckled and the white.
Here files of pins extend their shining rows,
Puff, powders, patches, Bibles, billet-doux.[7]
Now awful Beauty puts on all its arms;
The fair each moment rises in her charms,   20
Repairs her smiles, awakens every grace,
And calls forth all the wonders of her face.

---

7. **billet-doux** (bil'ē dü′), literally, "sweet letters"; love
letters.

"AT HAMPTON COURT" (CANTO III)

Close by those meads, forever crowned with flowers,
Where Thames[1] with pride surveys his rising towers,
There stands a structure of majestic frame[2]
Which from the neighboring Hampton takes its name.
Here Britain's statesmen oft the fall foredoom   5
Of foreign tyrants and of nymphs at home;
Here thou, great Anna![3] whom three realms obey,
Dost sometimes counsel take—and sometimes tea.[4]
Hither the heroes and the nymphs resort,
To taste awhile the pleasures of a court;   10
In various talk the instructive hours they passed,
Who gave the ball, or paid the visit last;
One speaks the glory of the British Queen,
And one describes a charming Indian screen;
A third interprets motions, looks, and eyes;   15
At every word a reputation dies.
Snuff, or the fan, supply each pause of chat,
With singing, laughing, ogling, and all that.
Meanwhile, declining from the noon of day,
The sun obliquely shoots his burning ray;   20
The hungry judges soon the sentence sign,
And wretches hang that jurymen may dine;
The merchant from the Exchange[5] returns in peace,
And the long labors of the toilet cease.

---

1. **Thames** (temz), London's river.
2. **structure of majestic frame,** Hampton Court.
3. **Anna,** Queen Anne (1665–1714).
4. **tea,** pronounced "tay."
5. **Exchange,** Stock Exchange.

# THOMAS GRAY

Thomas Gray (1716–1771) is best known for his meditation on death and human glory, "Elegy Written in a Country Churchyard." In that poem he celebrates the common person, evoking the melancholy atmosphere of the churchyard and the immortality of the individual soul. But Gray was also capable of the lighter touch, as the following poem shows. It is a wonderfully cheerful demonstration of the mock-heroic style, which we find also in the satires of Dryden and Pope.

Ode (On the Death of a Favorite Cat, Drowned in a Tub of Goldfishes)

'Twas on a lofty vase's side,
Where China's gayest art had dyed
  The azure flowers that blow;[1]
Demurest of the tabby kind,
The pensive Selima, reclined,   5
  Gazed on the lake below.

Her conscious tail her joy declared;
The fair round face, the snowy beard,
  The velvet of her paws,
Her coat, that with the tortoise vies,   10
Her ears of jet, and emerald eyes,
  She saw; and purred applause.

Still had she gazed; but 'midst the tide
Two angel forms were seen to glide,
  The genii[2] of the stream: 15
Their scaly armor's Tyrian hue[3]
Through richest purple to the view
  Betrayed a golden gleam.

The hapless nymph with wonder saw:
A whisker first and then a claw,   20
  With many an ardent wish,
She stretched in vain to reach the prize.
What female heart can gold despise?
  What cat's averse to fish?

Presumptuous maid! with looks intent   25
Again she stretched, again she bent,
  Nor knew the gulf between.
(Malignant Fate sat by and smiled)
The slippery verge her feet beguiled,
  She tumbled headlong in.   30

Eight times emerging from the flood
She mewed to every watery god,
  Some speedy aid to send.
No dolphin came, no Nereid stirred;[4]
Nor cruel Tom, nor Susan heard,[5]   35
  A favorite has no friend!

From hence, ye beauties, undeceived,
Know, one false step is ne'er retrieved,
  And be with caution bold.
Not all that tempts your wandering eyes   40
And heedless hearts, is lawful prize;
  Nor all that glisters,[6] gold.

---

1. **blow**, bloom.
2. **genii** (jē′nē ī), guardian spirits.
3. **Tyrian hue** (tir′ē ən hyü′), ancient Tyre was known for its purple dye. We would probably consider goldfish more red and gold than purple and gold.
4. **dolphin**, a dolphin rescued the legendary Greek poet and musician Arion from drowning; **nereid**, a sea nymph.
5. **Tom and Susan**, traditional names for servants.
6. **glisters** (glis′tərz), glistens.

Stourhead (Wiltshire, England), a replica of the Pantheon, is representative of the eighteenth century's return to a classic style of architecture.

MacFlecknoe

1. What is the major metaphor developed in these twenty-eight lines? Why is it useful for Dryden's satiric purpose?

2. How would you describe Dryden's satiric strategy in lines 15–28?

Absalom and Achitophel

1. What details show Dryden's hatred of Achitophel?

2. What details suggest his possible sympathy for or understanding of Achitophel?

3. How would you distinguish between the satire of *MacFlecknoe* and that of *Absalom and Achitophel?* Do you think that Dryden is using the same techniques in both poems?

Belinda Gets Dressed

1. What is the central metaphor of this passage?

2. What details indicate that Pope is satirizing the involved makeup and dressing process?

At Hampton Court

1. What values of the society are revealed in this description?

2. What is Pope's attitude toward these values? How do you know?

Ode (On the Death of a Favorite Cat . . .)

1. What picture of the cat is created in the first two stanzas?

2. What details in stanzas 3–6 contribute to the "grand" style? What details remind us of the less grand reality?

3. How seriously are we meant to take the last stanza?

FOIBLES

THE CONJURERS   *Hieronymus Bosch*

Durestring the eighteenth century, a popular view of the universe was expressed in the idea of "the great chain of being." At the top of the chain was God and under God were the angels. Next came humans, beneath humans the animals, and beneath animals, the plants. Literary scholars, such as Alexander Pope, often expressed the idea that humans are in a "middle state" between the divine and the material. We have something in our nature of both the angel and the animal. Consequently, being human, we have weaknesses, faults, and foibles. At times we can rise to the sublime heights of great nobility and courage, love and sacrifice. At other times, we become pretentious, hypocritical, absurd.

In trying to understand human nature, we are puzzled by inconsistencies in thoughts, actions, and feelings. Why do we yearn toward the good and do the bad? How can people fervently believe in and admire the sublime actions that are portrayed for them in their religions and in the lives of their heroes, and the next minute thoroughly enjoy making someone near at hand feel mean or inadequate?

All of us as we mature are quick to see the weaknesses or the foibles of others. We recognize how ridiculous is the vanity of the snob, the prejudice of the bigot, the hypocrisy of the churchgoer who cheats in business, the folly of the person who pretends to be what she or he is not. We wonder to ourselves why other people are so silly; often we fail to see our own foibles.

Artists in all fields have glorified the great in human nature, but they have also held weaknesses up for inspection. Sometimes they have even combined these aspects. Tragedy, as you have discovered, is often built around the one weakness within a noble person that ultimately causes his or her downfall. Comedy, on the other hand, almost always presents the ridiculous side of human nature, and its favorite subject has been human foibles. The great tragedies of Shakespeare, grand opera, the stories of ballets have often used comic scenes in which foibles are exposed to relieve the mounting emotional pressure. The great medieval cathedrals of Europe combine the sublime and the ridiculous, for they are encrusted with sculptured personifications of greed, lust, and gluttony set against images of saints yearning for perfection. There can be no doubt that all people are a blend of strengths and weaknesses.

The group of literary selections that follows is entitled FOIBLES. In this unit, you will have a chance to see how other writers representing many ages and cultures have used human weaknesses as the raw material for their art. And perhaps, in the process, you may come to recognize some of your own foibles and gain a certain tolerance for those of others.

MOLIÈRE

1622-1673

France's greatest comic playwright, Jean-Baptiste Poquelin, better known as Molière, was born in January, 1622, the son of a Parisian upholsterer. He was educated at the College of Clermont (a preparatory school run by the Jesuits), where one of his friends was Cyrano de Bergerac, a poet later to be immortalized in Rostand's romantic drama. Molière might have followed his father's career, or he might have become a notary (we know that he studied civil law), but he decided instead to become involved with the theatre. In 1643, he formed a company, the Illustre Théâtre, with his friends Madeleine, Geneviève, and Joseph Béjart, and six other actors. Since their first efforts were thoroughly unsuccessful, they left Paris and toured through France from 1645 to 1658, performing in provincial theaters.

This period was invaluable to Molière, as it gave him practice in everything from stage carpentry to play carpentry. We know that while traveling he must have seen productions of Italian touring companies that combined stock characters; clever, if conventionalized, plots; traditional comic routines (*lazzi*); and improvised dialogue—in short, the style of the commedia dell'arte. The vivacity and life of the characters, the humor of the plots, and the broad farce of the routines were transformed in Molière's plays by dialogue that was witty, topical, rhythmically controlled, and easily playable.

Molière's troupe of actors, of which he was now the director, returned to Paris in 1658. There they presented his short farce *The Doctor in Love*, which delighted King Louis XIV and finally brought success to the group. In the next fifteen years, Molière wrote some twenty-nine theatrical works, including fantastical court entertainments designed to be performed for

and by the court of Louis XIV in his great festivals at Versailles. But Molière's real achievements are the comedies, both in prose and verse, of which the most famous today are *The School for Wives* (1662), *Tartuffe* (written in 1664, but not allowed to be produced until 1669), *The Misanthrope* (1664–1666), *The Doctor in Spite of Himself* (1666), *The Miser* (1668), *The Would-Be Gentleman* (1670), *The Tricks of Scapin* (1671), and *The Imaginary Invalid* (1673).

These plays were performed by Molière's increasingly prestigious troupe, who were granted royal patronage in 1665. Molière himself played the leading role in many of the plays, which often contain autobiographical elements. *The School for Wives*, for example, shows us an older man who has brought up a young girl in seclusion so that she will be a perfectly submissive and innocent wife. The play opened less than a year after the marriage of the forty-year-old Molière and Armande Béjart, the twenty-year-old sister of Madeleine Béjart. Molière's lungs were affected by a severe illness in 1666. In *The Miser* we find Harpagon worrying about his catarrh and Frosine reassuring him, "Your cough is quite charming." And Molière's final appearance, onstage and in life, was in the fourth performance of *The Imaginary Invalid*, a play about a hypochondriac. The ailing Molière insisted on going on with the performance, suffered an attack in the last scene but finished the performance, and with an irony worthy of his own plays, died a few hours later.

The Miser

Like most of Molière's work, *The Miser* is based on situations and characters found in other plays. The story comes from one of Plautus's Roman comedies. The characterizations of the miser, the young lovers, the tricky servants, and the intriguing busybody have counterparts in the Italian commedia dell'arte, and Molière used some of the same names and even some of the same background material (the story of Marianne, for example) in other plays. But to recognize Molière's frequent borrowing and his repetition of devices is in no way to diminish his genius. Rather we delight in his ability to use familiar figures and stories and to make them unforgettably alive.

What are the sources of this theatrical vitality? Molière gives his characters qualities that are recognizably human—desires for love, power, and money—and then exaggerates and heightens those qualities until the characters become grandly ridiculous. We laugh at Harpagon's suspicions, his gullibility, and his obsessions because they seem absurd. We remember him because those desires are so powerful that they turn him from a human being into a machine who controls the life of everyone else on stage. Harpagon is not just a man who hoards money, but the epitome of avarice in its many contradictions. He has a houseful of servants, but orders a dinner for eight to serve ten. He suspects that his children and his servants are trying to steal his money, but he hides it in the garden for safekeeping. He constantly refers to his love for his money, but he is willing to seek marriage with a young (and undowried) girl. The contradictions are inherently funny, yet necessarily true. Harpagon's desires are our desires; we laugh at him and thus at ourselves.

The Style of the Play

The plays of the great French playwrights of the seventeenth century—Corneille, Racine, and Molière—follow some formal patterns that may seem strange to readers of English drama. The French playwrights imitated what they thought of as classical practice. They divided

Molière

plays into five acts, they limited the action to a single place, and they constructed the plot so that it took place in a single day. We see all these conventions in *The Miser*, which occurs at Harpagon's house in Paris. The action is continuous, with no time elapsing between acts. The scenes are, by convention, marked by the entrance of a new character. Some scenes therefore are very short, while others are more extended. The play requires very little in the way of setting or props, but the props mentioned are always used for comic effect. Molière does not need to write elaborate stage directions since the dialogue clearly indicates what is happening. Also, the wit of the actors can always invent new comic routines within the outlines of the sharply defined characters.

The Miser

Persons of the play

HARPAGON [Här pä gon], *father of Cléante and Élise, suitor for the hand of Marianne*

CLÉANTE [Klā änt], *his son, in love with Marianne*

ÉLISE [Ā lēz], *his daughter, in love with Valère*

VALÈRE [Vä lär], *son of Anselme and in love with Élise*

MARIANNE [Mä ryän], *in love with Cléante and courted by Harpagon*

ANSELME [Än selm], *father of Valère and Marianne*

FROSINE [Frō zēn], *an adventuress*

MASTER SIMON [Sē mon], *an intermediary*

MASTER JACQUES [Zhäk], *cook and coach driver to Harpagon*

BRINDAVOINE [Bren da vwan]
LA MERLUCHE [Lä Mer lūsh] } *servants to Harpagon*
DAME CLAUDE [Däm Klōd]

LA FLÈCHE [Lä Flesh], *valet to Cléante*

OFFICER

OFFICER'S CLERK

The scene is in Paris.

Act I

SCENE 1: VALÈRE, ÉLISE.

VALÈRE. Come, my dear Élise, surely you are not feeling sad, after giving me such generous assurance of your love? Here am I, the happiest of men, and I find you sighing! Is it because you regret having made me happy? Do you repent the promise which my ardour has won from you?

ÉLISE. No, Valère. I could never regret anything I did for you. I cannot even bring myself to wish things were other than as they are, though I must confess I am concerned about the outcome and more than a little afraid that I may love you more dearly than I ought.

VALÈRE. But what can you possibly have to fear from loving me, Élise?

ÉLISE. Alas! A hundred and one things: my father's anger, the reproaches of my family, what people may say about me, but most of all, Valère, a change in your affection for me. I dread the cruel indifference with which men so often requite an innocent love too ardently offered them.

VALÈRE. Ah! Do not be so unjust as to judge me by other men. Believe me capable of anything, Élise, rather than of failure in my duty to you. I love you too dearly, and mine is a love which will last as long as life itself.

ÉLISE. Ah, Valère, you all talk like that. Men are all alike in their promises. It is only in their deeds that they differ.

The Miser and Other Plays translated by John Wood (Penguin Classics, 1962). Copyright John Wood, 1953.

VALÈRE. If deeds alone show what we are, then at least wait and judge my love by mine. Do not look for faults which only exist in your own fond forebodings. I implore you not to let such wounding and unjust suspicions destroy my happiness! Give me time to convince you and you shall have a thousand proofs of the sincerity of my love.

ÉLISE. Ah, How easy it is to let ourselves be persuaded by those we love! I am convinced that you would never deceive me, Valère. I do believe you love me truly and faithfully. I have not the least wish to doubt you, and my only concern is that other people may find cause to blame me.

VALÈRE. And why should that trouble you?

ÉLISE. Ah, if only everyone could see you as I do, I should have nothing to fear. The qualities I see in you justify everything I do for you. My love is founded on knowledge of your virtues and sustained by my gratitude, a gratitude which Heaven itself enjoins.[1] How can I ever forget the dreadful danger which first brought us together, your noble courage in risking your life to snatch me from the fury of the waves, your tender solicitude when you had brought me to the shore and the unremitting ardour of your love which neither time nor adversity has diminished, a love for which you neglect your parents and your country, conceal your true rank and stoop to service in my father's household merely for the sake of being near me! These are the things which weigh with me, Valère, and justify, for me, my promises to you, but the justification may not seem sufficient to others—and I cannot be certain that they will share my feelings.

VALÈRE. Of all these things you have mentioned, only one gives me any claim on you, Élise, and that is my love. As for your scruples, surely your father has done everything he could to justify you in the eyes of the world! Surely his avarice and the miserable existence he makes his children lead, would justify still stranger things! Forgive me, my dear, for speaking of

him in this way, but you know that on this issue there is nothing good one can say of him. However, if only I can find my parents again, as I hope I may, we shall have little difficulty in gaining his consent. I grow impatient for news of them, and if I do not hear soon I shall set out in search of them myself.

ÉLISE. Oh no, Valère. Do not go away, I beseech you! Stay and give your whole attention to gaining my father's confidence.

VALÈRE. Cannot you see how I am endeavouring to do so? You know what adroitness and subservience I had to show to get into his service, what a mask of sympathy and conformity with his feelings I assumed in order to ingratiate myself with him, how in his presence I am forever playing a part with a view to gaining his favour. And am I not, indeed, making remarkable progress? I find that the best way to win people's favour is to pretend to agree with them, to fall in with their precepts, encourage their foibles and applaud whatever they do. One need have no fear of overdoing the subservience. One can play up to them quite openly, for, when it comes to flattery, the most cunning of men are the most easily deceived, and people can be induced to swallow anything, however absurd or ridiculous, provided it is sufficiently seasoned with praise. Such methods may impair one's integrity, but if one has need of people one must accommodate oneself to them, and if there is no other way of gaining their support, well then, the blame lies less with the flatterers than with those who want to be flattered.

ÉLISE. Why don't you try to win my brother's support in case the maidservant should take it into her head to betray us?

VALÈRE. No, I couldn't handle father and son at the same time. They are so utterly different that one could not be in the confidence of both simultaneously. Do what you can with your brother and make use of your mutual affection to win him to our side. He is coming in now. I will withdraw. Take this opportunity of speaking to him, but tell him only so much of our affairs as you think fit. (*Exits.*)

---

1. **enjoins,** commands.

ÉLISE. I don't know whether I can bring myself to take him into my confidence.

SCENE 2: CLÉANTE, ÉLISE.

[*Enter* CLÉANTE.]

CLÉANTE. I am delighted to find you alone, sister. I have been longing for a talk with you. I want to tell you a secret.

ÉLISE. Well, here I am, ready to listen, Cléante. What have you to tell me?

CLÉANTE. Lots of things, my dear, but—to sum it up in one word—I'm in love.

ÉLISE. *You* are in love?

CLÉANTE. Yes. I'm in love, and let me say before we go any further that I am fully aware that I am dependent on my father, that as a son I must submit to his wishes, that we should never give a promise of marriage without the consent of those who brought us into the world, that Heaven made them the arbiters[2] of our choice, that it is our duty never to bestow our affections except as they may decide, that, not being blinded by passion, they are less likely to be deceived and better able to see what is good for us than we are ourselves, that it behoves[3] us to trust to the light of their prudence rather than to our own blind desires, and that youthful impetuosity leads, as often as not, to disaster! I mention all this, my dear sister, to save you the trouble of saying it. The fact is that I am too much in love to listen to anything you have to say and I, therefore, ask you to spare your remonstrances.[4]

ÉLISE. And have you actually given her your promise?

CLÉANTE. No, but I am determined to do so, and I ask you, once again, not to try to dissuade me.

ÉLISE. Am I such a strange person as that, Cléante?

CLÉANTE. No, Élise, but you aren't in love. You know nothing of the power of the tender passion over the hearts of us lovers. I am afraid you may take too prudent a view.

ÉLISE. Oh, don't talk of my prudence! There is no one who is not imprudent at some time or other, and if I were to reveal all that is in my own heart you might find I was even less prudent than you are.

CLÉANTE. Ah, if only you were like me—if only you loved—

ÉLISE. Let us deal with your troubles first. Tell me who she is.

CLÉANTE. A new-comer to our neighbourhood—the most charming person in the world. I was completely carried away from the first moment I saw her. Her name is Marianne and she lives with her invalid mother, to whom she is wonderfully devoted. She cares for and consoles her in her sufferings with the most touching devotion. She lends a charm to everything she touches and a grace to everything she does. She is so gentle, so kind, so modest—so adorable. Oh, Élise, I only wish you had seen her!

ÉLISE. Oh, I can see her very well from your description, and the fact that you love her tells me sufficiently what sort of person she is.

CLÉANTE. I have discovered, indirectly, that they are not very well off, and that, even living modestly, as they do, they are hard put to make ends meet. Just think, my dear, what a pleasure it would be if I could restore her fortunes or even discreetly supplement the modest needs of a virtuous family. Imagine, on the other hand, my despair at my inability to enjoy such a pleasure, thanks to my father's avarice, or even to offer a single token of my love.

ÉLISE. Yes, I can see how galling it must be for you.

CLÉANTE. Ah, my dear, it's worse than you could ever imagine. Could anything be more cruel than this rigorous economy he inflicts on us, this unnatural parsimony[5] under which we perforce languish? What use will money be to us if it only comes when we are too old to enjoy it; if, to manage at all in the meantime, I have to run into debt on all sides, and, like

---

2. **arbiters,** decision makers.
3. **behoves,** it is necessary for.
4. **remonstrances,** arguments, usually in opposition.
5. **parsimony,** stinginess.

The Miser

you, am constantly reduced to going to tradesmen for help in order to clothe myself decently? I wanted to talk to you and ask you to help me to sound father about what I have in mind. If I find he is opposed to it, I'm determined to run away with my beloved and take whatever fortune Heaven may vouchsafe us. With this end in view I am trying to raise money everywhere. If you are in the same position as I am, my dear sister, and father opposes your wishes too, let us both leave him and free ourselves from the tyranny his intolerable avarice has so long imposed on us.

ÉLISE. He certainly gives us more and more cause every day to regret our dear mother's death.

CLÉANTE. I hear his voice. Let us go and discuss our plans somewhere else and later we can join forces in an attack on his obduracy.[6] (*Exit* CLÉANTE *with* ÉLISE.)

SCENE 3: HARPAGON, LA FLÈCHE.
[*Enter* HARPAGON *and* LA FLÈCHE.]

HARPAGON. Get out at once! I'll have no back answers! Go on! Clear out of my house, sworn thief and gallows-bird that you are!

LA FLÈCHE (*aside*). I never came across such a confounded old scoundrel. I reckon he is possessed of a devil, if you ask me!

HARPAGON. What are you muttering about?

LA FLÈCHE. What are you turning me out for?

HARPAGON. What right have you to ask me my reasons? Get out before I throw you out.

LA FLÈCHE. What have I done to you?

HARPAGON. Enough for me to want to be rid of you.

LA FLÈCHE. Your son—my master—told me to wait for him!

HARPAGON. Go wait in the street, then! Don't let me see you in the house any more, standing there keeping a watch on everything that goes on, and an eye for anything you can pick up. I want no spy for ever watching my affairs, a sneaking dog with his confounded eyes on

everything I do, devouring everything I possess and rummaging everywhere to see if there's anything he can steal.

LA FLÈCHE. And how the deuce do you think anyone is going to steal from you? Is it likely anyone is going to steal from you when you keep everything under lock and key and stand guard day and night?

HARPAGON. I'll lock up what I want and stand guard when I please. I never saw such a pack of prying scoundrels! They've an eye on everything one does! (*Aside*.) I'm only afraid he's got wind of my money. (*To* LA FLÈCHE.) You are just the man to go spreading it round that I have got money hidden, aren't you?

LA FLÈCHE. You have money hidden?

HARPAGON. No, you rogue—I never said so! (*Aside*.) Oh, it infuriates me! (*To* LA FLÈCHE.) All I'm asking is that you shan't go spreading malicious rumours that I have!

LA FLÈCHE. What does it matter to us whether you have or you haven't? It's all the same either way.

HARPAGON. So you'll argue, will you! (*Raising his fist*.) I'll teach you to argue! Once again, get out of here!

LA FLÈCHE. All right! I'm going.

HARPAGON. Wait! You are not taking anything with you?

LA FLÈCHE. What could I be taking?

HARPAGON. Come here! Let me see! Show me your hands.

LA FLÈCHE. There!

HARPAGON. Now the others.

LA FLÈCHE. The others?

HARPAGON. Yes, the others.

LA FLÈCHE. There you are!

HARPAGON (*pointing to his breeches*). Have you nothing in there?

LA FLÈCHE. See for yourself!

HARPAGON (*feeling at the bottom of his breeches*). These wide breeches are the very things for hiding stolen property. They deserve hanging—whoever makes such things.

LA FLÈCHE (*aside*). A fellow like this deserves to get what he expects. I only wish I could have the pleasure of robbing him.

---

6. **obduracy**, stubbornness.

339

HARPAGON. Eh?

LA FLÈCHE. What's that?

HARPAGON. What did you say about robbing?

LA FLÈCHE. I said, "Have a good look and make sure I am not robbing you."

HARPAGON. That's what I intend to do. (HARPAGON *feels in* LA FLÈCHE's *pockets*.)

LA FLÈCHE (*aside*). A plague on all misers and their miserly ways.

HARPAGON. What's that? What d'ye say?

LA FLÈCHE. What did I say?

HARPAGON. Yes, what did you say about misers and miserly ways?

LA FLÈCHE. I said a plague on all misers and their miserly ways!

HARPAGON. And who are you referring to?

LA FLÈCHE. Misers, of course.

HARPAGON. And who are they?

LA FLÈCHE. Who are they? Stingy old scoundrels.

HARPAGON. But who d'ye mean by that?

LA FLÈCHE. What are *you* worrying about?

HARPAGON. I am worrying about what I've a right to worry about.

LA FLÈCHE. Did you think I meant you?

HARPAGON. I think what I choose, but I want to know who you were talking to.

LA FLÈCHE. To—my hat.

HARPAGON. Yes, and I'll talk to your thick skull.

LA FLÈCHE. Can't I say what I like about misers?

HARPAGON. Yes, you can if you like, but I can put a stop to your impudent nonsense! Hold your tongue.

LA FLÈCHE. I mentioned no names.

HARPAGON. If you say a word more, I'll leather[7] you.

LA FLÈCHE. If the cap fits—I say—

HARPAGON. Will you be quiet?

LA FLÈCHE. Yes, if I must!

HARPAGON. Ah! You—

LA FLÈCHE (*shows a pocket in his jerkin*). Steady on! Here's another pocket! Will that satisfy you?

HARPAGON. Come on! Hand it over without my having to search you!

---

7. **leather,** whip.

LA FLÈCHE. Hand over what?

HARPAGON. Whatever it is you've taken from me!

LA FLÈCHE. I've taken nothing from you.

HARPAGON. Sure?

LA FLÈCHE. Certain!

HARPAGON. Be off, then! Go!

LA FLÈCHE. That's a nice sort of leave taking. (*Exits.*)

HARPAGON. I leave you to your conscience. (*Alone.*) He's a confounded nuisance, this scoundrelly valet. I hate the sight of the limping cur!

SCENE 4: ÉLISE, CLÉANTE, HARPAGON.

HARPAGON. It is a terrible worry having a large sum of money in the house. Much better have one's money well invested and keep no more than is needed for current expenses. It's difficult to find a safe hiding-place in the house. I've no confidence in strong boxes. I don't trust 'em. They are just an invitation to thieves, I always think—the first things they go for. All the same I'm not sure I was wise to bury in the garden the ten thousand crowns I was paid yesterday. Ten thousand crowns in gold is a sum which . . . (*Enter* ÉLISE *and* CLÉANTE *talking together in low voices*.) Oh Heavens! Have I given myself away? I let myself be carried away by my temper—I do believe I was talking aloud. (*To* CLÉANTE.) What is it?

CLÉANTE. Nothing, father.

HARPAGON. Have you been here long?

ÉLISE. No, we have only just come.

HARPAGON. Did you hear—er—

CLÉANTE. Hear what, father?

HARPAGON. Just now—

ÉLISE. What was it?

HARPAGON. What I have just been saying.

CLÉANTE. No.

HARPAGON. Yes, you did, you did! You did!

CLÉANTE. Pardon me, we heard nothing.

HARPAGON. I can see you overheard something. The fact is I was just saying to myself how difficult it is nowadays to get hold of any money and how fortunate anybody is who has ten thousand crowns by him.

CLÉANTE. We hesitated to come near you for fear of interrupting you.

HARPAGON. I'm very glad of the chance to explain to you, in case you got the wrong impression and imagined I was saying that I had ten thousand crowns.

CLÉANTE. We don't concern ourselves with your affairs.

HARPAGON. I only wish I had ten thousand crowns.

CLÉANTE. I don't believe—

HARPAGON. It would be a good thing for me if I had.

ÉLISE. Such things—

HARPAGON. I could well do with a sum like that.

CLÉANTE. I think—

HARPAGON. It would come in very useful.

ÉLISE. You are—

HARPAGON. I should have less cause to complain of hard times than I have.

CLÉANTE. Good Heavens, father! You have no cause to complain. Everybody knows you are well enough off!

HARPAGON. Me? Well off! What a lie! Nothing could be further from the truth! It's scandalous to spread such tales!

ÉLISE. Well, don't be angry.

HARPAGON. It's a queer thing when my own children betray me and turn against me.

CLÉANTE. Is it turning against you to say that you are well off?

HARPAGON. Yes. What with your saying things like that and your extravagant ways someone will be coming and cutting my throat one of these days in the belief that I'm made of money.

CLÉANTE. What extravagant ways have I got?

HARPAGON. What, indeed! What could be more scandalous than the sumptuous apparel you flaunt round the town? Only yesterday I was complaining of your sister—but you are far worse! It's a crying scandal! What you are wearing now, taking you as you stand, would add up to a nice competency.[8] I have told you a score of times already, my lad, I don't like your goings on at all: this aping[9] of the nobility and going about dressed up as you are can only mean that you are robbing me somehow.

CLÉANTE. But how can I be robbing you?

HARPAGON. How should I know? Where do you get the money to live as you do?

CLÉANTE. Where do I get the money? From cards. I happen to be lucky and I put my winnings on my back.

HARPAGON. That's no way to go on! No way at all! If you are lucky at cards you should take advantage of it and put your winnings into some sound investment. Then they'll be there when you want 'em. But what I would like to know, never mind anything else, is what's the use of all these ribbons that you are decked out with from head to foot? Wouldn't half a dozen pins do to fasten up your breeches? Why need you spend money on a wig, when you can wear your own hair—which costs nothing? I'm willing to bet that your perukes[10] and ribbons cost you twenty guineas at least, and twenty guineas invested bring in one pound thirteen shillings and elevenpence farthing a year at no more than eight per cent.

CLÉANTE. That's true enough.

HARPAGON. Well now, suppose we leave that and come to something else—Eh? (*Aside.*) I believe they are making signs to each other to steal my purse. (*To* CLÉANTE.) What do you mean by making signs like that?

ÉLISE. We are just arguing as to who should speak first. We both have something to tell you.

HARPAGON. Yes, and I have something to tell both of you.

CLÉANTE. We want to talk to you about marriage, father.

HARPAGON. Ay, and it's marriage I want to talk to you about.

ÉLISE. Oh, father!

HARPAGON. Why the "Oh, father"? Is it the word marriage or the idea of getting married yourself you are afraid of, my girl?

---

8. **competency,** means to live on.

CLÉANTE. The word marriage might well alarm both of us. It depends on what you understand by it. We are afraid that what *we* want may not agree with what *you* want.

HARPAGON. Now do be patient. Don't get alarmed. I know what is good for both of you. Neither of you shall have any cause to complain of what I am going to do for you. First of all, do you know a young lady named Marianne who lives not far from here?

CLÉANTE. Yes, father, I do.

HARPAGON (*to* ÉLISE). And you?

ÉLISE. I have heard of her.

HARPAGON. Well now, my boy, what is your opinion of this young lady?

CLÉANTE. She is a most charming person.

HARPAGON. Her looks?

CLÉANTE. Modest and intelligent.

HARPAGON. Her manner?

CLÉANTE. Admirable, beyond question.

HARPAGON. You think a girl like that is worth serious consideration?

CLÉANTE. I do, father.

HARPAGON. An eligible match, in fact?

CLÉANTE. Most eligible.

HARPAGON. And she looks as if she'd make a good housewife?

CLÉANTE. Without a doubt.

HARPAGON. And whoever marries her can count himself a lucky man, eh?

CLÉANTE. Assuredly.

HARPAGON. There's one little difficulty. I'm afraid she may not bring as much money as one would like.

CLÉANTE. Ah! What does money matter, father, when it is a question of marrying a good woman?

HARPAGON. Oh no, I don't agree with you there! But there *is* this to be said, that if she hasn't as much money as one would wish there may be some other way of making up for it.

CLÉANTE. Of course.

HARPAGON. Well now, I'm very pleased to find you agree with me, because her modest ways and gentle disposition have quite won my heart. Provided that I find she has *some* money—I've made up my mind to marry her.

CLÉANTE. Eh?

HARPAGON. What do you mean by "Eh"?

CLÉANTE. You have made up your mind to—what did you say?

HARPAGON. Marry Marianne.

CLÉANTE. You mean—you—you yourself?

HARPAGON. Yes. Me! Me! Me myself. What about it?

CLÉANTE. I feel faint. I must get out of here.

HARPAGON. It will pass off. Go into the kitchen and have a good drink—of cold water. (*Exit* CLÉANTE.) There! You see what these effeminate young men are! They haven't the strength of a chicken! Well, there you are, my girl, that is what I've decided for myself. For your brother I have a certain widow in mind. Someone came to talk to me about her this morning. As for you, yourself, I mean to bestow you on Seigneur Anselme.

ÉLISE. Seigneur Anselme!

HARPAGON. Yes, he's a man of ripe experience, prudent and discreet, not more than fifty years of age and reputed to be very rich.

ÉLISE (*curtseying*). If you please, father, I don't want to marry.

HARPAGON (*imitating her*). If *you* please, my pet, I want you to marry.

ÉLISE. Excuse me, father—

HARPAGON. Excuse *me*, my dear—

ÉLISE. I am Seigneur Anselme's very humble servant but, if you don't mind, I won't marry him.

HARPAGON. And I am your very humble servant, my dear, but, if you don't mind, you *will* marry him, and this very evening too.

ÉLISE. This evening!

HARPAGON. This evening!

ÉLISE. No, father, I won't.

HARPAGON. Yes, daughter, you will.

ÉLISE. No!

HARPAGON. Yes!

ÉLISE. I tell you I shan't!

HARPAGON. But I say you shall!

ÉLISE. I will never agree to it!

HARPAGON. But I shall make you agree to it!

ÉLISE. I'll kill myself rather than marry such a man.

HARPAGON. You won't kill yourself and you shall marry him. The impertinence! Who ever heard of a daughter talking like this to her father!

ÉLISE. Who ever heard of a father requiring his daughter to make such a marriage!

HARPAGON. It is a most suitable match. I am willing to bet that everyone will approve of my choice.

ÉLISE. And I am willing to bet that no reasonable person would do any such thing.

HARPAGON. Here comes Valère. Will you agree to let him judge between us?

ÉLISE. Yes, I agree.

HARPAGON. You'll accept his decision?

ÉLISE. Yes, I'll abide by whatever he says.

HARPAGON. That's settled, then.

SCENE 5: VALÈRE, HARPAGON, ÉLISE.
[*Enter* VALÈRE.]

HARPAGON. Come here, Valère! We want you to decide which of us is in the right—my daughter here, or myself.

VALÈRE. Oh, you sir, beyond question.

HARPAGON. But you don't know what we are talking about!

VALÈRE. No, but you *couldn't* be wrong. You are always in the right.

HARPAGON. I intend to marry her this evening to a man who is both wealthy and wise, and the silly chit[11] tells me to my face that she won't have him at any price. What d'ye say to that?

VALÈRE. What do I say to that?

HARPAGON. Yes.

VALÈRE. Ah well—I—

HARPAGON. Well?

VALÈRE. What I say is that fundamentally I agree with you—for of course you just must be right, but, on the other hand, she isn't altogether in the wrong.

HARPAGON. Why! Seigneur Anselme is an eligible match, well born, quiet, assured, prudent, and very well off and with no surviving children of his first marriage. What more could she want?

VALÈRE. That's true—though she might perhaps contend that it is rather precipitate[12] and that

she ought at least to be allowed time to see if she can reconcile herself to . . .

HARPAGON. No! An opportunity like this won't stand delay. What is more, there is a special, a unique advantage. He is willing to take her —without dowry!

VALÈRE. Without dowry?

HARPAGON. Yes.

VALÈRE. Oh! I say no more. There you are! One must agree—that's absolutely conclusive.

HARPAGON. It means a considerable saving for me.

VALÈRE. Of course, there's no gainsaying that. It is true that your daughter might contend that marriage is a more serious matter than people sometimes realize, that a lifetime's happiness or unhappiness may depend upon it and that one ought not to enter into a commitment for life without giving it serious consideration.

HARPAGON. But—without dowry!

VALÈRE. Yes, you are right! That's the important thing, of course—although there are people who would contend that in a case like this your daughter's own feelings should be considered, and that where there is such a great disparity of age, temperament, and opinions there is a risk that the marriage might turn out badly. . . .

HARPAGON. But—without dowry!

VALÈRE. Yes, one must admit there's no answer to that. There is no arguing against it. Not that there are not some fathers who would attach more importance to their daughter's happiness than the money they might have to part with and refuse to sacrifice it to mercenary considerations. They would rather seek to secure before everything else that union of mutual affection from which spring happiness, joy, and contentment—

HARPAGON. Without dowry!

VALÈRE. True. It is unanswerable. Without dowry! There's no countering that!

HARPAGON (*aside—looking offstage*). Ah, I thought I heard a dog barking. Can it be some-

---

11. **chit,** child.
12. **precipitate,** rushed.

one after my money? (*To* VALÈRE.) Don't go away. I'll be back directly. (*Goes out.*)

ÉLISE. Surely you don't mean what you are saying, Valère?

VALÈRE. If we are to get what we want from him we must avoid rubbing him the wrong way. It would ruin everything to oppose him directly. There are some people you can't deal with except by humouring them. Impatient of opposition, restive by nature, they never fail to shy at the truth and won't go about things in a common-sense fashion. The only way to lead them is to turn them gently in the direction you want them to go. Pretend to give your consent and you'll find it's the best way to get what you want.

ÉLISE. But this marriage, Valère?

VALÈRE. We will find some excuse for breaking it off.

ÉLISE. But how—when it is to take place this evening?

VALÈRE. You must pretend to be ill and have it postponed.

ÉLISE. But they will discover the truth when they call in the doctor.

VALÈRE. Not they! What do those fellows know about anything? Have whatever malady you like, they'll explain how you got it.

HARPAGON (*returning—to himself*). It's nothing, thank Heaven!

VALÈRE. If the worst comes to the worst we must take refuge in flight, that is, if you love me well enough, my dear Élise, to face—(*Seeing* HARPAGON.) Yes, it's a daughter's duty to obey her father. It's not for her to worry about what her husband looks like; when it's a case of— without dowry—she must take what she's given.

HARPAGON. Good! That's the way to talk.

VALÈRE. Forgive me, sir, for letting my feelings run away with me and taking the liberty of talking to her in this way.

HARPAGON. Not at all. I am delighted. I give you a free hand with her. (*To* ÉLISE.) It's no use running away. I invest him with full parental authority over you. You must do whatever he tells you.

VALÈRE (*to* ÉLISE). Now will you resist my remonstrances! (*To* HARPAGON.) I'll follow her and continue the homily[13] I was giving her.

HARPAGON. Do. I shall be grateful to you.

VALÈRE. It is as well to keep her on a tight rein.

HARPAGON. True. We must—

VALÈRE. Don't worry. I think I can deal with her.

HARPAGON. Do, by all means! I am just going to take a stroll in the town. I'll be back before long.

VALÈRE. Yes. Money is the most precious thing in all the world! You ought to thank Heaven you have such a good father. He knows the value of things. When a man offers to take a girl without dowry there's no point in looking any further. That's the only thing that matters. "Without dowry"—it counts for more than good looks, youth, birth, honour, wisdom, and probity.[14]

(*They go out together.*)

HARPAGON. Good lad! Spoken like an oracle! How lucky I am to have such a man in my service.

ACT I
EXPOSITION AND CHARACTERIZATION

1. What information about the Valère/Élise relationship is set up in Act I, Scene 1?

2. What do we learn about Valère's character and background in the first scene? Do later events in this act modify this impression of Valère?

3. What do we learn about Cléante's character and situation in Scene 2?

4. What indications are there about Harpagon's character in the first two scenes?

5. Harpagon, the main character, does not appear until Scene 3. What effects does this postponed entrance have?

6. Scene 3 is not an expository scene in the same way that Scenes 1 and 2 are. What, then, does it contribute to the play?

___

13. **homily,** sermon.
14. **probity,** integrity.

7. In Scene 4, we see the family together for the first time. How would you describe the relationship between the father and his children?

8. How is Harpagon's miserliness exhibited in his conversation with Valère in Scene 5?

9. What major plot complications are set up by the end of this act?

WORDS

A. In the first two scenes of this play, the language may seem excessively formal. But in the third scene, a change is immediately obvious. How would you account for this difference? Could the style of speaking have anything to do with the characters? How does the style influence your reaction to the characters? As you read the play, pay attention to differences in ways of speaking and to how these differences are related to characterization.

B. Look at Valère's speech in Scene 1, beginning "If deeds alone show what we are, then at least wait and judge my love by mine." Compare it with Harpagon's speech in Scene 4, beginning "That's no way to go on! No way at all!" What differences do you see in the kinds of words used by these two men?

Act II

SCENE 1: CLÉANTE, LA FLÈCHE.

CLÉANTE. Now, you scoundrel! where have you been hiding yourself? Didn't I tell you to . . .

LA FLÈCHE. Yes, sir, and I came in here with every intention of waiting for you, but your father, who's a most awkward old man to deal with, would chase me out willy-nilly. I very nearly got myself a hiding.

CLÉANTE. How is our affair progressing? Things have become more pressing than ever, and since I last saw you I have found out that my father is my rival in love.

LA FLÈCHE. Your father in love?

CLÉANTE. Yes, and I had the greatest difficulty in the world in preventing him from seeing how upset I was by the discovery.

LA FLÈCHE. Fancy his being in love! What the devil is he thinking about? Is he trying to take a rise out of everybody? What use is love to a fellow like him, anyway?

CLÉANTE. It must be a judgement on me—his getting an idea like this into his head!

LA FLÈCHE. But why do you conceal your own love affair from him?

CLÉANTE. To give him less cause for suspicion, to keep myself in a position to prevent this marriage of his if it comes to the point. What reply did they give you?

LA FLÈCHE. Upon my word, sir, borrowing money is a miserable business. Anyone who has to go through the money-lender's hands, as you have, must put up with some pretty queer things.

CLÉANTE. So nothing will come of it?

LA FLÈCHE. Oh no! Master Simon, the agent they put us in touch with, is a keen business-like fellow, and he's moving Heaven and Earth for you. He assures me he has taken quite a fancy to you.

CLÉANTE. So I shall get the fifteen thousand I'm asking for?

LA FLÈCHE. Yes—subject to a few trifling conditions you'll have to accept if you want it to go through.

CLÉANTE. Has he put you in touch with the actual lender?

LA FLÈCHE. Now really, sir, that isn't the way these things are done! He's even more anxious to conceal his identity than you are. There is more involved in these jobs than you think. They won't give his name and he is to have an opportunity of talking to you to-day at a house hired for the purpose, so that he can learn from your own lips about your means and your family. I have no doubt at all that the mere mention of your father's name will make everything easy.

CLÉANTE. Especially as my mother is dead and they can't stop me getting her money.

LA FLÈCHE. There are a few conditions here which he himself has dictated to our go-between. He wants you to see them before going any further. "Provided that the lender shall be satisfied as to the securities and that the borrower be of age and of a family with means sufficient, substantial and secure, free and quit of all encumbrance there shall be executed a proper and precise undertaking before a notary, of known probity, who to this end and purpose shall be nominated by the lender inasmuch as he is the more con-concerned that the instrument be executed in due form."

CLÉANTE. I have nothing to say against that.

LA FLÈCHE. "The lender, that his conscience may be free from all reproach, proposes to make his money available at no more than five and a half per cent."

CLÉANTE. Five and a half per cent! My goodness, but that's very reasonable. There's nothing to complain of there!

LA FLÈCHE. True. "But—whereas the lender aforesaid has not the sum in question by him and in order to oblige the borrower is himself obliged to borrow elsewhere at the rate of twenty per cent, the aforesaid borrower shall agree to meet this interest without prejudice to the five and a half per cent aforementioned in consideration of the fact that it is only to oblige the aforesaid borrower that the lender aforesaid undertakes to borrow the aforesaid amount."

CLÉANTE. What the devil! What sort of Jew or Turk[1] have we got hold of? That's more than twenty-five per cent!

LA FLÈCHE. True. That's what I said. You'd better think about it.

CLÉANTE. What's the use of thinking about it. I need the money, so I shall have to agree to everything.

LA FLÈCHE. That's what I told them.

CLÉANTE. Is there anything else?

LA FLÈCHE. Just one small clause. "Of the fifteen thousand francs which the borrower requires, the lender can only dispose of twelve thousand in cash, and for the other three thousand the borrower shall undertake to take over the effects, clothing, and miscellaneous objects as set out in the following inventory and priced by the aforesaid lender at the most moderate valuation possible."

CLÉANTE. What does that mean?

LA FLÈCHE. Listen to the inventory. "Item— one four-poster bed complete with hangings of Hungarian lace, very handsomely worked upon an olive-coloured material, together with six chairs and a counterpane[2] to match, the whole in very good condition and lined in red and blue shot silk; item—one tester bed[3] with hangings of good Aumale serge[4] in old rose with silk fringes and valance."

CLÉANTE. What does he expect me to do with that?

LA FLÈCHE. Wait. "Item—one set of hangings in tapestry representing the loves of Gombaut and Macaea;[5] item—one large table in walnut with twelve pedestal or turned legs with draw-out leaf at either end and fitted underneath with six stools."

CLÉANTE. Confound it! What use is that to me?

LA FLÈCHE. Patience, please. "Item—three muskets, inlaid in mother-of-pearl, with three assorted rests; item—one brick furnace with two retorts and three flasks, very useful for anyone interested in distilling; item—"

CLÉANTE. Oh! It's infuriating—

LA FLÈCHE. Now, now! "Item—one Bologna lute complete with strings or nearly so; item— one fox-and-goose board, one draughts-board,[6] one game of mother goose as derived from the ancient Greeks, very useful for passing the time when one has nothing else to do; item—one crocodile skin three feet six inches in length and stuffed with hay, a very attractive curio for suspension from the ceiling—all the aforementioned articles valued at upwards of four thousand five hundred francs and reduced to three thousand at the discretion of the lender."

---

1. **Jew or Turk**, Jewish and Turkish people were often money lenders and were sometimes accused of charging very high interest rates.

2. **counterpane**, bedspread.
3. **tester bed**, four-poster bed.
4. **Aumale serge**, coarse woven cloth.
5. **Gombaut and Macaea**, characters in a pastoral romance.
6. **draughts-board**, checkerboard.

CLÉANTE. Confound him and his discretion! The miserable rogue! Did you ever hear of such usury! Not content with charging outrageous interest, he must rook me three thousand francs for his collection of old junk. I shan't get two hundred for the lot, and yet I suppose I must just resign myself to agreeing to whatever he wants! He's in a position to make me put up with it. His dagger's at my throat, the scoundrel!

LA FLÈCHE. It seems to me, master, if you don't mind my saying so, that you are going the same road to ruin as Panurge[7]—drawing your money in advance, buying dear, selling cheap, and eating your corn in the blade.[8]

CLÉANTE. Well, what else can I do? That's what young men are driven to by the cursed niggardliness of their fathers. Can anyone wonder that their sons wish them dead!

LA FLÈCHE. I must admit that your father's behaviour would exasperate the mildest of men. I have no particular fancy for getting myself hanged, thank the Lord, and when I see some of my colleagues involving themselves in transactions of a certain sort I know when to keep out and steer clear of the little amusements which lead one too near the gallows, but I'm bound to say that I think his behaviour is a sheer invitation to robbery. I should even consider it a praiseworthy action to rob him.

CLÉANTE. Give me the inventory a moment, I'll have another look at it.

SCENE 2: MASTER SIMON, HARPAGON, CLÉANTE, LA FLÈCHE.

[*Enter* MASTER SIMON *and* HARPAGON.]

MASTER SIMON. Yes, as I was saying, sir, the young man is in need of money. His affairs are such that he needs it urgently, and he will agree to any conditions you like to make.

---

7. **Panurge**, friend of the giant Gargantua in Rabelais' comic epic, *Gargantua and Pantagruel.* The line following is a direct quotation of Rabelais' description of Panurge.
8. **eating your corn in the blade**, eating very young sweet corn and, by implication, not thinking ahead for later, hungrier days.

HARPAGON. And you feel certain, Master Simon, that there's not the least risk? You know your client's name, means, and family?

MASTER SIMON. No, I can't tell you exactly. It was only by chance that he was put in touch with me, but he will tell you it all himself, and his servant assures me that you'll be completely satisfied when you make his acquaintance. All I can tell you is that his family is very wealthy, his mother is dead, and that he'll guarantee, if need be, that his father will die within six months!

HARPAGON. Well, that's something! After all, it's only charitable to assist people when we can, Master Simon.

MASTER SIMON. Of course.

LA FLÈCHE (*to* CLÉANTE *in a whisper*). What's the meaning of this—our Master Simon talking to your father?

CLÉANTE (*to* LA FLÈCHE *in a whisper*). Someone must have told him who I was. Could *you* betray me?

MASTER SIMON. You *are* in a hurry! Who told you this was the meeting-place? (*To* HARPAGON) I didn't disclose your name and address to them, sir, but I think there's no great harm done. They are people of discretion and you can discuss things between you here.

HARPAGON. What's this?

MASTER SIMON. This gentleman is the person I was speaking of, sir, who wants to borrow fifteen thousand francs.

HARPAGON. So it's you, is it, you blackguard? You descend to this sort of thing, do you?

CLÉANTE. So it's you, is it, father? You stoop to this kind of trade, do you?

(MASTER SIMON *and* LA FLÈCHE *go out.*)

HARPAGON. So you are the man who is ruining himself by such outrageous borrowing?

CLÉANTE. And you are the man who is enriching himself by such criminal usury!

HARPAGON. How can you ever dare to face me after this?

CLÉANTE. How will you ever dare to face anyone at all?

HARPAGON. Aren't you ashamed to stoop to

Illustration from a nineteenth-century edition of The Miser

such extravagance, to involve yourself in such frightful expense, to squander in this disgraceful fashion the fortune your parents have toiled so hard to accumulate for you?

CLÉANTE. Don't you blush to disgrace your position by transactions of this kind, to sacrifice your honour and reputation to your insatiable lust for piling coin on coin and outdoing anything the most notorious usurers ever invented in the way of scandalous interest!

HARPAGON. Get out of my sight, you scoundrel! Get out of my sight!

CLÉANTE. I ask you, who commits the greater crime, the man who borrows to meet his necessities, or the one who extorts money from people which he doesn't need?

HARPAGON. Go away, I tell you! You make my blood boil. (*Exit* CLÉANTE.) I'm not sorry this has happened! It's a warning to me to keep a closer watch on him than ever.

SCENE 3: FROSINE, HARPAGON.

[*Enter* FROSINE.]

FROSINE. Sir—

HARPAGON. Just a minute. I'll come back and talk to you presently. (*Aside.*) It's time I had a look at my money! (*Exits.*)

SCENE 4: LA FLÈCHE, FROSINE.

[*Enter* LA FLÈCHE.]

LA FLÈCHE (*to himself*). It's a most peculiar business. He must have a regular furniture store somewhere. We didn't recognize any of the stuff in the inventory.

FROSINE. Ah, it's you, my poor La Flèche. Fancy meeting you!

LA FLÈCHE. Why, Frosine! What are you doing here?

FROSINE. Following my usual occupation—acting as go-between, making myself useful to people and picking up what I can from such small abilities as I possess. You have to live on your wits in this world, you know, and those of us who have no other resources must rely on scheming and hard work.

LA FLÈCHE. Have you some business with the master?

FROSINE. Yes, I'm handling a little transaction for him and hoping for some recompense.

LA FLÈCHE. From him? My goodness! You'll be clever if you get anything out of him! Money is hard to come by in this house I warn you.

FROSINE. But there *are* certain services which are wonderfully effective in opening the purse-strings.

LA FLÈCHE. Well I won't contradict you, but you don't know our Mr. Harpagon yet. He just isn't human at all, our Mr. Harpagon—he hasn't one scrap of humanity in him! He has the hardest heart and the closest fist of any man living. There's no service of any kind, sort, or description would make him grateful enough to put his hand in his pocket. Praise, compliments, fine words, friendliness, yes, as much as you like, but money—nothing doing! You may win his favour, be in his good graces—but nothing ever comes of it. He has such a dislike of the word "giving" that he won't even give you "good morning."

FROSINE. Good Heavens! As if I don't know how to get round men! Why, I know all there is to be known about stroking them the right way, arousing their sympathy, and finding their soft spots.

LA FLÈCHE. Not the slightest use here. Where money's involved I defy you to make any impression. On that score he's adamant—absolutely past praying for. You could be at death's door but *he* wouldn't budge. He puts money before reputation, honour, or virtue, and the mere sight of anyone asking for money is enough to throw him into a fit. It's like inflicting a mortal wound on him, taking his heart's blood, tearing out his very entrails, and if— but he's coming back. I must be off. . . . (*Exits.*)

SCENE 5: HARPAGON, FROSINE.

[*Enter* HARPAGON.]

HARPAGON (*to himself*). Everything is all right. (*To* FROSINE.) Well now, Frosine, what is it?

FROSINE. Goodness me, how well you are looking—the very picture of health.

HARPAGON. Who? Me!

FROSINE. I never saw you looking so fresh and so sprightly.

HARPAGON. Really?

FROSINE. Why, you've never looked so young in your life. I know fellows of twenty-five who are not half as youthful as you are.

HARPAGON. Nevertheless, I'm well over sixty, Frosine.

FROSINE. Well, what's sixty? What of it? It's the very flower of one's age. You are just coming to the prime of life.

HARPAGON. True, but I reckon I should be no worse for being twenty years younger.

FROSINE. What are you talking about! You need wish no such thing. You've the constitution to live to a hundred.

HARPAGON. Do you think so?

FROSINE. I'm certain. You have all the indications. Keep still a moment! Look what a sign of

longevity that is—the line between the eyes!

HARPAGON. Is that really so?

FROSINE. Of course. Give me your hand. Heavens! What a line of life!

HARPAGON. What d'ye mean?

FROSINE. You see where that line goes to?

HARPAGON. Well, what does that mean?

FROSINE. Upon my word. Did I say a hundred? You'll live to a hundred and twenty!

HARPAGON. No! Is it possible?

FROSINE. I tell you they'll have to knock you on the head! You'll see your children buried, ay, and your children's children.

HARPAGON. So much the better! And how is our little business getting on?

FROSINE. Need you ask? Did you ever know me to start a job and not finish it? I really have a wonderful talent for matchmaking. There's nobody I couldn't pair off, given a little time to arrange things. I really think, if I took it into my head, I could match the Grand Turk and the Venetian Republic! Not that there was anything very difficult about this little business of yours. I am friendly with the two ladies and have talked to them both about you and told the mother of the intentions you have formed in regard to Marianne from seeing her pass along the street and taking the air at her window.

HARPAGON. And her reply?

FROSINE. She was delighted by the proposal, and when I intimated that you would like her daughter to be present this evening at the signing of your own daughter's marriage contract she agreed without hesitation and put her in my charge.

HARPAGON. You see, I am committed to giving a supper for Seigneur Anselme, Frosine, and I shall be very pleased if she will join the party too.

FROSINE. Good. She is to visit your daughter after dinner and then go to the fair, which she wants to do, and return in time for supper.

HARPAGON. Very well. I'll lend them my carriage and they can go down together.

FROSINE. That's the very thing for her!

HARPAGON. Now, have you sounded the mother

as to what dowry she can give her daughter, Frosine? Have you told her she must make an effort to contribute something and put herself to some pinching and scraping on an occasion like this? After all, nobody is going to marry a girl unless she brings something with her.

FROSINE. Why, this girl will bring you twelve thousand a year.

HARPAGON. Twelve thousand a year!

FROSINE. Yes. In the first place she's been brought up on a very spare diet. She is a girl who is used to living on salad and milk, apples and cheese, so she'll need no elaborate table, none of your rich broths or eternal barley concoctions, nor any of the delicacies other women would require, and that's no small consideration. It might well amount to three thousand francs a year at least. Moreover, her tastes are simple; she has not any hankering after extravagant dresses, expensive jewellery, or sumptuous furnishings which young women of her age are so fond of—and this item alone means more than four thousand a year. Then, again, she has a very strong objection to playing for money, a most unusual thing in a woman nowadays. I know one woman in our neighbourhood who has lost twenty thousand francs at cards this year. Suppose we reckon only a quarter of that—five thousand a year for cards and four thousand on clothes and jewellery, that's nine thousand, and another three thousand on food—that gives you your twelve thousand a year, doesn't it?

HARPAGON. Yes, it's not bad, but all these calculations don't amount to anything tangible.

FROSINE. Come, come! Do you mean to say that a modest appetite, a sober taste in dress, and a dislike of card playing don't amount to anything tangible? Why, they are a marriage portion and an inheritance rolled into one!

HARPAGON. No. It's just nonsense to try and make a dowry out of the expenses she won't incur. I'll give no credit for anything I don't actually receive. I really must have something I can get my hands on.

FROSINE. Heavens, man! You'll get your hands on plenty. They've mentioned that they have money abroad somewhere. That will come to you.

HARPAGON. Well, we shall have to look into that, but there's another thing worrying me, Frosine. The girl is young, as you know, and young people generally prefer those of their own age and don't fancy other society. I am afraid she may not take to a man as old as I am, and that might lead to certain little domestic complications which wouldn't please me at all.

FROSINE. How little you know her! It's another thing I was going to mention. She can't bear young men at all and keeps all her affection for old ones.

HARPAGON. Does she really?

FROSINE. Yes! I only wish you could have heard her on the subject. She can't bear the sight of a young man. She declares that nothing gives her more pleasure than to see a fine old man with a venerable beard. The older men are the better she likes them, so don't go making yourself look younger than you are. She wants someone in the sixties at least. She was on the point of being married when she suddenly broke it off because the man let it out that he was no more than fifty-six and he didn't put spectacles on to sign the marriage contract.

HARPAGON. That was the only reason?

FROSINE. Yes, she says fifty-six isn't old enough for her, and she likes a nose that wears spectacles.

HARPAGON. Well, that's something entirely new to me!

FROSINE. You wouldn't believe the lengths she goes to. She has a few pictures and engravings in her room, and what do you think they are? Adonis,[9] Cephales, Paris, or Apollo? Not at all! Pictures of Saturn,[10] King Priam, the aged Nestor, and good old father Anchises borne on the shoulders of his son.

HARPAGON. Well, that *is* remarkable! I should never have thought it. I'm delighted to hear

---

9. **Adonis, etc.,** representatives of beautiful young men in Greek mythology.
10. **Saturn, etc.,** representatives of aged leaders in Greek mythology.

that her tastes run that way. I must say if I'd been a woman I should never have fancied young men.

FROSINE. I can well believe you. What poor stuff young men are for anyone to fall in love with— a lot of snotty-nosed infants and fresh-faced country bumpkins. To think of anyone feeling any attraction towards them!

HARPAGON. I can never understand it myself. I don't know how it is that women are so fond of them.

FROSINE. They must be completely mad to find young men attractive. It doesn't make sense! These young fops aren't men. How can anyone take to such creatures?

HARPAGON. That's what I'm always saying. What with their effeminate voices and their two or three wisps of beard turned up like cat's whiskers, their tow wigs,[11] their flowing breeches and unbuttoned coats!

FROSINE. Ay! They make a poor show compared with a man like you. You are something like a man, something worth looking at. You have the sort of figure women fall in love with, and you dress the part too.

HARPAGON. You think I'm attractive?

FROSINE. Why, you are quite irresistible. Your face is a picture. Turn round a little, if you please. What could be more handsome? Let me see you walk. There's a fine figure of a man —as limber and graceful as one could wish to see! Not a thing ails you.

HARPAGON. No, nothing very serious, Heaven be praised, except a bit of catarrh[12] that catches me now and again.

FROSINE. Oh, that's nothing. Your catarrh is not unbecoming. Your cough is quite charming.

HARPAGON. Tell me now, has Marianne ever seen me? Has she not noticed me passing by?

FROSINE. No, but we've talked a lot about you. I've described you to her and I've not failed to sing your praises and tell her how fortunate she would be to have such a husband.

---

11. **tow wigs**, blond wigs.
12. **catarrh**, severe head and throat congestion.

HARPAGON. You've done well. Thank you, Frosine.

FROSINE. I should like to make one small request to you, sir. (HARPAGON *looks grave.*) I'm involved in a lawsuit, and on the point of losing it for lack of a little money. You could easily ensure that I win my case if you were disposed to help me. You've no idea how pleased she will be to see you. (HARPAGON *looks cheerful.*) How delighted she will be with you. How she'll adore that old-fashioned ruff of yours! She will be absolutely charmed with your way of wearing your breeches pinned to your doublet. A lover with pinned-up breeches will be something quite out of the ordinary for her.

HARPAGON. I'm delighted to hear it.

FROSINE. This lawsuit is really a serious matter for me, sir—(HARPAGON *looks grave again.*) If I lose it I'm ruined, but a very little help would retrieve my position. I only wish you could have seen how delighted she was to hear me talking about you. (HARPAGON *looks cheerful again.*) As I recounted your good qualities, her eyes filled with pleasure and in the end I made her quite impatient to have the marriage all settled.

HARPAGON. You have been very kind, Frosine, and I can't say how much obliged I am to you.

FROSINE. I beseech you, sir, grant me the small assistance I'm asking. (HARPAGON *looks grave again.*) It will put me on my feet again and I shall be eternally grateful to you.

HARPAGON. Good-bye. I must finish my letters.

FROSINE. I do assure you, sir, I am in the most urgent need of your help.

HARPAGON. I'll give instructions for my carriage to be got ready to take you to the fair.

FROSINE. I wouldn't trouble you if I weren't absolutely obliged to.

HARPAGON. I'll see that we have supper early so that it won't upset any of you.

FROSINE. Please don't refuse me. You couldn't imagine, sir, how pleased—

HARPAGON. I'm off. There's somebody calling me. Until later—(*He goes.*)

FROSINE. May you rot, you stingy old cur! The skinflint held out against all my attempts. But

I won't give it up. I can always count on getting something handsome out of the other party, whatever happens.

ACT II
COMPLICATION: HARPAGON VS. CLÉANTE, FROSINE VS. HARPAGON

1. Act I focuses on two romantic problems. The reader might expect the second act to continue with these problems. Instead, Act II, Scene 1 concentrates on a different situation. What is it? Why does Molière take the play in this direction?

2. Frosine is a new character in the play. What do we find out about her in Scenes 4 and 5? Does she resemble anyone else in the play? What makes her different?

3. In what ways does the second act increase the tension in the father/son conflict?

4. What does Molière do to make Frosine's deception of Harpagon believable? What techniques does he employ? What difference does it make that Scene 5 comes after Harpagon's confrontation with Cléante?

Act III

SCENE 1: HARPAGON, CLÉANTE, ÉLISE, VALÈRE, DAME CLAUDE, MASTER JACQUES, BRINDAVOINE, LA MERLUCHE.

HARPAGON. Come along. Let us have you all in here. I want to give you your instructions for this evening and see that everybody has his job. Come here, Dame Claude, we'll start with you. (*She carries a broom.*) Good, I see you are ready for the fray. Your job is to clean up all round, and do be careful not to rub the furniture too hard. I'm afraid of your wearing it out. Then, I'm putting you in charge of the bottles during the supper. If there's a single one missing or if anything is broken I shall hold you responsible and take it out of your wages.

MASTER JACQUES (*aside*). A shrewd penalty!

HARPAGON (*to* DAME CLAUDE). Off you go! (*She goes.*) Now you, Brindavoine, and you, La Merluche, I give you the job of rinsing the glasses and serving the wine, but mind, only when people are thirsty. Don't do, as some scoundrelly servants do, egg people on to drink, putting the idea into their heads when they would never have thought of it otherwise. Wait till they have asked several times and always remember to put plenty of water with it.

MASTER JACQUES (*aside*). Yes, wine without water goes to the head.

LA MERLUCHE. Be we to take off our aprons, master?

HARPAGON. Yes, when you see the guests arriving, but take care not to spoil your clothes.

BRINDAVOINE. You mind, master, that there be a great blotch of lamp oil on one side of my doublet.

LA MERLUCHE. And my breeches be that torn behind, master, that, saving your presence, they'll see my . . .

HARPAGON. That's enough. See that you keep it against the wall. Face the company all the time—and you—hold your hat in front of you like this when you are serving the guests. (*He shows* BRINDAVOINE *how to keep his hat over his doublet to hide the oil stain.*) As for you, my girl (*To* ÉLISE), you are to keep an eye on what is cleared away from the tables and see that nothing is wasted. That's the proper job for daughters to do. In the meantime get yourself ready to welcome my mistress. She is coming to call on you and take you to the fair. Do you hear what I'm telling you?

ÉLISE. Yes, father.

HARPAGON. And you, my effeminate fop of a son, I'm willing to forgive you for what happened just now, but don't you be giving her any of your black looks either.

CLÉANTE. I give her black looks, father? Whatever for?

HARPAGON. Oh Lord! We know very well how children carry on when their fathers marry again and what the usual attitude towards a stepmother is! If you want me to forget your last escapade, I'd advise you to put on a cheerful face for the young lady and make her as welcome as ever you can.

CLÉANTE. I really can't promise to be glad that she should become my stepmother. I couldn't truthfully say that I am, but I can promise to obey you to the letter in putting on a cheerful face to receive her.

HARPAGON. Well, mind that you do.

CLÉANTE. You will find you have no cause to complain on that score.

HARPAGON. Very well! (CLÉANTE *goes out.*) Valère, I want your help in this. Now then, Master Jacques, come along; I've kept you until last.

MASTER JACQUES. Do you want to speak to your cook or your coachman, sir? I'm both the one and the other.

HARPAGON. I want both.

MASTER JACQUES. But which d'ye want first?

HARPAGON. The cook.

MASTER JACQUES. Just a minute, then, if you don't mind. (*He takes off his coachman's overcoat and appears dressed as a cook.*)

HARPAGON. What the deuce is the meaning of this ceremony?

MASTER JACQUES. At your service now, sir.

HARPAGON. I am committed to giving a supper to-night, Master Jacques—

MASTER JACQUES. Wonders never cease!

HARPAGON. Now tell me, can you give us something good?

MASTER JACQUES. Yes, if you give me plenty of money.

HARPAGON. What's this! It's always money. It seems to be all they can say. Money! Money! Money! It's the one word they know. Money! They are always talking of money. They can never do anything without money!

VALÈRE. I never heard such a fatuous[1] answer. As if there's anything in providing good food if you have plenty of money. It's the easiest thing in the world. Any fool can do that much. The man who is really good at his job can put on a good meal without spending money.

MASTER JACQUES. Put on a good meal without spending money!

VALÈRE. Yes.

MASTER JACQUES. Upon my word, Mr Steward, I would like you to show how it's done. You had better take on my job as cook since it seems you want to be managing everything.

HARPAGON. Be quiet! Just tell us what we shall need.

MASTER JACQUES. Ask Mr Steward there. He is the man who can put on a meal without spending money.

HARPAGON. Hey! I want an answer from *you*.

MASTER JACQUES. How many will you be at table?

HARPAGON. We shall be eight or ten, but reckon on eight. Provide for eight and there's always plenty for ten.

VALÈRE. Of course.

MASTER JACQUES. Right. You need to provide four sorts of soup and five main courses—soups, entrées—

HARPAGON. What! You are not feeding the whole town.

MASTER JACQUES. Roasts—

HARPAGON (*putting his hand over his mouth*). You scoundrel. You'll eat me out of house and home.

MASTER JACQUES. Entremets[2]—

HARPAGON. Still going on?

VALÈRE. Do you want them to burst themselves? Do you think the master is asking people to come and gorge themselves to death? Go study the rules of health! Ask the doctor whether there's anything does people more harm than overeating.

HARPAGON. How right he is!

VALÈRE. You need to learn, you, and folk like you, Master Jacques, that an overloaded table is a veritable death-trap. Anyone who is really concerned for the well-being of his guests should see that the meal that he offers them is distinguished by frugality. As the ancient philosopher has it, "One should eat to live and not live to eat."

1. **fatuous**, absurd; silly.

2. **entremets**, additional dishes, such as vegetables.

HARPAGON. Ah, well said, well said! Come, let me embrace you for that. It is the finest precept I've ever heard—"One should live to eat and not eat to"—that's not it—how does it go?

VALÈRE. "One should eat to live and not live to eat."

HARPAGON. Yes. (*To* MASTER JACQUES.) Do you hear that? (*To* VALÈRE.) Who was the great man who said that?

VALÈRE. I don't remember his name just now.

HARPAGON. Remember to write the words down for me! I'll have them engraved in letters of gold over the chimney-piece in the dining-room.

VALÈRE. I won't fail to do so. As for the supper, just leave it to me. I will see that everything is as it should be.

HARPAGON. Yes, do.

MASTER JACQUES. So much the better. I shall have the less to worry about.

HARPAGON. We must have things people don't go in for much these days, things which soon fill them up—some good thick stew with dumplings and chestnuts. Have plenty of that.

VALÈRE. You may rely on me.

HARPAGON. And now, Master Jacques, I must have my carriage cleaned.

MASTER JACQUES. Just a minute. This is the coachman's job. (*Puts on his coat again.*) You were saying, sir?

HARPAGON. I must have my carriage cleaned and the horses made ready to go to the fair.

MASTER JACQUES. Your horses, master? Upon my word, they are in no state for work. I can't say that they are down on their litter because the poor creatures haven't a scrap, and that's the truth of it. You keep them on such short commons[3] that they are no more than ghosts or shadows of horses.

HARPAGON. They are in a bad way, then—but they never do anything!

MASTER JACQUES. Because they never do anything are they never to eat anything? It would be far better for them to work more, poor creatures, if they could only eat in proportion. It fair breaks my heart to see them so thin—for the fact is, I'm fond of my horses and I suffer along with them. Not a day passes but I go short myself to feed them. A man must be very hard-hearted, master, not to have pity for his fellow-creatures.

HARPAGON. It's no great job to go as far as the fair.

MASTER JACQUES. No, I haven't the heart to drive them, master, and I should be ashamed to use the whip to them in the state they are in. How do you expect them to pull the coach when they can hardly drag themselves along?

VALÈRE. I will arrange for Le Picard next door to drive them, sir. We shall want his help in preparing the supper, too.

MASTER JACQUES. Right. I'd far rather they died under someone else's hand than mine.

VALÈRE. You are a great talker, Master Jacques.

MASTER JACQUES. And you are a great meddler, Master Steward!

HARPAGON. Be quiet!

MASTER JACQUES. I can't stand flatterers, master, and I can see that everything he does, all his everlasting prying into the bread and the wine and the wood and the salt and the candles is nothing but back-scratching, all done to curry favour with you. That's bad enough, but on top of it all I have to put up with hearing what folk say about you and, after all, I have a soft spot for you, in spite of myself. Next to my horses I think more of you than anybody else.

HARPAGON. Would you mind telling me what people say about me?

MASTER JACQUES. Yes, master—if I could be sure it wouldn't annoy you.

HARPAGON. Not in the least.

MASTER JACQUES. Excuse me, but I know very well you'll be angry.

HARPAGON. On the contrary. I shall enjoy it. I like to know what people are saying about me.

MASTER JACQUES. Well, since you will have it, master, I'll tell you straight then—they make a laughing stock of you everywhere; we have

---

3. **short commons,** small rations.

scores of jokes thrown at us about you; there's nothing folk like better than running you down and making game of your stinginess. One tale is that you've had special almanacs printed with double the numbers of fast days and vigils so that you can save money by making your household keep additional fasts; another is that you are always ready to pick a quarrel with your servants when they have a present due to them or when they are leaving your service so that you don't have to give them anything; one fellow tells how you had the law on your neighbour's cat for eating the remains of a leg of mutton, another how you were caught one night stealing oats from your own horses and how your coachman, the one before me, gave you a drubbing in the dark and you never said anything about it; in fact, I'll tell you what it is, there's no going anywhere without hearing you pulled to pieces. You are a butt and a byword for everybody, and nobody ever refers to you except as a miser, a skinflint, and a niggardly old usurer.

HARPAGON (*beating him*). And you are a silly, rascally, scoundrelly, impudent rogue!

MASTER JACQUES. Ah, well! Didn't I guess as much? You wouldn't believe me. I said you'd be angry if I told you the truth.

HARPAGON. I'll teach you to talk like that. (*He goes out.*)

SCENE 2: MASTER JACQUES, VALÈRE.

VALÈRE. You seem to have got a poor reward for your frankness, Master Jacques.

MASTER JACQUES. Upon my word, Mr Upstart, you are mighty self-important, but it's no affair of yours. Keep your laughter for your own hidings when you get 'em. Don't come laughing at mine.

VALÈRE. Ah, my dear Master Jacques, please don't be annoyed—

MASTER JACQUES (*aside*). He's climbing down. I'll put on a bold front and give him a beating if he's fool enough to be frightened. (*To* VALÈRE.) *You* may laugh, but I'd have you

know that I'm not laughing, and if you get me annoyed I'll make you laugh on the other side of your face. (*Drives him across stage, threatening him.*)

VALÈRE. Go easy!

MASTER JACQUES. How d'ye mean, go easy? Suppose I don't choose to go easy.

VALÈRE. Please—

MASTER JACQUES. You are an impudent fellow!

VALÈRE. My dear Master Jacques—

MASTER JACQUES. I don't care tuppence[4] for your dear Master Jacques. If I once take my stick to you I'll beat you black and blue.

VALÈRE. How d'ye mean, your stick! (VALÈRE *makes him retreat in his turn.*)

MASTER JACQUES. I didn't mean anything.

VALÈRE. Just understand, my dear fat-head, that if anyone's going to feel the stick you are the one!

MASTER JACQUES. I don't doubt it.

VALÈRE. And that you are only a good-for-nothing cook when all's said and done.

MASTER JACQUES. Yes, I know I am.

VALÈRE. And that you don't half know me yet.

MASTER JACQUES. Please forgive me!

VALÈRE. Did you say that you'd beat me?

MASTER JACQUES. It was only a joke.

VALÈRE. Well, I don't like your jokes. (*Beats him.*) Your jokes are in very bad taste. Just understand that. (*He goes out.*)

MASTER JACQUES. So much for sincerity! It's a poor sort of trade. From now on I've done with it. No more telling the truth. I can put up with my master. He's got some right to beat me, but as for this precious steward, I'll have my own back on him if I can.

SCENE 3: MARIANNE, FROSINE, MASTER JACQUES.

(*Enter* MARIANNE *and* FROSINE.)

FROSINE. Do you know if the master is in, Master Jacques?

---

4. tuppence, twopence; two pennies.

MASTER JACQUES. Ay, indeed he is. I know only too well.

FROSINE. Please tell him that we are here. (MASTER JACQUES *goes out.*)

SCENE 4: MARIANNE, FROSINE.

MARIANNE. What a strange position to be in, Frosine! I must say I am dreading the meeting.

FROSINE. Why? What is there to worry about?

MARIANNE. Oh, dear! How can you ask! Can't you imagine what a girl feels when she is about to confront the fate that's in store for her?

FROSINE. I agree that Harpagon isn't what you would choose if you wanted a pleasant sort of death, and I guess from your expression that your thoughts still turn to the young man you were telling me about.

MARIANNE. Yes, I won't pretend to deny it, Frosine. The respectful manner in which he paid his visits to us made a most favourable impression upon me.

FROSINE. But did you find out who he is?

MARIANNE. No, I don't know in the least, but I do know that he is very attractive, and that if I had my own choice I would as soon have him as another. Indeed he makes me loathe this husband they have chosen for me all the more.

FROSINE. Good Lord, yes! these young sparks are all attractive enough, and can tell a good tale, but most of them are as poor as church mice. You would do much better to take an old husband with plenty of money. I admit it may seem to fly in the face of nature and there may well be some distasteful things to put up with, but then it won't be for long. When he dies you may be sure he'll leave you in a position to choose one you like better, and he'll make up for everything.

MARIANNE. But it doesn't seem right, Frosine, that one should have to look forward to someone else dying before one can be happy. Moreover, death doesn't always fall in with our schemes.

FROSINE. Don't be silly. You only marry him on the strict understanding that he leaves you a widow before very long. That must be put in the contract. It would be most inconsiderate of him if he didn't die within, say, three months!—But here comes the man himself.

MARIANNE. Oh, Frosine! What a face!

SCENE 5: HARPAGON,
MARIANNE, FROSINE.

(*Enter* HARPAGON.)

HARPAGON. Don't be offended, my dear, if I come to meet you with my spectacles on. I know that your charms are striking enough, sufficiently visible; they need no glasses to discover them, but it is through glass that one observes the stars, you know, and you yourself are a star, I declare, the loveliest one in all the firmament. (*To* FROSINE.) Frosine, she doesn't say a word, and from what I can see she doesn't seem at all pleased to see me.

FROSINE. She is a little overcome. Young girls are always shy of showing their feelings at first.

HARPAGON. Perhaps you are right. (*To* MARIANNE.) Now my dearie, here is my daughter coming to greet you.

SCENE 6: ÉLISE, HARPAGON,
MARIANNE, FROSINE.

(*Enter* ÉLISE.)

MARIANNE. I fear I am late in paying my respects.

ÉLISE. On the contrary, I should have come to you first.

HARPAGON. You see what a big lass she is, but ill weeds do grow fast.

MARIANNE (*aside to* FROSINE). What a horrible man!

HARPAGON. What did my pretty one say?

FROSINE. She was saying how much she admires you.

HARPAGON. That's very kind of you, my pet.

MARIANNE (*aside*). Oh, what a creature!

HARPAGON. Very gratifying sentiments indeed!

MARIANNE (*aside*). I can bear it no longer.

SCENE 7: CLÉANTE, ÉLISE, HARPAGON, MARIANNE, FROSINE.

(*Enter* CLÉANTE.)

HARPAGON. This is my son. He has come to pay his respects too.

MARIANNE (*aside to* FROSINE). Ah, Frosine! What an encounter. This is the very young man I was telling you about.

FROSINE (*to* MARIANNE). How very remarkable!

HARPAGON. I see you are surprised to find I have a grown-up family, but I shall be rid of both of them before long.

CLÉANTE. I must say this is a most unexpected meeting. I was completely taken aback when my father told me of his intentions a little while ago.

MARIANNE. I am in the same position. The meeting is as much a surprise to me as to you. I was quite unprepared for such a coincidence.

CLÉANTE. Truly, madam, my father could have made no better choice, and it is indeed a pleasure to meet you. All the same I cannot bring myself to say that I should welcome your becoming my stepmother. I must admit that the honour is not one I appreciate. Indeed the title, if I may say so, is that last one I should wish you to assume. All this might appear rude to some people, but you, I am sure, will know in what sense to take it, understand how repugnant this marriage must be to me, and how contrary to all my intentions. In short, I am sure you will allow me to say, with my father's kind permission, that if I had my way this marriage would never take place.

HARPAGON. That's a fine way of paying your respects. What a tale to be telling her!

MARIANNE. My answer is that I feel as you do. If you are loath to see me as your stepmother I am no less opposed to having you as a stepson. Please do not think it is by any wish of mine that you are placed in such a dilemma. I should be grieved to cause you distress, and had I any freedom of choice I should never consent to a marriage which would cause you unhappiness.

HARPAGON. She's quite right. Answer a fool according to his folly. I must apologize, my dear, for my son's silliness. He is young and foolish and doesn't yet understand what he is saying.

MARIANNE. I am not the least offended, I assure you. On the contrary, it has been a pleasure to hear your son express his feelings so frankly. I value such an avowal coming from him. Had he spoken otherwise I should not esteem him so highly.

HARPAGON. It's very good of you to overlook his faults. He will get more sense as he grows older, and you'll find that his feelings will change.

CLÉANTE. Never, father! My feelings will not change. I ask the lady to believe that.

HARPAGON. You see what an absurd fellow he is. He gets worse and worse.

CLÉANTE. Would you have me be false to my love?

HARPAGON. Still at it? Kindly try a different tune!

CLÉANTE. Very well, then, since you wish me to speak in a different vein—permit me, madam, to put myself in my father's place and assure you that you are the most charming person I ever met, that the greatest happiness I could imagine would be to win your favour and that I would rather be your husband than the greatest king on earth. Yes, madam, to enjoy your love would be for me the height of good fortune, and that is indeed my only ambition. There is nothing that I would not do to achieve so enviable a purpose, and whatever the obstacles may be—

HARPAGON. Steady on, lad, if you don't mind.

CLÉANTE. I am addressing the lady on your behalf.

HARPAGON. Good Lord! I have a tongue of my own. I don't need you as my advocate. Here, bring some chairs.

FROSINE. No, I think it would be better if we set out for the fair at once, so as to get back earlier and have plenty of time to talk later.

HARPAGON. Have the horses put in the carriage, then. Please forgive me, my dear, for not having thought to provide some refreshment before you go.

CLÉANTE. I have arranged it, father. I told them to bring in a bowl of china oranges,[5] lemons, and sweetmeats. I had them ordered on your behalf.

HARPAGON (*in a whisper*). Valère!

VALÈRE (*to* HARPAGON). He's out of his mind!

CLÉANTE. Do you think there is not enough, father? The lady will perhaps excuse any deficiency.

MARIANNE. There was no need to have troubled.

CLÉANTE. Did you ever see a finer diamond, madam, than the one my father has on his finger?

MARIANNE. It *is* very brilliant.

CLÉANTE (*taking it from his father's finger and offering it to* MARIANNE). You need to look at it from close to.

MARIANNE. It is certainly exquisite, so full of fire.

CLÉANTE (*preventing* MARIANNE *from returning it*). No, no madam. It is in hands which are worthy of it now. My father has made a present of it to you.

HARPAGON. *I* have?

CLÉANTE. You do wish the lady to keep it for your sake, don't you, father?

HARPAGON (*aside to* CLÉANTE). What d'ye mean?

CLÉANTE (*aside*). What a question! (*To* MARIANNE). He means that I am to make you accept it.

MARIANNE. But I don't at all want to—

CLÉANTE. You really can't mean that! He would never hear of taking it back.

HARPAGON (*aside*). I can't bear it!

MARIANNE. It would be—

CLÉANTE (*still preventing her from returning it*). No, I assure you, he would be offended—

MARIANNE. Please—

CLÉANTE. Not at all!

HARPAGON (*aside*). Confound the—

CLÉANTE. You see how put out he is at your refusal.

HARPAGON (*aside*). You traitor!

CLÉANTE. You see! He's losing his patience.

HARPAGON (*whispers to* CLÉANTE, *threatening him*). You scoundrel!

CLÉANTE. It's not my fault, father; I'm doing the best I can to make her keep it, but she's very obstinate.

HARPAGON (*furious, whispers to* CLÉANTE). You blackguard!

CLÉANTE. You are making my father angry with me, madam.

HARPAGON (*as before*). You villain!

CLÉANTE. You will make him ill. Madam, please do not refuse any further.

FROSINE. Goodness, what a fuss! Keep the ring since the gentleman wants you to.

MARIANNE. Rather than cause further annoyance I will keep it for the time being, but I will find another occasion to return it.

SCENE 8: BRINDAVOINE, CLÉANTE, ÉLISE, HARPAGON, MARIANNE, FROSINE.

(*Enter* BRINDAVOINE.)

BRINDAVOINE. There's a man wanting to speak to you, sir.

HARPAGON. Tell him I'm busy. Tell him to come back another time.

BRINDAVOINE. He says he has some money for you.

HARPAGON. Excuse me. I'll be back presently.

SCENE 9: LA MERLUCHE, BRINDAVOINE, CLÉANTE, ÉLISE, HARPAGON, MARIANNE, FROSINE.

(*Enter* LA MERLUCHE, *running. He knocks* HARPAGON *over.*)

LA MERLUCHE. Master!

HARPAGON. Oh! He's killed me.

CLÉANTE. What is it, father? Are you hurt?

HARPAGON. The scoundrel must have been bribed to break my neck by people who owe me money.

---

5. **china oranges, etc.,** refreshments of fresh fruit and candy.

VALÈRE. It's nothing serious.

LA MERLUCHE. Master, I beg your pardon, I thought I was doing right to hurry.

HARPAGON. What did you come for, you scoundrel?

LA MERLUCHE. To tell you that your horses have cast their shoes.

HARPAGON. Have them taken to the smith at once.

CLÉANTE. While they are being shod I will do the honours of the house for you, father, and take the lady into the garden. I will have the refreshments taken out there.

HARPAGON. Valère, keep your eye on that stuff, and do, I implore you, save as much of it as you can so that it can go back to the shop.

VALÈRE. Very good, sir.

HARPAGON (*alone*). Oh what a scoundrel of a son! He's determined to ruin me!

ACT III
COMPLICATION: HARPAGON AS LOVER

1. At the beginning of Act III, we suddenly find many people on stage—more than we have seen before (or will see, until the end of the play). What are the theatrical effects thus achieved? What does Scene 1 add to the portrait of the miser?

2. What new plot complication is introduced in the first two scenes? Does it seem extraneous, or can you imagine how it will be connected to the other major plot conflicts?

3. The climax of the act is the meeting of Harpagon, Marianne, and Cléante. How has Molière created anticipation for this scene?

WORDS

One of the dramatist's chief advantages is that words spoken on stage may communicate on several levels at once. There is the literal meaning of the words, but more importantly, there is the meaning or feeling that the character conveys through inflection, through gesture, through eye contact. We call that second level the *subtext*, since the meaning lies beneath the words, though it is implied through the text. Scene 7 provides a brilliant example of subtext.

As you look at the scene, describe what Cléante is really saying to Marianne and what she is really saying to him. How does Cléante manage to make the same speech mean one thing for Marianne and another for Harpagon?

Act IV

SCENE 1: CLÉANTE, MARIANNE, ÉLISE, FROSINE.

CLÉANTE. We'll do better to go in here. There's no one here to worry about, so we can talk openly.

ÉLISE. My brother has told me about his love for you. I know how trying your position must be and I assure you that you have my whole sympathy.

MARIANNE. It is a great comfort to know that one has the support of such a person as yourself, and I do hope you will always maintain the same friendliness for me. It is such a consolation in adversity.

FROSINE. Upon my word, it is most unlucky for both of you that you didn't let me into your secrets a bit earlier. I could have saved you all this trouble. I would never have let matters go the way they have done.

CLÉANTE. What's the use! It's my ill luck! It just had to happen this way. (*To* MARIANNE.) What decisions have you come to, my dear?

MARIANNE. Alas! How can I come to any decisions? Dependent as I am on other people, what more can I do than hope for the best?

CLÉANTE. Is that all the help you can offer me? Just to hope for the best? No compassionate support? No helping hand? No positive token of your affection?

MARIANNE. What can I say? Put yourself in my place and tell me what I should do! Advise me! Command me! I will put myself in your hands, and I know that you will not ask more of me than honour and propriety permit.

CLÉANTE. But how can I do anything effective if you expect me to keep within the bounds of rigorous honour and scrupulous propriety?

MARIANNE. But what would you have me do? Even if I could disregard the scruples of my sex I must still consider my mother. She has always shown me the most tender affection. I could never bring myself to give her cause for sorrow. You must persuade her. Use every endeavour to gain her approval. I give you leave to say and do whatever you think necessary, and if the issue should depend on my declaring my love for you I shall be willing to avow to her all that I feel.

CLÉANTE. Frosine, dear Frosine, won't you help us out?

FROSINE. Goodness me! Need you ask? I should like to—with all my heart. I'm really quite kind-hearted, you know! I'm not hard by nature, and when I see people really and truly in love I'm only too willing to help them. The question is, what can we do?

CLÉANTE. Please, do think of something.

MARIANNE. Do make some suggestions.

ÉLISE. Find some way of undoing the mischief you've done.

FROSINE. It isn't so easy. (To MARIANNE.) Your mother isn't altogether unreasonable. She might be persuaded to transfer to the son what she intended to bestow on the father. (To CLÉANTE.) The real difficulty, as I see it, is that your father's your father!

CLÉANTE. Exactly!

FROSINE. What I mean is that he'll have a grievance if he finds his offer refused, and be in no mood to agree to your marriage. What we really need is that the refusal shall come from him. We must try to find some means of making him take a dislike to you, Marianne.

CLÉANTE. That's the idea.

FROSINE. Yes, I know it's the right idea. That's what we need, but how the deuce can we manage it? Wait a minute. Suppose we could produce someone, an elderly woman, say, with a touch of any sort of talent who could carry off the part of a lady of quality with the help of a few scratch retainers and some fancy title or other—a Marchioness or Viscountess of Lower Britany, should we say—I might contrive to make your father believe she was a wealthy woman with a hundred thousand crowns in ready money and landed property as well, and that she was head over heels in love with him—so anxious to marry him that she would be willing to hand over all her money under the terms of the marriage contract. I don't doubt he'd listen to that proposition, for though I know he loves you very much (to MARIANNE) he loves money better. Once he has swallowed the bait and agreed to all that you want it wouldn't matter that he found out the truth when he came to examine our Marchioness's possessions more closely!

CLÉANTE. It sounds a most ingenious notion.

FROSINE. Leave it to me. I've just remembered a friend of mine who is the very person we want.

CLÉANTE. You can count on my showing my gratitude, Frosine, if you can carry it off. Meanwhile, dear Marianne, let us make a start by winning over your mother. It would be a great deal accomplished if we could only break off the marriage. I do implore you to do all you can. Make use of her affection for you. Employ all your charm, and all the eloquence of looks and of speech that Heaven has endowed you with. Use all your gentle persuasions and tender entreaties, those endearing caresses of yours, and they will, I am sure, prove irresistible.

MARIANNE. I will do all I can. I won't forget anything you tell me.

SCENE 2: HARPAGON, CLÉANTE, MARIANNE, ÉLISE, FROSINE.

(Enter HARPAGON.)

HARPAGON (aside). Ha! My son kissing the hand of his stepmother to be! And the stepmother to be doesn't seem to be offering much objection. Is there more in this than meets the eye?

ÉLISE. Here comes father.

HARPAGON. The carriage is ready. You can set out as soon as you like.

CLÉANTE. I will go with them, father, as you are not going.

HARPAGON. No, you stay here. They will get along very well by themselves, and I need you here.

(ÉLISE, MARIANNE, *and* FROSINE *go out.*)

SCENE 3: HARPAGON, CLÉANTE.

HARPAGON. Well now, forget she's your stepmother and let me hear what you think of her?

CLÉANTE. What I think of her?

HARPAGON. Yes, her looks, her manners, her figure, her intelligence?

CLÉANTE. Oh—so so.

HARPAGON. Is that all you can say?

CLÉANTE. Well, frankly, she doesn't come up to what I expected. She's just a coquette—nothing more; her figure is not particularly graceful, her looks are no more than middling, and her intelligence is very ordinary. Don't think I'm trying to put you off, father. As stepmothers go I would as soon have her as anyone else.

HARPAGON. But you were telling her just now that—

CLÉANTE. Merely a few conventional compliments on your behalf, and purely to please you.

HARPAGON. So you wouldn't fancy her for yourself, then?

CLÉANTE. Me? Not in the least!

HARPAGON. I'm sorry about that. It cuts across an idea that was passing through my mind. Looking at her just now I began thinking about my age and the way people would talk about my marrying a girl so young, and I was on the point of giving up the idea, but as I had asked for her hand and pledged my word to her I would have let you have her, had you not taken a dislike to her.

CLÉANTE. You would have given her to me?

HARPAGON. Yes, to you.

CLÉANTE. In marriage?

HARPAGON. In marriage.

CLÉANTE. Listen. It's true that she's not exactly what I should choose, but, to please you, father, I am prepared to marry her if you want me to.

HARPAGON. No, I'm not so unreasonable as you think. I have no wish to make you marry a girl against your will.

CLÉANTE. No, but I'm willing to make the effort out of consideration for you.

HARPAGON. No, no! There's no happiness in marriage without love.

CLÉANTE. Well, perhaps that might come afterwards. They say that love often comes after marriage.

HARPAGON. No. I'm against taking chances where the man is concerned. I don't want to run any risk of things turning out badly. If you'd felt any inclination for her, that would have been fine and I'd have arranged for you to marry her instead of me, but, as it is, I'll stick to my original plan and marry her myself.

CLÉANTE. Very well, father, since that's how things stand I must disclose my real feelings and tell you our secret. The truth is that I have loved her since the first day I saw her. I was intending just now to ask your permission to marry her; it was only when you revealed your own feelings and for fear of displeasing you that I refrained from doing so.

HARPAGON. Have you visited her home?

CLÉANTE. Yes, father.

HARPAGON. Often?

CLÉANTE. Fairly often, considering what time there has been.

HARPAGON. And were you well received?

CLÉANTE. Very well, but without their knowing who I was. That was why Marianne was so surprised when she saw me just now.

HARPAGON. Did you tell her you loved her and that you intended to marry her?

CLÉANTE. Of course. I have even made some approach to her mother.

HARPAGON. And she entertained your proposals on her daughter's behalf?

CLÉANTE. Yes, she was very kind.

HARPAGON. And the daughter returns your affections?

CLÉANTE. If one may judge from appearances, I think she likes me a little.

HARPAGON (*aside*). I'm very pleased to have

found all this out. It is just what I wanted to know. (*To* CLÉANTE.) Right, my lad, you want to know what the position is? It's this. You'll just put this fancy of yours out of your head if you don't mind; you'll stop paying attentions to the lady I am intending to marry myself, and marry the woman I've chosen for you—and at once.

CLÉANTE. So that was your game, father! Very well! Since that's what things have come to, let me tell you this—I will never give up my love for Marianne, I will stop at nothing to prevent your having her, and even if you have the mother's consent I may find I have some resources on my side.

HARPAGON. What, you rascal! You have the audacity to trepass on my preserves!

CLÉANTE. It's you who are trespassing on mine. I was there first.

HARPAGON. Am I not your father? Aren't you bound to defer to my wishes?

CLÉANTE. This isn't a case where a son needs to defer to his father. Love is no respecter of persons.

HARPAGON. I'll make *you* respect *me*—with a stick!

CLÉANTE. You will do no good with threats.

HARPAGON. You shall give up Marianne.

CLÉANTE. Never!

HARPAGON. Bring me a stick—at once!

SCENE 4: MASTER JACQUES,
HARPAGON, CLÉANTE.

(*Enter* MASTER JACQUES.)

MASTER JACQUES. Now, now now, gentlemen! What *is* all this? What are you thinking about?

CLÉANTE. I'm beyond caring!

MASTER JACQUES. Steady, sir! Steady on!

HARPAGON. Talking to me like that! The impudence!

MASTER JACQUES (*to* HARPAGON). Now, master —please!

CLÉANTE. I won't budge an inch.

MASTER JACQUES (*to* CLÉANTE). What! To your father!

HARPAGON. Just let me get at him!

MASTER JACQUES. What! To your son! It would be different if you were talking to me!

HARPAGON. I'll make you the judge between us, Master Jacques, and prove that I'm right.

MASTER JACQUES. I agree. (*To* CLÉANTE.) Just stand a bit farther away.

HARPAGON. I am in love with a young lady and mean to marry her, and now this scoundrel here has the impudence to fall in love with her too, and he wants to marry her, although I've told him he can't.

MASTER JACQUES. Oh! That's wrong of him.

HARPAGON. Don't you agree that it's shocking for a son to set up as his father's rival? Isn't he in duty bound, in respect for his father, to refrain from interfering with my intentions?

MASTER JACQUES. Oh yes, you are right, but let me have a word with him. Stay there! (*He goes across stage to* CLÉANTE.)

CLÉANTE. Very well, since he has chosen you as the judge, I make no objection. It doesn't matter to me who it is, I'm quite willing to submit to your decision, Master Jacques.

MASTER JACQUES. That's very kind of you.

CLÉANTE. I'm in love with a young lady. She returns my affection and receives my offer of love sympathetically. Then my father decides to come along and upset everything by proposing to marry her himself.

MASTER JACQUES. Oh, that's very wrong of him!

CLÉANTE. Should he not be ashamed to be thinking of marriage at his age? Isn't it absurd for him to be falling in love? Wouldn't he do better to leave love-making to younger men, don't you think?

MASTER JACQUES. You are right. He can't really mean it! Just let me have a word with him. (*Goes across to* HARPAGON.) Now look, the lad isn't as bad as you make him out to be. He'll listen to reason. He says he knows the respect he owes to you—that he was carried away in the heat of the moment and that he is willing to do whatever you want, provided you show him more consideration and arrange for him to marry someone to his liking.

HARPAGON. Well then, Master Jacques, you can tell him that, on that understanding, he can count on me absolutely. I leave him free to choose any woman he likes—except Marianne.

MASTER JACQUES. Leave it to me. (*Crosses to* CLÉANTE.) Well now, your father is not so unreasonable as you make him out to be. He has given me to understand that it was your outburst of temper that annoyed him, and all he objects to is your method of going about things. He's ready to grant you anything you ask provided you do it nicely and show him the respect and obedience a son owes to his father.

CLÉANTE. Well then, Master Jacques, you can assure him that if only he will let me have Marianne he'll find me obedience itself and I'll do whatever he wishes in future.

MASTER JACQUES (*to* HARPAGON). It's all settled. He's satisfied with your promises.

CLÉANTE. Thank Heaven for that!

MASTER JACQUES. Gentlemen! It only remains for you to talk it over together. You are now in complete agreement. You were going to fall out merely because you were misunderstanding each other.

CLÉANTE. My dear Master Jacques, I shall be eternally grateful to you.

MASTER JACQUES. Don't mention it, sir.

HARPAGON. I'm very pleased with you indeed, Master Jacques, and you deserve some reward. (*He feels in his pocket.* MASTER JACQUES *holds out his hand, but* HARPAGON *pulls out his handkerchief and says*) Well, be off. I shan't forget, I assure you.

MASTER JACQUES. Thank you kindly, sir. (*He goes out.*)

SCENE 5: CLÉANTE, HARPAGON.

CLÉANTE. Father, I ask you to forgive me for having been so angry.

HARPAGON. It doesn't matter.

CLÉANTE. I am very sorry, I assure you.

HARPAGON. And I'm extremely pleased, for my part, to find you so reasonable.

CLÉANTE. It's very generous of you to forgive me so promptly.

HARPAGON. A father can always forgive his children's faults once they remember the duty they owe him.

CLÉANTE. What! Have you forgiven my outrageous behaviour?

HARPAGON. I *must* forgive it now that you show such obedience and respect.

CLÉANTE. I promise you, father, I shall remember your goodness to my dying day.

HARPAGON. And for my part I promise you shall have anything you want from me.

CLÉANTE. Why, father, what more can I ask now that you have given me Marianne?

HARPAGON. What's that?

CLÉANTE. I was saying how grateful I am, father, for what you have done for me. In giving me Marianne you have given me all I could wish for.

HARPAGON. Who said anything about giving you Marianne?

CLÉANTE. Why, you did, father!

HARPAGON. I did?

CLÉANTE. Of course!

HARPAGON. But it's you who promised to give her up.

CLÉANTE. Give her up?

HARPAGON. Yes.

CLÉANTE. Never!

HARPAGON. You've not given her up?

CLÉANTE. On the contrary, I'm more determined than ever to marry her.

HARPAGON. What! Are you starting all over again, you scoundrel!

CLÉANTE. Nothing shall ever make me change my mind.

HARPAGON. I'll see about that, you villain!

CLÉANTE. You can do what you like!

HARPAGON. Clear out of my sight!

CLÉANTE. With the greatest of pleasure.

HARPAGON. I've finished with you!

CLÉANTE. Right! Be finished, then.

HARPAGON. I renounce you!

CLÉANTE. Good!

HARPAGON. I disinherit you!

CLÉANTE. Anything you please.

HARPAGON. And I give you my curse!

CLÉANTE. Keep your gifts to yourself!

(*Exit* HARPAGON.)

SCENE 6: LA FLÈCHE, CLÉANTE.

LA FLÈCHE (*coming from the garden with a strong box*). Ah master, here you are, just in the nick of time. Quick! Follow me!

CLÉANTE. What is it?

LA FLÈCHE. Follow me, I tell you. We are in luck.

CLÉANTE. How d'ye mean?

LA FLÈCHE. Here's just what you are needing.

CLÉANTE. What is it?

LA FLÈCHE. I have had my eye on it all day.

CLÉANTE. But what is it?

LA FLÈCHE. Your father's treasure—I've lifted it!

CLÉANTE. How did you manage it?

LA FLÈCHE. I'll tell you about it, but let us be off. I can hear him shouting.

(*They go.*)

SCENE 7: HARPAGON.

HARPAGON (*calling "Stop, thief!" in the garden. He enters hatless*). Thieves! Robbers! Assassins! Murderers! Justice! Merciful Heavens! I'm done for! I'm murdered! They've cut my throat; they've taken my money! Whoever can it be? Where's he gone to? Where is he now? Where is he hiding? How can I find him? Which way shall I go? Which way shan't I go? Is he here? Is he there? Who's that? Stop! (*Catching his own arm.*) Give me my money back, you scoundrel! Ah, it's me! I'm going out of my mind! I don't know where I am or who I am or what I'm doing. Oh dear, my dear, darling money, my beloved, they've taken you away from me and now you are gone I have lost my strength, my joy and my consolation. It's all over with me. There's nothing left for me to do in the world. I can't go on living without you. It's the finish. I can't bear any more. I'm dying; I'm dead—and buried. Will nobody bring me to life again by giving me my beloved money back or telling me who has taken it? Eh? What d'ye say? There's nobody there! Whoever did it must have watched his opportunity well and chosen the very moment I was talking to my blackguard of a son. I must go. I'll de-

Illustration from a nineteenth-century edition of The Miser

mand justice. I'll have everyone in the house put to the torture, menservants, maidservants, son, daughter, everyone—myself included. What a crowd in here! I suspect the whole pack of 'em. They all look to me like the thief. Eh? What are they talking about over there? About the fellow that robbed me? What's that noise up there? Is the thief there? Please, I implore you, tell me if you know anything about him! Isn't he hiding among you? They are all looking at me. Now they are laughing. You'll see, they are all in it, beyond question, all involved in the robbery. Come on! Come quickly! Magistrates, police, provosts,[1] judges, racks, gibbets,[2] hangmen. I'll have everybody hanged, and, if I don't get my money back, I'll hang myself afterwards.

---

1. **provosts,** prison keepers.
2. **gibbets,** gallows.

ACT IV
COMPLICATION: CLÉANTE LOSES MARIANNE AND HARPAGON LOSES HIS CASH BOX

1. What are the possible solutions offered to Cléante's and Marianne's problems in Scene 1? How successful do you think they might be?

2. Most of the act focuses on the Harpagon/Cléante conflict (Scenes 3, 4, and 5). What are the stages of this conflict? Why is it different from their previous arguments?

3. Consider Scene 4, involving Harpagon, Cléante, and Master Jacques. To what extent does the scene depend on visualizing the stage and the space separating Harpagon and Cléante? What kinds of comic devices are used in this scene?

4. What has Molière done to prepare us for La Flèche's entrance with the money? What has he done to distract us from that possibility, so that it comes as a surprise?

5. Look at Harpagon's speech in the last scene of this act. How does this speech exemplify Harpagon's obsession? Does it make the audience at all sympathetic toward him, or does it just make him seem ridiculous?

Act V

SCENE 1: HARPAGON, *an* OFFICER *and his* CLERK.

OFFICER. You leave it to me! I know my job, thank the Lord! This isn't the first time I've had a case of theft to investigate. I only wish I'd as many bags of money as I've had people hanged.

HARPAGON. It's to the interest of every magistrate in the country to take hand in this case. If I don't get my money back I'll demand justice on justice itself.

OFFICER. We must go through the proper procedure. How much did you say there was in the box?

HARPAGON. Ten thousand crowns—in cash.

OFFICER. Ten thousand crowns!

HARPAGON. Ten thousand crowns!

OFFICER. A considerable theft.

HARPAGON. No punishment could be bad enough for a crime of this enormity. If it goes unpunished nothing, however sacred, will be safe.

OFFICER. In what denomination of coin was the money?

HARPAGON. In good *louis d'or* and *pistoles* of full weight.

OFFICER. And whom do you suspect of the theft?

HARPAGON. Everybody. Arrest the whole town and the suburbs as well.

OFFICER. If you'll take my advice, it's unwise to alarm people unduly. Let us try to go quietly and collect our evidence, and then— then we can proceed with the full rigour of the law to recover the sum you have lost.

SCENE 2: MASTER JACQUES, HARPAGON, OFFICER, CLERK.

MASTER JACQUES (*calling over his shoulder as he comes on stage*). I'll be coming back. Cut his throat at once and let them be singeing his feet for me and putting him in boiling water. Then string him up from the rafters.

HARPAGON. Who? The fellow who has stolen my money?

MASTER JACQUES. I was talking about the suckling pig your steward has just sent me. I mean to dress him for you according to my own special recipe.

HARPAGON. We aren't interested in all that. There are other things you have to talk to this gentleman about.

OFFICER. Now, don't be alarmed. I'm not the sort of fellow to get you into trouble. Everything shall be done quietly.

MASTER JACQUES. Is the gentleman one of your supper party?

OFFICER. In a case like this, friend, you must withhold nothing from your master.

MASTER JACQUES. Upon my word, sir, I'll show you all I know. I'll do the best that I can for you.

HARPAGON. We are not worrying about that!

MASTER JACQUES. If I don't give you as good a meal as I could wish, you must blame that steward of yours. He's clipped my wings with his economies.

HARPAGON. You scoundrel! It isn't supper we are concerned with. I want you to tell what you know about the money that has been stolen from me.

MASTER JACQUES. Has somebody stolen your money?

HARPAGON. Yes, you rogue, and I'll have you hanged if you don't give it back.

OFFICER. Good Heavens! Don't be so hard on him. I can see by the look of him that he is an honest fellow, and he'll tell you what you want to know without need to put him in jail. Now, my lad, if you confess you'll come to no harm and you will get a suitable reward from your master. Someone has taken his money during the day and you must know something about it.

MASTER JACQUES (*aside*). Here's the very thing for getting my own back on that steward of ours. Ever since he arrived he's been the favourite. They won't listen to anybody but him. Moreover, I haven't forgotten the beating I had a while back.

HARPAGON. What are you muttering about now?

OFFICER. Let him alone. He's getting ready to tell you what you are wanting to know. I wasn't mistaken when I said he was an honest fellow.

MASTER JACQUES. If you want to know, master, I believe that precious steward of yours has done it.

HARPAGON. Valère?

MASTER JACQUES. Yes.

HARPAGON. He who seemed so trustworthy?

MASTER JACQUES. That's the man. I suspect he's the fellow who has robbed you.

HARPAGON. On what grounds do you suspect him?

MASTER JACQUES. On what grounds?

HARPAGON. Yes.

MASTER JACQUES. I suspect him on the grounds —that I suspect him.

OFFICER. But you must indicate what evidence you have.

HARPAGON. Did you see him hanging about the spot where I had put my money?

MASTER JACQUES. Yes, I did that! Where was your money?

HARPAGON. In the garden.

MASTER JACQUES. Exactly. He was hanging about the garden when I saw him. What was your money in?

HARPAGON. In a cash box.

MASTER JACQUES. The very thing! He had a cash box. I saw him with it.

HARPAGON. What sort of a cash box? I can easily tell if it was mine.

MASTER JACQUES. What sort of cash box?

HARPAGON. Yes, yes, yes.

MASTER JACQUES. Well—a sort of—like a cash box.

OFFICER. Yes, of course, but describe it a little so that we can see whether—

MASTER JACQUES. It was a big one.

HARPAGON. Mine was a small one.

MASTER JACQUES. Ay, it was small if you are going by size, but I meant it was big in that it had a big lot of money in it.

OFFICER. What colour was it?

MASTER JACQUES. What colour?

OFFICER. Yes.

MASTER JACQUES. A sort of—what's the word? Can't you help me to describe it?

HARPAGON. Eh?

MASTER JACQUES. It wasn't red, was it?

HARPAGON. No, grey.

MASTER JACQUES. That's it, a greyish red. That's what I meant.

HARPAGON. There's no doubt about it. It's certainly the same one. Write it down, sir, write down his evidence. Oh Heavens! Whom can one trust after this? There's no certainty in anything any more. I shall begin to believe that I'm capable of robbing myself.

MASTER JACQUES. Here he comes, master. Whatever you do, don't go and tell him I told you.

SCENE 3: VALÈRE, HARPAGON,
OFFICER, CLERK,
MASTER JACQUES.

(*Enter* VALÈRE.)

HARPAGON. Come here! Come and confess to the foulest, most dastardly crime that was ever committed.

VALÈRE. What can I do for you, sir?

HARPAGON. What, you scoundrel! Don't you blush for your crime?

VALÈRE. What crime are you talking about?

HARPAGON. What crime am I talking about! You infamous wretch! As if you didn't know very well what I'm talking about. It's no use your trying to hide it. The secret is out. I've just heard the whole story. To think of your taking advantage of my kindness and getting yourself into my household on purpose to betray me and play a trick like this on me.

VALÈRE. Well, sir, since you know all about it I won't attempt to excuse or deny it.

MASTER JACQUES (*aside*). So ho. Have I guessed better than I thought?

VALÈRE. I have been meaning to speak to you about it. I was waiting for a favourable opportunity, but since things have turned out as they have I can only ask you not to be angry, but be good enough to hear what I have to say in justification.

HARPAGON. And what sort of justification can you give, you scoundrelly thief?

VALÈRE. Ah sir, I hardly deserve epithets of that kind. It is true that I have put myself in the wrong with you, but, after all, my fault is a pardonable one.

HARPAGON. Pardonable! A stab in the back! A mortal injury!

VALÈRE. Please don't be angry. When you have heard what I have to say, you'll see that there is less harm done than you think.

HARPAGON. Less harm done than I think. My very heart's blood, you scoundrel!

VALÈRE. On a question of blood, sir, you haven't done badly. My rank is such that I shall not disgrace your blood and there's nothing in all this that I can't make amends for.

HARPAGON. And that's exactly what I intend that you shall do—you shall return what you've stolen from me.

VALÈRE. Your honour shall be fully satisfied, sir.

HARPAGON. There's no question of honour! Tell me, what on earth led you to do such a thing?

VALÈRE. Do you really need to ask?

HARPAGON. Of course I need ask!

VALÈRE. It was that little god who is always forgiven, whatever he makes people do. Love, I mean.

HARPAGON. Love!

VALÈRE. Of course.

HARPAGON. A pretty sort of love! Upon my word! Love of my gold pieces.

VALÈRE. No, sir, it was not your wealth that tempted me, not in the least. That's not what dazzled me! Let me assure you I have no aspirations whatever where your wealth is concerned, provided you let me keep the one treasure I already possess.

HARPAGON. No, indeed! Jove! You shan't keep it. The impudence! Wanting to keep what he's stolen.

VALÈRE. Do you really call it stealing?

HARPAGON. Do I really call it stealing? A treasure like that!

VALÈRE. Yes, a treasure indeed, and beyond question the most precious you have, but not lost to you in becoming mine. On my bended knees I beg you to accord me this most cherished of treasures. Surely you can't refuse your consent.

HARPAGON. I'll do nothing of the sort. What on earth are you talking about?

VALÈRE. We are promised to each other and sworn never to be parted.

HARPAGON. A wonderful promise! A very remarkable compact, I must say!

VALÈRE. Yes, we are bound to one another for ever.

HARPAGON. I'll put a stop to that, I promise you.

VALÈRE. Death alone shall part us.

HARPAGON. He must have my money on the brain!

VALÈRE. I have already told you, sir, that I was not moved to do what I have done by material considerations. My motive was not what you think, but a far nobler one.

HARPAGON. He'll be telling me next that it's sheer Christian charity set him wanting my money. But I'll see to that, and the law shall give me satisfaction on you, you impudent scoundrel.

VALÈRE. Do as you please. I am resigned to bear whatever violence you may resort to, but I do ask you to believe that if any fault has been committed I alone am guilty. Your daughter is in no way to blame.

HARPAGON. I should think not, indeed! It would be a queer thing if my daughter were involved in a crime like this. But I want to be seeing you make restoration. Where's the hiding-place?

VALÈRE. There's no question of restoration or of hiding-place since we have not left the house.

HARPAGON (*aside*). Oh, my treasure! (*To* VALÈRE.) Not left the house, you say?

VALÈRE. No sir.

HARPAGON. Now tell me—you haven't been tampering—

VALÈRE. Never! There you wrong both of us. My love is pure and honourable, and though I am so deeply in love—

HARPAGON (*aside*). Deeply in love—with my cash box?

VALÈRE. I would die sooner than harbour a single thought unworthy of one so kind and so modest as—

HARPAGON (*aside*). Modest—my cash box?

VALÈRE. I have asked nothing more than the pleasure of feasting my eyes upon her. Nothing base or unworthy has ever profaned the love which her beauty inspires in me.

HARPAGON (*aside*). Beauty—my cash box? You might think he was a lover talking of his mistress.

VALÈRE. Dame Claude knows the truth of the matter, sir. She can bear witness.

HARPAGON. Ha, so my servant is in the plot, is she?

VALÈRE. Yes, sir, she was a witness to our vows. Once she found that my intentions were

Charles Dullin as Harpagon, holding his cash box.

honourable, she helped me to persuade your daughter to give me her promise and accept mine in return.

HARPAGON (*aside*). Fear of justice must have turned his brain! (*To* VALÈRE.) What has my daughter to do with it?

VALÈRE. I am just saying, sir, that I had the greatest difficulty in persuading her to accept my advances.

HARPAGON. Accept your advances? Who?

VALÈRE. Why, your daughter, sir. It was not until yesterday that she gave me her promise to marry me.

HARPAGON. *My* daughter has given her promise to marry *you*?

VALÈRE. Yes, sir—as I gave her mine in return.

HARPAGON. Heavens! Another disaster!

MASTER JACQUES (*to the* OFFICER). Write it down, mister. Write it all down!

HARPAGON. Trouble on trouble. Misfortune piled on misfortune. Come, sir, do your duty! Draw up the indictment and arrest him as a thief and a seducer as well.

VALÈRE. I have done nothing to deserve such a description when you know who I am—

SCENE 4: ÉLISE, MARIANNE, FROSINE, HARPAGON, VALÈRE, MASTER JACQUES, OFFICER, CLERK.

(*Enter* ÉLISE, MARIANNE, FROSINE.)

HARPAGON. Wretched girl! You are unworthy of a father like me. This is how you follow my precepts! You go and fall in love with a scoundrelly thief and promise to marry him without my consent. But you will both find you have made a mistake. (*To* ÉLISE.) I'll keep you within four walls in future (*to* VALÈRE) and you shall pay for your audacity on the gallows.

VALÈRE. The question won't be decided by your getting angry. I shall at least be heard before I'm condemned.

HARPAGON. I was wrong when I said the gallows. You shall be broken on the wheel.

ÉLISE (*on her knees to* HARPAGON). Father, be merciful, I implore you. Do not push your parental rights to the limit. Don't let yourself be carried away in the first flush of anger. Take time to consider what you are doing. Take the trouble to find out a little more about the man you are so incensed against. He is not what he seems. You will be less surprised that I have given him my promise when you learn that you owe it to him that you haven't lost me already. Yes, it was he, father, who saved me from drowning. It is to him you owe your daughter's life and—

HARPAGON. All that amounts to nothing at all. I'd rather he had left you to drown than do what he has done.

ÉLISE. Father, I implore you by your love for me as a father—

HARPAGON. I won't hear any more. Justice must take its course.

MASTER JACQUES (*aside*). Now you shall pay for that beating you gave me.

FROSINE (*aside*). Here's a fine kettle of fish.

SCENE 5: ANSELME, ÉLISE, MARIANNE, FROSINE, HARPAGON, VALÈRE, MASTER JACQUES, OFFICER, CLERK.

(*Enter* ANSELME.)

ANSELME. What is the trouble, Mr Harpagon? You seem very much upset.

HARPAGON. Ah, Mr Anselme. You see in me the most unlucky of men. All sorts of trouble and difficulty have arisen over the contract you have come to sign. I have suffered deadly blows both to my fortune and my reputation. This treacherous scoundrel here has wormed his way into my household in defiance of every sacred obligation, stolen my money and seduced my daughter.

VALÈRE. Who cares anything about your money that you keep making such a song about?

HARPAGON. They've got themselves engaged to be married—that's an insult to you, Mr Anselme. You must bring an action against him, at your own expense, and get your revenge for his insolence with all the rigour of the law.

ANSELME. I have no intention of forcing anyone to marry me. I make no claim to any affection which is already given elsewhere, but, in so far as your own interests may be involved, you can count on me to support them as my own.

HARPAGON. This gentleman here is a very honest officer who has assured me he'll not fail to do everything his duty requires. (*To the* OFFICER.) Charge him with everything he can be charged with and see that you make things black against him.

VALÈRE. I fail to see how loving your daughter can be accounted a crime! As for the punishment you think will be meted out to me for aspiring to her hand, when you know who I am—

HARPAGON. I don't give a rap for your stories. The world is full of self-styled nobility nowadays, impostors who take advantage of their own obscurity to assume the first illustrious name that comes into their heads!

VALÈRE. I should scorn to lay claim to anything that doesn't belong to me, let me tell you.

Anyone in Naples can bear witness to my birth and family.

ANSELME. Gently! Mind what you are saying. You are running more risk than you think. You are speaking in the presence of one who knows Naples well and will see through any tale you invent.

VALÈRE (*proudly putting on his hat*). I have nothing to fear. If you know Naples you know who Don Thomas d'Alburci was.

ANSELME. I knew him well! Few better!

HARPAGON. I care nothing for Don Thomas or Don Martin either! (*He notices two candles burning, and blows one out.*)

ANSELME. Please—let him speak. Let us hear what he has to say.

VALÈRE. I say that he was my father.

ANSELME. *Your* father?

VALÈRE. Yes.

ANSELME. Come now! You are joking. Try a fresh tale and you may do better. You will do yourself no good with this one.

VALÈRE. Take care what you say! This is no tale. I don't make statements that I cannot easily prove.

ANSELME. What! You dare pretend that you are Thomas d'Alburci's son?

VALÈRE. I do, and I will maintain it against all comers.

ANSELME. What astounding effrontery! Let me tell you that the man you refer to was lost at sea more than sixteen years ago with his wife and children while fleeing from the cruel persecutions which accompanied the disorders in Naples, when so many noble families were driven into exile.

VALÈRE. Yes, and let me tell *you* that his son, a boy of seven years of age, was saved from the wreck along with one servant by a Spanish ship, and that it is that son who is now speaking to you. Let me tell you also that the ship's captain took compassion upon me, brought me up as his own son, and that I have followed a career of arms from my earliest years. It is only recently that I learned that my father did not perish as I had always believed. I set out in search of him, and, passing through this town, I met, by a happy chance, my beloved Élise and fell under the spell of her beauty. Such was the effect of my love and her father's intransigence[1] that I decided to take service in his household and send someone else in search of my parents.

ANSELME. But what proof can you offer beyond your own word that this is not just a story built upon some foundation of truth?

VALÈRE. The Spanish captain, a ruby signet ring which belonged to my father, an agate bracelet my mother clasped on my own arm, and lastly, old Pedro himself, who escaped from the shipwreck along with me.

MARIANNE. Now I myself can vouch for the truth of what you have told us. I realize now that you are my brother.

VALÈRE. Can you be my sister?

MARIANNE. Yes. My heart was strangely moved from the very moment you began to speak. My mother—how overjoyed she will be to see you—has recounted our family misfortunes to me a thousand times. Heaven so willed that we too survived that unhappy shipwreck, but we did so at the cost of our liberty. The men who saved my mother and myself from a fragment of wreckage were corsairs. After ten years of slavery we regained our freedom by a stroke of good fortune and returned to Naples. There we found that our possessions had been sold and that there was no news of my father. We took ship thence to Genoa where my mother went to collect the miserable remnants of a despoiled inheritance. Fleeing from the inhumanity of her family she came to these parts, where she has since languished.

ANSELME. Oh Lord! How wonderful are the manifestations of thy power! How true it is that Heaven alone can accomplish miracles! Come to my arms, my children, and mingle your happiness with your father's.

VALÈRE. You are our father?

MARIANNE. It was you my mother so lamented?

———

1. **intransigence**, immovability.

ANSELME. Yes, my daughter. Yes, my son. I am Don Thomas d'Alburci. By the mercy of Heaven I was saved from the waves with all the money I had with me. For sixteen years I have believed you all drowned. After many wanderings I was about to seek to renew the consolations of domestic felicity by marriage to a good woman. Uncertain of my safety if I returned to Naples, I renounced my country forever and, having contrived to dispose of all I had there, I settled down in this place and sought, under the name of Anselme, to forget the misfortunes which the other name had brought upon me.

HARPAGON. Is this your son?

ANSELME. It is.

HARPAGON. Then I shall hold you responsible for paying me the ten thousand crowns he has stolen from me.

ANSELME. Stolen from you?

HARPAGON. Yes, this same fellow.

VALÈRE. Who told you that?

HARPAGON. Master Jacques.

MASTER JACQUES. Oh! You know I've never said a word!

HARPAGON. Oh, yes you did, and the officer here wrote it all down.

VALÈRE. Do you think me capable of such an action?

HARPAGON. Capable or incapable, I want my money back.

SCENE 6: CLÉANTE, LA FLÈCHE, ANSELME, ÉLISE, MARIANNE, FROSINE, HARPAGON, VALÈRE, MASTER JACQUES, OFFICER, CLERK.

(*Enter* CLÉANTE *and* LA FLÈCHE.)

CLÉANTE. Don't worry any more, father. Don't accuse anybody. I have news of your money. I come to tell you you can have it all back, provided you let me marry Marianne.

HARPAGON. Where is the money?

CLÉANTE. Don't you worry. It is where I can answer for it. It rests entirely with me. Just say what you want to do. Take your choice.

Either give me Marianne or give up your money.

HARPAGON. Is it all there?

CLÉANTE. Every bit. Decide whether you will agree to the marriage and join her mother in giving consent. She has left her daughter free to choose between us: you—or me.

MARIANNE. You are overlooking the fact that my mother's consent is now not sufficient. Heaven has restored my brother to me and my father. You need his consent now.

ANSELME. Heaven has not brought me back to you, dear children, to oppose your own wishes. Mr Harpagon, you must be aware that a young girl is likely to prefer a son to his father. Come then, don't force me to say what I would much rather not. Join me in giving consent to this double marriage.

HARPAGON. I can't decide until I see my cash box again.

CLÉANTE. You shall—safe and sound.

HARPAGON. I have no money for marriage portions.

ANSELME. Well, I have enough for both, so that needn't worry you.

HARPAGON. And you'll undertake to meet the costs of both marriages?

ANSELME. Yes, I agree. Now are you satisfied?

HARPAGON. Provided you buy me new clothes for the wedding.

ANSELME. Agreed. Come, let us go and enjoy the pleasures of this happy day.

OFFICER. Heh! Gentlemen, just a minute, if you don't mind. Who is going to pay for my depositions?

HARPAGON. We want nothing to do with your depositions.

OFFICER. Yes, but I don't intend to work for nothing, not likely!

HARPAGON. There's that fellow there! (*Pointing to* MASTER JACQUES.) Take him and hang him for payment.

MASTER JACQUES. Oh dear! What's a fellow to do! First I'm beaten for telling the truth and now they are going to hang me for telling lies.

ANSELME. Come, Mr Harpagon, we must forgive him his untruths.

HARPAGON. Will you pay the officer, then?

ANSELME. So be it, but let us go at once and share our joy with your mother.

HARPAGON. And let me go and see my beloved cash box again.

THE END

ACT V
RESOLUTION

1. Act V, Scene 3 is a scene constructed almost solely on a single misunderstanding. What is that misunderstanding? How does it contribute to the play's comedy? How does it relate to a major theme of the play?

2. The stage becomes progressively filled with people as the act continues; no one leaves and more people enter. What is the theatrical effect of the increasing number of people on stage?

3. Anselme's appearance is necessary to resolve a number of plot complications. How has his appearance been prepared for? Does it seem believable? If not, does it seem appropriate for the play?

4. Do you see any changes in Harpagon in the last scene?

I
LAUGHTER AND SERIOUS IDEAS

The Miser is a farce which asks us to laugh in order to recognize human failings. Yet when we consider this comic play in relation to the tragedies *Antigone* and *Macbeth*, we see a surprising similarity. Harpagon and Cléante are no less in conflict than are Antigone and Creon. Why, then, do we seriously regard the conflicts in *Antigone* but laugh at the conflict between Harpagon and Cléante? And, again, the selfish desire for power that drives Macbeth to murder can be compared with the selfish greed that pushes Harpagon into more and more extreme behavior. Yet Harpagon's actions are comic rather than tragic. How has Molière created a comedy based on the same themes that have been the stuff of tragedy? How does he make us laugh at Harpagon's antics? Are we laughing at ourselves?

II
IMPLICATIONS

1. Discuss the following quotations from the play. They were written more than 300 years ago, but are they still true today?

a. Valère: "The best way to win people's favor is to pretend to agree with them, to fall in with their precepts, encourage their foibles and applaud whatever they do."

b. Cléante: "What use will money be to us if it only comes when we are too old to enjoy it?"

c. Valère: "Yes, money is the most precious thing in all the world."

d. Valère: "One should eat to live and not live to eat."

e. Harpagon: "Would you mind telling me what people say about me." Master Jacques: ". . . you'll be angry." Harpagon: "On the contrary, I shall enjoy it. I like to know what people are saying about me."

f. Master Jacques: "I suspect him on the grounds —that I suspect him."

2. Molière presents a group of people, each of whom is trying to manipulate someone else. Consider the following characters and discuss whom each is trying to manipulate, why, and how. Does the manipulator play on the other person's foibles?

Harpagon   Cléante   Frosine
Valère   Master Jacques

3. Consider the following relationships in the play. Who wins out? With whom do you sympathize?

a. Father/son

b. Master/servant

c. Schemer/victim

4. What is your reaction to each of the following statements?

a. Valère is just as wily as Harpagon.

b. Molière seems to be saying that people do not change; they continuously repeat the same follies and foibles.

c. Harpagon's foibles make him suspicious of everyone else. This is a true picture of how our faults cause us to misjudge other people.

d. The play implies that you can get what you want by flattery.

e. Harpagon's final speech at the end of Act IV can be delivered in such a manner that it elicits the audience's sympathy, not laughter.

Dinner at the house of Moliere at Auteuil (a nineteenth-century engraving)

III
TECHNIQUES

Characterization

In the section on character development (see pages 233 and 234, *Macbeth*), characters were described as either round or flat. Surely we would use the term *flat* for most of the characters in *The Miser*, perhaps for all. But *flat* is an evaluative word that suggests that the author has failed to create depth in a character. Yet the literary tradition in which Molière wrote thrived on such flat, or stock, characters. In English comedies of a slightly earlier period, Ben Jonson created what he called the "humor" character. People were thought of as composed of four humors or temperaments, created by the prevalence of one of four bodily fluids. Thus Renaissance physicians and philosophers spoke of the sanguine and cheerful humor (blood); the

phlegmatic and sluggish humor (phlegm): the angry and quick-tempered humor (black bile); and the melancholy and depressed humor (yellow bile). Ideally, a well-balanced person would have the proper combination of fluids and character qualities. But an imbalance produced an obsessive or irrational person, and such a person is clearly a natural subject for comedy. Let us look at the relationship between the flat character and the creation of comic situations and relationships.

1. How would you define each of the major characters in the play? For each think of (1) an adjective that describes the character and (2) an objective that the character wants. Do you see any distinct categories emerging? How does Harpagon fit into these categories?

2. How are flat characters useful in creating comic situations? What makes them successful as comic characters?

3. What is our relationship to these characters? How involved do we become (or can we become) with their problems?

The Multiple Plot

The plot of *The Miser* contains several stories, unlike the plot of *Antigone* or the plot of *Macbeth*, which focuses with relentless clarity on the actions of two major figures in each play. Comedy, however, frequently uses a combination of stories about a number of different people. Farce is traditionally a densely plotted form. Why is this so?

1. How many separate plots can you find in this play?

2. How would we feel if there were only one story, for example, Harpagon's attempt to marry Marianne? What would happen to our feelings about the characters?

3. How do the multiple plots expand the thematic range of the play?

Organization of Incident

Because *The Miser* contains several subplots developing at once and because the action of the play occurs in one place within one day, it is impossible to present every detail of each plot on the stage. Choices must be made about which episodes to present and which ones to exclude from the stage. Some scenes need to be "set up" or prepared for by previous explanation. And Molière must decide when to drop one story and bring in another. To understand how Molière manages to get all the necessary information to us, and, at the same time, to construct a pattern of events for comic effect, consider the following questions.

1. What incidents does Molière choose to leave offstage? Why?

2. What scenes function as "set-up" scenes? Do they have any other function (such as giving time for other plots to develop or preventing the situation on stage from getting too serious)?

3. How would you justify the placement of the scene in which the money is stolen? Could it come earlier in the play or not?

IV
WORDS

A. We have already noted the use of two different types of language in the play, the conventionalized speech of the lovers and the more colloquial talk of Harpagon, Frosine, La Flèche, and Master Jacques. But everyone in the play shares a tendency to use words that are slightly elaborate and thus form part of the mask the character wears. How many of the following words can be understood from the context of the speech?

forebodings (I:1)	*precipitate* (I:5)
solicitude (I:1)	*disparity* (I:5)
unremitting (I:1)	*usury* (II:2)
subservience (I:1)	*insatiable* (II:2)
ingratiate (I:1)	*adamant* (II:4)
arbiters (I:2)	*frugality* (III:1)
vouchsafe (I:2)	*irresistible* (IV:1)
sumptuous (I:4)	*epithets* (V:3)

B. One of the problems that Molière faces in the play is that of describing Harpagon without repeating the same words over and over. In the middle of the play (Act III, Scene 1), we find a famous speech by Master Jacques which serves as a capsule description of Harpagon. What makes this speech successful as a piece of description? Why do we believe it?

WILLIAM MAKEPEACE THACKERAY

Like his great contemporary, Charles Dickens, Thackeray (1811–1863)
wrote about the teeming variety of life he found in England. Dickens had
his greatest success in describing the lower classes. Thackeray at his best
described "High Life." But both attacked the pretense, the sham, and the worship
of wealth they saw about them. Born in India, Thackeray returned to England
at the age of six, attended Charterhouse school and, later, Cambridge. Leaving
before he graduated, Thackeray traveled for a while through Europe and then took
a fling at the law, newspaper enterprises, and caricaturing. Although these activities
were short-lived, he drew on these experiences for his novels. When Thackeray
returned to London, he began contributing to *Fraser's Magazine* and *Punch*, willing
to write anything that would sell. In 1846 he published *The Book of Snobs*,
which established his reputation. This same year he began publication of *Vanity Fair*,
a work which ridiculed society's worship of wealth and rank and made the hero,
Becky Sharp, a familiar name to readers. This book established his reputation
as a first-rate novelist. *Pendennis, Henry Esmond* (considered one of the greatest
historical novels of all times), and *The Newcomes* followed. The need for money
forced Thackeray onto the lecture circuit. Unfortunately, he found both writing
and lecturing hard work and professed to enjoy neither. He kept hoping
for a government position which would relieve him from the necessity of working.
But his hope was never realized. For a few years before his death, he edited
the *Cornhill Magazine,* a well-known periodical of the time, and was
writing another novel when he died.

The Influence
of the Aristocracy on Snobs

Last Sunday week, being at church in this
city, and the service just ended, I heard two
Snobs conversing about the Parson. One was
asking the other who the clergyman was? "He
is Mr. So-and-so," the second Snob answered,
"domestic chaplain to the Earl of What-d'ye-
call'im." "Oh, is he?" said the first Snob, with a
tone of indescribable satisfaction.—The Parson's orthodoxy, and identity were at once settled in this Snob's mind. He knew no more
about the Earl than about the Chaplain, but he
took the latter's character upon the authority
of the former; and went home quite contented
with his Reverence, like a little truckling Snob.

This incident gave me more matter for reflection even than the sermon: and wonderment
at the extent and prevalence of Lordolatry[1] in
this country. What could it matter to Snob
whether his Reverence were chaplain to his
Lordship or not? What Peerage-worship there
is all through this free country! How we are all
implicated in it, and more or less down on our
knees.—And with regard to the great subject
on hand, I think that the influence of the Peerage upon Snobbishness has been more remarkable than that of any other institution. The

1. **Lordolatry** (lôr′dol′ə trē), worship of lords, of men
who have titles.

William Makepeace Thackeray

increase, encouragement, and maintenance of Snobs are among the "priceless services," as Lord John Russell[2] says, which we owe to the nobility.

It can't be otherwise. A man becomes enormously rich, or he jobs successfully in the aid of a Minister, or he wins a great battle, or executes a treaty, or is a clever lawyer who makes a multitude of fees and ascends the bench; and the country rewards him for ever with a gold coronet (with more or less balls or leaves) and a title, and a rank as legislator. "Your merits are so great," says the nation, "that your children shall be allowed to reign over us, in a manner. It does not in the least matter that your eldest son be a fool: we think your services so remarkable, that he shall have the reversion of your honours when death vacates your noble shoes. If you are poor, we will give you such a sum of money as shall enable you and the eld-

est-born of your race for ever to live in fat and splendour. It is our wish that there should be a race set apart in this happy country, who shall hold the first rank, have the first prizes and chances in all government jobs and patronages. We cannot make all your dear children Peers—that would make Peerage common and crowd the House of Lords uncomfortably—but the young ones shall have everything a Government can give: they shall get the pick of all the places: they shall be Captains and Lieutenant-Colonels at nineteen, when hoary-headed old lieutenants are spending thirty years at drill: they shall command ships at one-and-twenty, and veterans who fought before they were born. And as we are eminently a free people, and in order to encourage all men to do their duty, we say to any man of any rank—get enormously rich, make immense fees as a lawyer, or great speeches, or distinguish yourself and win battles—and you, even you, shall come into the privileged class, and your children shall reign naturally over ours."

How can we help Snobbishness, with such a prodigious national institution erected for its worship? How can we help cringing to Lords? Flesh and blood can't do otherwise. What man can withstand this prodigious temptation? Inspired by what is called a noble emulation,[3] some people grasp at honours and win them; others, too weak or mean, blindly admire and grovel before those who have gained them; others, not being able to acquire them, furiously hate, abuse, and envy. There are only a few bland and not-in-the-least-conceited philosophers, who can behold the state of society, viz., Toadyism, organised:—base Man-and-Mammon[4] worship, instituted by command of law:—Snobbishness, in a word, perpetuated,—and mark the phenomenon calmly. And of these

2. **Lord John Russell** (1792–1878), an earl, who named and led the newly formed Liberal party; twice prime minister.
3. **emulation** (em′yə lā′shən), ambition.
4. **Mammon** (mam′ən), a pagan god, sometimes an evil spirit, personifying the evils of wealth and miserliness.

The snobs of England, drawings by Thackeray for The Book of Snobs.

calm moralists, is there one, I wonder, whose heart would not throb with pleasure if he could be seen walking arm-in-arm with a couple of dukes down Pall Mall?[5] No: it is impossible, in our condition of society, not to be sometimes a Snob.

On one side it encourages the commoner to be snobbishly mean, and the noble to be snobbishly arrogant. When a noble marchioness writes in her travels about the hard necessity under which steamboat travellers labour of being brought into contact "with all sorts and conditions of people:" implying that a fellowship with God's creatures is disagreeable to her Ladyship, who is their superior:—when, I say, the Marchioness of —— writes in this fashion, we must consider that out of her natural heart it would have been impossible for any woman to have had such a sentiment; but that the habit of truckling and cringing, which all who surround her have adopted towards this beautiful and

5. **Pall Mall** (pel′ mel′) *or* (pôl′ môl′), a fashionable street in London.

asked of a certain young man the reason of the disturbance. How was I to know that this young gent was a prince? He had not his crown and sceptre on: he was dressed in a white jacket and felt hat: but he looked surprised at anybody speaking to him: answered an unintelligible monosyllable, and—*beckoned his aide-de-camp to come and speak to me.* It **is** our fault, not that of the great, that they should fancy themselves so far above us. If you *will* fling yourself under the wheels, Juggernaut[6] will go over you, depend upon it; and if you and I, my dear friend, had Kotoo[7] performed before us every day,—found people whenever we appeared grovelling in slavish adoration, we should drop into the airs of superiority quite naturally, and accept the greatness with which the world insisted upon endowing us.

Here is an instance, out of Lord L——'s travels, of that calm, good-natured, undoubting way in which a great man accepts the homage of his inferiors. After making some profound and ingenious remarks about the town of Brussels, his lordship says:—"Staying some days at the Hôtel de Belle Vue—a greatly overrated establishment, and not nearly so comfortable as the Hôtel de France—I made acquaintance with Dr. L——, the physician of the Mission. He was desirous of doing the honour of the place to me, and he ordered for us a *dîner en gourmand*[8] at the chief restaurateur's, maintaining it surpassed the Rocher at Paris. Six or eight partook of the entertainment, and we all agreed it was infinitely inferior to the Paris display, and much more extravagant. So much for the copy."

And so much for the gentleman who gave the dinner. Dr. L——, desirous to do his lord-

magnificent lady,—this proprietor of so many black and other diamonds,—has really induced her to believe that she is the superior of the world in general: and that people are not to associate with her except awfully at a distance. I recollect being once at the city of Grand Cairo, through which a European Royal Prince was passing India-wards. One night at the inn there was a great disturbance; a man had drowned himself in the well hard by: all the inhabitants of the hotel came bustling into the Court, and amongst others your humble servant, who

---

6. **Juggernaut** (jug′ər nôt), a Hindu god, the remover of sin. It was once erroneously supposed that his fanatical worshipers threw themselves beneath the wheels of the enormous car on which the god's image was dragged through the city.
7. **Kotoo** (kou′tou′), the act of kneeling and touching the forehead to the ground to show deep respect (now usually spelled *kowtow*).
8. **dîner en gourmand,** French for dinner fit for a judge of good food.

ship "the honour of the place," feasts him with the best victuals money can procure—and my lord finds the entertainment extravagant and inferior. Extravagant! it was not extravagant to *him;*—Inferior! Mr. L—— did his best to satisfy those noble jaws, and my lord receives the entertainment, and dismisses the giver with a rebuke. It is like a three-tailed Pasha[9] grumbling about an unsatisfactory backsheesh.[10]

But how should it be otherwise in a country where Lordolatry is part of our creed, and where our children are brought up to respect the "Peerage" as the Englishman's second Bible?

I
ARE WE ALL SNOBS?

For a year Thackeray wrote an essay each week attacking the snobs of his time . . . people wrote in suggesting all sorts of possibilities for his essays and, when he stopped, the public clamored for him to continue. How well this demonstrates that common foible of thinking ourselves perfect and yet recognizing instantly the defects in our neighbors. Few will admit to any snobbery in their own nature, but are quick to point it out in a friend.

Which statement below do you think best sums up this essay?

1. Thackeray is attacking the aristocrats for their foolish assumption that their rank makes them great and noble, deserving of adulation.

2. Thackeray is attacking the "little people" who by their worship make aristocrats arrogant and overbearing.

---

9. **a three-tailed Pasha** (pǝ shä′), a Turkish governor of high rank (here used in ridicule).
10. **backsheesh** (bak′shēsh′), a term used in Turkey and India meaning a tip or an alms (usually spelled *baksheesh*).

II
IMPLICATIONS

Give your reaction to the following statements. Try to justify your opinion by examples.

1. There are as many snobs today as in Thackeray's time, but they worship money, fame, science, athletics, and celebrities, instead of the nobility.

2. It is a foible in human nature that people need to stand in awe of somebody.

3. A person must be little in soul and mind to be a snob.

4. The amount of space devoted in American newspapers to the doings of European royalty shows that Thackeray's point of view is true for our time as well as for his.

III
TECHNIQUES

Setting

An essay of ideas such as this one does not ordinarily have setting as one of its elements. However in thinking back on the selection, do any scenes come to your mind? If so, how many impressions do you have of the background or setting? Now check and see how many of the details of the setting were actually presented and how many were provided by your own imagination out of the hints given.

Prose Style

Often the rhythm of language cues us to many things about a writer and a particular selection of writing. From listening to the sound quality and flow and arrangement of words in paragraph two of the selection, answer the following.

1. Could this selection possibly have been written in the twentieth century?

2. What would you imagine to be some qualities of the period in which this was written?

3. Is the writer serious or merely mock serious?

4. What kind of person might be writing in this kind of language?

5. What peculiarities of language structure or arrangement gave you clues for answering the above?

SAMUEL JOHNSON

One of the literary giants of the eighteenth century was Samuel Johnson (1709–1784). His brilliant, astonishing mind was housed in a caricature of a body. With his huge torso balanced on spindly legs and with a scrofulous face, Johnson shambled as he walked and twitched when he talked. He grimaced, muttered, sometimes suddenly roared out a phrase of the Lord's Prayer, sometimes slopped soup on dinner guests. As a student at Oxford he was so poor and ragged that he excited mirth and pity, both of which roused him to terrible fury. Yet those who knew him respected his fantastic abilities. For thirty years he had a desperate struggle with poverty, which affected his personality and manners. Because it was often necessary to wear dirty clothes, he never insisted upon clean ones; because he was so often hungry, he always ate ravenously like a starving beast; because dullards were often insulting, he developed a proud and insolent manner. By 1747 he had gained sufficient eminence for several book publishers to employ him to write a dictionary of the English language which took him almost eight years to complete. As a relief from the tedious task of writing definitions, he published a series of essays in the years from 1750–1752. Johnson published these essays every Tuesday and Saturday in a paper called *The Rambler*. At first, reception to the periodical was cool; some critics called his style monotonous. Eventually circulation rose from a few hundred to 13,000. When completed, the dictionary was hailed with praise, as was *Rasselas,* his only novel, which he dashed off in a week to pay his mother's funeral expenses. In 1762 Johnson was offered a pension by the government, which he quickly accepted. Now at last he was free to indulge his whim of sleeping late and spending his days conversing with friends. Johnson gathered some of the most brilliant thinkers of the time around him and formed The Literary Club. Goldsmith, the poet; Garrick, the actor and director; Gibbon, the historian; Burke, the politician; Sir William Jones, the linguist; Reynolds, the painter; and Boswell, the Scottish lawyer, were among its members. Though Boswell was resented by many, his writings have saved for later generations the brilliant wit and conversation of this group of people. Through Boswell's *Life* we know Johnson today more as a person than as a writer. His style, which to modern taste often seems elaborate and heavy, is nevertheless a great one for its precision and balance.

A Journey in a Stage-Coach

"... Tolle periculum,
Jam vaga prosiliet froenis natura remotis."
                                        Horace

"But take the danger and the shame away,
And vagrant nature bounds upon her prey."
                                   Francis (after Horace)

To the Adventurer

Sir,

It has been observed, I think, by Sir William Temple,[1] and after him by almost every other writer, that England affords a greater variety of characters than the rest of the world. This is ascribed to the liberty prevailing amongst us, which gives every man the privilege of being wise or foolish in his own way, and preserves

---

1. **Sir William Temple** (1628–1699) was an English essayist, diplomat, and statesman.

him from the necessity of hypocrisy or the servility of imitation.

That the position itself is true, I am not completely satisfied. To be nearly acquainted with the people of different countries can happen to very few; and in life, as in everything else beheld at a distance, there appears an even uniformity: the petty discriminations which diversify the natural character, are not discoverable but by a close inspection; we, therefore, find them most at home, because there we have most opportunities of remarking them. Much less am I convinced that this peculiar diversification, if it be real, is the consequence of peculiar liberty; for where is the government to be found that superintends individuals with so much vigilance as not to leave their private conduct without restraint? Can it enter into a reasonable mind to imagine, that men of every other nation are not equally masters of their own time or houses with ourselves, and equally at liberty to be parsimonious or profuse, frolic or sullen, abstinent or luxurious? Liberty is certainly necessary to the full play of predominant humours; but such liberty is to be found alike under the government of the many or the few, in monarchies or in commonwealths.

How readily the predominant passion snatches an interval of liberty, and how fast it expands itself when the weight of restraint is taken away, I had lately an opportunity to discover, as I took a journey into the country in a stage-coach; which, as every journey is a kind of adventure, may be very properly related to you, though I can display no such extraordinary assembly, as Cervantes has collected at Don Quixote's inn.

In a stage-coach, the passengers are for the most part wholly unknown to one another, and without expectation of ever meeting again when their journey is at an end; one should therefore imagine, that it was of little importance to any of them what conjectures the rest should form concerning him. Yet so it is, that as all think themselves secure from detection, all assume that character of which they are most desirous, and on no occasion is the gen-

DR. SAMUEL JOHNSON
Portrait by Sir Joshua Reynolds.
Reproduced by courtesy of the Trustees
of the Tate Gallery, London.

eral ambition of superiority more apparently indulged.

On the day of our departure, in the twilight of the morning, I ascended the vehicle with three men and two women, my fellow-travellers. It was easy to observe the affected elevation of mien with which every one entered, and the supercilious civility with which they paid their compliments to each other. When the first ceremony was despatched, we sat silent for a long time, all employed in collecting importance into our faces, and endeavouring to strike reverence and submission into our companions.

It is always observable, that silence propagates itself, and that the longer talk has been suspended, the more difficult it is to find anything to say. We began now to wish for conversation; but no one seemed inclined to descend from his dignity, or first to propose a topic of discourse. At last a corpulent gentleman, who had equipped himself for this expedition with a scarlet surtout and a large hat with a broad lace, drew out his watch, looked on it in

*"Postboys and Post-horses at the White Hart Inn,"
etching by T. Rowlandson.*

silence, and then held it dangling at his finger. This was, I suppose, understood by all the company as an invitation to ask the time of day, but nobody appeared to heed his overture; and his desire to be talking so far overcame his resentment, that he let us know of his own accord that it was past five, and that in two hours we should be at breakfast.

His condescension was thrown away; we continued all obdurate; the ladies held up their heads; I amused myself with watching their behaviour; and of the other two, one seemed to employ himself in counting the trees as we drove by them, the other drew his hat over his eyes and counterfeited a slumber. The man of benevolence, to show that he was not depressed by our neglect, hummed a tune, and beat time upon his snuff-box.

Thus universally displeased with one another, and not much delighted with ourselves,

we came at last to the little inn appointed for our repast; and all began at once to recompense themselves for the constraint of silence, by innumerable questions and orders to the people that attended us. At last, what every one had called for was got, or declared impossible to be got at that time, and we were persuaded to sit round the same table; when the gentleman in the red surtout looked again upon his watch, told us that we had half an hour to spare, but he was sorry to see so little merriment among us; that all fellow-travellers were for the time upon the level, and that it was always his way to make himself one of the company. "I remember," says he, "it was on just such a morning as this, that I and my Lord Mumble and the Duke of Tenterden were out upon a ramble: we called at a little house as it might be this; and my landlady, I warrant you, not suspecting to whom she was talking, was so jocular and facetious, and made so many merry answers to our questions, that we were all ready to burst with laughter.

At last the good woman happening to overhear me whisper to the duke and call him by his title, was so surprised and confounded that we could scarcely get a word from her; and the duke never met me from that day to this, but he talks of the little house, and quarrels with me for terrifying the landlady."

He had scarcely time to congratulate himself on the veneration which this narrative must have procured him from the company, when one of the ladies having reached out for a plate on a distant part of the table, began to remark "the inconveniences of travelling and the difficulty which they who never sat at home without a great number of attendants found in performing for themselves such offices as the road required; but that people of quality often travelled in disguise and might be generally known from the vulgar by their condescension to poor innkeepers, and the allowance which they made for any defect in their entertainment; that for her part, while people were civil and meant well, it was never her custom to find fault, for one was not to expect upon a journey all that one enjoyed at one's own house."

A general emulation seemed now to be excited. One of the men, who had hitherto said nothing, called for the last newspaper; and having perused it a while with deep pensiveness, "It is impossible," says he, "for any man to guess how to act with regard to the stocks: last week it was the general opinion that they would fall; and I sold out twenty thousand pounds in order to make a purchase; they have now risen unexpectedly; and I make no doubt but at my return to London I shall risk thirty thousand pounds amongst them again."

A young man, who had hitherto distinguished himself only by the vivacity of his looks and a frequent diversion of his eyes from one object to another, upon this closed his snuff-box, and told us that "he had a hundred times talked with the chancellor and the judges on the subject of the stocks; that, for his part, he did not pretend to be well acquainted with the principles upon which they were established, but had always heard them reckoned perni-

cious to trade, uncertain in their produce, and unsolid in their foundation; and that he had been advised by three judges, his most intimate friends, never to venture his money in the funds, but to put it out upon land-security till he could light upon an estate in his own country."

It might be expected, that upon these glimpses of latent dignity, we should all have begun to look round us with veneration; and have behaved like the princes of romance when the enchantment that disguises them is dissolved, and they discover the dignity of each other: yet it happened, that none of these hints made much impression on the company; every one was apparently suspected of endeavouring to impose false appearance upon the rest; all continued their haughtiness in hopes to enforce their claims; and all grew every hour more sullen because they found their representations of themselves without effect.

Thus we travelled on four days with malevolence perpetually increasing, and without any endeavour but to outvie each other in superciliousness and neglect; and when any two of us could separate ourselves for a moment we vented our indignation at the sauciness of the rest.

At length the journey was at an end, and time and chance, that strip off all disguises, have discovered that the intimate of lords and dukes is a nobleman's butler, who has furnished a shop with the money he has saved; the man who deals so largely in the funds, is a clerk of a broker in 'Change-alley; the lady who so carefully concealed her quality, keeps a cookshop behind the Exchange; and the young man who is so happy in the friendship of the judges, engrosses and transcribes for bread in a garret of the temple.[2] Of one of the women only I could make no disadvantageous detection,

---

2. **temple,** the site formerly occupied by the buildings of the Knights Templars, a famous order of knighthood founded in the twelfth century for service in the Holy Land. Since 1346, the Temple has been in the possession of doctors and lawyers. It was wrecked by Nazi bombs in World War II.

because she had assumed no character, but accommodated herself to the scene before her, without any struggle for distinction or superiority.

I could not forbear to reflect on the folly of practising a fraud which, as the event showed, had been already practised too often to succeed, and by the success of which no advantage could have been obtained; of assuming a character which was to end with the day; and of claiming upon false pretences honours which must perish with the breath that paid them.

But, Mr. Adventurer, let not those who laugh at me and my companions think this folly confined to a stage-coach. Every man in the journey of life takes the same advantage of the ignorance of his fellow-travellers, disguises himself in counterfeited merit, and hears those praises with complacency which his conscience reproaches him for accepting. Every man deceives himself, while he thinks he is deceiving others, and forgets that the time is at hand when every illusion shall cease, when fictitious excellence shall be torn away, and all must be shown to all in their real state.

I am, Sir,
Your humble servant,
Viator.[3]

I
A CROSS SECTION OF HUMANITY

One of the oldest foibles of human beings is the belief that you can fool others about who you are, what you are, and what you believe. Usually the individuals so engaged are only fooling themselves, for pretending usually leads nowhere. Yet on trains and planes and in hotel and motel lobbies strangers still try to impress each other even today with imagined and impossible personalities and backgrounds.

Are Johnson's evaluations of people and situations in his time still valid today? Or have people changed? Consider the following statements:

---

3. **Viator,** Latin for "traveler."

1. . . . as all think themselves secure from detection, all assume that character of which they are most desirous. . . .

2. . . . the longer talk has been suspended, the more difficult it is to find anything to say.

3. Every man deceives himself, while he thinks he is deceiving others. . . .

II
IMPLICATIONS

What is your opinion of the following statements? Base your answer on your own experiences and on the selection.

1. To assume a new face, a new personality, when among strangers is a common human foible.

2. People have always needed to hide what they are from others as well as from themselves.

3. Honesty is for fools and little children; adults are always "pretenders."

III
TECHNIQUES

Setting

How important is the setting in this essay? What do you know about a stagecoach trip after reading this selection? The kind of setting in which a number of different characters are forced to remain together in one place is a common device in fiction, plays, and films. Can you think of other examples of such a "closed" setting?

Prose Style

Johnson was often accused of using too many polysyllabic words, monotonous arrangement of sentences, and too many balanced epithets. These, of course, contributed to his so-called pompous style. In later years his style became more vigorous and less artificial. Consider the second and third paragraphs of the essay you read.

1. Is the language simple or does Johnson use long-winded, many-syllabled words?

2. How many lines do the sentences tend to run? Do you think they are long or short, involved or simple, easy to read or difficult to understand?

3. In paragraph two, Johnson balances comparisons with the word "or." Read them out loud. How does this use of "or" affect the rhythm of the prose?

AUGUST STRINDBERG

August Strindberg (1849–1912) had a strong influence on Swedish life
and letters. His early novels and especially his short stories are credited
with bringing about a long-overdue change in Swedish prose style, for Strindberg
wrote in an easy, almost colloquial style. His greatest influence, however, came
through his plays, and the devices he developed for their production. His early plays
were realistic, but later he revolted against realism and moved into a form called
"expressionism."[1] Seemingly his work had little effect on Swedish drama; however,
Sean O'Casey in Ireland, Luigi Pirandello in Italy, and Eugene O'Neill in America
followed Strindberg's lead. Strindberg had an unhappy childhood, marred,
he claimed, by emotional insecurity. His adult life was a reflection of this same
emotional seesaw. He married three times, but was never able to find serenity
in these relationships. His later writings display a hatred for women. He tried
being a free-lance journalist, a librarian, and finally a full time author.
His interests swerved from Christianity to atheism, to alchemy, and finally
to mysticism. He claimed that life is ruled by the righteous, punishing "Powers."
Strindberg was never accepted as a member by the Swedish Academy, but when he died,
Swedes hailed him as their "greatest writer."

Love and Bread

Falk, the Royal Secretary, was certainly not informed as to the market-price of grain when he rode out to the Major's to ask his daughter's hand.

"I love Louisa," began the Secretary.

"How much do you earn?" asked the old man.

"Barely twelve hundred crowns. But we love each other so dearly, dear uncle!"

"That does not concern me. Twelve hundred crowns is not enough."

"I have some extra work besides. Louisa knows my heart."

"Don't speak so childishly! How much do you earn by this extra work?"

"We met first at Boo, on the island Lidingö."[2]

"How much do you earn outside?" said the Major, gesticulating with his lead-pencil as if he would stab him with it.

"And our feelings, which"—

"How much do you earn outside!" The Major began to scrawl something on his blotting-paper.

"Oh! that surely will not fail, if we only first"—

"Will you answer me or not? How much do you earn outside? Figures are what I want—figures and facts."

"I make translations at ten crowns the folio. I give French lessons, too; and proofreading is promised me."

"Promises are not facts. Figures, my young man, figures. So! I put it down. How much translating have you to do?"

"How much? Ah, indeed, that I cannot precisely say!"

---

1. **expressionism,** the practice of seeking to show, in art, not objective reality but the emotions that objects and events arouse in the artist.
2. **Boo** (bō); **Lidingö** (lē dǐng′gǔ), an area of Stockholm.

385

"What! You cannot? You have translating to do, as you just said. Will you not tell me what it is?"

"I am translating Guizot's 'History of Civilization,'[3] twenty-five folios thick, into Swedish."

"Ten crowns the folio makes all together two hundred and fifty crowns. And then!"—

"Then—then—that no one can say beforehand."

"How? One cannot know beforehand? But one should know exactly. You think that marriage is only in order to pass time as pleasantly as possible! No, my young man. In a year come the children; and children must have food and clothing."

"But the children do not always come so immediately; when one loves as we love"—

"How the devil do you love, then?"

"How do we love each other?" At this he laid his hand on his heart and rolled his eyes.

"Do not the children come 'when one loves as you do,' you rascal? Indeed, that is delicious! Yet you are a good-enough sort of a fellow, and so I say you may be betrothed. Make use of your engagement time, though, so that you earn something, for hard times are facing us. The price of wheat is going up."

Secretary Falk became quite red in the face as he heard this conclusion, yet his joy at attaining Louisa was so great that he was moved to kiss the old man's hand. God in heaven, how happy he was! And how happy his Louisa! As they walked for the first time on the street arm in arm, every one looked at them. You would suppose that every one halted to form a guard of honor for their triumphal procession. On they swept, with glances uplifted proudly.

In the evening he came to her. They sat themselves down in the middle of the drawing-room and read proof. The old man thought he was a capable fellow; and when the work was done the bridegroom said to the bride, "Now we have earned three crowns!" A kiss sealed the deed. But on the next evening they went to the theatre and rode home. That cost ten crowns. Sometimes when he had evening les-

August Strindberg

sons to give—what does one not do for love?— he excused himself from the lessons and went to his Louisa. Then they went out and took a walk. The wedding day drew near; all was different then. They betook themselves to the Brunkeberger Place,[4] to choose furniture. They began with the most important. Louisa did not wish to be present when the beds were being bought; but as it turned out she went, all the same. They must be of walnut—each piece of solid walnut. And they must have red-bordered mattresses, with springs, of course, and the pillows filled with eider-down. Each must have its especial eider-down quilt, too. Louisa wanted

3. **The History of Civilization in Europe** was written in 1828 by François Guizot (gē zō´), 1787–1874.
4. **Brunkeberger Place,** a street in Stockholm. Other places in this story not identified in notes are located in Stockholm.

a blue one, because she was blond. Then they went to the house-furnisher. First, of course, they chose a red-shaded night-lamp and a bisque Venus; then table service of every variety; fine knives and forks, a couple of dozen; and cut-glass, with a monogram. At last in their turn came the kitchen dishes, and in that mamma must help. Dear God! what had not the poor bridegroom to do: Making out checks, running to the bank, going after workmen, looking up houses, and putting up curtains. He became in arrears with his work. Once he was married, however, he would make all that up. So he thought. They would only rent two rooms to start with. They had resolved to be "reasonable." And if it were only two rooms, they could furnish them so much more prettily. So he found a dwelling of two rooms, with kitchen and pantry, in the Regierung Strasse, on the first floor, for six hundred crowns. When Louisa let fall the remark that she would just as lief have three rooms and a kitchen on the fourth floor, he grew embarrassed. But what mattered it when one was fond of another? Louisa thought so too, finally. The rooms were soon furnished. The bedroom was like a little temple. The beds stood near each other like two chariots in which life's journey was to be made. And the sun shone on the blue coverlid, the snow-white sheets, and the pillows with their monograms embroidered by an old aunt. These were large letters of brier-rose, intertwined, as if in embrace, and whenever they met in a knot they kissed each other. A little alcove was arranged for the wife, with a Japanese screen, and in the drawing-room, which was dining-room, study, and reception-room as well, stood her upright piano, which had cost twelve hundred crowns. There also was his writing-desk of old walnut, a large plate-glass mirror, sofa, reading-table, and dining-table. It looked as if people who could lead a comfortable and cosy life lived there.

At last came the wedding! It was on a Saturday evening. Thereupon followed Sunday morning. What a life! Oh, how delightful it is to be married! What a glorious invention marriage is! Then one may do what he pleases. Then come the brothers and sisters to make their congratulations.

In the morning at nine o'clock the bedroom was still dark. The young groom did not wish to open the shutters yet. He lighted the red lamp again, and threw its magical light on the blue coverlid and upon the somewhat rumpled white sheets. The bisque Venus stood saucy and inviting in the rosy glow. There lay the pretty young wife, so delightfully languid, and as happy as if this were the first night of her life in which she had slept well. No wagons were to be heard on the streets, for the day was Sunday, and the bells rang so cheerily, so joyfully, as if they would call all mankind together to give thanks that man and wife were created. He whispered in her ear. She should turn over, so that he could go out and order breakfast. She buried her little head in the pillows, while he went behind the screen in order to put on the absolutely necessary things. He entered the drawing-room, where the sun threw a broad beaming ray upon the floor. At first, for a moment, he did not know whether it were spring, summer, autumn, or winter. He only knew that it was Sunday. His bachelor days seemed to him like a dark shadow from which he had escaped, and in his new dwelling he breathed the breath of his old home and his future family. Oh, how strong he felt! His future loomed up before him like a tottering hill. He threw himself against it: it broke in sand beneath his feet, and he set forward upon his way over chimney and housetop with his pure young bride in his arms.

Then he picked up his clothes lying scattered on the floor; his white cravat he found perched on a picture-frame, like a butterfly. He went into the kitchen. Oh, how splendidly the new copper utensils glimmered and glistened! And the tin cooking-kettles! All that belonged to him and to her! He called the cook. She received the direction to order a breakfast from the "Restaurant of the Three Romans" at once. It must be fine. The host already knew; she need only tell him.

He returned then to the bedroom door and knocked. "May I come?" A little shriek; then, "No, my love; wait just a minute." Now he lays the table himself. When the breakfast came he filled the new plates, he folded the napkins beautifully, and wiped the wineglasses. The bridal bouquet paraded in front of his wife's plate. And now out she comes in her embroidered morning-gown, and the sunbeams meet her. She is a little faint, only a little, so he pushes her in an easy-chair up to the table. Quick! a little Kümmel[5] in a liqueur glass; a bit of bread with caviare. That helps. Oh, how glorious! One may do everything one chooses, if one is but married. Only to think what mamma would say if she saw her daughter drinking schnapps![6] He waits on her, runs and springs as if he still were her betrothed. But the breakfast after such a night! And no one had the right to criticise him! Often enough already had he had such breakfasts. But what a difference! Discontent, restlessness, he puts behind him; and as he drank a glass of real porter with his oysters he could not despise bachelors enough. Only think of the stupid men who do not marry! Such egoists should be taxed, like dogs. The young wife ventured to demur, yet as gently and lovingly as possible, that the poor fellows who do not wish to marry are rather to be pitied. If they could, surely they would, all of them. That gave the Secretary a little stab at the heart. He became meditative for a moment. He had been so overflowing with spirits. All his happiness was based on a question of economics. And when—when— Bah! A glass of Burgundy. Work will soon begin. Then we shall see. Next comes the roast pheasant, and with it delicious cranberries and cucumbers.

The young wife, a little concerned about the luxurious meal, laid her trembling hand upon his arm and said, "Dear heart! can we allow ourselves that?" Luckily she said "we."

"One day is not every day," he replied. "Herring and potatoes we can eat later, and often enough."

"Do you really eat herring and potatoes?"

"Well, I should think so."

"Yes, when you have been out and come in with a heavy head; and a beefsteak à la Chateaubriand[7] follows."

"Do not talk about it. Your health! That was faultless, that pheasant, and such artichokes!"

"No, Gustave; you are quite reckless. Artichokes at this time of year! What will that cost?"

"Are they not good? That is the main point. And now a little glass of wine! more wine! Don't you think life is beautiful? Oh, glorious! glorious!"

Exactly at six o'clock, before the door stood an elegant carriage in livery. The young wife scarcely believed her eyes. And how lovely that was!—half lying side by side, and gently rocked, to ride to the park. Acquaintances they met on the way greeted them, and comrades waved their hands and seemed to say, "Ha, ha! you sly dog! You have married money." Oh, how little people looked down below there! And however uneven the road, how easy the ride on the upholstered springs! So it should always be.

It lasted so a whole month—balls, companies, dinners, suppers, theatres. Between whiles they were at home. That was really the best of all. How delightful after the supper to take his wife away from papa and mamma; to put her in a closed carriage right before their faces; to nod to the dear parents and bid them good-by; and then to say, "We will go home and do there just what pleases us"! At home a little supper followed, and then they sat and talked until morning. At home Gustave was always prudent; that is, in principle. One day the young wife wished to attempt smoked salmon, boiled potatoes, and oat soup. How good it tasted! Still Gustave was somewhat out of humor over this menu. On the next Friday, when it was to be salmon again, he came home

---

5. **Kümmel** (kim′əl), a liqueur flavored with caraway seed.
6. **schnapps** (shnäps), liquor.
7. **à la Chateaubriand** (ä lä shə tō′brē änd), with an elaborate sauce.

with a pair of woodcock. He stood in the door-way, exclaiming, "Can you imagine anything so unheard-of, Louisa?"

"What, then?"

"You will scarcely believe what I tell you. I bought both of these partridges at the market. Guess for how much?"

The young wife was so angry that she scarcely wished to guess.

"Only think, a crown the pair!"

Louisa had once bought a pair of partridges at eighty pfennig, but she did not mention it, so as not to hurt her husband's feelings.

"But anyhow, you will admit that they are cheap?"

She must agree, if only to please him. For the evening there was oatmeal, only to try it. After Gustave had eaten a partridge, he was sorry not to eat as much oatmeal as he had really meant to. He would gladly have shown that the porridge pleased him. He really ate oatmeal, only he could not endure milk with it. He would eat oatmeal every evening, if only his wife would not be displeased with him. After this, of course, there was an end of the oatmeal. He never had it served to him again. Six weeks passed, and the young wife grew ill. She had headaches and nausea, probably in consequence of a cold. But the nausea did not stop. Hm! Had she perhaps poisoned herself? Was it maybe the fault of the copper kettles? The doctor was called. He laughed and said it was all in order. What was in order? Something suspicious! How was that possible? No; it came from the bedroom paper. There was certainly arsenic in it. Send it to the chemist at once, and let it be analyzed. "Free from arsenic," wrote the chemist. That was remarkable—no arsenic in the wall-paper. The young wife's sickness continued. Gustave studied a medical book, and whispered something in her ear. Yes; see there, now we have it. Ha, ha! Only a warm foot-bath. Four weeks afterward the nurse declared that all was in order. In order—horrible! That is clear. But it came so quick. Still, now it was settled, how lovely it would be! Think, a child! Hurrah! They would be papa and mamma. What should they call it? A boy, of course; that was certain. But now Louisa took her husband aside and spoke earnestly to him. Since his marriage he had not busied himself with translating or proofreading. His salary alone was not sufficient. Yes, yes! they had lived in riot and revel. "Lord! one is never young but once. However, now all should be different."

On the next day the Secretary went to his old friend the notary, and begged him to go security for a loan. "When one is about to become a father, my dear sir, one must think of the increase in expenses."

"I agree with you perfectly," answered the notary; "on that account I have never ventured to marry. You are indeed a lucky fellow. You were able to do so."

The Secretary was ashamed to press his request. How could he have the face to ask this bachelor who had not ventured to marry on account of his small income for a loan for himself and his child? No; that he could not do.

When he came home in the evening, his wife told him two men had been there looking for him. "How did they look? Were they young? Did they wear eyeglasses? They surely were two lieutenants, good old friends from Vaxholm."

"They were not lieutenants. They looked much older."

"Indeed!" Now he knew. They were old friends from Upsala. Probably Dr. P. and Deputy O., who wished to see how the old fellow bore married life.

"No; they were not from Upsala. They were Stockholmers."

The maid was called. She thought they looked suspicious, and they had sticks.

"Sticks! Hm! Who could that be? We shall soon learn when they come again."

In the meantime he had been to the market, and had bought a can of strawberries at a bargain—at a really absurd price: "Only think, a can of pineapple strawberries for a crown and a half now—at this time of year!"

"Gustave! Gustave! What is going to become of us?"

"Don't be anxious. I have secured a new piece of work to-day."

"But the debts, Gustave."

"Trifles! Only wait till I secure a large loan."

"A loan? Then that will be a new debt."

"Yes; but at what terms! Let us not talk of such things. Were not the strawberries good? What? Would not a little glass of sherry go well afterward? What do you say? Lina, go to the wine-dealer for a bottle of sherry; genuine, mind."

After the mid-day sleep on the sofa, his wife begged to be allowed to say two words; but he must not be angry. Angry! He? Heaven forbid! Probably money for the house.

"Well, then. The grocer is not paid. The butcher gives us warning. The liveryman wants his money. All that is, in a word, extremely disagreeable."

"Nothing more? They shall have their money, every cent, to-morrow morning. What impudence! For such trifles to give warning! To-morrow they shall receive everything. Moreover, they will lose a customer. But now we will talk no more of that. We will take a little walk. No carriage! We will go in the cars to the Park to get a little fresh air."

So they rode to the Park, and took a private room in the Alhambra. The young men in the dining-room whispered. They thought it was a pair out for a lark. So jolly, so exciting! But the wife did not quite like it. And then the bill. What could they not have had at home for that money?

Months pass. The time draws near. A cradle is needed—underclothing and dresses for the little one. And so much. Herr Gustave is busy the whole day. The price of grain had really risen. Hard times were at hand. No translations, no proof-reading. The world had grown so material. They do not buy books any more. They use their money for bread. In what prosaic times we live. The ideal vanishes. Pheasants cannot be bought under two marks a pair. The liveryman will not drive for nothing any more,

for he also has a wife and children; and even the grocer wants money for his goods. Oh, what realists! At last the eventful day arrives, and the night is near. He must run and fetch the nurse. From the sick-bed he must go out into the hall to receive his creditors. He carries his daughter in his arms. Tears come to his eyes. He feels the responsibilities weighing upon him more heavily than his strength can bear, and he makes new resolutions; but his nerves are upset. He had secured a translation, but he could not stick to it, for he had to go out continually on errands.

He rushed with the joyful tidings to his father-in-law, who had come into the city. "I am a father!"

"Good! have you bread, too, for your child?"

"At present, no. The father-in-law must help."

"This time, yes; this time, but in the future nothing more. I have little more than you, and, besides, the other children must have something."

The invalid must have chicken to eat now, which he himself buys at the market, and genuine Johannisberger[8] at six crowns the bottle. The nurse receives a hundred crowns. Why should they give less than others do? The captain gave a hundred crowns, too. The young wife is soon on her feet again. Like a young girl once more, slender as a willow, a little pale, but that is becoming to her. The father-in-law comes and takes Herr Gustave aside. "Now be so good as not to come to me for a while with any more children," said he, "or otherwise you will be ruined."

"What a speech for a father! Are we not man and wife? Do we not love each other, and are we not to have children?"

"Yes; but also bread for your children. All young people love easily. But the responsibility!"

The father-in-law is a materialist too. Wretched times without any ideality!

---

8. **Johannisberger** (yō hän′is bérg′ər), an expensive wine.

The life of the house was undermined; but love did not allow itself to be repressed, for it was strong, and young intentions are weak. But creditors are not weak. Bankruptcy threatened. An attachment was imminent. The father-in-law came with a large wagon and carried off his daughter and grandchild. He forbade the son-in-law to show himself until he had bread for them and had paid his debts. To his daughter he said nothing. But as he rode away it seemed to him as if he had brought home a ruined maiden. He had lent out his pure child to a young man for a year, and now he had received her back again. Louisa would gladly have remained with her husband, but she could not live with her child upon the street. So Gustave must remain behind and look on while his home was made desolate. Even that did not belong to him, for it was not paid for. The two men with the eyeglasses took beds, copper and pewter, china, chandeliers,—everything, everything. And as he stood there alone in the empty room, how disheartening it was for him! If she had only stayed! But what could she do in those empty rooms? It was better so.

The bitter earnest of life began. He obtained a position on a morning paper as proof-reader. He had to be at the office at midnight, and stay there three hours. He retained his official position, because he had not yet come to bankruptcy, but he was cut off from advancement. At last it was granted him to see his wife and daughter once a week, but that only under surveillance. At night he slept in a little room near his father-in-law's. Sunday evening he had to go back to the city, for the paper was published early on Monday morning. Then he took leave of wife and child, who accompanied him to the garden gate, and he waved to them from afar, and felt so unhappy, so miserable, so humiliated. And she?

He had reckoned that it would take him twenty years to pay his debts. After that? After that he would still be unable to provide for wife and child. Upon what, then, is any hope to be based? On nothing. If his father-in-law should die, wife and child would have nothing at all.

He did not venture, therefore, to curse his only prop. Oh, how pitiless is life! It provides no sustenance for the children of men, while it gives food to all other created beings. And that this life cannot offer all men partridges and strawberries—really, it is too hard!

I
DEATH ON THE INSTALLMENT PLAN

This story has a direct bluntness of impact that is characteristic of much Scandinavian literature. The reader knows early in the story that there is almost no hope that the young couple can solve their problems. And sure enough, the writer continues weaving a steady downhill record of the couple's fortunes. There is never a moment that indicates any hope of change as the web of disaster closes more and more tightly around the couple. Yet in contrast to the directness of storytelling is the wealth of detail—the details of furnishing the apartment, the lushness of their food, the description of their evening in the restaurant. Thus, Strindberg combines two contrasting elements: a basically simple story and rich, lush details.

What does "Love and Bread" indicate about the following?

1. The elements in a society that put pressures on people to live beyond their incomes.

2. The weaknesses inside people that lead them to live beyond their incomes.

3. Where the blame rests when a couple lives beyond their means. Is the fault the husband's or the wife's? Or both?

II
IMPLICATIONS

What is your opinion about the following statements?

1. It is a common foible of young people to believe that love will solve all their problems.

2. Living beyond one's income is a common fault of society in America today.

3. It is the duty of a parent to prevent a child from making a disastrous marriage.

TECHNIQUES

Setting

Strindberg is most famous as a playwright, one of the finest of the modern period. A playwright uses props and setting to develop action and characters. Sometimes a particular piece of furniture, a casual knickknack will take on a special value that is important. What are some of the details (like props) which are used to help carry the meaning of the story? How does the setting itself become an important force in the story?

IV
WORDS

A. Use context clue procedures and your dictionary to discover the meanings of these words as used by each author:

1. Thackeray: *orthodoxy, prodigious, emulation, victuals.*

2. Johnson: *servility, supercilious, corpulent, obdurate, pernicious.*

3. Strindberg: *gesticulate, egoist, demur, prosaic.*

B. How does Strindberg's choice of words compare with the choice of the preceding authors?

C. A metaphor, as we have learned, is a comparison that is assumed rather than stated. In Johnson's essay, to what is the journey in the stage-coach being compared?

Thackeray speaks of himself and most common citizens as "more or less down on our knees." He speaks of what will happen when death "vacates the shoes" of a noble lord.

In the Strindberg selection one finds "gesticulating with his lead pencil as if he would stab him with it" and "You would suppose that every one halted to form a guard of honor for their triumphant procession. On they swept, with glances uplifted proudly." How often does Strindberg make comparisons in this way?

Notice such phrases as "like a dark shadow" and "like a tottering hill." Where else does Strindberg use simple similes like these? Does Strindberg attempt sustained comparison or simile?

VOLTAIRE

Francois Marie Arouet (1694–1778), using the pseudonym Voltaire, became one of the greatest writers of the Eighteenth Century and was known for his biting wit, his philosophical ideas, and his stand for justice. Coming from a cultured, middle-class family, Voltaire was steeped in the classics by his Jesuit teachers at the College of Louis-le-Grand in Paris. He first studied the law but early on gave it up to become a writer. Twice he was unjustly confined to the Bastille for insulting certain courtiers, an experience that strengthened his passion for justice. Upon being released in 1726, he went to England for three years. There he discovered William Shakespeare and English literature and came to admire both the freedom of thought in England and the English prosperity. After returning to France, he wrote classical tragedies which made him well known but which are no longer performed. He also published *Lettres philosophiques*, a collection of letters in which he praised England in contrast to France. This book was banned in Paris, causing Voltaire to flee to Cirey, a place close to the border where he could escape if imprisonment were threatened. Always a fighter for causes, Voltaire not only wrote intelligent, sometimes ironic works supporting justice, but also personally fought to save freethinkers or Protestants.

Voltaire's most remembered works are his famous tale *Candide*, a rollicking, entertaining satire that is also a complex inquiry into the nature of good and evil and is a series of tongue-in-cheek stories in which he presents many of his ideas. Maligned by his enemies, Voltaire was often forced in these stories to dissemble, pretending to be telling simple moral tales while attacking the foibles of his time with biting wit and amusing twists. One of these stories you are about to read.

Jeannot and Colin

Many trustworthy persons have seen Jeannot and Colin when they went to school at Issoire in Auvergne,[1] a town famous all over the world for its college and its kettles. Jeannot was the son of a dealer in mules, a man of considerable reputation; Colin owed his existence to a worthy husbandman who dwelt in the outskirts of the town, and cultivated his farm with the help of four mules, and who, after paying tolls and tallage, scutage and salt-duty, poundage,

Translated by R. Bruce Boswell from *Zadig and Other Stories*. Copyright 1929 by BOHN's Standard Library.

1. **Auvergne,** a former province in central France.

poll-tax, and tithes,[2] did not find himself particularly well off at the end of the year.

Jeannot and Colin were very handsome lads for natives of Auvergne; they were much attached to each other, and had little secrets together and private understandings, such as old comrades always recall with pleasure when they afterwards meet in a wider world.

Their schooldays were drawing near their end, when a tailor one day brought Jeannot a velvet coat of three colors with a waistcoat of Lyons silk to match in excellent taste; this suit of clothes was accompanied by a letter addressed to Monsieur de la Jeannotière. Colin admired the coat, and was not at all jealous; but Jeannot assumed an air of superiority which distressed Colin. From that moment Jeannot paid no more heed to his lessons, but was always looking at his reflection in the glass, and despised everybody but himself. Some time afterwards a footman arrived post haste, bringing a second letter, addressed this time to His Lordship the Marquis de la Jeannotière; it contained an order from his father for the young nobleman, his son, to be sent to Paris. As Jeannot mounted the chaise[3] to drive off, he stretched out his hand to Colin with a patronizing smile befitting his rank. Colin felt his own insignificance, and wept. So Jeannot departed in all his glory.

Readers who like to know all about things may be informed that Monsieur Jeannot, the father, had rapidly gained immense wealth in business. You ask how those great fortunes are made? It all depends upon luck. Monsieur Jeannotière had a comely person, and so had his wife; moreover her complexion was fresh and blooming. They had gone to Paris to prosecute a lawsuit which was ruining them, when Fortune, who lifts up and casts down human beings, at her pleasure, presented them with an introduction to the wife of an army-hospital contractor, a man of great talent, who could boast of having killed more soldiers in one year than the cannon had destroyed in ten. Jeannot took the lady's fancy, and Jeannot's wife captivated the gentleman. Jeannot soon became a partner in the business, and entered into other speculations. When one is in the current of the stream it is only necessary to let oneself drift, and so an immense fortune may sometimes be made without any trouble. The beggars who watch you from the bank, as you glide along in full sail, open their eyes in astonishment; they wonder how you have managed to get on; they envy you at all events, and write pamphlets against you which you never read. That was what happened to Jeannot senior, who was soon styled Monsieur de la Jeannotière, and, after buying a marquisate at the end of six months, he took the young nobleman his son away from school, to launch him into the fashionable world of Paris.

Colin, always affectionately disposed, wrote a kind letter to his old schoolfellow in order to offer his congratulations. The little marquis sent him no answer, which grieved Colin sorely.

The first thing that his father and mother did for the young gentleman was to get him a tutor. This tutor, who was a man of distinguished manners and profound ignorance, could teach his pupil nothing. The marquis wished his son to learn Latin, but the marchioness would not hear of it. They consulted the opinion of a certain author who had obtained considerable celebrity at that time from some popular works which he had written. He was invited to dinner, and the master of the house began by saying:

"Sir, as you know Latin, and are conversant with the manners of the Court——"

"I, sir! Latin! I don't know a word of it," answered the man of wit; "and it is just as well for me that I don't for one can speak one's own language better, when the attention is not divided between it and foreign tongues. Look at all our ladies; they are far more charming in conversation than men, their letters are written

2. **tallage . . . tithes,** Tallage and scutage were two taxes paid by a tenant to his feudal lord. Salt-duty was a tax levied in England on salt imported by aliens. Poundage was a tax paid on all goods exported and imported. A poll-tax gave the payer the right to vote in public elections. A tithe was a tax paid to support the church and the clergy.
3. **chaise** (shāz), an open, two-wheeled carriage drawn by a horse.

Voltaire in Prison
Culver Pictures

with a hundred times more grace of expression. They owe that superiority over us to nothing else but their ignorance of Latin."

"There now! Was I not right?" said the lady. "I want my son to be a man of wit, and to make his way in the world. You see that if he were to learn Latin, it would be his ruin. Tell me, if you please, are plays and operas performed in Latin? Are the proceedings in court conducted Latin, when one has a lawsuit on hand? Do ple make love in Latin?"

The marquis, confounded by t

ments, passed sentence, and it was decided that the young nobleman should not waste his time in studying Cicero, Horace, and Virgil.

"But what is he to learn then? For still, I suppose, he will have to know something. Might he not be taught a little geography?"

"What good will that do him?" answered the tutor. "When my lord marquis goes to visit his country-seat, will not his postillions[4] know the roads? There will be no fear of their going astray. One does not want a sextant in order to travel, and it is quite possible to make a journey between Paris and Auvergne without knowing anything about the latitude and longitude of either."

"Very true," replied the father; "but I have heard people speak of a noble science, which is, I think, called *astronomy*."

"Bless my soul!" rejoined the tutor. "Do we regulate our behavior in this world by the stars? Why should my lord marquis wear himself out in calculating an eclipse, when he will find it predicted correctly to a second in the almanac, which will moreover inform him of all the movable feasts, the age of the moon, and that of all the princesses in Europe?"

The marchioness was quite of the tutor's opinion, the little marquis was in a state of the highest delight, and his father was undecided.

"What then is my son to be taught?" said he.

"To make himself agreeable," answered the friend whom they had consulted; "for, if he knows the way to please, he will know everything worth knowing; it is an art which he will learn from her ladyship, his mother, without the least trouble to either of them."

The marchioness, at these words, smiled graciously upon the court ignoramus, and said:

"It is easy to see, sir, that you are a most mplished gentleman; my son will owe all his ᵒn to you. I imagine, however, that it ᵉ a bad thing for him to know a little

 ᵉ—what good would that do ᵈ. "Assuredly the only enter-
ᵗory is that of the passing

hour. All ancient histories, as one of our clever writers has observed, are admitted to be nothing but fables; and for us moderns it is an inextricable chaos. What does it matter to the young gentleman, your son, if Charlemagne instituted the twelve Paladins[5] of France, or if his successor had an impediment in his speech?"

"Nothing was ever said more wisely!" exclaimed the tutor. "The minds of children are smothered under a mass of useless knowledge; but of all sciences that which seems to me the most absurd, and the one best adapted to extinguish every spark of genius, is geometry. That ridiculous science is concerned with surfaces, lines, and points which have no existence in nature. In imagination a hundred thousand curved lines may be made to pass between a circle and a straight line which touches it, although in reality you could not insert so much as a straw. Geometry, indeed, is nothing more than a bad joke."

The marquis and his lady did not understand much of the meaning of what the tutor was saying; but they were quite of his way of thinking.

"A nobleman like his lordship," he continued, "should not dry up his brain with such unprofitable studies. If, some day, he should require one of those sublime geometricians to draw a plan of his estates, he can have them measured for his money. If he should wish to trace out the antiquity of his lineage, which goes back to the most remote ages, all he will have to do will be to send some learned Benedictine. It is the same with all the other arts. A young lord born under a lucky star is neither a painter, nor a musician, nor an architect, nor a sculptor; but he may make all these arts flourish by encouraging them with his generous approval. Doubtless it is much better to patronize than to practice them. It will be quite enough if my lord the young mar-

---

4. **postillions** (pō stil′yənz), those who guide the horses drawing a carriage.
5. **Charlemagne . . . Paladins,** According to legend, Charlemagne (742–814), king of the Franks, emperor of the Holy Roman Empire, was attended by twelve knights or peers, known as Paladins.

VIEW OF THE GRANDE CHARTREUSE NEAR GRENOBLE

Culver Pictures

quis has taste; it is the part of artists to work for him, and thus there is a great deal of truth in the remark that people of quality (that is, if they are very rich) know everything without learning anything, because, in point of fact and in the long run, they are masters of all the knowledge which they can command and pay for."

The agreeable ignoramus then took part in the conversation and said:

"You have well remarked, madame, that the great end of man's existence is to succeed in society. Is it, forsooth, any aid to the attainment of this success to have devoted oneself to the sciences? Does anyone ever think in select company of talking about geometry? Is a well-bred gentleman ever asked what star rises today with the sun? Does anyone at the supper table ever want to know if Clodion the Long-Haired[6] crossed the Rhine?"

"No, indeed!" exclaimed the Marchioness de la Jeannotière, whose charms had been her passport into the world of fashion; "and my son must not stifle his genius by studying all that trash. But, after all, what is he to be taught? For it is a good thing that a young lord should be able to shine when occasion offers, as my noble husband has said. I remember once hearing an abbé remark that the most entertaining science was something the name of which I have forgotten— it begins with a *b*."

"With a *b*, madame? It was not botany, was it?"

"No, it certainly was not botany that he mentioned; it began, as I tell you, with a *b*, and ended in *onry*."

"Ah, madame, I understand! It was blazonry or heraldry. That is indeed a most profound science; but it has ceased to be fashionable since the custom has died out of having one's coat-of-arms painted on the carriage doors; it was the most useful thing imaginable in a well-ordered state. Besides, that line of study would be endless, for at the present day there is not a barber who is without his armorial bearings, and you know that whatever becomes common loses its attraction."

Finally, after all the pros and cons of the dif-

ferent sciences had been examined and discussed, it was decided that the young marquis should learn dancing.

Dame Nature, who disposes everything at her own will and pleasure, had given him a talent which soon developed itself with prodigious success; it was that of singing street-ballads in a charming style. His youthful grace accompanying this superlative gift, caused him to be regarded as a young man of the highest promise.

He was a favorite with the ladies, and having his head crammed with songs, he had no lack of mistresses to whom to address his verses. He stole the line, "Bacchus with the Loves at play," from one ballad; and made it rhyme with "night and day" taken out of another, while a third furnished him with "charms" and "alarms." But inasmuch as there were always some feet more or less than were wanted in his verses, he had them corrected at the rate of twenty sovereigns a song. And *The Literary Year* placed him in the same rank with such sonneteers as Le Fare, Chaulieu, Hamilton, Sarrasin, and Voiture.

Her ladyship the marchioness then believed that she was indeed the mother of a genius, and gave a supper to all the wits of Paris. The young man's head was soon turned upside down; he acquired the art of talking without knowing the meaning of what he said, and perfected himself in the habit of being fit for nothing.

When his father saw him so eloquent, he keenly regretted that he had not had him taught Latin, or he would have purchased some high appointment for him in the Law. His mother, who was of more heroic sentiments, took upon herself to solicit a regiment for her son; in the meantime he made love—and love is sometimes more expensive than a regiment. He squandered his money freely, while his parents drained their purses and credit to a lower and lower ebb by living in the grandest style.

---

6. **Clodion the Long-Haired,** Clodion was king of the Salian Franks, a people who settled north of the Rhine.

A young widow of good position in their neighborhood, who had only a moderate income, was well enough disposed to make some effort to prevent the great wealth of the Marquis and Marchioness de la Jeannotière from going altogether, by marrying the young marquis and so appropriating what remained. She enticed him to her house, let him make love to her, allowed him to see that she was not quite indifferent to him, led him on by degrees, enchanted him, and made him her devoted slave without the least difficulty. She would give him at one time commendation and at another time counsel; she became his father's and mother's best friend. An old neighbor proposed marriage; the parents, dazzled with the splendor of the alliance, joyfully fell in with the scheme, and gave to their only son their most intimate lady friend.

The young marquis was thus about to wed a woman whom he adored, and by whom he was beloved in return. The friends of the family congratulated him, the marriage settlement was on the point of being signed, the bridal dress and the epithalamium[7] were both well under way.

One morning our young gentleman was on his knees before the charmer whom fond affection and esteem were so soon to make his own; they were tasting in animated and tender converse the first fruits of future happiness; they were settling how they should lead a life of perfect bliss when one of his lady mother's footmen presented himself, scared out of his wits.

"Here's fine news which may surprise you!" said he; "the bailiffs are in the house of my lord and lady, removing the furniture. All has been seized by the creditors. They talk of personal arrest, and I am going to do what I can to get my wages paid."

"Let us see what has happened," said the marquis, "and discover the meaning of all this."

"Yes," said the widow, "go and punish those rascals—go, quick!"

He hurried homewards, he arrived at the house, his father was already in prison, all the servants had fled, each in a different direction, carrying off whatever they could lay their hands upon. His mother was alone, helpless, forlorn, and bathed in tears; she had nothing left her but the remembrance of her former prosperity, her beauty, her faults, and her foolish extravagance.

After the son had condoled with his mother for a long time, he said at last:

"Let us not despair; this young widow loves me to distraction; she is even more generous than she is wealthy, I can assure you; I will fly to her for succor, and bring her to you."

So he returns to his mistress, and finds her conversing in private with a fascinating young officer.

"What! Is that you, my Lord de la Jeannotière? What business have you with me? How can you leave your mother by herself in this way? Go, and stay with the poor woman, and tell her that she shall always have my good wishes. I am in want of a waiting-woman now, and will gladly give her the preference."

"My lad," said the officer, "you seem pretty tall and straight; if you would like to enter my company, I will make it worth your while to enlist."

The marquis, stupefied with astonishment, and secretly enraged, went off in search of his former tutor, confided to him all his troubles, and asked his advice. He proposed that he should become, like himself, a tutor of the young.

"Alas! I know nothing; you have taught me nothing whatever, and you are the primary cause of all my unhappiness." And as he spoke he began to sob.

"Write novels," said a wit who was present; "it is an excellent resource to fall back upon in Paris."

The young man, in more desperate straits than ever, hastened to the house of his mother's father confessor; he was a Theatine monk of the very highest reputation, who directed the souls

---

7. **epithalamium** (ep′ə thə lā′mē əm), a poem or song in honor of a bride and bridegroom.

of none but ladies of the first rank in society. As soon as he saw him, the reverend gentleman rushed to meet him.

"Good gracious! My lord marquis, where is your carriage? How is your honored mother, the marchioness?"

The unfortunate young fellow related the disaster that had befallen his family. As he explained the matter further the Theatine assumed a graver air, one of less concern and more self-importance.

"My son, herein you may see the hand of Providence; riches serve only to corrupt the heart. The Almighty has shown special favor then to your mother in reducing her to beggary. Yes, sir, so much the better!—she is now sure of her salvation."

"But, Father, in the meantime are there no means of obtaining some succor in this world?"

"Farewell, my son! There is a lady of the Court waiting for me."

The marquis felt ready to faint. He was treated after much the same manner by all his friends, and learned to know the world better in half a day than in all the rest of his life.

As he was plunged in overwhelming despair, he saw an old-fashioned traveling-chaise, more like a covered tumbril[8] than anything else, and furnished with leather curtains, followed by four enormous wagons all heavily laden. In the chaise was a young man in rustic attire; his round and rubicund face had an air of kindness and good temper. His little wife, whose sunburnt countenance had a pleasing if not a refined expression, was jolted about as she sat beside him. The vehicle did not go quite so fast as a dandy's chariot; the traveler had plenty of time to look at the marquis, as he stood motionless, absorbed in his grief.

"Oh! good Heavens!" he exclaimed; "I believe that is Jeannot there!"

Hearing that name the marquis raised his eyes—the chaise stopped.

" 'Tis Jeannot himself! Yes, it is Jeannot!"

The plump little man with one leap sprang to the ground, and ran to embrace his old companion. Jeannot recognized Colin; signs of sorrow and shame covered his countenance.

"You have forsaken your old friend," said Colin; "but be you as grand a lord as you like, I shall never cease to love you."

Jeannot, confounded and cut to the heart, told him with sobs something of his history.

"Come into the inn where I am lodging, and tell me the rest," said Colin; "kiss my little wife, and let us go and dine together."

They went, all three of them, on foot, and the baggage followed.

"What in the world is all this paraphernalia? Does it belong to you?"

"Yes, it is all mine and my wife's; we are just come from the country. I am at the head of a large tin, iron, and copper factory, and have married the daughter of a rich tradesman and general provider of all useful commodities for great folks and small. We work hard, and God gives us his blessing. We are satisfied with our condition in life, and are quite happy. We will help our friend Jeannot. Give up being a marquis; all the grandeur in the world is not equal in value to a good friend. You will return with me into the country; I will teach you my trade, it is not a difficult one to learn; I will give you a share in the business and we will live together with light hearts in that corner of the earth where we were born."

Jeannot, overcome by this kindness, felt himself divided between sorrow and joy, tenderness and shame; and he said within himself:

"All my fashionable friends have proved false to me, and Colin whom I despised, is the only one who comes to my succor. What a lesson!"

Colin's generosity developed in Jeannot's heart the germ of that good disposition which the world had not yet choked. He felt that he could not desert his father and mother.

"We will take care of your mother," said Colin; "and as for the good man your father, who is in prison—I know something of business matters—his creditors, when they see that he has

8. **tumbril** (tum′brəl), a two-wheeled cart, especially one used on a farm for hauling and dumping manure.

nothing more, will agree to a moderate composition. I will see to all that myself."

Colin was as good as his word, and succeeded in effecting the father's release from prison. Jeannot returned to his old home with his parents, who resumed their former occupation. He married Colin's sister, who, being like her brother in disposition, rendered her husband very happy. And so Jeannot the father, and Jeannotte the mother, and Jeannot the son came to see that vanity is no true source of happiness.

I
SATIRIC JABS AT PEOPLE'S FOIBLES

On first reading, this story appears to be a typical *exemplum,* a tale used to point out a moral. Voltaire seems to be giving a recipe for happiness: Stay home, work hard, and good fortune is bound to be your lot. But is this really what the story is all about? What is Voltaire suggesting about a Frenchman's view of Auvergne when he says it is "noted for its college and its kettles," and when he calls Jeannot and Colin "very handsome lads for natives of Auvergne"? What is he implying by the tutor's ridiculous arguments against young Jeannot's taking any of the usual subjects, such as Latin or mathematics or geography, and convincing the parents to have the young man take dancing instead? And what does he intimate about their Paris friends who desert the family when the father loses all his money? Almost every paragraph takes a satiric jab at the foibles of the society of that time. Voltaire's comments are so sly that a second reading may be necessary to catch the full thrust of his meaning.

II
IMPLICATIONS

Do you agree or disagree with the following statements?

1. Voltaire is actually satirizing the hypocrisy of people, not their vanity, in this story.

2. The attitudes presented in the quotations below are still in evidence today.

a. "The minds of children are smothered under a mass of useless knowledge. . . ."

b. "The marquis and his lady did not understand much of the meaning of what the tutor was saying; but they were quite of his way of thinking."

c. " . . . it is much better to patronize [the arts] than to practice them."

d. " . . . whatever becomes common loses its attraction."

e. " . . . an army-hospital contractor . . . who could boast of having killed more soldiers in one year than the cannon had destroyed in ten."

III
TECHNIQUES

Setting

There is almost no physical description of setting in the story. Nevertheless, setting is important to the satire.

1. What are the two settings?

2. What is implied in the choice of these two places?

3. If you were writing a similar story today, what two places might you pick for your settings?

4. Would the story have had the same effect if it had taken place completely in Auvergne?

Prose Style

Look back at the first paragraph. Notice that the sentences immediately begin with the subject and the verb. Then there are long series of phrases or clauses that comment by innuendo on the simple fact stated by the subject and verb. Check to see if this is a stylistic characteristic running through the story.

IV
WORDS

A. Use the context and your dictionary to determine the meanings of the italicized words as used in these phrases in the story:

1. "The marchioness . . . smiled graciously upon the court *ignoramus*. . . ."

2. " ' . . . for us moderns it is an *inextricable* chaos.' "

3. " 'If he should wish to trace out the antiquity of his *lineage*, which goes back to the most remote ages. . . .' "

4. " . . . a talent which soon developed itself with *prodigious* success. . . ."

5. "The marquis, *stupefied* with astonishment. . . ."

6. " . . . whose sunburned *countenance* had a pleasing if not a refined expression. . . ."

B. Voltaire enlivens his writing by the use of metaphor. One such example is in the tutor's statement that " 'The minds of children are smothered under a mass of useless knowledge.' " What others can you find?

V
COMPOSITION

Voltaire's effective satire relies upon his choice of words throughout the story. For example, he describes Jeannot's behavior by saying Jeannot gave Colin "a patronizing smile befitting his rank." The choice of "patronizing" to describe the smile and the added phrase "befitting his rank" combine to provide a picture of a foolishly arrogant young man.

Write your own description of a possible action or attitude of one of the characters in the story. Choose words and phrases that evoke clearly the personality of the character in as few words as possible. Use one of these or one of your own:

1. Colin watching Jeannot leave for Paris.

2. Jeannot's mother speaking to a servant.

3. Jeannot's tutor asking Jeannot's parents for a raise.

JOSEPH ADDISON

Addison and Steele—In English letters these two names are linked tightly together. The two met at Charterhouse school, continued as friends through Oxford, and found mutual interests in their politics and writing. But Steele (1672–1729) was vivacious, eloquent, and cut a dashing figure in the London of his day. Addison (1672–1719) was quiet, gentle, shy, and by far the greater writer. Both men served in Parliament, but Addison was so shy that when he rose to make his first speech he was overcome with fright and sat down without uttering a word. He never again attempted to make a speech there. But when he took pen in hand it was a different matter. Words flowed. He received a pension from the government "to travel and qualify" himself for service to his majesty. The pension ceased when the Tories came to power in 1702, but in 1704 he was appointed to a post in the excise which he held for life. In 1709 Richard Steele wrote the first number of the *Tatler*. At first Addison only made suggestions, but he finally authored some 42 of the 271 numbers of the *Tatler*. When Addison became a contributor, the news element of the thrice-weekly periodical almost disappeared and the essay of opinion dominated each issue. Publication of the *Tatler* ceased in January of 1711, but two months later the *Spectator* took its place. The framework of this publication was an imaginary club: Mr. Spectator, a learned and thoughtful yet gently humorous individual, was the center of the group. Sir Roger de Coverley represented the old English country gentleman; Sir Andrew Freeport represented the London merchant class; the Templar stood for learning and wit. In an age of bitter strife, the *Spectator* stood for reason, moderation, and morality. Samuel Johnson, who was unfavorable to Addison's political party, generously said, "Whoever wishes to attain an English style must give his days and nights to the volumes of Addison." And Macauley added to this praise by saying that Addison was the "consummate painter of life and manners . . . a satirist who alone knew how to use ridicule without abusing it." Of the 555 papers of the *Spectator* published in the two years of its existence, Addison wrote 274 and Steele wrote about 281. Published daily, the paper reached a circulation in some issues of 20,000, which was fantastic for London at that time. Each issue had one main article, and when taken together they almost form a running narrative. It is, in effect, one predecessor of the modern novel.

Dissecting of a Beau's Head[1]

No. 275.
Tuesday, January 15, 1712.

I was yesterday engaged in an assembly of virtuosos, where one of them produced many curious observations which he had lately made in the anatomy of an human body. Another of the company communicated to us several wonderful discoveries which he had also made on the same subject by the help of very fine glasses. This gave birth to a great variety of uncommon remarks, and furnished discourse for the remaining part of the day.

---

1. **of a Beau's Head,** the personality and temperament of a man of fashion.

Joseph Addison

like it; so we found that the brain of a beau is not a real brain, but only something like it.

The pineal gland,[3] which many of our modern philosophers suppose to be the seat of the soul, smelt very strong of essence and orange-flower water, and was encompassed with a kind of horny substance, cut into a thousand little faces or mirrors which were imperceptible to the naked eye, insomuch that the soul, if there had been any here, must have been always taken up in contemplating her own beauties.

We observed a large antrum or cavity in the sinciput,[4] that was filled with ribands, lace and embroidery, wrought together in a most curious piece of net-work, the parts of which were likewise imperceptible to the naked eye. Another of these antrums or cavities was stuffed with invisible billetdoux, loveletters, pricked dances, and other trumpery of the same nature. In another we found a kind of powder,[5] which set the whole company a sneezing, and by the scent discovered itself to be right Spanish. The several other cells were stored with commodities of the same kind, of which it would be tedious to give the reader an exact inventory.

There was a large cavity on each side the head, which I must not omit. That on the right side was filled with fictions, flatteries, and falsehoods, vows, promises, and protestations; that on the left, with oaths and imprecations. There issued out a duct from each of these cells, which ran into the root of the tongue, where both joined together, and passed forward in one common duct to the tip of it. We discovered several little roads or canals running from the ear into the brain, and took particular care to trace them out through their several passages. One of them extended itself to a bundle of sonnets and little musical instruments. Others ended in several bladders which were filled either with wind or froth. But the large canal entered into a great cavity of the skull, from whence there went

The different opinions which were started on this occasion, presented to my imagination so many new ideas, that, by mixing with those which were already there, they employed my fancy all the last night, and composed a very wild extravagant dream.

I was invited methought to the dissection of a beau's head and of a coquette's heart, which were both of them laid on a table before us. An imaginary operator opened the first with a great deal of nicety, which, upon a cursory and superficial view, appeared like the head of another man; but upon applying our glasses to it, we made a very odd discovery, namely, that what we looked upon as brains, were not such in reality, but an heap of strange materials wound up in that shape and texture, and packed together with wonderful art in the several cavities of the skull. For, as Homer[2] tells us that the blood of the gods is not real blood, but only something

2. **Homer,** the great epic poet of ancient Greece.
3. **pineal gland** (pin'ē əl), small conical structure of unknown function in the brain.
4. **antrum . . . sinciput** (an'trəm) . . . (sin'sə pət), hole in the upper part of the skull.
5. **kind of powder,** snuff.

THE

SPECTATOR.

VOLUME the FIRST.

LONDON:

Printed for J. and R. TONSON and S. DRAPER.

The Spectator. Title page to the first volume of the famous periodical written by Joseph Addison and Richard Steele.

Bettmann Archives.

another canal into the tongue. This great cavity was filled with a kind of spongy substance, which the French anatomists call galimatias, and the English, nonsense. The skins of the forehead were extremely tough and thick, and what very much surprised us, had not in them any single blood vessel that we were able to discover, either with or without our glasses; from whence we concluded, that the party when alive must have been entirely deprived of the faculty of blushing.

The os cribriforme[6] was exceedingly stuffed, and in some places damaged with snuff. We could not but take notice in particular of that small muscle which is not often discovered in dissections, and draws the nose upwards, when it expresses the contempt which the owner of it

has, upon seeing anything he does not like, or hearing anything he does not understand. I need not tell my learned reader, this is that muscle which performs the motion so often mentioned by the Latin poets, when they talk of a man cocking his nose, or playing the rhinoceros.

We did not find anything very remarkable in the eye, saving only that the musculi amatorii, or, as we may translate it into English, the ogling muscles, were very much worn and decayed with use; whereas, on the contrary, the elevator, or the muscle which turns the eye towards heaven, did not appear to have been used at all.

_____

6. **os cribriforme,** a sieve-like mouth.

I have only mentioned in this dissection such new discoveries as we were able to make, and have not taken any notice of those parts which are to be met with in common heads. As for the skull, the face, and indeed the whole outward shape and figure of the head, we could not discover any difference from what we observe in the heads of other men. We were informed that the person to whom this head belonged, had passed for a man above five and thirty years; during which time he ate and drank like other people, dressed well, talked loud, laughed frequently, and on particular occasions had acquitted himself tolerably at a ball or an assembly; to which one of the company added, that a certain knot of ladies took him for a wit. He was cut off in the flower of his age by the blow of a paring shovel,[7] having been surprised by an eminent citizen, as he was tendering some civilities to his wife.

_____

7. **paring shovel,** breast plow.

I
LAUGHING AT STOCK CHARACTERS

Certain types of people in literature have been so stylized that their appearance in a selection immediately sets the audience to react with laughter. Called stock characters, they are such stereotypes as the city slicker, the country bumpkin, the nagging wife, the miser, the goof-off. Addison delighted in writing sketches for the _Spectator_ satirizing the society of his time. In this essay, he has made fun of the beau, or the dandy. He is a man of fashion, but what does Addison say he is when seen truly?

II
IMPLICATIONS

Discuss the following questions.

1. The framework for this satire is an imagined dissection of a head. What was your reaction to the device? Can you think of another framework that might work equally well?

2. What details are given about the head? Thinking of the head as the center of reason, intelligence, and the soul, what foible does each detail highlight?

3. Which of the traits might be applied to a woman as well as to a man?

The Coquette's Heart

No. 281.
Tuesday, January 22, 1712.

Having already given an account of the dissection of a beau's head, with the several discoveries made on that occasion, I shall here, according to my promise, enter upon the dissection of a coquette's heart, and communicate to the public such particularities as we observed in that curious piece of anatomy.

I should perhaps have waived this undertaking, had not I been put in mind of my promise by several of my unknown correspondents, who are very importunate with me to make an example of the coquette, as I have already done of the beau. It is therefore in compliance with the request of friends that I have looked over the minutes of my former dream, in order to give the public an exact relation of it, which I shall enter upon without further preface.

Our operator, before he engaged in this visionary dissection, told us that there was nothing in his art more difficult than to lay open the heart of a coquette, by reason of the many labyrinths and recesses which are to be found in it, and which do not appear in the heart of any other animal.

He desired us first of all to observe the pericardium, or outward case of the heart, which we did very attentively; and by the help of our glasses discerned in it millions of little scars, which seemed to have been occasioned by the points of innumerable darts and arrows, that from time to time had glanced upon the outward coat; though we could not discover the smallest orifice by which any of them had entered and pierced the inward substance.

Every smatterer in anatomy knows that this pericardium, or case of the heart, contains in it a thin reddish liquor, supposed to be bred from the vapors which exhale out of the heart and, being stopped here, are condensed into this watery substance. Upon examining this liquor, we found that it had in it all the qualities of that spirit which is made use of in the thermometer to show the change of weather.

Nor must I here omit an experiment one of the company assured us he himself had made with this liquor, which he found in great quantity about the heart of a coquette whom he had formerly dissected. He affirmed to us that he had actually inclosed it in a small tube made after the manner of a weatherglass; but that, instead of acquainting him with the variations of the atmosphere, it showed him the qualities of those persons who entered the room where it stood. He affirmed also that it rose at the approach of a plume of feathers, an embroidered coat, or a pair of fringed gloves; and that it fell as soon as an ill-shaped periwig, a clumsy pair of shoes, or an unfashionable coat came into his house. Nay, he proceeded so far as to assure us that upon his laughing aloud when he stood by it, the liquor mounted very sensibly, and immediately sank again upon his looking serious. In short, he told us that he knew very well by this invention whenever he had a man of sense or a coxcomb[1] in his room.

Having cleared away the pericardium, or the case, and liquor above mentioned, we came to the heart itself. The outward surface of it was extremely slippery, and the mucro,[2] or point, so very cold withal that upon endeavoring to take hold of it, it glided through the fingers like a smooth piece of ice.

The fibers were turned and twisted in a more intricate and perplexed manner than they are usually found in other hearts; insomuch that the whole heart was wound up together like a Gor-

---

1. **coxcomb** (koks′kōm), a fool; a conceited, foolish person.
2. **mucro** (mū′krō), a learned word for *tip* or *point*.

LE BILLET DOUX (*The Love Letter*)
Jean Honoré Fragonard

The Metropolitan Museum of Art
The Jules S. Bache Collection

dian knot,[3] and must have had very irregular and unequal motions, while it was employed in its vital function.

One thing we thought very observable, namely, that upon examining all the vessels which came into it, or issued out of it, we could not discover any communication that it had with the tongue.

We could not but take notice likewise that several of those little nerves in the heart which are affected by the sentiments of love, hatred, and other passions, did not descend to this before us from the brain, but from the muscles which lie about the eye.

Upon weighing the heart in my hand, I found it to be extremely light, and consequently very hollow, which I did not wonder at, when, upon looking into the inside of it, I saw multitudes of cells and cavities running one within another, as our historians describe the apartments of Rosamond's bower.[4] Several of these little hollows were stuffed with innumerable sorts of trifles, which I shall forbear giving any particular account of, and shall, therefore, only take notice of what lay first and uppermost, which, upon our

---

3. **Gordian knot** (gôr′dē ən), a knot that none could untie. Alexander the Great (356–323 B.C.) was told that whoever undid the knot would rule over the whole East. Alexander promptly cut the knot in two with his sword. Hence, the expression means to get out of a difficult position with one decisive step.

---

4. **Rosamond's bower,** the private apartment of Rosamond Clifford (*d.* about 1176), mistress of Henry II of England.

unfolding it, and applying our microscopes to it, appeared to be a flame-colored hood.

We are informed that the lady of this heart, when living, received the addresses of several who made love to her, and did not only give each of them encouragement, but made everyone she conversed with believe that she regarded him with an eye of kindness; for which reason we expected to have seen the impression of multitudes of faces among the several plaits and foldings of the heart; but to our great surprise not a single print of this nature discovered itself till we came into the very core and center of it. We there observed a little figure, which, upon applying our glasses to it, appeared dressed in a very fantastic manner. The more I looked upon it, the more I thought I had seen the face before, but could not possibly recollect either the place or time; when at length one of the company, who had examined this figure more nicely[5] than the rest, showed us plainly by the make of its face, and the several turns of its features, that the little idol which was thus lodged in the very middle of the heart was the deceased beau, whose head I gave some account of in my last Tuesday's paper.

As soon as we had finished our dissection, we resolved to make an experiment of the heart, not being able to determine among ourselves the nature of its substance, which differed in so many particulars from that in the heart of other females. Accordingly, we laid it into a pan of burning coals, when we observed in it a certain salamandrine[6] quality that made it capable of living in the midst of fire and flame, without being consumed or so much as singed.

As we were admiring this strange phenomenon, and standing round the heart in a circle, it gave a most prodigious sigh, or rather crack, and dispersed all at once in smoke and vapor. This imaginary noise, which methought was louder than the burst of a cannon, produced such a violent shake in my brain, that it dissipated the fumes of sleep, and left me in an instant broad awake.

I
LAUGHING AT STOCK CHARACTERS

In the previous essay, Addison made fun of certain males. The selection you have just read is a companion essay satirizing a particular type of woman, the coquette. She is a typical stock character who has appeared and reappeared in literature. By lampooning her foibles, Addison hoped to delight his readers. Why did Addison choose the coquette's heart to dissect rather than the head, as for the beau? What is he saying about the chief characteristic of the coquette's nature?

II
IMPLICATIONS

Discuss the following questions:

1. The framework for this satire is an imagined dissection of a heart. What was your reaction to the device? Can you think of another framework that might work equally well?

2. What details are given about the heart? Thinking of the heart as the center of emotions, what foible does each detail highlight?

3. Which of the traits might be applied to a man as well as a woman?

III
TECHNIQUES

Prose Style

Consider the first three paragraphs of each of Addison's essays. Study the sentences. Are they long, short, a combination of different lengths? Can you read them easily aloud?

1. Can you find a good adjective to describe the personality of Addison's style?

2. Look for examples of contrast and comparison. Are there many sentences in which Addison balances phrases and clauses against each other?

---

5. **nicely,** carefully, with marked discrimination.
6. **salamandrine** (sal′ə man′ drən), like a salamander which, according to legend, could live in fire.

FOIBLES

Painters as well as authors, comment on human follies and vices through comedy. The purpose of comic art, as of literary satire, is to correct such follies by holding them up to ridicule. Human foibles may be seen in a quick, affectionate caricature, like Lautrec's YVETTE GUILBERT BOWING TO THE PUBLIC, or in an elaborate composition such as Hogarth's CHAIRING THE MEMBER. The fun may be harmless, as in Brouwer's THE SMOKER, or it may have the sword thrust of Goya's UNTIL SHE DIES.

Costumes may change, but the gullibility of people remains constant. The action in La Tour's painting could take place in any large city in the world: A young blade consults a fortune teller, while her attractive assistants slyly relieve him of his watch and purse.

THE FORTUNE TELLER
Georges de La Tour

THE SMOKER
Adriaen Brouwer

People's blindness to their own limitations
is ridiculed in this caricature of amateur actors
preparing for a play. The fat man at the left
is dressed as Cupid, the god of love. Beside him
the little man rehearses as Alexander the Great. The
plump woman is preparing to play the youthful star.

When Brouwer painted this picture
in the early seventeenth century,
pipe smoking was still something
of a novelty in Europe.

DILETTANTI-THEATRICALS
or A PEEP AT THE GREEN ROOM
James Gillray

DEATH AND THE GLUTTON
Thomas Rowlandson

Gluttony, one of
the seven deadly sins,
is portrayed in this
scene from the series
THE ENGLISH DANCE
OF DEATH. Death shows
the wealthy glutton
that the sands of time
have run out for him.
   In the original
caption, the glutton
angrily replies:
"What? Do these savory
meats delight you?
Begone! And stay till
I invite you."

411

Yvette Guilbert was a popular singer and comedian in the French and English music halls at the turn of the century. An eccentric person, she powdered her face dead-white and dyed her hair bright orange. In building her repertoire, she made herself one of the world's leading authorities on late medieval poetry and song. Lautrec presents her without a trace of harshness, smiling on the foibles that brighten the world.

The ancient hag in Goya's etching is still trying to look like a girl. Her maid and two young men snicker in the background.

YVETTE GUILBERT BOWING TO THE PUBLIC
Henri de Toulouse Lautrec

UNTIL SHE DIES (HASTA LA MUERTE)
Francisco Goya y Lucientes
Courtesy of The National Gallery of Art,
Washington, D.C., Rosenwald Collection

THE BLIND LEADING THE BLIND
Pieter Brueghel, the Elder

Brueghel, in the illustration
of Matthew xv: 14, "And if the blind
lead the blind, both shall fall
into the ditch," is not poking fun
at affliction. Rather, he is
pointing out the folly of the ill-informed
who follow a leader equally ill-informed.

Gambling is a persistent
human foible. This mid-nineteenth century
member of the English upper classes has
apparently gone broke at the races.
He gestures in comic futility, hounded
by beggars and creditors, while his
wife dissolves in tears.

RACE AT MORNING
Sir John Millais
Courtesy of Ashmolean Museum

The hullabaloo that surrounded an English election
in the eighteenth century provided Hogarth with the subject
of this satirical painting. Friends carry
a newly elected Member of Parliament
through the streets of a town. Hired ruffians
attempt to break up the procession. Members of the opposition
look on with amusement from a nearby window.

THE ELECTION—CHAIRING THE MEMBER
William Hogarth

JUOZAS GRUŠAS

Juozas Grušas[1] (1901–   ), a versatile dramatist, novelist, and short story writer, is a respected playwright in his beloved Lithuania. He was graduated from the University of Kaunas, and for several years he edited a weekly newspaper. Then he began writing, mostly during the first half of the twentieth century—a time in Lithuanian history characterized by political and social upheaval. In 1935, Grušas achieved acclaim for his satirical novel *The Careerists*, which related the struggle between idealism and fortune hunting in modern Lithuania. Next, Grušas demonstrated his skill as a short story writer.. He then went on to write plays. His drama of psychological realism, *Father*, placed him in the first rank of Lithuanian dramatists. Many consider his *Herkos Mantas* the most successful modern Lithuanian play. Another outstanding drama, *Ruinous Intoxication* (1967), was published as *Love, Jazz and the Devil*. An exploration of youthful nihilism, it is Grušas's furthest step toward the theater of fantasy and the grotesque.

A Trip with Obstacles

translated from the Lithuanian by Stepas Zobarskas

Once there lived a farmer named Valiulis[2] who had gray hair like the first frost of the fall. As he finished his eighty-one years of life, he knew that he was about to die and leave behind his prosperous farm, his childless wife who was twenty years younger than he, the wide fields, and the blue sky with the white clouds.

He used to do all his work fast and on time, but as he grew older he became weaker, and he lost his speed. Now the poor fellow was getting ready to pass away without any show of temper or hurry. All winter long he kept coughing, mumbling, and scolding his wife:

"Now I'm going to die, this is my last day . . . it's enough . . . it's all gone. . . ."

His wife, a genuine daughter of the soil, did not tear her hair and weep over this. She knew that there had to be some kind of rule everywhere, and that everything had to run according to the plan established by their fathers, forefathers, and God. She had never read romantic poetry nor did she ever weep while watching a melodrama at some theater. She was ever faithful to her husband. Actually, nothing that ever happened on the farm took her off balance.

Even the death of her husband had to be, more or less, an everyday event. If he had to die, let him die—for all of us will do the same thing. What was really important was to die decently, at the proper time. Even the neighbors did not wish him to die during the harvest season or on one of the big holidays when people have enough other amusements. Taking so much time, he had to choose a more convenient, freer time. Could it be that while promising to die during Lent he would, without saying a word to anybody, pass away on Easter? Such a joke could only be executed by an irresponsible, immature person, but not by a serious-minded farmer.

Order was the main thing, and the farmer's wife knew it perfectly well. She was ready to meet her husband's death with the same matter of factness, as, let us say, that the publisher of a newspaper awaits the demise of a sick king,

---

1. **Juozas Grušas** (yü äz′äs grü′säs).
2. **Valiulis** (väl′yə lis).

a patriarch, a prophet, or some other distinguished citizen. The malt had been sprouted and ground, the hops were bought, a bundle of candles was brought down from upstairs, and a black coffin with silver edges had been bought and placed in the attic, over the pantry. Here it would stay in readiness, waiting for its quiet and decent inhabitant.

The priest had also been brought in a few times.

So everything was ready; one had only to push the button. But the unknown fingers still did not ring that mysterious bell. Death must have become so used to the place that she forgot her duties. The neighbors began to grow restless, and his wife was bored because of all this preparation.

However, destiny has always been a prankster. Sometimes it made a laughing stock of great

things, and sometimes it made too much noise because of some trivial detail. Destiny and death—two creatures that should be trusted the least.

Nevertheless, something very important was happening in the farmer's living room.

One night the tired wife heard a voice in her sleep: "Mortel,[3] Mortel, my soul!" but she could not wake up.

"Mortel, you old bag, are you lost?"

The wife raised her head, rubbed her eyes with her fists, and murmured in a lazy voice: "You won't even let me sleep peacefully. . . ."

"Light the candle—I'm dying."

"What?" His wife's voice became more sober, but she still couldn't understand what her old man was mumbling.

---

3. **Mortel** (môr′təl), wife.

"I'm going to die . . . please light the little candle."

His wife got up, lit the lamp and approached the old man's bed. He was breathing heavily, his chest was heaving, and his forehead was wet.

"What is it? Don't you feel well?"

"Give me the holy candle—I'm going to die," the old man repeated with his choking voice, rolling his eyes from one side to the other.

No more jokes: a man is dying. But the farmer's wife still can't believe it. She stands for a while, gazing at the sick man, but when she realizes that he's not about to change his mind, lazily she comes back to her bed and starts rummaging under her pillow, as if she were looking for the band of her stockings. Finally she takes out a large wax candle, a little burned down already, and places it into the sick man's hands. Her husband presses the candle in his palm, looks at the flame, blinks his eyes, and plunges deep into his thoughts.

His wife is looking around the room. Is she going to remain that way on the floor, waiting and freezing? Who on earth could understand what this old man wants?

She thinks: it would be a good idea to go to the barn and see whether her red-spotted cow hadn't calved yet. But she still feels too sleepy to do it, so she blows out the light, slips back into her bed and covers herself warmly. If something happens—she will get up again. It's so warm and pleasant in bed. She turns on her side and soon begins to snore.

The sick man feels sad. For a long time he looks at the floating yellowish flame and moans silently. Now he feels that death is approaching him like a black shadow. It's dark and quiet outside the window. The old clock is ticking on the wall, and perhaps it is counting the last minutes of his life. Those precious last minutes are slow and monotonous; they fall like the rain drops from the roof. Shall I die or not, shall I die or not, he thinks long and lazily, until he begins to feel sleepy. He closes his eyes and

sweet sleep comes in like a lukewarm wind of spring.

In the morning, the wife jumps out of her bed—she overslept; she puts on some of her clothes and lights the lamp. What is it? She had certainly not expected that! Even a man with nerves of iron could not stand this sight any longer without bursting into rage. The sick man was sleeping. His head thrown back, and he was breathing heavily, and the candle was all gone. Only a small piece was left in his palm as if it wanted to enrage the farmer's wife even more.

The wax had fallen on the linen sheets and on the bed. At this rate he will have all his candles burnt down, that good-for-nothing creature, and when he dies—there won't be a single candle left to put next to his coffin. Like a child, he could have burned himself! And how could he fall asleep with a death candle burning in his hands? She had never seen such a stupid man in all her life. The more she thought of it, the more she wanted to scold him.

"Father! You should be ashamed of yourself. You could have burned yourself!"

The old man opened his eyes, but lazily and unwillingly, he looked at his angry wife and closed them again. Then he raised his hand meekly, and let it fall down on the blanket as if it were a sock full of ashes.

His wife was silent. Such a move of his hand was more serious than one might think it was. She had realized that she started to blame him at the wrong time, and she asked him softly, "Do you feel weak?"

"Oh, very weak, very weak."

The sick man moaned, and again he fell asleep.

This time it had to be a serious matter. No doubt, this was his last moment. She had never seen him that way before. Now she felt death slowly approaching her dear husband, and sorrow squeezed her heart like a pair of pliers. Now everything seemed different from what it was last night when she had to light the candle. Then it was only a laughing matter. . . .

But she was not a milksop of a woman; she did not kill herself with sorrow. It was sad, surely, but after all, this was an easy time, it was Lent. And everything has been ready for a long time. To tell the truth, it won't be bad if he dies right now. He has been ready anyway for quite a while, and he could have died at such a time that no one could ever come to look at him. She was accustomed to the rules from her childhood, and she never made much fuss. As she remembers now, she even got married because of the same rules. Her parents wanted it that way; they told her to do so. Such was the order of the farm, and she did not raise any fuss, even though her groom was neither young nor good looking. The farm and the program arranged by the parents, grandparents and God, were more important to her.

As she was so meditating, the closest neighbor, Sauliene,[4] tiptoed in without even knocking at the door. That was the custom of this region. She was devoted and sharp-tongued and yet quite a pleasant woman. She shook off the snow from her shoes, hailed Jesus, and started warbling her own song: "So you're preparing, my little heart . . . I noticed that your oxen were strolling around loose, so I thought I'd drop in and tell you about it . . . and how is your patient? Does he feel any better? Maybe God will give . . . ."

The farmer's wife soon realized that the oxen must have been let loose by a new farm hand who was a good-for-nothing blockhead.

"That must be our servant. Wherever he goes he causes a havoc."

She dusted a bench with the corner of her apron and asked the guest to sit down. Then she started telling her about the patient.

"Maybe a day or two, but no longer . . . I had to light the candle last night. . . ."

The lady guest walked toward the sick man, looked at him and shrugged her shoulders; then she turned toward the neighbor and whispered:

"You see. . . ."

But she wanted to be precise in counting the days that had been left for him on this earthly trip.

She again gave a look of appraisal, like a good merchant evaluating his wares, then she leaned over and whispered in his ear, "Are you going to get up, dear neighbor?"

The sick man opened his sleepy eyes.

"Very weak, very weak . . . ."

The lady guest slapped her thighs with her hands, then she tugged the hostess to a corner of the room and began to scold, "You see, deary! And you're not ready yet. He's going to pass away any minute . . . today . . . just look at him . . . he can hardly catch his breath. Get the attendants, hurry up! And the time is so convenient now."

Valiuliene[5] felt warm all over. There was no doubt any more that her dear husband was going to die today. There was no use of talking any longer. Death was close as his palm. Sauliene was well at home in such matters.

When the guest had finally left, the farmer's wife took up her work. Everything had to be smooth and decent. The priest had been called only recently, and she would not worry about that. Now she had to call the attendants. He could not leave this world without them. And where was the beer? The attendants could let her husband die without any beer, and that would be quite all right but no one would ever go to a wake if he knew that he would not get a glass of beer there. That would be shameful for her whole house. What would the people say?

She ordered the servant, the blockheaded boy, to get some beer; the maid was sent to invite the women from the village. The farmer's wife herself began to work inside the house. She had to fix the patient's bed, to cover the table, clean the benches, scrub the floor, and keep the candles ready. The attendants might be expected soon.

When everything was ready, she breathed

---

4. **Sauliene** (sou′lyä nä).
5. **Valiuliene** (väl′yə lyä nä).

easier, just as a good mower does after he cuts a tract of wheat. At this moment she could not see any obstacles that might thwart the pale hand of death. She checked everything in the house once more, then she turned toward the sick husband.

"Well, how do you feel now?"

"The patient only moaned, gave a deep groan, scratched his chin, and mumbled, "I'll die . . . today perhaps. . . ."

"Poor soul . . . and how is your head, do you feel giddy?" She did not want to contradict him now; she only wanted to console him, without paying much attention to her words.

The women began to gather. There were those who knew how to sing from their prayer books, and those who were experts in helping people to die—they all came here. They were all cleanly dressed and in a holiday mood.

With their expert eyes, they looked over the sick man and tried to guess how many minutes were left for this poor fellow to live.

"So you're going to leave us, uncle?" they asked him as if he were preparing to go to Brazil.

The old man did not show much trust in the attendants. True, he was very much interested in them, and his sleepiness was all gone, but one could have guessed from his face that those ladies did not make a good impression on him. He gazed at them with his eyes wide open, hardly realizing why they all gathered around him. Then, instead of giving an answer, he only muttered through his nose: "Hm!"

"Poor dear old man. He can't even pronounce a word."

"We should stop talking to him."

"Neighbor, you take the lead. We're going to sing a litany now."

"Father, do you want me to light the candle?" asked his wife, deeply moved, and drying a couple of tears, although as you see, she had no intention of crying.

Now the patient fought back as if he were defending himself from the wasps. He kept waving both his hands and mumbling. All this ritual roused a serious worry in him.

Some of the good old women took interest in the candles, and the others looked at the pages of their prayer books. All began talking and waiting for the real festivity of the dying to start. Those who were standing a little farther away began to discuss the burial and the mass.

"You cannot do without the obsequies. It doesn't cost too much . . . for such a farmer!" a loud-mouthed woman shouted through the whole house.

The patient heard all this very clearly. All his "weakness" had disappeared like camphor. He turned on the other side and lay with his face toward the wall. Then he began to scratch the top of his head and again turned around. Finally, to make a bigger effect, he kicked his blanket on the floor. It was amazing how strong and spry he became. He was about to sit up and get out of his bed, but a few women attendants rushed toward him, put him back to bed, and covered him.

"He's raving, poor old dear man."

"It's hard to pass away."

"God, give him a happy death."

Now it was too much for him. The patient clenched his fists and was ready to deal a blow to the first one who would wish him a happy death. He would close his ears, so as not to hear anyone talk about it.

You know him, the old stinker, he has always been an intolerably stubborn person. Every time his wife used to tell him that he wouldn't die, he would swear that he wanted to pass away; now, when everybody was wishing him a happy death—as sure as he was alive—he did not want to leave this miserable world.

The situation really became gloomy.

And now, to everyone's surprise, the most vehement woman in the village, Simkiene,[6] walked in.

"What do you think you're doing here?" she asked them suddenly, and without wait-

---

6. **Simkiene** (sim′kyä nä).

ing for an answer, she turned toward the sick man. "Chase all these women out; you're not going to die! We are going to have a fight yet. Look, someone has broken open the gate to the exit road; now the people are moving toward the field, and they will soon drive through my rye field."

The sick farmer's eyes lighted up, and he even smiled a little.

"I told you to chase all these women out and get your gate fixed!"

Having said that, she walked out smilingly.

The death ritual was in vain. The women looked at one another and did not know what to do. Although they all had much experience with wakes, they had never met such an obstacle.

The sick man became more courageous, and he felt that he was not alone any more in the battle against the whole bunch of attendants. He was determined to open his mouth:

"Why did you gather here? Get out!"

What ingratitude! What an impudent man! The women felt very much insulted.

And his wife realized that a miracle was being performed. A moment ago he was near death, and now he's chasing all the attendants away. Later, when there will be a real need, there will be no way of reinviting them here. What a stinker! But she was careful and ready to yield. She only asked, "Would you like something to eat, father?"

"Yes, if you'd give me something . . . ."

She brought him some beet soup with sour cream. The sick man sat down and began to eat it. And he had quite a good appetite.

In the meantime the women attendants rushed through the door, one after the other. They did not like this joke.

When the sick man finished eating the soup, he dried his mustache.

"Would you like to have some more?" asked his wife, stroking his gray hair.

"Yes, if you'd give me something . . . ."

She brought him a second bowl, but this time she put in even more sour cream to make the soup tastier.

The minute she placed the bowl in front of her husband, the maid rushed in, all excited and screaming: "Hostess, the pantry is burning!"

The woman rushed to the window and saw the gray clouds of smoke coming out of the pantry's roof.

"Oh my Heaven!"

She put on her fur coat and dashed away, and as she ran, she scolded the boy who, while trying to make the beer, set the pantry on fire.

There was a big noise in the yard. The neighbors rushed in, shouting, screaming and clicking with the buckets. The pantry was in flames, and it seemed as if someone had poured gasoline on the straw roof. There was nothing one could do about it. The firemen only tried to guard the rest of the houses from the sparks. But the wind was blowing favorably and the rest of the farmstead was not in danger.

The people turned their heads. It was the sick man who was speaking to them. Having eaten the soup, he took his cane and walked out of the house. Now he was moving around lively, giving orders and urging the other men to help. He was carrying buckets of water and he was helping to put out the fire.

Now what do you think happened? He saw a wonderful thing—the roof of the pantry was all burned down, and his coffin in the attic was in flames. A real coffin, destined for his own use! The man felt as if the last stone had fallen from his chest. A smile brightened his face. My, what a successful day it had been! He nudged the neighbor who was standing next to him and pointed out:

"It's burning!"

I
A TRIP DISRUPTED

The reader is startled to find out that the journey the author is using as the crux of his tale is not the ordinary kind, from one geographical spot to another. Instead, the trip is from the state of being alive to that of being dead. Even more surprising is the discovery that there can be obstacles in this particular trip. Gradually we find ourselves enjoying the annoyance of the wife and neighbors as their plans go awry and feeling as delighted as the old man as we watch the coffin burning. Is the author satirizing a common human foible of being annoyed when things do not go as planned, even when it is something as final as death?

II
IMPLICATIONS

Discuss your reactions to the following statements.

1. Both Molière and Grušas, by highlighting only their characters' foibles, make them one-dimensional.

2. The neighbors' and friends' foibles are satirized as well as those of the principal characters.

3. An individual is an emotional cripple if he or she is unable to feel sympathy for the plight of another.

III
TECHNIQUES

Setting

Modern drama often uses a stage with little scenery, certain designated areas for the action, and a few props. The same is often true of folk stories. If you were staging this story as simply as possible, what would be the necessary props?

Prose Style

In the scene of the lighting of the candle, the author suddenly shifts tenses from the past to the present. Then he goes back to the past tense to tell the rest of the story. What could be the reason for this?

LAWRENCE DURRELL

Of Irish ancestry, Lawrence Durrell (1912–   ) was born in the Himalayan region
of India when India was still a part of the British Empire. Later the family moved
to England, and Durrell was sent to school for what he called "the long, sad river
of my adolescence." England provided a strong contrast with the free, open,
mountainous region of his childhood, and in fact he has chosen to live most of his life
away from England. England, he has written, "tried to destroy anything singular and unique
in me. My so-called upbringing was quite an uproar. I have always broken stable when I was
unhappy. The list of schools I've been to would be a yard long." During the 1930's,
Durrell began to write poetry, novels, and plays. His career was interrupted by the war,
during and after which he served England in several capacities in Greece, Crete, Egypt,
Argentina, and Yugoslavia. Service as English information officer on Cyprus forms
a background for the hilarious narrative "How to Buy a House." In it, the reader can see
that while Durrell laughs at the foibles of the Cypriots, he also admires their spontaneous,
dramatic ways—all of which are so un-English. In 1957 he published the first of four
novels collected as *The Alexandria Quartet*, set against the background of Egypt.
The success of these books brought him to the attention of the world, and he is often
listed among the most interesting of living novelists.

How to Buy a House

"Last of all came the Greeks and inquired of
the Lord for their gift.

" 'What gift would you like?' said the Lord.

" 'We would like the gift of Power,' said the
Greeks.

"The Lord replied: 'Ah, my poor Greeks, you
have come too late. All the gifts have been distributed. There is practically nothing left. The
gift of Power has been given to the Turks, the
Bulgarians the gift of Labour; the Jews of Calcu-
lation, the French of Trickery and the English of
Foolishness.'

"The Greeks waxed very angry at this and
shouted 'By what intrigue have we been overlooked?'

" 'Very well,' said the Lord. 'Since you insist,
you too shall have a present and not remain
empty-handed—may Intrigue be your lot,' said
the Lord."

(Bulgarian Folk-tale)

Sabri Tahir's office in the Turkish quarter of
Kyrenia bore a sun-blistered legend describing
him as a valuer[1] and estate agent, but his activities had proliferated[2] since the board was
painted and he was clearly many things besides. The centre of the cobweb was a dark
cool godown perched strategically upon a junction of streets, facing the little Turkish shrine
of some saint or warrior whose identity had
vanished from the record, but whose stone
tomb was still an object of veneration and pilgrimage for the faithful. It stood under a dusty
and desiccated pepper tree, and one could always find an *ex voto*[3] or two hanging beside it.

Beyond was a featureless empty field of nettles in which stood a couple of shacks full of
disembodied pieces of machinery and huge

---

1. **valuer**, an expert at judging the value of real estate,
an appraiser.
2. **proliferated** (prō lif'ə rā təd), grew by rapid addition
of new parts (here, new business interests).
3. **ex voto**, an offering made in consequence of a vow or
solemn promise.

heaps of uncut carob and olive, mingled with old railway sleepers and the carcasses of buses which always turned up here at the end of the trail, as if to some Elephants' Graveyard, to be turned into fuel. Sabri's Empire was still in an embryonic stage, though it was quite clear that he was speculating wisely. A circular saw moaned and gnashed all day in one of the shacks under the ministrations of two handsome Turkish youths with green headbands and dilapidated clothes; a machine for making cement blocks performed its slow but punctual evacuations, accompanied by a seductive crunch.

Sabri could watch all these diverse activities from the darkness of his shop where he sat for the greater part of the day before a Turkish coffee, unmoved, unmoving, but watchful. His desk was in the far corner against the wall, and to reach it one traversed a *terrain vague*[4] which resembled the basement of Maple's, so crowded was it with armchairs, desks, prams, cooking-stoves, heaters, and all the impedimenta of gracious living.

The man himself was perhaps forty years of age, sturdily built, and with a fine head on his shoulders. He had the sleepy good looks—a rare smile with perfect teeth, thoughtful brown eyes—which one sees sometimes in Turkish travel posters. But what was truly Turkish about him was the physical repose with which he confronted the world. No Greek can sit still without fidgeting, tapping a foot or a pencil, jerking a knee, or making popping noises with his tongue. The Turk has a monolithic poise, an air of reptilian concentration and silence. It is with just such an air that a chameleon can sit, hour after hour, upon a shrub, staring unwinkingly at the world, living apparently in that state of suspended judgement which is summed up by the Arabic word *kayf*.[5] I have seen Sabri loading logs, shouting at peasants, even running down a street; but never has he conveyed the slightest feeling of energy being expended. His actions and words had the smoothness of inevitability; they flowed from him like honey from a spoon.

Lawrence Durrell lived with his family on Corfu and other of the Greek islands of which he writes.

On that first morning when I stepped into the shadows of his shop, the headquarters of the empire, he was sitting dreamily at his desk mending a faulty cigarette-lighter. His good-morning was civil, though preoccupied and in-different; but as I approached he paused for one instant to snap finger and thumb and a chair materialized from the shadows behind him. I sat down. He abandoned his task and sat silent and unwinking before me. "Mr. Sabri," I said, "I need your help. I have been making inquiries in Kyrenia and on all sides I am told that you are the most untrustworthy man of business in the place—in fact, the biggest rogue."

He did not find the idea offensive so much as merely interesting. His shrewd eye sharpened a trifle, however, and he lowered his head to scan me more gravely. I went on. "Now knowing the Levant[6] as I do, I know that a reputation for being a rogue means one thing and one thing only. It means that one is *cleverer*

4. **terrain vague,** an indistinct land or area.
5. **kayf** (kīf), serene contemplation and deep repose.
6. **the Levant** (lə vant'), the eastern shore of the Mediterranean from Egypt to, and including, Turkey, Syria, and Lebanon.

than other people." I accompanied this with the appropriate gesture—for cleverness in the hand-language is indicated by placing the forefinger of the right hand slowly and portentously upon the temple: tapping slightly, as one might tap a breakfast-egg. (Incidentally, one has to be careful, as if one turns the finger in the manner of turning a bolt in a thread, the significance is quite different: it means to be "soft in the head" or to "have a screw loose.") I tapped my skull softly. "*Cleverer* than other people," I repeated. "So clever that the stupid are envious of one."

He did not assent or dissent from the proposition. He simply sat and considered me as one might a piece of machinery if one were uncertain of its use. But the expression in his eyes shifted slightly in a manner suggesting the faintest, most tenuous admiration. "I am here," I went on, convinced by this time that his English was good, for he had followed me unerringly so far, to judge by his face, "I am here as a comparatively poor man to ask you a favour, not to make you a business proposition. There is no money to be made out of me. But I want you to let me use your brains and experience. I'm trying to find a cheap village house in which to settle for a year or two—perhaps forever if I like it enough here. I can see now that I was not wrong; far from being a rogue you are obviously a Turkish gentleman, and I feel I can confide myself entirely to your care—if you will accept such a thing. I have nothing to offer except gratitude and friendship. I ask you as a Turkish gentleman to assist me."

Sabri's colour had changed slowly throughout this harangue and when I ended he was blushing warmly. I could see that I had scored a diplomatic stroke in throwing myself completely upon the iron law of hospitality which underpins all relations in the Levant. More than this, I think the magic word "gentleman" turned the trick in my favour for it accorded him an unaccustomed place in the consideration of strangers which he certainly merited, and which he thenceforward lived up to in his dealings with me. By a single tactful speech I had made a true friend.

He leaned forward at his desk, smiling now, and patted my hand gently, confidingly: "But of course, my dear," he said, "of course."

Then he suddenly threw up his chin and barked an order. A barefoot youth materialized from the shadows bearing Coca-Cola on a tray, apparently ordered by some invisible gesture a while before. "Drink," he said quietly, "and tell me what house you want."

"A village house, not a modern villa."

"How far away?"

"Not far. Among these hills."

"Old houses need doing up."

"If I can buy one cheaply I shall do it up."

"How much can you spend?"

"Four hundred pounds."

He looked grave at this and this was understandable, for the price of land had been soaring since the war, and indeed continued to soar until the time of my departure from the island when building plots in the centre of Nicosia[7] cost roughly the same as those in Washington. "My dear," he said thoughtfully, and stroked his moustache. "My dear." Outside the darkness of his shop the spring sunshine glistened on trees loaded with cold tangerines; a cold wind touched the fronds of the palm-trees, quick with the taste of snow from the Taurus[8] mountains across the water. "My dear," repeated Sabri thoughtfully. "Of course if you lived very far away it would be quite easy, but do you wish to be within reach of the capital?" I nodded. "If I run out of money then I shall have to work, and there is nothing to be found out of Nicosia." He nodded. "Somewhere not too far from Kyrenia you want an arty old house." That summed it up perfectly. Sabri took a thoughtful turn or two among the shadows and stubbed out his cigarette on the box. "Honestly, my dear," he said, "it will be a matter of luck. I do hear of things, but it is a matter of luck. And it is very difficult to find one person to deal

---

7. **Nicosia** (nik′ə sē′ə), the capital of Cyprus located in the west central part of the island.
8. **Taurus** (tôr′əs), mountains in Turkey.

with. You are at once in a bloody family, my dear." I did not then know what he meant. I was soon to learn.

"Do not be disappointed if you hear nothing from me for a while. What you ask is not easy, but I think I can do it. I will be working on it even if I am silent. Do you understand, my dear?" His handshake was warm.

I had hardly reached the main street on my way back to Panos' house when Renos the bootblack came out of a side street and took my arm. He was a tiny little wisp of a man with the sort of eyes one finds sewn on to rag dolls. "My friend," he said, "you have been to see Sabri." This is the favourite Mediterranean game, a tireless spying upon the movements of friends and acquaintances, and is common to all communities which do not read, whose whole life is built up by oral tradition and common gossip. "Yes," I said.

"Phew." He went through a pantomime in the hand-language, burning his fingers on hot coals and blowing upon them. This meant "You will be stung." I shrugged my shoulders. "What to do?" I said cheerfully. "Aie aie," said Renos, laying one hand to his cheek and rocking his head commiseratingly as if he had toothache. But he said no more.

By the time I got home Panos himself had been informed of my visit—doubtless by bush telegraph.[9] You have been to see Sabri," he said as I crossed the brilliant courtyard of the church and joined him on his balcony over the bewitching blueness of the spring sea. "About a house?" I nodded. "You have done well," he said. "Indeed I was going to suggest it."

"Clito says he is a rogue."

"Nonsense. His dealings with me have been perfectly honourable. He is a pretty sharp business man, of course, which is not usual among Turks who are always half asleep. But he is no more of a rogue than anyone else. In fact, Clito himself is a rogue, if it comes to that. He overcharged me for this bottle of Commanderia. Incidentally did you tell Sabri how much money you have?"

"No, I told him less than I actually had."

Panos chuckled admiringly. "I see you understand business in these parts. Everything gets gossiped about, so that whatever price you would be prepared to pay would soon be known to everyone. You did right to put it low."

I accepted a glass of sweet Commanderia and a pickled pimento from the coloured china plate; the two children were doing a puzzle in the sunshine. The beadle crashed at the church bell in a sudden desultory burst of mania and then left the silence to echo round us in wingbeats of aftersound.

"I hear," said Panos when the vibrations had died away, "that your brother was killed at Thermopylae[10] during the war."

"To be absolutely honest with you," I said, "I made the whole thing up in order to . . ."

"Tease Frangos!"

"Yes. I was afraid there would be a fight."

"Excellent. Capital." Panos was delighted by the subtlety of my imagination. He struck his knee delightedly as he laughed. "Capital," he repeated. "It is clear that as rogues go you are as bad as any of us." It was a compliment to be thus included in the rogues' gallery of Kyrenia.

That evening it was I who recited the geography lesson while Panos stood behind me, nodding approvingly as I picked out the salient points of the Kyrenia range with a forefinger, travelling gently over the blue spines of the hills from the point where Myrtou lay invisible among its hazy farms and vineyards to where Akanthou (equally invisible) drowsed among its fields of yellow-green barley. In truth, by now I had memorized the lesson so well that the very names of the places I had yet to visit communicated a sharp visual image of them. I could see the lemon-groves of Lapithos[11] and feel the dense cool air of its orchards: hear the sullen thunder of the headspring as it gushed into the valley from the mountain's summit.

---

9. **bush telegraph,** news conveyed by the beating of drums as in Africa.
10. **Thermopylae** (thər mop′ə lē). At this narrow Greek pass, a small army of Greeks held back the Persians' mighty forces. Through the centuries, the spot has been a battle ground.
11. **Lapithos.** All places mentioned here are in Cyprus.

The great double-combed crown of Hilarion stood almost directly behind us with its castle taking the last lion-gold rays of the evening upon its tawny flanks. Over the saddle below it ran the main road to Nicosia, piercing the range at its lowest point. East of us loomed other peaks whose sulky magnificence echoed each other, mingling like the notes of a musical chord: Buffavento, seat of the winds, with the silent and graceful Gothic abbey of Bellapaix below it in the foothills; Pendedactyl whose five-fingered peak recalled the fingerprints of the hero Dighenis; fading all of them, and inclining slowly eastward into the mist like the proud sails of some Venetian argosy, to where Cape Andreas drowsed in spindrift at the end of the long stone handle of the Karpass. The place names chimed as one spoke them like a carillon, Greek Babylas and Myrtou, Turkish Kasaphani, Crusader Templos. . . . The mixture was a heady one.

"Very good," said Panos at last, with a sigh of real pleasure. "You really do know it. But now you must visit it." I had intended to ere this, but my preoccupations about a house had quite consumed me, while problems of correspondence and the transport of luggage, money, etc. had made my mind too turbid for use. I had left it all lying there, so to speak, multiplying itself in my imagination, until I should be ready to go out and meet it. Apart from a few short excursions around Kyrenia in search of spring flowers and mushrooms I had been nowhere; indeed had done nothing except bathe and write letters. Life in an island, however rich, is circumscribed, and one does well to portion out one's experiences, for sooner or later one arrives at a point where all is known and staled by repetition. Taken leisurely, with all one's time at one's disposal Cyprus could, I calculate, afford one a minimum of two years reckoned in terms of novelty; hoarded as I intended to hoard it, it might last anything up to a decade.

That is why I wished to experience it through its people rather than its landscape, to enjoy the sensation of sharing a common life with the humble villagers of the place; and later to expand my field of investigation to its history —the lamp which illumines national character —in order to offer my live subjects a frame against which to set themselves. Alas! I was not to have time.

The month or so of spring weather with its promise of summer to follow proved fraudulent. One day we woke to a sky covered in ugly festoons of black cloud and saw drift upon drift of silver needles like arrows falling upon the ramparts of Kyrenia castle. Thunder clamoured and rolled, and the grape-blue semi-darkness of the sea was bitten out in magnesium flashes as the lightning clawed at us from Turkey like a family of dragons. The stone floors turned damp and cold, the gutters brimmed and mumbled all day as they poured a cascade of rain into the street. Below us the sea dashed huge waves across the front where not a week ago we had been sitting in shorts and sandals, drinking coffee and *ouzo,* and making plans for the summer. It was a thrilling change, for one could feel the luxuriant grass fattening under the olives, and the spring flowers unwrapping their delicate petals on the anemone-starred slopes below Clepini.

It was hardly a propitious moment for Sabri to arrive, but arrive he did one black afternoon, wearing as his only protection a spotted handkerchief over his head against the elements. He burst through Panos' front door between thunder-flashes like an apparition from the underworld, gasping: "My dear." His suit was liberally streaked with rain. "I have something for you to see—but *please*" (in anguish almost) "don't blame me if it is not suitable. I haven't seen it myself yet. But it *may* be . . ." He accepted a glass of wine in chilled fingers. "It is in the village of Bellapaix, but too far from the road. Anyway, will you come? I have a taxi. The owner is a rogue of course. I can guarantee *nothing.*"

I could see that he was most anxious that I should not judge his professional skill by what might turn out to be a mistake. Together we galloped across the rain-echoing courtyard and down the long flight of stairs by the church to where Jamal and his ancient taxi waited. The handles were off all the doors and there ensued a brief knockabout scene from a Turkish shadow-play among the three of us which finally resulted in our breaking into the vehicle at a weak point in its defences. (Jamal had to crawl through the boot, and half-way through the back seat, in order to unlatch for us.) Then we were off through a landscape blurred with rain and the total absence of windscreen wipers. Jamal drove with his head out of the window for the sake of safety. Outside, the rain-blackened span of mountains glittered fitfully in the lightning-flashes.

Just outside Kyrenia a road turned to the right and led away across a verdant strip of olive and carob land towards the foothills where Bellapaix stood in rain and mist. "Nevertheless," said Sabri thoughtfully, "it is a good day, for nobody will be out of doors. The café will be empty. We won't cause the gossips, my dear." He meant, I suppose, that in any argument over prices the influence of the village wiseacres would seriously affect the owner's views. A sale needed privacy; if the village coffee-shop undertook a general debate on a transaction there was no knowing what might happen.

I was prepared for something beautiful, and I already knew that the ruined monastery of Bellapaix was one of the loveliest Gothic survivals in the Levant, but I was not prepared for the breath-taking congruence of the little village which surrounded and cradled it against the side of the mountain. Fronting the last rise, the road begins to wind through a landscape dense with orange and lemon trees, and noisy with running water. Almond and peach-blossom graze the road, as improbably precise as the décor to a Japanese play. The village comes down to the road for the last hundred yards or so with its grey old-fashioned houses with arched vaults and carved doors set in old-fashioned mouldings. Then abruptly one turns through an arc of 150 degrees under the Tree of Idleness and comes to a stop in the main square under the shadow of the Abbey itself. Young cypresses bent back against the sky as they took the wind; the broad flower beds were full of magnificent roses among the almond trees. Yet it all lay deserted in the rain.

The owner of the house was waiting for us in a doorway with a sack over his head. He was a rather dejected-looking man whom I had already noticed maundering about the streets of Kyrenia. He was a cobbler by trade. He did not seem very exuberant—perhaps it was the weather—but almost without a word spoken led us up the boulder-strewn main street, slipping and stumbling amongst the wet stones. Irrigation channels everywhere had burst their banks and Sabri, still clad in his handkerchief, gazed gloomily about him as he picked his way among the compost heaps where the chickens browsed. "It's no good, my dear," he said after we had covered about a hundred yards without arriving at the house. "You could never get up here." But still the guide led on, and curiosity made us follow him. The road had now become very steep indeed and resembled the bed of a torrent; down the centre poured a cascade of water. "My dear," groaned Sabri, "it is a trout-stream." It certainly seemed like one. The three of us crept upwards, walking wherever possible on the facing-stones of the irrigation channel. "I am terribly sorry," said Sabri. "You will have a cold and blame me."

The atmosphere of the village was quite enthralling; its architecture was in the purest peasant tradition—domed Turkish privies in courtyards fanning out from great arched doors with peasant mouldings still bearing the faint traces of a Venetian influence; old Turkish screen-windows for ventilation. It had the purity and authenticity of a Cretan hamlet. And everywhere grew roses, and the pale clouds of almond and peach blossom; on the balconies grew herbs in window-boxes made from old petrol tins; and crowning every courtyard like a messenger from my Indian childhood spread the luxuriant green fan of banana-leaves, rattling like parchment in the wind. From behind

427

the closed door of the tavern came the mournful whining of a mandolin.

At the top of the slope where the village vanished and gave place to the scrubby outworks of the mountain behind, stood an old irrigation tank, and here our guide disappeared round a corner, drawing from his breast an iron key the size of a man's forearm. We scrambled after him and came upon the house, a large box-like house in the Turkish-Cypriot mode, with huge carved doors made for some forgotten race of giants and their oxen. "Very arty, my dear," said Sabri, noting the fine old windows with their carved screens, "but what a place"; and then he kicked the wall in an expert way so that the plaster fell off and revealed the mysteries of its construction to his practised eye. "Mud brick with straw." It was obviously most unsatisfactory. "Never mind," I said, stirred by a vague interior premonition which I could not put exactly into words. "Never mind. Let's look now we're here."

The owner swung himself almost off the ground in an effort to turn the great key in the lock which was one of the old pistol-spring type such as one sees sometimes in medieval English houses. We hung on to his shoulders and added our strength to his until it turned screeching in the lock and the great door fell open. We entered, while the owner shot the great bolts which held the other half of the door in position and propped both open with a faggot. Here his interest died, for he stayed religiously by the door, still shrouded in his sack, showing no apparent interest in our reactions. The hall was gloomy and silent—but remarkably dry considering the day. I stood for a while listening to my own heart beating and gazing about me. The four tall double doors were splendid with their old-fashioned panels and the two windows which gave internally on to the hall were fretted with wooden slats of a faintly Turkish design. The whole proportion and disposition of things here was of a thrilling promise; even Sabri glowed at the woodwork which was indeed of splendid make and in good condition.

The floor, which was of earth, was as dry as if tiled. Obviously the walls of the house offered good insulation—but then earth brick usually does if it is laid thickly enough. The wind moaned in the clump of banana trees, and at intervals I could still hear the whimper of the mandolin.

Sabri, who had by now recovered his breath, began to take a more detailed view of things, while I, still obscured by premonitions of a familiarity which I could not articulate, walked to the end of the hall to watch the rain rattling among the pomegranates. The garden was hardly larger than twenty square yards, but crammed with trees standing shoulder to shoulder at such close quarters that their greenery formed an almost unbroken roof. There were too many—some would have to go: I caught myself up with a start. It was early for me to begin behaving like the house's owner. Abstractedly I counted them again: six tangerines, four bitter lemons, two pomegranates, two mulberry trees and a tall leaning walnut. Though there were houses on both sides they were completely hidden by greenery. This part of the village with its steep slope was built up in tiers, balcony upon balcony, with the trees climbing up between. Here and there through the green one caught a glint of the sea, or a corner of the Abbey silhouetted against it.

My reverie was interrupted by a moan and I feared for a moment that Sabri had immolated himself in one of the rooms upon the discovery of some dreadful fact about the woodwork. But no. A heifer was the cause of the noise. It stood, plaintively chewing something in the front room, tethered to a ring in the wall. Sabri clicked his tongue disapprovingly and shut the door. "A bloody cow, my dear," he smiled with all the townsman's indulgence towards the peasant's quirks. "Inside of the house." There were two other rather fine rooms with a connecting door of old workmanship, and a couple of carved cupboards. Then came a landslide. "Don't open it!" shouted the owner and flew to the help of the gallant Sabri who was wrestling with a door behind which apparently struggled some huge animal—a camel perhaps or an elephant? "I forgot to tell you," panted the owner as we all three set our shoulders to the panels. The room was stacked breast-high with grain which had poured out upon Sabri as he opened the door. Together we got it shut but not before the observant Sabri had noticed how dry the grain was in its store. "This place is dry," he panted grudgingly. "So much I can say."

But this was not all; we were about to leave when the owner suddenly recollected that there was more to see and pointed a quavering finger at the ceiling in the manner of Saint John in the icons. "One more room," he said, and we now took a narrow outside staircase where the rain still drizzled, and climbed out upon a balcony where we both stood speechless. The view was indescribable. Below us, the village curved away in diminishing perspective to the green headland upon which the Abbey stood, its fretted head silhouetted against the Taurus range. Through the great arches gleamed the grey-gold fields of cherries and oranges and the delicate spine of Kasaphani's mosque. From this high point we were actually looking down upon Bellapaix, and beyond it, five miles away, upon Kyrenia whose castle looked absurdly like a toy. Even Sabri was somewhat awed by the view. Immediately behind, the mountain climbed into blue space, topped by the ragged outcrop and mouldering turrets of Buffavento. "What a position," I said feebly.

The balcony itself was simply a flat platform of earth with no balustrade. Up here in one corner of it was a rather lofty and elegant room, built on a bias, and empty of everything save a pair of shoes and a pile of tangerines. We returned to the balcony with its terrific panorama. The storm had begun to lift now and sun was struggling feebly to get out; the whole eastern prospect was suffused with the light which hovers over El Greco's Toledo.[12]

"But the balcony itself," said Sabri with genuine regret, "my dear, it will need concrete." "Why?" He smiled at me. "I must tell you how the peasant house is built—the roof. Come down." We descended the narrow outside stair

together, while he produced a notebook and pencil. "First the beams are laid," he said indicating the long series of magnificent beams, and at the same time scribbling in his book. "Then some reed mats. Then packets of osiers to fill the airspace, or perhaps dried seaweed. Then Carmi earth, then gravel. Finally it all leaks and you spend the whole winter trying to stop the leaks."

"But this house doesn't," I said.

"Some do sooner than others."

I pointed to the mason's signature upon the graven iron plaque which adorned the main door. It bore the conventional Orthodox cross embossed on it with the letters IE XR N (Jesus Christ Conquers) and the date 1897. Underneath, on the lower half of the plate, in the space reserved to record subsequent building or alteration was written only one date (9th September 1940), when presumably some restoration work had been undertaken. "Yes, I know, my dear," said Sabri patiently. "But if you buy this house you will have to rebuild the balcony. You are my friend, and so I shall insist for your own good."

We debated this in low tones on the way down the hill. Though the rain had slackened the village street was empty save for the little corner shop, a grocery store, where a thickset young man sat alone, amid sacks of potatoes and dry packets of spaghetti, playing patience on a table. He shouted good afternoon.

In the main square Jamal sat uneasily under the Tree of Idleness beneath an open umbrella, drinking coffee. I was about to engage the owner of the house in discussion as to the sort of price he had in mind for such a fine old relic when Sabri motioned me to silence. The coffee-house was gradually filling up with people and faces were turning curiously towards us. "You will need time to think," he said. "And I have told him you don't want to buy it at all, at any price. This will make the necessary despondence, my dear."

---

12. **El Greco** (el grek'ō), Spanish painter, flourishing about 1600, who painted a famous picture of the city of Toledo.

"But I'd like to have an idea of the price."

"My dear, he has no idea *himself*. Perhaps five hundred pounds, perhaps twenty pounds, perhaps ten shillings. He is completely vacant of ideas. In the bargaining everything will get cleared. But we must take time. In Cyprus time is everything."

I rode regretfully down the green winding ways to Kyrenia thinking deeply about the house which seemed more desirable in retrospect than it had in actual fact. Meanwhile Sabri talked to me in knowledgeable fashion about the drawbacks to buying out there. "You simply have not considered such problems," he said, "as water, for example. Have you?"

I had not, and I felt deeply ashamed of the fact. "Give me two days," said Sabri, "and I will find out about the land and water-rights of the property. Then we will ask the man and his wife for the big price-conversation at my office. You will see how tricky we are in Cyprus. And if you buy the house I will send you to a friend of mine to do the rebuilding. He is a rogue, of course, but just the man. I only ask, give me time."

That night when I told Panos that I had seen what might prove to be a suitable house for me at Bellapaix he was delighted, for he had lived there for several years, teaching at the local school. "They are the laziest people in the world," he said, "and the best-natured in Cyprus. And you have honey, and also in the valley behind the house nightingales, my friend."

He did not mention silk, almonds and apricots: oranges, pomegranates, quince. . . . Perhaps he did not wish to influence me too deeply.

Sabri meanwhile retired into silence and contemplation for nearly a week after this; I imagined him sharpening himself for the coming contest of wills by long silent fasts—broken perhaps by a glass of sherbet—or perhaps even prayer for long stretches. The skies turned blue and hard again, and the orange-trees in the Bishopric put out their gleaming suns. The season was lengthening once more into summer, one felt; was stretching itself, the days beginning to unfold more slowly, the twilights to linger. Once more the little harbour filled up with its crowds of chaffering fishermen darning their nets, and of yachtsmen dawdling over caulked seams and a final coat of paint.

Then at last the summons came; I was to present myself at Sabri's office the next morning at eight. Panos brought me the message, smiling at my obvious anxiety, and telling me that Sabri was rather despondent because it now appeared that the house was owned not by the cobbler but by his wife. It had been her dowry, and she herself was going to conduct the sale. "With women," said my friend, "it is always a Calvary to argue. A Golgotha."[13] Nevertheless Sabri had decided to go forward with the business. The intervening space of time had been valuable, however, because he had come into possession of a piece of vital information about the water supply. Water is so scarce in Cyprus that it is sold in parcels. You buy an hour here and an hour there from the owner of a spring—needless to say no quantity measure exists. The trouble lies here: that water-rights form part of property-titles of citizens and are divided up on the death of the owner among his dependants. This is true also of land and indeed of trees. Families being what they are, it is common for a single spring to be owned by upwards of thirty people, or a single tree to be shared out among a dozen members of a family. The whole problem, then, is one of obtaining common consent—usually one has to pay for the signatures of thirty people in order to achieve any agreement which is binding. Otherwise one dissident nephew and niece can veto the whole transaction. In the case of some trees, for example, one man may own the produce of the tree, another the ground on which it stands, a third the actual timber. As may be imagined, the most elementary litigation as-

---

13. **Golgotha** (gol′gə thə), literally, the place of the skull, another name for Calvary, the hill northwest of Jerusalem where criminals once were executed, and where Jesus died on the cross.

sumes gigantic proportions—which explains why there are so many lawyers in Cyprus.

Now Sabri had got wind of the fact that the Government was planning to install the piped water supply to the village which had been promised for so long; moreover that the plans were already being drawn up. The architect of the Public Works happened to be a friend of his so he casually dropped into his office and asked to see where the various water-points were to be placed. It was a stroke of genius, for he saw with delight that there was to be a public water-point outside the very front door of the old house. This more than offset the gloomy intelligence that the only water the cobbler owned was about an hour a month from the main spring—perhaps sixty gallons: whereas the average water consumption of an ordinary family is about forty gallons a *day*. This was a trump card, for the cobbler's water belonged in equal part to the rest of his wife's family—all eighteen of them, including the idiot boy Pipi whose signature was always difficult to obtain on a legal document. . . .

I found my friend, freshly shaven and spruce, seated in the gloom of his office, surrounded by prams, and absolutely motionless. Before him on the blotter lay the great key of the house, which he poked from 'ime to time in a reproachful way. He put his finger to his lips with a conspiratorial air and motioned me to a chair. "They are all here, my dear," he hissed, "getting ready." He pointed to the café across the road where the cobbler had gathered his family. They looked more like seconds. They sat on a semicircle of chairs, sipping coffee and arguing in low voices; a number of beards waggled, a number of heads nodded. They looked like a rugger scrum[14] in an American film receiving last-minute instructions from their captain. Soon they would fall upon us like a ton of bricks and gouge us. I began to feel rather alarmed. "Now, whatever happens," said Sabri in a low voice, tremulous with emotion, "do not surprise. You must never surprise. And you don't want the house at all, see?"

I repeated the words like a catechism. "I don't want the house. I absolutely don't want the house." Yet in my mind's eye I could see those great doors ("See," Sabri had said, "this is fine wood. From Anatolia.[15] In the old days they floated the great timbers over the water behind boats. This is Anatolian timber, it will last for ever"). Yes, I could see those doors under a glossy coat of blue paint. . . . "I don't want the house," I repeated under my breath, feverishly trying to put myself into the appropriate frame of mind.

"Tell them we are ready," said Sabri to the shadows and a bare-footed youth flitted across the road to where our adversaries had gathered. They hummed like bees, and the cobbler's wife detached herself from the circle—or tried to, for many a hand clutched at her frock, detaining her for a last-minute consideration which was hissed at her secretively by the family elders. At last she wrenched herself free and walked boldly across the road, entering Sabri's shrine with a loud "Good morning" spoken very confidently.

She was a formidable old faggot, with a handsome self-indulgent face, and a big erratic body. She wore the white headdress and dark skirt of the village woman, and her breasts were gathered into the traditional baggy bodice with a drawstring at the waist, which made it look like a loosely furled sail. She stood before us looking very composed as she gave us good morning. Sabri cleared his throat, and picking up the great key very delicately between finger and thumb—as if it were of the utmost fragility —put it down again on the edge of the desk nearest her with the air of a conjurer making his opening dispositions. "We are speaking about your house," he said softly, in a voice ever so faintly curdled with menace. "Do you know that all the wood is . . ." he suddenly shouted the last word with such force that I nearly fell off my chair, "rotten!" And picking

---

14. **a rugger scrum**, a Rugby or English football team.
15. **Anatolia** (an′ə tō′lē ə), literally, *sunrise;* i.e., *eastern land,* the part of Asia Minor east of the Aegean Sea.

up the key he banged it down to emphasize the point.

The woman threw up her head with contempt and taking up the key also banged it down in her turn exclaiming: "It is not."

"It *is*." Sabri banged the key.

"It is *not*." She banged it back.

"It *is*." A bang.

"It is *not*." A counter-bang.

All this was not on a very high intellectual level, and made me rather ill at ease. I also feared that the key itself would be banged out of shape so that finally none of us would be able to get into the house. But these were the opening chords, so to speak, the preliminary statement of theme.

The woman now took the key and held it up as if she were swearing by it. "The house is a good house," she cried. Then she put it back on the desk. Sabri took it up thoughtfully, blew into the end of it as if it were a six-shooter, aimed it and peered along it as if along a barrel. Then he put it down and fell into an abstraction. "And suppose we wanted the house," he said, "which we don't, what would you ask for it?"

"Eight hundred pounds."

Sabri gave a long and stagy laugh, wiping away imaginary tears and repeating "Eight hundred pounds" as if it were the best joke in the world. He laughed at me and I laughed at him, a dreadful false laugh. He slapped his knee. I rolled about in my chair as if on the verge of acute gastritis. We laughed until we were exhausted. Then we grew serious again. Sabri was still fresh as a daisy, I could see that. He had put himself into the patient contemplative state of mind of a chess player.

"Take the key and go," he snapped suddenly, and handing it to her, swirled round in his swivel chair to present her with his back; then as suddenly he completed the circuit and swivelled round again. "What!" he said with surprise. "You haven't gone." In truth there had hardly been time for the woman to go. But she was somewhat slow-witted, though obstinate as a mule: that was clear. "Right," she now said

in a ringing tone, and picking up the key put it into her bosom and turned about. She walked off stage in a somewhat lingering fashion. "Take no notice," whispered Sabri and busied himself with his papers.

The woman stopped irresolutely outside the shop, and was here joined by her husband who began to talk to her in a low cringing voice, pleading with her. He took her by the sleeve and led her unwillingly back into the shop where we sat pointedly reading letters. "Ah! It's you," said Sabri with well-simulated surprise. "She wishes to discuss some more," explained the cobbler in a weak conciliatory voice. Sabri sighed.

"What is there to speak of? She takes me for a fool." Then he suddenly turned to her and bellowed, "Two hundred pounds and not a piastre more."

It was her turn to have a paroxysm of false laughter, but this was rather spoiled by her husband who started plucking at her sleeve as if he were persuading her to be sensible. Sabri was not slow to notice this. "You tell her," he said to the man. "You are a man and these things are clear to you. She is only a woman and does not see the truth. Tell her what it is worth."

The cobbler, who quite clearly lacked spirit, turned once more to his wife and was about to say something to her, but in a sudden swoop she produced the key and raised it above her head as if she intended to bring it down on his hairless dome. He backed away rapidly. "Fool," she growled. "Can't you see they are making a fool of you? Let me handle this." She made another pass at him with the key and he tiptoed off to join the rest of her relations in the coffee-shop opposite, completely crushed. She now turned to me and extended a wheedling hand, saying in Greek, "Ah come along there, you an Englishman, striking a hard bargain with a woman. . . ." But I had given no indication of speaking Greek so that it was easy to pretend not to understand her. She turned back to Sabri, staring balefully, and banging the key down once more shouted "Six hundred," while Sabri in the same breath bellowed "Two hundred." The noise was deafening.

They panted and glared at each other for a long moment of silence like boxers in a clinch waiting for the referee to part them. It was the perfect moment for Sabri to get in a quick one below the belt. "Anyway, your house is mortgaged," he hissed, and she reeled under the punch. "Sixty pounds and three piastres," he added, screwing the glove a little to try to draw blood. She held her groin as if in very truth he had landed her a blow in it. Sabri followed up swiftly: "I offer you two hundred pounds plus the mortgage."

She let out a yell. "No. Never," and banged the key. "Yes, I say," bellowed Sabri giving a counter-bang. She grabbed the key (by now it had become, as it were, the very symbol of our contention. The house was forgotten. We were trying to buy this old rusty key which looked like something fitter for Saint Peter's keyring than my own). She grabbed the key, I say, and put it to her breast like a child as she said: "Never in this life." She rocked it back and forth, suckled it, and put it down again.

Sabri now became masterful and put it in his pocket. At this she let out a yell and advanced on him shouting: "You give me back my key and I shall leave you with the curses of all the saints upon you." Sabri stood up like a showman and held the key high above his head, out of her reach, repeating inexorably: "Two hundred. Two hundred. Two hundred." She snapped and strained like a hooked fish, exclaiming all the time: "Saint Catherine defend me. No. No." Then quite suddenly they both stopped, he replaced the key on the desk and sat down, while she subsided like a pan of boiling milk when it is lifted off the fire. "I shall consult," she said briefly in another voice and leaving the key where it was she took herself off across the road to where her seconds waited with towels and sponges. The first round was a draw, though Sabri had made one or two good points.

"What happens now?" I said, and he chuckled. "Just time for a coffee. I think, you know,

my dear," he added, "that we will have to pay another hundred. I feel it." He was like a countryman who can tell what the weather will be like from small signs invisible to the ordinary townsman. It was an enthralling spectacle, this long-drawn-out pantomime, and I was now prepared for the negotiations to go on for a week. "They don't know about the water," said Sabri. "They will let us have the house cheap and then try and sting us for the water-rights. We must pretend to forget about the water and buy the house cheaper. Do you see?" I saw the full splendour of his plan as it unfolded before us. "But," he said, "everything must be done today, now, for if she goes back to the village and makes the gossips nothing will be consummated." It seemed to me that she was already making the gossips in the café opposite, for a furious altercation had broken out. She was accusing her husband of something and he was replying waspishly and waving his arms.

After a while Sabri whispered: "Here she comes again," and here she came, rolling along with sails spread and full of the cargo of her misfortunes. She had changed her course. She now gave us a long list of her family troubles, hoping to soften us up; but by now I felt as if my teeth had been sharpened into points. It was clear that she was weakening. It was a matter of time before we could start winding her in. It was, in fact, the psychological moment to let out the line, and this Sabri Tahir now did by offering her another hundred ("a whole hundred," he repeated juicily in a honeyed voice) if she would clinch the deal there and then. "Your husband is a fool," he added, "and your family ignorant. You will never find a buyer if you do not take this gentleman. Look at him. Already he is weakening. He will go elsewhere. Just look at his face." I tried to compose my face in a suitable manner to play my full part in the pantomime. She stared at me in the manner of a hungry peasant assessing a turnip and suddenly sat herself down for the first time, bursting as she did so into heartrending sobs. Sabri was delighted and gave me a wink.

She drew her wimple round her face and went into convulsions, repeating audibly: "What are they doing to me? Destruction has overtaken my house and my line. My issue has been murdered, my good name dragged in the dust." Sabri was in a high good humour by this time. He leaned forward and began to talk to her in the voice of Mephistopheles[16] himself, filling the interstices between her sentences with his insinuations. I could hear him droning on "Mortgage . . . two hundred . . . husband a fool . . . never get such an opportunity." Meanwhile she rocked and moaned like an Arab, thoroughly enjoying herself. From time to time she cast a furtive glance at our faces to see how we were taking it; she could not have drawn much consolation from Sabri's for he was full of a triumphant concentration now; in the looming shadows he reminded me of some great killer shark—the flash of a white belly as it turned over on its back to take her. "We have not spoken of the water as yet," he said, and among her diminishing sobs she was still able to gasp out, "That will be another hundred."

"We are speaking only of the house," insisted Sabri, and at this a look of cunning came over her face. "Afterwards we will speak of the water." The tone in which he said this indicated subtly that he had now moved over on to her side. The foreigner, who spoke no Greek, could not possibly understand that without water-rights the house itself was useless. She shot a glance at me and then looked back at him, the look of cunning being replaced by a look almost of triumph. Had Sabri, in fact, changed sides? Was he perhaps also planning to make a killing, and once the house was bought. . . . She smiled now and stopped sobbing.

"All this can only be done immediately," said Sabri quietly. "Look. We will go to the widow and get the mortgage paper. We will pay her mortgage before you at the Land Registry. Then we will pay you before witnesses for the house." Then he added in a low voice: "After that the gentleman will discuss the water. Have you the papers?"

We were moving rather too swiftly for her. Conflicting feelings beset her; ignorance and doubt flitted across her face. An occasional involuntary sob shook her—like pre-ignition in an overheated engine which has already been switched off. "My grandfather has the title-deeds."

"Get them," said Sabri curtly.

She rose, still deeply preoccupied, and went back across the street where a furious argument broke out among her seconds. The white-bearded old man waved a stick and perorated. Her husband spread his hands and waggled them. Sabri watched all this with a critical eye. "There is only one danger—she must not get back to the village." How right he was; for if her relations could make all this noise about the deed of sale, what could the village coffee-shop not do? Such little concentration as she could muster would be totally scattered by conflicting counsels. The whole thing would probably end in a riot followed by an island-wide strike. . . .

I gazed admiringly at my friend. What a diplomat he would make! "Here she comes again," he said in a low voice, and here she came to place the roll of title-deeds on the table beside the key. Sabri did not look at them. "Have you discussed?" he said sternly. She groaned. "My grandfather will not let me do it. He says you are making a fool of me." Sabri snorted wildly.

"Is the house yours?"

"Yes, sir."

"Do you want the money?"

"Yes."

"Do you want it today?"

"Yes."

My friend leaned back in his chair and gazed up at the cobwebs in the roof. "Think of it," he said, his voice full of the poetry of commerce. "This gentleman will cut you a chekky. You will go to the Bank. There they will look with respect at it, for it will bear his name. They will open the safe. . . ." His voice trembled and she

---

16. **Mephistopheles** (mef′ə stof′ə lēz′), a devil who first appears in the late medieval Faust legend.

gazed thirstily at him, entranced by the story-book voice he had put on. "They will take from it notes, thick notes, as thick as a honeycomb, as thick as salami" (here they both involuntarily licked their lips and I myself began to feel hungry at the thought of so much edible money). "One . . . two . . . three," counted Sabri in his mesmeric voice full of animal magnetism. "Twenty . . . sixty . . . a hundred" gradually getting louder and louder until he ended at "three hundred." Throughout this recital she behaved like a chicken with her beak upon a chalk line. As he ended she gave a sigh of rapture and shook herself, as if to throw off the spell. "The mortgage will have been paid. The widow Anthi will be full of joy and respect for you. You and your husband will have *three hundred pounds*." He blew out his breath and mopped his head with a red handkerchief. "All you have to do is to agree. Or take your key."

He handed her the key and once more swivelled round, to remain facing the wall for a full ten seconds before completing the circle.

"Well?" he said. She was hovering on the edge of tears again. "And my grandfather?" she asked tremulously. Sabri spread his hands. "What can I do about your grandfather? Bury him?" he asked indignantly. "But act quickly, for the gentleman is going." At a signal from him I rose and stretched and said, "Well I think I . . ." like the curate in the Leacock[17] story.

"Quick. Quick. Speak or he will be gone," said Sabri. A look of intense agony came over her face. "O Saint Matthew and Saint Luke," she exclaimed aloud, tortured beyond endurance by her doubts. It seemed a queer moment to take refuge in her religion, but obviously the decision weighed heavily upon her. "O Luke, O Mark," she rasped, with one hand extended towards me to prevent me from leaving.

Sabri was now like a great psychologist who divines that a difficult transference is at hand. "She will come," he whispered to me, and putting his fingers to his mouth blew a shrill blast which alerted everybody. At once with a rumble Jamal, who had apparently been lurking down a side street in his car, grated to the door

in a cloud of dust. "Lay hold of her," Sabri said and grabbed the women by the left elbow. Following instructions I grabbed the other arm. She did not actually resist but she definitely rested on her oars and it was something of an effort to roll her across the floor to the taxi. Apparently speed was necessary in this *coup de main*[18] for he shouted: "Get her inside" and put his shoulder to her back as we propelled her into the back of the car and climbed in on top of her.

She now began to moan and scream as if she were being abducted—doubtless for the benefit of the grandfather—and to make dumb appeals for help through the windows. Her supporters poured out into the road, headed by a nonagenarian waving a plate and her husband who also seemed in tears. "Stop." "You can't do that," they cried, alerting the whole street. Two children screamed: "They are taking Mummy away," and burst into tears.

"Don't pay any attention," said Sabri now, looking like Napoleon on the eve of Wagram. "Drive, Jamal, drive." We set off with a roar, scattering pedestrians who were making their way to the scene of the drama, convinced perhaps that a shot-gun wedding was in progress. "Where are we going?" I said.

"Lapithos—the widow Anthi," said Sabri curtly. "Drive, Jamal, drive."

As we turned the corner I noticed with horror that the cobbler and his family had stopped another taxi and were piling into it with every intention of following us. The whole thing was turning into a film sequence. "Don't worry," said Sabri, "the second taxi is Jamal's brother and he will have a puncture. I have thought of everything."

In the brilliant sunshine we rumbled down the Lapithos road. The woman looked about her with interest, pointing out familiar landmarks with great good-humour. She had completely recovered her composure now and

---

17. **Leacock** (lē′kok), Stephen Leacock, a Canadian, famous for his books of humor.
18. **coup de main,** French idiom, helping hand.

smiled upon us both. It was obviously some time since she had had a car-ride and she enjoyed every moment of it.

We burst into the house of the widow Anthi like a bomb and demanded the mortgage papers; but the widow herself was out and they were locked in a cupboard. More drama. Finally Sabri and the cobbler's wife forced the door of the cupboard with a flat-iron and we straggled back into the sunshine and climbed aboard again. There was no sign of the second taxi as we set off among the fragrant lemon-groves towards Kyrenia, but we soon came upon them all clustered about a derelict taxi with a puncture. A huge shout went up as they saw us, and some attempt was made to block the road but Jamal, who had entered into the spirit of the thing, now increased speed and we bore down upon them. I was alarmed about the safety of the grandfather, for he stood in the middle of the road waving his stick until the very last moment, and I feared he would not jump out of the way in time. I closed my eyes and breathed deeply through my nose: so did Sabri, for Jamal had only one eye and was unused to speeds greater than twenty miles an hour. But all was well. The old man must have been fairly spry for when I turned round to look out of the back window of the car I saw him spread-eagled in the ditch, but quite all right if one could judge by the language he was using.

The clerks in the Registry Office were a bit shaken by our appearance for by this time the cobbler's wife had decided to start crying again. I cannot for the life of me imagine why—there was nobody left to impress; perhaps she wanted to extract every ounce of drama from the situation. Then we found she could not write—Grandfather was the only one who could write, and she must wait for him. "If he comes, all is lost again, my dear," said Sabri. We had to forcibly secure her thumbprint to the article of sale, which sounds easy, but in fact ended by us all being liberally coated with fingerprint ink.

She only subsided into normality when the ratified papers were handed to Sabri; and when I made out her cheque she positively beamed and somewhat to my surprise insisted on shaking hands with me, saying as she did so, "You are a good man, may you be pleased in the house."

It was in the most amiable manner that the three of us now sauntered out into the sunlight under the pepper trees. On the main road a dusty taxi had drawn up and was steadily disgorging the disgruntled remains of the defeated army. Catching sight of her they shouted vociferously and advanced in open order, waving sticks and gesticulating. The cobbler's wife gave a shriek and fell into her grandfather's arms, sobbing as if overtaken by irremediable tragedy. The old man, somewhat tousled by his expedition, and with grass in his eyebrows, growled protectively at her and thundered: "Have you done it?" She sobbed louder and nodded, as if overcome. The air was rent with execrations, but Sabri was quite unmoved. All this was purely gratuitous drama and could be taken lightly. With an expressive gesture he ordered Coca-Cola all round which a small boy brought from a barrow. This had the double effect of soothing them and at the same time standing as a symbolic drink upon the closing of a bargain—shrewdly calculated as were all his strokes. They cursed us weakly as they seized the bottles but they drank thirstily. Indeed the drive to Lapithos is a somewhat dusty one.

"Anyway," said the cobbler at last when they had all simmered down a bit, "we still have the water-rights. We have not yet discussed those with the gentleman." But the gentleman was feeling somewhat exhausted by now, and replete with all the new sensations of ownership. I possessed a house! Sabri nodded quietly. "Later on," he said, waving an expressive hand to Jamal, who was also drinking a well-earned Coca-Cola under a pepper tree. "Now we will rest." The family now saw us off with the greatest good humour, as if I were a bridegroom, leaning into the taxi to shake my hand and mutter blessings. "It was a canonical price," said the old greybeard, as a parting blessing. One could not say fairer than that.

"And now," said Sabri, "I will take you to a special place of mine to taste the *meltemi* wind —what is the time? Yes, in half an hour."

High upon the bastions of Kyrenia castle was a narrow balcony which served the police officers as a mess. Sabri, I discovered later, was a sergeant in the specials. Here, gazing across the radiant harbour-bar towards the Caramanian mountains, we sat ourselves down in solitude and space like a couple of emperors while a bewildering succession of cold beers found their way out on to the table-cloth, backed up by various saucers full of delicious Cypriot comestibles. And here Sabri's wind punctually arrived—the faintest breath of coolness, stirring across the waters of the harbour, ruffling them. "You see?" he said quietly, raising his cheek to it like a sail. He was obviously endowed with that wonderful Moslem quality which is called *kayf* —the contemplation which comes of silence and ease. It is not meditation or reverie, which presupposes a conscious mind relaxing: it is something deeper, a fathomless repose of the will which does not even pose to itself the question: "Am I happy or unhappy?"

He had been jotting on a slip of paper and now he handed it to me, saying: "Now your troubles begin, for you will have to alter the house. Here, I have costed it for you. A bathroom will cost you so much. The balcony, at so much a cubic foot, should cost you so much. If you sell the beams—they fetch three pounds each, and there are eighty—you should have so much in hand. This is only for your private information, as a check, my dear." He lit a cigarette and smiled gently. "Now the man you want to build for you is Andreas Kallergis. He is good and honest—though of course he is a rogue like me! But he will do you a solid job— for much can go wrong, you know. You will find the cost of cement brick there, and rendering per cubic metre."

I tried to express my gratitude but he waved his hand. "My dear Durrell," he said, "when one

is warm to me I am warm to him back. You are my friend now and I shall never change even if you do."

We drank deeply and in silence. "I was sent to you by a Greek," I said, "and now the Turk sends me back to a Greek."

He laughed aloud. "Cyprus is small," he said, "and we are all friends, though very different. This is Cyprus, my dear."

It seemed in that warm honey-gold afternoon a delectable island in which to spend some years of one's life.

I
"WE ARE ALL FRIENDS, THOUGH VERY DIFFERENT"

Haggling is expected as a part of the business pattern of Cyprus. In truth, each side thoroughly enjoys the battle of wits that takes place. To the Western mind, the custom is puzzling. Hence, it is amusing to see how Durrell is confused and distraught as the game of bargaining is played before him when he attempts to buy a house.

Consider the following and discuss:

1. What are the foibles Durrell is exploring?

2. How are these foibles amusing? Troubling? Incomprehensible?

3. How are Durrell's own foibles as an English citizen illuminated?

II
IMPLICATIONS

Does the story bear out or refute the following statements? How do you yourself feel about these statements?

1. Bargaining is a part of everyone's life.

2. The haggling of the Cypriots is without lasting rancor because they accept and understand that it is the custom in business dealings. In our society, haggling in business dealings is considered undignified.

3. Durrell is really amazed at the foibles of the Cypriots.

4. "But we must take time. In Cyprus time is everything," says Sabri. Do you think this attitude represents a foible or a virtue?

TECHNIQUES

Setting

What does the setting do for the story? How necessary are all the details to the story?

Tell everything that you know from Durrell's story about:

1. Sabri's "godown."
2. The locale of Kyrenia.
3. Jamal's taxicab.
4. The town of Bellapaix.

Prose Style

Reread the first four paragraphs of this essay. Then answer the following questions:

1. Are Durrell's sentences short or long? Or a mixture? How does this affect your ability to read the paragraphs?

2. Consider the following adjectives. Which ones best describe the kinds of words Durrell uses? Are the words precise or vague? Are they ordinary or unusual? Elaborate or simple? Give examples to support your answers.

3. What mood do you feel Durrell is trying to create: comic, tragic, romantic, realistic? How does Durrell create the mood of the essay?

4. In these four paragraphs explain how Durrell balances the following opposites:
   a. Action and inaction.
   b. Light and dark.
   c. Turks and Greeks.

In what way does this balancing contribute to the mood? How does it mark his style?

IV
WORDS

A. Words for context clue exercises for dictionary study: *disembodied, monolithic, harangue, propitious, maundering, icon, paroxysm, nonagenarian, execrations, comestible.*

B. In Durrell's story, explain the following figures of speech by naming the two things being compared.

a sun-blistered legend
disembodied pieces of machinery
the carcasses of buses
a circular saw . . . gnashed all day
the Turk has a monolithic poise
the price of land had been soaring
its castle taking the last lion-gold rays of the
    evening upon its tawny flanks

GIOVANNI BOCCACCIO

Giovanni Boccaccio[1] (1313–1375) is one of Italy's great literary figures. The son of an Italian merchant and a French woman, he was born in Paris, France, but later moved to Florence, Italy, with his father. Boccaccio had a miserable childhood and was constantly frustrated by his father's lack of sympathy for his writing. Sent to Naples at the age of fifteen, he worked for six years there in a commercial house and spent another six studying canon law. Fortunately for Boccaccio, King Robert, whose court was in Naples, enjoyed having literary men around him. The young poet thus gained easy entrance to the court, which impressed upon him its noble ideals of courage, self-control, and courtesy. After returning to Florence in 1340, Boccaccio wrote his finest works, culminating in *The Decameron*, a masterpiece composed between 1349 and 1351. The piece begins as seven women and three men flee to a country villa in the hills to escape the Black Death raging in Florence. During their stay, each person "reigns" for a day and controls the tone and subject matter of all the entertainment, from conversation to storytelling. Each person tells one story on each of ten different afternoons for a total of one hundred stories. The title, meaning "ten days' work," was created by Boccaccio from two Greek words: *deca* meaning "ten," and *hemera*, meaning "day." Owing to the influence of Petrarch, his great literary contemporary, Boccaccio stopped writing creative works and turned to scholarly pursuits. Never an expert at managing his money, Boccaccio lived his last years almost destitute. In failing health, he retired to Certaldo, where he died. He was buried in the church of SS. Michele e Jacopo, but his bones seem to have been scattered in 1783.

The Decameron

translated from the Italian by Richard Aldington

Federigo's Falcon

FIFTH DAY, NINTH TALE

Filomena had ceased speaking, and the queen, seeing that nobody was left to speak except Dioneo (who had his privilege) and herself, began cheerfully as follows:

It is now my turn to speak, dearest ladies, and I shall gladly do so with a tale similar in part to the one before, not only that you may know the power of your beauty over the gentle heart, but because you may learn yourselves to be givers of rewards when fitting, without allowing Fortune always to dispense them, since Fortune most often bestows them, not discreetly but lavishly.

You must know then that Coppo di Borghese Domenichi,[2] who was and perhaps still is one of

---

1. **Boccaccio** (bō kä′chē ō).
2. **Coppo di Borghese Domenichi** (kō′pō dē bôr gä′zə dō men ē′kē).

Giovanni Boccaccio

our fellow citizens, a man of great and revered authority in our days both from his manners and his virtues (far more than from nobility of blood), a most excellent person worthy of eternal fame, and in the fullness of his years, delighted often to speak of past matters with his neighbours and other men. And this he could do better and more orderly and with a better memory and more ornate speech than anyone else.

Among other excellent things, he was wont to say that in the past there was in Florence a young man named Federigo, the son of Messer Filippo Alberighi, renowned above all other young gentlemen of Tuscany[3] for his prowess in arms and his courtesy. Now, as most often happens to gentlemen, he fell in love with a lady named Monna Giovanna, in her time held to be one of the gayest and most beautiful women ever known in Florence. To win her love, he went to jousts[4] and tourneys,[5] made and gave feasts,

and spent his money without stint. But she, no less chaste than beautiful, cared nothing for the things he did for her nor for him who did them.

Now as Federigo was spending far beyond his means and getting nothing in, as easily happens, his wealth failed and he remained poor with nothing but a little farm, on whose produce he lived very penuriously, and one falcon which was among the best in the world. More in love than ever, but thinking he would never be able to live in the town anymore as he desired, he went to Campi where his farm was. There he spent his time hawking,[6] asked nothing of anybody, and patiently endured his poverty.

Now while Federigo was in this extremity it happened one day that Monna Giovanna's husband fell ill, and seeing death come upon him, made his will. He was a very rich man and left his estate to a son who was already growing up. And then, since he had greatly loved Monna Giovanna, he made her his heir in case his son should die without legitimate children; and so died.

Monna Giovanna was now a widow, and as is customary with our women, she went with her son to spend the year in a country house she had near Federigo's farm. Now the boy happened to strike up a friendship with Federigo, and delighted in dogs and hawks. He often saw Federigo's falcon fly, and took such great delight in it that he very much wanted to have it, but did not dare ask for it, since he saw how much Federigo prized it.

While matters were in this state, the boy fell ill. His mother was very much grieved, as he was her only child and she loved him extremely. She spent the day beside him, trying to help him, and often asked him if there was anything he wanted, begging him to say so, for if it were possible to have it, she would try to get it for him. After she had many times made this offer, the boy said:

"Mother, if you can get me Federigo's falcon, I think I should soon be better."

The lady paused a little at this, and began to think what she should do. She knew that Federigo had loved her for a long time, and yet had

---

3. **Tuscany** (tus′kə nē), a northwestern region of Italy.
4. **jousts** (justs) *or* (jousts), combats on horseback between knights using lances.
5. **tourneys** (tėr′nēz), tournaments.
6. **hawking**, a method of hunting birds by using a trained hawk.

never had one glance from her, and she said to herself:

"How can I send or go and ask for this falcon, which is, from what I hear, the best that ever flew, and moreover his support in life? How can I be so thoughtless as to take this away from a gentleman who has no other pleasure left in life?"

Although she knew she was certain to have the bird for the asking, she remained in embarrassed thought, not knowing what to say, and did not answer her son. But at length love for her child got the upper hand and she determined that to please him in whatever way it might be, she would not send, but go herself for it and bring it back to him. So she replied:

"Be comforted, my child, and try to get better somehow. I promise you that tomorrow morning I will go for it, and bring it to you."

The child was so delighted that he became a little better that same day. And on the morrow the lady took another woman to accompany her, and as if walking for exercise went to Federigo's cottage, and asked for him. Since it was not the weather for it, he had not been hawking for some days, and was in his garden employed in certain work there. When he heard that Monna Giovanna was asking for him at the door, he was greatly astonished, and ran there happily. When she saw him coming, she got up to greet him with womanly charm, and when Federigo had courteously saluted her, she said:

"How do you do, Federigo? I have come here to make amends for the damage you have suffered through me by loving me more than was needed. And in token of this, I intend to dine today familiarly with you and my companion here."

"Madonna,"[7] replied Federigo humbly, "I do not remember ever to have suffered any damage through you, but received so much good that if I was ever worth anything it was owing to your worth and the love I bore it. Your generous visit to me is so precious to me that I could spend again all that I have spent; but you have come to a poor host."

7. **Madonna,** my lady (in Italian).

So saying, he modestly took her into his house, and from there to his garden. Since there was nobody else to remain in her company, he said:

"Madonna, since there is nobody else, this good woman, the wife of this workman, will keep you company, while I go to set the table."

Now, although his poverty was extreme, he had never before realised what necessity he had fallen into by his foolish extravagance in spending his wealth. But he repented of it that morning when he could find nothing with which to do honour to the lady, for love of whom he had entertained vast numbers of men in the past. In his anguish he cursed himself and his fortune and ran up and down like a man out his senses, unable to find money or anything to pawn. The hour was late and his desire to honour the lady extreme, yet he would not apply to anyone else, even to his own workman; when suddenly his eye fell upon his falcon, perched on a bar in the sitting room. Having no one to whom he could appeal, he took the bird, and finding it plump, decided it would be food worthy such a lady. So, without further thought, he wrung its neck, made his little maid servant quickly pluck and prepare it, and put it on a spit to roast. He spread the table with the whitest napery, of which he had some left, and returned to the lady in the garden with a cheerful face, saying that the meal he had been able to prepare for her was ready.

The lady and her companion arose and went to table, and there together with Federigo, who served it with the greatest devotion, they ate the good falcon, not knowing what it was. They left the table and spent some time in cheerful conversation, and the lady, thinking the time had now come to say what she had come for, spoke fairly to Federigo as follows:

"Federigo, when you remember your former life and my chastity, which no doubt you considered harshness and cruelty, I have no doubt that you will be surprised at my presumption when you hear what I have come here for chiefly. But if you had children, through whom you could know the power of parental love, I am certain that you would to some extent excuse me.

"But, as you have no child, I have one, and I cannot escape the common laws of mothers. Compelled by their power, I have come to ask you—against my will, and against all good manners and duty—for a gift, which I know is something especially dear to you, and reasonably so, because I know your straitened fortune has left you no other pleasure, no other recreation, no other consolation. This gift is your falcon, which has so fascinated my child that if I do not take it to him, I am afraid his present illness will grow so much worse that I may lose him. Therefore I beg you, not by the love you bear me (which holds you to nothing), but by your own nobleness, which has shown itself so much greater in all courteous usage than is wont in other men, that you will be pleased to give it me, so that through this gift I may be able to say that I have saved my child's life, and thus be ever under an obligation to you."

When Federigo heard the lady's request and knew that he could not serve her, because he had given her the bird to eat, he began to weep in her presence, for he could not speak a word. The lady at first thought that his grief came from having to part with his good falcon, rather than from anything else, and she was almost on the point of retraction. But she remained firm and waited for Federigo's reply after his lamentation. And he said:

"Madonna, ever since it has pleased God that I should set my love upon you, I have felt that Fortune has been contrary to me in many things, and have grieved for it. But they are all light in comparison with what she has done to me now, and I shall never be at peace with her again when I reflect that you came to my poor house, which you never deigned to visit when it was rich, and asked me for a little gift, and Fortune has so acted that I cannot give it to you. Why this cannot be, I will briefly tell you.

"When I heard that you in your graciousness desired to dine with me and I thought of your excellence and your worthiness, I thought it right and fitting to honour you with the best food I could obtain; so, remembering the falcon you ask me for and its value, I thought it a meal worthy of you, and today you had it roasted on the dish and set forth as best I could. But now I see that you wanted the bird in another form, it is such a grief to me that I cannot serve you that I think I shall never be at peace again."

And after saying this, he showed her the feathers and the feet and the beak of the bird in proof. When the lady heard and saw all this, she first blamed him for having killed such a falcon to make a meal for a woman; and then she inwardly commended his greatness of soul which no poverty could or would be able to abate. But, having lost all hope of obtaining the falcon, and thus perhaps the health of her son, she departed sadly and returned to the child. Now, either from disappointment at not having the falcon or because his sickness must inevitably have led to it, the child died not many days later, to the mother's extreme grief.

Although she spent some time in tears and bitterness, yet, since she had been left very rich and was still young, her brothers often urged her to marry again. She did not want to do so, but as they kept on pressing her, she remembered the worthiness of Federigo and his last act of generosity, in killing such a falcon to do her honour.

"I will gladly submit to marriage when you please," she said to her brothers, "but if you want me to take a husband, I will take no man but Federigo degli Alberighi."

At this her brothers laughed at her, saying:

"Why, what are you talking about, you fool? Why do you want a man who hasn't a penny in the world?"

But she replied:

"Brothers, I know it is as you say, but I would rather have a man who needs money than money which needs a man."

Seeing her determination, the brothers, who knew Federigo's good qualities, did as she wanted, and gave her with all her wealth to him, in spite of his poverty. Federigo, finding that he had such a woman, whom he loved so much, with all her wealth to boot, as his wife, was more prudent with his money in the future, and ended his days happily with her.

The One-Legged Crane

SIXTH DAY, FOURTH TALE

Lauretta was silent, and they all praised Nonna; whereupon the queen ordered Neifile to follow next. And she said:

Amorous ladies, although quick wits often provide speakers with useful and witty words, yet Fortune, which sometimes aids the timid, often puts words into their mouths which they would never have thought of in a calm moment. This I intend to show you by my tale.

As everyone of you must have heard and seen, Currado Gianfigliazzi[8] was always a noble citizen of our city, liberal and magnificent, leading a gentleman's life, continually delighting in dogs and hawks, and allowing his more serious affairs to slide. One day near Peretola his falcon brought down a crane, and finding it to be plump and young he sent it to his excellent cook, a Venetian named Chichibio,[9] telling him to roast it for supper and see that it was well done.

Chichibio, who was a bit of a fool, prepared the crane, set it before the fire, and began to cook it carefully. When it was nearly done and giving off a most savoury odour, there came into the kitchen a young peasant woman, named Brunetta, with whom Chichibio was very much in love. Smelling the odour of the bird and seeing it, she begged Chichibio to give her a leg of it. But he replied with a snatch of song:

"You won't get it from me, Donna Brunetta, you won't get it from me."

This made Donna Brunetta angry, and she said:

"Believe me, if you don't give it me, you'll never get anything you want from me."

In short, they had high words together. In the end Chichibio, not wanting to anger his ladylove, took off one of the crane's legs, and gave it to her. A little later the one-legged crane was served before Currado and his guests. Currado was astonished at the sight, sent for Chichibio, and asked him what happened to the other leg of the crane. The lying Venetian replied:

"Sir, cranes only have one leg and one foot."

"What the devil d'you mean," said Currado angrily, "by saying they have only one leg and foot? Did I never see a crane before?"

"It's as I say, Sir," Chichibio persisted, "and I'll show it you in living birds whenever you wish."

Currado would not bandy further words from respect to his guests, but said:

"Since you promise to show me in living birds something I never saw or heard of, I shall be glad to see it tomorrow morning. But, by my life, if it turns out otherwise I'll have you tanned in such a way that you'll remember my name as long as you live."

When day appeared next morning, Currado, who had not been able to sleep for rage all night, got up still furious, and ordered his horses to be brought. He made Chichibio mount a pad, and took him in the direction of a river where cranes could always be seen at that time of day, saying:

"We'll soon see whether you were lying or not last night."

Chichibio, seeing that Currado was still angry and that he must try to prove his lie, which he had not the least idea how to do, rode alongside Currado in a state of consternation, and would willingly have fled if he had known how. But as he couldn't do that, he kept gazing round him and thought everything he saw was a crane with two legs. But when they came to the river, he happened to be the first to see a dozen cranes on the bank, all standing on one leg as they do when they are asleep. He quickly pointed them out to Currado, saying:

"Messer, you can see that what I said last evening is true, that cranes have only one leg and one foot; you have only to look at them over there."

"Wait," said Currado, "I'll show you they have two."

And going up closer to them, he shouted: "Ho! Ho!" And at this the cranes put down their other

---

8. **Gianfigliazzi** (jän'fē lē ät'zē).
9. **Chichibio** (kē kē'byō).

legs and, after running a few steps, took to flight. Currado then turned to Chichibio, saying:

"Now, you glutton, what of it? D'you think they have two?"

In his dismay Chichibio, not knowing how the words came to him, replied:

"Yes, messer, but you didn't shout 'ho! ho!' to the bird last night. If you had shouted, it would have put out the other leg and foot, as those did."

Currado was so pleased with this answer that all his anger was converted into merriment and laughter, and he said:

"Chichibio, you're right; I ought to have done so."

So with this quick and amusing answer Chichibio escaped punishment, and made his peace with his master.

I
THE OUTWITTED AND THE WITTY

Tales such as these have long been favorites with both storytellers and listeners. Federigo loves so passionately that he sacrifices his last possession to please his lady. The bumbling rogue lies his way out of a situation by the quickness of his wit. Why do we enjoy these two stories? Perhaps because we really admire these people even though we see the absurdity of their actions.

II
IMPLICATIONS

Although these two stories are light and amusing, we still find ideas to reflect upon. Consider, for example, the following statements:

1. According to *The Decameron*, to be truly noble we must accept life as it is without bitterness; we must accept, above all, the consequences of our own actions however contrary to expectation they may be. Such nobility is examined in both these tales.

2. We have a grudging admiration for an ingenious lie.

3. Love can cause a normally rational person to behave foolishly.

III
TECHNIQUES

Setting

Like *The Canterbury Tales*, these two stories are placed in a framework. They are told by wealthy aristocrats who have fled to a country house to escape the plague. In what way does this setting add meaning to each of the stories?

Prose Style

The style, even in translation, comes across as old-fashioned and leisurely because it contains long and highly modified sentences. Look at paragraph 4 of "Federigo's Falcon," beginning with the words, "Among other excellent things. . . ." Pick out the subject and predicate of each sentence. Note the number of modifiers that surround these basic parts.

ILSE AICHINGER

The underlying theme of Ilse Aichinger's[1] (1921–   ) works is always the
same—human bondage that all too often is accepted willingly or with
indifference. She was born in Vienna. Her childhood was a normal one until
1938. Then, her family suffered greatly, and she was forced to discontinue
her studies until after the war. During two years as a medical student,
Aichinger wrote her only novel, *The Greater Hope*, published in 1948. It holds
the germ of nearly all her later works. Her style of writing has not
changed over the years, though she has moved from novel to short story
to radio play to lyric poem and finally to dialogue that employs the Socratic
method. Many consider this dialogue technique her special contribution to
midcentury literature. Symbolism is strong in Aichinger's writing.
Relying heavily on dream elements, she often weaves hidden parables into her
stories. She makes frequent reference to colors, especially green. Becoming
increasingly critical of the complacency of some cultural groups,
Aichinger has collaborated in drawing up and presenting manifestos against
war. She lives in her native Austria with her husband, Gunter Eich.

The Bound Man

Sunlight on his face woke him, but made him
shut his eyes again; it streamed unhindered
down the slope, collected itself into rivulets,
attracted swarms of flies, which flew low over
his forehead, circled, sought to land, and were
overtaken by fresh swarms. When he tried to
whisk them away he discovered that he was
bound.

A thin rope cut into his arms. He dropped
them, opened his eyes again, and looked down
at himself. His legs were tied all the way up to
his thighs; a single length of rope was tied round
his ankles, crisscrossed all the way up his legs,
and encircled his hips, his chest and his arms.
He could not see where it was knotted.

He showed no sign of fear or hurry, though
he thought he was unable to move, until he discovered that the rope allowed his legs some free

play, and that round his body it was almost
loose. His arms were tied to each other but not
to his body, and had some free play, too. This
made him smile, and it occurred to him that
perhaps children had been playing a practical
joke on him.

He tried to feel for his knife, but again the
rope cut softly into his flesh. He tried again,
more cautiously this time, but his pocket was
empty. Not only his knife, but the little money
that he had on him, as well as his coat, was missing. His shoes had been taken too. When he
moistened his lips he tasted blood, which had
flowed from his temples down his cheeks, his
chin, his neck, and under his shirt. His eyes
were painful; if he kept them open for long he
saw reddish stripes in the sky.

He decided to stand up. He drew his knees
up as far as he could, rested his hands on the
fresh grass and jerked himself to his feet. An
elder branch stroked his cheek, the sun dazzled
him, and the rope cut into his flesh. He collapsed to the ground again, half out of his mind

1. **Ilse Aichinger** (il'sə īk'in gər).

"The Bound Man" from *The Bound Man and Other Stories* by Ilse
Aichinger. Copyright 1956 by Ilse Aichinger. Reprinted with the permission of Farrar, Straus & Giroux, Inc.

with pain, and then tried again. He went on trying until the blood started flowing from his hidden weals. Then he lay still again for a long while, and let the sun and the flies do what they liked.

When he awoke for the second time the elder bush had cast its shadow over him, and the coolness stored in it was pouring from between its branches. He must have been hit on the head. Then they must have laid him down carefully, just as a mother lays her baby behind a bush when she goes to work in the fields.

His chances all lay in the amount of free play allowed him by the rope. He dug his elbows into the ground and tested it. As soon as the rope tautened he stopped, and tried again more cautiously. If he had been able to reach the branch over his head he could have used it to drag himself to his feet, but he could not reach it. He laid his head back on the grass, rolled over, and struggled to his knees, then managed to stand up almost without effort.

A few paces away lay the path across the plateau, and among the grass were wild pinks and thistles in bloom. He tried to lift his foot to avoid trampling on them, but the rope round his ankles prevented him. He looked down at himself.

The rope was knotted at his ankles, and ran round his legs in a kind of playful pattern. He carefully bent and tried to loosen it, but, loose though it seemed to be, he could not make it

any looser. To avoid treading on the thistles with his bare feet he hopped over them like a bird.

The cracking of a twig made him stop. People in this district were very prone to laughter. He was alarmed by the thought that he was in no position to defend himself. He hopped on until he reached the path. Bright fields stretched far below. He could see no sign of the nearest village, and, if he could move no faster than this, night would fall before he reached it.

He tried walking, and discovered that he could put one foot before another if he lifted each foot a definite distance from the ground and then put it down again before the rope tautened. In the same way he could swing his arms a little.

After the first step he fell. He fell right across the path and made the dust fly. He expected this to be a sign for the long-suppressed laughter to break out, but all remained quiet. He was alone. As soon as the dust had settled he got up and went on. He looked down and watched the rope slacken, grow taut, and then slacken. He felt in control of himself again, and his impatience to reach the nearest village faded.

Hunger made him light-headed, and he seemed to be going so fast that not even a motorcycle could have overtaken him; alternately he felt as if he were standing still and that the earth was rushing past him, like a river flowing past a man swimming against the stream.

The moon had risen, and illuminated the bare, curved summit of the plateau, the path which was overgrown with young grass, the bound man making his way along it with quick, measured steps, and two hares, which ran across the hill just in front of him and vanished down the slope. Though the nights were still cool at this time of the year, before midnight the bound man lay down at the edge of the escarpment[2] and went to sleep.

In the light of morning the animal tamer who was camping with his circus in the field outside the village saw the bound man coming down the path, gazing thoughtfully at the ground. The bound man stopped and bent down. He held out one arm to help keep his balance and with the other picked up an empty wine bottle. Then he straightened himself and stood erect again. He moved slowly to avoid being cut by the rope, but to the circus proprietor what he did suggested the voluntary limitation of an enormous swiftness of movement. He was enchanted by its extraordinary gracefulness, and while the bound man looked about for a stone on which to break the bottle, so that he could use the splintered neck to cut the rope, the animal tamer walked across the field and approached him. The first leaps of a young panther had never filled him with such delight.

"Ladies and gentlemen, the bound man!" His very first movements let loose a storm of applause which caused the blood to rush to the cheeks of the animal tamer standing at the edge of the arena.

The bound man rose to his feet. His surprise whenever he did this was like that of a four-footed animal which has managed to stand on its hind legs. He knelt, stood up, jumped, and turned cartwheels. The spectators found it as astonishing as if they had seen a bird which voluntarily remained earthbound, and confined itself to hopping.

The bound man became an enormous draw.

---

2. **escarpment** (e skärp′mənt), cliff.

His absurd steps and little jumps, his elementary exercises in movement, made the rope-dancer superfluous. His fame grew from village to village, but the motions he went through were few and always the same; they were really quite ordinary motions, which he had continually to practice in the daytime in the half-dark tent in order to retain his shackled freedom. In that he remained entirely within the limits set by his rope he was free of it—it did not confine him, but gave him wings and endowed his leaps and jumps with purpose; just as the flights of birds of passage have purpose when they take wing in the warmth of summer and hesitantly make small circles in the sky.

All the children of the neighborhood started playing the game of "bound man." They formed rival gangs, and one day the circus people found a little girl lying bound in a ditch, with a cord tied round her neck so that she could hardly breathe. They released her, and at the end of the performance that night the bound man made a speech. He announced briefly that there was no sense in being tied up in such a way that you could not jump. After that he was regarded as a comedian.

Grass and sunlight, tent pegs into the ground and then pulled up again, and on to the next village. "Ladies and gentlemen, the bound man!" The summer mounted towards its climax. It bent its face deeper over the fish ponds in the hollows, taking delight in its dark reflection, skimmed the surface of the rivers.

Everyone who could walk went to see the bound man. Many wanted a close-up view of how he was bound. The circus proprietor announced after each performance that anyone who wanted to satisfy himself that the knots were real and the rope not made of rubber was at liberty to do so.

The bound man generally waited for the crowd in the area outside the tent. He laughed or remained serious, and held out his arms for inspection. Many took the opportunity to look him in the face, others gravely tested the rope, tried the knots on his ankles, and wanted to know exactly how the lengths compared with the length of his limbs.

They asked him how he had been robbed as well. Those who had done it must have been pressed for time, because they had tied him up somewhat too loosely for someone who was not supposed to be able to move and somewhat too tightly for someone who was expected to be able to move. When the circus proprietor asked him why he didn't make up a better story, he always answered that he hadn't made up that one, and blushed.

The difference between him and the other performers was that when the show was over he did not take off his rope. The result was that every movement that he made was worth seeing, and the villagers used to hang about the camp for hours, just for the sake of seeing him get up from in front of the fire and roll himself in his blanket.

The circus proprietor often remarked that there was no reason why he should not be untied after the evening performance and tied up again next day. He pointed out that the ropedancers, for instance, did not stay on their rope over night. But no one took the idea of untying him seriously.

For the bound man's fame rested on the fact that he was always bound, that whenever he washed himself he had to wash his clothes too and vice versa, and that his only way of doing so was to jump in the river just as he was every morning when the sun came out, and that he had to be careful not to go too far out for fear of being carried away by the stream.

The proprietor was well aware that what in the last resort protected the bound man from the jealousy of the other performers was his helplessness; he deliberately left them the pleasure of watching him groping painfully from stone to stone on the river bank every morning with his wet clothes clinging to him. When his wife pointed out that even the best clothes would not stand up indefinitely to such treatment (and the bound man's clothes were by no means of the best) he replied curtly that it was not going to last for ever.

That was his answer to all objections—it was for the season only. But when he said this he was not being serious; he was talking like a gambler who has no intention of giving up his vice. In reality he would have been prepared cheerfully to sacrifice his lions and his ropedancers for the bound man.

He proved this on the night when the ropedancers jumped over the fire. Afterwards he was convinced that they did it, not because it was midsummer's day, but because of the bound man, who as usual was lying and watching them, with that peculiar smile that might have been real or might have been only the effect of the glow on his face. In any case, no one knew anything about him, because he never talked about anything that had happened to him before he emerged from the wood that day.

But that evening two of the performers suddenly picked him up by the arms and legs, carried him to the edge of the fire and started playfully swinging him to and fro, while two others held out their arms to catch him on the other side. In the end they threw him, but too short. The two men on the other side drew back—they explained afterwards that they did so the better to take the shock.

The result was that the bound man landed at the very edge of the flames and would have been burned if the circus proprietor had not seized his arms and quickly dragged him away to save the rope, which was starting to get singed. He was certain that the object had been to burn the rope. He sacked the four men on the spot.

A few nights later the proprietor's wife was awakened by the sound of footsteps on the grass, and went outside just in time to prevent the clown from playing his last practical joke. He was carrying a pair of scissors. When asked for an explanation he insisted that he had had no intention of taking the bound man's life, but only wanted to cut his rope, because he felt sorry for him. But he was sacked too.

These antics amused the bound man, because he could have freed himself if he had wanted to whenever he liked, but perhaps he wanted to learn a few new jumps first. The children's rhyme, "We travel with the circus, we travel with the circus," sometimes occurred to him while he lay awake at night.

The circus proprietor dreaded the danger involved for the bound man by sleep. Attempts were continually made to release him while he slept. The chief culprits were sacked rope-dancers, or children who were bribed for the purpose. But measures could be taken to safeguard against these.

A much bigger danger was that which he represented to himself. In his dreams he forgot his rope, and was surprised by it when he woke in the darkness of morning. He would angrily try to get up, but lose his balance and fall back again. The previous evening's applause was forgotten, sleep was still too near, his head and neck too free. You had to make sure that at such moments no knife was within his reach. In the early hours of the morning the circus proprietor sometimes sent his wife to see whether the bound man was all right. If he was asleep she would bend over him and feel the rope. It had grown hard from dirt and damp. She would test the amount of free play it allowed him, and touch his tender wrists and ankles.

The most varied rumors circulated about the bound man. Some said he had tied himself up and invented the story of having been robbed, and toward the end of the summer that was the general opinion. Others maintained that he had been tied up at his own request, perhaps in league with the circus proprietor. The hesitant way in which he told his story, his habit of breaking off when the talk got round to the attack on him, contributed greatly to these rumors.

Those who still believed in the robbery-with-violence story were laughed at. Nobody knew what difficulties the circus proprietor had in keeping the bound man, and how often he said he had had enough and wanted to clear off, for too much of the summer had passed.

Later, however, he stopped talking about clearing off. When the proprietor's wife brought him his food by the river and asked him how long he proposed to remain with them, he did not answer. She thought he had got used, not to being tied up, but to not forgetting for a moment that he was tied up—the only thing that anyone in his position could get used to.

She asked him whether he did not think it ridiculous to be tied up all the time, but he answered that he did not. Such a variety of people—clowns, freaks, and comics to say nothing of elephants and tigers—traveled with circuses that he did not see why a bound man should not travel with a circus, too.

He told her about the movements he was practicing, the new ones he had discovered, and about a new trick that had occurred to him. He described to her how he always anticipated the effect of the rope and always restrained his movements in such a way as to prevent it from ever tautening; and she knew that there were days when he was hardly aware of the rope when he jumped down from the wagon and slapped the flanks of the horses in the morning, as if he were moving in a dream.

She watched him vault over the bars almost without touching them, and saw the sun on his face, and he told her that sometimes he felt as if he were not tied up at all. She answered that if he were prepared to be untied there would never be any need for him to feel tied up. He agreed that he could be untied whenever he felt like it.

The woman ended by not knowing whether she were more concerned with the man or with the rope that tied him. She told him that he could go on traveling with the circus without his rope, but she did not believe it. For what would be the point of his antics without his rope, and what would he amount to without it? Without his rope he would leave them, and the happy days would be over. She knew that his continued presence, and her conversations with him, of which the rope was the only subject, depended on it. Whenever she agreed that the rope had its advantages, he would start talking about how troublesome it was, and whenever he started talking about its advantages she would urge him to get rid of it. All this seemed as endless as the summer itself.

At other times she was worried at the thought that she was herself hastening the end by her talk. Sometimes she would get up in the middle of the night and run across the grass to where he slept. She wanted to shake him, wake him up and ask him to keep the rope. But then she would see him lying there; he had thrown off his blanket, and there he lay like a corpse, with his legs outstretched and his arms close together, with the rope tied round them. His clothes had suffered from the heat and the water, but the rope had grown no thinner. She felt that he would go on traveling with the circus until the flesh fell from him and exposed the joints. Next morning she would plead with him more ardently than ever to get rid of his rope.

The increasing coolness of the weather gave her hope. Autumn was coming and he would not be able to go on jumping into the river with his clothes on much longer. But the thought of losing his rope, about which he had felt indifferent earlier in the season, now depressed him.

The songs of the harvesters filled him with foreboding. "Summer has gone, summer has gone." But he realized that soon he would have to change his clothes, and he was certain that when he had been untied it would be impossible to tie him up again in exactly the same way. About this time the proprietor started talking about traveling south that year.

The heat changed without transition into quiet, dry cold. When the bound man jumped down from the wagon he felt the coldness of the grass under his feet.

One of these days a young wolf escaped. The circus proprietor kept quiet about it, to avoid spreading alarm, but the wolf soon started raiding cattle in the neighborhood. People at first believed that the wolf had been driven to these parts by the prospect of a severe winter, but the circus soon became suspect.

The circus people offered their aid in tracking down the beast, but all their efforts were vain. Eventually the circus was openly blamed for the damage and the danger, and spectators stayed away.

The bound man went on performing before half-empty seats without losing anything of his amazing freedom of movement. During the day he wandered among the surrounding hills under the thin-beaten silver of the autumn sky, and, whenever he could, lay down where the sun shone longest. Soon he found a place which the twilight reached last of all, and when at last it reached him he got up most unwillingly from the withered grass.

In coming down the hill he had to pass through a little wood, and one evening he saw the gleam of two little green lights. He knew that they came from no church window, and was not for a moment under any illusion about what they were.

He stopped. The animal came towards him through the thinning foliage. He could make out its shape, the slant of its neck, its tail which swept the ground, its receding head.

If he had not been bound, perhaps he would have tried to run away, but as it was he did not even feel fear. He stood calmly with dangling arms and looked down at the wolf's bristling coat under which the muscles played like his own underneath the rope. He thought the evening wind was still between him and the wolf when the beast sprang. The man took care to obey his rope.

Moving with the deliberate care that he had so often put to the test, he seized the wolf by the throat. Tenderness for a fellow creature arose in him, tenderness for the upright being concealed in the four-footed. In a movement that resembled the drive of a great bird—he felt a sudden awareness that flying would be possible only if one were tied up in a special way—he flung himself at the animal and brought it to the ground. He felt a slight elation at having lost the fatal advantage of free limbs which causes men to be worsted.

The freedom he enjoyed in this struggle

was having to adapt every movement of his limbs to the rope that tied him—the freedom of panthers, wolves, and the wild flowers that sway in the evening breeze. He ended up lying obliquely down the slope, clasping the animal's hindlegs between his own bare feet and its head between his hands. He felt the gentleness of the faded foliage stroking the back of his hands, and he felt his own grip almost effortlessly reaching its maximum, and he felt, too, how he was in no way hampered by the rope.

The circus proprietor's wife tried to persuade her husband to announce the death of the wolf without mentioning that it had been killed by the bound man. She said that even at the time of his greatest popularity people would have refused to believe him capable of it, and in their present angry mood, with the nights getting cooler, they would be more incredulous than ever.

The wolf had attacked a group of children at play that day, and nobody would believe that it had really been killed; for the circus proprietor had many wolves, and it was easy enough for him to hang a skin on the rail and allow free entry. But he was not to be dissuaded. He thought that the announcement of the bound man's act would revive the triumphs of the summer.

That evening the bound man's movements were uncertain. He stumbled in one of his jumps, and fell. Before he managed to get up he heard some low whistles and catcalls, rather like birds calling at dawn. He tried to get up too quickly, as he had done once or twice during the summer, with the result that he tautened the rope and fell back again. He lay still to regain his calm, and listened to the boos and catcalls growing into an uproar.

"Well, bound man, and how did you kill the wolf?" they shouted, and: "Are you the man who killed the wolf?" If he had been one of them he would not have believed it himself. He thought they had a perfect right to be angry: a circus at this time of year, a bound man, an escaped wolf, and all ending up with this.

Some groups of spectators started arguing with others, but the greater part of the audience thought the whole thing a bad joke. By the time he had got to his feet there was such a hubbub that he was barely able to make out individual words. He saw people surging up all round him. This sudden collapse of everything filled him with anger.

They wanted him to repeat his battle with the wolf. He said that such a thing had no place in a circus performance, and the proprietor declared that he did not keep animals to have them slaughtered in front of an audience. But the mob stormed the ring and forced them towards the cages.

The proprietor's wife made her way between the seats to the exit and managed to get round to the cages from the other side. She pushed aside the attendant whom the crowd had forced to open a cage door, but the spectators dragged her back and prevented the door from being shut. She shouted at them that they needn't believe in the bound man if they didn't want to, they had never deserved him—painted clowns were good enough for them.

The bound man felt as if the bursts of laughter were what he had been expecting ever since early May. What had smelt so sweet all through the summer now stank. But, if they insisted, he was ready to take on all the animals in the circus. He had never felt so much at one with his rope.

Gently he pushed the woman aside. Perhaps he would travel south with them after all. He stood in the open doorway of the cage, and he saw the wolf, a strong young animal, rise to its feet, and he heard the proprietor grumbling again about the loss of his exhibits.

He clapped his hands to attract the animal's attention, and when it was near enough he turned to slam the cage door. He looked the woman in the face. Suddenly he remembered the proprietor's warning to suspect of murderous intentions anyone near him who had a sharp instrument in his hand. At the same moment he felt the blade on his wrists, as cool as the water of the river in autumn.

The rope curled up in a tangle beside him while he struggled free. He pushed the woman back, but there was no point in anything he did now. Had he been insufficiently on his guard against those who wanted to release him, against the sympathy in which they wanted to lull him? If she had cut the cord at any other moment it would have been better than this.

He stood in the middle of the cage, and rid himself of the rope like a snake discarding its skin. It amused him to see the spectators shrinking back. Did they realize that he had no choice now? Or that fighting the wolf now would prove nothing whatever? At the same time he felt all his blood rush to his feet. He felt suddenly weak.

The rope, which fell at its feet like a snare, angered the wolf more than the entry of a stranger into its cage. It crouched to spring. The man reeled, and grabbed the pistol that hung ready at the side of the cage. Then, before anyone could stop him, he shot the wolf between the eyes. The animal reared, and touched him in falling.

On the way to the river he heard the footsteps of his pursuers—spectators, the ropedancers, the circus proprietor, and the proprietor's wife. He hid in a clump of bushes and listened to them hurrying past, and later on streaming in the opposite direction back to the camp. The moon shone on the meadow; in that light its color was that of both growth and death.

When he came to the river his anger died away. At dawn it seemed to him as if lumps of ice were floating in the water, and as if snow had fallen, obliterating memory.

I
WHY?

This story confronts the reader with a number of unanswered questions. Why is the man bound so loosely? Why does he wear the ropes continuously, even when offstage? Why is he so appealing to audiences? Why do people keep trying to cut the ropes? Why do the ropes remain new though his clothing begins to wear? Why is he nameless? Does he have no past? But largest of all looms the ultimate question: Is there a meaning? The discussion below may give you some answers.

II
IMPLICATIONS

Reflect on what you have read and consider your own experiences in discussing the statements that follow.

1. All human beings are *bound*.

2. The most important thing for people to learn is what they can do within their own limitations.

3. The story is a comment on the restrictions of freedom in a totalitarian country.

4. There are multiple explanations for why the people want to cut the rope.

5. In the last sentences of the story, the linking together of growth, death, and memory is the key to the story's meaning.

III
TECHNIQUES

Setting

1. The principal setting is a traveling circus. Is the circus ever described? What details are given? Do these total up to a setting?

2. What symbolic associations has the word *circus* garnered through its long existence?

Prose Style

A writing style may be stripped-down or rich, depending on the number of ideas and details that are put into a sentence or a paragraph. These qualities come through even in translation. How would you characterize the style of "The Bound Man"?

IV
WORDS

Sometimes it is interesting to try to write without using any modifiers. Immediately we become aware that we must find verbs that will carry the *quality* of action as well as the action itself. Here are a handful of such verbs used in this story.

grope	to search blindly or uncertainly
sack	(slang) to abruptly dismiss from a job
storm	to rush or attack suddenly and violently
obliterate	to destroy so as to leave no trace
whisk	to sweep with light strokes

HERMANN HESSE

Hermann Hesse[1] (1877–1962), a German novelist, was born at Calw in the Black Forest, the product of a Protestant family of preachers, physicians, and missionaries. He says of his life, "I was as a boy called to the ministry. I broke away from this career very early, was for a number of years a bookseller and dealer in antiques and have published many books since 1899. Since the success of my first novel, *Peter Camenzin* (1904), I have lived without any profession but literature. My books . . . brought me a reading public mostly of young men who have been drawn to me both personally and as a writer and to whom I have become a counselor. The difficulties which in the world today confront the individual and his building of a harmonious personality are felt, as I daily discover, to be very great, especially among young people within the authoritative churches and states. . . ." Hesse, who wrote not only novels but poetry, essays, and short stories, was awarded the Nobel Prize for Literature in 1946 for his novel *Magister Ludi*.
It was not until the 1960s that Hesse's work became popular with college students in this country and, a few years later, with high school students.

A Man by the Name of Ziegler

translated by Ralph Manheim

There was once a young man by the name of Ziegler, who lived on Brauergasse. He was one of those people we see every day on the street, whose faces we can never really remember, because they all have the same face: a collective face.

Ziegler was everything and did everything that such people always are and do. He was not stupid, but neither was he gifted; he loved money and pleasure, liked to dress well, and was as cowardly as most people: his life and activities were governed less by desires and strivings than by prohibitions, by the fear of punishment. Still, he had a number of good qualities and all in all he was a gratifyingly normal young man, whose own person was most interesting and important to him. Like every other man, he regarded himself as an individual, though in reality he was only a specimen, and like other men he regarded himself and his life as the center of the world. He was far removed from all doubts, and when facts contradicted his opinions, he shut his eyes disapprovingly.

As a modern man, he had unlimited respect not only for money, but also for a second power: science. He could not have said exactly what science was, he had in mind something on the order of statistics and perhaps a bit of bacteriology, and he knew how much money and honor the state accorded to science. He especially admired cancer research, for his father had died of cancer, and Ziegler firmly believed that science, which developed so remarkably since then, would not let the same thing happen to him.

Outwardly Ziegler distinguished himself by his tendency to dress somewhat beyond his means, always in the fashion of the year. For since he could not afford the fashions of the

1. **Hermann Hesse** (hėr′män hes′ə).

Reprinted with the permission of Farrar, Straus & Giroux, Inc. from *Stories of Five Decades* by Hermann Hesse, translated by Ralph Manheim. Translation copyright 1954, © 1972 by Farrar, Straus & Giroux, Inc.

Hermann Hesse

charge on Sunday mornings, and the zoo could be visited in the afternoon for a moderate fee.

Wearing his new suit with cloth buttons—he was very fond of it—he set out for the historical museum. He was carrying his thin, elegant, red-lacquered walking cane, which lent him dignity and distinction, but which to his profound displeasure he was obliged to part with at the entrance.

There were all sorts of things to be seen in the lofty rooms, and in his heart the pious visitor sang the praises of almighty science, which here again, as Ziegler observed in reading the meticulous inscriptions on the showcases, proved that it could be counted on. Thanks to these inscriptions, old bric-a-brac, such as rusty keys, broken and tarnished necklaces, and so on, became amazingly interesting. It was marvelous how science looked into everything, understood everything and found a name for it—oh, yes, it would definitely get rid of cancer very soon, maybe it would even abolish death.

In the second room he found a glass case in which he was reflected so clearly that he was able to stop for a moment and check up, carefully and to his entire satisfaction, on his coat, trousers, and the knot of his tie. Pleasantly reassured, he passed on and devoted his attention to the products of some early wood-carvers. Competent men, though shockingly naïve, he reflected benevolently. He also contemplated an old grandfather clock with ivory figures which danced the minuet when it struck the hour, and it too met with his patient approval. Then he began to feel rather bored; he yawned and looked more and more frequently at his watch, which he was not ashamed of showing, for it was solid gold, inherited from his father.

As he saw to his regret, he still had a long way to go until lunchtime, and so he entered another room. Here his curiosity revived. It contained objects of medieval superstition, books of magic, amulets, trappings of witchcraft, and in one corner a whole alchemist's[2]

month or season, it goes without saying that he despised them as foolish affectation. He was a great believer in independence of character and often spoke harshly, among friends and in safe places, of his employers and of the government. I am probably dwelling too long on this portrait. But Ziegler was a charming young fellow, and he has been a great loss to us. For he met with a strange and premature end, which set all his plans and justified hopes at naught.

One Sunday soon after his arrival in our town, he decided on a day's recreation. He had not yet made any real friends and had not yet been able to make up his mind to join a club. Perhaps this was his undoing. It is not good for man to be alone.

He could think of nothing else to do but go sightseeing. After conscientious inquiry and mature reflection he decided on the historical museum and the zoo. The museum was free of

---

2. **alchemist** (al′kə mist), medieval chemist who tried to transform the base metals into gold.

workshop, complete with forge, mortars, pot-bellied flasks, dried-out pig's bladders, bellows, and so on. This corner was roped off, and there was a sign forbidding the public to touch the objects. But one never reads such signs very attentively, and Ziegler was alone in the room.

Unthinkingly he stretched out his arm over the rope and touched a few of the weird things. He had heard and read about the Middle Ages and their comical superstitions; it was beyond him how the people of those days could have bothered with such childish nonsense, and he failed to see why such absurdities as witch-craft had not simply been prohibited. Alchemy, on the other hand, was pardonable, since the useful science of chemistry had developed from it. Good heavens, to think that these gold-makers' crucibles and all this magic hocus-pocus may have been necessary, because without them there would be no aspirin or gas bombs today!

Absentmindedly he picked up a small dark-colored pellet, rather like a pill, rolled the dry, weightless little thing between his fingers, and was about to put it down again when he heard steps behind him. He turned around. A visitor had entered the room. Ziegler was embarrassed at having the pellet in his hand, for actually he had read the sign. So he closed his hand, put it in his pocket, and left.

He did not think of the pellet again until he was on the street. He took it out and decided to throw it away. But first he raised it to his nose and sniffed it. It had a faint resinous smell that he found rather pleasing, so he put it back in his pocket.

Then he went to a restaurant, ordered, leafed through a few newspapers, toyed with his tie, and cast respectful or haughty glances at the guests around him, depending on how they were dressed. But when his meal was rather long in coming, he took out the alchemist's pill that he had involuntarily stolen, and smelled it. Then he scratched it with his fingernail, and finally, naïvely giving in to a childlike impulse, he put it in his mouth. It did not taste bad and dissolved quickly; he washed it down with a sip of beer. And then his meal arrived.

At two o'clock the young man jumped off the street car, went to the zoo, and bought a Sunday ticket.

Smiling amiably, he went to the primate house and planted himself in front of the big cage where the chimpanzees were kept. A large chimpanzee blinked at him, gave him a good-natured nod, and said in a deep voice: "How goes it, brother?"

Repelled and strangely frightened, Ziegler turned away. As he was hurrying off, he heard the ape scolding: "What's he got to be so proud about! The stupid fool!"

He went to see the long-tailed monkeys. They were dancing merrily. "Give us some sugar, old buddy!" they cried. And when he had no sugar, they grew angry, mimicked him, called him a cheapskate, and bared their teeth. That was more than he could stand; he fled in consternation and made for the deer, whom he expected to behave better.

A large stately elk stood close to the bars, looking him over. And suddenly Ziegler was stricken with horror. For since swallowing the magic pill, he understood the language of the animals. And the elk spoke with his eyes, two big brown eyes. His silent gaze expressed dignity, resignation, sadness, and with regard to the visitor a lofty and solemn contempt, a terrible contempt. In the language of these silent, majestic eyes, Ziegler read, he, with his hat and cane, his gold watch and his Sunday suit, was no better than vermin, an absurd and repulsive bug.

From the elk he fled to the ibex,[3] from the ibex to the chamois,[4] the llama,[5] and the gnu,[6] to the wild boars and bears. They did not all insult him, but without exception they despised him. He listened to them and learned from their conversations what they thought of people in general. And what they thought was most distressing. Most of all, they were surprised that these ugly, stinking, undignified bipeds with their foppish disguises should be allowed to run around loose.

He heard a puma talking to her cub, a conversation full of dignity and practical wisdom, such as one seldom hears among humans. He heard a beautiful panther expressing his opinions of this riffraff, the Sunday visitors, in succinct, well-turned, aristocratic phrases. He looked the blond lion in the eye and learned of the wonderful immensity of the wilderness, where there are no cages and no human beings. He saw a kestrel[7] perched proud and forlorn, congealed in melancholy, on a dead branch

and saw the jays bearing their imprisonment with dignity, resignation, and humor.

Dejected and wrenched out of all his habits of thought, Ziegler turned back to his fellow men in his despair. He looked for eyes that would understand his terror and misery; he listened to conversations in the hope of hearing something comforting, something understandable and soothing; he observed the gestures of the visitors in the hope of finding nobility and quiet, natural dignity.

But he was disappointed. He heard voices and words, he saw movements, gestures, and glances, but since he now saw everything as through the eyes of an animal, he found nothing but a degenerate, dissembling mob of bestial fops, who seemed to be an unbeautiful mixture of all the animal species.

In despair Ziegler wandered about. He felt hopelessly ashamed of himself. He had long since thrown his red-lacquered cane into the bushes and his gloves after it. But when he threw away his hat, took off his shoes and his tie, and shaken with sobs pressed against the bars of the elk's cage, a crowd collected, the guards seized him, and he was taken away to an insane asylum.

I

THE FOLLY OF PRETENTIONS

Notice that almost the first third of the story is devoted to a catalogue of Ziegler's characteristics, habits, and mind set. In fact, at one point the narrator apologizes for taking so long to describe Ziegler. He realizes he has been critical and attempts to soften his sharp comments by saying that Ziegler was really a charming young fellow. Reread the first four paragraphs and list Ziegler's foibles.

II

IMPLICATIONS

Reflect on the following quotations from the selection. What do they mean? Do you find them perceptive judgments of people in general?

---

3. **ibex** (ī′beks), type of horned wild goat.
4. **chamois** (sham′ē), small, goatlike antelope.
5. **llama** (lä′mə), animal related to the camel and found in South America.
6. **gnu** (nü) *or* (nyü), large African antelope.
7. **kestrel** (kes′trəl), small European falcon.

1. "He was one of those people we see every day on the street, whose faces we can never really remember, because they all have the same face: a collective face."

2. ". . . like other men he regarded himself and his life as the center of the world."

3. "As a modern man, he had unlimited respect not only for money, but also for a second power: science."

III
TECHNIQUES

Setting

Jonathan Swift in *Gulliver's Travels* wanted to have nonhumans comment on the absurdities of human beings. He used intelligent horses that could speak and had organized a society of their own. Recently, a French writer has used apes. Since Hesse, too, is using nonhumans as commentators in this story, what other setting might he have used? What makes the zoo a particularly good choice?

Prose Style

Read the second paragraph aloud. What positive comments does the narrator make about Ziegler? What negative ones? How are they arranged? What is the effect on the reader's feeling toward Ziegler?

SUMMING UP
Foibles

THE WORLD OF COMEDY

The writers in this unit have held up for view many common human foibles. Most have satirized and poked fun at these failings, for human weakness is the stuff of which comedy is made. Our natural instinct is to laugh at such trifling faults, yet in this laughter there is a common bond of humanity, for each of us recognizes that we share in these foibles to some degree. Instinctively we reach out in sympathy toward these characters in whom we see ourselves reflected.

Consider the material in FOIBLES. You have read a full-length play, autobiography, biography, essays, and short stories. Discuss the following.

1. How many of these employed humor?

2. Select the two characters with whom you felt the most sympathy and explain why.

3. Do the authors seemingly agree in their attitudes toward human foibles, or is there a wide difference of opinion?

4. What is the total effect of these selections, that is, what do they say to you about human foibles?

IMPLICATIONS

1. Open your book to the Table of Contents. For each selection in this unit, name the foible that is highlighted.

2. Do the selections in this unit confirm or contradict the ideas in the following statements? Use examples to support your opinions.

a. Foibles distort a person's behavior.

b. Foibles make a person interesting.

c. Most people are better known for their foibles than for their virtues.

TECHNIQUES

Setting

Consider the selections you have read in this unit.
1. In which selection is the setting most vivid?

2. In which piece did the setting have the most effect on the plot?

3. Did any of the settings contribute to the mood of the story?

4. Which selection used parts of the setting almost like props in a play?

Prose Style

1. How do the types of dialogue used by Strindberg and Johnson differ? How does dialogue affect the movement or rhythm of these pieces of writing?

2. Read several narrative passages from both "Federigo's Falcon" and "Love and Bread." Assuming that Boccaccio and Strindberg each used a style typical of his time, how has the style of writing changed over this 500-year period?

NINETEENTH-CENTURY BRITISH POETRY: Revolution and Imagination

The real break between the eighteenth century and the nineteenth century occurred almost twenty-five years before the turn of the century. In 1776, the American Revolution shocked England and Europe. And the French Revolution, beginning in 1789, increased the unrest of this period. It was difficult to retain a sense of stability when colonists revolted against their parent country or when French workers sacked the Bastille and beheaded the King. These political revolutions forced people to reexamine their beliefs. Moreover, since the mid-eighteenth century, the Industrial Revolution had been bringing changes to the lives of both city and country dwellers. Another big change was the revolution in scientific thought that occurred in the latter half of the century with the publication of Charles Darwin's *Origin of Species* (1859) and *The Descent of Man* (1871).

Considering these widely felt changes in the political, industrial, and scientific spheres, it is not surprising that English poetry also changed. William Blake, a major poet of the nineteenth century, reacted violently against repressive institutions. His later poetry broke away from familiar patterns and experimented with long, unrhymed lines.

This movement away from rhyme was strengthened by the efforts of Wordsworth and Coleridge. Together they assembled a collection of their poems entitled *Lyrical Ballads* (1798), which urged that poetry be written in everyday language. Moreover, Wordsworth and Coleridge accomplished a major change in the subject matter of English poetry by focusing on their feelings, experiences, and thoughts.

Poets before had done this, but never quite so clearly. In Wordsworth's long autobiographical poem, *The Prelude*, the poet himself becomes the central subject, and imagination is seen as his most important gift.

The centrality of the poet and of imagination is associated with the term *romantic*, a word often applied to the poetry of Blake, Wordsworth, Coleridge, Byron, Shelley, and Keats. The word is difficult to define but may be understood in contrast to *rational*, a word often applied to the ideas and the forms of eighteenth-century writers. Romanticism stresses love of the individual rather than love of the group. It places the value of nature over that of society. The Romantic poets express feelings rather than teach morality, and they rely on the imagination rather than on the mind.

As the nineteenth century wore on, the doubts caused by the various political revolutions and revolutions in thought became stronger. Imagination no longer seemed a strong-enough barrier against a world besieged with war, slums, poverty, and disease. One result was the emergence of the Victorian poets, who turned not only to themselves but to characters from other times. Among the major Victorian poets were Tennyson, Browning, Arnold, and Housman. Tennyson wrote his great work, *The Idylls of the King*, about England's legendary hero, King Arthur. Browning found inspiration in the Italian Renaissance and its often corrupt, but richly alive, figures. Arnold returned to classical sources. And Housman, although living in London, wrote about the countryside he remembered from his childhood.

Although the feelings of the poet were still of major importance, we sense that questions about the quality of life and where the world was going had become more pressing. After Wordsworth's death in 1850, Arnold wrote, "The last poetic voice is dumb." Arnold thus expressed his doubt that his own poetry, or that of anyone else, could achieve Wordsworth's depth of feeling. The revolutions of the late eighteenth century had promised much. But by the end of the nineteenth century, poets were expressing sorrow, doubt, and only a shaky faith.

WILLIAM BLAKE

The poetry of William Blake (1757–1827) is characterized by a constant balancing of opposites. For example, he wrote a series of poems called *Songs of Innocence* (1789) and five years later wrote *Songs of Experience* (1794). Indeed, the central metaphor for Blake's poetry may be found in the title of his visionary satire, *The Marriage of Heaven and Hell.* Blake felt that we must recognize the often integral relationships between opposites. In "Auguries of Innocence," an unfinished poem with couplet after couplet of paradoxes, Blake tells us:

> Man was made for Joy and Woe
> And when this we rightly know
> Thro the World we Safely go
> Joy and Woe are woven fine
> A clothing for the Soul divine

Both Joy and Woe are essential aspects of life; they are woven so closely together that they cannot be separated. Blake's vision of opposites pulled together found expression in visual art as well as in language. With a special engraving process known as *illuminated printing*, he often prepared drawings for his own poems.

The Lamb

Little Lamb, who made thee?
Dost thou know who made thee?
Gave thee life and bid thee feed,
By the stream and o'er the mead;
Gave thee clothing of delight,   5
Softest clothing wooly bright;
Gave thee such a tender voice,
Making all the vales rejoice!
Little Lamb, who made thee?
Dost thou know who made thee?   10

Little Lamb, I'll tell thee,
Little Lamb, I'll tell thee!
He is callèd by thy name,
For he calls himself a Lamb;
He is meek and he is mild,   15
He became a little child:
I a child and thou a lamb,
We are called by his name.
Little Lamb, God bless thee.
Little Lamb, God bless thee.   20

The Tyger

Tyger! Tyger! burning bright
In the forests of the night,
What immortal hand or eye
Could frame thy fearful symmetry?

In what distant deeps or skies   5
Burnt the fire of thine eyes?
On what wings dare he aspire?
What the hand, dare seize the fire?

And what shoulder, and what art
Could twist the sinews of thy heart?   10
And when thy heart began to beat,
What dread hand? and what dread feet?

What the hammer? what the chain?
In what furnace was thy brain?
What the anvil? what dread grasp   15
Dare its deadly terrors clasp?

When the stars threw down their spears,
And watered heaven with their tears,
Did he smile his work to see?
Did he who made the Lamb make thee?   20

Tyger! Tyger! burning bright
In the forests of the night,
What immortal hand or eye
Dare frame thy fearful symmetry?

London

I wander thro' each charter'd street,
Near where the charter'd Thames does flow.
And mark in every face I meet
Marks of weakness, marks of woe.

In every cry of every Man,   5
In every Infant's cry of fear,
In every voice, in every ban,
The mind-forg'd manacles I hear.

How the Chimney-sweeper's cry
Every black'ning Church appalls;   10
And the hapless Soldier's sigh
Runs in blood down Palace walls.

But most thro' midnight streets I hear
How the youthful Harlot's curse
Blasts the new born Infant's tear,   15
And blights with plagues the Marriàge hearse.

The Garden of Love

I went to the Garden of Love,
And saw what I never had seen:
A Chapel was built in the midst,
Where I used to play on the green.

And the gates of this Chapel were shut,   5
And "Thou shalt not" writ over the door;
So I turn'd to the Garden of Love,
That so many sweet flowers bore.

I saw it was filled with graves,
And tomb-stones where flowers should be: 10
And Priests in black gowns were walking their rounds,
And binding with briars my joys and desires.

The Lamb and *The Tyger*

1. "The Lamb" is part of a collection of poems Blake called *Songs of Innocence*, and "The Tyger" is a companion piece in a collection called *Songs of Experience*. What details in each poem would be associated with those two different qualities, innocence and experience?

2. Both poems begin with a question. How many questions are there in each poem? How many answers? In what ways is the difference important?

3. In what ways are these poems concerned with a religious question? Can you state the question? What is the answer in "The Lamb"? What is the answer in "The Tyger"?

4. In "The Tyger," what seems to be the central metaphor in stanzas 2–4? Why is this metaphor appropriate?

5. The first and last stanzas of "The Tyger" are identical, except for one word. How is the meaning altered by this word change? What is the effect of the repetition of the first stanza? What is the effect of repetition in "The Lamb"?

London

1. Look up the possible meanings of *charter'd*. How many meanings seem relevant to the poem?

2. Blake sets up a conflict between two groups in his society. What are these groups? By whom are they presented in the poem? Do you think Blake is fair to both groups?

3. Blake is describing eighteenth-century London. Is the description he gives of a huge city still a valid one? How does the London of Blake's time differ from today's New York, Chicago, or Los Angeles?

4. In lines 5–7, Blake repeats the words *in every*. How does this repetition affect the tone and meaning of the poem?

5. What are the sources of oppression suggested by the poem? Does Blake imply any solution?

The Garden of Love

1. Try reading this poem aloud. Listen to the sound of the words, to the rhymes, and to the rhythm of the stanzas. Do you notice any difference in these elements as you read the three stanzas? How might this difference be connected to Blake's notions about freedom and repression?

2. What is the central image of the last stanza? How is it related to the image suggested by the phrase, "The Garden of Love"?

Implications (Blake)

What might Blake say about the following statements? How do you feel?

1. It is more important to raise questions than to have answers.

2. Religion is an institution that deadens rather than revives the soul.

3. A person's mind can act to enslave or to set free.

WILLIAM WORDSWORTH

William Wordsworth (1770–1850) was born in England's Lake District and
from that sternly beautiful countryside gathered his poetic strength and vision.
He studied at Cambridge, traveled through Europe, came back to London to
live, and in 1791 returned to France. That visit to France was a turning point
in his life, both politically and personally. At first, like so many English
people, he was stirred and excited by the French Revolution. But the October
Massacres (1792) sickened him, and as he put it, he "yielded up moral
questions in despair." His nervous breakdown was also probably related to his
guilt at having to leave France and thus be parted from Annette Vallon and
their daughter Caroline. Wordsworth returned to England and through several
years of companionship with his sister Dorothy and his friend Coleridge
regained his delight in life and in poetry. In 1798, Wordsworth and
Coleridge published *Lyrical Ballads*, a collection famous for both its poems and
its preface. The preface argued that poetry should treat "incidents and
situations from common life," in "a selection of language really used" by
most people. The emphasis on poetry as "the spontaneous overflow of powerful
feelings" and the avoidance of a specialized and artificial poetic diction
were, in poetic terms, revolutionary ideas. Wordsworth had a long poetic
career. Between 1798 and 1799, he began work on a poetic self-examination,
which he thought he needed to write as a preliminary to another long
philosophical poem, *The Recluse*. That preliminary poem, fittingly called
The Prelude, turned out to be his major work. He finished it in 1802
and later revised sections of it (1850). The poem is over 8000 lines long
(4 times the length of *Macbeth*) and is divided into 14 books. Needless to say,
it is not just a poem but an epic—a spiritual autobiography that tries to find
answers to questions such as "Who am I?" "How and what did I learn from
Nature?" "How can I be a poet?" "What can I do when my imagination fails?"
The subject matter of this epic is thus not a Spenserian romance or
a Miltonic religious theme but, as the subtitle puts it, the "growth of a poet's
mind."

from The Prelude

BOOK I

Fair seedtime had my soul, and I grew up
Fostered alike by beauty and by fear:
Much favored in my birthplace,[1] and no less
In that beloved Vale[2] to which erelong
We were transplanted—there were we let loose   5
For sports of wider range. Ere I had told

---

1. **birthplace,** Cockermouth, in the Lake District.
2. **Vale** (vāl), Esthwaite, also in the Lake District.

Ten birthdays, when among the mountain slopes
Frost, and the breath of frosty wind, had snapped
The last autumnal crocus, 'twas my joy
With store of springes³ o'er my shoulder hung   10
To range the open heights where woodcocks run
Along the smooth green turf. Through half the night,
Scudding⁴ away from snare to snare, I plied
That anxious visitation—moon and stars
Were shining o'er my head. I was alone,   15
And seemed to be a trouble to the peace
That dwelt among them. Sometimes it befell
In these night wanderings, that a strong desire
O'erpowered my better reason, and the bird
Which was the captive of another's toil   20
Became my prey; and when the deed was done
I heard among the solitary hills
Low breathings coming after me, and sounds
Of undistinguishable motion, steps
Almost as silent as the turf they trod.   25

   Nor less, when spring had warmed the cultured⁵ Vale,
Moved we as plunderers where the mother bird
Had in high places built her lodge; though mean
Our object and inglorious, yet the end
Was not ignoble. Oh! when I have hung   30
Above the raven's nest, by knots of grass
And half-inch fissures⁶ in the slippery rock
But ill sustained, and almost (so it seemed)
Suspended by the blast that blew amain,⁷
Shouldering the naked crag, oh, at that time   35
While on the perilous ridge I hung alone,
With what strange utterance did the loud dry wind
Blow through my ear! the sky seemed not a sky
Of earth—and with what motion moved the clouds!

   Dust as we are, the immortal spirit grows   40
Like harmony in music; there is a dark
Inscrutable⁸ workmanship that reconciles
Discordant elements, makes them cling together
In one society. How strange that all
The terrors, pains, and early miseries,   45

-----

3. **springes** (sprinj′əz), traps, snares.
4. **scudding** (skud′ing), rushing.
5. **cultured,** cultivated.
6. **fissures** (fish′ərz), cracks.
7. **amain** (ə mān′), with full force.
8. **inscrutable** (in skrü′tə bəl), mysterious.

Regrets, vexations, lassitudes[9] interfused
Within my mind, should e'er have borne a part,
And that a needful part, in making up
The calm existence that is mine when I
Am worthy of myself! Praise to the end!   50
Thanks to the means which Nature deigned[10] to employ;
Whether her fearless visitings, or those
That came with soft alarm, like hurtless light
Opening the peaceful clouds; or she may use
Severer interventions, ministry   55
More palpable, as best might suit her aim.

   One summer evening (led by her) I found
A little boat tied to a willow tree
Within a rocky cave, its usual home.
Straight I unloosed her chain, and stepping in   60
Pushed from the shore. It was an act of stealth
And troubled pleasure, nor without the voice
Of mountain echoes did my boat move on;
Leaving behind her still, on either side,
Small circles glittering idly in the moon,   65
Until they melted all into one track
Of sparkling light. But now, like one who rows,
Proud of his skill, to reach a chosen point
With an unswerving line, I fixed my view
Upon the summit of a craggy ridge,   70
The horizon's utmost boundary; for above
Was nothing but the stars and the gray sky.
She was an elfin pinnace[11]; lustily
I dipped my oars into the silent lake,
And, as I rose upon the stroke, my boat   75
Went heaving through the water like a swan;
When, from behind that craggy steep till then
The horizon's bound, a huge peak, black and huge,
As if with voluntary power instinct,[12]
Upreared its head. I struck and struck again,   80
And growing still in stature the grim shape
Towered up between me and the stars, and still,
For so it seemed, with purpose of its own
And measured motion like a living thing,
Strode after me. With trembling oars I turned,   85

---

9. **lassitudes** (lasʹə tüdz), conditions of weariness or
indifference.
10. **deigned** (dānd), thought appropriate.
11. **pinnace** (pinʹis), light sailing ship.
12. **instinct** (inʹstingkt), inborn.

And through the silent water stole my way
Back to the covert[13] of the willow tree;
There in her mooring place I left my bark,[14]
And through the meadows homeward went, in grave
And serious mood; but after I had seen   90
That spectacle, for many days, my brain
Worked with a dim and undetermined sense
Of unknown modes of being; o'er my thoughts
There hung a darkness, call it solitude
Or blank desertion. No familiar shapes   95
Remained, no pleasant images of trees,
Of sea or sky, no colors of green fields;
But huge and mighty forms, that do not live
Like living men, moved slowly through the mind
By day, and were a trouble to my dreams.   100

---

13. **covert** (kuv′ərt), hiding.
14. **bark,** boat.

Composed upon Westminster Bridge

Earth has not anything to show more fair:
Dull would he be of soul who could pass by
A sight so touching in its majesty;
This City now doth, like a garment, wear
The beauty of the morning; silent, bare,   5
Ships, towers, domes, theaters, and temples lie
Open unto the fields, and to the sky;
All bright and glittering in the smokeless air.
Never did sun more beautifully steep
In his first splendor, valley, rock, or hill;   10
Ne'er saw I, never felt, a calm so deep!
The river glideth at his own sweet will:
Dear God! the very houses seem asleep;
And all that mighty heart is lying still!

1. Wordsworth describes three different episodes in this section. What do they have in common?

2. Lines 340–344 talk about the "dark / Inscrutable workmanship that reconciles / Discordant elements." How does this generalization apply to the specific events described before and after these lines?

3. Why is the boat-stealing episode described in greater detail and placed after the other descriptions? What makes this episode particularly memorable, for Wordsworth and for us?

Composed upon Westminster Bridge

1. Where is the poet standing? What time of day is it? How is the time related to the mood of the poem?

2. What lines convey the speaker's emotion?

3. Is this a poem about city life or nature?

4. How does Wordsworth's view of London differ from Blake's (see p. 460)?

Implications (Wordsworth)

What would Wordsworth think about the following statements? What do you think?

1. Pain and fear are necessary preliminaries to achieving a "calm existence."

2. Nature will give us strength if we are able to understand its lessons.

SAMUEL TAYLOR COLERIDGE

Samuel Taylor Coleridge (1772–1834) is frequently associated with Wordsworth. Indeed, the two poets' friendship produced one of the most important books in the history of English poetry, the *Lyrical Ballads* (1798). Their works sometimes intertwine, as in Coleridge's "Frost at Midnight" and Wordsworth's "Tintern Abbey" or in Wordsworth's "Immortality" ode and Coleridge's "Dejection: An Ode." Coleridge, however, is a much more intense poet—and with this greater intensity comes, perhaps inevitably, less steady writing. Wordsworth created a huge body of writing, some of it extremely fine, some of it pedestrian. Coleridge, however, is remembered primarily for a few poems: the superbly crafted and evocative "The Rime of the Ancient Mariner," the "conversation poems" such as "Frost at Midnight" and "This Lime-Tree Bower My Prison," and the strange and "unfinished" works such as "Christabel" and "Kubla Khan." Scholars have traced many of the details in this last poem to Coleridge's voluminous reading. Their artful emergence into Coleridge's dream-vision may perhaps be due to the opium he was taking (as he explains in a prefatory note). But the poem might equally well be the result of a dream or of his great genius. Even if we cannot explain "Kubla Khan" fully, it is a poem that haunts the mind, whether ours or that of the sleeping Coleridge.

Kubla Khan

Or, a Vision in a Dream, a Fragment

In Xanadu[1] did Kubla Khan[2]
A stately pleasure dome decree:
Where Alph,[3] the sacred river, ran

Through caverns measureless to man
  Down to a sunless sea.   5
So twice five miles of fertile ground
With walls and towers were girdled round:
And there were gardens bright with sinuous rills,
Where blossomed many an incense-bearing tree;
And here were forests ancient as the hills,   10
Enfolding sunny spots of greenery.

But oh! that deep romantic chasm which slanted
Down the green hill athwart[4] a cedarn cover!
A savage place! as holy and enchanted
As e'er beneath a waning moon was haunted   15
By woman wailing for her demon lover!
And from this chasm, with ceaseless turmoil seething,
As if this earth in fast thick pants were breathing,
A mighty fountain momently was forced:
Amid whose swift half-intermitted burst   20
Huge fragments vaulted like rebounding hail,
Or chaffy grain beneath the thresher's flail:
And 'mid these dancing rocks at once and ever
It flung up momently the sacred river.
Five miles meandering with a mazy motion   25
Through wood and dale the sacred river ran,
Then reached the caverns measureless to man,
And sank in tumult to a lifeless ocean:
And 'mid this tumult Kubla heard from far
Ancestral voices prophesying war!   30
  The shadow of the dome of pleasure
    Floated midway on the waves;
  Where was heard the mingled measure
    From the fountain and the caves.
It was a miracle of rare device,   35
A sunny pleasure dome with caves of ice!

A damsel with a dulcimer[5]
In a vision once I saw:
It was an Abyssinian[6] maid,

---

1. **Xanadu** (zan′ə dü), name taken from *Purchas's Pilgrimages*, of Kubla Khan's city.
2. **Kubla Khan** (kü′blə kän′), Mongol emperor of the thirteenth century, grandson of Genghis Khan.
3. **Alph** (alf), perhaps a combination of alpha, the first letter of the Greek alphabet, and Alpheus, an underground river mentioned in classical literature.

4. **athwart** (ə thwôrt′), across.
5. **dulcimer** (dul′sə mər), a harplike instrument.
6. **Abyssinian** (ab′ə sin′ē ən), literally Ethiopian. However, Abyssinia was frequently mentioned in legend as a possible site for the Garden of Eden.

And on her dulcimer she played,   40
Singing of Mount Abora.[7]
Could I revive within me
Her symphony and song,
    To such a deep delight 'twould win me,
That with music loud and long,   45
I would build that dome in air,
That sunny dome! those caves of ice!
And all who heard should see them there,
And all should cry, Beware! Beware!
His flashing eyes, his floating hair!   50
Weave a circle round him thrice,
And close your eyes with holy dread,
For he on honey-dew hath fed.
And drunk the milk of Paradise.

---

7. **Mount Abora,** perhaps a version of Milton's Mount
Amara, (*Paradise Lost*, IV, 280–282), referred to in
his description of the Garden of Eden.

GEORGE GORDON, LORD BYRON
PERCY BYSSHE SHELLEY

George Gordon, Lord Byron (1788–1824) and Percy Bysshe Shelley
(1792–1822) led extremely different lives, yet both can be seen as symbolic
figures who acted out their visions of what it meant to be a poet. Byron
created in his poetry the image of a romantically rebellious individual who
stood apart from society and challenged its beliefs and customs. And his own
life acted out that image. He became a favorite topic of London gossipers, who
speculated about his love life, his tempestuous marriage, and his poetry.
Shelley was also a rebel, although in a very different social sphere. He fought
against the fag system at Eton, by which the younger boys acted as servants to
the older ones. Later, he wrote a book, called *The Necessity of Atheism*,
that caused his expulsion from Oxford. Shelley also persuaded his first wife,
Harriet, to join him and Mary Godwin, who became his second wife, in a
strange triangular family. Byron and Shelley were both social exiles from
England, and from 1816 to 1822 they spent much time together in Switzerland
and Italy. Byron, in fact, was present at Shelley's funeral and cremation
(following Shelley's death from a boating accident). Byron died just two years
later, of a fever caught while fighting in Greece. The two poems printed here
reflect the different personalities of these poets. Both treat the question
of immortality. Yet Byron's poem is characteristically flippant, whereas
Shelley's poem is more serious in tone, more conscious of both the
magnificence of the past and the emptiness of the present.

On Fame

What are the hopes of man? Old Egypt's King
   Cheops[1] erected the first pyramid
And largest, thinking it was just the thing
   To keep his memory whole, and mummy hid;
But somebody or other rummaging,   5
   Burglariously broke his coffin's lid:
Let not a monument give you or me hopes,
Since not a pinch of dust remains of Cheops.

GEORGE GORDON, LORD BYRON

---

1. **Cheops** (kē′ops), second pharoah of the fourth dynasty of Egypt and builder of the great pyramids at Giza.

Ozymandias

I met a traveler from an antique land
Who said: Two vast and trunkless legs of stone
Stand in the desert. Near them, on the sand,
Half sunk, a shattered visage lies, whose frown,
And wrinkled lip, and sneer of cold command,   6
Tell that its sculptor well those passions read
Which yet survive, stamped on these lifeless things,
The hand that mocked them and the heart that fed:
And on the pedestal these words appear:
"My name is Ozymandias, king of kings: 10
Look on my works, ye Mighty, and despair!"
Nothing beside remains. Round the decay
Of that colossal wreck, boundless and bare
The lone and level sands stretch far away.

PERCY BYSSHE SHELLEY

Kubla Khan

1. What atmosphere is created by the first stanza? How do the images and the rhythm of the lines contribute to that feeling?

2. What changes do you find in the second stanza, both emotionally and rhythmically?

3. Suddenly in the third stanza, a speaker ("I") enters the poem. How do you explain the speaker's appearance? Who is the speaker? How is the third stanza connected to the previous two stanzas?

4. In the subtitle, Coleridge calls this poem "a vision in a dream" and "a fragment." Do you agree with either or both of these descriptions? Why? Is this really an unfinished poem?

On Fame

1. Consider and discuss the following propositions:

a. "Ozymandias" and "On Fame" make identical statements.

b. The poems differ in tone.

2. What effect is created by the word *burglariously?*

Ozymandias

After you are sure you understand the scene Shelley is describing, consider and discuss these statements.

1. Everyone feels a need to be remembered in some way.

2. Ozymandias succeeded in being remembered for something quite different from what he had intended.

3. The most enduring things a person can achieve are the creations of art.

4. It is significant that the scene is laid in a desert.

JOHN KEATS

When John Keats (1795–1821) was dying of tuberculosis, he asked that no name be put on his tombstone, only the epitaph, "Here lies one whose name was writ in water." Keats died at the age of twenty-five. Although he did not enjoy fame during his lifetime, he has been praised since then as one of England's greatest poets. At the age of twenty-three, during the year 1819, Keats wrote some of the finest and most enduring lyrics in English literature. His earlier works, especially a long romance called *Endymion*, had not been successful. In fact, critics attacked both it and the poet savagely, and contemporaries such as Byron and Shelley blamed Keats's early death in part on the harsh critical treatment he had received. What Keats's poetic career lacked in length, it made up in passionate intensity. He was a man in love with poetry, whether the poetry of Shakespeare, Homer, Spenser, or the natural world. In his poem "La Belle Dame sans Merci," Keats creates an atmosphere of death that is nevertheless filled with sensuously vivid images. "Ode to a Nightingale" is one of the great poems about life, death, and dreams—a poem as rich in its imagery as Coleridge's "Kubla Khan." In addition to "Ode to a Nightingale," Keats wrote four other odes during April and May of 1819: "Ode to Psyche," "Ode on a Grecian Urn," "Ode to Melancholy," and "To Autumn." The last of these is, for some, the richest of Keats's poems. It expresses an intensely felt experience of autumn and a gentle acceptance of the life and the death contained in that season.

La Belle Dame sans Merci [1]

O what can ail thee, Knight at arms,
    Alone and palely loitering?
The sedge[2] has withered from the Lake
    And no birds sing!

O what can ail thee, Knight at arms,   5
    So haggard, and so woebegone?
The squirrel's granary is full
    And the harvest's done.

I see a lily on thy brow
    With anguish moist and fever dew,   10
And on thy cheeks a fading rose
    Fast withereth too.

"I met a Lady in the Meads,[3]
    Full beautiful, a faery's child,
Her hair was long, her foot was light   15
    And her eyes were wild.

"I made a Garland for her head,
    And bracelets too, and fragrant Zone;[4]
She looked at me as she did love
    And made sweet moan.   20

"I set her on my pacing steed
    And nothing else saw all day long,
For sidelong would she bend and sing
    A faery's song.

"She found me roots of relish sweet,   25
    And honey wild, and manna[5] dew,
And sure in language strange she said
    'I love thee true.'

"She took me to her elfin grot[6]
    And there she wept and sighed full sore,   30
And there I shut her wild wild eyes
    With kisses four.

"And there she lullèd me asleep,
    And there I dreamed, Ah Woe betide!
The latest[7] dream I ever dreamt   35
    On the cold hill side.

"I saw pale Kings, and Princes too,
    Pale warriors, death-pale were they all;
They cried, 'La belle dame sans merci
    Hath thee in thrall!'[8]   40

"I saw their starved lips in the gloam[9]
    With horrid warning gaped wide,
And I awoke, and found me here
    On the cold hill's side.

"And this is why I sojourn here,   45
    Alone and palely loitering;
Though the sedge is withered from the Lake
    And no birds sing."

---

1. **La belle dame sans merci,** the beautiful lady without mercy. The title is taken from a medieval Provençal poem by Alain Chartier. In Keats's romantic poem *The Eve of St. Agnes,* the lover plays a setting of Chartier's poem on the lute to awaken his sleeping lady.
2. **sedge** (sej), flowering grass.
3. **Meads** (mēdz), meadows.
4. **Zone** (zōn), archaic word for belt.
5. **manna** (man′ə), the mysterious substance that fell from heaven to feed the wandering Israelites.
6. **grot** (grot), grotto or cave.
7. **latest,** last.
8. **thrall** (thrôl), captivity.
9. **gloam** (glōm), dusk (an archaic form).

Ode to a Nightingale

My heart aches, and a drowsy numbness pains
  My sense, as though of hemlock[1] I had drunk,
Or emptied some dull opiate to the drains
  One minute past, and Lethe-wards[2] had sunk:
'Tis not through envy of thy happy lot,   5
  But being too happy in thine happiness—
    That thou, light-wingéd Dryad[3] of the trees,
      In some melodious plot
  Of beechen green, and shadows numberless,
    Singest of summer in full-throated ease.   10

O, for a draught of vintage! that hath been
  Cooled a long age in the deep-delved earth,
Tasting of Flora[4] and the country green,
  Dance, and Provençal[5] song, and sunburnt mirth!
O for a beaker full of the warm South,   15
  Full of the true, the blushful Hippocrene,[6]
    With beaded bubbles winking at the brim,
      And purple-stainéd mouth;
  That I might drink, and leave the world unseen,
    And with thee fade away into the forest dim: 20

Fade far away, dissolve, and quite forget
  What thou among the leaves hast never known,
The weariness, the fever, and the fret
  Here, where men sit and hear each other groan;
Where palsy[7] shakes a few, sad, last gray hairs,   25
  Where youth grows pale, and specter-thin, and dies,
    Where but to think is to be full of sorrow
      And leaden-eyed despairs.
  Where Beauty cannot keep her lustrous eyes,
    Or new Love pine at them beyond tomorrow.   30

Away! away! for I will fly to thee,
  Not charioted by Bacchus and his pards,[8]
But on the viewless[9] wings of Poesy,
  Though the dull brain perplexes and retards:
Already with thee! tender is the night,   35
  And haply[10] the Queen-Moon is on her throne,
    Clustered around by all her starry Fays;[11]
      But here there is no light,
  Save what from heaven is with the breezes blown
    Through verdurous[12] glooms and winding mossy ways.   40

I cannot see what flowers are at my feet,
   Nor what soft incense hangs upon the boughs,
But, in embalméd darkness, guess each sweet
   Wherewith the seasonable month endows
The grass, the thicket, and the fruit tree wild;   45
   White hawthorn, and the pastoral eglantine;[13]
      Fast fading violets covered up in leaves;
        And mid-May's eldest child,
   The coming musk-rose, full of dewy wine,
      The murmurous haunt of flies on summer eves.   50

Darkling[14] I listen; and for many a time
   I have been half in love with easeful Death,
Called him soft names in many a muséd rhyme,
   To take into the air my quiet breath;
Now more than ever seems it rich to die,   55
   To cease upon the midnight with no pain,
      While thou art pouring forth thy soul abroad
        In such an ecstasy!
   Still wouldst thou sing, and I have ears in vain—
      To thy high requiem become a sod.   60

Thou wast not born for death, immortal Bird!
   No hungry generations tread thee down;
The voice I hear this passing night was heard
   In ancient days by emperor and clown:
Perhaps the selfsame song that found a path   65
   Through the sad heart of Ruth,[15] when, sick for home,
      She stood in tears amid the alien corn;
        The same that ofttimes hath
   Charmed magic casements, opening on the foam
      Of perilous seas, in faery lands forlorn.   70

---

1. **hemlock** (hem′lok), drug made from a poisonous herb.
2. **Lethe-wards** (lē′thē wərdz), towards the river Lethe, a mythical river in the Greek underworld, symbol of oblivion.
3. **Dryad** (drī′əd), wood-nymph.
4. **Flora** (flôr′ə), Roman goddess of spring.
5. **Provencal** (prov′ən säl′), of southern France, and specifically alluding to medieval troubadours.
6. **Hippocrene** (hip′ə krēn′), the fountain of the Muses; its waters were supposed to help poetic inspiration.
7. **palsy** (pôl′zē), shaking disease.
8. **Bacchus and his pards** (bak′əs) . . . (pärdz), Roman god of wine, frequently pictured in a leopard-drawn chariot.
9. **viewless,** not seen; invisible.
10. **haply,** perhaps.
11. **Fays** (fāz), fairies.
12. **verdurous** (vėr′jər əs), covered with vegetation.
13. **eglantine** (eg′lən tīn), sweetbriar (a wild rose).
14. **Darkling,** in darkness.
15. **Ruth,** the Biblical figure who left her own country (Moab) to accompany her mother-in-law, Naomi, back to Judah.

Forlorn! the very word is like a bell
  To toll me back from thee to my sole self!
Adieu![16] the fancy cannot cheat so well
  As she is famed to do, deceiving elf.
Adieu! adieu! thy plaintive anthem fades   75
  Past the near meadows, over the still stream,
      Up the hill side; and now 'tis buried deep
        In the next valley-glades:
Was it a vision, or a waking dream?
      Fled is that music:—Do I wake or sleep?   80

---

16. **Adieu** goodbye, in French.

To Autumn

Season of mists and mellow fruitfulness,
  Close bosom-friend of the maturing sun;
Conspiring with him how to load and bless
  With fruit the vines that round the thatch-eaves run;
To bend with apples the moss'd cottage trees,   5
  And fill all fruit with ripeness to the core;
      To swell the gourd, and plump the hazel shells
With a sweet kernel; to set budding more,
And still more, later flowers for the bees,
Until they think warm days will never cease,   10
      For Summer has o'er-brimmed their clammy cells.

Who hath not seen thee oft amid thy store?
  Sometimes whoever seeks abroad may find
Thee sitting careless on a granary floor,
  Thy hair soft-lifted by the winnowing wind;   15
Or on a half-reap'd furrow sound asleep,
  Drows'd with the fume of poppies, while thy hook
      Spares the next swath and all its twinèd flowers:
And sometimes like a gleaner thou dost keep
  Steady thy laden head across a brook;   20
  Or by a cider-press, with patient look,
      Thou watchest the last oozings hours by hours.

Where are the songs of Spring? Aye, where are they?
    Think not of them, thou hast thy music too,—
  While barrèd clouds bloom the soft-dying day,   25
    And touch the stubble-plains with rosy hue;
Then in a wailful choir the small gnats mourn
    Among the river sallows, borne aloft
        Or sinking as the light wind lives or dies;
And full-grown lambs loud bleat from hilly bourn;   30
    Hedge-crickets sing; and now with treble soft
The red-breast whistles from a garden-croft;
    And gathering swallows twitter in the skies.

La Belle Dame sans Merci

1. Who are the two speakers in the poem? Why are two speakers necessary? Why doesn't the poem return to the first speaker?

2. Keats is deliberately imitating an old form, the ballad, and he is purposely using old-fashioned language (as Spenser did). How does this poem remind you of the ballads in the first poetry section? What deliberately archaic words and phrases can you find? Why does Keats use them?

3. Keats changes the ballad stanza in a significant way by shortening the fourth line of each quatrain. What effect does that change have on our experience of the poem?

Ode to a Nightingale

1. What is the emotional condition of the speaker in stanza 1? How does the speaker connect that emotion to the nightingale's song?

2. In the second stanza, the speaker asks for drink, in order to "fade away" from the world. Why? Where does the speaker imagine the nightingale to be?

3. What atmosphere is created by the images in stanza 5? What is the importance of this stanza to the poem?

4. In stanza 6, the speaker feels it "rich to die." What changes of thought occur in stanzas 6, 7, and 8 that keep the speaker from satisfying this death wish?

5. The poem ends with a question. How would you answer it?

To Autumn

1. What relationship and what feeling does Keats create by personifying Autumn?

2. The meaning of the poem must be traced through its lush imagery. To what senses does the poet appeal in each stanza? What pictures are drawn in words?

3. What sound effects give this poem its solemn and stately movement?

4. What is the dominant impression of Autumn that this poem leaves with you?

5. What patterns are repeated in each stanza?

ALFRED, LORD TENNYSON

In some ways, Alfred, Lord Tennyson (1809–1892) is the most representative
Victorian poet. Reflected in his poetry and his life are both the great
doubts and the assured faith of that era. He studied at Cambridge, where his
dearest friend was Arthur Henry Hallam. Tennyson's early career
was not without problems. Critical response to his early work was negative,
and he suffered a further shock in 1833 when Hallam died suddenly
in Vienna. Moreover, Tennyson had financial troubles and had to postpone his
marriage. Matters did improve, though, beginning with his receipt
of a government pension in 1845. The tremendous success of *In Memoriam*,
a series of 131 poems about Hallam's death (published in 1850), as well
as his appointment as Poet Laureate furthered his transition to a new and
happy life. Tennyson's poems deal with a number of subjects, frequently
beginning with a figure or an episode from the past. His longest work,
The Idylls of the King, is a series of blank-verse narratives based on the
legends of King Arthur. For Tennyson, Arthur was the new order, coming to
lift the human race out of its beastly existence into a higher life.
He saw the failure of the Round Table as tragic because its promise of spiritual
greatness was not brought into reality. Yet the message of "Ulysses"
(a dramatic monologue also about a heroic figure from the past) is that perhaps
the finding and establishing of greatness is not as important as the
search itself.

Ulysses [1]

It little profits that an idle king,
By this still hearth, among these barren crags,
Matched with an aged wife, I mete and dole[2]
Unequal laws unto a savage race,
That hoard, and sleep, and feed, and know not me.   5
I cannot rest from travel; I will drink
Life to the lees. All times I have enjoyed
Greatly, have suffered greatly, both with those
That loved me, and alone; on shore, and when
Through scudding drifts the rainy Hyades[3]   10
Vext the dim sea. I am become a name;
For always roaming with a hungry heart
Much have I seen and known—cities of men
And manners, climates, councils, governments,
Myself not least, but honored of them all,—   15
And drunk delight of battle with my peers,
Far on the ringing plains of windy Troy.

---

1. **Ulysses** (yü lis′ēz), in Greek, Odysseus, king of
Ithaca, hero of Homer's *Odyssey*. Tennyson begins with
Ulysses at home, returned from the Trojan War.

2. **mete and dole,** measure out and give.
3. **Hyades** (hī′ə dēz′), stars in the constellation Taurus,
believed to signal rainfall.

I am a part of all that I have met;
Yet all experience is an arch wherethrough
Gleams that untraveled world whose margin fades   20
For ever and for ever when I move.
How dull it is to pause, to make an end,
To rust unburnished, not to shine in use!
As though to breathe were life! Life piled on life
Were all too little, and of one to me   25
Little remains; but every hour is saved
From that eternal silence, something more,
A bringer of new things; and vile it were
For some three suns to store and hoard myself,
And this gray spirit yearning in desire   30
To follow knowledge like a sinking star,
Beyond the utmost bound of human thought.
   This is my son, mine own Telemachus,
To whom I leave the scepter and the isle,
Well-loved of me, discerning to fulfill   35
This labor, by slow prudence to make mild
A rugged people, and through slow degrees
Subdue them to the useful and the good.
Most blameless is he, centered in the sphere
Of common duties, decent not to fail   40
In offices of tenderness, and pay
Meet[4] adoration to my household gods,
When I am gone. He works his work, I mine.
   There lies the port; the vessel puffs her sail;
There gloom the dark, broad seas. My mariners,   45
Souls that have toiled, and wrought, and thought with me,
That ever with a frolic welcome took
The thunder and the sunshine, and opposed
Free hearts, free foreheads—you and I are old;
Old age hath yet his honor and his toil.   50
Death closes all; but something ere the end,
Some work of noble note, may yet be done,
Not unbecoming men that strove with gods.
The lights begin to twinkle from the rocks;
The long day wanes; the slow moon climbs; the deep   55
Moans round with many voices. Come, my friends,
'Tis not too late to seek a newer world.
Push off, and sitting well in order smite
The sounding furrows; for my purpose holds
To sail beyond the sunset, and the baths   60
Of all the western stars, until I die.
It may be that the gulfs will wash us down;

---

4. **Meet**, fitting.

It may be we shall touch the Happy Isles,[5]
And see the great Achilles, whom we knew.
Though much is taken, much abides; and though   65
We are not now that strength which in old days
Moved earth and heaven, that which we are, we are,
One equal temper of heroic hearts,
Made weak by time and fate, but strong in will
To strive, to seek, to find, and not to yield.   70

---

5. **Happy Isles,** Elysium, the final resting place of those loved by the gods.

ROBERT BROWNING

Robert Browning (1812–1889) was a poet of immense vitality and gusto.
His early poetry, especially the long poem *Sordello* (1840), earned a reputation
for obscurity. His mature poetry, however, portrays exciting,
controversial characters, some based on historical figures, some products of
Browning's fertile imagination. Among these later works are: "Men and
Women" (1855), "Dramatis Personae" (1864), and the long narrative of a
seventeenth-century murder story, *The Ring and the Book* (1868 to 1869).
Browning's supreme achievement was in a form called the *dramatic
monologue*, in which a single person, not the poet, is presented speaking at a
critical moment to a silent companion. During the monologue the speaker
unwittingly reveals through words and actions aspects of personality that he or
she would want to keep hidden. Indeed, *The Ring and the Book*
consists of the dramatic monologues of twelve major characters connected with
a sensational murder and trial. Browning's most famous dramatic monologue is
the one we present here, "My Last Duchess." We get a vivid sense of the
speaker and his feelings and an equally clear picture of the wife
whose portrait he is proudly displaying. What makes the poem memorable is
its evocation of two conflicting attitudes in readers: Are we horrified by the
duke or do we admire his resolute arrogance?

My Last Duchess

FERRARA

That's my last Duchess painted on the wall,
Looking as if she were alive. I call
That piece a wonder, now: Frà Pandolf's[1] hands

---

1. **Frà Pandolf** (frä pän′dôlf), an imaginary work and painter.

Worked busily a day, and there she stands.
Will't please you sit and look at her? I said
"Frà Pandolf" by design, for never read
Strangers like you that pictured countenance,
The depth and passion of its earnest glance,
But to myself they turned (since none puts by
The curtain I have drawn for you, but I)
And seemed as they would ask me, if they durst,
How such a glance came there; so, not the first
Are you to turn and ask thus. Sir, 'twas not
Her husband's presence only, called that spot
Of joy into the Duchess' cheek: perhaps
Frà Pandolf chanced to say "Her mantle laps
Over my lady's wrist too much," or "Paint
Must never hope to reproduce the faint
Half-flush that dies along her throat": such stuff
Was courtesy, she thought, and cause enough
For calling up that spot of joy. She had
A heart—how shall I say?—too soon made glad,
Too easily impressed; she liked whate'er
She looked on, and her looks went everywhere.
Sir, 'twas all one! My favor at her breast,
The dropping of the daylight in the West,
The bough of cherries some officious fool
Broke in the orchard for her, the white mule
She rode with round the terrace—all and each
Would draw from her alike the approving speech,
Or blush, at least. She thanked men—good! but thanked
Somehow—I know not how—as if she ranked
My gift of a nine-hundred-years-old name
With anybody's gift. Who'd stoop to blame
This sort of trifling? Even had you skill
In speech—(which I have not)—to make your will
Quite clear to such an one, and say, "Just this
Or that in you disgusts me; here you miss,
Or there exceed the mark"—and if she let
Herself be lessoned so, nor plainly set
Her wits to yours, forsooth, and made excuse
—E'en then would be some stooping; and I choose
Never to stoop. Oh sir, she smiled, no doubt,
Whene'er I passed her; but who passed without
Much the same smile? This grew; I gave commands;
Then all smiles stopped together. There she stands
As if alive. Will't please you rise? We'll meet
The company below, then. I repeat,
The Count your master's known munificence
Is ample warrant that no just pretense

Of mine for dowry will be disallowed;
Though his fair daughter's self, as I avowed
At starting, is my object. Nay, we'll go
Together down, sir. Notice Neptune, though,
Taming a sea horse, thought a rarity,   55
Which Claus of Innsbruck² cast in bronze for me!

---

2. **Neptune,** the god of the sea; **Claus** (klous) **of Innsbruck** (inz′brŭk), an imaginary sculptor of Innsbruck in the Tyrol in Austria, a town noted for bronzework.

ELIZABETH BARRETT BROWNING

Elizabeth Barrett Browning (1806–1861) was for some time a more famous poet than her husband, Robert Browning. As a small child she fell from her pony, badly injuring her spine. For many years thereafter her life was spent as an invalid, writing poetry. In 1845, the dashing Robert Browning met her, fell in love with her, and persuaded her to elope with him to Italy. The emotional record of her growing love for Browning and her fears and doubts about her ill health and unworthiness of such love were recorded in a series of forty-four sonnets. After their marriage and a trip to Italy, where her health improved, she finally showed the sonnets to her husband, and he insisted that they be published. Because the sonnets were deeply personal, she decided to present them as translations, calling them *Sonnets from the Portuguese*.

from Sonnets from the Portuguese

8

What can I give thee back, O liberal
And princely giver, who hast brought the gold
And purple of thine heart, unstained, untold,
And laid them on the outside of the wall
For such as I to take or leave withal,   5
In unexpected largesse? Am I cold,
Ungrateful, that for these most manifold
High gifts, I render nothing back at all?
Not so; not cold—but very poor instead.
Ask God, who knows. For frequent tears have run   10
The colors from my life, and left so dead
And pale a stuff, it were not fitly done
To give the same as pillow to thy head.
Go farther! let it serve to trample on.

Is it indeed so? If I lay here dead,
Wouldst thou miss any life in losing mine?
And would the sun for thee more coldly shine
Because of grave-damps falling round my head?
I marveled, my Beloved, when I read   5
Thy thought so in the letter. I am thine—
But . . . *so* much to thee? Can I pour thy wine
While my hands tremble? Then my soul, instead
Of dreams of death, resumes life's lower range.
Then, love me, Love! look on me—breathe on me!   10
As brighter ladies do not count it strange,
For love to give up acres and degree,
I yield the grave for thy sake, and exchange
My near sweet view of Heaven, for earth with thee!

Ulysses

1. What different motives does Ulysses have for wanting to leave Ithaca? Which seem to be the most important?

2. Why is Telemachus brought into the poem?

3. Is Ulysses looking for death (he speaks of touching the Happy Isles and of seeing Achilles)? If not, what is he looking for?

My Last Duchess

1. What words immediately give you the clue to the identity of the speaker? Who is the listener?

2. What do you learn about the duke from the words in parentheses in lines 9 and 10?

3. What are the complaints that the duke had about his wife?

4. What is implied by the words "I gave commands; then all smiles stopped together"? What may have happened?

5. Since the envoy's master is wealthy, what is the effect of the duke's confession that the woman's "self" is his real object?

6. What final bit of information do you gain about the duke through his pointing out the sculpture of Neptune and the sea horse?

7. What was most threatened in the duke: his pride or his faith in love?

8. To what extent is this poem intended to reveal something about the individual personality?

9. The duke lists four things (besides the painter's remarks) which would bring to the duchess a blush of pleasure. What have they in common? What irony is there in the relation of the first of these to the other three?

10. What tones of voice does the duke employ?

Sonnets from the Portuguese

1. What view of self is presented by the speaker of "Sonnet 8"? What view of the beloved? How is color imagery used in the poem?

2. Assuming that the speaker of "Sonnet 23" is the same person, what change in attitude do you see? What has caused this change?

MATTHEW ARNOLD

Matthew Arnold (1822–1888) was a poet and a critic. He wrote volumes of poetry and a series of essays on literary and social topics while at the same time earning his living as an inspector of schools. Arnold went to Oxford, where he received a fine classical education that served him well throughout his life, for he constantly looked to the classics for symbols of permanence and stability. In his poem "To a Friend," he named Homer, Epictetus (the Stoic philosopher), and Sophocles as the three writers to whom he turned for mental and moral support. Sophocles is mentioned again in "Dover Beach." In that poem Arnold finds consolation in the thought that the sadness of the sea was also heard by Sophocles so very long ago. Arnold's turning to the past and his praise of classical writers reflect his dissatisfaction with the present, a feeling shared by many Victorians. The impact of the revolutions in industry and science was not comforting, and Arnold, like other Victorians, sought refuge in faith.

Dover Beach

The sea is calm tonight.
The tide is full, the moon lies fair
Upon the straits—on the French coast the light
Gleams and is gone; the cliffs of England stand,
Glimmering and vast, out in the tranquil bay.   5
Come to the window, sweet is the night air!
Only, from the long line of spray
Where the sea meets the moon-blanched land,
Listen! you hear the grating roar
Of pebbles which the waves draw back, and fling,   10
At their return, up the high strand,
Begin, and cease, and then again begin,
With tremulous cadence slow, and bring
The eternal note of sadness in.

Sophocles long ago   15
Heard it on the Aegean, and it brought
Into his mind the turbid ebb and flow
Of human misery; we
Find also in the sound a thought,
Hearing it by this distant northern sea.[1]   20

The Sea of Faith
Was once, too, at the full, and round earth's shore
Lay like the folds of a bright girdle furled.
But now I only hear
Its melancholy, long, withdrawing roar,   25
Retreating, to the breath
Of the night wind, down the vast edges drear
And naked shingles of the world.

---

1. **northern sea**, the North Atlantic as it flows through the English Channel.

Ah, love let us be true
To one another! for the world, which seems   30
To lie before us like a land of dreams,
So various, so beautiful, so new,
Hath really neither joy, nor love, nor light,
No certitude, nor peace, nor help for pain;
And we are here as on a darkling plain   35
Swept with confused alarms of struggle and flight,
Where ignorant armies clash by night.

A. E. HOUSMAN

A. E. Housman (1859–1936) is known primarily for one book,
A Shropshire Lad, written in a burst of creative energy in 1895. Housman was
then Professor of Latin at University College, London. Before that time,
though, he had failed his honors exam at Oxford and had spent ten years
working as a clerk in the Patent Office. During those years, Housman studied
Greek and Latin and finally received his university position. In 1911, he was
appointed to the Chair of Latin at Cambridge and served in that capacity until
his death. The poems in *A Shropshire Lad* are remarkable for their surface
simplicity and their hidden irony. We might expect that a Latin professor
would fill his poems with classical allusions, but Housman instead turned to
scenes of his childhood, using natural images, peasant characters, and
small events as the subjects of his poems. The true subjects, however, are the
attitudes that Housman implies or suggests through a gentle irony. When you
read the poems, you will find that there is often a difference between
what you expect and what you get—or between what you know and what the
character knows. The poems are carefully crafted and deceptively simple.

With Rue
My Heart Is Laden

With rue my heart is laden
  For golden friends I had,
For many a rose-lipt maiden
  And many a lightfoot lad.

By brooks too broad for leaping   5
  The lightfoot boys are laid;
The rose-lipt girls are sleeping
  In fields where roses fade.

Loveliest of Trees

Loveliest of trees, the cherry now
Is hung with bloom along the bough,
And stands about the woodland ride
Wearing white for Eastertide.

Now, of my threescore years and ten,   5
Twenty will not come again,
And take from seventy springs a score,
It only leaves me fifty more.

And since to look at things in bloom
Fifty springs are little room,   10
About the woodlands I will go
To see the cherry hung with snow.

When I Was
One-and-Twenty

When I was one-and-twenty
  I heard a wise man say,
"Give crowns and pounds and guineas
  But not your heart away;
Give pearls away and rubies   5
  But keep your fancy free."
But I was one-and-twenty,
  No use to talk to me.

When I was one-and-twenty
  I heard him say again,   10
"The heart out of the bosom
  Was never given in vain;
'Tis paid with sighs a plenty
  And sold for endless rue."
And I am two-and-twenty,   15
  And oh, 'tis true, 'tis true.

To an Athlete
Dying Young

The time you won your town the race
We chaired[1] you through the market-place,
Man and boy stood cheering by,
And home we brought you shoulder-high.

To-day, the road all runners come,   5
Shoulder-high we bring you home,
And set you at your threshold down,
Townsman of a stiller town.

Smart lad, to slip betimes away
From fields where glory does not stay,   10
And early though the laurel[2] grows
It withers quicker than the rose.

Eyes the shady night has shut
Cannot see the record cut,
And silence sounds no worse than cheers   15
After earth has stopped the ears:

Now you will not swell the rout
Of lads that wore their honours out,
Runners whom renown outran
And the name died before the man.   20

So set, before its echoes fade,
The fleet foot on the sill of shade,
And hold to the low lintel up
The still-defended challenge-cup.

And round the early-laurelled head   25
Will flock to gaze the strengthless dead,
And find unwithered on its curls
The garland briefer than a girl's.

---

1. **chaired,** carried in joy and triumph in or as if in a chair.
2. **the laurel,** a symbol of victory, the laurels of the athlete are for the day only.

Dover Beach

1. What starts the poet on his meditation?

2. What does Arnold mean by the "Sea of Faith"? When was it at the full? What does he mean when he says it is withdrawing?

3. State in your own words the human condition as Arnold describes it in this poem. What single positive value does he still cling to?

Think through and discuss the following propositions about the Housman poems:

With Rue My Heart Is Laden

1. The basic idea of the poem, "I am sad because so many of my friends are dead," is commonplace, but the poem makes it fresh.

2. The only expression of emotion is in line 1.

3. With the exception of line 1 and the last word of the poem, all of the words have good or pleasant connotations.

4. The irony exists in the contrast between what is being said and the choice of words and rhythm in which it is being said.

Loveliest of Trees

1. All the loveliness of spring is suggested by the description of only one object.

2. The poem suggests the characteristic human restlessness during spring that Chaucer suggested in the opening lines of "The Prologue" to *The Canterbury Tales.*

3. In spite of the joy in spring, the poem is tinged with melancholy.

4. Joy is enhanced by our knowledge that it cannot last.

When I Was One-and-Twenty

1. The advice given in stanza 2 differs slightly in its content from that given in stanza 1.

2. The irony lies in the fact that the reader is led to expect that the speaker is an old person.

To an Athlete Dying Young

1. "Shoulder-high" has a different meaning in stanza 1 from that in stanza 2.

2. The words "smart lad" are meant by the speaker as a sincere expression of admiration.

3. It is better to die young than to live to "see the record cut."

4. The poem implies that people who die in a moment of victory will be longer remembered than those who live out their lives.

CRITICS OF SOCIETY

Literature is one of the most effective ways of commenting on society and protesting against injustices. From early times, particularly in societies where people did not have freedom of speech, stories and rhymes were used as a means of ridiculing the ruling class. A writer could pretend to be talking about animals or imaginary people in a distant land and, using this smoke screen, comment on personal dissatisfactions with present-day reality. Some of the Mother Goose rhymes were originally written and passed on by word of mouth as social commentary. Little Jack Horner, for example, refers to a Lord Horner who pulled a particularly shady deal during Elizabethan times. The American blacks used spirituals built on Biblical themes to express their own plight as slaves.

Why do writers use fiction, poems, and drama to talk about social problems? Why not make simple, direct statements of fact? For one thing, a story catches and holds the reader's imagination and emotions in a way that speeches, statistics, and haranguing cannot. In his novels, Dickens dramatized the scandal of debtor's prisons in such a way that English law was reformed. Harriet Beecher Stowe's story of Uncle Tom fired the imagination of the American people and helped light the fuse of the War between the States. Upton Sinclair presented the conditions in the slaughterhouses of Chicago with such vividness in *The Jungle,* that the public demanded and got the government to inspect the food industries. Writers who are also critics of society often say nothing that is new, but they present their facts in such a way as to reach a large audience. They know how to use language to speak so effectively to people that their consciences press them to action.

Literature strives always to get to the innermost feelings of human beings and to show the complexity and variety possible in life. The social protest of the writer is only significant when the situation is presented in such a way that it has universal meaning and is not limited to a small local concern. Consequently, the great writer who turns to social criticism is careful to avoid certain pitfalls:

THREE JUDGES
Georges Rouault
Courtesy of the Museum of
Modern Art, New York,
Sam A. Lewisohn Bequest

1. Sentimentality: If the characters are too obvious and one-sided, if the "good" people are too pure and innocent and the "bad" people are completely evil, the work becomes melodramatic—a tearjerker. This is the case with *Uncle Tom's Cabin*. To the modern reader the book is a curiosity, a fragment of history, not an example of good fiction.

2. Oversimplification: The writer becomes so eager to solve a social problem that he or she presents the problem in terms that are too simple. One side (or party) is totally right, the other side is totally wrong. This insults the reader who knows that people and problems are complex, and that social problems cannot be solved in a few moments.

3. Didacticism: Being deeply moved by the problem and eager that the reader not miss the point, the writer stops in the flow of the story to preach a little sermon, instead of letting the story speak for itself.

4. Too narrow or local a concern: If a writer deals with a very specific problem that is subsequently solved, the work loses its impact except as a historic document. The great writers of social criticism start from a special situation, but they see that whatever evil causes the situation—selfishness, stupidity, dishonesty—is deep within human nature. Thus, the work they produce becomes universal in its impact; it is read by later generations and applies to situations yet unknown.

HENRIK JOHAN IBSEN

1828-1906

Anyone who wishes to understand me fully must know Norway. The spectacular but severe landscape which people have around them in the north, and the lonely, shut-off life—the houses often lie miles from each other—force them not to bother about other people, but only their own concerns, so that they become reflective and serious, they brood and doubt and often despair. In Norway every other person is a philosopher. And those dark winters, with the thick mists outside—ah, they long for the sun![1]

So spoke Henrik Ibsen, Norway's great poet and dramatist who has often been called the first great modern playwright. Considering his feeling that the landscape itself had affected him, it should be no surprise to discover that Ibsen was withdrawn, little given to the social life of his time, and intent on perfecting his skill in playwriting.

Born into a merchant's family in the small town of Skien on the east coast of Norway, Ibsen had his childhood scarred at age eight by his father's financial failure. At fifteen, Ibsen was apprenticed to an apothecary in a small town and found himself doing practically everything while his employer spent his time socializing. For relief, the lonely boy turned to writing poetry and reading avidly any books of poetry and theology he could find.

After a short period during which he studied for the university, Ibsen accepted the post of "theater-poet" for the newly organized theater at Bergen. There he learned all aspects of the dramatic craft, for he was at times not only the theater-poet but also the producer, manager, adviser, and designer. And finally he wrote dramas for the theater to pro-duce. His last play for this group was *Love's Comedy,* which attacked the stupidity of the majority and caused a burst of public indignation. This kind of reaction was to become all too familiar to Ibsen, who delighted in attacking society's favorite ideas.

After he married Susanna Thorensen in 1857, Ibsen and his wife went to Christiania hoping to better their financial situation. Instead, things took a turn for the worse, and in 1864, after receiving a small grant from the government, Ibsen left for Italy determined to express his sense of the injustice of his native land toward its writers. From this anger came two of his great poetic dramas, *Brand,* a grim story of a minister who refuses to compromise, and *Peer Gynt,* a fantasy describing the adventures of a young man. The next years of Ibsen's life are remarkable only for his steady output of a play every two years. He broke from this pattern only once: Angered by the public's reception of *Ghosts,* he wrote *An Enemy of the People* which was produced only a year later.

Ibsen was always in crisis, the center of tumultous conflict. In one of his letters he said:

I maintain that a fighter at the intellectual outposts can never gather a majority around him. In ten years, perhaps, the majority may occupy the standpoint which Dr. Stockmann held at the public meeting. But during those ten years the Doctor will not have been standing still; he will still be at least ten years ahead of the majority. The majority, the mass, the multitude, can never overtake him; he can never have the majority with

---

1. Ibsen in conversation, quoted by Felix Philipp.

Henrik Ibsen

him. As for myself, at all events, I am conscious of this incessant progression. At the point where I stood when I wrote each of my books, there now stands a fairly compact multitude; but I myself am there no longer; I am elsewhere, and, I hope, further ahead.[2]

Critics indicate that Dr. Stockmann in *An Enemy of the People* was created to present the playwright's own views. But Ibsen was too skilled a writer to make the doctor a copy of himself. In the letter that accompanied the manuscript of the play to the publisher, Ibsen said:

I have enjoyed writing this piece, and I feel quite lost and lonely now that it is out of hand. Dr. Stockmann and I got on excellently together; we agree on so many subjects. But the Doctor is a more muddleheaded person than I am, and he

has, moreover, several other characteristics because of which people will stand hearing a good many things from him which they may not have taken in such very good part had they been said by me.

Not until 1892 did Ibsen return to Norway to live. By then he was famous and financially secure, and his own people had at last accepted him.

An Enemy of the People

The ideas proposed by Ibsen in *An Enemy of the People* had concerned him in his conversations and letters for years. But they shocked his audience. They may even have the power to shock today. Some of the incidents in the play were based on actual happenings. A young German poet had told Ibsen about his father's discovery that a German spa was the source of a cholera outbreak. But when his findings were made public, the citizens stoned the man's house and forced him to flee the community. The great fourth act of *An Enemy of the People* is a close paraphrase of a newspaper transcript of a public meeting in which a Norwegian chemist attempted to expose the terrible conditions of the Oslo steam kitchens and the treatment of the city's poor.

But the ultimate greatness of the play rests on the complicated character of Dr. Stockmann, a part that only the greatest actors have been able to portray. Ibsen in a letter to the director said, "... Hot headed people are in general more slightly built. [Ibsen himself was a very short man.] He [the actor playing the part of Stockmann] must make himself as thin and small as possible. Above all [in the staging] truthfulness to nature—the illusion that everything is real and that one is sitting and watching something that is actually taking place in real life—this is the feeling I wish to convey."

2. From a letter to Brandes, a drama critic, written six months after *An Enemy of the People* was produced.

AN ENEMY OF THE PEOPLE

Characters

DR. THOMAS STOCKMANN, *Medical Officer of the Municipal Baths*

MRS. STOCKMANN, *his wife*

PETRA, *their daughter, a teacher*

EJLIF
MORTEN } *their sons*

(aged 13 and 10 respectively)

PETER STOCKMANN, *the Doctor's elder brother; Mayor of the Town and Chief Constable, Chairman of the Baths' Committee, etc., etc.*

MORTEN KIIL, *a tanner*

(Mrs. Stockmann's adoptive father)

HOVSTAD, *editor of the "People's Messenger"*

BILLING, *sub-editor*

CAPTAIN HORSTER

ASLAKSEN, *a printer*

Men of various conditions and occupations, some few women, and a troop of schoolboys—the audience at a public meeting

The action takes place in a coast town in southern Norway.

Act I

SCENE—DR. STOCKMANN'S *sitting-room. It is evening. The room is plainly but neatly appointed and furnished. In the right-hand wall are two doors; the farther leads out to the hall, the nearer to the doctor's study. In the left-hand wall, opposite the door leading to the hall, is a door leading to the other rooms occupied by the family. In the middle of the same wall stands the stove, and, further forward, a couch with a looking-glass hanging over it and an oval table in front of it. On the table, a lighted lamp, with a lampshade. At the back of the room, an open door leads to the dining-room.*

BILLING *is seen sitting at the dining table, on which a lamp is burning. He has a napkin tucked under his chin, and* MRS. STOCKMANN *is standing by the table handing him a large plateful of roast beef. The other places at the table are empty, and the table somewhat in disorder, a meal having evidently recently been finished.*

MRS. STOCKMANN. You see, if you come an hour late, Mr. Billing, you have to put up with cold meat.

BILLING (*as he eats*). It is uncommonly good, thank you—remarkably good.

MRS. STOCKMANN. My husband makes such a point of having his meals punctually, you know—

BILLING. That doesn't affect me a bit. Indeed, I almost think I enjoy a meal all the better when I can sit down and eat all by myself and undisturbed.

MRS. STOCKMANN. Oh well, as long as you are enjoying it—. (*Turns to the hall door, listening.*) I expect that is Mr. Hovstad coming too.

BILLING. Very likely.

PETER STOCKMANN *comes in. He wears an overcoat and his official hat, and carries a stick.*

PETER STOCKMANN. Good evening, Katherine.

MRS. STOCKMANN (*coming forward into the sitting-room*). Ah, good evening—is it you? How good of you to come up and see us!

PETER STOCKMANN. I happened to be passing, and so—(*looks into the dining-room*). But you have company with you, I see.

MRS. STOCKMANN (*a little embarrassed*). Oh, no—it was quite by chance he came in. (*Hurriedly.*) Won't you come in and have something, too?

PETER STOCKMANN. I! No, thank you. Good

gracious—hot meat at night! Not with my digestion.

MRS. STOCKMANN. Oh, but just once in a way—

PETER STOCKMANN. No, no, my dear lady; I stick to my tea and bread and butter. It is much more wholesome in the long run—and a little more economical, too.

MRS. STOCKMANN (*smiling*). Now you mustn't think that Thomas and I are spendthrifts.

PETER STOCKMANN. Not you, my dear; I would never think that of you. (*Points to the Doctor's study.*) Is he not at home?

MRS. STOCKMANN. No, he went out for a little turn after supper—he and the boys.

PETER STOCKMANN. I doubt if that is a wise thing to do. (*Listens.*) I fancy I hear him coming now.

MRS. STOCKMANN. No, I don't think it is he. (*A knock is heard at the door.*) Come in! (HOVSTAD *comes in from the hall.*) Oh, it is you, Mr. Hovstad!

HOVSTAD. Yes, I hope you will forgive me, but I was delayed at the printer's. Good evening, Mr. Mayor.

PETER STOCKMANN (*bowing a little distantly*). Good evening. You have come on business, no doubt.

HOVSTAD. Partly. It's about an article for the paper.

PETER STOCKMANN. So I imagined. I hear my brother has become a prolific contributor to the "People's Messenger."

HOVSTAD. Yes, he is good enough to write in the "People's Messenger" when he has any home truths to tell.

MRS. STOCKMANN (*to* HOVSTAD). But won't you—? (*Points to the dining-room.*)

PETER STOCKMANN. Quite so, quite so. I don't blame him in the least, as a writer, for addressing himself to the quarters where he will find the readiest sympathy. And, besides that, I personally have no reason to bear any ill will to your paper, Mr. Hovstad.

HOVSTAD. I quite agree with you.

PETER STOCKMANN. Taking one thing with another, there is an excellent spirit of toleration in the town—an admirable municipal spirit. And it all springs from the fact of our having a great common interest to unite us—an interest that is in an equally high degree the concern of every right-minded citizen—

HOVSTAD. The Baths, yes.

PETER STOCKMANN. Exactly—our fine, new, handsome Baths. Mark my words, Mr. Hovstad—the Baths will become the focus of our municipal life! Not a doubt of it!

MRS. STOCKMANN. That is just what Thomas says.

PETER STOCKMANN. Think how extraordinarily the place has developed within the last year or two! Money has been flowing in, and there is some life and some business doing in the town. Houses and landed property are rising in value every day.

HOVSTAD. And unemployment is diminishing.

PETER STOCKMANN. Yes, that is another thing. The burden of the poor rates has been lightened, to the great relief of the propertied classes; and that relief will be even greater if only we get a really good summer this year, and lots of visitors—plenty of invalids, who will make the Baths talked about.

HOVSTAD. And there is a good prospect of that, I hear.

PETER STOCKMANN. It looks very promising. Enquiries about apartments and that sort of thing are reaching us every day.

HOVSTAD. Well, the doctor's article will come in very suitably.

PETER STOCKMANN. Has he been writing something just lately?

HOVSTAD. This is something he wrote in the winter; a recommendation of the Baths—an account of the excellent sanitary conditions here. But I held the article over, temporarily.

PETER STOCKMANN. Ah,—some little difficulty about it, I suppose?

HOVSTAD. No, not at all; I thought it would be better to wait till the spring, because it is just at this time that people begin to think seriously about their summer quarters.

PETER STOCKMANN. Quite right; you were perfectly right, Mr. Hovstad.

HOVSTAD. Yes, Thomas is really indefatigable when it is a question of the Baths.

PETER STOCKMANN. Well—remember, he is the Medical Officer to the Baths.

HOVSTAD. Yes, and what is more, they owe their existence to him.

PETER STOCKMANN. To him? Indeed! It is true I have heard from time to time that some people are of that opinion. At the same time I must say I imagined that I took a modest part in the enterprise.

MRS. STOCKMANN. Yes, that is what Thomas is always saying.

HOVSTAD. But who denies it, Mr. Stockmann? You set the thing going and made a practical concern of it; we all know that. I only meant that the idea of it came first from the doctor.

PETER STOCKMANN. Oh, ideas—yes! My brother has had plenty of them in his time—unfortunately. But when it is a question of putting an idea into practical shape, you have to apply to a man of different mettle, Mr. Hovstad. And I certainly should have thoughts that in this house at least—

MRS. STOCKMANN. My dear Peter—

HOVSTAD. How can you think that—?

MRS. STOCKMANN. Won't you go in and have something, Mr. Hovstad? My husband is sure to be back directly.

HOVSTAD. Thank you, perhaps just a morsel. (*Goes into the dining-room.*)

PETER STOCKMANN (*lowering his voice a little*). It is a curious thing that these farmers' sons never seem to lose their want of tact.

MRS. STOCKMANN. Surely it is not worth bothering about! Cannot you and Thomas share the credit as brothers?

PETER STOCKMANN. I should have thought so; but apparently some people are not satisfied with a share.

MRS. STOCKMANN. What nonsense! You and Thomas get on so capitally together. (*Listens.*) There he is at last, I think. (*Goes out and opens the door leading to the hall.*)

DR. STOCKMANN (*laughing and talking outside*). Look here—here is another guest for you, Katherine. Isn't that jolly! Come in, Captain Horster; hang your coat up on this peg. Ah, you don't wear an overcoat. Just think, Katherine; I met him in the street and could hardly persuade him to come up! (CAPTAIN HORSTER *comes into the room and greets* MRS. STOCKMANN. *He is followed by* DR. STOCKMANN.) Come along in, boys. They are ravenously hungry again, you know. Come along, Captain Horster; you must have a slice of beef. (*Pushes* HORSTER *into the dining-room.* EJLIF *and* MORTEN *go in after them.*)

MRS. STOCKMANN. But, Thomas, don't you see—?

DR. STOCKMANN (*turning in the doorway*). Oh, is it you, Peter? (*Shakes hands with him.*) Now that is very delightful.

PETER STOCKMANN. Unfortunately I must go in a moment—

DR. STOCKMANN. Rubbish! There is some toddy just coming in. You haven't forgotten the toddy, Katherine?

MRS. STOCKMANN. Of course not; the water is boiling now. (*Goes into the dining-room.*)

PETER STOCKMANN. Toddy too!

DR. STOCKMANN. Yes, sit down and we will have it comfortably.

PETER STOCKMANN. Thanks, I never care about an evening's drinking.

DR. STOCKMANN. But this isn't an evening's drinking.

PETER STOCKMANN. It seems to me—. (*Looks towards the dining-room.*) It is extraordinary how they can put away all that food.

DR. STOCKMANN (*rubbing his hands*). Yes, isn't it splendid to see young people eat? They have always got an appetite, you know! That's as it should be. Lots of food—to build up their strength! They are the people who are going to stir up the fermenting forces of the future, Peter.

PETER STOCKMANN. May I ask what they will find here to "stir up," as you put it?

DR. STOCKMANN. Ah, you must ask the young

people that—when the time comes. We shan't be able to see it, of course. That stands to reason—two old fogies, like us—

PETER STOCKMANN. Really, really! I must say that is an extremely odd expression to—

DR. STOCKMANN. Oh, you mustn't take me too literally, Peter. I am so heartily happy and contented, you know. I think it is such an extraordinary piece of good fortune to be in the middle of all this growing, germinating life. It is a splendid time to live in! It is as if a whole new world were being created around one.

PETER STOCKMANN. Do you really think so?

DR. STOCKMANN. Ah, naturally you can't appreciate it as keenly as I. You have lived all your life in these surroundings, and your impressions have got blunted. But I, who have been buried all these years in my little corner up north, almost without ever seeing a stranger who might bring new ideas with him—well, in my case it has just the same effect as if I had been transported into the middle of a crowded city.

PETER STOCKMANN. Oh, a city—!

DR. STOCKMANN. I know, I know; it is all cramped enough here, compared with many other places. But there is life here—there is promise—there are innumerable things to work for and fight for; and that is the main thing. (*Calls.*) Katherine, hasn't the postman been here?

MRS. STOCKMANN (*from the dining-room*). No.

DR. STOCKMANN. And then to be comfortably off, Peter! That is something one learns to value, when one has been on the brink of starvation, as we have.

PETER STOCKMANN. Oh, surely—

DR. STOCKMANN. Indeed I can assure you we have often been very hard put to it, up there. And now to be able to live like a lord! Today, for instance, we had roast beef for dinner—and, what is more, for supper too. Won't you come and have a little bit? Or let me show it you, at any rate? Come here—

PETER STOCKMANN. No, no—not for worlds!

DR. STOCKMANN. Well, but just come here then. Do you see, we have got a table-cover?

PETER STOCKMANN. Yes, I noticed it.

DR. STOCKMANN. And we have got a lamp shade too. Do you see? All out of Katherine's savings! It makes the room so cosy. Don't you think so? Just stand here for a moment—no, no, not there—just here, that's it! Look now, when you get the light on it altogether—I really think it looks very nice, doesn't it?

PETER STOCKMANN. Oh, if you can afford luxuries of this kind—

DR. STOCKMANN. Yes, I can afford it now. Katherine tells me I earn almost as much as we spend.

PETER STOCKMANN. Almost—yes!

DR. STOCKMANN. But a scientific man must live in a little bit of style. I am quite sure an ordinary civil servant spends more in a year than I do.

PETER STOCKMANN. I daresay. A civil servant—a man in a well-paid position—

DR. STOCKMANN. Well, any ordinary merchant, then! A man in that position spends two or three times as much as—

PETER STOCKMANN. It just depends on circumstances.

DR. STOCKMANN. At all events I assure you I don't waste money unprofitably. But I can't find it in my heart to deny myself the pleasure of entertaining my friends. I need that sort of thing, you know. I have lived for so long shut out of it all, that it is a necessity of life to me to mix with young, eager, ambitious men, men of liberal and active minds; and that describes every one of those fellows who are enjoying their supper in there. I wish you knew more of Hovstad—

PETER STOCKMANN. By the way, Hovstad was telling me he was going to print another article of yours.

DR. STOCKMANN. An article of mine?

PETER STOCKMANN. Yes, about the Baths. An article you wrote in the winter.

DR. STOCKMANN. Oh, that one! No, I don't intend that to appear just for the present.

PETER STOCKMANN. Why not? It seems to me that this would be the most opportune moment.

DR. STOCKMANN. Yes, very likely—under normal conditions. (Crosses the room.)

PETER STOCKMANN (following him with his eyes). Is there anything abnormal about the present conditions?

DR. STOCKMANN (standing still). To tell you the truth, Peter, I can't say just at this moment—at all events not tonight. There may be much that is very abnormal about the present conditions—and it is possible there may be nothing abnormal about them at all. It is quite possible it may be merely my imagination.

PETER STOCKMANN. I must say it all sounds most mysterious. Is there something going on that I am to be kept in ignorance of? I should have imagined that I, as Chairman of the governing body of the Baths—

DR. STOCKMANN. And I should have imagined that I—. Oh, come, don't let us fly out at one another, Peter.

PETER STOCKMANN. Heaven forbid! I am not in the habit of flying out at people, as you call it. But I am entitled to request most emphatically that all arrangements shall be made in a business-like manner, through the proper channels, and shall be dealt with by the legally constituted authorities. I can allow no going behind our backs by any roundabout means.

DR. STOCKMANN. Have I ever at any time tried to go behind your backs!

PETER STOCKMANN. You have an ingrained tendency to take your own way, at all events; and that is almost equally inadmissible in a well-ordered community. The individual ought undoubtedly to acquiesce in subordinating himself to the community—or, to speak more accurately, to the authorities who have the care of the community's welfare.

DR. STOCKMANN. Very likely. But what the deuce has all this got to do with me?

PETER STOCKMANN. That is exactly what you never appear to be willing to learn, my dear Thomas. But, mark my words, some day you will have to suffer for it—sooner or later. Now I have told you. Good-bye.

DR. STOCKMANN. Have you taken leave of your senses? You are on the wrong scent altogether.

PETER STOCKMANN. I am not usually that. You must excuse me now if I—(calls into the dining-room). Good night, Katherine. Good night, gentlemen. (Goes out.)

MRS. STOCKMANN (coming from the dining-room). Has he gone?

DR. STOCKMANN. Yes, and in such a bad temper.

MRS. STOCKMANN. But, dear Thomas, what have you been doing to him again?

DR. STOCKMANN. Nothing at all. And, anyhow, he can't oblige me to make my report before the proper time.

MRS. STOCKMANN. What have you got to make a report to him about?

DR. STOCKMANN. Hm! Leave that to me, Katherine.—It is an extraordinary thing that the postman doesn't come.

HOVSTAD, BILLING and HORSTER have got up from the table and come into the sitting-room. EJLIF and MORTEN come in after them.

BILLING (stretching himself). Ah!—one feels a new man after a meal like that.

HOVSTAD. The mayor wasn't in a very sweet temper tonight, then.

DR. STOCKMANN. It is his stomach; he has a wretched digestion.

HOVSTAD. I rather think it was us two of the "People's Messenger" that he couldn't digest.

MRS. STOCKMANN. I thought you came out of it pretty well with him.

HOVSTAD. Oh yes; but it isn't anything more than a sort of truce.

BILLING. That is just what it is! That word sums up the situation.

DR. STOCKMANN. We must remember that Peter is a lonely man, poor chap. He has no home comforts of any kind; nothing but everlasting business. And all that infernal weak tea wash that he pours into himself! Now then, my boys, bring chairs up to the table. Aren't we going to have that toddy, Katherine?

MRS. STOCKMANN (*going into the dining-room*). I am just getting it.

DR. STOCKMANN. Sit down here on the couch beside me, Captain Horster. We so seldom see you—. Please sit down, my friends. (*They sit down at the table.* MRS. STOCKMANN *brings a tray, with a spirit-lamp, glasses, bottles, etc., upon it.*)

MRS. STOCKMANN. There you are! This is arrack, and this is rum, and this one is the brandy. Now every one must help himself.

DR. STOCKMANN (*taking a glass*). We will. (*They all mix themselves some toddy.*) And let us have the cigars. Ejlif, you know where the box is. And you, Morten, can fetch my pipe. (*The two boys go into the room on the right.*) I have a suspicion that Ejlif pockets a cigar now and then!—but I take no notice of it. (*Calls out.*) And my smoking-cap too, Morten. Katherine, you can tell him where I left it. Ah, he has got it. (*The boys bring the various things.*) Now, my friends, I stick to my pipe, you know. This one has seen plenty of bad weather with me up north. (*Touches glasses with them.*) Your good health! Ah, it is good to be sitting snug and warm here.

MRS. STOCKMANN (*who sits knitting*). Do you sail soon, Captain Horster?

HORSTER. I expect to be ready to sail next week.

MRS. STOCKMANN. I suppose you are going to America?

HORSTER. Yes, that is the plan.

MRS. STOCKMANN. Then you won't be able to take part in the coming election.

HORSTER. Is there going to be an election?

BILLING. Didn't you know?

HORSTER. No, I don't mix myself up with those things.

BILLING. But do you not take an interest in public affairs?

HORSTER. No, I don't know anything about politics.

BILLING. All the same, one ought to vote, at any rate.

HORSTER. Even if one doesn't know anything about what is going on?

BILLING. Doesn't know! What do you mean by that? A community is like a ship; every one ought to be prepared to take the helm.

HORSTER. Maybe that is all very well on shore; but on board ship it wouldn't work.

HOVSTAD. It is astonishing how little most sailors care about what goes on on shore.

BILLING. Very extraordinary.

DR. STOCKMANN. Sailors are like birds of passage; they feel equally at home in any latitude. And that is only an additional reason for our being all the more keen, Hovstad. Is there to be anything of public interest in tomorrow's "Messenger"?

HOVSTAD. Nothing about municipal affairs. But the day after tomorrow I was thinking of printing your article—

DR. STOCKMANN. Ah, devil take it—my article! Look here, that must wait a bit.

HOVSTAD. Really? We had just got convenient space for it, and I thought it was just the opportune moment—

DR. STOCKMANN. Yes, yes, very likely you are right; but it must wait all the same. I will explain to you later. (PETRA comes in from the hall, in hat and cloak and with a bundle of exercise books under her arm.)

PETRA. Good evening.

DR. STOCKMANN. Good evening, Petra; come along.

Mutual greetings; PETRA *takes off her things and puts them down on a chair by the door.*

PETRA. And you have all been sitting here enjoying yourselves, while I have been out slaving!

DR. STOCKMANN. Well, come and enjoy yourself too!

BILLING. May I mix a glass for you?

PETRA (*coming to the table*). Thanks, I would rather do it; you always mix it too strong. But I forgot, father—I have a letter for you. (*Goes to the chair where she has laid her things.*)

DR. STOCKMANN. A letter? From whom?

PETRA (*looking in her coat pocket*). The postman gave it to me just as I was going out—

DR. STOCKMANN (*getting up and going to her*). And you only give it to me now!

PETRA. I really had not time to run up again. There it is!

DR. STOCKMANN (*seizing the letter*). Let's see, let's see, child! (*Looks at the address.*) Yes, that's all right!

MRS. STOCKMANN. Is it the one you have been expecting so anxiously, Thomas?

DR. STOCKMANN. Yes, it is. I must go to my room now and—. Where shall I get a light, Katherine? Is there no lamp in my room again?

MRS. STOCKMANN. Yes, your lamp is all ready lit on your desk.

DR. STOCKMANN. Good, good. Excuse me for a moment—. (*Goes into his study.*)

PETRA. What do you suppose it is, mother?

MRS. STOCKMANN. I don't know; for the last day or two he has always been asking if the postman has not been.

BILLING. Probably some country patient.

PETRA. Poor old dad!—he will overwork himself soon. (*Mixes a glass for herself.*) There, that will taste good!

HOVSTAD. Have you been teaching in the evening school again today?

PETRA (*sipping from her glass*). Two hours.

BILLING. And four hours of school in the morning—

PETRA. Five hours.

MRS. STOCKMANN. And you have still got exercises to correct, I see.

PETRA. A whole heap, yes.

HORSTER. You are pretty full up with work too, it seems to me.

PETRA. Yes—but that is good. One is so delightfully tired after it.

BILLING. Do you like that?

PETRA. Yes, because one sleeps so well, then.

MORTEN. You must be dreadfully wicked, Petra.

PETRA. Wicked?

MORTEN. Yes, because you work so much. Mr. Rörlund says work is a punishment for our sins.

EJLIF. Pooh, what a duffer you are, to believe a thing like that!

MRS. STOCKMANN. Come, come, Ejlif!

BILLING (*laughing*). That's capital!

HOVSTAD. Don't you want to work as hard as that, Morten?

MORTEN. No, indeed I don't.

HOVSTAD. What do you want to be, then?

MORTEN. I should like best to be a Viking.

EJLIF. You would have to be a pagan then.

MORTEN. Well, I could become a pagan, couldn't I?

BILLING. I agree with you, Morten! My sentiments, exactly.

MRS. STOCKMANN (*signalling to him*). I am sure that is not true, Mr. Billing.

BILLING. Yes, I swear it is! I am a pagan, and I am proud of it. Believe me, before long we shall all be pagans.

MORTEN. And then shall be allowed to do anything we like?

BILLING. Well, you see, Morten—.

MRS. STOCKMANN. You must go to your room now, boys; I am sure you have some lessons to learn for tomorrow.

EJLIF. I should like so much to stay a little longer—

MRS. STOCKMANN. No, no; away you go, both of you.

The boys say good night and go into the room on the left.

HOVSTAD. Do you really think it can do the boys any harm to hear such things?

MRS. STOCKMANN. I don't know, but I don't like it.

PETRA. But you know, mother, I think you really are wrong about it.

MRS. STOCKMANN. Maybe, but I don't like it—not in our own home.

PETRA. There is so much falsehood both at home and at school. At home one must not speak, and at school we have to stand and tell lies to the children.

HORSTER. Tell lies?

PETRA. Yes, don't you suppose we have to teach them all sorts of things that we don't believe?

BILLING. That is perfectly true.

PETRA. If only I had the means I would start a school of my own, and it would be conducted on very different lines.

BILLING. Oh, bother the means—!

HORSTER. Well, if you are thinking of that, Miss Stockmann, I shall be delighted to provide you with a schoolroom. The great big old house my father left me is standing almost empty; there is an immense dining-room downstairs—

PETRA (*laughing*). Thank you very much; but I am afraid nothing will come of it.

HOVSTAD. No, Miss Petra is much more likely to take to journalism, I expect. By the way, have you had time to do anything with that English story you promised to translate for us?

PETRA. No, not yet; but you shall have it in good time.

DR. STOCKMANN *comes in from his room with an open letter in his hand.*

DR. STOCKMANN (*waving the letter*). Well, now the town will have something new to talk about, I can tell you!

BILLING. Something new?

MRS. STOCKMANN. What is this?

DR. STOCKMANN. A great discovery, Katherine.

HOVSTAD. Really?

MRS. STOCKMANN. A discovery of yours?

DR. STOCKMANN. A discovery of mine. (*Walks

497

up and down.) Just let them come saying, as usual, that it is all fancy and a crazy man's imagination! But they will be careful what they say this time, I can tell you!

PETRA. But, father, tell us what it is.

DR. STOCKMANN. Yes, yes—only give me time, and you shall know all about it. If only I had Peter here now! It just shows how we men can go about forming our judgments, when in reality we are as blind as any moles—

HOVSTAD. What are you driving at, Doctor?

DR. STOCKMANN (*standing still by the table*). Isn't it the universal opinion that our town is a healthy spot?

HOVSTAD. Certainly.

DR. STOCKMANN. Quite an unusually healthy spot, in fact—a place that deserves to be recommended in the warmest possible manner either for invalids or for people who are well—

MRS. STOCKMANN. Yes, but my dear Thomas—

DR. STOCKMANN. And we have been recommending it and praising it—I have written and written, both in the "Messenger" and in pamphlets—

HOVSTAD. Well, what then?

DR. STOCKMANN. And the Baths—we have called them the "main artery of the town's life-blood," the "nerve-center of our town," and the devil knows what else—

BILLING. "The town's pulsating heart" was the expression I once used on an important occasion—

DR. STOCKMANN. Quite so. Well, do you know what they really are, these great, splendid, much-praised Baths, that have cost so much money—do you know what they are?

HOVSTAD. No, what are they?

MRS. STOCKMANN. Yes, what are they?

DR. STOCKMANN. The whole place is a pest-house!

PETRA. The Baths, father?

MRS. STOCKMANN (*at the same time*). Our Baths!

HOVSTAD. But, Doctor—

BILLING. Absolutely incredible!

DR. STOCKMANN. The whole Bath establishment is a whited, poisoned sepulcher, I tell you— the gravest possible danger to the public health! All the nastiness up at Mölledal, all that stinking filth, is infecting the water in the conduit-pipes leading to the reservoir; and the same cursed, filthy poison oozes out on the shore too—

HORSTER. Where the bathing-place is?

DR. STOCKMANN. Just there.

HOVSTAD. How do you come to be so certain of all this, Doctor?

DR. STOCKMANN. I have investigated the matter most conscientiously. For a long time past I have suspected something of the kind. Last year we had some very strange cases of illness among the visitors—typhoid cases, and cases of gastric fever—

MRS. STOCKMANN. Yes, that is quite true.

DR. STOCKMANN. At the time, we supposed the visitors had been infected before they came; but later on, in the winter, I began to have a different opinion; and so I set myself to examine the water, as well as I could.

MRS. STOCKMANN. Then that is what you have been so busy with?

DR. STOCKMANN. Indeed I have been busy, Katherine. But here I had none of the necessary scientific apparatus; so I sent samples, both of the drinking-water and of the sea-water, up to the University, to have an accurate analysis made by a chemist.

HOVSTAD. And have you got that?

DR. STOCKMANN (*showing him the letter*). Here it is! It proves the presence of decomposing organic matter in the water—it is full of infusoria. The water is absolutely dangerous to use, either internally or externally.

MRS. STOCKMANN. What a mercy you discovered it in time.

DR. STOCKMANN. You may well say so.

HOVSTAD. And what do you propose to do now, Doctor?

DR. STOCKMANN. To see the matter put right— naturally.

HOVSTAD. Can that be done?

DR. STOCKMANN. It must be done. Otherwise the Baths will be absolutely useless and wasted. But we need not anticipate that; I have a very clear idea what we shall have to do.

MRS. STOCKMANN. But why have you kept this all so secret, dear?

DR. STOCKMANN. Do you suppose I was going to run about the town gossiping about it, before I had absolute proof? No, thank you. I am not such a fool.

PETRA. Still, you might have told us—

DR. STOCKMANN. Not a living soul. But tomorrow you may run round to the old Badger—

MRS. STOCKMANN. Oh, Thomas! Thomas!

DR. STOCKMANN. Well, to your grandfather, then. The old boy will have something to be astonished at! I know he thinks I am cracked —and there are lots of other people think so too, I have noticed. But now these good folks shall see—they shall just see—! (*Walks about, rubbing his hands.*) There will be a nice upset in the town, Katherine; you can't imagine what it will be. All the conduit-pipes will have to be relaid.

HOVSTAD (*getting up*). All the conduit-pipes—?

DR. STOCKMANN. Yes, of course. The intake is too low down; it will have to be lifted to a position much higher up.

PETRA. Then you were right after all.

DR. STOCKMANN. Ah, you remember, Petra—I wrote opposing the plans before the work was begun. But at that time no one would listen to me. Well, I am going to let them have it, now! Of course, I have prepared a report for the Baths Committee; I have had it ready for a week, and was only waiting for this to come. (*Shows the letter.*) Now it shall go off at once. (*Goes into his room and comes back with some papers.*) Look at that! Four closely written sheets!—and the letter shall go with them. Give me a bit of paper, Katherine—something to wrap them up in. That will do! Now give it to—to—(*stamps his foot*)—what the deuce is her name?— give it to the maid, and tell her to take it at once to the Mayor.

MRS. STOCKMANN *takes the packet and goes out through the dining-room.*

PETRA. What do you think uncle Peter will say, father?

DR. STOCKMANN. What is there for him to say? I should think he would be very glad that such an important truth has been brought to light.

HOVSTAD. Will you let me print a short note about your discovery in the "Messenger"?

DR. STOCKMANN. I shall be very much obliged if you will.

HOVSTAD. It is very desirable that the public should be informed of it without delay.

DR. STOCKMANN. Certainly.

MRS. STOCKMANN (*coming back*). She has just gone with it.

BILLING. Upon my soul, Doctor, you are going to be the foremost man in the town!

DR. STOCKMANN (*walking about happily*). Nonsense! As a matter of fact I have done nothing more than my duty. I have only made a lucky find—that's all. Still, all the same—

BILLING. Hovstad, don't you think the town ought to give Dr. Stockmann some sort of testimonial?

HOVSTAD. I will suggest it, anyway.

BILLING. And I will speak to Aslaksen about it.

DR. STOCKMANN. No, my good friends, don't let us have any of that nonsense. I won't hear of anything of the kind. And if the Baths Committee should think of voting me an increase of salary, I will not accept it. Do you hear, Katherine?—I won't accept it.

MRS. STOCKMANN. You are quite right, Thomas.

PETRA (*lifting her glass*). Your health, father!

HOVSTAD *and* BILLING. Your health, Doctor! Good health!

HORSTER (*touches glasses with* DR. STOCKMANN). I hope it will bring you nothing but good luck.

DR. STOCKMANN. Thank you, thank you, my dear fellows! I feel tremendously happy! It is a splendid thing for a man to be able to feel that he has done a service to his native town and to his fellow-citizens. Hurrah, Katherine!

He puts his arms round her and whirls her round and round, while she protests with laughing cries. They all laugh, clap their hands, and cheer the DOCTOR. *The boys put their heads in at the door to see what is going on.*

DISCUSSION FOR UNDERSTANDING

1. In this act you have met most of the characters in the play. What do you know about the following people?

a. Peter Stockmann

b. Dr. Stockmann

c. Mrs. Stockmann

d. Petra

2. How are the Baths important to the town's economy?

3. To whom does Dr. Stockmann make the announcement that the Baths are polluted? What is their reaction?

4. Why is Dr. Stockmann so pleased with his findings?

5. What two people does he single out to be notified immediately?

Act II

SCENE—*The same. The door into the dining-room is shut. It is morning.* MRS. STOCKMANN, *with a sealed letter in her hand, comes in from the dining-room, goes to the door of the* DOCTOR'S *study, and peeps in.*

MRS. STOCKMANN. Are you in, Thomas?

DR. STOCKMANN (*from within his room*). Yes, I have just come in. (*Comes into the room.*) What is it?

MRS. STOCKMANN. A letter from your brother.

DR. STOCKMANN. Aha, let us see! (*Opens the letter and reads:*) "I return herewith the manuscript you sent me"—(*Reads on in a low murmur.*) Hm!—

MRS. STOCKMANN. What does he say?

DR. STOCKMANN (*putting the papers in his pocket*). Oh, he only writes that he will come up here himself about midday.

MRS. STOCKMANN. Well, try and remember to be at home this time.

DR. STOCKMANN. That will be all right; I have got through all my morning visits.

MRS. STOCKMANN. I am extremely curious to know how he takes it.

DR. STOCKMANN. You will see he won't like its' having been I, and not he, that made the discovery.

MRS. STOCKMANN. Aren't you a little nervous about that?

DR. STOCKMANN. Oh, he really will be pleased enough, you know. But, at the same time, Peter is so confoundedly afraid of anyone's doing any service to the town except himself.

MRS. STOCKMANN. I will tell you what, Thomas —you should be good natured, and share the credit of this with him. Couldn't you make out that it was he who set you on the scent of this discovery?

DR. STOCKMANN. I am quite willing. If only I can get the thing set right. I—

MORTEN KIIL *puts his head in through the door leading from the hall, looks round in an enquiring manner, and chuckles.*

MORTEN KIIL (*slyly*). Is it—is it true?

MRS. STOCKMANN (*going to the door*). Father! —is it you?

DR. STOCKMANN. Ah, Mr. Kiil—good morning, good morning!

MRS. STOCKMANN. But come along in.

MORTEN KIIL. If it is true, I will; if not, I am off.

DR. STOCKMANN. If what is true?

MORTEN KIIL. This tale about the water supply. Is it true?

DR. STOCKMANN. Certainly it is true. But how did you come to hear it?

MORTEN KIIL (*coming in*). Petra ran in on her way to the school—

DR. STOCKMANN. Did she?

MORTEN KIIL. Yes; and she declares that—. I thought she was only making a fool of me, but it isn't like Petra to do that.

DR. STOCKMANN. Of course not. How could you imagine such a thing!

MORTEN KIIL. Oh well, it is better never to trust

anybody; you may find you have been made a fool of before you know where you are. But it is really true, all the same?

DR. STOCKMANN. You can depend upon it that it is true. Won't you sit down? (*Settles him on the couch.*) Isn't it a real bit of luck for the town—

MORTEN KIIL (*suppressing his laughter*). A bit of luck for the town?

DR. STOCKMANN. Yes, that I made the discovery in good time.

MORTEN KIIL (*as before*). Yes, yes, yes!—But I should never have thought you the sort of man to pull your own brother's leg like this!

DR. STOCKMANN. Pull his leg!

MRS. STOCKMANN. Really, father dear—

MORTEN KIIL (*resting his hands and his chin on the handle of his stick and winking slyly at the* DOCTOR). Let me see, what was the story? Some kind of beast that had got into the water-pipes, wasn't it?

DR. STOCKMANN. Infusoria—yes.

MORTEN KIIL. And a lot of these beasts had got in, according to Petra—a tremendous lot.

DR. STOCKMANN. Certainly; hundreds of thousands of them, probably.

MORTEN KIIL. But no one can see them—isn't that so?

DR. STOCKMANN. Yes; you can't see them.

MORTEN KIIL (*with a quiet chuckle*). Darn—it's the finest story I have ever heard!

DR. STOCKMANN. What do you mean?

MORTEN KIIL. But you will never get the Mayor to believe a thing like that.

DR. STOCKMANN. We shall see.

MORTEN KIIL. Do you think he will be fool enough to—?

DR. STOCKMANN. I hope the whole town will be fools enough.

MORTEN KIIL. The whole town! Well, it wouldn't be a bad thing. It would just serve them right, and teach them a lesson. They think themselves so much cleverer than we old fellows. They hounded me out of the council; they did, I tell you—they hounded me out. Now they shall pay for it. You pull their legs too, Thomas!

DR. STOCKMANN. Really, I—

MORTEN KIIL. You pull their legs! (*Gets up.*) If you can work it so that the Mayor and his friends all swallow the same bait, I will give ten pounds to a charity—like a shot!

DR. STOCKMANN. That is very kind of you.

MORTEN KIIL. Yes, I haven't got much money to throw away, I can tell you; but if you can work this, I will give five pounds to a charity at Christmas.

HOVSTAD *comes in by the hall door.*

HOVSTAD. Good morning! (*Stops.*) Oh, I beg your pardon—

DR. STOCKMANN. Not at all; come in.

MORTEN KIIL (*with another chuckle*). Oho!—is he in this too?

HOVSTAD. What do you mean?

DR. STOCKMANN. Certainly he is.

MORTEN KIIL. I might have known it! It must get into the papers. You know how to do it, Thomas! Set your wits to work. Now I must go.

DR. STOCKMANN. Won't you stay a little while?

MORTEN KIIL. No, I must be off now. You keep up this game for all it is worth; you won't repent it, I'm cursed if you will!

He goes out; MRS. STOCKMANN *follows him into the hall.*

DR. STOCKMANN (*laughing*). Just imagine—the old chap doesn't believe a word of all this about the water supply.

HOVSTAD. Oh, that was it, then?

DR. STOCKMANN. Yes, that was what we were talking about. Perhaps it is the same thing that brings you here?

HOVSTAD. Yes, it is. Can you spare me a few minutes, Doctor?

DR. STOCKMANN. As long as you like, my dear fellow.

HOVSTAD. Have you heard from the Mayor yet?

DR. STOCKMANN. Not yet. He is coming here later.

HOVSTAD. I have given the matter a great deal of thought since last night.

DR. STOCKMANN. Well?

501

HOVSTAD. From your point of view, as a doctor and a man of science, this affair of the water-supply is an isolated matter. I mean, you do not realize that it involves a great many other things.

DR. STOCKMANN. How, do you mean?—Let us sit down, my dear fellow. No, sit here on the couch. (HOVSTAD *sits down on the couch,* DR. STOCKMANN *on a chair on the other side of the table.*) Now then. You mean that—?

HOVSTAD. You said yesterday that the pollution of the water was due to impurities in the soil.

DR. STOCKMANN. Yes, unquestionably it is due to that poisonous morass up at Mölledal.

HOVSTAD. Begging your pardon, doctor, I fancy it is due to quite another morass altogether.

DR. STOCKMANN. What morass?

HOVSTAD. The morass that the whole life of our town is built on and is rotting in.

DR. STOCKMANN. What the deuce are you driving at, Hovstad?

HOVSTAD. The whole of the town's interests have, little by little, got into the hands of a pack of officials.

DR. STOCKMANN. Oh, come!—they are not all officials.

HOVSTAD. No, but those that are not officials are at any rate the officials' friends and adherents; it is the wealthy folk, the old families in the town, that have got us entirely in their hands.

DR. STOCKMANN. Yes, but after all they are men of ability and knowledge.

HOVSTAD. Did they show any ability or knowledge when they laid the conduit-pipes where they are now?

DR. STOCKMANN. No, of course that was a great piece of stupidity on their part. But that is going to be set right now.

HOVSTAD. Do you think that will be all such plain sailing?

DR. STOCKMANN. Plain sailing or no, it has got to be done, anyway.

HOVSTAD. Yes, provided the press takes up the question.

DR. STOCKMANN. I don't think that will be nec-essary, my dear fellow, I am certain my brother—

HOVSTAD. Excuse me, doctor; I feel bound to tell you I am inclined to take the matter up.

DR. STOCKMANN. In the paper?

HOVSTAD. Yes. When I took over the "People's Messenger" my idea was to break up this ring of self-opinionated old fossils who had got hold of all the influence.

DR. STOCKMANN. But you know you told me yourself what the result had been; you nearly ruined your paper.

HOVSTAD. Yes, at the time we were obliged to climb down a peg or two, it is quite true; because there was a danger of the whole project of the Baths coming to nothing if they failed us. But now the scheme has been carried through, and we can dispense with these grand gentlemen.

DR. STOCKMANN. Dispense with them, yes; but we owe them a great debt of gratitude.

HOVSTAD. That shall be recognized ungrudg-ingly. But a journalist of my democratic tendencies cannot let such an opportunity as this slip. The bubble of official infallibility must be pricked. This superstition must be destroyed, like any other.

DR. STOCKMANN. I am whole-heartedly with you in that, Mr. Hovstad; if it is a superstition, away with it!

HOVSTAD. I should be very reluctant to bring the Mayor into it, because he is your brother. But I am sure you will agree with me that truth should be the first consideration.

DR. STOCKMANN. That goes without saying. (*With sudden emphasis.*) Yes, but—but—

HOVSTAD. You must not misjudge me. I am neither more self-interested nor more ambi-tious than most men.

DR. STOCKMANN. My dear fellow—who suggests anything of the kind?

HOVSTAD. I am of humble origin, as you know; and that has given me opportunities of know-ing what is the most crying need in the hum-bler ranks of life. It is that they should be allowed some part in the direction of public affairs, Doctor. That is what will develop their faculties and intelligence and self-respect—

DR. STOCKMANN. I quite appreciate that.

HOVSTAD. Yes—and in my opinion a journalist incurs a heavy responsibility if he neglects a favorable opportunity of emancipating the masses—the humble and oppressed. I know well enough that in exalted circles I shall be called an agitator, and all that sort of thing; but they may call what they like. If only my conscience doesn't reproach me, then—

DR. STOCKMANN. Quite right! Quite right, Mr. Hovstad. But all the same—devil take it! (*A knock is heard at the door.*) Come in!

ASLAKSEN *appears at the door. He is poorly but decently dressed, in black, with a slightly crumpled white neckcloth; he wears gloves and has a felt hat in his hand.*

ASLAKSEN (*bowing*). Excuse my taking the liberty, Doctor—

DR. STOCKMANN (*getting up*). Ah, it is you, Aslaksen!

ASLAKSEN. Yes, Doctor.

HOVSTAD (*standing up*). Is it me you want, Aslaksen?

ASLAKSEN. No; I didn't know I should find you here. No, it was the Doctor I—

DR. STOCKMANN. I am quite at your service. What is it?

ASLAKSEN. Is what I heard from Mr. Billing true, sir—that you mean to improve our water-supply?

DR. STOCKMANN. Yes, for the Baths.

ASLAKSEN. Quite so, I understand. Well, I have come to say that I will back that up by every means in my power.

HOVSTAD (*to the* DOCTOR). You see!

DR. STOCKMANN. I shall be very grateful to you, but—

ASLAKSEN. Because it may be no bad thing to have us small tradesmen at your back. We form, as it were, a compact majority in the town—if we choose. And it is always a good thing to have the majority with you, Doctor.

DR. STOCKMANN. That is undeniably true; but I confess I don't see why such unusual precautions should be necessary in this case. It seems to me that such a plain, straightforward thing—

ASLAKSEN. Oh, it may be very desirable, all the same. I know our local authorities so well; officials are not generally very ready to act on proposals that come from other people. That is why I think it would not be at all amiss if we made a little demonstration.

HOVSTAD. That's right.

DR. STOCKMANN. Demonstration, did you say? What on earth are you going to make a demonstration about?

ASLAKSEN. We shall proceed with the greatest moderation, Doctor. Moderation is always my aim; it is the greatest virtue in a citizen—at least, I think so.

DR. STOCKMANN. It is well known to be a characteristic of yours, Mr. Aslaksen.

ASLAKSEN. Yes, I think I may pride myself on that. And this matter of the water-supply is of the greatest importance to us small tradesmen. The Baths promise to be a regular goldmine for the town. We shall all make our living out of them, especially those of us who are householders. That is why we will back up the project as strongly as possible. And as I am at present Chairman of the Householders' Association—

DR. STOCKMANN. Yes—?

ASLAKSEN. And, what is more, local secretary of the Temperance Society—you know, sir, I suppose, that I am a worker in the temperance cause?

DR. STOCKMANN. Of course, of course.

ASLAKSEN. Well, you can understand that I come into contact with a great many people. And as I have the reputation of a temperate and law-abiding citizen—like yourself Doctor—I have a certain influence in the town, a little bit of power, if I may be allowed to say so.

DR. STOCKMANN. I know that quite well, Mr. Aslaksen.

ASLAKSEN. So you see it would be an easy matter for me to set on foot some testimonial, if necessary.

DR. STOCKMANN. A testimonial?

ASLAKSEN. Yes, some kind of an address of thanks from the townsmen for your share in a matter of such importance to the community. I need scarcely say that it would have to be drawn up with the greatest regard to moderation, so as not to offend the authorities—who, after all, have the reins in their hands. If we pay strict attention to that, no one can take it amiss, I should think!

HOVSTAD. Well, and even supposing they didn't like it—

ASLAKSEN. No, no, no; there must be no discourtesy to the authorities, Mr. Hovstad. It is no use falling foul of those upon whom our welfare so closely depends. I have done that in my time, and no good ever comes of it. But no one can take exception to a reasonable and frank expression of a citizen's views.

DR. STOCKMANN (shaking him by the hand). I can't tell you, dear Mr. Aslaksen, how extremely pleased I am to find such hearty support among my fellow-citizens. I am delighted—delighted! Now, you will take a small glass of sherry, eh?

ASLAKSEN. No, thank you; I never drink alcohol of that kind.

DR. STOCKMANN. Well, what do you say to a glass of beer, then?

ASLAKSEN. Nor that either, thank you, Doctor. I never drink anything as early as this. I am going into town now to talk this over with one or two householders, and prepare the ground.

DR. STOCKMANN. It is tremendously kind of you, Mr. Aslaksen; but I really cannot understand the necessity for all these precautions. It seems to me that the thing should go of itself.

ASLAKSEN. The authorities are somewhat slow to move, Doctor. Far be it from me to seem to blame them—

HOVSTAD. We are going to stir them up in the paper tomorrow, Aslaksen.

ASLAKSEN. But not violently, I trust, Mr. Hovstad. Proceed with moderation, or you will do nothing with them. You may take my advice; I have gathered my experience in the school of life. Well, I must say goodbye, Doctor. You know now that we small tradesmen are at your back at all events, like a solid wall. You have the compact majority on your side, Doctor.

DR. STOCKMANN. I am very much obliged, dear Mr. Aslaksen. (Shakes hands with him.) Goodbye, goodbye.

ASLAKSEN. Are you going my way, towards the printing-office, Mr. Hovstad?

HOVSTAD. I will come later; I have something to settle up first.

ASLAKSEN. Very well. (Bows and goes out; STOCKMANN follows him into the hall.)

HOVSTAD (as STOCKMANN comes in again). Well, what do you think of that, Doctor? Don't you think it is high time we stirred a little life into all this slackness and vacillation and cowardice?

DR. STOCKMANN. Are you referring to Aslaksen?

HOVSTAD. Yes, I am. He is one of those who are floundering in a bog—decent enough fellow though he may be, otherwise. And most of the people here are in just the same case—see-sawing and edging first to one side and then to the other, so overcome with caution and scruple that they never dare to take any decided step.

DR. STOCKMANN. Yes, but Aslaksen seemed to me so thoroughly well-intentioned.

HOVSTAD. There is one thing I esteem higher than that; and that is for a man to be self-reliant and sure of himself.

DR. STOCKMANN. I think you are perfectly right there.

HOVSTAD. That is why I want to seize this opportunity, and try if I cannot manage to put a little virility into these well-intentioned people for once. The idol of Authority must be shattered in this town. This gross and inexcusable blunder about the water-supply must be brought home to the mind of every municipal voter.

DR. STOCKMANN. Very well; if you are of opinion that it is for the good of the community, so be it. But not until I have had a talk with my brother.

HOVSTAD. Anyway, I will get a leading article ready; and if the Mayor refuses to take the matter up—

DR. STOCKMANN. How can you suppose such a thing possible?

HOVSTAD. It is conceivable. And in that case—

DR. STOCKMANN. In that case I promise you—. Look here, in that case you may print my report—every word of it.

HOVSTAD. May I? Have I your word for it?

DR. STOCKMANN (*giving him the manuscript*). Here it is; take it with you. It can do no harm for you to read it through, and you can give it me back later on.

HOVSTAD. Good, good! That is what I will do. And now goodbye, Doctor.

DR. STOCKMANN. Goodbye, goodbye. You will see everything will run quite smoothly, Mr. Hovstad—quite smoothly.

HOVSTAD. Hm!—we shall see. (*Bows and goes out.*)

DR. STOCKMANN (*opens the dining-room door and looks in*). Katherine! Oh, you are back, Petra?

PETRA (*coming in*). Yes, I have just come from the school.

MRS. STOCKMANN (*coming in*). Has he not been here yet?

DR. STOCKMANN. Peter? No. But I have had a long talk with Hovstad. He is quite excited about my discovery. I find it has a much wider bearing than I at first imagined. And he has put his paper at my disposal if necessity should arise.

MRS. STOCKMANN. Do you think it will?

DR. STOCKMANN. Not for a moment. But at all events it makes me feel proud to know that I have the liberal-minded independent press on my side. Yes, and—just imagine—I have had a visit from the Chairman of the Householders' Association!

MRS. STOCKMANN. Oh! What did he want?

DR. STOCKMANN. To offer me his support too. They will support me in a body if it should

be necessary. Katherine—do you know what I have got behind me?

MRS. STOCKMANN. Behind you? No, what have you got behind you?

DR. STOCKMANN. The compact majority.

MRS. STOCKMANN. Really? Is that a good thing for you, Thomas?

DR. STOCKMANN. I should think it was a good thing. (*Walks up and down rubbing his hands.*) By Jove, it's a fine thing to feel this bond of brotherhood between oneself and one's fellow citizens!

PETRA. And to be able to do so much that is good and useful, father!

DR. STOCKMANN. And for one's own native town into the bargain, my child!

MRS. STOCKMANN. That was a ring at the bell.

DR. STOCKMANN. It must be he, then. (*A knock is heard at the door.*) Come in!

PETER STOCKMANN (*comes in from the hall*). Good morning.

DR. STOCKMANN. Glad to see you, Peter!

MRS. STOCKMANN. Good morning, Peter. How are you?

PETER STOCKMANN. So so, thank you. (*To* DR. STOCKMANN.) I received from you yesterday, after office hours, a report dealing with the condition of the water at the Baths.

DR. STOCKMANN. Yes. Have you read it?

PETER STOCKMANN. Yes, I have.

DR. STOCKMANN. And what have you to say to it?

PETER STOCKMANN (*with a sidelong glance*). Hm!—

MRS. STOCKMANN. Come along, Petra. (*She and* PETRA *go into the room on the left.*)

PETER STOCKMANN (*after a pause*). Was it necessary to make all these investigations behind my back?

DR. STOCKMANN. Yes, because until I was absolutely certain about it—

PETER STOCKMANN. Then you mean that you are absolutely certain now?

DR. STOCKMANN. Surely you are convinced of that.

PETER STOCKMANN. Is it your intention to bring this document before the Baths Committee as a sort of official communication?

DR. STOCKMANN. Certainly. Something must be done in the matter—and that quickly.

PETER STOCKMANN. As usual, you employ violent expressions in your report. You say, amongst other things, that what we offer visitors in our Baths is a permanent supply of poison.

DR. STOCKMANN. Well, can you describe it any other way, Peter! Just think—water that is poisonous, whether you drink it or bathe in it! And this we offer to the poor sick folk who come to us trustfully and pay us at an exorbitant rate to be made well again!

PETER STOCKMANN. And your reasoning leads you to this conclusion, that we must build a sewer to draw off the alleged impurities from Mölledal and must relay the water-conduits.

DR. STOCKMANN. Yes. Do you see any other way out of it? I don't.

PETER STOCKMANN. I made a pretext this morning to go and see the town engineer, and, as if only half seriously, broached the subject of these proposals as a thing we might perhaps have to take under consideration some time later on.

DR. STOCKMANN. Some time later on!

PETER STOCKMANN. He smiled at what he considered to be my extravagance, naturally. Have you taken the trouble to consider what your proposed alterations would cost? According to the information I obtained, the expenses would probably mount up to fifteen or twenty thousand pounds.

DR. STOCKMANN. Would it cost so much?

PETER STOCKMANN. Yes; and the worst part of it would be that the work would take at least two years.

DR. STOCKMANN. Two years? Two whole years?

PETER STOCKMANN. At least. And what are we to do with the Baths in the meantime? Close them? Indeed we should be obliged to. And do you suppose any one would come near the place after it had got about that the water was dangerous?

DR. STOCKMANN. Yes, but, Peter, that is what it is.

PETER STOCKMANN. And all this at this juncture—just as the Baths are beginning to be known. There are other towns in the neighborhood with qualifications to attract visitors for bathing purposes. Don't you suppose they would immediately strain every nerve to divert the entire stream of strangers to themselves? Unquestionably they would; and then where should we be? We should probably have to abandon the whole thing, which has cost us so much money—and then you would have ruined your native town.

DR. STOCKMANN. I—should have ruined—!

PETER STOCKMANN. It is simply and solely through the Baths that the town has before it any future worth mentioning. You know that just as well as I.

DR. STOCKMANN. But what do you think ought to be done, then?

PETER STOCKMANN. Your report has not convinced me that the condition of the water at the Baths is as bad as you represent it to be.

DR. STOCKMANN. I tell you it is even worse!—or at all events it will be in summer, when the warm weather comes.

PETER STOCKMANN. As I said, I believe you exaggerate the matter considerably. A capable physician ought to know what measures to take—he ought to be capable of preventing injurious influences or of remedying them if they become obviously persistent.

DR. STOCKMANN. Well? What more?

PETER STOCKMANN. The water supply for the Baths is now an established fact, and in consequence must be treated as such. But probably the Committee, at its discretion, will not be disinclined to consider the question of how far it might be possible to introduce certain improvements consistently with a reasonable expenditure.

DR. STOCKMANN. And do you suppose that I will have anything to do with such a piece of trickery as that?

PETER STOCKMANN. Trickery!!

DR. STOCKMANN. Yes, it would be a trick—a fraud, a lie, a downright crime towards the public, towards the whole community!

PETER STOCKMANN. I have not, as I remarked

before, been able to convince myself that there is actually any imminent danger.

DR. STOCKMANN. You have! It is impossible that you should not be convinced. I know I have represented the facts absolutely truthfully and fairly. And you know it very well, Peter, only you won't acknowledge it. It was owing to your action that both the Baths and the water-conduits were built where they are; and that is what you won't acknowledge— that miserable blunder of yours. Pooh!—do you suppose I don't see through you?

PETER STOCKMANN. And even if that were true? If I perhaps guard my reputation somewhat anxiously, it is in the interests of the town. Without moral authority I am powerless to direct public affairs as seems, to my judgment, to be best for the common good. And on that account—and for various other reasons too—it appears to me to be a matter of

importance that your report should not be delivered to the Committee. In the interests of the public, you must withhold it. Then, later on, I will raise the question and we will do our best, privately; but nothing of this unfortunate affair—not a single word of it— must come to the ears of the public.

DR. STOCKMANN. I am afraid you will not be able to prevent that now, my dear Peter.

PETER STOCKMANN. It must and shall be prevented.

DR. STOCKMANN. It is no use, I tell you. There are too many people that know about it.

PETER STOCKMANN. That know about it? Who? Surely you don't mean those fellows on the "People's Messenger"?

DR. STOCKMANN. Yes, they know. The liberal-minded independent press is going to see that you do your duty.

PETER STOCKMANN (*after a short pause*). You

507

are an extraordinarily independent man, Thomas. Have you given no thought to the consequences this may have for yourself?

DR. STOCKMANN. Consequences?—for me?

PETER STOCKMANN. For you and yours, yes.

DR. STOCKMANN. What the deuce do you mean?

PETER STOCKMANN. I believe I have always behaved in a brotherly way to you—have always been ready to oblige or to help you?

DR. STOCKMANN. Yes, you have, and I am grateful to you for it.

PETER STOCKMANN. There is no need. Indeed, to some extent I was forced to do so—for my own sake. I always hoped that, if I helped to improve your financial position, I should be able to keep some check on you.

DR. STOCKMANN. What!! Then it was only for your own sake—!

PETER STOCKMANN. Up to a certain point, yes. It is painful for a man in an official position to have his nearest relative compromising himself time after time.

DR. STOCKMANN. And do you consider that I do that?

PETER STOCKMANN. Yes, unfortunately, you do, without even being aware of it. You have a restless, pugnacious, rebellious disposition. And then there is that disastrous propensity of yours to want to write about every sort of possible and impossible thing. The moment an idea comes into your head, you must needs go and write a newspaper article or a whole pamphlet about it.

DR. STOCKMANN. Well, but is it not the duty of a citizen to let the public share in any new ideas he may have?

PETER STOCKMANN. Oh, the public doesn't require any new ideas. The public is best served by the good, old-established ideas it already has.

DR. STOCKMANN. And that is your honest opinion?

PETER STOCKMANN. Yes, and for once I must talk frankly to you. Hitherto I have tried to avoid doing so, because I know how irritable you are; but now I must tell you the truth, Thomas. You have no conception what an amount of harm you do yourself by your impetuosity. You complain of the authorities, you even complain of the government—you are always pulling them to pieces; you insist that you have been neglected and persecuted. But what else can such a cantankerous man as you expect?

DR. STOCKMANN. What next! Cantankerous, am I?

PETER STOCKMANN. Yes, Thomas, you are an extremely cantankerous man to work with—I know that to my cost. You disregard everything that you ought to have consideration for. You seem completely to forget that it is me you have to thank for your appointment here as medical officer to the Baths—

DR. STOCKMANN. I was entitled to it as a matter of course!—I and nobody else! I was the first person to see that the town could be made into a flourishing watering-place, and I was the only one who saw it at that time. I had to fight single-handed in support of the idea for many years; and I wrote and wrote—

PETER STOCKMANN. Undoubtedly. But things were not ripe for the scheme then—though, of course, you could not judge of that in your out-of-the-way corner up north. But as soon as the opportune moment came I—and the others—took the matter into our hands—

DR. STOCKMANN. Yes, and made this mess of all my beautiful plan. It is pretty obvious now what clever fellows you were!

PETER STOCKMANN. To my mind the whole thing only seems to mean that you are seeking another outlet for your combativeness. You want to pick a quarrel with your superiors—an old habit of yours. You cannot put up with any authority over you. You look askance at anyone who occupies a superior official position; you regard him as a personal enemy, and then any stick is good enough to beat him with. But now I have called your attention to the fact that the town's interests are at stake—and, incidentally, my own too. And therefore I must tell you, Thomas, that you will find me inexorable with regard to what I am about to require you to do.

DR. STOCKMANN. And what is that?

PETER STOCKMANN. As you have been so indiscreet as to speak of this delicate matter to outsiders, despite the fact that you ought to have treated it as entirely official and confidential, it is obviously impossible to hush it up now. All sorts of rumors will get about directly, and everybody who has a grudge against us will take care to embellish these rumors. So it will be necessary for you to refute them publicly.

DR. STOCKMANN. I! How? I don't understand.

PETER STOCKMANN. What we shall expect is that, after making further investigations, you will come to the conclusion that the matter is not by any means as dangerous or as critical as you imagined in the first instance.

DR. STOCKMANN. Oho!—so that is what you expect!

PETER STOCKMANN. And, what is more, we shall expect you to make public profession of your confidence in the Committee and in their readiness to consider fully and conscientiously what steps may be necessary to remedy any possible defects.

DR. STOCKMANN. But you will never be able to do that by patching and tinkering at it—never! Take my word for it, Peter; I mean what I say, as deliberately and emphatically as possible.

PETER STOCKMANN. As an officer under the Committee, you have no right to any individual opinion.

DR. STOCKMANN (*amazed*). No right?

PETER STOCKMANN. In your official capacity, no. As a private person, it is quite another matter. But as a subordinate member of the staff of the Baths, you have no right to express any opinion which runs contrary to that of your superiors.

DR. STOCKMANN. This is too much! I, a doctor, a man of science, have no right to—!

PETER STOCKMANN. The matter in hand is not simply a scientific one. It is a complicated matter, and has its economic as well as its technical side.

DR. STOCKMANN. I don't care what it is! I intend to be free to express my opinion on any subject under the sun.

PETER STOCKMANN. As you please—but not on any subject concerning the Baths. That we forbid.

DR. STOCKMANN (*shouting*). You forbid—! You! A pack of—

PETER SROCKMANN. *I* forbid it—I, your chief; and if I forbid it, you have to obey.

DR. STOCKMANN (*controlling himself*). Peter—if you were not my brother—

PETRA (*throwing open the door*). Father, you shan't stand this!

MRS. STOCKMANN (*coming in after her*). Petra, Petra!

PETER STOCKMANN. Oh, so you have been eavesdropping.

MRS. STOCKMANN. You were talking so loud, we couldn't help—

PETRA. Yes, I was listening.

PETER STOCKMANN. Well, after all, I am very glad—

DR. STOCKMANN (*going up to him*). You were saying something about forbidding and obeying?

PETER STOCKMANN. You obliged me to take that tone with you.

DR. STOCKMANN. And so I am to give myself the lie, publicly?

PETER STOCKMANN. We consider it absolutely necessary that you should make some such public statement as I have asked for.

DR. STOCKMANN. And if I do not—obey?

PETER STOCKMANN. Then we shall publish a statement ourselves to reassure the public.

DR. STOCKMANN. Very well; but in that case I shall use my pen against you. I stick to what I have said; I will show that I am right and you are wrong. And what will you do then?

PETER STOCKMANN. Then I shall not be able to prevent your being dismissed.

DR. STOCKMANN. What—?

PETRA. Father—dismissed!

MRS. STOCKMANN. Dismissed!

PETER STOCKMANN. Dismissed from the staff of the Baths. I shall be obliged to propose that you shall immediately be given notice, and shall not be allowed any further participation in the Baths' affairs.

DR. STOCKMANN. You would dare to do that?

PETER STOCKMANN. It is you that are playing the daring game.

PETRA. Uncle, that is a shameful way to treat a man like father!

MRS. STOCKMANN. Do hold your tongue, Petra!

PETER STOCKMANN (*looking at* PETRA). Oh, so we volunteer our opinions already, do we? Of course. (*To* MRS. STOCKMANN.) Katherine, I imagine you are the most sensible person in this house. Use any influence you may have over your husband, and make him see what this will entail for his family as well as—

DR. STOCKMANN. My family is my own concern and nobody else's!

PETER STOCKMANN. —for his own family, as I was saying, as well as for the town he lives in.

DR. STOCKMANN. It is I who have the real good of the town at heart! I want to lay bare the defects that sooner or later must come to the light of day. I will show whether I love my native town.

PETER STOCKMANN. You, who in your blind obstinacy want to cut off the most important source of the town's welfare?

DR. STOCKMANN. The source is poisoned, man! Are you mad? We are making our living by retailing filth and corruption! The whole of our flourishing municipal life derives its sustenance from a lie!

PETER STOCKMANN. All imagination—or something even worse. The man who can throw out such offensive insinuations about his native town must be an enemy to our community.

DR. STOCKMANN (*going up to him*). Do you dare to—!

MRS. STOCKMANN (*throwing herself between them*). Thomas!

PETRA (*catching her father by the arm*). Don't lose your temper, father!

PETER STOCKMANN. I will not expose myself to violence. Now you have had a warning; so reflect on what you owe to yourself and your family. Goodbye. (*Goes out.*)

DR. STOCKMANN (*walking up and down*). Am I to put up with such treatment as this? In my own house, Katherine! What do you think of that!

MRS. STOCKMANN. Indeed it is both shameful and absurd. Thomas—

PETRA. If only I could give uncle a piece of my mind—

DR. STOCKMANN. It is my own fault. I ought to have flown out at him long ago!—shown my teeth!—bitten! To hear him call me an enemy to our community! Me! *I* shall not take that lying down, upon my soul!

MRS. STOCKMANN. But, dear Thomas, your brother has power on his side—

DR. STOCKMANN. Yes, but I have right on mine, I tell you.

MRS. STOCKMANN. Oh yes, right—right. What is the use of having right on your side if you have not got might?

PETRA. Oh, mother!—how can you say such a thing!

DR. STOCKMANN. Do you imagine that in a free country it is no use having right on your side? You are absurd, Katherine. Besides, haven't I got the liberal-minded, independent press to lead the way, and the compact majority behind me? That is might enough, I should think!

MRS. STOCKMANN. But, good heavens, Thomas, you don't mean to—?

DR. STOCKMANN. Don't mean to what?

MRS. STOCKMANN. To set yourself up in opposition to your brother.

DR. STOCKMANN. In God's name, what else do you suppose I should do but take my stand on right and truth?

PETRA. Yes, I was just going to say that.

MRS. STOCKMANN. But it won't do any earthly good. If they won't do it, they won't.

DR. STOCKMANN. Oho, Katherine! Just give me time, and you will see how I will carry the war into their camp.

MRS. STOCKMANN. Yes, you carry the war into their camp, and you get your dismissal—that is what you will do.

DR. STOCKMANN. In any case I shall have done my duty towards the public—towards the community. I, who am called its enemy!

MRS. STOCKMANN. But towards your family, Thomas? Towards your own home! Do you think that is doing your duty towards those you have to provide for?

PETRA. Ah, don't think always first of us, mother.

MRS. STOCKMANN. Oh, it is easy for you to talk; you are able to shift for yourself, if need be. But remember the boys, Thomas; and think a little too of yourself, and of me—

DR. STOCKMANN. I think you are out of your senses, Katherine! If I were to be such a miserable coward as to go on my knees to Peter and his crew, do you suppose I should ever know an hour's peace of mind all my life afterwards?

MRS. STOCKMANN. I don't know anything about that; but Heaven preserve us from the peace of mind we shall have, all the same, if you go on defying him! You will find yourself again without the means of subsistence, with no income to count upon. I should think we had had enough of that in the old days. Remember that, Thomas; think what that means.

DR. STOCKMANN (*collecting himself with a struggle and clenching his fists*). And this is what this slavery can bring upon a free, honorable man! Isn't it horrible, Katherine?

MRS. STOCKMANN. Yes, it is sinful to treat you so, it is perfectly true. But, good heavens, one has to put up with so much injustice in this world.—There are the boys, Thomas! Look at them! What is to become of them? Oh, no, no, you can never have the heart—.

EJLIF and MORTEN have come in while she was speaking, with their school books in their hands.

DR. STOCKMANN. The boys—! (*Recovers himself suddenly.*) No, even if the whole world goes to pieces, I will never bow my neck to this yoke! (*Goes towards his room.*)

MRS. STOCKMANN (*following him*). Thomas—what are you going to do!

DR. STOCKMANN (*at his door*). I mean to have the right to look my sons in the face when they are grown men. (*Goes into his room.*)

MRS. STOCKMANN (*bursting into tears*). God help us all!

PETRA. Father is splendid! He will not give in.

The boys look on in amazement; PETRA *signs to them not to speak.*

DISCUSSION FOR UNDERSTANDING

1. At the end of Act I, Dr. Stockmann has sent his report of the pollution to his brother, the Mayor. How long a period of time do you think has elapsed between Act I and the beginning of Act II?

2. Throughout Act II a number of people react to the news in characteristic patterns. What is the reaction of each of the following? What does it reveal about them as people?

a. Morten Kiil

b. Hovstad

c. Aslaksen

d. Peter Stockmann

3. Do any of these people see the real issue?

4. What arguments does Mrs. Stockmann use at the end of the act?

5. Does anyone really seem to understand Dr. Stockmann?

Act III

SCENE—*The editorial office of the "People's Messenger." The entrance door is on the left-hand side of the back wall; on the right-hand side is another door with glass panels through which the printing-room can be seen. Another door in the right-hand wall. In the middle of the room is a large table covered with papers, newspapers and books.*

In the foreground on the left a window, before which stand a desk and a high stool. There are a couple of easy chairs by the table, and other chairs standing along the wall. The room is dingy and uncomfortable; the furniture is old, the chairs stained and torn. In the printing-room the compositors are seen at work, and a printer is working a hand-press. HOVSTAD *is sitting at the desk, writing.* BILLING *comes in from the right with* DR. STOCKMANN's *manuscript in his hand.*

BILLING. Well, I must say!

HOVSTAD (*still writing.*) Have you read it through?

BILLING (*laying the manuscript on the desk*). Yes, indeed I have.

HOVSTAD. Don't you think the Doctor hits them pretty hard?

BILLING. Hard? Bless my soul, he's crushing! Every word falls like—how shall I put it?—like the blow of a sledge-hammer.

HOVSTAD. Yes, but they are not the people to throw up the sponge at the first blow.

BILLING. That is true; and for that reason we must strike blow upon blow until the whole of this aristocracy tumbles to pieces. As I sat in there reading this, I almost seemed to see a revolution in being.

HOVSTAD (*turning round*). Hush!—Speak so that Aslaksen cannot hear you.

BILLING (*lowering his voice*). Aslaksen is a chicken-hearted chap, a coward; there is nothing of the man in him. But this time you will insist on your own way, won't you? You will put the Doctor's article in?

HOVSTAD. Yes, and if the Mayor doesn't like it—

BILLING. That will be the devil of a nuisance.

HOVSTAD. Well, fortunately we can turn the situation to good account, whatever happens. If the Mayor will not fall in with the Doctor's project, he will have all the small tradesmen down on him—the whole of the Householders' Association and the rest of them. And if he does fall in with it, he will fall out with the whole crowd of large shareholders in the Baths, who up to now have been his most valuable supporters—

BILLING. Yes, because they will certainly have to fork out a pretty penny—

HOVSTAD. Yes, you may be sure they will. And in this way the ring will be broken up, you see, and then in every issue of the paper we will enlighten the public on the Mayor's incapability on one point and another, and make it clear that all the positions of trust in the town, the whole control of municipal affairs, ought to be put in the hands of the Liberals.

BILLING. That is perfectly true! I see it coming —I see it coming; we are on the threshold of a revolution!

A knock is heard at the door.

HOVSTAD. Hush! (*Calls out.*) Come in! (DR. STOCKMANN *comes in by the street door.* HOVSTAD *goes to meet him.*) Ah, it is you, Doctor! Well?

DR. STOCKMANN. You may set to work and print it, Mr. Hovstad!

HOVSTAD. Has it come to that, then?

BILLING. Hurrah!

DR. STOCKMANN. Yes, print away. Undoubtedly it has come to that. Now they must take what they get. There is going to be a fight in the town, Mr. Billing!

BILLING. War to the knife, I hope! We will get our knives to their throats, Doctor!

DR. STOCKMANN. This article is only a beginning. I have already got four or five more sketched out in my head. Where is Aslaksen?

BILLING (*calls into the printing-room*). Aslaksen, just come here for a minute!

HOVSTAD. Four or five more articles, did you say? On the same subject?

DR. STOCKMANN. No—far from it, my dear fellow. No, they are about quite another matter. But they all spring from the question of the water-supply and the drainage. One thing leads to another, you know. It is like beginning to pull down an old house, exactly.

BILLING. Upon my soul, it's true; you find you

are not done till you have pulled all the old rubbish down.

ASLAKSEN (*coming in*). Pulled down? You are not thinking of pulling down the Baths surely, Doctor?

HOVSTAD. Far from it, don't be afraid.

DR. STOCKMANN. No, we meant something quite different. Well, what do you think of my article, Mr. Hovstad?

HOVSTAD. I think it is simply a masterpiece—

DR. STOCKMANN. Do you really think so? Well, I am very pleased, very pleased.

HOVSTAD. It is so clear and intelligible. One need have no special knowledge to understand the bearing of it. You will have every enlightened man on your side.

ASLAKSEN. And every prudent man too, I hope?

BILLING. The prudent and the imprudent—almost the whole town.

ASLAKSEN. In that case we may venture to print it.

DR. STOCKMANN. I should think so!

HOVSTAD. We will put it in tomorrow morning.

DR. STOCKMANN. Of course—you must not lose a single day. What I wanted to ask you, Mr. Aslaksen, was if you would supervise the printing of it yourself.

ASLAKSEN. With pleasure.

DR. STOCKMANN. Take care of it as if it were a treasure! No misprints—every word is important. I will look in again a little later; perhaps you will be able to let me see a proof. I can't tell you how eager I am to see it in print, and see it burst upon the public—

BILLING. Burst upon them—yes, like a flash of lightning!

DR. STOCKMANN. —and to have it submitted to the judgment of my intelligent fellow-townsmen. You cannot imagine what I have gone through today. I have been threatened first with one thing and then with another; they have tried to rob me of my most elementary rights as a man—

BILLING. What! Your rights as a man!

DR. STOCKMANN. —they have tried to degrade me, to make a coward of me, to force me to put personal interests before my most sacred convictions—

BILLING. That is too much—I'm hanged if it isn't.

HOVSTAD. Oh, you mustn't be surprised at anything from that quarter.

DR. STOCKMANN. Well, they will get the worst of it with me; they may assure themselves of that. I shall consider the "People's Messenger" my sheet-anchor now, and every single day I will bombard them with one article after another, like bomb-shells—

ASLAKSEN. Yes, but—

BILLING. Hurrah!—it is war, it is war!

DR. STOCKMANN. I shall smite them to the ground—I shall crush them—I shall break down all their defenses, before the eyes of the honest public! That is what I shall do!

ASLAKSEN. Yes, but in moderation, Doctor—proceed with moderation—

BILLING. Not a bit of it, not a bit of it! Don't spare the dynamite!

DR. STOCKMANN. Because it is not merely a question of water-supply and drains now, you know. No—it is the whole of our social life that we have got to purify and disinfect—

BILLING. Spoken like a deliverer!

DR. STOCKMANN. All the incapables must be turned out, you understand—and that in every walk of life! Endless vistas have opened themselves to my mind's eye today. I cannot see it all quite clearly yet, but I shall in time. Young and vigorous standard-bearers—those are what we need and must seek, my friends; we must have new men in command at all our outposts.

BILLING. Hear, hear!

DR. STOCKMANN. We only need to stand by one another, and it will all be perfectly easy. The revolution will be launched like a ship that runs smoothly off the stocks. Don't you think so?

HOVSTAD. For my part I think we have now a prospect of getting the municipal authority into the hands where it should lie.

ASLAKSEN. And if only we proceed with moderation, I cannot imagine that there will be any risk.

DR. STOCKMANN. Who the devil cares whether there is any risk or not! What I am doing, I am doing in the name of truth and for the sake of my conscience.

HOVSTAD. You are a man who deserves to be supported, Doctor.

ASLAKSEN. Yes, there is no denying that the Doctor is a true friend to the town—a real friend to the community, that he is.

BILLING. Take my word for it, Aslaksen, Dr. Stockmann is a friend of the people.

ASLAKSEN. I fancy the Householders' Association will make use of that expression before long.

DR. STOCKMANN (*affected, grasps their hands*). Thank you, thank you, my dear staunch friends. It is very refreshing to me to hear you say that; my brother called me something quite different. By Jove, he shall have it back, with interest! But now I must be off to see a poor devil—. I will come back, as I said. Keep a very careful eye on the manuscript, Aslaksen, and don't for worlds leave out any of my notes of exclamation! Rather put one or two more in! Capital, capital! Well, goodbye for the present—goodbye, goodbye!

They show him to the door, and bow him out.

HOVSTAD. He may prove an invaluably useful man to us.

ASLAKSEN. Yes, so long as he confines himself to this matter of the Baths. But if he goes farther afield, I don't think it would be advisable to follow him.

HOVSTAD. Hm!—that all depends—

BILLING. You are so infernally timid, Aslaksen!

ASLAKSEN. Timid? Yes, when it is a question of the local authorities, I am timid, Mr. Billing; it is a lesson I have learnt in the school of experience, let me tell you. But try me in higher politics, in matters that concern the government itself, and then see if I am timid.

BILLING. No, you aren't, I admit. But this is simply contradicting yourself.

ASLAKSEN. I am a man with a conscience, and that is the whole matter. If you attack the government, you don't do the community any harm, anyway; those fellows pay no attention to attacks, you see—they go on just as they are, in spite of them. But *local* authorities are different; they *can* be turned out, and then perhaps you may get an ignorant lot into office who may do irreparable harm to the householders and everybody else.

HOVSTAD. But what of the education of citizens by self-government—don't you attach any importance to that?

ASLAKSEN. When a man has interests of his own to protect, he cannot think of everything, Mr. Hovstad.

HOVSTAD. Then I hope I shall never have interests of my own to protect!

BILLING. Hear, hear!

ASLAKSEN (*with a smile*). Hm! (*Points to the desk.*) Mr. Sheriff Stensgaard was your predecessor at that editorial desk.

BILLING (*spitting*). Bah! That turncoat.

HOVSTAD. I am not a weathercock—and never will be.

ASLAKSEN. A politician should never be too certain of anything, Mr. Hovstad. And as for you, Mr. Billing, I should think it is time for you to be taking in a reef or two in your sails, seeing that you are applying for the post of secretary to the Bench.

BILLING. I—!

HOVSTAD. Are you, Billing?

BILLING. Well, yes—but you must clearly understand I am doing it only to annoy the bigwigs.

ASLAKSEN. Anyhow, it is no business of mine. But if I am to be accused of timidity and of inconsistency in my principles, this is what I want to point out: my political past is an open book. I have never changed, except perhaps to become a little more moderate, you see. My heart is still with the people; but I don't deny that my reason has a certain bias towards the authorities—the local ones, I mean. (*Goes into the printing-room.*)

BILLING. Oughtn't we to try and get rid of him, Hovstad?

HOVSTAD. Do you know anyone else who will advance the money for our paper and printing bill?

BILLING. It is an infernal nuisance that we don't possess some capital to trade on.

HOVSTAD (*sitting down at his desk*). Yes, if we only had that, then—

BILLING. Suppose you were to apply to Dr. Stockmann?

HOVSTAD (*turning over some papers*). What is the use? He has got nothing.

BILLING. No, but he has got a warm man in the background, old Morten Kiil—"the Badger," as they call him.

HOVSTAD (*writing*). Are you so sure *he* has got anything?

BILLING. Good Lord, of course he has! And some of it must come to the Stockmanns. Most probably he will do something for the children, at all events.

HOVSTAD (*turning half round*). Are you counting on that?

BILLING. Counting on it? Of course I am not counting on anything.

HOVSTAD. That is right. And I should not count on the secretaryship to the Bench either, if I were you; for I can assure you—you won't get it.

BILLING. Do you think I am not quite aware of that? My object is precisely *not* to get it. A slight of that kind stimulates a man's fighting power—it is like getting a supply of fresh bile—and I am sure one needs that badly enough in a hole-and-corner place like this, where it is so seldom anything happens to stir one up.

HOVSTAD (*writing*). Quite so, quite so.

BILLING. Ah, I shall be heard of yet!—Now I shall go and write the appeal to the House-holders' Association. (*Goes into the room on the right.*)

HOVSTAD (*sitting at his desk, biting his pen-holder, says slowly*). Hm!—that's it, is it?

(*A knock is heard.*) Come in! (PETRA *comes in by the outer door.* HOVSTAD *gets up.*) What, you!—here?

PETRA. Yes, you must forgive me—

HOVSTAD (*pulling a chair forward*). Won't you sit down?

PETRA. No, thank you; I must go again in a moment.

HOVSTAD. Have you come with a message from your father, by any chance?

PETRA. No, I have come on my own account. (*Takes a book out of her coat pocket.*) Here is the English story.

HOVSTAD. Why have you brought it back?

PETRA. Because I am not going to translate it.

HOVSTAD. But you promised me faithfully—

PETRA. Yes, but then I had not read it. I don't suppose you have read it either?

HOVSTAD. No, you know quite well I don't understand English; but—

PETRA. Quite so. That is why I wanted to tell you that you must find something else. (*Lays the book on the table.*) You can't use this for the "People's Messenger."

HOVSTAD. Why not?

PETRA. Because it conflicts with all your opinions.

HOVSTAD. Oh, for that matter—

PETRA. You don't understand me. The burden of this story is that there is a supernatural power that looks after the so-called good people in this world and makes everything happen for the best in their case—while all the so-called bad people are punished.

HOVSTAD. Well, but that is all right. That is just what our readers want.

PETRA. And are you going to be the one to give it to them? For myself, I do not believe a word of it. You know quite well that things do not happen so in reality.

HOVSTAD. You are perfectly right; but an editor cannot always act as he would prefer. He is often obliged to bow to the wishes of the public in unimportant matters. Politics are the most important thing in life—for a news-paper, anyway; and if I want to carry my public with me on the path that leads to liberty and progress, I must not frighten them away. If they find a moral tale of this sort in the serial at the bottom of the page, they will be all the more ready to read what is printed above it; they feel more secure, as it were.

PETRA. For shame! You would never go and set a snare like that for your readers; you are not a spider!

HOVSTAD (*smiling*). Thank you for having such a good opinion of me. No; as a matter of fact that is Billing's idea and not mine.

PETRA. Billing's!

HOVSTAD. Yes; anyway he propounded that theory here one day. And it is Billing who is so anxious to have that story in the paper; I don't know anything about the book.

PETRA. But how can Billing, with his emancipated views—

HOVSTAD. Oh Billing is a many-sided man. He is applying for the post of secretary to the Bench, too, I hear.

PETRA. I don't believe it, Mr. Hovstad. How could he possibly bring himself to do such a thing?

HOVSTAD. Ah, you must ask him that.

PETRA. I should never have thought it of him.

HOVSTAD (*looking more closely at her*). No? Does it really surprise you so much?

PETRA. Yes. Or perhaps not altogether. Really, I don't quite know—

HOVSTAD. We journalists are not much worth, Miss Stockmann.

PETRA. Do you really mean that?

HOVSTAD. I think so sometimes.

PETRA. Yes, in the ordinary affairs of everyday life, perhaps; I can understand that. But now, when you have taken a weighty matter in hand—

HOVSTAD. This matter of your father's, you mean?

PETRA. Exactly. It seems to me that now you must feel you are a man worth more than most.

HOVSTAD. Yes, today I do feel something of that sort.

PETRA. Of course you do, don't you? It is a splendid vocation you have chosen—to smooth the way for the march of unappreciated truths, and new and courageous lines of thought. If it were nothing more than because you stand fearlessly in the open and take up the cause of an injured man—

HOVSTAD. Especially when that injured man is —ahem!—I don't rightly know how to—

PETRA. When that man is so upright and so honest, you mean?

HOVSTAD (*more gently*). Especially when he is your father, I meant.

PETRA (*suddenly checked*). *That?*

HOVSTAD. Yes, Petra—Miss Petra.

PETRA. Is it *that*, that is first and foremost with you? Not the matter itself? Not the truth?— not my father's big generous heart?

HOVSTAD. Certainly—of course—that too.

PETRA. No, thank you; you have betrayed yourself, Mr. Hovstad, and now I shall never trust you again in anything.

HOVSTAD. Can you really take it so amiss in me that it is mostly for your sake—?

PETRA. What I am angry with you for, is for not having been honest with my father. You talked to him as if the truth and the good of the community were what lay nearest to your heart. You have made fools of both my father and me. You are not the man you made yourself out to be. And that I shall never forgive you—never!

HOVSTAD. You ought not to speak so bitterly, Miss Petra—least of all now.

PETRA. Why not now, especially?

HOVSTAD. Because your father cannot do without my help.

PETRA (*looking him up and down*). Are you that sort of man too? For shame!

HOVSTAD. No, no, I am not. This came upon me so unexpectedly—you must believe that.

PETRA. I know what to believe. Goodbye.

ASLAKSEN (*coming from the printing-room, hurriedly and with an air of mystery*). Hovstad! —(*Sees* PETRA.) Oh, this is awkward—

PETRA. There is the book; you must give it to

some one else. (*Goes towards the door.*)

HOVSTAD (*following her*). But, Miss Stock-mann—

PETRA. Goodbye. (*Goes out.*)

ASLAKSEN. I say—Mr. Hovstad—

HOVSTAD. Well, well!—what is it?

ASLAKSEN. The Mayor is outside in the printing-room.

HOVSTAD. The Mayor, did you say?

ASLAKSEN. Yes, he wants to speak to you. He came in by the back door—didn't want to be seen, you understand.

HOVSTAD. What can he want? Wait a bit—I will go myself. (*Goes to the door of the printing-room, opens it, bows and invites* PETER STOCK-MANN *in.*) Just see, Aslaksen, that no one—

ASLAKSEN. Quite so. (*Goes into the printing-room.*)

PETER STOCKMANN. You did not expect to see me here, Mr. Hovstad?

HOVSTAD. No, I confess I did not.

PETER STOCKMANN (*looking round*). You are very snug in here—very nice indeed.

HOVSTAD. Oh—

PETER STOCKMANN. And here I come, without any notice, to take up your time!

HOVSTAD. By all means, Mr. Mayor. I am at your service. But let me relieve you of your— (*takes* STOCKMANN's *hat and stick and puts them on a chair*). Won't you sit down?

PETER STOCKMANN (*sitting down by the table*). Thank you. (HOVSTAD *sits down.*) I have had an extremely annoying experience today, Mr. Hovstad.

HOVSTAD. Really? Ah well, I expect with all the various business you have to attend to—

PETER STOCKMANN. The Medical Officer of the Baths is responsible for what happened to-day.

HOVSTAD. Indeed? The Doctor?

PETER STOCKMANN. He has addressed a kind of report to the Baths Committee on the subject of certain supposed defects in the Baths.

HOVSTAD. Has he indeed?

PETER STOCKMANN. Yes—has he not told you? I thought he said—

HOVSTAD. Ah, yes—it is true he did mention something about—

ASLAKSEN (*coming from the printing-room*). I ought to have that copy—

HOVSTAD (*angrily*). Ahem!—there it is on the desk.

ASLAKSEN (*taking it*). Right.

PETER STOCKMANN. But look there—that is the thing I was speaking of!

ASLAKSEN. Yes, that is the Doctor's article, Mr. Mayor.

HOVSTAD. Oh, is *that* what you were speaking about?

PETER STOCKMANN. Yes, that is it. What do you think of it?

HOVSTAD. Oh, I am only a layman—and I have only taken a very cursory glance at it.

PETER STOCKMANN. But you are going to print it?

HOVSTAD. I cannot very well refuse a distinguished man—

ASLAKSEN. I have nothing to do with editing the paper, Mr. Mayor—

PETER STOCKMANN. I understand.

ASLAKSEN. I merely print what is put into my hands.

PETER STOCKMANN. Quite so.

ASLAKSEN. And so I must—(*moves off towards the printing-room*).

PETER STOCKMANN. No, but wait a moment, Mr. Aslaksen. You will allow me, Mr. Hovstad?

HOVSTAD. If you please, Mr. Mayor.

PETER STOCKMANN. You are a discreet and thoughtful man, Mr. Aslaksen.

ASLAKSEN. I am delighted to hear you think so, sir.

PETER STOCKMANN. And a man of very considerable influence.

ASLAKSEN. Chiefly among the small tradesmen, sir.

PETER STOCKMANN. The small tax-payers are the majority—here as everywhere else.

ASLAKSEN. That is true.

PETER STOCKMANN. And I have no doubt you know the general trend of opinion among them, don't you?

ASLAKSEN. Yes, I think I may say I do, Mr. Mayor.

PETER STOCKMANN. Yes. Well, since there is such a praiseworthy spirit of self-sacrifice among the less wealthy citizens of our town—

ASLAKSEN. What?

HOVSTAD. Self-sacrifice?

PETER STOCKMANN. It is pleasing evidence of a public-spirited feeling, extremely pleasing evidence. I might almost say I hardly expected it. But you have a closer knowledge of public opinion than I.

ASLAKSEN. But, Mr. Mayor—

PETER STOCKMANN. And indeed it is no small sacrifice that the town is going to make.

HOVSTAD. The town?

ASLAKSEN. But I don't understand. Is it the Baths—?

PETER STOCKMANN. At a provisional estimate, the alterations that the Medical Officer asserts to be desirable will cost somewhere about twenty thousand pounds.

ASLAKSEN. That is a lot of money, but—

PETER STOCKMANN. Of course it will be necessary to raise a municipal loan.

HOVSTAD (getting up). Surely you never mean that the town must pay—?

ASLAKSEN. Do you mean that it must come out of the municipal funds?—out of the ill-filled pockets of the small tradesmen?

PETER STOCKMANN. Well, my dear Mr. Aslaksen, where else is the money to come from?

ASLAKSEN. The gentlemen who own the Baths ought to provide that.

PETER STOCKMANN. The proprietors of the Baths are not in a position to incur any further expense.

ASLAKSEN. Is that absolutely certain, Mr. Mayor?

PETER STOCKMANN. I have satisfied myself that it is so. If the town wants these very extensive alterations, it will have to pay for them.

ASLAKSEN. But, hang it all—I beg your pardon—this is quite another matter, Mr. Hovstad!

HOVSTAD. It is, indeed.

PETER STOCKMANN. The most fatal part of it is that we shall be obliged to shut the Baths for a couple of years.

HOVSTAD. Shut them? Shut them altogether?

ASLAKSEN. For two years?

PETER STOCKMANN. Yes, the work will take as long as that—at least.

ASLAKSEN. We won't stand for that, Mr. Mayor! What are we householders to live upon in the meantime?

PETER STOCKMANN. Unfortunately that is an extremely difficult question to answer, Mr. Aslaksen. But what would you have us do? Do you suppose we shall have a single visitor in the town, if we go about proclaiming that our water is polluted, that we are living over a plague spot, that the entire town—

ASLAKSEN. And the whole thing is merely imagination?

PETER STOCKMANN. With the best will in the world, I have not been able to come to any other conclusion.

ASLAKSEN. Well then I must say it is absolutely unjustifiable of Dr. Stockmann—I beg your pardon, Mr. Mayor—

PETER STOCKMANN. What you say is lamentably true, Mr. Aslaksen. My brother has unfortunately always been a headstrong man.

ASLAKSEN. After this, do you mean to give him your support, Mr. Hovstad?

HOVSTAD. Can you suppose for a moment that I—?

PETER STOCKMANN. I have drawn up a short *résumé* of the situation as it appears from a reasonable man's point of view. In it I have indicated how certain possible defects might suitably be remedied without outrunning the resources of the Baths Committee.

HOVSTAD. Have you got it with you, Mr. Mayor?

PETER STOCKMANN (*fumbling in his pocket*). Yes, I brought it with me in case you should—

ASLAKSEN. Good Lord, there he is!

PETER STOCKMANN. Who? My brother?

HOVSTAD. Where? Where?

ASLAKSEN. He has just gone through the printing-room.

PETER STOCKMANN. How unlucky! I don't want

to meet him here, and I had still several things to speak to you about.

HOVSTAD (*pointing to the door on the right*). Go in there for the present.

PETER STOCKMANN. But—?

HOVSTAD. You will only find Billing in there.

ASLAKSEN. Quick, quick, Mr. Mayor—he is just coming.

PETER STOCKMANN. Yes, very well; but see that you get rid of him quickly. (*Goes out through the door on the right, which* ASLAKSEN *opens for him and shuts after him.*)

HOVSTAD. Pretend to be doing something, Aslaksen. (*Sits down and writes.* ASLAKSEN *begins foraging among a heap of newspapers that are lying on a chair.*)

DR. STOCKMANN (*coming in from the printing-room*). Here I am again. (*Puts down his hat and stick.*)

HOVSTAD (*writing*). Already, Doctor? Hurry up with what we were speaking about, Aslaksen. We are very pressed for time today.

DR. STOCKMANN (*to* ASLAKSEN). No proof for me to see yet, I hear.

ASLAKSEN (*without turning round*). You couldn't expect it yet, Doctor.

DR. STOCKMANN. No, no; but I am impatient, as you can understand. I shall not know a moment's peace of mind till I see it in print.

HOVSTAD. H'm!—It will take a good while yet, won't it, Aslaksen?

ASLAKSEN. Yes, I am almost afraid it will.

DR. STOCKMANN. All right, my dear friends; I will come back. I do not mind coming back twice if necessary. A matter of such great importance—the welfare of the town at stake —it is no time to shirk trouble. (*Is just going, but stops and comes back*). Look here— there is one thing more I want to speak to you about.

HOVSTAD. Excuse me, but could it not wait till some other time?

DR. STOCKMANN. I can tell you in half a dozen words. It is only this. When my article is read tomorrow and it is realized that I have been quietly working the whole winter for the welfare of the town—

HOVSTAD. Yes, but, Doctor—

DR. STOCKMANN. I know what you are going to say. You don't see how on earth it was any more than my duty—my obvious duty as a citizen. Of course it wasn't; I know that as well as you. But my fellow citizens, you know—! Good Lord, think of all the good souls who think so highly of me—!

ASLAKSEN. Yes, our townsfolk have had a very high opinion of you so far, Doctor.

DR. STOCKMANN. Yes, and that is just why I am afraid they—. Well, this is the point; when this reaches them, especially the poorer classes, and sounds in their ears like a summons to take the town's affairs into their own hands for the future—

HOVSTAD (*getting up*). Ahem! Doctor, I won't conceal from you the fact—

DR. STOCKMANN. Ah!—I knew there was something in the wind! But I won't hear a word of it. If anything of that sort is being set on foot—

HOVSTAD. Of what sort?

DR. STOCKMANN. Well, whatever it is—whether it is a demonstration in my honor, or a banquet, or a subscription list for some presentation to me—whatever it is, you must promise me solemnly and faithfully to put a stop to it. You too, Mr. Aslaksen; do you understand?

HOVSTAD. You must forgive me, Doctor, but sooner or later we must tell you the plain truth—

He is interrupted by the entrance of MRS. STOCKMANN, *who comes in from the street door.*

MRS. STOCKMANN (*seeing her husband*). Just as I thought!

HOVSTAD (*going towards her*). You too, Mrs. Stockmann?

DR. STOCKMANN. What on earth do *you* want here, Katherine?

MRS. STOCKMANN. I should think you know very well what I want.

HOVSTAD. Won't you sit down? Or perhaps—

MRS. STOCKMANN. No, thank you; don't trouble. And you must not be offended at my coming to fetch my husband; I am the mother of three children, you know.

DR. STOCKMANN. Nonsense!—we know all about that.

MRS. STOCKMANN. Well, one would not give you credit for much thought for your wife and children today; if you had had that, you would not have gone and dragged us all into misfortune.

DR. STOCKMANN. Are you out of your senses, Katherine! Because a man has a wife and children, is he not to be allowed to proclaim the truth—is he not to be allowed to be an actively useful citizen—is he not to be allowed to do a service to his native town!

MRS. STOCKMANN. Yes, Thomas—in reason.

ASLAKSEN. Just what I say. Moderation is everything.

MRS. STOCKMANN. And that is why you wrong us, Mr. Hovstad, in enticing my husband away from his home and making a dupe of him in all this.

HOVSTAD. I certainly am making a dupe of no one—

DR. STOCKMANN. Making a dupe of me! Do you suppose *I* should allow myself to be duped!

MRS. STOCKMANN. It is just what you do. I know quite well you have more brains than anyone in the town, but you are extremely easily duped, Thomas. (*To* HOVSTAD.) Please do realize that he loses his post at the Baths if you print what he has written—

ASLAKSEN. What!

HOVSTAD. Look here, Doctor—

DR. STOCKMANN (*laughing*). Ha—ha!—just let them try! No, no—they will take good care not to. I have got the compact majority behind me, let me tell you!

MRS. STOCKMANN. Yes, that is just the worst of it—your having any such horrid thing behind you.

DR. STOCKMANN. Rubbish, Katherine!—Go home and look after your house and leave me to look after the community. How can you be so afraid, when I am so confident and happy? (*Walks up and down, rubbing his hands.*) Truth and the People will win the

fight, you may be certain! I see the whole of the broadminded middle class marching like a victorious army—! (*Stops beside a chair.*) What the deuce is that lying there?

ASLAKSEN. Good Lord!

HOVSTAD. Ahem!

DR. STOCKMANN. Here we have the topmost pinnacle of authority! (*Takes the Mayor's official hat carefully between his finger-tips and holds it up in the air.*)

MRS. STOCKMANN. The Mayor's hat!

DR. STOCKMANN. And here is the staff of office too. How in the name of all that's wonderful—?

HOVSTAD. Well, you see—

DR. STOCKMANN. Oh, I understand. He has been here trying to talk you over. Ha—ha!—he made rather a mistake there! And as soon as he caught sight of me in the printing-room—. (*Bursts out laughing.*) Did he run away, Mr. Aslaksen?

ASLAKSEN (*hurriedly*). Yes, he ran away, Doctor.

DR. STOCKMANN. Ran away without his stick or his—Fiddlesticks! Peter doesn't run away and leave his belongings behind him. But what the deuce have you done with him? Ah!—in there, of course. Now you shall see, Katherine!

MRS. STOCKMANN. Thomas—please don't—!

ASLAKSEN. Don't be rash, Doctor.

DR. STOCKMANN *has put on the Mayor's hat and taken his stick in his hand. He goes up to the door, opens it, and stands with his hand to his hat at the salute.* PETER STOCKMANN *comes in, red with anger.* BILLING *follows him.*

PETER STOCKMANN. What does this tomfoolery mean?

DR. STOCKMANN. Be respectful, my good Peter. I am the chief authority in the town now. (*Walks up and down.*)

MRS. STOCKMANN (*almost in tears*). Really, Thomas!

PETER STOCKMANN (*following him about*). Give me my hat and stick.

DR. STOCKMANN (*in the same tone as before*). If you are chief constable, let me tell you that I am the Mayor—I am the master of the whole town, please understand!

PETER STOCKMANN. Take off my hat, I tell you. Remember it is part of an official uniform.

DR. STOCKMANN. Pooh! Do you think the newly awakened lion-hearted people are going to be frightened by an official hat? There is going to be a revolution in the town tomorrow, let me tell you. You thought you could turn me out; but now I shall turn you out—turn you out of all your various offices. Do you think I cannot? Listen to me. I have triumphant social forces behind me. Hovstad and Billing will thunder in the "People's Messenger," and Aslaksen will take the field at the head of the whole Householders' Association—

ASLAKSEN. That I won't, Doctor.

DR. STOCKMANN. Of course you will—

PETER STOCKMANN. Ah!—may I ask then if Mr. Hovstad intends to join this agitation?

HOVSTAD. No, Mr. Mayor.

ASLAKSEN. No, Mr. Hovstad is not such a fool as to go and ruin his paper and himself for the sake of an imaginary grievance.

DR. STOCKMANN (*looking round him*). What does this mean?

HOVSTAD. You have represented your case in a false light, Doctor, and therefore I am unable to give you my support.

BILLING. And after what the Mayor was so kind as to tell me just now, I—

DR. STOCKMANN. A false light! Leave that part of it to me. Only print my article; I am quite capable of defending it.

HOVSTAD. I am not going to print it. I cannot and will not dare not print it.

DR. STOCKMANN. You dare not? What nonsense! —you are the editor; and an editor controls his paper, I suppose!

ASLAKSEN. No, it is the subscribers, Doctor.

PETER STOCKMANN. Fortunately, yes.

ASLAKSEN. It is public opinion—the enlightened public—householders and people of that kind; they control the newspapers.

DR. STOCKMANN (*composedly*). And I have all these influences against me?

ASLAKSEN. Yes, you have. It would mean the absolute ruin of the community if your article were to appear.

DR. STOCKMANN. Indeed.

PETER STOCKMANN. My hat and stick, if you please. (DR. STOCKMANN *takes off the hat and lays it on the table with the stick.* PETER STOCKMANN *takes them up.*) Your authority as mayor has come to an untimely end.

DR. STOCKMANN. We have not got to the end yet. (*To* HOVSTAD.) Then it is quite impossible for you to print my article in the "People's Messenger"?

HOVSTAD. Quite impossible—out of regard for your family as well.

MRS. STOCKMANN. You need not concern yourself about his family, thank you, Mr. Hovstad.

PETER STOCKMANN (*taking a paper from his pocket*). It will be sufficient, for the guidance of the public, if this appears. It is an official statement. May I trouble you?

HOVSTAD (*taking the paper*). Certainly; I will see that it is printed.

DR. STOCKMANN. But not mine. Do you imagine that you can silence me and stifle the truth! You will not find it so easy as you propose. Mr. Aslaksen, kindly take my manuscript at once and print it as a pamphlet—at my expense. I will have four hundred copies—no, five—six hundred.

ASLAKSEN. If you offered me its weight in gold, I could not lend my press for any such purpose, Doctor. It would be flying in the face of public opinion. You will not get it printed anywhere in the town.

DR. STOCKMANN. Then give it me back.

HOVSTAD (*giving him the manuscript*). Here it is.

DR. STOCKMANN (*taking his hat and stick*). It shall be made public all the same. I will read it out at a mass meeting of the townspeople. All my fellow-citizens shall hear the voice of truth!

PETER STOCKMANN. You will not find any public body in the town that will give you the use of their hall for such a purpose.

ASLAKSEN. Not a single one, I am certain.

BILLING. I'm hanged if you will find one.

MRS. STOCKMANN. But this is too shameful! Why should every one turn against you like that?

DR. STOCKMANN (angrily). I will tell you why. It is because all the men in this town are old women—like you; they all think of nothing but their families, and never of the community.

MRS. STOCKMANN (putting her arm into his). Then I will show them that an—an old woman can be a man for once. I am going to stand by you, Thomas!

DR. STOCKMANN. Bravely said, Katherine! It shall be made public—as I am a living soul! If I can't hire a hall, I shall hire a drum, and parade the town with it and read it at every street-corner.

PETER STOCKMANN. You are surely not such an arrant fool as that!

DR. STOCKMANN. Yes, I am.

ASLAKSEN. You won't find a single man in the whole town to go with you.

BILLING. No, I'm hanged if you will.

MRS. STOCKMANN. Don't give in, Thomas. I will tell the boys to go with you.

DR. STOCKMANN. That is a splendid idea!

MRS. STOCKMANN. Morten will be delighted; and Ejlif will do whatever he does.

DR. STOCKMANN. Yes, and Petra!—and you too, Katherine!

MRS. STOCKMANN. No, I won't do that; but I will stand at the window and watch you, that's what I will do.

DR. STOCKMANN (puts his arms round her and kisses her). Thank you, my dear! Now you and I are going to try a fall, my fine gentlemen! I am going to see whether a pack of cowards can succeed in gagging a patriot who wants to purify society! (He and his wife go out by the street door.)

PETER STOCKMANN (shaking his head seriously). Now he has sent her out of her senses, too.

DISCUSSION FOR UNDERSTANDING

1. Before Peter Stockmann arrives, how does each of the following react to Dr. Stockmann's article?

   a. Billing, the assistant editor

   b. Hovstad, the editor

   c. Aslaksen, the printer

2. What job has Billing applied for? How does Billing explain this action?

3. Why does Hovstad continue to use Aslaksen as his printer when he does not agree with him politically?

4. Why does Petra refuse to translate the English story?

5. What reasons does Hovstad give for printing it?

6. What is the real reason that Hovstad is supporting Dr. Stockmann? How does Petra react to this revelation?

7. What discouraging facts does the Mayor tell the newspaper editors? How does Aslaksen react? What is the crux of the Mayor's article?

8. Why does Mrs. Stockmann come to the newspaper office? What is her attitude towards her husband's article?

9. In the confrontation between the Mayor and the Doctor, what does the Doctor find has happened to the editor's and the printer's support? What is Mrs. Stockmann's attitude now?

10. What is the final piece of bad news for the Doctor?

Act IV

SCENE—A big old-fashioned room in CAPTAIN HORSTER's house. At the back folding-doors, which are standing open, lead to an ante-room. Three windows in the left-hand wall. In the middle of the opposite wall a platform has been erected. On this is a small table with two candles, a water-bottle and glass, and a bell. The room is lit by lamps placed between the windows. In the foreground on the left there is a table with candles and a chair. To the right is a door and *some chairs standing near it. The room is nearly filled with a crowd of townspeople of all sorts, a few women and schoolboys being amongst them. People are still streaming in from the back, and the room is soon filled.*

1ST CITIZEN (*meeting another*). Hullo, Lamstad! You here too?

2ND CITIZEN. I go to every public meeting, I do.

3RD CITIZEN. Brought your whistle too, I expect!

2ND CITIZEN. I should think so. Haven't you?

3RD CITIZEN. Rather! And old Evensen said he was going to bring a cow-horn, he did.

2ND CITIZEN. Good old Evensen! (*Laughter among the crowd*).

4TH CITIZEN (*coming up to them*). I say, tell me what is going on here tonight.

2ND CITIZEN. Dr. Stockmann is going to deliver an address attacking the Mayor.

4TH CITIZEN. But the Mayor is his brother.

1ST CITIZEN. That doesn't matter; Dr. Stockmann's not the chap to be afraid.

3RD CITIZEN. But he is in the wrong; it said so in the "People's Messenger."

2ND CITIZEN. Yes, I expect he must be in the wrong this time, because neither the Householders' Association nor the Citizens' Club would lend him their hall for his meeting.

1ST CITIZEN. He couldn't even get the loan of the hall at the Baths.

2ND CITIZEN. No, I should think not.

A MAN IN ANOTHER PART OF THE CROWD. I say —who are we to back up in this?

ANOTHER MAN, BESIDE HIM. Watch Aslaksen, and do as he does.

BILLING (*pushing his way through the crowd, with a writing-case under his arm*). Excuse me, gentlemen—do you mind letting me through? I am reporting for the "People's Messenger." Thank you very much! (*He sits down at the table on the left.*)

A WORKMAN. Who was that?

SECOND WORKMAN. Don't you know him? It's Billing, who writes for Aslaksen's paper.

CAPTAIN HORSTER *brings in* MRS. STOCKMANN *and* PETRA *through the door on the right.* EJLIF *and* MORTON *follow them in.*

HORSTER. I thought you might all sit here; you can slip out easily from here, if things get too lively.

MRS. STOCKMANN. Do you think there will be a disturbance?

HORSTER. One can never tell—with such a crowd. But sit down, and don't be uneasy.

MRS. STOCKMANN (*sitting down*). It was extremely kind of you to offer my husband the room.

HORSTER. Well, if nobody else would—

PETRA (*who has sat down beside her mother*). And it was a plucky thing to do, Captain Horster.

HORSTER. Oh, it is not such a great matter as all that.

HOVSTAD *and* ASLAKSEN *make their way through the crowd.*

ASLAKSEN (*going up to* HORSTER). Has the Doctor not come yet?

HORSTER. He is waiting in the next room. (*Movement in the crowd by the door at the back.*)

HOVSTAD. Look—here comes the Mayor!

BILLING. Yes, I'm hanged if he hasn't come after all!

PETER STOCKMANN *makes his way gradually through the crowd, bows courteously, and takes up a position by the wall on the left. Shortly afterwards* DR. STOCKMANN *comes in by the right-hand door. He is dressed in a black frock-coat, with a white tie. There is a little feeble applause, which is hushed down. Silence is obtained.*

DR. STOCKMANN (*in an undertone*). How do you feel, Katherine?

MRS. STOCKMANN. All right, thank you. (*Lowering her voice.*) Be sure not to lose your temper, Thomas.

DR. STOCKMANN. Oh, I know how to control myself. (*Looks at his watch, steps on to the platform, and bows.*) It is a quarter past—so I will begin. (*Takes his manuscript out of his pocket.*)

ASLAKSEN. I think we ought to elect a chairman first.

DR. STOCKMANN. No, it is quite unnecessary.

SOME OF THE CROWD. Yes—yes!

PETER STOCKMANN. I certainly think too that we ought to have a chairman.

DR. STOCKMANN. But I have called this meeting to deliver a lecture, Peter.

PETER STOCKMANN. Dr. Stockmann's lecture may possibly lead to a considerable conflict of opinion.

VOICES IN THE CROWD. A chairman! A chairman!

HOVSTAD. The general wish of the meeting seems to be that a chairman should be elected.

DR. STOCKMANN (*restraining himself*). Very well—let the meeting have its way.

ASLAKSEN. Will the Mayor be good enough to undertake the task?

THREE MEN (*clapping their hands*). Bravo! Bravo!

PETER STOCKMANN. For various reasons, which you will easily understand, I must beg to be excused. But fortunately we have amongst us a man who I think will be acceptable to you all. I refer to the President of the Householders' Association, Mr. Aslaksen.

SEVERAL VOICES. Yes—Aslaksen! Bravo Aslaksen!

DR. STOCKMANN *takes up his manuscript and walks up and down the platform.*

ASLAKSEN. Since my fellow-citizens choose to entrust me with this duty, I cannot refuse.

Loud applause. ASLAKSEN *mounts the platform.*

BILLING (*writing*). "Mr. Aslaksen was elected with enthusiasm."

ASLAKSEN. And now, as I am in this position, I should like to say a few brief words. I am a quiet and peaceable man, who believes in discreet moderation, and—and—in moderate discretion. All my friends can bear witness to that.

SEVERAL VOICES. That's right! That's right, Aslaksen!

ASLAKSEN. I have learnt in the school of life and experience that moderation is the most valuable virtue a citizen can possess—

PETER STOCKMANN. Hear, hear!

ASLAKSEN. —And moreover that discretion and moderation are what enable a man to be of most service to the community. I would therefore suggest to our esteemed fellow-citizen, who has called this meeting, that he should strive to keep strictly within the bounds of moderation.

A MAN BY THE DOOR. Three cheers for the Moderation Society!

A VOICE. Shame!

SEVERAL VOICES. Sh!—Sh!

ASLAKSEN. No interruptions, gentlemen, please! Does anyone wish to make any remarks?

PETER STOCKMANN. Mr. Chairman.

ASLAKSEN. The Mayor will address the meeting.

PETER STOCKMANN. In consideration of the close relationship in which, as you all know, I stand to the present Medical Officer of the Baths, I should have preferred not to speak this evening. But my official position with regard to the Baths and my solicitude for the vital interests of the town compel me to bring forward a motion. I venture to presume that there is not a single one of our citizens present who considers it desirable that unreliable and exaggerated accounts of the sanitary conditions of the Baths and the town should be spread abroad.

SEVERAL VOICES. No, no! Certainly not! We protest against it!

PETER STOCKMANN. Therefore I should like to propose that the meeting should not permit the Medical Officer either to read or to comment on his proposed lecture.

DR. STOCKMANN (*impatiently*). Not permit—! What the devil—!

MRS. STOCKMANN (*coughing*). Ahem!—ahem!

DR. STOCKMANN (*collecting himself*). Very well. Go ahead!

PETER STOCKMANN. In my communication to the "People's Messenger," I have put the essential facts before the public in such a way that every fair-minded citizen can easily form his own opinion. From it you will see that the main result of the Medical Officer's proposals—apart from their constituting a vote of censure on the leading men of the town—would be to saddle the ratepayers with an unnecessary expenditure of at least some thousands of pounds.

Sounds of disapproval among the audience, and some catcalls.

ASLAKSEN (*ringing his bell*). Silence, please, gentlemen! I beg to support the Mayor's motion. I quite agree with him that there is something behind this agitation started by the Doctor. He talks about the Baths; but it is a revolution he is aiming at—he wants to get the administration of the town put into new hands. No one doubts the honesty of the Doctor's intentions—no one will suggest that there can be any two opinions as to that. I myself am a believer in self-government for the people, provided it does not fall too heavily on the taxpayers. But that would be the case here; and that is why I will see Dr. Stockmann hanged—I beg your pardon—before I go with him in the matter. You can pay too dearly for a thing sometimes; that is my opinion.

Loud applause on all sides.

HOVSTAD. I, too, feel called upon to explain my position. Dr. Stockmann's agitation appeared to be gaining a certain amount of sympathy at first, so I supported it as impartially as I could. But presently we had reason to suspect that we had allowed ourselves to be misled by misrepresentation of the state of affairs—

DR. STOCKMANN. Misrepresentation—!

HOVSTAD. Well, let us say a not entirely trustworthy representation. The Mayor's statement has proved that. I hope no one here has any doubt as to my liberal principles; the attitude of the "People's Messenger" towards important political questions is well known to every one. But the advice of experienced and thoughtful men has convinced me that in purely local matters a newspaper ought to proceed with a certain caution.

ASLAKSEN. I entirely agree with the speaker.

HOVSTAD. And, in the matter before us, it is now an undoubted fact that Dr. Stockmann has public opinion against him. Now, what is an editor's first and most obvious duty, gentlemen? Is it not to work in harmony with his readers? Has he not received a sort of tacit mandate to work persistently and assiduously for the welfare of those whose opinions he represents? Or is it possible I am mistaken in that?

VOICES FROM THE CROWD. No, no! You are quite right!

HOVSTAD. It has cost me a severe struggle to break with a man in whose house I have been lately a frequent guest—a man who till today has been able to pride himself on the undivided goodwill of his fellow-citizens —a man whose only, or at all events whose essential, failing is that he is swayed by his heart rather than his head.

A FEW SCATTERED VOICES. That is true! Bravo, Stockmann!

HOVSTAD. But my duty to the community obliged me to break with him. And there is another consideration that impels me to oppose him, and, as far as possible, to arrest him on the perilous course he has adopted; that is, consideration for his family—

DR. STOCKMANN. Please stick to the water-supply and drainage!

HOVSTAD. —consideration, I repeat, for his wife and his children for whom he has made no provision.

MORTEN. Is that us, mother?

MRS. STOCKMANN. Hush!

ASLAKSEN. I will not put the Mayor's proposition to the vote.

DR. STOCKMANN. There is no necessity! Tonight I have no intention of dealing with all that filth down at the Baths. No; I have something quite different to say to you.

PETER STOCKMANN (*aside*). What is coming now?

A DRUNKEN MAN (*by the entrance door*). I am a taxpayer! And therefore I have a right to speak too! And my entire—firm—inconceivable opinion is—

A NUMBER OF VOICES. Be quiet, at the back there!

OTHERS. He is drunk! Turn him out! (*They turn him out.*)

DR. STOCKMANN. Am I allowed to speak?

ASLAKSEN (*ringing his bell*). Dr. Stockmann will address the meeting.

DR. STOCKMANN. I should like to have seen anyone, a few days ago, dare to attempt to silence me as has been done tonight! I would have defended my sacred rights as a man, like a lion! But now it is all one to me; I have something of even weightier importance to say to you.

The crowd presses nearer to him, MORTEN KIIL *conspicuous among them.*

DR. STOCKMANN (*continuing*). I have thought and pondered a great deal, these last few days—pondered over such a variety of things that in the end my head seemed too full to hold them—

PETER STOCKMANN (*with a cough*). Ahem!

DR. STOCKMANN. —but I got them clear in my mind at last, and then I saw the whole situation lucidly. And that is why I am standing here tonight. I have a great revelation to make to you, my fellow-citizens! I will impart to you a discovery of a far wider scope than the trifling matter that our water-supply is poisoned and our medicinal Baths are standing on pestiferous soil.

A NUMBER OF VOICES (*shouting*). Don't talk about the Baths! We won't hear you! None of that!

DR. STOCKMANN. I have already told you that what I want to speak about is the great discovery I have made lately—the discovery that all the sources of our *moral* life are poisoned and that the whole fabric of our civic community is founded on the pestiferous soil of falsehood.

VOICES OF DISCONCERTED CITIZENS. What is that he says?

PETER STOCKMANN. Such an insinuation—!

ASLAKSEN (*with his hand on his bell*). I call upon the speaker to moderate his language.

DR. STOCKMANN. I have always loved my native town as a man only can love the home of his youthful days. I was not old when I went away from here; and exile, longing and memories cast as it were an additional halo over both the town and its inhabitants. (*Some clapping and applause.*) And there I stayed, for many years, in a horrible hole far away up north. When I came into contact with some of the people that lived scattered about among the rocks, I often thought it would of been more service to the poor half-starved creatures if a veterinary doctor had been sent up there, instead of a man like me. (*Murmurs among the crowd.*)

BILLING (*laying down his pen*). I'm hanged if I have ever heard—!

HOVSTAD. It is an insult to a respectable population!

DR. STOCKMANN. Wait a bit! I do not think anyone will charge me with having forgotten my native town up there. I was like one of the eider-ducks brooding on its nest, and what I hatched was—the plans for these Baths. (*Applause and protests.*) And then when fate at last decreed for me the great happiness of coming home again—I assure you, gentlemen, I thought I had nothing more in the world to wish for. Or rather, there was one thing I wished for—eagerly, untiringly, ardently—and that was to be able to be of service to my native town and the good of the community.

PETER STOCKMANN (*looking at the ceiling*). You chose a strange way of doing it—ahem!

DR. STOCKMANN. And so, with my eyes blinded to the real facts, I revelled in happiness. But yesterday morning—no, to be precise, it was yesterday afternoon—the eyes of my mind were opened wide, and the first thing I realized was the colossal stupidity of the authorities—. (*Uproar, shouts and laughter. MRS. STOCKMANN coughs persistently.*)

PETER STOCKMANN. Mr. Chairman!

ASLAKSEN (*ringing his bell*). By virtue of my authority—!

DR. STOCKMANN. It is a petty thing to catch me up on a word, Mr. Aslaksen. What I mean is only that I got scent of the unbelievable piggishness our leading men had been responsible for down at the Baths. I can't stand leading men at any price!—I have had enough of such people in my time. They are like billy-goats in a young plantation; they do mischief everywhere. They stand in a free man's way, whichever way he turns, and what I should like best would be to see them exterminated like any other vermin—. (*Uproar.*)

PETER STOCKMANN. Mr. Chairman, can we allow such expressions to pass?

ASLAKSEN (*with his hand on his bell*). Doctor—!

DR. STOCKMANN. I cannot understand how it is that I have only now acquired a clear conception of what these gentry are, when I had almost daily before my eyes in this town such an excellent specimen of them— my brother Peter—slow-witted and hidebound in prejudice—. (*Laughter, uproar and hisses. MRS. STOCKMANN sits coughing assiduously. ASLAKSEN rings his bell violently.*)

THE DRUNKEN MAN (*who has got in again*). Is it me he is talking about? My name's Petersen, all right—but devil take me if I—

527

ANGRY VOICES. Turn out that drunken man! Turn him out. (*He is turned out again.*)

PETER STOCKMANN. Who was that person?

1ST CITIZEN. I don't know who he is, Mr. Mayor.

2ND CITIZEN. He doesn't belong here.

3RD CITIZEN. I expect he is a navvy from over at (*the rest is inaudible*).

ASLAKSEN. He had obviously had too much beer.—Proceed, Doctor; but please strive to be moderate in your language.

DR. STOCKMANN. Very well, gentlemen, I will say no more about our leading men. And if anyone imagines, from what I have just said, that my object is to attack these people this evening, he is wrong—absolutely wide of the mark. For I cherish the comforting conviction that these parasites—all these venerable relics of a dying school of thought—are most admirably paving the way for their own extinction; they need no doctor's help to hasten their end. Nor is it folk of that kind who constitute the most pressing danger to the community. It is not they who are most instrumental in poisoning the sources of our moral life and infecting the ground on which we stand. It is not they who are the most dangerous enemies of truth and freedom amongst us.

SHOUTS FROM ALL SIDES. Who then? Who is it? Name! Name!

DR. STOCKMANN. You may depend upon it I shall name them! That is precisely the great discovery I made yesterday. (*Raises his voice.*) The most dangerous enemy of truth and freedom amongst us is the compact majority—yes, the rotten compact Liberal majority—that is it! Now you know! (*Tremendous uproar. Most of the crowd are shouting, stamping and hissing. Some of the older men among them exchange stolen glances and seem to be enjoying themselves.* MRS. STOCKMANN *gets up, looking anxious.* EJLIF *and* MORTEN *advance threateningly upon some schoolboys who are playing pranks.* ASLAKSEN *rings his bell and begs for silence.* HOVSTAD *and* BILLING *both*

talk at once, but are inaudible. At last quiet is restored.)

ASLAKSEN. As chairman, I call upon the speaker to withdraw the ill-considered expressions he has just used.

DR. STOCKMANN. Never, Mr. Aslaksen! It is the majority in our community that denies me my freedom and seeks to prevent my speaking the truth.

HOVSTAD. The majority always has right on its side.

BILLING. And truth too, by God!

DR. STOCKMANN. The majority *never* has right on its side. Never, I say! That is one of these social lies against which an independent, intelligent man must wage war. Who is it that constitute the majority of the population in a country? Is it the clever folk or the stupid? I don't imagine you will dispute the fact that at present the stupid people are in an absolutely overwhelming majority all the world over. But, good Lord!—you can never pretend that it is right that the stupid folk should govern the clever ones! (*Uproar and cries.*) Oh, yes—you can shout me down, I know! but you cannot answer me. The majority has *might* on its side—unfortunately; but *right* it has *not*. I am in the right—I and a few other scattered individuals. The minority is always in the right. (*Renewed uproar.*)

HOVSTAD. Aha!—so Dr. Stockmann has become an aristocrat since the day before yesterday!

DR. STOCKMANN. I have already said that I don't intend to waste a word on the puny, narrow-chested, short-winded crew whom we are leaving astern. Pulsating life no longer concerns itself with them. I am thinking of the few, the scattered few amongst us, who have absorbed new and vigorous truths. Such men stand, as it were, at the outposts, so far ahead that the compact majority has not yet been able to come up with them; and there they are fighting for truths that are too newly-born into the world of consciousness to have any considerable number of people on their side as yet.

HOVSTAD. So the Doctor is a revolutionary now!

DR. STOCKMANN. Good heavens—of course I am, Mr. Hovstad! I propose to raise a revolution against the lie that the majority has the monopoly of the truth. What sort of truths are they that the majority usually supports? They are truths that are of such advanced age that they are beginning to break up. And if a truth is as old as that, it is also in a fair way to become a lie, gentlemen. (*Laughter and mocking cries.*) Yes, believe me or not, as you like; but truths are by no means as long-lived as Methuselah—as some folk imagine. A normally constituted truth lives, let us say, as a rule seventeen or eighteen, or at most twenty years; seldom longer. But truths as aged as that are always worn frightfully thin, and nevertheless it is only then that the majority recognizes them and recommends them to the community as wholesome moral nourishment. There is no great nutritive value in that sort of fare, I can assure you; and, as a doctor, I ought to know. These "majority truths" are like last year's cured meat—like rancid, tainted ham; and they are the origin of the moral scurvy that is rampant in our communities.

ASLAKSEN. It appears to me that the speaker is wandering a long way from his subject.

PETER STOCKMANN. I quite agree with the Chairman.

DR. STOCKMANN. Have you gone clean out of your senses, Peter? I am sticking as closely to my subject as I can; for my subject is precisely this, that it is the masses, the majority—this infernal compact majority—that poisons the sources of our moral life and infects the ground we stand on.

HOVSTAD. And all this because the great, broad-minded majority of the people is prudent enough to show deference only to well-ascertained and well-approved truths?

DR. STOCKMANN. Ah, my good Mr. Hovstad, don't talk nonsense about well-ascertained truths! The truths of which the masses now approve are the very truths that the fighters at the outposts held to in the days of our grandfathers. We fighters at the outposts nowadays no longer approve of them; and I do not believe there is any other well-ascertained truth except this, that no community can live a healthy life if it is nourished only on such old marrowless truths.

HOVSTAD. But instead of standing there using vague generalities, it would be interesting if you would tell us what these old marrowless truths are, that we are nourished on.

Applause from many quarters.

DR. STOCKMANN. Oh, I could give you a whole string of such abominations; but to begin with I will confine myself to one well-approved truth, which at bottom is a foul lie, but upon which nevertheless Mr. Hovstad and the "People's Messenger" and all the "Messenger's" supporters are nourished.

HOVSTAD. And that is—?

DR. STOCKMANN. That is, the doctrine you have inherited from your forefathers and proclaim thoughtlessly far and wide—the doctrine that the public, the crowd, the masses, are the essential part of the population—that they constitute the People—that the common folk, the ignorant and incomplete element in the community, have the same right to pronounce judgment and to approve, to direct and to govern, as the isolated, intellectually superior personalities in it.

BILLING. Well, hang me if ever I—

HOVSTAD (*at the same time, shouting out*). Fellow-citizens, take good note of that!

A NUMBER OF VOICES (*angrily*). Oho!—we are not the People! Only the superior folk are to govern, are they!

A WORKMAN. Turn the fellow out, for talking such rubbish!

ANOTHER. Out with him!

ANOTHER (*calling out*). Blow your horn, Evensen!

A horn is blown loudly, amidst hisses and an angry uproar.

DR. STOCKMANN (*when the noise has somewhat abated*). Be reasonable! Can't you stand hearing the voice of truth for once? I don't in the least expect you to agree with me all at once; but I must say I did expect Mr. Hovstad to admit I was right, when he had recovered his composure a little. He claims to be a freethinker—

VOICES (*in murmurs of astonishment*). Freethinker, did he say? Is Hovstad a freethinker?

HOVSTAD (*shouting*). Prove it, Dr. Stockmann! When have I said so in print?

DR. STOCKMANN (*reflecting*). No, confound it, you are right!—you have never had the courage to. Well, I won't put you in a hole, Mr. Hovstad. Let us say it is I that am the freethinker, then. I am going to prove to you, scientifically, that the "People's Messenger" leads you by the nose in a shameful manner when it tells you that you—that the common people, the crowd, the masses, are the real essence of the People. That is only a newspaper lie, I tell you! The common people are nothing more than the raw material of which a People is made. (*Groans, laughter and uproar.*) Well, isn't that the case? Isn't there an enormous difference between a well-bred and an ill-bred strain of animals? Take, for instance, a common barn-door hen. What sort of eating do you get from a shrivelled up old scrag of a fowl like that? Not much, do you! And what sort of eggs does it lay? A fairly good crow or a raven can lay pretty nearly as good an egg. But take a well-bred Spanish or Japanese hen, or a good pheasant or a turkey—then you will see the difference. Or take the case of dogs, with whom we humans are on such intimate terms. Think first of an ordinary common cur—I mean one of the horrible, coarse-haired, low-bred curs that do nothing but run about the streets and befoul the walls of the houses. Compare one of these curs with a poodle whose sires for many generations have been bred in a gentleman's house, where they have had the best of food and had the opportunity of hearing soft voices and music. Do you not think that the poodle's brain is developed to quite a different degree from that of the cur? Of course it is. It is puppies of well-bred poodles like that, that showmen train to do incredibly clever tricks—things that a common cur could never learn to do even if it stood on its head. (*Uproar and mocking cries.*)

A CITIZEN (*calls out*). Are you going to make out we are dogs, now?

ANOTHER CITIZEN. We are not animals, Doctor!

DR. STOCKMANN. Yes, but, bless my soul, we *are*, my friend! It is true we are the finest animals anyone could wish for; but, even amongst us, exceptionally fine animals are rare. There is a tremendous difference between poodle-men and cur-men. And the amusing part of it is, that Mr. Hovstad quite agrees with me as long as it is a question of four-footed animals—

HOVSTAD. Yes, it is true enough as far as they are concerned.

DR. STOCKMANN. Very well. But as soon as I extend the principle and apply it to two-legged animals, Mr. Hovstad stops short. He no longer dares to think independently, or to pursue his ideas to their logical conclusion; so he turns the whole theory upside down and proclaims in the "People's Messenger" that it is the barn-door hens and street curs that are the finest specimens in the menagerie. But that is always the way, as long as a man retains the traces of common origin and has not worked his way up to intellectual distinction.

HOVSTAD. I lay no claim to any sort of distinction. I am the son of humble countryfolk, and I am proud that the stock I come from is rooted deep among the common people he insults!

VOICES. Bravo, Hovstad! Bravo! Bravo!

DR. STOCKMANN. The kind of common people

I mean are not only to be found low down in the social scale; they crawl and swarm all around us—even in the highest social positions. You have only to look at your own fine, distinguished Mayor! My brother Peter is every bit as plebeian as anyone that walks in two shoes—(*laughter and hisses*).

PETER STOCKMANN. I protest against personal allusions of this kind.

DR. STOCKMANN (*imperturbably*). —and that, not because he is, like myself, descended from some old rascal of a pirate from Pomerania or thereabouts—because that is who we are descended from—

PETER STOCKMANN. An absurd legend. I deny it!

DR. STOCKMANN. —but because he thinks what his superiors think and holds the same opinions as they. People who do that are, intellectually speaking, common people; and that is why my magnificent brother Peter is in reality so very far from any distinction—and consequently also so far from being liberal-minded.

PETER STOCKMANN. Mr. Chairman—!

HOVSTAD. So it is only the distinguished men that are liberal-minded in this country? We are learning something quite new! (*Laughter.*)

DR. STOCKMANN. Yes, that is part of my new discovery too. And another part of it is that broad-mindedness is almost precisely the same thing as morality. That is why I maintain that it is absolutely inexcusable in the "People's Messenger" to proclaim, day in and day out, the false doctrine that it is the masses, the crowd, the compact majority, that have the monopoly of broad-mindedness and morality—and that vice and corruption and every kind of intellectual depravity are the result of culture, just as all the filth that is draining into our Baths is the result of the tanneries up at Mölledal! (*Uproar and interruptions.* DR. STOCKMANN *is undisturbed, and goes on, carried away by his ardor, with a smile.*) And yet this same "People's Messenger" can go on preaching that the masses ought to be elevated to higher conditions of life! But, bless my soul, if the "Messenger's" teaching is to be depended upon, this very raising up the masses would mean nothing more or less than setting them straight-way upon the paths of depravity! Happily the theory that culture demoralizes is only an old falsehood that our forefathers believed in and we have inherited. No, it is ignorance, poverty, ugly conditions of life, that do the devil's work! In a house which does not get aired and swept every day—my wife Katherine maintains that the floor ought to be scrubbed as well, but that is a debatable question—in such a house, let me tell you, people will lose within two or three years the power of thinking or acting in a moral manner. Lack of oxygen weakens the conscience. And there must be a plentiful lack of oxygen in very many houses in this town, I should think, judging from the fact that the whole compact majority can be unconscientious enough to wish to build the town's prosperity on a quagmire of falsehood and deceit.

ASLAKSEN. We cannot allow such a grave accusation to be flung at a citizen community.

A CITIZEN. I move that the Chairman direct the speaker to sit down.

VOICES (*angrily*). Hear, hear! Quite right! Make him sit down!

DR. STOCKMANN (*losing his self-control*). Then I will go and shout the truth at every street corner! I will write it in other towns' newspapers! The whole country shall know what is going on here!

HOVSTAD. It almost seems as if Dr. Stockmann's intention were to ruin the town.

DR. STOCKMANN. Yes, my native town is so dear to me that I would rather ruin it than see it flourishing upon a lie.

ASLAKSEN. This is really serious. (*Uproar and catcalls.* MRS. STOCKMANN *coughs, but to no purpose; her husband does not listen to her any longer.*)

531

HOVSTAD (*shouting above the din*). A man must be a public enemy to wish to ruin a whole community!

DR. STOCKMANN (*with growing fervor*). What does the destruction of a community matter, if it lives on lies! It ought to be razed to the ground, I tell you! All who live by lies ought to be exterminated like vermin! You will end by infecting the whole country; you will bring about such a state of things that the whole country will deserve to be ruined. And if things come to that pass, I shall say from the bottom of my heart: Let the whole country perish, let all these people be exterminated!

VOICES FROM THE CROWD. That is talking like an out-and-out enemy of the people!

BILLING. There sounded the voice of the people, by all that's holy!

THE WHOLE CROWD (*shouting*). Yes, yes! He is an enemy of the people! He hates his country! He hates his own people!

ASLAKSEN. Both as a citizen and as an individual, I am profoundly disturbed by what we have had to listen to. Dr. Stockmann has shown himself in a light I should never have dreamed of. I am unhappily obliged to subscribe to the opinion which I have just heard my estimable fellow-citizens utter; and I propose that we should give expression to that opinion in a resolution. I propose a resolution as follows: "This meeting declares that it considers Dr. Thomas Stockmann, Medical Officer of the Baths, to be an enemy of the people." (*A storm of cheers and applause. A number of men surround the* DOCTOR *and hiss him.* MRS. STOCKMANN *and* PETRA *have got up from their seats.* MORTEN *and* EJLIF *are fighting the other schoolboys for hissing; some of their elders separate them.*)

DR. STOCKMANN (*to the men who are hissing him*). Oh, you fools! I tell you that—

ASLAKSEN (*ringing his bell*). We cannot hear you now, Doctor. A formal vote is about to be taken; but, out of regard for personal feelings, it shall be by ballot and not verbal. Have you any clean paper, Mr. Billing?

BILLING. I have both blue and white here.

ASLAKSEN (*going to him*). That will do nicely; we shall get on more quickly that way. Cut it up into small strips—yes, that's it. (*To the meeting.*) Blue means no; white means yes. I will come round myself and collect votes. (PETER STOCKMANN *leaves the hall.* ASLAKSEN *and one or two others go round the room with the slips of paper in their hats.*)

1ST CITIZEN (*to* HOVSTAD). I say, what has come to the Doctor? What are we to think of it?

HOVSTAD. Oh, you know how headstrong he is.

2ND CITIZEN (*to* BILLING). Billing, you go to their house—have you ever noticed if the fellow drinks?

BILLING. Well, I'm hanged if I know what to say. There are always spirits on the table when you go.

3RD CITIZEN. I rather think he goes quite off his head sometimes.

1ST CITIZEN. I wonder if there is any madness in his family?

BILLING. I shouldn't wonder if there were.

4TH CITIZEN. No, it is nothing more than sheer malice; he wants to get even with somebody for something or other.

BILLING. Well, certainly he suggested a rise in his salary on one occasion lately, and did not get it.

THE CITIZENS (*together*). Ah!—then it is easy to understand how it is!

THE DRUNKEN MAN (*who has got amongst the audience again*). I want a blue one, I do! And I want a white one too!

VOICES. It's that drunken chap again! Turn him out!

MORTEN KIIL (*going up to* DR. STOCKMANN). Well, Stockmann, do you see what these monkey tricks of yours lead to?

DR. STOCKMANN. I have done my duty.

MORTEN KIIL. What was that you said about the tanneries at Mölledal?

DR. STOCKMANN. You heard well enough. I said they were the source of all the filth.

MORTEN KIIL. My tannery too?

DR. STOCKMANN. Unfortunately your tannery is by far the worst.

MORTEN KIIL. Are you going to put that in the papers?

DR. STOCKMANN. I shall conceal nothing.

MORTEN KIIL. That may cost you dear, Stockmann. (*Goes out.*)

A STOUT MAN (*going up to* CAPTAIN HORSTER, *without taking any notice of the ladies*). Well, Captain, so you lend your house to enemies of the people?

HORSTER. I imagine I can do what I like with my own possessions, Mr. Vik.

THE STOUT MAN. Then you can have no objection to my doing the same with mine.

HORSTER. What do you mean, sir?

THE STOUT MAN. You shall hear from me in the morning. (*Turns his back on him and moves off.*)

PETRA. Was that not your owner, Captain Horster?

HORSTER. Yes, that was Mr. Vik the ship-owner.

ASLAKSEN (*with the voting-papers in his hands, gets up on to the platform and rings his bell*). Gentlemen, allow me to announce the result. By the votes of every one here except one person—

A YOUNG MAN. That is the drunk chap!

ASLAKSEN. By the votes of every one here except a tipsy man, this meeting of citizens declares Dr. Thomas Stockmann to be an enemy of the people. (*Shouts and applause.*) Three cheers for our ancient and honorable citizen community! (*Renewed applause.*) Three cheers for our able and energetic Mayor, who has so loyally suppressed the promptings of family feeling! (*Cheers.*) The meeting is dissolved. (*Gets down.*)

BILLING. Three cheers for the Chairman!

THE WHOLE CROWD. Three cheers for Aslaksen! Hurrah!

DR. STOCKMANN. My hat and coat, Petra! Captain, have you room on your ship for passengers to the New World?

HORSTER. For you and yours we will make room, Doctor.

DR. STOCKMANN (*as* PETRA *helps him into his coat*). Good. Come, Katherine! Come, boys!

MRS. STOCKMANN (*in an undertone*). Thomas, dear, let us go out by the back way.

DR. STOCKMANN. No back ways for me, Katherine. (*Raising his voice.*) You will hear more of this enemy of the people, before he shakes the dust off his shoes upon you! I am not so forgiving as a certain Person; I do not say: "I forgive you, for ye know not what ye do."

ASLAKSEN (*shouting*). That is a blasphemous comparison, Dr. Stockmann!

BILLING. It is! It's dreadful for an earnest man to listen to.

A COARSE VOICE. Threatens us now, does he!

OTHER VOICES (*excitedly*). Let's go and break his windows! Duck him in the fjord!

ANOTHER VOICE. Blow your horn, Evensen. Pip, pip!

Horn-blowing, hisses, and wild cries. DR. STOCKMANN *goes out through the hall with his family,* HORSTER *elbowing a way for them.*

THE WHOLE CROWD (*howling after them as they go*). Enemy of the People! Enemy of the People!

BILLING (*as he puts his papers together*). Well, I'm hanged if I go and drink toddy with the Stockmanns tonight!

The crowd press towards the exit. The uproar continues outside; shouts of "Enemy of the People!" are heard from without.

DISCUSSION FOR UNDERSTANDING

1. Where does Dr. Stockmann hold his meeting? What do you learn from the crowd's comments before the meeting begins?

2. How do the newspaper editors and the Mayor set out to muzzle the Doctor?

3. What is the gist of Dr. Stockmann's talk?

4. How does the crowd react to the speech?

5. What does Morten Kiil ask his son-in-law?

6. How may the meeting affect Captain Horster?

7. What request does Dr. Stockmann make of Horster?

8. How does Dr. Stockmann's departure from the meeting give you new insight about him?

Act V

SCENE—DR. STOCKMANN's *study. Bookcases, and cabinets containing specimens, line the walls. At the back is a door leading to the hall; in the foreground on the left, a door leading to the sitting-room. In the right-hand wall are two windows, of which all the panes are broken. The* DOCTOR's *desk, littered with books and papers, stands in the middle of the room, which is in disorder. It is morning.* DR. STOCK-MANN *in dressing-gown, slippers and a smoking-cap, is bending down and raking with an umbrella under one of the cabinets. After a little while he rakes out a stone.*

DR. STOCKMANN (*calling through the open sitting-room door*). Katherine, I have found another one.

MRS. STOCKMANN (*from the sitting-room*). Oh, you will find a lot more yet, I expect.

DR. STOCKMANN (*adding the stone to a heap of others on the table*). I shall treasure these stones as relics. Ejlif and Morten shall look at them every day, and when they are grown up they shall inherit them as heirlooms. (*Rakes about under a bookcase*). Hasn't—what the deuce is her name?—the girl, you know—hasn't she been to fetch the glazier, yet?

MRS. STOCKMANN (*coming in*). Yes, but he said he didn't know if he would be able to come today.

DR. STOCKMANN. You will see he won't dare to come.

MRS. STOCKMANN. Well, that is just what Randine thought—that he didn't dare to, on account of the neighbors. (*Calls into the sitting-room.*) What is it you want, Randine? Give it to me. (*Goes in, and comes out again directly.*) Here is a letter for you, Thomas.

DR. STOCKMANN. Let me see it. (*Opens and reads it.*) Ah!—of course.

MRS. STOCKMANN. Who is it from?

DR. STOCKMANN. From the landlord. Notice to quit.

MRS. STOCKMANN. Is it possible? Such a nice man—

DR. STOCKMANN (*looking at the letter*). Does not dare do otherwise, he says. Doesn't like doing it, but dare not do otherwise—on account of his fellow-citizens—out of regard for public opinion. Is in a dependent position—dare not offend certain influential men—

MRS. STOCKMANN. There, you see, Thomas!

DR. STOCKMANN. Yes, yes, I see well enough; the whole lot of them in the town are cowards; not a man among them dares do anything for fear of the others. (*Throws the letter on to the table.*) But it doesn't matter to us, Katherine. We are going to sail away to the New World, and—

MRS. STOCKMANN. But, Thomas, are you sure we are well advised to take this step?

DR. STOCKMANN. Are you suggesting that I should stay here, where they have pilloried me as an enemy of the people—branded me—broken my windows! And just look here, Katherine—they have torn a great rent in my black trousers too!

MRS. STOCKMANN. Oh, dear!—and they are the best pair you have got!

DR. STOCKMANN. You should never wear your best trousers when you go out to fight for freedom and truth. It is not that I care so much about the trousers, you know; you can always sew them up again for me. But that the common herd should dare to make this attack on me, as if they were my equals—that is what I cannot, for the life of me, swallow!

MRS. STOCKMANN. There is no doubt they have behaved very ill to you, Thomas; but is that sufficient reason for our leaving our native country for good and all?

DR. STOCKMANN. If we went to another town, do you suppose we should not find the common people just as insolent as they are here? Depend upon it, there is not much to choose between them. Oh, well, let the curs snap—that is not the worst part of it. The worst is that, from one end of this country to the other, every man is the slave of his Party. Although, as far as that goes, I dare say it is not much better in the free West either; the compact majority, and liberal public opinion, and all that infernal old bag of tricks are probably rampant there too. But there things are done on a larger scale, you see. They may kill you, but they won't put you to death by slow torture. They don't squeeze a free man's soul in a vise, as they do here. And, if need be, one can live in solitude. (*Walks up and down.*) If only I knew where there was a virgin forest or a small South Sea island for sale, cheap—

MRS. STOCKMANN. But think of the boys, Thomas.

DR. STOCKMANN (*standing still*). What a strange woman you are, Katherine! Would you prefer to have the boys grow up in a society like this? You saw for yourself last night that half the population are out of their minds; and if the other half have not lost their senses, it is because they are mere brutes, with no sense to lose.

MRS. STOCKMANN. But, Thomas dear, the imprudent things you said had something to do with it, you know.

DR. STOCKMANN. Well, isn't what I said perfectly true? Don't they turn every idea topsy-turvy? Don't they make a regular hotch-potch of right and wrong? Don't they say that the things I know are true, are lies? The craziest part of it all is the fact of these "liberals," men of full age, going about in crowds imagining that they are the broadminded party! Did you ever hear anything like it, Katherine!

MRS. STOCKMANN. Yes, yes, it's mad enough of them, certainly; but—(PETRA *comes in from the sitting-room*). Back from school already?

PETRA. Yes. I have been given notice of dismissal.

MRS. STOCKMANN. Dismissal?

DR. STOCKMANN. You too?

PETRA. Mrs. Busk gave me my notice; so I thought it was best to go at once.

DR. STOCKMANN. You were perfectly right, too!

MRS. STOCKMANN. Who would have thought Mrs. Busk was a woman like that!

PETRA. Mrs. Busk isn't a bit like that, mother; I saw quite plainly how it hurt her to do it. But she didn't dare do otherwise, she said; and so I got my notice.

DR. STOCKMANN (*laughing and rubbing his hands*). She didn't dare do otherwise, either! It's delicious!

MRS. STOCKMANN. Well, after the dreadful scenes last night—

PETRA. It was not only that. Just listen to this, father!

DR. STOCKMANN. Well?

PETRA. Mrs. Busk showed me no less than three letters she received this morning—

DR. STOCKMANN. Anonymous, I suppose?

PETRA. Yes.

DR. STOCKMANN. Yes, because they didn't dare to risk signing their names, Katherine!

PETRA. And two of them were to the effect that a man who has been our guest here, was declaring last night at the Club that my views on various subjects are extremely emancipated—

DR. STOCKMANN. You did not deny that, I hope?

PETRA. No, you know I wouldn't. Mrs. Busk's own views are tolerably emancipated, when we are alone together; but now that this report about me is being spread, she dare not keep me on any longer.

MRS. STOCKMANN. And some one who had been a guest of ours! That shows you the return you get for your hospitality, Thomas!

DR. STOCKMANN. We won't live in such a disgusting hole any longer. Pack up as quickly as you can, Katherine; the sooner we can get away, the better.

MRS. STOCKMANN. Be quiet—I think I hear some one in the hall. See who it is, Petra.

PETRA (opening the door). Oh, it's you, Captain Horster! Do come in.

HORSTER (coming in). Good morning. I thought I would just come in and see how you were.

DR. STOCKMANN (shaking his hand). Thanks—that is really kind of you.

MRS. STOCKMANN. And thank you, too, for helping us through the crowd, Captain Horster.

PETRA. How did you manage to get home again?

HORSTER. Oh, somehow or other. I am fairly strong, and there is more sound than fury about these folk.

DR. STOCKMANN. Yes, isn't their swinish cowardice astonishing? Look here, I will show you something! There are all the stones they have thrown through my windows. Just look at them! I'm hanged if there are more than two decently large bits of hardstone in the whole heap; the rest are nothing but gravel—wretched little things. And yet they stood out there bawling and swearing that they would do me some violence; but as for *doing* anything—you don't see much of that in this town.

HORSTER. Just as well for you this time, doctor!

DR. STOCKMANN. True enough. But it makes one angry all the same; because if some day it should be a question of a national fight in real earnest, you will see that public opinion will be in favor of taking to one's heels, and the compact majority will turn tail like a flock of sheep, Captain Horster. That is what is so mournful to think of; it gives me so much concern, that—. No! It is ridiculous to care about it! They have called me an enemy of the people, so an enemy of the people let me be!

MRS. STOCKMANN. You will never be that, Thomas.

DR. STOCKMANN. Don't swear to that, Katherine. To be called an ugly name may have the same effect as a pin-scratch in the lung. And that hateful name—I can't get quit of it. It is sticking here in the pit of my stomach, eating into me like a corrosive acid. And no magnesia will remove it.

PETRA. Bah!—you should only laugh at them, father.

HORSTER. They will change their minds some day, Doctor.

MRS. STOCKMANN. Yes, Thomas, as sure as you are standing here.

DR. STOCKMANN. Perhaps, when it is too late. Much good may it do them! They may wallow in their filth then and rue the day when they drove a patriot into exile. When do you sail, Captain Horster?

HORSTER. Hm!—that was just what I had come to speak about—

DR. STOCKMANN. Why, has anything gone wrong with the ship?

HORSTER. No; but what has happened is that I am not to sail in it.

PETRA. Do you mean that you have been dismissed from your command?

HORSTER (smiling). Yes, that's just it.

PETRA. You too.

MRS. STOCKMANN. There, you see, Thomas!

DR. STOCKMANN. And that for the truth's sake! Oh, if I had thought such a thing possible—

HORSTER. You mustn't take it to heart; I shall be sure to find a job with some ship-owner or other, elsewhere.

DR. STOCKMANN. And that is this man Vik—a wealthy man, independent of every one and everything—! Shame on him!

HORSTER. He is quite an excellent fellow other-

wise; he told me himself he would willingly
have kept me on, if only he had dared—

DR. STOCKMANN. But he didn't dare? No, of
course not.

HORSTER. It is not such an easy matter, he
said, for a party man—

DR. STOCKMANN. The worthy man spoke the
truth. A party is like a sausage machine; it
mashes up all sorts of heads together into
the same mincemeat—fatheads and block-
heads, all in one mash!

MRS. STOCKMANN. Come, come, Thomas dear!

PETRA (*to* HORSTER). If only you had not come
home with us, things might not have come
to this pass.

HORSTER. I do not regret it.

PETRA (*holding out her hand to him*). Thank
you for that!

HORSTER (*to* DR. STOCKMANN). And so what I
came to say was that if you are determined
to go away, I have thought of another
plan—

DR. STOCKMANN. That's splendid!—if only we
can get away at once.

MRS. STOCKMANN. Hush!—wasn't that some
one knocking?

PETRA. That is uncle, surely.

DR. STOCKMANN. Aha! (*Calls out.*) Come in!

MRS. STOCKMANN. Dear Thomas, promise me
definitely—

PETER STOCKMANN *comes in from the hall.*

PETER STOCKMANN. Oh, you are engaged. In
that case, I will—

DR. STOCKMANN. No, no, come in.

PETER STOCKMANN. But I wanted to speak to
you alone.

MRS. STOCKMANN. We will go into the sitting-
room in the meanwhile.

HORSTER. And I will look in again later.

DR. STOCKMANN. No, go in there with them,
Captain Horster; I want to hear more
about—

HORSTER. Very well, I will wait, then. (*He follows* MRS. STOCKMANN *and* PETRA *into the
sitting-room.*)

DR. STOCKMANN. I daresay you find it rather
draughty here today. Put your hat on.

PETER STOCKMANN. Thank you, if I may. (*Does
so.*) I think I caught cold last night; I stood
and shivered—

DR. STOCKMANN. Really? I found it warm
enough.

PETER STOCKMANN. I regret that it was not in
my power to prevent those excesses last
night.

DR. STOCKMANN. Have you anything particular
to say to me besides that?

PETER STOCKMANN (*taking a big letter from
his pocket*). I have this document for you,
from the Baths Committee.

DR. STOCKMANN. My dismissal?

PETER STOCKMANN. Yes, dating from today.
(*Lays the letter on the table.*) It gives us
pain to do it; but, to speak frankly, we
dared not do otherwise on account of public opinion.

DR. STOCKMANN (*smiling*). Dared not? I seem
to have heard that word before, today.

PETER STOCKMANN. I must beg you to understand your position clearly. For the future
you must not count on any practice whatever in the town.

DR. STOCKMANN. Devil take the practice! But
why are you so sure of that?

PETER STOCKMANN. The Householders' Association is circulating a list from house to
house. All right-minded citizens are being
called upon to give up employing you; and
I can assure you that not a single head of a
family will risk refusing his signature. They
simply dare not.

DR. STOCKMANN. No, no; I don't doubt it. But
what then?

PETER STOCKMANN. If I might advise you, it
would be best to leave the place for a little
while—

DR. STOCKMANN. Yes, the propriety of leaving
the place *has* occurred to me.

PETER STOCKMANN. Good. And then, when you
have had six months to think things over,
if, after mature consideration, you can per-

suade yourself to write a few words of regret, acknowledging your error—

DR. STOCKMANN. I might have my appointment restored to me, do you mean?

PETER STOCKMANN. Perhaps. It is not at all impossible.

DR. STOCKMANN. But what about public opinion, then? Surely you would not dare to do it on account of public feeling.

PETER STOCKMANN. Public opinion is an extremely mutable thing. And, to be quite candid with you, it is a matter of great importance to us to have some admission of that sort from you in writing.

DR. STOCKMANN. Oh, that's what you are after, is it! I will just trouble you to remember what I said to you lately about foxy tricks of that sort!

PETER STOCKMANN. Your position was quite different then. At that time you had reason to suppose you had the whole town at your back—

DR. STOCKMANN. Yes, and now I feel I have the whole town *on* my back—(*flaring up*). I would not do it if I had the whole world on my back—! Never—never, I tell you!

PETER STOCKMANN. A man with a family has no right to behave as you do. You have no right to do it, Thomas.

DR. STOCKMANN. I have no right! There is only one single thing in the world a free man has no right to do. Do you know what that is?

PETER STOCKMANN. No.

DR. STOCKMANN. Of course you don't, but I will tell you. A free man has no right to soil himself with filth; he has no right to behave in a way that would justify his spitting in his own face.

PETER STOCKMANN. This sort of thing sounds extremely plausible, of course; and if there were no other explanation for your obstinacy—. But as it happens that there is—

DR. STOCKMANN. What do you mean?

PETER STOCKMANN. You understand very well what I mean. But, as your brother and as a man of discretion, I advise you not to build too much upon expectations and prospects that may so very easily fail you.

DR. STOCKMANN. What in the world is all this about?

PETER STOCKMANN. Do you really ask me to believe that you are ignorant of the terms of Mr. Kiil's will?

DR. STOCKMANN. I know that the small amount he possesses is to go to an institution for indigent old workpeople. How does that concern me?

PETER STOCKMANN. In the first place, it is by no means a small amount that is in question. Mr. Kiil is a fairly wealthy man.

DR. STOCKMANN. I had no notion of that!

PETER STOCKMANN. Hm!—hadn't you really? Then I suppose you had no notion, either, that a considerable portion of his wealth will come to your children, you and your wife having a life-rent of the capital. Has he never told you so?

DR. STOCKMANN. Never, on my honor! Quite the reverse; he has consistently done nothing but fume at being so unconscionably heavily taxed. But are you perfectly certain of this, Peter?

PETER STOCKMANN. I have it from an absolutely reliable source.

DR. STOCKMANN. Then, thank Heaven, Katherine is provided for—and the children too! I must tell her this at once—(*calls out*) Katherine, Katherine!

PETER STOCKMANN (*restraining him*). Hush, don't say a word yet!

MRS. STOCKMANN (*opening the door*). What is the matter?

DR. STOCKMANN. Oh, nothing, nothing; you can go back. (*She shuts the door.* DR. STOCKMANN *walks up and down in his excitement.*) Provided for!—Just think of it, we are all provided for. And for life! What a blessed feeling it is to know one is provided for!

PETER STOCKMANN. Yes, but that is just exactly what you are not. Mr. Kiil can alter his will any day he likes.

DR. STOCKMANN. But he won't do that, my dear Peter. The "Badger" is much too delighted at my attack on you and your wise friends.

PETER STOCKMANN (*starts and looks intently at him*). Ah, that throws a light on various things.

DR. STOCKMANN. What things?

PETER STOCKMANN. I see that the whole thing was a combined maneuver on your part and his. These violent, reckless attacks that you have made against the leading men of the town, under the pretence that it was in the name of truth—

DR. STOCKMANN. What about them?

PETER STOCKMANN. I see that they were nothing else than the stipulated price for that vindictive old man's will.

DR. STOCKMANN (*almost speechless*). Peter—you are the most disgusting plebeian I have ever met in all my life.

PETER STOCKMANN. All is over between us. Your dismissal is irrevocable—we have a weapon against you now. (*Goes out.*)

DR. STOCKMANN. For shame! For shame! (*Calls out.*) Katherine, you must have the floor scrubbed after him! Let—what's her name —you know, the girl who has always got soot on her nose—

MRS. STOCKMANN (*in the sitting-room*). Hush, Thomas, be quiet!

PETRA (*coming to the door*). Father, grandfather is here, asking if he may speak to you alone.

DR. STOCKMANN. Certainly he may. (*Going to the door.*) Come in, Mr. Kiil. (MORTEN KIIL *comes in.* DR. STOCKMANN *shuts the door after him.*) What can I do for you? Won't you sit down?

MORTEN KIIL. I won't sit. (*Looks around.*) You look very comfortable here today, Thomas.

DR. STOCKMANN. Yes, don't we!

MORTEN KIIL. Very comfortable—plenty of fresh air. I should think you have got enough today of that oxygen you were talking about yesterday. Your conscience must be in splendid order today, I should think.

DR. STOCKMANN. It is.

MORTEN KIIL. So I should think. (*Taps his chest.*) Do you know what I have got here?

DR. STOCKMANN. A good conscience, too, I hope.

MORTEN KIIL. Bah!—No, it is something better than that. (*He takes a thick pocket-book from his breast-pocket, opens it and displays a packet of papers.*)

DR. STOCKMANN (*looking at him in astonishment*). Shares in the Baths?

MORTEN KIIL. They were not difficult to get today.

DR. STOCKMANN. And you have been buying—?

MORTEN KIIL. As many as I could pay for.

DR. STOCKMANN. But, my dear Mr. Kiil—consider the state of the Baths' affairs!

MORTEN KIIL. If you behave like a reasonable man, you can soon set the Baths on their feet again.

DR. STOCKMANN. Well, you can see for yourself that I have done all I can, but—. They are all mad in this town!

MORTEN KIIL. You said yesterday that the worst of this pollution came from my tannery. If that is true, then my grandfather and my father before me, and I myself, for many years past, have been poisoning the town like three destroying angels. Do you think I am going to sit quiet under that reproach?

DR. STOCKMANN. Unfortunately I am afraid you will have to.

MORTEN KIIL. No, thank you. I am jealous of my name and reputation. They call me "the Badger," I am told. A badger is a kind of pig, I believe; but I am not going to give them the right to call me that. I mean to live and die a clean man.

DR. STOCKMANN. And how are you going to set about it?

MORTEN KIIL. You shall cleanse me, Thomas.

DR. STOCKMANN. I!

MORTEN KIIL. Do you know what money I have bought these shares with? No, of course you can't know—but I will tell you. It is the money that Katherine and Petra and the boys will have when I am gone.

Because I have been able to save a little bit after all, you know.

DR. STOCKMANN (*flaring up*). And you have gone and taken Katherine's money for *this!*

MORTEN KIIL. Yes, the whole of the money is invested in the Baths now. And now I just want to see whether you are quite stark, staring mad, Thomas! If you still make out that these animals and other nasty things of that sort come from my tannery, it will be exactly as if you were to flay broad strips of skin from Katherine's body, and Petra's, and the boys'; and no decent man would do that—unless he were mad.

DR. STOCKMANN (*walking up and down*). Yes, but I *am* mad; I *am* mad!

MORTEN KIIL. You cannot be so absurdly mad as all that, when it is a question of your wife and children.

DR. STOCKMANN (*standing still in front of him*). Why couldn't you consult me about it, before you went and bought all that trash?

MORTEN KIIL. What is done cannot be undone.

DR. STOCKMANN (*walks about uneasily*). If only I were not so certain about it—! But I am absolutely convinced that I am right.

MORTEN KIIL (*weighing the pocketbook in his hand*). If you stick to your mad idea, this won't be worth much, you know. (*Puts the pocketbook in his pocket.*)

DR. STOCKMANN. But, hang it all! it might be possible for science to discover some prophylactic, I should think—or some antidote of some kind—

MORTEN KIIL. To kill these animals, do you mean?

DR. STOCKMANN. Yes, or to make them innocuous.

MORTEN KIIL. Couldn't you try some rat's-bane?

DR. STOCKMANN. Don't talk nonsense! They all say it is only imagination, you know. Well, let it go at that! Let them have their own way about it! Haven't the ignorant, narrow-minded curs reviled me as an enemy of the people?—and haven't they been ready to tear the clothes off my back too?

MORTEN KIIL. And broken all your windows to pieces!

DR. STOCKMANN. And then there is my duty to my family. I must talk it over with Katherine; she is great on those things.

MORTEN KIIL. That is right; be guided by a reasonable woman's advice.

DR. STOCKMANN (*advancing towards him*). To think you could do such a preposterous thing! Risking Katherine's money in this way, and putting me in such a horribly painful dilemma! When I look at you, I think I see the devil himself—.

MORTEN KIIL. Then I had better go. But I must have an answer from you before two o'clock—yes or no. If it is no, the shares go to a charity, and that this very day.

DR. STOCKMANN. And what does Katherine get?

MORTEN KIIL. Not a halfpenny. (*The door leading to the hall opens and* HOVSTAD *and* ASLAKSEN *make their appearance.*) Look at those two!

DR. STOCKMANN (*staring at them*). What the devil!—have *you* actually the face to come into my house?

HOVSTAD. Certainly.

ASLAKSEN. We have something to say to you, you see.

MORTEN KIIL (*in a whisper*). Yes or no—before two o'clock.

ASLAKSEN (*glancing at* HOVSTAD). Aha! (MORTEN KIIL *goes out.*)

DR. STOCKMANN. Well, what do you want with me? Be brief.

HOVSTAD. I can quite understand that you are annoyed with us for our attitude at the meeting yesterday—

DR. STOCKMANN. Attitude, do you call it? Yes, it was a charming attitude! I call it weak, womanish—shameful!

HOVSTAD. Call it what you like, we could not do otherwise.

DR. STOCKMANN. You *dared* not do otherwise—isn't that it?

HOVSTAD. Well, if you like to put it that way.

ASLAKSEN. But why did you not let us have word of it beforehand?—just a hint to Mr. Hovstad or to me?

DR. STOCKMANN. A hint? Of what?

ASLAKSEN. Of what was behind it all.

DR. STOCKMANN. I don't understand you in the least.

ASLAKSEN (*with a confidential nod*). Oh yes, you do, Dr. Stockmann.

HOVSTAD. It is no good making a mystery of it any longer.

DR. STOCKMANN (*looking first at one of them and then at the other*). What the devil do you both mean?

ASLAKSEN. May I ask if your father-in-law is not going round the town buying up all the shares in the Baths?

DR. STOCKMANN. Yes, he has been buying Bath shares today; but—

ASLAKSEN. It would have been more prudent to get some one else to do it—some one less nearly related to you.

HOVSTAD. And you should not have let your name appear in the affair. There was no need for anyone to know that the attack on the Baths came from you. You ought to have consulted me, Dr. Stockmann.

DR. STOCKMANN (*looks in front of him; then a light seems to dawn on him and he says in amazement:*) Are such things conceivable? Are such things possible?

ASLAKSEN (*with a smile*). Evidently they are. But it is better to use a little *finesse*, you know.

HOVSTAD. And it is much better to have several persons in a thing of that sort; because the responsibility of each individual is lessened, when there are others with him.

DR. STOCKMANN (*composedly*). Come to the point, gentlemen. What do you want?

ASLAKSEN. Perhaps Mr. Hovstad had better—

HOVSTAD. No, you tell him, Aslaksen.

ASLAKSEN. Well, the fact is that, now we know the bearings of the whole affair, we think we might venture to put the "People's Messenger" at your disposal.

DR. STOCKMANN. Do you dare do that now?

What about public opinion? Are you not afraid of a storm breaking upon our heads?

HOVSTAD. We will try to weather it.

ASLAKSEN. And you must be ready to go off quickly on a new tack, Doctor. As soon as your invective has done its work—

DR. STOCKMANN. Do you mean, as soon as my father-in-law and I have got hold of the shares at a low figure?

HOVSTAD. Your reasons for wishing to get the control of the Baths are mainly scientific, I take it.

DR. STOCKMANN. Of course; it was for scientific reasons that I persuaded the old "Badger" to stand in with me in the matter. So we will tinker at the conduit-pipes a little, and dig up a little bit of the shore, and it shan't cost the town a sixpence. That will be all right—eh?

HOVSTAD. I think so—if you have the "People's Messenger" behind you.

ASLAKSEN. The Press is a power in a free community, Doctor.

DR. STOCKMANN. Quite so. And so is public opinion. And you, Mr. Aslaksen—I suppose you will be answerable for the Householders' Association?

ASLAKSEN. Yes, and for the Temperance Society. You may rely on that.

DR. STOCKMANN. But, gentlemen—I really am ashamed to ask the question—but, what return do you—?

HOVSTAD. We should prefer to help you without any return whatever, believe me. But the "People's Messenger" is in a rather shaky condition; it doesn't go really well; and I should be very unwilling to suspend the paper now, when there is so much work to do here in the political way.

DR. STOCKMANN. Quite so; that would be a great trial to such a friend of the people as you are. (*Flares up.*) But I am an enemy of the people, remember! (*Walks about the room.*) Where have I put my stick? Where on earth is my stick?

HOVSTAD. What's that?

ASLAKSEN. Surely you never mean—?

DR. STOCKMANN (*standing still*). And suppose I don't give you a single penny of all I get out of it? Money is not very easy to get out of us rich folk, please to remember!

HOVSTAD. And you please to remember that this affair of the shares can be represented in two ways!

DR. STOCKMANN. Yes, and you are just the man to do it. If I don't come to the rescue of the "People's Messenger," you will certainly take an evil view of the affair; you will hunt me down, I can well imagine—pursue me—try to throttle me as a dog does a hare.

HOVSTAD. It is a natural law; every animal must fight for its own livelihood.

ASLAKSEN. And get its food where it can, you know.

DR. STOCKMANN (*walking about the room*). Then you go and look for yours in the gutter; because I am going to show you which is the strongest animal of us three! (*Finds an umbrella and brandishes it above his head*). Ah, now—!

HOVSTAD. You are surely not going to use violence!

ASLAKSEN. Take care what you are doing with that umbrella.

DR. STOCKMANN. Out of the window with you, Mr. Hovstad!

HOVSTAD (*edging to the door*). Are you quite mad!

DR. STOCKMANN. Out of the window, Mr. Aslaksen! Jump, I tell you! You will have to do it, sooner or later.

ASLAKSEN (*running round the writing-table*). Moderation, Doctor—I am a delicate man—I can stand so little—(*calls out*) help, help!

MRS. STOCKMANN, PETRA and HORSTER *come in from the sitting-room.*

MRS. STOCKMANN. Good gracious, Thomas! What is happening?

DR. STOCKMANN (*brandishing the umbrella*). Jump out, I tell you! Out into the gutter!

HOVSTAD. An assault on an unoffending man! I call you to witness, Captain Horster. (*Hurries out through the hall.*)

ASLAKSEN (*irresolutely*). If only I knew the way about here—. (*Steals out through the sitting-room.*)

MRS. STOCKMANN (*holding her husband back*). Control yourself, Thomas!

DR. STOCKMANN (*throwing down the umbrella*). Upon my soul, they have escaped after all.

MRS. STOCKMANN. What did they want you to do?

DR. STOCKMANN. I will tell you later on; I have something else to think about now. (*Goes to the table and writes something on a calling-card.*) Look there, Katherine; what is written there?

MRS. STOCKMANN. Three big No's; what does that mean?

DR. STOCKMANN. I will tell you that too, later on. (*Holds out the card to* PETRA). There, Petra; tell sooty-face to run over to "the Badger's" with that, as quickly as she can. Hurry up! (PETRA *takes the card and goes out to the hall.*)

DR. STOCKMANN. Well, I think I have had a visit from every one of the devil's messengers today! But now I am going to sharpen my pen till they can feel its point; I shall dip it in venom and gall; I shall hurl my ink-pot at their heads!

MRS. STOCKMANN. Yes, but we are going away, you know, Thomas.

PETRA *comes back.*

DR. STOCKMANN. Well?

PETRA. She has gone with it.

DR. STOCKMANN. Good.—Going away, did you say? No, I'll be hanged if we are going away! We are going to stay where we are, Katherine!

PETRA. Stay here?

MRS. STOCKMANN. Here, in the town?

DR. STOCKMANN. Yes, here. This is the field of battle—this is where the fight will be. This is where I shall triumph! As soon as I have had my trousers sewn up I shall go out and look for another house. We must have a roof over our heads for the winter.

HORSTER. That you shall have in my house.

DR. STOCKMANN. Can I?

HORSTER. Yes, quite well. I have plenty of room, and I am almost never at home.

MRS. STOCKMANN. How good of you, Captain Horster!

PETRA. Thank you!

DR. STOCKMANN (*grasping his hand*). Thank you, thank you! That is one trouble over! Now I can set to work in earnest at once. There is an endless amount of things to look through here, Katherine! Luckily I shall have all my time at my disposal; because I have been dismissed from the Baths, you know.

MRS. STOCKMANN (*with a sigh*). Oh yes, I expected that.

DR. STOCKMANN. And they want to take my practice away from me too. Let them! I have got the poor people to fall back upon, anyway—those that don't pay anything; and, after all, they need me most, too. But, by Jove, they will have to listen to me; I shall preach to them in season and out of season, as it says somewhere.

MRS. STOCKMANN. But, dear Thomas, I should have thought events had showed you what use it is to preach.

DR. STOCKMANN. You are really ridiculous, Katherine. Do you want me to let myself be beaten off the field by public opinion and the compact majority and all that devilry? No, thank you! And what I want to do is so simple and clear and straightforward. I only want to drum into the heads of these curs the fact that the liberals are the most insidious enemies of freedom—that party programs strangle every young and vigorous truth—that considerations of expediency turn morality and justice upside down

543

—and that they will end by making life here unbearable. Don't you think, Captain Horster, that I ought to be able to make people understand that?

HORSTER. Very likely; I don't know much about such things myself.

DR. STOCKMANN. Well, look here—I will explain! It is the party leaders that must be exterminated. A party leader is like a wolf, you see—like a voracious wolf. He requires a certain number of smaller victims to prey upon every year, if he is to live. Just look at Hovstad and Aslaksen! How many smaller victims have they not put an end to—or at any rate maimed and mangled until they are fit for nothing except to be householders or subscribers to the "People's Messenger"! (*Sits down on the edge of the table.*) Come here, Katherine—look how beautifully the sun shines today! And this lovely spring air I am drinking in!

MRS. STOCKMANN. Yes, if only we could live on sunshine and spring air, Thomas.

DR. STOCKMANN. Oh, you will have to pinch and save a bit—then we shall get along. That gives me very little concern. What is much worse is, that I know of no one who is liberal-minded and high-minded enough to venture to take up my work after me.

PETRA. Don't think about that, father; you have plenty of time before you.—Hullo, here are the boys already!

EJLIF *and* MORTEN *come in from the sitting-room.*

MRS. STOCKMANN. Have you got a holiday?

MORTEN. No; but we were fighting with the other boys between lessons—

EJLIF. That isn't true; it was the other boys were fighting with us.

MORTEN. Well, and then Mr. Rörlund said we had better stay at home for a day or two.

DR. STOCKMANN (*snapping his fingers and getting up from the table*). I have it! I have it, by Jove! You shall never set foot in the school again!

THE BOYS. No more school!

MRS. STOCKMANN. But, Thomas—

DR. STOCKMANN. Never, I say. I will educate you myself; that is to say, you shan't learn a blessed thing—

MORTEN. Hooray!

DR. STOCKMANN. —but I will make liberal-minded and high-minded men of you. You must help me with that, Petra.

PETRA. Yes, father, you may be sure I will.

DR. STOCKMANN. And my school shall be in the room where they insulted me and called me an enemy of the people. But we are too few as we are; I must have at least twelve boys to begin with.

MRS. STOCKMANN. You will certainly never get them in this town.

DR. STOCKMANN. We shall. (*To the boys*). Don't you know any street urchins—regular ragamuffins—?

MORTEN. Yes, father, I know lots!

DR. STOCKMANN. That's capital! Bring me some specimens of them. I am going to experiment with curs, just for once; there may be some exceptional heads amongst them.

MORTEN. And what are we going to do, when you have made liberal-minded and high-minded men of us?

DR. STOCKMANN. Then you shall drive all the wolves out of the country, my boys!

EJLIF *looks rather doubtful about it;* MORTEN *jumps about crying "Hurrah!"*

MRS. STOCKMANN. Let us hope it won't be the wolves that will drive you out of the country, Thomas.

DR. STOCKMANN. Are you out of your mind, Katherine? Drive me out! Now—when I am the strongest man in the town!

MRS. STOCKMANN. The strongest—now?

DR. STOCKMANN. Yes, and I will go so far as to say that now I am the strongest man in the whole world.

MORTEN. I say!

DR. STOCKMANN (*lowering his voice*). Hush! You mustn't say anything about it yet; but I have made a great discovery.

MRS. STOCKMANN. Another one?

DR. STOCKMANN. Yes. (*Gathers them round him, and says confidentially:*) It is this, let me tell you—that the strongest man in the world is he who stands most alone.

MRS. STOCKMANN (*smiling and shaking her head*). Oh, Thomas, Thomas!

PETRA (*encouragingly, as she grasps her father's hands*). Father!

DISCUSSION FOR UNDERSTANDING

1. What actions have the townspeople taken against the Stockmanns?

2. What is Mrs. Stockmann's attitude towards leaving the town?

3. What does Dr. Stockmann anticipate he may find in the New World?

4. What news does Captain Horster bring?

5. What is Peter Stockmann's mood when he first talks to his brother? What brings about a change in his attitude?

6. What news does Morten Kiil give the Doctor? What is his ultimatum?

7. What is Aslaksen's and Hovstad's conclusion about Kiil's buying of the stock? What is their proposition? How does the Doctor react?

8. What help does Captain Horster offer the family?

9. Whom does Dr. Stockmann now expect to treat medically in the town? What will his price be?

10. Whom does Dr. Stockmann proclaim as the strongest person in the world?

I
THE KNIFE OF SATIRE

An Enemy of the People is a social satire which holds up flaws of people or society for the amusement of the audience. Hence, the play is labeled a comedy, and some critics have called it the most good humored of Ibsen's writings. These designations may take today's readers by surprise, for the subject of this drama seems so grimly serious. But as we reflect, we see the amusing contradictions presented by the characters' actions: Morten Kiil's agitation as he urges his son-in-law to make the officials squirm; the absurd take-over of the public meeting called by Dr. Stockmann to present his own case; the good Doctor's irrepressible rashness and utter blindness to the possible reactions of the public to his news. Yet, through the gentle humor comes a bitter indictment of human nature, in which concern for one's pocketbook takes precedence over the social good.

Considering their attitudes as presented in the play, how do you think Dr. Stockmann and his brother would react to each of the following statements? In your opinion how would most people react to the statements today?

1. An employee should hold the same opinion as his or her employer.

2. The public should not be exposed to new ideas. The old ones are good enough.

3. Too much culture demoralizes and destroys a people.

4. Might is more important than right in an ideological struggle.

5. To change a social situation, all that is necessary is to inform the public of the need for change.

II
IMPLICATIONS

The following statements were made by characters in the play. What is your reaction to the idea presented in each? Is it valid today or has society changed?

1. Aslaksen: "Officials are not generally very ready to act on proposals that come from other people."

2. Billing: "All the same, one ought to vote, at any rate." Horster: "Even if one doesn't know anything about what is going on?"

3. Dr. Stockmann: "They [the young people] are the people who are going to stir up the fermenting forces of the future, Peter."

4. Aslaksen: "If you attack the government, you don't do the community any harm anyway; those fellows pay no attention to attacks, you see —they go on just as they are, in spite of them."

5. Dr. Stockmann: "The most dangerous enemy

of truth and freedom amongst us is the compact majority. . . ."

6. Dr. Stockmann: "The majority never has right on its side."

7. Dr. Stockmann: "You should never wear your best trousers when you go out to fight for freedom and truth."

8. Aslaksen: "The Press is a power in a free community, Doctor."

9. Dr. Stockmann: "The strongest man in the world is he who stands most alone."

III
TECHNIQUES

Author's Purpose

An author may have a certain purpose in mind when writing. Some authors wish to criticize society, some, to amuse their audience, some, to tell a good story, and some to comment about human relationships. An author's purpose is a deciding factor in the selection of characters, in the selection of events which move the plot ahead, and even in the choice of language.

In the introduction to this unit on page 487, there are four points listed as pitfalls in the writing of a piece of literature intended as a criticism of some flaw in society. Consider the following and give your opinion of Ibsen's handling of the "pitfalls."

1. *Sentimentality:* Are the following characters sentimentalized?

a. Mrs. Stockmann

b. Dr. Stockmann

c. Peter Stockmann, the mayor

2. *Oversimplification:* What is the problem presented in the play? Is one side totally right or wrong?

3. *Didacticism:* Has Ibsen stopped the flow of action to preach? Do you understand something after reading the play that you didn't grasp earlier?

4. *Too narrow or local a concern:* Is the problem presented here outmoded or contemporary? Is it local or of general human concern? Will the problem continue to be a human dilemma?

Irony

Irony is such a universal literary device that it would be hard to think of a major writer who does not use it. There are two main kinds: verbal irony and dramatic irony. In verbal irony, words seem to mean one thing but really mean the opposite. For example, if someone scrapes the fender of your car you might exclaim, "Just the touch I wanted." But what you really mean, of course, is "Terrible! How awful!" A famous example of verbal irony in literature is Antony's assertion to the Roman crowd in *Julius Caesar* that "Brutus is an honorable man."

Dramatic irony results when events turn out in an entirely different way from either the intention or expectation of those involved, and the reader or the audience is in on what is going to happen. Joanna's life in Hardy's story, "To Please His Wife" has an ending different from her intention. Macbeth misinterprets the witches' prophesies and events proceed in an order that he never anticipated. These are examples of dramatic irony.

Think back to the action in *Enemy of the People*. What is ironic about:

1. Dr. Stockmann's feeling about his town?

2. the Doctor's expectations about the town's reaction to his news?

3. Hovstad's reason for publishing the English novel?

4. Mrs. Stockmann's inheritance?

5. the Doctor's brother being the Mayor?

6. Horster's being fired?

IV
WORDS
A. Most English words have their origin in another language and another age. Write a definition for each word, using the etymological (word-history) information as a clue to meaning.

1. *pestiferous*	derived from Latin *pestis*, a plague and *ferre*, to bear
2. *pugnacious*	derived from Latin *pugnare*, to fight
3. *morass*	derived from Dutch *moeras*, a marsh
4. *adherents*	derived from Latin *ad-*, to and *haerere*, to stick
5. *sepulcher*	derived from Latin *sepelire*, to bury

6. *conduit*   derived from Latin *conducere,* to lead or bring together

7. *acquiesce*   derived from French *acquiescer,* to yield to

8. *invective*   derived from Latin *invehere,* to attack with words

B. A word can have several different meanings. The factor determining the meaning of a given word at a given time is the context of the sentence in which it is found. Select the definition for the italicized word in each sentence.

1. And there is another consideration that impels me to oppose him, and, as far as possible, to *arrest* him on the perilous course he has adopted. **a.** *to seize or take into custody by authority of the law* **b.** *to stop or check the motion, course, or spread of* **c.** *to catch and keep (one's attention, sight, and so on).*

2. You will not find any public *body* in the town that will give you the use of their hall for such a purpose. **a.** *the whole material part of a human, animal, or plant* **b.** *the main part of a speech or document* **c.** *group of persons considered together; collection of persons or things: a body of troops.*

3. I cannot understand how it is that I have only now acquired a clear *conception* of what these gentry are. **a.** *a mental impression or image; general notion; concept* **b.** *a conceiving or being conceived in the womb* **c.** *the beginning of some process, or chain of events.*

4. I cherish the comforting *conviction* that these parasites are most admirably paving the way for their own extinction. **a.** *act of proving or declaring guilt* **b.** *act of convincing (a person)* **c.** *firm belief.*

JONATHAN SWIFT

Jonathan Swift (1667–1745) was one of the most brilliant satirists ever to use
the English language. Born in Ireland of English parents, Swift attended
Trinity College, Dublin. In his youth, he was secretary at Moor Park to Sir
William Temple. Here he raged at his inferior position. He quarreled with Temple
in 1694 and left for Ireland, where he was ordained as a minister of the Church
of England. But soon tiring of his country parish, he returned to Moor Park
where he read avidly in the well-stocked library. His friendship with the adopted
daughter (Esther Johnson) of Sir William took root and she became the Stella of his
Journal to Stella. While at Moor Park he wrote *A Tale of a Tub* and *The Battle
of the Books*. In later years he commented about *A Tale of a Tub*, "Good God, what
a genius I had when I wrote that book." Most critics agree. In 1713 Swift became
the Dean of St. Patrick's Cathedral in Dublin, a position which he held
for thirty-two years. More English than Irish in his thinking, Swift's reception
by the Irish was a cold one. However, he took up the Irish cause, speaking out
with sharp, bruising irony in defense of the Irish position and giving much of his
income to the poor. In 1726 he published *Gulliver's Travels*, a bitter satire on the
failings of humanity. Instead of repelling its readers, its fanciful inventions
fascinated them. Astonishingly, parts of this harsh satire have survived
as a favorite children's story. Who has not heard of Gulliver's capture by the
tiny Lilliputians? In 1729 he solemnly published "A Modest Proposal." Some people
took the brilliant dead-pan irony of his preposterous proposal seriously,
clearly indicating the brutal attitude of the English toward the Irish.
In later years, a lifelong disability became pronounced and from 1738
until his death Swift suffered periods of insanity.

A Modest Proposal

FOR PREVENTING
THE CHILDREN OF POOR PEOPLE
FROM BEING A BURDEN
TO THEIR PARENTS OR COUNTRY,
AND FOR MAKING THEM BENEFICIAL
TO THE PUBLIC.

It is a melancholy object to those who walk through this great town, or travel in the country, when they see the streets, the roads, and cabin-doors crowded with beggars of the female sex, followed by three, four or six children, *all in rags*, and importuning every passenger for an alms. These mothers, instead of being able to work for their honest livelihood, are forced to employ all their time in strolling, to beg sustenance for their helpless infants, who, as they grow up, either turn thieves for want of work, or leave their dear Native Country to fight for the Pretender in Spain, or sell themselves to the Barbadoes.[1]

I think it is agreed by all parties that this prodigious number of children in the arms, or on the backs, or at the heels of their mothers and frequently of their fathers, is in the present de-

---

1. That is, to fight as mercenary soldiers for a claimant to the Spanish throne or to sell themselves as indentured servants in **Barbadoes** (bär bā′dōz) in the West Indies.

plorable state of the kingdom a very great additional grievance; and therefore whoever could find out a fair, cheap, and easy method of making these children sound useful members of the commonwealth would deserve so well of the public as to have his statue set up for a preserver of the nation.

But my intention is very far from being confined to provide only for the children of professed beggars; it is of a much greater extent, and shall take in the whole number of infants at a certain age who are born of parents in effect as little able to support them as those who demand our charity in the streets.

As to my own part, having turned my thoughts, for many years, upon this important subject, and maturely weighed the several schemes of other projectors, I have always found them grossly mistaken in their computation. It is true a child, just dropped from its dam, may be supported by her milk for a solar year with little other nourishment, at most not above the value of two shillings, which the mother may certainly get, or the value in scraps, by her lawful occupation of begging, and it is exactly at one year old that I propose to provide for them, in such a manner as, instead of being a charge upon their parents, or the parish, or wanting food and raiment for the rest of their lives, they shall, on the contrary, contribute to the feeding and partly to the clothing of many thousands. . . .

The number of souls in this kingdom being usually reckoned one million and a half, of these I calculate there may be about two hundred thousand couples whose wives are breeders, from which number I subtract thirty thousand couples who are able to maintain their own children, although I apprehend there cannot be so many under the present distresses of the kingdom, but this being granted, there will remain an hundred and seventy thousand breeders. I again subtract fifty thousand for those women who miscarry, or whose children die by accident or disease within the year. There only remain an hundred and twenty

Jonathan Swift, author of Gulliver's Travels.

thousand children of poor parents annually born: the question therefore is, how this number shall be reared, and provided for, which, as I have already said, under the present situation of affairs, is utterly impossible by all the methods hitherto proposed, for we can neither employ them in handicraft, or agriculture; we neither build houses (I mean in the country), nor cultivate land: they can very seldom pick up a livelihood by stealing till they arrive at six years old, except where they are of towardly parts, although, I confess they learn the rudiments much earlier, during which time they can however be properly looked upon only as *probationers,* as I have been informed by a principal gentleman in the County of Cavan,[2] who protested to me that he never knew above one or two instances under the age of six, even in a

_____

2. **Cavan** (kav′ən), a county in north Ireland.

part of the kingdom so renowned for the quickest proficiency in that art.

I am assured by our merchants that a boy or girl, before twelve years old, is no saleable commodity, and even when they come to this age, they will not yield above three pounds, or three pounds and half-a-crown at most on the Exchange, which cannot turn to account either to the parents or the kingdom, the charge of nutriment and rags having been at least four times that value.

I shall now therefore humbly propose my own thoughts, which I hope will not be liable to the least objection.

I have been assured by a very knowing American of my acquaintance in London, that a young healthy child well nursed is at a year old a most delicious, nourishing, and wholesome food, whether stewed, roasted, baked, or boiled, and I make no doubt that it will equally serve in a fricassee, or a ragout.

I do therefore humbly offer it to public consideration, that of the hundred and twenty thousand children already computed, twenty thousand may be reserved for breed, whereof only one fourth part to be males, which is more than we allow to sheep, black-cattle, or swine. . . . That the remaining hundred thousand may at a year old be offered in sale to the persons of quality, and fortune, through the kingdom, always advising the mother to let them feed plentifully in the last month, so as to render them plump, and fat for a good table. A child will make two dishes at an entertainment for friends, and when the family dines alone, the fore or hind quarter will make a reasonable dish, and seasoned with a little pepper or salt will be very good boiled on the fourth day, especially in winter.

I have reckoned upon a medium, that a child just born will weigh 12 pounds, and in a solar year if tolerably nursed increaseth to 28 pounds.

I grant this food will be somewhat dear, and therefore very proper for landlords, who, as they have already devoured most of the parents, seem to have the best title to the children. . . .

I have already computed the charge of nursing a beggar's child (in which list I reckon all cottagers, labourers, and four-fifths of the farmers) to be about two shillings *per annum*,[3] rags included, and I believe no gentleman would repine to give ten shillings for the carcass of a good fat child, which, as I have said, will make four dishes of excellent nutritive meat, when he hath only some particular friend or his own family to dine with him. Thus the Squire will learn to be a good landlord, and grow popular among his tenants, the mother will have eight shillings net profit, and be fit for work till she produces another child.

Those who are more thrifty (as I must confess the times require) may flay the carcass; the skin of which, artificially dressed, will make admirable gloves for ladies, and summer boots for fine gentlemen.

As to our City of Dublin, shambles may be appointed for this purpose, in the most convenient parts of it, and butchers we may be assured will not be wanting, although I rather recommend buying the children alive, and dressing them hot from the knife, as we do roasting pigs.

A very worthy person, a true lover of this country, and whose virtues I highly esteem, was lately pleased, in discoursing on this matter, to offer a refinement upon my scheme. He said that many gentlemen of this kingdom, having of late destroyed their deer, he conceived that the want of venison might be well supplied by the bodies of young lads and maidens, not exceeding fourteen years of age, nor under twelve, so great a number of both sexes in every country being now ready to starve, for want of work and service: and these to be disposed of by their parents if alive, or otherwise by their nearest relations. But with due deference to so excellent a friend, and so deserving a patriot, I cannot be altogether in his sentiments; for as

_____
3. **per annum** (per an′əm), Latin for "per year."

The Potato Famine in Ireland, 1846.
Starving peasants at the gate of a workhouse,
scene from a contemporary woodcut.

to the males, my American acquaintance assured me from frequent experience that their flesh was generally tough and lean, like that of our schoolboys, by continual exercise, and their taste disagreeable, and to fatten them would not answer the charge. Then as to the females, it would, I think with humble submission, be a loss to the public, because they soon would become breeders themselves: And besides, it is not improbable that some scrupulous people might be apt to censure such a practice (although indeed very injustly) as a little bordering upon cruelty, which, I confess, hath always been with me the strongest objection against any project, however so well intended.

But in order to justify my friend, he confessed that this expedient was put into his head by the famous Psalmanazar,[4] a native of the island Formosa, who came from thence to London, above twenty years ago, and in conversation told my friend that in his country when any young person happened to be put to death, the executioner sold the carcass to persons of quality, as a prime dainty, and that, in his time, the body of a plump girl of fifteen, who was crucified for an attempt to poison the emperor, was sold to his Imperial Majesty's Prime Minister of State, and other great Mandarins of the Court, in joints from the gibbet, at four hundred crowns. Neither indeed can I deny that if the same use were made of several plump young girls in this town, who, without one single groat to their fortunes, cannot stir abroad without a chair, and appear at the playhouse,

---

4. **Psalmanazar** (sal'mə na'zər) was a French citizen who came to London where he pretended to be from **Formosa** (fôr mō'sə), an island off China north of the Philippines.

and assemblies in foreign fineries, which they never will pay for, the kingdom would not be the worse.

Some persons of a desponding spirit are in great concern about that vast number of poor people, who are aged, diseased, or maimed, and I have been desired to employ my thoughts what course may be taken to ease the nation of so grievous an encumbrance. But I am not in the least pain upon that matter, because it is very well known that they are every day dying, and rotting, by cold, and famine, and filth, and vermin, as fast as can be reasonably expected. And as to the younger labourers they are now in almost as hopeful a condition. They cannot get work, and consequently pine away for want of nourishment, to a degree, that if at any time they are accidentally hired to common labour, they have not strength to perform it; and thus the country and themselves are happily delivered from the evils to come.

I have too long digressed, and therefore shall return to my subject. I think the advantages by the proposal which I have made are obvious and many, as well as of the highest importance.

For first, as I have already observed, it would greatly lessen the number of Papists,[5] with whom we are yearly over-run, being the principal breeders of the nation, as well as our most dangerous enemies, and who stay at home on purpose with a design to deliver the kingdom to the Pretender,[6] hoping to take their advantage by the absence of so many good Protestants, who have chosen rather to leave their country than stay at home, and pay tithes against their conscience to an Episcopal curate.

Secondly, The poorer tenants will have something valuable of their own, which by law be made liable to distress, and help to pay their landlord's rent, their corn and cattle being already seized, and *money a thing unknown.*

Thirdly, Whereas the maintenance of an hundred thousand children, from two years old, and upwards, cannot be computed at less than ten shillings a piece *per annum,* the nation's stock will be thereby increased fifty thousand pounds *per annum,* besides the profit of a new dish, introduced to the tables of all gentlemen of fortune in the kingdom, who have any refinement in taste, and the money will circulate among ourselves, the goods being entirely of our own growth and manufacture.

Fourthly, The constant breeders, besides the gain of eight shillings sterling *per annum,* by the sale of their children, will be rid of the charge of maintaining them after the first year.

Fifthly, This food would likewise bring great custom to taverns, where the vintners will certainly be so prudent as to procure the best receipts for dressing it to perfection, and consequently have their houses frequented by all the fine gentlemen, who justly value themselves upon their knowledge in good eating; and a skilful cook, who understands how to oblige his guests, will contrive to make it as expensive as they please.

Sixthly, This would be a great inducement to marriage, which all wise nations have either encouraged by rewards, or enforced by laws and penalties. It would increase the care and tenderness of mothers toward their children, when they were sure of a settlement for life, to the poor babes, provided in some sort by the public to their annual profit instead of expense. We should see an honest emulation among the married women, which of them could bring the fattest child to the market, men would become as fond of their wives, during the time of their pregnancy, as they are now of their mares in foal, their cows in calf, or sows when they are ready to farrow, nor offer to beat or kick them (as it is too frequent a practice). . . .

Many other advantages might be enumerated: For instance, the addition of some thousand carcasses in our exportation of barrelled beef; the propagation of swine's flesh, and improvement in the art of making good bacon, so much wanted among us by the great destruction of pigs, too frequent at our tables, which are no way comparable in taste or mag-

---

5. **Papist** (pā′pist), Catholic.
6. **the Pretender,** the Catholic claimant to the throne of England at the time.

nificence to a well-grown, fat yearling child, which roasted whole will make a considerable figure at a Lord Mayor's feast, or any other public entertainment. But this and many others I omit, being studious of brevity.

Supposing that one thousand families in this city would be constant customers for infants' flesh, besides others who might have it at merry-meetings, particularly weddings and christenings, I compute that Dublin would take off annually about twenty thousand carcasses, and the rest of the kingdom (where probably they will be sold somewhat cheaper) the remaining eighty thousand.

I can think of no one objection that will possibly be raised against this proposal, unless it should be urged that the number of people will be thereby much lessened in the kingdom. This I freely own, and was indeed one principal design in offering it to the world. I desire the reader will observe, that I calculate my remedy for this one individual *Kingdom of Ireland, and for no other that ever was, is, or, I think, ever can be upon earth.* Therefore let no man talk to me of other expedients: *Of taxing our absentees at five shillings a pound: Of using neither clothes, nor household furniture, except what is of our own growth and manufacture: Of utterly rejecting the materials and instruments that promote foreign luxury: Of curing the expensiveness of pride, vanity, idleness, and gaming in our women: Of introducing a vein of parsimony, prudence, and temperance: Of learning to love our Country, wherein we differ even from* LAPLANDERS, *and the inhabitants of* TOPINAMBOO:[7] *Of quitting our animosities and factions, nor act any longer like the infidels, who were murdering one another at the very moment their city was taken: Of being a little cautious not to sell our country and consciences for nothing: Of teaching landlords to have at least one degree of mercy toward their tenants. Lastly, of putting a spirit of honesty, industry, and skill into our shopkeepers, who, if a resolution could now be taken to buy only our native goods, would immediately unite to cheat and exact upon us in the price, the measure, and*

the goodness, nor could ever yet be brought to make one fair proposal of just dealing, though often and earnestly invited to it.

Therefore I repeat, let no man talk to me of these and the like expedients, till he hath at least some glimpse of hope that there will ever be some hearty and sincere attempt to put them in practice.

But as to myself, having been wearied out for many years with offering vain, idle, visionary thoughts, and at length utterly despairing of success, I fortunately fell upon this proposal, which as it is wholly new, so it hath something solid and real, of no expense and little trouble, full in our own power, and whereby we can incur no danger in *disobliging* ENGLAND. For this kind of commodity will not bear exportation, the flesh being of too tender a consistence to admit a long continuance in salt, *although perhaps I could name a country which would be glad to eat up our whole nation without it.*

After all I am not so violently bent upon my own opinion as to reject any offer, proposed by wise men, which shall be found equally innocent, cheap, easy, and effectual. But before something of that kind shall be advanced in contradiction to my scheme, and offering a better, I desire the author, or authors, will be pleased maturely to consider two points. First, as things now stand, how they will be able to find food and raiment for an hundred thousand useless mouths and backs. And secondly, there being a round million of creatures in human figure, throughout this kingdom, whose whole subsistence put into a common stock would leave them in debt two millions of pounds sterling; adding those, who are beggars by profession, to the bulk of farmers, cottagers, and labourers with their wives and children, who are beggars in effect. I desire those politicians, who dislike my overture, and may perhaps be so bold to attempt an answer, that they will first ask the parents of these mortals whether they would not at this day think it a great happiness

---

7. **Topinamboo,** a fictitious country.

to have been sold for food at a year old, in the manner I prescribe, and thereby have avoided such a perpetual scene of misfortunes as they have since gone through, by the oppression of landlords, the impossibility of paying rent without money or trade, the want of common sustenance, with neither house nor clothes to cover them from the inclemencies of the weather, and the most inevitable prospect of entailing the like, or greater miseries upon their breed for ever.

I profess in the sincerity of my heart that I have not the least personal interest in endeavouring to promote this necessary work, having no other motive than the *public good of my country, by advancing our trade, providing for infants, relieving the poor, and giving some pleasure to the rich.* I have no children by which I can propose to get a single penny; the youngest being nine years old, and my wife past child-bearing.

I
SAVAGE INDIGNATION

Reactions to Swift's "proposal" ranged from shocked amazement to ready acceptance. Swift felt that the absentee English landlords and the English Parliament stripped Ireland of any possibility of a reasonable existence. The decent people of England had to be made aware of the situation, and his bitter essay shook his readers.

II
IMPLICATIONS

Do you agree or disagree with the following statements?

1. Swift's essay is so bitter that it loses its impact.

2. There is enough common sense in this essay to make the "proposal" acceptable to some people.

3. Swift is not so much concerned with the starving Irish as he is with attacking the British who rejected him.

III
TECHNIQUES
Author's Purpose

Does one of the following statements express your opinion of why Swift wrote "A Modest Proposal"? Do you think a combination of the following would come closer to his purpose? Do you have other ideas of his purpose?

1. Swift wrote this as a protest against English absentee landlordism.

2. Swift wrote this to make the English aware of Ireland's terrible poverty.

3. Swift was crying out against the increase of Catholics in Ireland.

4. How well do you think Swift fulfilled his purpose? Find out if his bitter criticism led to any reform.

Irony

What irony do you find in the title?

1. Are the last six points given by Swift as a reason for his proposal dramatic or verbal irony?

2. In the following quotations, Swift is saying one thing, but you, the reader, know that what he says is not his real intent. He is saying it tongue-in-cheek, daring you to believe him. What makes the following statements ironic?

a. I have been assured by a very knowing American of my acquaintance in London, that a young healthy child well nursed is at a year old a most delicious, nourishing, and wholesome food. . . .

b. I grant this food will be somewhat dear, and therefore very proper for landlords, who, as they have already devoured most of the parents, seem to have the best title to the children.

c. . . . the skin of which, artificially dressed, will make admirable gloves for ladies. . . .

JOHN GALSWORTHY

John Galsworthy (1867–1933) showed a tremendous versatility
in his ability to use drama, poetry, the novel, the essay, and the short story
as his mediums. Like many writers before him, Galsworthy was trained in another field,
in his case law, which he dropped in favor of writing. But he was always interested
in the subject of justice and his writing often contained critical judgment
on the social injustices of his time. His most important work is considered to be
The Forsyte Saga, a series of novels that follow the fortunes of a moneyed family
through several generations. In fact, the main character of the series,
Soames Forsyte, became so well known that when he died (in a book, of course),
the London *Times* announced his death in newspaper headlines. A later series
of novels about the Forsyte family, published in one volume as *A Modern Comedy,*
reflects Galsworthy's touching concern with the beauty of youth
and with the great changes taking place in twentieth-century England. These later novels
are not as successful as the original *Forsyte Saga.* The author acts as an observer
of the modern scene but finds it bewildering and unpleasant. His plays,
like his other writings, investigated social and ethical problems. In these writings
he was scrupulous about presenting both sides of the question, even at the expense
of dramatic impact. Galsworthy was awarded the British Order of Merit in 1929
and the Nobel Prize for Literature in 1933.

Quality

I knew him from the days of my extreme youth, because he made my father's boots; inhabiting with his elder brother two little shops let into one, in a small by-street—now no more, but then most fashionably placed in the West End.[1]

That tenement had a certain quiet distinction; there was no sign upon its face that he made for any of the Royal Family—merely his own German name of Gessler Brothers; and in the window a few pairs of boots. I remember that it always troubled me to account for those unvarying boots in the window, for he made only what was ordered, reaching nothing down, and it seemed so inconceivable that what he made could ever have failed to fit. Had he bought them to put there? That, too, seemed inconceivable. He would never have tolerated in his house leather on which he had not worked himself. Besides, they were too beautiful—the pair of pumps, so inexpressibly slim, the patent leathers with cloth tops, making water come into one's mouth, the tall brown riding boots with marvellous sooty glow, as if, though new, they had been worn a hundred years. Those pairs could only have been made by one who saw before him the Soul of Boot—so truly were they prototypes incarnating the very spirit of all foot-gear. These thoughts, of course, came to me later, though even when I was promoted to him, at the age of perhaps fourteen, some inkling haunted me of the dignity of himself and brother. For to make boots—such boots as he made—seemed to me then, and still seems to me, mysterious and wonderful.

1. **West End**—of London.

John Galsworthy, portrait by Randall Davey.

I remember well my shy remark, one day, while stretching out to him my youthful foot: "Isn't it awfully hard to do, Mr. Gessler?"

And his answer, given with a sudden smile from out of the sardonic redness of his beard: "Id is an Ardt!"

Himself, he was a little as if made from leather, with his yellow crinkly face, and crinkly reddish hair and beard, and neat folds slanting down his cheeks to the corners of his mouth, and his guttural and one-toned voice; for leather is a sardonic substance, and stiff and slow of purpose. And that was the character of his face, save that his eyes, which were grey-blue, had in them the simple gravity of one secretly possessed by the Ideal. His elder brother was so very like him—though watery, paler in every way, with a great industry—that sometimes in the early days I was not quite sure of him until the interview was over. Then I knew that it was he, if the words, "I will ask my brudder," had not been spoken; and that, if they had, it was his elder brother.

When one grew old and wild and ran up bills, one somehow never ran them up with Gessler Brothers. It would not have seemed becoming to go in there and stretch out one's foot to that blue iron-spectacled glance, owing him for more than—say—two pairs, just the comfortable reassurance that one was still his client.

For it was not possible to go to him very often—his boots lasted terribly, having something beyond the temporary—some, as it were, essence of boot stitched into them.

One went in, not as into most shops, in the mood of: "Please serve me, and let me go!" but restfully, as one enters a church; and, sitting on the single wooden chair, waited—for there was never anybody there. Soon, over the top edge of that sort of well—rather dark, and smelling soothingly of leather—which formed the shop, there would be seen his face, or that of his elder brother, peering down. A guttural sound, and the tip-tap of bast slippers beating the narrow wooden stairs, and he would stand before one without coat, a little bent, in leather apron, with sleeves turned back, blinking—as if awakened from some dream of boots, or like an owl surprised in daylight and annoyed at this interruption.

And I would say: "How do you do, Mr. Gessler? Could you make me a pair of Russian leather boots?"

Without a word he would leave me, retiring whence he came, or into the other portion of the shop. And I would continue to rest in the wooden chair, inhaling the incense of his trade. Soon he would come back, holding in his thin, veined hand a piece of gold-brown leather. With eyes fixed on it, he would remark: "What a beaudiful biece!" When I, too, had admired it, he would speak again. "When do you wand dem?" And I would answer: "Oh! As soon as you conveniently can." And he would say: "Tomorrow fordnighd?" Or if he were his elder brother: "I will ask my brudder!"

Then I would murmur: "Thank you! Goodmorning, Mr. Gessler." "Goot-morning!" he would reply, still looking at the leather in his hand. And as I moved to the door, I would hear the tip-tap of his bast slippers restoring him, up the stairs, to his dream of boots. But if it were some new kind of foot-gear that he had not yet made me, then indeed he would observe ceremony—divesting me of my boot and holding it long in his hand, looking at it with eyes at once critical and loving, as if recalling the glow with which he had created it, and rebuking the way in which one had disorganized this masterpiece. Then, placing my foot on a piece of paper, he would two or three times tickle the outer edges with a pencil and pass his nervous fingers over my toes, feeling himself into the heart of my requirements.

I cannot forget that day on which I had occasion to say to him: "Mr. Gessler, that last pair of town walking-boots creaked, you know."

He looked at me for a time without replying, as if expecting me to withdraw or qualify the statement, then said:

"Id shouldn'd 'ave greaked."

"It did, I'm afraid."

"You goddem wed before dey found demselves?"

"I don't think so."

At last he lowered his eyes, as if hunting for memory of those boots, and I felt sorry I had mentioned this grave thing.

"Zend dem back!" he said; "I will look at dem."

A feeling of compassion for my creaking boots surged up in me, so well could I imagine the sorrowful long curiosity of regard which he would bend on them.

"Zome boods," he said slowly, "are bad from birdt. If I can do noding wid dem, I dake dem off your bill."

Once (once only) I went absent-mindedly into his shop in a pair of boots bought in an emergency at some large firm's. He took my order without showing me any leather, and I could feel his eyes penetrating the inferior integument of my foot. At last he said:

"Dose are nod my boods."

The tone was not one of anger, nor of sorrow, not even of contempt, but there was in it something quiet that froze the blood. He put his hand down and pressed a finger on the place where the left boot, endeavouring to be fashionable, was not quite comfortable.

"Id 'urds you dere," he said. "Dose big virms 'ave no self-respect. Drash!" And then, as if something had given way within him, he spoke long and bitterly. It was the only time I ever heard him discuss the conditions and hardships of his trade.

"Dey get id all," he said, "dey get id by advertisement, nod by work. Dey dake it away from us, who lofe our boods. Id gomes to this—bresently I haf no work. Every year id gets less—you will see." And looking at his lined face I saw things I had never noticed before, bitter things and bitter struggle—and what a lot of grey hairs there seemed suddenly in his red beard!

As best I could, I explained the circumstances of the purchase of those ill-omened boots. But his face and voice made so deep an impression that during the next few minutes I ordered many pairs. Nemesis[2] fell! They lasted more terribly than ever. And I was not able conscientiously to go to him for nearly two years.

When at last I went I was surprised to find that outside one of the two little windows of his shop another name was painted, also that of a bootmaker—making, of course, for the Royal Family. The old familiar boots, no longer in dignified isolation, were huddled in the single window. Inside, the now contracted well of the one little shop was more scented and darker than ever. And it was longer than usual, too, before a face peered down, and the tip-tap of the bast slippers began. At last he stood before me, and gazing through those rusty iron spectacles, said:

"Mr. ———, isn't it?"

"Ah! Mr. Gessler," I stammered, "but your boots are really *too* good, you know! See, these are quite decent still!" And I stretched out to him my foot. He looked at it.

"Yes," he said, "beople do nod wand good boods, id seems."

---

2. **Nemesis** (nem'ə sis), a spirit of vengeful retribution.

To get away from his reproachful eyes and voice I hastily remarked: "What have you done to your shop?"

He answered quietly: "Id was too exbensif. Do you wand some boods?"

I ordered three pairs, though I had only wanted two, and quickly left. I had, I do not know quite what feeling of being part, in his mind, of a conspiracy against him; or not perhaps so much against him as against his idea of boot. One does not, I suppose, care to feel like that; for it was again many months before my next visit to his shop, paid, I remember, with the feeling: "Oh! well, I can't leave the old boy—so here goes! Perhaps it'll be his elder brother!"

For his elder brother, I knew, had not character enough to reproach me, even dumbly.

And, to my relief, in the shop there did appear to be his elder brother, handling a piece of leather.

"Well, Mr. Gessler," I said, "how are you?"

He came close, and peered at me.

"I am breddy well," he said slowly, "but my elder brudder is dead."

And I saw that it was indeed himself—but how aged and wan! And never before had I heard him mention his brother. Much shocked, I murmured: "Oh! I am sorry!"

"Yes," he answered, "he was a good man, he made a good bood; but he is dead." And he touched the top of his head, where the hair had suddenly gone as thin as it had been on that of his poor brother, to indicate, I suppose, the cause of death. "He could nod ged over losing de oder shop. Do you wand any boods?" And he held up the leather in his hand: "Id's a beaudiful biece."

I ordered several pairs. It was very long before they came—but they were better than ever. One simply could not wear them out. And soon after that I went abroad.

It was over a year before I was again in London. And the first shop I went to was my old friend's. I had left a man of sixty, I came back to one of seventy-five, pinched and worn and tremulous, who genuinely, this time, did not at first know me.

"Oh! Mr. Gessler," I said, sick at heart; "how splendid your boots are! See, I've been wearing this pair nearly all the time I've been abroad; and they're not half worn out, are they?"

He looked long at my boots—a pair of Russian leather, and his face seemed to regain steadiness. Putting his hand on my instep, he said:

"Do dey vid you here? I 'ad drouble wid dat bair, I remember."

I assured him that they had fitted beautifully.

"Do you wand any boods?" he said. "I can make dem quickly; id is a slack dime."

I answered: "Please, please! I want boots all round—every kind!"

"I will make a vresh model. Your food must be bigger." And with utter slowness, he traced my foot, and felt my toes, only once looking up to say:

"Did I dell you my brudder was dead?"

To watch him was painful, so feeble had he grown; I was glad to get away.

I had given those boots up, when one evening they came. Opening the parcel, I set the four pairs out in a row. Then one by one I tried them on. There was no doubt about it. In shape and fit, in finish and quality of leather, they were the best he had ever made me. And in the mouth of one of the Town walking-boots I found his bill. The amount was the same as usual, but it gave me quite a shock. He had never before sent it in till quarter day.[3] I flew down-stairs, and wrote a cheque, and posted it at once with my own hand.

A week later, passing the little street, I thought I would go in and tell him how splendidly the new boots fitted. But when I came to where his shop had been, his name was gone. Still there, in the window, were the slim pumps, the patent leathers with cloth tops, the sooty riding boots.

---

3. **quarter day,** quarterly, one of four days scheduled throughout the year for billing and collecting.

I went in, very much disturbed. In the two little shops—again made into one—was a young man with an English face.

"Mr. Gessler in?" I said.

He gave me a strange, ingratiating look.

"No, sir," he said, "no. But we can attend to anything with pleasure. We've taken the shop over. You've seen our name, no doubt, next door. We make for some very good people."

"Yes, yes," I said; "but Mr. Gessler?"

"Oh!" he answered; "dead."

"Dead! But I only received these boots from him last Wednesday week."

"Ah," he said; "a shockin' go. Poor old man starved 'imself."

"Good God!"

"Slow starvation, the doctor called it! You see he went to work in such a way! Would keep the shop on, wouldn't have a soul touch his boots except himself. When he got an order, it took him such a time. People won't wait. He lost everybody. And there he'd sit, goin' on and on—I will say that for him—not a man in London made a better boot! But look at the competition! He never advertised! Would 'ave the best leather, too, and do it all 'imself. Well, there it is. What could you expect with his ideas?"

"But starvation——!"

"That may be a bit flowery, as the sayin' is—but I know myself he was sittin' over his boots day and night, to the very last. You see I used to watch him. Never gave 'imself time to eat; never had a penny in the house. All went in rent and leather. How he lived so long I don't know. He regular let his fire go out. He was a character. But he made good boots."

"Yes," I said, "he made good boots."

And I turned and went out quickly, for I did not want that youth to know that I could hardly see.

I
THE PASSING OF AN ERA

Stories of social criticism and protest are seldom jolly in their tone. There is a brooding despair that permeates the lines and shakes the reader out of comfortable complacency. Galsworthy's tremendous concern for justice seeps through the story.

What do you learn about the characters and people in general from the following lines?

1. The Gesslers:

a. For to make boots—such boots as he made—seemed to me then, and still seems to me, mysterious and wonderful.

b. "Isn't it awfully hard to do, Mr. Gessler?" ..."Id is an Ardt!"

2. The narrator of the story:

a. ... some inkling haunted me of the dignity of himself and brother.

b. I had, I do not know quite what feeling of being part, in his mind, of a conspiracy against him. ...

II
IMPLICATIONS

Considering this selection and your own experiences, what is your opinion of the following statements?

1. Society today is not interested in the quality of a product, but only in cost and the speed of production.

2. The Gessler brothers failed because of their inability to adapt and not because of any wrong on society's part.

3. Justice does not play a part in an individual's success.

III
TECHNIQUES
Author's Purpose

Which of the following best expresses your idea of Galsworthy's purpose? Try to find support in the story for your opinion.

1. His purpose is to criticize the Gesslers for not adapting to the times.

2. His purpose is to criticize society for not helping people of Gessler's ilk.

Irony

How does the ending demonstrate dramatic irony? Why is this ending appropriate? What would be the effect on the story if it ended happily?

Is there anything ironic in the statement—"not a man in London made a better boot!"—when you know that Mr. Gessler starved to death?

KATHERINE MANSFIELD

The writing of Katherine Mansfield (1888–1923) has often been compared
to that of the Russian short-story writer Chekhov; certainly there was
a similarity in temperament. She had the ability to respond completely to life
about her. Though she suffered greatly, for during her last years she waged
a losing battle with tuberculosis, she never lost her ability to take delight
in life. There is about her writing a certain instinctive quality that makes her work
difficult to imitate. Her most cherished criticism came from a printer who set in type
one of her stories and said: "My but those kids are *real!*" Born in Wellington,
New Zealand, of a family that had lived in Australia and New Zealand for three
generations, she went to the village school with the milk boy and the washerwoman's
daughter. When she was thirteen she was sent to Queen's College in England
to be educated and became involved in editing the college magazine. After five years
she returned to New Zealand, but felt like an unhappy exile there and finally persuaded
her parents to let her return to London. She struggled at her writing and had to play
minor parts in traveling opera companies in order to survive. In 1911 she published
a collection of short stories, *In a German Pension.* The book was tremendously
successful, but unfortunately the publisher went bankrupt which meant no royalties
for Mansfield. In 1918 she married John Middleton Murray, a critic of some note,
and when he became editor of the magazine *The Athenaeum*, she wrote literary criticism
for it. *The Garden Party*, a group of short stories published in 1922,
was a great success, but Mansfield had scant time to enjoy the recognition,
for she died in January the following year.

Life of Ma Parker

When the literary gentleman, whose flat old Ma Parker cleaned every Tuesday, opened the door to her that morning, he asked after her grandson. Ma Parker stood on the doormat inside the dark little hall, and she stretched out her hand to help her gentleman shut the door before she replied. "We buried 'im yesterday, sir," she said quietly.

"Oh, dear me! I'm sorry to hear that," said the literary gentleman in a shocked tone. He was in the middle of his breakfast. He wore a very shabby dressing-gown and carried a crumpled newspaper in one hand. But he felt awkward. He could hardly go back to the warm sitting-room without saying something— something more. Then because these people set such store by funerals he said kindly, "I hope the funeral went off all right."

"Beg parding, sir?" said old Ma Parker huskily.

Poor old bird! She did look dashed. "I hope the funeral was a—a—success," said he. Ma Parker gave no answer. She bent her head and hobbled off to the kitchen, clasping the old fish bag that held her cleaning things and an apron and a pair of felt shoes. The literary gentlemen raised his eyebrows and went back to his breakfast.

"Overcome, I suppose," he said aloud, helping himself to the marmalade.

Ma Parker drew the two jetty spears out of her toque[1] and hung it behind the door. She unhooked her worn jacket and hung that up

1. **jetty spears out of her toque**, broad black hat pins from her hat.

too. Then she tied her apron and sat down to take off her boots. To take off her boots or to put them on was an agony to her, but it had been an agony for years. In fact, she was so accustomed to the pain that her face was drawn and screwed up ready for the twinge before she'd so much as untied the laces. That over, she sat back with a sigh and softly rubbed her knees. . . .

"Gran! Gran!" Her little grandson stood on her lap in his button boots. He'd just come in from playing in the street.

"Look what a state you've made your gran's skirt into—you wicked boy!"

But he put his arms round her neck and rubbed his cheek against hers.

"Gran, gi' us a penny!" he coaxed.

"Be off with you; Gran ain't got no pennies."

"Yes, you 'ave."

"No, I ain't."

"Yes, you 'ave. Gi' us one!"

Already she was feeling for the old, squashed, black leather purse.

"Well, what'll you give your gran?"

He gave a shy little laugh and pressed closer. She felt his eyelid quivering against her cheek. "I ain't got nothing," he murmured. . . ."

The old woman sprang up, seized the iron kettle off the gas stove and took it over to the sink. The noise of the water drumming in the kettle deadened her pain, it seemed. She filled the pail, too, and the washing-up bowl.

It would take a whole book to describe the state of that kitchen. During the week the literary gentleman "did" for himself. That is to say, he emptied the tea leaves now and again into a jam jar set aside for that purpose, and if he ran out of clean forks he wiped over one or two on the roller towel. Otherwise, as he explained to his friends, his "system" was quite simple, and he couldn't understand why people make all this fuss about housekeeping.

"You simply dirty everything you've got, get a hag in once a week to clean up, and the thing's done."

Katherine Mansfield, whose collection of short stories completed before her early death continues to gather praise.

The result looked like a gigantic dustbin. Even the floor was littered with toast crusts, envelopes, cigarette ends. But Ma Parker bore him no grudge. She pitied the poor young gentleman for having no one to look after him. Out of the smudgy little window you could see an immense expanse of sad-looking sky, and whenever there were clouds they looked very worn, old clouds, frayed at the edges, with holes in them or dark stains like tea.

While the water was heating, Ma Parker began sweeping the floor. "Yes," she thought, as the broom knocked, "what with one thing and another I've had my share. I've had a hard life."

Even the neighbours said that of her. Many a time, hobbling home with her fish bag she

561

heard them, waiting at the corner, or leaning over the area railings, say among themselves, "She's had a hard life, has Ma Parker." And it was so true she wasn't in the least proud of it. It was just as if you were to say she lived in the basement-back at Number 27. A hard life . . .

At sixteen she'd left Stratford and come up to London as kitching-maid. Yes, she was born in Stratford-on-Avon. Shakespeare, sir? No, people were always arsking her about him. But she'd never heard his name until she saw it on the theatres.

Nothing remained of Stratford except that "sitting in the fireplace of a evening you could see the stars through the chimley," and "Mother always 'ad 'er side of bacon 'anging from the ceiling." And there was something—a bush, there was—at the front door, that smelt ever so nice. But the bush was very vague. She'd only remembered it once or twice, in the hospital, when she'd been taken bad.

That was a dreadful place—her first place. She was never allowed out. She never went up-stairs except for prayers morning and evening. It was a fair cellar. And the cook was a cruel woman. She used to snatch away her letters from home before she'd read them, and throw them in the range because they made her dreamy. . . . And the beetles! Would you be-lieve it?—until she came to London she'd never seen a black beetle. Here Ma always gave a little laugh, as though—not to have seen a black beetle! Well! It was as if to say you'd never seen your own feet.

When that family was sold up she went as "help" to a doctor's house, and after two years there, on the run from morning till night, she married her husband. He was a baker.

"A baker, Mrs. Parker!" the literary gentle-man would say. For occasionally he laid aside his tomes and lent an ear, at least, to this product called Life. "It must be rather nice to be married to a baker!"

Mrs. Parker didn't look so sure.

"Such a clean trade," said the gentleman.

Mrs. Parker didn't look convinced.

"And didn't you like handing the new loaves to the customers?"

"Well, sir," said Mrs. Parker, "I wasn't in the shop above a great deal. We had thirteen little ones and buried seven of them. If it wasn't the 'ospital it was the infirmary, you might say!"

"You might, *indeed*, Mrs. Parker!" said the gentleman, shuddering, and taking up his pen again.

Yes, seven had gone, and while the six were still small her husband was taken ill with con-sumption. It was flour on the lungs, the doctor told her at the time. . . . Her husband sat up in bed with his shirt pulled over his head, and the doctor's finger drew a circle on his back.

"Now, if we were to cut him open *here*, Mrs. Parker," said the doctor, "you'd find his lungs chock-a-block with white powder. Breathe, my good fellow!" And Mrs. Parker never knew for certain whether she saw or whether she fancied she saw a great fan of white dust come out of her poor dead husband's lips. . . .

But the struggle she'd had to bring up those six little children and keep herself to herself. Terrible it had been! Then, just when they were old enough to go to school her husband's sister came to stop with them to help things along, and she hadn't been there more than two months when she fell down a flight of steps and hurt her spine. And for five years Ma Parker had another baby—and such a one for crying—to look after. Then young Maudie went wrong and took her sister Alice with her; the two boys emigrimated, and young Jim went to India with the army, and Ethel, the youngest, mar-ried a good-for-nothing little waiter who died of ulcers the year little Lennie was born. And now little Lennie—my grandson. . . .

The piles of dirty cups, dirty dishes, were washed and dried. The inkblack knives were cleaned with a piece of potato and finished off with a piece of cork. The table was scrubbed, and the dresser and the sink that had sardine tails swimming in it . . .

He'd never been a strong child—never from the first. He'd been one of those fair babies that everybody took for a girl. Silvery fair curls he had, blue eyes, and a little freckle like a diamond on one side of his nose. The trouble she and Ethel had had to rear that child! The things out of the newspapers they tried him with! Every Sunday morning Ethel would read aloud while Ma Parker did her washing.

"Dear Sir,—Just a line to let you know my little Myrtil was laid out for dead. . . . After four bottils . . . gained 8 lbs. in 9 weeks, *and is still putting it on.*"

And then the egg-cup of ink would come off the dresser and the letter would be written, and Ma would buy a postal order on her way to work next morning. But it was no use. Nothing made little Lennie put it on. Taking him to the cemetery, even, never gave him a colour; a nice shake-up in the bus never improved his appetite.

But he was gran's boy from the first. . . .

"Whose boy are you?" said old Ma Parker, straightening up from the stove and going over to the smudgy window. And a little voice, so warm, so close, it half stifled her—it seemed to be in her breast under her heart—laughed out, and said, "I'm gran's boy!"

At that moment there was a sound of steps, and the literary gentleman appeared, dressed for walking.

"Oh, Mrs. Parker, I'm going out."

"Very good, sir."

"And you'll find your half-crown in the tray of the ink-stand."

"Thank you, sir."

"Oh, by the way, Mrs. Parker," said the literary gentleman quickly, "you didn't throw away any cocoa last time you were here—did you?"

"No, sir."

"*Very* strange. I could have sworn I left a teaspoonful of cocoa in the tin." He broke off. He said softly and firmly, "You'll always tell me when you throw things away—won't you, Mrs. Parker?" And he walked off very well pleased with himself, convinced, in fact, he'd shown Mrs. Parker that under his apparent carelessness he was as vigilant as a woman.

The door banged. She took her brushes and cloths into the bedroom. But when she began to make the bed, smoothing, tucking, patting, the thought of little Lennie was unbearable. Why did he have to suffer so? That's what she couldn't understand. Why should a little angel child have to arsk for his breath and fight for it? There was no sense in making a child suffer like that.

. . . . From Lennie's little box of a chest there came a sound as though something was boiling. There was a great lump of something bubbling in his chest that he couldn't get rid of. When he coughed the sweat sprang out on his head; his eyes bulged, his hands waved, and the great lump bubbled as a potato knocks in a saucepan. But what was more awful than all was when he didn't cough he sat against the pillow and never spoke or answered, or even made as if he heard. Only he looked offended.

"It's not your poor old gran's doing it, my lovey," said old Ma Parker, patting back the damp hair from his little scarlet ears. But Lennie moved his head and edged away. Dreadfully offended with her he looked—and solemn. He bent his head and looked at her sideways as though he couldn't have believed it of his gran.

But at the last . . . Ma Parker threw the counterpane over the bed. No, she simply couldn't think about it. It was too much—she'd had too much in her life to bear. She'd borne it up till now, she'd kept herself to herself, and never once had she been seen to cry. Never by a living soul. Not even her own children had seen Ma break down. She'd kept a proud face always. But now! Lennie gone—what had she? She had nothing. He was all she'd got from life, and now he was took too. Why must it all have happened to me? she wondered. "What have I done?" said old Ma Parker. "What have I done?"

As she said those words she suddenly let fall her brush. She found herself in the kitchen. Her misery was so terrible that she pinned on her hat, put on her jacket and walked out of the flat like a person in a dream. She did not know what she was doing. She was like a person so dazed by the horror of what has happened that he walks away—anywhere, as though by walking away he could escape. . . .

It was cold in the street. There was a wind like ice. People went flitting by, very fast; the men walked like scissors; the women trod like cats. And nobody knew—nobody cared. Even if she broke down, if at last, after all these years, she were to cry, she'd find herself in the lockup as like as not.

But at the thought of crying it was as though little Lennie leapt in his gran's arms. Ah, that's what she wants to do, my dove. Gran wants to cry. If she could only cry now, cry for a long time, over everything, beginning with her first place and the cruel cook, going on to the doctor's, and then the seven little ones, death of her husband, the children's leaving her, and all the years of misery that led up to Lennie. But to have a proper cry over all these things would take a long time. All the same, the time for it had come. She must do it. She couldn't put it off any longer; she couldn't wait any more. . . . Where could she go?

"She's had a hard life, has Ma Parker." Yes, a hard life, indeed! Her chin began to tremble; there was no time to lose. But where? Where?

She couldn't go home; Ethel was there. It would frighten Ethel out of her life. She couldn't sit on a bench anywhere; people would come asking her questions. She couldn't possibly go back to the gentleman's flat; she had no right to cry in strangers' houses. If she sat on some steps a policeman would speak to her.

Oh, wasn't there anywhere where she could hide and keep herself to herself and stay as long as she liked, not disturbing anybody, and nobody worrying her? Wasn't there anywhere in the world where she could have her cry out —at last?

Ma Parker stood, looking up and down. The

icy wind blew out her apron into a balloon. And now it began to rain. There was nowhere.

I
FOR THE DIGNITY
OF THE INDIVIDUAL

This is a cry from the heart . . . a cry against the terrible indifference of people toward one another. The literary gentleman really doesn't care a hoot about Ma Parker's troubles. Neither do her neighbors or acquaintances. Society has turned its back on this poor, hardworking woman and left her isolated in a cocoon of sorrow and pain. She remains a curiosity piece . . . interesting but unimportant.

Katherine Mansfield in her *Journal* has made the statement, "At the end, *truth* is the only thing worth having." What is the "truth" in this particular story?

II
IMPLICATIONS

Do you think the following statements are true? Or false? Or somewhere in between?

1. Most people are calloused and indifferent to anybody else's troubles.

2. Poverty saps personal initiative and thus inhibits an individual from overcoming difficulties.

3. The poor do not even have a place where they can grieve in private.

III
TECHNIQUES
Author's Purpose

Consider Katherine Mansfield's purpose: to tell the truth as she saw it. What was your reaction to this story? What is the social injustice attacked in this story?

Irony

How are the following ironic?

1. Ma Parker's answer to the literary gentleman's question about Lennie.

2. His asking her about the cocoa.

3. Her finding herself walking aimlessly with no place to go and cry.

Social Protest in Art

Is the artist's only task to create things of beauty?
Those who think so cry, *"Art for art's sake."*

   This gallery of paintings and drawings by great Western artists attests to widespread and passionate involvement of artists in the affairs of society. Like writers, these artists have cried out against injustice, corruption, and the ravages of war.

   Although the great Spanish painter Goya was official First Painter to the King of Spain, his sympathies were with the common person. Often he painted the Spanish aristocrats as fools and common men and women as aristocrats. He witnessed the savage scene below during the French invasion of Spain in 1808. Napoleon had named his brother, Joseph Bonaparte, King of Spain. The citizens of Madrid rebelled, but the resistance was repressed. On May third, French troops shot citizens who had taken part in the uprising.

THE EXECUTION OF THE CITIZENS OF MADRID ON THE THIRD OF MAY, 1808
Francisco Goya y Lucientes

Like many artists and writers, Daumier spent time in prison for criticism of the government. In this lithograph, he maliciously portrays the members of the French legislature as aged, self-satisfied, and overstuffed. Evil and stupidity mark every face.

THE LEGISLATIVE BODY
Honoré Daumier
Courtesy of The National Gallery of Art,
Washington, D.C., Rosenwald Collection

In his youth, van Gogh lived among the poor miners of Belgium. In sympathy, he lived as they did, even sleeping on the floor to provide a bed for those who had none. Of THE POTATO EATERS he wrote: "I have tried to emphasize that those people, eating their potatoes in the lamplight, have dug the earth with those very hands they put in the dish, and so it speaks of manual labor, and how they have honestly earned their food . . . Painting peasant life is a serious thing, and I should reproach myself if I did not try to make pictures which will rouse serious thoughts in those who think seriously about art and about life."

THE POTATO EATERS
Vincent van Gogh

An illiterate farmer, Emiliano Zapata was one of the
key figures of the Mexican Revolution of 1910–1917.
With the cry, "Land and Liberty," he led the Indian
peasants who supported Madero against the dictator
Porfirio Diaz, "The Iron Man of Mexico," who
had neglected the social needs of Mexicans.

ZAPATISTAS
José Clemente Orozco

Käthe Kollwitz' etching was made as an illustration for Hauptmann's play *The Weavers.* Driven by poverty, women pass paving stones to men during an attempt to storm the gates of a great house. Scenes like this occurred throughout Europe during the Industrial Revolution.

RIOT *Käthe Kollwitz*
Courtesy of The National Gallery of Art,
Washington, D.C., Rosenwald Collection

During the Battle of Britain in World War II, the German Luftwaffe pounded London with nightly bombing raids. The British sculptor Henry Moore protests against the destruction of the city in this chalk drawing dating from the year of crisis, 1940.

THE MORNING AFTER THE BLITZ
Henry Moore
Courtesy of Wadsworth Antheneum,
Hartford, Conn.

Dali's surrealist painting is full of protest against atomic war.
The mushroom cloud hovering above the world may be a symbol of destruction. On the
right, groups of people resembling a scientist's model of a molecular structure stand, like
the nations of the world, each with a rifle pointed at the other's head.
On the left is another model of molecular action, which by a trick
of the eye resembles armies crossing a battlefield.

GALACIDALACIDESOXIRIBUNUCLEICACID
Salvador Dali

SLAWOMIR MROŻEK

Born in Poland, Slawomir Mrożek[1] (1930–   ) spent his adolescence in that country during the postwar period of tense political conflict. The boy received a "stiff and unquestioning" Catholic education from his parents. As he learned the English language, he devoured English and American literature. Following attempts at studying architecture, Oriental culture, and painting, he left the University of Krakow to work as a caricaturist on a leading humor magazine. His inventive, subtly subversive cartoons, attracted national interest. Mrożek's first volume of satirical stories was a best-seller. Because of the resemblance between these very short stories and his cartoons, Mrożek earned a reputation for building fantastic anecdotes. His work depicts a disjointed, alienated world ruled by political systems that reduce laws and logic to absurdity—and people to mechanical objects. A quiet and withdrawn man, Mrożek views the world sadly. After a political break with his country in 1968, his stories and plays were banned and his books were taken out of Polish libraries. Still, outside Poland, Mrożek is considered one of the most talented contemporary Polish writers. He currently lives in voluntary exile in Paris with his wife.

Two Polish Tales

translated from the Polish by Konrad Syrop

On a Journey

Just after B—— the road took us among damp, flat meadows. Only here and there the expanse of green was broken by a stubble field. In spite of mud and potholes the chaise was moving at a brisk pace. Far ahead, level with the ears of the horses, a blue band of the forest was stretching across the horizon. As one would expect at that time of the year, there was not a soul in sight.

Only after we had traveled for a while did I see the first human being. As we approached his features became clear; he was a man with an ordinary face and he wore a Post Office uniform. He was standing still at the side of the road, and as we passed he threw us an indifferent glance. No sooner had we left him behind than I noticed another one, in a similar uniform, also standing motionless on the verge. I looked at him carefully, but my attention was immediately attracted by the third and then the fourth still figure by the roadside. Their apathetic eyes were all fixed in the same direction, their uniforms were faded.

Intrigued by this spectacle I rose in my seat so that I could glance over the shoulders of the cabman; indeed, ahead of us another figure was standing erect. When we passed two more of them my curiosity became irresistible. There they were, standing quite a distance from each other, yet near enough to be able to see the next

1. **Slawomir Mrożek** (slä′vo mir mro′zhek).

"On a Journey" and "Children" by Slawomir Mrożek from *The Elephant* by Slawomir Mrozek. Translated from the Polish by Konrad Syrop. Reprinted by permission of Grove Press, Inc. Copyright © 1962 by MacDonald & Co., Publishers, Ltd.

man, holding the same posture and paying as much attention to us as road signs do to passing travelers. And as soon as we passed one, another came into our field of vision. I was about to open my mouth to ask the coachman about the meaning of those men, when, without turning his head, he volunteered: "On duty."

We were just passing another still figure, staring indifferently into the distance.

"How's that?" I asked.

"Well, just normal. They are standing on duty," and he urged the horses on.

The coachman showed no inclination to offer any further elucidation; perhaps he thought it was superfluous. Cracking his whip from time to time and shouting at the horses, he was driving on. Roadside brambles, shrines and solitary willow trees came to meet us and receded again in the distance; between them, at regular intervals, I could see the now familiar silhouettes.

"What sort of duty are they doing?" I inquired.

"State duty, of course. Telegraph line."

"How's that? Surely for a telegraph line you need poles and wires!"

The coachman looked at me and shrugged his shoulders.

"I can see that you've come from far away," he said. "Yes we know that for a telegraph you need poles and wires. But this is wireless telegraph. We were supposed to have one with wires but the poles got stolen and there's no wire."

"What do you mean, no wire?"

"There simply isn't any," he said, and shouted at the horses.

Surprise silenced me for the moment but I had no intention of abandoning my inquiries.

"And how does it work without wires?"

"That's easy. The first one shouts what's needed to the second, the second repeats it to the third, the third to the fourth and so on until the telegram gets to where it's supposed to. Just now they aren't transmitting or you'd hear them yourself."

"And it works, this telegraph?"

"Why shouldn't it work? It works all right.

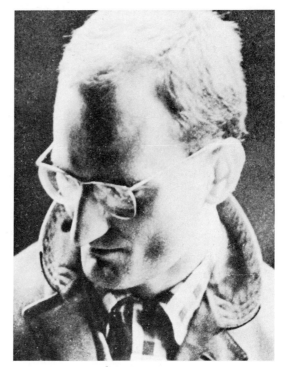

Sławomir Mrożek

But often the message gets twisted. It's worst when one of them has had a drink too many. Then his imagination gets to work and various words get added. But otherwise it's even better than the usual telegraph with poles and wires. After all live men are more intelligent, you know. And there's no storm damage to repair and great saving on timber, and timber is short. Only in the winter there are sometimes interruptions. Wolves. But that can't be helped."

"And those men, are they satisfied?" I asked.

"Why not? The work isn't very hard, only they've got to know foreign words. And it'll get better still; the postmaster has gone to Warsaw to ask for megaphones for them so that they don't have to shout so much."

"And should one of them be hard of hearing?"

"Ah, they don't take such-like. Nor do they take men with a lisp. Once they took on a chap that stammered. He got his job through influence but he didn't keep it long because he was blocking the line. I hear that by the twenty-

kilometers stone[2] there's one who went to a drama school. He shouts most clearly."

His arguments confused me for a while. Deep in thought, I no longer paid attention to the men by the road verge. The chaise was jumping over potholes, moving towards the forest, which was now occupying most of the horizon.

"All right," I said carefully, "but wouldn't you prefer to have a new telegraph with poles and wires?"

"Good heavens, no." The coachman was shocked. "For the first time it's easy to get a job in our district—in the telegraph, that is. And people don't have to rely only on their wages either. If someone expects a cable and is particularly anxious not to have it twisted, then he takes his chaise along the line and slips something into the pocket of each one of the tele-

graph boys. After all a wireless telegraph is something different from one with wires. More modern."

Over the rattle of the wheels I could hear a distant sound, neither a cry nor a shout, but a sort of sustained wailing.

"Aaaeeeaaauuueeeaaaeeeaayayay."

The coachman turned in his seat and put his hand to his ear.

"They are transmitting," he said. "Let's stop so that we can hear better."

When the monotonous noise of our wheels ceased, total silence enveloped the fields. In that silence the wailing, which resembled the cry of birds on a moor, came nearer to us. His hand cupped to his ear, the telegraph man nearby made ready to receive.

"It'll get here in a moment," whispered the coachman.

Indeed. When the last distant "ayayay" died

---

2. **twenty-kilometers stone,** 12½-mile marker.

away, from behind a clump of trees came the prolonged shout:

"Fa . . . th . . . er dea . . . d fu . . . ner . . . al Wed . . . nes . . . day."

"May he rest in peace," sighed the coachman and cracked his whip. We were entering the forest.

Children

That winter there was plenty of snow.

In the square children were making a snow man.

The square was vast. Many people passed through it every day and the windows of many offices kept it under constant observation. The square did not mind, it just continued to stretch into the distance. In the very center of it the children, laughing and shouting, were engaged in the making of a ridiculous figure.

First they rolled a large ball. That was the trunk. Next came a smaller ball—the shoulders. An even smaller ball followed—the head. Tiny pieces of coal made a row of suitable buttons running from top to bottom. The nose consisted of a carrot. In other words it was a perfectly ordinary snow man, not unlike the thousands of similar figures which, the snow permitting, spring up across the country every year.

All this gave the children a great deal of fun. They were very happy.

Many passers-by stopped to admire the snow man and went on their way. Government offices continued to work as if nothing had happened.

The children's father was glad that they should be getting exercise in the fresh air, acquiring rosy cheeks and healthy appetites.

In the evening, when they were all at home, someone knocked at the door. It was the news agent who had a kiosk[3] in the square. He apolo-

gized profusely for disturbing the family so late and for troubling them, but he felt it his duty to have a few words with the father. Of course, he knew the children were still small but that made it all the more important to keep an eye on them, in their own interest. He would not have dared to come were it not for his concern for the little ones. One could say his visit had an educational purpose. It was about the snow man's nose the children had made out of a carrot. It was a red nose. Now, he, the news agent, also had a red nose. Frostbite, not drink, you know. Surely there could be no earthly reason for making a public allusion to the color of his nose. He would be grateful if this did not happen again. He really had the upbringing of the children at heart.

The father was worried by this speech. Of course children could not be allowed to ridicule people, even those with red noses. They were probably still too young to understand. He called them, and, pointing at the news agent, asked severely: "Is it true that with this gentleman in mind, you gave your snow man a red nose?"

The children were genuinely surprised. At first they did not see the point of the question. When they did, they answered that the thought had never crossed their minds.

Just in case, they were told to go to bed without supper.

The news agent was grateful and made for the door. There he met face to face with the Chairman of the Co-operative. The father was delighted to greet such a distinguished person in his house.

On seeing the children, the Chairman chided: "Ah, here are your brats. You must keep them under control, you know. Small, but already impertinent. What do you think I saw from the window of my office this afternoon? If you please, they were making a snow man."

"If its about its nose—"

"Nose, fiddlesticks! Just imagine, first they made one ball of snow, then another and yet another. And then what do you think? They put one ball on top of the other and the third on top of both of them. Isn't it exasperating?"

---

3. **kiosk** (kē osk'), small building with one or more open sides, usually used as a newsstand.

The father did not understand and the Chairman went on angrily: "You don't see! But it's crystal clear what they meant. They wanted to say that in our Co-operative one thief sits on top of another. And that's libel. Even when one writes such things to the papers one has to produce some proof, and all the more so when one makes a public demonstration in the square."

However, the Chairman was a considerate, tolerant man. He would make allowances for youth and thoughtlessness. He would not insist on a public apology. But it must not happen again.

Asked if, when putting one snowball on top of the other, they wished to convey that in the Co-operative one thief was sitting on top of another, the children replied in the negative and burst into tears. Just in case, however, they were ordered to stand in a corner.

That was not the end of the day. Sleigh bells could be heard outside and soon two men were at the door. One of them was a fat stranger in a sheepskin coat, the other—the President of the local National Council himself.

"It's about your children," they announced in unison from the door.

These calls were becoming a matter of routine. Both men were offered chairs. The President looked askance at the stranger, wondering who he might be, and decided to speak first.

"I'm astonished that you should tolerate subversive activities in your own family. But perhaps you are politically ignorant? If so, you'd better admit it right away."

The father did not understand why he should be politically ignorant.

"One can see it at a glance by your children's behavior. Who makes fun of the People's authority? Your children do. They made a snow man outside the window of my study."

"Oh, I understand," whispered the father, "you mean that one thief—"

"Thief, my foot. But do you know the meaning of the snow man outside the window of the President of the National Council? I know very well what people are saying about me. Why don't your brats make a snow man outside Adenauer's window, for instance? Well, why not?

You don't answer. That silence speaks volumes. You'll have to take the consequences."

On hearing the word "consequences" the fat stranger rose and furtively tiptoed out of the room. Outside, the sleigh bells tinkled and faded into the distance.

"Yes, my dear sir," the President said, "you'd better reflect on all these implications. And one more thing. It's entirely my private affair that I walk about the house with my fly undone and your children have no right to make fun of it. Those buttons on the snowman, from top to bottom, that's ambiguous. And I'll tell you something: if I like, I can walk about my house without my trousers and it's none of your children's business. You'd better remember that."

The accused summoned his children from the corner and demanded that they confess. When making the snow man had they had the President in mind and, by adorning the figure with buttons from top to bottom had they made an additional joke, in very bad taste, alluding to the fact that the President walks about his house with his fly undone?

With tears in their eyes the children assured him that they had made the snow man just for fun, without any ulterior motive. Just in case, however, apart from being deprived of their supper and sent to the corner, they were now made to kneel on the hard floor.

That night several more people knocked at the door but they obtained no reply.

The following morning I was passing a little garden and I saw the children there. The square having been declared out of bounds the children were discussing how best to occupy themselves in the confined space.

"Let's make a snow man," said one.

"An ordinary snow man is no fun," said another.

"Let's make the news agent. We'll give him a red nose, because he drinks. He said so himself last night," said the third.

"And I want to make the Co-op."

"And I want to make the President, silly fool.

And we'll give him buttons because he walks with his fly undone."

There was an argument but in the end the children agreed; they would make all of them in turn.

They started working with gusto.

I
TONGUE IN CHEEK

These stories, like Swift's satire, are told in a straightforward, serious manner. Notice the first paragraph of "On a Journey." It describes a cold, wintry landscape and gives no hint of the ridiculous telegraph line which is about to emerge. So the "tone" of the story contrasts with the absurdity of the content. This contrast heightens our pleasure in much the same way as do unexpected punch lines from a straight-faced comedian.

II
IMPLICATIONS

Do you agree or disagree with the following statements?

1. Human power is preferable to mechanical power.

2. People tend to be unduly sensitive about their weaknesses and watch for anything that seems to make fun of them.

III
TECHNIQUES

Author's Purpose

Which of the following is Mrożek criticizing in "On a Journey"?

1. The absurd ways a government tries to save money.

2. Mechanization of the modern age.

3. Society's way of solving problems.

Irony

In "On a Journey," what is ironic about the coach driver's answer to the question of whether this kind of telegraph works?

What is ironic about the ending of "Children"?

WILLIAM SANSOM

Born in England, William Sansom (1912–1976) was writing from the age
of seven. He did not attend college, but instead traveled abroad and, at some time
in his life, lived in most of the countries of Europe, including France, Germany,
Spain, and Hungary. He produced his first serious work while serving in the ranks
of the London Fire Service during World War II. In 1946 and 1947 the Society
of Authors in London awarded him two literary scholarships. He wrote not only short
stories, but novels, essays, and travel articles. Sansom has been called a magician
by some critics, because one is never quite sure if he is making the unreal world real
or tinging the real world with unreality. He gives the reader a refracted view
of life with distortions and sudden bursts of light. Some of his short stories
are close to being "contrived shockers." What saves them from this fate is the
fact that they contain a larger meaning which removes from them the charge of being
mere tricks. He has a remarkable ability to create mood, showing evidence of a keen eye,
sharp ears, and a good nose . . . he can make you *smell* the smells of a country lane
or a city alley. Said one reviewer of Sansom's characters, "They embark on a voyage
of the spirit, but generally the home port is misery."

The Long Sheet

Have you ever wrung dry a wet cloth; wrung it bone-white dry—with only the grip of your fingers and the muscles of your arms? If you have done this, you will understand better the situation of the captives at Device Z when the warders set them the task of the long sheet.

You will remember how, having stretched the cloth between your hands, you begin by twisting one end—holding the other firmly so that the water is corkscrewed from its hiding place. At first the water spurts out easily, but later you will find yourself screwing with both hands in different directions, whitening your knuckles, straining every fiber of your diaphragm—and all to extract the smallest drop of moisture! The muscle of your arm swells like an egg—yet the wet drop remains a pinhead! As you work, the cloth will gradually change from a gray color to the whiteness of dried

bone, yet even then the cloth will be wet! Still you will knot your muscles; still you will wrench away at the furtive damp. Then—at last!—you will believe the cloth to be dry . . . but in the next second the tip of a finger will quiver tragically as it touches some cold, hidden veil of damp clinging deep down in the interlaced threads.

Such, then, was the task of the captives.

They were placed in a long steel box of a room with no windows and no doors. The room was some six feet wide and six feet high, but it ran one hundred feet in length. It resembled thus a rectangular tunnel with no entrance and no exit, yet the sensation inside was not really that of a tunnel. For instance, a quantity of light flowed through thick glass panels set at intervals along the ceiling; these were the skylights, and through these the captives had been dropped into the box. Again, the impression of living in a tunnel was offset by a system of cubicle walls that separated the captives into groups. These cubicle walls were made

From *Fireman Flower* by William Sansom, published by The Hogarth Press.
Copyright © by William Sansom, 1944.

from the same riveted steel as the main walls: there was no communication from cubicle to cubicle except through a half-foot of space left between the top of the wall and the ceiling. Thus each group of captives occupied, as it were, a small room. There were twenty-two captives. They were grouped in unequal number within four cubicles.

Through the entire length of this system, raised three feet from the ground, passing through the very center of each room, ran a long wound sheet. It was made from coarse white linen bundled into a loose cylinder of cloth some six inches in diameter.

When the captives were first thrown into their cubicles, the long sheet was heavy with water. The warders had soaked the material so thoroughly that in the folds the water had gathered into lakes. The warders then issued their instructions. The captives were to wring the sheet dry. It would not do to wring the sheet to what we would normally call a "dry" state—as of clothes ready for airing. On the contrary—this sheet must be purged of *every* moisture. It must be wrung as dry as a bone. This, the warders concluded, might take a long time. It might even take months of hard work. In fact, they had taken special care to treat the linen so that it would be durable over a lengthy period. But when the task was finally completed, then the men and women would be granted their freedom. They would be released.

As the grave faces of the warders disappeared and the glass skylights slid shut, the captives smiled for the first time. For months they had lived with the fear of death, they had shrunk in ceaseless apprehension of the terrible devices that awaited them. And now that future had devolved into the wringing of a simple sheet! A long sheet, it was true, but child's play in comparison with what they had expected. Thus they sank to the steel floor in relief. Few laid a hand on the sheet that day.

But after three months the captives began to realize the true extent of their task. By this time each group in each cubicle had wrung

William Sansom

the worst water from their section of the sheet. Yet with all their sweating and straining they could not rid the cloth of its last dampness.

It was apparent that the warders had no intention of presenting them with a simple task. For through vents near the roof, hot steam was injected mechanically into the cubicles as long as daylight lasted. This steam naturally moistened the sheet afresh. The steam was so regulated that it hindered rather than prevented the fulfillment of the wringing. Thus there was always less steam entering than moisture wrung from the sheet at a normal rate of working. The steam injection merely meant that for every ten drops of water wrung seven new drops would settle upon the sheet, so that eventually the captives would still be able to wring the sheet dry. This device of the warders was introduced solely to complicate the task. It seemed that the warders were acting in two ways; daily they encouraged the efforts of the captives with promises of release, but daily they turned on the steam cocks.

In the cubicles the air was thick with steam. It was the air of a laundry, where steam catches in the throat, where it is sometimes difficult to breathe, where the smell of hot, wet cloth sickens the heart. The steel walls sweated. Condensed water trickled in winding trails down the gray plate. Beads of moisture clustered at the rivet heads. The long sheet spattered a few drops into the central gutter in the floor as the captives twisted against time. Both men and women worked half-naked. Since the sheet was positioned three feet from the ground, they were forced to stoop. If they sat at their work, then their arms grew numb in the raised attitude at which they had to be maintained. There was nothing for it but to stoop. In the hot air they sweated, yet they dared not lean over the sheet for fear their sweat should fall on the hungry cloth. Their muscles knotted, their backs cried out as they twisted. The end was far, but there was an end. That meant that there was hope. This knowledge lent fire to the struggling ambition that lived in their human hearts. They worked.

Yet some were not always equal to the task.

Room Three—
Those Who Sought Outside

There were four rooms. Take Room Three. This housed five people—two married couples and a young Serbian grocer. All five of them wanted freedom. They worked earnestly at their task. That the task was in essence unproductive did not worry them. At least, it would produce their freedom. It was thus artificially productive. These five people set about the problem in a normal businesslike way. Previously, they had been used to habitual hours, a life of steady formula. This they now applied to the new business of wringing. Set hours were allotted to each person. It was as if they commuted regularly from their suburbia (the steel sleeping corner) to the office (the long sheet). They worked in relays, in four-hour stretches throughout the day and night.

However, as I have said, they were not equal to the task. The framework of habit overcame them. Like so many who live within a steady, comfortable routine, they allowed the routine around the work to predominate in importance above the work itself. They arrived at the long sheet punctually, and with consciences thus satisfied, they put insufficient effort into the actual work. Furthermore, when they had fulfilled the routine assiduously for a period, one or the other would congratulate his conscience and really believe that he deserved a "little relaxation," and he would take the afternoon off. Such was the force of his emphasis on obedience to the letter that he was convinced the law would not suffer. Thus the real work of wringing suffered. New moisture crept in where his hands were weak. These people had set about the quest for freedom in the right way, but they were unhappily convinced of their righteousness.

. . . One of the women became pregnant. Her child was born in the steam box, but, under the influence of Room Three's routine, that child could never be free. The influence, the constriction, and the hopeless task of the parents would keep the child in the steam box for life. The child would never have the chance to learn to wring with effect.

Room Two—
Those Who Sought In and Out
and Around

In another of the rooms—Room Two—there were five men. Their names and their professions do not matter. It is how they attacked the long sheet that matters. They attacked it in five different ways.

Here were five individualists, five who were forced by the set of their minds to approach their problems in various ways of their own. Day after day they labored in the hot, damp steel cubicle, each twisting the long cylinder of cloth with different reasonings.

One man had been frightened by a sheet when he was young. On some indefinite day of his childhood, a new nurse had appeared. Her black eyes had burned with a powerful scorn; her small lascivious teeth and huge drooping cheeks had threatened him in the candlelight. On her first day the new nurse had made a little white monster from a white sheet. It had two little heads and a shapeless flowing body. The little heads were sharp, and always bobbing. The nurse had come silently into the night nursery when it was dark. Lighting a candle on the floor behind the end of the bed, she had quietly raised her little white monster so that the boy could just see it above his toes. Then she had begun a strident sing-song crowing, like the harsh crowing of Punch.[1] The boy had awaked to this sound, and had seen the sharp bobbing heads of the little monster.

Now, some thirty years later, the man has forgotten the scene, but somehow his hands cannot touch the long sheet without a great sensation of uneasiness. His hands do not touch the white cloth well. Consequently, he is forever making excuses to avoid working on the sheet. He feigns illness. . . . He has mutilated his hands. . . . Oh, there is no end to the devices the fellow had invented from his sadness! But whatever he does cannot eradicate the awful uneasiness that clouds the far reaches of his mind. At the moment of writing, this man is still in the steel cubicle. He will never be free.

Another of the men in Room Two was a simple quiet fellow. The others took no interest in him, he was too simple a fellow. Yet a most amazing thing—his section of the sheet was white and quite dry. There was a good reason for this. Without any conscious knowledge, without planning and scheming, he had naturally gone at his wringing the good way. He was accustomed to wring sitting astride the cloth. In this position, his legs squeezed at the cloth too. Thus, without questioning, he surrendered his *whole* body to the task. His heart, too, for he was such a simple fellow. This man's sheet was dry. But the others never even noticed. He was such a simple fellow.

There was one man in Room Two whose *métier* in life had always been the short cut. As previously in business, in love, in all relationships, he attempted to apply the short cut system to the most important task of all—the

wringing of the long sheet. He tried out a great many tricks and petty deceptions. He blocked up the pipe through which the guards pumped the steam. The next morning, like a mushroom, another pipe had grown at the side of the first. He tried feigning madness. The warders threw buckets of cold water down through the skylight. Some of this water splashed on to the sheet, destroying a whole month's work. The other men nearly killed him for this. Once he bribed one of the warders to send him a pot of white enamel. With this he painted the sheet white. The enamel dried hard. The sheet seemed dry! But the next day the warders came to chip the enamel off. They punished him with a traveling hose jet. This jet traveled inconsequently about the room. To save the water hitting the sheet, the man had to intercept the jet with his body. He was kept running and jumping and squatting for a whole day—until toward evening he dropped exhausted and rolled into the central gutter. The warders, of course, can never be bribed.

Then there was another man who can best be described as a fumbler. He worked hard and earnestly. He was up at the wringing well before the others, he seldom lay down till long after the skylights were dark and the air cleared of steam. But he fumbled. His mind co-ordinated imperfectly with his body. Although he felt that he concentrated his whole effort, psychic and physical, on the job of wringing— his mind would wander to other things. He never knew that this happened, but his hands did. They stopped wringing, they wrung the wrong way—and the fatal drops of moisture accumulated. He could never understand this. He thought his mind was always on the job. But instead his mind settled too often on matters only near to the job, not the job in essence. For a small instance—his mind might wander to the muscle on his left forearm. He might see that it bulges at a downward screw of the wet linen. He watches this bulge as he works. The

---

1. **Punch**, a common character in English Punch-and-Judy or puppet shows.

bulge then absorbs his interest to such an extent that he makes greater play with this left arm to stimulate further the bulge of muscle. In compensation the right arm slackens its effort. The wringing becomes uneven and inefficient. Yet all this time he himself in honesty believes that he is concentrating upon his job. The muscle is, in fact, part of the job. Yet it is only a facet, not the full perspective. He fumbles because he does not see clearly: and to wring dry the long sheet a man must give his whole thought in calm and complete clarity.

The fifth man in Room Two was a good worker: that is, he had found the way to wring effectively, and at times his portion of the sheet was almost dry. But he was perverted. This man liked to wring the sheet almost dry—then stand by and watch the steam settle into the folds once more! He liked to watch the fruits of his labor rot. In this way he freed himself from the task. He freed himself by attaining his object, and then treating it with the scorn he imagined it deserved. He felt himself master of the work—but in reality he never became the master of his true freedom. There was no purity in this man. His freedom was false.

Room Four—
Those Who Never Sought at All

Room Number Four housed more captives than the others. Seven people were crowded into this one cell of steam and steel. There were three women, one girl of twelve, and three men. These people seldom did much work. They were a source of great disappointment to the warders. To these people the effort was not worth eventual freedom. The immensity of the task had long ago disheartened them. Their minds were not big enough to envisage the better future. They had enough. They had their breeding and their food. The state of life held no interest for them. Vaguely, they would have preferred better conditions. But at the cost of toil and thought—no. These people were squalid and small. Their desire for freedom had been killed by a dull acceptance of their im-

potence. This also became true of the little girl of twelve. She had no alternative but to follow the others.

The warders never played their favorite trick on Room Four, for the simple reason that the trick would have had no effect. The trick was to release into the cells small squadrons of saturated birds. The birds flew into the cells and scattered water from their wings everywhere. The birds flew in all directions and the captives ran wildly here and there in hysterical efforts to trap them before they splashed water onto the sacred sheet. The warders considered that the element of chance implicit in these birds was a healthy innovation. Otherwise, life for the captives would have been too ordered. There must be risk, said the warders. And so from time to time, with no warning, they injected these little wet birds and the captives hastened to protect the purity of their work against the interference of fate. If they could not catch the birds in time, they learnt in this manner how to accept misfortune: and in patience they redoubled their efforts to retrieve the former level of their work.

But into Room Four the birds never flew. The trick would never have affected the inhabitants, who lived at the low ebb of misfortune already. Perhaps the real tragedy of these dispirited people was not their own misfortune, to which they had grown accustomed, but that their slackness had its effect on those whose ambitions were pure and strong. The slackness was contagious. In this way. The sheet was so wet in Room Four that the water seeped through into Room One. And in Room One lived the most successful of all the captives.

Room One—
Those Who Sought Inside

There were five of them in cubicle One. Four men and one woman. They were successful no more for their method of wringing than for their attitude toward wringing. At first, when they had been dropped through the skylight, when they saw the long sheet, when they slowly accustomed themselves to the idea of what lay before them, they were profoundly shocked. Unlike the others, they thought death preferable to such senseless and unproductive labor. But they were good people. Soon they saw beyond the apparent drudgery. Soon they had passed through and rejected the various phases experienced and retained by the other rooms. They had known the defeat of Room Four, the individual terrors and escapes of Room Two, the veneer of virtue beneath which the inhabitants of Room Three purred with such alarming satisfaction. No, it was not so very long before these good people saw beyond the apparent and thenceforth set themselves to work with body and soul, gently but with strength, humbly yet fearlessly, towards the only end of value —freedom.

First, these people said "Unproductive? The long sheet of senseless drudgery? Yes—but why not? In whatever other sphere of labor could we ever have produced ultimately anything? It is not the production that counts, but the life lived in the spirit during production. Production, the tightening of the muscles, the weaving of the hands, the pouring forth of shaped materials—this is only an employment for the nervous body, the dying legacy of the hunter's will to movement. Let the hands weave, but at the same time let the spirit search. Give the long sheet its rightful place—and concentrate on a better understanding of the freedom that is our real object."

At the same time, they saw to it that the sheet was wrung efficiently. They arranged a successful rota system. They tried various methods and positions with their hands. Examining every detail, they selected in every way the best approach. They did not overtax themselves. They did not hurry themselves. They worked with a rhythmic resilience, conserving this energy for the exertion of that. They allowed no extremes. They applied themselves with sincerity and a good will.

Above all they had faith. Their attitude was broad—but led in one direction. Their endeavor was freedom. They feared neither work

nor weakness. These things did not exist for them; their existence was a material through which they could achieve, by calm and sensitive understanding, the goal of perfect freedom.

Gradually these people achieved their end. In spite of the steam, in spite of the saturated birds, in spite of the vaporous contagion seeping through from the room of the defeated, in spite of the long hours and the heat and the squared horizon of rusting steel—their spirit prevailed and they achieved the purity they sought. One day, seven years later, the wet gray sheet dawned a bright white—dry as desert ivory, dry as marble dust.

They called up through the skylight to the warders. The grave faces appeared. Coldly the warders regarded the white sheet. There were nods of approbation.

"Freedom?" said the captives.

The guards brought out their great hoses and doused the white sheet sodden gray with a huge pressure of water.

"You already have it," they answered. "Freedom lies in an attitude of the spirit. There is no other freedom." And the skylights silently closed.

I
THE NIGHTMARE OF LIFE

What makes a story such as this one remain so vividly in the reader's mind and imagination? Few people who read it ever forget it. First there is the bizarre situation of the cubicles with the long sheet and the task set each group. The reader is horrified by the devilish ingenuity of the situation. Next the story shows how each set of people goes to work. Somewhere among the groups, most readers find their own work habits detailed, so that they have a shuddering kind of identity with the prisoners. But the ending comes with such unexpected suddenness and with such diabolical results that the reader's thought processes are shaken. If the people in the room had gained their physical freedom, the story would have been a nice, little moral tale. But the ending is a worrisome one, sending the reader into endless speculations about the author's meaning.

The prisoners are placed in four rooms . . . each set represents a different mind-set and attitude. Just what is Sansom criticizing in each group? What people in the American scene do you feel belong in each one of the particular categories? What is the intent of the titles for the rooms?

Room Three—Those Who Sought Outside.
Room Two—Those who Sought In and Out and Around.
Room Four—Those Who Never Sought at All.
Room One—Those Who Sought Inside.

II
IMPLICATIONS

What is your opinion of the following statements?

1. The people who are seeking security, who are always looking after their own privileges, are the most to be pitied, for they are confined by their own weaknesses.

2. Freedom means different things to different people.

3. The organization of society is cruel, and real freedom is only for those in control.

4. Most people live and die in cubicles of their own making, spending their lives doing things just as senseless as the wringing out of the sheet.

5. Freedom of mind and spirit is the only real freedom.

III
TECHNIQUES

Author's Purpose

What was Sansom's purpose in this story? Decide what you think he was criticizing or ridiculing? Try to find elements in the story to support your idea. Consider the following interpretations. How close do they come to your interpretation?

1. The warders represent the supreme authority . . . God; the cubicle is the world; the people represent the different segments of society.

2. The warders represent the business leaders; the people are the workers in the cubicles; the cubicles are the classes of society.

3. The people in each cubicle are there through their own attitudes and abilities; the cubicle is devised in their own minds; the task is representa-tive of the useless jobs we are forced to perform in life; the warders are our natures, which complicate the task.

Irony

This is a telling example of bitter dramatic irony. It comes so suddenly, so unexpectedly that the reader is caught by surprise. What would have been the effect if the tale had ended with the people in Room One gaining their freedom?

IV
WORDS

A. Use these words to begin your context clue and dictionary study.

1. From "A Modest Proposal": *sustenance, raiment, ragout, scrupulous, digress, curate.*

2. From "Quality": *prototype, incarnate, integument.*

3. From "Life of Ma Parker": *tomes.*

4. From "The Long Sheet": *furtive, lascivious, veneer, approbation.*

B. In "A Modest Proposal" what do you understand by the following: *Barbadoes, Formosa, Mandarin?*

What does Galsworthy mean by saying, "Nemesis fell"?

ÉMILE ZOLA

Émile Zola (1840–1902) wrote with blunt realism, portraying the seamy side of life, which shocked but intrigued his readers, who were used to romantic tales.
Zola was born in Paris, but the family soon moved to the town of Aix-en-Provence, and here his father died when Zola was only eight. The family's sole inheritance seems to have been a lawsuit against the municipality of Aix. Returning to Paris when he was eighteen, Zola attended the Lycée de Paris for two years. After working as a clerk in a publishing house and writing in his spare time, he gave up his job in order to write full time. In 1867 he launched an ambitious project that was to take him twenty-two years to complete: a history of the Rougon-Marquart family, tracing the descendants of a mentally ill woman through the different levels of society. His characters are helpless victims of their heredity and environment, unable to break away from their tragic fates. Vivid description and swift-paced style made the books popular with the public, who did not seem to mind the brutality and ugliness deplored by critics. In 1898 a certain Captain Dreyfus of the French Army was accused of selling military secrets to Germany.
He was convicted and immediately shipped off to the penal colony on Devil's Island. After studying the case, Zola became convinced that Dreyfus had been the victim of a conspiracy by guilty army officials. He promptly wrote a letter which began, "I accuse." This letter, published in a newspaper, set forth his views on the case. The result was a suit for libel against Zola by the accused army officials.
Zola was found guilty and immediately appealed the case. But the trial had the desired effect: the details of the Dreyfus case were brought to light.
The French people demanded a retrial for Dreyfus. In the second trial, Captain Dreyfus was found innocent. Three years later Zola died. He had just finished writing a novel, *Vérité*, which centered on the Dreyfus trial, and he was preparing to write a sequel. The French Government honored Zola by giving him a public funeral.

The Attack on the Mill

I

There was a great merry-making at old Merlier's mill that beautiful summer evening—three tables had been placed in the yard end to end, for the use of the guests who were expected. All the country round knew that the Merlier girl, Françoise,[1] was that day to be betrothed to Dominique,[2]—a lad who they said was somewhat lazy, but whom all the women for miles about used to gaze at with glistening eyes,—so good-looking he was.

Old Merlier's mill was a delightful place. It stood right in the middle of Rocreuse,[3] just where the high-road makes an elbow. The village has only one street—two rows of buildings, one row on each side of the road;—but there at the turn, the meadows widen, and the tall

1. **Françoise** (frän swäz′).
2. **Dominique** (dom′i nēk′).
3. **Rocreuse** (rō kruz′).

583

*Émile Zola at his desk,
portrait by Edouard Manet.*

trees that follow the course of the Morelle[4] cover the further end of the valley with magnificent shade. There is not a more beautiful spot in all Lorraine.[5] To right and left deep woods, century-old trees ascend the gentle slopes, filling the horizon with a sea of green; while southward extends the marvellous fertile plain, unfolding to the infinite its surface of lands and fields enclosed by hedges. But the peculiar charm of Rocreuse is the coolness of that green hollow even in the hottest days of July and August. The Morelle descends from the Gagny[6] woods; and it really seems to bear along with it the coolness of the foliage under which it flows for many miles; it carries with it the murmuring noises, the frigid and dreamy shadows of the forest. Nor is the river the only source of coolness. All kinds of running waters sing under the trees; at almost every step

springs gush up. Following some narrow pathway, you feel as though there were subterranean lakes under your feet, breaking up through the moss, and finding the smallest fissures at the foot of a tree, or the least crevice between the rocks, before they burst out in crystal fountains. So numerous and so loud are the whispering voices of all these springs, that they drown the songs of the bullfinches. You could imagine yourself in some enchanted park, with cascades falling upon every side.

Below, the fields are soaked. Gigantic chestnut trees make black shadows. Bordering the meadows, long curtains of poplar trees display their rustling hangings in line. There are two lanes of enormous plane trees which ascend, across fields, to the old ruined château[7] of Gagny. In that continually watered soil the grasses and herbs grow thickly. It is like a garden,—a flower-bed between two planted mounds,—but a natural flower-garden in which the meadows are the lawns, and the giant trees take the place of ornamental shrubs. When the sun falls perpendicularly at noon, the shadows become blueish; the lighted plants slumber in the heat, while trembling breaths of cold air pass under the foliage.

And here it was that old Merlier's mill used to make its lively *tic-tac* sound in that spot of wildly beautiful nature. The building itself, made of plaster and planks, seemed old as the world. It was half steeped in the Morelle, which rounds out at that point into a clear basin. A dam had been contrived, and the water fell from the height of a few yards upon the mill-wheel, which crackled as it turned with the asthmatic cough of a faithful servant-woman grown old in the house. When folks advised old Merlier to replace it, he used to shake his head and declare that a young wheel would be lazy and would not understand the works so well; and he would continue to mend the old

4. **Morelle**, a river.
5. **Lorraine** (lə rān′), a Rhineland region of Europe contested by France and Germany.
6. **Gagny** (gän′yē), east of Paris.
7. **château** (sha tō′), castle.

one with whatever came to hand,—barrel staves, rusty iron, zinc, or lead. The wheel looked all the merrier, with its profile thus made strange, and bedecked with weeds and mosses. When the water whipped it with silver waves, it covered itself with pearls;—its strange carcass turned beneath a dazzling array of mother-of-pearl necklaces.

The portion of the mill that dipped down into the river, looked like a barbaric ark that had been grounded there. One-half of the building, at least, was built upon piles. The water flowed under the flooring, and there were holes, famous in that part of the country by reason of the enormous eels and crawfish that were caught in them. Below the fall the water was clear as a mirror; and when it was not disturbed by the foam of the wheel, shoals of big fish could be seen swimming about, slowly as sailing squadrons. A broken stairway descended to the river, near a stake to which a boat was fastened. There was a wooden gallery above the wheel. Irregularly placed windows pierced the walls. It was all one jumble of angles, little walls, afterthought construction, beams and gables, which gave the mill the look of an old dismantled citadel. But ivy had grown, and all sorts of climbing plants had closed up the larger cracks and gaps, and had flung a green mantle over the old building. The young ladies who passed that way used to make sketches of old Merlier's mill for their albums.

On the side by the road the house was more solid. A stone gate opened into the great yard, flanked on the right and left by sheds and stables. Near the well, there was an immense elm which covered half the yard with its shadow. In the background the house displayed the four windows of its second story, topped by a dovecot. Father Merlier's only outward show consisted in having this facade whitewashed once every ten years. It had only just been whitewashed; and at midday, when the sun shone fully upon it, it dazzled the village.

Old father Merlier had been Mayor of Rocreuse for twenty years. He was esteemed for the fortune which he had been shrewd enough to gather. He was popularly believed to be worth about eighty thousand francs, scraped together sou by sou. When he had married Madeleine Guillard, who brought him the mill for her dowry, he had nothing in the world except his two arms. Now, his wife was dead; he remained a widower, and lived all alone with his daughter Françoise. No doubt he might have taken a rest at last, and have allowed the old millwheel to slumber in its moss; but then he would have felt wearily lonesome, and the house would have seemed dead. So he kept on working still, just for the pleasure of it. Father Merlier was then a tall old man, with a long taciturn face,—a man who never laughed, but who was at bottom really a jolly fellow. He had been chosen for Mayor partly on account of his money, and partly on account of the fine appearance he knew how to make when performing a marriage ceremony.

Françoise Merlier was just eighteen. She was slight, and not considered one of the handsomest girls in the country. Until the age of fifteen she had even been ugly. Nobody at Rocreuse could understand how it was that the daughter of "father" Merlier and "mother" Merlier, both so well-to-do, grew up so scrawny and with such a sad face. But at fifteen, although remaining delicate, she suddenly bloomed out with the prettiest little face in the world. She had black hair and black eyes and a bright, rosy complexion;—her little mouth was always smiling; she had dimples in her cheeks, and a clear forehead that seemed to be wreathed with sunlight. Although weakly compared with other girls in that part of the country, she was not thin,—far from it: in calling her weakly people only meant to say that she could not lift a sack of wheat. She had become quite dimpled in her teens, and finally grew round and dainty as a quail. Still, her father's long spells of silence had made her thoughtful while yet very young. If she laughed constantly, it was only to please other people: at heart she was a very serious girl.

Of course the whole country courted her, even more for her money than her pleasing ways. And she had ended by making a choice which scandalized everybody. On the other side of the Morelle lived a tall lad called Dominique Penquer. He was not from Ro-creuse. Ten years previously he had arrived from Belgium, as the heir of an uncle who owned a little property on the borders of the forest of Gagny, just opposite the mill, only a few rifle-shots' distance off. He then said that he had just come to sell that property, and then intended to return home. But it seemed that the country charmed him; for he never left it. He was seen cultivating his little field, harvesting his little crop of vegetables, on which he lived. He fished, he hunted; several times the guards were on the point of arresting him, and institu-ting proceedings against him. So free a way of living, the resources whereof the country people could not very well understand, finally earned him a bad reputation. He was suspected, in a vague sort of way, of being a poacher. At all events he was lazy; for he was often seen lying in the grass asleep, when he ought to have been working. The building he lived in, and the last trees of the forest, did not look at all like the dwelling place of an honest man. If he had been found to have weird relations with the wolves of the ruins of Gagny, the old gossips would not have been a bit surprised. Nevertheless the young girls ventured to take his part some-times; for he was really superb—the great sinis-ter fellow, supple and tall like a poplar, and very white-skinned, with a light beard and hair that looked like gold in the sun. Now, one fine morning, Françoise had told her father that she loved Dominique, and that she would never consent to marry any other lad.

One may well imagine what a blow that was to old Merlier! He said nothing, according to his custom. His face remained as thoughtful as usual; but that interior good humor of his no longer shone in his eyes. Father and daughter pouted at each other for a whole week. Fran-çoise also became quite grave. What worried old Merlier most of all was how that rascal of a poacher could have managed to bewitch his daughter. Dominique had never come to the mill. The miller set himself to watch; and at last he saw the young man, on the other side of the Morelle, lying in the grass, and pretending to sleep. Françoise could see him from her room. The thing was clear enough now; they had fallen in love by dint of making eyes at each other over the mill-wheel.

Meanwhile eight days more rolled by. Fran-çoise became graver and graver. Still father Merlier said nothing. At last one evening, with-out a word, he brought Dominique to the mill himself. Françoise was just setting the table. She did not appear at all surprised, and simply laid another knife, fork and plate on the table; but the little dimples in her cheeks showed themselves again; and her laugh was heard once more. Father Merlier had been that morning to Dominique's tumble-down house on the edge of the woods. The two men had talked there for more than three hours, with closed doors and windows. No one ever learned what they said to each other. But it was certain that when father Merlier was leaving, he had already begun to treat Dominique like a son. No doubt the old man had found the lad he went to see a really fine fellow, instead of a mere idler hiding in the grass to make love to the girls.

All Rocreuse was in uproar at the news. The women, standing in the doors, could not stop talking about the craziness of father Merlier in introducing a scamp into his house. Merlier let them say all they pleased. Perhaps he remem-bered his own marriage. Neither did he have a sou when he married Madeleine and her mill; but that had not prevented him from being a good husband. Besides Dominique put a stop to all the gossip, by going so heartily to work that the whole country wondered at him. It so happened that the miller's hired lad had been drafted into the army, and Dominique would not have them hire another in his place. He carried in the sacks himself, drove the cart, fought with the old wheel when she needed coaxing to make her turn—and all this with such good will that folks came to look at him working, just for the pleasure of the thing. Father Merlier laughed with his own silent laugh. He felt quite proud to have discovered the character of the lad. There is nothing like love for giving courage to young folks.

And in the midst of all this hard work, Françoise and Dominique were worshiping each other. They never spoke; but they gazed at one another with smiling tenderness. So far, old Merlier had never so much as hinted at the subject of marriage; and both, respecting this silence, patiently awaited the old man's pleasure. At last, one day, about the middle of July, he had their table set in the middle of the yard, under the big elm tree, and sent an invitation to all his friends in Rocreuse to drop in that evening and have a glass of wine with him. When the yard was thronged, and everybody's glass was ready, old Merlier lifted his own very high, and said:—

" . . . . I have the pleasure of announcing to you that Françoise will be married to this good fellow here, in a month from to-day,—on the feast of Saint Louis."

Then all clinked their glasses together, noisily. Everybody laughed. But father Merlier, raising his voice, continued:—

"Dominique, kiss your fiancée! Must be done!"

And they kissed each other, both turning very red, while everybody laughed louder than before. It was quite a merry time. A little cask was emptied. Then, when all except intimate friends were gone, there was a quiet little chat. Night came—a starry and very clear night. Dominique and Françoise, sitting upon a bench beside one another, said nothing. An old peasant talked about war having been declared by the Emperor against Prussia. All the village lads were gone already. Troops had passed by only the evening before. There was going to be some hard fighting.

"Bah!" cried old Merlier, with the egotism of a happy man, "Dominique is a stranger; he will not have to go. And then if the Prussians come, he will be here to defend his wife."

The idea that the Prussians could possibly come seemed an immense joke. The Prussians! They were going to get a good licking, and in short order.

"I've seen them already! I've seen them already!" repeated the old peasant in his hollow voice.

There was silence for a time. Then glasses were touched once more. Françoise and Dominique had heard nothing; they had taken each other's hand gently, behind the bench where nobody could see them; and that seemed to them so nice that they remained there dreaming, with eyes fixed upon the dark sky.

What a splendid, lukewarm night it was! The village, on either side of the white road, slumbered with childlike tranquillity. Afar off no sound could be heard except the occasional crowing of a cock that had awakened too soon. From the great neighboring woods came long breaths of wind at intervals, passing over the roofs like caresses. The meadows, with their black shadows, assumed a majestic and solemn look; while all the springs, all the running waters that gushed up in the darkness, seemed like the cool and rhythmic breathing of the slumbering country. From time to time the old mill-wheel, dozing, seemed to dream like those old hunting dogs which bark in their sleep; it made crackling noises, talking to itself, rocked by the fall of the Morelle, whose smooth surface gave out a sound musical and sustained as that of organ-pipes. Never did a deeper peace rest upon a spot more blessed by nature.

II

Just a month later, on the eve of the feast-day of Saint Louis, Rocreuse was terror-stricken. The Prussians had beaten the Emperor, and were advancing by forced marches upon the village. For more than a week people passing by along the road had been announcing the coming of the Prussians: "They are at Lormiere!" . . . . . "They are at Novelles,"—and hearing of the rapidity of their coming, the Rocreuse folks expected every morning to see the Prussians descending from the Gagny woods. Still they did not come. This frightened the people still more. They were certainly going to fall upon the village in the middle of the night and murder everybody.

The night before, a little before daybreak, there had been an alarm. The inhabitants had been awakened by a great noise of men marching along the road. The women had already fallen upon their knees and were making the sign of the cross, when somebody peeping cautiously through a closed window-shutter, had recognized the red trousers. It was a French detachment. The captain had at once asked for the Mayor of the village, and had remained in the mill, after a chat with old Merlier.

The sun rose gayly that morning. It would be hot at noon. A blond brightness glowed above the woods; while, below, above the meadows, white mists arose. The scrubbed and pretty village awoke in the coolness; and the country, with its rivers and springs, had the moist loveliness of a bouquet of flowers. But no one smiled at the beauty of the day. The captain was seen to walk round and round the mill, inspect the neighboring houses, cross to the other side of the river and study the country with a field-glass;—father Merlier, who accompanied him, appeared to be giving him explanations. Then the captain had posted soldiers behind walls, behind trees, and in hollows. The body of the detachment camped in the mill-yard. So there was going to be fighting? And when Merlier came back, he was questioned. He gave a long nod, without speaking. Yes, there was going to be a fight.

Françoise and Dominique were then in the yard, watching him. At last he took his pipe out of his mouth, and uttered the simple words:

"Ah, my poor children, I cannot marry you tomorrow."

Dominique, with compressed lips, and a wrinkle of anger upon his forehead, raised himself upon his toes once in awhile to fix his eyes upon the Gagny woods, as if he wanted to see the Prussians coming. Françoise, very pale and serious, went and came, furnishing the soldiers whatever they needed. They made soup in a corner of the yard, and cracked jokes while the meal was being prepared.

Meanwhile the captain appeared to be delighted. He had visited the rooms, and the great hall of the mill which looked out upon the river. Now he was sitting by the well, talking with father Merlier:

"Why, this is a regular fortress," he said. "We can hold our own until evening. . . . The bandits are late. They ought to have been here already."

The miller remained grave. He imagined that he could see his mill flaming like a torch. But he uttered no word of complaint, judging that to be useless. He opened his lips only to reply:—

"You ought to make them hide the boat behind the mill-wheel. There is a little hole there it fits into. Perhaps it might be of use" . . . .

The captain gave an order. This captain was a handsome man of forty, tall, with a kindly face. The sight of Françoise and Dominique together seemed to delight him. He interested himself in them, as if he had forgotten all about the coming fight. He followed Françoise with his eyes; and his manner plainly showed that he thought her charming. Then turning to Dominique he asked brusquely:—

"So you are not in the army, my lad?"

"I am a stranger," answered the young man.

The captain seemed to think very poorly of this apology. He winked his eyes and smiled. Françoise was pleasanter company than a cannon. Thus seeing him smile, Dominique added:—

"I am a stranger; but I can hit an apple at five hundred meters. . . . . . See, there is my hunting rifle behind you."

"You can find use for it," replied the captain simply.

Françoise had drawn near; and Dominique, regardless of all present, took and pressed her hands within his own, as if putting herself under his protection. The captain had smiled again; but he did not utter a word. He remained seated, with his sword between his legs, —his eyes vaguely fixed as if dreaming.

It was already 10 o'clock. The heat was intense. A heavy silence fell upon the place. Under the shadow of the sheds in the yard the soldiers began to eat their soup. No sound came from the village, whose inhabitants had barricaded their houses, doors and windows. One dog, left alone in the street, howled dismally. From the woods and the meadows, wilting under the heat, came a distant and prolonged murmur, made up of all kinds of sounds. A cuckoo sang. Then the silence became vaster.

And suddenly, on the slumbering air, burst the report of a rifle. The captain leaped to his feet; the soldiers abandoned their plates of soup only half emptied. Within a few seconds all were at their posts of combat; the mill was manned from top to bottom. Meanwhile the captain who had directed his telescope along the road, had seen nothing; the road stretched away to right and left, desolate and very white. A second shot rang out,—and still there was nothing,—not even a shadow. But turning the other way, the captain perceived, on the Gagny side, between two trees, a light fleck of smoke rising up, like a piece of transparent cloth. The wood otherwise seemed deep and sweet as usual.

"The rascals have taken to the forest," he said. "They know we are here."

Then the fusillade continued, and became hotter and hotter,—between the French soldiers stationed all about the mill, and the Prussian soldiers hiding behind the trees. The bullets whistled over the Morelle without causing any loss on either side. The shooting was irregular; every bush sent forth its flash, and still nothing could be seen except the thin wreaths of smoke, softly swaying in the wind. So it went on for nearly two hours. The captain hummed a tune; carelessly Françoise and Dominique, who had remained in the yard, got up from time to time, to peep over the low wall. They were very much interested in a little soldier posted on the bank on the Morelle, behind the carcass of an old boat. He was lying flat upon his belly, watching, shooting from time to time; after each shot he would slide back into a ditch just behind him, to reload; and his movements were so funny, so cunning, and so supple, that one could not help smiling at him. He must

have seen some Prussian at last, for he suddenly rose to his feet and took aim; but before he could fire, he uttered a cry, turned round once, and rolled into the ditch, where his legs quivered for a moment with rigid convulsions like the legs of a chicken after being killed. The little soldier had just received a bullet in the chest. He was the first dead. Françoise instinctively seized Dominique's hand, and pressed it with a nervous squeeze.

"Don't stay there!" cried the captain: "the shots are coming this way."

And in fact a little sharp thud was heard in the old elm; and the end of a broken branch fell down, swinging by a shred. But the two young people did not move, nailed to the spot by the excitement of the spectacle. At the edge of the wood a Prussian had suddenly emerged, as if from a piece of stage scenery, beating the air with his hands, and at last falling back. And nothing moved. The two dead men seemed to be sleeping under the great sun; not a soul was visible in all the slumbering country. The very crackling of the fusillade ceased. Only the Morelle was now heard, with its clear murmur.

Merlier looked at the captain with an air of surprise, as if to ask him whether it was all over.

"Now comes the heavy attack," muttered the captain. "Take care! don't stay there!"

He had scarcely spoken when a frightful volley was discharged. The great elm was almost cut down;—a shower of leaves fell whirling. Luckily the Prussians had fired a little too high. Dominique dragged, almost carried Françoise away; while father Merlier followed them, crying:

"Go into the little cellar; the walls are solid!"

But they did not listen to him; they entered the great hall where a dozen soldiers were waiting in silence behind the closed shutters, watching through the chinks. The captain alone remained in the yard, crouching behind the low wall, while the furious volleys continued. The soldiers he had stationed outside, yielded the ground foot by foot. Still one after the other, they came in, crawling on all fours, when the enemy dislodged them from their hiding places. Their orders were to gain time, and not to show themselves, so that the Prussians should not know how large a force they had to deal with. Another hour passed. And when a sergeant came in at last, stating there were only two or three men still out, the officer pulled out his watch, muttering:

"Half-past two. . . . Come! we must hold out four hours."

He ordered the great yard gate to be closed; and all was made ready for a vigorous resistance. As the Prussians were upon the other side of the Morelle, there was no fear of an immediate assault. There was indeed a bridge about two kilometers off; but the Prussians had probably no suspicion of its existence, and it was not at all likely that they would attempt to ford the river. So the officer simply stationed sentinels to watch the road. All the defense was concentrated upon the country side of the mill.

The fusillade had stopped again. Under the sunlight the mill seemed dead. Not a shutter was opened; no sound issued from the interior. Meanwhile, little by little, the Prussians showed themselves at the edge of the Gagny woods. They strained their heads forward; grew bolder, advanced. In the mill several soldiers were already taking aim; but the captain cried:—

"No, no! Wait. . . . Let them come nearer!"

They advanced very cautiously, watching the mill with a suspicious air. The silent, dismal old building, with its curtains of ivy, inspired them with uneasiness. Nevertheless they approached. When about fifty had reached the meadow in front, the French captain uttered the simple phrase:

"Let go!"

A rending crash was heard: a rattling fire of isolated shots followed. Françoise, trembling from head to foot, had instinctively lifted her hands to her ears;—Dominique peeped out behind the soldiers; and when the smoke had partly cleared away, he saw three Prussians lying on their backs in the middle of the meadow.

The others had flung themselves behind the willows and poplars. And the siege began.

For more than an hour the mill was riddled with bullets. They whipped the old walls like a tempest of hail. They could be heard flattening when they struck the stones, and falling back in the water. They buried themselves in the woodwork with a hollow thud. From time to time a loud crack told that the mill-wheel had received a shot. The soldiers inside were now sparing of their shots; they only fired when it was possible to take aim. From time to time the captain looked at his watch. And as a bullet splintered its way through a shutter and plunged into the ceiling, he muttered—

"Four o'clock. We shall never be able to hold out!"

And little by little, that terrible fusillade began to shake the old mill. One shutter fell into the water, as full of holes as a piece of lace; and it had to be replaced by a mattress. Old Merlier risked his life almost every moment in order to make an estimate of the damage done to his poor wheel, whose every crack went to his heart. Ah! the wheel was well done for, this time; he could never mend it again. Dominique had begged Françoise to retire: but she wished to remain with him; she was sitting behind a great oaken chest which sheltered her. But a bullet entered the chest, making its sides utter a deep sound. Then Dominique placed himself in front of Françoise. He had not yet fired a shot; he held his rifle in his hand, not being able to approach the windows whose whole breadth was occupied by the soldiers. At every volley, the whole floor shook.

"Look out! attention there!" suddenly shouted the captain.

He had just seen a great dark mass issue from the woods. At the same moment an awful platoon firing began. It was as if a storm had burst over the house. Another shutter was carried away; and the bullets came in through the yawning hole. Two soldiers rolled upon the floor. One remained motionless; he was pushed against the wall because he was in the way. The other writhed, begging them to kill him;

but no one listened to him, the bullets were showering in, every one was looking out for himself and trying to find some loophole to return the fire through. A third soldier was wounded—this one uttered no sound, he let himself fall over the edge of a table, his eyes wild and fixed. Face to face with these three dead, Françoise, seized with horror, had mechanically pushed away her chair to sit down upon the floor, against the wall; she thought she would be a smaller mark there, and less in danger. Meanwhile they had taken all the mattresses in the house, and had half plugged the window with them. The room began to fill with rubbish, broken weapons, wrecked furniture.

"Five o'clock!" said the captain. "Hold out! . . . . They are going to try to cross the water."

Just then Françoise uttered a cry. A bullet, ricocheting, had grazed her forehead. Some drops of blood appeared. Dominique looked at her for a moment; then approaching the window, he fired his first shot, and thereafter never ceased. He loaded and fired, taking no heed of anything going on around him, only that from time to time, he glanced at Françoise. Furthermore, he never hurried himself, and took careful aim. The Prussians following the line of poplar-trees, tried to cross the Morelle at last, as the captain had predicted; but, as soon as the first of them showed himself, he fell dead, shot through the head by Dominique. The captain who watched this sharpshooting, was astonished. He complimented the young man,—telling him that he would think himself lucky to have a number of sharpshooters equally skillful. Dominique did not hear him. A bullet touched his shoulder; another bruised his arm. And he kept on firing.

Two more fell dead. The mattresses torn to atoms could no longer stop up the windows. A last heavy volley seemed to tear the mill away. The place was no longer tenable. But the officer repeated:—

"Hold out!—Half an hour more."

Now he began to count the time by minutes. He had promised his superior officers that he would keep the enemy in check until evening;

and he would not retreat the length of a shoe-sole before the hour he had fixed. He retained his amiable manner; smiled at Françoise in order to reassure her. He had taken up the rifle of a dead soldier, and was firing also.

There were now only four soldiers in the room. The Prussians showed themselves in heavy force upon the other side of the river, and it was evident they might pass the river at any moment. Several minutes passed. The captain remained obstinate; he would not give the order to retreat. A sergeant rushed in, saying:

"They are on the road!—they are going to attack us from the rear!"

The Prussians must have found the bridge. The captain pulled out his watch.

"Five minutes more," he replied. "They cannot get here in less than five minutes."

Then at 6 o'clock, precisely, he at last consented to withdraw his men, by a little door which opened into an alley. They threw themselves into a ditch, and following its bed, gained the Sauval[8] forest. The captain had saluted old Merlier very politely before leaving, with excuses. And he had even added:—

"Amuse them! . . . . We shall come back."

Meanwhile Dominique had remained alone in the hall. He was still firing, hearing nothing, understanding nothing. He only felt the furious desire to defend Françoise. The soldiers were going, and he had not the least suspicion of it. He kept on, taking aim, and killing his man at every shot. Suddenly, there was a great noise. The Prussians, advancing from the rear, had just entered the mill-yard. He fired once more, and they rushed upon him while his rifle was still smoking.

Four men seized him. Others shouted around him in some frightful language. They were on the point of killing him then and there. Françoise threw herself before them, begging them. But an officer entered, and ordered the prisoner to be brought to him. After exchanging a few words in German with the soldiers, he

---

8. **Sauval** (sō′väl).

turned to Dominique, and said to him roughly, but in very good French:

"You shall be shot within two hours."

III

It was a rule laid down by the staff of the German army that every Frenchman not belonging to the regular army, and captured with weapons in his possession, should be shot. The volunteer companies themselves were not recognized as belligerents. By making a few terrible examples among the peasantry who sought to defend their homes, the Germans hoped to prevent a general uprising, which they feared. The officer, a tall, bony man, about fifty years old, subjected Dominique to a brief questioning. Although he spoke French with great purity, he had all the German stiffness of manners.

"You are a native of this country?"

"No; I am a Belgian."

"Why did you take up arms? All this ought not to concern you?"

Dominique did not answer. At that moment the officer noticed Françoise standing by, very pale, listening; her slight wound made a red stripe on her white forehead. He looked at each of the young people in turn, seemed to understand, and contented himself with adding:

"You do not deny that you fired?"

"I fired just as much as I could," tranquilly answered Dominique.

This statement was unnecessary, for he was black with powder, covered with sweat, and spotted with the drops of blood which had flowed from the wound in his shoulder, grazed by a bullet.

"Very well," repeated the officer. "You shall be shot in two hours."

Françoise uttered no cry. She clasped her hands and lifted them in a gesture of dumb despair. The officer observed the gesture. Two soldiers had led Dominique into a neighboring room, where they had orders to keep him constantly under their eyes. The young girl had let herself fall upon a chair, her limbs were yielding under her; she could not weep, she was smothering with emotion. Meanwhile the officer continued to watch her. Finally he spoke to her:—

"Is that lad your brother?" he asked.

She answered no by a movement of her head. He remained as stiff as ever, without a smile. Then, after a brief silence, he continued:

"He has lived in this part of the country a long time?"

She answered yes, by another sign.

"Then he must be very well acquainted with the neighboring woods?"

This time she spoke.

"Yes, sir," she replied, looking at him with some surprise.

He said nothing further, and simply turned upon his heel ordering them to bring the Mayor of the village to him. But Françoise had arisen, with a slight flush upon her face—fancying she understood the purpose of his questions, and feeling a return of hope. She ran to find her father.

Just as soon as the firing was over, old Merlier had hurriedly descended by way of the wooden gallery to look at his wheel. He adored his daughter; he had the most solid friendship for Dominique, his future-son-in-law; but his wheel also occupied a large place in his heart. Since the "little ones" as he called them had got out of the mess safe and sound, he could now devote himself to this other affection, which had suffered considerably, indeed. And leaning over the great wooden carcass he studied the nature of its wounds with a heart-broken look on his face. Five paddle-boards had been knocked into smithereens; the central framework was riddled. He poked his fingers into the bullet-holes to find how deep they were; he tried to imagine how all these damages could be repaired. Françoise found him already engaged in plugging up chinks with rubbish and moss.

"Father," she said, "they want you!"

And she burst out crying at last as she told him what she had just heard. Old Merlier shook his head. They could not shoot people like that! He must see about it. And he re-entered the mill with his customary silent and peaceful expression. When the officer demanded provisions for the men, he replied that the folks of Rocreuse were not accustomed to brutal treatment, and that nothing could be obtained from them if violence was used. He would take everything upon himself; but only on condition that he was allowed to act without the least interference. At first the officer seemed provoked by this cool manner of speech; but finally he yielded to the sharp, brief offers of the old man. He even called him back, to ask:—

"What is the name of those woods opposite?"

"The Sauval woods."

"And how far do they extend?"

The miller looked fixedly at him.

"I do not know," he replied.

And he departed. An hour later the war contribution of provisions and money demanded by the officer was in the mill-yard. Night approached. Françoise anxiously watched the movements of the soldiers. She remained near the door of the room in which Dominique was confined. About 7 o'clock she saw the officer enter the prisoner's room; and for a quarter of an hour she could hear their voices, rising higher as they talked. Then the officer re-appeared at the threshold for a moment, to give an order in German, which she did not understand; but when twelve men took their places in line in the yard, with their rifles, a trembling seized her; she felt as though she were about to die. All hope was over, then: the execution was going to take place. The twelve men stood there for about ten minutes; the voice of Dominique continued to grow louder, as in a tone of violent refusal. Finally the officer came out, slamming the door brutally after him, with the words:

"Very well, think over it. . . . . . I will give you until to-morrow morning."

And with a wave of his hand he bade the twelve men break ranks. Françoise remained in stupefaction. Old Merlier who had continued to smoke his pipe, and had been watching the platoon with an air of simple curiosity, now advanced to take her by the arm, with paternal gentleness. He led her to her room.

"Keep yourself quiet," he said;—"try to sleep. It will be daylight to-morrow, and we shall see."

As he went to bed, he looked in on her by way of precaution. It was a principle with him that women were good for nothing, and always spoiled everything when they meddled in important business. Meanwhile Françoise did not lie down. She remained a long time seated upon her bed, listening to all the noises in the house. The German soldiers, camping in the yard, sang and laughed; they must have continued eating and drinking until 11 o'clock, for the noise never ceased even for an instant. Even in the mill itself, heavy steps could be heard from time to time; they were relieving the sentries no doubt. But the noises which she could hear in the room immediately below her own, interested her most of all. Several times she lay down upon the floor, and pressed her ear over the chinks in the planking. The room below was the very room in which Dominique was confined. He must have been walking backward and forward between the wall and the window; for she could hear the regular cadence of his steps for a long time; then a great silence came—he must have sat down. Moreover all the other noises ceased; everybody was sleeping. When the whole house seemed to have sunk into a heavy slumber, she opened her window as gently as possible and leaned over the sill. Outside the night was serene and warm. The thin crescent of the moon, sinking behind the Sauval woods, illuminated the country faintly, as with the gleam of a night-light. The lengthened shadows of the tall trees barred the meadows with black, while the grass on the unshaded places seemed to have the softness of green velvet. But Françoise paid little heed to the mysterious charms of the night. She was examining the country roundabout, looking for the sentries stationed along the shore by the Germans. She could see their shadows distinctly, in a line, far along the Morelle. There was only one in front of the mill, on the other side of the river, standing by a willow whose branches dipped into the water. Françoise could see him plainly. He was a tall youth, who stood motionless with face turned toward the sky, like a shepherd in revery.

Then when she had carefully inspected the neighborhood, she turned from the window, and sat down upon her bed again. Thus she remained sitting for an hour, absorbed in thought. Then she listened again:—not a breath could be heard in the house. She returned to the window and glanced out; but perhaps one of the horns of the moon which still shone behind the trees, made her uneasy, for she continued to wait. At last the hour seemed to have come. The night was perfectly black: she could not see the sentry opposite; the country stretched away like a vast pool of ink. She strained her ears to listen a moment; then decided what to do. There was, very near the window, a ladder of iron bars let into the wall, leading up from the wheel to the granary, by which the millers used to go up to visit certain parts of the machinery;—but afterward the mechanism had been modified and the ladder had long ago disappeared under the thick masses of ivy that covered this side of the building.

Françoise bravely climbed over the balustrade of her window, clutched one of the iron bars, and swung herself over the void. She began to descend. Her petticoats made it difficult. Suddenly a stone detached itself from the wall and fell into the Morelle with a loud plash. She stopped; an icy trembling seized her. But she soon reflected that the continual rumble of the waterfall must at a distance drown all the noises she could make; and she continued her descent more boldly, feeling the ivy with her feet, making sure of the iron rungs. When she got as far as the room which had been converted into a prison for Dominique, she stopped. An unforeseen difficulty almost caused her to lose all her courage. The window of the lower room was not directly below the window of her own;—it was far away from the ladder, and when she reached out her hand she felt nothing but the wall. Must she then climb back, without being able to carry out her project? Her arms were getting tired,—the murmur of the Morelle underneath began to make her dizzy. Then she broke off little bits of plaster from the wall, and threw them at Dominique's window. He did not hear:—perhaps he was asleep. She still sought for crumbs of plaster; she tore the skin of her fingers. And she felt her strength leaving her; she was on the very point of falling backward,—when Dominique opened his window, at last, gently.

"It is I," she whispered,—"thy hand!—take me, quick! I am falling."

It was the first time that she had addressed him as "thou." He caught her, leaning out, and lifted her into the room. There she had a nervous crisis of tears, trying to smother her sobs, lest they should hear her. Then, with an immense effort, she regained her calm.

"You are guarded?" she asked, in a whisper.

Dominique, still bewildered at seeing her thus, simply nodded, and pointed to the door. A sound of snoring could be heard without: the sentry, yielding to sleep, must have lain down upon the floor across the threshold, thinking that the prisoner could not move without awaking him.

"You must escape!" she said. "I have come to beg you to fly, and to bid you adieu."

But he did not seem to hear her. He repeated:—

"What! it is you! it is you . . . . Oh! how you frightened me! You might have killed yourself."

He seized her hands and kissed them.

"How I love you, Françoise! . . . You are as brave as you are good! I had only one fear. I was afraid I should die without being able to see you again. But you are here; and now they can shoot me. When I have been a quarter of an hour with you, I shall be ready."

Little by little, he had drawn her to him; and she nestled her head upon his shoulder. Danger had drawn them closer to each other. They forgot all in that embrace.

"Ah! Françoise," continued Dominique in his caressing voice;—"to-day is St. Louis' day—the longed-for day of our marriage. Nothing could separate us; we are here alone, faithful to the rendezvous. Is it not so?—this is our wedding morning."

"Yes, yes," she repeated, "our wedding morning."

They kissed each other, quivering. But suddenly she disengaged herself from his embrace; the terrible reality loomed up before her.

"You must fly! you must escape!" she stammered,—"don't lose a moment!"

And as he reached out his arms in the darkness to draw her to him again, she addressed him once more with the thee-and-thou of intimate affection:

"Oh! I pray thee, listen to me! . . . If thou diest, I shall die. In one hour more it will be day. I desire thee to fly at once."

Then she rapidly explained her plan. The iron ladder descended to the wheel; he could descend by the paddles and get into the little boat which was placed in a recess below. It would then be easy for him to get to the other side of the river and escape.

"But there must be sentries?" he said.

"Only one, opposite, at the foot of the first willow-tree."

"And if he should see me?—if he should give the alarm?"

Françoise shuddered. She slipped into his hand a knife she had brought with her. There was a silence.

"And your father?—and you?" replied Dominique. "Ah! no; I cannot fly. Perhaps when I had gone, the soldiers would massacre you all. . . . You do not know what kind of men they are. . . . They offered to pardon me, if I would agree to guide them through the Sauval forest. When they find me gone, they are capable of doing anything."

The young girl did not waste time in argument. For answer to all his reasoning she simply repeated:

"If you love me, go! . . . If you love me, Dominique, do not stay here one moment longer."

Then she promised to return to her room. They would never know that she had helped him. Finally she caught him in her arms and kissed him, in order to coax him—kissed him with a strange burst of passionate affection.

He was conquered. He only asked one question more:—

"Swear to me that your father knows what you are doing, and that he wishes me to escape."

"It was my father who sent me to you," boldly replied Françoise.

She lied. At that moment she only felt one immense desire—to know that he was in safety, to save herself from the hideous thought that the sunrise would be the signal for his death. When he should be far away, anything might happen to her,—whatever might come would seem sweet to her, so that she could only know that he lived. The egotism of her affection wanted him to live at any cost.

"Very well," returned Dominique, "I shall do as you please."

Then they ceased speaking to each other. Dominique reopened the window. But a sudden noise chilled them both. The door was shaken, and it seemed to them that it was going to be opened. Evidently some one going the rounds had heard their voices. And both stood there, pressing close to each other, in unspeakable agony. The door was again shaken; but it did not open. Both uttered a sigh of relief; it was only the soldier lying across the threshold, who had turned over in his sleep. Silence fell; and the snoring recommenced.

Dominique absolutely insisted that Françoise should first return to her room. He took her in his arms; he bade her a mute farewell. Then he aided her to seize the ladder, and clung to it himself. But he refused to descend one step until he felt assured that she was in her room. When Françoise had re-entered her chamber, she let fall, in a voice low as a breath of wind, the words:—

"*Au revoir,*—I love thee!"

She remained at the window, leaning out; she tried to follow Dominique with her eyes, and could not see him;—the willow alone made a pale spot against the darkness. For a moment she could hear Dominque's body rubbing against the ivy. Then the wheel cracked; and a light lapping sound told her that the young man had found the boat. Another moment, and she

595

could distinguish the dark silhouette of the boat against the gray surface of the Morelle. Then a terrible anguish again seized her by the throat. At every instant she fancied that she heard the alarm cry of a sentry; the least noises, scattering through the darkness, seemed the hurried tread of soldiers, the clash of arms, the sound of the cocking of rifles. Yet the minutes passed; the country preserved its sovereign peace. Dominique must have reached the other bank. Françoise could see nothing more. The silence became majestic. And she heard a trampling of feet,—a hoarse cry,—the fall of a heavy body. Then the silence became deeper than ever. And cold as though she had felt Death pass by her, she remained face to face with the thick darkness.

IV

At early dawn, an outburst of voices shook the mill. Father Merlier had opened the door for Françoise. She went down into the yard, pale and very calm. But there, she could not repress a shudder upon seeing before her the corpse of a Prussian soldier, extended upon the ground, near the well, with a cloak spread under him.

Soldiers were standing round the body, gesticulating, shouting in furious tones. Several shook their fists in the direction of the village. Meanwhile the officer had summoned old Merlier before him, as the mayor of the commune.

"See here!" he said to him, in a voice choked by anger,—"here is one of our men who was found murdered by the river-bank. . . . We must make a severe example, and I expect you to aid us in discovering the murderer."

"Whatever you wish," replied the miller, calmly. "Only it will not be very easy."

The officer had bent down to lift a corner of the cloak, which concealed the dead man's face. Then a horrible wound was seen. The sentinel had been struck in the throat, and the weapon remained in the wound. It was a kitchen knife with a black handle.

Luckily his anger prevented him from noticing the profound alteration of Françoise's face. She had been obliged to sit down upon the stone bench, near the well. In spite of herself, she could not take her eyes from that corpse, lying on the ground, almost at her feet. It was a tall and handsome lad, with fair hair and blue eyes, who resembled Dominique. The resemblance made her heart sick. She thought that the dead man might have left, far away in Germany, some sweetheart who would weep for him. And she recognized her own knife in the dead man's throat. She had killed him!

"Look at this knife," said the officer to father Merlier,—"perhaps it will aid us in our investigations."

The old man started. But he recovered himself immediately, and answered without moving a muscle of his face.

"Everybody has that kind of knives in this part of the country. . . . Perhaps your man was tired of fighting, and did the business for himself. That's plain enough!"

"Silence!" shouted the officer in fury. "I do not know what keeps me from setting fire to the four corners of the village."

Meanwhile the officer was talking of punishing Rocreuse with terrible penalties, when all of a sudden some soldiers ran up to him. The escape of Dominique had just been discovered. This caused the greatest excitement. The officer visited the spot at once, looked out of the window which had been left open, understood, and came back exasperated.

Father Merlier seemed very much annoyed by Dominique's flight.

"The imbecile!" he muttered,—"he spoils everything."

Françoise, who heard him, was seized with anguish. Her father, indeed, never suspected that she had helped Dominique. He shook his head, saying to her in an under tone:

"Now we are in a nice fix!"

"It was that rascal! it was that rascal!" shouted the officer. "He must have got to the woods. . . . But he must be caught for us, or the whole village shall pay for him!"

And, suddenly turning to the miller:

"Here! you must know where he is hiding."

Old Merlier laughed with his silent laugh, pointing to the vast stretch of wooded slopes beyond.

"How could you find a man there?" he asked.

"Oh! there are hollows enough that you know. I will give you ten men. You shall lead them."

"I am perfectly willing, only it will take us at least eight days to scour all the woods in the neighborhood."

The old man's coolness enraged the officer. He saw, in fact, how ridiculous the idea of such a search was. Just then he noticed Françoise seated upon the bench, pale and trembling. The anxious look of the young girl impressed him. He remained silent a moment, examining Françoise and the miller by turns. At last he asked the old man, brutally—

"Is not that fellow your daughter's lover?"

Old Merlier became livid: one would have thought him about to leap at the officer's throat to strangle him. He stiffened himself;—he gave no answer. Françoise hid her face with her hands.

"Yes, that is just it!" continued the Prussian. "Either you or your daughter aided him to escape. You are his accomplice. . . . For the last time, will you give him up or not?"

The miller did not answer. He turned, and looked away off, indifferently, as if the officer were not speaking to him at all. This excited the anger of the officer to the highest pitch.

"Very well, then," he shouted, "you shall be shot in his place."

And he ordered out the platoon to execute the sentence. Old Merlier preserved his usual calm. He only shrugged his shoulders the least bit; this sort of dramatic performance seemed to him in very bad taste. Doubtless he never dreamed that a man could be shot so easily as all that. Then when the platoon was in position, he gravely observed:—

"So, this is serious? . . . I am quite willing. If you must absolutely shoot some one, just as well shoot me as anybody else."

But Françoise had arisen, wild with terror, stammering:—

"Mercy, sir! do not hurt my father! . . . Kill me in his place. It was I who helped Dominique to escape. I alone am guilty."

"Shut up, child," shouted father Merlier. "What are you lying for? . . . She was locked up in her room all night, sir. She lies! I assure you she lies!"

"No, I am not lying," the young girl answered hotly. "I climbed down by the window; I urged Dominique to fly. It is the truth. . . . the whole truth!"

The old man had become very pale. He saw clearly in her eyes that she was not lying; and the story terrified him. Ah! these children, with their hearts, how they spoil everything! Then he became angry.

"She is mad! Don't listen to her. She is telling you a lot of stupid lies. . . . Come, let's end this business!"

She wanted to protest again. She knelt down; she clasped her hands. The officer quietly looked on at this painful scene.

"My God," he cried at last, "I take your father only because I don't have the other man. . . . Try to find the other; and I will let your father go."

She looked at him a moment, with eyes made big by the atrocity of the proposition.

"It is horrible," she muttered. "How could I find Dominique now? He is gone—I don't know where."

"Very well, choose! Either he or your father?"

"Oh, my God! how can I choose!. . . . But even if I knew where Dominique was, I could not choose!. . . . Ah! You are tearing my heart out! I would rather die at once. Yes, it would be sooner over. Kill me, I pray you,—I beg you, kill me! . . ."

This scene of despair and tears put the officer out of patience at last. He shouted:

"Enough of this! I wish to be just. I am willing to give you two hours more. . . . If, in two hours your lover is not here, your father shall pay for him."

And he bade them take father Merlier to the room which had been used as a prison for Dominique. The old man asked for some tobacco and began to smoke. Upon his impassive face no trace of emotion was legible. But when he was alone, even as he smoked, two great tears trickled slowly down his cheeks. His poor, dear child, how she was suffering!

Françoise had remained in the centre of the yard. Prussian soldiers passed by laughing. Some flung words at her, uttered jests she did not understand. She gazed at the door through which her father had just disappeared. And, with slow gesture, she raised her hand to her forehead, as if to keep it from bursting.

The officer turned upon his heel, repeating:

"You have two hours!—try to use them!"

She had two hours. The words buzzed through her brain. Then, mechanically, she left the yard, she walked straight before her. Where was she to go? What was she to do? She did not even try to adopt a plan, feeling only too well the futility of her efforts. Still, she would have liked to see Dominique. They could have put their minds together; they would perhaps have been able to find a way out. And with her thoughts thus all confused she descended the bank of the Morelle, which she crossed just below the lock, at a place where there were big stones. Her feet brought her under the first willow, at the corner of the meadow. As she bent down, she saw a pool of blood that made her turn pale. That was indeed the place. And she followed Dominique's track in the trampled grass. He must have run,—there was a line of great footsteps cutting across the meadow. Then, further off, she lost these tracks. But in a neighboring field she thought she found them again. This brought her to the edge of the woods, where all signs disappeared.

Nevertheless Françoise went forward under the trees. It helped her to be alone. She sat down a moment. Then remembering that the hour was passing away, she rose up again. How long was it since she had left the mill? Five minutes?—half-an-hour? She had lost all knowledge of time. Perhaps Dominique had gone to hide in a thicket she knew of,—where they had walked together one afternoon. She went to the thicket, looked through every part of it. Only a thrush flew away, uttering his sweet sad cry. Then she thought that he might have taken refuge in a certain rocky hollow, where he used to lie in watch for game; but the rocky hollow was empty. What was the use of looking for him?—she would never find him; —and then, little by little, the desire to find him increased with passionate force; she walked faster. The idea suddenly occurred to her that he might have climbed up a tree. Then she walked on with uplifted eyes,—and, in order that he might know she was near him, she called him every fifteen or twenty steps she took. Cuckoos answered her; breezes playing through the trees made her imagine that he was there and was coming down. But she even fancied that she saw him,—she paused, with a rising in her throat, an impulse to run away. What was she going to say to him? Had she come there only to bring him back and have him shot? Oh! no; she would not speak of those things at all. She would call out to him to run away,—not to remain in the neighborhood. Then the thought of her father waiting for her caused her a sharp pang. She threw herself upon the ground, weeping, and crying aloud:

"My God; my God! why am I here?"

She was mad to have come there! And, as if smitten with terror, she ran, she sought to leave the forest. Three times she lost her way, and she thought that she would never be able to find the mill again, when she came out upon a meadow, exactly opposite the village of Rocreuse. As soon as she saw the village, she stopped. Was she indeed to return alone?

She was still standing there, when a voice called her gently:

"Françoise! Françoise!"

And she saw Dominique's head peering above the edge of a ditch. God was good to her! She had found him! Then Heaven indeed willed that he should die! She smothered a cry, and let herself glide down into the ditch.

"Thou wert looking for me?" he asked.

"Yes," she answered, her head whirling, not knowing what she said.

"Ah! what is the matter?"

She lowered her eyes, she stammered:

"Why, nothing. . . . I was uneasy, I wanted to see you."

Then, set at rest, he told her that he had not been able to make up his mind to go away. He was frightened about them. Those villains of Prussians were quite capable of revenging themselves upon women and old men. Well, everything was all right; and he added, laughing:

"The wedding will be eight days from now— that's all."

Then as she remained agitated as ever, he became serious again:

"But what is the matter with thee? thou art hiding something from me?"

"No, I swear to thee! I ran to get here."

He kissed her, telling her it would be very imprudent for both her and himself to talk any longer; and he was about to climb out of the ditch in order to re-enter the forest. She held him back. She was trembling.

"Listen; thou wouldst perhaps do well to remain where thou art. No one is looking for thee; fear nothing."

"Françoise, thou art hiding something from me!" he repeated.

Again she swore she was hiding nothing from him. Only, she would rather know that he was near her. And she stammered other reasons. She seemed to him to act so strangely that he would now have refused to go away. Besides he believed the French would return. The troops had been seen on the other side of Sauval.

"O let them hurry! Let them come as soon as possible!" she exclaimed, with fervor.

At that moment 11 o'clock sounded from the steeple of Rocreuse. The strokes came, clear and distinct. She rose in terror. Two hours had passed since she left the mill.

"Listen," she said quickly, "if we have need of thee, I shall go up to my room, and shake my handkerchief."

And she departed, running, while Dominique, very uneasy, stretched himself over the edge of the ditch in order to watch the mill. As she was going into Rocreuse, Françoise met an old beggar, Bontemps, who knew the country well. He greeted her: he had just seen the miller in the midst of the Prussians;—then making the sign of the cross, and muttering broken words, he went on his way.

"The two hours are over!" said the officer, when Françoise appeared.

Old Merlier was there, sitting on the bench near the well. He was still smoking away. The young girl again begged, wept, knelt. She wanted to gain a little time. The hope of seeing the French return, had increased within her; and even while lamenting, she fancied that she could hear afar off the cadenced tread of an army. Oh! if they would only come!—if they could only save them all!

"Listen, sir! One hour, one hour more. . . . You can surely give us one hour!"

But the officer remained inflexible. He even ordered two men to take hold of her and take her away, so that they could proceed quietly with the execution of the old man. Then a frightful struggle took place in the heart of Françoise. She could not leave her father to be murdered thus. No! no!—she would rather die with Dominique; and she was rushing toward her room,—when Dominique himself entered the yard.

The officer and the soldiers uttered a cry of triumph. But he, as though there were no one there except Françoise, walked directly to her, quite calm, slightly severe.

"This is bad!" he said. "Why did you not bring me back? I had to find out how things were from old Bontemps. Well, I am here!"

V

It was 3 o'clock. Huge black clouds had slowly filled the sky,—the tail of some neighboring storm. The yellow horizon, the copper-colored rags of clouds above, had changed the valley of Rocreuse, so gay by sunlight, into a murderous-looking place full of sinister shadow. The Prussian officer had contented himself by locking up Dominique, without saying anything about the fate reserved for him. Since midday Françoise had been suffering in terrible agony. She would not leave the yard in spite of her father's urging. She was waiting for the French. But the hours were passing slowly by, night was approaching; and she suffered all the more on finding that all the time gained did not appear to promise any change in the frightful thing that was to happen.

Nevertheless, about 3 o'clock the Prussians made their preparations to depart. For a moment the officer had shut himself up with Dominique as on the evening before. Françoise understood that the life of the young man was at stake. Then she joined her hands; she prayed. Father Merlier, beside her, maintained the dumb rigidity of an old peasant, who never struggles against the fate of circumstances.

"Oh my God! oh my God," stammered Françoise,—"they are going to kill him!"

The miller drew her to him, and took her upon his knees, like a child.

At the same moment the officer came out, while behind him, two men led out Dominique.

"Never! never!" shouted the latter,—"I am quite ready to die!"

"Think well," returned the officer. "The service you refuse me, will be supplied by another. I offer you your life; I am generous. . . . It is merely a question of guiding us to Montredon through the woods. There must be pathways."

Dominique returned no answer.

"Then you remain obstinate?"

"Kill me, and finish the matter," he replied.

Françoise, with clasped hands, begged him from afar off. She forgot everything; she would even have counseled him to be a coward. But father Merlier seized her hands, lest the Prussians should see that wild womanly gesture.

"He is right," he murmured. "Better to die!"

The platoon was there for the execution. The officer expected Dominique to weaken. He still reckoned upon changing his resolution. There was a silence. Afar off, violent claps of thunder were heard. A heavy heat crushed down the country. And in that silence the cry rang out:

"The French! the French!"

It was they, indeed. On the Sauval road at the edge of the woods, the line of red trousers could be seen. There was an extraordinary excitement in the mill. The Prussian soldiers ran hither and thither, with gutteral exclamations. From without not a single shot had yet been fired.

"The French! the French!" cried Françoise, clapping her hands.

She was like a mad woman. She had escaped from her father's embrace, and laughed, tossing her arms in air. They were coming at last, and they were coming in time; for Dominique was still standing there!

A terrible platoon volley which burst upon her ears like a thunderclap, caused her to turn. The officer had just said:

"First of all, let us settle this business!"

And with his own hands pushing Dominique against the wall of a shed, he had given the word of command to fire. When Françoise had turned, Dominique was lying on the ground, his breast riddled by twelve bullets.

She did not weep. She stood there stupidly. Her eyes became fixed; and she went to sit down under the shed, a few steps away from the body. She stared at it. Sometimes she made a vague and childish gesture with her hand. The Prussians had seized old Merlier as a hostage.

It was a fine fight. Rapidly the officer posted his men, knowing that he could not retreat without being crushed. It was just as well to sell his life dearly. Now it was the Prussians who were defending the mill, and the French who were attacking it. The fusillade began with unparalleled violence. For one whole hour it never ceased. Then a heavy crash was heard, and a round shot smashed a main branch of the ancient elm-tree. The French had cannon! A battery, trained just above the ditch where

Dominique had hidden, swept the Rocreuse highroad. The fight could not now last long.

Ah! the poor mill! Cannon-shot pierced it through and through. One-half of the roof was carried away. Two walls crumbled down. But it was especially upon the Morelle side that the disaster became lamentable. The ivy, torn from the quivering walls, hung down like rags; the river carried away debris of all kinds; and, through a breach could be seen Françoise's room, with its bed, whose white curtains had been carefully drawn. The old wheel received two cannon-shot, one after the other, and uttered a last groan; the paddleboards were carried away by the current; the carcass crushed in.

The merry mill had given up its ghost!

Then the French stormed the mill. There was a furious fight with cold steel. Under the rust-colored sky the valley of slaughter filled itself with dead. The vast meadows wore a weird look, with their great isolated trees, their curtains of poplars which sported them with shade. To right and left the forests were like the walls of a circus hemming in the combatants, while the springs, the fountains, and running waters uttered a sound of sobbing in the panic of the land.

Under the shed Françoise had not moved,— crouching before the body of Dominique. Father Merlier had just been killed upon the spot by a spent bullet. Then when the Prussians had been exterminated, and the mill was burning, the French captain entered first into the yard. Since the beginning of the campaign, it was the only success he had been able to win. So, inflamed with his triumph, making taller his tall stature, he laughed in his amiable, hand-some-cavalier way. And beholding Françoise, stunned, between the corpses of her husband and of her father, in the midst of the smoking ruins of the mill, he saluted her gallantly with his sword, crying:

"Victory! victory!"

I

A SENSELESS WASTE

After finishing the last page of "The Attack on the Mill," the reader's first emotion is sorrow over the senselessness of what has happened. Zola has aroused sympathy for the young couple from the beginning. The girl has blossomed into a beauty only recently. Her fiancé seems on the verge of a real reformation of character. The father has devoted his life to his daughter and his mill and has been sensible in not opposing the young couple's engagement. Suddenly, these simple people are the center of events that are not important to them. And they, as people, are not important to the events. Though readers may keep hoping that a miracle will happen, they know instinctively that the characters are doomed. This kind of story shows Zola's basic feelings that people are caught in a web of cause-effect relationships that will inevitably control their lives despite their own best efforts. Each detail of the plot leads inexorably to the next, despite our desire to change the tragic direction for the characters. This viewpoint, that the world in which we live irrevocably influences our destiny, is part of the style called *naturalistic* writing, of which Zola was a leading exponent. Other writers in this manner are de Maupassant, James Joyce, and Eugene O'Neill.

II

IMPLICATIONS

What does Zola's story seem to imply about society? With this in mind, react to the following propositions:

1. In war the innocent inevitably suffer.

2. It is impossible to make plans for the future.

3. No matter how hard you work, you may lose everything because of things over which you have no control.

4. Character is destiny.

5. Happiness is only an occasional interlude in a basic drama of pain.

6. There is a parallel between the destruction of the mill and the destruction of the romance.

III

TECHNIQUES

Author's Purpose

It is useful in getting at the central purpose of a piece of writing to ask questions about various details within it. Try answering the following.

1. What aspects of the setting does Zola emphasize in the first section? How do these things contrast with what happens later in the story?

2. How does Dominique change after his betrothal? How does this change in attitude affect the situation he eventually finds himself in?

3. What are the thoughts that Françoise has about the dead Prussian soldier? In what ways is he like her own sweetheart?

4. All in all, what would you say is the purpose of Zola in constructing the story as he did?

Irony

What is ironic about each of the following?

1. Dominique's change of character in which he settles down and becomes a hard-working young man.

2. The fact that the attack on the mill takes place on the particular day it does.

3. Father Merlier's great care of the mill and the mill-wheel.

4. The appearance of the man whom Dominique kills.

5. The kind of town and landscape in which the events take place.

6. Dominique's nationality.

7. The final words of the story: "Victory! victory!"

IV
WORDS

A. At this point, near the close of your twelfth-grade course, you should have acquired curiosity about words and a habit of adding new words to your vocabulary. We suggest one principle: If you encounter a word for a second time in your reading or other activities, there is good reason to suppose that you will meet with it again and that you had better learn it now.

B. Merlier's mill, we are told in the second paragraph of the story, stood "where the high-road makes an elbow." The mill-wheel, as we are told, "crackled as it turned with the asthmatic cough of a faithful servant-woman grown old in the house." Merlier declared "that a young wheel would be lazy." We have here a sequence of metaphors involving comparisons between people on the one hand and things on the other. "The Attack on the Mill" contains many such figures. How many can you find?

The following story is an anonymous Russian folktale. Although it was originally written in the seventeenth century, it reveals truths about human nature and human foibles that are still true today.

The Judgments of Shemyaka

translated from the Russian by Bernard Guilbert Guerney

Once upon a time, in a certain land and region, there lived two brothers, tillers of the soil both. One was well off, the other poor as poor can be; the one that was well off used to help out the poor one for many years and long, yet could not abide him because of his poverty.

So one day the poor brother came to the one that was well off and begged for the loan of a horse, to haul a load of firewood to keep him warm through the winter, but the brother that was well off was loath to lend his horse to the one that was poor, saying: "Thou hast borrowed much, brother, yet couldst never repay."

Yet when the poor brother did get the horse at last, what does he do but ask for the loan of a horsecollar as well! Whereupon the brother that was well off waxed wroth at him and fell to railing at his poverty, saying: "What, thou hast not even a horsecollar?" But give him one he would not.

So the poor brother left the one that was well off, got out his sledge, hitched the horse thereto by its tail, drove to the forest, chopped a lot of wood and loaded the sledge with it, as much as the horse could draw. When he got home he opened the gates and gave the horse the whip, but he had forgotten to remove the bottom bar on the gates, so that the horse ran the sledge full tilt against it and tore its tail right out.

And when the poor brother brought back the horse, the brother that was well off, seeing that his horse now lacked a tail, fell to upbraiding his poor brother, because he had maimed his

horse all for nothing and, refusing to take the animal back, started off for town to lodge a complaint against his poor brother before Shemyaka the Judge. As for the poor brother, when he saw the brother that was well off setting out to lodge a complaint against him, he decided to go along, knowing that otherwise a summons would come for him, and he would have to pay the expenses of the sumner[1] on top of everything else.

With the darkness coming on and the town still far off, when they reached a certain hamlet the well-off brother decided to lodge with the priest, whom he knew; as for the poor brother, he also went to the same priest's house, but climbed up on a sort of unrailed balcony and laid him down there. And the well-off brother started telling the priest of the mishap that had befallen his horse, and why he was on his way to town, after which he and the priest fell to their supper; however, they never called the poor brother to join them. But the poor brother became so taken up in watching what his brother and the priest were eating that he tumbled off the balcony and, falling upon a cradle, crushed the priest's little boy to death.

So the priest, too, started off to town to lodge a complaint against the poor brother for having been the cause of his little son's death, and the poor brother tagged right along.

As they were crossing a bridge that led into the town, a certain citizen thereof happened to be passing through the moat below, bringing his

1. **sumner,** summoner.

sick father to the public baths. In the meanwhile the poor brother, pondering on the utter ruin that would be brought upon him by his brother and the priest, and deciding to put an end to himself, cast himself headlong off the bridge, thinking he would be smashed to death in the moat below. But it was the sick old man he landed on, causing him to die before the eyes of his son, who laid hold of the poor brother and dragged him off before the judge.

Now the poor brother, mulling over how he might get out of his scrape, and what he could give the judge, yet having nought upon him, struck on the idea of picking up a stone and, wrapping it in a kerchief, he placed it in his cap as he took his place before the judge.

So then his well-off brother laid a complaint against him before Judge Shemyaka, seeking damages for his horse. And, having heard the complaint to the end, Shemyaka spake to the poor brother, saying: "Make answer." But the poor brother, knowing not what answer to make, took the wrapped stone out of his cap and, showing the bundle to the judge, bowed low before him. Whereupon the judge, thinking the defendant was offering him a reward if the decision went his way, spake unto the rich brother: "Since he hath plucked out thy horse's tail, thou art not to take thy horse back from him until such time as it hath grown a new tail; but when the said horse shall have grown a new tail, then wilt thou take the said horse back from him."

And thereafter the second suit began: the priest sought to have the poor brother executed for having crushed his son to death; but the poor brother, even as before, took the same stone wrapped in a kerchief and showed the bundle to the judge. The judge saw this, and again thinking that the defendant was promising him another bag of gold for a second favorable decision, spake unto the priest: "Since he hath crushed thy son to death, thou shalt even let him have thy wife, until such time as he shall have begotten a son upon her, when thou shalt take from him thy wife and the child."

And thereupon the third suit began, concerning the poor brother's having cast himself off the bridge and, by falling on the sick old man, having killed the townsman's father. But the poor man, once more taking out of his cap the stone wrapped in a kerchief, showed it to the judge for the third time. And the judge, looking forward to a third bag of gold for a third decision favorable to the defendant, spake unto the man whose father had been killed: "Go thou up on the bridge, while the slayer of thy father shall take his place below it, and do thou cast thyself down upon him in thy turn, slaying him even as he hath slain thy father."

The trials over, the plaintiffs left the courtroom together with the defendant.

Now when the well-off brother approached the poor one and asked him for the return of the horse, the latter answered him, saying: "According to the decision, as soon as that horse will have grown back its tail, I shall surely give it back to thee." Whereupon the rich brother offered him five rubles,[2] and seventeen bushels and a little over of grain, and a milch goat, and the poor brother promised to give him back the horse, even without a tail, and the two brothers made up their differences and lived in amity to the end of their days, even as all brethren should.

And when the poor brother approached the priest, asking him to turn his wife over to him, according to Shemyaka's decision, that he might beget a child upon her and, having begotten the same, give both wife and child back to him, the priest fell to pleading with him not to take his wife from him, and the poor man at last agreed to accept fifty rubles from the priest, and twenty-three bushels and a little over of grain, and a cow with a calf, and a mare with a foal, and they made up their difference and lived in amity to the end of their days.

And in the same way the poor brother spake unto the third plaintiff: "In accordance with the decision, I shall take my place under the bridge; see that thou go up on the bridge and cast thyself down upon me, even as I did upon thy father." But the other bethought himself: "I may

_____

2. **five rubles,** around two and one-half dollars.

cast myself down, right enough, but what if I not only miss him but kill myself into the bargain?" And he began making peace with the other, and gave him two hundred rubles, and all but a little short of twenty-nine bushels of grain, and a bull, and they made up their difference and lived in amity to the end of their days.

And thus did the poor brother collect payment from all three.

As for Judge Shemyaka, he sent one of his men out to the defendant, and bade him bring back the three bags the poor brother had shown him; but when the judge's man began asking for these three bags: "Give me that which thou didst show to the judge, which is in those three bags thou hadst in thy cap; he told me to take it from thee," the poor brother did take out of his cap the stone in the kerchief and, unwrapping the kerchief, showed him the stone, whereupon the judge's man asked him: "Wherefore showest thou me a stone?" Whereupon the defendant told him: "That was for the judge. I showed him the stone that he might not decide against me, for had he done so I would have let him have it over his head."

And the messenger went back and told this to the judge. And Judge Shemyaka, having heard his messenger out, spake, saying: "I thank and praise my God that I decided in his favor, for had I not done so he would have brained me."

And the poor man went thence, and home, rejoicing and praising God.

I
THE RASCAL WINS OUT AGAIN
The characterization of the clever rogue has always intrigued readers. This character is found throughout literature, from great epics like *The Odyssey* to folk stories like "Jack and the Bean Stalk." Even contemporary TV series and motion pictures make use of this stock character. Often, as in this story, the rogue seems a bumbling fool but in reality has a native shrewdness that wins out in the end.

II
IMPLICATIONS
Discuss the following.

1. Shemyaka follows the principle of making the punishment fit the crime.

2. Consider the situations given below and decide what punishment Shemyaka would have meted out to the culprit.

a. Accidentally spilling a soft drink on a teacher's new cashmere sweater.

b. Accidentally tripping your best friend and breaking his or her ankle.

c. While riding your three-speed bike you run into someone on a ten-speed bike. The other person's bike is slightly damaged. Yours is okay.

III
TECHNIQUES
Author's Purpose

Is the following statement true or false?

Folk stories have no other purpose than to delight the reader.

Irony

The punishments are all obviously ironic, but what is the final irony in the story?

YEFIM DAVIDOVICH ZOZULYA

Yefim Davidovich Zozulya[1] (1891–   ) was born in Moscow. During his childhood he lived in Lodz, Poland, a textile-manufacturing city where his father owned a store. In later life Yefim recalled Lodz as a city of narrow streets, of bad air, and of stuffy bourgeois attitudes. At the age of fourteen, Zozulya became involved with radicals and participated in the 1905 revolution. Arrested three times, he finally was sent to prison. There he began to write. Following the revolution, he moved to Odessa, where his writing was published for the first time when he was only twenty. He then worked in St. Petersburg and in Moscow as a journalist and a reporter. But Zozulya's early recognition by the Soviet Republic was later withdrawn, and his name was stricken from the *Great Soviet Encyclopedia*. "A Tale About Ak and Humanity" delves into the philosophy of human values and thus gains universality. Departing from the usual method of short story presentation, it becomes a grotesque fantasy calling to mind the mood of much modern painting and music.

A Tale About Ak and Humanity

translated by John Cournos

I. THE PLACARDS

The houses and the streets had an ordinary appearance. And, above them, the unchanging sky was azure. And the gray masks of the pavement stone were, as always, impenetrable and indifferent, while maddened men, from whose faces tears dropped into pails of paste, were adorning the walls with placards.

Their text was simple, pitiless and irrevocable. Here it is:

To all without exclusion:

An examination of the inhabitants of the town with regard to their right to live is being carried out by districts by special commissions consisting of three members of the Courts of the Higher Decisions. Inhabitants, acknowledged to be superfluous (unnecessary), are obliged to depart from life within twenty-four hours. The right of appeal is allowed within that time. The appeal must be made in writing and will be delivered to the Central Court of the Higher Decisions. A reply will be given within three hours. Superfluous human beings, unable either from weakness of will or from love of living to depart from life, will be dealt with by the Courts of the Higher Decisions, who will call on friends, neighbors, or special armed companies to execute the sentence.

Remarks. 1. The inhabitants of the town, with complete obedience, are obliged to submit to the acts and regulations of the members of the Courts of the Higher Decisions. Truthful answers must be given to all questions. An official report will be given of the characteristics of every person judged to be superfluous.

2. This decree will be carried out with irrevocable severity. Human rubbish, hindering the reconstruction of life on the basis of justice and happiness, must be pitilessly destroyed. This decree concerns, without exclusion, all citizens—men and women, rich and poor.

3. The departure from town of any person whatsoever while the examination with regard to the right to live is in progress is absolutely forbidden.

1. **Yefim Davidovich Zozulya** (yef ēm′ dä vid′ō vich zo zùl′yä).

From *Short Stories out of Soviet Russia*, translated by John Cournos. Copyright, 1929, 1957 by E. P. Dutton & Co., Inc. Reprinted by permission of the publisher, E. P. Dutton, Inc.

II. THE FIRST WAVES
OF PERTURBATION

"Have you read?"

"Have you read?"

"Have you read? !"

"Have you read? ! ! Have you read? ! !"

"Have you seen? ! ! Have you heard? ! !"

"Have you read? ! !"

Crowds began to gather all over the town. Traffic became congested. From sudden weakness pedestrians leaned against house walls. Many wept. Some had fainting spells. Towards evening their number reached a tremendous figure.

"Have you read? ! !"

"How terrible? Who's ever heard of such a thing!"

"Why, we ourselves elected the Courts of the Higher Decisions! We ourselves gave them full powers!"

"Yes, that's true."

"We ourselves are to blame for the monstrous situation."

"Yes, that's true. We are to blame. That's because we ourselves wanted to create a better life. But who could have thought that the Courts would approach the question in so simple and terrible a manner?"

"But what names have been chosen for the composition of the Courts! Oh, what names!"

"How do you know? Have they published a list of the members?"

"I've heard from an acquaintance. Ak has been chosen Chairman."

"Oh, you don't say! Ak? That's a piece of good fortune!"

"Yes. Yes. It's a fact!"

"What good fortune! He's a magnificent personality."

"Of course! We must not be too anxious: he's sure to weed out the human rubbish. We need not fear injustice."

"Dear citizen, what do you think? Will I be left among the living? I am a decent sort of man. Do you know, once during the wreck of a ship twenty passengers saved themselves in a boat.

But the boat could not stand such a huge load, and all were threatened with death. In order that fifteen might be saved, it was necessary that five should fling themselves into the sea. I was one of the five. I volunteered to do it. Don't look so incredulously. Now I'm old and feeble. Haven't you really heard of this happening? The papers were full of it at the time. My four comrades perished. A chance saved me. What do you think? Will they spare me?"

"And me, citizens? And me? I gave away all my possessions to the poor. That was long ago. I have documents to prove it."

"I don't know, really. All depends on the point of view of the Courts of the Higher Decisions."

"Allow me to inform you, esteemed citizens, that primitive usefulness to neighbors by no means justifies the existence of human beings on earth. Why, in that case, every stupid wet nurse would have the right to live. That's an old notion. You're behind the times!"

"What, then, is the value of a human being?"

"Yes, what is his value?"

"I don't know."

"Oh, you don't know! Why do you poke your muzzle here with your opinions if you don't know?"

"I'm sorry. I only said what I thought."

"Citizens! Citizens! Look! Look! They're running! What a confusion! A panic!"

"Oh, heavens! Heavens! . . . Ah! . . . Save yourselves! Save yourselves!"

"Stop! Don't run!"

"Don't make the panic worse!"

"Stop!"

III. THE FUGITIVES

The crowds ran in the streets. Red-cheeked young men ran, with terror-stricken faces. Modest clerks serving in offices and establishments. Bridegrooms in clean cuffs. Choir singers from amateur societies. Dandies. Tellers of anecdotes. Billiard players. Evening visitors to the moving pictures. Career-pursuers, evil-

doers, sharpers, with white foreheads and curly hair. Hypocritical rakes. Wicked drunkards. Jolly fellows, hooligans, Adonises, visionaries, lovers, cyclists. Broad-shouldered squabblers, squabbling from having nothing else to do, talkers, deceivers, long-haired hypocrites, petty grief indulgers, with dark sad eyes, behind whose sadness, concealed by youth, lay cold emptiness. Young churls with full, smiling lips, vainglorious adventurers, scandalmongers, good-hearted failures, clever profligates.

Corpulent, voracious, lazy women also ran. And lean shrews, nagging, boring women, tedious females, wives of fools and wise men, gossipers, betrayers, the envious and the greedy, now distorted with fear. Proud she-fools, the good-for-nothing good, those who from boredom dyed their hair, the colorless libertines, the lonely, the helpless, the brazen, the begging, the supplicating, who, from terror, had lost all outward decorum.

Stooped old men ran. And squat men, small men, tall men, and handsome and malformed men.

Men who managed houses, pawnbrokers, ironmongers, carpenters, artisans, jailers, grocers, good-natured publicans, decorous gray-haired lackeys, respectable fathers of families, those who had battened up dupes of their baseness, venerable sharps and fat scoundrels.

They ran in a dense, impetuous, ruthless mass. Loads of rags enveloped their bodies and extremities. Hot steam poured from their mouths. Curses and wails resounded through the concealed indifference of the abandoned edifices.

Many ran carrying possessions. With twisted fingers they dragged pillows, boxes, drawers. They seized their precious gems, their children, their money. They shouted, then returned, lifting their arms in terror, and then ran again.

But they were all turned back. All. Such beings as themselves shot at them, ran in front of them, beat them with sticks, fists, stones; there was biting too, and terrible outcries; the crowds fell back, leaving behind their killed and wounded.

Towards evening the town resumed its normal appearance. The trembling bodies of the inhabitants returned to their homes and flung themselves on their beds. A brief poignant hope desperately struggled in tight, feverish skulls.

IV. A SIMPLE PROCEDURE

"Your name?"

"Boss."

"How old are you?"

"Thirty."

"Occupation?"

"I make cigarettes."

"Tell the truth!"

"I am telling the truth. I've worked honestly at my trade for fourteen years and supported my family."

"Where is your family?"

"Here they are. This is my wife. This is my son."

"Doctor, examine the Boss family."

"I have done so."

"Well, what can you tell us about them?"

"Citizen Boss is anaemic. General condition, average. His wife suffers with headaches and rheumatism. The boy is healthy."

"Good. You may go, doctor. Citizen Boss, what are your pleasures? What do you love?"

"I love people and life generally."

"Be more precise, citizen Boss. To the point."

"I love. . . . Well, what do I love? . . . I love my son. . . . He is so clever with the fiddle. . . . I love my meals, though to be sure, I'm not a glutton. . . . I am fond of women. . . . It is pleasant to look at handsome women and girls passing in the street. I love, when I'm tired in the evening, to rest. . . . I love making cigarettes. . . . I can make five hundred an hour. . . . I love life."

"Be calm, citizen Boss! Stop whimpering. What do you say, psychologist?"

"Claptrap, colleague! Rubbish! The most ordinary creatures. A poor existence. Temperament semi-phlegmatic, semi-sanguine. Activity feeble. Class—the last. Hope for betterment —none. Passivity—seventy-five percent. Mrs. Boss—still lower. The boy is commonplace, but perhaps . . . . How old is your son, citizen Boss? Stop whimpering!"

"Thirteen."

"Don't be alarmed. For the time being your son will remain among the living. As for you . . . . In any case, that is none of my affair. Render your decision, colleague!"

"In the name of the Courts of the Higher Decisions, with the object of cleansing life of superfluous human rubbish, of indifferent beings, I order you, citizen Boss, and your wife, to depart from this life within twenty-four hours. Be quiet! Don't bawl! Sanitary officer, calm the woman! Call the guard! It doesn't look as if they'll manage it without assistance."

V. CHARACTERISTICS OF THE SUPERFLUOUS PRESERVED IN THE GRAY CABINET

The Gray Cabinet was situated in the corridor in the department of the Courts of the Higher Decisions. This cabinet had the usual appearance: it was a solid, pensively stupid affair, like most cabinets. It was neither in width nor in height more than seven feet, but it was the grave of several thousand human beings. It was marked with the brief inscription:

Catalogue of the Superfluous.

The catalogue was divided into several sections, and among others were:

The Indiscriminately Impressionable.
Petty Partisans.
The Passive.
Without Equilibrium.

and so forth.

The characteristics were stated briefly and objectively. In some instances, to be sure, there were sharp remarks, but these were, inevitably, red-penciled by Ak, who added his commentary to the effect that it was not necessary to abuse the superfluous.

Here are some specimen records of the characteristics of the superfluous:

Superfluous Male No. 14,741.

Health average. He visits acquaintances, without being either useful or interesting to them. He is free with advice. In the bloom of his strength he had seduced a girl, then cast her off. He regards the acquisition of furniture after marriage as the most important function in life. His brain is drowsy, lymphatic. He has no capacity for work. To the question what he considered to be the most interesting thing he had encountered in life, he told of his visit to the restaurant "Quisisana" in Paris. A common creature. Category of the lower strata. Heart feeble. Within 24 hours.

Superfluous Male No. 14,623.

A worker in a cooper's[2] shop. Class—mediocre. Has no love for his work. His mind in everything works along lines of least resistance. Physically, well; but spiritually, he suffers from a common disease: the fear of life. The fear of freedom. When free, during holidays, he stupefies himself with alcohol. During the revolution he exhibited some energy: he wore a red ribbon, and hoarded potatoes and everything else he could get hold of. He was afraid of falling short. He prided himself on his proletarian[3] origin. He took no active share in the revolution: he was afraid. He loves sour cream. He beats children. The tempo of his life is uniformly dispirited. Within 24 hours.

Superfluous Male No. 15,201.

He knows eight languages, but says that it is tedious to listen even to one. He is fond of ingenious trifles. Very self-confident. His self-confidence is based on his knowledge of languages. Demands esteem. Indulges in gossip. Towards real animate life indifferent, like an ox. Afraid of beggars. Sweet-tempered in his relations out of fear. Is fond of killing flies and other insects. Rarely experiences joy. Within 24 hours.

Superfluous Female No. 4,356.

Scolds her servants out of boredom. Secretly skims the cream from the milk and the fat top layer from the bouillon. Reads shilling-shockers. For days on end lounges on the couch. Her greatest dream: to have a frock with yellow sleeves and slit sides. For twelve years she was loved by a gifted inventor. She did not know his occupation, and thought he was an electrician. She abandoned him and married a tradesman in leather. No children. Is often capricious and hysterical without cause. Wakes in the night to order a samovar[4] and a snack. A wholly superfluous creature. Within 24 hours.

VI. AT WORK

An army of specialists had gathered round Ak and the Courts of the Higher Decisions. It consisted of doctors, psychologists, observers and writers. They all worked with extraordinary speed. There were occasions when at a given hour the specialists speeded a good hundred persons on the way to the other world. And into the Gray Cabinet there flew a hundred records of characteristics, in which the lucidity of expression vied with the firm assurance of the authors.

From morning till night the work went on apace in the chief department. House commissions came and went. Companies of executors of sentences came and went, while behind the desks, as in an immense editorial office, dozens of human beings were sitting and writing, with quick, firm, unreflecting hands.

Ak looked at all this with narrow, strong, impenetrable eyes, and thought his own thoughts, from which his body grew more and more hunched, and his large, impetuous, stubborn head more and more gray,

Something rose up between him and his servants, something erected itself as it were between his tense, sleepless thought and the blind, unreflecting hands of the executors.

---

2. **cooper** (kü′pər), one who makes or repairs wooden barrels.
3. **proletarian** (prō′lə ter′ē ən), the proletariat was the lowest social class; the common people; laborers.

4. **samovar** (sam′ə vär), an urn used to boil water for tea.

VII. AK'S DOUBTS

One day the members of the Courts of the Higher Decisions came into the department with the intention of delivering their reports.

They did not find Ak in his usual place. They sought and did not find him. They sent out messengers, called on the telephone without success.

Only after two hours they found him by chance in the Gray Cabinet.

Ak was sitting in the Cabinet on the death warrants of the superfluous, with an intense expression of thought in his eyes, unusual even for him.

"What are you doing here?" they asked Ak.

"As you see, I am thinking," answered Ak, wearily.

"But why in the Cabinet?"

"It's the most fitting place. I am thinking of human beings, and to think of human beings profitably it is best to do it in the immediate proximity of the decrees of their destruction. Only sitting on the documents of the destruction of man is it possible to learn something of his extraordinary strange life."

Someone laughed shallowly and emptily.

"Don't you laugh!" said Ak warningly, waving someone's record of characteristics in his hand. "Don't you laugh! I think the Courts of the Higher Decisions are passing through a crisis. An examination of the records of those who have perished has led me to seek new paths towards progress. You have all learned, quickly and malignantly, to prove the superfluity of this or that existence. Even the least gifted among you is ready, in a few phrases, to demonstrate this with conviction. And here am I sitting and thinking, 'Is your way just?'"

Once more Ak lapsed into thought, then sighed bitterly, and said quietly:

"What's to be done? Where's the issue? When one examines the lives of the living, one arrives at the conclusion that three-fourths of them should be rooted out of existence. But when one examines those who have perished, a doubt comes; wouldn't it have been better if one had loved them and pitied them? That's where, in my opinion, is the blind alley of the human question, the blind alley of human history."

Again Ak lapsed into a sad silence, and he dug into the mountain of records of the condemned dead, and unhealthily began to pore over their officially painful brevity.

The members of the Courts departed. No one contradicted. In the first place, because it was useless to contradict Ak; in the second, because no one dared to contradict him. But they all felt that a new decision was ripening, and they nearly all felt dissatisfied: here was a matter which had become a matter of custom, everything was clear and definite, and now it looked as if it all would have to be changed for something else. But for what?

What else has this man's brain contrived, this brain which had such a fabulous power over the town?

VIII. THE CRISIS

Ak vanished.

He always vanished when he fell into meditation. They sought him everywhere and did not find him. Someone said that Ak was sitting outside the town and weeping. Others said that Ak was running about his garden on all fours and gnawing the earth.

The activity of the Courts of the Higher Decisions weakened. The work ceased to run smoothly with the disappearance of Ak. The inhabitants simply put up iron bars across their doors and would not let the servants of the Courts in. In some districts the questions of the members of the Courts as regards the right to live were answered with laughter, and it even happened that the superfluous seized the members of the Courts of the Higher Decisions and examined them as to their right to live and wrote mock records of characteristics, which in no wise differed from those preserved in the Gray Cabinet.

Chaos possessed the town. Superfluous, good-for-nothing inhabitants who had not yet been executed became so brazen as to appear in the streets and to make good cheer with their neighbors, to give themselves up to all sorts of diversions, and even to enter into marriage.

Congratulations were exchanged in the streets:

"Ended! Ended! Hurrah!"

"The examinations of the right to live have come to an end!"

"Don't you think, citizen, life's become very pleasant? There's less human rubbish about. Why, one can breathe now!"

"Aren't you ashamed, citizen? You really think that those who've left this life hadn't a right to it? Oh, I know some who haven't the right to live even a single hour, but they're still alive and will go on living! On the other hand, how many really decent people have perished? If you only knew!"

"That's nothing. Mistakes are unavoidable. Tell me, do you know what's become of Ak?"

"I don't know."

"Ak is sitting on a tree outside town and weeping."

"Ak is running about on all fours and gnawing the earth."

"Let him weep."

"Let him go on gnawing."

"You are rejoicing prematurely, citizens! Prematurely, I say. Ak is returning this evening, and the Courts of the Higher Decisions will resume their work."

"How do you know?"

"I know. There's still an awful lot of human rubbish left. It's necessary to clean up things thoroughly. Thoroughly."

"You're very hard, citizen."

"Fiddlesticks!"

"Citizens! Citizens! Look! Look!"

"New placards are being put up."

"Look!"

"Citizens! What a joy! What good fortune!"

"Citizens, read!"

"Read!"

"Read! Read!"

"Read!"

IX. THE NEW PLACARDS

Men were running breathlessly round the streets, with pails full of paste. Packets of huge rose-tinted placards were being unfurled and, with a joyous crackle, were being pasted onto walls of houses. Their text was precise, clear and simple:

To all without exclusion:

From the moment of the publication of this decree all inhabitants of the town are allowed to live. Live, multiply and fill the earth. The Courts of the Higher Decisions have fulfilled their stern obligations and will hereafter be called the Courts of the Higher Delicacy. You are all excellent citizens, and your rights to life are indisputable.

The Courts of the Higher Delicacy will appoint special commissions consisting of three members whose duty it shall be to pay daily visits to homes and to congratulate their occupants on the fact of their existence and to note their observations in special "Joyous Records."

The members of these commissions shall have the right to question citizens as to the manner of their life, and citizens, if they so desire, may answer in detail. The latter is desirable. The joyous observations shall be preserved in the Rose-tinted Cabinet for posterity.

X. NORMAL LIFE RESUMED

The doors, the windows, the balconies were all opened. Loud human voices, laughter, singing and music resounded from them. Stout, incapable girls began to play on the piano. Gramophones dinned from morning till night. Fiddles, clarinets and guitars also made themselves audible. In the evening men took off their coats, sat themselves on the balconies, and, stretching out their legs, sighed with pleasure. The traffic in the streets grew animated. Young men, taking young women out with them, went driving in cabs and motorcars. The cafés and confectionary shops were full of customers enjoying pastries and cool drinks. Trinket shops which sold mirrors did a bustling business. Men and women bought mirrors and enjoyed their reflections. Artists and photographers were overrun with orders for portraits. The portraits were put into frames and adorned the walls. In one instance they caused a murder, which the newspapers made much of. It happened like this. A young man hired a furnished room and demanded that the portraits of the parents of his landlord and landlady be removed. The landlord and the landlady were offended and killed the young man, and threw him out of a fifth-story window onto the street.

Feelings of personal dignity and self-love developed tremendously. Collisions and quarrels became a common occurrence. Such colloquies as the following became the rule:

"It is evident that you're alive only because of some mistake. The Courts of the Higher Decisions did their work carelessly."

"Yes, very carelessly, when they left such as you alive."

Generally speaking, these quarrels went unnoticed in the normal course of life. Human beings improved their table, cooked all sorts of jams. Warm knit apparel became in demand, as every one held his health in high regard.

The members of the Courts of the Higher Delicacy regularly visited homes and asked their occupants how they managed.

Many replied that they managed very well, and even tried to convince their questioners of this.

"Just look!" they said, smiling with self-satisfaction and rubbing their hands. "We are pickling some cucumbers, he-he! And we have some pickled herrings, too. Our larder is better than it was, thank heavens. . . ."

Others complained of inconveniences and lamented the fact that the work of the Courts of the Higher Decisions had been cut prematurely short.

"Last evening I was in a tram, and just think of it! There wasn't a single unoccupied place. . . . What a disgrace! Both my wife and I had to stand up. There're a good many superfluous people left. They nudge you everywhere—the devil

take them! A pity they weren't removed when there was the chance!"

Still others were perturbed for different reasons.

"Just consider! Neither on Wednesday nor on Thursday did any congratulate me on my existence. Shameless, I say! And what will you say to that? Is it, then, necessary for me to come to you to be congratulated, eh?"

XI. THE END OF THE TALE

In Ak's office, as before, the work went on apace: men were sitting there and writing. The Rose-tinted Cabinet was full of joyous records and observations. Carefully and in detail were described the birthdays, the marriages, the journeys, the dinners and the suppers, the love stories, indeed all manner of happenings, and some of the records bore the character and appearance of short stories and novels. The inhabitants requested the members of the Courts of the Higher Delicacy to publish them in the form of books, and they had plenty of reading.

Ak was silent.

He grew only more and more hunched and more and more gray.

Sometimes he got into the Rose-tinted Cabinet and remained sitting there a long time, just as he had done before in the Gray Cabinet.

Once he jumped out of the Rose-tinted Cabinet with the cry:

"It's necessary to kill them! To kill them! To kill them!"

But, on seeing the white fingers of his servants hurrying speedily across the paper, describing the living with the same zeal with which they had formerly described the dead, Ak waved a hand, ran out of the office and disappeared.

He disappeared forever.

There were many legends concerning the disappearance of Ak, and all sorts of rumors, but Ak was never again found.

And the human beings, of whom there were so many in town, whom at first Ak wanted to kill and afterwards pitied, and whom later he again wanted to kill, human beings among whom are many good people and not a little rubbish, continue to this day to live as if there had been no Ak at all, as if there had been no one to raise the question as regards one's right to live.

I
HOW AWFUL! HOW AWFUL!

Using the same direct and unemotional language of Swift's "A Modest Proposal," Yefim Zozulya presents a bizarre fantasy that horrifies the reader. "How awful!" one thinks, that the Courts of the Higher Decisions should presume to decide whether a person is superfluous to society. But when the observations of the Courts of the Higher Delicacy show how self-centered, quarrelsome, and odious humans are, one again thinks, "How awful." Obviously, those who judged and those who remained alive after their judgments are equally pernicious and bigoted. The story seems to be suggesting that human society cannot improve as long as human nature remains as it now is.

II
IMPLICATIONS

Discuss your reactions to the following.

1. To determine the worth of a person's life, the Courts of the Higher Decisions ask not only the usual biographical information but also such questions as: What are your pleasures? Your loves? Your ambitions? Your relationships with others? The most memorable event in your life? Try answering these questions yourself. Do the answers give a fair picture of an individual's value?

2. Define the human frailties epitomized in each of the four case studies.

3. React to Ak's statement: "When one examines the lives of the living, one arrives at the conclusion that three-fourths of them should be rooted out of existence. But when one examines those who have perished, a doubt comes. . . ."

4. Ak is really a great person.

III
TECHNIQUES

Author's Purpose

The author of this selection is Russian. Do you think he intends to criticize only Russian society or humankind in general?

Irony

What is ironic about the following situations?

1. The people have elected Ak and have great trust in him.

2. The officials scorn primitive usefulness to a neighbor.

3. The Joyous Records are filled with complaints.

4. In quarrels, the people say such things as: "It is evident that you're alive only because of some mistake. The Courts of the Higher Decisions did their work carelessly."

IV
WORDS

There is a tendency in officialdom to invent new phrases for things to make them acceptable to the populace. This practice is sometimes called "double speak." What is the actual definition of the following?

1. Courts of the Higher Decisions

2. depart from life

3. human rubbish

4. primitive usefulness

5. Courts of the Higher Delicacy

SUMMING UP

Critics of Society

THE WRITER AND THE STATE

The great eighteenth-century politician Edmund Burke declared, "Writers, especially when they act in a body and with one direction, have great influence on the public mind." Robert Browning went further, declaring, "It is the glory and the good of Art, that Art remains the one way possible of speaking truths." Again and again we see that the force of ideas given shape and strength by the writer's skill is greater than the force of governments and armies.

Great writers have been exiled, gagged, jailed or murdered in attempts to silence their voices: the Italian poet Dante; the modern Russian novelist Boris Pasternak, author of *Dr. Zhivago*; the Russian Jewish storyteller Isaac Babel; the German Thomas Mann. Sometimes the pressures are subtle; sometimes, as in the case of Nazi Germany or Stalinist Russia, harsh as bullets.

The pieces of writing in CRITICS OF SOCIETY have ranged from humorous satire to bitter irony. Each in its way has held some flaw in society up to the revealing light of ridicule. In the glare of criticism, faults are silhouetted so that we see them as dark shadows against the light.

IMPLICATIONS

Consider the following and discuss your reactions.

1. For each selection in this unit, explain what the author was criticizing.

2. Criticism is inherently ugly and produces bitter, depressing literature.

3. Galsworthy is so involved with his theme of social justice that he has not made his portrayal of the old shoemaker a realistic one.

4. Making fun of society is easy but does little to reform evils.

5. A folktale or fantasy is a good vehicle for social criticism because the writer can remain objective and detached.

6. Swift makes his essay more effective by pretending to advocate something that is completely unbelievable.

TECHNIQUES

Author's Purpose

If the purpose of the writers in this unit is to hold up for critical scrutiny some facet of society, discuss and decide which selections in this unit do the best job of the following:

1. Making clear and obvious what was being criticized.

2. Making you want to help the situation.

3. Making you sympathetic with the characters.

4. Making you puzzle over possible meanings.

5. Shaking you up and giving you a new viewpoint.

Irony

First think through and decide what your own opinion is about the following questions. Then discuss them.

1. Which selection makes the best use of verbal irony?

2. Which has the most telling example of dramatic irony?

3. Which type, verbal irony or dramatic irony, is used more in these selections?

4. Which type of irony has the greater effect on you emotionally? Which mentally?

5. Why do you think irony is such a common literary device?

WRITING FROM READING

1. Try your hand at writing your own "Modest Proposal." Think of an absolutely outrageous proposition: for example, that people are forbidden to eat all yellow or green fruits and vegetables; that no one is permitted to have a pet; that children are delegated to run the military; that schools should teach only sports; etc. Write your proposal in a straightforward, serious way bringing forth all the logical arguments you can to support your proposition.

2. Consider this sentence. _____ is like a _____. Fill in the first blank with a social issue, such as war, poverty, political corruption, civil rights, women's liberation, etc. In the second blank, put in the first *object* that comes to your mind no matter how ridiculous it may seem. Now write three or more short statements about the second word. These statements should have some connection with the social problem. Let's take an example: *War* is like an *apple*. An apple is red. It decays. It often has worms. It satisfies certain appetites. Now using the ideas you have jotted down, write an extended simile. Take turns reading some of these aloud. How many of them are ironic?

TWENTIETH-CENTURY BRITISH POETRY:
The Present and the Past

William Butler Yeats compared the writing of the twentieth century with earlier English literature in his short poem "Three Movements":

> Shakespearean fish swam the sea, far away
>   from land;
> Romantic fish swam in nets coming to the hand;
> What are all those fish that lie gasping on
>   the strand?

Yeats viewed Shakespeare and other Elizabethan poets as being bold, free, and adventurous. He pictured Romantic poets as being somewhat more closely related to the common person—catchable, accessible. And he saw himself and other writers of his time as struggling, "gasping on the strand." The change Yeats describes through the metaphor is based on one of modern poetry's most striking characteristics— its sense that the world has lost greatness and faith and that poetry is left to utter desperately that loss.

The causes for such a feeling are many and complex. Certainly the doubts that had troubled Tennyson and Arnold still trouble twentieth-century writers. Moreover, revolution had turned into bloody, messy war: the constant fighting in Ireland, the Spanish Civil War, the two world wars, and Vietnam. The Industrial Revolution had brought technology to nineteenth-century England, but in the twentieth century, the changes caused by that technology have come more quickly. To many observers, human beings seem prisoners of their creations; machines control their lives, and sophisticated war machines kill them.

Modern poets often respond to these social and political changes by turning to the past, but in two contradictory ways. First, just as Renaissance poets rediscovered the richness of classical literature, so modern poets have rediscovered their own literary heritage, especially medieval and Renaissance poetry. They include in their poems specific allusions to earlier literature, and they borrow many earlier poetic forms, frequently using heavy alliteration and striking, even bizarre, images.

But even as they turn to the past for images of a greatness that once existed, they also reject the past. They feel, as Yeats puts it, "Myself I must remake," and that remaking calls for new forms, new language, new thoughts. So the second relationship to the past involves a breaking away from older forms. When Gerard Manley Hopkins, writing out of traditional Catholic beliefs and using a form as structured as the sonnet, praises "God's grandeur," he invents his own rhythms to do so. T. S. Eliot, like Browning, writes a memorable dramatic monologue, "The Love Song of J. Alfred Prufrock." But instead of the structured couplets characteristic of Browning, we find fragments of lines and images whose connections *we* must find. The lines sometimes rhyme and sometimes do not. Some lines are long and some are short. Pattern in the old sense does not exist because the belief in a stable, meaningful world that can be portrayed in stable patterns also does not exist.

We cannot sum up twentieth-century poetry, in part because the century is not over, but even more because each poet creates a new form and a new voice. We can say only that reading modern poetry demands careful attention to language, imagery, and style—sometimes to see the reflection of the past, sometimes to see the new shape of the present.

GERARD MANLEY HOPKINS

Although Gerard Manley Hopkins lived from 1844 to 1889, there are reasons
to consider him a twentieth-century rather than a nineteenth-century
poet. First of all, his work did not appear during his lifetime. In fact, it
remained unpublished until 1918, when his friend Robert Bridges brought out
an edition of his poetry. Moreover, the poems are noticeably experimental.
Hopkins devised a new system of marking rhythmic stresses, and he was fond
of making up new words. The strangeness of his language, imagery,
and rhythm is counterbalanced by the traditional quality of other poetic
devices. Hopkins uses a great deal of alliteration and assonance, techniques
we find often in medieval poetry. And since he was a Jesuit priest, the beliefs
too are traditional. Poem after poem begins in contemplation of a
natural image and then turns to the maker of the natural world.
Hopkins believed strongly in the individual distinctiveness of every living
thing. He gave the name *inscape* (a Hopkins-coined word, related to
landscape) to that quality that makes each living being different and special.
As we look at the following poems, we see an "oddness" in unusual
words and in Hopkins's "sprung rhythm." We also should see that delight in
and celebration of the distinctive inscape which, for Hopkins, reminds
us that in our differences we are all still the same.

God's Grandeur

The world is charged with the grandeur of God.
   It will flame out, like shining from shook foil;[1]
   It gathers to a greatness, like the ooze of oil
Crushed.[2] Why do men then now not reck his rod?
Generations have trod, have trod, have trod;   5
   And all is seared with trade; bleared, smeared with toil;
   And wears man's smudge and shares man's smell: the soil
Is bare now, nor can foot feel, being shod.

And for all this, nature is never spent;
   There lives the dearest freshness deep down things;   10
And though the last lights off the black West went
   Oh, morning, at the brown brink eastward, springs—
Because the Holy Ghost over the bent
   World broods with warm breast and with ah! bright wings.

---

1. **shook foil,** shaken foil. See page 618 of this book.
2. **oil Crushed,** the reference is to crushing olives in
making olive oil.

Spring and Fall

To a Young Child

Margaret, are you grieving
Over Goldengrove unleaving?
Leaves, like the things of man, you
With your fresh thoughts care for, can you?
Ah! as the heart grows older   5
It will come to such sights colder
By and by, nor spare a sigh
Though worlds of wanwood leafmeal¹ lie;
And yet you will weep and know why.
Now no matter, child the name: 10
Sorrow's springs are the same.
Nor mouth had, no nor mind, expressed
What heart heard of, ghost² guessed:
It is the blight man was born for,
It is Margaret you mourn for.   15

---

1. **wanwood leafmeal,** two words coined by Hopkins.
Wanwood means "pale or dim forests." The paleness
could be due to the light colors of the autumn leaves
or to the effect of the light filtered through the leaves.
Leafmeal could, by analogy with "piecemeal," be
"leaf by leaf," or it could mean "leaf mold."
2. **ghost,** archaic word for spirit or soul.

God's Grandeur

1. The images in the poem seem strange symbols
of grandeur—the light from a piece of metal foil that
is shaken, and the gathering of oil from crushed
olives. Discuss: It is much more forceful for the poet
to have used unusual comparisons than familiar
ones.

2. What, according to Hopkins, have human
beings done to the Earth?

3. How does the poem go about illustrating the
proposition stated in the first line: "The world is
charged with the grandeur of God"?

4. Hopkins wrote in what he called *sprung rhythm,* a kind of meter quite different from that used
in the other poems in this book. Still, there is a strong
pattern to the sound. Read the poem aloud, discovering the strong beats that come naturally from the
phrasing. You should find five beats to a line, even
though the number of syllables varies. Notice how the
sprung rhythm springs in particular on the word *ah!*
in the last line.

Spring and Fall

1. Why does autumn produce sad thoughts? What
natural details are given emotional connotations?

2. What do you understand the last two lines of
the poem to mean?

WILLIAM BUTLER YEATS

Perhaps more than any other poet of our century, William Butler Yeats (1865–1939) expressed the combined passions of public issues and private longings. An Irish citizen, he helped found the Irish National Theatre and searched in Gaelic mythology for characters and symbols for his plays. Yeats also served as a senator of the Irish Free State. He was also a keen lover of Oriental art, a mystic, and a constructor of elaborately personal symbolic systems. Many of Yeats's poems begin with himself or his reaction to a particular situation. In "The Wild Swans at Coole," for example, we begin with the poet looking back at his life nineteen years earlier, and we share the sensation of time passing. A complex poet, Yeats combined symbols from Oriental and Greek mythologies. Sometimes he made up his own symbols, and he changed stanza forms, rhythms, and vocabulary from poem to poem. This complexity was needed to express his intense and varying emotions. In a late poem called "The Circus Animals' Desertion," Yeats describes himself as an old man, a "broken man," deserted by the ideas, the themes, the plays, and the poems of his earlier years. But, as the last stanza tells us, he resolves to begin again. And the place where one begins is, in his words, "the foul rag-and-bone shop of the heart." This phrase gives us a clue to Yeats's artistry and vision. For one thing, it is startlingly accurate if we consider the physical heart as surrounded first by the body's bones and then by the rags we wear. The phrase also displays contradictory emotions, describing simultaneous beauty and ugliness. It is therefore representative of Yeats's style, a style that speaks directly of all experience.

The Lamentation of the Old Pensioner

Although I shelter from the rain
Under a broken tree,
My chair was nearest to the fire
In every company
That talked of love or politics,   5
Ere Time transfigured me.

Though lads are making pikes[1] again
For some conspiracy,
And crazy rascals rage their fill
At human tyranny,   10
My contemplations are of Time
That has transfigured me.

There's not a woman turns her face
Upon a broken tree,
And yet the beauties that I loved   15
Are in my memory;
I spit into the face of Time
That has transfigured me.

---

1. **pikes** (pīks), weapons consisting of a metal spearhead on a long wooden shaft.

An Irish Airman Foresees His Death[1]

I know that I shall meet my fate
Somewhere among the clouds above;
Those that I fight I do not hate,
Those that I guard I do not love;
My country is Kiltartan Cross,[2]   5
My countrymen Kiltartan's poor,
No likely end could bring them loss
Or leave them happier than before.
Nor law, nor duty bade me fight,
Nor public men, nor cheering crowds,   10
A lonely impulse of delight
Drove to this tumult in the clouds;
I balanced all, brought all to mind,
The years to come seemed waste of breath,
A waste of breath the years behind   15
In balance with this life, this death.

---

1. The airman is Major Robert Gregory, son of Yeats's
friend, Lady Augusta Gregory; she helped Yeats found
the Irish Literary Theatre. Gregory was killed in 1917,
flying over Italy. Although an Irishman, he was a member of England's Royal Flying Corps.
2. **Kiltartan Cross,** Kiltartan was a village on Lady Gregory's estate, thus Kiltartan Cross would be the village
square (frequently marked by a cross) and Kiltartan's
poor are the poor of Ireland.

The Wild Swans
at Coole

The trees are in their autumn beauty,
The woodland paths are dry
Under the October twilight the water
Mirrors a still sky;
Upon the brimming water among the stones   5
Are nine-and-fifty swans.

The nineteenth autumn has come upon me
Since I first made my count;
I saw, before I had well finished,
All suddenly mount   10
And scatter wheeling in great broken rings
Upon their clamorous wings.

I have looked upon those brilliant creatures,
And now my heart is sore.
All's changed since I, hearing at twilight,   15
The first time on this shore,
The bell-beat of their wings above my head,
Trod with a lighter tread.

Unwearied still, lover by lover,
They paddle in the cold   20
Companionable streams or climb the air;
Their hearts have not grown old;
Passion or conquest, wander where they will,
Attend upon them still.

But now they drift on the still water,   25
Mysterious, beautiful;
Among what rushes will they build,
By what lake's edge or pool
Delight men's eyes when I awake some day
To find they have flown away?   30

Reprinted with permission of The Macmillan Company from *Collected Poems* by W. B. Yeats. Copyright 1919 The Macmillan Company. Renewed 1946 by Bertha Georgie Yeats.

The Lamentation of the Old Pensioner

1. In what sense has time transfigured the old pensioner?

2. Why does the speaker spit into the face of time.

3. What specific historical event is the poet referring to in lines 7–10? What is their wider meaning?

4. In the last stanza, lines 13–18, the poet contrasts tranquillity with violence. What effect does this have on the readers? Does line 17 succeed as a line of poetry, or does its violence stop readers—forcing them to disregard the poem as a whole?

An Irish Airman Foresees His Death

1. The speaker lists a number of reasons why he is *not* fighting. What are they and why does he put the explanation in the negative?

2. What is the real reason for his action that eventually leads to his death?

3. The last four lines speak of balance; how many different kinds of balance are reflected in these lines? How is balance crucial for an understanding of the poem?

The Wild Swans at Coole

1. What has happened to the poet during the nineteen years since he first counted the swans? What has happened to the swans?

2. What is the season of the year? How does it reflect the theme of the poem?

3. What is implied by the following lines: " . . . when I awake some day / To find they have flown away"?

D. H. LAWRENCE

D. H. Lawrence (1885–1930) brought to English literature the passionate feelings of a rebel. Lawrence was born and educated in Nottingham and taught school for a time in London. But he lived abroad for most of his life. Lawrence's novels emphasize the individual's right to have personal passions and to remain true to these personal desires. Lawrence does not use standard line lengths or rhyme schemes; each poem creates its own shape, as in the undulating lines of "Snake." And the poem asks us to rebel too, against our instinctive fears and learned prejudices.

Snake

A snake came to my water trough
On a hot, hot day, and I in pajamas for the heat,
To drink there.

In the deep, strange-scented shade of the great dark carob tree[1]
I came down the steps with my pitcher 5
And must wait, must stand and wait, for there he was at the trough
    before me.

He reached down from a fissure in the earth-wall in the gloom
And trailed his yellow-brown slackness soft-bellied down, over the
    edge of the stone trough
And rested his throat upon the stone bottom,
And where the water had dripped from the tap, in a small clearness, 10
He sipped with his straight mouth,
Softly drank through his straight gums, into his slack long body,
Silently.

Someone was before me at my water trough,
And I, like a second-comer, waiting. 15

He lifted his head from his drinking, as cattle do,
And looked at me vaguely, as drinking cattle do,
And flickered his two-forked tongue from his lips, and mused a moment,
And stooped and drank a little more,
Being earth-brown, earth golden from the burning bowels of the earth, 20
On the day of Sicilian July, with Etna[2] smoking.

The voice of my education said to me
He must be killed,
For in Sicily the black black snakes are innocent, the gold are venomous.

And voices in me said, If you were a man 25
You would take a stick and break him now, and finish him off.

But must I confess how I liked him,
How glad I was he had come like a guest in quiet, to drink at my
    water trough
And depart peaceful, pacified, and thankless
Into the burning bowels of this earth? 30

---

1. **carob tree,** an evergreen of the Mediterranean regions.
2. **Etna,** volcano on Sicily.

Was it cowardice, that I dared not kill him?
Was it perversity, that I longed to talk to him?
Was it humility, to feel so honored?
I felt so honored.

And yet those voices: 35
If you were not afraid, you would kill him!

And truly I was afraid, I was most afraid,
But even so, honored still more
That he should seek my hospitality
From out the dark door of the secret earth. 40

He drank enough
And lifted his head, dreamily, as one who has drunken,
And flickered his tongue like a forked night on the air, so black,
Seeming to lick his lips,
And looked around like a god, unseeing, into the air, 45
And slowly turned his head,
And slowly, very slowly, as if thrice adream
Proceeded to draw his slow length curving round
And climb the broken bank of my wall-face.

And as he put his head into that dreadful hole, 50
And as he slowly drew up, snake-easing his shoulders, and entered further,
A sort of horror, a sort of protest against his withdrawing into that
　　horrid black hole,
Deliberately going into the blackness, and slowly drawing himself after,
Overcame me now his back was turned.

I looked round, I put down my pitcher, 55
I picked up a clumsy log
And threw it at the water trough with a clatter.
I think it did not hit him;
But suddenly that part of him that was left behind convulsed in
　　undignified haste,
Writhed like lightning, and was gone 60

Into the black hole, the earth-lipped fissure in the wall-front
At which, in the intense still noon, I stared with fascination.

And immediately I regretted it.
I thought how paltry,[3] how vulgar, what a mean act!
I despised myself and the voices of my accursed human education. 65

And I thought of the albatross[4]
And I wished he would come back, my snake.

For he seemed to me again like a king,
Like a king in exile, uncrowned in the underworld,
Now due to be crowned again. 70

And so, I missed my chance with one of the lords
Of life.
And I have something to expiate:
A pettiness.

3. **paltry** (pôl′ trē), almost worthless, petty.
4. **albatross** (al′bə trôs), The albatross was killed by Coleridge's Ancient Mariner; the impulsive slaying haunted his life.

"The Snake" by D. H. Lawrence, from *The Complete Poems of D. H. Lawrence*, edited by Vivian de Sola Pinto and F. Warren Roberts. Copyright © 1964, 1971 by Angelo Ravagli and C. M. Weekley, Executors of the Estate of Frieda Lawrence. Reprinted by permission of Viking Penguin Inc.

T. S. ELIOT

T. S. Eliot (1888–1965) had both American and English ties. He was born in
St. Louis, Missouri, and was educated at Harvard. But he settled
in London in 1915 and acquired British citizenship in 1927. To many people,
he is the one poet who clearly expresses the sense of loss and
fragmentation of the modern world—a view that is apparent from the titles of
poetic works such as *The Waste Land* and "The Hollow Men." Within
his poems we find quotations from other authors. There are frequent allusions
to Dante, Shakespeare, Goethe, and other Western writers as well as to
Oriental culture and Eastern writers. Eliot alludes to so many great works of
the past both to search for help and to remind us of the spiritual,
intellectual, and emotional poverty of our own time. Nowhere
is that poverty shown more devastatingly than in "The Love Song
of J. Alfred Prufrock," the long poem that follows this introduction. The poem
is a dramatic monologue (the "you" being addressed is probably the speaker
himself). In it a middle-aged man with a ridiculous, slightly pompous
name talks about himself. He speaks to us perhaps as the speaker of the
poem's epigraph speaks to Dante—thinking that he is safe because no one
will ever repeat his words. The reference to Dante puts the poem in the
context of being in hell. This is a modern version of hell, though, made up of
constant trivial chatter (Michelangelo is reduced to meaningless talk)
and an overwhelming sense of absurdity. Other great figures are evoked—
John the Baptist, Lazarus whom Christ raised from the dead, and
Hamlet—and always Prufrock feels his inadequacy. For Eliot, one possible
answer to the meaninglessness he saw about him lay in faith. It is
not accidental that Eliot, like Gerard Manley Hopkins, was a devoutly religious
person. "The Journey of the Magi" shows us the combination of the
modern questioning attitude and traditional faith, as the speaker
tries to fathom the mystery of Christ's birth. Eliot's poems demand
careful reading; he often does not make transitions but forces us to connect one
image to another, one stanza to another. He breaks up our expectations
of formal pattern by giving us unrhymed lines and then suddenly
shifting back into rhyme. The form of the poetry reflects the uneasiness
of the poet's outlook; the world is for him, in spite of faith, a difficult
place to comprehend. His poetry must, if it is to be honest, mirror
that complex difficulty.

The Love Song of J. Alfred Prufrock

S'io credesse che mia risposta fosse
a persona che mai tornasse al mondo,
questa fiamma staria senza più scosse.
Ma per cio che giammai di questo fondo
non torno vivo alcun, s'i'odo il vero,
Senza tema d'infamia ti rispondo.[1]

Let us go then, you and I,
When the evening is spread out against the sky
Like a patient etherized upon a table;
Let us go, through certain half-deserted streets,
The muttering retreats   5
Of restless nights in one-night cheap hotels
And sawdust[2] restaurants with oyster shells:
Streets that follow like a tedious argument
Of insidious intent
To lead you to an overwhelming question . . .   10
Oh, do not ask, "What is it?"
Let us go and make our visit.

In the room the women come and go
Talking of Michelangelo.
The yellow fog that rubs its back upon the windowpanes,   15
The yellow smoke that rubs its muzzle on the windowpanes
Licked its tongue into the corners of the evening,
Lingered upon the pools that stand in drains,
Let fall upon its back the soot that falls from chimneys,
Slipped by the terrace, made a sudden leap,   20
And seeing that it was a soft October night,
Curled once about the house, and fell asleep.

And indeed there will be time
For the yellow smoke that slides along the street,
Rubbing its back upon the windowpanes;   25
There will be time, there will be time
To prepare a face to meet the faces that you meet;
There will be time to murder and create,
And time for all the works and days of hands
That lift and drop a question on your plate;   30
Time for you and time for me,
And time yet for a hundred indecisions,
And for a hundred visions and revisions,
Before the taking of a toast and tea.

---

1. The epigraph to this poem comes from Dante's *Inferno*, Canto 27, lines 61–66. The speaker is a man in the eighth circle of hell (the ninth being the lowest). He tells Dante and Virgil that he is willing to talk about himself because he is sure that they won't return to the world. The lines translate as follows:

    If I thought my answer were given
    to anyone who would ever return to the world,

this flame would stand still without moving any
    further.
But since never from this abyss
has anyone ever returned alive, if what I hear is
    true,
without fear of infamy I answer thee.
2. **sawdust,** with sawdust on the floors.

In the room the women come and go   35
Talking of Michelangelo.

And indeed there will be time
To wonder, "Do I dare?" and, "Do I dare?"
Time to turn back and descend the stair,
With a bald spot in the middle of my hair—   40
(They will say: "How his hair is growing thin!")
My morning coat, my collar mounting firmly to the chin,
My necktie rich and modest, but asserted by a simple pin—
(They will say: "But how his arms and legs are thin!")
Do I dare   45
Disturb the universe?
In a minute there is time
For decisions and revisions which a minute will reverse.

For I have known them all already, known them all—
Have known the evenings, mornings, afternoons,   50
I have measured out my life with coffee spoons;
I know the voices dying with a dying fall
Beneath the music from a farther room.
    So how should I presume?
And I have known the eyes already, known them all—   55
The eyes that fix you in a formulated phrase,
And when I am formulated, sprawling on a pin,
When I am pinned and wriggling on the wall,
Then how should I begin
To spit out all the butt-ends of my days and ways?   60
    And how should I presume?

And I have known the arms already, known them all—
Arms that are braceleted and white and bare
(But in the lamplight, downed with light brown hair!)
Is it perfume from a dress   65
That makes me so digress?
Arms that lie along a table, or wrap about a shawl.
    And should I then presume?
    And how should I begin?

                    •   •   •   •   •

Shall I say, I have gone at dusk through narrow streets   70
And watched the smoke that rises from the pipes
Of lonely men in shirt-sleeves, leaning out of windows? . . .

I should have been a pair of ragged claws
Scuttling across the floors of silent seas.

                    •   •   •   •   •

And the afternoon, the evening, sleeps so peacefully!   75
Smoothed by long fingers,
Asleep . . . tired . . . or it malingers,
Stretched on the floor, here beside you and me.
Should I, after tea and cakes and ices,
Have the strength to force the moment to its crisis?   80
But though I have wept and fasted, wept and prayed,
Though I have seen my head (grown slightly bald) brought in
        upon a platter[3]
I am no prophet—and here's no great matter;
I have seen the moment of my greatness flicker,
And I have seen the eternal Footman hold my coat, and snicker,   85
And in short, I was afraid.
And would it have been worth it, after all,
After the cups, the marmalade, the tea,
Among the porcelain, among some talk of you and me,
Would it have been worth while,   90
To have bitten off the matter with a smile,
To have squeezed the universe into a ball
To roll it toward some overwhelming question,
To say: "I am Lazarus[4] come from the dead,
Come back to tell you all, I shall tell you all"—   95
If one, settling a pillow by her head,
    Should say: "That is not what I meant at all.
        That is not it, at all."

And would it have been worth it, after all,
Would it have been worth while,   100
After the sunsets and the dooryards and the sprinkled streets,
After the novels, after the teacups, after the skirts that trail
        along the floor—
And this, and so much more?—
It is impossible to say just what I mean!
But as if a magic lantern threw the nerves in patterns on a screen: 105
Would it have been worth while
If one, settling a pillow or throwing off a shawl,
And turning toward the window, should say:
    "That is not it at all,
        That is not what I meant, at all."   110

          •   •   •   •   •

---

3. This is a reference to the story of John the Baptist.
See the New Testament, Matthew 4:11.
4. Lazarus was raised from the dead. See the New
Testament, John 11.

No! I am not Prince Hamlet[5] nor was meant to be;
Am an attendant lord, one that will do
To swell a progress,[6] start a scene or two,
Advise the prince; no doubt, an easy tool,
Deferential, glad to be of use,   115
Politic, cautious, and meticulous;
Full of high sentence,[7] but a bit obtuse;
At times, indeed, almost ridiculous—
Almost, at times, the Fool.

I grow old . . . I grow old . . .   120
I shall wear the bottoms of my trousers rolled.

Shall I part my hair behind? Do I dare to eat a peach?
I shall wear white flannel trousers, and walk upon the beach.
I have heard the mermaids singing, each to each.

I do not think that they will sing to me.   125

I have seen them riding seaward on the waves
Combing the white hair of the waves blown back
When the wind blows the water white and black.

We have lingered in the chambers of the sea
By sea-girls wreathed with seaweed red and brown   130
Till human voices wake us, and we drown.

---

5. **Hamlet,** since he was a prince of Denmark, whatever Hamlet said was of importance.
6. **to swell a progress,** to add to a procession.
7. **full of high sentence,** full of wise observations.

Journey of the Magi [1]

'A cold coming we had of it,
Just the worst time of the year
For a journey, and such a long journey:
The ways deep and the weather sharp,
The very dead of winter.'[2]   5
And the camels galled, sore-footed, refractory,[3]
Lying down in the melting snow.
There were times we regretted
The summer palaces on slopes, the terraces,

And the silken girls bringing sherbet. 10
Then the camel men cursing and grumbling
And running away, and wanting their liquor and women,
And the night-fires going out, and the lack of shelters,
And the cities hostile and the towns unfriendly
And the villages dirty and charging high prices: 15
A hard time we had of it.
At the end we preferred to travel all night,
Sleeping in snatches,
With the voices singing in our ears, saying
That this was all folly. 20

Then at dawn we came down to a temperate valley,
Wet, below the snow line, smelling of vegetation;
With a running stream and a water-mill beating the darkness,
And three trees on the low sky,
And an old white horse galloped away in the meadow. 25
Then we came to a tavern with vine-leaves over the lintel,
Six hands at an open door dicing for pieces of silver,
And feet kicking the empty wine-skins.
But there was no information, and so we continued
And arrived at evening, not a moment too soon 30
Finding the place; it was (you may say) satisfactory.

All this was a long time ago, I remember,
And I would do it again, but set down
This set down
This: were we led all that way for 35
Birth or Death? There was a Birth, certainly,
We had evidence and no doubt. I had seen birth and death,
But had thought they were different; this Birth was
Hard and bitter agony for us, like Death, our death.
We returned to our places, these Kingdoms, 40
But no longer at ease here, in the old dispensation,⁴
With an alien people clutching their gods.
I should be glad of another death.

---

1. **Magi** (mā′jī), the three wise men who journeyed to Bethlehem to witness the birth of Jesus.
2. Eliot consciously adapted lines from a sermon preached in 1622 by Bishop Lancelot Andrewes: "Last, we consider the *time* of their coming, the season of the year. It was no *summer Progress*. A cold coming they had of it, at this time of the year; just, the worst time of the year, to take a journey, and specially a long journey, in. The ways deep, the weather sharp, the days short, the sun farthest off . . . the very dead of *Winter*."
3. **refractory** (ri frak′tər ē), stubborn.
4. **old dispensation**, the former system of belief, now made old by the birth of Jesus, which brought the new dispensation.

Snake

1. Notice the way in which Lawrence uses long lines and short lines. What effects can you describe for such lines as "And must wait, must stand and wait, for there he was at the trough before me" (6), "A sort of horror, a sort of protest against his withdrawing into that horrid black hole" (52), "I felt so honored" (34), and "A pettiness" (74)?

2. What words suggest the instinctive horror Lawrence feels for the snake? What words suggest more positive feelings? What are those feelings?

3. What are the different voices that speak to Lawrence?

4. Why does he throw a log at the snake?

5. How do you understand the reference, "And I thought of the albatross"?

6. Is it an overstatement to call the snake "a king in exile" and "one of the lords of life"?

The Love Song of J. Alfred Prufrock

Consider and discuss these propositions:

1. Prufrock is haunted by the pettiness and triviality of his life.

2. Prufrock thinks of himself as a slightly ridiculous figure.

3. He still has some desires and ambitions left, but his own timidity prevents him from achieving them.

4. Discuss the implications of the following lines:

a. "Do I dare/Disturb the universe?"

b. "I have measured out my life with coffee spoons."

c. "I should have been a pair of ragged claws/ Scuttling across the floors of silent seas."

d. "It is impossible to say just what I mean!"

e. "I am Lazarus, come from the dead."

The Journey of the Magi

1. The sermon that provides the starting point for this poem describes the journey of the Magi from the third-person point of view. Eliot changes to the first-person point of view. What is the effect of this change?

2. There are three locations in the poem—the place where the Magi live, the road, and the place being sought. How does the poem evoke the different quality of these places?

3. What symbolic implications do you find in lines 24–28?

4. The speaker asks: "were we led all that way for/ Birth or Death?" What is the poem's answer?

5. How would you interpret the last line of the poem?

POETRY AND WAR

The revolutions that shook the nineteenth century to its intellectual and spiritual foundations had their twentieth-century counterparts in World War I and World War II. Those events changed forever the attitude toward war. If President Woodrow Wilson could claim that America entered World War I "to make the world safe for democracy," that pious hope would be shattered when Hitler's armies marched into Poland twenty years later. And the horrors of World War II created scars yet unhealed—whether for the survivors of the Nazi concentration camps or of Hiroshima and Nagasaki. The poems in this section are antiwar poems that protest the inhumanity of war. They also argue that we should not create peaceful, comforting illusions to shield ourselves from that inhumanity. The first two poems are specifically about World War I. The first, "Dulce et decorum est" is by Wilfred Owen (1893–1918), who died at the age of twenty-five, a week before the Armistice. The poem ends with Horace's famous saying, "It is sweet and fitting to die for one's country." It also describes vividly the horror of that dying. Alice

Meynell (1847–1922), who devoted her life to humanitarian causes as well as to writing, presents another view of the war in "Summer in England, 1914." She contrasts the beauty of the summer with the ugly reality of war. Stephen Spender (1909–   ), a British poet, editor, and critic (who was a close friend of W. H. Auden), takes us to World War II where he shows us how even a "winner" is implicated in the horrors of war: "Responsibility: The Pilots Who Destroyed Germany in the Spring of 1945." Thom Gunn (1929–   ) was too young to fight in World War II, but he uses an image from that war to talk about one of war's most frightening consequences: the deadening of human sensitivity and compassion.

Dulce et decorum est

Bent double, like old beggars under sacks,
Knock-kneed, coughing like hags, we cursed through sludge,
Till on the haunting flares we turned our backs,
And towards our distant rest began to trudge.
Men marched asleep. Many had lost their boots,   5
But limped on, blood-shod. All went lame, all blind;
Drunk with fatigue; deaf even to the hoots
Of gas shells dropping softly behind.

Gas! Gas! Quick, boys!—An ecstasy of fumbling,
Fitting the clumsy helmets just in time,   10
And flound'ring like a man in fire or lime.
Dim through the misty panes and thick green light,
As under a green sea, I saw him drowning.

In all my dreams before my helpless sight   15
He plunges at me, guttering,[1] choking, drowning.
If in some smothering dreams, you too could pace
Behind the wagon that we flung him in,
And watch the white eyes wilting in his face,
His hanging face, like a devil's sick of sin,   20
If you could hear, at every jolt, the blood
Come gargling from the froth-corrupted lungs
Bitten as the cud
Of vile, incurable sores on innocent tongues,—
My friend, you would not tell with such high zest   25
To children ardent for some desperate glory,
The old lie: Dulce et decorum est
Pro patria mori.
WILFRED OWEN

---

1. **guttering,** melting away like the wax of a candle.

Summer in England, 1914

On London fell a clearer light;
　Caressing pencils of the sun
Defined the distances, the white
　Houses transfigured one by one,
The "long, unlovely street"[1] impearled.[2]　　　　5
Oh, what a sky has walked the world!

Most happy year! And out of town
　The hay was prosperous, and the wheat;
The silken harvest climbed the down:[3]
　Moon after moon was heavenly-sweet,　　　　10
Stroking the bread within the sheaves,
Looking 'twixt apples and their leaves.

And while this rose made round her cup,
　The armies died convulsed. And when
This chaste young silver sun went up　　　　15
　Softly, a thousand shattered men,
One wet corruption, heaped the plain,
After a league-long[4] throb of pain.

Flower following tender flower; and birds,
　And berries; and benignant[5] skies　　　　20
Made thrive[6] the serried[7] flocks and herds. —
　Yonder are men shot through the eyes.
　　Love, hide thy face
From man's unpardonable race.

ALICE MEYNELL

---

1. **"long unlovely street"** The line appears in Tennyson's
In Memoriam.
2. **impearled** (im pėrld'), adorned as if with pearls, here
made lovely by the bright light.
3. **down**, archaic form of hill (as in *dune*).
4. **league-long**, as long as a league (3 miles).
5. **benignant** (bi nig'nənt), kindly.
6. **thrive**, flourish.
7. **serried** (ser'ēd), compact, densely packed together.

Responsibility:
The Pilots Who Destroyed Germany
in the Spring of 1945

I stood on a roof top and they wove their cage
Their murmuring, throbbing cage, in the air of blue crystal,
I saw them gleam above the town like diamond bolts
Conjoining invisible struts of wire,
Carrying through the sky their geometric cage   5
Woven by senses delicate as a shoal of flashing fish.

They went. They left a silence in our streets below
Which boys gone to schoolroom leave in their playground.
A silence of asphalt, of privet hedge, of staring wall.
In the glass emptied sky their diamonds had scratched   10
Long curving finest whitest lines.

These the day soon melted into satin ribbons
Falling over heaven's terraces near the golden sun.

Oh that April morning they carried my will
Exalted expanding singing in their aeriel cage.   15
They carried my will. They dropped it on a German town.
My will expanded and tall buildings fell down.

Then, when the ribbons faded and the sky forgot,
And April was concerned with building nests and being hot
I began to remember the lost names and faces.   20

Now I tie the ribbons torn down from those terraces
Around the most hidden image in my lines,
And my life, which never paid the price of their wounds,
Turns thoughts over and over like a propellor
Assumes their guilt, honours, repents, prays for them.   25

STEPHEN SPENDER

Innocence

He ran the course and as he ran he grew,
And smelt his fragrance in the field. Already,
Running he knew the most he ever knew,
The egotism of a healthy body.

Ran into manhood, ignorant of the past: 5
Culture of guilt and guilt's vague heritage,
Self-pity and the soul; what he possessed
Was rich, potential, like the bud's tipped rage.

The Corps developed, it was plain to see,
Courage, endurance, loyalty and skill   10
To a morale firm as morality,
Hardening him to an instrument, until

The finitude of virtues that were there
Bodied within the swarthy uniform
A compact innocence, child-like and clear,   15
No doubt could penetrate, no act could harm.

When he stood near the Russian partisan
Being burned alive, he therefore could behold
The ribs wear gently through the darkening skin
And sicken only at the Northern cold,   20

Could watch the fat burn with a violet flame
And feel disgusted only at the smell,
And judge that all pain finishes the same
As melting quietly by his boots it fell.

THOM GUNN

Reprinted by permission of Farrar, Straus and Giroux, Inc. "Innocence" from
Selected Poems 1950–1975 by Thom Gunn, Copyright © 1961, 1971, 1979 by
Thom Gunn.

Dulce et decorum est

1. What attitude toward war is Owen attacking?

2. Whom does the poet mean by "you" in the last stanza?

3. Does Owen give the last two lines the same meaning that the original author (Horace) gave them?

Summer in England, 1914

1. How does Meynell convey a sense of happiness and prosperity in the first two stanzas?

2. What words describe the results of war?

3. What is the effect of the short line, "Love, hide thy face" (line 23)?

Responsibility

1. How does the speaker feel that he is different from the pilots? How is he like them?

2. What is the change of attitude in the speaker from the first part of the poem to the final stanza? What caused the change?

3. Why is the poem called "Responsibility"?

4. What do the figures of speech "cage," "ribbons," and "diamond bolts" symbolize?

Innocence

1. Is innocence a desirable quality?

2. What is a synonym for innocence (for example, blamelessness or ignorance)?

3. How is the boy of the poem innocent?

4. The poet says "no doubt could penetrate, no act could harm" his innocence. Explain.

5. Consider the following statements and decide whether the poem substantiates or refutes them:

a. Because of his good traits most people would consider the boy a desirable kind of person.

b. After watching the torture of the partisan, the boy is still innocent.

c. Thom Gunn states that there is no more dangerous kind of person than the unthinking "tool" who obeys orders innocently and without questioning.

QUESTIONS FOR DISCUSSION: POETRY AND WAR

1. Sometimes violent feelings do not necessarily lead to good poetry but just to polemic or propaganda. How do these poems avoid becoming merely angry or emotional?

2. Does the modern poet have a responsibility to write about war?

3. What relationships do you see between these poems?

STEVIE SMITH

Stevie Smith (1902–1971) was named Florence Margaret at birth. Because
she was so small, though, she acquired the nickname *Stevie*, borrowed from
a famous jockey of the period. She lived in London for most of her life,
writing poems illustrated with her own drawings and working in a publisher's
office for many years. Her poems are, on the surface, much simpler
than those of Eliot or Yeats. She uses familiar language and familiar poetic
forms. But it is that very ordinary quality that throws into sharp focus her
caustic observations on the modern world. In the poem given here, note how
Smith repeats phrases, adding new meaning with each repetition.
The poem delivers a frightening twist at the end as we recognize the
inescapable trap created for the characters and for ourselves.

Not Waving But Drowning

Nobody heard him, the dead man,
But still he lay moaning:
I was much further out than you thought
And not waving but drowning.

Poor chap, he always loved larking[1]
And now he's dead
It must have been too cold for him his heart gave way,
They said.

Oh, no no no, it was too cold always
(Still the dead one lay moaning)
I was much too far out all my life
And not waving but drowning.

---

1. **larking** (lärk′ing), playing around.

Stevie Smith, *Selected Poems*. Copyright © Stevie Smith 1962. Reprinted by permission of New Directions Publishing Corporation.

Not Waving But Drowning

1. Much of the poem depends on the use of familiar phrases whose meanings are altered. How does Smith change the meaning?

2. How would you describe the formal structure of the poem? What does that structure contribute to the poem's effect?

635

W. H. AUDEN

W. H. (Wystan Hugh) Auden (1907–1973), like Eliot, had loyalties to both England and America. He was born in York and attended Oxford but left England in 1939 for the United States. He later became a U. S. citizen, although in 1972 he was invited back to live at his old college at Oxford. Like many modern poets, Auden looks to the past and finds in it a vision missing in the modern world. Praise for the past is seen in the opening line of "Musée des Beaux Arts." The idea that one might write a poem about a painting—as Auden does about Brueghel's *The Fall of Icarus* (see page 643)—recurs in the modern period, for poets frequently find excellence in art. The second major quality of Auden's philosophy is a view of the world as mechanized and increasingly deadened. His poem "The Unknown Citizen" is an amusing, yet serious, account of what we have become through technology. In Stevie Smith's poem, the modern individual is "not waving, but drowning." In Auden's poem, the person is also dead, though now the metaphor is one of being imprisoned, within both the marble monument and the mechanized world.

Musée des Beaux Arts

About suffering they were never wrong,
The Old Masters: how well they understood
Its human position; how it takes place
While someone else is eating or opening a window or just walking dully along;
How, when the aged are reverently, passionately waiting   5
For the miraculous birth, there always must be
Children who did not specially want it to happen, skating
On a pond at the edge of the wood:
They never forgot
That even the dreadful martyrdom must run its course   10
Anyhow in a corner, some untidy spot
Where the dogs go on with their doggy life and the torturer's horse
Scratches its innocent behind on a tree.

In Brueghel's *Icarus*,[1] for instance: how everything turns away
Quite leisurely from the disaster; the plowman may   15
Have heard the splash, the forsaken cry,
But for him it was not an important failure; the sun shone
As it had to on the white legs disappearing into the green
Water; and the expensive delicate ship that must have seen
Something amazing, a boy falling out of the sky,   20
Had somewhere to get to and sailed calmly on.

---

1. See p. 643 for Brueghel's painting. (In early Greek legend, **Icarus** (ikʹər əs) ignored his father's warnings about protecting his wax wings from the melting heat of the sun. He tumbled from the sky to drown in the ocean.)

The Unknown Citizen
JS/07/M/378
This Marble Monument
Is Erected by the State

He was found by the Bureau of Statistics to be
One against whom there was no official complaint,
And all the reports on his conduct agree
That, in the modern sense of an old-fashioned word, he was a saint,
For in everything he did he served the Greater Community.   5
Except for the war till the day he retired
He worked in the factory and never got fired,
But satisfied his employers, Fudge Motors Inc.
Yet he wasn't a scab or odd in his views,
For his Union reports that he paid his dues,   10
(Our report on his Union shows it was sound)
And our Social Psychology workers found
That he was popular with his mates and liked a drink.
The Press are convinced that he bought a paper every day
And that his reactions to poetry were normal in every way.   15
Policies taken out in his name prove that he was fully insured,
And his Health Card shows he was once in hospital but left it cured.
Both Producers Research and High-Grade Living declare
He was fully sensible to the advantages of the Installment Plan
And had everything necessary to the Modern Man,   20
A gramophone, a radio, a car, and a frigidaire.
Our researchers into public opinion are content
That he held the proper opinions for the time of year.
When there was peace, he was for peace; when there was war, he went.
He was married and added five children to the population,   25
Which our Eugenists say was the right number for a parent of his generation,
And our teachers report that he never interfered with their education.
Was he free? Was he happy? The question is absurd:
Had anything been wrong, we certainly should have heard.

DYLAN THOMAS

Dylan Thomas (1914–1953) might well have spoken the line he gives to one of his characters in the verse play, *Under Milk Wood:* "Oh, isn't life a terrible thing, thank God!" The sense of life's danger, its terror, its wonder, and its joy fill Thomas's poetry, just as they filled his life. He left his native Wales at the age of twenty, already having published his first book of poems. He went to London, married Caitlin Macnamara, and continued writing poems—and drinking. One might almost think of him as a Romantic poet misplaced in the twentieth century, since, like Byron and Shelley, he was a well-known public figure. In his later years, Thomas frequently gave poetry readings in America and was famous for his magnificent performances, whether drunk or sober, whether on lecture platforms or in bars. More importantly, like Keats and like D. H. Lawrence, Thomas was in love with language and the sensory images it could evoke. There is passion in Thomas's poetry, for sensory description and for people and the quality with which they live. One of his most famous poems, "Do Not Go Gentle into That Good Night," written during the illness that finally took his father, attacks fiercely the notion of dying easily or gently. "In My Craft or Sullen Art" presents the familiar modern consciousness—the poet viewed as poet and making us highly aware that poetry is a crafted, shaped art.

Do Not Go Gentle into That Good Night

Do not go gentle into that good night.
Old age should burn and rave at close of day;
Rage, rage against the dying of the light.

Though wise men at their end know dark is right,
Because their words have forked no lightning they   5
Do not go gentle into that good night.

Good men, the last wave by, crying how bright
Their frail deeds might have danced in a green bay,
Rage, rage against the dying of the light.

Wild men who caught and sang the sun in flight,   10
And learn, too late, they grieved it on its way,
Do not go gentle into that good night.

Grave men, near death, who see with blinding sight
Blind eyes could blaze like meteors and be gay,
Rage, rage against the dying of the light.   15

And you, my father, there on the sad height,
Curse, bless, me now with your fierce tears, I pray.
Do not go gentle into that good night.
Rage, rage against the dying of the light.

In My Craft or Sullen Art

In my craft or sullen art
Exercised in the still night
When only the moon rages
And the lovers lie abed
With all their griefs in their arms,   5
I labour by singing light
Not for ambition or bread
Or the strut and trade of charms
On the ivory stages
But for the common wages   10
Of their most secret heart.

Not for the proud man apart
From the raging moon I write
On these spindrift[1] pages
Nor for the towering dead   15
With their nightingales and psalms
But for the lovers, their arms
Round the griefs of the ages,
Who pay no praise or wages
Nor heed my craft or art.   20

1. **spindrift,** spray blown from a rough sea or surf.

Musée des Beaux Arts

1. What is the relationship between the first and second stanzas of this poem?

2. To whom does the "they" in line 9 refer?

3. What is the difference in attitude between the "aged" and the "children"?

The Unknown Citizen

1. What does the title mean?

2. Who is speaking in this poem? What is the speaker's concept of the good life?

3. What is Auden attacking?

Do Not Go Gentle into That Good Night

1. In stanza 1, what is the meaning of "good night," "close of day," and "dying light"?

2. What four types of people are mentioned?

3. What has each kind of person failed to accomplish or understand?

4. Is the poet saying that the way to die is to protest against it with every bit of strength that you have?

In My Craft or Sullen Art

The structure of this poem is as follows: There are 20 lines in the poem, and each line has 7 syllables (except lines 11, 14, and 20, which have 6 syllables). The rhyme scheme is abcdebdecca abcdeecca.

1. Examine the three lines that are each six syllables. How are all three linked in relationship to meaning?

2. What is the basic irony of this poem?

SOME MODERN THEMES

The titles of the three poems in this section might almost be seen as representative of a number of important ideas in modern poetry. Elizabeth Jennings (1926–) worked as a librarian and a publisher's reader before becoming a poet. The title of her poem, "Answers," should be read in the context of the poem's insistence on answers that are small rather than large. Jennings shows that the modern poet frequently is aware of the individual's smallness in relation to the world, particularly a world overwhelmed by war and technology. The concern with identity and the way in which it can change is reflected in Jenny Joseph's (1932–) poem "Warning." She tells us of the number of faces we have, meaning not merely the one we see in the mirror but also the "faces" shown through our behavior. The warning in the poem is to all those people who seem unable to accept behavior in themselves or in others that differs from stereotypes. Dannie Abse (1923–), the Welsh poet and physician, also treats the problem of identity, but in a far less cheerful manner than Jenny Joseph. The "duality" of his poem's title is not easy to resolve. We see reflected in the frequent opposites of the poem the problems faced by all poets from early medieval times to the present. The words and the problems are still the same: love, hate, death, and God.

Answers

I kept my answers small and kept them near;
Big questions bruised my mind but still I let
Small answers be a bulwark to my fear.

The huge abstractions I kept from the light;
Small things I handled and caressed and loved.   5
I let the stars assume the whole of night.

But the big answers clamored to be moved
Into my life. Their great audacity
Shouted to be acknowledged and believed.

Even when all small answers build up to   10
Protection of my spirit, still I hear
Big answers striving for their overthrow

And all the great conclusions coming near.
ELIZABETH JENNINGS

Warning

When I am an old woman I shall wear purple
With a red hat which doesn't go, and doesn't suit me,
And I shall spend my pension on brandy and summer gloves
And satin sandals, and say we've no money for butter.
I shall sit down on the pavement when I'm tired   5
And gobble up samples in shops and press alarm bells
And run my stick along the public railings
And make up for the sobriety of my youth.
I shall go out in my slippers in the rain
And pick the flowers in other people's gardens   10
And learn to spit.
You can wear terrible shirts and grow more fat
And eat three pounds of sausages at a go
Or only bread and pickle for a week
And hoard pens and pencils and beermats and things in boxes.   15

But now we must have clothes that keep us dry
And pay our rent and not swear in the street
And set a good example for the children.
We will have friends to dinner and read the papers.

But maybe I ought to practice a little now?   20
So people who know me are not too shocked and surprised
When suddenly I am old and start to wear purple.
JENNY JOSEPH

"Warning" by Jenny Joseph from *New Poems*, 1963, by Jenny Joseph.
Reprinted by permission of the author.

Duality

Twice upon a time,
there was a man who had two faces,
two faces but one profile:
not Jekyll and Hyde, not good and bad,
and if one were cut, the other would bleed— 5
two faces different as hot and cold.

At night, hung on the hooks on the wall
above that man's minatory[1] head,
one wants brass where one wants gold,
one sees white and one sees black, 10
and one mouth eats the other
until the second sweet mouth bites back.

They dream their separate dreams
hanging on the wall above the bed.
The first voice cries: "He's not what he seems," 15
but the second one sighs: "He is what he is,"
the one shouts "wine" and the other screams "bread,"
and so they will all his raving days
until they die on his double-crossed head.

At signposts he must wear them both. 20
Each would go their separate ways
as the East or the West wind blows—
and dark and light they both would praise,
but one would melt, the other one freeze.

I am that man twice upon this time: 25
my two voices sing to make one rhyme.
Death I love and Death I hate,
(I'll be with you soon and late).
Love I love and Love I loathe,
God I mock and God I prove, 30
yes, myself I kill, myself I save.

Now, now, I hang these masks on the wall.
Oh Christ, take one and leave me all
lest four tears from two eyes fall.
DANNIE ABSE

---

1. **minatory** (min′ə tôr′ē), menacing, threatening.

From *Collected Poems* 1918–1976. Published by Hutchinson. © in this collection by Dannie Abse 1977.

THE FALL OF ICARUS   *Pieter Brueghel, the Elder*

The art critic Thomas Craven has said
that Breughel's painting *"The Fall of Icarus"* is "the greatest conception
of indifference in painting." W. H. Auden describes
this same painting in "Musée des Beaux Arts" (The Museum of Fine Arts).

Answers

1. What things seem to frighten the speaker? Is the fear justified?

2. Why is the last line placed by itself?

Warning

1. How do you feel about the behavior described in the first eleven lines? Is it irresponsible? Is it natural?

2. What details suggest "appropriate" behavior? What is the poet's attitude toward such behavior?

Duality

1. Consider the following implications of the title of the poem:

a. The quality of character is twofold.

b. The world is ruled by the antagonistic forces of good and evil.

2. Make a list of the actions, characteristics, and feelings of each of the two faces. Then discuss what the poet seems to be saying about the duality of human nature.

643

KNOW THYSELF

Human beings are complex creatures. We often lose our way and must grope for answers to the question "Who Am I?" Our picture of self may evolve from many sources: a sudden glimpse of our image in a store window, comments of friends and family, stored memories or quick impressions. We may try constantly to classify our own strengths and weaknesses, but the picture is never complete. And, too often, the picture becomes distorted.

Writers from all ages and cultures have repeated that if we do not first have self-knowledge, we cannot know other people and cannot begin to find our own place in the world. The Greeks inscribed the words KNOW THYSELF above the temple of the oracle at Delphi. The Spaniard, Cervantes, counseled in Don Quixote, "Make it thy business to know thyself which is the most difficult lesson in the world."

In modern times, the study of psychology has had a great influence on literature. Writers have gone more deeply into the unconscious minds of their characters in a new attempt to portray the eternal struggle to gain self-insight.

The following writers take us inside the minds of their characters. The crucial action they relate is often the making of a decision or a new evaluation of inner experience. Some of the selections are fiction; others are autobiographical essays. In both cases, the writers portray moments of doubt and moments of understanding. Through such writings, readers may sharpen their own self-portraits.

The tragic artist Vincent van Gogh painted
for only ten years at the end of his life.
During this time a succession of penetrating
self-portraits bear witness to his increasing
agitation, terror and madness.
This series of portraits traces the last
few years before his death in 1890. After
attempting to murder his friend Gauguin,
van Gogh, beset by guilt, cut off part of
his own ear. The second painting, reflecting
the style of the painter Gauguin, records
the self-inflicted damage. In 1889 as he
descended rapidly to his death, he paints
himself gaunt and brooding with harsh brush
strokes and morbid colors.

FRANZ KAFKA

1883-1924

Born in Prague, Czechoslovakia, to middle-class German parents, Franz Kafka became one of the great literary figures of his age. He seems early to have lost his self-confidence and to have developed a deep, troubling sense of guilt. Kafka fell victim to the conditions of his life: he was raised in the midst of Czech people yet spoke only German; he was Jewish; and he lived in a family of extroverts headed by a domineering, capricious father. All his life, Kafka struggled to please his father, whom he admired for his stolid strength yet hated for his insensitivity. When discussing ideas with friends, Kafka's words flowed freely, but in the presence of his father, he stuttered. Near the end of his life, Kafka wrote to his father, saying, "You began to have that mysterious quality which all tyrants have whose privilege is based on their personality, not on reason." Still later, in another letter, he added, "My writings are all about you."

His parents owned and operated a small wholesale dress firm whose logo was a black crow (appropriate because in Czech, *kafka* means crow). The boy and his three sisters, as in other shopkeepers' families, were expected to help in the shop whenever possible. His mother, Julie, a brilliant woman, much preferred to work side by side with her husband in their business than to stay at home and care for her family. Her son resented her continuous absence from their home.

Kafka's education began in a German-speaking elementary school, from which he graduated to a German-speaking secondary school that accepted only the best students. From there, he went to law school as his father wished, although Kafka, himself, favored the study of literature. After graduation, and at his father's insistence, Kafka took a well-paying governmental insurance post. But trying to write all night and work all day disintegrated his health. To remedy his splitting headaches and frayed nerves, Kafka tried vegetarianism, which brought no relief.

The year 1912 was important for Kafka. In August, he met "Fräulein F. B." whom he described in his diary as a "wholesome, merry, robust young woman." Though he loved her deeply, they never married because Kafka believed that his personality was not suited to marriage. In September, he wrote *The Judgment* in one sitting between ten o'clock in the evening and six o'clock the next morning. In October, he produced the long, opening chapter of *Amerika*, which Max Brod, his editor, published as a separate prize-winning story. And in November, Kafka finished *The Metamorphosis*, his greatest short piece. While writing it, he felt a terrible inwardness and urgency, as if the frozen ice of creativity had broken. He once wrote: "The books we need are of the kind that act upon us like a misfortune, that make us suffer like the death of someone we love more than ourselves, that make us feel as though we were on the verge of suicide or lost in a forest remote from all human habitation—a book should serve as the ax for the frozen sea within us."

Critics and readers alike are intrigued with the strange combinations that appear in Kafka's works; his simple, straightforward words are in sharp contrast to the bizarre events they report; his very real people and their very normal behavior are set down in a nightmarish world; his characters have a terrible need to establish order in the disordered, irrational events besetting them. Interestingly

Franz Kafka

enough, the brilliant Einstein claimed that he couldn't read Kafka "because the human mind isn't complicated enough." Yet almost everyone else who reads Kafka has few doubts about understanding exactly what Kafka is suggesting. That is, perhaps, a sign of Kafka's skill as a writer.

During the last year of his life, the few moments of happiness that Kafka knew came from his romance with Dora Dyman and his association with Max Brod, his friend and editor. Dying from tuberculosis, which was diagnosed in 1917, he instructed Brod to burn all his manuscripts after his death. Brod was caught in a moral dilemma, but he finally ignored Kafka's instructions and brought out three unfinished novels and many sketches and stories. This saved the great body of Kafka's work.

For Franz Kafka, the nightmarish world with its guilt-ridden dreams ended in a sanitorium on June 3, 1924. In answer to his doctor's promise to leave him, Kafka replied, "But I am leaving you." Then he died.

The Metamorphosis

The Metamorphosis, like Kafka's other works, is autobiographical and centers on the conflict between father and son. When Kafka had finished the story, he read it aloud to his friends, laughing uproariously. Neither his friends nor subsequent readers have had a similar reaction. Before the story was published, Kafka wrote Brod, begging that the illustrator not attempt to draw the insect, itself. "Not that, please, not that! . . . I wish to request it as a result of my better understanding of the story as is natural. The insect itself cannot be drawn. It cannot be drawn even as if seen from a distance."

The title, with its double meaning, adds further dimension to the story. *Metamorphosis* can mean a sudden change or transformation usually brought about by sorcery or magic. Fairy stories abound with such instances: a prince turned into a toad, a pumpkin changed into a coach, a rat changed to a coach driver.

But *metamorphosis* has a scientific meaning as well. It is used to describe the change of a tadpole into a frog or a maggot into a fly or a caterpillar into a butterfly. Metamorphosis in this sense is the change from the immature to the adult stage, completing the life cycle. Both of these meanings should be considered when reading the story.

Kafka once said that the supreme question of life was to determine what was real in the world. The world he presents in *The Metamorphosis* is a normal one except for one bizarre difference that imparts a strange and eerie dimension to reality. Certainly the opening sentence is one of the most dramatic beginnings in all literature, instantly pitching the reader into a macabre situation.

THE METAMORPHOSIS

As Gregor Samsa awoke one morning from uneasy dreams he found himself transformed in his bed into a gigantic insect. He was lying on his hard, as it were armor-plated, back and when he lifted his head a little he could see his dome-like brown belly divided into stiff arched segments on top of which the bed quilt could hardly keep in position and was about to slide off completely. His numerous legs, which were pitifully thin compared to the rest of his bulk, waved helplessly before his eyes.

What has happened to me? he thought. It was no dream. His room, a regular human bedroom, only rather too small, lay quiet between the four familiar walls. Above the table on which a collection of cloth samples was unpacked and spread out—Samsa was a commercial traveler—hung the picture which he had recently cut out of an illustrated magazine and put into a pretty gilt frame. It showed a lady, with a fur cap on and a fur stole, sitting upright and holding out to the spectator a huge fur muff into which the whole of her forearm had vanished!

Gregor's eyes turned next to the window, and the overcast sky—one could hear rain drops beating on the window gutter—made him quite melancholy. What about sleeping a little longer and forgetting all this nonsense, he thought, but it could not be done, for he was accustomed to sleep on his right side and in his present condition he could not turn himself over. However violently he forced himself towards his right side he always rolled on to his back again. He tried it at least a hundred times, shutting his eyes to keep from seeing his struggling legs, and only desisted when he began to feel in his side a faint dull ache he had never experienced before.

Oh drat, he thought, what an exhausting job I've picked on! Traveling about day in, day out. It's much more irritating work than doing the actual business in the office, and on top of that there's the trouble of constant traveling, of worrying about train connections, the bad and irregular meals, casual acquaintances that are always new and never become intimate friends. Well, they can take it all! He felt a slight itching up on his belly; slowly pushed himself on his back nearer to the top of the bed so that he could lift his head more easily; identified the itching place which was surrounded by many small white spots the nature of which he could not understand and made to touch it with a leg, but drew the leg back immediately, for the contact made a cold shiver run through him.

He slid down again into his former position. This getting up early, he thought, makes one quite stupid. A man needs his sleep. Other commercials live like harem women. For instance, when I come back to the hotel of a morning to write up the orders I've got, these others are only sitting down to breakfast. Let me just try that with my chief; I'd be sacked on the spot. Anyhow, that might be quite a good thing for me, who can tell? If I didn't have to hold my hand because of my parents I'd have given notice long ago, I'd have gone to the chief and told him exactly what I think of him. That would knock him endways from his desk! It's a queer way of doing, too, this sitting on high

at a desk and talking down to employees, especially when they have to come quite near because the chief is hard of hearing. Well, there's still hope; once I've saved enough money to pay back my parents' debts to him—that should take another five or six years—I'll do it without fail. I'll cut myself completely loose then. For the moment, though, I'd better get up, since my train goes at five.

He looked at the alarm clock ticking on the chest. Heavenly Father! he thought. It was half-past six o'clock and the hands were quietly moving on, it was even past the half-hour, it was getting on toward a quarter to seven. Had the alarm clock not gone off? From the bed one could see that it had been properly set for four o'clock; of course it must have gone off. Yes, but was it possible to sleep quietly through that ear-splitting noise? Well, he had not slept quietly, yet apparently all the more soundly for that. But what was he to do now? The next train went at seven o'clock; to catch that he would need to hurry like mad and his samples weren't even packed up, and he himself wasn't feeling particularly fresh and active. And even if he did catch the train he wouldn't avoid a row with the chief, since the firm's porter would have been waiting for the five o'clock train and would have long since reported his failure to turn up. The porter was a creature of the chief's, spineless and stupid. Well, supposing he were to say he was sick? But that would be most unpleasant and would look suspicious, since during his five years' employment he had not been ill once. The chief himself would be sure to come with the sick-insurance doctor, would reproach his parents with their son's laziness and would cut all excuses short by referring to the insurance doctor, who of course regarded all mankind as perfectly healthy malingerers. And would he be so far wrong on this occasion? Gregor really felt quite well, apart from a drowsiness that was utterly superfluous after such a long sleep, and he was even unusually hungry.

As all this was running through his mind at top speed without his being able to decide to leave his bed—the alarm clock had just struck a quarter to seven—there came a cautious tap at the door behind the head of his bed. "Gregor," said a voice—it was his mother's—"it's a quarter to seven. Hadn't you a train to catch?" That gentle voice! Gregor had a shock as he heard his own voice answering hers, unmistakably his own voice, it was true, but with a persistent horrible twittering squeak behind it like an undertone, that left the words in their clear shape only for the first moment and then rose up reverberating round them to destroy their sense, so that one could not be sure one had heard them rightly. Gregor wanted to answer at length and explain everything, but in the circumstances he confined himself to saying: "Yes, yes, thank you, Mother, I'm getting up now." The wooden door between them must have kept the change in his voice from being noticeable outside, for his mother contented herself with this statement and shuffled away. Yet this brief exchange of words had made the other members of the family aware that Gregor was still in the house, as they had not expected, and at one of the side doors his father was already knocking, gently, yet with his fist. "Gregor, Gregor," he called, "what's the matter with you?" And after a little while he called again in a deeper voice: "Gregor! Gregor!" At the other side door his sister was saying in a low, plaintive tone: "Gregor? Aren't you well? Are you needing anything?" He answered them both at once: "I'm just ready," and did his best to make his voice sound as normal as possible by enunciating the words very clearly and leaving long pauses between them. So his father went back to his breakfast, but his sister whispered: "Gregor, open the door, do." However, he was not thinking of opening the door, and felt thankful for the prudent habit he had acquired in traveling of locking all doors during the night, even at home.

His immediate intention was to get up quietly without being disturbed, to put on his clothes and above all eat his breakfast, and only then to consider what else was to be done, since in bed, he was well aware, his meditations would come to no sensible conclusion. He remembered that often enough in bed he had felt small aches and pains, probably caused by awkward postures, which had proved purely imaginary once he got up, and he looked forward eagerly to seeing this morning's delusions gradually fall away. That the change in his voice was nothing but the precursor of a severe chill, a standing ailment of commercial travelers, he had not the least possible doubt.

To get rid of the quilt was quite easy; he had only to inflate himself a little and it fell off by itself. But the next move was difficult, especially because he was so uncommonly broad. He would have needed arms and hands to hoist himself up; instead he had only the numerous little legs which never stopped waving in all directions and which he could not control in the least. When he tried to bend one of them it was the first to stretch itself straight; and did he succeed at last in making it do what he wanted, all the other legs meanwhile waved the more wildly in a high degree of unpleasant agitation. "But what's the use of lying idle in bed," said Gregor to himself.

He thought that he might get out of bed with the lower part of his body first, but this lower part, which he had not yet seen and of which he could form no clear conception, proved too difficult to move; it shifted so slowly; and when finally, almost wild with annoyance, he gathered his forces together and thrust out recklessly, he had miscalculated the direction and bumped heavily against the lower end of the bed, and the stinging pain he felt informed him that precisely this lower part of his body was at the moment probably the most sensitive.

So he tried to get the top part of himself out first, and cautiously moved his head towards the edge of the bed. That proved easy enough, and despite its breadth and mass the bulk of his body at last slowly followed the movement of his head. Still, when he finally got his head free over the edge of the bed he felt too scared to go on advancing, for after all if he let himself fall in this way it would take a miracle to keep his head from being injured. And at all costs he must not lose consciousness now, precisely now; he would rather stay in bed.

But when after a repetition of the same efforts he lay in his former position again, sighing, and watched his little legs struggling against each other more wildly than ever, if that were possible, and saw no way of bringing any order into this arbitrary confusion, he told himself again that it was impossible to stay in bed and that the most sensible course was to risk everything for the smallest hope of getting away from it. At the same time he did not forget meanwhile to remind himself that cool reflection, the coolest possible, was much better than desperate resolves. In such moments he focused his eyes as sharply as possible on the window, but unfortunately, the prospect of the morning fog, which muffled even the other side of the narrow street, brought him little encouragement and comfort. "Seven o'clock already," he said to himself when the alarm clock chimed again, "seven o'clock already and still such a thick fog." And for a little while he lay quiet, breathing lightly, as if perhaps expecting such complete repose to restore all things to their real and normal condition.

But then he said to himself: "Before it strikes a quarter past seven I must be quite out of this bed, without fail. Anyhow, by that time someone will have come from the office to ask for me, since it opens before seven." And he set himself to rocking his whole body at once in a regular rhythm, with the idea of swinging it out of the bed. If he tipped himself out in that way he could keep his head from injury by lifting it at an acute angle when he fell. His back seemed to be hard and was not likely to suffer from a fall on the carpet. His biggest worry was the loud crash he would not be able to help making, which would probably cause anxiety, if not terror, behind all the doors. Still, he must take the risk.

When he was already half out of the bed—the new method was more a game than an effort, for he needed only to hitch himself across by rocking to and fro—it struck him how simple it would be if he could get help. Two strong people—he thought of his father and the servant girl—would be amply sufficient; they would only have to thrust their arms under his convex back, lever him out of the bed, bend down with their burden and then be patient enough to let him turn himself right over on to the floor, where it was to be hoped his legs would then find their proper function. Well, ignoring the fact that the doors were all locked, ought he really to call for help? In spite of his misery he could not suppress a smile at the very idea of it.

He had got so far that he could barely keep his equilibrium when he rocked himself strongly, and he would have to nerve himself very soon for the final decision since in five minutes' time it would be a quarter past seven—when the front door bell rang. "That's someone from the office," he said to himself, and grew almost rigid, while his little legs only jigged about all the faster. For a moment everything stayed quiet. "They're not going to open the door," said Gregor to himself, catching at some kind of irrational hope. But then of course the servant girl went as usual to the door with her heavy tread and opened it. Gregor needed only to hear the first good morning of the visitor to know immediately who it was—the chief clerk himself. What a fate, to be condemned to work for a firm where the smallest omission at once gave rise to the gravest suspicion! Were all employees in a body nothing but scoundrels, was there not among them one single loyal devoted man who, had he wasted only an hour or so of the firm's time in a morning, was so tormented by conscience as to be driven out of his mind and actually incapable of leaving his bed? Wouldn't it really have been sufficient to send an apprentice to inquire—if any inquiry were necessary at all—did the chief clerk himself have to come and thus indicate to the entire family, an innocent family, that this suspicious circumstance could be investigated by no one less versed in affairs than himself? And more through the agitation caused by these reflections than through any act of will Gregor swung himself out of bed with all his strength. There was a loud thump, but it was not really a crash. His fall was broken to some extent by the carpet, his back, too, was less stiff than he thought, and so there was merely a dull thud, not so very startling. Only he had not lifted his head carefully enough and had hit it; he turned it and rubbed it on the carpet in pain and irritation.

"That was something falling down in there," said the chief clerk in the next room to the left. Gregor tried to suppose to himself that something like what had happened to him today might some day happen to the chief clerk; one really could not deny that it was possible. But as if in brusque reply to this supposition the chief clerk took a couple of firm steps in the next-door room and his patent leather boots creaked. From the right-hand room his sister was whispering to inform him of the situation: "Gregor, the chief clerk's here." "I know," muttered Gregor to himself; but he didn't dare to make his voice loud enough for his sister to hear it.

"Gregor," said his father now from the left-hand room, "the chief clerk has come and wants to know why you didn't catch the early train. We don't know what to say to him. Besides, he wants to talk to you in person. So open the door, please. He will be good enough to excuse the untidiness of your room." "Good morning, Mr. Samsa," the chief clerk was calling amiably meanwhile. "He's not well," said his mother to the visitor, while his father was still speaking through the door, "he's not well, sir, believe me. What else would make him miss a train! The boy thinks about nothing but his work. It makes me almost cross the way he never goes out in the evenings; he's been here the last eight days and has stayed at home every single evening. He just sits there quietly at the table reading a newspaper or looking through railway timetables. The only amusement he gets is doing fretwork. For instance, he spent two or three evenings cutting out a little picture frame; you would be surprised to see how pretty it is; it's hanging in his room; you'll see it in a minute when Gregor opens the door. I must say I'm glad you've come, sir; we should never have got him to unlock the door by ourselves; he's so obstinate; and I'm sure he's unwell, though he wouldn't have it to be so this morning." "I'm just coming," said Gregor slowly and carefully, not moving an inch for fear of losing one word of the conversation. "I can't think of any other explanation, madam," said the chief clerk, "I hope it's nothing serious. Although on the other hand I must say that we men of business—fortunately or unfortunately—very often simply have to ignore any slight indisposition, since business must be attended to." "Well, can the chief clerk come in now?" asked Gregor's father impatiently, again knocking on the door. "No," said Gregor. In the left-hand room a painful silence followed this refusal, in the right-hand room his sister began to sob.

Why didn't his sister join the others? She was probably newly out of bed and hadn't even begun to put on her clothes yet. Well, why was she crying? Because he wouldn't get up and let the chief clerk in, because he was in danger of losing his job, and because the chief would begin dunning his parents again for the old debts? Surely these were things one didn't need to worry about for the present. Gregor was still at home and not in the least thinking of deserting the family. At the moment, true, he was lying on the carpet and no one who knew the condition he was in could seriously expect him to admit the chief clerk. But for such a small discourtesy, which could plausibly be explained away somehow later on, Gregor could hardly be dismissed on the spot. And it seemed to Gregor that it would be much more sensible to leave him in peace for the present than to trouble him with tears and entreaties. Still, of course, their uncertainty bewildered them all and excused their behavior.

"Mr. Samsa," the chief clerk called now in a louder voice, "what's the matter with you? Here you are, barricading yourself in your room, giving only 'yes' and 'no' for answers, causing your parents a lot of unnecessary trouble and neglecting—I mention this only in passing—neglecting your business duties in an incredible fashion. I am speaking here in the name of your parents and of your chief, and I beg you quite seriously to give me an immediate and precise explanation. You amaze me, you amaze me. I thought you were a quiet, dependable person, and now all at once you seem bent on making a disgraceful exhibition of yourself. The chief did hint to me early this morning a possible explanation for your disappearance—with reference to the cash payments that were entrusted to you recently—but I almost pledged my solemn word of honor that this could not be so. But now that I see how incredibly obstinate you are, I no longer have the slightest desire to take your part at all. And your position in the firm is not so unassailable. I came with the intention of telling you all this in private, but since you are wasting my time so needlessly I don't see why your parents shouldn't hear it too. For some time past your work has been most unsatisfactory; this is not the season of the year for a business boom, of course, we admit that, but a season of the year for doing no business at all, that does not exist, Mr. Samsa, must not exist."

"But, sir," cried Gregor, beside himself and in his agitation forgetting everything else,

"I'm just going to open the door this very minute. A slight illness, an attack of giddiness, has kept me from getting up. I'm still lying in bed. But I feel all right again. I'm getting out of bed now. Just give me a moment or two longer! I'm not quite so well as I thought. But I'm all right, really. How a thing like that can suddenly strike one down! Only last night I was quite well, my parents can tell you, or rather I did have a slight presentiment. I must have showed some sign of it. Why didn't I report it at the office! But one always thinks that an indisposition can be got over without staying in the house. Oh sir, do spare my parents! All that you're reproaching me with now has no foundation; no one has ever said a word to me about it. Perhaps you haven't looked at the last orders I sent in. Anyhow, I can still catch the eight o'clock train, I'm much the better for my few hours' rest. Don't let me detain you here, sir; I'll be attending to business very soon, and do be good enough to tell the chief so and to make my excuses to him!"

And while all this was tumbling out pell-mell and Gregor hardly knew what he was saying, he had reached the chest quite easily, perhaps because of the practice he had had in bed, and was now trying to lever himself upright by means of it. He meant actually to open the door, actually to show himself and speak to the chief clerk; he was eager to find out what the others, after all their insistence, would say at the sight of him. If they were horrified then the responsibility was no longer his and he could stay quiet. But if they took it calmly, then he had no reason either to be upset, and could really get to the station for the eight o'clock train if he hurried. At first he slipped down a few times from the polished surface of the chest, but at length with a last heave he stood upright; he paid no more attention to the pains in the lower part of his body, however they smarted. Then he let himself fall against the back of a near-by chair, and clung with his little legs to the edges of it. That brought him into control of himself again and he stopped speaking, for now he could listen to what the chief clerk was saying.

"Did you understand a word of it?" the chief clerk was asking; "surely he can't be trying to make fools of us?" "Oh dear," cried his mother, in tears, "perhaps he's terribly ill and we're tormenting him. Grete! Grete!" she called out then. "Yes Mother?" called his sister from the other side. They were calling to each other across Gregor's room. "You must go this minute for the doctor. Gregor is ill. Go for the doctor, quick. Did you hear how he was speaking?" "That was no human voice," said the chief clerk in a voice noticeably low beside the shrillness of the mother's. "Anna! Anna!" his father was calling through the hall to the kitchen, clapping his hands, "get a locksmith at once!" And the two girls were already running through the hall with a swish of skirts—how could his sister have got dressed so quickly?—and were tearing the front door open. There was no sound of its closing again; they had evidently left it open, as one does in houses where some great misfortune has happened.

But Gregor was now much calmer. The words he uttered were no longer understandable, apparently, although they seemed clear enough to him, even clearer than before, perhaps because his ear had grown accustomed to the sound of them. Yet at any rate people now believed that something was wrong with him, and were ready to help him. The positive certainty with which these first measures had been taken comforted him. He felt himself drawn once more into the human circle and hoped for great and remarkable results from both the doctor and the locksmith, without really distinguishing precisely between them. To make his voice as clear as possible for the decisive conversation that was now imminent he coughed a little, as quietly as he could, of course, since this noise too might not sound like a human cough for all he was able to judge. In the next room meanwhile there was complete silence. Perhaps his parents were sitting at the table with the chief clerk, whispering, perhaps they were all leaning against the door and listening.

Slowly Gregor pushed the chair towards the door, then let go of it, caught hold of the door for support—the soles at the end of his little legs were somewhat sticky—and rested against it for a moment after his efforts. Then he set himself to turning the key in the lock with his mouth. It seemed, unhappily, that he hadn't really any teeth—what could he grip the key with?—but on the other hand his jaws were certainly very strong; with their help he did manage to set the key in motion, heedless of the fact that he was undoubtedly damaging them somehow, since a brown fluid issued from his mouth, flowed over the key and dripped on the floor. "Just listen to that," said the chief clerk next door; "he's turning the key." That was a great encouragement to Gregor; but they should all have shouted encouragement to him, his father and mother too: "Go on, Gregor," they should have called out, "keep going, hold on to that key!" And in the belief that they were all following his efforts intently, he clenched his jaws recklessly on the key with all the force at his command. As the turning of the key progressed he circled round the lock, holding on now only with his mouth, pushing on the key, as required, or pulling it down again with all the weight of his body. The louder click of the finally yielding lock literally quickened Gregor. With a deep breath of relief he said to himself: "So I didn't need the locksmith," and laid his hand on the handle to open the door wide.

Since he had to pull the door towards him, he was still invisible when it was really wide open. He had to edge himself slowly round the near half of the double door, and to do it very carefully if he was not to fall plump upon his back just on the threshold. He was still carrying out this difficult maneuver, with no time to observe anything else, when he heard the chief clerk utter a loud "Oh!"—it sounded like a gust of wind—and now he could see the man, standing as he was nearest to the door, clapping one hand before his open mouth and slowly backing away as if driven by some invisible steady pressure. His mother—in spite of the chief clerk's being there her hair was still undone and sticking up in all directions—first clasped her hands and looked at his father, then took two steps towards Gregor and fell on the floor among her outspread skirts, her face quite hidden on her breast. His father knotted his fist with a fierce expression on his face as if he meant to knock Gregor back into his room, then looked uncertainly round the living room, covered his eyes with his hands and wept till his great chest heaved.

Gregor did not go now into the living room, but leaned against the inside of the firmly shut wing of the door, so that only half his body was visible and his head above it bending sideways to look at the others. The light had meanwhile strengthened; on the other side of the street one could see clearly a section of the endlessly long, dark gray building opposite—it was a hospital—abruptly punctuated by its row of regular windows; the rain was still falling, but only in large singly discernible and literally singly splashing drops. The breakfast dishes were set out on the table lavishly, for breakfast was the most important meal of the day to Gregor's father, who lingered it out for hours over various newspapers. Right opposite Gregor on the wall hung a photograph of himself on military service, as a lieutenant, hand on sword, a carefree smile on his face, inviting one to respect his uniform and military bearing. The door leading to the hall was open, and one could see that the front door stood open too, showing the landing beyond and the beginning of the stairs going down.

"Well," said Gregor, knowing perfectly that he was the only one who had retained any composure, "I'll put my clothes on at once, pack up my samples and start off. Will you only let me go? You see, sir, I'm not obstinate, and I'm willing to work; traveling is a hard life, but I couldn't live without it. Where are you going, sir? To the office? Yes? Will you give a true account of all this? One can be temporarily incapacitated, but that's just the moment for remembering former services and bearing in mind that later on, when the incapacity has been got over, one will certainly work with all the more industry and concentration. I'm loyally bound to serve the chief, you know that very well. Besides, I have to provide for my parents and my sister. I'm in great difficulties, but I'll get out of them again. Don't make things any worse for me than they are. Stand up for me in the firm. Travelers are not popular, I know. People think they earn sacks of money and just have a good time. And there seems to be no particular reason to revise this prejudice. But you, sir, have a more comprehensive view of affairs than the rest of the staff, yes, let me tell you in confidence, a more comprehensive view than the chief himself, who, being the owner, lets his judgment easily be swayed against one of his employees. And you know very well that the traveler, who is never seen in the office almost the whole year round, can so easily fall a victim to gossip and ill luck and unfounded complaints, which he mostly knows nothing about, except when he comes back exhausted from his rounds, and only then suffers in person from their evil consequences, which he can no longer trace back to the original causes. Sir, sir, don't go away without a word to me to show that you think me in the right at least to some extent!"

But at Gregor's very first words the chief clerk had already backed away and only stared at him with parted lips over one twitching shoulder. And while Gregor was speaking he did not stand still one moment but stole away towards the door, without taking his eyes off Gregor, yet only an inch at a time, as if obeying some secret injunction to leave the room. He was already at the hall, and the suddenness with which he took his last step out of the living room would have made one believe he had burned the sole of his foot. Once in the hall he stretched his right arm before him towards the staircase, as if some supernatural power were waiting there to deliver him.

Gregor perceived that the chief clerk must on no account be allowed to go away in this frame of mind if his position in the firm were not to be endangered to the utmost. His parents did not understand this so well; they had convinced themselves in the course of years that Gregor was settled for life in this firm, and besides they were so preoccupied with their immediate troubles that all foresight had forsaken them. Yet Gregor had this foresight. The chief clerk must be detained, soothed, persuaded and finally won over; the whole future of Gregor and his family depended on it! If only his sister had been there! She was intelligent; she had begun to cry while Gregor was still lying quietly on his back. And no doubt the chief clerk, so partial to ladies, would have been guided by her; she would have shut the door of the flat and in the hall talked him out of his horror. But she was not there, and Gregor would have to handle the situation himself. And without remembering that he was still unaware what powers of movement he possessed, without even remembering that his words in all possibility, indeed in all likelihood, would again be unintelligible, he let go the wing of the door, pushed himself through the opening, started to walk towards the chief clerk, who was already ridiculously clinging with both hands to the railing on the landing; but immediately, as he was feeling for a support, he fell down with a little cry upon all his numerous legs. Hardly was he down when he experienced for the first time this morning a sense of physical comfort; his legs had firm ground under them; they were completely obedient, as he noted with joy; they even strove to carry him forward in whatever direction he chose; and he was inclined to believe that a final relief from all his sufferings was at hand. But in the same moment as he found himself on the floor, rocking with suppressed eagerness to move, not far from his mother, indeed just in front of her, she, who had seemed so completely crushed, sprang all at once to her feet, her arms and fingers outspread, cried: "Help, for Heaven's sake, help!" bent her head down as if to see Gregor better, yet on the contrary kept backing senselessly away; had quite forgotten that the laden table stood behind her; sat upon it hastily, as if in absence of mind, when she bumped into it; and seemed altogether unaware that the big coffee pot beside her was upset and pouring coffee in a flood over the carpet.

"Mother, Mother," said Gregor in a low voice, and looked up at her. The chief clerk, for the moment, had quite slipped from his mind; instead, he could not resist snapping his jaws together at the sight of the streaming coffee. That made his mother scream again, she fled from the table and fell into the arms of his father, who hastened to catch her. But Gregor had now no time to spare for his parents; the chief clerk was already on the stairs; with his chin on the banisters he was taking one last backward look. Gregor made a dash, to be as sure as possible of overtaking him; the chief clerk must have divined his intention, for he leaped down several steps and vanished; he was still yelling "Ugh!" and it echoed through the whole staircase. Unfortunately, the flight of the chief clerk seemed completely to upset Gregor's father, who had remained relatively calm until now, for instead of running after the man himself, or at least not hindering Gregor in his pursuit, he seized in his right hand the walking stick which the chief clerk had left behind on a chair, together with a hat and greatcoat, snatched in his left hand a large newspaper from the table and began stamping his feet and flourishing the stick and the newspaper to drive Gregor back into his room. No entreaty of Gregor's availed, indeed no entreaty was even understood, however humbly he bent his head his father only stamped on the floor the more loudly. Behind his father his mother had torn open a window, despite the cold weather, and was leaning far out of it with her face in her hands. A strong draught set in from the street to the staircase, the window curtains blew in, the newspapers on the table fluttered, stray pages whisked over the floor. Pitilessly Gregor's father drove him back, hissing and crying "Shoo!" like a savage. But Gregor was quite unpracticed in walking backwards, it really was a slow business. If he only had a chance to turn round he could get back to his room at once, but he was afraid of exasperating his father by the slowness of such a rotation and at any moment the stick in his father's hand might hit him a fatal blow on the back or on the head. In the end, however, nothing else was left for him to do since to his horror he observed that in moving backwards he could not even control the direction he took; and so, keeping an anxious eye on his father all the time over his shoulder, he began to turn round as quickly as he could, which was in reality very slowly. Perhaps his father noted his good intentions, for he did not interfere except every now and then to help him in the maneuver from a distance with the point of the stick. If only he would have stopped making that unbearable hissing noise! It made Gregor quite lose his head. He had turned almost completely round when the hissing noise so distracted him that he even turned a little the wrong way again. But when at last his head was fortunately right in front of the doorway, it appeared that his body was too broad simply to get through the opening. His father, of course, in his present mood was far from thinking of such a thing as opening the other half of the door, to let Gregor have enough space. He had merely the fixed idea of driving Gregor back into his room as quickly as possible. He would never have suffered Gregor to make the circumstantial preparations for standing up on end and perhaps slipping this way through the door. Rather, he was now making more noise than ever to urge Gregor forward, as if no obstacle impeded him; to Gregor, anyhow, the noise in his rear sounded no longer like the voice of one single father; this was really no joke, and Gregor thrust himself—come what might—into the doorway. One side of his body rose up, he was tilted at an angle in the doorway, his flank was quite bruised, horrid blotches stained the white door, soon he was stuck fast and, left to himself, could not have moved at all, his legs on one side fluttered trembling in the air, those on the other were crushed painfully to the floor—when from behind his father gave him a strong push which was literally a deliverance and he flew far into the room, bleeding freely. The door was slammed behind him with the stick, and then at last there was silence.

DISCUSSION FOR UNDERSTANDING

1. Describe Gregor Samsa at the beginning of the story.
2. What details are given about Gregor and his job?
3. What is the evidence that Gregor does not accept his change as permanent?
4. How does Gregor open the door?
5. How do his parents and the Chief Clerk react on seeing Gregor?
6. How does Gregor get back to his room?

II

Not until it was twilight did Gregor awake out of a deep sleep, more like a swoon than a sleep. He would certainly have waked up of his own accord not much later, for he felt himself sufficiently rested and well-slept, but it seemed to him as if a fleeting step and a cautious shutting of the door leading into the hall had aroused him. The electric lights in the street cast a pale sheen here and there on the ceiling and the upper surfaces of the furniture, but down below, where he lay, it was dark. Slowly, awkwardly trying out his feelers, which he only now learned to appreciate, he pushed his way to the door to see what had been happening there. His left side felt like one single long, unpleasantly tense scar, and he had actually to limp on his two rows of legs. One little leg, moreover, had been severely damaged in the course of that morning's events—it was almost a miracle that only one had been damaged—and trailed uselessly behind him.

He had reached the door before he discovered what had really drawn him to it: the smell of food. For there stood a bowl filled with fresh milk in which floated little sops of white bread. He could almost have laughed with joy, since he was now still hungrier than in the morning, and he dipped his head almost over the eyes straight into the milk. But soon in disappointment he withdrew it again; not only did he find it difficult to feed because of his tender left side—and he could only feed with the palpitating collaboration of his whole body—he did not like the milk either, although milk had been his favorite drink and that was certainly why his sister had set it there for him, indeed it was almost with repulsion that he turned away from the bowl and crawled back to the middle of the room.

He could see through the crack of the door that the gas was turned on in the living room, but while usually at this time his father made a habit of reading the afternoon newspaper in a loud voice to his mother and occasionally to his sister as well, not a sound was now to be heard. Well, perhaps his father had recently given up this habit of reading aloud, which his sister had mentioned so often in conversation and in her letters. But there was the same silence all around, although the flat was certainly not empty of occupants. "What a quiet life our family has been leading," said Gregor to himself, and as he sat there motionless staring into the darkness he felt great pride in the fact that he had been able to provide such a life for his parents and sister in such a fine flat. But what if all the quiet, the comfort, the contentment were now to end in horror? To keep himself from being lost in such thoughts Gregor took refuge in movement and crawled up and down the room.

Once during the long evening one of the side doors was opened a little and quickly shut again, later the other side door too; someone had apparently wanted to come in and then thought better of it. Gregor now stationed himself immediately before the living room door, determined to persuade any hesitating visitor to come in or at least to discover who it might be; but the door was not opened again and he waited in vain. In the early morning, when the doors were locked, they had all wanted to come in, now that he had opened one door and the other had apparently been opened during the day, no one came in and even the keys were on the other side of the doors.

It was late at night before the gas went out in the living room, and Gregor could easily tell that his parents and his sister had all stayed awake until then, for he could clearly hear the three of them stealing away on tiptoe. No one was likely to visit him, not until the morning, that was certain; so he had plenty of time to meditate at his leisure on how he was to arrange his life afresh. But the lofty, empty room in which he had to lie flat on the floor filled him with an apprehension he could not account for, since it had been his very own room for the past five years—and with a half-unconscious action, not without a slight feeling of shame, he scuttled under the sofa, where he felt comfortable at once, although his back was a little cramped and he could not lift his head up, and his only regret was that his body was too broad to get the whole of it under the sofa.

He stayed there all night, spending the time partly in a light slumber, from which his hunger kept waking him up with a start, and partly in worrying and sketching vague hopes, which all led to the same conclusion, that he must lie low for the present and, by exercising patience and the utmost consideration, help the family to bear the inconvenience he was bound to cause them in his present condition.

Very early in the morning, it was still almost night, Gregor had the chance to test the strength of his new resolutions, for his sister, nearly fully dressed, opened the door from the hall and peered in. She did not see him at once, yet when she caught sight of him under the sofa—well, he had to be somewhere, he couldn't have flown away, could he?—she was so startled that without being able to help it she slammed the door shut again. But as if regretting her behavior she opened the door again immediately and came in on tiptoe, as if she were visiting an invalid or even a stranger. Gregor had pushed his head forward to the very edge of the sofa and watched her. Would she notice that he had left the milk standing, and not for lack of hunger, and would she bring in some other kind of food more to his taste? If she did not do it of her own accord, he would rather starve than draw her attention to the fact, although he felt a wild impulse to dart out from under the sofa, throw himself at her feet and beg her for something to eat. But his sister at once noticed, with surprise, that the bowl was still full, except for a little milk that had been spilt all round it, she lifted it immediately, not with her bare hands, true, but with a cloth and carried it away. Gregor was wildly curious to know what she would bring instead, and made various speculations about it. Yet what she actually did next, in the goodness of her heart, he could never have guessed at. To find out what he liked she brought him a whole selection of food, all set out on an old newspaper. There were old, half-decayed vegetables, bones from last night's supper covered with a white sauce that had thickened; some raisins and almonds; a piece of cheese that Gregor would have called uneatable two days ago; a dry roll of

bread, a buttered roll, and a roll both buttered and salted. Besides all that, she set down again the same bowl, into which she had poured some water, and which was apparently to be reserved for his exclusive use. And with fine tact, knowing that Gregor would not eat in her presence, she withdrew quickly and even turned the key, to let him understand that he could take his ease as much as he liked. Gregor's legs all whizzed towards the food. His wounds must have healed completely, moreover, for he felt no disability, which amazed him and made him reflect how more than a month ago he had cut one finger a little with a knife and had still suffered pain from the wound only the day before yesterday. Am I less sensitive now? he thought, and sucked greedily at the cheese, which above all the other edibles attracted him at once and strongly. One after another and with tears of satisfaction in his eyes he quickly devoured the cheese, the vegetables and the sauce; the fresh food, on the other hand, had no charms for him, he could not even stand the smell of it and actually dragged away to some little distance the things he could eat. He had long finished his meal and was only lying lazily on the same spot when his sister turned the key slowly as a sign for him to retreat. That roused him at once, although he was nearly asleep, and he hurried under the sofa again. But it took considerable self-control for him to stay under the sofa, even for the short time his sister was in the room, since the large meal had swollen his body somewhat and he was so cramped he could hardly breathe. Slight attacks of breathlessness afflicted him and his eyes were starting a little out of his head as he watched his unsuspecting sister sweeping together with a broom not only the remains of what he had eaten but even the things he had not touched, as if these were now of no use to anyone, and hastily shoveling it all into a bucket, which she covered with a wooden lid and carried away. Hardly had she turned her back when Gregor came from under the sofa and stretched and puffed himself out.

In this manner Gregor was fed, once in the early morning while his parents and the servant girl were still asleep, and a second time after they had all had their midday dinner, for then his parents took a short nap and the servant girl could be sent out on some errand or other by his sister. Not that they would have wanted him to starve, of course, but perhaps they could not have borne to know more about his feeding than from hearsay, perhaps too his sister wanted to spare them such little anxieties wherever possible, since they had quite enough to bear as it was.

Under what pretext the doctor and the locksmith had been got rid of on that first morning Gregor could not discover, for since what he said was not understood by the others it never struck any of them, not even his sister, that he could understand what they said, and so whenever his sister came into his room he had to content himself with hearing her utter only a sigh now and then and an occasional appeal to the saints. Later on, when she had got a little used to the situation—of course she could never get completely used to it—she sometimes threw out a remark which was kindly meant or could be so interpreted. "Well, he liked his dinner today," she would say when Gregor had made a good clearance of his food; and when he had not eaten, which gradually happened more and more often, she would say almost sadly: "Everything's been left standing again."

But although Gregor could get no news directly, he overheard a lot from the neighboring rooms, and as soon as voices were audible, he would run to the door of the room concerned and press his whole body against it. In the first few days especially there was no conversation that did not refer to him somehow, even if only indirectly. For two whole days there were family consultations at every mealtime about what should be done; but also between meals the same subject was discussed, for there were always at least two members of the family at home, since no one wanted to be alone in the flat and to leave it quite empty was unthinkable. And on the very first of these days the household cook—it was not quite clear what and how much she knew of the situation—went down on her knees to his mother and begged leave to go, and when she departed, a quarter of an hour later, gave thanks for her dismissal with tears in her eyes as if for the greatest benefit that could have been conferred on her, and without any prompting swore a solemn oath that she would never say a single word to anyone about what had happened.

Now Gregor's sister had to cook too, helping her mother; true, the cooking did not amount to much, for they ate scarcely anything. Gregor was always hearing one of the family vainly urging another to eat and getting no answer but: "Thanks, I've had all I want," or something similar. Perhaps they drank nothing either. Time and again his sister kept asking his father if he wouldn't like some beer and offered kindly to go and fetch it herself, and when he made no answer suggested that she could ask the concierge to fetch it, so that he need feel no sense of obligation, but then a round "No" came from his father and no more was said about it.

In the course of that very first day Gregor's father explained the family's financial position and prospects to both his mother and his sister. Now and then he rose from the table to get some voucher or memorandum out of the small safe he had rescued from the collapse of his business five years earlier. One could hear him opening the complicated lock and rustling papers out and shutting it again. This statement made by his father was the first cheerful information Gregor had heard since his imprisonment. He had been of the opinion that nothing at all was left over from his father's business, at least his father had never said anything to the contrary, and of course he had not asked him directly. At that time Gregor's sole desire was to do his utmost to help the family to forget as soon as possible the catastrophe which had overwhelmed the business and thrown them all into a state of complete despair. And so he had set to work with unusual ardor and almost overnight had become a commercial traveler instead of a little clerk, with of course much greater chances of earning money, and his success was immediately translated into good round coin which he could lay on the table for his amazed and happy family. These had been fine times, and they had never recurred, at least not with the same sense of glory, although later on Gregor had earned so much money that he was able to meet the expenses of the whole household and did so. They had simply got used to it, both the family and Gregor; the money was gratefully accepted and gladly given, but there was no special uprush of warm feeling. With his sister alone had he remained intimate, and it was a secret plan of his that she, who loved music, unlike himself, and could play movingly on the violin, should be sent next year to study at the Conservatorium, despite the great expense that would entail, which must be made up in some other way. During his brief visits home the Conservatorium was often mentioned in the talks he had with his sister, but always merely as a beautiful dream which could never come true, and his parents discouraged even these innocent references to it; yet Gregor had made up his mind firmly about it and meant to announce the fact with due solemnity on Christmas Day.

Such were the thoughts, completely futile in his present condition, that went through his head as he stood clinging upright to the door and listening. Sometimes out of sheer weariness he had to give up listening and let his head fall negligently against the door, but he always had to pull himself together again at once, for even the slight sound his head made was audible next door and brought all conversation to a stop. "What can he be doing now?" his father would say after a while, obviously turning towards the door, and only

then would the interrupted conversation gradually be set going again.

Gregor was now informed as amply as he could wish—for his father tended to repeat himself in his explanations, partly because it was a long time since he had handled such matters and partly because his mother could not always grasp things at once—that a certain amount of investments, a very small amount it was true, had survived the wreck of their fortunes and had even increased a little because the dividends had not been touched meanwhile. And besides that, the money Gregor brought home every month— he had kept only a few dollars for himself— had never quite been used up and now amounted to a small capital sum. Behind the door Gregor nodded his head eagerly, rejoiced at this evidence of unexpected thrift and foresight. True, he could really have paid off some more of his father's debts to the chief with this extra money, and so brought much nearer the day on which he could quit his job, but doubtless it was better the way his father had arranged it.

Yet this capital was by no means sufficient to let the family live on the interest of it; for one year, perhaps, or at the most two, they could live on the principal, that was all. It was simply a sum that ought not to be touched and should be kept for a rainy day; money for living expenses would have to be earned. Now his father was still hale enough but an old man, and he had done no work for the past five years and could not be expected to do much; during these five years, the first years of leisure in his laborious though unsuccessful life, he had grown rather fat and become sluggish. And Gregor's old mother, how was she to earn a living with her asthma, which troubled her even when she walked through the flat and kept her lying on a sofa every other day panting for breath beside an open window? And was his sister to earn her bread, she who was still a child of seventeen and whose life hitherto had been so pleasant, consisting as it did in dressing herself nicely, sleeping long, helping in the housekeeping, going out to a few modest entertainments and above all playing the violin? At first whenever the need for earning money was mentioned Gregor let go his hold on the door and threw himself down on the cool leather sofa beside it, he felt so hot with shame and grief.

Often he just lay there the long nights through without sleeping at all, scrabbling for hours on the leather. Or he nerved himself to the great effort of pushing an armchair to the window, then crawled up over the window sill and, braced against the chair, leaned against the window panes, obviously in some recollection of the sense of freedom that looking out of a window always used to give him. For in reality day by day things that were even a little way off were growing dimmer to his sight; the hospital across the street, which he used to execrate for being all too often before his eyes, was now quite beyond his range of vision, and if he had not known that he lived in Charlotte Street, a quiet street but still a city street, he might have believed that his window gave on a desert waste where gray sky and gray land blended indistinguishably into each other. His quick-witted sister only needed to observe twice that the armchair stood by the window; after that whenever she had tidied the room she always pushed the chair back to the same place at the window and even left the inner casements open.

If he could have spoken to her and thanked her for all she had to do for him, he could have borne her ministrations better; as it was, they oppressed him. She certainly tried to make as light as possible of whatever was disagreeable in her task, and as time went on she succeeded, of course, more and more, but time brought more enlightenment to Gregor too. The very way she came in distressed him. Hardly was she in the room when she rushed to the window, without even taking time to shut the door, careful as she was usually to shield the sight of Gregor's room from the others, and as if she were almost suffocating tore the casements open with hasty fingers, standing then in the open draught for a while even in the bitterest cold and drawing deep breaths. This noisy scurry of hers upset Gregor twice a day; he would crouch trembling under the sofa all the time, knowing quite well that she would certainly have spared him such a disturbance had she found it at all possible to stay in his presence without opening the window.

On one occasion, about a month after Gregor's metamorphosis, when there was surely no reason for her to be still startled at his appearance, she came a little earlier than usual and found him gazing out of the window, quite motionless, and thus well placed to look like a bogey. Gregor would not have been surprised had she not come in at all, for she could not immediately open the window while he was there, but not only did she retreat, she jumped back as if in alarm and banged the door shut; a stranger might well have thought that he had been lying in wait for her there meaning to bite her. Of course he hid himself under the sofa at once, but he had to wait until midday before she came again, and she seemed more ill at ease than usual. This made him realize how repulsive the sight of him still was to her, and that it was bound to go on being repulsive, and what an effort it must cost her not to run away even from the sight of the small portion of his body that stuck out from under the sofa. In order to spare her that, therefore, one day he carried a sheet on his back to the sofa—it cost him four hours' labor—and arranged it there in such a way as to hide him completely, so that even if she were to bend down she could not see him. Had she considered the sheet unnecessary, she would certainly have stripped it off the sofa again, for it was clear enough that this curtaining and confining of himself was not likely to conduce to Gregor's comfort, but she left it where it was, and Gregor even fancied that he caught a thankful glance from her eye when he lifted the sheet carefully a very little with his head to see how she was taking the new arrangement.

For the first fortnight his parents could not bring themselves to the point of entering his room, and he often heard them expressing their appreciation of his sister's activities, whereas formerly they had frequently scolded her for being as they thought a somewhat useless daughter. But now, both of them often waited outside the door, his father and his mother, while his sister tidied his room, and as soon as she came out she had to tell them exactly how things were in the room, what Gregor had eaten, how he had conducted himself this time and whether there was not perhaps some slight improvement in his condition. His mother, moreover, began relatively soon to want to visit him, but his father and sister dissuaded her at first with arguments which Gregor listened to very attentively and altogether approved. Later, however, she had to be held back by main force, and when she cried out: "Do let me in to Gregor, he is my unfortunate son! Can't you understand that I must go to him?" Gregor thought that it might be well to have her come in, not every day, of course, but perhaps once a week; she understood things, after all, much better than his sister, who was only a child despite the efforts she was making and had perhaps taken on so difficult a task merely out of childish thoughtlessness.

Gregor's desire to see his mother was soon fulfilled. During the daytime he did not want to show himself at the window, out of consideration for his parents, but he could not crawl very far around the few square yards of floor space he had, nor could he bear lying quietly at rest all during the night, while he was fast losing any interest he had ever taken in food, so that for mere recreation he had formed the habit of crawling crisscross over the walls and ceiling. He especially enjoyed hanging suspended from the ceiling; it was much better than lying on the floor; one could breathe more freely; one's body swung and rocked lightly; and in the almost blissful ab-

sorption induced by this suspension it could happen to his own surprise that he let go and fell plump on the floor. Yet he now had his body much better under control than formerly, and even such a big fall did him no harm. His sister at once remarked the new distraction Gregor had found for himself—he left traces behind him of the sticky stuff on his soles wherever he crawled—and she got the idea in her head of giving him as wide a field as possible to crawl in and of removing the pieces of furniture that hindered him, above all the chest of drawers and the writing desk. But that was more than she could manage all by herself; she did not dare ask her father to help her; and as for the servant girl, a young creature of sixteen who had had the courage to stay on after the cook's departure, she could not be asked to help, for she had begged as a special favor that she might keep the kitchen door locked and open it only on a definite summons; so there was nothing left but to apply to her mother at an hour when her father was out. And the old lady did come, with exclamations of joyful eagerness, which, however, died away at the door of Gregor's room. Gregor's sister, of course, went in first, to see that everything was in order before letting his mother enter. In great haste Gregor pulled the sheet lower and rucked it more in folds so that it really looked as if it had been thrown accidentally over the sofa. And this time he did not peer out from under it; he renounced the pleasure of seeing his mother on this occasion and was only glad that she had come at all. "Come in, he's out of sight," said his sister, obviously leading her mother in by the hand. Gregor could now hear the two women struggling to shift the heavy old chest from its place, and his sister claiming the greater part of the labor for herself, without listening to the admonitions of her mother who feared she might overstrain herself. It took a long time. After at least a quarter of an hour's tugging his mother objected that the chest had better be left where it was, for in the first place it was too heavy and could never be got out before his father came home, and standing in the middle of the room like that it would only hamper Gregor's movements, while in the second place it was not at all certain that removing the furniture would be doing a service to Gregor. She was inclined to think to the contrary; the sight of the naked walls made her own heart heavy, and why shouldn't Gregor have the same feeling, considering that he had been used to his furniture for so long and might feel forlorn without it. "And doesn't it look," she concluded in a low voice—in fact she had been almost whispering all the time as if to avoid letting Gregor, whose exact whereabouts she did not know, hear even the tones of her voice, for she was convinced that he could not understand her words—"doesn't it look as if we were showing him, by taking away his furniture, that we have given up hope of his ever getting better and are just leaving him coldly to himself? I think it would be best to keep his room exactly as it has always been, so that when he comes back to us he will find everything unchanged and be able all the more easily to forget what has happened in between."

On hearing these words from his mother Gregor realized that the lack of all direct human speech for the past two months together with the monotony of family life must have confused his mind, otherwise he could not account for the fact that he had quite earnestly looked forward to having his room emptied of furnishing. Did he really want his warm room, so comfortably fitted with old family furniture, to be turned into a naked den in which he would certainly be able to crawl unhampered in all directions but at the price of shedding simultaneously all recollection of his human background? He had indeed been so near the brink of forgetfulness that only the voice of his mother, which he had not heard for so long, had drawn him back from it. Nothing should be taken out of his room; everything must stay as it was; he

could not dispense with the good influence of the furniture on his state of mind; and even if the furniture did hamper him in his senseless crawling round and round, that was no drawback but a great advantage.

Unfortunately his sister was of the contrary opinion; she had grown accustomed, and not without reason, to consider herself an expert in Gregor's affairs as against her parents, and so her mother's advice was now enough to make her determined on the removal not only of the chest and the writing desk, which had been her first intention, but of all the furniture except the indispensable sofa. This determination was not, of course, merely the outcome of childish recalcitrance and of the self-confidence she had recently developed so unexpectedly and at such cost; she had in fact perceived that Gregor needed a lot of space to crawl about in, while on the other hand he never used the furniture at all, so far as could be seen. Another factor might have been also the enthusiastic temperament of an adolescent girl, which seeks to indulge itself on every opportunity and which now tempted Grete to exaggerate the horror of her brother's circumstances in order that she might do all the more for him. In a room where Gregor lorded it all alone over empty walls no one save herself was likely ever to set foot.

And so she was not to be moved from her resolve by her mother, who seemed moreover to be ill at ease in Gregor's room and therefore unsure of herself, was soon reduced to silence and helped her daughter as best she could to push the chest outside. Now, Gregor could do without the chest, if need be, but the writing resk he must retain. As soon as the two women had got the chest out of his room, groaning as they pushed it, Gregor stuck his head out from under the sofa to see how he might intervene as kindly and cautiously as possible. But as bad luck would have it, his mother was the first to return, leaving Grete clasping the chest in the room next door where she was trying to shift it all by herself, without of course moving it from the spot. His mother however was not accustomed to the sight of him, it might sicken her and so in alarm Gregor backed quickly to the other end of the sofa, yet could not prevent the sheet from swaying a little in front. That was enough to put her on the alert. She paused, stood still for a moment and then went back to Grete.

Although Gregor kept reassuring himself that nothing out of the way was happening, but only a few bits of furniture were being changed round, he soon had to admit that all this trotting to and fro of the two women, their little ejaculations and the scraping of furniture along the floor affected him like a vast disturbance coming from all sides at once, and however much he tucked in his head and legs and cowered to the very floor he was bound to confess that he would not be able to stand it for long. They were clearing his room out; taking away everything he loved; the chest in which he kept his fret saw and other tools was already dragged off; they were now loosening the writing desk which had almost sunk into the floor, the desk at which he had done all his homework when he was at the commercial academy, at the grammar school before that, and, yes, even at the primary school—he had no more time to waste in weighing the good intentions of the two women, whose existence he had by now almost forgotten, for they were so exhausted that they were laboring in silence and nothing could be heard but the heavy scuffling of their feet.

And so he rushed out—the women were just leaning against the writing desk in the next room to give themselves a breather—and four times changed his direction, since he really did not know what to rescue first, then on the wall opposite, which was already otherwise cleared, he was struck by the picture of the lady muffled in so much fur and quickly crawled up to it and pressed himself to the glass, which was a good surface to hold on to and comforted his hot belly. This picture at least, which was entirely hidden

beneath him, was going to be removed by nobody. He turned his head towards the door of the living room so as to observe the women when they came back.

They had not allowed themselves much of a rest and were already coming; Grete had twined her arm round her mother and was almost supporting her. "Well, what shall we take now?" said Grete, looking round. Her eyes met Gregor's from the wall. She kept her composure, presumably because of her mother, bent her head down to her mother to keep her from looking up, and said, although in a fluttering, unpremeditated voice: "Come, hadn't we better go back to the living room for a moment?" Her intentions were clear enough to Gregor, she wanted to bestow her mother in safety and then chase him down from the wall. Well, just let her try it! He clung to his picture and would not give it up. He would rather fly in Grete's face.

But Grete's words had succeeded in disquieting her mother, who took a step to one side, caught sight of the huge brown mass on the flowered wallpaper, and before she was really conscious that what she saw was Gregor screamed in a loud, hoarse voice: "Oh no, oh no!" fell with outspread arms over the sofa as if giving up and did not move. "Gregor!" cried his sister, shaking her fist and glaring at him. This was the first time she had directly addressed him since his metamorphosis. She ran into the next room for some aromatic essence with which to rouse her mother from her fainting fit. Gregor wanted to help too—there was still time to rescue the picture—but he was stuck fast to the glass and had to tear himself loose; he then ran after his sister into the next room as if he could advise her, as he used to do; but then had to stand helplessly behind her; she meanwhile searched among various small bottles and when she turned round started in alarm at the sight of him; one bottle fell on the floor and broke; a splinter of glass cut Gregor's face and some kind of corrosive medicine splashed him; without pausing a moment longer Grete gathered up all the bottles she could carry and ran to her mother with them; she banged the door shut with her foot. Gregor was now cut off from his mother, who was perhaps nearly dying because of him; he dared not open the door for fear of frightening away his sister, who had to stay with her mother; there was nothing he could do but wait; and harassed by self-reproach and worry he began now to crawl to and fro, over everything, walls, furniture and ceiling, and finally, in his despair, when the whole room seemed to be reeling round him, fell down on to the middle of the big table.

A little while elapsed, Gregor was still lying there feebly and all around was quiet, perhaps that was a good omen. Then the doorbell rang. The servant girl was of course locked in her kitchen, and Grete would have to open the door. It was his father. "What's been happening?" were his first words; Grete's face must have told him everything. Grete answered in a muffled voice, apparently hiding her head on his breast: "Mother has been fainting, but she's better now. Gregor's broken loose." "Just what I expected," said his father, "just what I've been telling you, but you women would never listen." It was clear to Gregor that his father had taken the worst interpretation of Grete's all too brief statement and was assuming that Gregor had been guilty of some violent act. Therefore Gregor must now try to propitiate his father, since he had neither time nor means for an explanation. And so he fled to the door of his own room and crouched against it, to let his father see as soon as he came in from the hall that his son had the good intention of getting back into his room immediately and that it was not necessary to drive him there, but that if only the door were opened he would disappear at once.

Yet his father was not in the mood to perceive such fine distinctions. "Ah!" he cried as soon as he appeared, in a tone which sounded at once angry and exultant. Gregor drew his head back from the door and lifted it to look at his father. Truly, this was not the father he had imagined to himself; admittedly he had been too absorbed of late in his new recreation of crawling over the ceiling to take the same interest as before in what was happening elsewhere in the flat, and he ought really to be prepared for some changes. And yet, and yet, could that be his father? The man who used to lie wearily sunk in bed whenever Gergor set out on a business journey; who welcomed him back of an evening lying in a long chair in a dressing gown; who could not really rise to his feet but only lifted his arms in greeting, and on the rare occasions when he did go out with his family, on one or two Sundays a year and on high holidays, walked between Gregor and his mother, who were slow walkers anyhow, even more slowly than they did, muffled in his old greatcoat, shuffling laboriously forward with the help of his crook-handled stick which he set down most cautiously at every step and, whenever he wanted to say anything, nearly always came to a full stop and gathered his escort around him? Now he was standing there in fine shape; dressed in a smart blue uniform with gold buttons, such as bank messengers wear; his strong double chin bulged over the stiff high collar of his jacket; from under his bushy eyebrows his black eyes darted fresh and penetrating glances; his onetime tangled white hair had been combed flat on either side of a shining and carefully exact parting. He pitched his cap, which bore a gold monogram, probably the badge of some bank, in a wide sweep across the whole room on to a sofa and with the tail-ends of his jacket thrown back, his hands in his trouser pockets, advanced with a grim visage towards Gregor. Likely enough he did not himself know what he meant to do; at any rate he lifted his feet uncommonly high, and Gregor was dumbfounded at the enormous size of his shoe soles. But Gregor could not risk standing up to him, aware as he had been from the very first day of his new life that his father believed only the severest measures suitable for dealing with him. And so he ran before his father, stopping when he stopped and scuttling forward again when his father made any kind of move. In this way they circled the room several times without anything decisive happening, indeed the whole operation did not even look like a pursuit because it was carried out so slowly. And so Gregor did not leave the floor, for he feared that his father might take as a piece of peculiar wickedness any excursion of his over the walls or the ceiling. All the same, he could not stay this course much longer, for while his father took one step he had to carry out a whole series of movements. He was already beginning to feel breathless, just as in his former life his lungs had not been very dependable. As he was staggering along, trying to concentrate his energy on running, hardly keeping his eyes open; in his dazed state never even thinking of any other escape than simply going forward; and having almost forgotten that the walls were free to him, which in this room were well provided with finely carved pieces of furniture full of knobs and crevices—suddenly something lightly flung landed close behind him and rolled before him. It was an apple; a second apple followed immediately; Gregor came to a stop in alarm; there was no point in running on, for his father was determined to bombard him. He had filled his pockets with fruit from the dish on the sideboard and was now shying apple after apple, without taking particularly good aim for the moment. The small red apples rolled about the floor as if magnetized and cannoned into each other. An apple thrown without much force grazed Gregor's back and glanced off harmlessly. But another following immediately landed right on his back and sank in; Gregor wanted to drag himself forward, as if this startling, incredible pain could be left behind him; but he felt as if nailed to the spot and flattened himself out in a complete derangement of all his senses. With his last conscious look he saw the door

of his room being torn open and his mother rushing out ahead of his screaming sister, in her underbodice, for her daughter had loosened her clothing to let her breathe more freely and recover from her swoon, he saw his mother rushing towards his father, leaving one after another behind her on the floor her loosened petticoats, stumbling over her petticoats straight to his father and embracing him, in complete union with him—but here Gregor's sight began to fail—with her hands clasped round his father's neck as she begged for her son's life.

DISCUSSION FOR UNDERSTANDING

1. What changes have taken place in Gregor's food preferences, healing ability, vision, sleep needs?

2. How does Grete act toward Gregor?

3. What does Gregor find out about the family's financial situation?

4. Why does Grete decide to move the furniture from Gregor's room? Why does his mother object? What is Gregor's reaction to this?

5. What happens when Gregor tries to save his furniture?

6. Describe the scene between Gregor and his father.

III

The serious injury done to Gregor, which disabled him for more than a month—the apple went on sticking in his body as a visible reminder, since no one ventured to remove it—seemed to have made even his father recollect that Gregor was a member of the family, despite his present unfortunate and repulsive shape, and ought not be treated as an enemy, that, on the contrary, family duty required the suppression of disgust and the exercise of patience, nothing but patience.

And although his injury had impaired, probably for ever, his powers of movement, and for the time being it took him long, long minutes to creep across his room like an old invalid—there was no question now of crawling up the wall—yet in his own opinion he was sufficiently compensated for this worsening of his condition by the fact that towards evening the living-room door, which he used to watch intently for an hour or two beforehand, was always thrown open, so that lying in the darkness of his room, invisible to the family, he could see them all at the lamp-lit table and listen to their talk, by general consent as it were, very different from his earlier eavesdropping.

True, their intercourse lacked the lively character of former times, which he had always called to mind with a certain wistfulness in the small hotel bedrooms where he had been wont to throw himself down, tired out, on damp bedding. They were now mostly very silent. Soon after supper his father would fall asleep in his armchair; his mother and sister would admonish each other to be silent; his mother, bending low over the lamp, stitched at fine sewing for an underwear firm; his sister, who had take a job as a salesgirl, was learning shorthand and French in the evenings on the chance of bettering herself. Sometimes his father woke up, and as if quite unaware that he had been sleeping said to his mother: "What a lot of sewing you're doing today!" and at once fell asleep again, while the two women exchanged a tired smile.

With a kind of mulishness his father persisted in keeping his uniform on even in the house; his dressing gown hung uselessly on its peg and he slept fully dressed where he sat, as if he were ready for service at any moment and even here only at the beck and call of his superior. As a result, his uniform, which was not brand-new to start with, began to look dirty, despite all the loving care of the mother and sister to keep it clean, and Gregor often spent whole evenings gazing at the many greasy spots on the garment, gleaming with gold buttons always in a high state of polish, in which the old man sat sleeping

in extreme discomfort and yet quite peacefully.

As soon as the clock struck ten his mother tried to rouse his father with gentle words and to persuade him after that to get into bed, for sitting there he could not have a proper sleep and that was what he needed most, since he had to go on duty at six. But with the mulishness that had obsessed him since he became a bank messenger he always insisted on staying longer at the table, although he regularly fell asleep again and in the end only with the greatest trouble could be got out of his armchair and into his bed. However insistently Gregor's mother and sister kept urging him with gentle reminders, he would go on slowly shaking his head for a quarter of an hour, keeping his eyes shut, and refuse to get to his feet. The mother plucked at his sleeve, whispering endearments in his ear, the sister left her lessons to come to her mother's help, but it had no effect on Gregor's father. He would only sink down deeper in his chair. Not until the two women hoisted him up by the armpits did he open his eyes and look at them both, one after the other, usually with the remark: "This is a life. This is the peace and quiet of my old age." And leaning on the two of them he would heave himself up, with difficulty, as if he were a great burden to himself, suffer them to lead him as far as the door and then wave them off and go on alone, while the mother abandoned her needlework and the sister her pen in order to run after him and help him further.

Who could find time, in this overworked and tired-out family, to bother about Gregor more than was absolutely needful? The household was reduced more and more; the servant girl was turned off; a gigantic bony charwoman with white hair flying round her head came in morning and evening to do the rough work; everything else was done by Gregor's mother, as well as great piles of sewing. Even various family ornaments, which his mother and sister used to wear with pride at parties and celebrations, had to be sold, as Gregor discovered of an evening from hearing them all discuss the prices obtained. But what they lamented most was the fact that they could not leave the flat which was much too big for their present circumstances, because they could not think of any way to shift Gregor. Yet Gregor saw well enough that consideration for him was not the main difficulty preventing the removal, for they could have easily shifted him in some suitable box with a few air holes in it; what really kept them from moving into another flat was rather their own complete hopelessness and the belief that they had been singled out for a misfortune such as had never happened to any of their relations or acquaintances. They fulfilled to the utmost all that the world demands of poor people, the father fetched breakfast for the small clerks in the bank, the mother devoted her energy to making underwear for strangers, the sister trotted to and fro behind the counter at the behest of customers, but more than this they had not the strength to do. And the wound in Gregor's back began to nag at him afresh when his mother and sister, after getting his father into bed, came back again, left their work lying, drew close to each other and sat cheek by cheek; when his mother, pointing towards his room, said: "Shut that door now, Grete," and he was left again in darkness, while next door the women mingled their tears or perhaps sat dry-eyed staring at the table.

Gregor hardly slept at all by night or by day. He was often haunted by the idea that next time the door opened he would take the family's affairs in hand again just as he used to do; once more, after this long interval, there appeared in his thoughts the figures of the chief and the chief clerk, the commercial travelers and the apprentices, the porter who was so dull-witted, two or three friends in other firms, a chambermaid in one of the rural hotels, a sweet and fleeting memory, a cashier in a milliner's shop, whom he had wooed earnestly but too slowly—they all ap-

peared, together with strangers or people he had quite forgotten, but instead of helping him and his family they were one and all unapproachable and he was glad when they vanished. At other times he would not be in the mood to bother about his family, he was only filled with rage at the way they were neglecting him, and although he had no clear idea of what he might care to eat he would make plans for getting into the larder to take the food that was after all his due, even if he were not hungry. His sister no longer took thought to bring him what might especially please him, but in the morning and at noon before she went to business hurriedly pushed into his room with her foot any food that was available, and in the evening cleared it out again with one sweep of the broom, heedless of whether it had been merely tasted, or—as most frequently happened—left untouched. The cleaning of his room, which she now did always in the evenings, could not have been more hastily done. Streaks of dirt stretched along the walls, here and there lay balls of dust and filth. At first Gregor used to station himself in some particularly filthy corner when his sister arrived, in order to reproach her with it, so to speak. But he could have sat there for weeks without getting her to make any improvement; she could see the dirt as well as he did, but she had simply made up her mind to leave it alone. And yet, with a touchiness that was new to her, which seemed anyhow to have infected the whole family, she jealously guarded her claim to be the sole caretaker of Gregor's room. His mother once subjected his room to a thorough cleaning, which was achieved only by means of several buckets of water—all this dampness of course upset Gregor too and he lay widespread, sulky and motionless on the sofa—but she was well punished for it. Hardly had his sister noticed the changed aspect of his room that evening than she rushed in high dudgeon into the living room and, despite the imploringly raised hands of her mother, burst into a storm of weeping, while her parents—her father had of course been startled out of his chair—looked on at first in helpless amazement; then they too began to go into action; the father reproached the mother on his right for not having left the cleaning of Gregor's room to his sister; shrieked at the sister on his left that never again was she to be allowed to clean Gregor's room; while the mother tried to pull the father into his bedroom, since he was beyond himself with agitation; the sister, shaken with sobs, then beat upon the table with her small fists; and Gregor hissed loudly with rage because not one of them thought of shutting the door to spare him such a spectacle and so much noise.

Still, even if the sister, exhausted by her daily work, had grown tired of looking after Gregor as she did formerly, there was no need for his mother's intervention or for Gregor's being neglected at all. The charwoman was there. This old widow, whose strong bony frame had enabled her to survive the worst a long life could offer, by no means recoiled from Gregor. Without being in the least curious she had once by chance opened the door of his room and at the sight of Gregor, who, taken by surprise, began to rush to and fro although no one was chasing him, merely stood there with her arms folded. From that time she never failed to open his door a little for a moment, morning and evening, to have a look at him. At first she even used to call him to her, with words which apparently she took to be friendly, such as: "Come along, then, you old dung beetle!" or "Look at the old dung beetle, then!" To such allocutions Gregor made no answer, but stayed motionless where he was, as if the door had never been opened. Instead of being allowed to disturb him so senselessly whenever the whim took her, she should rather have been ordered to clean out his room daily, that charwoman! Once, early in the morning—heavy rain was lashing on the windowpanes, perhaps a sign that spring was on the way—Gregor was so exasperated when she began addressing him again that he ran at her, as if to attack her, although slowly and feebly enough. But the charwoman instead of showing fright merely lifted high a chair that happened to be beside the door, and as she stood there with her mouth wide open it was clear that she meant to shut it only when she brought the chair down on Gregor's back. "So you're not coming any nearer?" she asked, as Gregor turned away again, and quietly put the chair back into the corner.

Gregor was now eating hardly anything. Only when he happened to pass the food laid out for him did he take a bit of something in his mouth as a pastime, kept it there for an hour at a time and usually spat it out again. At first he thought it was chagrin over the state of his room that prevented him from eating, yet he soon got used to the various changes in his room. It had become a habit in the family to push into his room things there was no room for elsewhere, and there were plenty of these now, since one of the rooms had been let to three lodgers. These serious gentlemen—all three of them with full beards, as Gregor once observed through a crack in the door—had a passion for order, not only in their own room but, since they were now members of the household, in all its arrangements, especially in the kitchen. Superfluous, not to say dirty, objects they could not bear. Besides, they had brought with them most of the furnishings they needed. For this reason many things could be dispensed with that it was no use trying to sell but that should not be thrown away either. All of them found their way into Gregor's room. The ash can likewise and the kitchen garbage can. Anything that was not needed for the moment was simply flung into Gregor's room by the charwoman, who did everything in a hurry; fortunately Gregor usually saw only the object, whatever it was, and the hand that held it. Perhaps she intended to take the things away again as time and opportunity offered, or to collect them until she could throw them all out in a heap, but in fact they just lay wherever she happened to throw them, except when Gregor pushed his way through the junk heap and shifted it somewhat, at first out of necessity, because he had not room enough to crawl, but later with increasing enjoyment, although after such excursions, being sad and weary to death, he would lie motionless for hours.

Since the lodgers often ate their supper at home in the common living room, the living-room door stayed shut many an evening, yet Gregor reconciled himself quite easily to the shutting of the door, for often enough on evenings when it was opened he had disregarded it entirely and lain in the darkest corner of his room, quite unnoticed by the family. But on one occasion the charwoman left the door open a little and it stayed ajar even when the lodgers came in for supper and the lamp was lit. They set themselves at the top end of the table where formerly Gregor and his father and mother had eaten their meals, unfolded their napkins and took knife and fork in hand. At once his mother appeared in the other doorway with a dish of meat and close behind her his sister with a dish of potatoes piled high. The food steamed with a thick vapor. The lodgers bent over the food set before them as if to scrutinize it before eating, in fact the man in the middle, who seemed to pass for an authority with the other two, cut a piece of meat as it lay on the dish, obviously to discover if it were tender or should be sent back to the kitchen. He showed satisfaction, and Gregor's mother and sister, who had been watching anxiously, breathed freely and began to smile.

The family itself took its meals in the kitchen. None the less, Gregor's father came into the living room before going into the kitchen and with one prolonged bow, cap in hand, made a round of the table. The lodgers all stood up and murmured something in their beards. When they were alone again they ate their food in almost complete silence. It seemed remarkable to Gregor that among the various noises coming from the table he could always distinguish the sound of their masticating teeth, as if this were a sign to Gregor that one needed teeth in order to eat, and that with toothless jaws even of the finest make one could do nothing. "I'm hungry enough," said Gregor sadly to himself, "but not for that kind of food. How these lodgers are stuffing themselves, and here am I dying of starvation!"

On that very evening—during the whole of his time there Gregor could not remember ever having heard the violin—the sound of violin playing came from the kitchen. The lodgers had already finished their supper, the one in the middle had brought out a newspaper and given the other two a page apiece, and now they were leaning back at ease reading and smoking. When the violin began to play they pricked up their ears, got to their feet, and went on tiptoe to the hall door where they stood huddled together. Their movements must have been heard in the kitchen, for Gregor's father called out: "Is the violin playing disturbing you, gentlemen? It can be stopped at once." "On the contrary," said the middle lodger, "could not Fräulein Samsa come and play in this room, beside us, where it is much more convenient and comfortable?" "Oh certainly," cried Gregor's father, as if he were the violin player. The lodgers came back into the living room and waited. Presently Gregor's father arrived with the music stand, his mother carrying the music and his sister with the violin. His sister quietly made everything ready to start playing; his parents, who had never let rooms before and so had an exaggerated idea of the courtesy due to lodgers, did not venture to sit down on their own chairs; his father leaned against the door, the right hand thrust between two buttons of his livery coat, which was formally buttoned up; but his mother was offered a chair by one of the lodgers and, since she left the chair just where he had happened to put it, sat down in a corner to one side.

Gregor's sister began to play; the father and mother, from either side, intently watched the movements of her hands. Gregor, attracted by the playing, ventured to move forward a little until his head was actually inside the living room. He felt hardly any surprise at his growing lack of consideration for the others; there had been a time when he prided himself on being considerate. And yet just on this occasion he had more reason than ever to hide himself, since owing to the amount of dust which lay thick in his room and rose into the air at the slightest movement, he too was covered with dust; fluff and hair and remnants of food trailed with him, caught on his back and along his sides; his indifference to everything was much too great for him to turn on his back and scrape himself clean on the carpet, as once he had done several times a day. And in spite of his condition, no shame deterred him from advancing a little over the spotless floor of the living room.

To be sure, no one was aware of him. The family was entirely absorbed in the violin playing; the lodgers, however, who first of all had stationed themselves, hands in pockets, much too close behind the music stand so that they could all have read the music, which must have bothered his sister, had soon retreated to the window, half whispering with downbent heads, and stayed there while his father turned an anxious eye on them. Indeed, they were making it more than obvious that they had been disappointed in their expectation of hearing good or enjoyable violin playing, that they had had more than enough of the performance and only out of courtesy suffered a continued disturbance of their peace. From the way they all kept blowing the smoke of their cigars high in the air through nose and mouth one could divine their irritation. And yet Gregor's sister was playing so beautifully. Her face leaned sideways, intently and sadly her eyes followed the notes of music. Gregor crawled a little farther forward and lowered his head to the ground so that it might be possible for his eyes to meet hers. Was he an animal, that music had such an effect upon him? He felt as if the way were opening before him to the unknown nourishment he craved. He was determined to push forward till he reached his sister, to pull at her skirt and to let her know that she was to come into his room with her violin, for no one here appreciated her playing as he would appreciate it. He would never let her out of his room, at least, not so long as he lived; his frightful appearance would become, for the first time, useful to him; he would watch all the doors of his room at once and spit at intruders; but his sister should need no constraints, she should stay with him of her own free will; she should sit beside him on the sofa, bend down her ear to him and hear him confide that he had had the firm intention of sending her to the Conservatory, and that, but for his mishap, last Christmas—surely Christmas was long past?—he would have announced it to everybody without allowing a single objection. After this confession his sister would be so touched that she would burst into tears, and Gregor would then raise himself to her shoulder and kiss her on the neck, which, now that she went to business, she kept free of any ribbon or collar.

"Mr. Samsa!" cried the middle lodger, to Gregor's father, and pointed, without wasting any more words, at Gregor, now working himself slowly forwards. The violin fell silent, the middle lodger first smiled to his friends with a shake of the head and then looked at Gregor again. Instead of driving Gregor out, his father seemed to think it more needful to begin by soothing down the lodgers, although they were not at all agitated and apparently found Gregor more entertaining than the violin playing. He hurried towards them and, spreading out his arms, tried to urge them back into their own room and at the same time to block their view of Gregor. They now began to be really a little angry, one could not tell whether because of the old man's behavior or because it had just dawned on them that all unwittingly they had such a neighbor as Gregor next door. They demanded explanations of his father, they waved their arms like him, tugged uneasily at their beards, and only with reluctance backed towards their room. Meanwhile Gregor's sister, who stood there as if lost when her playing was so abruptly broken off, came to life again, pulled herself together all at once after standing for a while holding violin and bow in nervelessly hanging hands and staring at her music, pushed her violin into the lap of her mother, who was still sitting in her chair fighting asthmatically for breath, and ran into the lodgers' room to which they were now being shepherded by her father rather more quickly than before. One could see the pillows and blankets on the beds flying under her accustomed fingers and being laid in order. Before the lodgers had actually reached their room she had finished making the beds and slipped out. The old man seemed once more to be so possessed by his mulish self-assertiveness that he was forgetting all the respect he should show to his lodgers. He kept driving them on and driving them on until in the very door of the bedroom the middle lodger stamped his foot loudly on the floor and so brought him to a halt. "I beg to announce," said the lodger, lifting one hand and looking also at Gregor's mother and sister, "that because of the disgusting conditions prevailing in this household and family"—here he spat on the floor with emphatic brevity—"I give you notice on the spot. Naturally I won't pay you a penny for the days I have lived here, on the contrary I shall consider bringing an action for damages against you, based on claims—believe me—that will be easily susceptible of proof." He ceased and stared straight in front of him, as if he expected something. In fact his two friends at once rushed into the breach with these words: "And we too give notice on the spot." On that he seized the door-handle and shut the door with a slam.

Gregor's father, groping with his hands, staggered forward and fell into his chair; it looked as if he were stretching himself there for his ordinary evening nap, but the marked jerkings of his head, which was as if uncontrollable, showed that he was far from asleep. Gregor had simply stayed quietly all the time on the spot where the lodgers had espied him. Disappointment at the failure of his plan, perhaps also the weakness arising from extreme hunger, made it impossible for him to move. He feared, with a fair degree of certainty, that at any moment the general tension would discharge itself in a combined attack upon him, and he lay waiting. He did not react even to the noise made by the violin as it fell off his mother's lap from under her trembling fingers and gave out a resonant note.

"My dear parents," said his sister, slapping her hand on the table by way of introduction, "things can't go on like this. Perhaps you don't realize that, but I do. I won't utter my brother's name in the presence of this creature, and so all I say is: we must try to get rid of it. We've tried to look after it and to put up with it as far as is humanly possible, and I don't think anyone could reproach us in the slightest."

"She is more than right," said Gregor's father to himself. His mother, who was still choking for lack of breath, began to cough hollowly into her hand with a wild look in her eyes.

His sister rushed over to her and held her forehead. His father's thoughts seemed to have lost their vagueness at Grete's words, he sat more upright, fingering his service cap that lay among the plates still lying on the table from the lodgers' supper, and from time to time looked at the still form of Gregor.

"We must try to get rid of it," his sister now said explicitly to her father, since her mother was coughing too much to hear a word, "it will be the death of both of you, I can see that coming. When one has to work as hard as we do, all of us, one can't stand this continual torment at home on top of it.

673

At least I can't stand it any longer." And she burst into such a passion of sobbing that her tears dropped on her mother's face, where she wiped them off mechanically.

"My dear," said the old man sympathetically, and with evident understanding, "but what can we do?"

Gregor's sister merely shrugged her shoulders to indicate the feeling of helplessness that had now overmastered her during her weeping fit, in contrast to her former confidence.

"If he could understand us," said her father, half questioningly; Grete, still sobbing, vehemently waved a hand to show how unthinkable that was.

"If he could understand us," repeated the old man, shutting his eyes to consider his daughter's conviction that understanding was impossible, "then perhaps we might come to some agreement with him. But as it is—"

"He must go," cried Gregor's sister, "that's the only solution, Father. You must just try to get rid of the idea that this is Gregor. The fact that we've believed it for so long is the root of all our trouble. But how can it be Gregor? If this were Gregor, he would have realized long ago that human beings can't live with such a creature, and he'd have gone away on his own accord. Then we wouldn't have any brother, but we'd be able to go on living and keep his memory in honor. As it is, this creature persecutes us, drives away our lodgers, obviously wants the whole apartment to himself and would have us all sleep in the gutter. Just look, Father," she shrieked all at once, "he's at it again!" And in an excess of panic that was quite incomprehensible to Gregor she even left her mother, literally thrusting the chair from her as if she would rather sacrifice her mother than stay so near to Gregor, and rushed behind her father, who also rose up, being simply upset by her agitation, and half-spread his arms out as if to protect her.

Yet Gregor had not the slightest intention of frightening anyone, far less his sister. He

had only begun to turn round in order to crawl back to his room, but it was certainly a startling operation to watch, since because of his disabled condition he could not execute the difficult turning movements except by lifting his head and then bracing it against the floor over and over again. He paused and looked round. His good intentions seemed to have been recognized; the alarm had only been momentary. Now they were all watching him in melancholy silence. His mother lay in her chair, her legs stiffly outstretched and pressed together, her eyes almost closing for sheer weariness; his father and his sister were sitting beside each other, his sister's arm around the old man's neck.

Perhaps I can go on turning round now, thought Gregor, and began his labors again. He could not stop himself from panting with the effort, and had to pause now and then to take breath. Nor did anyone harass him, he was left entirely to himself. When he had completed the turn-round he began at once to crawl straight back. He was amazed at the distance separating him from his room and could not understand how in his weak state he had managed to accomplish the same journey so recently, almost without remarking it. Intent on crawling as fast as possible, he barely noticed that not a single word, not an ejaculation from his family, interfered with his progress. Only when he was already in the doorway did he turn his head round, not completely, for his neck muscles were getting stiff, but enough to see that nothing had changed behind him except that his sister had risen to her feet. His last glance fell on his mother, who was now quite overcome by sleep.

Hardly was he well inside his room when the door was hastily pushed shut, bolted and locked. The sudden noise in his rear startled him so much that his little legs gave beneath him. It was his sister who had shown such haste. She had been standing ready waiting and had made a light spring forward, Gregor had not even heard her coming, and she cried "At last!" to her parents as she turned the key in the lock.

"And what now?" said Gregor to himself, looking round in the darkness. Soon he made the discovery that he was now unable to stir a limb. This did not surprise him, rather it seemed unnatural that he should ever actually have been able to move on these feeble little legs. Otherwise he felt relatively comfortable. True, his whole body was aching, but it seemed that the pain was gradually growing less and would finally pass away. The rotting apple in his back and the inflamed area around it, all covered with soft dust, already hardly troubled him. He thought of his family with tenderness and love. The decision that he must disappear was one that he held to even more strongly than his sister, if that were possible. In this state of vacant and peaceful meditation he remained until the tower clock struck three in the morning. The first broadening of light in the world outside the window entered his consciousness once more. Then his head sank to the floor of its own accord and from his nostrils came the last faint flicker of his breath.

When the charwoman arrived early in the morning—what between her strength and her impatience she slammed all the doors so loudly, never mind how often she had been begged not to do so, that no one in the whole apartment could enjoy any quiet sleep after her arrival—she noticed nothing unusual as she took her customary peep into Gregor's room. She thought he was lying motionless on purpose, pretending to be in the sulks; she credited him with every kind of intelligence. Since she happened to have the long-handled broom in her hand she tried to tickle him up with it from the doorway. When that too produced no reaction she felt provoked and poked at him a little harder, and only when she had pushed him along the floor without meeting any resistance was her attention aroused. It did not take her long to establish

the truth of the matter, and her eyes widened, she let out a whistle, yet did not waste much time over it but tore open the door of the Samsas' bedroom and yelled into the darkness at the top of her voice: "Just look at this, it's dead; it's lying here dead and done for!"

Mr. and Mrs. Samsa started up in their double bed and before they realized the nature of the charwoman's announcement had some difficulty in overcoming the shock of it. But then they got out of bed quickly, one on either side, Mr. Samsa throwing a blanket over his shoulders, Mrs. Samsa in nothing but her nightgown; in this array they entered Gregor's room. Meanwhile the door of the living room opened, too, where Grete had been sleeping since the advent of the lodgers; she was completely dressed as if she had not been to bed, which seemed to be confirmed also by the paleness of her face. "Dead?" said Mrs. Samsa, looking questioningly at the charwoman, although she could have investigated for herself, and the fact was obvious enough without investigation. "I should say so," said the charwoman, proving her words by pushing Gregor's corpse a long way to one side with her broomstick. Mrs. Samsa made a movement as if to stop her, but checked it. "Well," said Mr. Samsa, "now thanks be to God." He crossed himself, and the three women followed his example. Grete, whose eyes never left the corpse, said: "Just see how thin he was. It's such a long time since he's eaten anything. The food came out again just as it went in." Indeed, Gregor's body was completely flat and dry, as could only now be seen when it was no longer supported by the legs and nothing prevented one from looking closely at it.

"Come in beside us, Grete, for a little while," said Mrs. Samsa with a tremulous smile, and Grete, not without looking back at the corpse, followed her parents into their bedroom. The charwoman shut the door and opened the window wide. Although it was so early in the morning a certain softness was preceptible in the fresh air. After all, it was already the end of March.

The three lodgers emerged from their room and were surprised to see no breakfast; they had been forgotten. "Where's our breakfast?" said the middle lodger peevishly to the charwoman. But she put her finger to her lips and hastily, without a word, indicated by gestures that they should go into Gregor's room. They did so and stood, their hands in the pockets of their somewhat shabby coats, around Gregor's corpse in the room where it was now fully light.

At that the door of the Samsas' bedroom opened and Mr. Samsa appeared in his uniform, his wife on one arm, his daughter on the other. They all looked a little as if they had been crying; from time to time Grete hid her face on her father's arm.

"Leave my house at once!" said Mr. Samsa, and pointed to the door without disengaging himself from the women. "What do you mean by that?" said the middle lodger, taken somewhat aback, with a feeble smile. The two others put their hands behind them and kept rubbing them together, as if in gleeful expectation of a fine set-to in which they were bound to come off the winners. "I mean just what I say," answered Mr. Samsa, and advanced in a straight line with his two companions towards the lodger. He stood his ground at first quietly, looking at the floor as if his thoughts were taking a new pattern in his head. "Then let us go, by all means," he said, and looked up at Mr. Samsa as if in a sudden access of humility he were expecting some renewed sanction for this decision. Mr. Samsa merely nodded briefly once or twice with staring eyes. Upon that the lodger really did go with long strides into the hall, his two friends had been listening and had quite stopped rubbing their hands for some moments and now went scuttling after him as if afraid that Mr. Samsa might get into the hall before them and cut them off from their leader. In the hall they all three took their

hats from the rack, their sticks from the umbrella stand, bowed in silence and quitted the apartment. With a suspiciousness which proved quite unfounded Mr. Samsa and the two women followed them out to the landing; leaning over the banister they watched the three figures slowly but surely going down the long stairs, vanishing from sight at a certain turn of the staircase on every floor and coming into view again after a moment or so; the more they dwindled, the more the Samsa family's interest in them dwindled, and when a butcher's boy met them and passed them on the stairs coming up proudly with a tray on his head, Mr. Samsa and the two women soon left the landing and as if a burden had been lifted from them went back into their apartment.

They decided to spend this day in resting and going for a stroll; they had not only deserved such a respite from work, but absolutely needed it. And so they sat down at the table and wrote three notes of excuse, Mr. Samsa to his board of management, Mrs. Samsa to her employer and Grete to the head of her firm. While they were writing, the charwoman came in to say that she was going now, since her morning's work was finished. At first they only nodded without looking up, but as she kept hovering there they eyed her irritably. "Well?" said Mr. Samsa. The charwoman stood grinning in the doorway as if she had good news to impart to the family but meant not to say a word unless properly questioned. The small ostrich feather standing upright on her hat, which had annoyed Mr. Samsa ever since she was engaged, was waving gaily in all directions. "Well, what is it then?" asked Mrs. Samsa, who obtained more respect from the charwoman than the others. "Oh," said the charwoman, giggling so amiably that she could not at once continue, "just this, you don't need to bother about how to get rid of the thing next door. It's been seen to already." Mrs. Samsa and Grete bent over their letters again, as if preoccupied; Mr. Samsa, who perceived that she was eager to begin describing it all in detail, stopped her with a decisive hand. But since she was not allowed to tell her story, she remembered the great hurry she was in, being obviously deeply huffed: "Bye, everybody," she said, whirling off violently, and departed with a frightful slamming of doors.

"She'll be given notice tonight," said Mr. Samsa, but neither from his wife nor his daughter did he get any answer, for the charwoman seemed to have shattered again the composure they had barely achieved. They rose, went to the window and stayed there, clasping each other tight. Mr. Samsa turned in his chair to look at them and quietly observed them for a little. Then he called out: "Come along, now, do. Let bygones be bygones. And you might have some consideration for me." The two of them complied at once, hastened to him, caressed him and quickly finished their letters.

Then they all three left the apartment together, which was more than they had done for months, and went by tram into the open country outside the town. The tram, in which they were the only passengers, was filled with warm sunshine. Leaning comfortably back in their seats they canvassed their prospects for the future, and it appeared on closer inspection that these were not at all bad, for the jobs they had got, which so far they had never really discussed with each other, were all three admirable and likely to lead to better things later on. The greatest immediate improvement in their condition would of course arise from moving to another house; they wanted to take a smaller and cheaper but also better situated and more easily run apartment than the one they had, which Gregor had selected. While they were thus conversing, it struck both Mr. and Mrs. Samsa, almost at the same moment, as they became aware of their daughter's increasing vivacity, that in spite of all the sorrow of recent times, which had made her cheeks pale, she had bloomed into a pretty girl with a good figure. They grew quieter and half unconsciously exchanged glances of complete agreement, having come to the conclusion that it would soon be time to find a good husband for her. And it was like a confirmation of their new dreams and excellent intentions that at the end of their journey their daughter sprang to her feet first and stretched her young body.

DISCUSSION FOR UNDERSTANDING

1. In the month since Gregor's injury, what has happened to each of the following: the father? the mother? Grete? Gregor?

2. What are the attitudes of the family and the charwoman toward Gregor?

3. What happens when Grete plays the violin?

4. What are Grete's reasons for getting rid of Gregor? Does Gregor agree or disagree?

5. How do the Samsas feel about Gregor's death?

I
THE REAL AND THE UNREAL

Perhaps the thing that most startles readers of *The Metamorphosis* is the juxtaposition of the unreal and real. The unreal is the metamorphosis of Gregor into a huge and unpleasant insect. We learn of this in the calm, matter-of-fact first sentence of the story. From then on, everything is almost clinically realistic. Never forgetting the monstrousness of the metamorphosis, itself, we nevertheless recognize what our own feelings would be if we were involved in the situation, either as Gregor or as someone living with him. Kafka thus forces us to consider the whole spectrum of problems facing individuals learning to know themselves.

The story explores a series of identity crises. How is Gregor affected by each of the following?

1. Physical appearance
2. Family relationships
3. Physical surroundings
4. Response to the arts
5. Food preferences
6. Ability to communicate

II
IMPLICATIONS

What is your reaction to the following statements? Use both *The Metamorphosis* and your own experiences to support your opinion.

1. It is natural to assume, as Gregor does, that even after a change, things will go on as usual.

2. The real metamorphosis is what happens to the family, not what happens to Gregor.

3. The father's treatment of Gregor represents the usual father-son relationship.

4. Gregor's sister is the only member of the family who seems *human* in her treatment of Gregor.

5. The charwoman, although uneducated and probably not too bright, is basically the most admirable person in the story.

6. The family is better off because of Gregor's metamorphosis.

Many people have tried to work out an interpretation for the story. You should certainly try to do so, too. Consider the following as possibilities. What are the strengths and weaknesses of each?

1. Gregor has tried to usurp his father's rightful place as head of the family and is therefore punished.

2. This is the story of the treatment of minority-group people by the majority.

3. Every family (or group) must make one of its members an insect in order to operate successfully.

4. Our technological society crushes the humanity from a person.

5. People have no time for a member of society who cannot keep up physically or mentally.

6. This is the story of the rejection of an individual's appeals for love in the modern world.

7. People react to the exterior of others, not to what they really are inside.

III
TECHNIQUES

In this unit, you are asked to consider two elements in the writer's craft: selection of incident and organization.

Selection of Incident

We have all known a storyteller who, halfway through a tale, says, "Oh, that reminds me. . . ." He or she then goes off on a tangent, the story becomes filled with irrelevant details, and it loses its impact. Skillful authors avoid this pitfall by including only those incidents which move the story forward. Obviously the writer can't record everything the characters do day after day—to do so would make an intolerably long and dull book.

Careful selection of meaningful incidents brings about a tight plot. An incident may help portray a character's personality and thus prepare the reader for later events. Sometimes an incident fills the reader in on what happened earlier or spurs interest in what is to follow. Each detail the writer creates and presents to the reader must have some purpose; it must add to the total picture.

Some writers use relatively few incidents but concentrate on what is going on in the minds of characters as they react to these incidents. Others, like Kafka in *The Metamorphosis*, literally cram their stories with incidents. Notice that Gregor is never much worried about the metamorphosis from his personal point of view. Instead, he worries about his job and about his effect on others. A myriad of detailed incidents piled up one upon another move the story along.

1. Suppose a television writer created a character who woke in the morning to find a greatly changed body. Typically what would the character do?

2. How is Kafka's selection of incidents different from this?

3. In the first section, what are the three phases in Gregor's reaction to his situation? What effect do these incidents create?

4. What are the incidents that show other people's reactions?

5. Consider the first section. What incident is most vivid for you?

Organization

Having selected which incidents and details to use, the writer must then decide how to arrange them. The most usual form of arrangement is chronological order—that is, the events are put down in the order in which they occur in time. But some writers begin with the present and at some later point go back in time to fill the reader in on earlier happenings. Other stories shuttle back and forth in time. This interruption of the present to introduce an element from the past is called *flashback*.

Another form of organization is *stream of consciousness*. In this structure, the order of events is determined by the character's thought processes. The order is logical only in so far as one thought links to another thought in the character's mind.

1. How much time elapses in each of the sections? Are the incidents arranged chronologically or in some other pattern?

2. A modern play is often divided into three acts that are designated as: the situation, the development or complication, and the resolution. *The Metamorphosis* is divided into three parts. Does it basically follow the three-act play pattern?

IV

WORDS

When reading, do you tend to skip over words whose meaning is vague or unknown, letting the rest of the context carry you along? You shouldn't, because studying the meanings of new words encountered in your reading is one of the best ways to build vocabulary. Following are some unusual words used in *The Metamorphosis*. Test your grasp of their meaning by using them in sentences of your own.

1. Gregor must now try to *propitiate* his father. To appease, to conciliate, to make favorably inclined.

2. advanced with a grim *visage*   The face or look of a person or animal.

3. He could have borne her *ministrations*. The act of serving or helping a person, as with food, care, or advice.

4. He used to *execrate* the hospital.   To abhor, to curse, to detest utterly.

5. a perfectly healthy *malingerer*   One who shirks a duty by pretending illness or injury.

6. words were *reverberating* around him Echoing, resounding, repeatedly reflected.

7. a childish *recalcitrance*   The act of stubborn rebellion or obstinate resistance to authority.

MASSIMO BONTEMPELLI

Massimo Bontempelli[1] (1878–1960), Italian novelist and critic, was born in Como, Italy. He taught school for a few years, but he was so anxious to express his own thoughts that he decided to make writing his career. He became a contributor to several well-known newspapers and magazines. In 1926, with the French writer Malaparte, he established a review to publicize happenings in Italy and Europe. James Joyce was one of its foreign editors. Bontempelli described his position as the difficult one of trying to find what he called "magical realism," or reality within surrealism. (Surrealism attempts to portray the working of the subconscious mind and is characterized by unnatural combinations and juxtapositions of material.) His short stories appeared in English translations during the mid-1930s and again in the mid-1950s. Some of them, such as "Pictures on Skulls" and "Avenging Film," delved into the mysterious. Bontempelli died in Rome in 1960.

Mirrors

translated from the Italian by Eduardo Corsi

Talking of mirrors it is necessary that I relate another experience. I know that I shall be accused of abusing this theme, but patience, my friend. Rather I would prefer not to have some malicious person think that I spend most of my life before a mirror. On the contrary it is because I so seldom use this baffling contrivance that it still deigns to create for me the strange illusions it denies to those who make of it as constant and ordinary an article of use.

About eight days ago, on a morning toward noon, my landlady woke me up with a telegram. After a few willing efforts I managed to put myself in a condition to read it. It was a telegram from Vienna. It was addressed to me, to me alone, and it was correctly addressed. This is what it said:

"Leave for Rome day after to-morrow stop *arrivederci* stop Massimo."

I was in Vienna two months ago, for fifteen days. I tried to recall all the persons I had met there during those fifteen days. There was an old Hungarian friend of mine called Tibor, and some others named Fritz, Richard and John. I thought and thought again, but I could think of no other Massimo in Vienna but myself.

There was just one conclusion and it was a clear one. Since I was the only Massimo I could think of in Vienna, the Massimo who sent me that telegram was myself.

It was my telegram therefore.

I understand—I shouted.

But the reader, on the other hand, cannot as yet have understood.

I shall explain. But before I do so it is necessary that I tell my reader of some of the other experiences I have had in this matter of telegrams. A single example will suffice. I was arranging my belongings in my room one day when, as luck would have it, I noticed that my umbrella was gone. I looked for it everywhere. More than once (as we are in the habit of doing in such cases, as if once were not enough) I

---

1. **Massimo Bontempelli** (mäs′sē mō bon′tem pel ē).

Reprinted from *Great Stories of All Nations*, Maxim Lieber & Blanche Colton Williams (eds.). Copyright 1934 by Tudor Publishing Company.

looked for it in the corner where I usually kept it, but in vain. I finally resigned myself to the loss and went about my business: we lose greater things in life than an umbrella.

I had almost forgotten it when, two days later, I received the following telegram: "Shall arrive to-night Umbrella." I gave it little thought, and at night I retired peacefully. The following morning the first thing to attract my attention was my umbrella. Sure enough there it was, in the very corner where I had looked for it many times.

Of course, I know perfectly well that it is not an uncommon thing (even if science has not as yet explained it) to find a lost article in the very place where one has looked for it many times before. And there is really no use in talking about it. But to have a lost article announce its return by telegram, that is not so common.

With this example in mind, the thing that struck me intuitively in reading that telegram from Vienna, and which I am about to explain, ought to seem quite natural even to the most materialistic of my readers.

But here we have got to go back a bit.

Two months ago in Vienna I was standing before a mirror fixing my tie. I was getting ready to take my train back to Rome. There were political demonstrations going on throughout the city at the time.

As I have said, I was standing before a mirror fixing my tie. Suddenly a tremendous explosion shook the house and smashed my mirror into bits.

I realised it was a bomb, and I went on fixing my tie without a mirror. When I was through, I took my bag, drove to the station, and left. A few days later I was in Rome. It was late at night, so I immediately undressed and went to bed.

The next morning I stood before the mirror with my shaving brush in one hand a towel in the other, when to my great surprise I saw nothing there. To be more precise, there was everything there but me. I could see a soap-soaked brush dangling to and fro, and a towel equally agitated, as if it had suddenly gone mad in the empty space. But I, I was not to be seen. Neither my face nor my image was there.

Massimo Bontempelli

Realising at once what had happened, I broke into laughter.

All those who use a mirror, the women especially, must have noticed, I believe, that the moment they pull themselves away from it, from the mirror into which they are looking, they feel a slight sense of discomfort. There is a little jerk in the parting. Well, this results from the very light, imperceptible effort we all make when tearing ourselves away, when withdrawing the image that is there.

Now this is exactly what happened to me on that day in Vienna. My mirror broke so instantly, it was smashed and destroyed so suddenly, that I was not quick enough to withdraw my image, to pull it back before it vanished.

Naturally, hurried as I was to get away, I paid little attention to the incident at the time. I first realised what had happened when I found myself facing a mirror here in Rome, or two days later, as I have said.

And so for these past two months I have been without my image. It was somewhat of a nuisance at first, especially for my tie and beard. But I learned to get on without it. I learned to make my tie by memory, and as to my beard I shaved it by ear with a Gillette.

I took the mirror down from its accustomed place and put it away in my trunk.

The only thing I had to be very careful about was not to have anyone see me standing before any of the mirrors along the streets, in the cafés, or in the homes of others. People are easily surprised, you know. They would want to know why and how, and then I should have to explain. I should have to discuss metaphysics[2] and other such annoyances.

For this reason, though the loss itself may have been anything but serious, I was happy to receive that telegram eight days ago. I understood at once (and by this time I presume that even the densest of my readers has understood) that that telegram had been sent to me by my own image so that I might be informed of its homecoming.

Naturally, I did not hasten to look at myself in the mirror. Not at all. I did not want to give my image the satisfaction of knowing that I care very much about it, that I have been waiting for it impatiently, that I cannot do without it. Since it left Vienna eight days ago, even admitting that it travelled on a very fast train, it should have reached here at least four days ago. But I did not show myself until yesterday. It was only yesterday that I went after the mirror in my trunk, whistling an air from Aida[3] as I did so. I restored it to its place in the bathroom without even looking at it. Then with the utmost tranquillity and indifference I adjusted my collar and tie and took a glimpse at myself. There I was: there was my image, not a whit changed. I had had a vague fear that I might find it a little disturbed, somewhat resentful of my indifference, and probably tired from the long trip and its

many experiences. Instead it seemed to be in the finest condition, and as indifferent and tranquil as its owner.

I
HOW IMPORTANT IS YOUR IMAGE?

Psychologists can demonstrate that most of us do not really have an accurate picture of what we look like. We tend either to over- or underestimate our facial features. Have you noticed how seldom people are satisfied with snapshots of themselves? Suppose that you were blind and had no way of gaining a visual image of yourself. Would it make a difference in your self-identity?

II
IMPLICATIONS

Are the ideas implied by the quotations that follow valid or false?

1. "Rather I would prefer not to have some malicious person think that I spend most of my life before a mirror."

2. ". . . it is not an uncommon thing (even if science has not as yet explained it) to find a lost article in the very place where one has looked for it many times before."

3. "All those who use a mirror . . . must have noticed, I believe, that the moment they pull themselves away from it, from the mirror into which they are looking, they feel a slight sense of discomfort."

4. "I did not want to give my image the satisfaction of knowing that I care very much about it, that I have been waiting for it impatiently, that I cannot do without it."

III
TECHNIQUES

Selection of Incident

The incident with the umbrella seems to intrude into the story. What does the author gain by including it?

Organization

This story provides an example of a particular type of organization. Can you identify its organizational method?

---

2. **metaphysics** (met'ə fiz'iks), a branch of philosophy concerned with the nature of being.
3. **Aida** (ä ē'dä), a famous Italian opera.

ANTON CHEKHOV

Anton Chekhov (1860–1904) was the son of a poverty-ridden shopkeeper
in Russia who was fanatically religious and beat his children at the slightest whim.
Looking back, Chekhov said, "There was no childhood in my childhood." At nineteen,
in order to support himself and his family while he attended medical school,
Chekhov wrote little sketches and humorous pieces for the cheap humor magazines.
After he had finished his medical course, he met Suvorin, the owner of *New Time*,
a great daily newspaper. When he invited Chekhov to contribute longer tales
at a better rate of pay, Chekov turned seriously to writing, which he found
more congenial than a medical career. His writing changed at this time,
and a deep pessimism came to the fore. His main interest lay with the characters,
and he liked to show how a mood or relationship between people changed
because of the minute pinpricks of life. Often a seemingly insignificant happening
can turn a life in a completely different direction. Perhaps more than any other
Russian writer, Chekhov illustrates the comment that "a Russian story is always
the story of the undoing of a life." Critics have noted a sense of scientific
objectivity in Chekhov. He presents his people's pettiness, weakness, faults,
but does not moralize about them. The theme of futility, the inability
of his characters to come to grips with reality, is common to all of Chekhov's plays.
He abandoned false melodrama and involved plot, in an attempt to present life
as truthfully as possible. In the theater, his plays, such as *The Cherry Orchard*
and *The Three Sisters,* are performed all over the world. Chekhov was still
a young man when he died in Germany of tuberculosis.

After the Theater

When she came back with Mummy from the theater where they saw *Eugene Onegin*,[1] Nadia Zelenin went to her room, hurriedly thrust off her dress, let down her hair and in only a petticoat and white blouse sat quicker still to the table to write a letter like Tatiana's.

"I love you," she wrote down, "but you do not love me, do not love me!"

She wrote it down and began to laugh.

She was only sixteen and so far was in love with no one. She knew that Gorni, the officer, and Gruzdev, the student, were in love with her but now, after the opera, she wished to feel doubt of their love. To be unloved and unhappy—how interesting that was! When one loves greatly but the other is indifferent, there is something beautiful in that, affecting and poetic. Onegin is interesting because he is not in love at all and Tatiana fascinating because she loves so much, but if they loved each other just the same and both were happy, then, very likely, they would seem boring.

"Do stop declaring that you love me," Nadia went on, thinking of Gorni. "I cannot believe you. You are very clever, well-educated and earnest, you have immense talent and perhaps a

"After the Theater" and "The Trick" reprinted from *The Sinner from Toledo and Other Stories* by Anton Chekhov, translated by Arnold Hinchliffe. Fairleigh Dickinson University Press. © 1972 by Associated University Presses.

1. **Eugene Onegin,** an opera by Peter I. Tchaikovsky. In the opera, Tatiana writes a letter to Onegin declaring her love. Onegin rebuffs Tatiana but then returns too late to try to win her love after she is married to a prince.

Anton Chekhov, 1889

brilliant future awaits you, while I am a dull girl of no account and you know perfectly well I would only be a hindrance in your life. True, you were attracted by me and thought that in me you had found your ideal but it was a mistake and now you ask yourself in despair: 'What did I meet this girl for?' And only your kind nature prevents you from admitting that to yourself."

Nadia felt sorry for herself, began to cry and went on:

"It is hard for me to leave Mummy and my brother or I would put on a nun's dress and go away wherever my eyes may lead me. And you would be free and come to love another. Ah, if only I were dead!"

Through tears she could not make out what she wrote; and on the table, floor and ceiling little rainbows flickered as if she were looking through a prism. She could not write and leaned back in the chair and began to think about Gorni.

My God, how interesting men were, how fascinating! She remembered what a lovely look there was on Gorni's face, fawning, guilty and gentle, when they argued about music and what an effort he exerted to keep the sound of passion from his voice. In a society where indifference and chill arrogance are counted signs of breeding and of noble manners men have to hide their passion. And hide it he did, but unsuccessfully and everybody clearly knew that he loved music passionately. Endless debate about music and the bold assertions of the ignorant always put him under strain and he was apprehensive, shy and reticent. He played magnificently like a professional pianist and, had he not become an officer, would indeed be a famous musician.

The tears dried about her eyes. She remembered that Gorni declared his love for her at a symphony concert and then again downstairs near the cloak room, with draughts blowing all over the place.

"I'm very glad," she wrote, "that at last you've been introduced to Grusdev. He is a very clever man and you are certain to like him. He was with us yesterday and stayed till two o'clock. We were all delighted and I was sorry you hadn't come. He said a lot of wonderful things."

Nadia laid her arms on the table and rested her head on them, her hair covering the letter. She remembered that Grusdev was in love with her as well and had as much right to a letter as Gorni. For that matter wouldn't it be better to write to Grusdev?

Quite without reason joy stirred in her breast: small at first, it rolled there like a rubber ball, then grew broader and larger and gushed like a wave. She forgot Gorni and Grusdev now, her thoughts became confused and her joy grew and grew, spreading from her breasts into her arms and legs, and it seemed as if a light, fresh breeze puffed about her head, ruffling her hair. Her shoulders trembled with a quiet laughter, and the table trembled too, and the glass round the lamp; and tears spattered on the letter from her eyes. It wasn't in her power to stop this laughter and to show herself she wasn't laughing without reason, she hastened to think of something funny.

"What a funny poodle!" she said, feeling as if the laughter would choke her. "What a funny poodle!"

She remembered how after tea the previous evening Grusdev had played with Maxim, the poodle, and then told a story about a very clever poodle who chased a raven in a yard and the raven looked back at him and said:

"Oh, you rascal!"

Not knowing he was up against a learned raven, the poodle was terribly bewildered, retreated in confusion, then began to bark.

"No, I'd better be in love with Grusdev!" Nadia decided and tore up the letter.

She began to think of the student and of his love and of her own love but then it seemed her thoughts ran off in all directions and she thought about everything: Mummy, the street, her pencil, the piano.

She brooded with delight and found everything splendid and wonderful, and her joy let her know that this was still not all, that in a little time it would be better still. Spring soon, summer, going to Gorbiki with Mummy, Gorni coming on leave and he would walk with her in the garden and make love. And Grusdev coming too. He would play croquet with her and skittles, tell her funny and astonishing things. A passionate longing came upon her for the garden, for darkness, clear sky and stars. Again her shoulders trembled with laughter and it seemed there was a scent of wormwood in the room and a twig tapped at the window.

She went to her bed and sat down; and not knowing what to do with the great joy that oppressed her, looked at the holy image hanging at her bedhead and said:

"God! God! God!"

The Trick

A clear winter noon . . .

A frost, hard and crackling, and Nadenka, holding me under the arm, had silver rime on curls at her temples and the down of her upper lip. We stood on a high hill and from our feet a slope, reflecting the sun like a mirror, stretched all the way down. Beside us was a little sledge upholstered in bright red cloth.

"Let's slide down, Nadejda Petrovna," I pleaded. "Just once. I assure you, we'll come through safe and sound."

But Nadenka was afraid. All the way down from her tiny galoshes to the bottom of the icy slope seemed a terrifying abyss, immeasurably deep. Her heart sank and her breathing stopped when she looked down or when I merely suggested sitting in the sledge. If she took a risk and hurtled into the abyss, what then? She'd die, lose her senses.

"I beg you," I said. "There's no need to be afraid. That's mean-spirited, you know, cowardice!"

At last Nadenka gave in and I saw from her face that she did it with fear for her life. I seated her, pale and trembling, in the sledge, clutched her hand and down we sped together into the abyss.

The sledge flew like a bullet. The cleaving air whipped, howling, into our faces, whistled in our ears, tore and tweaked at us in hurtful spite and tried to rive the heads from our shoulders. The wind's force took away our power to breathe. It was as if the devil himself had clutched us in his claws and with a roar was rushing us to hell. Everything about us blurred together in a single, headlong-rushing strip. Only a moment more, it seemed, and we would perish!

"I love you, Nadia!" I whispered.

The sledge began to move more quietly, more quietly, the roar of wind and the whirr of runners less fierce, we were free to breathe again and there we were, at last, at the bottom. Nadenka seemed neither alive nor dead. She was white, scarcely breathing. . . . I helped her up.

"I'll not go again for anything," she said, looking at me with wide eyes full of horror. "Not for anything on earth! I nearly died!"

After a little time she recovered and looked inquiringly into my eyes: had I said those four

words or did she only seem to hear them in the wind? And I stood beside her, smoking, and carefully examining my glove.

She took me by the arm and for a long time we walked about the hill. Clearly the puzzling question gave her no peace. Were those words spoken or weren't they? Yes or no? Yes or no? It was a matter of pride, of honor, of life and happiness, of great consequence, the greatest on earth. Impatiently, sadly and with a searching expression, Nadenka looked into my face, responding absent-mindedly as she waited, wondering if I'd speak. Oh, what a play of expression on that dear face, what indeed! I saw her struggle with herself; she had to say something, ask a certain question but couldn't find words, was ill at ease, alarmed, disturbed by joy. . . .

"Do you know something?" she said, not looking at me.

"What?" I asked.

"Let's do it once more . . . slide down."

We climbed the steps to the hill top. Again I seated Nadenka, pale and trembling, in the sledge and again we hurtled down into the terrifying abyss; the wind roared again and the runners whirred, and again, when noise and speed were fiercest, I whispered:

"I love you, Nadia!"

As the sledge came to a halt, Nadenka glanced back at the hill we'd sped down and then looked a long time into my face and listened intently to my indifferent and impassive voice; and everything about her, even her muff and hood, all of her figure expressed extreme bewilderment.

Her face was saying: "What on earth was it? Who pronounced *those* words? Did he, or did I only seem to hear them?"

The uncertainty made her agitated, put her quite out of patience. The poor girl made no reply to questions and she frowned, on the edge of tears.

"Shall we go home?" I asked.

"But . . . but I like tobogganing . . ." she said, blushing. "Shall we go once again?"

She "liked" tobogganing: all the same, sitting in the sledge, she was pale and trembling, just as before, could scarcely breathe for fear.

We went down for the third time and I saw how she looked into my face, watching my lips. But I put a handkerchief to my lips and coughed, and when we were half way down, I managed to murmur:

"I love you, Nadia!"

And so the enigma was enigma still. Nadenka was silent, preoccupied. . . .

I saw her home from the rink. She endeavored to move more quietly, slowing her steps and never ceasing to wonder whether I'd speak those words. And I saw how her spirit was troubled and what control she had to exercise to keep from saying:

"It can't really be the wind that spoke those words. And I don't want it to be the wind!"

Next morning I received a note: "If you're going today to the rink, then call for me. N."

And from then on I began to go there with Nadenka every day and every time we hurtled down in the sledge I whispered the very same words:

"I love you, Nadia!"

Quickly Nadenka became addicted to the words as if to wine or morphia. She couldn't live without them. It was true that hurtling down the slope was terrifying from the very first but fear and danger gave peculiar force to fascinating words of love which from the very first remained a strange enigma troubling her soul. There were only two suspects indeed: the wind and I. Which of them confessed their love she did not know, but clearly it was all the same to her. This drinking cup or that, it's all the same if only you get drunk.

For some reason once at midday I went to the rink. Mingling with a crowd, I saw Nadenka go to the hill as if she were looking for me. . . . Then she went timidly up the steps. She was afraid to slide down alone, so afraid. She was white as snow and trembled as if she were going to execution. But go she did, her mind made up, without a backward glance.

Clearly she had decided at last to make the test: would she hear those wonderfully sweet words if I were not there?

I saw how, blanching, mouth wide with hor-

ror, she sat in the sledge, closed her eyes and with a last farewell to earth set off.

"Zzzzzz . . ." zoomed the runners. Whether Nadenka heard the words I do not know. I only saw how weak and exhausted she was as she got out of the sledge. And her face showed clearly that she herself did not know if she heard anything or not. Her fear as she swept down took away her power to hear, to distinguish sounds and understand. . . .

But then March was upon us and Spring. The sun grew warmer, our icy slope darkened, losing its sheen and finally melted away. We stopped tobogganing. There was nowhere anymore for poor Nadenka to hear those words, nor anyone to say them either, for the wind was silent and I was going to Petersburg, for a long time, perhaps forever.

It happened that before I left, a couple of days before, I was sitting at twilight in a little garden separated from the place where Nadenka lived by a high nailed fence. It was cold enough still, snow still about by the muck heap and the trees dead; but Spring was in the air for all that, and rooks cawed loudly as they settled to their nests at nightfall. I went up to the fence and looked a long time through a crack. . . .

I watched as Nadenka came out on the porch and turned a mournful, yearning glance at the sky. . . . The spring wind blew straight into her pale, dejected face. . . . It reminded her of the wind that roared at us on the slope when she heard those four words, and her face went sad, most sad, a tear running on her cheek. . . . And the poor girl stretched out both arms as if imploring the wind to bring those words again. And with the wind I whispered:

"I love you, Nadia!"

My God, the effect on her! She cried out, smiled with all her face and stretched her arms into the wind, delighted, joyful, so beautiful.

And I went to pack. . . .

That was all a long time ago. Nadenka is married now: they gave her or she gave herself—it's all the same—to a secretary for wardship of estates and she's three children already. But she's not forgotten how she went with me to the rink and how the wind carried the words, "I love you, Nadia!" It is now the happiest, most endearing and beautiful memory of her life. . . .

And now, as I've grown older, I really don't know why I said those words, for what reason I played the trick.

I
FOOLING ONESELF

As they examine their emotions, both young women in these stories fool themselves. How do they do it? Do they fool themselves intentionally or unintentionally? How does this help them know themselves?

II
IMPLICATIONS

1. The following lines from the two stories are thought-provoking. Discuss whether you agree or disagree with the implications suggested by these statements.

a. "When one loves greatly but the other is indifferent, there is something beautiful in that, affecting and poetic."

b. "In a society where indifference and chill arrogance are counted signs of breeding and of noble manners men have to hide their passion."

c. ". . . fear and danger gave peculiar force to fascinating words of love. . . ."

2. In the last paragraph of "After the Theater," what is meant by "the great joy that oppressed her"? Can joy be oppressive?

3. Do you agree or disagree?

a. Romance cannot thrive on happiness.

b. Nadia was basically an unhappy person.

c. Nadenka believed that the wind whispered to her.

d. The narrator in "The Trick" was cruel to Nadenka.

III
TECHNIQUES

Selection of Incident

The two stories are very different in their time span. "After the Theater" takes place in probably about an hour, but "The Trick" covers most of a winter season. Yet each story only covers one event. Chekhov has chosen the incidents carefully for each story.

1. How would "After the Theater" be different if Chekhov had begun it while Nadia was still at the opera?

2. Why does "The Trick" need to take place over a period of time? Would it have worked as well if Chekhov had told about only one trip down the slope?

Organization

1. "After the Theater" takes the main character through a variety of moods. Are the shifts in Nadia's reactions handled smoothly or awkwardly? Why do you think Chekhov organized this story around one evening's time but with many changes in the characters', feelings?

2. "The Trick" is a flashback told in the first person. How would the effect of the story be different if it had been set in the present? How would the effect be different if the narrator himself were not in the story?

JAMES JOYCE

James Joyce (1882–1941), born in Dublin, and educated under the Jesuits,
left Ireland in a spirit of rebellion when he was only twenty-two years old.
He felt suffocated in the "provincial" atmosphere of his native land. Yet, though he
lived and wrote in Paris, Zurich, and Trieste, he never really left Dublin. That city,
its people, and the Irish version of the English language provided the setting,
characters, and language for everything Joyce wrote. His first major publication
was *Dubliners*, a book of short stories from which "Eveline" is taken. His attitudes
toward Ireland and toward the responsibility of the artist are shown in a statement
he made about *Dubliners:* "My intention was to write a chapter in the moral history
of my country and I chose Dublin for the scene because that city seemed to me
the center of paralysis. . . . I have written it for the most part in a style
of scrupulous meanness. . . ." In *A Portrait of the Artist as a Young Man,*
Joyce wrote a thinly disguised autobiographical account of his own young manhood
in Dublin. The keystone of Joyce's reputation is his long novel *Ulysses,* the action
of which takes place on a single day in the Dublin of the writer's youth.
But into this single day, Ireland's history, much of the history of Europe,
and the entire lives of the characters are packed. Joyce managed this by the use
of a *stream-of-consciousness* technique, in which his characters' thoughts, memories,
and associations are put down as they might pass through their minds. There is
no apparent logic or design to the flow of thought other than the free associations
happening in the mind. Joyce had severe eye trouble through most of his life,
underwent many operations, and lived his final years in near blindness.
He and his family lived for years on the edge of poverty, so great was his devotion
to his art.

Eveline

She sat at the window watching the evening invade the avenue. Her head was leaned against the window curtains and in her nostrils was the odour of dusty cretonne. She was tired.

Few people passed. The man out of the last house passed on his way home; she heard his footsteps clacking along the concrete pavement and afterwards crunching on the cinder path before the new red houses. One time there used to be a field there in which they used to play every evening with other people's children. Then a man from Belfast[1] bought the field and built houses in it—not like their little brown houses but bright brick houses with shining roofs. The children of the avenue used to play together in that field—the Devines, the Waters, the Dunns, little Keogh the cripple, she and her brothers and sisters. Ernest, however, never played: he was too grown up. Her father used often to hunt them in out of the field with his blackthorn stick; but usually little Keogh used to keep *nix*[2] and call out when he saw her father coming. Still they seemed to have been rather happy then. Her father was not so bad then; and besides, her mother was alive. That

"Eveline" from *Dubliners* by James Joyce. Originally published in 1916 by B. W. Huebsch. Definitive Text Copyright © 1967 by the Estate of James Joyce. Reprinted by permission of Viking Penguin Inc.

1. **Belfast** (bel′fast), a seaport in northern Ireland.
2. **to keep nix,** to keep a quiet lookout.

James Joyce

was a long time ago; she and her brothers and sisters were all grown up; her mother was dead. Tizzie Dunn was dead, too, and the Waters had gone back to England. Everything changes. Now she was going to go away like the others, to leave her home.

Home! She looked round the room, reviewing all its familiar objects which she had dusted once a week for so many years, wondering where on earth all the dust came from. Perhaps she would never see again those familiar objects from which she had never dreamed of being divided. And yet during all those years she had never found out the name of the priest whose yellowing photograph hung on the wall above the broken harmonium beside the coloured print of the promises made to Blessed Margaret Mary Alacoque.[3] He had been a school friend of her father. Whenever he showed the photograph to a visitor her father used to pass it with a casual word:

"He is in Melbourne now."

She had consented to go away, to leave her home. Was that wise? She tried to weigh each side of the question. In her home anyway she had shelter and food; she had those whom she had known all her life about her. Of course she

had to work hard, both in the house and at business. What would they say of her in the Stores when they found out that she had run away with a fellow? Say she was a fool, perhaps; and her place would be filled up by advertisement. Miss Gavan would be glad. She had always had an edge on her, especially whenever there were people listening.

"Miss Hill, don't you see these ladies are waiting?"

"Look lively, Miss Hill, please."

She would not cry many tears at leaving the Stores.

But in her new home, in a distant unknown country, it would not be like that. Then she would be married—she, Eveline. People would treat her with respect then. She would not be treated as her mother had been. Even now, though she was over nineteen, she sometimes felt herself in danger of her father's violence. She knew it was that that had given her the palpitations. When they were growing up he had never gone for her, like he used to go for Harry and Ernest, because she was a girl; but latterly he had begun to threaten her and say what he would do to her only for her dead mother's sake. And now she had nobody to protect her. Ernest was dead and Harry, who was in the church decorating business, was nearly always down somewhere in the country. Besides, the invariable squabble for money on Saturday nights had begun to weary her unspeakably. She always gave her entire wages—seven shillings—and Harry always sent up what he could but the trouble was to get any money from her father. He said she used to squander the money, that she had no head, that he wasn't going to give her his hard-earned money to throw about the streets, and much more, for he was usually fairly bad on Saturday night. In the end he would give her the money and ask her had she any intention of buying Sunday's dinner. Then she had to rush out as quickly as she could and do her marketing, holding her black leather

---

3. **Margaret Mary Alacoque** (ä lä kok′), 1647–1697, a canonized French nun.

purse tightly in her hand as she elbowed her way through the crowds and returning home late under her load of provisions. She had hard work to keep the house together and to see that the two young children who had been left to her charge went to school regularly and got their meals regularly. It was hard work—a hard life—but now that she was about to leave it she did not find it a wholly undesirable life.

She was about to explore another life with Frank. Frank was very kind, manly, open-hearted. She was to go away with him by the night-boat to be his wife and to live with him in Buenos Ayres where he had a home waiting for her. How well she remembered the first time she had seen him; he was lodging in a house on the main road where she used to visit. It seemed a few weeks ago. He was standing at the gate, his peaked cap pushed back on his head and his hair tumbled forward over a face of bronze. Then they had come to know each other. He used to meet her outside the Stores every evening and see her home. He took her to see *The Bohemian Girl* and she felt elated as she sat in an unaccustomed part of the theater with him. He was awfully fond of music and sang a little. People knew that they were court-ing and, when he sang about the lass that loves a sailor, she always felt pleasantly confused. He used to call her Poppens out of fun. First of all it had been an excitement for her to have a fellow and then she had begun to like him. He had tales of distant countries. He had started as a deck boy at a pound a month on a ship of the Allan Line going out to Canada. He told her the names of the ships he had been on and the names of the different services. He had sailed through the Straits of Magellan and he told her stories of the terrible Patagonians.[4] He had fallen on his feet in Buenos Ayres, he said, and had come over to the old country just for a holiday. Of course, her father had found out the affair and had forbidden her to have any-thing to say to him.

"I know these sailor chaps," he said.

One day he had quarrelled with Frank and after that she had to meet her lover secretly.

The evening deepened in the avenue. The white of two letters in her lap grew indistinct. One was to Harry; the other was to her father. Ernest had been her favourite but she liked Harry too. Her father was becoming old lately, she noticed; he would miss her. Sometimes he could be very nice. Not long before, when she had been laid up for a day, he had read her out a ghost story and made toast for her at the fire. Another day, when their mother was alive, they had all gone for a picnic to the Hill of Howth.[5] She remembered her father putting on her mother's bonnet to make the children laugh.

Her time was running out but she continued to sit by the window, leaning her head against the window curtain, inhaling the odor of dusty cretonne. Down far in the avenue she could hear a street organ playing. She knew the air. Strange that it should come that very night to remind her of the promise to her mother, her promise to keep the home together as long as she could. She remembered the last night of her mother's illness; she was again in the close dark room at the other side of the hall and outside she heard a melancholy air of Italy. The organ-player had been ordered to go away and given sixpence. She remembered her father strutting back into the sickroom saying:

"Those Italians! coming over here!"

As she mused the pitiful vision of her mother's life laid its spell on the very quick of her being—that life of commonplace sacrifices closing in final craziness. She trembled as she heard again her mother's voice saying con-stantly with foolish insistence:

"Derevaun Seraun! Derevaun Seraun!"

She stood up in a sudden impulse of terror. Escape! She must escape! Frank would save her. He would give her life, perhaps love, too. But she wanted to live. Why should she be un-happy? She had a right to happiness. Frank would take her in his arms, fold her in his arms. He would save her.

---

4. **Patagonians** (pat'ə gō'nē ənz), the inhabitants of the country near the Straits of Magellan at the tip of South America.

5. **Howth** (hōth), a seaport north of Dublin Bay.

She stood among the swaying crowd in the station at the North Wall. He held her hand and she knew that he was speaking to her, saying something about the passage over and over again. The station was full of soldiers with brown baggages. Through the wide doors of the sheds she caught a glimpse of the black mass of the boat, lying in beside the quay wall, with illumined portholes. She answered nothing. She felt her cheek pale and cold and, out of a maze of distress, she prayed to God to direct her, to show her what was her duty. The boat blew a long mournful whistle into the mist. If she went, tomorrow she would be on the sea with Frank, steaming towards Buenos Ayres. Their passage had been booked. Could she still draw back after all he had done for her? Her distress awoke a nausea in her body and she kept moving her lips in silent fervent prayer.

A bell clanged upon her heart. She felt him seize her hand:

"Come!"

All the seas of the world tumbled about her heart. He was drawing her into them: he would drown her. She gripped with both hands at the iron railing.

"Come!"

No! No! No! It was impossible. Her hands clutched the iron in frenzy. Amid the seas she sent a cry of anguish!

"Eveline! Evvy!"

He rushed beyond the barrier and called to her to follow. He was shouted at to go on but he still called to her. She set her white face to him, passive, like a helpless animal. Her eyes gave him no sign of love or farewell or recognition.

I
A NEW LIFE

Most men and women simply drift along with a vague picture of self until a tremendous moment of pressure forces them to assess what they are. It is just such a moment of choice that forces Eveline to reject a picture of herself as someone who can make a romantic gesture. She comes to know herself as afraid of living life to the full.

II
IMPLICATIONS

1. Use these questions to explore some of the far-reaching implications of the brief story.

a. What suggestion is there of how Eveline will pass the rest of her life?

b. How is the world Joyce portrays in "Eveline" a reflection of the "paralysis" he wishes to examine in *Dubliners*? What sort of paralysis did he mean?

2. Do you agree or disagree with these statements:

a. One's first duty is to oneself.

b. Eveline was unable to escape from her dreary life because in reality it suited her.

c. Eveline's character is so weak that she would have been just as unhappy in Buenos Ayres (Aires) as in Dublin.

d. Happiness belongs to those who are strong enough to take it.

III
TECHNIQUES

Selection of Incident

The American novelist Henry James remarked that character is the action or plot of a story. Good writers do not just *tell* the reader that a character is good or bad, brave or cowardly, greedy or generous. Rather, they use action and incident to *reveal* character. An incident is not chosen because it is interesting in itself, but because it tells us something about the characters.

"Eveline" is a good example of the interaction of plot and character. Each little incident that Eveline remembers reveals something about herself and the small world she lives in—a world which has become part of her. All these small moments bring the story forward to the great moment in which she is unable to break with her old life. What does each of the following incidents show about Eveline:

1. The children playing games in the fields?

2. Her thoughts about her job at the Stores?

3. The Saturday night squabble over money?

4. Her romance with Frank?

5. Her mother's death?

6. Her inability to follow Frank through the the gate at the dock?

KNOW THYSELF

Self-Portraits

The self-portrait is the painter's equivalent of the personal essay or autobiographical sketch. In the long history of Western art, many artists have left records of their own appearance. Rembrandt, Goya, and van Gogh painted themselves over and over again in many moods, costumes, and lights. This gallery of self-portraits records the attempts of eleven European painters to know themselves, or at least to capture one aspect of themselves on canvas.

SELF-PORTRAIT
BEFORE EASEL
Paul Gauguin

Morisot's self-portrait reflects her belief in the fleeting moment, her reducing of all things to allusion. Her view of self is misty, ephemeral, yet self-aware—the gaze is unflinching.

SELF-PORTRAIT
Berthe Morisot
The Art Institute of Chicago

In their efforts to know themselves through the self-portrait, painters may go beyond a mere recording of their features. These painters dramatized themselves through the use of theatrical settings. Albrecht Dürer painted himself in a long wig. Ensor, the Belgian, donned a plumed hat for the self-portrait on the opposite page. The masks may represent his many selves, or may suggest his reaction to the world around him.

Was di Chirico in his enigmatic portrait—brooding and troubled before a bust of himself—implying a sad discrepancy between the artist and the person?

SELF-PORTRAIT
AT THE AGE OF TWENTY-EIGHT
Albrecht Dürer

SELF-PORTRAIT
Giorgio di Chirico
Courtesy of The Toledo Museum of Art,
Gift of Edward Drummond Libbey

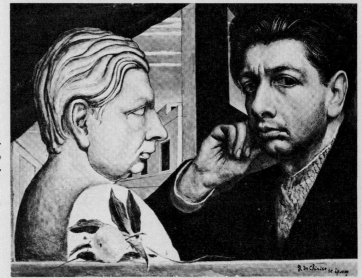

SELF-PORTRAIT
WITH MASKS
James Ensor

SELF-PORTRAIT
WITH HIS WIFE,
ISABELLA BRANDT
Peter Paul Rubens

Here, two painters present an aspect of themselves through family relationship and background. Rubens was clearly proud of the fact that he was a prosperous painter and that he had married a wealthy woman.

In contrast, the twentieth-century painter Gorky painted this wistful self-portrait from an old daguerreotype taken shortly after he and his mother had arrived in the New World as immigrants from Turkish Armenia.

THE ARTIST AND HIS MOTHER
Arshile Gorky
Courtesy of Whitney Museum of American Art,
Collection of the Whitney Museum
of American Art, New York, gift of
Julian Levy for Maro and Natasha Gorky
in memory of their father.

I AND THE VILLAGE *Marc Chagall*
Courtesy of Museum of Modern Art

Chagall, a Russian who has lived
most of his adult life in France, has
become a world-famous painter.
He probes his own beginnings
in this dreamlike re-creation
of the Russian village of his childhood.
While Chagall emphasizes
his simple peasant roots, the other two
artists on this page see themselves
as urbanized and sophisticated.

One of the landmarks of Western art
is the uncompromising realism
of Rembrandt's self-portrait
on the opposite page.

SELF-PORTRAIT
IN TUXEDO
Max Beckmann

SELF-PORTRAIT
Francisco Goya y Lucientes
*Courtesy of The National Gallery
of Art, Washington, D.C.,
Rosenwald Collection*

697

SELF-PORTRAIT *Rembrandt van Rijn*
Courtesy of The National Gallery of Art,
Washington, D.C., Rosenwald Collection

THE PERSONAL ESSAY

The next group of selections are examples of the personal essay, the most easygoing and conversational of literary forms. The personal essayist begins with an interesting idea, some personally engaging notion; but the idea is seldom pursued along a straight line. Like any good conversationalist, the essayist lets one idea trigger another, wandering off onto any path that seems appealing, but always returning to the starting point. Think of an essay as good talk polished and raised to a higher level of style than is possible in impromptu speech. But remember that, for all its apparent formlessness, the good essay *does* make a point— often a very serious one—and it probably has more of a planned structure than at first meets the reader's eye.

When did the essay begin? The word "essay" was first used by the sixteenth-century French writer, Montaigne; it means an "attempt" or "experiment"—in other words an attempt to take up a subject and examine it from a personal point of view. Of course, writers had attempted to deal with ideas for centuries; but these "essays" of Montaigne had something quite new in them—the personal element. In these pieces, both long and short, Montaigne showed a frankness, an interest in the quirks of his own personality, an attempt to come to *know himself* and to share his self-examination with the reader.

The following quotation is excerpted from Montaigne's essay on "The Inconstancy of Our Actions."

There is some apparency to judge a man by the most common conditions of his life, but seeing the natural instability of our customs and opinions, I have often thought that even good Authors do ill and take a wrong course, willfully to opinionate themselves about framing a constant and solid contexture of us. They choose a universal air, and following that image, range and interpret all a man's actions; which, if they cannot wrest sufficiently, they remit them into dissimulation. Augustus hath escaped their hands, for there is so apparent, so sudden and continual a variety of actions found in him, through the course of his life, that even the boldest Judges and strictest censurers have been fain to give him over and leave him undecided. There is nothing I so hardly believe to be in man as constancy, and nothing so easy to be found in him as inconstancy. He that should distinctly and part by part judge of him, should often jump to speak truth. View all antiquity over, and you shall find it a hard matter to choose out a dozen of men that have directed their life unto one certain, settled, and assured course, which is the surest drift of wisdom.

Essays are limited in subject only by the writers' reactions to their own inner and outer worlds. An American essayist, Christopher Morley, said, "No matter how personal or trifling the topic may be, there is always a tendency to generalize, to walk around the subject of experience and view it from several vantages. So an essay can never be more than an attempt, for it is an excursion into the endless."

The personal essay is usually short, and it does not attempt to arrive at a definitive or complete analysis of an idea. The style is informal, with a strong personal flavor closely resembling the elements of good conversation. In reading the selections that follow, imagine yourself sitting down with these witty and educated people (three are English, one Spanish) and just listening to them talk—about themselves.

J. B. PRIESTLEY

The following essays, in which J. B. Priestley looks at himself in terms
of the things that give him pleasure, are taken from a book full of such pieces,
called *Delight*. Priestley, a novelist, dramatist, and critic, born in 1894,
describes himself as follows: "I have always been a grumbler. All the records,
going back to earliest childhood, establish this fact. Probably I arrived here
a malcontent, convinced that I had been sent to the wrong planet. (And I feel
even now there is something in this.) I was designed for the part, for I have
a sagging face, a weighty underlip, what I am told is 'a saurian eye,' and a rumbling
but resonant voice from which it is difficult to escape. Money could not buy
a better grumbling outfit. In the West Riding of Yorkshire, where I spent
my first nineteen years, all local customs and prejudices favor the grumbler.
To a good West Riding type there is something shameful about praise, that soft
Southern trick. But fault-finding and blame are constant and hearty. The edge
of criticism up there is sharpened every morning. So the twilight of Victoria
and the brief but golden afternoon of Edward the Seventh discovered Jackie Priestley
grumbling away, a novice of course but learning fast. A short spell of the wool trade—
and in no trade do you hear more complaints and bitter murmurs—developed
my technique. Then came the First World War, in which I served with some
of the dourest unwearying grumblers that even the British Army has ever known, and was
considered to hold my own with the best of them. After that, a rapidly ripening
specimen, I grumbled my way through Cambridge, Fleet Street,[1] and various fields
of literature and dramatic enterprise. I have grumbled all over the world,
across seas, on mountains, in deserts. I have grumbled as much at home as abroad,
and so I have been the despair of my womenfolk. . . . So my long-suffering kinsfolk,
my patient friends, may a glimmer of that delight which has so often possessed me,
but perhaps too frequently in secret, now reach you from these pages."

After Finishing Some Work

After finishing a piece of work that has
been long and rather difficult, I have a sense
of satisfaction that can expand into delight.
This does not come from surveying the work
done, for at these times I am rarely sure of
the value of what I have just created, am more
doubtful if my first intention has been fulfilled,
and may even wonder gloomily, while I hold
the work in mind, if I have not been wasting
time and energy. No, the delight springs from
a sense of release. I have been in prison with
this one idea, and now, I feel, I am free. Tomorrow, ten times the size of last Tuesday, is
suddenly rich with promise. Time and space
are both extended. I catch a glimpse of fifty
new ideas, flickering like lizards among the
masonry of my mind; but I need not bother
about them. I am now the master and not the

Reprinted by permission of A. D. Peters and Company.

1. **Fleet Street** is a center for London journalism.

slave. I can go to China, learn the clarinet, read Gibbon again, study metaphysics, grow strange flowers in hothouses, lie in bed, lunch and dine with old friends and brilliant acquaintances, look at pictures, take the children to concerts, tidy up the study, talk properly to my wife. What a world this is to be free and curious in! What a wealth of sunlight and starlight and firelight! And so for a little while, before the key grates in the lock again, there I am, out and free, with mountains of treasure before my dazzled eyes. Yes, there comes a moment—just a moment—of delight.

J. B. Priestley

My First Article

When I was sixteen I was already writing articles and offering them to any kind of editor whose address I could discover. These articles were of two kinds. The first, which I signed portentously "J. Boynton Priestley," were serious, very serious indeed, and were full of words like "renaissance" and "Significance" and "aftermath," and suggested that their author was about a hundred and fifty years old. And nobody wanted them. They could not be given away. No editor had a body of readers old enough for such articles. The other kind were skits and burlesques and general funny work, written from the grimly determined humorous standpoint of the school magazine. One of these was accepted, printed and paid for by a London humorous weekly. I had arrived. (And my father, not to be found wanting on such an occasion, presented me with one of his fourpenny cigars, with which, as I fancy he guessed, I had been secretly experimenting for some months.) The issue of the weekly containing my article burst upon the world. Riding inside a tram from Duckworth Lane to Godwin Street,

Bradford,[1] I saw a middle-aged woman opening this very copy of the weekly, little knowing, as I made haste to tell myself, that one of its group of brilliant contributors was not two yards away. I watched her turn the pages. She came to *the* page; she hesitated; she stopped; she began to read my article. Ah—what delight! But mine, of course, not hers. And not mine for long, not more than a second, for then there settled on her face an expression I have noticed ten thousand times since, and have for years now tried not to notice—the typical expression of the reader, the audience, the customer, the patron. How shall I describe this curious look? There is in it a kind of innocence —and otherwise I think I would have stopped writing years ago—but mixed a trifle sourly with this admirable innocence is a flavoring of wariness, perhaps a touch of suspicion itself. "Well, what have we here?" it inquires dubiously. And then the proud and smirking Poet and Maker falls ten thousand feet in dubiety. So ever since that tramride I have never caught a glimpse of the reader, the audience, the customer, the patron, without instantly trying to wedge myself into the rocks above the black tarn of doubt. As I do this, there is the flash of a blue wind—and the bird of delight has flown.

---

1. **Bradford** is west of Leeds in western Yorkshire.

Waking to Smell Bacon, etc.

Waking just in time to smell coffee and bacon and eggs. And how rarely it happens! If there should be coffee and bacon and eggs (not all your eggs, of course) to smell, then it is long odds against our waking—or at least against *my* waking—just in time to smell them. If we should happen to waken bang on breakfast, the nit[1] is probably fifty to one against there being bacon *and* eggs *and* coffee all hot and suitably odorous. We live in a world of fantastic events and staggering coincidences. The papers are full of them. After listening to an hour of our talk these days, Sinbad the Sailor would roll out in disgust, calling us a pack of liars. Few of us ask to be immersed day after day in all this farfetchedness. Most of us could do with a smaller, plainer but more companionable world. We plan, we toil, we suffer—in the hope of what? A camelload of idols' eyes? The title deeds of Radio City?[2] The Empire of Asia? A trip to the moon? No, no, no, no. Simply to wake just in time to smell coffee and bacon and eggs. And, again I cry, how rarely it happens! But when it does happen—then what a moment, what a morning, what delight!

---

1. **nit,** an English dialect form for "nut," here meaning "odds."
2. **Radio City,** an extensive cluster of impressive buildings on Sixth Avenue in New York City.

Giving Advice

Giving advice, especially when I am in no position to give it and hardly know what I am talking about, I manage my own affairs with as much care and steady attention and skill as— let us say—a drunken Irish tenor. I swing violently from enthusiasm to disgust. I change policies as a woman changes hats. I am here today and gone tomorrow. When I am doing one job, I wish I were doing another. I base my judgments on anything—or nothing. I have never the least notion what I shall be doing or where I shall be in six months time. Instead of holding one thing steadily, I try to juggle with six. I cannot plan, and if I could I would never stick to the plan. I am a pessimist in the morning and an optimist at night, am defeated on Tuesday and insufferably victorious by Friday. But because I am heavy, have a deep voice and smoke a pipe, few people realize that I am a flibbertigibbet on a weathercock. So my advice is asked. And then, for ten minutes or so, I can make Polonius[1] look a trifler. I settle deep in my chair, two hundred pounds of portentousness, and with some first-rate character touches in the voice and business with pipe, I begin: "Well, I must say that in your place ——" And inside I am bubbling with delight.

----

1. **Polonius** (pə lō′nē əs), a character in Shakespeare's *Hamlet* who gives much pompous advice to his son and daughter.

Other People's Weaknesses

What delight we give other people by confessing to absurd weaknesses! For example, I cannot endure being tossed about in small boats, where I sweat with terror. Again, the sight and sound of a bat or a bird fluttering and banging about in a room fill me with disgust that can leap to fear and panic. When I have admitted this, I have seen people light up for the first time in their converse with me. At last I have succeeded in pleasing them. Until then, apparently, I have been insufferable. And I behave in the same fashion. I delight in J's terror of public speaking, in M's horror of spiders, in A's fear of being left alone in any old house, in H's rejection of all flying, in W's shuddering withdrawal from any cat. We like to feel that there is an equitable rationing system for this nonsense, and that we are all at times still children huddling together in the dark. A man or woman whose personality had not a speck of such weakness would be intolerable, not one of us at all, a sneering visitor from some other planet. Now and again they turn up, and we are delighted to see them go.

Dreams

Now and again I have had horrible dreams, but not enough of them to make me lose my delight in dreams. To begin with, I like the idea of dreaming, of going to bed and lying still and then, by some queer magic, wandering into another kind of existence. As a child I could never understand why grown-ups took dreaming so calmly when they could make such a fuss about any holiday. This still puzzles me. I am mystified by people who say they never dream and appear to have no interest in the subject. It is much more astonishing than if they said they never went out for a walk. Most people—or at least most Western Europeans—do not seem to accept dreaming as part of their lives. They appear to see it as an irritating little habit, like sneezing or yawning. I have never understood this. My dream life does not seem as important as my waking life, if only because there is far less of it, but to me it *is* important. As if there were at least two extra continents added to the world, and lightning excursions running to them at any moment between midnight and breakfast. Then again, the dream life, though queer and bewildering and unsatisfactory in many respects, has its own advantages. The dead are there, smiling and talking. The past is there, sometimes all broken and confused but occasionally as fresh as a daisy. And perhaps, as Mr. Dunne tells us, the future is there too, winking at us. This dream life is often overshadowed by huge mysterious anxieties, with luggage that cannot be packed and trains that refuse to be caught; and both persons and scenes there are not as dependable and solid as they are in waking life, so that Brown and Smith merge into one person while Robinson splits into two, and there are thick woods outside the bathroom door and the dining room is somehow part of a theater balcony; and there are moments of desolation or terror in the dream world that are worse than anything we have known under the sun. Yet this other life has its interests, its gaieties, its satisfactions, and, at certain rare intervals, a serene glow or a sudden ecstasy, like glimpses of another form of existence altogether, that we cannot match with open eyes. Daft or wise, terrible or exquisite, it is a further helping of experience, a bonus after dark, another slice of life cut differently, for which, it seems to me, we are never sufficiently grateful. Only a dream! Why only? It was there, and you had it. "If there were dreams to sell," Beddoes[1] inquires, "what would you buy?" I cannot say offhand, but certainly rather more than I could afford.

---

1. **Beddoes** (bed′ōz), English dramatist and poet (1803–1849).

THE BLOCKHEAD *Francisco Goya*

No School Report

We fathers of families have one secret little source of delight that is closed to other men. As we read the school reports upon our children, we realize with a sense of relief that can rise to delight that—thank Heaven—nobody is reporting in this fashion upon us. What a nightmare it would be if our personalities were put through this mincing machine! I can imagine my own report: *"Height and weight at beginning of term—5 feet, 9 inches: 13 stone, 10 lbs. At end of term—5 feet, 8 inches: 14 stone, 2 lbs.* Note: Through greed and lack of exercise, J. B. is putting on weight and is sagging. He must get out more and eat and drink less. *Conduct*—Not satisfactory. J. B. is increasingly irritable, inconsiderate, and uncooperative. He is inclined to blame others for faults in himself. He complains of lack of sleep but persists in remaining awake to finish rubbishy detective stories. He smokes far too much, and on several occasions has been discovered smoking in bed. There is no real harm in him but at the present time he tends to be self-indulgent, lazy, vain and touchy. He should be encouraged to spend some weeks this summer with the Sea Scouts or at a Harvest Camp. *Eng. Lang. & Lit.:* Fair but inclined to be careless. *French:* A disappointing term. *History:* Has not made the progress here that we expected of him. Should read more. *Mathematics:* Very poor. *Art:* Has made some attempts both at oils and watercolor but shows little aptitude. Has been slack in his Appreciation and did not attend Miss Mulberry's excellent talks on the Italian Primitives. *Music:* Fair, but will not practice. *Natural History:* Still professes an interest but finds it impossible to remember names of birds, butterflies, flowers. Has not joined in the Rambles this term. *Chemistry:* Clearly has no interest in this subject. *Physics:*

705

Poor, though occasionally shows interest. Fails to comprehend basic laws. *Physical Culture:* Sergeant Beefer reports that J. B. has been frequently absent and is obviously far from keen. A bad term. *General Report:* J. B. is not the bright and helpful member of our little community that he once promised to be. He lacks self-discipline and does not try to cultivate a cheery outlook. There are times when he still exerts himself—e.g., he made a useful contribution to the end of term production of *A Comedy of Errors*[1]—but he tends to be lazy and egotistical. His housemaster has had a talk with him, but I suggest that stronger parental guidance would be helpful, and is indeed nec-

essary." And then I would be asked to see my father, and would find him staring and frowning at this report, and then he would stare and frown at me and would begin asking me, in his deep and rather frightening voice, what on earth was the matter with me. But it can't happen, not this side of the grave. I am knee-deep in the soggy world of graying hair and rotting teeth, of monstrous taxes and over-drafts, of vanishing friends and fading sight; but at least, I can tell myself delightedly, nobody is writing a school report on me.

---

1. *A Comedy of Errors,* one of Shakespeare's comedies.

I
SECRET PLEASURES

As Priestley has moved through life he has caught little glimpses of his true self in these moments of sheer delight. But, unfortunately, those about him have had a very different picture: They thought of him as a "grumbler." So in these brief vignettes Priestley has attempted to reveal his secret delights and in the process he reveals much about himself. But he also helps readers learn something about themselves. As you read, you probably reacted by saying, "Yes, I have known that feeling," and a pleasurable twinge makes you smile. Thus your picture of yourself is more clear.

Try to pin down in your own words what the following lines reveal about Priestley. Do you share these feelings or these traits with him?

1. After finishing a piece of work that has been long and rather difficult, I have a sense of satisfaction that can expand into delight. . . . I have been in prison with this one idea, and now, I feel, I am free.

2. So ever since that tramride I have never caught a glimpse of the reader, the audience, the customer, the patron, without instantly trying to wedge myself into the rocks above the black tarn of doubt.

3. Most of us could do with a smaller, plainer but more companionable world.

4. A man or woman whose personality had not a speck of such weakness would be intolerable. . . .

II
IMPLICATIONS

Would you agree or disagree with the following statements? Explain your reasoning.

1. One of the best ways to know yourself is to tally up the things you take delight in or the things you dislike. You can learn to know yourself better by tallying the things you like rather than the things you dislike.

2. Most of us build our own picture of self by little everyday judgments rather than by blinding moments of revelation.

III
TECHNIQUES

Selection of Incident

1. What kinds of incidents does Priestley use in an essay to support his picture of a particular delight? Do you feel he has been selective?

2. Do you actually share his remembered delights with him?

Organization

1. Take any three essays and decide what the pattern of organization is in each. Are they all alike? Does it matter how he arranges examples in them?

2. All of us have moments when we feel twinges of delight. Take any one of your private delights and, using Priestley's pattern of organization, write an essay describing it.

JUAN RAMÓN JIMÉNEZ

Juan Ramón Jiménez (1881–1958) was born in the south of Spain, in the Andalusian village of Moguer, which is the setting of *Platero*[1] *and I.* He studied to become a painter in Seville, but soon abandoned painting for poetry and published his first book of poems in Madrid. Later, he returned to live in his native town, and it is this period of his life that is reflected in *Platero,* a book that is loved as a classic throughout the Spanish-speaking world. This collection of essays, which tend toward poetry in their sensitive use of language, reflects the isolation of the poet from the common life of the village around him. He rides around on his little donkey, Platero (*plata* means silver), observing life around him, talking to the little donkey, his only friend. In his later years, Jiménez lived in self-exile in Puerto Rico, in protest against the policies of the Franco government in Spain. He was awarded the Nobel Prize in 1956. The following essays are only a handful of those in the complete text of *Platero and I: An Andalusian Elegy.* The subtitle is important, for it tells the reader both the setting for the essays and the writer's emotional attitude toward them.

Platero

translated by William and Mary Roberts

Platero is small, downy, smooth—so soft to the touch that one would think he were all cotton, that he had no bones. Only the jet mirrors of his eyes are hard as two beetles of dark crystal.

I let him run loose and he goes off to the meadow; softly, scarcely touching them, he brushes his nose against the tiny flowers of pink, sky-blue and golden yellow. I call him gently: "Platero?" and he comes to me at a gay little trot as though he were laughing, lost in a clatter of fancy.

He eats everything I give him. He likes tangerines, muscatel grapes, all amber-colored, and purple figs with their crystal point of honey.

He is tender and loving as a little boy, as a little girl; but strong and firm as a stone. When I ride him on Sunday through the lanes at the edge of the town, the men from the country, clean-dressed and slow-moving, stand still to watch him.

"He is made of steel."

He is made of steel. Both steel and quicksilver.

Reprinted by permission of William and Mary Roberts, translators of *Platero y yo* by Juan Ramón Jiménez. New York: New American Library, 1961.

1. **Platero** (plä tä′rō).

White Butterflies

Night is coming on, misty and purple. Vague green and mauve lights persist beyond the church tower. The road rises enveloped in shadow, in bellflowers, the scent of grass, songs, weariness, and longing. Suddenly a dark man, with a cap and swordstick, his ugly face showing red for a moment in the glow of his cigar, comes down toward us from a wretched hut, buried among coal sacks. Platero shies in alarm.

"Any merchandise?"

"Look . . . white butterflies."

The man wants to thrust his iron stick in the little basket, and I do not prevent it. I open the saddlebag and he can see nothing. And so the stuff for dreams passes free and guileless, paying no tribute to the tax collectors.

Juan Ramón Jiménez

The Crazy Man

Dressed in mourning, with my beard cut like a Nazarene's[1] and my narrow-brimmed hat, I must present a strange figure riding on Platero's soft gray back.

When on the way to the vineyards I cross the last streets, bright with whitewash and sun, the gypsy children come running after us, shaggy and oily-smooth, showing tense brown bellies through their red, green and yellow rags. They give long shrill cries of:

"The crazy man! The crazy man! The crazy man!"

Already the green fields lie before us. Facing the vast pure sky of burning indigo, my eyes—how far removed from what I hear!—open nobly, receiving into their calm that nameless quietude, that divine, harmonious serenity which lives in the endlessness of the horizon.

There in the distance, among the high garden patches, a few sharp-pitched cries persist, finely veiled, intermittent, panting, tedious:

"The cra-azy man! The cra-azy man!"

---

1. **Nazarene** (naz′ə rēn′), a person from Nazareth in the Holy Land.

The Grape Harvest

How few donkeys have come bringing grapes this year, Platero! In vain do the handbills say in large letters: AT SIX REALES.[1] Where are those donkeys from Lucena and Almonte and Palos,[2] laden with liquid gold as taut and flowing as the blood in your body and mine—

those great droves of beasts of burden waiting hours and hours while the wine presses were emptied? The grape juice flowed in the streets

---

1. **reales** (rā ä′lās), a Spanish unit of money.
2. **Lucena, Almonte, Palos,** towns in southern Spain.

and women and children filled their pitchers, crocks and earthen jars.

How gay the wine cellars were at that time, Platero, especially the tithe cellars. Beneath the great walnut tree which had pushed down the roof, the cellar keepers sang, with a fresh, sonorous and heavy cadence, as they washed the wine vats; the men who decanted the wine would go by, barelegged, with jugs of light and dark grape juice, sparkling and foaming; there at the back, under the shed, the barrel-makers struck full, resounding blows, standing in the clean, fragrant wood shavings. As I rode in on Almirante through one door and out by the other—two opposite doors, each giving gaily to the other its stamp of life and light—I could sense the affection of the workmen.

Twenty wine presses worked day and night. What madness, what dizziness, what burning optimism! This year, Platero, all the windows of the wine presses are closed, and the press in the corral, with two or three workmen, is sufficient and more.

And now, Platero, you must do something, for you are not going to be an idler forever.

The other heavy-laden donkeys have been looking at Platero who is free and loafing; so that they may not dislike him or think badly of him, I go with him to the next pressing floor, load him with grapes, and lead him very slowly among them to the wine press. Then I take him away from there inconspicuously.

The Little Girl

The little girl was Platero's delight. As soon as he saw her coming toward him between the lilacs, with her little white dress and her rice-straw hat, calling to him lovingly, "Platero, Platerillo,"[1] the silly ass tried to break his rope and jumped about like a little boy and brayed madly.

With perfect confidence she would go back and forth beneath him, give him light taps with her foot, and put her white flower of a hand in that great pink mouth armed with large yellow teeth; or catching the ears which he lowered to within her reach, she would call him by all the tender variations of his name: "Platero! Platerón! Platerillo! Platerete!"

During the long days when the little girl was gliding downstream in her snowy-white crib toward death, no one thought of Platero. She in her delirium would call him sadly, "Platerillo!" From the dark house full of sighs, one could hear at times the distant, doleful call of her friend. Melancholy summer!

What splendor God put on you, O afternoon of the burial! September, in its rose and gold, was drawing to a close. How the bells echoed in the cemetery in the full-blown sunset, road to glory! Lonely and downcast, I returned along the walls and entered the house by the gate of the corral. Fleeing from people, I went to the stable and sat down to weep with Platero.

---

1. **Platerillo**, little Platero.

The Old Donkey

At last he walks so wearily,
    that he strays at every step.
(The Gray Colt of the Mayor of Vélez)
ROMANCERO GENERAL

I do not know how I can leave here, Platero. Who has abandoned him there, poor thing, with no one to lead or help him?

He must have got out of the boneyard. I think that he cannot either hear or see us. You saw him this morning in this same enclosure, beneath the white clouds. Covered, in his sad withered misery, by moving islands of flies and illuminated by a radiant sun, he was quite foreign to the wonderful beauty of the winter's day. He would turn slowly, disorientated, lame in all four legs, and come around again to the same spot. He has done nothing except change direction. This morning he was facing west and now he is facing east.

How crippling old age is, Platero! There is that poor friend, free to go and yet staying, although Spring is moving toward him. Or can it be that he is dead, like Bécquer,[1] while still standing? A child could draw his outline, motionless against the evening sky.

You see him now. I tried to push him and he will not move. Nor does he pay any attention to calls. It seems as if the death struggle has rooted him to the ground.

He will die of the cold tonight, Platero, in this high field where the north wind sweeps. I do not know how I can leave here; I do not know what to do, Platero.

---

1. **Bécquer**, (1836–1870) Spanish poet.

711

Carnival

Rain, sun and cold. The twisting colored papers are blown in parallel lines along the sidewalk by the bitter wind of the afternoon, and the shivering maskers turn anything into pockets for their blue-cold hands.

When we reach the square, a group of women dressed as lunatics, with long white shirts and garlands of green leaves in their flowing black hair, pull Platero into the center of their riotous circle and whirl gaily about him.

Confused, Platero pricks up his ears, raises his head, and, like a scorpion surrounded by fire, tries nervously to escape in any direction. But he is so small that the lunatics are not afraid of him and continue whirling and singing and laughing around him. The children, seeing him captive, bray to make him bray. The whole square is now an insolent concert of brass, braying, laughter, songs, tambourines and mortars.

At last, making up his mind like a man, Platero breaks through the circle and comes trotting and crying to me, his rich trappings in disarray. Like me he wants to have nothing to do with Carnival. We were not made for this sort of thing.

How handsome Platero looks today! It is Carnival Monday, and the children who have dressed in costume have put Moorish trappings on him, all heavily worked in arabesques of red, blue, white and yellow.

Melancholy

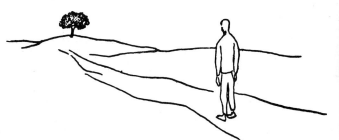

This afternoon I went with the children to visit Platero's grave in the orchard at La Piña, beneath the sheltering pine. All around, April had decked the damp ground with great yellow iris.

Up above in the treetops, their green dyed zenith-blue, the titmice were singing and their slight trills, gay and flowering, floated off through the golden air of the mild afternoon like a clear dream of new love.

As we drew near, the children gradually stopped their shouting. Quiet, serious, their shining eyes on mine, they now flooded me with anxious questions.

"Platero, my friend," I said to the earth, "if you are now in a field in heaven as I think you are, carrying youthful angels on your soft, furry back, I wonder if perhaps you have forgotten me. Tell me, Platero, do you still remember me?"

As if in answer to my question, a delicate white butterfly which I had not seen before flew insistently from iris to iris, like a soul.

I
A POET'S ISOLATION

A melancholy sadness pervades this whole series of essays. The mood is gentle, soft, a little sad, as the silvery donkey and the poet wander through the landscape of Andalusia. The muted tones seem to reflect the poet's own personality. How different from the boisterous, outgoing, lusty approach to life reflected in Priestley's *Delight*!

II
IMPLICATIONS

1. Clearly, Jiménez used Platero as his own alter ego. As he talks to the donkey he discovers his own feelings and attitudes about life. The speaker in these little dialogues is a man who has come to know himself and his place in the world. What insights into his life and personality are revealed in the following lines:

a. He is made of steel. Both steel and quicksilver.

b. "The cra-azy man!"

c. And now, Platero, you must do something, for you are not going to be an idler forever.

d. Like me he wants to have nothing to do with Carnival. We were not made for this sort of thing.

2. Do you agree or disagree?

a. In spite of the fact that there is a tone of sadness in Jiménez's essays, they reflect a mind at peace with itself, the mind of a man who knows who he is and is comfortable in that knowledge.

b. "This world is a comedy to those that think; a tragedy to those that feel."

c. The author's feeling for his donkey is too sentimental.

III
TECHNIQUES
Selection of Incident

In "White Butterflies," "The Crazy Man," and "Carnival," Jiménez selects three incidents in which he comes in direct contact with his fellow townspeople. What is the purpose behind the selection of these three incidents?

What picture of himself is Jiménez trying to communicate to the reader?

Organization

These little essays flow along like pure poetry. Can you detect any common shape or pattern in them? Does each one rise to a climax? Does the last sentence in each essay serve as a summing up?

713

E. M. FORSTER

Edward Morgan Forster (1879–1970), an English novelist and essayist,
was educated at King's College, Cambridge, where he continued to live
for most of his life. His first novel was published in 1905 and was quickly followed
by several others. His most successful book, *A Passage to India* (1924), reflected
Forster's experiences as a young man in what was at that time a colony of England.
This book was Forster's last novel, for although more than four decades
passed until his death, he never again turned to the novel form.
After *A Passage to India,* he produced only a few books of essays, memoirs,
and criticism. This sudden abandonment of the novel by one of its masters has been
a source of mystery to modern readers. In most of his works Forster contrasts
two kinds of people: those who are ruled by convention, and those who live
by their own instincts. He has the ability to observe society and report its foibles
with understanding and wit. He also is able to convey a sense of the other world
where instincts hold sway.

My Wood

A few years ago I wrote a book which dealt in part with the difficulties of the English in India. Feeling that they would have had no difficulties in India themselves, the Americans read the book freely. The more they read it the better it made them feel, and a cheque to the author was the result. I bought a wood with the cheque. It is not a large wood—it contains scarcely any trees, and it is intersected, blast it, by a public footpath. Still, it is the first property that I have owned, so it is right that other people should participate in my shame, and should ask themselves, in accents that will vary in horror, this very important question: What is the effect of property upon the character? Don't let's touch economics; the effect of private ownership upon the community as a whole is another question—a more important question, perhaps, but another one. Let's keep to psychology. If you own things, what's their effect on you? What's the effect on me of my wood?

In the first place, it makes me feel heavy. Property does have this effect. Property produces men of weight, and it was a man of weight who failed to get into the Kingdom of Heaven. He was not wicked, that unfortunate millionaire in the parable, he was only stout; he stuck out in front, not to mention behind, and as he wedged himself this way and that in the crystalline entrance and bruised his well-fed flanks, he saw beneath him a comparatively slim camel passing through the eye of a needle and being woven into the robe of God. The Gospels all through couple stoutness and slowness. They point out what is perfectly obvious, yet seldom realized: that if you have a lot of things you cannot move about a lot, that furniture requires dusting, dusters require servants, servants require insurance stamps, and the whole tangle of them makes you think twice before you accept an invitation to dinner or go for a bathe in the Jordan. Sometimes the Gospels proceed further and say with Tolstoy that property is sinful; they approach the difficult ground of asceticism here, where I cannot follow them. But as to the immediate effects of property on people, they just show straightforward logic. It produces men of weight. Men of weight cannot, by

From *Abinger Harvest,* copyright, 1936, © 1964, by E. M. Forster. Reprinted by permission of Harcourt Brace Jovanovich, Inc.

definition, move like the lightning from the East unto the West, and the ascent of a fourteen-stone bishop into a pulpit is thus the exact antithesis of the coming of the Son of Man. My wood makes me feel heavy.

In the second place, it makes me feel it ought to be larger.

The other day I heard a twig snap in it. I was annoyed at first, for I thought that someone was blackberrying, and depreciating the value of the undergrowth. On coming nearer, I saw it was not a man who had trodden on the twig and snapped it, but a bird, and I felt pleased. My bird. The bird was not equally pleased. Ignoring the relation between us, it took fright as soon as it saw the shape of my face, and flew straight over the boundary hedge into a field, the property of Mrs. Henessy, where it sat down with a loud squawk. It had become Mrs. Henessy's bird. Something seemed grossly amiss here, something that would not have occurred had the wood been larger. I could not afford to buy Mrs. Henessy out, I dared not murder her, and limitations of this sort beset me on every side. Ahab[1] did not want that vineyard —he only needed it to round off his property, preparatory to plotting a new curve—and all the land around my wood has become necessary to me in order to round off the wood. A boundary protects. But—poor little thing—the boundary ought in its turn to be protected. Noises on the edge of it. Children throw stones. A little more, and then a little more, until we reach the sea. Happy Canute![2] Happier Alexander![3] And after all, why should even the world be the limit of possession? A rocket containing a Union Jack,[4] will, it is hoped, be shortly fired at the moon. Mars. Sirius.[5] Beyond which . . . But these immensities ended by saddening me. I could not suppose that my wood was the destined nucleus of universal dominion—it is so very small and contains no mineral wealth beyond the blackberries. Nor was I comforted when Mrs. Henessy's bird took alarm for the second time and flew clean away from us all, under the belief that it belonged to itself.

E. M. Forster

In the third place, property makes its owner feel that he ought to do something to it. Yet he isn't sure what. A restlessness comes over him, a vague sense that he has a personality to express —the same sense which, without any vagueness, leads the artist to an act of creation. Sometimes I think I will cut down such trees as remain in the wood, at other times I want to fill up the gaps between them with new trees. Both impulses are pretentious and empty. They are not honest movements towards money-making or beauty. They spring from a foolish desire to express myself and from an inability to enjoy what I have got. Creation, property, enjoyment form a sinister trinity in the human mind. Creation and enjoyment are both very, very good, yet they are often unattainable without a material basis, and at such moments property

---

1. **Ahab** (ā'hab), See I Kings 21:2–6 in the King James Bible.
2. **Canute** (kə nüt'), a Dane who conquered and united England (1016–1035) and became king of Denmark (1018–1035) and later of Norway and a wide area around the Baltic Sea.
3. **Alexander the Great** established an empire around the Mediterranean Sea.
4. **Union Jack,** flag of the United Kingdom (Britain).
5. **Sirius** (sir' ē əs), the brightest star in the heavens, in Canis Major.

pushes itself in as a substitute, saying, "Accept me instead—I'm good enough for all three." It is not enough. It is, as Shakespeare said of lust, "The expense of spirit in a waste of shame"; it is "Before, a joy proposed; behind, a dream." Yet we don't know how to shun it. It is forced on us by our economic system as the alternative to starvation. It is also forced on us by an internal defect in the soul, by the feeling that in property may lie the germs of self-development and of exquisite or heroic deeds. Our life on earth is, and ought to be, material and carnal. But we have not yet learned to manage our materialism and carnality properly; they are still entangled with the desire for ownership, where (in the words of Dante[6]) "Possession is one with loss."

And this brings us to our fourth and final point: the blackberries.

Blackberries are not plentiful in this meagre grove, but they are easily seen from the public footpath which traverses it, and all too easily gathered. Foxgloves, too—people will pull up the foxgloves, and ladies of an educational tendency even grub for toadstools to show them on the Monday in class. Other ladies, less educated, roll down the bracken in the arms of their gentlemen friends. There is paper, there are tins. Pray, does my wood belong to me or doesn't it? And, if it does, should I not own it best by allowing no one else to walk there? There is a wood near Lyme Regis,[7] also cursed by a public footpath, where the owner has not hesitated on this point. He has built high stone walls each side of the path, and has spanned it by bridges, so that the public circulate like termites while he gorges on the blackberries unseen. He really does own his wood, this able chap. Dives[8] in Hell did pretty well, but the gulf dividing him from Lazarus could be traversed by vision, and nothing traverses it here. And perhaps I shall come to this in time. I shall wall in and fence out until I really taste the sweets of property. Enormously stout, endlessly avaricious, pseudocreative, intensely selfish, I shall weave upon my forehead the quadruple crown of possession until those nasty Bolshies[9]

come and take it off again and thrust me aside into the outer darkness.

I
POSSESSOR OR POSSESSED?

One's views on any subject are determined by the angle from which one observes. Thus the "haves" and the "have nots" hold different views about the merits of owning property. Often, when a "have not" becomes a "have," political opinions change sharply.

In this essay Forster describes how he discovered some telling things about himself and humankind in general as a result of his first experience as a property owner.

II
IMPLICATIONS

1. Is Forster either "for" or "against" the ownership of private property? Or does he commit himself to neither side? What, in your own words, is the point he is trying to make?

2. At some time in your life you have owned something that had value for you. Did you feel toward your property as Forster did toward his? Compare his reactions with your own:

a. . . . it makes me feel heavy.

b. . . . it makes me feel it ought to be larger.

c. . . . property makes its owner feel that he ought to do something to it.

III
TECHNIQUES

Organization

Forster has organized his essay by presenting a series of his own reactions to his ownership of the woods. Try rearranging these reactions. Does any other arrangement lead to the same point? Is the effect of the essay changed? Do you find that Forster has placed his reactions in a natural order?

---

6. **Dante** (dän′tā), (1265–1321) Italian poet, author of *The Divine Comedy*.
7. **Lyme Regis** (līm′ rē′jis), a resort town in Dorset in southern England.
8. **Dives** (dī′vēz), (from the Latin word for *rich*) the rich man in the parable about the beggar Lazarus who was "carried by the angels to Abraham's bosom."
9. **Bolshies** (bōl′shēz), Bolsheviks, members of the majority party of the Russian revolutionary movement who seized power under Lenin in 1917.

CHARLES LAMB

Charles Lamb (1775–1834) was a man who was able to face what he was
and what he could become without bitterness or despair. The son of a poor family,
he attended a charity school, Christ's Hospital, where he met Samuel Coleridge
and formed a lifelong friendship that had lasting effects on Lamb's enthusiasm
for writing. At fourteen he was faced with the realization that an incurable
speech impediment would prevent him from winning a University scholarship,
since these generally were offered only to prospective clergy. He worked
for nearly six months at the South Sea House, using the experience thirty years later
as a point of departure in his famous *Essays of Elia.* In April
of 1792 he began work in the accountant's office of the East India House, where he
stayed for thirty-three years. During this time, he produced some 100 folios
of official documents which he often referred to as his "true works." In 1796
calamity struck: Lamb's sister Mary, in a moment of insanity, stabbed their mother
to death. Rather than let her be shunted off to a life of restraint
in an asylum, Lamb persuaded the authorities to put her in his care. This was
no light assignment, for though Mary Lamb was charming and perceptive
during her lucid periods, Lamb had to watch for the signs
of returning violence. Knowing that insanity might run in the family,
Lamb himself did not marry. Together the Lambs wrote *Tales from Shakespeare,*
Charles summarizing the tragedies and Mary the comedies. In 1820
he contributed the first of his *Essays of Elia* to the newly founded *London Magazine.*
These essays were gathered together as a book in 1823. Lamb's essays
are noted for their delightful humor, their pervasive quality of pleasantness,
and their moments of pathos. Some critics attacked his style as
antique and artificial, but Lamb was so steeped in the Shakespearean period
that it was natural to him to copy the style of the older writers. Here, then,
is an essay that looks backward into memories to assess the values of an individual.

Old China

I have an almost feminine partiality for old
china. When I go to see any great house, I inquire for the china closet, and next for the picture gallery. I cannot defend the order of preference, but by saying that we have all some
taste or other, of too ancient a date to admit of
our remembering distinctly that it was an
acquired one. I can call to mind the first play,
and the first exhibition, that I was taken to; but
I am not conscious of a time when china jars
and saucers were introduced into my imagination.

I had no repugnance then—why should I
now have?—to those little, lawless, azure-tinc-
tured grotesques, that under the notion of men
and women float about, uncircumscribed by
any element, in that world before perspective—
a china teacup.

I like to see my old friends—whom distance
cannot diminish—figuring up in the air (so they
appear to our optics), yet on terra firma[1] still—
for so we must in courtesy interpret that speck

_____
1. **terra firma** (ter′ə fĕr′mə), earth.

Charles Lamb

of deeper blue, which the decorous artist, to present absurdity, had made to spring up beneath their sandals.

I love the men with women's faces, and the women, if possible, with still more womanish expressions.

Here is a young and courtly mandarin, handing tea to a lady from a salver—two miles off. See how distance seems to set off respect! And here the same lady, or another—for likeness is identity of teacups—is stepping into a little fairy boat, moored on the hither side of this calm garden river, with a dainty mincing foot, which in a right angle of incidence (as angles go in our world) must infallibly land her in the midst of a flowery mead—a furlong off on the other side of the same strange stream!

Farther on—if far or near can be predicated of their world—see horses, trees, pagodas, dancing the hays.[2]

Here—a cow and rabbit couchant, and co-extensive—so objects show, seen through the lucid atmosphere of fine Cathay.[3]

I was pointing out to my cousin last evening, over our Hyson[4] (which we are old-fashioned

enough to drink unmixed still of an afternoon), some of these *speciosa miracula*[5] upon a set of extraordinary old blue china (a recent purchase) which we were now for the first time using; and could not help remarking how favorable circumstances had been to us of late years that we could afford to please the eye sometimes with trifles of this sort—when a passing sentiment seemed to overshade the brows of my companion. I am quick at detecting these summer clouds in Bridget.[6]

"I wish the good old times would come again," she said, "when we were not quite so rich. I do not mean that I want to be poor; but there was a middle state"—so she was pleased to ramble on—"in which I am sure we were a great deal happier. A purchase is but a purchase, now that you have money enough and to spare. Formerly it used to be a triumph. When we coveted a cheap luxury (and, O! how much ado I had to get you to consent in those times!)—we were used to have a debate two or three days before, and to weigh the *for* and *against*, and think what we might spare it out of, and what saving we could hit upon, that should be an equivalent. A thing was worth buying then, when we felt the money that we paid for it.

"Do you remember the brown suit, which you made to hang upon you, till all your friends cried shame upon you, it grew so threadbare—and all because of that folio Beaumont and Fletcher,[7] which you dragged home late at night from Barker's in Covent Garden?[8] Do you remember how we eyed it for weeks before we could make up our minds to the purchase, and had not come to a determination till it was

2. **the hays** (hāz), an English country dance.
3. **Cathay** (ka thā′), China.
4. **Hyson** (hī′sən), a Chinese green tea.
5. **speciosa miracula,** splendid wonders.
6. **Bridget** was Lamb's nickname for his sister.
7. **Beaumont and Fletcher,** a folio volume, one of single rather than folded leaves stitched together, of the plays of Beaumont and Fletcher (Elizabethan dramatists). Lamb was much interested in the Elizabethan theater
8. **Covent** (kuv′ ənt) **Garden,** a section of London.

near ten o'clock of the Saturday night, when you set off from Islington,[9] fearing you should be too late—and when the old bookseller with some grumbling opened his shop, and by the twinkling taper (for he was setting bedwards) lighted out the relic from his dusty treasures—and when you lugged it home, wishing it were twice as cumbersome—and when you presented it to me—and when we were exploring the perfectness of it (*collating*, you called it)—and while I was repairing some of the loose leaves with paste, which your impatience would not suffer to be left till daybreak—was there no pleasure in being a poor man? or can those neat black clothes which you wear now, and are so careful to keep brushed, since we have become rich and finical, give you half the honest vanity with which you flaunted it about in that overworn suit—your old corbeau[10]—for four or five weeks longer than you should have done, to pacify your conscience for the mighty sum of fifteen—or sixteen shillings was it?—a great affair we thought it then—which you had lavished on the old folio. Now you can afford to buy any book that pleases you, but I do not see that you ever bring me home any nice old purchases now.

"When you came home with twenty apologies for laying out a less number of shillings upon that print after Leonardo,[11] which we christened the 'Lady Blanch'; when you looked at the purchase, and thought of the money—and thought of the money, and looked again at the picture—was there no pleasure in being a poor man? Now, you have nothing to do but to walk into Colnaghi's, and buy a wilderness of Leonardos. Yet do you?

"Then, do you remember our pleasant walks to Enfield, and Potter's Bar, and Waltham,[12] when we had a holiday—holidays, and all other fun, are gone now we are rich—and the little hand-basket in which I used to deposit our day's fare of savory cold lamb and salad—and how you would pry about at noontide for some decent house, where we might go in and produce our store—only paying for the ale that you must call for—and speculate upon

the looks of the landlady, and whether she was likely to allow us a tablecloth—and wish for such another honest hostess as Izaak Walton has described many a one on the pleasant banks of the Lea, when he went a-fishing—and sometimes they would prove obliging enough, and sometimes they would look grudgingly upon us—but we had cheerful looks still for one another, and would eat our plain food savorily, scarcely grudging Piscator[13] his Trout Hall? Now—when we go out a day's pleasuring, which is seldom, moreover, we *ride* part of the way—and go into a fine inn, and order the best of dinners, never debating the expense—which, after all, never has half the relish of those chance country snaps, when we were at the mercy of uncertain usage, and a precarious welcome.

"You are too proud to see a play anywhere now but in the pit.[14] Do you remember where it was we used to sit, when we saw the *Battle of Hexham,* and the *Surrender of Calais,* and Bannister and Mrs. Bland in the *Children in the Wood*[15]—when we squeezed out our shilling apiece to sit three or four times in a season in the one-shilling gallery—where you felt all the time that you ought not to have brought me—and more strongly I felt obligation to you for having brought me—and the pleasure was the better for a little shame—and when the curtain drew up, what cared we for our place in the house, or what mattered it where we were sitting, when our thoughts were with Rosalind in Arden, or with Viola at the Court of Illyria.[16]

---

9. **Islington** (iz′ling tən), a section of north London.
10. **corbeau** (kôr bō′), a coat of very dark green cloth (from the French word for raven).
11. **Leonardo,** Leonardo da Vinci; etchings were commonly made to copy renowned paintings.
12. . . . **Waltham** (wôl′thəm), all northern suburbs of London.
13. **Piscator** (pis′kə tôr), the chief character in *The Compleat Angler,* a book about fishing in and near the Lea River in southeast England written by Izaak Walton in 1653.
14. **the pit,** the orchestra seats rather than the balcony.
15. Titles of plays attended by the Lambs.
16. . . . **Illyria,** Rosalind is the heroine of Shakespeare's *As You Like It,* Viola that of *Twelfth Night.*

You used to say that the gallery was the best place of all for enjoying a play socially—that the relish of such exhibitions must be in proportion to the infrequency of going—that the company we met there, not being in general readers of plays, were obliged to attend the more, and did attend, to what was going on, on the stage—because a word lost would have been a chasm, which it was impossible for them to fill up. With such reflections we consoled our pride then—and I appeal to you whether, as a woman, I met generally with less attention and accommodation than I have done since in more expensive situations in the house? The getting in indeed, and the crowding up those inconvenient staircases, was bad enough—but there was still a law of civility to woman recognized to quite as great an extent as we ever found in the other passages—and how a little difficulty overcome heightened the snug seat and the play, afterwards! Now we can only pay our money and walk in. You cannot see, you say, in the galleries now. I am sure we saw, and heard too, well enough then—but sight, and all, I think, is gone with our poverty.

"There was pleasure in eating strawberries, before they became quite common—in the first dish of peas, while they were yet dear—to have them for a nice supper, a treat. What treat can we have now? If we were to treat ourselves now—that is, to have dainties a little above our means, it would be selfish and wicked. It is the very little more that we allow ourselves beyond what the actual poor can get at that makes what I call a treat—when two people living together, as we have done, now and then indulge themselves in a cheap luxury, which both like; while each apologizes, and is willing to take both halves of the blame to his single share. I see no harm in people making much of themselves, in that sense of the word. It may give them a hint how to make much of others. But now—what I mean by the word—we never do make much of ourselves. None but the poor can do it. I do not mean the veriest poor of all, but persons as we were, just above poverty.

"I know what you were going to say, that it is mighty pleasant at the end of the year to make all meet—and much ado we used to have every Thirty-first Night of December to account for our exceedings—many a long face did you make over your puzzled accounts, and in contriving to make it out how we had spent so much—or that we had not spent so much—or that it was impossible we should spend so much next year—and still we found our slender capital decreasing—but then, betwixt ways, and projects, and compromises of one sort or another, and talk of curtailing this charge, and doing without that for the future—and the hope that youth brings, and laughing spirits (in which you were never poor till now), we pocketed up our loss, and in conclusion, with 'lusty brimmers' (as you used to quote it out of *hearty cheerful Mr. Cotton*,[17] as you called him), we used to welcome in 'the coming guest.' Now we have no reckoning at all at the end of the old year—no flattering promises about the new year doing better for us."

Bridget is so sparing of her speech on most occasions that when she gets into a rhetorical vein, I am careful how I interrupt it. I could not help, however, smiling at the phantom of wealth which her dear imagination had conjured up out of a clear income of poor ———— hundred pounds a year. "It is true we were happier when we were poorer, but we were also younger, my cousin. I am afraid we must put up with the excess, for if we were to shake the superflux into the sea, we should not much mend ourselves. That we had much to struggle with, as we grew up together, we have reason to be most thankful. It strengthened and knit our compact closer. We could never have been what we have been to each other, if we had always had the sufficiency which you now complain of. The resisting power—those natural dilations of the youthful spirit, which circumstances cannot straiten—with us are long since passed away. Competence to age is supplementary youth, a sorry supplement indeed, but I

_____

17. **Charles Cotton** (1630–1687), a favorite poet of Lamb, author of the quoted poem, *The New Year.*

fear the best that is to be had. We must ride where we formerly walked: live better and lie softer—and shall be wise to do so—than we had means to do in those good old days you speak of. Yet could those days return—could you and I once more walk our thirty miles a day —could Bannister and Mrs. Bland again be young, and you and I be young to see them— could the good old one-shilling gallery days return[18]—they are dreams, my cousin, now—but could you and I at this moment, instead of this quiet argument, by our well-carpeted fireside, sitting on this luxurious sofa—be once more struggling up those inconvenient staircases, pushed about, and squeezed, and elbowed by the poorest rabble of poor gallery scramblers— could I once more hear those anxious shrieks of yours—and the delicious *Thank Heaven, we are safe*, which always followed when the topmost stair, conquered, let in the first light of the whole cheerful theater down beneath us—I know not the fathom line that ever touched a descent so deep as I would be willing to bury more wealth in than Croesus had, or the great R——[19] is supposed to have, to purchase it. And now do just look at that merry little Chinese waiter holding an umbrella, big enough for a bed-tester, over the head of that pretty insipid half Madonnaish chit of a lady in that very blue summerhouse."

---

18. **gallery days return,** that is, could we return to the times when we enjoyed the gallery seats in the theater for only a shilling.
19. **Croesus** (krē′səs), an early king in Asia Minor famed for his wealth. **R——**, Nathan Rothschild (roth′chĭld), (1777–1836) founder of the London branch of a great European banking company.

out that they are no longer young and what was a delight in their youth might become a torment in their old age. Lamb's comments about old china at the beginning and the end of the essay act as a framework for his rambling thoughts.

II
IMPLICATIONS

1. The following quotations reveal some discoveries that Bridget has made about herself and her brother. How true are they of people in general? And of yourself?

a. "A purchase is but a purchase, now that you have money enough and to spare. Formerly it used to be a triumph."

b. "Now, you have nothing to do but to walk into Colnaghi's, and buy a wilderness of Leonardos. Yet do you?"

2. Do you agree or disagree:

a. Delving back into memories of bygone times is a good way to find out what you are.

b. Bridget is not satisfied with what she has become.

c. The delights of being poor are more fun to remember than actually to live through.

III
TECHNIQUES
Selection of Incident

What do each of the following incidents reveal about the characters of Bridget and her brother? Do you think her memories tend to "rose-tint" the past? Do the incidents convince you that her argument is valid?

1. The Beaumont and Fletcher folio

2. The print they called Lady Blanch

3. The holiday expeditions

4. Their viewing of the plays from the one-shilling gallery

5. Their little food extravagances

6. Their struggle at the year's end to make the accounts balance

Organization

This essay is neatly framed by Lamb's remarks about old china. He starts on this subject which triggers Bridget's memories of the past, and he finally pulls the conversation back to this subject. What does this do to the main body of the essay?

I
"A MIDDLE STATE"

Lamb and his sister are both gentle people who reveal some of their quiet reflections of self in this essay. Though they have known bitter and grim days, what shines through their memories of this period are its particular delights. Bridget is willing to believe that it would be better for them if they were still poor, but Lamb realistically points

SHELAGH DELANEY

Shelagh Delaney (1939–   ) achieved international success
as a writer at an age when many Americans are still in school. With the help
of the English director Joan Littlewood, her first play, *A Taste of Honey*,
was a success in London, then in New York, and eventually became a movie. It reflects
the working-class world of the north of England, where Shelagh grew up. In looking
to the English lower classes for her material, she joined a movement that was strong
in England during the 1950's and 1960's—often referred to as the "Angry Young Men."
These young writers were in revolt against literature devoted exclusively
to upper-class values. Stories such as the following (taken from Shelagh Delaney's
autobiography, *Sweetly Sings the Donkey*) reflect this turning away
from an interest in the doings of "ladies and gentlemen" toward the life
of the average urban English citizen.

Pavan for a Dead Prince

A death while bringing sorrow and some-times joy brought something else with it when I was a child—sightseers. It was customary then—and still is—for friends, relations and any other interested parties to visit the bodies of the dear departed before the burning, burying or embalming took place. Most people only bothered to view for the last time corpses of people they had known well in life but some were not so particular and went to see anyone's corpse whether known to them or not in life. One woman who called herself my mother's friend though my mother despised her and never pretended not to, had this dead-watching down to a fine art. Every night she would go through the Death Columns in the newspaper with a fine-tooth comb making note of any lately deceased persons who sounded interesting enough to merit a trip:

"Frederick Corny—aged ninety-five—a great age that is—Maria Moravia—aged six years—God rest her soul—a baby—sounds foreign to mmmm . . ."

Into the pages of a small red book she would copy their names and addresses and later on, suitably composed, would go to their homes and ask to see. Her request was rarely, if ever, refused.

This visitor was always showing this anxious interest in death. When I was little I used to think it was a good-luck token to see a dead body like touching a sailor's collar or seeing a pin and picking it up but as I got older I realized it was a hobby, always received reservedly in our house. She talked while my mother worked and my father read.

"A child. That's all she was. A baby. She looked beautiful. I'll swear she wasn't dead. Catholic family. Candles all round the coffin. Her cheeks were so rosy and her lips were so red."

And my father would wink at me and my mother would spit on the iron. The spit hissed at the iron's heat and bounced off it like lead shot.

He left school when he was fourteen years old and went to work with his father down the mines. Every night the pair of them came home

Reprinted by permission of G. P. Putnam's Sons, Inc. from *Sweetly Sings the Donkey* by Shelagh Delaney, © 1963, by Shelagh Delaney Productions Ltd.

Shelagh Delaney

They wolf-whistled him on the street. They'd line up and wait while he took his pick. They wrote him love letters which small boys delivered by hand, thereby earning themselves a penny or sometimes a sixpence depending on the pressure of the passion involved. Whenever he took a girl out it was a foregone conclusion that they would go dancing. He loved to dance. To watch him dance and to dance with him was a treat.

On a Saturday night in a mild September he took me to see a troupe of performing Spanish Gipsies who had turned up all of a sudden at the local bughut[2] under the auspices of an organization bent on bringing a bit of culture to the working classes. We eyed the poster pasted outside the theatre. *Genuine Spanish Gipsies* it said. We looked at each other and then back to the poster. Conchita. José. Maria. Yerma. We looked at the photographs. Neither of us objected strongly to somebody assuming that we came from a class short on culture but to be considered brainless into the bargain was, we felt, in bad taste. But we paid our money and we took our chance. As soon as those Genuine Spanish Gipsies pranced onto the stage all our suspicions solidified. There wasn't a pinprick's worth of Spanish blood between the lot of them. I have Spanish blood in my own veins— a bit watered down now since the day my great-grandmother blew in from Barcelona on the arm of my great-grandfather, a seafaring gentleman from this fair city—and it can always detect itself in others. We didn't hold the deception against them however. The company consisted of a small tight man with hair like a distraught steel-wool panscrub, a tall thin woman, a short medium-weight woman, a large stout woman and a boy who played a guitar when he was not trying to beat it to death. The tall woman was a grotesque clown who arched her back and ground her teeth together, the short woman's performance was memorable

from the pit together covered in coal dust. Every speck of it had to be washed away before they were allowed to set foot inside their house. Stripped right down to the waist—out in the backyard in all kinds of weather—they'd pour buckets of water over each other until the dirt disappeared. By the time Benjamin had finished scrubbing himself he shone. He was a big lad to start with and the longer he heaved the coal the bigger he became. He wasn't big in the style of muscle-bound apemen who go in for dynamic tension and take part in this year's Adonis[1] or Mr. Universe contests. The power of his body was elegant and graceful and subtle. Girls fell for him left, right and center.

---

1. **Adonis** (ə don′is), a handsome Greek youth who serves as a prototype for masculine beauty.
2. **bughut**, meeting hall.

for the way she flashed her large mouthful of snow-white china choppers[3] about in the spotlight, the fat woman hammered her way from one corner of the stage to the other, holding her skirts high above her tree-trunk legs with one hand while tinkling tiny golden bells attached to the fingertips of the other, the man— taut sinister and dramatic in black—twitted bulls, fought duels, tamed wild horses and wild women, polished off glasses of wine and tossed his head so enthusiastically it was a wonder it didn't fly off its handle. Although we had never seen such dancing before it didn't take a professor to tell us that it wasn't a very good exhibition we were watching. We had the time of our lives though. Probably because the dancers enjoyed themselves so much. The audience cheered sometimes booed catcalled and made rude remarks but the dancers did not mind and gave as good as they got. At the end of the show the small man was transported and danced the soles off his leather boots in his ecstasy. We clapped him up until our hands were red raw and went to bed that night well satisfied for once with our dose of culture.

We lived in the same street in houses that faced each other head on. All the houses in the street, whether they were on the right-hand side where the sun shone or on the left-hand side that was always in shadow, were identical. Two rooms up two rooms down no bathroom no garden and one backyard each. My bedroom and Benjamin's bedroom were directly opposite and sometimes if we did not draw the curtains we could see each other in bed and many a time we talked to each other through our windows across the narrow street. When I was getting ready for bed one night I looked across into Benjamin's room. What was he doing? At first I thought he was having a bad attack of Saint Vitus's dance but I watched and wondered for a while longer and then it suddenly struck me. All that hip wriggling, heel stamping, hand clapping and head tossing. He was working out a Spanish dance routine. I kept him secretly under observation for a long time and night after night he kept at it. He was dedicated. It was very interesting. I never mentioned anything to him about his gipsy dancing and he never mentioned it to me.

At Eastertime he got rheumatic fever. He went into the hospital and stayed there for months. In due course he came home and I went to see him. All the shine had gone off him. There isn't much you can say to somebody you love who has been very ill. You can tell them how sorry you are that they have been sick. You can tell them how much you have missed them while they've been away. You can tell them how much you would miss them if they went away for good. You can wish them well soon but somehow the words that come out of poor mouths at such times never sound anything like what you wanted them to so I said nothing. The fever had weakened Benjamin's heart and he wasn't allowed to do anything strenuous for fear of overstraining it. For weeks he had to stay in his bed which his father had brought downstairs and pushed up against the window so that he could see what was going on in the street. He saw all sorts of things through that window. How much of it was true and how much of it he made up because he was bored I don't know but he told me a lot and I always felt that I knew everybody's business better than they knew it themselves. Some people said it was a mistake for me to see him as often as I did, maintaining that my presence did him more harm than good. Maybe it did. I don't know. I wouldn't go and sit with him when other people were visiting. They always got on my nerves with their pity. I suppose it was pitiful that Benjamin had to lie around all day instead of being on the go but he didn't need reminding of it all the time.

"You'll soon be on your feet again, son."

"Doctors don't know nothing. Especially the National Health Service Wallahs.[4] You'll be cutting a rug at Madame Jones's Ballroom with

---

3. **china choppers,** false teeth.
4. **Wallahs** (wol'əz), agents.

the rest of them this time next year," they would jovially say.

Looking at them I used to think that they were the pitiful ones in actual fact with their horrible hypocrite hope. The trouble with me was that I had had no practice in visiting the sick. The small refinements of sickroom procedure escaped me. I would be ushered into the presence of my pale and pajama'd lover, his bowl of fruit, jug of orange juice and the smell of disinfectant as chaperon; my intentions were always honorable. I started off those evenings all sweetness patience and good nature but it was ten to one that before very long our tempers, which matched each other step for step for violence, quickness and complete unreasonableness, would smash the peace up into blazing quarrels. And I would get myself gone bearing all the blame. And then if it wasn't a ferocious and remorseless argument that got the invalid dangerously worked up it would be too much laughing that caused the trouble. Everything had to be extreme with that boy. I'd say something funny and before either of us knew where we were we'd be rolling about holding our stomachs and wiping tears of laughter from our eyes. Reproachful looks from his mother would drive me away. O you can't win, I said it then and I say it now.

The day came when he was allowed to leave his bed. At last. He was thrilled to bits. He had gone very thin. I held one of his hands up to the light once because I felt sure it would be transparent. His face was white and his eyes seemed bent on burrowing their way out through the back of his head. He was allowed to walk round the park twice a day.

"Big thrill," he said when told.

The park was very small and very barren. The trees were encrusted with the filth that passes for fresh air in all industrial cities. A valiant grass covered the ground like a threadbare carpet. Fiendish flower thieves and murderers disguised as tiny children and little old ladies stalked the city gardens. Twice a day round this he went as quickly as his legs could carry him for he hated the place. There were

better places but far away and he wasn't allowed to make the journey. His mining days had gone for good, the doctor said, and his dancing days were over too. He was fed up.

"You'll have to do something else, that's all," I said to him one night.

"Such as what?" he asked.

"Such as stopping sulking just for five minutes."

"You'd sulk worse than me if you were in my place."

"I know I would. Are you going to spend the rest of your life sitting here in idleness and misery?"

"Yes."

"Well, so long as you don't expect me to sit here with you it's all right."

"I thought you loved me."

"I do."

"You don't show it."

"What would you like me to do?"

"Comfort me in my trouble. Treat me nice. I'm delicate."

"I'll comfort you with a big hard brick one of these days. Right in your left eye. You could read books."

"I don't like reading."

"You could paint."

"I can't paint."

"Why don't you take up knitting and sewing then?"

"And you go down the mines digging coal."

"You're not taking me seriously."

"O I am."

He loathed his weak heart. He would stand with his hand on his breast reciting carefully and with feeling every swear word he knew. . . .

We were walking home from the pictures one night after seeing a good film about an internationally famous ravishingly beautiful female concert pianist who discovered she was dying of T.B. when he invited me to an exhibition of Spanish flamenco dancing in his bedroom.

"And who's going to flamenco?" I wondered.

"Ferdinando Jones here."

"You'll be reclining in a small plot of land in Saint James's Church of England Cemetery if you're not careful," I told him.

"I know I will," he said and hopped skipped and jumped along a hopscotch chart that a child had chalked out on the pavement. "But there's one dance left in the old man yet you know."

The exhibition was an event cloaked in necessary mystery. He had to give it when his parents were out of the house. If they had discovered his intentions they would have gone mad. I was sworn to secrecy and promised on my mother's life not to tell a single soul. On the night in question he led me by the hand up to his bedroom. He draped a thick dark heavy army blanket over the window to spite nosy Parkers[5] who were always on the peep. He stopped up all cracks and spaces in walls and door where sound was likely to get through. He set his gramophone in motion.

"I hope this build-up's justified, Benjamin."

"It'll be something you'll remember all your life. It'll be the high spot of your existence and mine too."

At first he made jokes about himself but the more engrossed he became in what he was doing the less self-conscious he was about doing it. He was completely absorbed. He danced like a demon. He danced for all he was worth, generating a radiance around himself. I got drunk on the sound of the guitar and the sight of him. His face shone and I felt again the incredible fierce frightening desire for something beautiful that we had shared with each other. Then it stopped. We stared at each other. We glared at each other. We hated each other then like deadly enemies. He lost his breath. Falling across the bed he lay still on it and stared at the ceiling through wide-open eyes. It occurred to me without fear or surprise that he was going to die. Whether he would die there and then I didn't know and that didn't matter. He would die. I put my hand over his thundering heart and placed my mouth against the pulse in his throat and watched the ritual beginning.

"Not years." He had got his breath back and was able to speak. "Not years."

"Do you think I'm daft?" he asked me.

"Why?"

"For dancing like that?"

"Why should you be daft?"

"Did I look funny?"

---

5. **nosy Parkers,** British slang for prying busybodies.

"Do you care?"

"No."

"You didn't look funny. You looked lovely."

"If anyone found out I liked that sort of dancing they'd think I was a fool."

"Only people who think that anything they aren't interested in and know nothing about is stupid and useless."

"Before I was ill I'd been practicing. It was after seeing them fake Spaniards that night. Do you remember? I enjoyed watching them. I like dancing that way. Means more. Doesn't it? Don't you think so? You can put more feeling into a flamenco than you can put into a fox-trot I'm telling you."

The Procession formed up. Quiet men and women—sightseers feigning sorrow to conceal curiosity—all bowed grave and dignified and moved into the ceremonial. Doffed caps. Wet eyes. Deepest sympathy. Silence. Whispers—

—a tragic

—a young lad like that

—good die young

—his poor mother

—what a waste.

But his face had shone again.

"What's funny, kid?"

"Nothing."

I
LIFE WITHOUT COMPROMISE

In these few pages Shelagh Delaney has caught vividly the strange web that life presents . . . all of us are caught between what we want life to be and what life really is. So Benjamin chooses not to compromise. The doctors tell him that in order to "live," he must give up the mines, athletics, the dance. He refuses such a life.

His last moments are filled with flamboyant action as he tastes once again that "something beautiful" that haunts us all.

II
IMPLICATIONS

1. Even though Shelagh and Benjamin know that the traveling dancers they saw are "fake" it doesn't seem to bother them. Why not?

2. Can you find any indications in the story that Shelagh is a "rebel" against the world she lives in?

3. Do you agree or disagree with these propositions:

a. When you know the things you want from life it is better to die than compromise.

b. It would have been better for Benjamin to seek a goal that contributes more to society than does Spanish dancing.

c. In most people there is a deep desire for something beautiful.

III
TECHNIQUES

Selection of Incident

Quickly jot down the scenes as you remember them. Then answer the following:

1. Why does the author begin with a discussion of funerals?

2. What was your reaction to Benjamin's attempts at dancing?

3. In what scene did you sense that the mood of the story was darkening?

4. How vivid is the funeral?

Organization

Consider this story's pattern. First you have the completely separate discussion of death, then the girl's romance with Benjamin, and finally just a few lines from Benjamin's funeral. The main vibrant part of the story, is, in effect, bracketed by death. How did this:

1. make the central moments stand out?

2. set the tone for the story?

CHARLES DICKENS

Charles Dickens (1812–1870) was the son of a man of wavering fortunes, whom he referred to as "the prodigal father." During one period, Dickens' father had a little money, and Charles had a brief chance to attend school.

But John Dickens soon went deep into debt and moved his family from place to place to escape his creditors. At last, when the senior Dickens was thrown into debtors' prison, his wife tried to support the children by running a little school in their home. She was forced to put Charles to work in a warehouse, pasting labels on pots of stove blacking. This was the darkest period of Charles's youth. Yet even while he was living through the scarring experience (vividly retold in *David Copperfield*) he was storing away pictures of the people he met. His ne'er-do-well father appears in *David Copperfield* as Mr. Micawber. Later, Charles became a solicitor's clerk (where he soaked up the world of law and lawyers that was to reappear in many of his novels) and taught himself shorthand. He then became a reporter, and began writing sketches of London life published in newspapers over the signature of "Boz." The sketches were a success, and a publisher asked Dickens to write comments for a series of humorous drawings by the well-known artist Seymour. Dickens invented the Pickwick Club for the purpose, and soon his zany stories were more popular than the drawings. Dickens' years of struggle were over. For the next thirty years, Dickens was the most popular novelist in England and America. He worked furiously, turning out such masterpieces as *Oliver Twist, Great Expectations,* and *Hard Times.* The names of his characters became household words on two continents. Into Dickens' pages crowd thieves, lawyers, gentry, journalists, snobs—rich and poor, cruel and kind. His imagination gave birth to the greatest collection of eccentric characters ever conceived by a writer. But Dickens continued to see the novel as a means of social reform, exposing the evils of child labor, debtors' prisons, the dishonest schemes of financiers, and the red tape of the law. The selection that follows is a story from a group of Christmas tales.

The Poor Relation's Story

He was very reluctant to take precedence of so many respected members of the family, by beginning the round of stories they were to relate as they sat in a goodly circle by the Christmas fire; and he modestly suggested that it would be more correct if "John our esteemed host" (whose health he begged to drink) would have the kindness to begin. For as to himself, he said, he was so little used to lead the way that really—but as they all cried out here, that he must begin, and agreed with one voice that he might, could, would, and should begin, he left off rubbing his hands, and took his legs out from under his arm-chair, and did begin.

I have no doubt (said the poor relation) that I shall surprise the assembled members of our family, and particularly John, our esteemed host, to whom we are so much indebted for the great hospitality with which he has this day entertained us, by the confession I am going to make. But if you do me the honour to be surprised at anything that falls from a person so

Charles Dickens

count of not being as sharp as he could have wished in worldly matters. That, through life, I have been rather put upon and disappointed, in a general way. That I am at present a bachelor of between fifty-nine and sixty years of age, living on a limited income in the form of a quarterly allowance, to which I see that John our esteemed host wishes me to make no further allusion.

The supposition as to my present pursuits and habits is to the following effect.

I live in a lodging in the Clapham Road—a very clean back room, in a very respectable house—where I am expected not to be at home in the day-time, unless poorly;[1] and which I usually leave in the morning at nine o'clock, on pretence of going to business. I take my breakfast—my roll and butter, and my half-pint of coffee—at the old established coffee-shop near Westminster Bridge; and then I go into the City[2]—I don't know why—and sit in Garraway's Coffee House, and on 'Change, and walk about, and look into a few offices and counting-houses where some of my relations or acquaintances are so good as to tolerate me, and where I stand by the fire if the weather happens to be cold. I get through the day in this way until five o'clock, and then I dine: at a cost, on the average, of one and threepence.[3] Having still a little money to spend on my evening's entertainment, I look into the old-established coffee-shop as I go home, and take my cup of tea, and perhaps my bit of toast. So, as the large hand of the clock makes its way round to the morning hour again, I make my way round to the Clapham Road again, and go to bed when I get to my lodging—fire being expensive, and being objected to by the family on account of its giving trouble and making a dirt.

Sometimes, one of my relations or acquaintances is so obliging as to ask me to dinner. Those are holiday occasions, and then I gen-

unimportant in the family as I am, I can only say that I shall be scrupulously accurate in all I relate.

I am not what I am supposed to be. I am quite another thing. Perhaps, before I go further, I had better glance at what I *am* supposed to be.

It is supposed, unless I mistake,—the assembled members of our family will correct me if I do, which is very likely (here the poor relation looked mildly about him for contradiction),—that I am nobody's enemy but my own. That I never met with any particular success in anything. That I failed in business because I was unbusiness-like and credulous—in not being prepared for the interested designs of my partner. That I failed in love, because I was ridiculously trustful—in thinking it impossible that Christiana could deceive me. That I failed in my expectations from my Uncle Chill, on ac-

1. **unless poorly,** unless sick.
2. **the City,** the original area of the City of London. Other references in this passage are to places and things in London.
3. One shilling and threepence.

erally walk in the Park. I am a solitary man, and seldom walk with anybody. Not that I am avoided because I am shabby; for I am not at all shabby, having always a very good suit of black on (or rather Oxford mixture, which has the appearance of black and wears much better); but I have got into a habit of speaking low, and being rather silent, and my spirits are not high, and I am sensible that I am not an attractive companion.

The only exception to this general rule is the child of my first cousin, little Frank. I have a particular affection for that child, and he takes very kindly to me. He is a diffident boy by nature; and in a crowd he is soon run over, as I may say, and forgotten. He and I, however, get on exceedingly well. I have a fancy that the poor child will in time succeed to my peculiar position in the family. We talk but little; still, we understand each other. We walk about, hand in hand; and without much speaking he knows what I mean, and I know what he means. When he was very little indeed, I used to take him to the windows of the toy-shops, and show him the toys inside. It is surprising how soon he found out that I would have made him a great many presents if I had been in circumstances to do it.

Little Frank and I go and look at the outside of the Monument—he is very fond of the Monument—and at the Bridges, and at all the sights that are free. On two of my birthdays, we have dined on à-la-mode beef,[4] and gone at half-price to the play, and been deeply interested. I was once walking with him in Lombard Street, which we often visit on account of my having mentioned to him that there are great riches there—he is very fond of Lombard Street—when a gentleman said to me as he passed by, "Sir, your little son has dropped his glove." I assure you, if you will excuse my remarking on so trivial a circumstance, this accidental mention of the child as mine quite touched my heart and brought the foolish tears into my eyes.

When little Frank is sent to school in the country, I shall be very much at a loss what to do with myself, but I have the intention of walking down there once a month and seeing him on a half holiday. I am told he will then be at play upon the Heath; and if my visits should be objected to, as unsettling the child, I can see him from a distance without his seeing me, and walk back again. His mother comes of a highly genteel family, and rather disapproves, I am aware, of our being too much together. I know that I am not calculated to improve his retiring disposition; but I think he would miss me beyond the feeling of the moment if we were wholly separated.

"Mr. Gummidge casts a damp on our departure," from an early edition of David Copperfield *illustrated by "Phiz," the pseudonym of Hablot Knight Browne.*

When I die in the Clapham Road, I shall not leave much more in this world than I shall take out of it; but, I happen to have a miniature of a bright-faced boy, with a curling head and an open shirt-frill waving down his bosom (my mother had it taken for me, but I can't believe that it was ever like), which will be worth nothing to sell, and which I shall beg may be given to Frank. I have written my dear boy a little letter with it, in which I have told him that I felt very sorry to part from him, though bound to confess that I knew no reason why I should remain here. I have given him some short advice, the best in my power, to

---

4. **à-la-mode beef,** beef pot roast.

take warning of the consequences of being no-body's enemy but his own; and I have endeavoured to comfort him for what I fear he will consider a bereavement, by pointing out to him, that I was only a superfluous something to every one but him; and that having by some means failed to find a place in this great assembly, I am better out of it.

Such (said the poor relation, clearing his throat and beginning to speak a little louder) is the general impression about me. Now, it is a remarkable circumstance which forms the aim and purpose of my story, that this is all wrong. This is not my life, and these are not my habits. I do not even live in the Clapham Road. Comparatively speaking, I am very seldom there. I reside mostly, in a—I am almost ashamed to say the word, it sounds so full of pretension—in a Castle. I do not mean that

"Oliver amazed at the Dodger's mode of 'going to work.'" Drawing for early edition of Oliver Twist *by illustrator George Cruikshank.*

it is an old baronial habitation, but still it is a building always known to every one by the name of a Castle. In it, I preserve the particulars of my history; they run thus:

It was when I first took John Spatter (who had been my clerk) into partnership, and when I was still a young man of not more than five-and-twenty, residing in the house of my Uncle Chill, from whom I had considerable expectations, that I ventured to propose to Christiana. I had loved Christiana a long time. She was very beautiful, and very winning in all respects. I rather mistrusted her widowed mother, who I feared was of a plotting and mercenary turn of mind; but I thought as well of her as I could, for Christiana's sake. I never had loved any one but Christiana, and she had been all the world, and O, far more than all the world, to me, from our childhood!

Christiana accepted me with her mother's consent, and I was rendered very happy indeed. My life at my Uncle Chill's was of a spare, dull kind, and my garret chamber was as dull, and bare, and cold, as an upper prison room in some stern northern fortress. But, having Christiana's love, I wanted nothing upon earth. I would not have changed my lot with any human being.

Avarice was, unhappily, my Uncle Chill's master-vice. Though he was rich, he pinched, and scraped, and clutched, and lived miserably. As Christiana had no fortune, I was for some time a little fearful of confessing our engagement to him; but, at length I wrote him a letter, saying how it all truly was. I put it into his hand one night, on going to bed.

As I came down-stairs next morning, shivering in the cold December air; colder in my uncle's unwarmed house than in the street, where the winter sun did sometimes shine, and which was at all events enlivened by cheerful faces and voices passing along; I carried a heavy heart towards the long, low breakfast-room in which my uncle sat. It was a large room with a small fire, and there was a great bay window in it which the rain had marked in the night as if with the tears of houseless people. It stared upon a raw yard, with a cracked stone pavement, and some rusted iron railings half uprooted, whence an ugly out-building, that had once been a dissecting-room (in the time of the great surgeon who had mort-gaged the house to my uncle), stared at it.

We rose so early always, that at that time of the year we breakfasted by candle-light. When I went into the room, my uncle was so contracted by the cold, and so huddled to-gether in his chair behind the one dim candle, that I did not see him until I was close to the table.

As I held out my hand to him, he caught up his stick (being infirm, he always walked about the house with a stick), and made a blow at me, and said, "You fool!"

"Uncle," I returned, "I didn't expect you to be so angry as this." Nor had I expected it, though he was a hard and angry old man.

"You didn't expect!" said he; "when did you ever expect? When did you ever calculate, or look forward, you contemptible dog?"

"These are hard words, uncle!"

"Hard words? Feathers, to pelt such an idiot as you with," said he. "Here! Betsy Snap! Look at him!"

Betsy Snap was a withered, hard-favoured, yellow old woman—our only domestic—al-ways employed, at this time of the morning, in rubbing my uncle's legs. As my uncle ad-jured her to look at me, he put his lean grip on the crown of her head, she kneeling beside him, and turned her face towards me. An in-voluntary thought connecting them both with the dissecting-room, as it must often have been in the surgeon's time, passed across my mind in the midst of my anxiety.

"Look at the snivelling milksop!" said my uncle. "Look at the baby! This is the gentleman who, people say, is nobody's enemy but his own. This is the gentleman who can't say no. This is the gentleman who was making such large profits in his business that he must needs take a partner, t'other day. This is the gentle-man who is going to marry a wife without a

"I make the acquaintance of the Mowchers."
Another illustration by "Phiz" for
Dickens' David Copperfield.

penny, and who falls into the hands of Jezebels[5] who are speculating on my death!"

I knew, now, how great my uncle's rage was; for nothing short of his being almost beside himself would have induced him to utter that concluding word, which he held in such re-pugnance that it was never spoken or hinted at before him on any account.

"On my death," he repeated, as if he were defying me by defying his own abhorrence of the word. "On my death—death—Death! But I'll spoil the speculation. Eat your last under this roof, you feeble wretch, and may it choke you!"

You may suppose that I had not much appe-tite for the breakfast to which I was bidden in these terms; but I took my accustomed seat. I saw that I was repudiated henceforth by my

---

5. **Jezebel** (jez′ə bəl), a coarse, scheming woman, such as Jezebel in Kings, Chapter 9, in the Bible.

uncle; still I could bear that very well, possessing Christiana's heart.

He emptied his basin of bread and milk as usual, only that he took it on his knees with his chair turned away from the table where I sat. When he had done, he carefully snuffed out the candle; and the cold, slate-coloured, miserable day looked in upon us.

"Now, Mr. Michael," said he, "before we part, I should like to have a word with these ladies in your presence."

"As you will, sir," I returned; "but you deceive yourself and wrong us cruelly, if you suppose that there is any feeling at stake in this contract but pure, disinterested, faithful love."

To this, he only replied, "You lie!" and not one other word.

Illustration of a Christmas party,
drawing by "Phiz"
from early edition.

We went, through half-thawed snow and half-frozen rain, to the house where Christiana and her mother lived. My uncle knew them very well. They were sitting at their breakfast, and were surprised to see us at that hour.

"Your servant, ma'am," said my uncle to the mother. "You divine the purpose of my visit, I dare say, ma'am. I understand there is a world of pure, disinterested, faithful love cooped up here. I am happy to bring it all it wants, to make it complete. I bring you your son-in-law, ma'am—and you your husband, miss. The gentleman is a perfect stranger to me, but I wish him joy of his wise bargain."

He snarled at me as he went out, and I never saw him again.

It is altogether a mistake (continued the poor relation) to suppose that my dear Christiana, over-persuaded and influenced by her mother, married a rich man, the dirt from whose carriage wheels is often, in these changed times, thrown upon me as she rides by. No, no. She married me.

The way we came to be married rather sooner than we intended, was this. I took a frugal lodging and was saving and planning for her sake, when, one day, she spoke to me with great earnestness, and said:

"My dear Michael, I have given you my heart. I have said that I loved you, and I have pledged myself to be your wife. I am as much yours through all changes of good and evil as if we had been married on the day when such words passed between us. I know you well, and know that if we should be separated, and our union broken off, your whole life would be shadowed, and all that might, even now, be stronger in your character for the conflict with the world would then be weakened to the shadow of what it is!"

"God help me, Christiana!" said I. "You speak the truth."

"Michael!" said she, putting her hand in mine, in all maidenly devotion, "let us keep apart no longer. It is but for me to say that I can live contented upon such means as you have, and I well know you are happy. I say so from my heart. Strive no more alone; let us strive together. My dear Michael, it is not right that I should keep secret from you what you do not suspect, but what distresses my whole life. My mother; without considering that what you have lost, you have lost for me, and on the assurance of my faith; sets her heart on riches, and urges another suit upon me, to my misery. I cannot bear this, for to bear it is to be untrue to you. I would rather share your struggles than look on. I want no better home than you can give me. I know that you will aspire and labour with a higher courage if I am wholly yours, and let it be so when you will!"

I was blest, indeed, that day, and a new world opened to me. We were married in a very little while, and I took my wife to our happy home. That was the beginning of the residence I have spoken of; the Castle we have ever since inhabited together dates from that time. All our children have been born in it. Our first child—now married—was a little girl, whom we called Christiana. Her son is so like little Frank, that I hardly know which is which.

The current impression as to my partner's dealings with me is also quite erroneous. He did not begin to treat me coldly, as a poor simpleton, when my uncle and I so fatally quarrelled; nor did he afterwards gradually possess himself of our business and edge me out. On the contrary, he behaved to me with the utmost good faith and honour.

Matters between us took this turn:—On the day of my separation from my uncle, and even before the arrival at our counting-house of my trunks (which he sent after me, *not* carriage paid), I went down to our room of business, on our little wharf, overlooking the river; and there I told John Spatter what had happened. John did not say, in reply, that rich old relatives were palpable facts, and that love and sentiment were moonshine and fiction. He addressed me thus:

"Michael," said John, "we were at school together, and I generally had the knack of getting on better than you, and making a higher reputation."

"You had, John," I returned.

"Although," said John, "I borrowed your books and lost them; borrowed your pocket-money, and never repaid it; got you to buy my damaged knives at a higher price than I had given for them new; and to own to the windows that I had broken."

"All not worth mentioning, John Spatter," said I, "but certainly true."

"Mrs. Gamp proposes a toast."
Another demonstration of the detail
with which "Phiz" illustrated.

"When you were first established in this infant business, which promises to thrive so well," pursued John, "I came to you, in my search for almost any employment, and you made me your clerk."

"Still not worth mentioning, my dear John Spatter," said I; "still, equally true."

"And finding that I had a good head for business, and that I was really useful *to* the business, you did not like to retain me in that capacity, and thought it an act of justice soon to make me your partner."

"Still less worth mentioning than any of those other little circumstances you have recalled, John Spatter," said I; "for I was, and am, sensible of your merits and my deficiencies."

"Now, my good friend," said John, drawing my arm through his, as he had had a habit of doing at school; while two vessels outside the windows of our counting-house—which were shaped like the stern windows of a ship—went lightly down the river with the tide, as John and I might then be sailing away in company, and in trust and confidence, on our voyage of life; "let there, under these friendly circumstances, be a right understanding between us. You are too easy, Michael. You are nobody's enemy but your own. If I were to give you that damaging character among our connection, with a shrug, and a shake of the head, and a sigh; and if I were further to abuse the trust you place in me—"

"Marley's Ghost."
Drawing for early edition of
A Christmas Carol.

"But you never will abuse it at all, John," I observed.

"Never!" said he, "but I am putting a case— I say, and if I were further to abuse that trust by keeping this piece of our common affairs in the dark, and this other piece in the light, and again this other piece in the twilight, and so on, I should strengthen my strength, and weaken your weakness, day by day, until at last I found myself on the high road to fortune, and you left behind on some bare common, a hopeless number of miles out of the way."

"Exactly so," said I.

"To prevent this, Michael," said John Spatter, "or the remotest chance of this, there must be perfect openness between us. Nothing must be concealed, and we must have but one interest."

"My dear John Spatter," I assured him, "that is precisely what I mean."

"And when you are too easy," pursued John, his face glowing with friendship, "you must allow me to prevent that imperfection in your nature from being taken advantage of by any one; you must not expect me to humour it—"

"My dear John Spatter," I interrupted, "I *don't* expect you to humour it. I want to correct it."

"And I, too!" said John.

"Exactly so!" cried I. "We both have the same end in view; and, honourably seeking it, and fully trusting one another, and having but one interest, ours will be a prosperous and happy partnership."

"I am sure of it!" returned John Spatter. And we shook hands most affectionately.

I took John home to my Castle, and we had a very happy day. Our partnership throve well. My friend and partner supplied what I wanted, as I had foreseen that he would; and, by improving both the business and myself, amply acknowledged any little rise in life to which I had helped him.

I am not (said the poor relation, looking at the fire as he slowly rubbed his hands) very rich, for I never cared to be that; but I have

*"Restoration of mutual confidence
between Mr. and Mrs. Micawber."
Early illustration for* David Copperfield.

enough, and am above all moderate wants and anxieties. My Castle is not a splendid place, but it is very comfortable, and it has a warm and cheerful air, and is quite a picture of Home.

Our eldest girl, who is very like her mother, married John Spatter's eldest son. Our two families are closely united in other ties of attachment. It is very pleasant of an evening, when we are all assembled together—which frequently happens—and when John and I talk over old times, and the one interest there has always been between us.

I really do not know, in my Castle, what loneliness is. Some of our children or grandchildren are always about it, and the young voices of my descendants are delightful—O, how delightful!—to me to hear. My dearest and most devoted wife, ever faithful, ever loving, ever helpful and sustaining and consoling, is the priceless blessing of my house; from whom all its other blessings spring. We are rather a musical family, and when Christiana sees me, at any time, a little weary or depressed, she steals to the piano and sings a gentle air she used to sing when we were first betrothed. So weak a man am I, that I cannot bear to hear it from any other source. They played it once, at the Theatre, when I was there with little Frank; and the child said, wondering, "Cousin

Michael, whose hot tears are these that have fallen on my hand!"

Such is my Castle, and such are the real particulars of my life therein preserved. I often take little Frank home there. He is very welcome to my grandchildren, and they play together. At this time of the year—the Christmas and New Year time—I am seldom out of my Castle. For, the associations of the season seem to hold me there, and the precepts of the season seem to teach me that it is well to be there.

"And the Castle is—" observed a grave, kind voice among the company.

"Yes. My Castle is," said the poor relation, shaking his head as he still looked at the fire, "is in the Air. John our esteemed host suggests its situation accurately. My Castle is in the Air! I have done. Will you be so good as to pass the story."

<hr />

I
A CASTLE IN THE AIR

The mood of "The Poor Relation's Story" is quiet, reflective. The storyteller is much like the poet in *Platero and I*. He has come to know his inadequacies well. No longer caught up in a struggle to change himself, he has sunk back into dreams and found in them a strange peace. The result for the reader is a deep feeling of pathos. Perhaps Dickens is saying that only in a dream world can individuals truly know themselves and be at peace.

II
IMPLICATIONS

1. Take any one of the following lines and explain in your own words why you think it is the best expression of the poor relation's evaluation of himself.

   a. "I am not what I am supposed to be."

   b. "I am nobody's enemy but my own."

   c. "Yes. My Castle is . . . is in the Air."

2. Give your reaction to the following statements:

a. People who are unsuccessful in life are more likely to "know themselves" than are successful individuals.

b. Individuals who recognize personal faults and do nothing about them are always their "own enemies."

c. Most people find it easier to be sympathetic with someone who is truly bad than with someone like the poor relation, who is simply "weak."

d. Dreams are the escape valve for the overburdened mind, allowing it to release pressures by ignoring or forgetting them.

III
TECHNIQUES
Selection of Incident

Dickens' friend, the novelist Wilkie Collins, had a formula for the writing of successful fiction: "Make 'em laugh, make 'em cry, make 'em wait." The "'em" he referred to was the reading public. Consider the incidents in this story. Do you think Dickens' made use of this formula?

1. Does Dickens use the incidents here to reveal character or to move toward the climax?

2. Dickens, in his stories, moved from attacking the particular evils of society such as the poor law and the iniquities of private schools to an all-out attack on the evils of money. Are there incidents in this story that point out the evils of money?

Organization

Dickens, in effect, tells the same story twice. Is the retelling as detailed as the first telling? Are the details simplified or more elaborate? Does he use as many incidents in the second sequence?

Consider now the effect of this kind of arrangement. What is your picture of the poor relation at the end of the first story? What is your picture of him when he has finished the dream story? How does the second story change your impression of the poor relation?

IV
WORDS

Style may be defined as an individual or distinctive manner of expression. That which individualizes or sets apart a single writer, a group of writers, or the writers of a certain period is style. If you carefully consider the preceding selections you will feel or see differences in the ways the writers express themselves. There may be many such differences. Some concern grammatical matters, such as sentence patterns and arrangements of modifiers. In this series of exercises, we can notice differences in connection with vocabulary. In which of these selections is the wording relatively simple? Where do monosyllabic words predominate? Does their use make for simplicity of style and ease of reading? Which authors use many polysyllabic words? Do these words always make for great complexity?

A. Beginning with context clues, learn the following words as used by these authors:

1. Chekhov: *capricious, emaciation, ethereal, terrestrial*

2. Joyce: *palpitations, nausea*

3. Priestley: *saurian, dour, dubiety, daft*

4. Jiménez: *quietude, sonorous, cadence, arabesque*

5. Forster: *asceticism, antithesis, avaricious*

6. Lamb: *tinctured, decorous, mandarin, finical, rhetorical*

7. Delaney: *dynamic, catcall*

8. Dickens: *genteel, baronial, mercenary*

B. Look up the meaning of the following terms.
In "The Bet": *Byron, Mont Blanc, Pan.*
In "Eveline": *The Bohemian Girl, Patagonians.*
In Priestley's essays: *the West Riding of Yorkshire, Victoria, Edward the Seventh, Fleet Street, Sinbad the Sailor, Polonius, A Comedy of Errors.*

C. Joyce starts his story with the picture of Eveline "watching the evening invade the avenue." Where else does Joyce use figurative language?

In connection with figurative language, how do the beginnings and endings of Priestley's short essays differ? What is the effect of his procedure?

Of Platero, Jiménez says, "the jet mirrors of his eyes are hard as two beetles of dark crystals." This is a bold figure. Would it be true or not to say that Jiménez has used bolder figurative language than have the other authors in this section? Explain.

MAX AUB

Although Max Aub[1] was born in Paris, France, in 1903, he has become a naturalized Spanish citizen and writes only in Spanish. Aub has been called a "virtuoso" because his talents extend equally to the writing of poetry, short stories, essays, novels, and drama. Aub first gained recognition in the 1920s as an avant-garde dramatist. But in the 1930s he turned to the novel as his major form of expression. His masterpiece, *El laberinto magico* (*The Magic Labyrinth*), 1943, is a leviathan work consisting of a collection of twenty-seven novels and sketches set in the politically torn and physically devastated Spain of the civil war. His 1958 work, *Jusep Torres Campalan* (the title is the name of the main character), is almost as ambitious an accomplishment as his other mammoth work. It is a fictitious account that professes to explore the life of an actual, though minor and unknown, Spanish painter. Aub even supplies the reader with catalogues of the artist's works, technical criticism, and a few reproductions. In recognition of his prodigious accomplishments in literature, Aub has represented Spain as the cultural assistant in the Spanish Embassy in Paris, served as secretary of the National Council of Theaters, and acted as director of Spain's Theaters and Movies.

The Launch

translated from the Spanish by Elizabeth Mantel

He said he was born in Bermeo,[2] but the truth was that he came from a little town across the mouth of the Mundaca river, a settlement which was known by no name, or by many names, which is the same thing. The beaches and cliffs of this area were all that he knew of the world. For him, the Machichaco, Potorroari and Uguerriz marked Ultima Thule;[3] for him, Sollube was Olympus; Bermeo, Paris; and the Atalaya mall, the Elysian Fields. The wide expanse of his world, his Sahara, was the Laida, and the end of his world to the east was the steep, flat-topped reddish Ogoño. Beyond was Elanchove and the gentlemen of Lequeitio, in hell. His mother was the daughter of an overseer in an arms factory in Guernica. His father was a miner from Matamoros: he did not live long.

They called him "El Chirto," perhaps because he was half crazy. When he became ill he left the Franco-Belgian mines of Somorrostro, and went to work in a sawmill factory. There, among the woodplaning and dovetailing machines, Erramón Churrimendi[4] grew up.

He was fond of the little steamboats, the tunny boats, the pretty little sardine fishing smacks; the fishing tackle: the trotlines, the sieves, the fish traps, the nets. The world was the sea, and the only living beings were the hake, the eels, the sea bass, and the tunny. And he loved to catch moving fish in the water with a deep fisherman's net, to fish for anchovies and sardines with

---

1. **Max Aub** (mäks′ oub′).
2. **Bermeo** (ber mā′ō), fishing port in the Vizcaya (Biscay) province of northern Spain on the Bay of Biscay. All other towns, unless otherwise noted, are in the vicinity of Bermeo.
3. **Ultima Thule** (ul′tə mə thü′lē), the end of the world.
4. **Erramon Churrimendi** (er ä mōn′ chü rē men′dē).

a light, or at dusk; and to catch the bonito and tuna with a spinning tackle.

But he no sooner put his feet in a boat than he became seasick. And there was nothing he could do about it. He tried all the official medicines, and all the recondite ones, and all advice, spoken and whispered. He followed the advice of Don Pablo, of the drugstore; of Don Saturnio, of the City Council; of Cándida, Don Timoteo's maid; of the doctor from Zarauz, who was a native of Bermeo. To no avail. He had only to put one foot in a boat, and he became seasick. He tried a hundred stratagems: he would get aboard on an empty stomach, or after a good breakfast, sober, or drunk, or without having slept; he even tried the magic cures of Sebastiana, the woman from the edge of town; he tried crosses, lemons, the right foot, the left foot, at 7:00 A.M. on the dot, at low tide and at high tide, on the right day of the week. He went after Mass, after several "Our Fathers," and he tried pure will power and even in his sleep he heard: "I'll never be seasick again, I'll never be seasick again. . . ." But nothing helped. As soon as he put his foot on a moving plank, his insides turned round and round, he lost all sense of balance, and he was forced to huddle in the corner of the boat to keep out of the others' way, hoping to stay unnoticed. He spent some terrible moments. But he was not among those who despair, and for many years he repeatedly dared the adventure. Because, naturally, the people were laughing at him—not much, but they were laughing at him. He took to wine. What else could he do? Chacolí wine is a remedy. Erramón never married, the idea never even occurred to him. Who would marry him? He was a good man. Everyone admitted that. He was not even guilty of anything. But he got seasick. The sea made sport of him, and without any right.

He slept in a cabin by the estuary. It belonged to him. There was a beautiful oak there—if I say *there was*, it's for a good reason.

It *was* really a splendid tree, with a tall trunk and high branches. A tree the likes of which there are not many. It was his tree, and every day, every morning, every evening, on passing by, the man would touch it as if it were a horse's croup or the side of a beautiful woman. Sometimes he even spoke to it. It seemed to him that the bark was warm and that the tree was grateful to him. The roughness of the tree perfectly matched the rough skin on the man's hand. There was a perfect understanding between him and the tree.

Erramón was a methodical man. So long as there was variety in his work he did whatever he was asked, willingly and tidily. He was asked to do a hundred odd chores: to repair nets, to dig, to help in the sawmill, which had been his father's; to him it was all the same whether he raised a thatch or calked, or earned his few pesetas[5] by helping to bring in the fish. He never said no to anything. Erramón also sang, and sang well. He was greatly respected in the tavern. One of his Basque[6] songs went something like this:

> All the Basques are alike,
> All save one.
> And what's the matter with that one?
> That's Erramón,
> And he's like all the rest.

One night Erramón dreamed that he was not seasick. He was alone in a little boat, far out on the sea. He could see the coastline clearly in the distance. Only the red Ogoño shone like a fake sun which was sinking in the middle of the earth. Erramón was happier than he had ever been in his life. He lay down in the bottom of the boat and began to watch the clouds. He could feel the incessant rocking motion of the sea. The clouds were flying swiftly by, pushed by a wind which greeted him without stopping; and the circling sea gulls were shouting his welcome:

"Erramón, Erramón!"

And again:

"Erramón, Erramón!"

The clouds were like lace doves. Erramón closed his eyes. He was on the water and he was

---

5. **peseta** (pə sā′tə), Spanish bronze coin worth about 17 cents U.S.
6. **Basque** (bask), member of a people of northern Spain and southern France.

not seasick. The waves rocked him in their hammock back and forth, back and forth, up and down, in a sweet cradling motion. All his youth was about his neck, and yet, at that moment, Erramón had no memories, no other desire than to continue forever just as he was. He caressed the sides of his boat. Suddenly his hands were speaking to him. Erramón raised his head in surprise. He was not mistaken! His boat was made of the wood of his oak tree!

So shocking was the effect that he woke up.

From that moment on, Erramón's life began to change completely. It entered his head that if he made a boat out of his tree he would never again become seasick. In order to prevent himself from committing this crime, he drank more chacolí than usual; but he could not sleep. He turned over and over in his bed, hounded by the stars. He listened to his dream. He tried to convince himself of the absurdity of all this:

"If I've always been seasick, I'll continue being seasick."

He turned over on his left side.

He got up to look at his tree, and caressed it.

"Will I end by winning or losing?"

But deep inside he knew he should not do it, that it would be a crime. Was it his tree's fault that he got seasick? But Erramón could not resist the temptation for long. One morning he himself, aided by Ignacio, the one from the sawmill, cut down the tree. When the tree fell, Erramón felt very sad and alone as if the most beloved member of his family had died. It was hard for him now to recognize his cabin, it was so lonely. Only with his back to it, facing the estuary, did he feel easy.

Every afternoon he went to see how his tree was changing into a boat. This took place on the beach where his friend Santiago, the boatwright, was building it. The whole thing was made of the trunk; the keel, the floor timbers, the frame, the stem, the beams, even the seats and the oars, and a mast, just in case.

And so it was that one August morning when the sea did not seem like one, it was so calm, Erramón plowed outward on it with his new boat. It was a marvelous boat, it flew at the slightest urging of the man; he dipped the oars gently, throwing back his shoulders before he slightly contracted his arms, which made the boat fly. For the first time Erramon felt drunk, ecstatic. He drew away from the shore. He dipped the right oar a few times to make a turn, then the other in order to zigzag through the water. Then he drew the oars in and began to caress the wood of his boat. Slowly, the boards were letting in a little water. Erramón raised his hands to his forehead to dampen it a little. The silence was absolute; not a cloud, not a breeze, not even a sea gull. The land had disappeared, submerged. Erramón put his hands on the gunwale to caress it. Again he removed his hands wet. He was a little surprised: splashes on the wood had long since dried in the sun. He glanced over the inside of the boat: from every part water was slowly seeping in. On the bottom there was already a small puddle. Erramón did not know what to do. Again he passed his hands over the sides of his boat. There was no question about it; the wood was gradually letting water in. Erramón looked around; a slight uneasiness was beginning to gnaw his stomach. He had himself helped in calking the boat and was sure that the work had been well done. He bent down to inspect the seams: they were dry. It was the wood that was letting the water in! Without thinking, he raised his hand to his mouth. The water was sweet!

Desperately, he began to row. But despite his frantic efforts the boat did not move. It seemed to him that his boat was caught among the branches of a giant underwater tree, held as if in a hand. He rowed as hard as he could, but the boat did not budge. And now he could see with his own eyes how the wood of his tree was exuding clean, fresh water! Erramón fell to his knees and began to bail with his hands, because he had no bucket.

But the hull continued to ooze more and more water. It was already a spring with a thousand holes. And the sea seemed to be sprouting branches.

Erramón crossed himself.

He was never seen again on the shores of Biscay. Some said that he had been seen around

San Sebastian, others that he was seen in Bilbao.[7] A sailor spoke of an enormous octopus which had been seen about that time. But no one could give any information about him with any certainty. The oak tree began to grow again. The people shrugged their shoulders. The rumor spread that he was in America. Then, nothing.

I
AMBIGUITIES ENRICH INTERPRETATION

The title of this story is ambiguous. *Launch* is a noun that describes a kind of boat—any large, open boat—exactly the kind that Erramón builds. But *launch* is also a verb, meaning to set in motion with force, to slide a boat into the water for the first time, to begin or to initiate. Do both meanings of the word operate in this story? As you discuss the following implications, see if you gain a clearer interpretation of the title.

II
IMPLICATIONS

What reactions are generated by the following statements? Use either your experiences or the story for support.

1. There are two major symbols in the selection —the sea and the oak tree. What are the possible implications of each? What are Erramón's reactions to each?

2. Oscar Wilde wrote, "Each man kills the thing he loves," but this story suggests that the thing you love may kill you as well.

3. There are some weaknesses that a person should learn to live with.

4. There is no reason for Erramón's desperate urge to go to sea.

III
TECHNIQUES
Selection of Incident

On first reading, "The Launch" appears to be a very simple story. But on closer study, it is filled with casual incidents that explode with revelations about Erramón. What does each of the following reveal about Erramón?

1. The first sentence

2. The long list of cures for seasickness that he tries (three paragraphs in this short, short story)

3. The song he sings

4. The last few sentences

Organization

There are only two scenes in which there is step-by-step action. The remainder of the story consists of generalized statements and exposition.

1. What are the two scenes?

2. At which points in the story do they occur?

3. How much space do they occupy in the story?

4. Do you prefer a story consisting primarily of action scenes?

5. Would such a pattern of organization have been possible here?

---

7. **San Sebastian . . . Bilboa,** major seaports on the Bay of Biscay.

FRANK O'CONNOR

Frank O'Connor (1903–1966) was born in Cork, Ireland, the only son of a hard-working, hard-drinking laboring man whom he said he hated and loved, but of whom he was mostly jealous. He loved his mother intensely, and when for political reasons he changed his name from Michael John O'Donovan it was his mother's maiden name O'Connor that he chose for his last name. His family was so poor that he attended school only briefly. "I had to content myself with a make-believe education and the curious thing is that it was the make-believe that succeeded," said O'Connor. At the age of twelve he turned out his first collection of poems, biographies, and essays on history. While in his teens, O'Connor joined the Irish Republican Army (IRA). He was arrested and put in prison. While there he studied to be a librarian, and when released he became involved with the Irish Literary revival. "Story telling is the nearest thing one can get to the quality of a pure lyric poem," wrote O'Connor. "It doesn't deal with problems; it doesn't have any solutions to offer; it just states the human condition. . . ." One biographer has said, "O'Connor strove throughout his career to achieve . . . a form which captured a human event in all its complexities and which embraced the past, present and future. This goal determined the form a story was to take." "Judas" is an example of just such a story.

Judas

I'll forget a lot of things before I forget that night. As I was going out the mother said: "Sure, you won't be late, Jerry?" and I only laughed at her and said: "Am I ever late?" As I went down the road I was thinking it was months since I had taken her to the pictures. You might think that funny, Michael John, but after the father's death we were thrown together a lot. And I knew she hatèd being alone in the house after dark.

At the same time I had troubles of my own. You see, Michael John, being an only child, I never knocked round with girls the way others did. All the chaps in the office went with girls, or at any rate they let on they did. They said: "Who was the old doll I saw you with last night, Jerry? Aha, Jerry, you'd better mind yourself, boy, or you'll be getting into trouble!" Paddy Kinnane, for instance, talked like that, and he never saw

how it upset me. I think he thought it was a great compliment. It wasn't until years after that I began to suspect that Paddy's acquaintance with dolls was about of one kind with my own.

Then I met Kitty Doherty. Kitty was a hospital nurse, and all the chaps in the office said a fellow should never go with hospital nurses—they knew too much. I knew when I met Kitty that that was a lie. She was a well-educated, superior girl; she lived up the river in a posh locality, and her mother was on all sorts of councils and committees. She was small and wiry; a good-looking girl, always in good humor, and when she talked, she hopped from one thing to another like a robin on a frosty morning.

Anyway, she had me dazzled. I used to meet her in the evenings up the river road, as if I was walking there by accident and very surprised to see her. "Fancy meeting you!" I'd say, or "Well, well, isn't this a great surprise?" Then we'd stand talking for half an hour and I'd see her home. Several times she asked me in, but I was too nervous. I knew I'd lose my head, break the china, use some dirty word, and then go home and cut my throat. Of course, I never asked her to come to the pictures or anything like that. I knew she was above that. My only hope was that if I waited long enough I might be able to save her from drowning, the white slave traffic, or something of the sort. That would show in a modest, dignified way how I felt about her. Of course, I knew at the same time I ought to stay at home more with the mother, but the very thought that I might be missing an opportunity like that would be enough to spoil a whole evening on me.

This night in particular I was nearly distracted. It was three weeks since I'd seen Kitty. You know what three weeks are at that age. I was sure that at the very least the girl was dying and asking for me and that no one knew my address. A week before, I'd felt I simply couldn't bear it any longer, so I made an excuse and went down to the post office. I rang up the hospital and asked for her. I fully expected them to say that she was dead, and I got a shock when the girl at the other end asked my name. "I'm afraid," I said, "I'm a stranger to Miss Doherty, but I have an important message for her." Then I got completely panic-stricken. What could a girl like Kitty make of a damned deliberate lie like that? What else was it but a trap laid by an old and cunning hand. I held the receiver out and looked at it. "Moynihan," I said to it, "you're mad. An asylum, Moynihan, is the only place for a fellow like you." Then I heard her voice, not in my ear at all, but in the telephone booth as if she were standing before me, and I nearly dropped the receiver with terror. I put it to my ear and asked in a disguised voice: "Who is that speaking, please?" "This is Kitty Doherty," she said rather impatiently. "Who are you?" "I am Monsieur Bertrand," said I, speaking in what I hoped was a French accent. "I am afraid I have de wrong number." Then I put down the receiver carefully and thought how nice it would be if only I had a penknife handy to cut my throat with. It's funny, but from the

moment I met Kitty I was always coveting sharp things like razors and penknives.

After that an awful idea dawned on my mind. Of course, I should have thought of it before, but, as you've probably guessed, I wasn't exactly knowledgeable. I began to see that I wasn't meeting Kitty for the very good reason that Kitty didn't want to meet me. That filled me with terror. I examined my conscience to find out what I might have said to her. You know what conscience is at that age. I remembered every remark I'd made and they were all brutal, indecent or disgusting. I had talked of Paddy Kinnane as a fellow who "went with dolls." What could a pure-minded girl think of a chap who naturally used such a phrase except—what, unfortunately, was true—that he had a mind like a cesspit.

It was a lovely summer evening, with views of hillsides and fields between the gaps in the houses, and that raised my spirits a bit. Maybe I was wrong, maybe she hadn't found out the sort I was and wasn't avoiding me, maybe we might meet and walk home together. I walked the full length of the river road and back, and then started off to walk it again. The crowds were thinning out as fellows and girls slipped off up the lanes or down to the river. As the streets went out like lamps about me I grew desperate. I saw clearly that she was avoiding me; that she knew I wasn't the quiet, good-natured chap I let on to be but a volcano of brutality and lust. "Lust, lust, lust!" I hissed to myself, clenching my fists.

Then I glanced up and saw her on a tram.[1] I forgot instantly about the lust and smiled and waved my cap at her, but she was looking ahead and didn't see me. I ran after the car, intending to jump on it, to sit on one of the back seats on top and then say as she was getting off: "Fancy meeting you here!" (Trams were always a bit of a problem. If you sat beside a girl and paid for her, it might be considered forward; if you didn't, it looked mean. I never quite knew.) But as if the driver knew what was in my mind, he put on

---

1. **tram,** a streetcar; a passenger car running on rails.

speed and away went the tram, tossing and screeching down the straight, and I stood panting in the middle of the road, smiling as if missing a tram was the best joke in the world and wishing all the time I had the penknife and the courage to use it. My position was hopeless. Then I must have gone a bit mad, for I started to race the tram. There were still lots of people out walking, and they stared after me, so I lifted my fists to my chest in the attitude of a professional runner and dropped into a comfortable stride which I hoped vaguely would delude them into the belief that I was in training for a big race.

Between the running and the halts I just managed to keep the tram in view all the way through town and out at the other side. When I saw Kitty get off and go up a hilly street I collapsed and was just able to drag myself after her. When she went into a house on a terrace I sat on the curb with my head between my knees till the panting stopped. At any rate I felt safe. I could now walk up and down before the house till she came out, and accost her with an innocent smile and say: "Fancy meeting you!"

But my luck was dead out that night. As I was walking up and down out of range of the house I saw a tall chap come strolling up at the opposite side and my heart sank. It was Paddy Kinnane.

"Hullo, Jerry," he chuckled with that knowing grin he put on whenever he wanted to compliment you on being discovered in a compromising situation, "what are you doing here?"

"Ah, just waiting for a chap I had a date with, Paddy," I said, trying to sound casual.

"Begor," said Paddy, "you look to me more like a man that was waiting for an old doll. Still waters run deep. . . . What time are you supposed to be meeting him?"

"Half-eight," I said at random.

"Half-eight?" said Paddy in surprise. " 'Tis nearly nine now."

"I know," said I, "but as I waited so long I may as well give him another few minutes."

"Ah, I'll wait along with you," said Paddy, leaning against the wall and taking out a packet of fags. "You might find yourself stuck by the end of the evening. There's people in this town and they have no consideration for anyone."

That was Paddy all out; no trouble too much for him if he could do you a good turn.

"As he kept me so long," I said hastily, "I don't think I'll bother with him. It only struck me this very minute that there's a chap up the Asragh road that I have to see on urgent business. You'll excuse me, Paddy. I'll tell you about it another time."

And away I went hell for leather to the tram. When I reached the tram stop below Kitty's house I sat on the river wall in the dusk. The moon was rising, and every quarter of an hour the trams came grunting and squeaking over the old bridge and then went black out while the conductors switched the trolleys. I stood on the curb in the moonlight searching for Kitty. Then a bobby came along, and as he seemed to be watching me, I slunk slowly off up the hill and stood against a wall in the shadow. There was a high wall at the other side too, and behind it the roofs of a house shining in the moon. Every now and then a tram would come in and people would pass in the moonlight, and the snatches of conversation I caught were like the warmth from an open door to the heart of a homeless man. It was quite clear now that my position was hopeless. The last tram came and went, and still there was no Kitty and still I hung on.

Then I heard a woman's step. I couldn't even pretend to myself that it might be Kitty till she shuffled past me with that hasty little walk of hers. I started and called out her name; she glanced over her shoulder and, seeing a man emerging from the shadow, took fright and ran. I ran too, but she put on speed and began to outdistance me. At that I despaired. I stood on the pavement and shouted after her at the top of my voice.

"Kitty!" I cried. "Kitty, for God's sake, wait for me!"

She ran a few steps further and then halted, turned, and came back slowly down the path.

"Jerry Moynihan!" she whispered, lifting her two arms to her breasts as if I had found her with nothing on. "What in God's name are you doing here?"

I was summoning up strength to tell her that I just happened to be taking a stroll in that direction and was astonished to see her when I realized the improbability of it and began to cry instead. Then I laughed. I suppose it was nerves. But Kitty had had a bad fright and now that she was getting over it she was as cross as two sticks.

"What's wrong with you, I say," she snapped. "Are you out of your senses or what?"

"Well, you see," I stammered awkwardly, half in dread I was going to cry again, "I didn't see you in town."

"No," she replied with a shrug, "I know you didn't. I wasn't out. What about it?"

"I thought it might be something I said to you," I said desperately.

"No," said Kitty candidly, "it wasn't anything to do with you. It's Mother."

"Why?" I asked almost joyously. "Is there something wrong with her?"

"I don't mean that," said Kitty impatiently. "It's just that she made such a fuss, I felt it wasn't worth it."

"But what did she make a fuss about?" I asked.

"About you, of course," said Kitty in exasperation. "What did you think?"

"But what did I do?" I asked, clutching my head. This was worse than anything I'd ever imagined. This was terrible.

"You didn't do anything," said Kitty, "but people were talking about us. And you wouldn't come in and be introduced to her like anyone else. I know she's a bit of a fool, and her head is stuffed with old nonsense about her family. I could never see that they were different to anyone else, and anyway, she married a commercial[2] herself, so she has nothing much to boast about. Still, you needn't be so superior. There's no obligation to buy, you know."

I didn't. There were cold shivers running through me. I had thought of Kitty as a secret between God, herself, and me and that she only knew the half of it. Now it seemed I didn't even know the half. People were talking about us! I was superior! What next?

"But what has she against me?" I asked despairingly.

"She thinks we're doing a tangle, of course," snapped Kitty as if she was astonished at my stupidity, "and I suppose she imagines you're not grand enough for a great-great-grandniece of Daniel O'Connell.[3] I told her you were a different sort of fellow entirely and above all that sort of thing, but she wouldn't believe me. She said I was a deep, callous, crafty little intriguer and that I hadn't a drop of Daniel O'Connell's blood in my veins." Kitty began to giggle at the thought of herself as an intriguer.

"That's all she knows," I said bitterly.

"I know," said Kitty with a shrug. "The woman has no sense. And anyway she has no reason to think I'm telling lies. Cissy and I always had fellows, and we spooned with them all over the shop under her very nose, so why should she think I'm lying to her now?"

At that I began to laugh like an idiot. This was worse than appalling. This was a nightmare. Kitty, whom I had thought so angelic, talking in cold blood about "spooning" with fellows all over the house. Even the bad women in the books I'd read didn't talk about love in that cold-blooded way. Madame Bovary[4] herself had at least the decency to pretend that she didn't like it. It was like another door opening on the outside world, but Kitty thought I was laughing at her and started to apologize.

"Of course I had no sense," she said. "You're the first fellow I ever met that treated me properly. The others only wanted to fool around with me, and now because I don't like it, Mother thinks I'm getting stuck-up. I told her I liked you better than any fellow I knew, but that I'd grown out of all that sort of thing."

"And what did she say to that?" I asked fiercely. It was—how can I describe it?—like a man who'd lived all his life in a dungeon getting

---

2. **a commercial,** a commercial traveler, a salesperson.
3. **Daniel O'Connell** (1775–1847), a great Irish nationalist.
4. **Madame Bovary,** heroine of the novel of the same name by Gustave Flaubert (1857).

into the sunlight for the first time and afraid of every shadow.

"Ah, I told you the woman was silly," said Kitty, getting embarrassed.

"Go on!" I shouted. "I want to know everything. I insist on knowing everything."

"Well," said Kitty with a demure little grin, "she said you were a deep, designing guttersnipe who knew exactly how to get round feather-pated little idiots like me. . . . You see," she added with another shrug, "it's quite hopeless. The woman is common. She doesn't understand."

"But I tell you she does understand," I shouted frantically. "She understands better than you do. I only wish to God I was deep and designing so that I'd have some chance with you."

"Do you really?" asked Kitty, opening her eyes wide. "To tell you the truth," she added after a moment, "I thought you were a bit keen the first time, but then I didn't know. When you didn't kiss me or anything, I mean."

"God," I said bitterly, "when I think of what I've been through in the past couple of weeks!"

"I know," said Kitty, biting her lip. "I was the same." And then we said nothing for a few moments.

"You're sure you're serious?" she asked suspiciously.

"I tell you, girl," I shouted, "I was on the point of committing suicide."

"What good would that be?" she asked with another shrug, and then she looked at me and laughed outright—the little jade!

It is all as clear in my mind as if it had happened last night. I told Kitty about my prospects. She didn't care, but I insisted on telling her. It was as if a stone had been lifted off my heart, and I went home in the moonlight singing. Then I heard the clock strike, and the singing stopped. I remembered the mother at home, waiting, and began to run again. This was desperation too, but a different sort.

The door was ajar and the kitchen in darkness. I saw her sitting before the fire by herself, and just as I was going to throw my arms about her, I smelt Kitty's perfume round me and was afraid to go near her. God help us, as if it would have told her anything!

"Hallo, Mum," I said with a laugh, rubbing my hands, "you're in darkness."

"You'll have a cup of tea?" she said.

"I might as well," said I.

"What time is it?" she said, lighting the gas. "You're very late."

"Ah, I met a fellow from the office," I said, but at the same time I was stung by the complaint in her tone.

"You frightened me," she said with a little whimper. "I didn't know what happened to you. What kept you at all?"

"Oh, what do you think?" I said, goaded into retorting. "Drinking and blackguarding as usual."

I could have bitten my tongue off when I'd said it; it sounded so cruel, as if some stranger had said it instead of me. She turned to me for a moment with a frightened stare as if she was seeing the stranger too, and somehow I couldn't bear it.

"God Almighty," I said, "a fellow can have no life in his own house," and away with me upstairs.

I lit the candle, undressed and got into bed. I was wild. A chap could be a drunkard and blackguard and not be made to suffer more reproach than I was for being late one single night. That, I felt, was what you got for being a good son.

"Jerry," she called from the foot of the stairs, "will I bring you up your cup?"

"I don't want it now, thanks," I said.

I heard her give a heavy sigh and turn away. Then she locked the two doors front and back. She didn't wash up, and I knew my cup of tea was standing there on the table with a saucer on top in case I changed my mind. She came slowly up the stairs, and she walked like an old woman. I blew out the candle before she reached the landing in case she came in to ask me if I wanted anything else, and the moonlight came in at the attic window and brought me memories of Kitty. But every time I tried to imagine her face while she grinned up at me, waiting for me to kiss her, it was the mother's face that came up with that look like a child's when you strike him the first time—as if he suddenly saw the stranger in you. I remembered all our life together from the night the father—God rest him!—died; our early Mass on Sunday; our visits to the pictures; our plans for the future, and Christ, Michael John, it was as if I was inside her mind and she sitting by the fire, waiting for the blow to fall! And now it had fallen, and I was a stranger to her, and nothing I ever did could make us the same to each other again. There was something like a cannon ball stuck in my chest, and I lay awake till the cocks started crowing. Then I couldn't bear it any longer. I went out on the landing and listened.

"Are you awake, Mother?" I asked in a whisper.

"What is it, Jerry?" she said in alarm, and I knew she hadn't slept any more than I had.

"I only came to say I was sorry," I said, opening the room door, and then as I saw her sitting up in bed under the Sacred Heart lamp, the cannon ball burst inside me and I began to bawl like a kid.

"Oh, child, child," she cried out, "what are you crying for at all, my little boy?" and she spread out her arms to me. I went to her and she hugged me and rocked me just as she did when I was only a nipper. "Oh, oh, oh," she was saying to herself in a whisper, "my storeen bawn,[5] my little man!"—all the names she hadn't called me since I was a kid. That was all we said. I couldn't bring myself to tell her what I'd done, and she wouldn't confess to me that she was jealous; all she could do was to try and comfort me for the way I'd hurt her, to make up to me for the nature she'd given me. "My storeen bawn," she said. "My little man!"

I

THE STRANGER WITHIN

After his encounter with his mother upon returning home from seeing Kitty, Jerry describes

---

5. **storeen bawn,** Irish for little fair-haired treasure.

the mother's face as having "that look like a child's, when you strike him the first time—as if he suddenly saw the stranger in you." What is this stranger within? Is it what we are becoming or what we actually are? Through the story Jerry is torn by his thoughts and feelings: his sense of duty toward his mother; his feelings about girls; his fear of going into Kitty's house; his awe of his friends' experiences with "dolls"; the possibility of having offended Kitty. What does the story seem to say about the inner turmoil experienced in the teenage years?

II

IMPLICATIONS

Discuss the following by exploring what the story indicates about each and how you interpret the statement.

1. The turmoil and stress of the teenage years comes from not knowing oneself.

2. A young person today would not feel the guilt and distress that Jerry does toward his mother.

3. Growing to adulthood makes every child a Judas toward his or her parents.

4. In moments of stress individuals often learn something surprising about themselves.

III

TECHNIQUES

Selection of Incident

After the narrator establishes the attraction of Jerry for Kitty, there are six major incidents, almost like separate scenes in a play. What does each of these reveal about Jerry?

1. Calling the hospital

2. Following the tram

3. Waiting outside the house for Kitty to come out and meeting Paddy there

4. Talking with Kitty after the chase

5. Finding his mother waiting up for him

6. The next morning

Organization

The narrator is telling the story about an event in his life to someone called Michael John. So the story itself is a flashback though it does not return to the present at the end. What does this pattern allow the author to do that he could not do if the story had been told in a straight, chronological order?

DINO BUZZATI

Dino Buzzati[1] (1906–1972) was born near the Dolomite Mountains of northern Italy. His love for the fierce beauty of that landscape is lyrically expressed in his writing. Although Buzzati had earned a law degree in Milan (where he spent all of his adult life), he turned to writing and journalism. His first novel, *Barnabò of the Mountains*, was published when he was twenty-seven. *The Tartar Steppe*, his third novel, made him famous in Italy. This book represents the most powerful of his major themes: the loneliness and absurdity we feel in the face of death and the ludicrous devices we use to blunt our awareness of death's inevitability. Throughout the novel, Buzzati's impeccable prose communicates a subdued sense of terror.

After *The Tartar Steppe*, Buzzati stopped writing novels and turned to short stories. Twenty years later, several collections of his stories appeared that present the same themes. Remaining a bachelor throughout his life, he enjoyed skiing, mountaineering, and painting. Three years before his death he created a pop-art cartoon strip of the myth of Orpheus and Eurydice, set in a futuristic city. It became very popular in Italy, especially with young people.

Seven Stories

translated from the Italian by Ben Johnson

One March morning, at the end of a day's journey by train, Giuseppe Corte[2] arrived in the city where the famous nursing home was located. He had a slight fever, but chose nonetheless to walk from the station to the hospital, carrying his overnight bag himself.

Detected in an early stage and negligible though his infection was, Giuseppe Corte had been counseled to seek treatment at the renowned sanitorium, to which sufferers from his disease were the only ones admitted. This thereby guaranteed exceptional competence on the part of the doctors and the soundest disposition of facilities within the hospital itself.

As he caught sight of it from a distance—recognizable from a photograph he had once seen in a prospectus—Giuseppe Corte was most favorably impressed. With a façade of projecting wings, the white seven-storied structure bore a vague resemblance to a hotel. It was surrounded by a border of tall trees.

After a brief physical examination, with promise of a more careful, more thorough one to follow, Giuseppe Corte was assigned to a cheerful room on the seventh and uppermost floor. His furniture there, like the wallpaper, was bright and clean, and the armchairs were of wood with cushions of a polychrome material. His view dominated one of the loveliest quarters of the city. All was tranquil, hospitable, and reassuring.

Giuseppe Corte slipped into bed at once and, turning on the light above the bolster, began to read a book he had brought with him. Presently a nurse entered to ask if there was anything he desired.

No, nothing at all; but he quickly seized upon the opportunity to engage the girl in conversation, to question her about the nursing home.

---

1. **Dino Buzzati** (dē′nō bṳts ä′tē).
2. **Giuseppe Corte** (jə sep′ē kôr′tä).

It was thus that he came to hear of its unique arrangement. The patients were distributed on various floors depending on the gravity of their cases. On the seventh—that is, on the top floor —were those whose infections were very slight. The sixth handled cases which, if not grave, could by no means be neglected. Cases treated on the fifth floor were serious; and so on, all the way down, floor by floor. The condition of patients on the second, for instance, was extremely critical. And the first was reserved for those for whom there could be no hope.

This singular stratification, apart from greatly accelerating the hospital service, insured mildly infected patients against being disturbed by neighbors in agony, and guaranteed in each ward a homogeneous atmosphere. Moreover, it lent itself to a perfect graduation of treatment, the achievement of optimum results.

It followed, then, that the patients were divided into seven progressive castes. Each floor was like a little world in itself, with its own rules and special traditions which were meaningless on other floors. And since each section was under the direction of a different doctor, there had developed, though on a very minor scale, subtle differences in the method of treatment, despite the fact that the director general had established in the institution one fundamental procedure.

When the nurse left, Giuseppe Corte, feeling that his temperature had subsided to normal, went to the window and looked out, not so much to view the city, new though it was to him, as in hopes of catching a glimpse of other patients through the windows on the floors below. The structure of the building, with its projecting wings and recesses, lent itself to this sort of observation. Mostly Giuseppe Corte's attention was focused on the windows of the first floor, which looked to him to be very far away and were seen only slantwise. But there was nothing of interest. Nearly all the windows were shuttered tight with gray sliding blinds.

Corte then noticed that a man had appeared at a window next to his. The two men looked at each other for some time with a growing sense

Dino Buzzati

of fellow feeling, but neither knew just how to break the silence.

At length Giuseppe Corte summoned courage enough to ask: "Have you just arrived yourself?"

"Oh, no," answered the other. "I've been here for two months now. . . ." He was silent for a moment or so, and then, uncertain how to continue, added: "I was looking at my brother."

"Your brother?"

"Yes, explained the stranger. "We entered together—quite an exceptional case, ours; but he got worse. Just think, he's already on the fourth!"

"The fourth?"

"Yes, the fourth floor," explained the man, enunciating these words with accents of such commiseration and horror as to evoke in Giuseppe Corte a feeling almost of terror.

"Is it really so serious on the fourth floor?" he ventured cautiously.

"Goodness," said the other, slowly shaking his head, "they're not desperate, those cases, but there's precious little to rejoice about."

"But then," pursued Corte with the playfully

detached manner of one who alludes to tragic events of no concern to him, "well, if they're that serious on the fourth floor, whom do they put on the first?"

"Oh," said the other, "the first is for patients who are dying—actually dying. In fact, down there the doctors don't have a thing to do. The only person who's kept busy is the priest. Naturally—"

"But there's hardly anybody there, anyway," interrupted Corte, as if eager for confirmation; "nearly all the rooms are closed."

"True, there aren't many at the moment, but they had a number this morning," replied the stranger, with a subtle smile. "Wherever you see that the blinds are drawn, it means that someone has just died. Anyway, you can see, can't you, that the shutters on the other floors are all open? . . . But you'll excuse me now," he said, slowly withdrawing. "It's growing a bit chilly, I feel. I'm going back to bed. I wish you luck . . . the best of luck!"

The man disappeared from the sill and the window was closed energetically; a light came on in his room. Giuseppe Corte remained at his window, motionless, his eyes fixed on the drawn blinds of the first floor; he stared at them with morbid intensity, trying to imagine the funereal secrets of that dreadful floor where patients were assigned to die; and a sense of relief pervaded him, knowing that he was so far away. Evening settled over the city. One by one, lights appeared at the thousand windows of the sanatorium; from a distance one might have mistaken it for a hotel party. Only on the first floor, at the foot of the precipice, were there windows, scores of them, that remained blind and dark.

The results of his thorough physical examination reassured Giuseppe Corte. Inclined as a rule to expect the worst, he was already inwardly prepared for a harsh verdict, and would not, indeed, have been surprised if they had declared that he would have to be sent to the floor below. In fact, his fever, though his general condition continued good, had shown no signs of subsiding. The doctor, however, chose to speak to him in terms that were amicable and encouraging. There was certainly, he said, an incipient trace of the disease, but it was very slight and would no doubt clear up in two or three weeks.

"Then I'm to remain on the seventh?" Giuseppe Corte had asked, anxious, at this juncture.

"Why, of course!" the doctor had replied, patting him in a friendly fashion on the shoulder. "Where did you expect to go?" Certainly not to the fourth?" he laughed, as if this were the worst, the most absurd of possibilities.

Giuseppe Corte, in fact, remained in the room to which he had originally been assigned. He came to know some of his fellow patients in the hospital on those rare occasions, in the afternoon, when he was permitted out of bed. He attended scrupulously to his treatment, doing his very utmost to hasten recovery; yet, despite his efforts, his condition seemed to remain unchanged.

About ten days had elapsed when the chief attendant of the seventh floor introduced himself to Giuseppe Corte. He wanted to know if Corte would grant him a favor, a purely personal favor; a lady with two children was scheduled to arrive the following day; they happened to have two free rooms on either side of Corte's, but they needed a third. Would Signor Corte mind moving to another, but equally comfortable, room?

Giuseppe Corte had, naturally, no objections; one room or another was quite the same to him, and there was a chance that he might find himself with a new and prettier nurse.

"Thanks ever so much," said the chief attendant, bowing lightly. "But from a person like you, I admit, so kind and gentlemanly a gesture scarcely surprises me. In an hour, then, if that is suitable to you, we'll proceed with the transfer. You realize that you'll have to go down to the next floor," he added offhand, as if this were a detail hardly worth mentioning. "Unfortunately, we do not have any other vacant rooms on this floor. But this is a temporary arrangement," he went on quickly, observing that

Corte, suddenly sitting up in bed, was about to protest. "An absolutely temporary arrangement. Just as soon as we have a free room, and I believe we shall within two or three days, you'll be able to come back up."

"I must say," said Giuseppe Corte, smiling, to make it quite clear that he was no child, "I must say that a transfer of this sort does not please me in the least."

"But it is not being made on any medical grounds whatever; I understand perfectly what you mean, but this is no more than a gesture of courtesy toward a lady who does not wish to be separated from her children. . . . Really," he added, laughing aloud, "you mustn't even think that there are other reasons."

"Very well," said Giuseppe Corte. "Only it looks to me like a bad sign."

Thus Signor Corte went to the sixth floor. And although convinced that his transfer was in no way due to a worsening of his condition, he felt uneasy at the thought that between him and the world at large, the world of healthy people, an obstacle had been interposed. On the seventh floor, at the port of arrival, one still had contact somehow with the society of man; it might even be considered a kind of annex to the everyday world. But on the sixth, one had then entered the hospital proper: the mentality of the doctors, of the nurses, and of the patients themselves was already a little different. Here, it was admitted, was a ward for real, genuinely ill patients, slight though their infections were. In fact, from his first discussions there, with patients in the neighboring rooms, with attendants and doctors, Giuseppe Corte remarked the way the seventh floor was dismissed as a joke, as a place reserved for amateur patients suffering largely from imaginary complaints; only on the sixth did the hospital, so to speak, really begin.

And Giuseppe Corte understood that before returning upstairs to his rightful level, according with the characteristics of his particular case, he would encounter, certainly, some difficulties; to return to the seventh floor, he would have to set in motion a complicated organism, however slight was the effort required of it; doubtless, had he not spoken up, no one would have dreamed of returning him to the floor of the "amateurs."

He was determined therefore not to yield on any of his rights, and not to let himself fall a prey to habit. He was fond of pointing out to his ward mates that he would be with them for only a few days, that it had been merely his desire to accommodate a lady that accounted for his presence there, and that as soon as they had an empty room upstairs he was leaving them. His listeners would nod assent, but skeptically.

Giuseppe Corte's convictions were bolstered, however, by the opinion of his new doctor. The doctor himself admitted that Corte could perfectly well be assigned to the seventh floor; his infection was ab-so-lute-ly neg-li-gi-ble—syllabizing the words to give them due importance; fundamentally, though, he believed that Signor Corte stood to benefit more from the treatment on the sixth—

"I don't care to hear such talk as that," interrupted the patient determinedly at this point. "You said that the seventh floor is where I belong, and I want to go back!"

"No one has suggested anything but," the doctor returned. "Mine was purely and simply the advice not of your doc-tor, but of a gen-u-ine friend! Your infection, may I repeat, is very slight—it would not be an exaggeration to say that you're not even ill; in my judgment, however, yours is distinguished from analogous cases by the rather sizable area infected. Let me explain: the intensity of your infection is hardly worth mention, but the affected area is considerable; the destructive process in the cells"—it was Giuseppe Corte's first occasion to hear this sinister expression in the hospital—"the destructive process in your cells is absolutely in its initial stage; perhaps it has not even begun, but it may—mind you, only *may* —it may attack simultaneously over a vast area of the organism. It is for this reason alone that, in my opinion, you can be treated more effectively here, on the sixth floor, where the thera-peutic methods are of a more specific and intensive nature than upstairs."

One day it was reported that, after prolonged discussion with his colleagues, the director general of the institution had decided to alter the subdivisional status of the patients. The grade, so to speak, of each patient was to be lowered a half point. If, say, the patients on each floor were divided, according to the gravity of their cases, into two categories (this subdivision was actually made by the respective ward doc-tors, but for their own guidance), the lower half was automatically to be transferred to the floor below. For instance, half the patients on the sixth floor, those cases that were somewhat more advanced than the others, would proceed to the fifth; and the more slightly infected pa-tients on the seventh would go to the sixth. Giuseppe Corte was delighted: in such a com-plete shake-up, his return to the seventh floor would be more easily effected.

Upon mentioning this hope of his to the nurse, he received, however, a rude surprise. He was certainly scheduled for transfer, he learned, but not to the seventh; rather, to the floor below. For reasons which were beyond the nurse to explain, he had been included in the more serious half of the inmates on the sixth floor, and he would, therefore, have to proceed to the fifth.

Once recovered from the first shock, Giu-seppe Corte gave vent to his fury. They had played a low trick on him! he screamed; he wanted to hear no further talk of a transfer downstairs! he was going home! he stood on his rights! and the hospital was not permitted to ignore so blatantly the doctors' diagnoses!

He was still raging when the doctor came puffing in to calm him. He advised Corte not to excite himself, unless he wanted his tempera-ture to rise, and he explained that there had been a misunderstanding, or in any case a partial one. He again admitted that Giuseppe Corte's rightful place was on the seventh floor, but added that his opinion of Corte's case—a purely personal opinion, naturally—was a little at variance with this judgment. Actually, Corte's infection might in a certain sense, of course, be classified in grade six, considering the mag-nitude of morbid manifestation. He himself, however, was utterly at a loss to explain why Corte had been included in the lower half of the sixth floor. Except, perhaps the administra-tive secretary, who had just that morning telephoned to ask about Corte's exact position —perhaps the secretary had made an error. Or more likely, the administration itself had "stepped down" his own recommendations, for, though an expert doctor, he was felt to be too lenient. In conclusion, the doctor counseled Corte not to let himself become overwrought, and to submit to the transfer with good grace; after all, it was not the floor to which a patient was assigned that mattered, but the actual status of his disease.

And, added the doctor, as regarded his treat-ment, Giuseppe Corte would have no cause for regret; the doctor on the floor below was certainly more experienced: it was almost dog-matic that the ability of the doctors gradually increased—at least that's what the directors thought—as one descended. His room would be no less comfortable and elegant. The view was equally spacious: only from the third floor was it obstructed by the girdle of trees.

Gripped by an evening fever, Giuseppe Corte listened carefully, but with a growing sense of weariness, to the various points the doctor raised by way of justifying the transfer. Eventually, Corte realized that he simply lacked strength and, still more, the will to oppose this unjust action. And he let himself be carried to the floor below.

Giuseppe Corte's sole comfort—a cold one, however—once he was installed on the fifth floor, lay in his knowledge that there was uni-versal agreement, among the doctors, nurses, and patients alike, that his was the least serious case in the entire ward. Within the confines of the fifth floor, in any case, he could consider himself by far the most fortunate inmate. Yet on the other hand, rankling in his brain was the thought that, interposed between him and the normal world, there were now *two* barriers.

Spring advanced and the air grew warmer, but Giuseppe Corte had ceased to enjoy, as in the early days, lounging at the window; perfectly ridiculous though his fears were, a peculiar shudder convulsed him whenever he looked at the windows of the first floor—most of them always closed—now that they were considerably nearer.

His condition appeared to be unchanged. But after he had spent three days on the fifth floor a rash broke out on his right leg, which, in the days that followed, showed no signs of healing. It was an infection, the doctors informed him—in no way related to his principal one: something, in fact, that could befall the healthiest person in the world. And it would require, that he might be rid of it in a few days, intensive digamma-ray treatments.

"But that can be done here, can't it?" asked Giuseppe Corte.

"Certainly," replied the doctor with pride. "Our hospital is equipped to handle any eventuality. There's only one inconvenience."

"An inconvenience?" said Giuseppe Corte with a vague presentiment.

"An inconvenience only in a manner of speaking," said the doctor, correcting himself. "I mean that this particular apparatus is located on the fourth floor. And I certainly wouldn't advise your making such a trek three times a day."

"Then there's nothing to be done, is there?"

"Well, I would recommend that you agree to move to the fourth floor until the rash clears up."

"*No!*" Giuseppe Corte exploded. "I'm fed up with forever going downstairs. I'd die first!"

"Suit yourself," said the doctor, conciliatory, not wishing to irritate the patient; "but as your attending doctor, please note that I shall not permit you to climb the stairs three times a day."

And the worst of it was that his eczema, instead of healing, slowly began to spread. Constantly tossing in bed, unable to rest, Giuseppe Corte endured it, furious, for three days before

finally having to yield. Then, voluntarily, he requested that the doctor have them proceed with the digamma-ray treatments, that he be transferred to the floor below.

Down there, Corte noted with unconfessed delight that he stood out as an exception. The other patients, their cases decidedly more serious than his, were not allowed up for a minute, whereas he was able to indulge in the luxury of strolling from his bed to the digamma-ray room, to the compliments and marvel even of the nurses.

He was careful to explain to his new doctor the highly specialized nature of his case, of a patient, that is, who actually belonged on the seventh floor but found himself on the fourth. And as soon as his rash was cured, he had every intention of returning upstairs. He would accept absolutely no more excuses. He, whose proper place was still on the seventh!

"The seventh, the *seventh!*" exclaimed the doctor, smiling; he had just finished examining Corte. "You patients are eternally exaggerating! May I be the first to state that you ought to be pleased with your condition. By your progress chart, I see there has been no marked worsening. Still, between this and talk of the seventh floor—you'll pardon me if I am brutally frank—there's a considerable difference! You *are* one of our least critical cases; this I quite admit, but you are a sick man all the same."

"Well," said Giuseppe Corte, his face reddening, "well, you—on what floor would you put me?"

"Heavens, it's not that easy to say. I've given you only a cursory examination. I should have to watch your progress for a week or more before hazarding an opinion."

"Agreed. But you know more or less," persisted Corte.

The doctor pretended for a moment to lose himself in thought, allowing Corte time to compose himself; then, nodding his head, he said deliberately, "Heavens. All right, to satisfy you, we might actually put you on the sixth. Yes . . . yes," he added, as if persuading himself, "the sixth might do very well."

This, the doctor believed, would please his patient; instead, a look of dismay darkened Giuseppe Corte's face: it was apparent now that the doctors had deceived him; for here, this new one, obviously more competent and honest than the others, would *really* put him —it was perfectly clear—not on the seventh, but on the fifth, and perhaps in the *lower* fifth! His temperature that evening was high.

Giuseppe Corte's residence on the fourth floor marked his most tranquil period since his arrival at the hospital. The doctor was a particularly likable person, friendly and attentive, and on numerous occasions spent entire hours discussing a wide range of subjects with his patient. Giuseppe Corte enjoyed their sessions together, during which he sought topics relating to his accustomed life as an attorney and man of the world; he sought to convince himself that he still fitted into the company of healthy men, that he still had ties with the world of business, that he was still concerned with current happenings. All this he sought—but without success. And, unfailingly their discussions would eventually return to his disease.

Meanwhile, his desire for improvement, any improvement whatever, had become obsessive. Although the digamma rays had arrested the spread of his eczema, they had not, unfortunately, succeeded in removing it entirely. Each day Giuseppe Corte would dwell at length on this with the doctor, making at the same time an effort to appear strong, even ironical— again without success.

"Tell me, doctor," he asked one day, "how is the destructive process in my cells getting along?"

"My word, what an ugly expression!" said the doctor, gently chiding him. "Where did you ever pick that up? It is not at all seemly— not at all!—especially from a patient. Please, I don't wish to hear such talk as that again from you."

"Very well, but you haven't given me an answer yet," objected Corte.

"Oh, I shall give you an answer at once," said the doctor civilly. "The destructive pro-cess in your cells, to repeat your horrible expression, remains in your case at a minimum —at an absolute minimum. Although I might be tempted to call it obstinate."

"Obstinate—do you mean chronic?"

"You mustn't try to put words into my mouth. I mean simply obstinate. But anyway, this applies to most cases. Even the mildest of infections may often require long and vigorous treatment."

"But tell me, doctor, when may I look for some improvement?"

"When? . . . Really, predictions in these cases are somewhat difficult to make. . . . But look," he added after a reflective pause, "I notice that you have a real mania to recover . . . and if I were not afraid of making you angry I would offer you a little advice—"

"Please, doctor, don't hesitate. . . ."

"Very well, then. I shall put it in the clearest possible terms. If I had this disease of yours— even the very mildest form of it—and found myself in this sanatorium, which is perhaps the best anywhere, I would ask on the very first day—on the very first day, mind you—to be assigned to one of the lower floors. I would see to it that I was sent directly to the—"

"First?" suggested Corte with a forced smile.

"Oh, no, not to the first!" replied the doctor, gently ironic, "my word, no. But to the third or even, certainly, to the second. I guarantee you that the treatment down there is vastly superior, the facilities are more complete, more efficacious, the personnel more competent. You're aware, of course, who the guiding spirit of the hospital is?"

"Professor Dati, isn't it?"

"Quite true, Professor Dati. It was he who devised the method that is practiced here, he who designed the entire hospital. . . . Well, Professor Dati, the master himself, is located, so to speak, between the first and second floors. His force as director radiates from that point. But I assure you, his influence does not extend up beyond the third floor; above the third, one might say that even his orders diminish, lose consistency, go astray. The heart of the hospital is downstairs, and downstairs is where one must be to receive the best treatment."

"In other words," said Giuseppe Corte, his voice quavering, "you recommend—"

"Consider one other thing," the doctor ran on dauntlessly, "consider that in your particular case there is your eczema that would need attention. A matter of no importance, I assure you, but rather irksome, and something which, in time, could weaken your morale; and you, of course, recognize that serenity of mind is essential to recovery. The digamma-ray treatments which I have been giving you have been only partially successful. Now why? It may be pure chance; however, it may be that the rays have not been sufficiently intense. Well, then, the apparatus down on the third floor is considerably more powerful. The likelihood of getting rid of your eczema would be vastly increased. Then, once recovery has begun, you see, you have already cleared the most difficult hurdle. Once you have started up, it's quite unlikely that you'll slip back again. When you really feel better, there is nothing to prevent your rising back to us or still higher, according to your 'merits,' to the fifth, sixth—even, I daresay, to the seventh—"

"And you believe that this would really hasten the cure?"

"Why, there can be no doubt of it! I have already told you what I should do if *I* were in your shoes."

The doctor presented arguments of this nature daily. And the moment ultimately came when the patient, no longer able to endure the eczema, and notwithstanding an instinctive reluctance to descend to the realm of even more serious cases, decided to act upon the doctor's advice and was transferred to the floor below.

As soon as he arrived, he detected in the ward a special note of gaiety, in both the nurses and the attending doctor, despite the fact that there, on the third floor, cause for concern about the patients under treatment was a good deal greater. In fact, with each passing day he

remarked that the gaiety increased: his curiosity aroused, he waited a while, until he had gained a degree of confidence in the nurse, and then asked her why it was that they were all so gay.

"Oh, don't you know?" answered the nurse. "In three days we're going on vacation."

"Vacation?"

"Yes. For fifteen days the third floor will be closed down and the staff is to be let off. Each floor takes its turn."

"But the patients, what about them?"

"There are relatively few, so two floors will be combined."

"You mean they'll put the patients of the third and fourth floors together?"

"No, no," said the nurse, correcting him: "the third and second. The patients up here will all be sent downstairs."

"Downstairs?" said Corte, pale as clay. "You mean, then, that I'll have to go down to the second?"

"Of course. Is there anything so unusual about that? When we come back, in a fortnight's time, you'll all return to your rooms up here. It doesn't seem such a dreadful thing to me."

Yet Giuseppe Corte—some mysterious instinct gave him notice—was assailed by fear. But since he could scarcely prevent the staff from taking its vacation, and convinced that the new digamma-ray treatments were proving beneficial—his eczema had almost completely cleared up—he did not dare object to the new transfer. However, when he reached the second floor he insisted, despite the nurses' banter, on having a notice tacked to the door that read: GIUSEPPE CORTE OF THE THIRD FLOOR—TRANSIENT.

This delusion of his was without precedent in the history of the sanatorium, but the doctors said nothing, fully aware that in a nervous temperament such as Corte's the slightest annoyance was liable to produce shock.

It was a question now merely of waiting for fifteen days—not one day more or one day less. Giuseppe Corte set to counting them with dogged avidity as he lay abed, motionless for hours on end, his eyes focused on the furniture which, on that floor, was not modern and gay as in the upper wards, but was heavier, more solemn and severe in style. And occasionally he pricked up his ears, for he seemed to hear from the floor below—from the floor of the dying, the "death cell"—the indistinct rattle of death throes.

All this, naturally, had a tendency to depress him. And his increased uneasiness seemed to aggravate his illness: his temperature rose, his debility sank to new depths. From the window —it was now midsummer and the window was nearly always open—neither the rooftops nor any of the houses of the city were visible: only the green wall of trees surrounding the hospital.

Seven days passed. One afternoon around two, the chief attendant and three nurses pushing a stretcher suddenly entered. "Well, are we ready for the transfer?" asked the attendant in a tone of good-natured jest.

"What transfer?" asked Corte in a pinched voice. "What sort of joke is this? Don't those of us of the third floor still have a week before being sent back?"

"The third floor?" said the chief attendant, as if not quite understanding. "I have instructions to take you to the first. Look." And he held out a printed form ordering the patient's transfer to the floor below. It was signed by no less a personage than Professor Dati himself.

All Giuseppe Corte's terror and uncontainable fury erupted into a long outburst that echoed down through the ward. "Calm yourself. For goodness' sake, calm yourself!" the nurses entreated. "There are other patients here who are not well." But that alone could hardly have been expected to quiet him.

Finally he noticed the doctor in charge of the ward, a very kind and well-mannered person. Informed of the transfer, he looked at the form and asked Corte what was happening. Then he turned angrily to the chief attendant and declared that there was some mistake, that he had not given any order to this effect, that for some time there had been an insufferable amount of confusion, and that he was kept completely in the dark about everything. . . . Having thus taken his subordinate to task, he turned politely to Corte, begging him to accept his deepest apologies.

"Unfortunately, however," added the doctor, "unfortunately, Professor Dati left only an hour ago on a short holiday and will not be back for a couple of days. I am very, very sorry about this, but the Professor's orders cannot be countermanded. I assure you, though, he will be the first deplore such an error! I can't understand how it could have happened!"

By now Giuseppe Corte was in the throes of a pitiable fit of trembling. He had lost complete control of himself. He was like a child, terror had so overwhelmed him. His sobs filled the room.

And thus, by virtue of a monstrous error, he arrived at the last station. In the ward of the dying, he who actually, in light of his condition, according even to the diagnoses of the most uncompromising doctors, ought to have been assigned to the sixth, if not the seventh floor! The situation was so grotesque, really, that he felt at times a desire to roar with laughter.

The heat of the summer's afternoon crept slowly across the city. Lying abed, he gazed at the green of the trees through the window, with the sensation of having arrived in an unreal world, a world created of absurd sterilized-tile walls, of cold mortuary passages, of white soulless figures. He had even a notion that the trees, which he thought he discerned through the window, were also unreal: he became finally convinced of it, in fact, after noticing that the leaves did not move.

This idea so upset him that he rang for the nurse and asked to be given his glasses, which he did not normally wear in bed; only then was he able to set his mind a little at rest: aided by his glasses, he was able to establish that the trees, after all, were real, and that the leaves, if ever so slightly, occasionally did flutter a little in the thin breeze.

After the nurse left, a quarter-hour of deep silence ensued. Six floors, six terrible walls, although the result simply of a clerical error, lay upon Giuseppe Corte with their implacable weight. How many years—yes, now he must really think in terms of years—how many years would it take to regain the heights of that precipice?

But why now had the room suddenly begun to darken? It was still midafternoon. With great effort, for he felt himself to be paralyzed by a curious languor, Giuseppe Corte looked at his watch which lay on the night table beside the bed. It was three-thirty. Then he turned, facing the other way. He saw that the blinds, obedient to some mysterious command, were slowly drawing to, shutting off the light.

I
SLOW RETREAT FROM THE WORLD

To be frightened and uneasy in the sterile, strange world of a hospital is a very human trait. Most readers are intrigued, yet horrified, by the persuasive arguments of the medical personnel that lead Corte step by step downward toward the first floor. The persuasions run the gamut from appeals to his generosity, to suggestions that he will get better care, to possible administrative blunders. The reader watches fascinated as Corte allows himself to be moved further and further from the world.

II
IMPLICATIONS

What ideas do the following statements trigger for you?

1. The story can be interpreted literally or symbolically.

2. The disease you think of first in reading the story is the thing most troubling you at the time you read it.

3. We tend to change and become the way we are classified by others.

4. There is no good reason why Corte does not simply walk out and leave the sanatorium.

5. Corte is really destroyed by his own fear of the first floor.

6. There are indications that Corte is personally insecure.

III
TECHNIQUES

Selection of Incident

The story is built around Corte's six moves to lower floors in the hospital. How are the reasons for these handled so that they do not become monotonous for the reader?

Organization

Which of the following dominates the external organization of the story: the characters, the setting, the theme?

SUMMING UP
Know Thyself
THE MASKS OF THE SELF

The stories and essays in this section have shown that to "know thyself" is not a simple process. It is a continuing challenge that deepens and broadens as one moves through life. We have seen men and women who had a false concept of themselves, and so fell into misadventures. We have seen others who came to grips with a decision, and in the course of making the decision gained new knowledge of themselves. Other selections have reflected minds that have found peace through sound self-evaluation. Once people know and accept themselves for what they are, they open the road to a rewarding life, for they can operate securely and successfully within their known limits.

Where in this theme, KNOW THYSELF, have the authors presented characters who exemplify the following situations?

1. People who discover that they cannot act against their inner nature.

2. People who attempt to build up their own egos.

3. People who do not really know themselves.

4. People who discover something about themselves that they did not previously know.

5. People who truly know themselves.

IMPLICATIONS

How do the selections in this section either support or negate these statements?

1. People try to hide their weaknesses even from themselves.

2. Knowledge of self is essential to be a free person.

3. Learning about one's self can change behavior.

4. Self-knowledge gives a person confidence in facing a crisis.

5. To know oneself completely is an impossible task.

TECHNIQUES

In discussing the following questions, refer to the selections in this section.

Selection of Incident

1. Which selections are stripped down to a bare minimum of incident? Which selections are jammed with incident? Do you prefer one kind of writing to another? Why?

2. Choosing one or two selections, show how the selection of incidents affected the mood of the piece.

3. Which selection in this theme seemed the most tightly plotted? That is, in which does everything selected seem absolutely necessary to the movement of the writing?

Organization

1. In the preceding group of selections, which stories present events in chronological order? Which selections use a "stream-of-consciousness" pattern?

2. Which stories employ the flashback technique?

3. Take one of the essays, and make an outline of it. In the course of making the outline, do you learn something about the structure of the essay which you had not seen in reading it?

IV
WRITING FROM READING

1. Look back at the Priestley essays. Pick one of the topics he wrote about or select some small but important pleasure in your own life such as getting a good grade, making a team, the smell of a particular season or time of day, a sight you always enjoy, etc. Write a short essay in which you try to present exactly what there is about this particular thing that gives you delight.

2. Write a list of twenty or more statements about yourself. Include your height, weight, strengths, weaknesses, your likes and dislikes, your relationships with other people, etc. Then ask yourself in writing whether this list sums you up? What is left out?

3. Imagine that you have metamorphosed into an insect, reptile, animal, bird, or fish. Write a description of yourself as you discover your new form. Choose the incidents to show the problems and advantages of your new shape.

Handbook of
Literary Terms

Definitions given here refer only to the meaning of the word as related to works of literature.

Abstract Terms: Terms that describe ideas, concepts, qualities, or generalities as opposed to *concrete terms* which refer to concrete or specific objects. For example, *martyr* is an idea or concept (an abstract term); *girl* is a generalization; *Joan of Arc* is a concrete term. The language of science and philosophy frequently uses abstract terms, whereas literature tends to use more concrete language, such as is seen in metaphor and image.

Absurd, Theater of the: A kind of drama that presents life as ridiculous and unreal. It usually depends on strange settings, distorted dialogue, and mindless plots that create a sense of madness. Instead of a logical story line, it uses a series of images that show people confused and struggling in a chaotic, uncaring, incomprehensible world. The first true example of *The Theater of the Absurd* was Eugene Ionesco's *The Bald Soprano* (1950). Other playwrights attracted to the movement are Jean Cocteau, Samuel Beckett, Edward Albee, Harold Pinter, and Luigi Pirandello.

Act: A main division of a play, usually indicating a stage in the unfolding development of the action. In the time of Shakespeare, dramas followed the classic Greek and Roman tradition of five acts. In the twentieth century, the most usual division has been three acts. Late in the nineteenth century a new form developed, the one-act play.

Allegory: An extended metaphor, usually a narrative, in which objects and persons refer to meaning outside the narrative. *The Faerie Queene* and *Pilgrim's Progress* are both allegories. Allegory differs from *symbolism* which also suggests other levels of meaning but does not structure the whole narrative to carry the extended meaning. Parables, fables, apologue, and exemplum are some of the possible kinds of allegories.

Alliteration: Repetition of the same initial consonant or vowel sounds in words that appear in fairly close order.

Allusion: A brief and often indirect reference to a famous historical or literary event or person. Allusion is used to enhance the meaning of a passage by evoking other associations.

Amphitheater: An oval or round structure or sloping ground rising outward from an open space at the center.

Anapest: A three-syllable poetic foot consisting of two unaccented syllables followed by one accented syllable.

Archaic: From an earlier period, and rare in current times.

Archetype: An image, type, or story pattern that has occurred so frequently in myth, religion, or folklore that it arouses associations in the unconscious that create strong, though perhaps illogical, responses. Northrop Frye defines it as "a symbol, usually an image, which recurs often enough in literature to be recognizable as an element of one's literary experience as a whole."

Assonance: Similarity in sound of vowels followed by different consonants. It differs from *rhyme* which has the vowel and consonant alike. *Mate* and *fate* rhyme; *pain* and *maim* have assonance.

Atmosphere: The prevailing mood or tone a piece of literature creates in the reader's mind.

Autobiography: The narration of a person's life story written by the individual.

Balanced Sentence: A sentence in which parts are set one against the other by position so as to emphasize a contrast in meaning. (*The higher one climbs, the farther the fall.*)

Ballad: A verse narrative (often sung) that has come down through the oral tradition. A ballad is usually composed in a four-line stanza with a refrain that adds stress and impact.

Biography: An account of a person's life written by another individual. In some, the writer attempts to use only facts and documented materials. In others, the biographer imagines the subject's actions, speeches, or even thoughts in the various situations of the subject's life.

Blank Verse: A characteristic English form of poetry, blank verse consists of unrhymed lines of five iambic feet. It is perhaps the most flexible meter in English poetry. Blank verse was used by Shakespeare in his plays.

Caesura: A pause in a verse line, usually near the middle.

Canto: A section of a long narrative poem.

Catalogue: To list details one after another in order to illustrate a point.

Catharsis: The release of emotions that have been building up within the spectator while watching the struggle of a tragic hero.

Characterization: The word portrait of a person in a piece of writing created by (1) direct description, (2) the character's actions and words, and (3) what others say about that person. Also *Character Development*.

Chorus: One or more persons in a play who comment on the action that is taking place. The stage manager in the drama *Our Town* is an example of a modern chorus figure.

Chronological Organization: An ordering of the happenings in a literary selection according to the time they occurred, beginning with the earliest and coming up to the latest.

Classics: The literature of ancient Greece and Rome; or literature that imitates its qualities; or literature that has gained a lasting recognition (usually works written before 1900).

Classic Unities: Principles of dramatic construction

emerging from the ancient Greek theater in regard to *time, place,* and *action.* These principles stated that time represented in a play should not exceed 24 hours, that setting should be in a single place, and that action should deal with only one event.

Climax: The point of highest interest and greatest audience emotional response. It may also be the turning point of the action in which the conflicting issues are resolved toward one possible action. In drama, climax designates the turning point in the action's intensity, the point at which the action reverses from rising action to falling action.

Colloquial: Informal conversational use of language which is not acceptable in more formal speech or writing.

Comedy: A narrative or drama, intended to amuse the audience and usually ending happily.

Commedia Dell'arte: Italian improvised comedy, based on a plot outline and stock characters.

Concrete Terms: The opposite of *abstract terms,* generally using specific or particular words to describe something that has actual existence and can be seen or heard or touched.

Conflict: The struggle that grows out of the interplay of two or more forces in a story. This struggle may be against other people, against nature, or within the character. Without conflict, there is no drama, interest, or suspense.

Connotations: The emotional sensations or images that a word brings to mind as opposed to its dictionary or *denotational* meaning.

Convention: A device, style, or subject that has through repeated use become an accepted technique. Examples of convention are the stanza form, a soliloquy in a play, or the use of stock characters.

Couplet: Two lines of verse with end-rhymes. The heroic couplet is two lines of rhymed iambic pentameter. Dryden and Pope used this form.

Critic: One who estimates and passes judgment on the value and quality of literary works.

Dactyl: A three-syllable poetic foot consisting of one accented syllable followed by two unaccented syllables.

Denotation: The literal, exact meaning of a word that excludes its emotional associations. See *Connotations.*

Densely Plotted: A narrative or drama with a plot that contains a great number of incidents.

Description: One of the four types of composition (*argument, exposition, narration,* and *description*). It is most effective when its details are selected with a purpose and point of view in mind and when its images are clear and definite. The words of color, sound, and motion should capture the view or sensation for the reader.

Dialect: A regional variety of a language distinguished from others by slight variations in pronunciation, grammar, and vocabulary. Dialect is usually caused by geographical, cultural, or ethnic factors.

Dialogue: Conversation between two or more people in a piece of writing.

Diction: The choice and use of words in speech or writing. A simple list of words is vocabulary, but the accurate use of words to express a particular, specific meaning is good diction.

Didacticism: A characteristic of a literary work whose main purpose is to give guidance in moral, ethical, or religious matters.

Drama: The necessary elements of a drama are a story, told in action, and dialogue by players who impersonate the characters of the story. All drama developed from religious ceremonies. *Comedy* grew out of the Greek Dionysian rites celebrating fertility; *tragedy* arose from the Dionysian rites dealing with life and death; the Medieval drama began in rites honoring events of the Christian religion.

Dramatic Irony: See *Irony.*

Dramatic Monologue: A lyric poem that catches a character in a dramatic situation. The inner workings of the speaker's mind are revealed through the words spoken or thought. There is a clearly identified, silent person who is being addressed. An example is Browning's "My Last Duchess," p. 478.

Elegy: A formal, poetic lament for the dead.

Empathy: A literal projection of the reader into the physical and emotional sensations of a character, such as subconsciously flexing one's muscles when reading about great physical exertion.

End-Stopped: A verse line in which the grammatical structure and the meaning are completed at the end of the line.

Epic: A long narrative poem about a great hero on whose actions depends the fate of a nation or race. The story line for the epics may have been drawn from the pool of stories sung or told during the time when the oral tradition was the most important way of recording literature. Even this type of *folk epic* was eventually written down by one individual, even though the person's name is now unknown. *Beowulf* is an example of this type. Homer is the known author of two important epics, *The Odyssey* and *The Illiad.*

Epigram: Any succinct, pointed saying such as "Man proposes, but God disposes." The word in ancient Greece meant an inscription, especially an epitaph. Then it grew to mean a poem summing up the heart of an inscription. Hence it grew to mean a compressed, pointed, clear comment. Ben Jonson is considered one of the greatest writers of epigrams in the English language.

Essay: A brief, nonfictional prose discussion of a restricted topic. Literally, it is an "attempt." Essays are often divided into the formal and the informal. The formal are sober, serious, dignified, and logical. The informal tend to be personal, narrative, and often humorous.

Exemplum: A tale or anecdote used by medieval preachers and some later writers to point out a moral or to illustrate a doctrine. "Jeannot and Colin" (p. 393) is an example of an exemplum.

Existentialism: A body of ethical thought that centers about the uniqueness and isolation of individual experience in a universe which is indifferent or even hostile to human beings. It regards human existence as unexplainable while emphasizing the freedom of choice and responsibility for the consequences of one's acts. Sartre and Ionesco are *existentialists*.

Exposition: In drama, the introductory section that gives the audience necessary background information.

Farce: A comic drama with exaggerated characters, broad humor, and a complicated plot.

Fiction: A piece of writing created by the writer's imagination. It is most often prose, such as short stories, novels, and dramas, though epics and narrative poems may also be considered forms of fiction.

First Person Narrative: A story or poem in which the narrator is a character or an observer. It can be identified by the use of the first person pronouns *I* and *we*.

Flashback: Scenes or incidents in a narrative that happen prior to the opening scene and interrupt the chronological order.

Flat Character: A character who is presented with a single or very limited set of qualities, sometimes called *two-dimensional*.

Foot: A unit of rhythm in a verse line, usually with one stressed and one or more unstressed syllables.

Form: The style, the diction, the organization of a piece of writing as separated from its subject matter.

Formal Writing: Serious, dignified, logically organized writing.

Genre: Literally, "kind" or "type." A literary form such as the novel or a larger category such as tragedy.

Gothic: Reference to a literary type characterized by mystery, magic, horror, and often romance.

Hero/Heroine: The central character in a work of fiction or drama, and the focal point of a reader's or spectator's concern. May be referred to as the *protagonist*.

Hexameter: A verse line of six metrical feet.

Humor: One of two major types of writing (wit and humor) which is intended to create laughter. The term came from an early medical theory that the four fluids (humours) in the body controlled one's disposition and if not balanced could create eccentric behavior. From such behavior came the meaning of today's word.

Hyperbole: An exaggerated statement as a figure of speech.

Iamb: A two-syllable poetic foot consisting of one unaccented syllable followed by one accented syllable.

Identification: The entering into the very being of a character so that the reader experiences vicariously the same feelings as the character.

Imagery: Concrete sensory description, frequently extended to nonsensory objects.

Incident: An individual event that when strung together with others constitutes a narrative.

Irony: Occurs when an effect is produced that is different from what might have been expected. In *verbal irony*, the intended meaning of words contrasts sharply with their literal meaning. In *dramatic irony,* the audience or reader knows something that the character does not; therefore, speeches and actions are understood differently by the audience than by the characters. In fiction, irony is often produced when the actions of a character lead that character progressively further away from a desired goal, as in Hardy's "To Please His Wife" (p. 270).

Latinate: Literally, derived from Latin; hence, often long and difficult words.

Lyric: A kind of poetry that explores emotions and sensations, is generally brief, and creates a single impression for the reader. The word itself comes from the word *lyre*, a musical instrument, and the sound patterns of this poetry often come close to sounding like music.

Melodrama: A plot that is developed through heavy use of suspense and sensational episodes, with little regard to motivations. The aim is to keep the audience on tenterhooks of emotion, such as joy, pity, horror, or anger.

Metaphor: A figure of speech in which a comparison is implied between two essentially unlike things.

Meter: Regular rhythmic pattern in poetry.

Mock-Heroic: A grand literary style used for trivial subject matter.

Modern: Generally refers to writing of the twentieth century, which, characteristically, may break with the old, accepted forms, may emphasize individual experimentation, and may use psychological methods to explore disillusionment or alienation.

Mood: The tone that prevails in a piece of literature—humorous, serious, lighthearted, etc.

Morality Play: A form of poetic drama which developed in the late fourteenth century and differed from the other religious plays by having abstract virtues and vices such as mercy, shame, greed, and contentment presented as characters struggling for the souls of human beings.

Narrator: The person telling a story. Sometimes it is a character in the story; other times it is the author.

Nobel Prize: A monetary award made annually in each of six fields. One Nobel Prize is given for the most eminent piece of literature. The prize, first awarded in 1901, was made possible by a Swedish chemist and engineer, Alfred Bernhard Nobel.

Novel: An extended prose-fiction narrative having a central plot.

Objectivity: The attempt on the part of writers to keep their personal sentiments and opinions out of their writing. It gives a quality of impersonality to the work.

Octave: The first eight lines of an Italian sonnet.

Ode: An enthusiastic, exalted, lyrical verse dealing with a dignified theme.

Onomatopoeia: A word so formed that it sounds like the thing to which it refers. Examples are *moo, buzz,* and *snap*.

Parody: A composition that burlesques or satirizes a serious work by a ridiculous imitation.

Pastoral: A poem about the shepherds and rustic life, often highly romanticized.

Pentameter: A verse line of five metrical feet.

Personification: A figure of speech in which inanimate or nonhuman figures are given human attributes.

Playwright: Literally, a maker of plays; one who writes plays.

Plot: A series of interrelated actions progressing from a beginning through a series of happenings to a logical and natural outcome.

Point of View: The term describes the point of observation the author is using in the story. If the writer acts as all-knowing and is free to move about in time and place and make comments at will, the point of view is called *omniscient*. If the writer uses a character in the story to tell the incidents from observation, own thoughts, or previous or present knowledge of events, it is called a *first person narrator* point of view. The writer may also choose to write the story in the third person from one character's point of view, and this is labeled a *limited* point of view.

Prologue: A preface or introduction most frequently used in a drama.

Prose: A literary piece of writing that does not have meter or rhythm. It states its ideas in a connected way, has a particular style springing from its author's abilities and choices, and depends on diction and sentence structure to create variety. The purposes of the various types of prose writing control the way it is written. In all cultures, prose has developed more slowly than verse.

Prose Style: Style is to writing what personality is to a human being. Words like *plain, ornate, crisp,* or *earthy* are sometimes used to describe a particular style of writing. A style may be described by counting length of sentences, choice of nouns and verbs, number of modifiers, etc., but this method is seldom used.

Psychological Organization: A pattern of narration following the thoughts of characters rather than their external movements.

Purpose: The intent of a work, such as to amuse, to terrify, to mystify, to arouse pity, to instruct, etc.

Quatrain: A four-line stanza, often rhymed *a b a b*.

Realism: A movement in literature in the nineteenth century that arose in reaction to romanticism. It demands "the truthful treatment of materials," generally centering on the surface details, ordinary actions, and minor catastrophes of middle-class society. The realist concentrates on the here and now—on specific actions and consequences that can be verified by experience. The realist tries to find the scientific laws controlling the action in contrast to the romanticist who rises above the moment to find the ideal.

Realistic Drama: Plays in which the characters, the setting, and the action purport to be like those found in real life. The movement in England began in the last decades of the nineteenth century. Inspired by Ibsen and French playwrights, Pinero and Galsworthy began writing problem plays for the British stage while Wilde and Shaw lightened the theater-goer's fare with their witty comedies and biting satire.

Refrain: A group of words, usually a phrase or a sentence, repeated at intervals in a poem, usually at the end of a stanza.

Renaissance: Literally, rebirth. The period in English literature from 1500 to 1642.

Rhyme: Similar or identical sounds at the end of words.

Rhyme Scheme: The pattern of rhymes in a stanza or poem, indicated by letters. Thus, the rhyme scheme for the couplet is *a a*.

Rhythm: A systematic repetition of elements in writing by sound, by words, and even by events.

Romantic Period: In English literature, the period 1798–1832.

Round Character: A character who has many, often contradictory, qualities; sometimes called *three-dimensional*.

Run-on Lines: A line of poetry in which the grammatical structure and the meaning continue into the next verse line.

Satire: A work written with a critical attitude, with humor, and with wit in the hope of bringing about a change in human institutions or human foibles.

Scansion: The process of dividing verse into metric feet by noting the accented and unaccented syllables thus determining the meter of a poem.

Scene: In English drama, a scene is defined as continuous action in an unchanged locality. In French drama, a scene consists of a continuous grouping of characters; whenever a character enters or exits, the scene changes.

Semantics: The study of meaning; the relationship between a sign (usually a word) and what it means.

Sestet: The last six lines of an Italian sonnet.

Set: The scenery, properties, etc., used on a stage as a background for a play. The materials may be realistic or abstract.

Setting: The physical location of the events in a narration. Setting may include the geographical location, the socioeconomic background, the historical period, and the cultural environment. One approach to literary study insists that fiction is made up of four parts: setting, plot, characterization, and effect.

Short Story: A short fictional narrative using a limited number of characters and built around a single incident or issue designed to produce a single effect.

Simile: A figure of speech in which a comparison between two unlike things is expressed using the word *like* or *as*.

Slant Rhyme: An imperfect rhyme, a common device

of contemporary poetry. Usually assonance or consonance is deliberately used.

Soliloquy: A speech, usually in a play, delivered by the character alone on the stage and intended to reveal to the audience what he or she is thinking or to give information which is important for understanding the action.

Sonnet: A lyric poem of fourteen lines that follows a conventional pattern. The two most important forms are the Italian sonnet (*abbaabbacdecde*) and the English sonnet (*ababcdcdefefgg*). Renaissance poets (and later ones) often wrote a sequence of sonnets, frequently chronicling a love story.

Speaker: The imagined voice that is telling the story or poem; in dialogue, the character who is speaking.

Spondee: A two-syllable poetic foot consisting of two accented syllables.

Stage Action: The movements and gestures of actors on a stage during a scene.

Stanza: A grouping of two or more verse lines in a poem; the pattern of a stanza is formed by the length of the lines, the rhythm, the meter, and the rhyme scheme.

Stock Character: A conventional character with prescribed characteristics that the reader recognizes in given forms of literature: in fairy tales, the cruel stepmother and Prince Charming; in Shakespeare's works, the disguised romantic heroine, the buffoon, the witty fool; in Gothic romances, the beautiful but poor and virtuous heroine. Every type of fiction and drama—romances, detective stories, comedy, space fiction—develop their own stock characters.

Stream of Consciousness: A form of writing that attempts to follow the uninterrupted, uneven, and endless flow of thoughts of one or more of the characters.

Subplot: This is a secondary or minor story which may have a direct relationship to the central plot explaining or expanding it or may simply be extraneous and introduced for zest or emphasis. At times, writers create three and four subplots which may be called *multiple plots*. See Act III, Scenes 1 and 2, and also p. 374, *The Miser*.

Subtext: In drama, the emotion of meaning implied by the dialogue, assisted by gesture and tone, which is not the literal meaning of the words themselves. See Act I, Scene 5, P. 343, *The Miser*.

Symbol: An image which both stands for itself and evokes an abstract meaning.

Tale: At one time no distinction was made between tale and short story, but today *tale* is used rather loosely for any short narrative, either true or fictitious, and *short story* for a piece that is more consciously constructed.

Theme: The dominant idea, perception, or impression that a work of literature conveys through its characters, images, and action. Usually the theme is not stated directly. This text has grouped selections according to a dominant theme expressed in them. Each adds a new facet or dimension to the reader's understanding of the theme.

Tone: The pitch or quality of voice that the reader imagines the author is using in speaking about the subject. The tone might be loud, soft, happy, somber, angry, bored, etc. The writer conveys tone by rhythm, choice of words, images, length of sentences, and even punctuation. Tone may also be used to describe the writer's attitude toward the reader.

Tragedy: A drama that deals with casually related events that lead to catastrophe for a person of importance, usually destroying the protagonist. See *Antigone*, p. 4.

Tragic Flaw: The defect or imperfection in the tragic hero which leads to that character's downfall. See *Antigone*, p. 5, column 2.

Trochee: A two-syllable poetic foot consisting of one accented syllable followed by one unaccented syllable.

Villain: A character in a narrative or drama who is capable of base acts or is already the perpetrator of such and who opposes the hero. In a drama, the villain is called the *antagonist*.

Glossary

This Glossary contains those relatively common yet difficult words used in the selections contained in this book. Many of the words occur two or more times in the book. The definitions are in accord with how the words are used in the selections.

Technical, archaic, obscure, and foreign words are footnoted with the selections as they occur.

The pronunciation symbols used in this Glossary follow the system used in the Thorndike/Barnhart *Advanced Dictionary* (1979). For words having more than one pronunciation, the first pronunciation is the one used here, and regional pronunciations may therefore vary from some pronunciations in this Glossary.

Syllable division and stress marks for primary and secondary accent marks used in the pronunciations also follow the system used in the *Advanced Dictionary*, including the practice of putting stress marks after the syllables stressed.

The following abbreviations are used to indicate parts of speech:

n.	noun
v.	verb
adj.	adjective
adv.	adverb

abate (ə bāt′) *v.* Put an end to; stop.

abhorrence (ab hôr′əns) *n.* A feeling of loathing; revulsion.

abides (ə bīdz′) *v.* Remains or stays.

abjure (ab jür′) *v.* Deny or give up.

abominations (ə bom′ə nā′shənz) *n.* Things that arouse strong disgust.

absorption (ab sôrp′shən) *n.* Great interest in something.

abstinent (ab′stə nənt) *adj.* Very plain; restricted.

abstractedly (ab strak′id lē) *adv.* Absent-mindedly; in a preoccupied manner.

abstractions (ab strak′shənz) *n.* Ideas, beliefs, questions, etc.

abstrusest (ab strüs′əst) *adj.* Most hard to understand; most difficult.

absurdities (ab sėr′də tēz) *n.* Senseless or ridiculous practices or ideas.

absurdity (ab sėr′də tē) *n.* Condition of being ridiculous; senseless.

abyss (ə bis′) *n.* Chasm; anything too deep to be measured.

accelerating (ak sel′ə rāt′ing) *v.* Speeding up; hastening.

accentuate (ak sen′chü āt) *v.* Emphasize or stress.

accomplice (ə kom′plis) *n.* A person who helps another in wrongdoing.

accrue (ə krü′) *v.* Increase gradually, like the interest on money.

accusations (ak′yə zā′shənz) *n.* Charges of wrongdoing.

acquiescence (ak′wē es′ns) *n.* Consent given without making objections; agreement.

adamant (ad′ə mənt) *adj.* Firm and unyielding; immovable.

adherents (ad hir′ənts) *n.* Faithful supporters or followers; allies.

admonition (ad′mə nish′ən) *n.* Earnest advice; a warning.

admonitions (ad′mə nish′ənz) *n.* Advice against something; gentle scolding or reproof.

adroitness (ə droit′nəs) *n.* Resourcefulness in reaching one's objective; skillfulness.

adversaries (ad′vər ser′ēz) *n.* Persons opposing or resisting another or others; opponents; enemies.

adversity (ad vėr′sə tē) *n.* Misfortune; hardship; distress.

advocate (ad′və kit) *n.* A person who favors or recommends a proposal, belief, etc.; a supporter.

affectation (af′ek tā′shən) *n.* Behavior that is not natural, but assumed to impress others; pretense.

agape (ə gāp′) *adj.* Open-mouthed with wonder or surprise.

aghast (ə gast′) *adj.* Struck with horror; dumbfounded; horrified.

agitation (aj′ə tā′shən) *n.* A violent moving or shaking. Also, a disturbed, upset, or troubled state.

agitator (aj′ə tā′tər) *n.* A person who stirs up public feeling for or against something.

alleged (ə lejd′) *adj.* Declared as a fact, often with the suggestion that the person's truthfulness is in question.

allocutions (al ə kyü′shənz) *n.* Encouraging remarks.

allotted (ə lot′əd) *v.* Given as a share, task, duty, etc.; assigned.

allusions (ə lü′zhənz) *n.* Act of referring indirectly to something; slight mentions; hints.

altercation (ôl′tər kā′shən) *n.* An angry dispute; a noisy quarrel.

alternately (ôl′tər nit lē) *adv.* One after the other by turns.

amateur (am′ə chər) *adj.* Being or doing something for pleasure, not for money or as a profession.

hat, āge, fär; let, ēqual, tėrm; it, īce; hot, ōpen, ôrder; oil, out; cup, půt, rüle; ch, child; ng, long; sh, she; th, thin; ŦH, then; zh, measure; ə represents *a* in about, *e* in taken, *i* in pencil, *o* in lemon, *u* in circus.

764

ambiguous (am big′yü əs) *adj*. Being so expressed that either of two meanings is possible; having more than one interpretation or explanation.

amendment (ə mend′mənt) *n*. Act of making a correction or improvement.

amends (ə mendz′) *n*. Something given or paid to make up for a wrong or an injury done; compensation.

amity (am′ə tē) *n*. Peace and friendship; friendliness.

amplifying (am′plə fī ing) *v*. Making greater, stronger, louder, etc.

amply (am′plē) *adv*. Abundantly; adequately; enough.

amulets (am′yə lits) *n*. Lockets, carved images, or other small objects worn as magic charms against evil, disease, etc.

analogous (ə nal′ə gəs) *adj*. Similar in certain qualities, circumstances, or uses; comparable.

anathemas (ə nath′ə məz) *n*. Denunciations of persons or things as evil. Also, solemn curses.

ancestral (an ses′trəl) *adj*. Of or from one's ancestors.

anguish (ang′gwish) *n*. Extreme mental pain or suffering.

anonymous (ə non′ə məs) *adj*. Whose name is not known; nameless; unknown.

anthropomorphic (an′thrə pə môr′fik) *adj*. Attributing human form or qualities to gods, animals, or things.

anticipated (an tis′ə pāt əd) *v*. Taken care of ahead of time; considered in advance.

antithesis (an tith′ə sis) *n*. The direct opposite.

apathy (ap′ə thē) *n*. Lack of interest in or desire for activity; indifference.

apothecary (ə poth′ə ker′ē) *n*. Druggist; pharmacist.

appalls (ə pôlz′) *v*. Fills with consternation and horror; terrifies.

apparition (ap′ə rish′ən) *n*. Ghost or phantom.

approbation (ap′rə bā′shən) *n*. Favorable opinion; approval.

aptitude (ap′tə tüd) *n*. Natural capacity; talent; ability.

arabesques (ar′ə besks′) *n*. Elaborate and fanciful designs of flowers, leaves, geometrical figures, etc.

arable (ar′ə bəl) *adj*. Suitable for producing crops which require plowing and tillage.

arbitrary (är′bə trer′ē) *adj*. Determined by chance.

arbitrate (är′bə trāt) *v*. Settle a dispute; give a decision.

arduous (är′jü əs) *adj*. Hard to do; requiring much effort; difficult.

arrant (ar′ənt) *adj*. Thoroughgoing; downright; complete.

arrears (ə rirz′) *n*. Behind in payments, work, etc.

artifice (är′tə fis) *n*. A clever device or trick.

asceticism (ə set′ə siz′əm) *n*. Unusual or extreme self-denial or severe discipline over oneself, especially for religious reasons.

askance (ə skans′) *adv*. With suspicion and disapproval.

asperity (a sper′ə tē) *n*. Harshness or sharpness of temper, especially as shown in tone or manner.

assailable (ə sāl′ə bəl) *adj*. Capable of being attacked and overcome.

assiduously (ə sij′ü əs lē) *adv*. Carefully and attentively; diligently.

assurance (ə shůr′əns) *n*. Certainty; confidence.

astute (ə stüt′) *adj*. Shrewd, especially with regard to one's own interests; wise.

atrocity (ə tros′ə tē) *n*. A very cruel or brutal act; monstrous wickedness or cruelty.

attenuated (ə ten′yü āt əd) *v*. Weakened or reduced.

attribute (at′rə byüt) *n*. A quality considered as belonging to a person or thing; characteristic.

audacity (ô das′ə tē) *n*. Rude boldness; impudence.

audible (ô′də bəl) *adj*. Loud enough to be heard.

augury (ô′gyər ē) *n*. Art or practice of foretelling events by interpreting such signs and omens as the flight of birds, thunder and lightning, etc.

auspices (ô′spə siz) *n*. Patronage; approval or support.

authenticity (ô′then tis′ə tē) *n*. Genuineness.

avarice (av′ər is) *n*. Too great a desire for money or property; greed for wealth.

avaricious (av′ə rish′əs) *adj*. Greatly desiring money or property; greedy for wealth.

averse (ə vèrs′) *adj*. Opposed; having a strong or fixed dislike.

avidity (ə vid′ə tē) *n*. Great eagerness.

azure (azh′ər) *n*. The clear blue color of the unclouded sky.

baffling (baf′ling) *adj*. Puzzling; bewildering.

balefully (bāl′fə lē) *adv*. In a hatefully injurious manner; woefully.

balustrade (bal′ə strād) *n*. A row of short posts or columns topped by a rail.

bandy (ban′dē) *v*. Give and take; exchange (words).

baronial (bə rō′nē əl) *adj*. Suitable for a nobleman; splendid, stately, and grand.

bearing (ber′ing) *n*. The way a person manages the whole body, including one's gestures, mannerisms, posture, and way of holding the head and the way one walks and sits.

beau (bō) *n*. A man who pays too much attention to the way he dresses and to the fashion of his clothes; a dandy.

bedecked (bi dekt′) *adj*. Decorated.

beguile (bi gīl′) *v*. While away (time) pleasantly.

behest (bi hest′) *n*. A command; an order.

belie (bi lī′) *v*. Show to be false; prove to be mistaken; give a wrong idea or impression of.

belligerents (bə lij′ər ənts) *n*. Persons engaged in waging war.

bereaved (bi rēvd′) *adj*. Being left alone and desolate; deprived.

bereavement ((bi rēv′mənt) *n*. A loss causing sorrow; loss of a relative or friend by death.

beseeching (bi sēch′ing) *v*. Begging; imploring; asking earnestly.

blasphemous (blas′fə məs) *adj*. Saying or using mocking words about God or sacred things.

blatantly (blāt′nt lē) *adv*. Outrageously; flagrantly.

boorish (bůr′ish) *adj*. Rude; ill-bred or ill-mannered.

brandished (bran′disht) *adj*. Being waved or shaken threateningly.

brevity (brev′ə tē) *n.* Shortness in speech or writing; conciseness.

brusque (brusk) *adj.* Abrupt in manner or speech; blunt.

bulwark (bủl′wərk) *n.* Person, place, or thing that is a protection.

burlesques (bər lesks′) *n.* Literary compositions that treat serious subjects in a ridiculous manner or trivial subjects as if they were important.

cadence (kād′ns) *n.* Rhythm; rise and fall of the voice.

calamitous (kə lam′ə təs) *adj.* Dreadful; ruinous.

callous (kal′əs) *adj.* Unfeeling; insensitive; hardhearted.

candidly (kan′did lē) *adj.* Frankly; straight-forwardly.

canonical (kə non′ə kəl) *adj.* Authorized; accepted; legal.

cantankerous (kan tang′kər əs) *adj.* Hard to get along with because of a nature that is ready to make trouble and oppose anything suggested; headstrong; quarrelsome.

canvassed (kan′vəst) *v.* Examined carefully; discussed.

capricious (kə prish′əs) *adj.* Likely to change suddenly without reason; changeable; fickle.

carillon (kar′ə lon) *n.* A melody played on a set of bells arranged for such playing.

carousal (kə rou′zəl) *n.* A noisy revel or drinking party.

catapult (kat′ə pult) *n.* An ancient weapon for shooting stones, arrows, etc.

celestial (sə les′chəl) *adj.* Having to do with the heavens; heavenly.

censure (sen′shər) *v.* Express disapproval of; find fault with; criticize.

certitude (sėr′tə tüd) *n.* Certainty; sureness.

chagrin (shə grin′) *n.* A feeling of disappointment, failure, or humiliation; annoyance.

chaise (shāz) *n.* A light, open carriage, usually with a folding top.

chameleon (kə mē′lē ən) *n.* A small lizard that can change the color of its skin to blend with the surroundings.

chaos (kā′os) *n.* Very great confusion; complete disorder.

chide (chīd) *v.* Reproach or blame; scold.

chignon (shē′nyon) *n.* A large knot or roll of hair worn at the back of the head by women.

chivalry (shiv′əl rē) *n.* The rules and customs of knights in the Middle Ages that included bravery, courtesy, honor, protection of the weak, etc.

chronic (kron′ik) *adj.* Lasting a long time; never stopping.

cincture (singk′chər) *n.* An encircling band of some sort such as a necklace or belt.

circumscribed (sėr′kəm skrībd′) *adj.* Limited; restricted.

citadel (sit′ə dəl) *n.* A strongly fortified place; a fortress.

cleave (klēv) *v.* Hold fast; cling.

coagulate (kō ag′yə lāt) *v.* Become more dense; thicken.

collaboration (kə lab′ə rā′shən) *n.* Act of working together.

collapse (kə laps′) *n.* A breakdown or failure.

collective (kə lek′tiv) *adj.* Taken all together; as a whole.

colloquies (kol′ə kwēz) *n.* Conversations; a talking together.

colossal (kə los′əl) *adj.* Of huge size; gigantic; vast.

comeliness (kum′lē nis) *n.* Pleasant appearance; attractiveness.

comestibles (kə mes′tə bəlz) *n.* Things to eat.

commend (kə mend′) *v.* Speak well of; praise.

commiseratingly (kə miz′ə rāt′ing lē) *adv.* Sympathetically; feelingly, for another's troubles.

commiseration (kə miz′ə rā′shən) *n.* An expression of sorrow for another's suffering or trouble; sympathy for (something).

competence (kom′pə təns) *n.* Ability; fitness.

complacently (kəm plā′snt lē) *adv.* With self-satisfaction; in a self-satisfied manner.

compromising (kom′prə mīz ing) *v.* Exposing oneself to suspicion, criticism, danger, etc.

conceivable (kən sē′və bəl) *adj.* Being imaginable; capable of being thought of.

conception (kən sep′shən) *n.* An idea; an impression.

concierge (kon′sē erzh′) *n.* A person living in an apartment who serves as doorkeeper, landlord's representative, and janitor.

conciliatory (kən sil′ē ə tôr′ē) *adj.* Tending to win over, soothe, or reconcile.

condoled (kən dōld′) *v.* Expressed sympathy for; sympathized with.

conduit (kon′dü it) *n.* A channel or pipe for carrying liquids long distances.

confiscated (kon′fə skāt əd) *v.* Took and kept.

confounded (kon found′əd) *v.* Confused; surprised and puzzled.

congruence (kən grü′əns) *n.* Harmony; agreeableness.

connive (kə nīv′) *v.* Give aid to wrongdoing by not telling about it or by helping it secretly.

conscientiously (kon′shē en′shəs lē) *adv.* Carefully, to make it right; painstakingly.

consign (kən sīn′) *v.* Hand over; put for safekeeping.

consistency (kən sis′tən sē) *n.* Firmness; stiffness.

conspiratorial (kən spir′ə tôr′ē əl) *adj.* Having to do with secret plans, plots, or intrigues.

consternation (kon′stər nā′shən) *n.* Paralyzing terror.

constituents (kən stich′ü ənts) *n.* Voters in a particular district.

constitute (kon′stə tüt) *v.* Make up; form; comprise.

contemptible (ken temp′tə bəl) *adj.* Worthless; despicable; deserving scorn; mean; low.

contrivance (kən trī′vəns) *n.* Thing invented; device.

---

hat, āge, fär; let, ēqual, tėrm; it, īce; hot, ōpen, ôrder; oil, out; cup, pùt, rüle; ch, child; ng, long; sh, she; th, thin; ᵺ, then; zh, measure; ə represents *a* in about, *e* in taken, *i* in pencil, *o* in lemon, *u* in circus.

contrived (kən trīvd') v. Planned or plotted; managed.

converted (kən vėrt'əd) v. Changed.

conveyance (kən vā'əns) n. A legal document showing transfer of ownership of property; a deed.

convulsions (kən vul'shənz) n. Spasms; violent, involuntary contracting and relaxing of the muscles.

coquette (kō ket') n. A woman who tries to attract men merely to please her vanity; a flirt.

coronets (kôr'ə nets') n. Small crowns, especially those worn by nobility below the rank of king.

corporal (kôr'pər əl) adj. Being or having a body.

corpulent (kôr'pyə lənt) adj. Large or bulky of body; fat.

counterfeit (koun'tər fit) v. Imitate; pretend.

countermanded (koun'tər mand əd) v. Withdrawn or canceled.

covetousness (kuv'ə təs nəs) adj. Desiring things that belong to others.

credulous (krej'ə ləs) adj. Too ready to believe; easily deceived.

crucial (krü'shəl) adj. Very important or decisive.

cubicle (kyü'bə kəl) n. A very small room or apartment.

culls (kulz) v. Selects; picks out.

culprits (kul'prits) n. Persons guilty of a fault or crime; offenders.

cursory (kėr'sər ē) adj. Without attention to details; hasty and superficial.

daft (daft) adj. Without sense or reason; silly; foolish. Also, crazy or insane.

dastardly (das'tərd lē) adj. Mean and cowardly; sneaking.

debility (di bil'ə tē) n. A being weak; weakness; feebleness.

deceased (di sēst') adj. No longer living; dead.

decorous (dek'ər əs) adj. Acting properly; in good taste; well-behaved; dignified.

decorum (di kôr'əm) n. Proper behavior.

decree (di krē') v. Command; order; decide.

deference (def'ər əns) n. Great respect.

deficiencies (di fish'ən sēz) n. Lack of things needed or required.

deficiency (di fish'ən sē) n. Lack of something needed or required; a shortage.

definite (def'ə nit) adj. Exact; fixed.

degenerate (di jen'ər it) adj. Showing a decline in physical, mental, or moral qualities.

deign (dān) v. Condescend to give; lower oneself.

deigned (dānd') v. Thought fit (to do something); stooped (to do something); lowered oneself.

delectable (di lek'tə bəl) adj. Very pleasing; delightful.

delirium (di lir'ē əm) n. A temporary disorder of the mind that occurs during fevers, insanity, etc., characterized by restlessness, excitement, etc.

delusive (di lü'siv) adj. Misleading the mind or judgment; deceptive.

demur (di mėr') v. Take exception; raise objections.

denounce (di nouns') v. Give information against; accuse. Also, express strong disapproval of.

deplore (di plôr') v. Regret deeply.

depositions (dep'ə zish'əns) n. Sworn statements in writing.

depravity (di prav'ə tē) n. Wickedness; extremely bad behavior.

depreciating (di prē'shē āt ing) v. Lessening or lowering the value of.

desecrated (des'ə krāt əd) adj. Being treated with scorn and disrespect; ruined.

desiccated (des'ə kāt əd) adj. Shriveled and dried up.

despondence (di spon'dəns) n. Discouragement; dejection.

despondent (di spon'dənt) adj. Discouraged; dejected.

desultorily (des'əl tôr'ə lē) adv. In a manner lacking aim or method; aimlessly.

deterred (di tėrd') v. Discouraged or prevented from acting or proceeding as planned.

deviates (dē'vē āts) v. Turns aside.

devotees (dev'ə tēz) n. Persons who are strongly devoted to something; enthusiasts.

diffident (dif'ə dənt) adj. Lacking self-confidence; shy; bashful.

digressed (də grest') v. Turned aside from the main subject; wandered from.

dilapidated (də lap'ə dā'tid) adj. Fallen into ruin or disrepair; shabby.

dilemma (də lem'ə) n. A difficult choice; a predicament. Also, a situation requiring a choice between two alternatives, which are or appear equally unfavorable.

diminutive (də min'yə tiv) adj. Very small; tiny; minute.

direst (dīr'əst) adj. The most dreadful, fearful, or terrible.

discernment (də zėrn'mənt) n. Keeness in seeing and understanding.

disconcerted (dis'kən sėrt'əd) adj. Being taken unawares; disturbed so suddenly or so badly as to lose for a moment one's self-possession.

disconsolate (dis kon'sə lit) adj. Without hope; forlorn; unhappy.

disdain (dis dān') n. A feeling of scorn; contempt.

dismays (dis māz') v. Troubles greatly; makes afraid.

disoriented (dis ôr'ē ən təd) adj. Losing one's bearings; confused as to time, place, identity, etc.

disparaging (dis par'ij ing) v. Speaking slightingly of; belittling.

disparity (dis par'ə tē) n. Lack of equality; the difference.

dispense (dis pens') v. Distribute; give out.

dispersed (dis pėrst') adj. Scattered in all directions.

dissection (di sek'shən) n. Act of cutting apart an animal, plant, etc., in order to examine or study the structure.

dissembling (di sem'bəl ing) adj. Hiding one's real feelings, thoughts, plans, etc.; pretending.

dissension (di sen'shən) n. Disagreement in opinion that produces strife; discord.

distemper (dis tem'pər) n. An infectious disease of dogs and other animals.

distinguished (dis ting'gwisht) adj. A being set off from others of the same kind because of outstanding qualities; famous; well-known.

distraught (dis trôt′) *adj.* Very distressed; distracted; frantic.

divination (div′ə nā′shən) *n.* Act of foreseeing the future or discovering what is hidden or obscure by supernatural or magical means.

dogma (dôg′mə) *n.* Any system of principles; doctrine.

dogmatic (dôg mat′ik) *adj.* Positive and emphatic in asserting opinions; stubborn.

domicile (dom′ə sīl) *n.* A dwelling place; a house; one's home.

dowry (dou′rē) *n.* Money or property that a woman brings to her husband when she marries him.

dubiety (dü bī′ə tē) *n.* Doubtfulness; uncertainty.

dubiously (dü′bē əs lē) *adv.* Doubtfully; uncertainly.

dudgeon (duj′ən) *n.* A feeling of great anger or resentment.

dunning (dun′ing) *v.* Demanding payment of a debt from someone again and again.

dupe (düp) *n.* One who is being deluded or tricked.

dynamic (dī nam′ik) *adj.* Active; energetic; powerful; vigorous.

ecstatically (ek stat′ik lē) *adv.* With overwhelming joy or delight; joyously.

edict (ē′dikt) *n.* A decree or law proclaimed by a king or other ruler on his sole authority.

effectually (ə fek′chü əl ē) *adv.* In a manner to produce the desired result.

efficacious (ef′ə kā′shəs) *adj.* Producing the desired results; effective.

effrontery (ə frun′tər ē) *n.* Shameless boldness; impudence; insolence.

egoists (ē′gō ists) *n.* Persons who seek the welfare of themselves only; vain, selfish persons.

egotistical (ē′gō tis′tə kəl) *adj.* Talking too much about oneself; conceited.

ejaculations (i jak′yə lā′shənz) *n.* Remarks said suddenly and briefly; exclamations.

elated (i lā′tid) *adj.* In high spirits; joyful or proud.

elation (i lā′shən) *n.* Joy or happiness; great satisfaction.

elegance (el′ə gəns) *n.* Refinement; good taste; grace and beauty.

eligible (el′ə jə bəl) *adj.* Properly qualified; desirable; suitable.

elucidation (i lü′sə dā′shən) *n.* An explanation; a making clear.

emaciation (i mā′shē ā′shən) *n.* A thin, gaunt, wasted condition.

embarked (em bärkt′) *v.* Went on board a ship. Also, began an undertaking; started.

embellish (em bel′ish) *v.* Make more interesting by adding real or imaginary details.

eminently (em′ə nənt lē) *adv.* Outstandingly; with renown for a characteristic or quality.

emulation (em′yə lā′shən) *n.* A copying or imitating in order to equal or excel; act of trying to equal or excel; competition; rivalry.

encumbrance (en kum′brəns) *n.* Hindrance; burden.

engendering (en jen′dər ing) *v.* Bringing into existence; producing.

engrossed (en grōst′) *adj.* Being occupied wholly by something; giving all one's attention to something.

enmity (en′mə tē) *n.* Hostility or hatred; ill will.

ensued (en süd′) *v.* Followed what happened before.

entail (en tāl′) *v.* Make necessary or require.

enthralling (en thrôl′ing) *adj.* Fascinating; charming; most interesting.

enticing (en tīs′ing) *v.* Tempting; luring.

entombed (en tümd′) *v.* Buried; placed in a tomb.

entreaties (en trē′tēz) *n.* Earnest requests; pleas.

entreaty (en trē′tē) *n.* An earnest request; a prayer or an appeal.

enumerated (i nü′mə rāt′əd) *v.* Named one by one; listed.

enunciating (i nun′sē āt ing) *v.* Speaking clearly and distinctly.

envisage (en viz′ij) *v.* Form a mental picture of.

equilibrium (ē′kwə lib′rē əm) *n.* Mental poise; steadiness of character.

equitable (ek′wə tə bəl) *adj.* Fair; just.

equivalent (i kwiv′ə lənt) *n.* Something equal in value, or in any other quality, to another.

eradicate (i rad′ə kāt) *v.* Get rid of entirely; destroy completely; eliminate.

erroneous (ə rō′nē əs) *adj.* Wrong; mistaken; incorrect.

erudite (er′u dīt) *adj.* Having much knowledge; scholarly; learned.

escapade (es′kə pād) *n.* Wild adventure or prank.

espouse (e spouz′) *v.* Marry.

esteemed (e stēmd′) *adj.* Thinking highly of; highly valued.

estimable (es′tə mə bəl) *adj.* Worthy of respect; deserving high regard; honorable.

estranged (e strānjd′) *adj.* Being turned from affection for a person to indifference, dislike, or hatred; keeping apart from a person.

estuaries (es′chü er′ēz) *n.* The mouth of a river.

eternal (i tėr′nl) *adj.* Lasting throughout all time; timeless; everlasting.

eternity (i tėr′nə tē) *n.* All time; a seemingly endless period of time.

ethereal (i thir′ē əl) *adj.* Light; airy; delicate. Also, heavenly.

etherized (ē′thə rīzd′) *adj.* Being made unconscious with ether, or anesthetic.

eugenisists (yü jen′ə sists) *n.* Experts in the science of improving the human race by a careful selection of parents in order to develop healthier and more intelligent children.

excavations (ek′skə vā′shənz) *n.* Places uncovered by digging, especially ancient places.

---

hat, āge, fär; let, ēqual, tėrm; it, īce; hot, ōpen, ôrder; oil, out; cup, put, rüle; ch, child; ng, long; sh, she; th, thin; ŦH, then; zh, measure; ə represents *a* in about, *e* in taken, *i* in pencil, *o* in lemon, *u* in circus.

exclusion (ek sklü′zhən) *n*. Condition of being shut out or kept out.

execrate (ek′sə krāt) *v*. Loath intensely; detest; call down curses upon.

execrations (ek′sə krā′shənz) *n*. Curses; loud expressions of hatred.

exemplary (eg zem′plər ē) *adj*. Worth imitating; admirable; serving as a model or pattern.

exercising (ek′sər sīz ing) *v*. Using actively; applying; employing.

exhorting (eg zôrt′ing) *v*. Urging strongly; advising or warning earnestly.

exorbitant (eg zôr′bə tənt) *adj*. Excessive; unreasonable.

expediency (ek spē′dē ən sē) *n*. Personal advantage; self-interest.

expiate (ek′spē āt) *v*. Make amends for a wrong, sin, etc.; atone for.

explicitly (ek splis′it lē) *adv*. Plainly; clearly; definitely.

exquisite (ek′skwi zit) *adj*. Very lovely; delicate.

exterminated (ek stėr′mə nāt əd) *v*. Destroyed completely.

extinction (ek stingk′shən) *n*. A doing away with completely; a wiping out; destruction

extorts (ek stôrts′) *v*. Obtains by threats, force, fraud, or illegal use of authority.

extremity (ek strem′ə tē) *n*. Very great danger or need.

exuberant (eg zü′bər ənt) *adj*. Very abundant; lavish.

fabulous (fab′yə ləs) *adj*. Not believable; amazing.

falcon (fôl′kən) *n*. Any of various hawks trained to hunt and kill other birds and small game.

fallow (fal′ō) *adj*. Plowed and left unseeded for a season or more.

feigning (fān′ing) *v*. Making believe; pretending.

felicity (fə lis′ə tē) *n*. Great happiness; bliss.

fell (fel) *adj*. Fierce; savage; ruthless; deadly; destructive.

fervor (fėr′vər) *n*. Enthusiasm or earnestness; intense emotion.

fictitious (fik tish′əs) *adj*. Assumed in order to deceive; false.

filial (fil′ē əl) *adj*. Due from a son or daughter toward a father or mother.

finesse (fə nes′) *n*. The skillful handling of a delicate situation to one's advantage; subtle or tactful strategy.

finical (fin′ə kəl) *adj*. Too dainty or particular; too precise; fussy.

firmament (fėr′mə mənt) *n*. The heavens; the sky.

fissure (fish′ər) *n*. A long, narrow opening; a split; a crack.

flaunt (flônt) *v*. Show off to impress others; display in such a way as to attract notice.

flounces (flouns′əs) *n*. Wide ruffles.

foible (foi′bəl) *n*. A weak point; weakness; a little fault or failing.

fops (fops) *n*. Vain men who are very fond of fine clothes and have affected manners; dandies.

forebodings (fôr bō′dingz) *n*. Feelings that something bad is going to happen.

forfeit (fôr′fit) *adj*. Lost or given up as a penalty.

forlorn (fôr lôrn′) *adj*. Left alone and neglected; deserted; friendless; forsaken.

formulated (fôr′myə lāt əd) *adj*. Being made or forced to fit a rule for doing something, especially as used by those who do not know the reason on which the rule is based.

forsaken (fôr sā′kən) *adj*. Deserted; abandoned.

fossils (fos′əlz) *n*. Very old persons, set in their ways.

fostered (fô′stərd) *v*. Reared; cherished.

fraudulent (frô′jə lənt) *adj*. Dishonest; deceitful.

frenzy (fren′zē) *n*. A state of near madness; a frantic condition.

frivolous (friv′ə ləs) *adj*. Lacking in seriousness or sense; silly; foolish.

frugality (frü gal′ə tē) *n*. Avoidance of waste; thrift; economy.

fundamental (fun′də men′tl) *adj*. Of or forming a foundation or basis; essential; basic.

furled (fėrld) *v*. Rolled or folded up.

furtive (fėr′tiv) *adj*. Secret; sly; stealthy.

fusillade (fyü′zə lād′) *n*. A rapid or continuous discharge of many firearms at the same time.

gadfly (gad′flī′) *n*. Person who goads others to action by irritating or annoying remarks.

gallery (gal′ər ē) *n*. A balcony.

galling (gôl′ing) *adj*. Bitter and hateful; irritating.

garish (ger′ish) *adj*. Glaringly bright; gaudy.

genteel (jen tēl′) *adj*. Belonging to polite society; well-bred; well-mannered.

germinated (jėr′mə nāt əd) *v*. Grown or developed.

glib (glib) *adj*. Speaking too smoothly or easily to be believed; insincere.

gratuitous (grə tü′ə təs) *adj*. Without reason or cause; unnecessary; uncalled-for.

groping (grōp′ing) *v*. Searching blindly or uncertainly.

grossly (grōs′lē) *adv*. Clearly; plainly; glaringly.

guileless (gīl′lis) *adj*. Without deceit or trickery; honest; frank; straightforward.

hallowed (hal′ōd) *v*. and *adj*. Made holy; honored or observed as holy.

hallucination (hə lü′sn nā′shən) *n*. A seeing or hearing things that exist only in a person's imagination; an imaginary thing seen or heard.

haphazard (hap′haz′ərd) *adv*. By chance; at random; without plan.

harangue (hə rang′) *n*. A noisy, forceful speech.

harass (har′əs) *v*. Trouble by repeated attacks; torment; annoy; disturb.

harbinger (här′bən jər) *n*. One that goes ahead to announce another's coming.

havoc (hav′ək) *n*. Very great destruction; ruin.

hideous (hid′ē əs) *adj*. Very ugly; frightful; horrible.

homage (hom′ij) *n*. Dutiful respect; honor.

homogeneous (hō′mə jē′nē əs) *adj*. Similar; of uniform character or nature throughout.

humility (hyü mil′ə tē) *n*. Humbleness of mind; meekness.

hypocrisy (hi pok′rə sē) *n*. A pretending to be what

one is not; pretense. Also, an outward show of goodness.

icons (ī′konz) *n*. Pictures or images of Jesus, an angel, or a saint, usually painted on wood or ivory.

ignoble (ig nō′bəl) *adj*. Dishonorable; disgraceful.

ignoramus (ig′nə rā′məs) *n*. A person who knows little or nothing.

ignorance (ig′nər əns) *n*. A lack of knowledge.

illumination (i lü′mə nā′shən) *n*. A lighting up; light.

imbecile (im′bə səl) *n*. A very stupid or foolish person.

immensity (i men′sə tē) *n*. Very great size or extent; vastness.

imminent (im′ə nənt) *adj*. Likely to happen soon; about to occur.

immolated (im′ə lāt əd) *v*. Killed oneself as a sacrifice.

immortal (i môr′tl) *adj*. Divine; having to do with living forever; never dying; everlasting.

impartially (im pär′shəl ē) *adv*. Fairly; justly; without more favor to one side than to the other.

impassive (im pas′iv) *adj*. Without feeling or emotion; unmoved; calm.

impediments (im ped′ə mənts) *n*. Hindrances; obstructions.

impenetrable (im pen′ə trə bəl) *adj*. Impossible to explain or understand; incomprehensible.

imperceptible (im′pər sep′tə bəl) *adj*. That cannot be seen or felt; invisible.

imperceptibly (im′pər sep′tə blē) *adv*. In a manner so gradual as to be unnoticed.

imperialism (im pir′ē ə liz′əm) *n*. Policy of extending rule of one country over other countries.

impertinent (im pèrt′n ənt) *adj*. Disrespectful and rude.

imperturbably (im′pər tèrb′ə blē) *adv*. Calmly; unexcitedly.

impetuosity (im pech′ü os′ə te,) *n*. Sudden, rash, or hasty acts; impulsiveness.

impious (im′pē əs) *adj*. Wicked; ungodly; lacking reverence for God.

implacable (im plā′kə bəl) *adj*. Unforgiving; unrelenting; unyielding.

implications (im′plə kā′shənz) *n*. Indirect suggestions; hints; things understood though not said.

implicit (im plis′it) *adj*. Meant, but not clearly expressed or distinctly stated.

importuning (im′pôr tün′ing) *v*. Asking urgently or repeatedly; asking again and again.

importunities (im′pôr tü′nə tēz) *n*. Acts of asking again and again.

imprecations (im′prə kā′shənz) *n*. Curses; a calling down of evil, etc., upon someone or something.

impregnable (im preg′nə bəl) *adj*. Able to resist attack.

impressionable (im presh′ə nə bəl) *adj*. Easily influenced.

improbability (im prob′ə bil′ə tē) *n*. An unlikelihood; something not likely to be true.

inadmissible (in′əd mis′ə bəl) *adj*. Not to be permitted; not allowable.

incapacitated (in′kə pas′ə tāt əd) *adj*. Being deprived of ability, power, or fitness; disabled.

incarnating (in kär′nāt ing) *v*. Putting into concrete form; personifying.

incensed (in senst′) *v*. Made very angry; filled with rage.

incessantly (in sès′nt lē) *adv*. Continually or repeatedly without interruption; unceasingly.

incipient (in sip′ē ənt) *adj*. Just beginning; in an early stage.

inclemencies (in klem′ən sēz) *n*. Harshnesses; severities.

inconceivable (in′kən sē′və bəl) *adj*. Impossible to imagine; hard to believe.

indefatigable (in′di fat′ə gə bəl) *adj*. Never getting tired or giving up; tireless.

indictment (in dīt′mənt) *n*. A formal written accusation of a crime; an accusation of wrongdoing.

indignation (in′dig nā′shən) *n*. Anger at something unworthy, unjust, unfair, or mean; resentment.

indigo (in′də gō) *n*. and *adj*. Deep violet blue.

indiscriminately (in′dis krim′ə nit lē) *adv*. Without making distinctions between good and bad, etc.

indispensable (in′dis pen′sə bəl) *adj*. Absolutely necessary; essential.

indisputable (in′dis pyü′tə bəl) *adj*. Too evident to be called into question; undoubted; certain; unquestionable; undeniable.

inducement (in düs′mənt) *n*. Something that influences or persuades.

inexorably (in ek′sər ə blē) *adv*. Unyieldingly.

inextricable (in ek′strə kə bəl) *adj*. That cannot be disentangled or solved.

infallibility (in fal′ə bil′ə tē) *n*. Inability to make a mistake; never wrong.

infernal (in fèr′nl) *adj*. Of or having to do with hell; hellish; fiendish; outrageous.

infirmity (in fèr′mə tē) *n*. Sickness; illness.

ingenious (in jē′nyəs) *adj*. Cleverly planned or made.

ingrained (in grānd′) *adj*. Deeply and firmly fixed.

ingratiate (in grā′shē āt) *v*. Bring oneself into favor; make oneself acceptable.

ingratiating (in grā′shē āt ing) *adj*. Trying to make oneself acceptable.

injunction (in jungk′shən) *n*. An authoritative or emphatic order; a command.

innocuous (i nok′yü əs) *adj*. Not hurtful or injurious; harmless.

insatiable (in sā′shə bəl) *adj*. Never satisfied; extremely greedy.

insidious (in sid′ē əs) *adj*. Secretly harmful; working secretly or subtly; seeking to entrap or ensnare.

insinuations (in sin′yü ā′shənz) *n*. Indirect hints or suggestions meant to discredit someone.

insipid (in sip′id) *adj*. Lacking interest or spirit; dull.

hat, āge, fär; let, ēqual, tėrm; it, īce; hot, ōpen, ôrder; oil, out; cup, pùt, rüle; ch, child; ng, long; sh, she; th, thin; ᴛн, then; zh, measure; ə represents *a* in about, *e* in taken, *i* in pencil, *o* in lemon, *u* in circus.

insolence (in'sə ləns) n. Bold rudeness; insulting behavior or speech.

insufferably (in suf'ər ə blē) adv. Unbearably; detestably.

insufficiently (in'sə fish'ənt lē) adv. Inadequately.

integrity (in teg'rə tē) n. Honesty or sincerity; uprightness.

interdiction (in'tər dik'shən) n. Formal order forbidding something.

interim (in'tər im) n. The time between. adj. For the meantime; temporary.

interpreter (in ter'prə tər) n. Person whose business is translating, especially from a foreign language.

interrogation (in ter'ə gā'shən) n. A questioning.

interstices (in tėr'stə sēz') n. Gaps or openings.

intimated (in'tə māt əd) v. Suggested something in a delicate manner, so that others understand without being told.

intrigued (in trēgd') adj. Exciting the curiosity and interest of.

intriguer (in trē'gər) n. A plotter or schemer.

intrusion (in trü'zhən) n. An entry without permission; coming unasked and unwanted.

intuitively (in tü'ə tiv lē) adv. Instinctively; without reasoning.

invariable (in ver'ē ə bəl) adj. Unchanging; constant.

invective (in vek'tiv) n. A violent attack in words; verbal abuse.

inveigle (in vē'gəl) v. Entice; wheedle.

invested (in vest'əd) v. Installed in office with a ceremony.

invincible (in vin'sə bəl) adj. Unable to be conquered; impossible to overcome; unbeatable.

irately (ī'rāt lē) adv. Angrily; furiously.

irrational (i rash'ə nəl) adj. Contrary to reason; unreasonable.

irremediable (ir'i mē'dē ə bəl) adj. That cannot be corrected or put right; incurable.

irreparable (i rep'ər ə bəl) adj. That cannot be repaired, put right, or made good.

irresistible (ir'i zis'tə bəl) adj. Too great to be withstood; overwhelming.

irresolutely (i rez'ə lüt lē) adv. Undecidedly; unsurely; uncertainly; in a manner indicating unsureness of mind.

irrevocable (i rev'ə kə bəl) adj. Not able to be taken back, canceled, withdrawn, etc; final.

isolated (ī'sə lāt əd) adj. Being set apart or separate from others; solitary.

jocund (jok'ənd) adj. Cheerful; merry; gay.

joust (just) or (joust) v. Fight with lances on horseback. Knights used to joust with each other for sport.

knell (nel) n. A warning sign of death, failure, etc.

labyrinths (lab'ə rinths') n. Many winding passages so arranged that it is hard to find one's way from point to point.

lamentable (lam'ən tə bəl) adj. To be regretted or pitied; deplorable.

languished (lang'gwisht) adj. Being weakened or weary; drooped.

languor (lang'gər) n. Lack of energy; weakness; weariness.

largesse (lär'jis) n. A generous giving.

latent (lāt'nt) adj. Hidden; concealed; not developed.

laudable (lô'də bəl) adj. Worthy of praise.

lenient (lē'nyənt) adj. Mild or gentle; not harsh or stern; merciful.

libation (lī bā'shən) n. The wine, water, etc., poured out as an offering to a god.

libel (lī'bəl) n. Any false or damaging statement about a person; a slander.

loath (lōth) adj. Unwilling or reluctant.

loftily (lôf'tə lē) adv. In a haughty, overbearing manner; grandly.

lofty (lôf'tē) adj. Exalted or dignified; grand.

longevity (lon jev'ə tē) n. Long life.

lucid (lü'sid) adj. Clear in intellect; rational; sane.

lustrous (lus'trəs) adj. Shining; glossy; radiant.

madrigals (mad'rə gəlz) n. Songs, especially love songs.

maimed (māmd) adj. Disabled; crippled.

majesty (maj'ə stē) n. Stately appearance; grandeur.

malevolence (mə lev'ə ləns) n. The wish that evil will happen to others; ill will; spite.

malingerers (mə ling'gər ərz) n. Persons who pretend to be sick, injured, etc., in order to escape work; shirkers.

malingers (mə ling'gərz) v. Pretends to be sick, injured, etc., to escape work or duty; shirks.

malodorous (mal ō'dər əs) adj. Smelling bad.

manacles (man'ə kəlz) n. Handcuffs; anything that chains or binds; restraints.

mandarin (man'dər ən) n. A high-ranking official in ancient China.

mandate (man'dāt) n. An order or command; an instruction to act on behalf of another or others.

maneuver (mə nü'vər) n. A well-planned action or movement.

manifestation (man'ə fə stā'shən) n. Something that becomes apparent to the eye or mind.

massacre (mas'ə kər) v. Kill needlessly or cruelly.

masticating (mas'tə kāt ing) v. Chewing thoroughly.

materialistic (mə tir'ē ə lis'tik) adj. Worldly; being more interested in things of the world than of spiritual needs.

maundering (môn'dər ing) v. Moving and acting in an aimless, confused manner.

meandering (mē an'dər ing) v. Following a winding course.

mediocre (mē'dē ō'kər) adj. Neither good nor bad; of average quality; ordinary.

melancholy (mel'ən kôl'e) adj. Causing sadness; depressing; deplorable. n. condition of sadness and low spirits; gloominess; dejection.

mellow (mel'ō) adj. Soft and full-flavored from ripeness.

menagerie (mə naj'ər ē) n. A collection of wild or strange animals. Also, the place where such animals are kept.

mercenary (mėr'sə ner'ē) adj. Acting with money as the motive; money-loving.

mesmeric (mez mer′ik) *adj.* Producing a dreamlike state; hypnotic.

metamorphosis (met′ə môr′fə sis) *n.* A change of form or structure or shape; a transformation.

methodical (mə thod′ə kəl) *adj.* Systematic; orderly.

meticulous (mə tik′yə ləs) *adj.* Extremely or excessively careful about small details.

mettle (met′l) *n.* Quality of disposition or temperament.

millenniums (mə len′ē əmz) *n.* Periods of a thousand years each.

minions (min′yənz) *n.* Darlings; favorites.

ministrations (min′ə strā′shənz) *n.* Help; aid.

miscreants (mis′krē ənts) *n.* Base or wicked persons; villains; rascals.

mobilized (mō′bə līzd) *adj.* Organized and prepared for war.

modes (mōdz) *n.* The ways in which things are done; methods.

monotonous (mə not′n əs) *adj.* Not varying; without change; uniform.

morass (mə ras′) *n.* A piece of low, soft, wet ground; a swamp; a marsh.

morbid (môr′bid) *adj.* Unwholesome or unhealthy. Also, diseased.

municipal (myü nis′ə pəl) *adj.* Of or having to do with the affairs of a city, town, or other district having local self-government.

mused (myüzd) *v.* Completely absorbed in thought; pondered.

mutable (myü′tə bəl) *adj.* Capable of or liable to change; changeable.

naïvely (nä ēv′lē) *adj.* In a simple, childlike manner; artlessly.

nausea (nô′zē ə) *n.* A feeling a person has when about to vomit.

negligible (neg′lə jə bəl) *adj.* Not worth noticing; unimportant; insignificant.

niggardliness (nig′ərd lē nəs) *n.* Stinginess; miserliness.

nonagenarian (non′ə jə ner′ē ən) *n.* Person who is 90 years old or between 90 and 100 years old.

nonpareil (non′pə rel′) *n.* Person or thing having no equal.

obdurate (ob′dər it) *adj.* Stubborn or unyielding; obstinate.

oblivion (ə bliv′ē ən) *n.* Condition of being entirely forgotten.

obsequies (ob′sə kwēz) *n.* Funeral rites or ceremonies.

obsequiously (əb sē′kwē əs lē) *adv.* Flatteringly; servilely.

obsession (əb sesh′ən) *n.* A thought or intention that overcomes all others; influence of a feeling, idea, or impulse to an unreasonable or unhealthy extent.

obsolete (ob′sə lēt) *adj.* Old-fashioned; out-of-date.

obstinately (ob′stə nit lē) *adv.* Stubbornly.

obtruded (əb trüd′əd) *v.* Thrust forward; stuck out.

obtuse (əb tüs′) *adj.* Slow in understanding; dull; slow-witted.

offensive (ə fen′siv) *adj.* Insulting; being extremely unpleasant.

officious (ə fish′əs) *adj.* Offering unwanted help; interfering; meddlesome.

ominous (om′ə nəs) *adj.* Threatening; foretelling misfortune.

omnipotent (om nip′ə tənt) *adj.* Having all power; almighty.

omniscient (om nish′ənt) *adj.* Knowing everything; having complete or infinite knowledge.

opaline (ō′pə līn) *adj.* Having a play of colors resembling a rainbow.

opiate (ō′pē it) *n.* Medicine that soothes, dulls pain, induces sleep, etc., especially one containing opium.

opportune (op′ər tün′) *adj.* Timely; suitable; just right.

oppressive (ə pres′iv) *adj.* Close; sultry. Also, hard to bear; burdensome.

optimist (op′tə mist) *n.* One who looks on the bright side of things.

optimum (op′tə məm) *adj.* Best or most favorable.

orifice (ôr′ə fis) *n.* An opening or hole.

ornate (ôr nāt′) *adj.* Characterized by the use of elaborate figures of speech, flowery language, etc.

orthodoxy (ôr′thə dok′sē) *n.* The holding of correct or generally accepted religious beliefs. Also, conforming to established customs and traditions.

overindulged (ō′vər in duljd) *adj.* Allowing oneself to have, use, or enjoy something pleasant for too long a time.

pagan (pā′gən) *n.* One who worships many gods or no gods; heathen.

palfrey (pôl′frē) *n.* A gentle riding horse, especially one used by ladies.

pallor (pal′ər) *n.* Lack of color from fear, illness, death, etc.; paleness.

palpable (pal′pə bəl) *adj.* Readily seen or heard and recognized; obvious; actual; real.

palpitating (pal′pə tāt ing) *adj.* Throbbing; beating.

palpitations (pal′pə tā′shənz) *n.* Rapid beatings of the heart; tremblings.

panoply (pan′ə plē) *n.* A complete suit of armor; complete equipment or covering; any splendid array.

panorama (pan′ə ram′ə) *n.* A wide, unbroken view of a surrounding region.

paradox (par′ə doks) *n.* Person or thing that seems to be full of contradictions.

paraphernalia (par′ə fər nā′lyə) *n.* Personal belongings.

parasites (par′ə sīts) *n.* Persons who live on others without making any useful and fitting return; hangers-on.

---

hat, āge, fär; let, ēqual, tėrm; it, īce; hot, ōpen, ôrder; oil, out; cup, pùt; rüle; ch, child; ng, long; sh, she; th, thin; ᵺ, then; zh, measure; ə represents *a* in about, *e* in taken, *i* in pencil, *o* in lemon, *u* in circus.

parasol (par′ə sôl) *n*. A light umbrella used as a protection from the sun.

parched (pärcht) *adj*. Being hot and dried up; shriveled.

parley (pär′lā) *n*. A conference or informal talk.

paroxysm (par′ək siz′əm) *n*. A sudden outburst of emotion.

parsimonious (pär′sə mō′nē əs) *adj*. Too economical; stingy; miserly.

partiality (pär′shē al′ə tē) *n*. A particular liking; great fondness; preference.

partisans (pär′tə zənz) *n*. Supporters of a person, party, or cause and whose support may be based on feeling rather than on reasoning.

patriarch (pā′trē ärk) *n*. A church leader of high rank.

patronizing (pā′trə nīz ing) *adj*. Treating in a haughty, condescending manner.

pavan (pav′ən) *n*. A slow, stately dance and also the music for it.

pedagogue (ped′ə gog) *n*. Teacher of children; a schoolmaster.

peerless (pir′lis) *adj*. Without equal; matchless.

penitents (pen′ə tənts) *n*. Persons who are sorry for their sin or wrongdoing, especially those who confess their wrongdoing.

pensive (pen′siv) *adj*. Thoughtful in a serious or sad way.

penuriously (pi nùr′ē əs lē) *adv*. In extreme want; in great poverty.

perdition (pər dish′ən) *n*. Damnation; loss of one's soul and the joys of heaven.

perforce (pər fôrs′) *adv*. By necessity; necessarily.

perilous (per′ə ləs) *adj*. Dangerous; risky.

pernicious (pər nish′əs) *adj*. Fatal; deadly.

perorated (per′ə rāt əd) *v*. Talked in a grand manner as if making a public speech.

perpendicularly (pèr′pən dik′yə lər lē) *adv*. In an upright position; vertically.

perpetuated (pər pech′ü āt əd) *v*. Preserved forever; caused to be continuous.

perplexity (pər plek′sə tē) *n*. Puzzlement; bewilderment; great confusion.

persecutes (pèr′sə kyüts) *v*. Causes to suffer repeatedly; torments.

persevered (pèr′sə vird′) *v*. Continued steadily (in doing something hard); persisted.

perspective (pər spek′tiv) *n*. A method of drawing which gives a correct idea of distance, and of the relation in size of one object to another.

perturbation (pèr′tər bā′shən) *n*. A thing, act, or event that causes disturbance or agitation; condition of being greatly disturbed; great distress; worry; anxiety.

perturbed (pər tèrbd′) *adj*. Greatly troubled; uneasy; distressed.

perused (pə rüzd′) *v*. Read especially thoroughly and carefully.

pervaded (pər vād′əd) *v*. Spread throughout; filled.

perversity (pər vèr′sə tē) *n*. Contrariness; waywardness.

pessimist (pes′ə mist) *n*. A person inclined to look on the dark side of things or to see all the difficulties and disadvantages.

pestiferous (pe stif′ər əs) *adj*. Bringing disease or infection.

phenomenon (fə nom′ə non) *n*. A rare circumstance that can be observed; a marvel.

phlegmatic (fleg mat′ik) *adj*. Not easily aroused to feeling or action; indifferent.

pilloried (pil′ər ēd) *v*. Exposed to public ridicule, contempt, or abuse.

plague (plāg) *v*. Vex; annoy; bother.

plaintiffs (plān′tifs) *n*. Persons beginning a lawsuit.

plaintive (plān′tiv) *adj*. Mournful; sad.

plateau (pla tō′) *n*. A large, high plain in the mountains or at a height considerably above sea level; a tableland.

plausibly (plô′zə bə lē) *adv*. Apparently true or reasonable.

plebian (pli bē′ən) *adj*. Belonging or having to do with common people; common; vulgar.

portentousness (pôr ten′təs nəs) *n*. Great importance.

potent (pōt′nt) *adj*. Having great power; powerful; strong.

prating (prāt′ing) *n*. Empty or foolish talk.

precarious (pri ker′ē əs) *adj*. Doubtful; uncertain; dependent on chance or circumstance.

precedence (pres′ə dəns) *n*. The act of going first; the lead.

precedent (pres′ə dənt) *n*. An example; an action serving as an example or reason for a later action.

precept (prē′sept) *n*. Rule of action or behavior; a maxim.

precursor (pri kèr′sər) *n*. Forerunner; predecessor; one who goes before.

predominate (pri dom′ə nāt) *v*. Be greater in power or influence; control; be master of.

prejudicial (prej′ə dish′əl) *adj*. Harmful; detrimental; damaging.

prelate (prel′it) *n*. Clergyman of high rank.

prematurely (prē′mə chùr′lē) *adv*. Too hastily; too soon.

premonition (prē′mə nish′ən) *n*. Notification or warning of what is to come; forewarning.

preoccupied (prē ok′yə pīd) *adj*. Absorbed; engrossed.

preposterous (pri pos′tər əs) *adj*. Absurd; ridiculous; senseless.

prerogative (pri rog′ə tiv) *n*. A right or privilege that nobody else has; special right or privilege such as may derive from an official position, office, etc.

presentiment (pri zen′tə mənt) *n*. A vague sense or feeling of approaching misfortune.

presumption (pri zump′shən) *n*. Forwardness; unpleasant boldness.

presumptuous (pri zump′chü əs) *adj*. Too bold; forward; acting without permission or right.

pretension (pri ten′shən) *n*. A doing things for show or to make a fine appearance.

pretentious (pri ten′shəs) *adj*. Making claims to excellence or importance.

pretext (prē′tekst) *n*. A false reason concealing the real reason; misleading excuse.

prevarication (pri var′ə kā′shən) *n*. Turning aside from the truth; a falsehood; a lie.

pristine (pris′tēn′) *adj*. Original.

probationers (prō bā′shə nərz) *n*. Persons who are learning a trade or profession; pupils.

prodigious (prə dij′əs) *adj*. Enormous; monstrous; marvelous; wonderful.

profligates (prof′lə gits) *n*. Very wicked or extravagant persons.

profoundly (prə found′lē) *adv*. Very deeply; greatly; thoroughly.

profusion (prə fyü′zhən) *n*. Great abundance; lavishness.

prolific (prə lif′ik) *adj*. Highly productive.

prominent (prom′ə nənt) *adj*. Standing out; projecting.

propensity (prə pen′sə tē) *n*. A natural inclination; a tendency; a liking for something.

propitiate (prə pish′ē āt) *v*. Pacify; reduce the anger of; win over.

propitious (prə pish′əs) *adj*. Favorable.

proprietor (prə prī′ə tər) *n*. An owner.

propriety (prə prī′ə tē) *n*. Proper behavior; seemliness.

prosaic (prō zā′ik) *adj*. Ordinary; not exciting; dull.

prospects (pros′pekts) *n*. Outlook for the future.

prospectus (prə spek′təs) *n*. A printed description of something; an advertising brochure.

prototypes (prō′tə tīps) *n*. The first or primary types of anything; the originals or models.

protracted (prō trakt′əd) *adj*. Prolonged; lengthened.

provoked (prə vōkt′) *adj*. Angry; vexed; irritated.

proximity (prok sim′ə tē) *n*. The nearness or closeness; the neighborhood.

pseudocreative (sü′dō krē ā′tiv) *adj*. Being falsely original or inventive; pretending to be original or inventive.

pugnacious (pug nā′shəs) *adj*. Fond of fighting; quarrelsome.

punctilious (pungk til′ē əs) *adj*. Very careful and exact; paying strict attention to details of conduct.

punctuated (pungk′chü āt əd) *adj*. Interrupted now and then.

punitive (pyü′nə tiv) *adj*. Inflicting punishment.

purgation (pėr′gā′shən) *n*. Suffering or punishment.

quagmire (kwag′mīr) *n*. A difficult or precarious position. Also, soft, muddy ground; a bog.

quietude (kwī′ə tüd) *n*. Stillness; calmness.

quiver (kwiv′ər) *n*. Case to hold arrows.

quondam (kwon′dəm) *adj*. Former; that once was.

railing (rāl′ing) *v*. Complaining bitterly; using violent and reproachful language.

rampant (ram′pənt) *adj*. Passing beyond restraint or usual limits; unchecked; widespread.

rancid (ran′sid) *adj*. Stale; spoiled.

range (rānj) *v*. Wander; rove; roam.

rebuking (ri byük′ing) *v*. Expressing disapproval of something.

recalcitrance (ri kal′sə trəns) *n*. Refusal to submit, conform, or comply; disobedience.

receded (ri sēd′əd) *v*. Withdrew or moved backward.

recesses (rē′ses əs) *n*. Niches or openings.

recompense (rek′əm pens) *n*. Reward; payment.

reconciled (rek′ən sīld) *adj*. No longer opposed to each other; becoming friends again. *v*. No longer opposed.

reconciles (rek′ən sīlz) *v*. Brings into agreement or harmony.

recondite (rek′ən dīt) *adj*. Little known; obscure.

redress (rē′dres) *n*. A setting right; relief; a remedy.

refute (ri fyüt′) *v*. Prove a statement to be wrong; show something to be false or incorrect.

regime (ri zhēm′) *n*. A system or set of rules for living.

relevant (rel′ə vənt) *adj*. Bearing upon or connected with the matter in hand; to the point.

relish (rel′ish) *n*. Keen enjoyment.

reluctance (ri luk′təns) *n*. Unwillingness.

remnants (rem′nənts) *n*. Small parts that are left; fragments.

renunciation (ri nun′sē ā′shən) *n*. A giving up entirely of something; a delcaring that one gives up something; a rejection.

replete (ri plēt′) *adj*. Filled or full; gorged.

repudiated (ri pyü′dē āt əd) *v*. Rejected; cast off; disowned.

repugnance (ri pug′nəns) *n*. Strong dislike, distaste, or aversion.

repugnant (ri pug′nənt) *adj*. Disagreeable or offensive; distasteful; objectionable.

repulsive (ri pul′siv) *adj*. Causing strong dislike or aversion; hateful; very displeasing.

reputed (ri pyü′tid) *adj*. Accounted or supposed to be such.

requite (re kwīt′) *v*. Pay back; reward; repay.

resigned (ri zīnd′) *adj*. Submitting to or accepting what comes without complain.

resilience (ri zil′ē əns) *n*. Power of recovering readily; cheerfulness; springiness.

respite (res′pit) *n*. Time of relief and rest.

resplendent (ri splen′dənt) *adj*. Glorious; splendid; shining.

retribution (ret′rə byü′shən) *n*. A deserved punishment; return for evil done; a reckoning.

retrospect (ret′rə spekt) *n*. Thinking about the past; when looking back.

revelled (rev′əld) *v*. Took great pleasure (in).

reverberating (ri vėr′bə rāt′ing) *v*. Echoing back; resounding.

reveres (ri virz′) *v*. Loves and respects deeply; honors greatly.

revoke (ri vōk′) *v*. Take back; withdraw.

rhetorical (ri tôr′ə kəl) *adj*. Having to do with making a speech and using language skillfully.

rive (rīv) *v*. Tear apart; split.

hat, āge, fär; let, ēqual, tėrm; it, īce; hot, ōpen, ôrder; oil, out; cup, put, rüle; ch, child; ng, long; sh, she; th, thin; ŦH, then; zh, measure; ə represents *a* in about, *e* in taken, *i* in pencil, *o* in lemon, *u* in circus.

774

rite (rīt) *n*. A formal procedure or act in a religious or other observance.

rogue (rōg) *n*. A rascal; a scoundrel.

rubicund (rü'bə kund) *adj*. Reddish; ruddy.

rudiments (rü'də mənts) *n*. Part to be learned first; the beginning; something in an early stage.

rue (rü) *v*. Be sorry for; regret. *n*. Sorrow; regret.

rumination (rü'mə nā'shən) *n*. Meditation; reflection; deep thought.

rummaging (rum'ij ing) *v*. Searching in a disorderly way; ransacking.

sacked (sakt) *v*. Dismissed from employment; fired.

sacristy (sak'ri stē) *n*. Place where the sacred vessels, robes, etc., of a church are kept; vestry.

sardonic (sär don'ik) *adj*. bitterly sarcastic, scornful, or mocking.

sated (sāt'əd) *v*. Satisfied fully.

satellites (sat'l īts) *n*. Followers of a person of importance; hangers-on.

sauntered (sôn'tərd) *v*. Strolled; walked slowly.

scandalized (skan'dl īzd) *v*. Offended by doing something thought to be wrong or improper; shocked.

scepter (sep'tər) *n*. The rod or staff carried by a ruler as a symbol of royal power or authority.

scruples (skrü'pəlz) *n*. Feelings of doubt about what one ought to do; uneasy feelings that keep one from doing something.

scrupulous (skrü'pyə ləs) *adj*. Very careful to do what is right; conscientious.

scrutinize (skrüt'n īz) *v*. Examine carefully; inspect carefully.

scurvy (skėr'vē) *n*. A terrible disease due to lack of fresh vegetables.

secular (sek'yə lər) *adj*. Not religious or sacred; worldly.

sepulcher (sep'əl kər) *n*. Place of burial; tomb; grave.

serenely (sə rēn'lē) *adv*. Calmly; in an untroubled manner.

servility (sėr'vil'ə tē) *n*. Attitude or behavior fit for a slave; base obedience.

shackled (shak'əld) *v*. Enslaved; held fast; restrained.

shagreen (shə grēn') *n*. Kind of untanned leather having a granular surface and usually dyed green.

shying (shī'ing) *v*. Throwing; flinging.

sinister (sin'ə stər) *adj*. Harmful; threatening; dishonest.

skeptical (skep'tə kəl) *adj*. Inclined to doubt; not believing easily.

skeptically (skep'tə kəl ē) *adv*. Doubtfully; questioningly.

skits (skits) *n*. Short written pieces that contain humor or satire.

slithery (sliᴛʜ'ər ē) *adj*. Slippery; crawly.

smack (smak) *v*. Have a taste, trace, or touch (of something).

smirking (smėrk'ing) *adj*. Smiling in a conceited, self-satisfied way.

sobriety (sə brī'ə tē) *n*. Seriousness; moderateness; quietness.

solicitous (sə lis'ə təs) *adj*. Showing care or concern; anxious; concerned.

solicitude (sə lis'ə tüd) *n*. Anxious care; anxiety; concern.

sonorous (sə nôr'əs) *adj*. Full and rich in sound.

sorties (sôr'tēz) *n*. Excursions; sudden attacks.

sovereign (sov'rən) *n*. Person having the greatest rank or power.

spectacle (spek'tə kəl) *n*. A splendid display; something presented to view as noteworthy, beautiful, etc.

speculations (spek'yə lā'shənz) *n*. Guesses; conjectures.

speculative (spek'yə lā'tiv) *adj*. Of or involving buying or selling at a large risk.

spontaneously (spon tā'nē əs lē) *adv*. Naturally and freely and not planned beforehand.

squander (skwon'dər) *v*. Spend foolishly; waste foolishly.

stipulated (stip'yə lāt əd) *v*. Demanded as a condition of agreement; arranged for as a condition of agreement.

stomacher (stum'ə kər) *n*. An ornamental covering for the stomach and bodice, formerly worn by a woman under the lacing of the bodice.

straitened (strāt'nd) *adj*. Impoverished; difficult.

straits (strāts) *n*. Difficulty; need; distress.

strand (strand) *n*. Shore; land bordering a sea, lake, or river.

stratagems (strat'ə jəmz) *n*. Careful, often complicated schemes for gaining an advantage.

stratification (strat'ə fə kā'shən) *n*. An arrangment in layers or levels.

stupefaction (stü'pə fak'shən) *n*. A dazed or senseless condition; overwhelming amazement, shock, etc.

subservience (səb sėr'vē əns) *n*. Slavish politeness and obedience.

subterranean (sub'tə rā'nē ən) *adj*. Underground.

succeeding (sək sēd'ing) *adj*. Following after.

succession (sək sesh'ən) *n*. Order or arrangement of persons having the right to take the place of another.

succinct (sək singkt') *adj*. Expressed briefly and clearly; brief; concise.

succor (suk'ər) *n*. Help; aid.

suffice (sə fīs') *v*. Be enough; be sufficient.

suffused (sə fyüzd') *v*. Overspread; spread throughout with (something).

sumptuous (sump'chü əs) *adj*. Lavish and costly; magnificent; rich.

sundry (sun'drē) *adj*. Different; various; several.

supercilious (sü'pər sil'ē əs) *adj*. Haughty, proud, and contemptuous; disdainful; showing scorn because of feeling oneself superior.

superfluous (sü pėr'flü əs) *adj*. Needless; unnecessary.

superlative (sə pėr'lə tiv) *adj*. Of the highest kind; above all others; supreme; unequalled.

surcease (sər sēs') *n*. An end.

surfeited (sėr'fit əd) *adj*. Having eaten or drunk to excess; gluttonous.

surveillance (sər vā'ləns) *n*. Watch kept over a person.

susceptible (sə sep'tə bəl) *adj*. Open to; capable of being affected by.

swoon (swün) *n*. A faint.

symbolic (sim bol'ik) *adj*. Being represented by something that stands for an idea, condition, etc.

symmetry (sim′ə trē) *n.* Pleasing proportions; harmony.

tacit (tas′it) *adj.* Implied or understood without being openly expressed.

taciturn (tas′ə tèrn′) *adj.* Speaking very little; silent.

tactician (tak tish′ən) *n.* A person skilled in planning, especially of military operations.

tangible (tan′jə bəl) *adj.* Real; actual; whose value can be accurately appraised.

taunt (tônt) *v.* Jeer at; mock; ridicule.

tempestuous (tem pes′chü əs) *adj.* Strong; violent.

tenuous (ten′yü əs) *adj.* Thin or slight; slender.

terrestrial (tə res′trē əl) *adj.* Of the earth; not of the heavens.

testimonial (tes′tə mō′nē əl) *n.* Gift, banquet, or the like, extended to someone as a token of esteem, admiration, gratitude, etc.

thralls (thrôlz) *n.* Persons in bondage.

throttle (throt′l) *v.* Choke or strangle; suppress a person's activities.

tinctured (tingk′chərd) *adj.* Colored or tinted.

tolerate (tol′ə rāt) *v.* Bear; endure; put up with.

tomes (tōmz) *n.* Books, especially large, heavy books.

tram (tram) *n.* A streetcar; a passenger car running on rails.

tranquil (trang′kwəl) *adj.* Calm; peaceful; quiet.

transfigured (tran sfig′yərd) *v.* Made more beautiful or glorious; changed in form or appearance.

transfixed (tran sfikst′) *v.* Pierced through.

transgressed (trans grest′) *v.* Broke a law, command, etc.

transition (tran zish′ən) *n.* A change or passing from one condition to another.

transparent (tran sper′ənt) *adj.* Transmitting light so that objects beyond or behind can be seen distinctly; being easy to see through.

traverses (trav′ərs əs) *v.* Cuts through; crosses from one side to the other.

treble (treb′əl) *n.* A shrill, high-pitched voice, sound, or note.

tremendous (tri men′dəs) *adj.* Very great; enormous.

tremulous (trem′yə ləs) *adj.* Trembling; quivering.

trinity (trin′ə tē) *n.* A group of three.

trivial (triv′ē əl) *adj.* Not important; insignificant.

truckling (truk′ling) *v.* Cringing; submitting tamely.

turbid (tèr′bid) *adj.* Confused; disordered.

tussle (tus′əl) *n.* Severe struggle or hard contest.

ulterior (ul tir′ē ər) *adj.* Beyond what is seen or expressed; hidden.

unauthorized (un ô′thə rīzd) *adj.* Illegal.

unique (yü nēk′) *adj.* Having no like or equal; being the only one of its kind.

unintelligible (un′in tel′ə jə bəl) *adj.* Not able to be understood.

unison (yü′nə sən) *n.* Agreement; accord.

unmerited (un mer′it əd) *adj.* Undeserved.

unparalleled (un par′ə ləld) *adj.* Unequaled; matchless.

unpremeditated (un′prē med′ə tāt′əd) *adj.* Unplanned or unconsidered beforehand.

unremitting (un′ri mit′ing) *adj.* Never stopping; not slackening; maintained steadily.

unwarranted (un wôr′ənt əd) *adj.* Having no right or authority.

upbraiding (up brād′ing) *v.* Finding fault with; scolding.

urbane (èr′bān′) *adj.* Courteous, refined or elegant; polite; well-mannered.

usurped (yü zèrpt′) *v.* seized or held by force or without right.

usury (yü′zhər ē) *n.* An extremely high or unlawful rate of interest.

utterance (ut′ər əns) *n.* Expression in words or sounds; speaking.

vacillation (vas′ə lā′shən) *n.* A wavering in mind or opinion; uncertainty.

vainglorious (vān′glôr′ē əs) *adj.* Excessively proud or boastful; arrogant.

vehemently (vē′ə mənt lē) *adv.* In a manner showing strong feeling; passionately.

vellicating (vel′ə kāt′ing) *adj.* Twitching.

veneer (və nir′) *n.* Surface appearance or show.

venerated (ven′ə rāt′əd) *v.* Respected highly.

vented (vent′əd) *v.* Let out; expressed freely.

verge (vèrj) *n.* The edge or shoulder of a road.

veriest (ver′ē ist) *adj.* Utmost.

veritable (ver′ə tə bəl) *adj.* True; real; actual; genuine; authentic.

verity (ver′ə tē) *n.* Truth; a true statement or fact.

vies (vīz) *v.* Contends in rivalry; competes.

vigilant (vij′ə lənt) *adj.* Keeping steadily on the alert; watchful; wide-awake.

vindicate (vin′də kāt) *v.* Defend successfully against opposition; uphold.

virtuosos (vèr′chü ō′sōz) *n.* Persons skilled in the techniques of a special art or profession.

visage (viz′ij) *n.* Face; appearance.

visionary (vizh′ə ner′ē) *adj.* Not practical; fanciful.

vivacity (vī vas′ə tē) *n.* Liveliness; sprightliness; animation; gaiety.

vociferation (vō sif′ə rā′shən) *n.* Loud, noisy cries or shouts.

vociferously (vō sif′ər əs lē) *adv.* Loudly and noisily.

voraciously (və rā′shəs lē) *adj.* Greedily; gluttonously.

vouchsafe (vouch sāf′) *v.* Be willing to grant or give.

vulnerable (vul′nər ə bəl) *adj.* Defenseless; open to attack.

waived (wāvd) *v.* Gave up; refused.

wariness (wer′ē nis) *n.* Caution; care; watchfulness.

wassails (wos′əlz) *n.* Drinking parties and revelries.

weals (wēlz) *n.* Marks or ridges on the skin made by a stick or whip.

wheedle (hwē′dl) *v.* Coax; persuade by pleasant words, flattery, or false promises.

winnowing (win′ō ing) *v.* Blowing chaff from grain; sifting.

winsomeness (win′səm nəs) *n.* Quality of being charming, attractive, and pleasing.

wit (wit) *n.* Intelligence, good sense, etc.

wretchedness (rech′id nəs) *n.* Condition of being very unfortunate, unhappy, miserable, etc.

General Index

Literary Types Index

Autobiography and Biography

Drama

Essays

Poetry

Short Story

Literary
Terms Index

Fine Art Index

Illustration Sources

Librairie Espagnole: 707, 708T, 709, 710, 712, 713
Little, Brown & Co.: 577
Lord Moyne, from the portrait by Henry Lamb in the Collection of Lord Moyne by whose kind permission it is here reproduced: 87

Magnum: 287
Metropolitan Museum of Art: 17L, Gift of Samuel Ward, 1875; 17R, Rogers Fund, 1906; 41C, Joseph Pulitzer Bequest, Purchase, 1926; 42B, Fletcher Fund, 1927; 245, Wolfe Fund, 1931; 382, Rogers Fund, 1922; 408, The Jules S. Bache Collection, 1949; 410, Rogers Fund, 1960
Arnoldo Mondadori, photo by Dino Buzzati: 749
Musée des Beaux-Arts, Brussels: 643
Museum of Modern Art: 567

NBC-TV: 181
National Gallery of Art, Washington, D.C.: 549, 705
National Portrait Gallery: 119, 271, 376, 404, 690, 718

National Tourist Organization of Greece: 4–7, 14, 32, 44T, 242
New England Merchants National Bank of Boston: 569
New York Public Library: 152, 157, 256, 321, 335, 373, 377, 378, 440, 681
W. W. Norton & Co., New York: 237

Photo Researchers: 100, Calvin Larson; 318, Hans Wamuth; 574, John Henry Sullivan, Jr.
Photographie Giraudon: 332, 412R, 696TR
Princeton University Museum and R. V. Schoder: 26

Radio Times Hulton Picture Library: 551, 715
Royal Norwegian Embassy Information Service: 489
St. Louis Public Library: 729–736
Schocken Books, Inc.: 647, from Franz Kafka: Eine Biographie by Max Brod, copyright 1946 by Schocken Books, Inc.
R. Schoder, S. J.: 39BL, Archaeological Museum, Athens; 39BR,

Olympia Museum; 40, Archaeological Museum, Athens; 41T, British Museum; 41B, Glypotek, Munich; 42T, Louvre; 44B, Istanbul Archaeological Museum; 45BL, British Museum; 45R, Istanbul Archaeological Museum
Shostal: 43T
Simon and Schuster: 399, photographed by Ira Rosenberg
Sovfoto: 684
Stratford Shakespearean Festival Foundation of Canada: 8, photos by Peter Smith
Martha Swope: 495, 507, 525, 543

Tarshish Books, Publishers, Jerusalem (Dr. M. Spitzer): 648, Jose Bergner's drawings to Franz Kafka
Théâtre National Polulaire, Paris: 186, 187, 199, 221
Trans World Airlines: 39T, 43B

Viking Press: 248

Warburg Institute, London: 411TR

Author Time Line

496–406 B.C.	Sophocles	(Greek)
427–347 B.C.	Plato	(Greek)
1313–1375	Giovanni Boccaccio	(Italian)
1340–1400	Geoffrey Chaucer	(British)

1500

1503–1542	Sir Thomas Wyatt	(British)
1517–1547	Henry Howard, Earl of Surrey	(British)
1552–1618	Sir Walter Raleigh	(British)
1552–1599	Edmund Spenser	(British)
1564–1593	Christopher Marlowe	(British)
1564–1616	William Shakespeare	(British)
1572–1631	John Donne	(British)
1572–1637	Ben Jonson	(British)
1591–1674	Robert Herrick	(British)
1593–1633	George Herbert	(British)

1600

1608–1674	John Milton	(British)
1618–1658	Richard Lovelace	(British)
1621–1678	Andrew Marvell	(British)
1622–1673	Molière	(French)
1631–1700	John Dryden	(British)
1667–1745	Jonathan Swift	(British)
1672–1719	Joseph Addison	(British)
1688–1744	Alexander Pope	(British)
1694–1778	Voltaire	(French)

1700

1709–1784	Samuel Johnson	(British)
1716–1771	Thomas Gray	(British)
1757–1827	William Blake	(British)
1770–1850	William Wordsworth	(British)
1772–1834	Samuel Taylor Coleridge	(British)
1775–1834	Charles Lamb	(British)
1788–1824	George Gordon, Lord Byron	(British)
1792–1822	Percy Bysshe Shelley	(British)
1795–1821	John Keats	(British)

1800

1806–1861	Elizabeth Barrett Browning	(British)
1809–1892	Alfred, Lord Tennyson	(British)
1811–1863	William Makepeace Thackeray	(British)
1812–1889	Robert Browning	(British)
1812–1870	Charles Dickens	(British)
1822–1888	Matthew Arnold	(British)
1828–1906	Henrik Johan Ibsen	(Norwegian)
1828–1910	Leo Tolstoy	(Russian)
1840–1928	Thomas Hardy	(British)
1840–1902	Émile Zola	(French)
1844–1889	Gerard Manley Hopkins	(British)
1847–1922	Alice Meynell	(British)
1849–1912	August Strindberg	(Swedish)
1850–1893	Guy de Maupassant	(French)
1859–1936	A. E. Housman	(British)
1860–1904	Anton Chekhov	(Russian)
1865–1939	William Butler Yeats	(Irish)
1867–1933	John Galsworthy	(British)
1867–1963	Edith Hamilton	(American)
1867–1936	Luigi Pirandello	(Italian)
1869–1954	Martin Andersen Nexø	(Danish)
1870–1916	Saki (H. H. Munro)	(British)
1873–1954	Sidonie Gabrielle Colette	(French)
1877–1962	Hermann Hesse	(German)
1878–1960	Massimo Bontempelli	(Italian)
1879–1970	E. M. Forster	(British)
1881–1958	Juan Ramón Jiménez	(Spanish)
1882–1941	James Joyce	(Irish)
1882–1941	Virginia Woolf	(British)
1883–1924	Franz Kafka	(Austrian)
1885–1930	D. H. Lawrence	(British)
1888–1965	T. S. Eliot	(British)
1888–1923	Katherine Mansfield	(British)
1890–1938	Karel Čapek	(Czechoslovakian)
1891–	Yefim Davidovich Zozulya	(Russian)
1893–1918	Wilfred Owen	(British)
1894–	J. B. Priestley	(British)

1900

1901–	Juozas Grušas	(Lithuanian)
1902–1971	Stevie Smith	(British)
1903–	Max Aub	(Spanish)
1903–1950	George Orwell (Eric Blair)	(British)
1903–1966	Frank O'Connor	(Irish)
1903–1966	Evelyn Waugh	(British)
1904–	Graham Greene	(British)

1906–1972	Dino Buzzati	(Italian)	1921–	Ilse Aichinger	(Austrian)
1907–1973	W. H. Auden	(British)	1923–	Dannie Abse	(British)
1908–1968	Giovanni Guareschi	(Italian)	1925–	John Wain	(British)
1909–	Stephen Spender	(British)	1926–	Elizabeth Jennings	(British)
1912–	Lawrence Durrell	(British)	1929–	Thom Gunn	(British)
1912–1976	William Sansom	(British)	1930–	Slawomir Mrożek	(Polish)
1913–1960	Albert Camus	(French)	1932–	Jenny Joseph	(British)
1914–1953	Dylan Thomas	(British)	1939–	Shelagh Delaney	(British)